The Greenwood Encyclopedia
of World Folklore and Folklife

VOLUME 1

Topics and Themes, Africa, Australia and Oceania

VOLUME 2

Southeast Asia and India, Central and East Asia, Middle East

VOLUME 3

Europe

VOLUME 4

North and South America

The Greenwood Encyclopedia of World Folklore and Folklife

VOLUME 3
Europe

Edited by William M. Clements

Thomas A. Green, Advisory Editor

GREENWOOD PRESS
Westport, Connecticut • London

Library of Congress Cataloging-in-Publication Data

The Greenwood encyclopedia of world folklore and folklife / edited by William
   M. Clements.
       p.   cm.
   Includes bibliographical references and index.
   ISBN 0–313–32847–1 (set : alk. paper)—ISBN 0–313–32848–X
(v. 1 : alk. paper)—ISBN 0–313–32849–8 (v. 2 : alk. paper)—
ISBN 0–313–32850–1 (v. 3 : alk. paper)—ISBN 0–313–32851–X
(v. 4 : alk. paper)
   1. Folklore—Encyclopedias.   2. Manners and customs—Encyclopedias.
I. Clements, William M., 1945–   .
   GR35.G75   2006
   398'.03—dc22   2005019219

British Library Cataloguing in Publication Data is available.

Library of Congress Catalog Card Number: 2005019219
ISBN: 0–313–32847–1 (set)
         0–313–32848–X (vol. 1)
         0–313–32849–8 (vol. 2)
         0–313–32850–1 (vol. 3)
         0–313–32851–X (vol. 4)

First published in 2006

Greenwood Press, 88 Post Road West, Westport, CT 06881
An imprint of Greenwood Publishing Group, Inc.
www.greenwood.com

Printed in the United States of America

The paper used in this book complies with the
Permanent Paper Standard issued by the National
Information Standards Organization (Z39.48–1984).

10 9 8 7 6 5 4 3 2 1

Contents

Foreword   ix
Thomas A. Green

Preface   xi

Acknowledgments   xv

Comprehensive List of Entries   xvii

Europe   1

Britain and Ireland   **1**
England   1
Ireland   22
Isle of Man   41
Scotland   52
Wales   69

Nordic Countries   **80**
Denmark   80
Finland   90
Finnish-Swedish   97
Greenland   103
Iceland   111
Norway   123
Sámi   134
Sweden   144

Western Europe   **157**
France: Peoples and Regions   157
France Overview   157
Brittany   170
Iberian Peninsula: Peoples and Regions   177
Spain Overview   177
Basque   189

Catalan	195
Galicia	202
Sephardim	211
The Low Countries	**223**
Flanders (Belgium)	223
The Netherlands	233
Central Europe	**249**
Austria	249
Germany	260
Hungary	273
Slovakia	285
Slovenia	295
Switzerland	306
Eastern Europe	**320**
Albania	320
Ashkenazim	330
Croatia	341
Georgia	352
Latvia	362
Macedonia	370
Poland	378
Roma	395
Russia	408
Serbia	425
Ukraine	437
The Mediterranean	**450**
Italy: Peoples and Regions	450
Italy Overview	450
Piedmont and Val d'Aosta	469
Sicily	480
Other Mediterranean Countries	493
Greece	493
Malta	502
Cumulative Index	**513**

Foreword

In many ways, *The Greenwood Encyclopedia of World Folklore and Folklife* represents the completion of a two-volume work published in 1997, *Folklore: An Encyclopedia of Beliefs, Customs, Tales, Music, and Art*. As editor of that encyclopedia, I endeavored to bring together a set of general entries on folklore forms, methods, and theories. Attempting to confine such diverse topics within a two-volume work often compelled those of us who took on the task to violate a guiding principle of folkloristics—the consideration of cultural contexts. To paraphrase a disclaimer included in the Preface to *Folklore*: the variety and wealth of the world's traditions demanded a severely abridged treatment of the subjects.

This concern returned to haunt me in the person of my former editor, Gary Kuris, who had changed presses and saw the opportunity to build on our earlier collaboration. Other obligations compelled me to pass along the editorial duties to William Clements, who had played a major role in the original project. Unable to resist involvement in such an ambitious and meaningful enterprise, I accepted the role of advisory editor. Thanks to Bill, this role has allowed me to be associated with what I believe will prove to be an extraordinary research tool, while requiring very little effort on my part.

Thus, almost a decade after the publication of *Folklore*, Greenwood Publishing Group, in this four-volume *Greenwood Encyclopedia of World Folklore and Folklife*, has provided a venue for redressing the omissions of that earlier project. These volumes flesh out the relatively economical treatments of concepts, forms, and theories with specific discussions of folklore in context; comparisons of art forms and lifeways within the various culture areas of the world; and consideration of topics that transcend cultural, social, and disciplinary borders. As such, the vision of folklore as a culturally situated phenomenon, arising from and contributing to the lives of its bearers, becomes fully apparent.

THOMAS A. GREEN
Texas A&M University

Preface

The term "folk-lore" entered the English language in 1846 when William J. Thoms, writing as Ambrose Merton, proposed it as a "good Saxon substitute" for the Latinate "popular antiquities," which British enthusiasts for the beliefs, behaviors, and objects of the "olden time" were using to denominate their interest. Thoms's contribution was a word (one that had been occasionally in use before his coinage); what it referred to already existed. And, in fact, other European languages had already found their own words for what Thoms was calling "folklore." (The hyphen disappeared in the twentieth century.) Germans were already studying *Volkskunde*, for example, by the time "folklore" appeared over the name Ambrose Merton.

The term may be English and of fairly recent coinage, but the kind of cultural material that it has come to encompass exists in every society, and many societies have been taking an interest in their folklore (by whatever name they refer to it) for quite some time. *The Greenwood Encyclopedia of World Folklore and Folklife* is an attempt to assess this cultural material on an international basis and also to provide some idea of what has been done in each of the represented groups by both group members and outsiders to document, analyze, preserve, and revitalize it.

Like language, religion, politics, and economics, folklore is a cultural universal found everywhere in the world. That fact—and the fact that the materials of folklore often show remarkable similarities in different places and at different times—makes a survey of folklore materials on a worldwide basis especially relevant. Moreover, although the foundations of folklore study—at least in Europe—lay in romantic nationalism, a tradition of internationalism also exists. One need only think of such compendiums as Frazer's *The Golden Bough* (1890 and many subsequent editions), which, although driven by a view of culture that few serious folklorists would endorse today, nevertheless brings together a vast amount of folklore material from all over the world. The first edition of Stith Thompson's monumental *Motif-Index of Folk-Literature* (1932–1937; 2nd edition, 1955–1958) catalogued narrative elements from a range of traditional genres from throughout the world. The *Funk and Wagnalls Standard Dictionary of Folklore, Mythology, and Legend* (1949)—famous among folklorists for its twenty-one different definitions of the term "folklore"—has unsystematic worldwide coverage. Beginning in the 1960s, the University of Chicago Press's Folktales of the World series also adopted the globe as its bailiwick. Each of the twenty or so volumes in that series focuses on the narrative traditions of a particular country (for example, Japan, China, Mexico, France, England, Israel, and India). In 1961, Richard M. Dorson edited *Folklore Research around the World*, a collection of essays that assessed the state of folklore scholarship in several different countries. When he inaugurated the *Journal of the Folklore Institute* (now *Journal of Folklore Research*) at Indiana University, he intended that its coverage be international. Of course, these few examples do not exhaust the attempts by folklorists to highlight what Dorson, in an essay entitled "The Techniques of the Folklorist," called "international relations" in folklore. They do, however, suggest the academic tradition out of which the current work emerges. As far as I know, a vision such as that of Thomas Green and the editors of Greenwood Publishing Group has not found expression in any previous work; the purpose of these four volumes is to survey the world's folklore heritages in a way that emphasizes the international nature of folklore in general and of specific folklore materials, while placing folklore within particular cultural milieus.

The aim of this encyclopedia is to examine folklore within the broad contexts of culture areas and the more narrow contexts of specific societies. To that end, the goal was to sample from every continent and subcontinent and to represent as many of the specific societies on those land masses as seemed feasible. The result is a series of substantial essays by specialists in the folklore of particular groups.

Given that both the specific nature of the folklore and the availability of resources on each topic vary from society to society, contributors had considerable latitude in what they felt to be important to represent the folklore of their societies and in how they decided to present it. However, they were given the following template—intended to be more suggestive than prescriptive—with ten areas that they might attend to in their essays:

1. *Geographical Setting*. The topography, climate, and other features of the physical and natural environment that help to shape the society's culture.
2. *Sociocultural Features*. Subsistence activities, political organization, social organization, and other aspects of the culture that will help readers understand how folklore works in the society.
3. *Ethnohistorical Information*. Migration patterns, political developments, watershed events, and interactions with other societies.
4. *Belief System*. Worldview and traditional religion (including medical practices).
5. *Verbal Art*. Myth, legend, folktale, and other oral forms, approached from an indigenous perspective.
6. *Musical Art*. Vocal and instrumental.
7. *Sports and Games*.
8. *Graphic and Plastic Arts*. Arts, crafts, architecture, clothing, and foodways.
9. *Effects of Modernization and Globalization*.
10. *References and Bibliographical Essay*. A brief history of the study of the society's folklore with a list of works from which the entry has drawn and recommendations for additional reading.

Contributors were encouraged to think not just in terms of folklore "texts" but of the processes of storytelling, singing, and performing folklore.

The four-volume *Greenwood Encyclopedia of World Folklore and Folklife* contains 205 entries written by more than 200 folklore scholars from around the world. To facilitate the comparison of geographically related countries and cultures, the volumes are broken down into the following regional subdivisions:

Volume 1: Topics and Themes, Africa, Australia and Oceania

Volume 2: Southeast Asia and India, Central and East Asia, Middle East

Volume 3: Europe

Volume 4: North and South America

Volume 1 opens with an alphabetically arranged collection of thirty-nine short essays on processes, research tools, social and intellectual movements, and concepts important for understanding folklore on an international, intercultural basis. These introductory entries should equip the reader to appreciate the dynamic nature of folklore through time and as it passes across cultural boundaries. Volume 1 then proceeds to a series of entries on the peoples and cultures of Africa, Australia, and Oceania, which, like all the entries in the other three volumes, are listed alphabetically within a series of regional subdivisions (e.g., Southern Africa, Western and Central Africa, Polynesia).

Most entries run between 3,000 and 5,000 words, although those for older and more complex cultures and societies (e.g., China, India) are often longer. Useful subheads (e.g., Geography and History; Myths, Legends, and Folktales; Music and Songs; Challenges of the Modern World) divide the entries into topical sections, allowing readers quickly to find the aspect or genre of a group's folklore that may be of most interest to them. Written in a clear, readable style, the entries are also based on the best and latest scholarship, offering detailed, current information on the folklore and folklife of particular peoples and cultures. The *Encyclopedia* can thus serve a variety of users, from students (both high school and undergraduate) requiring information for projects and papers in a wide variety of subjects and interdisciplinary classes, to general readers or travelers interested in knowing more about a particular culture or custom, to folklore specialists needing to stay current with the latest work on peoples and cultures beyond or related to their own areas of expertise. By promoting cultural diversity and stressing the interconnectedness of peoples and cultures around the globe, the *Encyclopedia* can also help any user who wishes better to understand his or her own cultural heritage and the influences neighboring and even more distant groups have had on its development. Most entries also help readers understand how the emerging global society and economy have and are affecting the customs and beliefs of peoples around the world.

The *Encyclopedia* also contains maps located at the start of the relevant geographical section and numerous photographs of the peoples and artifacts of a culture. Volume 4 contains a number of additional features, including a glossary that briefly defines some of the terms that recur throughout the entries. The purpose of the glossary is to give the reader a point of departure for understanding some of the language of folklore studies and anthropology used by the authors, and most of these terms merit the much more extended treatments they have received elsewhere, in such works as Thomas A. Green's *Folklore: An Encyclopedia of Beliefs, Customs, Tales,*

Music, and Art (1997). Volume 4 also includes a geographical guide of peoples and cultures to help readers put an unfamiliar culture in geographical context, and a highly selective general bibliography that identifies works offering intercultural perspectives on folklore.

Besides concluding with extensive bibliographies of important information resources, the entries are also cross-referenced, with entry names highlighted in **boldface** type when they are first mentioned in the entry or listed in a "See also" line at the end of the text. To make the cross-references useful across the set, each volume contains a listing of the entries found in the other volumes so that users can quickly identify where to find the entry for a highlighted reference. Each volume also contains a volume-specific table of contents and a complete subject index to the set.

Acknowledgments

Obviously, this work is a team effort. Most of the members of that team are named in the Editors and Contributors section in Volume 4 and appear with their contributions throughout the work. I want to call special attention here to individuals whose contributions might otherwise be unclear and underestimated: Thomas A. Green, who had the idea for this encyclopedia; Gary Kuris, vice president, Editorial, and George Butler, senior acquisitions editor, of Greenwood Publishing Group, who contacted me and helped to devise the formal proposal for the project; John Wagner, senior development editor at Greenwood Publishing Group, who has been the principal editor for this project, with whom I have been in almost daily contact for the last several years, and whose influence is felt in every aspect of the work; Charles R. Carr and Clyde A. Milner II, administrators at Arkansas State University, who arranged for me to have help from graduate assistants and other amenities; William Allen, Jennifer Majors, Cliff Stamps, and Diane Unger, who provided technical assistance; and Frances M. Malpezzi, who helped to keep the work focused during the three years that it has been the major professional aspect of my life. I would also like to thank Tom Brennan for preparation of the maps. The production staff at Westchester Book Group also deserves thanks: production editors Rebecca A. Homiski and Carla L. Talmadge; copyeditors Jamie Nan Thaman, Frank Saunders, Carol Lucas, and Krystyna Budd; and Enid Zafran, who prepared the index.

I also believe I was particularly fortunate in my formal folklore education in having instructors whose view of folklore was truly international. These include Richard M. Dorson, who, though an Americanist, never lost sight of the importance of thinking of folklore globally; Warren E. Roberts, whose work in historic-geographic folktale studies and in material folk culture had a strong international flavor; Linda Dégh, who brought a continental perspective to the Indiana University Folklore Institute in the late 1960s; and John C. Messenger, an anthropologist whose fieldwork has taken him to Nigeria and to the west of Ireland. They and others reminded us that folklore cannot be understood only by looking at it within the context of a single culture. I hope that this work will impress that point on its readers.

Comprehensive List of Entries

VOLUME 1
**Topics and Themes, Africa,
Australia and Oceania**

*Topics and Themes in
World Folklore*
Antiquarianism
Archives
Bibliography
Colonialism
Creolization
Cultural Evolution
Cultural Relativism
Culture Area
Diaspora
Diffusion
Ethnicity
Ethnography
Ethnopoetics
Fieldwork
Folklorism
Frontier
Gender
Globalization
Hero
Hybridity
Invented Tradition
Modernization
Motif
Museums
Nationalism
Nativism
Oikotypification
Performance Theory
Popular Culture
Primitivism
Public Folklore
Race
Repertoire

Text
Tourism
Translation
Trickster
Type
Worldview

Africa
Abanyole
Baule
Benin
Berber
Ga
Igbo
Ijo
Jie
Lunda
Madagascar and the Comoros
Mascarene Islands
Nuer
San
Shona
Swahili
Tuareg
Wolof
Xhosa
Yoruba
Zande
Zulu

Australia and Oceania
Australia (British)
Australian Aborigines
Guam
Hawai'i
Kiribati
Malaita
Marquesas Islands
Marshall Islands
New Caledonia

Palau
Samoa
Tonga
Trobriand Islands
Tuvalu
Vanuatu

VOLUME 2
**Southeast Asia and India,
Central and East Asia,
Middle East**

Southeast Asia and India
Assam
Bali
Bangladesh
Bhutan
Bihar
Duna
Gaddi
Haryana
Iban
India Overview
Isaan
Kadazandusun
Kaliai
Karnataka
Kashmir
Kewa
Khasi-Jaintia
Malay
Maluku
Nagaland
Nepal
Orissa
Semai
Sri Lanka
Tairora
Uttar Pradesh

Central and East Asia
Ainu (Japan)
China Overview
Chinese Abroad
Japan Overview
Kazakh
Korea
Manchu
Mongol
Siberia
Taiwan (Republic of China)
Tajik
Uyghur
Uzbek

Middle East
Armenia
Israel
Kurds
Lebanon
Palestine
Persia
Turkey
Yemen

VOLUME 3
Europe

Europe
Albania
Ashkenazim
Austria
Basque
Brittany
Catalan
Croatia
Denmark
England
Finland
Finnish-Swedish
Flanders (Belgium)

France Overview
Galicia
Georgia
Germany
Greece
Greenland
Hungary
Iceland
Ireland
Isle of Man
Italy Overview
Latvia
Macedonia
Malta
Norway
Piedmont and Val d'Aosta
Poland
Roma
Russia
Sámi
Scotland
Sephardim
Serbia
Sicily
Slovakia
Slovenia
Spain Overview
Sweden
Switzerland
The Netherlands
Ukraine
Wales

VOLUME 4
North and South America

North America
African American
Apache
Appalachia

Cherokee
Cheyenne
Choctaw
Haida
Hopi
Iroquois
Kiowa
Lakota
Mississippi Delta
Navajo
Nez Perce
Ojibwe
Seminole
Tlingit
Western Inuit and Yupik

South and Central America and the Caribbean
Caipira (Brazil)
Candoshi
Cuba
Ecuador
Haiti
Island Carib (Dominica)
Jamaica
Kaingang
Maya
Mexico
Nahua
Otomí
Peru
Quechua
Rarámuri
Sertão (Brazil)
Shuar
Sibundoy
Suriname Maroon
Xavante
Yanomami

Europe

Britain and Ireland

ENGLAND

GEOGRAPHY AND HISTORY

The folklore of England as compared with that of other parts of Britain, let alone **Ireland** and many countries of Continental Europe, looks scanty and fragmented. The chief reason is that the Industrial Revolution and mass education came early to this country, disrupting traditional patterns of work and relaxation, causing much movement of population, and gradually destroying older customs and beliefs.

However, this was not the first event to cause a major break in tradition. The Celtic culture of the Britons, who once formed the whole population of the island, was largely supplanted by that of the incoming Anglo-Saxons in the fifth century C.E. It is clearly very relevant to **Wales** and parts of **Scotland**, but how far it affected English folklore is a contested issue. The Norman Conquest of 1066 was even more disruptive. A French-speaking ruling class imposed its language, architecture, culture, and fashions for several hundred years, and a great deal of native English lore was lost. Pre-Conquest heroic legend, for example, survives almost wholly through a single poem, the 3,000-line epic *Beowulf*. The Norman hierarchy also deleted many saints who had been venerated by the Anglo-Saxons from the church calendar, though some were later restored. However, the English language did survive with a much modified grammar and copious additions of French words. Likely, medieval English customs were similarly influenced by the French.

In the sixteenth century, the Reformation brought radical changes to religious beliefs and rituals and hence to the activities of daily life. Monasteries and convents were closed and their property confiscated; the cult of saints and the Virgin Mary, pilgrimages, relics, holy water, blessed candles, religious amulets, prayers for the dead, Latin prayers, and much else were forbidden; saints' days and certain other holy days were abolished; and a determined effort was made to prevent sports and games on Sundays and in churchyards and to break all links between religion and communal festive culture. Protestants argued correctly that such customs were based on Catholic practice, and since they viewed Catholics as idolaters, not Christians, they stressed every possible parallel with the only two pagan cultures they knew about: the Old Testament gentiles and classical Greeks and Romans. They condemned the Maypole as "a stinking idol," Christmas gifts and the custom of decking houses with greenery as survivals of the Roman midwinter Saturnalia, and so forth. They also condemned festivals for encouraging drunkenness and public disorder. It is obviously true that most calendar customs do involve celebrations (for example, extra food and drink, dancing, bonfires, parades, and disguises) that have

Countries of Europe.

nothing to do with the religious meaning of the event (if any), but it is a logical error to label everything that is not explicitly "Christian" as "pagan." The appropriate category in this case is simply "secular."

This severity was carried further by the Puritan party after their victory in the English Civil War in the 1640s. Regarding Catholicism as a form of pagan idolatry, they tried to destroy all customs and festivals surviving from the Middle Ages if they could not be endorsed by biblical texts. Even the celebration of Christmas was forbidden for some years. However, the death of Cromwell and the restoration of Charles II to the throne brought immediate reversal of these policies, leading to a vigorous return of secular merrymaking, notably on May Day and at Christmas, encouraged by local gentry as a mark of loyalty to the monarchy.

In the eighteenth century, however, the social elite became increasingly hostile and contemptuous in their attitude toward traditional customs and disengaged themselves from communal festivity. The result seems to have been the fragmentation of what were previously national customs into localized forms and their restriction to underprivileged and marginalized groups such as farm laborers, urban milk-sellers, chimney sweeps, and eventually children.

The Victorian period saw two opposite trends. On the one hand, educational and social reformers deplored the persistence of superstitions, folk medicine, fear of witchcraft, and public rowdiness and drunkenness often seen at working-class celebrations. Their disapproval led to the suppression of various violent or cruel sports such as street football, bullbaiting, and cockfighting, which had been a regular feature of seasonal events. Attempts were also made to suppress or modify events that attracted large and potentially dangerous crowds, notably the bonfires of 5 November. This sometimes led to violent fights between participants and the police. On the other hand, some influential writers (including Sir Walter Scott and Washington Irving) gave glowing descriptions of the supposed Golden Age of "Merrie England" in Elizabethan

England, Scotland, Wales, and the Isle of Man.

times, with squire, parson, and common people all united in simple customs and innocent merriment. Inspired by nostalgic enthusiasm, local gentry, writers, schoolteachers, and clergy encouraged the "revival" of folk festivals, provided they were well organized and stripped of any subversive or unseemly elements. May Day and Christmas were radically transformed to suit this romantic image.

Victorian scholars, embarking on recording and interpreting the various genres of folklore, devoted much time and energy to debates about their origins. The prevailing theory was that of "survivalism": that many beliefs, rituals, myths, and customs had originated in pre-historic times and could best be understood by comparison with contemporary "primitive" societies in Africa or Australia, for example. It was thought that people in English rural communities had passed on the belief or performed the custom unchanged for generations but had no idea what it truly meant. This theory, long abandoned by all anthropologists, historians, and folklorists, unfortunately remains a taken-for-granted assumption among many journalists and popular writers. Currently, it is reflected in the common notion that the best place to look for the origin of a folk belief or tradition is in pagan religion. Examining this issue is thus a necessary task for today's English folklorist.

RELIGION

The religion that has shaped English culture for 1,500 years is Christianity—first in its Catholic, later in its Protestant form. Much English folklore echoes biblical stories, supports Christian morality, or presents modified secular equivalents to old church festivals and customs. The Bible could be quoted in support of folk belief in certain aspects of the supernatural (ghosts, witches, dragons, giants, and demons, though not fairies); folk medicine, healing charms, and divination drew heavily on Christian symbols; and the religious power ascribed to churches, holy wells, sacred names, biblical phrases, or blessed objects was also a source of protection and health. Many beliefs older and more widespread than Christianity still fit easily into its framework. Devout Christians, for instance, interpreted omens and premonitory dreams as messages from God. When something with pre-Christian or non-Christian parallels is found in a Christian community, that does not mean that paganism is still remembered and practiced there.

A fair amount is known about the Roman, Celtic, and Anglo-Saxon religions current in England before the coming of Christianity, and many attempts both by scholars and at the popular level have been made to relate them to known folklore. Demonstrable links are few. The names of Germanic gods appear in the days of the week, in some place-names, and in one or two early medical charms, but their myths have vanished. Surviving early hero-legends—for example, about Beowulf—contain marvels, but nothing religious. Medieval literature, especially the Arthurian romances, has clear parallels with Welsh and Irish tales of heroes and marvels, but these themes did not come directly to England. Probably originating in **Brittany**, they were mediated through French literature from the twelfth century onward. Yet claims for pre-Christian origins have a powerful appeal. In the later twentieth and twenty-first centuries many people see pagan beliefs (especially Celtic ones) as admirable and romantic and Christian tradition as repressive and dull.

CELTIC INFLUENCE

The issue of Celtic influence on English folklore is complex. Both Ireland and the areas of Britain where Celtic languages are, or were, once spoken—that is, Wales, the Scottish Highlands and Islands, and Cornwall—have rich, well-documented folklore, but the reason is debated. Victorian scholars assumed that Celts formed a distinct racial group with an inborn tendency toward anything mystical, poetic, or "superstitious," so folklore collectors paid particular attention to these areas and interpreted their finds accordingly. On the other hand, it could be argued that for geographical reasons the "Celtic" regions were less affected than lowland England and Scotland by the socioeconomic effects of nineteenth-century industrialization and so kept their traditions relatively stable. If a nationwide systematic survey could have been carried out in, say, 1700, how great a difference would there have been between the folklore recorded in Sussex and in Skye?

The question is unanswerable but warns us not to assume too easily that when a localized custom or belief in England resembles a more widespread one in Celtic areas, it must either be inherited from the native Britons of pre-Roman times or adopted from Celtic communities. The matter has to be considered in a European context, for the true distribution of the item may be far wider than appears at first. Irish and Scottish folklore is easily available for comparison in England, whereas that of **France**, **Germany**, or Scandinavia is known only to specialists. What looks "Celtic" from an English perspective may, in fact, be inherited from a broader European folk culture. Each custom or belief dubbed "Celtic" must be individually and carefully assessed. Thus, Halloween can reasonably be called a Celtic festival because sound evidence shows that it spread into England from Scotland in the late nineteenth century and was also observed in Wales and Ireland. May Day, however, is medieval and was vigorously celebrated in France (which then had a strong cultural influence on England), so its parallels with Irish and Scottish Beltane are not especially significant.

SUPERSTITION AND FAIRY LORE

It has always been tempting to assume that superstitions have ancient roots, and certainly some mentioned in classical Greek and Roman writers can be traced down the centuries and are still current—for example, the belief that all good or bad things come in threes. Romantic explanations are commonly put forward for well-known English beliefs: that saying "touch wood" to avert bad luck is a survival of primitive tree-worship (or of medieval devotion to relics of the Cross); that the bad luck of thirteen people sitting together at a meal dates from Christ's Last Supper; that thirteen itself has something to do with the moon or with witch covens. But the corpus of English superstition (which is large) has been assembled and investigated with scholarly rigor, and it turns out that though there have indeed been superstitions at all periods, individual ones arise, flourish, and then die out at a fairly rapid rate. Those that can be documented in the fifteenth or sixteenth century such as the use of holed stones and horseshoes as protection from witchcraft count as "old" by scholarly standards. Many of those best known today are surprisingly recent. "Thirteen at a meal" is first mentioned as a death omen in 1695; thirteen as a general unlucky number in the 1850s; and Friday the Thirteenth in 1913 (or possibly 1873, though that reference is ambiguous). Touching wood is recorded in the early nineteenth century but simply as a gesture and phrase used in a children's chasing game. As a superstition, it begins to arouse comment toward the end of that century. Of course, it is always possible that the items had existed for some time before they happened to be recorded in print, but in an intensely literate culture, where both clergy and schoolmasters campaigned vigorously against "ignorant credulity," a widespread belief is unlikely to have gone entirely unobserved for many decades, let alone centuries. In this context, absence of evidence does come fairly close to being evidence of absence.

Alongside superstitions in the narrow sense (beliefs involving luck, fate, omens, divinations, and similar supernatural concepts) exists a large body of what might be called semi-scientific lore, or, less charitably, "old wives' tales"—that cobwebs staunch bleeding, that copper rings cure cramp or rheumatism, that sleeping in the light of the full moon makes you mad, that lions cannot stand the smell of a pregnant woman, that a dried kingfisher hung on a string serves as a weathervane, and many more. In most cases, these exemplify folkloric "devolution": the situation where a theory (or custom or art form) previously accepted among the educated elite has been discarded by them but survives lower down the social scale. The older ones are now dead or dying, but no doubt future generations will find "old wives' tales" to laugh at among our present ideas.

Robin Goodfellow, a shape-changing trickster. Belief in fairies was widespread in rural districts in the seventeenth century and survived into the nineteenth. (© Mary Evans Picture Library/The Image Works)

The traditional folk beliefs of Europe include a wide range of supernatural beings: fairies (under various names), giants, water spirits, dragons, witches, ghosts, and the Devil. In English lore, giants and dragons are seen as figures of a remote and fantastic past and do not command serious belief. They appear only in fairy tales and in local legends, usually humorous in tone and often claiming to explain some landscape feature. The Devil's position is paradoxical. In official religion he is a powerfully evil tempter, and in folk tradition he sometimes dramatically punishes sinners even in this world—for example, by arriving visibly to carry them off to Hell. His sinister aspects are mostly found in connection with witchcraft. But the folk Devil is more often a stupid figure whose wicked plans fail because of his own clumsiness or because he is outwitted by ordinary humans. Such tales are common in local legends about the formation of the landscape, in stories of magicians who make the Devil serve them, and in comic anecdotes where the Devil is tricked or loses a wager.

Belief in fairies had a more direct impact on daily life. It was widespread in rural districts in the seventeenth century and survived more patchily into the nineteenth. By the twentieth century, it was extinct. The word "fairy" is a medieval borrowing from French, displacing the native English term "elf," which is now purely a literary word. Local names include puck, pixy, hob, and brownie. These beings could be helpful or harmful, according to circumstances. Their moral ambiguity is expressed in the traditional "explanation" that they were once angels who refused to take sides when Lucifer rebelled against God and so, being too good for Hell and too bad for Heaven, were thrown down to earth. In folk belief, the most "friendly" type was the household brownie (or puck or pixy), which lived in one's house or farm, bringing good luck and helping with the work in exchange for small offerings of food. But if anyone mocked him or spied on him, he would leave, and the luck would go with him. Goblins, called "knockers," were similarly helpful in tin mines and lead mines.

Fairies encountered in woods, marshes, or dark lanes were more alarming. Some were shape-changing tricksters like Robin Goodfellow in late medieval and Elizabethan tradition. He would appear as a horse, tempting weary travelers to ride him and then toss them into a river and gallop off with a loud "Ho, ho!" Yet he also could be a helpful household fairy. Shakespeare's Puck in *A Midsummer Night's Dream* similarly combines mischief and helpfulness. For most of the play he is a woodland

Engraving of Puck and the fairies, from Shakespeare's *A Midsummer Night's Dream*. For most of the play Puck is a woodland trickster, but at the end he arrives to sweep the house and bless it. (© North Wind/North Wind Picture Archives)

trickster but at the end arrives to sweep the house and bless it. Pixies were notorious for making people lose their way. The Will-o-the-Wisp or Lantern Man led them to dangerous bogs or cliffs. Some fairies lured people to join their dances and then carried them away into fairyland, from which they might or might not return unharmed.

The greatest fear was that fairies would steal a human baby and substitute one of their own race, a changeling that would remain small, sickly, and mentally deficient. This idea served to explain many real-life cases of physical or mental abnormality in babies and might lead to their being ill-treated by their parents, since it was held that beating or burning a changeling or putting it out of doors on a cold night would force the fairies to remove it and restore the real human child. Fortunately, the belief had grown rare by the nineteenth century.

The most long-lasting fairy lore is that used deliberately by adults to regulate the behavior of children, usually by a threat that if they go near some dangerous place or stay out after dark, a supernatural being will "get them." People still living remember being taught to fear Jenny Greenteeth, a murderous creature lurking in deep stagnant pools in Lancashire and Cheshire, or the twittering hytersprites in Norfolk woods. There were fairy rewards, too. Just as an Elizabethan servant-girl thought that fairies would put sixpence in her shoe at night if she worked hard, so modern children who bravely make no fuss over losing a milk tooth are told that if they put it under their pillow, the fairies will replace it with money. "Oberon's Palace," a poem by Robert Herrick from 1648, contains an early allusion to children's teeth being taken to fairyland, and memories of the practice are common from the 1890s onward. Nowadays, under American influence, it is no longer "fairies" in general but "*the* Tooth Fairy" who comes.

Other alarming creatures appeared in rural lore. There were phantom Black Dogs (often shaggy and with glowing eyes), some of which could change shape and had regional names such as Shuck, Guytrash, or Padfoot. They always appeared singly, usually patrolling a specified lane, or at the same churchyard, pool, or mound. Some appeared as omens of death, while others were harmless, even friendly. They are especially common in the traditions of East Anglia, the northern counties, and the southwest. In popular religion, the Devil sometimes appears as a black dog. Other phantom animals were said to guard buried treasures and scare away treasure-seekers. Ravens, hens, calves, horses, and snakes might assume this role but, surprisingly, not dogs. Finally, the Wild Hunt, more often heard than seen, had a ghostly or demonic huntsman leading a pack of phantom hounds across the sky on stormy nights. Some said this was the Devil pursuing damned souls; others that it was a man who blasphemously declared he preferred hunting to Heaven and so must hunt forever.

WITCHCRAFT AND POPULAR MAGIC

Belief in witchcraft has passed through several phases in England. In Anglo-Saxon, the word "witch" applied to anyone who could cast spells, whether harmful or helpful. This neutral use was still possible in the sixteenth century as an alternative to "wise-woman/wise man" for someone who provided magical healing, but in most contexts "witchcraft" meant using magic to harm humans, farm animals, or property. In Europe in the late fifteenth century theologians and lawyers developed a theory that witches got their power by making a pact with Satan and should be systematically prosecuted. The first English Act of Parliament making witchcraft a crime was in 1542, and others followed in 1563 and 1604. The first two stipulated the death penalty by hanging for murder by magic and imprisonment, fines, or pillorying for lesser offenses. The 1604 Act further made it a capital crime to "consult, covenant with, employ, feed, or reward any evil or wicked spirit." Nevertheless, witch trials in England (unlike those in Scotland and on the Continent) concentrated on showing that the witch had done actual harm, not on accusations of Devil-worship. The number of trials peaked in the 1580s and again in the 1640s but decreased sharply after 1660. The last, in 1717, ended in acquittal as most had done over previous decades. The Witchcraft Act was repealed in 1736. Full court records are missing from several regions, but the number of persons hanged probably totaled fewer than 500, though others died in prison.

Although the church or state exerted no pressure to prosecute witches, some local magistrates were more ready than others to do so. One lawyer, Matthew Hopkins, is notorious for conducting England's only large witch hunt in East Anglia in 1645/1646, in which nearly 250 people were arrested or investigated and probably about 100 hanged. Normally, accusations arose from quarrels between neighbors, often after years of mounting suspicion. Almost 90 percent of those accused were women, often elderly, sometimes with bad reputations, and generally poorer and less "respectable" than their accusers. A common scenario was that the suspect woman had asked a more prosperous neighbor for some small gift, loan, or favor and had shown anger when this was refused. The neighbor would then think that any sickness or misfortune in her household was magical revenge for her lack of generosity and would bring a case against the supposed witch.

Some trials were reported in pamphlets, which are more elaborate and dramatic than the actual evidence presented in court, aiming not only to convince their readers but also to shock them. They include traditional stereotyped anecdotes and beliefs: that witches have familiars that feed on their blood; that they make a pact with Satan in the form of a black man or black dog, have sexual relations with him, and feast with him at a Sabbath; that they can change themselves into hares and change others into horses, which they ride to the Sabbath. Such pamphlets reinforced and spread these ideas, most of which (apart from the Sabbath) recur frequently in folklore down to the early twentieth century and even today.

Fear of witchcraft remained strong and widespread in the nineteenth century, though prosecution was no longer possible. Physical attacks on alleged witches are recorded, especially in the earlier part of the century. Sometimes these took the form of "swimming" the suspect—that is, dunking her repeatedly—a procedure based on an old form of ordeal that was supposed to reveal whether she was guilty or not. Sometimes the suspect would be scratched or cut in the face, since it was said that one could break a witch's power by drawing blood from her "above the breath." When people were prosecuted for such acts of violence, public sympathy was often on their side.

Regional folklorists have noted many material charms to protect a house from witchcraft such as holed stones, twigs of mountain ash ("rowan"), horseshoes, colored glass balls, and carved posts by the chimney. People who believed that an evil spell had already taken hold on them or their possessions could perform a counterspell, usually after taking advice from a "cunning man." One was to make a "witch bottle," which required filling a bottle with the sick person's urine, nails, pins, thorns, or threads, corking it tightly, and either burying it or putting it to heat by the fire. This would torture the witch by preventing her from passing water and force her to lift her own spell to free herself from the pain. Such bottles have been found buried under hearths and thresholds in East Anglia and in ditches and streams in London. To halt disease among farm animals caused by witchcraft, the usual counterspell was to cut the heart from one of the animals, stick pins or thorns in it, and either boil it or hang it up in a chimney to dry slowly, this being done at midnight in complete silence with all doors and windows shut. This, too, would cause acute pain for the witch.

Local legends are full of anecdotes about witches keeping mice, toads, or (less commonly) cats as familiars, halting horses, preventing cream from being churned into butter, and letting themselves be chased by hounds while in the form of hares. The notion of riding a broomstick through the air is far more common as a stereotype in children's literature than in actual folk tradition, but it does occur. As recorded in folklore collections, these local tales mostly sound quaint and lighthearted, presumably reflecting both a change in attitude by tellers of later generations and the mediating influence of the collector.

Information about "cunning men," "conjurers," "wizards," and "wisewomen" gives more direct insight into the world of popular magic. They were familiar figures in rural communities up to the end of the nineteenth century and until the eighteenth had been common in towns, too. They were people who were known to have magical skills, sometimes combined with knowledge of herbal and other traditional forms of medicine. They would be employed to heal the sick and the bewitched, tell fortunes, cast horoscopes, identify thieves, practice clairvoyance, provide charms, induce love, and so on. The ability to counteract witchcraft is central to defining their role as contrasted with the wider group of "charmers" who cured natural afflictions such as warts by secret "blessings."

Cunning folk were paid in money or small gifts but generally had some regular occupation, too. Normally, they presented themselves as learned specialists in a particular form of knowledge. Many owned printed works or handwritten notebooks on astrology, conjuration, herbal medicine, dream interpretation, prophecies, and collections of magical recipes. Their literacy was an important factor in their prestige. Surviving written charms mostly combine occult and astrological symbols with fragments of Christian prayers. Magical ability was sometimes said to run in families. The seventh child of a seventh child was widely thought to be able to cure certain specified illnesses. A few cunning folk in earlier centuries claimed to have received their skill as a gift from fairies. Victorian folklorists were given information and anecdotes about some of the more famous ones in various districts, while Owen Davies (2003) has recently provided a far more thorough picture by systematic research into court records, press reports, and press advertisements.

Ghost Lore

Belief in ghosts persists in various forms throughout English folklore from its earliest records to the present day. The first evidence is archeological from pre-Christian Romano-British and Anglo-Saxon graves where corpses were laid face down or decapitated (the head often being placed between the feet), bound, or crushed under boulders. This might be a way of dishonoring the corpse but could also be intended to prevent the dead from "walking." If so, it implies a belief that the "undead" can emerge physically from their graves, and this was explicitly stated by two writers in the 1190s (William of Newburgh and Walter Map). However, the standard medieval view of ghosts, in England as in the rest of Europe, was shaped by the Catholic doctrine of Purgatory. They were "suffering souls" paying the penalty for past sins and not yet allowed into Heaven. They appeared to the living to ask for prayers and masses to help them on their way.

Theologians of the Reformation denied the doctrine of Purgatory, some arguing that alleged apparitions of ghosts were always devils in disguise, while others replied that to deny the possibility of ghosts was to deny the afterlife, a cornerstone of Christianity. Learned writers debating this point in the sixteenth and seventeenth centuries often cited contemporary accounts of ghosts, usually dignified and purposeful, coming to redress wrongs or bring warnings. They also described destructive spirits, which would now be called poltergeists, but regarded these as minor demons, not ghosts. In the eighteenth century, the elite were predominantly rationalists, dismissing ghost-lore as an ignorant superstition of the lower classes.

In Victorian times, collectors found strong, but very diverse, beliefs about ghosts to be current. The **archives** of the Spiritualist Church and the Society of Psychical Research are filled with personal testimonies from people who believed they had experienced the presence of the dead, whether their own departed loved ones or anonymous spirits. Folklorists did not usually publish personal material of this kind out of respect for their informants' privacy but recorded a wide range of communal, public ghost-lore linked to specific sites. Some spirits were anonymous and stereotyped (a headless horseman, a monk, a White Lady); some were historical persons (Anne Boleyn, a Roman legion); and some were local people who had died violently or tragically (especially murder victims, murderers, and suicides) or who had been so wicked in their lives that they could not rest in their graves. It is difficult to assess the degree of belief involved because most folklore collectors were amused by these "foolish superstitions" and were more concerned with recording the stories than inquiring into the attitudes of the tellers.

Many stories that developed from the mass of local ghost-lore are detailed, dramatic narratives. In some tales a scholarly parson (or a group of parsons) masters a troublesome spirit, driving it away to the Red Sea or imprisoning it in a bottle thrown into a local pool. Other tales tell of skulls that must always be kept in the house where they used to live and that will make trouble if they are moved; of spectral re-enactments of past tragedies; of phantom coaches in which the ghost of some wicked squire or lady must ride forever; or of banished ghosts creeping homeward at the rate of one cock-stride per year. Such local legends, originally collected from oral tradition, now pass to and fro between orality and print, since booklets on the ghost-lore of particular districts have found a keen market among tourists.

During the twentieth century English ghost-lore became even more varied. Interest in psychic and occult theories increased, as did the taste for fictional tales of the supernatural, often with sinister and malevolent ghosts, leading to hugely popular horror novels and films. For some people, these have raised strong fear of the occult powers of the dead. Press reports recount people asking for their houses to be exorcised. Some people genuinely fear haunted houses, haunted woods, and the like, yet "ghost walks" in historic towns are successful tourist attractions. For an old house to have a ghost can be a matter of pride for the owners, and for the bereaved, feeling the continued presence of a loved one is a source of deep personal consolation.

MYTHS, LEGENDS, AND STORYTELLING

Belief in the supernatural provides rich material for narrative, but it is by no means the only source available. Legends are extremely common throughout England, and their contents vary, some involving the supernatural and others being realistic or humorous. The one constant factor is that they are firmly linked to the landmarks, buildings, or history of the place where they are told. Some preserve fairly accurate memories of actual events, while in others, the "history" is so heavily overlaid with standard folk motifs that establishing any underlying facts becomes a contentious issue (as in traditions about Robin Hood or Lady Godiva). Other legends describe a startling, but not impossible, event, which tellers may well think is true, though folklorists recognize it as a recurrent story-pattern found in many places, a "migratory

Hand-colored woodcut of an old Englishwoman telling folk stories to young girls in a cottage. (© North Wind/North Wind Picture Archives)

legend." Some stories are told only for fun, but other narratives are readily accepted as true—for example, those about secret tunnels, buried treasures, and haunted places. Where a story is blatantly impossible, people may re-interpret it in order to find a "grain of truth" in it, explaining, for instance, that a dragon's death "really" refers to the defeat of an attack by Viking ships. Sadly, there has been no systematic field recording of English legends from oral narrators, and the older printed sources are scattered and vary greatly in quality.

Legends are abundant, but native versions of international fairy tales are rare, probably due to the fact that at the very period when someone might have decided to collect and print them, foreign tales flooded onto the market—French ones in the seventeenth and eighteenth centuries, those of the Brothers Grimm and Hans Christian Andersen in the nineteenth. "Cinderella," "Red Riding Hood," "Snow White," "The Little Mermaid," and others were immediately adopted into English culture, together with Aladdin and Sinbad from the *Arabian Nights*. The native stories that did get printed in cheap eighteenth-century chapbooks were comic ones: "Jack the Giant-Killer," "Jack and the Beanstalk," and "Tom Thumb," for example. Victorian collectors discovered a few English equivalents for Continental fairy tales, all of high quality. Tom Tit Tot is our Rumplestiltskin, Cap o' Rushes our Catskin, the Rose Tree our Juniper Tree, Mr. Fox our Robber Bridegroom. But the crop is meager unless one turns to the repertoire of Gypsy storytellers, who are as closely linked to Scotland as to England.

The performance context of English folktales in past generations is poorly documented, early collectors seeming hardly aware of oral storytelling as an art form or social activity. Certainly, there were no formal gatherings such as were common in

Ireland and Scotland, and only one group of professional storytellers is known, the wandering Cornish "droll-tellers" of the early nineteenth century. (Gypsies told stories only among themselves.) One informal, but influential, form of transmission occurred when nannies and nursemaids from working-class families told stories to the middle-class children under their care, either to entertain them or to warn them against bad behavior. Charles Dickens vividly retells the bloodthirsty tales with which his nurse used to terrify him, claiming that they were absolutely true. One is a gruesome variation on the theme of the ogre bridegroom (AT 311), and another concerns a carpenter who sold himself to the Devil in the form of a huge rat. Transmission also occurred in a wide variety of informal situations, as it still does: during visits to some place with a traditional legend attached, in pubs, at Christmas family gatherings, and as after-dinner anecdotes. There are occasional mentions of storytelling in workhouses, prisons, and barracks and one intriguing reference to knitting parties in Lancashire and Yorkshire in the 1830s where the old men would retell "old stories and traditions of the dale." But no coherent picture emerges.

SONGS

Song has been more systematically collected and studied from the 1880s onward. Previously, Thomas Percy's important collection *Reliques of Early English Poetry* (1765) included many traditional ballads, but as texts without tunes. Readers and literary scholars admired them as poetry, with little awareness of musical quality and performance. Francis James Child's monumental collection (1882–1898) established 305 ballads from both England and Scotland as the authoritative corpus of British ballads. Many are known in America, too, and many have European analogues, especially in Scandinavia. Their topics include love stories (often tragic), encounters with fairies or the dead, skirmishes on the border between England and Scotland, and the adventures of Robin Hood. Some can be proven to have been current in the seventeenth century. The more popular among them were collected repeatedly from different regions in the nineteenth and twentieth centuries.

Cecil Sharp, an energetic collector whose views dominated English folk music and folk dance studies from about 1900 until long after his death in 1924, took quite the opposite approach to folksong. For Sharp tunes were far more important than words. He defined a genuine folksong as being orally transmitted within rural communities of uneducated people, freely varying without reference to any printed version. It must not be influenced either by commercialized popular music or by the "art" music of the elite. This, he argued, was England's true national music. Sharp did not merely collect and publish. He inspired and guided an enthusiastic revival movement, involving both fieldwork and the performance of traditional songs in schools (arranged with piano accompaniment) and at concerts by trained singers. He became a dominant member of the Folk-Song Society. He was not, however, the only important scholar in the field: Sabine Baring-Gould, Lucy Broadwood, and Frank Kidson all made major contributions. Their work inspired many English composers of the early twentieth century to use traditional tunes in their music.

Apart from the early ballads mentioned above, the bulk of English songs date from the late eighteenth and the nineteenth centuries, and (contrary to Sharp's theories) their texts show much influence from popular entertainment and from cheap printed media, the broadside and the chapbook. Their subjects are various. Songs about love and sex are numerous, but so are those about seafaring, war, crime, drink, poaching, and farm life. On sailing ships, shanties were sung to assist in certain types of rhythmic work. In tone, the folksongs range from the lyrical or sentimental to the jocular, but few are blatantly coarse. Both collectors and singers themselves filtered out any "unsuitable" material. It is almost certain, however, that bawdy songs were performed in closed male groups and that handwritten copies circulated. Since the 1960s uncensored versions have been often published.

A fresh surge of interest in folksong began in the 1950s, encouraged by left-wing political groups and by American examples (notably, the work of Alan Lomax) and drawing on a large-scale British Broadcasting Corporation project to record an archive of dialect speech and local song throughout Britain. This led to the "Second Revival," when the stress was on participation and amateur performance in the informal setting of a club. New collectors set out, discovering fresh material and previously unknown singers and musicians. Meanwhile, some were creating their own songs in traditional idiom, so that for the first time one had "folksongs" by known, named authors. From the 1960s onward, the "folk scene" was increasingly influenced by commercial recording companies and by a popular taste for rock and pop music, leading to various hybrid performance styles using microphones and electronic instruments. This evolution still continues.

DANCE

The story of English folk dance is equally complex. There are two basic categories: "social dances," which can be danced by anyone at any time just for mutual enjoyment, and the "ceremonial dances," which are performed as displays by one specialized group at a special time and in special costume. Social dances are so much affected by changes in fashion and by class differences that styles come and go quite rapidly. In the Middle Ages, the circle dance ("carol") was the norm and was still popular in Elizabethan times. After it fell out of fashion, it still lived on in children's games and in the belief that fairies (and witches) liked to dance in a ring. Other old figures include serpentine chains of linked dancers and Thread the Needle, now seen in the children's games of the Big Ship Sails and Oranges and Lemons.

Later came what Cecil Sharp labeled "country dances," in which couples of dancers combined with other couples in various formations. They were very popular in fashionable society in the seventeenth century, and it is a matter for debate whether (as Sharp maintained) the upper class had appropriated a rural style of dancing or whether the reverse was true—that the fashion spread from the towns to the villages. Referring to Dorset at the beginning of the nineteenth century, Thomas Hardy wrote that "country dances" belonged to one class of village people, the tradesmen, small farmers, and upper servants, who did not mix socially with manual workers. The latter had their own gatherings where they did reels, jigs, and long dances. In Victorian times, fashionable society adopted many Continental dances such as waltzes, quadrilles, and the polka, and these, too, eventually spread down the social scale. But Cecil Sharp and the English Folk Dance Society, which he founded in 1911, led a vigorous campaign to revive "country dancing." This proved very successful up to World War II but then was followed by a craze for the livelier American style of square dancing. Currently, a "barn dance" or "ceilidh" will consist of a mixture of English, American, Scottish, and Irish dances.

The working class, both urban and rural, also practiced "step dancing"—the main feature being rhythmic stamping and foot movements within a limited space. It included the solo hornpipe and jig and reels for three or four couples. In parts of northern England, the dancers wore wooden-soled working shoes ("clogs") with metal tips, which enhanced the sound. Step dancing and clog dancing competitions were held.

The two major forms of English ceremonial dancing are the morris and the sword dance—the former subdivided into three or four regional styles. They are display dances, almost always restricted to males and primarily associated with festival dates such as Whitsun or May Day. References prove that morris dancing was known in the late fifteenth century and very common in the sixteenth and seventeenth. Several features that characterize it today were already present: small bells strapped to the dancers' legs, costumes bedecked with ribbons, and handkerchiefs to be waved or sticks to be clashed during the dance. The music at this time was pipe and tabor (a small drum) and, in later periods, fiddle or concertina. Ceremonial dances were on the verge of extinction before Sharp began recording them and launched his revival movement. Many contemporary performing teams can claim unbroken tradition going back into the nineteenth century.

The most widespread type is the Cotswold Morris. The earliest references are to performances at Court and in London civic pageantry, but during the sixteenth century it spread to towns and villages along the Thames Valley and throughout southern England, usually as part of a Church Ale—an annual fund-raising event organized by a parish church, involving food and drink, sports, competitions, and entertainments. The Puritans of the seventeenth century objected strongly to Ales in general and morris dancing in particular. Cromwell's government banned the custom, but it returned after the restoration of Charles II in 1660. Documentation is patchy, but, apparently, dance teams flourished in many places in the eighteenth century, performing at fairs, in public houses, and at the homes of local gentry. By the end of the century, however, attitudes had shifted again. Upper-class landowners generally regarded working-class recreations as encouraging idleness and drunkenness, and most ceased to patronize their local dancers. Rural poverty in Victorian times further eroded the custom. The team that Cecil Sharp happened to see at Headington (Oxfordshire) on Boxing Day in 1899 was one of the very few left by that time.

The "sword dance" does not involve real swords, only flexible strips of wood or metal. Each dancer holds the handle of his own sword in one hand and the point of his neighbor's in the other so that the whole team remains linked throughout the figure. Sometimes the dance culminates with six swords being interwoven in a star shape called "the lock" and held aloft. Linked sword dances are widespread in Europe, where they date from the late fourteenth century. In England, however, they appear only in the mid-eighteenth century and are confined to Yorkshire, Northumberland, and County Durham.

PLAYS AND THEATER

By far the most widespread folk performance in the nineteenth century was a short comic play in rhyme, of which hundreds of versions are known. Though it is conventionally called the Mummers' Play, the performers were known by many local names (Guizers, Tipteerers, Paper Boys, and so on). They were rural working-class men and youths who toured their district during the Christmas and New Year period (or, in certain districts, at Easter or Halloween), acting their play at the houses of the better-off, in pubs, and in the street and collecting money after each performance. No stage was required, only a few yards of open space.

The most common type is the Hero Combat Play. It opens with a presenter (for example, Father Christmas), who calls on the characters to step forward one by one. The first is the **hero**, usually called "King George" or "St. George," who boasts of his achievements. Another boastful character arrives (sometimes more than one). They exchange taunts and challenges and fight till one is wounded or killed. The presenter laments over the fallen warrior and calls for a doctor, who (sometimes accompanied by a cheeky assistant) after some arguments and nonsense patter revives the dead or wounded man. One or more extra characters arrive to ask the audience for food and money, and the performance often ends with a general song or dance. The second basic type is the Sword-Dance Play, in which dancers of the type described above incorporate a scene of one of their number being "beheaded" by having the "lock" placed around his neck and then being revived. The third is the Plough or Wooing Play of the East Midlands, featuring comic lovemaking between a "Lady" (played by a man) and her wooers, including a Fool, as well as the fight, death, and revival sequence of the Combat Play. It was performed on Plough Monday (the Monday after 6 January) by farm laborers who dragged a plow around with them.

The performance style, as reported by nineteenth-century observers, was not naturalistic. The players would line up at one edge of the acting area, and each would step forward to declaim his lines in a stiff, monotonous tone, pace up and down, do conventional fighting movements, and then step back into line when his part was over. At this period, it was normal for all the players to be dressed alike. Some teams decorated their working smocks with ribbons and rosettes and blackened their faces. Others covered themselves in strips of rag or wallpaper dangling from their hats and jackets, which formed a cheap, but very effective, disguise. Later, some teams tried to dress appropriately for the character enacted. The Doctor would wear a top hat, Father Christmas a red gown, the fighters various types of military gear, according to what the teams could obtain. This is how most of the revival mummers now dress, though some village teams keep the old disguises traditional to their area—for example, the Paper Boys at Marshfield (Gloucestershire).

The custom has been much studied and its age and significance hotly debated. Confusion can arise because the term "mumming" can also be used to mean simply donning a disguise without any form of dramatic performance and challenging people to guess one's identity. This type of amusement ranges from the elaborate masquerades of medieval aristocrats to simple house-visiting by youths with blackened faces, as in Yorkshire villages in the nineteenth century. In this sense, "mumming" has medieval origins. But the actual Mummers' Play, as now known, is not mentioned anywhere before the middle of the eighteenth century. Nothing about it appears in early parish records; it was not attacked by Puritan writers; and it is not described by early antiquarians. Current scholarly opinion holds that it originated in the eighteenth century and was spread through cheap printed chapbooks.

Nevertheless, many writers, both popular and scholarly, have taken for granted that the play must be very old—in its actions, at least, since the words are relatively modern in style. One theory was that it dated to the Crusades because one of George's adversaries is often called the Turkish Knight. Another, held by many scholars up to the 1970s and still widespread at a popular level, sees it as a relic of some pre-Christian fertility ritual with the death-and-resurrection of a central character symbolizing and magically ensuring the renewal of vegetation after the winter. This would imply an origin no later than the sixth century C.E. It is hard to believe that such a colorful public entertainment could exist for about 1,200 years without anybody commenting on it.

CALENDAR CUSTOMS

Dating is a recurrent problem in the study of calendar customs. The theory of pagan origins, typified by Sir James Frazer's hugely influential anthropological work *The Golden Bough* (1890–1915), dominated English folklore scholarship up to the second half of the twentieth century. It is always open to the objection that in this country there is virtually no evidence to bridge the gap between antiquity and, at best, the late Middle Ages or, more commonly, the Early Modern period for the item under discussion. On the other hand, recurrent similarities between English customs and their Continental counterparts raise tantalizing suggestions of a common origin, possibly in medieval times. Our May Day Jack-in-the-Green, for instance, was an urban street custom, unknown before the late eighteenth century, performed by chimney sweeps to raise money for themselves. Yet spring guising customs in which performers are wholly concealed under greenery can be cited from various parts of Europe. How and when did the sweeps pick up the idea?

All books on regional folklore include a section on calendar customs—that is, those that take place once a year at a particular date or season—but such customs are by no means stable. Historical "evidence" for them may be only brief snapshots from different times and places. Lovers' customs for St. Valentine's Day, for example, are first mentioned in the fourteenth century, and allusions appear in Shakespeare's *Hamlet*, Pepys's

An 1848 print showing an English family gathered around the Christmas tree. (Courtesy Library of Congress)

diary, Thomas Hardy's *Far from the Madding Crowd*, and, of course, folklore collections. Yet the differences are sharp. Ophelia's song in *Hamlet* is about a girl visiting a man by night; Pepys and his friends drew lots to be one another's Valentines and gave presents openly; and in Hardy and in modern practice, people send anonymous love tokens or cards. A custom may be highly popular throughout society at one period, only to fade away and be confined to children and marginalized groups of adults and then undergo a vigorous revival in modified form and become widely known again. That is what happened to May Day celebrations between the fifteenth and twentieth centuries.

Another problem is that currently the traditional calendar is changing fast, with some public customs being transferred from fixed dates to the nearest weekend or Bank Holiday while others are spread over a longer period. Popular events are held on different dates in different places to avoid conflicts. Customary foods for certain festivals are on sale long before the festival itself. Some customs (including well-dressing, rush-bearing, and harvest feasts) are necessarily seasonal but not tied to a specific date. It is impossible to summarize the topic both briefly and accurately, but an outline of major traditions would be as follows:

Christmas season (25 December to 6 January). Older customs include cessation of normal work; festive food and hospitality; decoration of houses and churches with greenery; music and dancing; house-to-house performances, including the Mummers' Play, sword dancing, guising, and wassailing (wishing good luck to the householders). Among modern customs (mid-nineteenth-century onward) are the Christmas tree, cards, carol singing, present-giving, and Father Christmas as gift-bringer for children (since the 1870s and increasingly called "Santa Claus" in the twentieth century).

Twelfth Night (6 January). Practices include a large rich cake containing one bean (whoever gets the slice with the bean in it is "king"); spiced drink served in a large "wassail bowl"; "wassailing" apple trees—that is, drinking in the orchard and pouring some ale on their roots to ensure a good crop; and "wassailing" cows.

Plough Monday (Monday following 6 January). A decorated plow was dragged around the villages by farmworkers in procession. Dancing, singing, or performing the Mummers' Play also occurred.

St. Valentine's Day (14 February). See previous page.

Shrove Tuesday (the day before Lent begins, so the date varies). Older customs include lavish food, especially pancakes; rowdy sports such as mass street football and stoning live cocks; children visiting houses, demanding food, and pelting the door with stones if refused. Races between women tossing pancakes are occasionally mentioned from 1870 onward and became widespread after 1945.

Mothering Sunday (the middle Sunday in Lent). The older custom was that servants and apprentices were allowed the day off to go home and see their mothers. A special food was a simnel cake. This is now widely called Mother's Day, though still always a Sunday, and involves sending flowers and gifts to one's mother.

Easter. People would climb hills before dawn to watch the sunrise, believing it would "dance" to celebrate the Resurrection of Christ. In northern counties, eggs were hardboiled and decorated. Children then rolled them downhill as a game. A modern custom is eating chocolate eggs.

April Fools' Day (1 April). In the seventeenth century, this was a festival when adults tried to hoax one another but later became a children's custom only.

May Day. Older customs included gathering flowers and greenery for garlands to decorate oneself or one's house or to display for money; erecting a felled and decorated tree as a Maypole; sports, games, morris dancing; "Robin Hood" plays. Eighteenth-century observances were characterized by dancing and the display of "garlands" of silver items by female urban milk-sellers; urban sweeps' Jack-in-the-Green; and the Padstow hobbyhorse procession and dance. Victorian customs included children displaying garlands and/or dolls, the ribboned Maypole dance, and the Queen of the May.

Whitsun (seventh Sunday after Easter). Feasts, sports, fairs, morris dancing, and floral decoration of churches and (in some regions) wells marked this event, though most practices are now transferred to the Spring Bank Holiday (last Monday in May).

Royal Oak Day or Oak Apple Day (29 May). Instituted in 1661 to celebrate Charles II's escape after the Battle of Worcester by hiding in an oak tree and his Restoration in 1660, this occasion was observed by decking houses and churches with oak branches. Later, children wore oak leaves.

Corpus Christi (Thursday after Trinity Sunday). Before the Reformation, this was marked by elaborate religious and civic processions and pageants with plays on biblical themes. Afterward, the civic pageantry was transferred to Midsummer Day.

Midsummer Eve and Day (23–24 June). Older customs were bonfires and torchlight parades on the eve with feasting and dancing; houses decked with flowers, then large civic processions on the day. These had mostly ceased by the nineteenth century except in Cornwall.

Halloween (31 October). This was once observed by the joyful ringing of church bells for the eve of All Saints' Day (1 November) and the tolling of those bells as a call to pray for the dead on the eve of All Souls' Day (2 November). Modern customs include love divinations, games with apples and nuts, and costumed and masked children house-visiting with turnip or pumpkin lanterns for trick-or-treat.

Bonfire Night or Guy Fawkes Night (5 November). Instituted in 1606 to celebrate the foiling of Guy Fawkes's Gunpowder Plot in 1605, this occasion was observed with church services, bell-ringing, and bonfires as well as fireworks, torchlight parades, rolling blazing tar-barrels, and burning effigies of religious or political opponents. Partially suppressed in the nineteenth century because of danger, the event has been observed more recently either at domestic parties with fireworks and small bonfires or in controlled public displays.

As can be seen, customs linked to different dates may, nevertheless, be similar in what is actually done. One recurrent practice is for participants to go from one house (or pub or public place) to another to sing, dance, and/or display their costumes or something they have made in order to collect money (or food and drink). Examples include the Mummers' Play, carolling, the display of May garlands by Victorian children, and trick-or-treat by modern children. Other customs feature processions, which can be only a small group of dancers or costumed characters or a large communal parade. Buildings are decorated—in early times with vegetation (flowers and green branches or evergreens, according to season), later with flags, streamers, and lights. Organized competitive sports, fairs, music, dancing, and festive eating and drinking have always been popular features.

CELEBRATIONS

The major life-cycle customs in modern England focus on weddings, funerals, birthdays, and wedding anniversaries. In the seventeenth and eighteenth centuries, the only birthdays celebrated were those of the Royal Family, but the fashion seems to have spread rapidly in the early nineteenth at first for children and later for adults. It involves gifts, cards, and usually a party. Celebrating a "Golden" or "Silver" wedding began in the Victorian period. Weddings and funerals, however, have always existed and have always followed the same formula: a journey (often processional) in which members of the community escort the bride and groom (or the corpse) to the designated place where the change of status is officially recorded and enacted, followed by a return to a more homely environment where participants share food and drink. Considerable variation of detail within this framework reflects changes in religious outlook, differences of wealth and social status, increased mobility (both social and geographical), and changes in fashion. Funerals are much simpler now than in Victorian times, while weddings are much more elaborate and expensive.

CHILDREN'S FOLKLORE

The study of English children's folklore began in the nineteenth century with J. O. Halliwell's work on nursery rhymes and tales (1849) and Alice Bertha Gomme's two-volume collection of games (1894, 1898). It is now one of the best-documented topics, thanks to a series of substantial books produced by Peter and Iona Opie from the 1950s to the 1990s, based upon nationwide questionnaires and fieldwork. *The Lore and Language of Schoolchildren* (1959) covers jokes, tricks, taunts, rhymes, riddles, customs, and beliefs. Their other books deal with various types of games. The Opies highlighted the crucial distinction between the rhymes and games deliberately taught to small children by adults in the home or the infant school and what children learn directly from one another—generally without the approval or even knowledge of adults. This body of childlore was purely oral in transmission, circulating rapidly and showing both continuity and variation, yet some items were several centuries old. For instance, medieval and Elizabethan pictures show some games still current today. The work of the Opies is not only of great interest in itself but typifies the change of approach to folklore study in the latter part of the twentieth century in England. Meticulous and very detailed research has now replaced romantic speculation in every area, and the results have been very fruitful.

BIBLIOGRAPHY

Briggs, Katharine M. 1970–1971. *A Dictionary of British Folk-Tales in the English Language*, Parts A and B. 4 volumes. London: Routledge and Kegan Paul.

———. 1978. *The Vanishing People*. London: Batsford.

Cass, Eddie. 2001. *The Lancashire Pace-Egg Play: A Social History*. London: FLS Books.

Cawte, E. C. 1978. *Ritual Animal Disguise*. Ipswich: Brewer.

Chandler, Keith. 1993. *Ribbons, Bells and Squeaking Fiddles: The Social History of Morris Dancing in the English South Midlands 1660–1900*. Enfield Lock: Hisarlik.

Child, Francis James. 1965 (1882–1898). *The English and Scottish Popular Ballads*. 5 volumes. New York: Dover.

Corrsin, Stephen D. 1997. *Sword Dancing in Europe: A History*. Enfield Lock: Hisarlik.

Davies, Owen. 1999. *Witchcraft, Magic and Culture 1736–1951*. Manchester: Manchester University Press.

———. 2003. *Cunning-Folk: Popular Magic in English History*. London: Hambledon and London.

Duffy, Eamon. 1992. *The Stripping of the Altars: Traditional Religion in England 1400–1580*. New Haven, CT: Yale University Press.

Hole, Christina. 1976. *British Folk Customs*. London: Hutchinson.

Hutton, Ronald. 1994. *The Rise and Fall of Merry England: The Ritual Year, 1400–1700*. Oxford: Oxford University Press.

———. 1996. *The Stations of the Sun: A History of the Ritual Year in Britain*. Oxford: Oxford University Press.

Judge, Roy. 2000. *The Jack-in-the-Green*. Revised edition. London: Folklore Society.

Knight, Stephen. 1994. *Robin Hood: A Complete Study of the English Outlaw*. Oxford: Blackwell.

Merrifield, Ralph. 1987. *The Archaeology of Ritual and Magic*. London: BCA.

Opie, Iona, and Peter Opie. 1951. *The Oxford Dictionary of Nursery Rhymes*. Oxford: Oxford University Press.

———. 1959. *The Lore and Language of Schoolchildren*. Oxford: Oxford University Press.

———. 1969. *Children's Games in Street and Playground*. Oxford: Oxford University Press.

———. 1985. *The Singing Game*. Oxford: Oxford University Press.

———. 1997. *Children's Games with Things*. Oxford: Oxford University Press.

Opie, Iona, and Moira Tatem. 1989. *A Dictionary of Superstitions*. Oxford: Oxford University Press.

Philip, Neil. 1992. *The Penguin Book of English Folktales*. London: Penguin.

Roud, Steve. 2003. *The Penguin Guide to the Superstitions of Britain and Ireland*. London: Penguin.

Sharp, Cecil J. 1907. *English Folk-Song: Some Conclusions*. London: Simpkin and Novello.

Sharpe, James. 1996. *Instruments of Darkness: Witchcraft in England 1550–1750*. London: Hamish Hamilton.

Shuel, Brian. 1985. *The National Trust Guide to the Traditional Customs of Britain*. Exeter: Webb and Bower.

Simpson, Jacqueline, and Steve Roud. 2000. *A Dictionary of English Folklore*. Oxford: Oxford University Press.

Thomas, Keith. 1971. *Religion and the Decline of Magic*. London: Weidenfeld and Nicolson.

Vickery, Roy. 1995. *A Dictionary of Plant Lore*. Oxford: Oxford University Press.

Westwood, Jennifer. 1985. *Albion: A Guide to Legendary Britain*. London: Granada.

Westwood, Jennifer, and Jacqueline Simpson. 2005. *The Penguin Guide to the Legends of England*. London: Penguin.

Jacqueline Simpson

IRELAND

GEOGRAPHY AND HISTORY

Few places offer a greater wealth of traditional verbal art, custom, and material culture than Ireland. For many, Ireland brings to mind both accurate and romanticized images of country people dancing at crossroads, singing ballads in pubs, and telling tales in thatched houses nestled among stone walls and green fields. This association of Ireland with its folklore and folklife was consciously cultivated by nineteenth- and twentieth-century nationalists who bolstered the cause of an Ireland independent of Great Britain by bearing witness to a distinct and distinctive Irish culture. Folklore has been so central to Irish national identity that in 1937 citizens of the newly independent state in the south of Ireland elected a folklorist, Douglas Hyde, to be their first president. While folk traditions continue to have their political uses in Ireland, more generally and perhaps more importantly folklore and folklife offer shared

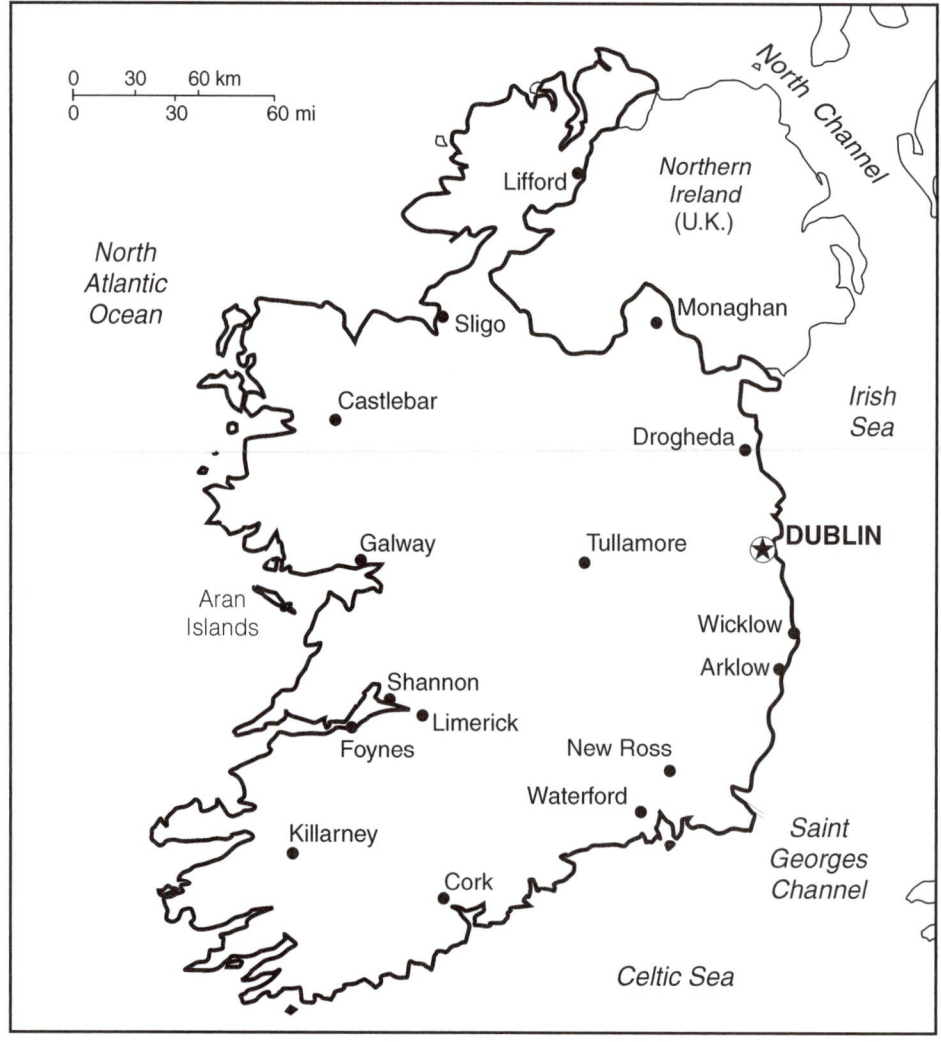

Ireland.

resources for cultural expression, social interaction, and satisfaction of fundamental material needs.

Paraphrasing Irish folklorist Kevin Danaher, Irish folklore and folklife consist of the sayings and doings of ordinary people. The often-studied stories and songs along with the shared beliefs, customs, and subsistence technologies that constitute Irish folk tradition have been passed down through the generations mainly by word of mouth and imitation of example. Certain stories, holiday observances, and architectural forms, for example, have their roots in the far distant, even pre-historic past. Although much of Irish folk tradition is of great antiquity, the main focus here is on folklore and folklife that are a legacy of the late eighteenth through early twentieth centuries because these traditions have more immediately shaped the lives and worldviews of the people of Ireland in the present and recent past.

Proper appreciation of Irish folklore and folklife begins with an understanding of Irish geography and history. Evergreen and damp, the island of Ireland has an area of 84,512 square kilometers and lies in the relatively warm Atlantic Gulf Stream off the west coast of Britain on the fringe of Northwest Europe. Ireland is mostly ringed by mountains except on the central eastern coast. These mountains give way inland to low and flat midlands punctuated by hills and bogs that make the west generally less accessible and fertile than the east. One is never more than sixty miles from the coast, so from the earliest era of human settlement to the present, seafaring and fishing have always been prominent aspects of Irish life and have inspired a wealth of lore about what lies beneath the waves. The majority of Irish people over time, however, have subsisted through mixed agriculture and pastoralism, particularly cattle-raising.

Although Ireland had been home to hunters and gatherers as early as 8,000 years ago and later to a more complex farming culture about 5,000 years ago, folklorists have paid more attention to a later group of settlers, the Celts, whose contributions to traditional Irish culture remain evident. As early as the fifth century B.C.E., Celtic tribes from Central Europe began to settle Ireland, bringing with them iron, rich oral traditions, and a language that developed into modern Irish Gaelic, still spoken in pockets along the western coast. The Celts lived in rural, dispersed settlements of extended families, and they established the four provinces that remain today: Ulster, Munster, Leinster, and Connacht in the north, south, east, and west, respectively. Although folklore and early literature refer to a High King ruling over roughly 150 smaller kingdoms, this office was never a fully developed political reality.

A lack of strong central authority made Celtic society in Ireland vulnerable to foreign conquest, yet the Roman Empire never invaded Ireland as it did Britain. Broader European influence entered Ireland through trade and most significantly, in the fifth century C.E., through Christian missionaries. The slow process of converting the Celts was begun by missionaries such as St. Patrick, Ireland's patron, but as in other parts of Europe much pre-Christian religious belief and practice survived. Pre-Christian holidays and pilgrimage sites were simply incorporated into the new religion.

Starting in the late eighth century, Vikings from Scandinavia invaded and later settled in Ireland, establishing the island's first towns. This wave of settlement was followed by the Normans from **England** in the twelfth century. Like the Vikings, the Normans assimilated into Irish culture over time, but they also laid the groundwork for the eventual conquest of Ireland by England. If the Norman Conquest can be described as incomplete, subsequent sixteenth- and seventeenth-century British rulers made more concerted efforts to control and Anglicize Ireland. British colonization restricted local Irish autonomy not only in political and economic terms but also in cultural and religious terms. After the sixteenth-century Protestant Reformation in England, later waves of British colonizers in Ireland were Protestants, whereas the Irish remained Roman Catholic. This religious divide provided successive British regimes with justifications for conquest in the name of the new religion, and securing Ireland as a Protestant colony became essential to stopping Catholic **Spain** and later **France** from using Ireland as a back door into Britain. A British policy of relocation, known as Plantation, forced the native Irish onto less productive land in the west and replaced these dispossessed Catholics with English and Scottish Protestant settlers or "planters." In addition to privileging Protestantism over Catholicism, Anglicization during the era of Plantation included generally successful efforts to stamp out the Irish language in favor of English and to supplant Irish customs and laws with British.

By the late eighteenth century, rural Ireland had become a peasant society governed by a landlord system that ensured Protestant political dominance. All but 5 percent of the land was owned by descendants of wealthier English and Scottish planters, and Irish Catholics were hard-pressed to raise the cash necessary to pay rents on land their ancestors had owned. From the late eighteenth century through the late nineteenth century, four-fifths of the island's population were Irish Catholic tenant farmers and landless laborers, subordinate to upper-class Protestant landlords and their agents. Although some scholars dislike the pejorative connotations of the term "peasantry," in this era the majority of Ireland's population fit a strict definition of the term, which denotes rural dwellers subject to a ruling class and entirely dependent on the land for subsistence.

The late eighteenth-century introduction of the potato—a nutritious and prolific food source—from America allowed the rural poor to subsist on the smallest and least productive plots of land, and the potato combined with widespread early marriage led to a dramatic population explosion by the mid-nineteenth century. The near universal dependence on potatoes left this peasant society vulnerable, and when the Irish Potato Famine of 1845–1851 struck, roughly 1 million people died of disease and starvation while another 1 million people were forced to emigrate to North America, England, and **Australia**. Due to continued emigration, Ireland's mid-nineteenth-century population of 8 million was nearly halved by the early twentieth century.

Once the British government was persuaded to begin dismantling the landlord system in the late nineteenth century, the attention of many Irish men and women turned to self-rule. Oscillating between political agitation and armed rebellion, Irish Catholics and a significant number of sympathetic Protestant intellectuals looked to Irish folklore for inspiration in their struggle for national independence. Eventually, a failed rebellion in 1916 followed by a protracted and bloody guerrilla war resulted in a political compromise that partitioned the island into two nation-states. Twenty-six counties in the south split from Britain, later becoming the present-day Republic of Ireland, and six northeastern counties, where the descendants of Protestant British colonizers formed the majority, remained part of the United Kingdom as the province of Northern Ireland. Having roots in the sixteenth- and seventeenth-century era of Plantation, violent conflict between Catholics and Protestants continues sporadically in contemporary Northern Ireland, where certain genres of folklore such as the political ballad play a major role in reinforcing opposing Irish and British ethnic, sectarian, and political identities.

Most traditions that folklorists study today are a living legacy of the late-eighteenth- through early-twentieth-century peasant society that emerged in the wake of British colonization. Focusing briefly on rel-

During the late eighteenth through early twentieth centuries, most Irish people lived in solitary, rectangular houses that were typically one room wide and roofed with thatch, or occasionally with slate. (Courtesy Library of Congress)

evant material aspects of this peasant society, we should note that during this period most people lived in solitary, rectangular houses that were typically one room wide and roofed with thatch or occasionally with slate. Directed away from prevailing winds, entry doors opened onto a central kitchen/living room dominated by an open-hearth fire used for both cooking and heating. Daytime domestic chores and nighttime socializing revolved around these hearths, which burned dried peat turf cut from the bogs. Common in many poorer parts of the west were byre dwellings shared by people and their livestock. Only a drain separated the human and animal ends of the house. The most modest homes consisted of the kitchen/living room alone, and the poorest, landless laborers built their one-room homes out of mud and sod. More prosperous tenant farmers used stone and enlarged their homes by adding bedrooms on either side of the kitchen along a lateral axis. Even more prosperous tenant farmers, landlords' agents, and landlords expanded their homes with second stories rather than building perpendicular to the lateral axis of the house.

These solitary houses tended to be scattered across a landscape of enclosed fields that gave way to shared, open grazing land in higher elevations. This settlement pattern and landscape organization were relatively recent and partly a product of the landlord system. In previous eras clusters of houses and open fields had been the norm, yet despite greater dispersal of the population after the late eighteenth century, subsistence continued to depend heavily on neighborly cooperation. In general, a strong ethic of loyalty to kin and local social networks combined with a guarded suspicion of external authority. Given that urban centers were scarce, individual farmers and landless laborers alike needed to be well versed in several agrarian

Nineteenth-century Pattern Day celebrations, which honor a patron saint. (From Mrs. S. C. Hall, *Sketches of Irish Character* [London: M. A. Nattali, 1844], p. 211)

"Ceili," or a nighttime visit among neighbors in mid-nineteenth-century County Waterford. (From Mr. and Mrs. S. C. Hall, *Ireland, Its Scenery, Character, etc.* [London: Virtue, 1845], volume 1, p. 316)

skills, and specialist craftsmen such as tinkers and tailors were generally itinerant. Massive assemblies of people for trade and socializing were possible only on occasions such as market fairs and patterns as well as annual pilgrimages to holy sites associated with local saints.

Calendar Customs

Fairs and patterns were some of the many highlights in the yearly cycle of festive events that included Christian holidays such as Christmas and Easter and holidays with pre-Christian origins such as May Day (Bealtaine), First Harvest (Lúghnasa), and Halloween (Samhain)—a roster of calendar customs encyclopedically treated in Danaher (1972). Except for the solemn, penitential period of Lent, most Irish holidays were occasions for feasting, music, and dancing. Traditional Irish music, which has enjoyed a popular revival in recent decades, is played on fiddles, flutes, tin whistles, concertinas, accordions, and uillean pipes (a type of bagpipe). The variety of rhythms and meters in traditional Irish music such as reels, jigs, and hornpipes is meant to accompany different forms of dance still practiced today in venues ranging from community halls to Broadway stages. Popular in the past at holiday festivities, weddings, and wakes, Irish dance focuses primarily on footwork and consists of several forms of solo and group or social dances. Breathnach (1971) usefully surveys Irish music and dance.

During the winter months, more intimate social gatherings of neighbors took place on an almost nightly basis around the turf fires in certain local homes, known in English as ceili, raking, or rambling houses. There, hosts were known in more prosperous times for providing food, tea, and tobacco, and guests would repay the hospitality with entertaining conversation, story, and song. Wakes, weddings, patterns, and various gatherings of people for shared labor also provided ideal environments for several forms of traditional verbal art. Yet the ceili house provided, and in some areas still provides, the primary social context for the wealth of folklore for which people in both Irish- and English-speaking communities are rightfully renowned.

SONGS, HEROIC TALES, AND FOLKTALES

Looking first to the Irish-language tradition, the earliest form of song, surviving until the 1940s, was the lay, a chanted poem recalling the deeds of heroic warriors such as Fionn Mac Cumhaill (Finn MacCool). In addition, at wakes well into the nineteenth century, women in Irish-speaking areas sang formulaic, but often improvised, keens or laments for the dead. A third genre popular in the Irish language was the lyric love song. Unlike narrative genres that report a sequence of linked events, these lyric songs only allude to an underlying story while emphasizing emotion. In English-speaking areas, Irish singers adopted many English and Scottish ballads and, like their early American counterparts, altered these imported ballads to fit the local scene. These fictional narrative songs often deal with themes such as troubled family relationships, star-crossed lovers, and murdered brides. Sometimes referred to as "come-all-ye's," later ballads composed in Ireland from the eighteenth century disseminated through printed broadsides and oral tradition. These later Irish ballads often served a journalistic function by treating historical events and thereby complementing legends in Irish storytelling tradition.

Traditionally, Irish folk narrative was categorized either as *scéalaíocht* or *seanchas*, and both main classes of narrative can be broken down into numerous other genres of story. In general, *scéalaíocht* consists of longer, more complex, and often multi-episodic stories of heroes, mythological beings, and magical happenings. *Seanchas* consists of shorter, realistic, and usually single-episode stories including accounts of personal experiences and locally or nationally relevant past events. Overall, *scéalaíocht* functioned as art, whereas *seanchas* functioned as historical lore. These two classes of narrative and the genres they include persisted in English-speaking communities even if the Irish Gaelic terms did not.

In some cases, the star performers of a given community could tell stories from both classes of narrative, but more often a storyteller would specialize in either *scéalaíocht* or *seanchas* and be known as a *scéalaí* or *seanchaí*, respectively. Because *seanchas* depends more on accurate reporting than artful telling, almost any adult, regardless of age or gender, could be a *seanchaí* (shanachie in English). The *scéalaí*, however, was held to higher esthetic standards for performance and linguistic dexterity and, especially in Irish-speaking areas, was more highly regarded than the *seanchaí*. With a few documented exceptions, men tended to dominate the *scéalaí* role. Note, however, that early antiquarians and folklorists were, by and large, men focused on storytelling in predominantly male realms such as the fireside ceili. Therefore, women telling *scéalaíocht*

Folklorist and storyteller. (From Patrick Kennedy, *Legendary Fictions of the Irish Celts* [London: Macmillan, 1891], frontispiece)

in female social circles and to children may well have been more widespread than the written record indicates. In addition to resident male and female storytellers, itinerant beggars, peddlers, and tradesmen were highly valued both for bringing news from the wider world and for disseminating *scéalaíocht* and *seanchas* unknown in the local community. The important role of the Irish storyteller has been well treated in Delargy (1969 [1945]) and Zimmerman (2001), while the English-language repertoire of storytellers in Ireland is treated by Harvey (1992).

Less commonly told today, *scéalaíocht* includes heroic tales composed in Ireland and local versions or oikotypes of internationally known folktales. Looking first to the native tradition of *scéalaíocht*, *scéalta gaisce* (stories of heroism) describe various quasi-historical Irish warriors and kings performing valiant deeds such as battling monsters and rescuing abducted women. Though composed and set in Ireland, *scéalta gaisce* include some international motifs such as certain magical objects, helpful animals, and supernatural adversaries. Two other, more unified bodies of heroic narrative known as the Ulster Cycle and the Fenian Cycle recall the exploits of two groups of warriors and kings. Although thematically and stylistically similar to *scéalta gaisce*, the Ulster and Fenian Cycles were considered by Irish storytellers and audiences to be separate genres.

Fionn Mac Cumhaill comes to aid the Fianna. (© Mary Evans Picture Library/The Image Works)

Tales from the Ulster Cycle recall the deeds of the Red Branch warriors of Ireland's northern province. Set in the pre-Christian past and recorded later by Christian scribes, these tales offer a window into the Celtic Iron Age, when all wealth was measured in cattle and the warrior-aristocracies of small kingdoms were constantly at war. The central story of this cycle, the *Táin Bó Cualigne* (The Cattle Raid of Cooley), relates how Cúchulainn, the champion of Ulster, single-handedly keeps at bay an army from Connacht until the Red Branch warriors recover from a curse to help Cúchulainn defend Ulster and their king's prized bull. Although certain tales from this cycle were told in nineteenth-century Ulster and Gaelic-speaking **Scotland**, the Ulster Cycle is more thoroughly preserved in early Irish literature than in oral tradition.

The Fenian Cycle is also extensively recorded in early medieval manuscripts, but these stories appear to have been of later composition and much more popular in oral tradition, especially in Leinster and Munster. Also known in Irish as *finnscéalta*, these stories tell of the exploits of Fionn Mac Cumhaill and the Fianna, his roving band of young warriors-in-training. Hundreds of tales recall how the Fianna excelled at hunting and put down tyrannical giants, destructive dragons, and bewitching hags. Equally popular are tales of the Fianna defending Ireland from foreign and supernatural invasions. For example, in a tale known as the Battle of the Sheaves, the Fianna chase a deer into a field of grain. Fionn orders his men to harvest the field, helping its owner while flushing out the deer. Unexpectedly, the Lochlannach (historically Vikings, here supernatural invaders from beyond the North Sea) attack the unarmed Fianna, who are forced to defend themselves with nothing but newly bound sheaves. So strong are the Fianna that not one of them is injured, and once one of their band retrieves their weapons, they unleash their full force and slay the remaining invaders.

Fionn himself is a complex figure. He is a warrior, poet, and seer of the future who uses both strength and wit to prevail. In a contest with an English giant, for example, Fionn unearths a sod of turf in Ulster so large that, once flung into the Irish Sea, it becomes the Isle of Man and the remaining crater becomes Lough Neagh. Yet in another tale, despite Fionn's reputation for bravery and strength, he hides in fear from a much stronger giant seeking to challenge him to a fight. Once the giant arrives at his home, Fionn jumps into a cradle dressed as a baby. As the giant waits for the baby's "father" to return, he plays with the "baby," who nearly bites off the giant's finger. Not wanting to meet the father of such a child, the giant flees for his life. Fionn's more serious and perhaps darker side is portrayed in a series of tales about his pursuit of Diarmaid and Gráinne. Fionn is engaged to the much younger Gráinne, but she falls in love with the handsome Diarmaid, one of Fionn's favorite warriors. Diarmaid and Gráinne flee the infuriated Fionn, who hounds them all over Ireland and Scotland. In the end, Diarmaid, as prophesied, is gored by a magical boar. The only cure for Diarmaid is a drink of water from Fionn's hands. Overcome by jealousy, Fionn twice brings and spills the water. When Fionn returns with water a third time, Diarmaid is dead. Gráinne reluctantly agrees to marry Fionn, and the mismatched couple lives an unhappy life together.

In addition to these three native genres of heroic tales (*scéalta gaisce*, the Ulster Cycle, and the Fenian Cycle), *scéalaíocht* includes what folklorists would identify as folktales—fictional narratives told for the entertainment of adults and often the education of children. About one-third of the international tale types listed in the Aarne-Thompson tale type index have been recorded in Ireland. Most numerous are the "ordinary folk-tales" listed as types 300-1199, and of these the most popular in Irish tradition were local versions of wonder tales or Märchen such as "Cinderella." Known in Irish as *sean sgéalta* or "old stories," wonder tales are set in a timeless and geographically vague fantasy world, and these tales usually follow the adventures of a young protagonist through strange adventures. The protagonist eventually overcomes his or her obstacles through luck, magic, and personal qualities such as bravery, cleverness, kindness, or patience.

For adults, the vicarious enjoyment of a magical world in which wishes are fulfilled and all problems are eventually resolved may have helped compensate for—or at least distract them from—the shortcomings of everyday life. For children, the younger **heroes** of wonder tales provided examples of proper behavior and models for growing into maturity. In more recent generations, wonder tales have faded as a form of entertainment for adults. Nevertheless, adults still use them with children to teach moral lessons about the importance of generosity, for example. Certain tales involving menacing creatures such as water horses or witches also provide adults an extra means of control to stop children from wandering near lakes or walking the roads at night, for example.

MYTHS AND HAGIOGRAPHIES

Now known mostly through early Irish literature, a Mythological Cycle once existed in Celtic oral tradition and described the successive waves of gods and humans who settled Ireland. Echoes of this mythology are found in the Ulster Cycle, Fenian Cycle, and later fairy beliefs and legends. Yet after the dawn of Christianity in Ireland, biblical literature and, in oral tradition, tales of early Irish saints served as stories of sacred beginnings. Legends of the saints qualify as *seanchas* rather than *scéalaíocht*. From the perspective of a nineteenth-century Irish storyteller, the ancient past is worth remembering in an artfully told story, but mythical pre-history ends, and truthful, though no less marvelous, history begins with Sts. Patrick, Brigit, and Colmcille.

Hagiographies, or biographies of the saints, were written in Irish Gaelic and Latin from the seventh century through the Middle Ages, and as with the Ulster and Fenian Cycles, written and oral versions of stories influenced each other. Popular in the oral traditions of Irish peasant society were legends of local Irish saints converting Celtic chieftains and establishing the first places of worship. St. Patrick, for example, is said to have lit a fire at Easter on the Hill of Slane, proclaiming the good news of Christ's sacrifice and Resurrection. According to legend, Patrick's provocation draws the attention of the High King of Ireland's druids, holy men of the old religion. The druids are unable to extinguish the fire, which Patrick defends as the unquenchable light of the true faith. After defeating the druids in magical combat, Patrick converts the High King and uses the three-petaled shamrock, a contemporary symbol of Ireland, to explain how the Holy Trinity is three divine beings in one. According to a later legend set in Kildare, St. Brigit asks a local chieftain to donate land for her mission. The arrogant chieftain scoffs and tells her she can have no more land than her cloak can cover. Undeterred, Brigit then lays her cloak on the ground, and it miraculously spreads to encompass the entire area on which her famous monastery was built.

Scores of local saints are credited with banishing demonic serpents and monsters in the name of Christ and with blessing herbs or holy wells to provide people with cures for common ailments. Despite performing countless miracles, healings, and other superhuman feats, many early Irish saints are depicted in folklore as being overwhelmed by all-too-human emotions. In one legend, St. Patrick is fed up with the difficult work of proselytizing, and he orders a servant boy to take note of anything he says while napping. The saint's sleep talk consists of withering curses against the stubborn pagan Irish, but the

Popular in the oral traditions of Irish peasant society were legends of local Irish saints like St. Patrick—pictured here—converting Celtic chieftains and establishing the first places of worship. (Courtesy Library of Congress)

quick-thinking boy deflects each curse through prayer. When Patrick awakes and hears what has transpired, he congratulates the boy for nothing less than saving Ireland. Like St. Patrick, St. Colmcille is also known for his fiery temper. In one of the better-known legends about him, Colmcille copies without permission a set of the Gospels loaned to him. A case is brought before the High King, who rules that Colmcille must return both the Gospels and his copy. Infuriated and unwilling to relinquish the books, Colmcille rallies an army of his kinsmen against the High King and wins a great battle, but he soon regrets the vast slaughter he has caused. In penance he vows never to set eyes on Ireland again, then sets sail for Scotland to convert as many souls as were killed in the battle fought for his sake.

SUPERNATURAL LORE

Having turned our attention from *scéalaíocht* to one genre of *seanchas*, the saint's legend, we should note that although *seanchas* serve primarily as history rather than art, they also recount mysterious and fantastical events that may or may not be believed by storytellers and audiences. Such is the case with firsthand accounts and second-hand legends of encounters with fairies, ghosts, and other supernatural phenomena. Supernatural legends and personal experience narratives (memorates)—forms of *seanchas*—were, and are, quite often understood to be truthful reports of actual events. However, even when people question their factuality, these stories of mystery require people to examine the nature of reality. In *scéalaíocht* the supernatural is taken for granted, even expected. In *seanchas*, the supernatural comes as a surprise. Accounts of the supernatural in legend may not be verifiable, but information is offered for contemplation, and the issue of belief must be entertained.

Perhaps the most famous examples of Irish supernatural legend are stories of the fairies. Fairy lore preserves elements of pre-Christian belief and worldview and serves as one aspect of Irish folk religion, unofficial belief and practice that both complement and compete with official Christian theology. There are two common explanations for the origin of the fairies or *sí*. In some places, these Otherworldly beings are thought to be the descendants of the *Tuatha Dé Danann*, a race of gods central to the old Mythological Cycle who retained many of their powers but were driven underground when humans took over Ireland. More commonly, the origin of the fairies is tied to Judeo-Christian mythology. In the beginning, we are told, a great war occurred between the angels. Those who sided with Michael the Archangel prevailed, and God cast down the angels who sided with Lucifer into Hell. However, another group of angels took neither side. These neutral angels were cast out of Heaven, too, but God relented and allowed them to live suspended between Heaven and Hell. According to this explanation, these angels became what we now refer to as fairies or the *sí*.

As characterized in supernatural legend, the world of the *sí*, the Otherworld, is separate from our own, yet the boundaries between our world and the Otherworld are open at certain times and places. In the old Celtic calendar, Bealtaine (the night of 30 April through 1 May) and Samhain (the night of 31 October through 1 November) divided the year into dark and light halves. Along with the daily moments of dawn, dusk, and midnight, Bealtaine and Samhain are considered magical, temporal thresholds. Neither light nor dark, neither today nor tomorrow, neither this half of the year nor the next, these moments allow fairies to slip from the Otherworld and into our own. In spatial terms, the boundaries between the human and fairy worlds are most permeable at special locations. Throughout Ireland are megalithic dolmens, usually consisting of three standing stones capped with massive flat stones. Historically, these served as the burial chambers of a pre-Celtic Neolithic farming culture. Also dotting the Irish landscape are the foundations of Celtic Iron Age ring forts. Fairy lore depicts both types of archeological remains as portals into the Otherworld. People must take care not to disturb these and other sites associated with the fairies. For example, gathering wood from a ring fort—also known as a *rath*, *lios*, or fairy fort—is sure to result in bad luck.

Fearful reverence for the fairies is reflected in the fact that, traditionally, the fairies are not referred to directly but with names such as *na daoine maithe* (the good people) or *na daoine uaisle* (the noble people). In all cases, interaction with the fairies must proceed with caution because one's conduct may be rewarded or punished. For example, one legend tells of a man who begins building his house on a fairy path only to find his work undone each night. Offering to save the fairies the trouble of repeatedly knocking down his house, he rebuilds elsewhere and is rewarded with a pot of gold. In another often-told fairy legend, a good-natured hunchback hears the fairies singing one night, and he politely joins in, adding to their song. The fairies are so pleased with his contribution and his deferential manner that they remove his hunch. Hearing of this, a second, more mercenary hunchback seeks out the fairies, and when he adds to their song, he is brash and impatient for his reward. In response, the fairies angrily swarm around the insolent hunchback and fix a second hunch to his back as punishment.

As this nighttime gathering of singing fairies indicates, most fairies are depicted in legend as social creatures. Quite often they appear as thousands of tiny flying people traveling in a large group known as the fairy host, or *slua sí*. In the Otherworld the fairies have their own leaders, farmers, and herders, and in general their society parallels that of the Irish peasantry. Still, the fairies covet certain members of human society including young children, midwives, women of childbearing age, and talented musicians and sportsmen. Consequently, a wealth of legend describes the fairies taking or "sweeping" a person away to the Otherworld, sometimes leaving a changeling or old, sickly fairy in his or her place. Also popular in supernatural legends are accounts of people rescuing their loved ones from the Otherworld and chasing off changelings through prayer, the help of priests, or threatening the fairy substitute with an object made of iron, a substance over which the *sí* have no power.

Supernatural legends also describe a number of solitary (rather than social) fairies, including the selkie (a mysterious seal-woman) and the pooka (a **trickster** in the form of a horse, pig, or dog). Best known of these individual fairies is the leprechaun, a shoemaker who appears as a small man no taller than a few feet. He guards buried treasure and can be quite clever in keeping it hidden from humans. In one very popular legend, a young man captures the leprechaun, who, under threat of violence, discloses the location of his pot of gold in a field. The man quickly releases the leprechaun in order to mark the treasure's location by driving a stick into the ground. Before running home to fetch a spade, the man takes the extra precaution of tying a ribbon to the stick and saying an *Ave Maria* over it. The leprechaun is powerless to remove the stick because it has been consecrated with a Christian prayer. Nevertheless, when the man returns, the field is filled with thousands of identical sticks and ribbons, and he is outwitted and defeated.

Nearly as famous as the leprechaun is another solitary fairy known as the banshee, an Anglicization of *bean sí* or fairy woman. In most legends, the banshee is depicted as an eerie Otherworld messenger heard to cry out near the home of a person fated to die. In other stories she is heard at the site of an impending death. More often heard than seen, her other name is *bean caointe*, or keening woman. Although belief in the fairies in general has faded, belief in the banshee remains strong. In December 1998, I recorded the following description of the banshee from Patrick James McGrath, near Pettigo, County Donegal:

The banshee. (From Thomas Crofton Croker, *Fairy Legends and Traditions of the South of Ireland* [London: William Tegg, 1862], p. 110)

> You see, the banshee is a spirit, associated with the fairies. It never had a body, but sometimes it can appear as a little old woman combing her long hair, sad and weeping, weeping bitterly. Oh, Tommy Haughey and Dennis McGrath was people who heard it the night before the Haughey children were drowned in the lough. See, they were the old Celtic race of people, too, the Haugheys. The banshee always keens for the Macs and the Os, people with the old Celtic names O'Haughey, McGrath, and the like. Earlier on the Haugheys had dropped the O from their name, but they were the same race of people the banshee follows. Oh, there's something to that, now.

McGrath's description identifies most of the banshee's best-known characteristics. He also reiterates the widespread belief that the banshee is connected in particular to old Irish families rather than those of later English and Scottish planters. These families with Celtic origins are usually identified by the Mac- or O- prefixes of their surnames, and the banshee's connection to them reflects her origin in earlier Celtic mythology. Contemporary folklore does little to explain the motif of the banshee combing her long hair. Some storytellers explain that she uses the comb to rip out her hair in anguish. Others explain that the combing itself creates the keening sound associated with her. Whatever the significance of the comb, it is clearly important to the banshee. In one widespread legend, a man encounters the banshee, she drops her comb in haste, and he takes it. The next night, he awakes to high-pitched screeching and frantic clawing at his door. Realizing the banshee has returned, the man picks up her comb with iron tongs and passes it out his window. The banshee snatches her comb and is gone. When the man retrieves his tongs, he finds that they have been horribly twisted.

As the example of the banshee demonstrates, fairy lore overlaps with legends and beliefs concerning the dead. Several stories depict the dead as dancing with the fairies when and where thresholds to the Otherworld are open. Such stories reflect in Irish folklore a conflation of the fairy Otherworld with the older Celtic concept of *Tír na nÓg* (Land of the Young), a timeless land where souls of the dead live in perpetual youth. Of course, the fairies are not the only supernatural beings depicted in *seanchas*, and, especially today, as belief in the fairies wanes, stories about ghosts take precedence in supernatural legend. Traditionally, Samhain, later known as Halloween, was considered a time for not only fairies but also the souls of the dead to wander the earth. The Catholic Church incorporated this belief by establishing 2 November (the day after All Saints' Day) as All Souls' Day, a time of remembering and praying for the dead. In the wake of Christian influence, ghost legends often tell of souls who return on Halloween or All Souls' Day to ask favors from the living, especially prayers to release them from the spiritual limbo of Purgatory and allow them to ascend to Heaven.

Irish legends about ghosts appearing at other times or haunting the locations of their deaths are comparable to those in other European countries, but they often reflect features of the local scene. Patrick James McGrath, who described the banshee, also tells a local story about the ghost of Bob Gowdy. Gowdy was a poor Protestant with a small family, but he died young, at home, in the mid-1700s. His mostly agreeable ghost lingered in the Gowdy home, making sure, for instance, that his children stayed tucked in at night. Over the generations he continued to haunt the house and was generally kind to its occupants. However, during the mid-1800s, the house was occupied by "Ribbonman" McSorley, a member of a militant Catholic secret society seeking to end the landlord system. Apparently, the old and new tenants did not get along. At dusk Gowdy's ghost would annoy McSorley by blowing out his candle, and, eventually, their argument came to blows. As McGrath describes the fight, each time McSorley would land a punch "it was like driving your fist into a bag of wool," but each time the ghost returned the punch "McSorley got the full force of a sledgehammer." McSorley took ill and died within the year, and the house lay empty until a priest exorcised Gowdy's spirit, casting it into a nearby outcropping of rock. As McGrath concludes the story, "And that was that. Bob Gowdy was laid to rest then. An old story. Whether it's true or whether it's not, I'll not tell you. But that's how I got the story. There'd have to be something about it, I think. It's 'true enough,' as the saying goes."

LEGENDS

Major genres of *seanchas* or historical lore, legends of the saints recall sacred beginnings that underpin faith, and legends of fairies and ghosts recall later events that impel belief. But the greater part of *seanchas* involves the historical legend. Whether organized around past events, the places where they took place, or the individuals involved, the historical legend chronicles human behavior in the social, rather than supernatural, realm, behavior that begs contemplation. Stories in this genre are often unverifiable, but for the *seanchaí* and his or her audience, factuality is more often taken for granted in historical rather than supernatural legends. At stake are how ordinary and extraordinary people have interacted in the past and how these memorable dramas speak to us in the present.

Unlike a written academic history, legends that revolve around significant events in Irish history do not often attempt to tell the whole story on a national scale. Rather, they offer insights into the local experience and put a human face on the historian's quantifiable data. In one legend set in County Kerry during the height of the Famine, a woman is faced with the pitiful task of having to bury her daughter, a victim of disease brought on by starvation. After the burial, a neighbor woman calls the mother into her home to share what food she has. Shattered, the mother manages only to say, "Thank God it wasn't the food we buried." It is open to an audience's interpretation whether the mother's words reflect her numbed shock, make use of dark humor as a coping mechanism, or convey an understated, yet devastating, criticism of a neighbor whose assistance has come too late. However one may interpret it, the statement is undeniably arresting and underscores—in a way that mere statistics cannot convey—the desperation of common people facing the horror of the Famine. Whether or not this incident ever took place, whether or not these particular words were ever spoken, this legend eloquently addresses a larger tragedy, and it forces us in the present to feel some fraction of the darkness experienced by people in the past.

Settled in a given place, people often mentally organize the past in terms of where rather than when events took place, and in Ireland especially a large body of historical legend is brought to mind by specific sites. Traditionally, this subgenre of historical legend is referred to as *dinnsenchas* or "place lore." It includes both explanations of place-names and accounts of past events that occurred at given locations. For example, in County Fermanagh, a river crossing known as Biscuit Ford is near a field known as the Red Meadow. Hugh Nolan, this community's star historian, tells a story set in the sixteenth century that explains how these locations got their names. Resisting the Plantation of Ulster, the Irish Catholic Maguire clan sets siege to the English army occupying their ancestral stronghold of Enniskillen Castle. At a crossing in the Arney River, allies of the Maguires successfully ambush reinforcements that the English had called from Dublin. During the battle, the Irish overturn the English supply wagons midstream, and a steady stream of biscuits (small, dry cakes of bread) flows from the wagons, giving the ford its name. In a nearby meadow, the Irish force cuts down the retreating reinforcements, and the slaughter is so bloody that afterward the field becomes known as the Red Meadow.

As *dinnsenchas*, this legend fulfills its function of explaining the origin of two local place-names. Yet there is more to the legend that offers commentary on choices people must face in the present. As Nolan tells the story, the reinforcements that the English sent for included Irishmen conscripted into the English army, so the Irish victory is simultaneously a defeat, a slaughter of fellow countrymen, to be followed by a series of greater defeats resulting in Plantation. How does this story use the past to speak of the present? In 1972, when this story was recorded by Henry Glassie, Northern Ireland was consumed by civil war pitting Irish Catholics against their

Protestant neighbors and an occupying British army. Those who called for a ceili with Hugh Nolan included young Catholic men—labeled by some as terrorists—who made the bombs that killed both friend and foe. Nolan's account of the Battle of Biscuit Ford offers such men neither solutions nor directives, only a tragic theme, familiar throughout Irish history, to contemplate. Oppressed, one may have an obligation to stand up for one's rights, but neighbors and innocents die when people resort to armed struggle in their own land. Nolan's story requires men of violence to think twice, to be aware that when they disobey God's commandment not to kill, victory cannot be separated from defeat.

Offering commentary on both past and present, the historical legends reviewed thus far have revolved around important events ordered in time or located in place. Another type of historical legend takes as its primary subject the actions of historical figures. In these personal historical legends, heroes and anti-heroes abound. For instance, in the early to mid-1800s Daniel O'Connell organized the rural poor in nonviolent opposition to anti-Catholic legislation, and folklore portrays him as a figure with enough wit and eloquence to outmaneuver the entire British establishment on behalf of a subject people. By way of contrast, in the mid-seventeenth century Oliver Cromwell led a merciless campaign of British conquest throughout Ireland, and folklore portrays him as an arch-villain before whom the Devil himself bows down. After the likes of Cromwell broke the back of Catholic resistance, but before O'Connell the Liberator gave the Irish peasantry true cause for optimism, the Irish outlaw loomed large in people's imaginations, providing the material needed for popular commentary on social justice. Known in successive periods as tories, rapparees, or highwaymen, Irish outlaws emerged from the multitudes of the dispossessed to harass and rob Protestant planters, landlords, and their agents. As historical actors, these outlaws posed a relatively minor threat to British authority in Ireland, yet as symbolic figures in legends (and ballads), they allowed the Irish peasantry vicarious enjoyment of triumph in the midst of continual disappointment.

One example from many, Redmond O'Hanlon was born into an Irish Catholic family of landowners dispossessed by Cromwell. As a young man he took to the hills of his native Ulster to form a band of tories celebrated in folklore as no less heroic than the pre-Christian Fianna. In one of many legends told about O'Hanlon, he comes upon a poor widow who is crying because her landlord has threatened to evict her for failure to pay rent. O'Hanlon gives her the rent money and instructs her to get a receipt. After the landlord collects the rent and rides for home, O'Hanlon intercepts him. Holding the landlord at gunpoint, O'Hanlon retrieves the money and threatens the landlord with violence should he ever again ask the widow for rent. No one is injured, and the outlaw leaves the widow with a substantial, involuntary donation from her cowed landlord.

Combing through Irish folklore collected over the past two centuries, one finds that these same actions have also been attributed to other outlaws, including James Freney, Michael Collier, William Brennan, and Richard Power. Farther afield, the same legend is told of outlaws in Scotland, South Africa, **Australia**, and the United States. In fact, all over the world, the outlaw is portrayed in the folklore of oppressed people as their champion who robs the rich to supply the poor. Once recognized, these patterns call into question the factuality of outlaw legends, but the key issue raised by these legends is not whether the events depicted actually happened. More important is what these stories reveal about the experience, values, and concerns of the people who tell them. Outlaw legends come from people hobbled by failure but quite sure of what is right and wrong. From the perspective of the Irish peasantry, official law under the landlord system is oppressive and bereft of moral authority. By breaking the law, the outlaw becomes a folk hero rather than a mere criminal. Symbolizing the virtue of loyalty to kin and community, outlaw legends articulate a popular sense of social justice and condemn the inequity of the British colonial system. Later nationalists interested in stirring the masses to support an independent Ireland took a special interest in outlaw lore.

Recalling aspects of the past that are relevant to us in the present, *seanchas* remains popular today. Depending on the interests of contemporary audiences, certain stories may be forgotten while others may be invented or adopted, but *seanchas* as a category of storytelling promises to continue. Indeed, recently a young man in County Tyrone told me a story that cast the ghost of a Scottish soldier killed in Northern Ireland as the internationally known Vanishing Hitchhiker of urban legend. In contrast to *seanchas* in its many forms, *scéalaíocht* told in English and Irish is in decline. In the midst of **modernization** and changing tastes, parents may amuse and educate their children with folktales, but most adults turn to the mass media for the entertainment offered by fantasy. Today a primary audience for those who can tell traditional *Märchen* and hero tales is, in fact, folklorists. Yet there remains one final branch of traditional Irish storytelling that has no native label but nonetheless thrives whenever and wherever people gather for conversation. This branch of narrative includes the mostly humorous genres of tall tale, local character anecdote, and joke.

TALL TALES

Also popular in the United States, the tall tale is a fictional folk narrative that begins within the frame of a realistic story but builds through exaggeration toward implausible fantasy. For example, Patrick James McGrath tells a story about a character known as the Buffer in his community on the Donegal-Tyrone border. The story begins plausibly with the Buffer traveling to the port city of Derry to catch a boat for Scotland, a common experience in the recent past for many Irish Catholics who migrated at least temporarily to earn higher wages. The Buffer misses his boat and, lacking the funds for lodging, decides to spend the night inside one of the famous, massive cannons on the fortified walls of Derry. By a fluke, the cannon is fired, but all turns out well for the Buffer, who lands in Glasgow for no money at all.

Using traditional plots and motifs, many tall tales are already well known to their audiences, so the effectiveness and humor of these stories depend on the imaginations and verbal talents of their narrators rather than on the originality of their material. In other cases, a tall tale may be invented on the spot as a form of expressive lying, also known as "codding," intended to test the gullibility of an audience. Such was the case when County Tyrone man Paddy Hilley told a group of adults and youngsters sitting up at a wake the following story about a local bachelor, Willie McHugh, who died in the 1950s. Apparently, McHugh was a miserly, old-fashioned sort who lived with his livestock in a rough, filthy house. As Paddy tells it, one day Willie was taken into the hospital, but the nurses were compelled to bathe him before anything else. They stripped off his clothes and scrubbed him with brushes, but the dirt was stubborn. Finally, one nurse got the idea that they might have better luck scraping him with spoons. In the end, "the nurses were beat." As Hilley said, "They were scraping probably fifteen minutes, when they come on another shirt." During that particular performance, most of the adults had figured out that Hilley's story was a fictional tall tale, but both they and Hilley took great delight from the wide-eyed looks of the youngsters, who believed Hilley's every word.

ANECDOTES AND JOKES

Today many people in rural areas continue to swap entertaining stories at ceilis, but the art of storytelling is perhaps best preserved at wakes such as the one where Patrick Hilley told his tall tale. When neighbors convene to console bereaved relatives, televisions and radios are silenced, and people pay their respects with a prayer over the deceased's body, then pass the time in conversation. At the contemporary wakes of elderly people who have died a natural death, sadness is mixed with the older, more raucous spirit of the traditional wake, and people sit up all night, entertaining each other with tall tales, jokes, and especially local character anecdotes. Local character anecdotes are brief, often humorous biographical sketches about noteworthy or eccentric community members. These stories are told as true, but they often incorporate traditional, migratory motifs and punch lines. For instance, an anecdote Billy McGrath tells about Joe Byrne of Ardara, County Donegal, places Byrne in a battle of wits with his hateful sister-in-law. At the climax of the story, the sister-in-law tells him, "Joe Byrne, if I was married to you, I would give you poison." "You know this," Byrne replies, "if I was married to you, I would surely take it." The same words have been attributed to Winston Churchill, George Bernard Shaw, and Samuel Johnson in similar situations. By telling the anecdote as if it were nonfiction, Billy McGrath's objective is not deception, as in some tall tales. His goal is to establish the sort of person Joe Byrne is by telling us the sort of thing Joe Byrne would say.

Through anecdotes an actual individual comes to exemplify one of a number of recurring character types that are appreciated by storytellers and audiences alike as distinctive to their local community. Some character types such as the gossip, the fool, or the rough bachelor introduced in Patrick Hilley's tall tale are remembered for a laugh, and a certain amount of good-natured criticism is implied. Other character types such as clever talkers, resourceful tricksters, and wily smugglers are remembered for their wit, which reflects brightly on themselves and the community that generates them. Identifying the foibles and virtues of a range of local characters, anecdotes popular in a given parish or town catalog shared values and serve as a community study initiated by locals long before any ethnographer arrived on the scene.

Like local character anecdotes, jokes also provide humorous entertainment while offering keen observations about human nature. However, unlike anecdotes, jokes are told and received as fictions, and they are not tied to any specific community. Both of these differences allow jokes to touch upon subjects such as adultery that are too sensitive for purportedly nonfictional anecdotes, which portray one's own neighbors.

Most jokes popular in Ireland are similar to those in other countries, but one cycle of jokes native to Ireland deserves attention. In wide circulation over the last fifty years, scores of "Paddy and the Yank" jokes reflect the amusement and annoyance Irish people experience when American tourists or even their own emigrant relations put on airs of sophistication when they visit the "Old Country." These jokes invariably depict an American (the Yank) who is brash and boastful and an Irishman (Paddy) who, though poorer and less educated, uses superior wit to deflate the Yank's sense of self-importance. One of the most popular of these jokes portrays the Yank bragging to Paddy about the size of his ranch back in Texas. As Patrick McElhill of Ederney, County Fermanagh, tells it, the Yank pushes back his cowboy hat and says, "Why, it takes me two whole days just to drive around it in my car!" Unimpressed, Paddy replies, "Aye, I'd an old car like that one time, but I had the good sense to get rid of her."

If certain genres of storytelling such as tales about heroic kings and warriors, for example, no longer resonate as much as they did in the past, other genres such as jokes and anecdotes about local characters flourish in response to the tastes and concerns of present generations. The currency of specific examples of folklore may fade, but folklore as a process of human expression and interaction will always exist, enfolding past example and present context. Scholars have only recently adopted this less pessimistic perspective on folklore as a process of adapting tradition to changing circumstances rather than as a dying commodity.

STUDIES OF IRISH FOLKLORE

Useful histories of the study of Irish folklore include Dorson's foreword to O'Sullivan (1966) and the introduction to Glassie (1985). Ó Giolláin has recently (2000) published a book-length treatment of the philosophical and political underpinnings of Irish folklore studies over the last 250 years. Influenced by Romanticism, late eighteenth- and nineteenth-century antiquarians collected folklore, in part, because they viewed traditional ways of life to be authentic and praiseworthy but doomed in the face of modernization. Growing out of travel literature while developing a literary form of **ethnography**, key texts in this vein include Croker (1969 [1824], 1998 [1825]). After Croker and until the late nineteenth century, Irish folklore was most often represented for educated audiences by the literary sketches and novels of authors such as Samuel Lover (1831), William Carleton (1990 [1843–1844]), and Patrick Kennedy (1989 [1875]). Later literary greats such as Lady Augusta Gregory (1904), William Butler Yeats (1986 [1888]), and John Millington Synge (1992 [1907]) collected folklore and borrowed from it in composing some of their best prose, poetry, and drama. Influenced as much by **nationalism** as by Romanticism, many late nineteenth- through mid-twentieth-century collectors also considered their work a patriotic act of rescuing the relics of a Golden Age of Irish Culture that pre-dated British colonization. In the late nineteenth century, Douglas Hyde in particular championed efforts to collect folklore in the Irish-speaking west. He considered the language to be essential to Irish identity and Irish-language folklore to be most characteristic of the cultural distinctiveness that supported the nationalist case for Irish self-determination. In addition to privileging Irish-language materials in a nationalistic era, Hyde is responsible for another turning point in the collection and representation of Irish folklore. Hyde (1890) ushered in an era of publishing direct transcriptions of folklore texts and faithful translations in an effort to be more "scientific."

Committed to preserving Irish national identity, James Delargy (Séamus Ó Duilearga) answered Hyde's call for more rigorous study and pioneered the institutionalization of folklore studies in a newly independent Ireland. Having edited the Irish folklore journal *Béaloideas* since 1927, Delargy became head of the Irish Folklore Commission, established in 1935 by the Irish government. The commission employed the first full-time, professional folklorists in Ireland, who have amassed more than 2 million manuscript pages now housed in the Department of Irish Folklore at University College Dublin. Sent by Delargy to study archiving and the historic-geographic method in Sweden, Sean O'Sullivan (Seán Ó Suilleabháin) wrote *A Handbook of Irish Folklore* (1942), which has been used as a guide by collectors ever since. O'Sullivan's other classics include a collection of Irish folktales (1966), an overview of custom and belief (1967), and, with Reidar Christiansen, an index of Irish folktale types (1967). Following Delargy and O'Sullivan, other excellent Irish folklorists who have authored book-length studies include Danaher (1972), Lysaght (1996), and Ó Catháin (1982). In general, scholars in Northern Ireland have concentrated more on the material dimensions of Irish peasant society that have survived into the twentieth century. This Northern scholarship is presented in the journal *Ulster Folklife*, and the best single work in this tradition is Evans (1957). Although folklorists continue to conduct productive archival research and document Irish folklore in danger of extinction, they have also expanded their mission from salvage ethnography to an examination of culture as it is reflected in, and constituted by, folklore performed in contemporary settings. The best example of this ethnographic approach to folklore in use is Henry Glassie's monumental study of one County Fermanagh community (1982).

BIBLIOGRAPHY

Breathnach, Breandán. 1971. *Folk Music and Dances of Ireland*. Cork: Mercier Press.

Buttimer, Neil, Colin Rynne, and Helen Guerin, eds. 2000. *The Heritage of Ireland*. Cork: Collins Press.

Carleton, William. 1990 (1843–1844). *Traits and Stories of the Irish Peasantry*. 2 volumes. Savage, MD: Barnes and Noble.

Casey, Daniel J., and Robert E. Rhodes, eds. 1977. *Views of the Irish Peasantry 1800–1916*. Hamden, CT: Archon.

Croker, T. Crofton. 1969 (1824). *Researches in the South of Ireland*. Shannon: Irish University Press.

———. 1998 (1825). *Fairy Legends and Traditions of the South of Ireland*. Cork: Collins Press.

Danaher, Kevin. 1972. *The Year in Ireland*. Cork: Mercier Press.

Delargy, James (Séamus Ó Duilearga). 1969 (1945). *The Gaelic Story-Teller*. Chicago: University of Chicago Press.

Evans, E. Estyn. 1957. *Irish Folk Ways*. New York: Routledge.

Glassie, Henry. 1982. *Passing the Time in Ballymenone*. Philadelphia: University of Pennsylvania Press.

————. 1985. *Irish Folktales*. New York: Penguin.

Gregory, Lady Augusta. 1904. *Gods and Fighting Men*. London: John Murray.

Harvey, Cloddagh Brennan. 1992. *Contemporary Irish Traditional Narrative: The English Language Tradition*. Berkeley: University of California Press.

Hyde, Douglas. 1890. *Beside the Fire*. London: David Nutt.

Kennedy, Patrick. 1989 (1875). *The Banks of Boro*. Enniscorthy: Duffrey Press.

Lover, Samuel. 1831. *Legends and Stories of Ireland*. Dublin: W. F. Wakeman.

Lysaght, Patricia. 1996. *The Banshee*. Dublin: O'Brien Press.

Ó Catháin, Séamas. 1982. *Irish Life and Lore*. Cork: Mercier Press.

Ó Giolláin, Diarmuid. 2000. *Locating Irish Folklore: Tradition, Modernity, Identity*. Cork: Cork University Press.

Ó hEochaidh, Seán, Máire Mac Néill, and Séamas Ó Catháin, eds. 1977. *Fairy Legends from Donegal*. Dublin: Dundalgan Press.

Ó hÓgáin, Dáithí. 1991. *Myth, Legend & Romance: An Encyclopaedia of the Irish Folk Tradition*. New York: Prentice Hall.

O'Sullivan, Sean (Seán Ó Súilleabháin). 1942. *A Handbook of Irish Folklore*. Dublin: Educational Company of Ireland.

————. 1966. *Folktales of Ireland*. Chicago: University of Chicago Press.

————. 1967. *Irish Folk Custom and Belief*. Dublin: Three Candles.

O'Sullivan, Sean, and Reidar Christiansen. 1967. *The Types of the Irish Folktale*. Folklore Fellows Communications 188. Helsinki: Suomalainen Tiedeakatemia.

Shields, Hugh. 1993. *Narrative Singing in Ireland*. Dublin: Irish Academic Press.

Synge, John Millington. 1992 (1907). *The Aran Islands*. New York: Penguin.

Yeats, William Butler. 1986 (1888). *Irish Fairy and Folk Tales*. New York: Dorset Press.

Zimmerman, Georges Denis. 2001. *The Irish Storyteller*. Dublin: Four Courts Press.

Ray Cashman

ISLE OF MAN

GEOGRAPHY AND HISTORY

Less than thirty-three by thirteen miles in area, the Isle of Man is a small island located in the center of the British Isles. Although geographically at the center, it is not part of the United Kingdom but rather is a British Crown Dependency with its own government. The island's history, culture, and folklore exhibit a unique mixture of the influences of the surrounding countries of **England**, **Ireland**, **Scotland**, and **Wales**. As a result many aspects of Manx culture and its folklore may be viewed as variations of those found in the broader British and Irish context, while others are distinctive to the Isle of Man.

The island has been described as a microcosm of the British Isles in terms of its physical geography because of its wide variety of topography and landforms. These range from a central mountain massif, upland moorlands, undulating pastoral hills to the south, and flat northern glacial plains to sheer rocky cliffs and long, sandy cliffs and beaches. The island's central position in the Irish Sea and the Gulf Stream means that it has a temperate maritime climate with mild winter and summer temperatures.

The island has been continuously occupied since the Mesolithic period (8000 B.C.E.). A major difference, though, between Manx history and that of lowland mainland Britain is that neither the Romans nor the Anglo-Saxons colonized the island. Instead, the defining culture on the island from 500 B.C.E. to 800 C.E. was the "Celtic" Iron Age and the subsequent arrival of Christianity after 500 C.E. The first major external cultural influence to affect the island came with the Viking raids in the late eighth century, resulting in permanent Norse settlements. The significance of the Norse period is shown by the number of "Norse" survivals still to be found, including place-names, surnames, political institutions such as Tynwald (the Manx Parliament), settlement patterns, and archeological sites.

The island's location in the middle of the Irish Sea made it both a target and a stronghold for its Norse occupants, and its highly strategic location made it an important maritime trading center throughout its history. It has also ensured that neighboring powers have wanted to rule the island and thereby establish and control a major stronghold on this significant maritime route. Following the collapse of the Norse kingdom, the island became a pawn in the power struggles between the English and the Scottish Crowns during the thirteenth and fourteenth centuries. The island achieved political stability only in 1405, when Sir John Stanley was appointed the hereditary King of Man as a reward for his loyal duty to, and support of, the English Crown. The title later became Lord of Man, as Stanley decided he would rather be a "Great Lord rather than a Petty King." The Stanleys were not permanently resident on the island but maintained large estates in northern England. They did, though, establish "royal" residences at the island's two medieval castles, Peel Castle and Castle Rushen. A point of debate is whether this English-speaking population would have had much significant interaction with, or cultural impact upon, the wider and numerically much larger Gaelic-speaking Manx population.

The island's reliance on commercial trade, viewed as smuggling or the "running trade" by the British and Irish Exchequers because the island imposed lower taxes, was brought to an abrupt halt in 1765 with the passing of the "Mischief Act" and the Revestment (purchase) of the Lord of Man's hereditary rights to the island's taxes and duties by the British Crown. The island's trading economy collapsed almost immediately and took a considerable period of time to re-establish itself over the next century. The nineteenth century was characterized by the growth and development of transport links between the island and Britain, beginning with the establishment of a regular packet service by the Isle of Man Steam Packet Company in 1830. The improved transport links and later harbor facilities also helped to improve conditions for the island's existing staple industries of farming, fishing, and lead mining and also underpinned the success of a new industrial base of tourism. The tourist industry was eventually to eclipse financially all the other industries. Though recognized as a fundamental part of the Manx economy, it has also been viewed and blamed for the decline and loss of "traditional" Manx culture—in particular, the decline of the Manx Gaelic language. The seasonal influx of tourists was seen as a necessary financial evil but also as a corrupting and diluting influence on the Manx. Although tourism continued to be an important part of the Manx economy through the early part of the twentieth century, by the 1960s it had begun to decline in absolute terms—along with the majority of other British tourist resorts—in the face of competition by cheaper foreign package holidays. The decline of the tourist industry was accompanied by ongoing decline in the island's primary industries of farming and fishing.

Migration from the island, a common feature of island life since the early nineteenth century, reached its zenith in the 1950s and led to the island's population reaching its lowest figure since the 1840s. The political solution to the economic and population decline was the introduction by the Tynwald of various tax policies to attract investment and new residents to the island. Since the 1980s, Tynwald policy has been to establish and maintain the island as an offshore finance center. Its success, however, has led to allegations that the finance sector is a factor in causing negative and detrimental cultural change on the island in the same way that **tourism** was viewed a century before.

FUNCTIONS OF MANX FOLKLORE

The earliest published account of Manx folklore is *A Description of the Isle of Man* by George Waldron (1731), which concentrates predominantly on what are now considered the classic myths and legends of the island and the importance of fairy belief to the Manx population. It contains the most archetypal of Manx folktales, which are Manx variations of common and well-known British and European folktales. These include the accounts of *Moddey Dhoo* (Black Dog) of Peel Castle, descriptions of the subterranean mansions and giant believed to be found under Castle Rushen, and tales of fairies who intrude on human life in a variety of ways and who will steal babies and leave fairy changelings in their place. Subsequent collection and publication of Manx folklore resulted from commercial antiquarianism, as folklore was used to provide "local color" for tourist guidebooks and tours of the Isle of Man through the nineteenth and twentieth centuries. This may still be viewed as an important function of Manx folklore, which has been used as the basis for an official tourist board publicity campaign and for a road safety campaign for the international TT motorcycle races.

Another contemporaneous and continuing function of Manx folklore has been as both symbol and embodiment of Manx cultural identity. As a result, collecting and publishing of Manx folklore material were considered an important part of the Manx "cultural revival" at the turn of the nineteenth and twentieth centuries, together with the preservation and promotion of the rapidly declining Manx Gaelic language. Unfortunately, several generations of Manx folklorists believed that it was already too late to collect anything of real importance and that the most authentic material had already been lost, an opinion that pervaded until the late twentieth century.

Published accounts of Manx folklore tend to emphasize the existence of a static and timeless corpus of Manx folklore as part of a "traditional" Manx way of life that has been lost or is being lost due to rapid cultural changes resulting from cultural **globalization** and homogenization. This ahistorical view of the island's culture ignores both the dynamic nature of Manx folklore, past and present, and also the new and modified forms of folklore to be found on the island in the twenty-first century.

FAIRY LORE

Fairy belief has permeated all aspects of Manx folklore. This ranges from the wide variety of supernatural creatures found on the Isle of Man to the importance of fairies as either the perpetrators of ill-wishing and the evil eye or as the providers of cures and remedies for such afflictions. The human counterparts of the fairies with regard to ill-wishing and healing are the associated figures of witches, wisewomen, and fairy doctors, who were viewed almost as emissaries of the fairies, since their powers were frequently thought to have emanated from the fairy realm. The influence of fairies and fairy belief on the island also extended to how the Manx perceived and interpreted the landscape around them and can be seen in several Manx calendar customs and elements of occupational folklore. It is even given as the source for some of the island's traditional music.

The Manx fairy is not the typical gossamer-winged creature of traditional European fairy tales or modern-day children's cartoons, but rather a small, humanlike creature dressed in green or blue with a red, peaked cap. In keeping with fairy belief throughout Europe, Manx fairies were considered to be sociable creatures who occupied a parallel dimension. Although they only occasionally came into direct contact with humans, the island's landscape was interpreted as evidence of extensive fairy activity. Therefore, prehistoric burial mounds were seen as fairy hills and portals to underground fairy kingdoms, where great feasts and banquets were held. Large tracts of the island were considered to be the traditional hunting grounds of the fairy host or the sites of great battles between rival bands of fairies. As with many supernatural creatures, it was considered dangerous to talk about fairies directly since it would unnecessarily attract their attention and notice. It is still common practice to use a variety of euphemisms when referring to fairies. These include *Themselves* and *Mooinjer Veggey* (Manx Gaelic for the "little people"). The attitude of the Manx to *Themselves* has traditionally been one of vigilant caution since fairies have an ambivalent reputation of being both mischievous and neither intrinsically good nor evil. Instead, they are seen as being opportunistic, and, if treated well, they will be helpful. But if they feel themselves to be in any way affronted, intentionally or not, they will react in a malignant and potentially violent manner. The need to be polite is still recognized on the island, and as a result Manx residents and visitors alike are careful to say "Hello" to *Themselves* as they cross the Fairy Bridge on the main Douglas to Castletown road. This is a widespread custom that is still commonly practiced, though it is often no more than a slight raising of the hand as the bridge is crossed—a gesture frequently seen on the island's public transport or when traveling in a group. Although the original and "authentic" Fairy Bridge is farther downstream on the old foot track, it is worth noting that the Fairy Bridge tradition can be traced back only to the nineteenth century. The practice of telling people to say hello to the fairies is extremely popular among the island's coach and taxi drivers and, one suspects, earlier charabanc drivers. Therefore, it is possible that one of the most popular Manx customs is the product of nineteenth-century tourism rather than a centuries-old Manx fairy belief. But this does not make it any less authentic as an expression of Manx folklore.

In the local souvenir shops one can buy postcards of the Fairy Bridge and even small pixie figures for charm bracelets (which have been dipped in the stream at the Fairy Bridge to make them more effective). The folklore surrounding the bridge is evolving all the time. A recent development has been the hanging of small messages and plaques on the thorn tree adjacent to the bridge. On closer inspection these are requests made to the fairies for good luck, in particular, success with the lottery. This is an interesting development of an older folkloric tradition of hanging rags on a thorn tree by a well or spring known for its healing properties. The logic behind this use of sympathetic magic holds that as a rag that had been used to apply the healing water to an ailment rotted away, so the ailment would also disappear. In the case of the Fairy Bridge, several of the messages and requests are written on plastic plaques or sheets of headed notepaper put into plastic bags so they will not deteriorate with the weather. The tradition seems to date from about 1997–1998, with a dramatic increase being witnessed during the Tynwald period (the annual open-air sitting of the Manx Parliament on Old Midsummer's Day), and several of the messages were written on hotel notepaper, apparently by visiting overseas delegates of the Commonwealth Parliamentary Association. One assumes that it began with one specific group and is now becoming more universally practiced, though many local residents disapprove of the custom and think the notes should be removed.

A Manx fairy good luck charm for sale in the window of a tourist souvenir shop, Douglas, Isle of Man, 1990s. The charm has been dipped in the stream at the Fairy Bridge to enhance its effectiveness. (Photograph by Yvonne Creswell)

A considerable proportion of Manx folklore revolves around placating *Themselves* through the observance of numerous positive preventive procedures, the provision of a variety of protective barriers, and finally a range of cures and remedies if all else has failed. The first line of defense was to leave food and fresh water by the *chiollagh* (open hearth) as a supper for *Themselves* before going to bed. It was felt to be equally important never to throw wastewater out the door at night before first calling a warning to *Themselves* so that they would not be soaked with it. These apparently meaningless superstitions may be viewed as having important and pragmatic reasons underlying them. The abstract concept of fairy belief is made more concrete and real by the physical ritual of leaving out food for *Themselves*, thereby reinforcing the belief particularly for young children. The belief that *Themselves* regularly entered the family home and could be found in the middle of the night sitting around the hearth may have been one that parents wanted consciously to foster to discourage children from getting out of bed in the middle of the night and going near an extremely dangerous and unguarded turf (peat) fire in the dark. This was particularly true of the traditional single-storied Manx cottage, where children slept in a cock loft with only a ladder for access. The use of existing folklore beliefs, for example, fairies and

St. Trinian's Church. Legend holds that a *buggane* removed its roof.

supernatural creatures lurking in dangerous places such as deep pools and near steep cliffs, as a form of verbal control of children is well documented throughout the world, and several examples can be found in Manx folklore.

The fairy hosts were only one part of the island's bestiary of supernatural creatures, though they were the most numerous. In contrast to the communal and sociable fairies, there was the *phynnodderee*, the solitary fairy. The *phynnodderee* was distinguished by his great height and his naked and hairy appearance. He was the equivalent of the house elf or brownie and was closely associated with specific farms where he would work prodigiously, doing the work of several farm laborers. The *phynnodderee* was, however, easily offended and would leave a farm immediately when given a gift of a set of clothes. In contrast to the hardworking, but temperamental, *phynnodderee*, the Manx *buggane* was a truly malevolent, hobgoblinlike creature whose most famous feat was the repeated tearing off of the roof of St. Trinian's Church. The latter has been an essential tale in Manx tourist guides since the mid-nineteenth century and is still one of the best known on the Isle of Man, though it does not appear in Waldron's eighteenth-century account of Manx folklore. Therefore, it may be possible that the tale of the *buggane* of St. Trinian's was created or developed specifically for the tourist industry to provide a colorful explanation to answer the questions of curious tourists about the origins of the roofless church. Other supernatural creatures would initially appear to be perfectly normal, and only on closer inspection would their true nature become apparent. These included the *glashtin*, the water horse, and the *tarroo ushtey*, the water bull. Each was known to be immensely powerful and to frequent dangerous stretches of water, where they drowned their unsuspecting victims. As a result, children would be told not to play near various streams and rivers for fear of being taken by the *glashtin* or *tarroo ushtey*—another potential example of using folklore to control and modify the behavior of children in dangerous situations.

Indeed, many of the island's folktales relating to the fairies may be regarded as cautionary tales for both children and adults. They are similar in form to modern urban folk and contemporary legends, since they are usually geographically and temporally specific and often relate to a named or known individual. They highlight the inherent dangers of certain behavior such as laziness in traditional examples of trying to profit as an individual from dealing with *Themselves* rather than maintaining the common good of the community. It may also be noted that less scrupulous storytellers or even whole communities may have exploited these fears and concerns. As a result, it should be considered that a section of Manx coastline now known to have been used by smugglers was also the site of a series of caves that were traditionally home to the "fairy coopers," who worked throughout the night making their barrels and whom it was extremely unlucky to disturb or to see. Strange lights seen at night off this coast were also said to be examples of the "fairy fishing fleet." In the same area, a phantom coach might be seen with a headless driver, an omen of impending death for all who saw it. Therefore, it is not surprising that few would admit to seeing a coach in the middle of the night near the "big house," home to the local magistrate, merchant, and gentleman "smuggler."

The level of protection required against fairies depended on who occupied a house and also varied throughout the year. The most vulnerable members of a household were newborn babies and their mothers. Consequently, several Manx tales tell of babies and young women being taken by *Themselves* and a fairy changeling being left in their places. The traditional remedies were to ensure that neither was left alone, but if this was not possible, then a pair of iron tongs would be placed across the cradle because iron was considered a highly potent material against the power of fairies. Another form of protection was to sew the most powerful of Manx herbs, Vervain, into the child's nightgown. But the most effective, long-term form of protection was considered to be baptism, the first rite of passage. If a child or woman were taken by the fairies, the Manx attitude was generally to care for the fairy changeling and hope that the human might be finally returned. The changeling child or the "child that ceases to thrive" is now thought to be a pre-medical explanation for children with a variety of pediatric developmental conditions such as autism and, in the cases of women, may potentially be post-natal depression. The fairy changeling interpretation may be viewed as a relatively humane response to a condition that in many societies would be viewed as a punishment from the god(s) and result in the condemnation of the parents by the community.

CALENDAR CUSTOMS

The potentially most dangerous point in the Manx calendar, as in the rest of upland pastoral Britain, was a time when lowland, arable Britain was celebrating fertility with wild festivities: the beginning of May and the summer. For pastoral communities, this is a vulnerable time when the dairy cows are put out for summer grazing. Therefore, May Eve, the beginning of summer and the end of winter, may be viewed as liminal or threshold periods, dangerous times when the spirits were considered to be at their most active and potent and when increased levels of protection were seen as being essential. Traditionally, this involved laying yellow primroses and kingcups on the doorstep to protect the threshold into the house and making *crosh cuirns* (rowan or mountain ash crosses) to be hung over the door as an added form of protection. The *crosh cuirns* were also hung over the doors to the cowhouse and even tied to the tails of the cows to prevent them from being ill-wished and ceasing to produce milk. As well as the intimate family-oriented aspects of Manx folklore practiced on May Eve, it was also traditional for the younger members of the community to go up to the hills and set the gorse alight and then for the cattle to be driven through the smoldering ashes of the burnt gorse. Although the latter is frequently noted by

Manx folklorists as a traditional custom, its apparent function as a protective and/or cleansing ritual may have been misconstrued. An early nineteenth-century Manx newspaper account notes that an outside commentator reported on the burning of the gorse as being a superstitious ritual. In reality its function was to burn off the dead vegetation and to "clean" the cattle after a winter being kept in the cowhouse. The hot ash cleansed the hooves, and the smoke killed parasites in their coats before they were turned out into the summer pastures. The custom probably also provided the young people involved with a considerable amount of amusement. Since the superstitious and ritualistic explanation has been maintained as the "authentic" interpretation in subsequent folklore publications, contrary to the actual newspaper account of the time, it highlights the dangers when folklorists interpret actions without actually asking the participants what they are doing and why. Although the function of a *crosh cuirn* as protection for one's cattle or household from evil spirits is no longer necessary, these crosses are still made and put over a front door on May Eve. The action has remained the same through time, though its function has changed, the *crosh cuirn* now being a badge or emblem of Manx cultural identity. *Crosh cuirns* are most typically found in the home of older Manx people who are proud of their Manx antecedents or younger people, not necessarily Manx, who are Manx Gaelic speakers and are involved in cultural activities such as Manx music and dance.

The traditional element of juvenile mischief, superseded by cultural revival and modern Manx cultural identity, can also be seen in the Manx calendar customs surrounding Halloween, known in the Manx context as *Hop tu naa*, and the Christmas period of *Y Kegeesh Ommydagh* or Foolish Fortnight. Historically, *Hop tu naa* has been considered the Celtic New Year, marking the end of the summer and the beginning of winter. It was a time when people could celebrate that the harvest had been safely gathered and that all necessary preparations had been made for the winter ahead. In the nineteenth century, 31 October was known as *Thump the Door Night* on the Isle of Man, and boys would go out with cabbage stalks and turnips and *thump* people's doors until they came out to hear them sing the *Hop tu naa* song, which survives in many variants in both English and Manx Gaelic. When they had been rewarded with apples and maybe some sweets and the odd penny, they would then go on to the next house. The boys would also indulge in mischief by swapping people's field and house gates and playing practical jokes on neighbors. While the young boys went out singing, the girls would stay at home and practice divination by trying to look into the future to find out whom they were going to marry. Divination rites included sitting in front of a mirror with a candle and looking intently into the mirror until one saw one's future husband's face. Another custom involved peeling an apple and throwing the apple skin over the shoulder, the shape of the fallen apple skin assuming the form of the first letter of the future husband's name. Girls might also make a *soddag valloo* (dumb cake), a cake made of flour, eggs (shells and all), salt, and soot, which had to be made and eaten in silence. The makers then had to walk backwards to bed, where they would dream that night of their future husband. Folklorists have concentrated on the highly ritualistic elements of making the cake, in particular the potentially highly symbolic ingredients and the inversions and reversals of normal behavior. In practice, though, attempts by a group of young women to make and eat such a disgusting concoction in silence were probably not the solemn ritual normally envisaged but highly enjoyable and entertaining affairs, particularly for older married women who did not have to eat the cake.

By the early twentieth century divination does not appear to have been practiced, which may be the result of wider societal changes regarding young women and the changing form of courtship rituals. But it may also relate to whether in a post–World War I era, divination was felt to be an appropriate and acceptable parlor game. Instead of young boys, mixed-gender groups of children would go out in the evening with a carved turnip lantern singing versions of the *Hop tu naa* song. Making a turnip lantern was, and still appears to be, gender-specific, with fathers hollowing out the lantern with the children, while mothers helped decorate the lantern with a face carved on one side and maybe stars and moons and other patterns on the other side. Twentieth-century changes to Manx *Hop tu naa* have included the development of *guising*, the use of costumes. Although common in Scotland and Ireland at Halloween, costumes were not traditionally an element of Manx *Hop tu naa*. Most children now go out in costumes, dressed up as witches and ghouls and assorted monsters, and carry torches or plastic lanterns rather than turnips with candles. However, many still sing the *Hop tu naa* song and, like their predecessors, wait expectantly for sweets and hopefully some money. The importance and relevance of money have equally not changed, as its function was to purchase fireworks for Bonfire Night on 5 November.

Although for children *Hop tu naa* still fulfills its original function of providing an opportunity for relatively unregulated fun, enjoyment, and legitimized begging, it now has an additional function of providing an important benchmark for the state of Manx cultural identity. Heated discussion has taken place since the 1990s in the Manx press as to whether 31 October is being celebrated on the island as American "Trick or Treat," English "Halloween," or Manx *Hop tu naa*. As a result there have been a resurgence in the use of the term *Hop tu naa* and a proliferation of *Hop tu naa* events staged by Manx cultural bodies to stem what is perceived as a domination of the Manx calendar custom by "foreign" Halloween customs and growing commercialization.

The Christmas period, "Foolish Fortnight" or *Y Kegeesh Ommydagh*, lasted for twelve days and nights and began on

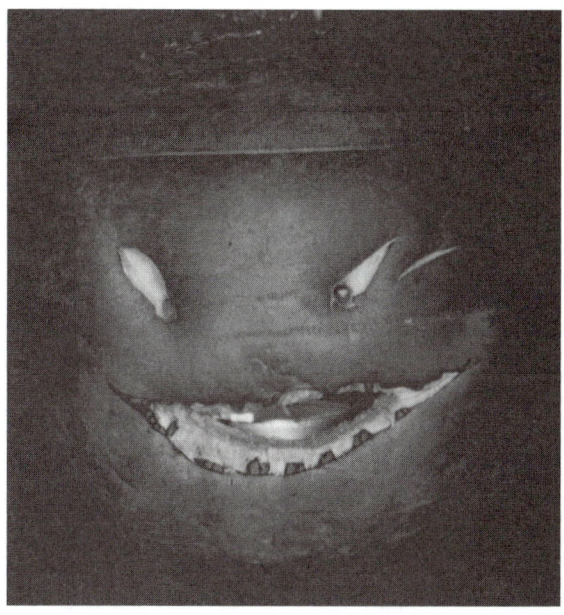

A carved *Hop tu naa* turnip lantern. (Photograph by Yvonne Cresswell)

The photographer's son costumed as a character from a television program about to go door-to-door singing the *Hop tu naa* song "Jinny the Witch" and collecting sweets and money. (Photograph by Yvonne Cresswell)

Christmas Eve with the *Oie'l Voirrey* or *Verree* service (Eve of the Feast of Mary) held in the parish churches. Originally, this was an informal church service, which could last several hours while individuals or small groups would sing *carvals* (Manx carols) they had written for the entertainment and often unintended amusement of the congregation. The *carvals* were written and sung in Manx Gaelic and now constitute one of the most important collections of Manx literature. By the 1890s, these relatively riotous gatherings of young people had been replaced by more sober affairs of organized services with choirs and "traditional" Christmas carols sung in English. The tradition of the *Oie'l Voirrey* is still maintained in some rural chapels with the staging of popular sacred music concerts, though they are now held anytime in the winter months rather than specifically on Christmas Eve.

Another essential part of a Manx Christmas were the White Boys, who performed a mummers' play about St. George and his battle with a Turkish knight, a greatly modified version of the St. George and the dragon hero/combat play. The characters wore white "dresses" bedecked with ribbons, colored papers, and tinsel and matching tall, conical cardboard hats while the "doctor," who miraculously cures the Turkish knight killed by St. George, is dressed all in black. The "doctor" collects contributions from the crowd and also berates (and beats) the audience with an inflated pig's bladder on a stick if they approach too closely to the "stage."

The highlight of St. Stephen's Day (also known as Boxing Day) has been Hunt the Wren, a custom once widespread throughout the British Isles. Originally, it was quite a bloodthirsty ritual as gangs of youths would scour the countryside looking for a wren to trap and kill, but now a more humane option is to use an artificial bird. The wren then became the centerpiece for a "bush," composed of two wooden hoops set at right angles and placed on top of a pole and covered with ribbons and evergreens. The "bush" would then be carried from house to house while the group sang the "Hunt the Wren" song and hoped to collect some money or treats for their troubles. The song charts the progress of the poor wren being hunted, caught, cooked, and then eaten. The many suggestions for why the poor wren should be singled out for such treatment include its being a commemoration of the martyrdom of St. Stephen or revenge on the wren because it is the reincarnation of an enchantress who lured men to their death by drowning. The feathers of the wren are distributed among the "wren" boys as a good luck charm, being particularly potent against witchcraft and to prevent shipwreck, an important concern for Manx fishermen.

Both the White Boys and Hunt the Wren have undergone similar developments throughout the nineteenth and twentieth centuries. From being acceptable forms of recreation for young men, they increasingly became socially unacceptable, together with the associated concept of "legitimized begging." By the early decades of the twentieth century only young boys could participate in the activities, and then by the 1920s the White Boys play was no longer performed in the public streets but became rather an object of cultural heritage to be performed in the sanitized context and environment of the local **museum**. The latter part of the twentieth century saw another major change as individuals involved in Manx language, music, dance, and politics revived the tradition of performing the White Boys play in the local streets, public houses, and even shopping centers on the Saturday before Christmas. There are also increasing numbers of groups going out on 26 December to perform Hunt the Wren at various places around the island.

The motivations for these individuals and groups to participate in Manx folklore are probably as numerous as the people involved: raising money for charity, a desire to maintain and promote Manx heritage and traditions, spending time with friends, or raising public awareness of a distinct Manx cultural identity. Though these functions and others may be fulfilled by participation in Manx folklore activities, a major strand is still one of enjoyment and the sense of community given by a shared set of beliefs. Therefore, although Manx folklore may appear to change dramatically through time in terms of its form, context, and even apparent function, the element of fun and provision of a sense of community for its participants can still be found even in a rapidly changing world.

STUDIES OF MANX FOLKLORE

Many books have been published on Manx folklore. Other important sources on the subject include *Yn Lioar Manninagh*, which the Isle of Man Natural History and Antiquarian Society published between 1889 and 1905, the society's current run of *Proceedings* (which began in 1906), the *Manx Museum Journal* (1924–1980), a series of thirty-three volumes published by the Manx Society published between 1858 and 1894, and the periodical *Manx Life* (1971–1996).

BIBLIOGRAPHY

Broderick, George. 1991 (1981–1982). *Manx Stories and Reminiscences of Ned Beg Hom Ruy (Edward Faragher of Cregneash 1831–1908)*. Douglas: Yn Cheshaght Ghailckagh.

Callow, Edward. 1994 (1882). *The Phynodderree and Other Legends*. Ceredigion, Wales: Llanerch.

Cashen, William. 1993 (1912). *William Cashen's Manx Folklore*, edited by Stephen Miller. Onchan: Chiollagh.

Clague, John. 1911. *Manx Reminiscences*. Castletown: M. J. Blackwell.

Craine, David. 1955. *Manannan's Isle: A Collection of Manx Historical Essays*. Douglas: Manx Museum and National Trust.

Crellin, A. M. 1994. *Manx Folklore: Fairy Legends, Customs & Superstitions*, edited by Stephen Miller. Onchan: Chiollagh.

Cubbon, William. 1933. *A Bibliographical Account of Works Relating to the Isle of Man*. London: Oxford University Press. 1:397–410, 496–504.

Douglas, Mona. 1964. *This Is Ellan Vannin: A Miscellany of Manx Life and Lore*. Douglas: Times Press.

———. 1966. *This Is Ellan Vannin Again*. Douglas: Times Longbooks.

———. 1970. *We Call It Ellan Vannin*. Douglas: Times Longbooks.

———. 1994. *Manx Folk-Song, Folk Dance, Folklore: Collected Writings*, edited by Stephen Miller. Onchan: Chiollagh.

Fraser, Maxwell. 1948. *In Praise of Manxland*. London: Methuen.

Gill, W. Walter. 1929. *A Manx Scrapbook*. London: Arrowsmith.

———. 1932. *A Second Manx Scrapbook*. London: Arrowsmith.

———. 1963. *A Third Manx Scrapbook*. London: Arrowsmith.

Harrison, Stephen. 1986. Voice of the People: The Work of the Manx Folk Life Survey. In *100 Years of Heritage*. Douglas: Manx Museum and National Trust. 190–205.

Kelly, I. M. 1989. *Twas Thus and Thus They Lived*. Castletown: I. M. Kelly.

Kermode, E. 1985 (1885). *Celtic Customs*. Peel: Frank Quayle.

Killip, Kathleen. 1975. *Saint Bridget's Night*. London: Hamish Hamilton.

———. 1980. *Twisting the Rope and Other Folktales from the Isle of Man*. London: Hodder and Stoughton.

Killip, Margaret I. 1975a. *The Folklore of the Isle of Man*. London: Rowman and Littlefield.

Kinrade, Thomas. 1993 (1945). *Life at the Lhen*, edited by Stephen Miller. Onchan: Chiollagh.

Miller, Stephen, ed. 1994. *Manx Folkways: A Gleaning of Writings No 1 (1894–1911)*. Onchan: Chiollagh.

Moore, A. W. 1895. Further Notes on Manx Folklore. *The Antiquary* 31:5–9, 39–43, 72–76, 106–109, 142–146, 176–178, 198–201, 229–233, 265–270, 293–296, 344–346.

———. 1994 (1891). *The Folk-Lore of the Isle of Man*. Ceredigion, Wales: Llanerch.

Morrison, Sophia. 1991 (1911). *Manx Fairy Tales*. Douglas: Manx Experience.

Paton, C. I. 1942. *Manx Calendar Customs*. London: Folk-Lore Society.

Penrice, Harry. 1996. *Fables, Fantasies and Folklore of the Isle of Man*. Douglas: Manx Experience.

Quayle, George E. 1973. *Legends of a Life Time: Manx Folklore*. Douglas: Courier-Herald Printers.

Rhys, Sir John. 1901. *Celtic Folklore, Welsh and Manx*. Oxford: Clarendon Press.

Roeder, Charles. 1897. Contributions to the Folk-Lore of the IOM. *Yn Lioar Manninagh* 3.4:129–191.

———. 1904. *Manx Notes and Queries*. Douglas: S. K. Broadbent.

Rydings, Egbert. 1895. *Manx Tales*. London: John Heywood.

Train, Joseph. 1845. *An Historical and Statistical Account of the Isle of Man, from the Earliest Times to the Present Date*. 2 volumes. Douglas: M. A. Quiggin.

Waldron, George. 1865 (1731, 1744). *A Description of the Isle of Man*. Douglas: Manx Society.

Wentz, W. Y. Evans. 1911. *The Fairy Faith in the Celtic Countries*. London: Oxford University Press.

Wood, G. W. 1894. On the Classification of Proverbs and Sayings in the Isle of Man. *Folklore* 31:229–274.

Yvonne Cresswell

SCOTLAND

GEOGRAPHY AND HISTORY

Scotland is a land of borders, both internal and external. There are boundaries between the Gaelic and Scots languages, Highland and Lowland areas, the Islands and the Mainland, the Central Belt (Edinburgh and Glasgow), and "the Borders" (between Scotland and **England**). In some ways Scotland has always been defined by its relationship with England. The "debatable lands" between the two countries remained unfixed and dangerous territory until recent centuries.

Settlements such as Skara Brae in Orkney attest that Iron Age Scotland was a prosperous place, with a milder climate than today that allowed for the widespread cultivation of grain crops. (Bere, *Hordeum sativum*, an ancestor of modern barley, is still grown in Orkney.) With the cooling of the climate and social changes, settlement areas have altered, but there remains little land that has not been shaped by human and domesticated animal habitation.

Scotland is replete with megalithic monuments, from standing stone alignments such as Callanish and Stenness to dwellings and tombs—some, like Maeshowe in Orkney, with much later Viking graffiti to the effect of "Leif was here." Some highly decorated stones feature Pictish motifs on one side with later Christian symbols added on the other.

Since the Iron Age, Scotland's housing stock has been almost exclusively stone-built. The Western Isles were known into the twentieth century for their "black houses," chimneyless, thick-walled, rough-stone, thatched ovals divided into two or three chambers by wooden partitions. Basic furniture included sideboards, low stools or benches (designed to avoid the pall of peat smoke, which seeped slowly through the chimneyless roof), and box beds, which helped retain warmth. Later houses include the two-story farmhouses still in use all over the country, often built to commercially available plans following World War I and frequently accompanied by substantial stone-built byres, or barns, with an L- or U-shaped floor plan. The urban setting was notorious for its tenements, now often replaced by tower blocks and detached bungalows. At the upper end of the scale are Scotland's tower houses and castles, originating as defensive structures in the eleventh and twelfth centuries and adapted into country estate houses as the country was pacified and the nobility's affluence increased. Housing improvements culminated in the huge, rambling, impractical shooting lodges on the great Highland estates (now often converted to outdoor centers or abandoned, their roofs removed after World War II, to avoid property taxes).

Scotland's climate is harsh and unforgiving. The west coast bears the brunt of the Atlantic gales, getting twice as much rain as the eastern seaboard. Nevertheless, agriculture has been the mainstay of Scotland's economy for millennia, a characteristic development being the crofting system. A croft is a rural smallholding allowing limited cultivation—usually on very poor soil in need of much backbreaking improvement—and some stock-raising on a small scale. Crofters' basic subsistence is supplemented by fishing, barter, and migrant labor (for example, in the oil industry, forestry, and military and domestic service).

In contrast to the rural nation, the Central Belt was the heartland of Scottish industrialization: coal mining, steel production, milling, and weaving. Among its most striking innovations is the model town of New Lanark, now a World Heritage Site, developed by the visionary industrialist Robert Owen in his time as manager (1800–1825). Housing, health care, schooling, and affordable food were provided; child labor and corporal punishment were eradicated.

The best-known regional division is that between Highlands and Lowlands. The mountains of the west coast rise thousands of feet directly from sea level to the Cuillin peaks in the Isle of Skye and the hills of Applecross. Farther south rises Ben Nevis, Scotland's highest mountain, and to the east, the Cairngorm massif, now one of the few great wilderness areas in Western Europe, sloping down to the North Sea on the Aberdeenshire coast. The Highlands, to the north and west, are more mountainous in general, but the "Highland line" has always been political, linguistic, and social rather than strictly geographical, defined by the relationship between Gaelic Highland culture and the Lowland Scots.

Apart from scattered references by Roman chroniclers and poets and early Christian missionaries from Columban Iona or Northumbria between the third and eighth centuries, little is known about the Pictish and Brythonic tribes that inhabited the north and south of Scotland 2,000 years ago. Broadly speaking, Scotland's people today are of either Irish (Gaelic) origin via the circa fifth-century colony of Dal Riada in southwest Scotland or Scandinavian-Anglo-Germanic origin via migration from the south and Viking invasions around the coastline in the eighth and ninth centuries. Throughout the last 1,500 years, these two societies have effectively competed for dominance.

Though Gaelic has been spoken in every area of Scotland at one time or another, it has never been the lingua franca of the whole country at any one time. Instead, political power in the middle of the last millennium was balanced between the kings of Scotland and the Lord of the Isles, who ruled vast stretches of the west coast Highlands and Islands. **Norway** ruled the northern isles of Orkney and Shetland for many centuries, but they were gradually absorbed into the Scottish realm in the thirteenth to sixteenth centuries. Norn, the local derivative of Old Norse, was spoken in the northern isles until the fifteenth century.

The dramatic decline of Highland (Gaelic) power really began in 1493, when James IV abolished the Lordship of the Isles, which for centuries had ruled over Scotland's western islands almost as a nation unto itself. In 1603, upon the death of Elizabeth I of England, Scotland's Stuart king, Elizabeth's cousin James VI, was invited south to take up the throne as James I and VI. A century later, in 1707, the Scottish parliament was disbanded and all power ceded to London as much through monetary chicanery as any popular or political will. In 1688, the Catholic monarch, James II and VII, fled Britain in the face of invasion by William of Orange, invited from Holland by a small committee of peers and commoners anxious to restore the religious oppression opposed by James. Fifty-eight years of rebellion and conflict followed, culminating in the decisive Battle of Culloden in 1746, which brought to an end the Stuart dynasty, a Catholic monarchy, and the patriarchal clan system of the Highlands and Islands. There followed a brutal repression and demilitarization of Highland culture, which, coupled with the potato famine of the 1840s, led to massive emigration to the United States, Canada, **Australia**, and New Zealand, sometimes funded by landlords—some of them eager to use the land for sheep farming. Reform finally came with the 1884 Crofters Holding Act (Scotland), but by this time Gaelic culture was severely debilitated.

Lowland culture was also changing dramatically. Agricultural developments of the eighteenth century (improved drainage, technology, and ideas of land use) led to higher productivity, an amalgamation of farms with occasional evictions, and the concomitant exploitation of a mobile workforce on short-term contracts. Emigration due to hardship and economic opportunity was widespread both overseas and to the growing factories of the Central Belt, draining the countryside of its population.

As the British Empire expanded, the demand for people and products skyrocketed. Scotland's warlike traditions were harnessed overseas in the new Highland Regiments, established post-Culloden to afford an outlet for restless youth, while the workforce that remained behind provided food and industrial products to fuel the expansion.

Following loyal service in conflicts around the world, particularly in World Wars I and II, the movement for self-rule gathered momentum in fits and starts, headlined by the 1951 retrieval from the Coronation Chair in London's Westminster Abbey of the "Stone of Destiny," the coronation stone of Scottish kings, stolen in 1297 by England's Edward I, Hammer of the Scots. Even the stone itself is surrounded by myth; it is said by some to have been brought from the Holy Land and perhaps even to have been Jacob's Pillow:

> Oh the Dean o' Westminster wis a powerful man,
> He held a' the strings o' the state in his hand.
> But with a' this great business it flustered him nane,
> Till some rogues ran away wi' his wee magic stane.

Many say the returned stone is a replica, the genuine article still hidden near Perth. The movement for political autonomy foundered with successive governments, but in the 1980s the British government undertook deindustrialization on a massive scale, closing mines and foundries across the country and leaving whole communities without focus or support. This social devastation finally awakened Scotland's political muscle, and in the 1997 election the incumbent Conservative government failed to gain a single seat in Scotland. In 1998 the country regained its parliament, disbanded since 1707. Scotland is therefore an ancient and a new nation, building a new self-image and identity out of multiform and multicultural traditions.

SUPERNATURAL LORE

Though broadly speaking a Christian country, Scotland's layers of belief run deep. The Pictish tribes were Christianized in the middle of the first millennium, but traces of pagan and other pre-Christian beliefs survive today, deeply embedded in tradition. Incompatible beliefs co-exist quite comfortably in most people's experience, and such is the case with the widespread acceptance of supernatural phenomena such as second sight, fairies, or, more recently, UFO sightings within a culture of devout Christian belief.

Second sight is a form of psychic ability that runs in families, according to tradition, through the seventh son of a seventh son. Documented incidents are numerous and have a long history. Many narratives are still to be heard in various communities, particularly among Highlanders and Traveling folk (Scotland's itinerant workers, dealers, hawkers, and craftsmen). Typical unsought phenomena include visions of phantom funerals and experiences of death omens (lights, a tap, or a sharp bang), while intentional actions include infinite forms of divination—for example, with coggies, small wooden bowls filled with water, or hazelnuts in a fire, which upon cracking reveal the identity of a person's future partner.

Scottish tradition, both Highland and Lowland, has a huge range of magical, supernatural beings that include brownies (helpful spirits who must be appeased with offerings of food or milk), elves, and fairies. Other beings include water creatures such as kelpies, the *each-uisge* (water-horse), selkies (seals that take human form), and mermaids. Experiences of this supernatural world are frequently recorded with detailed descriptions of fairies' appearance, habits, and habitation. The most famous account perhaps is Rev. Robert Kirk's *Secret Commonwealth of Elves, Fauns and Fairies* of 1691. Kirk was the seventh son of a minister and had second sight himself. *The Secret Commonwealth* reflects no conflict whatsoever between Kirk's Christian belief and his experience of the fairy Otherworld. It is the first systematic attempt to describe that world and its quality of time-out-of-time, where a terrestrial century is perceived as but a moment in the company of fairies.

These older fairies of tradition abduct children and mortal women: "[W]omen are yet alive who tell they were taken away when in child-bed to nurse fayrie Children," Kirk notes. They adopt local customs of dress; they live and die; they have rulers but no religion; and they have "bodies of congealed air." Fairies were often accused of abducting human children and leaving their own to be breast-fed in their place. This may have been an explanation of sudden changes in a baby's development, but there were also numerous ways of exposing the impostor, ranging from pricking to throwing the baby on the fire, at which point a changeling baby would vanish up the chimney. Fairies are said to move on the quarter days, one of which is Halloween. (Even today Scotland conducts its business of rent paying or commencement of leases on the quarter days.)

Like many cultures bounded by sea, legends of supernatural water beings are widespread, though particularly so in Shetland, the Orkneys, and the Outer Hebrides. Tales and songs tell of a seal emerging from the sea, taking on the shape of a woman, rolling up her skin, and secreting it behind a rock. An observer hides the skin, traps the being in human form, and often takes her as his wife. She bears him children but is often cheerless. After many years, she finds the skin and is compelled to return to the sea, from where she floats near the shore, keeping watch on her family but never to return to land. Often, the genders are reversed, and sometimes the husband, in seal form, is shot by the woman's suitor:

> It shall come to pass on a summer's day,
> When the sun shines hot on every stone,
> That I shall take my little young son,
> And teach him for to swim the foam.
>
> And thou shalt marry a proud gunner,
> And a proud gunner I'm sure he'll be,
> And the very first shot that ever he'll shoot,
> He'll kill both my young son and me.

No Scottish tradition of the cycle of life—birth, death, or marriage—is complete without a dram of whiskey, sometimes more than one. Courtship rituals of former times included bundling, sharing a bed with a bolster separating the couple, and the *rèiteach*, a Highland betrothal ceremony involving euphemistic bargaining between the groom and the bride's father. One still-flourishing ritual is the blackening, in which the prospective groom or bride is captured by "friends" and covered with oil, treacle, flour, feathers, dirt, shoe polish, and any other sticky material that can be found. The victim is paraded around the streets to the accompaniment of raucous singing and noise, then often chained to a railing and left on public display for some time. Extreme examples have included oil workers tethered on the upper deck of an oil rig on cold North Sea nights.

FOLKTALES

In the verbal arts, the full range of narrative and song is represented. Both language traditions (including the dialects of Shetland and Orkney) feature international wonder (fairy) tales, historical and place-name legends, jokes, riddles, and proverbs.

The place of performance for most narrative and song in the Highland tradition is the *céilidh*, or visiting house. There are Lowland equivalents, of course, and such evenings would usually turn out to be mixtures of stories, gossip, jokes, songs, and general chat. In fact, most communities had houses known for storytelling, songs, or lively repartee—sometimes all three—but there does seem to have been a degree of specialization (a tradition carried on in emigrant Gaelic communities in Cape Breton and Quebec).

Scottish tradition has for many centuries moved flexibly from oral to written and back again with great ease, evolving, adapting, and re-forming throughout. Such a case is that of the international wonder tales, which often borrow episodes from written sources and, just as often, become sources themselves for written versions. In Lowland Scots culture, the wonder tales are best represented among the Traveling people with textured, multi-episodic narratives sometimes lasting a whole evening, enriched by the use of the Travelers' secret language, the cant.

Storytellers' styles vary widely, of course, from the conversational and subdued to the dramatic and physical, the tales expanding or contracting as the audience and the context vary. Some tellers such as Duncan Macdonald of South Uist told tales lasting many hours with little more than a dozen variations in diction between renditions (and a seventeenth-century manuscript, which may have been his family's original source).

Among the oldest narratives are the Fenian tales, recounting the exploits of the legendary Irish hero Fionn MacCumhail (Finn MacCool) and his Irish/Scottish band of warriors. The stories sometimes appear in ballad form. They reflect a Highland society that even as late as the eighteenth century glorified the chivalric code of the warrior. Probably the most common types of narrative in Highland lore are the numerous legends of clan history and origins, coupled with the stories associated with local supernatural fairy traditions.

SONGS AND BALLADS

Song is fundamental to Scotland's identity: from Murrayfield stadium, where international rugby matches are preceded by 60,000 people singing "Flower of Scotland" by Roy Williamson, to the opening of the new Scottish parliament, where Robert Burns's paean to the common man, "A Man's a Man for A' That," was sung in front of the queen:

> The rank is but the guinea's stamp,
> The Man's the gowd for a' that.
>
> Then let us pray that come it may,
> As come it will for a' that,
> That sense and worth, o'er a' the earth,
> Shall bear the gree, and a' that.
> For a' that, an' a' that,
> It's comin' yet for a' that,
> That man to man, the world o'er,
> Shall brithers be for a' that.

We may also look to songs as a barometer of people's emotional response to social change.

As recently as 1904, when he began collecting songs, schoolmaster Gavin Greig expected to rescue a few sad remains of tradition but found more than 3,000 songs within a few-mile radius of his home. Traditions often exist beneath the surface of society, a phenomenon dramatically illustrated again by the "discovery" of the Traveler singing tradition in the 1950s by Hamish Henderson and other collectors. Many Travelers continue a tradition of singing and storytelling within extended family units and more recently in storytelling and traditional music festivals around the world.

Broadly defined, the Scottish ballad is a song that tells a story, though the term is not generally used by singers themselves, who often refer to ballads as big, or heavy, songs. Ballads often deal with fundamental themes of power, hegemony, and injustice, death and vengeance, cultural identity and gender rivalry—all within a context of symmetric plot patterning and a detached narrative style that allows listeners to infer meaning and symbolism from their own experience and their familiarity with the tradition. "The Dowie Dens o Yarrow," a classic tragic ballad from the Borders, is also popular in Aberdeenshire. Traveler Jane Turriff sings a distinctive version:

> He's gan tae his lady gaen
> As he has done before-o,
> Sayin, "Madam, I maun keep a tryst
> On the dowie dens o Yarrow."

She pleads for him to stay at home, but he keeps the tryst and meets her brothers.

> "I come nae here tae howk or hound
> Nor tae drink the wine sae clear-o,
> Nor come I here tae pairt ma land
> Bit I'll fight wi you on Yarrow.
>
> "Noo it's fower he's hurt, an five he's slain
> On the bloody dens o Yarrow,
> Till a cowardly man cam him behind
> An pierced his body through-o."

The woman's brother is sent home with the news, but she is already on the way.

> "I dreamt a dreary dream yestreen.
> God keep us a' fae sorrow.
> I dreamt I pu'ed the birk sae green
> On the dowie dens o Yarrow."

> "Oh sister, I will read your dream,
> And I know it has come sorrow.
> Your true love, he lies dead an gone.
> He wis killed, he wis killed in Yarrow."

The classic ballads encompass narratives of history, romance, and humor in two- or four-line stanzas, often following the "ballad rhythm" of four and three stresses per line. They are intended to be sung and possibly, in the past, also chanted rather than read. Codified in 1882–1898 in *The English and Scottish Popular Ballads* by Harvard University scholar Francis James Child and characterized by him as moribund or dead in oral tradition, the ballads are still very much alive, sung both by those who were raised with traditional song and by revival performers.

Scottish singing style varies from the very emotional to the positively detached. There are no firm boundaries of style along cultural, racial, or geographic lines, except that, in the main, Gaelic singing is more highly decorated. The one constant is that singers get "the wey o a sang," internalizing it and, as singer Jeannie Robertson put it, "tak it oot bonnie," not necessarily with a beautiful voice but rather with due attention to the story, the emotion, and those who passed the song on. Traditional singers are often called untrained, but within tradition teaching and training certainly do occur. Most of this is less overt than in formal Western musical training, but the understanding of what makes a good singer, a good song, and a good performance is clear and often expressed. In some cases, guidance is made explicit, either with advice on how to sing—"Ye're grippin in your voice. Sing oot"—or, for example, with assessments of another's lack of vocal expression: "It's like an egg withoot salt."

While the ballads receive the lion's share of scholarship and kudos, they are far outnumbered in Scottish tradition by various forms of lyric song. Chief among the known composers of such popular songs are Robert Burns, Walter Scott, Allan Cunningham, Allan Ramsay, Robert Tannahill, and Lady Nairne, along with Neil Macleod and William Ross in the Gaelic tradition, but an equal number of anonymous creations are still to be found.

Social song making is one of the liveliest areas of creativity in both Lowlands and Highlands: local poets composing songs of entertainment but also of social control and public censure regarding local events and characters. Meaning is created in the space between listener and singer, and while composers would naturally want to sing about such issues, their audience would expect it, too. Also of great importance is the huge body of occupational songs and worksongs, perhaps best exemplified by the Scots "bothy ballads" and the Gaelic "waulking songs," respectively.

The so-called bothy ballads (not technically ballads at all) are songs of the farm servants of the Lowlands. Definitions range from the strict (songs about farmwork) to the broad (any song sung by the farmworkers in the small bothies, farm outbuildings, in which they lived). At the end of the eighteenth century and into the nineteenth, improved Scottish farms required hired hands to work the land. Farm servants were hired at twice-yearly regional fairs (held at Whitsunday and Martinmas) for a six-month "fee." "Arles" of a coin or two were passed and a whiskey drunk to seal the bargain. The servant would report to the farm the next day, living in a bothy, or a chaamer, from French *chambre*, a room within the main farmhouse. Conditions were harsh and basic and the diet often plain (sometimes oatmeal brose, a kind of unboiled porridge, three times a day), leading in some cases to rickets. In the nineteenth century, the system was blamed for higher than normal rates of illegitimacy, though it held sway with improved conditions until World War II.

The songs themselves often complain forthrightly about workers' conditions and the parsimonious farmer, adhering to a formulaic pattern of feeing with promises of fine horses and kind treatment, followed often by disappointment: "Bit fin I got tae the Barnyards, / There wis naethin there bit skin an bane" ("The Barnyards o Delgatie"). Often, the compositions are rich catalogs of farm life, beginning with the feeing process, enumerating the social hierarchy, and ending with the lad's eventual departure for a new farm.

While the ballads are full of heroic deeds and occasional supernatural happenings, the bothy songs portray scenes of backbreaking labor, social inequality, and draconian conditions. In "Sleepy Toon," for example, the lads are ordered to salvage their dinner from rain-soaked sacks of oatmeal. They defy the farmer, but they must see out the term or break their fee, making them virtually unemployable come next feeing fair. In such cases the end of the six-month term was a blessed relief, and the songs reflect the freedom of the hiring fair:

> We'll maybe see aul Adam there,
> A-suppin at his brose,
> I'll gie a lien o ma hankie,
> For tae dicht his snottery nose.

Some say the bothy songs could be sung at the next fair to warn prospective workers away from particular farms, but their chief function was surely to pass the time and to provide often humorous catharsis in an oppressive and constrictive social system.

From the late nineteenth century onward, the tradition was in transition as conditions improved. The bothy life became romanticized or made humorous; the tradition softened; and the form was absorbed by the music hall, source of the examples most commonly sung today such as "Nicky Tams": "I'll niver forget the happy days, / I wore ma nicky tams." Yet even in concert or competition settings the bothy songs tap into an important vein of Northeast Scottish identity.

In the Gaelic-speaking areas, social song making is even more widespread and active. Any community would have had at least one local song maker, some of whose songs have become well known nationally and internationally, such as "*Gruagach òg an fhuilt bhàin*" (Fair-haired Young Girl).

Since the demise of the clan system with its professional poets, vernacular poetry has been a key form of social interaction in Gaelic society. The land agitation songs of Màiri Mhòr nan Oran (Mary Macpherson) are sung as historical fact as well as markers of identity and political allegiance. The still-popular songs of Duncan Bàn Macintyre and a composition about a mad bull making fools of the local "heroes" who went out to tame him were sung side by side at local *cèilidhs*, the one harking back to a high point of Gaelic nature poetry, the other a gentle, teasing satire about local happenings. Since topics were usually ephemeral, local songs often had a short life. Sometimes, however, they would prove popular and be taken up by local people and learned, sung, and traded. These are not static documents but a living means of firsthand communication.

The crucial measure of this creative tradition is the composer's treatment of her subject and her skill at fitting words to the chosen melody, whether it be of Lowland or Highland origin. (Gaelic and Scots melodic traditions borrow freely from each other.) The traditional composer certainly considers the tone and atmosphere of a melody as it relates to the subject matter of the song, but the music's originality is not a separate concern.

In the last half century, Gaelic song making has altered dramatically, and while several composers still make songs about local events, places, and people, creative composition has generally shifted to the professional and semi-professional stage. With inexorable Anglicization, swift economic development, and a more fluid movement of migrant laborers (for example, in the two-weeks-on, two-weeks-off pattern of the oil industry), audiences no longer have the necessary cultural background. The songs are thus diminished in both meaning and significance. Emigrant communities of Gaels in Canada, the United States, and New Zealand maintained communities of critical mass for some time, but even these are now too fragmented to sustain social song making in Gaelic as a living art.

The oldest songs in the Gaelic tradition are the "Ossianic" ballads, so called after the bard—Oisean, Oisín in Irish—who accompanied the legendary warriors. These formulaic, syllabic-meter parallels to the prose narratives can be found as far back as the twelfth century in Irish and were popular in Scotland in the Middle Ages. Half-chanted, half-sung, they could be found in oral tradition into the 1980s, such as this version of "*Latha dha'n Fhin am Beinn Iongnaidh*" sung by Mrs. Archie Macdonald:

> A day when the Fenians were in the Mountain of Marvels
> All of the Fenians, the fierce men,
> They sent Caoilte because of his swiftness
> Ahead of them to act as guide.

By far the largest category of Gaelic songs consists of those used in the traditional work of the croft, both men's and women's: milking, spinning, reaping, rowing, churning, and, particularly, waulking, or fulling, the tweed when fresh off the loom. Today, most commercial dairies play music in their milking parlors to help relax the cows. Fifty years ago, in the island of Barra, Kate Nicholson sang this song for the same purpose:

> Turn the cows, turn the cows,
> Turn the cows, laddie,
> And you will get a loveable wife
> And the generous cattle fold beside MacIntosh.

The most numerous Gaelic songs are those used for waulking, the rhythmic work of pounding the loosely woven cloth to tighten the threads, making it thicker and virtually waterproof. This body of song is thought to be composed largely by women and the work done exclusively by them as well (though Gaelic emigrants in Canada included men in the work). The songs are normally in the form of a choral call and response between the leader and the other women. Annie Nicholson led a group:

Leader:	*Hì rì hoireann ó*	There is sorrow,
All:	*Hì rì hoireann ó*	there is sorrow,
Leader:	*Tha mulad, tah mulad,*	there is grief on me.
	tha lionn dubh orm fhein	
All:	*Hì rì rirì oho*	My spirited noble young man is the
	Roho hi hoireann ó.	root of it.

The songs were sometimes improvised satires about local people and issues. Other examples contain fragments of Ossianic ballads or other songs drafted to fulfill a new function.

Religious song is another important area of both Highland and Lowland tradition, one of the most distinctive and dramatic expressions being the Gaelic Presbyterian psalm tradition. It has its origins in the translation of the Metrical Psalms of David into Gaelic, using tunes in the English ballad-meter, which is foreign to Gaelic-language tradition. In order to help non-literate congregations take part, a Precentor would "line out" the words of each line or verse of the psalm before the congregation joined in. It was unnecessary, then, to know the words or to be able to read, though the words and tunes soon became familiar. But this is only half the story. Because of the highly ornamented style of singing in Gaelic, singers would decorate their own melodic lines individually. With each singer creating his or her own variations and arriving at the main melody notes only roughly simultaneously, powerful, cyclical waves of sound are created.

MUSIC

One of Scotland's most obvious exports is instrumental music, chiefly known through the Highland bagpipe, though there are strong vernacular and formalized traditions of fiddle and accordion (piano and some button) as well. In the last twenty years, the bellows-driven Scottish small pipes have undergone a revival from near extinction. Scotland is also home to the harp, or *clàrsach*, its earliest iconic instrument, used for melody playing and also perhaps by minstrels to accompany heroic or clan poetry. According to recent research, it is probable that the gut-strung harp originated in Scotland and passed thence to **Ireland**. As well as the "native" Scottish instruments of bagpipe and harp, many others have been adopted over the centuries, including harmonica, piano, mandolin, bouzouki, banjo, and guitar. (Samuel Johnson reports having heard the last in Skye in 1773.)

Instrumentation varies from solo melody playing, to the eighteenth-century tradition of fiddle and cello and from ensembles with fiddle, two accordions, and drums, to the full pipes and drums of the competition circuit.

The piping tradition includes functional tunes such as marches (for retreat or advance) and presentation tunes such as the complex *pìobaireachd* (pibroch), a series of evermore complex variations on a fundamental theme, or *ùrlar*. Scottish tunes, though, are principally composed for dancing. Nowadays they are often lumped under the "Celtic" music rubric but are only partly Celtic because the Eastern and Lowland traditions owe much to English, Continental, Scandinavian, and Germanic tradition as well. While sharing basic musical structures with Irish dance tunes—jigs, reels, airs—Scotland has also developed the distinctive Strathspey form, a marked, stately form of reel in 2/4 or 4/4, known in Northern Ireland as a "Highland." Prominent composers on the fiddle include James Oswald (1711–1769), Niel Gow (1727–1807), his son Nathaniel (b. 1763), William Marshall (1748–1833), and dancing master-fiddler-composer James Scott Skinner (1843–1927), "the Strathspey King," who successfully toured America on several occasions.

DANCES AND SONG COMPETITIONS

Scottish dances are mostly done by couples who stand either in opposing lines or in square sets of four couples in settings ranging from village halls to the Shetland house dances, with styles adapted to the cramped physical space. Sometimes if a fiddler had too many drams, someone would "diddle" the tunes orally, using nonsense syllables. Both Highlands and Lowlands feature mouth tunes, *puirt-a-beul*, tongue twisters that make linguistic, but not necessarily narrative, sense.

Traditional dances include the Three-, Four-, and Eightsome Reels, Strip the Willow, and the Dashing White Sergeant; couples dances include the Military Two-step, the Canadian Barn Dance, and the St. Barnard's Waltz, each customarily done twice in a row before the band proceeds to the next dance. In 1923, Jean Milligan, a trained teacher, set about codifying and "correcting" Scottish traditional dance, giving rise to the worldwide Royal Scottish Country Dance Society movement. In recent decades, vernacular dance has made a comeback with "ceilidh dances" nearly every Friday and Saturday night in most major towns and cities.

Solo dance also appears in the form of Highland Dance and Hebridean Dance, both of which are strictly codified and choreographed forms of display. Traditional Scottish step dance (analogous to the Irish, but with a more relaxed upper body) has recently undergone a revival with added influence of dancers from emigrant communities in Cape Breton and Newfoundland.

To the outsider, one of the most notable aspects of Scottish traditional music and song must be the competitive element. From the huge range of events at the Gaelic Royal National Mòd, to the wide array of competitions conducted by the Traditional Music and Song Association, the contest circuit is one of the most common places to hear a particular kind of traditional music. Though in some ways ossifying tradition, competitions have undoubtedly brought forth many "source singers" and also encouraged hundreds to take part in traditions new to them.

SPORTS AND GAMES

Scotland is obsessed with football (soccer), like most of the world. Memories of past achievements linger and lead the "Tartan Army" of fans on to celebrate the years of glorious failure since the disastrous 1978 World Cup campaign:

> We're on the march wi Ally's Army,
> We're going tae the Argentine,
> And we'll really shake them up,
> When we win the World Cup,
> Cause Scotland has the greatest football team.

Success comes rarely, but the reputation of a good-natured, fun-loving army is genuine enough.

There are strong followings also for rugby, particularly in the Borders, where a wedding commonly used to be followed by a scrum among the groomsmen, still dressed in their finery, with the ball kicked into play by the bride in her ankle-length white dress. The Gaelic game is *camanachd*, or shinty, a cross between hurling, lacrosse, and field hockey, which can become very physical. Many regional teams have fanatical followings. To an international audience, the most recognizably Scottish pastimes are the Highland Games, thought to have their origin in off-duty military pastimes and rural, agricultural fairs but now to be found around the world as well as throughout Scotland. Here they are often very local events, but some such as Braemar and Lonach attract a tourist audience. In the United States, Canada, and New Zealand such games have expanded, drawing upward of 50,000 spectators; even Moscow has an annual Highland Games. Competitions are held for piping, Highland dancing, and athletics, among which are hill races, the hammer throw, a sheaf toss, and, most distinctively, the tossing of the caber, in which a substantial log must be carried and thrown end-over-end in one powerful throw.

CALENDAR CUSTOMS

The traditional Scottish year is replete with calendar customs: Burns Night on 25 January, Shrovetide Ba' games in Border villages in February, Easter, the quarter day of Whitsunday, Beltane (30 April), Lammas in August, Halloween (or *Samhuinn*), Martinmas quarterday, St. Andrew's Night (30 November), and Hogmanay (31 December [11 January, according to the old calendar]). The quarter days themselves go back to the old Celtic cyclical year of Samhuinn (the Celtic New Year), Imbolg, Beltane, and Lughnasa, or Lammas, the harvest festival.

Among the most distinctive of celebrations remaining today are the Hogmanay fire festivals ranging from the Biggar and Wick Bonfires and the Comrie Flambaux to the Stonehaven Fireballs and the Burning of the Clavie and the best-known Up-Helly-aas, various Viking fire festivals in Shetland at the end of January.

At midnight on Hogmanay in Stonehaven, around fifty strong men and women swing blazing baskets of burning wood and paraffin round their heads while walking up and down the main street. The swingers follow a ritual route and procedures, and their midwinter fire festival is as old as any, though the present revival appears to be about 150 years old.

Shetland's Up-Helly-aas take place in villages around the islands with floats and skits depicting local events and characters. The largest event in Lerwick includes the burning of a full-size replica longship, surrounded by men in Viking costume, led by a Guizer Jarl elected each year to head the ceremony.

At Burghead, on 11 January, Aul Eel or Old Yule—New Year's Eve before the change from Julian to Gregorian calendars in 1752—a burning half barrel is carried high through the streets, its bottom resting on one of the crew's head and shoulders. The Clavie is documented as early as 1655, and over the centuries, the church has had varying attitudes, ranging from early condemnation as a heathen and idolatrous custom, to acceptance. The ritual shares much with the Fireballs, but there are significant differences, the most obvious being that membership of the crew is male only, and there is only one Clavie. There is status attached to being on the crew, for which one must be a Burghead native.

Even making the Clavie is steeped in tradition, following long-standing rules and rituals. The route never varies, weaving through the old town, perhaps around its ancient boundaries, and stopping at hotels and particular houses to throw a burning barrel stave or fragment in the door to bring luck to the house. Perhaps in former days such burning splinters were used to re-light hearth fires for the New Year.

Eventually, the procession winds its way to Doorie Hill at the heart of the old Pictish fort, where the Clavie post is wedged into a stone pillar and immolated in waves of tar and creosote, thrown by the crew to the cheers of a crowd often several thousand strong. The conflagration continues until the barrel, weakened by burning and sometimes a few taps from an adze, collapses. The crew moves in, breaking up the remains and distributing pieces to onlookers, keeping what they need to give or to send to their own families and friends. The post is retrieved, complete with nail, and carried from house to house with the crew as they "first foot" around the village on a habitual route. First footing is a feature of Hogmanay all across Scotland. After midnight, one visits friends or relatives and receives a welcoming dram of whiskey. A dark-haired first footer is deemed to presage good fortune for the New Year.

Similar barrel-burning rituals once took place in Argyll, Galloway, and Wigtownshire, and a revival festival occurs in Northumberland, but today, the Clavie is unique. Burghead natives—"Brochers"—around the world stop and think of home on Clavie Night, and in former days, fishermen unable to return home burned small herring barrels, suspended over the ship's side by chains. In the past, many other parts of Scotland had fire festivals, too. Queen Victoria herself was partial to a good fire and had Beltane fires lit on hilltops across the country in celebration of the old Celtic festival. Remnants of the ancient practice in which she was taking part can be seen in place-names such as Tullybelton—from the Gaelic for Beltane Hill.

Traditionally, Hogmanay would also see guising, costumed children and sometimes adults going door-to-door:

Rise up aul wife an shak yer feathers;
Dinna think that we are beggars;
We're only bairnies come tae play;
Rise up an gie's wir Hogmanay.

Some communities would perform a traditional resurrection play, the Galoshins, last surviving in the Borders, in which stock characters act out a heroic battle, the hero of which is killed and later resurrected by the mysterious doctor figure. The play closes with Wee Keekum Funny collecting coins from the assembled audience.

Internationally, nothing matches (Robert) Burns Night, in honor of Scotland's most celebrated poet. On 25 January dinners are held in **Japan**, **Russia**, North America, and points between. The ritual is closely adhered to: the piping-in of the haggis, recitation of Burns's tongue-in-cheek "Address to a Haggis," the "Immortal Memory" (reflections on Burns and his poetry), a "Toast to the Lasses," and a "Reply to the Toast to the Lasses." Recently, a number of "Jean Armour" nights, named after Burns's long-suffering wife, have been held in response to the perceived chauvinist, womanizing aspects of the poet's life and letters.

CHALLENGES OF THE MODERN WORLD

Because tradition survives by adaptation, it comes as no surprise that Scottish folklore has grafted itself into numerous hybrids with modern innovations, giving it new life and relevance to younger generations. Scottish wedding customs are regularly drawn on and adapted into modern hybrid ceremonies. One of the best known of these old traditions is handfasting, in which a couple would agree at a fair or market to live together for a year and a day, returning to the gathering to cement the marriage or to go their separate ways without stigma. Notably, any child born to the handfasted couple would be the financial responsibility of the male. "Celtic Christianity" is a growing and very marketable concept, though it has little or nothing to do with the early Celtic church of historical record, being rather a blend of old and New Age mysticism, mixed with the sketchy, little-known details of druidism and the like.

In the 1930s, Sorley Maclean, a poet from the Isle of Skye, along with a handful of others—Donald Macaulay, George Campbell Hay, and Iain Crichton Smith—re-invented Gaelic poetry in twentieth-century forms. Maclean in particular was strongly influenced by the visceral, living Gaelic tradition that surrounded him in his youth. On the Lowland side, folksong and poetry have blended well, with numerous composers such as Hamish Henderson, Iain Mackintosh, and Archie Fisher bringing twentieth-century (sometimes political) concerns into the traditional song form.

Instrumental music has also evolved dramatically, with innovators such as Martyn Bennett blending archive recordings of traditional song with techno, house, and drum 'n' bass rhythms, not to mention taking the Highland bagpipe into the realms of jazz. Ensembles, beginning with the like of the Battlefield Band and recently such inventive groups as Shooglenifty and the Cauld Blast Orchestra, have varied forms with the addition of an element of free-form improvisation and an array of instruments not normally associated with traditional music in Scotland.

Calendar customs are alive and well, too. Edinburgh's Hogmanay street party draws headline acts and half a million people to the capital. The Calton Hill Beltane attracts crowds of around 5,000. From humble (part Arts Council-funded) beginnings as a kind of performance art project attended by around 200 people, the event has grown into a massive spectacle. It now features an amalgam of traditions new and old: the ancient Beltane purifying bonfires, an English-style May Queen, a woad-painted man, drumming ensembles, various pageants and a performance of the Galoshins play, acted out with twenty-five-foot-high puppets.

As Scotland acclimatizes to its new parliament and reassesses its place in the world, it is time to reassess its legends, myths, and beliefs about itself. Hamish Henderson unflinchingly undertakes this examination and affirms Scotland's desire for tolerance:

> Nae mair will oor bonnie callants
> Mairch tae war when oor bragarts croosely craw,
> Nor wee weans fae pitheid an clachan
> Mourn the ships sailin doon the Broomielaw.
> Broken faimlies in lands we've hairriet
> Will curse "Scotland the Brave" nae mair, nae mair.
> Black an white ane til ither mairriet
> Maks the vile barracks o their maisters bare.
>
> So come a' ye at hame wi freedom;
> Niver heed whit the hoodies croak for doom.
> In your hoose a' the bairns o Adam
> Shall find breid, barley bree an paintit room.
> When Maclean meets wi his freins in Springburn,
> A' the roses an geans'll turn tae bloom,
> An the black boy fae yont Nyanga
> Dings the fell gallows o the burghers doon.

STUDIES OF SCOTTISH FOLKLORE

For a general history of Scotland, see Lynch (1992), and for reflections on modern Scottish identity, see McCrone (1992). For sketches of Scotland's cultural life, see Henderson (1992). General reference guides include Daiches (1993) and Thomson (1994). Linguistic issues are introduced in the highly readable pamphlets by Thomson (1984) and McClure (1997 [1988]). Place-names are thoroughly addressed in Nicolaisen (2001). For general folklore material, see the School of Scottish Studies magazine *Tocher*, which contains transcribed fieldwork interviews from the school's archives. For cycle-of-life customs, start with Bennett (1992 [1991]). For calendar customs, see Banks (1937–1946), Livingstone (1997), and Macneill (1957–1968). Specialist studies include Brown (1998). For narrative, both Scots and Gaelic, one could do no better than Bruford and Macdonald (1994). See also Williamson (1987) and Campbell (1994 [1860–1862]). For belief traditions, see Campbell (1900 and 1974). Henderson and Cowan (2001) offers a diachronic survey.

On Scottish music, see Purser (1992), Collinson (1966), and Johnson (1972). On fiddle and dance music in particular, see Johnson (1997 [1984]), Alburger (1996 [1983]), and Emmerson (1971). On dance, see Flett and Flett (1964). For a good reader on oral traditions with introductory material, see Buchan (1984). For song in particular, these compact discs (CDs) offer a cross-section of Scottish tradition: Alan Lomax's *World Library of Folk and Primitive Music—V. 3: Scotland* and the School of Scottish Studies "Scottish Tradition Series" (Greentrax CDTRAX 9001–9020), which surveys a range of material in some detail. Scotland's modern, commercial music scene is also well represented on CD. McKean (1997) discusses the world of Gaelic social song making in detail and includes a CD of the songs. The eight-volume *Greig-Duncan Folk-Song Collection*, edited by Shuldham-Shaw and Lyle (1981–2002), features over 3,000 songs from a small corner of Northeast Scotland, while Child (1882–1898) and Lyle (1995) focus on the ballad in particular. Gaelic tradition is well represented in Campbell (1933 and 1990). Shaw (1999) is a beautiful tribute to a people, a community, and a culture now long gone.

BIBLIOGRAPHY

Alburger, Mary Anne. 1996 (1983). *Scottish Fiddlers and Their Music*. Edinburgh: Hardie Press.

Banks, Mary Macleod. 1937–1946. *British Calendar Customs*. 4 volumes. London: Folk-Lore Society.

Bennett, Margaret. 1992 (1991). *Scottish Customs from the Cradle to the Grave*. Edinburgh: Polygon.

Brown, Callum. 1998. *Up-helly-aa: Custom, Culture, and Community in Shetland*. Manchester: Manchester University Press.

Bruford, Alan, and Donald A. Macdonald. 1994. *Scottish Traditional Tales*. Edinburgh: Polygon.

Buchan, David. 1984. *Scottish Tradition*. London: Routledge.

Buchan, Norman, ed. 1962. *101 Scottish Songs*. Glasgow: Collins.

Campbell, John Francis. 1994 (1860–1862). *Popular Tales of the West Highlands*. New edition. Edinburgh: Birlinn.

Campbell, John Gregorson. 1900. *Superstitions of the Highlands & Islands of Scotland*. Glasgow: James MacLehose.

———. 1974. *Witchcraft and Second Sight in the Highlands and Islands of Scotland*. East Ardsley, UK: EP Press.

Campbell, John Lorne. 1933. *Highland Songs of the Forty-Five*. Edinburgh: J. Grant.

———. 1990. *Songs Remembered in Exile*. Aberdeen: Aberdeen University Press.

Child, Francis James, ed. 1882–1898. *The English and Scottish Popular Ballads*. 10 volumes. Boston: Houghton.

Collinson, Francis. 1966. *The Traditional and National Music of Scotland*. London: Henley.

Daiches, David. 1993. *New Companion to Scottish Culture*. Edinburgh: Polygon.

Emmerson, George S. 1971. *Rantin' Pipe and Tremblin' String: A History of Scottish Dance Music*. London: Dent.

Flett, J. M., and T. M. Flett. 1964. *Traditional Dancing in Scotland*. London: Routledge and Kegan Paul.

Henderson, Hamish. 1992. *Alias MacAlias*. Edinburgh: Polygon.

Henderson, Lizanne, and Edward J. Cowan. 2001. *Scottish Fairy Belief: A History*. East Linton: Tuckwell Press.

Johnson, David. 1972. *Music and Society in Lowland Scotland in the Eighteenth Century*. London: Oxford University Press.

———. 1997 (1984). *Scottish Fiddle Music in the Eighteenth Century*. Edinburgh: Mercat.

Johnston, Calum, and Annie Johnston. 1995. *Scottish Tradition Series Vol. 13—Calum and Annie Johnston* (sound recording). Greentrax CTRAX9013.

Kirk, Robert. 1976 (1691). *The Secret Commonwealth of Elves, Fauns and Fairies*. Cambridge: Brewer.

Livingstone, Sheila. 1997. *Scottish Festivals*. Edinburgh: Birlinn.

Lomax, Alan, ed. N.d. *World Library of Folk and Primitive Music—V. 3: Scotland* (sound recording). Rounder CDROUN 1743.

Lyle, Emily. 1995. *Scottish Ballads*. New York: Barnes and Noble.

Lynch, Michael. 1992. *Scotland: A New History*. London: Pimlico.

Macneill, F. Marian. 1957–1968. *The Silver Bough*. 4 volumes. Glasgow: MacLellan.

McClure, J. Darrick. 1997 (1988). *Why Scots Matters*. Revised edition. Saltire Pamphlets No. 10, new series. Edinburgh: Saltire Society.

McCrone, David. 1992. *Understanding Scotland: The Sociology of a Stateless Nation*. London: Routledge.

McKean, Thomas A. 1997. *Hebridean Songmaker: The Life and Songs of Iain Macneacail*. Edinburgh: Polygon.

Nicolaisen, W.F.H. 2001. *Scottish Place Names: Their Study and Significance*. New edition. Edinburgh: John Donald.

Purser, John. 1992. *Scotland's Music*. Edinburgh: Mainstream.

Scottish Tradition 2: Music from the Western Isles. N.d. (sound recording). Greentrax CDTRAX 9002.

Shaw, Margaret Fay. 1999. *Folksongs and Folklore of South Uist*. 2nd edition. Edinburgh: Birlinn.

Shuldham-Shaw, Patrick, and Emily Lyle, eds. 1981–2002. *Greig-Duncan Folk-Song Collection*. 8 volumes. Aberdeen and Edinburgh: Aberdeen University Press and Mercat.

Thomson, Derick. 1984. *Why Gaelic Matters: A Short Discussion of the History and Significance of Gaelic and Its Related Arts in Scottish Life*. Saltire Pamphlets No. 5. Edinburgh: Saltire Society.

———. 1994. *Companion to Gaelic Scotland*. Glasgow: Gairm.

Turriff, Jane. 1996. *Singin Is Ma Life* (sound recording). Springthyme SPRCD 1038.

Williamson, Duncan. 1987. *The Thorn in the King's Foot*. Harmondsworth: Penguin.

Thomas A. McKean

WALES

GEOGRAPHY AND HISTORY

Bounded on the west by the Irish Sea and on the east roughly by Offa's Dyke, Wales is a land of mountains and high plateaus, cut through by deep valleys with low-lying arable land around the edges. It has a moderate climate, tempered by the Gulf Stream–warmed sea in winter and by the high altitude in summer and is noted for heavy rainfall, especially in winter. The terrain and climate have been exceptionally instrumental in shaping not only the economy but also the social organization and history of Wales. In the uplands, where grazing was good but the land poor, settlements were generally scattered, though there was some clustering around royal courts and religious houses. Each valley, both isolated and linked by the surrounding uplands, developed to a certain extent its own culture and government within a broader culture. (*Cantrefi*, the native political units, were autonomous and royal by Welsh law.) In the valley floors and the lowlands along the coasts, it was possible to have a mixed economy of keeping cattle and growing grain crops, making it possible to establish more permanent settlements. This was a transhumant culture, with the cattle taken to the uplands for the summer months. The steep mountain and valley terrain of the interior made it extremely difficult to cross Wales. The coastal areas and a central corridor of lowland extending eastward from Shrewsbury became the points of contact with outsiders, whether through commerce or invasion.

The Welsh are descendants of the Brythons, one of the Celtic branches to settle **Ireland** and Britain in successive waves from Continental Europe in the fifth, third, and first centuries B.C.E. Speakers of Goidelic (q-Celtic) settled in Ireland, where their language developed into Irish Gaelic and thence into Scottish and Manx Gaelic. British (Brythonic, p-Celtic) speakers settled in mainland Britain, where their language developed into Welsh, Cornish, Breton, and Cumbrian (as well as other forms of northern British now lost). Never a single unified people, the Celts were linguistically and culturally linked, and despite tribal divisions the Britons recognized their commonality. At the time of the first Roman subjugation in the first century, the Britons inhabited Britain south of the Antonine Wall. After the collapse of Roman rule toward the end of the fifth century, Anglo-Saxon invasions and settlements colonized most of the area now known as **England**, gradually replacing the language (Brittonic was still spoken in eastern England as late as 700), and pushed the Britons back until British kingdoms remained only on the edges—in the north of Britain (south of the Clyde and the Forth), in Wales, and in Cornwall. Though separated geographically (by land, though not by sea), they remained connected and continued to share traditions. The struggles of the northern kingdoms in the sixth and seventh centuries against the Anglo-Saxons and among themselves became the heroic age of Welsh history and tradition. Although Cornwall was absorbed into Wessex by the tenth century, and most of the northern British kingdoms were overcome in the seventh century, Strathclyde persisted until the late eleventh century. Before its absorption into **Scotland**, it served as a conduit of the northern traditions, preserving and transmitting them to Wales.

In the Middle Ages, Wales comprised a number of small, autonomous kingdoms that, while politically separate, shared for the most part a common language, literature, legal system, and view of themselves as *Cymry* ("compatriots"; *Welsh* is a Saxon term meaning "foreigners"). Although these kingdoms might vie with each other, they also joined together to resist incursions by the English kingdoms of Wessex and Northumbria and later by the Normans. Throughout the Middle Ages, before and after the Norman Conquest, the native Welsh princes' making and breaking of alliances, with a particularly adept prince occasionally coming to the fore, created frequent shifts in power, especially between the kingdoms of Gwynedd in the north and Deheubarth in the south. The contentiousness of this period has led to the stereotype, mentioned as early as Gerald of Wales in the twelfth century and accepted even by some in the present century, that the Welsh are always fighting among themselves and that their lack of unity has (rightly) cost them their own kingdom. The Norman Conquest had been rapid and appeared completed by the end of the eleventh century, but much of the twelfth century saw a national reawakening so that, by the end of the century, the major Welsh kingdoms—Gwynedd, Deheubarth, and Powys (mid-Wales)—had reached a balance with the Norman Marcher (border) lordships. The conquest was political rather than cultural, maintaining a division between Englishry around the Norman castles and their boroughs and Welshry, where Welsh law and custom functioned, but there was interaction in matters of economics, literature, and sociopolitical developments in both the Marcher lordships and the native princedoms. In the thirteenth century, Llywelyn I and his grandson Llywelyn II in Gwynedd worked toward a united Wales, to be led by one prince of Wales, who would in turn pay homage and serve as intermediary to the English Crown, a goal achieved for a short time (1255–1267) but destroyed during the Welsh wars of England's Edward I in 1277 and 1282, when Llywelyn II was betrayed into an ambush and killed. That date, 1282, marking the end of Welsh independence, and Llywelyn II, now known to Welsh people as *Llywelyn ein llyw olaf* (our last leader), figure prominently in Welsh national consciousness. One legend about the period tells of Llywelyn reversing the shoes on his horse to mislead the English but then being betrayed by the blacksmith, and the site of his death near Cilmeri has become a rallying point in nationalist activity. The Treaty of Rhuddlan (1284) created the king's domain of the Principality of Wales, under which Wales was governed according to English economic and administrative systems. Some aspects of local governance were the responsibility of a developing class of native administrators, who used the opportunity to increase their wealth and influence. These *uchelwyr* (gentry) became the dominant class in fourteenth- to sixteenth-century Welsh society and assumed the role of patrons of Welsh literature, as had the native princes before them.

This was a period of considerable hardship for the Welsh, a period of economic and social unrest during which they chafed under English rule, which had denied them rights while imposing heavy taxes. The early history of the Britons had provided a mythological basis underlying subsequent Welsh history and legend: that the Welsh were once overlords of the island of Britain and will be again one day, as symbolized by the Crown in London. Under oppression, many people clung to, and perhaps comforted themselves with, the prophecies, to be accomplished by *y mab darogan* (the son of prophecy), a redeemer-hero who, coming from afar or awakening from a long sleep, shall restore the nation to its former glories. Wales has had eight major redeemer heroes, of whom King Arthur was the fourth. A reference to him in *Y Gododdin* (which tells of a sixth-century battle and is the oldest extant Welsh poem) indicates he was a warrior of great prowess, and *Englynion y Beddau*, a ninth-century poem, suggests he has no known grave, a motif common to redeemer-heroes. In the fourteenth century, two other redeemer-heroes arose. Owain Lawgoch (Red hand), great-nephew of Llywelyn II, living in exile as a mercenary in France, twice raised troops to retake Wales but was twice forced to turn back, once in 1369 by storms and again in 1372 at the command of the king of France. Nonetheless, in Wales his coming had been prophesied, and there are references to people arming themselves to assist in his fight. Then in 1400 Owain Glyndŵr arose, claiming the title Prince of Wales (he is the last Welsh-recognized Welsh prince of Wales) and leading the Welsh in a war against the English that lasted fifteen years and almost succeeded in re-establishing Welsh independence. Invoking the prophesies of *y mab darogan*, Glyndŵr (Owen Glendower in Shakespeare's *Henry IV*, Part I) was at first successful, setting up an embryonic modern state with its own parliament and plans for an independent Welsh church and a university system, but eventually England's greater resources gave them victory. Glyndŵr disappeared and was perceived by some as never having died. This is certainly the predominant view in Welsh legendry, which tells of Glyndŵr as well as Arthur and Owain Lawgoch each sleeping in a cave until the time is right to emerge and save the nation. The caves that each is said to be sleeping in are various and located all over Wales, and sometimes a single cave is named for more than one hero—all indications of a vital tradition. Arthur, who has been to a large extent appropriated by the English, and Owain Lawgoch, who never got very far, are the subjects of a few other legends, while Owain Glyndŵr, who has become a primary symbol of modern Welsh nationalism, has an especially full legendry, with local legends in the places where he lived and fought. After 1415, Wales once again suffered under English rule. The next redeemer-hero was recognized in Henry Tudor, descended from one of the *uchelwr* families through his grandfather Owen Tudor, who married the widow of England's Henry V. When Henry Tudor returned from exile in France, he came through Wales, gathering the Welsh, who helped him to victory at Bosworth Field, thus ending the War of the Roses and leading to his being crowned Henry VII of England. Although some regarded Welsh hopes at regaining the Crown fulfilled, time led others to doubt it. In the 1536 Act of Union, Wales was assimilated to England. While the gentry became increasingly Anglicized, and the structure of traditional Welsh society disintegrated, most Welsh people still spoke Welsh and continued Welsh customs in food, dress, calendar customs, and agricultural practices. The next major upheaval came in the nineteenth century with industrialization and the advent of Nonconformity.

RELIGION

Celtic religion was oral, leaving little trace, now recoverable mainly from material remains (dedications, inscriptions, votive offerings), descriptions by classical authors, references in medieval vernacular literature, and historical-linguistic exploration of names of deities. In medieval Wales, which shared with other Celtic cultures such matters as a cosmological five-part system (the center and four directions) and a tripartite learned class (druids, bards, and seers in Gaul and early Ireland) who preserved and transmitted traditional knowledge, the *cyfarwyddiaid* (knowledgeable ones, understood in Middle Welsh as storytellers) were responsible for a wide range of lore: mythology, origin legends, history, religion. Court poets, who were also knowledgeable in these areas, used the lore not only in praising rulers but also in guiding them politically and reminding both them and their people of the rights and responsibilities of each. In medieval Wales, the roles of poets, storytellers, lawyers, and healers overlapped. Despite the wealth of lore that must have existed, little, especially of narrative, has been preserved. Middle Welsh prose literature may use traditional information but is shaped by an individual's artistic sensibility, not by a folk esthetic. Apart from glimpses in the literature, the best source for traditional narrative lore is the Triads of the Island of Britain, a collection in which references to heroes and their legends are arranged into groups of three, such as the "Three Unfortunate Counsels of the Island of Britain" or the "Three Golden Shoemakers of the Island of Britain."

Christianity had been introduced into Britain by the mid-third century and was widespread by the fifth- and sixth-century "age of saints," when hermits and monastic founders were active in the west and north of Britain. Stories, originally oral, about these men and a few women were eventually (mostly after the eleventh century) recorded in poetry and church *Vitae*, and many of the stories continue as local legends known only in the immediate vicinity of a saint's activity and especially in connection to geomorphic features such as a stone where the saint knelt or a spring that he raised. One saint, however, stands out, with legends known throughout the country: St. David (Dewi), patron saint of Wales, whose pre-eminence was recognized by the tenth century, when he was called on in the poem *Armes Prydein* to lead the warriors in driving out the Saxons. His church at St. Davids, over the centuries, was repeatedly at the forefront in claims of independence for the Welsh Church from Canterbury. Important enough that he has survived even the Protestant Reformation,

Welsh girls in Glamorgan wear traditional attire and hold Welsh flags for St. David's Day on 1 March. (© Tim Graham/CORBIS)

his feast day, *Gwyl Dewi Sant* (1 March), is celebrated in Wales in churches and chapels, by rugby clubs and choirs. People wear leeks and daffodils (symbols of both David and Wales) and hold feasts in his honor. Outside Wales, it is celebrated by ex-patriots and Welsh descendants, especially by those who gather in St. David's Societies, designed to foster Welsh sensibilities. A few of David's legends are widely known (not just in the vicinity of his churches), most especially one that tells how in a preaching contest to see who would be proclaimed the foremost saint in Britain, the ground rose under David as he spoke, marking him clearly as the best. That mound is still to be seen as the ground upon which his church Llanddewibrefi was built.

The Protestant Reformation did not have much immediate effect in Wales, though most Welsh people accepted the shift as their previously Catholic churches became Anglican (the Established Church). However, Nonconformity slowly gained ground, and in the nineteenth century, especially after 1811, when the Methodists, who had for almost a century been gradually drifting away, officially broke with the Anglican Church, Methodism and Nonconformity grew until Wales was a mainly Nonconformist nation with a strong chapel culture (now in decline). One of the folkloric contributions of Welsh Nonconformist worship is the *cymanfa ganu*, a festival of hymn singing. Once an important feature of chapel life, it could range anywhere on the spectrum from a serious worship service to a social gathering. Outside Wales, the *cymanfa ganu*, no longer necessarily attached to a chapel or church, often serves as a celebration of Welshness. Nonconformists also developed their own narrative lore with, for example, a rich fund of anecdotes about their preachers, such as the pre-eminent preacher John Elias: one time as he mimed shooting a fiery arrow, the mesmerized crowd parted to avoid the arrow's shaft. The Methodist view of the Welsh as a people thirsting for religious knowledge is illustrated by a historical legend about Mary Jones, who, having carefully saved her pennies, walked barefoot some twenty-five miles over the mountains to buy a Bible from Thomas Charles, a key editor of the Welsh Bible, who later presented her efforts to acquire a Bible as a motivating factor in the development of the British and Foreign Bible Society. Shifting religious attitudes over the centuries are naturally reflected in folklore as it is continually re-created. Wells that had been the site of pre-Christian rites or of a saint's healing miracles and then perhaps wishing or cursing wells as memory of the saints faded fell into disrepute in the nineteenth century and have mainly been forgotten (except in the way that any fountain might currently attract coins). Gwyn ap Nudd, originally a lord of the Otherworld, was re-interpreted as a king of devils and then of fairies.

The rise of Nonconformity is tied in with other forces of social change of the nineteenth century, especially the Industrial Revolution. In the first half of the century, the expansion of coal mines and industrialization mainly in the south drew much of the population away from the still rural north and mid-Wales. The Anglican Church, bound to established parishes and church buildings, was not as flexible as the Nonconformists, who adjusted more readily to the frontier atmosphere, meeting wherever people gathered. As people moved away from their home areas and the traditional controls of their home communities, they created new communities in which their new religious organizations and workers' organizations collaborated in giving a new structure to society. Wales had had a very rich traditional life built around the agricultural cycle and the church's feast days, much of which was replaced as people created new traditions to serve their new needs. Moreover, much of the native tradition was purposely destroyed by the Nonconformists, who were offended by what they saw as the frivolity of music, dance, storytelling, and games along with any festivals, which seemed too irreligious or too Anglican. Railroads, which both carried people away from the north and brought in new products and ideas, also undermined the older traditions. Furthermore, English workers, attracted by the new job opportunities, joined the Welsh workers, who were themselves being mixed together from every part of Wales, effecting changes in language and thereby in the oral culture.

POETRY AND STORYTELLING

Wales has a deep oral and literary tradition of poetry, stemming from the learned classes of the early Celts and early medieval Wales, which appears in folk tradition in a number of ways, of which the *eisteddfod* is one of the most significant. The *eisteddfod*, originally an assembly of poets and musicians who gathered to regulate professional matters, can be traced at least to 1176. In Elizabethan times it was used by the authorities to regulate "rhymsters" and "vagabonds" but fell into disuse. Revived in the eighteenth century as a meeting of poets, it became a more popular and public event in the nineteenth century when used by yr *Hen Bersoniaid Llengar* (the Old Literary Clerics) and other men with literary and antiquarian interests who were concerned with preserving traditional Welsh culture, which they did in part by means of regional literary societies. Combined also with neo-druidic ceremonies invented by Iolo Morganwg, the National Eisteddfod, though not in itself folkloric, has become since the late nineteenth century a major festival, an annual, weeklong celebration of the arts of poetry, prose, music, and dance along with a great deal of national pride. As well as helping to honor and preserve certain Welsh traditions and serving as an acknowledgment of Welshness, the Eisteddfod has also given rise to its own folklore, especially anecdotes about events on the competition field or in the campgrounds. Local and regional *eisteddfodau* are held at all levels from schoolchildren through adults. The highest honor of any *eisteddfod* goes to the winning poet. The special role of poets, guardians of knowledge, is perhaps further indicated by the belief that anyone who spends the night alone on top of Cadair Idris, a mountain in north Wales, will come down mad, blind, or a poet. An evening's entertainment might involve a friendly competition exchanging extempore verses in a traditional form.

Wales also has a storytelling tradition dating back to the earliest periods. Although whatever it may once have had of magic tales has for the most part disappeared (possibly destroyed by Nonconformist disapproval as well as the disappearance through socioeconomic change of storytelling occasions), humorous tales, animal tales, and other of the shorter genres persist. Welsh narrative tradition's greatest wealth is in its legendry: religious legends about saints and Nonconformists, supernatural legends about ghosts and fairies, historical legends about noted people and events, and contemporary legends, frequently shared with other cultures, about contaminated food, microwaves, and acquired immunodeficiency syndrome (AIDS). Though many of the legends are highly localized, some enjoy widespread usage, such as the one about *Cantre'r Gwaelod* (the lowland cantref), which was drowned when the drunken keeper of the sea dyke opened the gates. Nothing remains except the ringing of a church bell from under Cardigan Bay on calm evenings. Similar legends are told about various lakes in Wales. A legend, invented in the eighteenth century to explain the village name Bedd Gelert, has become well established, telling how Prince Llywelyn, finding his son's cradle overturned and his hound Gelert with a bloody muzzle, precipitately slew the dog, only to discover the child safe where he lay next to a dead wolf. The prince buried his faithful dog in Bedd Gelert ("Gelert's Grave"). The legend of Devil's Bridge tells that when an old woman's cow became stranded on the other side of a ravine, the Devil agreed to build a bridge in one night in exchange for the soul of the first living being to cross. The woman "tested" the bridge's construction by throwing a piece of bread on it, and her little dog ran to fetch the bread, thus frustrating the Devil.

Songs and Music

Wales is often called the Land of Song. As early as the twelfth century, Gerald of Wales praised the Welsh for their skills on the harp, pipes, and crwth (a stringed instrument) and for their multi-part singing. All instrumental music suffered under the Methodist Revival, but the harp, which was played in the homes of the common people after the Middle Ages when gentry became too Anglicized to patronize traditional Welsh culture, has recovered its place as Wales's most characteristic instrument. By the end of the eighteenth century, the triple harp (originally Italy's baroque harp) with its three rows of strings (sharps and flats in the middle row) had become predominant. The pedal harp became more popular once again in the nineteenth century, but there are efforts more recently to revive the triple harp along with the related traditions of improvisation and traditional Welsh dance music. The Welsh are still noted for their part-singing, whether in chapel or in competitive male choirs. The arts of harp and voice are brought together in *cerdd dant* (string art) or *penillion* (stanza singing), in which the singer (originally extemporaneously) sings verses in countermelody to a tune played on the harp.

English and Modern Influences

The Welsh and English had interacted with each other for centuries, especially along the border, but cultural assimilation was accelerated first in the nineteenth century with the arrival of English workers and the railroads and then in the twentieth century with broadcast media and a deluge of popular culture. Generalizations about Welsh folk culture are complicated by the fact that some native Welsh people use Welsh as their hearth language (that is, mother tongue), while some use only English, and there are by now generations of non-native Welsh living in Wales. Furthermore, nationalism plays a part within populations of both Welsh and non-Welsh speakers, producing lore such as anecdotes about specific events in the nationalist struggle or the custom of placing one postage stamp (with its picture of the queen) upside down to demonstrate disapproval. Most aspects of culture are the same for all of these groups, though there are obvious exceptions connected to language such as the abundance of Welsh proverbs and verses. Nonetheless, the result of assimilation is that many aspects of food, dress, and custom are the same in Wales and in England. Ideas of a cooked breakfast (for example, with eggs, fried meat, grilled tomatoes, toast, and marmalade) or afternoon tea (with sponges, jam rolls, and small sandwiches) or wedding cake (a fruitcake) are essentially the same. Nonetheless, Wales does have certain foods special to itself: *cawl* (soup, especially as made with leeks and meat), Welsh cakes (small griddle cakes), *bara brith* (speckled bread, a loaf cake made with raisins or currants), or, along the south coast, *bara lawr* (laver bread, cooked seaweed). Most of the more elaborate community, seasonal, and calendar customs have vanished. For example, the Welsh, who used to put more emphasis on New Year's than on Christmas, now celebrate Christmas and Boxing Day much as the English currently do (with an increasing use of Christmas trees, turkey, and plum pudding) rather than with groups of children or grown men going door-to-door claiming coins or food and drink while singing verses, performing small dramas, and dancing. Some of these older customs such as wassailing and hunting the wren were shared with English peasants, but some such as the *Mari Lwyd* (Gray

Mary), which involved the group of singers and a leader carrying a horse's skull (on a pole with the carrier hidden beneath a white cloth) that would snap at people until treats were provided and which has disappeared except for a few isolated cases or in revival, were special to Wales.

Industrialization and a globalized economy have made most forms of traditional material culture unnecessary, but some have been kept going or been revived in support of national identity and the tourist trade. The Welsh costume of a red skirt and tall black hat, a nineteenth-century invention partially derived from earlier peasant dress, is worn by children at self-consciously Welsh events such as St. David's Day pageants and at tourist spots, and eighteenth-century farmworkers' dress appears as "folk dancing" costume. Love spoons, intricately carved wooden spoons with features such as chain links and caged balls, were in the seventeenth through nineteenth centuries commonly given by the carver as a token of affection and are now sold as decorations, as are corn dollies, which once used to carry the luck of the harvest over into the next year. The distinctive and complex double-weave patterns of

Welsh costume, ca. 1900. Today this costume of a red skirt and tall black hat— a nineteenth-century invention—is worn by children at Welsh events such as St. David's Day pageants and at tourist spots. (Courtesy Library of Congress)

Welsh tapestry appear as placemats, change purses, and coats. The coracle, a small, flat-bottomed, wicker-work boat covered with hide, was once used all over Wales but is now licensed in just a few places for salmon fishing (and to provide picturesque postcards).

As with any living tradition, there is a continual mixing of old with new. Older traditions, such as turning the silver in one's pocket upon hearing the first cuckoo of spring to ensure good luck for the year or interpreting a wild bird in the house as a sign of death, persist in small ways, and it is still useful to know how to lay a peat or a coal fire. People still share remarks about the miserliness of Cardis (people from the county of Ceredigion) or the Welsh propensity for splitting off into new chapels. On the other hand, contemporary Welsh people, no longer playing games in the churchyard, now share with other nations the culture of rugby, cricket, and football (soccer)—though they are noted for giving matches a distinctive Welsh touch with the variety and quality of the songs sung by fans.

Edward Lhuyd, in the late seventeenth century, included folklore in his collection of cultural, natural, and historical information from around Wales, and antiquarians collected some folklore in the eighteenth century, but the major studies began in the nineteenth century, tied in with romantic nationalism. Welsh antiquarians and nationalists sought to preserve every aspect of Welsh tradition they could find. These materials were printed in journals and in books by such scholars as the Anglican minister Elias Owen (1896) and the Oxford professor John Rhys (1901). The Welsh Folk Museum, founded by Iorwerth C. Peate and opened in 1948, has actively preserved and recorded many aspects of folklore, though most extensively on material culture and dialects and generally with a view to that which is passing or already vanished from current usage. Their findings, along with other twentieth-century research, have been published in many booklets and also in major works (in English) by Owen (1959), Peate (1972), Jenkins (1976), and others. Relatively little work on contemporary Welsh folklore has been done, and the little there is has been published mostly in Welsh.

BIBLIOGRAPHY

Bromwich, Rachel, ed. 1978. *Trioedd Ynys Prydein/The Welsh Triads*. Cardiff: University of Wales Press.

Gerald of Wales. 1978. *The Journey through Wales and the Description of Wales*, translated by Lewis Thorpe. Harmondsworth: Penguin.

Grooms, Chris. 1993. *The Giants of Wales: Cewri Cymru*. Welsh Studies 10. Lewistown, PA: Edwin Mellen Press.

Gwyndaf, Robin. 1989. *Chwedlau Gwerin Cymru / Welsh Folk Tales*. Cardiff: National Museum of Wales.

Henken, Elissa R. 1987. *Traditions of the Welsh Saints*. Woodbridge: D. S. Brewer.

———. 1991. *Welsh Saints: A Study in Patterned Lives*. Woodbridge: D. S. Brewer.

———. 1996. *National Redeemer: Owain Glyndŵr in Welsh Tradition*. Cardiff and Ithaca, NY: University of Wales Press and Cornell University Press.

Huws, John Owen. 1996. *Y Nain yn y Carped*. Llanrwst: Gwasg Carreg Gwalch.

Jenkins, J. Geraint. 1976. *Life and Tradition in Rural Wales*. London: J. M. Dent.

Jones, Francis. 1992 (1954). *The Holy Wells of Wales*. Cardiff: University of Wales Press.

Owen, Elias. 1976 (1896). *Welsh Folk-Lore: A Collection of the Folk-Tales and Legends of North Wales*. East Ardsley: EP Publishing.

Owen, Trefor M. 1959. *Welsh Folk Customs*. Cardiff: National Museum of Wales, Welsh Folk Museum.

———. 1991. *The Customs and Traditions of Wales. A Pocket Guide*. Cardiff: University of Wales Press.

Peate, Iorwerth C. 1972. *Tradition and Folk Life: A Welsh View*. London: Faber and Faber.

Rhys, John. 1980 (1901). *Celtic Folklore: Welsh and Manx*. London: Wildwood House.

Elissa R. Henken

Nordic Countries

DENMARK

GEOGRAPHY AND HISTORY

Approximately 5.5 million people live in Denmark, a Scandinavian country consisting of 43,000 square kilometers of land, spread over a peninsula and many islands. Geohistorically, the country is a farmland with farming and fishing as its fundamen-

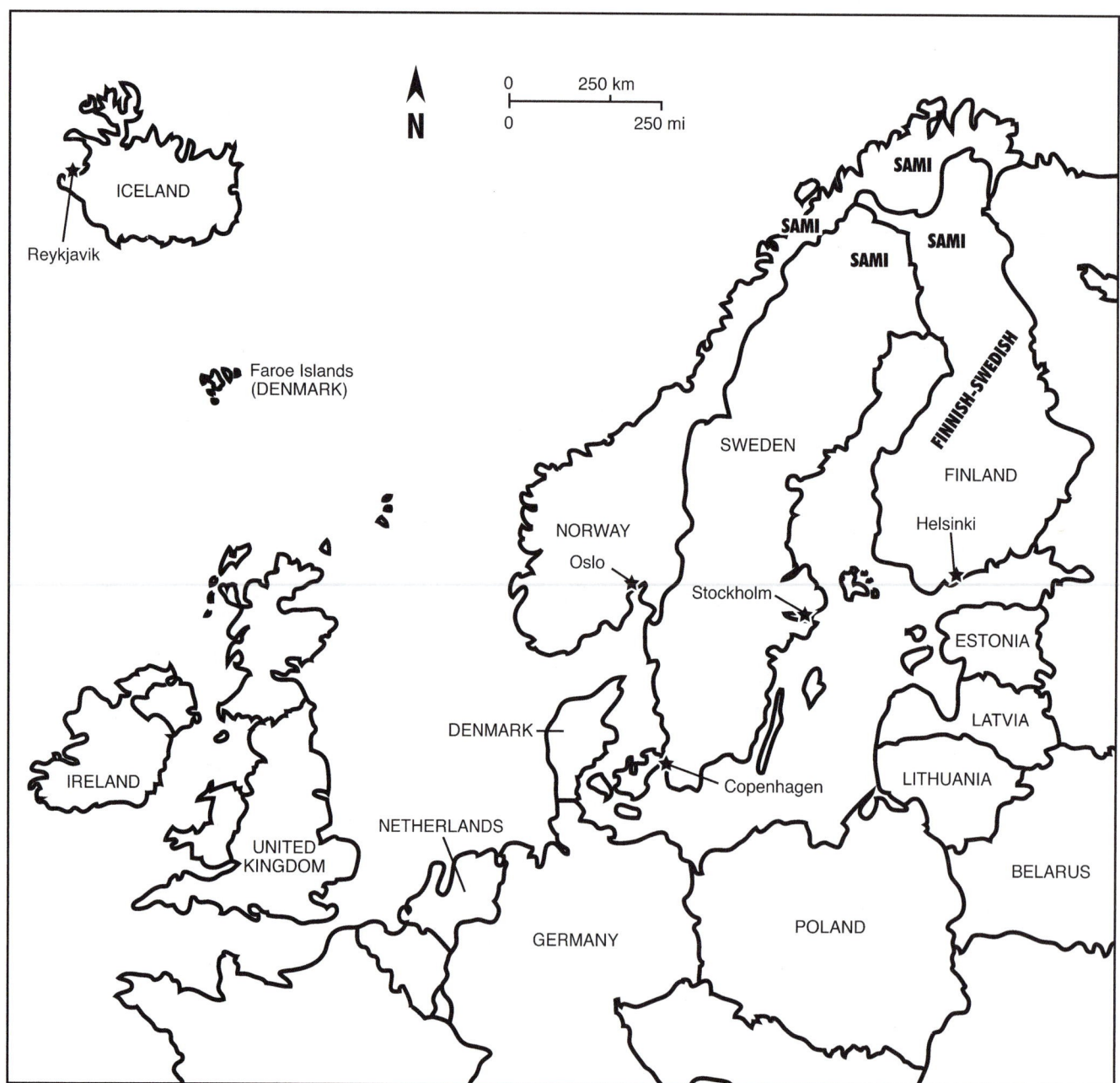

Nordic Countries.

tals. Today, though farming is still important, most Danes work in business, technology, education, and communications. Politically, Denmark is a democratic monarchy. The language is Danish, a close relative of Swedish and Norwegian and more distantly kin to languages spoken on the Faroe Islands and **Iceland**. There are many different Danish dialects, which once were so diverse that it was difficult for people from different regions to communicate. Today this is hardly the case because of the influence of the mass media. Within the last generation the English influence has been so significant, especially among youngsters, that a new composite speech called Danglish has developed.

Contemporary Danes think of Denmark as a homogeneous country, where most of the population is descended from the ancient Danes. However, immigration from other parts of Europe has affected the population, and the standard language among the ruling class has been periodically influenced by Latin, French, and German. During the first part of the twentieth century, Jews and Poles were significant ethnic minorities, and since 1970 larger ethnic communities of people from Chile, Yugoslavia, the Middle East, and Somalia, and Inuit people from **Greenland**—among others— have become part of the Danish population.

Due to its vast coastal line, Denmark was settled by Stone Age people at around 7000 B.C.E., and they left their marks through stone axes, stone knives, and other tools, which can still be found on beaches and fields, providing Danes with a historical identity that is displayed in many museums all around the country as well as on shelves and windowsills in people's homes. From 4000 B.C.E. people started cultivating the land, laying the basis for a rural culture that has been the main influence on what has been considered traditional Danish folklore.

The Viking period (700 C.E.–1000 C.E.) also played an important part in Danish identity. Viewed as a time filled with adventure, travel, and warfare, the Viking period left remains such as wooden ships, gold and silver jewelry, and weapons. Though the violent and powerful perception of the Viking age has been modified, the Viking remains one of the symbols of power and might for Danes. Today at soccer matches, fans wear Viking helmets and paint their faces with the colors of the Danish flag, sometimes even wearing robes made of the flag.

The national legend of the Danish flag, called Dannebrog, holds that it fell down from God in Heaven in 1219 to help one of the first Danish kings, Valdemar the Victorious, in combat in Estonia. After that event Denmark became what is considered the first empire of Northern Europe. Particularly since the middle of the nineteenth century, the Dannebrog has been an important symbol of national pride, not only in public life but in Danish personal identity. Today at most birthday parties the Dannebrog is hoisted on a pole in the garden and on the dinner table, gifts are wrapped in paper with printed with Dannebrogs, and a layered cake with small Dannebrogs on top is served. At very special birthdays—for instance, when somebody turns thirty, fifty, or sixty—song sheets with Dannebrogs on top are distributed to the celebrants of the occasion.

During its history the size of Denmark has varied. It was ruled by chiefs and later kings, subsidized by the nobility and landlords. The present monarchy derives from the tenth century. In 1849 Denmark was supplied with a democratic constitution, providing civil rights to all persons with citizenship (excluding women, young and poor people, and immigrants). During the Middle Ages till 1864, Denmark lost wars and land to its neighbors. But as the country was decreasing, the national identity was increasing, influenced also by the Enlightenment and especially the Romantic period. When urbanization and later industrialization slowly entered the country in the nineteenth century, many interests converged to create a national Danish history and identity. These civic interests searched for evidences of national identity in pre-history and among contemporary peasants because they were considered repositories of ancient traditions, customs, and beliefs.

One of the concerned citizens who participated in the creation of the democratic constitution in 1849 was N.S.F. Grundtvig, a Christian priest who was part of a nationwide movement for education, enlightenment, and community for rural people. He founded the folk high school, a people's institution for the education of unlearned peasants' young children. The folk high schools still exist. Young people can "learn for their life," according to one of the mottoes, while they live together for three to nine months. (Today, these schools include "family high schools," "sports high schools," and "senior high schools," where one- or two-week courses are offered to specialized audiences.) Talking and singing were important elements in Grundtvig's folk movement. He celebrated the "word alive" as an instrument of enlightenment for ordinary people and wrote a prodigious number of religious and national songs, which endure as an important part of Danish culture. N.F.S. Grundtvig's son Svend adhered to the romantic idea of valuing peasants' knowledge and culture as a precious relic of the Danish Golden Age. Consequently, Svend Grundtvig is one of the founding collectors of Danish folklore, since he helped to initiate nationwide interest in the subject and encouraged collectors around the country to contact and interview peasants to document their way of life. The folk high schools became local centers, which encouraged collecting Danish folklore during the last part of the nineteenth and early twentieth centuries.

Evald Tang Kristensen, a schoolteacher, was inspired by the younger Grundtvig to start collecting folklore in 1867, when he was a young man in his twenties. Kristensen spent his whole life (he died at the age of eighty-six in 1929) collecting ballads, folksongs, fairy tales, proverbs, dialect usages, legends, rhymes, jingles, plays, riddles, narratives about popular beliefs, healing practices, daily life, and customs. He wandered about the country to collect folklore through direct contact with ordinary people. His favorite sources were in Jutland—especially the poorest people—because he often found they knew the body of old folklore. He published seventy-two books, including more than 7,000 pages concerning daily life and folklore, and thirteen volumes containing approximately 22,000 legends. Moreover, many of his writings and letters are still unpublished and preserved in the Danish Folklore Archives. Many collectors of folklore were busy by the end of the nineteenth century, but no one approached the level of activity of Kristensen, whose large collection contains the basic knowledge of traditional Danish folklore. We should note, then, that much of what we know of traditional Danish folklore comes from a particular time (the nineteenth century) and people (the poor peasants of Jutland).

RELIGION

Religious beliefs can be traced back to Norse mythology and the cult of Thor, widespread in Scandinavia. The religious system consisted of many gods, among them Odin, Thor, Frej, Freja, Tyr, and the trickster Loki. Each god was responsible for specific phenomena in nature and human life. Many of the gods' names are still used daily in the Danish language in place-names and in the names of the weekdays: Tirsdag (Tuesday), Onsdag (Wednesday), Torsdag (Thursday), and Fredag (Friday). As some of the Vikings traveled abroad, they ravaged and settled in **England**, which explains the resemblance between English and Danish terms for the weekdays.

Tenth-century Viking smith's mold for casting both Christian crosses and Thor's hammers. Such amulets were widely used throughout Scandinavia, and several burials have provided evidence of people wearing both Christian and pagan symbols. (© 2004 Werner Forman/TopFoto/The Image Works)

Denmark was Christianized during the reign of King Harald Blåtand (Bluetooth) in the tenth century. As a monument to the new religion, Harald Blåtand raised a runic stone in 960, celebrating his parents and himself and announcing the Christian baptism of Denmark. In 1536 a nationwide Lutheran Reformation replaced the influence of Catholicism. Christianity was not so much an individual preference in Denmark as it was forced upon ordinary people. The Lutheran Church became an integral part of the Danish Constitution in 1849. It remains a state church today. Other religions are allowed, but Lutheranism has overall priority. This creates problems connected with other religions, whose members, for instance, are forced to follow the Danish registration practice for newborn babies, which has been under the jurisdiction of the Lutheran Church for several hundred years. Also in public schools, the vacation schedule conforms to the Christian holy days, though almost 10 percent of the students are not of Danish origin.

However, the Danish folk belief system has been a conglomeration of Catholicism, Protestantism, paganism, and animism. Christian theologians fought against what was considered paganism, especially in the seventeenth century, when witch hunting was at its peak in Denmark. It is estimated that 1,000 accused witches were executed on bonfires in Denmark. Most were elderly women, and the last woman to be officially accused of being a witch was Anne Palles in 1693. She had, however, a dispensation from King Christian V, specifying that she was to be beheaded before being burnt. Not until 1866 did the article on witches disappear from Danish law.

SUPERNATURAL LORE

Folk beliefs center on creatures and elements in nature and black and white magic. Nature was considered to be inhabited by different creatures living in water, hills, trees, and forests: pixies, trolls, and elves of different kinds. It was important to respect these creatures and their habitats, for they could punish or disturb the disrepectful.

Another category of belief-creatures existed between the human and the Otherworld. These were mainly ghosts, werewolves, and small, animal-like women, called mares, who rode men (and occasionally women) at night and gave them nightmares. Many of these creatures were being punished for improper behavior as humans. For instance, it was believed that a pregnant woman could prevent herself from pain in labor by climbing through a hole in a magic tree or through the skin of a dead horse. Pain in labor, however, was God's judgment at the expulsion from Paradise. Hence, it was sinful to try to prevent the pain. Nature itself would punish the woman through her newborn child, who would be a werewolf if male and a mare if female. Since werewolves and mares were a threat to ordinary people, everybody tried to prevent pregnant women from acting in this un-Christian way. Moreover, pregnant women had best stay indoors from dusk till dawn because of the threat from werewolves. A werewolf is a man who is condemned to turn into a wolf at night, and one of the ways for him to be rescued is to find a pregnant woman and eat the heart of her unborn child. Many of these folk beliefs had moral content, especially stressing women as sexually threatening beings capable of reproduction.

Beliefs about the mare and the witch seem to converge in many instances, especially references to "rides" either on a man or on a horse at night. But beliefs about witches are much more widespread and complex than those about the mare. The witch is connected with both healing traditions and religious practices with either black or white magic. Witches could steal from people without being present, they could bring on diseases and even death for people and animals, and they could practice healing by means of magic or herbal medicine. Before the scientific era of the nineteenth century, healing traditions in the public sphere were connected to religious practices. Priests were regarded most favorably as healers through the use of prayer. The folklore record also notes Christian priests practicing white magic—for instance, releasing wandering souls and ghosts from their destiny. In the folk healing practices, different kinds of people and things played a role. Barbers and other skilled men could use a knife on the human body, herbalists of different kinds made and sold ointments and extracts, and wisemen and wisewomen knew all sorts of good advice—for instance, magic connected to certain numbers, words, objects, and elements in nature.

During the eighteenth and nineteenth centuries, medical doctors trained at the university gained the full license to practice healing, as supported by the enlightened state, and the various other healing practices were condemned as non-scientific and "alternative." At the periphery, however, many kinds of healing practices and belief systems have survived. In the first half of the twentieth century, body-and-nature reformism was practiced with gymnastics, open-air activities, naturism, vegetarianism, and other concerns about digestion and health. Also, occultism, in particular clairvoyance and elevation sessions, held a certain appeal. The influence of astrology increased during the second half of the twentieth century, along with such traditions as fortune-telling, tarot, numerology, clairvoyant healing, and shamanism. In 2002 the number of nurses and medical doctors graduating from Danish universities was actually less than the number of graduates from schools of alternative healing.

In many cases, healing practices continue to converge with religious beliefs. Recently, a few Christian priests in Denmark have performed exorcisms, recalling the white magic practiced by priests in pre-modern times. The minister for ecclesiastical affairs, who is usually an educated Christian theologian, has to approve every religion practiced in Denmark. In 2003, the cult of Thor was accepted by the minister as a legitimate organized religion.

SONGS AND FOLKTALES

Performances of music, song, dance, and verbal art have occurred within the context of the above-mentioned social activities. In Denmark, a large collection of medieval ballads dates from 1550 to 1700. These ballads were probably connected primarily with the higher classes. Other kinds of songs and melodies used by the commonfolk have been collected since the nineteenth century. The old songs tended to be very long and to have a refrain, which everybody sang, while one person sang the narrative lines. Some of these songs were used as the melody line for a chain dance. Songs also accompany some games. Also telling riddles, jokes, and fairy tales has been connected to social activity. Fairy tales from folk tradition inspired Hans Christian. Andersen in his writings. A rich tradition of proverbs collected by Peder Laale and Peder Syv dates from the sixteenth and seventeenth centuries. Evald Tang Kristensen collected a vast amount of material—everything from fairy tales, proverbs, and riddles, to songs and melodies.

Since the early nineteenth century and the adoption of the constitution, singing nationalistic songs praising Danish history, the land, and nature has become popular. Denmark has many such songs, more widely known in the past than they are now. Singing at Christmas Eve remains popular. This includes a tradition of walking around the Christmas tree hand in hand, while singing songs from the early nineteenth century, which celebrate the story of Jesus' birth.

For more creative outlets of singing and verbal performances, the party tradition in Danish culture demands that people sit around a table for hours, eating, drinking, and taking turns in performing speeches and singing songs together. Many songs are composed for the occasion in praise of the person(s) honored by the occasion. This distinctively Danish custom contrasts with other traditions that blend elements from many cultures.

CALENDAR CUSTOMS

Social activities and festivities in pre-modern Denmark were organized according to the human life cycle and the yearly round of agricultural activities. Many gatherings centered on collective work such as harvesting, construction, and the making of clothing. Neighbors joined the work process, and once tasks were completed, the host offered a meal and something to drink. These working parties could be held all year round depending upon the tasks that needed to be done. Other social activities closely connected to the cycle of the year were Shrovetide, Midsummer's Eve, the harvest celebration, and Christmas.

Springtime was an especially busy period with parties for the youngsters, who were often organized in youth groups. The festival traditions for Danish youth vary both in content and in time of the year, but primarily such celebrations occurred during the period between Christmas and Midsummer's Eve. At some occasions, the youth met to play at rather informal "play-sessions," and their play activities often involved physical contact between the sexes. Physical activities such as running, catching, or hiding were popular. Dancing was, of course, a popular activity, but this required a musician and cost money, which the youngsters seldom had.

Gatherings during winter or early spring necessitated an indoor site. Often the richest farmers had big rooms in their houses exclusively for the purpose of festivity. The youngsters might borrow such a room, or farmers might take turns in hosting them. Often the males in the youth group had the responsibility of getting a room and something to drink, while the females brought the food. Some were supposed to be better equipped than others, complete with a musician. In such cases, youths—perhaps only the males—went around to the farms in the area to beg for money or for food for the party. The youngsters might walk or, if they were males only, ride horses, and often they were costumed as mummers who would perform at each farm in exchange for food or money. Youngsters could express their dislike toward certain adult members of the village by not visiting their homes.

Some winter social traditions did not involve a gathering by the whole group of youngsters, but only small groups of mummers, probably only males, who visited the houses in the neighborhood, were offered something to eat and performed with their identities unknown. Disguised like this, they could challenge certain social rules. The popularity of a farmer's house could be measured by the number of mummers' visits. A similar tradition at New Year's had people wandering around in the dark playing pranks, which could consist of making loud noises, throwing dust inside houses, or pulling carriages apart.

Earlier folkloristic interpretations of some of these games assigned them to what were considered old, pagan traditions such as worshipping the Devil or good and evil forces in nature supposedly to attract fertility in agricultural practice and human life. Shrovetide in February is one of these events, which has been connected with pre-Christian beliefs and traditions. According to this interpretation, youngsters played "King Winter" and "King Summer." These beings were supposed to fight until King Summer won, enabling the sun and the summer to come. Shrovetide is related to Carnival, called Fastelavn, which means—with a heavy influence from a German dialect—the night before fast. Documentation from the seventeenth century and later reports that youngsters mummed at Shrovetide, touring the neighborhood in a large group, begging for food and money for the party in the evening, and playing certain games during the day. The games played outside could be rough and violent. For instance, some involved a live cock, which was supposed to be caught and/or killed. This is seen as a survival of a pre-Christian attempt to catch fertility for the year to come, since the cock connoted male fertility (reinforced by the Danish slang *kok*, once used to mean the male sexual organ).

Another animal connected to Shrovetide is the black cat, though only a few documents in the archives mention a black cat especially at Shrovetide. The black cat plays a role in many legends from all over the country, as it supposedly represents either the Devil or a witch. However, the black cat has survived as a symbol of Shrovetide, while the cock is forgotten. The cruelty to the cock from the past has been replaced by the practice of placing a black cat inside a barrel, which is hung up and beaten to pieces. Of course, the cat is not present when this custom is practiced today among children only, but the story connected to this tradition relates that a cat used to be inside the barrel. Nowadays barrels are decorated with cartoon black cats.

Later in the year, as spring approached, bringing more daylight, the youngsters would meet at outdoor celebrations involving physical games, dancing, and singing. Often these games were oriented toward organizing the sexes into couples. In some areas of Denmark, a chosen chief, *gadebasse*, had charge of organizing the couples each year. In parts of Denmark, these events culminated in evening bonfires during the period between April and July. This custom came to be interpreted to be a special Danish tradition at Midsummer's Eve, and modern Danes perceive it as a very old Danish tradition on the day of St. John, 24 June. Today Danes meet, eat and drink, and light a bonfire, after which a nationalist hymn is sung. The symbol of a witch figures into contemporary Midsummer's Eve customs, because witches were supposed to fly to their biggest witches' Sabbath of the year at Bloksbjerg at this time. Today, the bonfire often features the burning of a witch in effigy—perhaps a vestige of the witch burnings of four centuries ago. However, the burning witch figure is viewed more as catharsis than with empathy. The witch atop the bonfire at Midsummer's Eve is rather new, deriving from the twentieth century, but it has spread due to older beliefs associated with magic, which was believed to be operative on the longest day in the year.

The other half of the year, from summer till December, did not have as concentrated a program of social activities to celebrate the cycle of the year except for the harvesting parties. The Protestant Christian calendar parallels the pre-Christian seasonal round: spring is filled with holidays, while the fall has none. However, a well-known hypothesis has it that the Christian calendar is based upon the previous pagan religious celebrations.

Annual celebratory traditions today are influenced by re-interpretations of old Danish traditions and influences from other cultures. Christmas is primarily a tradition reserved for family celebration—the one exception being the *julefrokost*, a Christmas lunch. Everybody with a job participates in a *julefrokost* with his or her colleagues, often from Friday afternoon until late at night. The tradition derives from the last half of the twentieth century but is widespread and involves considerable food, drink, and narratives about sexual excesses. A traditional *julefrokost* consists basically of pickled herring eaten on rye bread with beer and schnapps. Other dishes may be added. Every Friday night during the month of December frenetic traffic clogs streets and roads in Danish cities, and all cabs are occupied.

For the children, Christmas begins on 1 December with the opening of Christmas calendars. Children open one slot on the calendar each day, receiving a little gift from inside. On television special programs called "Christmas calendars" are shown every day, often involving pixies, princesses, Santa Claus, and *risengrød*, a porridge made with rice. This dish used to be the luxury food that people ate for Christmas some 100 years ago. It is made with white rice, once rare and expensive. Today, *risengrød* is connected to pixies and is one of many traditional Christmas dishes. Christmas Day in Denmark is celebrated on Christmas Eve, 24 December. In the days between Christmas Eve and New Year's Eve, families gather and have *julefrokost*.

While the Christmas holidays are reserved for family, New Year's Eve is a celebration mainly with friends.

After Shrovetide, today only a children's celebration, comes Valentine's Day, which is slowly entering Danish culture. Easter is a Christian holiday but is currently not celebrated to the extent of other days. The workers' International Day on 1 May is a public event, when people meet in parks according to political affiliation. (According to the old calendar, 1 May was called *Valborgs Dag* and involved an outdoor party for the youth in many areas of Denmark.) The Carnival preceding Lent, complete with people dancing the samba in the streets, is relatively new, beginning in Copenhagen in the 1980s. After Midsummer's Eve, no scheduled celebrations occur according to the calendar until Christmas. But new traditions are emerging, such as Ramadan, celebrated by Muslims living in Denmark, and Halloween, which has recently become a popular event among children and youth.

CELEBRATIONS

In pre-modern Denmark, other social activities and festivities focused on the life cycle. Three big events were celebrated: baptisms, weddings, and funerals. These celebrations concentrated on the individual, focusing primarily upon his or her position in the community. They usually involved a church and priest with afterward a gathering of people for eating and drinking. For pregnant women, a fourth religious tradition called *kirketagning*, which means re-acceptance as a Christian person, occurred. After having given birth, a woman was considered like a pagan and until she was re-accepted by God—represented by the priest in the church—six weeks later remained in great danger, unprotected from evil forces. The same would be true for her baby until it was baptized.

Today many additional social activities celebrate the individual as an individual and his or her position in the community. Birthdays, for example, are important for both children and adults, and for adults, the birthdays ending with a zero are highlighted. The Christian confirmation for children aged thirteen to fourteen years, graduations, jubilees, and anniversaries are celebrated. Housewarming is another social activity marking a significant life event. Marriage and its connected pre-party, *polterabend*, have become more emphasized within the last twenty years. Narratives about *polterabends* tend to focus upon excessive actions—friends making fun of the person who is to be married, maybe even committing acts of vandalism, or terrorizing the groom to the extent of preventing him from arriving for the ceremony on time. Most *polterabends*, though, are probably more innocent.

STUDIES OF DANISH FOLKLORE

Most publications dealing with Danish folklore are in Danish. For a general overview, see Steensberg (1982) or Troels-Lund (1929). More about verbal art can be found in Jonsen, Svale, and Danielson (1978). For old Danish proverbs, see Kjær and Sørensen (1983–1988) and Hansen and Behrend (1929). Kristensen has published many important works, especially a collection of legends (1980). An extensive collection of folksongs is Grundtvig and others (1966–1976). For more information about Danish folk music, see Koudal (1992) and Møller (1976). Sound recordings include Knudsen and Nørgaard (1963). Publications about festival and play include Ellekilde (1943) and Piø (n.d.). Both are short guides to the traditional festivals of the year in peasant Denmark. A very thorough and informative guide in English to Danish folklore traditions of the year appears at link "Traditions & Food" at the Web site www.denmark.dk. Two important books about games with songs are Nielsen (1981) and Thyregod (1931). Belief systems and medical practices can be studied in Rørbye (2002), which deals with the medical system and its alternatives from a folkloristic-historical perspective. A book treating witchcraft is Ankarloo and Henningsen (1993). The history of Danish folklore studies provides the subject for Holbek and Knudsen (1971), Holbek (1987), and Kofod (1989). The Web site of the Danish Folklore Archive is www.dafo.dk.

BIBLIOGRAPHY

Ankarloo, Bengt, and Gustav Henningsen, eds. 1993. *Early Modern European Witchcraft: Centres and Peripheries.* Oxford: Clarendon.

Ellekilde, Hans. 1943. *Danske højtidsskikke.* Copenhagen: J. H. Schultz Forlag.

Grundtvig, Sven, and others, eds. 1966–1976. *Danmarks gamle Folkeviser I–XII.* Copenhagen: Universitets-Jubilæets Danske Samfund.

Hansen, Aage, and Chr. Behrend. 1929. *Peder Laale's danske Ordsprog.* Copenhagen: Munksgaard.

Holbek, Bengt. 1987. *Interpretation of Fairy Tales: Danish Folkore in a European Perspective.* Helsinki: Suomalainen tiedeakatemia.

Holbek, Bengt, and Thorkild Knudsen. 1971. Evald Tang Kristensen. (1843–1929). In *Leading Folklorists of the North,* edited by Dag Strömbäck. Oslo: Universitetsforlaget. 239–257.

Jonsen, Bengt R., Solheim Svale, and Eva Danielson, eds. 1978. *The Types of the Scandinavian Medieval Ballad: A Descriptive Catalogue.* Stockholm: Skrifter utgivna av Svenskt Visarkiv, 5.

Kjær, Iver, and John Kousgård Sørensen, eds. 1983–1988. *Danske ordsprog.* Copenhagen: C. A. Reitzel.

Knudsen, Thorkild, and Anelise Nørgaard. 1963. *Dansk folkemusik* (sound recording). RCA DFS 451–455.

Kofod, Else Marie. 1989. *De vilde svaner og andre folkeeventyr: sidestykker til syv af H.C. Andersens eventyr.* Copenhagen: Foreningen Danmarks folkeminders skrifter Bd. 86.

Koudal, Jens Henrik. 1992. *Musiketnologi og folkemusikforskning i Danmark.* Copenhagen: DSF NYT.

Kristen, Evald Tang. 1980. *Danske sagn som de har lydt in folkemunde: udelukkende efter utrykte kilder,* edited by Johannes E. Tang Kristensen, Bengt Holbek, and Erik Ho. Copenhagen: Nyt Nordisk Forlag Arnold Busck.

Møller, Dorthe Falcon. 1976. Folk Music Instruments in Danish Iconographic Sources. *Studia instrumentorum musicae popularis* 4:73–76.

Nielsen, Svend. 1981. *Danske sanglege.* Gråsten: Drama.

Piø, Iørn. N.d. *Det festlige år.* Copenhagen: Sesam.

Rørbye, Birgitte. 2002. *Mellem sundhed og sygdom: om fortid, fremskridt og virkelige læger: en narrativ kulturanalyse,* edited by Anne Leonora Blaakilde. Copenhagen: MTF.

Steensberg, Axel, ed. 1982. *Dagligliv i Danmark i 17., 18., 19. og 20. århundrede.* 8 volumes. Copenhagen: Nyt Nordisk Forlag Arnold Busck.

Tang Kristensen, Evald. 1980. *Danske Sagn som de har lydt i folkemunde.* 8 volumes. Copenhagen: Nyt Nordisk Forlag Arnold Busck.

Thyregod, Tvermose S. 1931. *Danmarks Sanglege.* Copenhagen: Danmarks Folkeminder 38.

Troels-Lund, Troels Frederik. 1929. *Dagligt liv i Norden i det sekstende aarhundrede.* 14 volumes. Copenhagen: Gyldendalske Boghandel, Nordisk Forlag.

Anne Leonora Blaakilde

FINLAND

GEOGRAPHY AND HISTORY

The Republic of Finland is a Nordic country located in Northeastern Europe. It shares land borders with **Sweden, Norway,** and **Russia**; to the west is the Gulf of Bothnia, to the southwest the Baltic Sea, and to the southeast the Gulf of Finland, across which is the country of Estonia, with which Finland shares some linguistic characteristics. Finland is a land dominated by lakes—a grand total of 187,888, one of which, Lake Saimaa, is Europe's fifth largest. The landscape features few hills, being mostly flatland of which over two-thirds is still boreal forest. In addition, there are some 179,584 islands off the southwestern and southern coast, most notably the archipelago of the Åland Islands, which fall under Finnish sovereignty. Southern Finland is characterized by a temperate climate, but the northern quarter of Finland lies above the Arctic Circle; the Province of Lapland, in particular, is known for its harsh winters.

Archeologists believe that Finland was settled during the Stone Age around 8500 B.C.E. by hunter-gatherers who possibly spoke the Finno-Ugric language, which is not a part of the Indo-European language group. Successive waves of migration from these people pushed the indigenous **Sámi** (also known as Lapps), who speak a related language, into the harsher northern climes. Theories as to the origin of these ancestors of the Finns vary widely, with some researchers placing them in Southern Europe during the last Ice Age, while others postulate an origin in Siberia. However, modern genetic research finds the Finnish people most closely related to the Flemings of Belgium.

After 3200 B.C.E., a group of immigrants of the Battle Axe (or Cord-Ceramic) Culture settled in southern Finland. This brought more advanced agricultural and animal husbandry practices to the area. These migrants were likely of Indo-European stock. As Finland passed into the Bronze Age (1500–500 B.C.E.), further influence from regional cultures, most notably the Baltic peoples, resulted in the eventual divergence of the Finnish and Sámi languages. The Iron Age began in Finland in approximately 500 B.C.E., and trade with Scandinavia and Russia increased, but Finland would not begin to develop even the beginnings of a centralized society or a real sense of national identity until well into the late Middle Ages.

Christianity established itself in Finland in the eleventh century, but it was not until the thirteenth century that the church managed to stabilize. At this time, many secular rulers sought to exert their power in Finland. In the middle of the thirteenth century, the rather young Kingdom of Sweden managed to subdue most of the land, though the Republic of Novgorod in northwestern Russia established its rule in Karelia, a region that still retains significant ethnic and linguistic ties to Finland proper. As with the French language in England after 1066, Swedish became the language of the educated upper classes, while Finnish remained the language of the peasantry. (Swedish still remains an official language of the country, though it is spoken only as a primary language by a minority of people.) Thus began Finland's long rule by the Swedish kingdom. During the reign of King Gustav Vasa (1521–1560), the city of Helsinki was founded, and Protestantism became the official state religion for Sweden and its holdings. His death marked the beginning of a warlike phase for Sweden as his three sons, in successive reigns, fought at various times Estonia, **Poland**, **Denmark**, and Russia. The Club War (or Cudgel War) of 1596–1597 was a peasant rebellion protesting the effect of this militarism on the average Finnish people—most notably drafts and high taxes. It was suppressed with great ferocity by Swedish forces.

In the eighteenth century, Finland served as the stage for conflict between Russia and Sweden. Russian forces twice occupied virtually the whole of Finland in the periods from 1714 to 1721 and 1742 to 1743. These times of Russian occupation are known to the Finns as the "Greater Wrath" and "Lesser Wrath." In 1808, the armies of Tsar Alexander I finally conquered Finland, which remained an autonomous Grand Duchy in union with the Russian Empire until 1917, when Finland declared its independence following the Bolshevik Revolution. It was during this period of occupation that Finland developed a strong nationalist movement, with the government promoting the Finnish language over Swedish and Russian. The major cultural milestone of this period was the publication of the *Kalevala*, a collation of numerous folksongs collected from people living in the northern Karelia region. This work went on to become the national epic of the Finnish people. In 1892, the Finnish language achieved legal equality with Swedish.

Following independence, Finland suffered through a brief civil war between different strata of society—the "Whites," consisting of the educated classes and independent farmers, both of whom were largely supported by Imperial **Germany**, and the "Reds," rural and industrial workers who were backed by the Russian Bolsheviks. In part, Finland now served as a battleground between two opponents in World War I. However, the Treaty of Brest-Litovsk (3 March 1918), which marked Russia's exit from the war, spelled defeat for the Reds. On 3 April, German troops landed at Hanko, and the last of the Red fortifications fell the next month. Had Germany itself not fallen later that year, it is likely that Finland may have found itself ruled by yet another imperial master. The war polarized Finnish society and alienated the emergent nation from its Scandinavian neighbors, who had made the transition to democratic societies without so much bloodshed. In the period between world wars, Finland frequently changed its national allegiances, at one time even courting the favor of Nazi Germany. On 30 November 1939, the Soviet Union attacked Finland in what has come to be known as the Winter War. Finnish resistance, along with some limited Swedish support, helped to force a peace treaty upon the Soviets in March 1940, in which Finland ceded a portion of its land and industrial capacity. (Many historians have argued that the poor showing of the Soviet Union in Finland convinced Adolf Hitler to launch Operation Barbarossa in 1941.) After Germany occupied Norway, the government of Finland sought a closer bond with Hitler's regime. The goal of the Finnish government was to keep their nation independent, and an alliance with Germany seemed the surest way of countering attempted Soviet influence, for their eastern neighbor was exhibiting toward Finland much the same behavior that it had toward the Baltic states before launching a conquest of them. The Continuation War began on 25 June 1941, with the Soviets invading in response to perceived Finnish intransigence on transferring nickel mining rights in the Petsamo region from a British-Canadian company to a Soviet company. With extensive German assistance, Finland was able to force a cease-fire upon the Soviet Union on 4 September 1944. To this day, Finnish cooperation with Nazi Germany remains controversial. Following the conclusion of the Continuation War, the Finns, in compliance with their cease-fire with the Soviet Union, turned on their German former allies to drive them from the land in what is now called the Lapland War, since most of it took place in the northern part of the country.

During the Cold War era, Finland remained a neutral player on the world stage, seeking friendship with both the Soviet Union and its Scandinavian neighbors. Finland developed a welfare-state system similar to those of other Northern European countries. Following the dissolution of the Soviet Union in 1991, Finland abrogated its 1947 and 1948 treaties with that country and, in 1995, voted to join the European Union.

ELIAS LÖNNROT AND THE *KALEVALA*

The emergence of a modern Finnish national identity owed much to those individuals who preserved and promulgated the country's folklore. In this, Elias Lönnrot stands akin to a Finnish Homer for his compilation and editing of the *Kalevala*. Regarded as Finland's national epic, the *Kalevala* is distinctive from other such epics—for example, *The Iliad*, the *Niebelugenlied*, or the *Mahābhārata*—in that as a unified text the *Kalevala* is of comparatively recent origin, although the various poems that constitute it represent an oral tradition that reaches back into Finland's pre-Christian past.

Elias Lönnrot (1804–1884), a physician by profession, possessed a great love for the traditional stories of his native Finland and traveled extensively to collect stories and songs, primarily in the region of Karelia. He believed these stories constituted a once-continuous epic of the Finnish people, and his work in bringing together the *Kalevala* had the goal of reconstructing this native epic. In 1835, he published what is now known as the "old" *Kalevala*, a collection of thirty-two tales gathered from 1829 onward and edited to make a continuous story. In

A cartoon by A. W. Linsén (1847) depicting Elias Lönnrot on a field trip to collect the songs that eventually comprised the *Kalevala*. (From Francis Peabody Magoun Jr., trans., *The Kalevala or Poems of the Kaleva District* [Cambridge, MA: Harvard University Press, 1963], p. 343)

1849 Lönnrot published what is now the canonical version of the *Kalevala*, having incorporated another eighteen tales collected with the assistance of a younger song-collector, David E. D. Europaeus (1820–1884). Lönnrot's purpose in assembling this collection was to give to the Finnish people, long dominated by foreign powers that viewed the country as an intellectual backwoods, a pride in their language and history. In the preface to the 1835 edition, he wrote, "In these poems one meets the Finnish language and Finnish poetics in perhaps a purer form than in any other book. . . . These [poems] are not by any means on a par with those of the Greeks and Romans, but it is quite all right if they at least show that our forebears were not unenlightened in their intellectual efforts—and the songs at least show that." In this, the *Kalevala* became a rallying point for such nationalistic sentiments, lending itself to the cry, "*Suomi yoi sanoa itselleen: minullakin on historia!*" (Finland can [now] say for itself: I, too, have history!). The influence of the *Kalevala* cannot be understated. Indeed, it even gained a wide audience beyond Finland: for example, J.R.R. Tolkien cited the *Kalevala* as one of the primary influences on his *Lord of the Rings* trilogy.

The title of this work, *Kalevala*, refers to the legendary region—the Kaleva district—in which most of the action of the epic takes place. The epic begins with Lönnrot's prelude in the model of rune singers, an invocation expressing his desire to tell his people's stories:

> It is my desire,   it is my wish
> to set out to sing,   to begin to recite,
> to let a song of our clan glide on,   to sing a family lay.
> The words are melting in my mouth,   utterances dropping out,
> coming to my tongue,   being scattered about on my teeth.

From there the reader is introduced to Väinämöinen, the primary hero of the work, in the context of an ancient creation myth. Väinämöinen's mother, Ilmatar ("a virgin, maiden of the air, lovely woman, a spirit of nature"), leaves the "vast wastes of the air" where she lives for the wide-open sea. There she is impregnated by the wind and conceives Väinämöinen but is unable to give birth to him. He remains in her womb for thirty years. During that time, Ilmatar inadvertently creates the earth and the heavens when she breaks open an egg that a magical bird had laid upon her upraised knee. With this raw creation now before her, Ilmatar spends her time sculpting the various features of the land and sea before her son finally forces his way out of her womb. He floats upon the waters for eight years before coming to "a nameless land, a treeless land." After living there many years, he gets Sampsa, the "Spirit of Arable, lad of the field," to sow a variety of trees and plants. Väinämöinen himself begins the practice of agriculture when he finds a few grains of barley on the seashore and fells a clearing in which to plant them. In that clearing, he leaves a single birch tree for birds to perch upon. An eagle comes down and, pleased that Väinämöinen has left for him a perch, strikes fire for the man in order that he might burn over his field and sow the seeds. As he sows, Väinämöinen sings:

"Woman living under the earth,   old ruler of the soil, mistress of
   the earth!
Now make the turf grow,   the rich soil force up grass.
The land will not lack vital strength,   never, never at all
so long as there may be favor from those who gave it,   permission
   from the daughters of Nature.

"Rise, land, from slumbering,   Creator's grass, from sleeping!
Let stems grow stems,   and stalks grow stalks.
Send up shoots by the thousand,   spread sprouts by the hundred
as a result of my plowing, my sowing,   especially of my toil.

"O Ukko, god on high   or heavenly father,
holder of power in the clouds,   ruler of the cloud patches!
Hold folk assemblies in the clouds,   open meetings in the upper
   stories of the sky.
Make a cloud spring up in the east,   raise up a cloudbank in the
   northwest,
send others from the west,   drive others from the south.
Shed rain gently from the heavens,   sprinkle honey from the
   clouds
on the sprouting shoots,   on the murmuring crops."

This prayer to the earth and the various powers that exist within it offers a look into
Finland's pre-Christian religion. Certainly, there exists a hierarchy of gods, with
Ukko, apparently analogous to other sky gods such as Odin and Zeus, at the pinnacle, but an animistic worldview can be recognized, too. Väinämöinen invokes the
power of the "woman living under the earth" and the various "daughters of Nature"
to aid in his work to grow his barley. Throughout the epic, Väinämöinen encounters
various gnomes and nymphs that represent the power of nature. Later in the
Kalevala, Väinämöinen performs tasks that can be labeled shamanistic: in a singing
contest with young Joukahainen, he uses the magical power of song to bewitch his
opponent and slowly sink him into a fen. Later, he uses a special song to try to heal
a wound to his knee.

The *Kalevala* incorporates a number of story cycles, though they all exist within
the same continuity. Lemminkäinen's story comprises primarily poems 11 to 15, in
which, after casting aside one woman, Kyllikki, who broke an oath to him, he sets off
for North Farm (*Pohjoha*) in order to woo a maiden there. There he scatters every
man save Soppy Hat, a cattle herder, and demands of the dame of North Farm,
Louhi, her daughter. In response, she sets him many tasks, including the capture of
the Elk of Hiisi (the Devil), and it is while doing these tasks that he is killed by
Soppy Hat, chopped to pieces, and then thrown in the river. Lemminkäinen's
mother is told by the sun what happened to him and asks Ilmarinen to make for her
a rake with which to sift the river for her son's body parts. (Ilmarinen appeared earlier in the *Kalevala* when Väinämöinen, in an attempt also to win Louhi's daughter,
coerced him to forge the Sampo, a three-sided mill that grinds out grain, salt, and

money in unlimited quantities.) After she collects all of her son's body parts, she fits them together with special charms and restores him to life by means of an ointment retrieved from the Creator's storehouse by a bee.

The climax of the *Kalevala* comes when the three *Kalevala* heroes, Väinämöinen, Ilmarinen, and Lemminkäinen, venture together back to North Farm in order to retrieve the Sampo. On the way to North Farm, Väinämöinen kills a huge pike, which they then cook and eat, leaving only a pile of bones. Out of these bones, Väinämöinen fashions a *kantele*, a five-stringed harp, which he plays to the complete joy of all of nature; neither of his companions, however, can play the instrument. As with the opening creation story, this, too, is an etiological component of the *Kalevala*, explaining the origin of what has long been a very popular Finnish folk instrument famous for its bell-like sound and closely related to similar instruments in the Baltic states and Russia.

During a long martial and magical battle between the men of Kaleva and Louhi of North Farm, the Sampo is destroyed and the *kantele* lost. The *Kalevala* ends with the tale of Marjatta, who becomes pregnant after eating a lingonberry and is thus shunned by her family, who refuse to believe this miracle. She asks an old man to christen her son, but he refuses to do so until an inquiry can be made into the identity of the boy's father. Väinämöinen's judgment is called for, and he rules that as the boy supposedly came from the earth, "begotten of a berry from the ground," he should be buried in the ground himself. At this, the boy, just half a month old, speaks, upbraiding Väinämöinen for his foolishness. The old man secretly baptizes the boy as the King of Karelia, which upsets Väinämöinen, who then sets out for the sea, leaving this world but, like King Arthur lying in Avalon, promising to return when his people need him:

> "Let time pass,   one day go, another come;
> they will need me again,   be looking, waiting for me
> to fetch a new Sampo,   to prepare a new instrument,
> fetch a new moon,   free a new sun
> when there is no moon, no sun   nor any worldly joy."

As Tina Karina Ramnarine observes, despite the nature of the *Kalevala* as a compilation of the songs of many, many Finnish folksingers, "[I]t was the work of Lönnrot as an *individual* which was used to build a national identity." Early on, those most interested in studying the *Kalevala* were educated Finns who perceived the work within the context of a nationalist discourse. Believing that their national epic was now resurrected by Lönnrot, many folklorists ceased their collecting activities or limited them to "rounding out" the *Kalevala*. Interest in the original, unedited tales themselves lagged. Only when the poems of Ossian (a supposed Celtic Homer whose work was "translated" by Scottish poet James Macpherson) were exposed as a fraud did scholars begin looking into the oral originals behind the *Kalevala* in order to prove them genuine. They did indeed find such poems still existing in great abundance among the Finnish people, though with each new find, it became more and more difficult to view them as part of a unified national epic. That aspect of the

Kalevala, it was realized, was solely the creation of Lönnrot. This realization forced scholars to re-focus their research on the unedited folksongs rather than the heavily edited *Kalevala*.

JULIUS LEOPOLD KROHN AND THE STUDY OF FOLKLORE

The most important scholar to undertake a critical examination of the original tales constituting the *Kalevala* was Julius Leopold Krohn (1835–1888), who in 1885 published the enormously influential *Suomalaisen kirjallisuuden historia: I. Kalevala* (The History of Finnish Literature: I. The Kalevala), in which he presented a new interpretation of the poems heavily influenced by evolutionary theory. This book literally laid the scholarly foundation for the study of folklore, moving it well beyond the limits of nationalist discourse. Krohn made three central claims in this book: (1) that the stories in the *Kalevala* were not likely Finnish in origin, given that the central stories were familiar to other cultures; (2) that the poems, in their final "Finnish" form, originated not in Karelia, where they were collected, but rather in western Finland, given the presence in the poems of certain dialectical markers; and (3) that it was in the migration from abroad and through Finland that the larger poems and poetic cycles evolved, having originally come to the country as mere germ cells.

The method for studying folklore that arose from the work of Julius Krohn and his son Kaarle (1863–1933)—who in 1898 was appointed professor of Finnish and comparative folklore at the University of Helsinki, thus becoming the world's first professor in the discipline—is known as the historical-geographical or "Finnish" method. The underlying assumption of this method is that all variants of a particular piece of folklore—say, a folksong—are genetically related in some manner. By collecting them and pinpointing their geographical provenance, one can determine the manner in which the item of folklore diffused throughout a region and trace it back to its source, perhaps even reconstructing the original version. As William A. Wilson notes, this method struck a blow to German Romanticism and "the broken-down-myth theory of scholars like the Grimms, who had argued that present folklore was a decayed and fragmented remnant of earlier mythological and artistic wholes." In this worldview, the distant past was the repository of the most perfect forms of these songs and stories, which underwent degradation as humankind developed civilized societies and which survived only in fragmentary form, having devolved as humankind evolved. In contrast, the Krohns argued that such folklore began its life as a set of mere motifs and poetic units and then evolved into the larger poems and epic cycles found at present by folklorists. The period of the greatest development of a particular folksong or folktale was the present, not the distant past.

For many decades, the "Finnish" method remained the most influential method applied to the study of folklore, both nationally and internationally, and the work of the Krohns reverberates across the globe today. Likewise, research into the *Kalevala*—in terms of poetic meter, mythology, and other features—continued to be the primary focus of Finnish folklore scholarship until the 1960s. A significant part of that scholarship today is directed toward the study of contemporary and popular culture, with professors such as Leea Virtanen (b. 1934) examining the folklore of children, though Finnish mythology and folk belief still remain the most popular subject of study, as researchers tackle older archival materials with new frameworks for their investigations. The University of Helsinki, Joensuu University, the University of Turku, the University of Jyväskylä, and Åbo Academy in Turku all offer classes or degrees in folklore, testifying to the continued fascination the Finnish people have with the subject.

BIBLIOGRAPHY

Haavio, Martti. 1967. *Suomalainen mytologia*. Porvoo: W. Söderström.

Krohn, Julius. 1885. *Suomalaisen kirjallisuuden historia: 1. Kalevala*. Helsinki: Weilin ja Göösin tehdas- . . . kustantama.

Krohn, Kaarle. 1966. *Die folkloristiche Arbeitsmethode: Bergründet von Julius Krohn und weitergeführt von nordischen Forschern*. Oslo: Instituttet for ammenlingnende Kulturforskning.

Kuusi, Matti, Keith Bosley, and Michael Branch, eds. 1977. *Finnish Folk Poetry—Epic: An Anthology in Finnish and English*. Helsinki: Finnish Literature Society.

Magoun, Francis Peabody, Jr., trans. 1963. *The Kalevala, or Poems of the Kaleva District*. Cambridge: Harvard University Press.

Pentikäinen, Juha. 1999. *Kalevala Mythology*. Bloomington: Indiana University Press.

Ramnarine, Tina Karina. 1996. Folklore and the Development of National Identity in Finland. *Europa*, Number 1, Article 6 (www.intellectbooks.com/europa/number1/ramnarin.htm).

Schoolfield, George C., ed. 1988. *A History of Finland's Literature*. Lincoln: University of Nebraska Press.

Singleton, Fred. 1998. *A Short History of Finland*. Cambridge: Cambridge University Press.

Virtanen, Leea, and Thomas Dubois. 2001. *Finnish Folklore (Studia Fennica Folkloristica)*. Seattle: University of Washington Press.

Wilson, William A. 1976. *Folklore and Nationalism in Modern Finland*. Bloomington: Indiana University Press.

Guy Lancaster

FINNISH-SWEDISH

GEOGRAPHY AND HISTORY

The Swedish-speaking population of contemporary Finland is believed to have migrated to the area sometime between the twelfth and fourteenth centuries C.E., when the land was incorporated into the kingdom of **Sweden**. Their traditional settlement area is on the western coast in the province of Nyland (Finnish: *Uusimaa*), southwestern **Finland**, the Åland Islands, and Ostrobothnia. When Sweden ceded Finland to **Russia** in 1809, a sense of distinctive national character developed, originally geared only to Finnishness and the Finnish language. In the 1880s, however, a similar rallying of Swedish cultural resources, which continues to the present day, began. Thus, Finnish-Swedes have their own schools, institutions, mass media, theaters, and associations as well as a university, diocese, and political party. Though not a minority in the legal sense—both Finnish and Swedish are official languages in Finland—Finnish-Swedes often conceive of themselves as one.

The collection of Finnish-Swedish folklore, which started somewhat later than corresponding efforts among Finnish sources due to the exclusive emphasis on Finnish culture, began in the 1860s and 1870s and was associated with the growing awareness of Finnish-Swedish ethnic identity. The aim of collection was to legitimize the existence of Swedish culture in Finland.

SUPERNATURAL LORE

The Finnish-Swedish belief system as documented in the late 1800s and early 1900s consisted of both supernatural or magical and historical elements. The traditions of supranormal beings and magical folk medicine belonged to the former domain, while historical legends, for example, were included in the latter. Finnish-Swedish folk belief has many parallels in Swedish and Scandinavian tradition. The designations applied to different creatures are often the same, and belief legends in particular are of international stock. The species and character of supernatural beings vary according to ecological and economic conditions and to the sphere thought to be inhabited by each creature. In maritime and fishing communities the mermaid and merman dominated the belief tradition, while the supernatural beings of the forest—the troll and the *rå*—were prevalent in inland areas where farming and hunting were the chief means of subsistence. Generally, the creatures living in the wilds were viewed as more dangerous than ones living in man-made environments—for instance, the usually benevolent brownie. The fear of envy and anti-social behavior comes to the fore

In Finnish-Swedish maritime and fishing communities the mermaid and merman dominated the belief tradition. (Print Collection, Miriam and Ira D. Wallach Division of Art, Prints and Photographs, The New York Public Library, Astor, Lenox and Tilden Foundations)

in traditions about witches and the nightmare who threatened the well-being of individuals and society as a whole. Unlike the case in Sweden, though, elves do not seem to figure much in Finnish-Swedish folk belief.

Recent studies have demonstrated the importance of Christianity in shaping folk belief. The stories of the Bible disseminated in sermons, confirmation classes, Sunday school lessons, private reading, and—until the 1870s—schoolbooks for elementary school pupils furnished models for the description of supernatural beings and the Otherworld. Supranormal creatures may mimic biblical personages, for example, and the Otherworld can be portrayed in terms likening it to the Garden of Eden. The relationship between official religion and folk belief can be rather complicated, and it is seldom a question of the latter's blatant rejection or submissive acceptance of the tenets of the former.

As for folk medicine, diseases were believed to be caused by a variety of agents—supranormal beings, the dead, witches and wizards, or jealous people. Sometimes the disease was considered a punishment for insults against these agents, and illnesses caused by humans were connected with black magic and the evil eye, tongue, or thought. Professional healers used a multiplicity of methods of diagnosis, most involving some form of divination. The cure could be effected through a wide array of procedures, the most striking of which was the magic formula, but sacrifice, transference of the disease to other entities, and returning it to the sender were also common.

Love magic was also a much-discussed form of magic, but the extent to which it was actually utilized is hard to determine. It was said to be employed to attract a lover as well as to separate an established couple. Substances taken from the practitioner's own body were fed to the victim, or pins were stuck in the victim's clothes. Lovers could be separated through rituals involving "cold" and "hard" objects; these qualities were supposed to be transferred to the lovers' relationship. Though focused on love to a considerable degree, traditions of divination applied to other aspects of life: predicting the fate of a newborn child, revealing a future spouse, presaging a household's wealth or poverty, foretelling luck in husbandry or hunting, or anticipating the death of the elderly.

LEGENDS AND FOLKTALES

Historical legends about the founding settlements, the development of homesteads and villages, important persons, wars, epidemics and famine, religion and the church, law and order, communications, and subsistence reflect a popular understanding of history and its effects at the local and individual level. Legends were as important for the folk worldview as the supranormal traditions since they influenced the perception of the status of the group and its relation to the outside world.

The Finnish-Swedish narrative tradition is quite international, and many folktales and legends can be found in international type indices. The wonder tale dominates archive collections, but jocular tales also seem to have been appreciated. Fables and tales of the stupid ogre are somewhat less frequent. As elsewhere, the personal experience story is the foremost genre of contemporary narrative tradition. Since it is intimately connected to personal identity, it has been regarded as a very modern form. Legends have retained their popularity as urban legends, but the old jocular tale has largely been replaced by the shorter joke. With the introduction of a broader definition of folklore, the folkloric nature of media narratives such as television programs and news reports has become conspicuous.

SONGS, BALLADS, AND DANCE

The Finnish-Swedish ballad belongs to the Scandinavian tradition, and along with the jocular songs, ballads are believed to be the oldest songs still in use at the beginning of the twentieth century. The love song is a genre cherished by many, while other genres have been directed toward particular audiences or have been embraced by different occupational groups. Lullabies and singing games were sung for and by children, whereas shanties, soldiers' songs, prisoners' songs, and emigrants' songs reflect the concerns of specific groups—even though they were also performed by musicians not affiliated with the groups. Being a singer—especially a ballad singer—could be prestigious and an important part of the person's identity. The same is true for instrumental musicians, specialized narrators, and healers. Since the mid-twentieth century Swedish and international popular music has displaced traditional music. Nevertheless, it is still performed in the context of the folk music and world music movements. The safeguarding of traditional music closely relates to preservation of folk dance.

Dance was once an integral part of village life. It functioned as entertainment at late-night gatherings and as a reward for work. Many cooperative enterprises were undertaken with dancing in the evening as the anticipated conclusion of the working day. Ceremonial dances were considered very important for the proper celebration of a wedding. Dancing was also common at child weddings, a traditional form of charity at which a dance was arranged for the benefit of a poor girl and her family. Participants paid a small sum to dance with the "bride." Reel, minuet, quadrille, waltz, and polka were popular dances. The present-day repertoire of dances at adult social gatherings consists of waltz, foxtrot, and other types of couple dancing, while young people have adopted individual dancing styles such as disco and rave. Folk dance in the sense of dances current in pre-industrialized society is nowadays practiced as a specialized pastime by teams of dancers, and the activities are very much focused on the esthetic aspects of the dance since they are performed in public.

CHILDREN'S LORE

Children's lore is a fairly well researched facet of Finnish-Swedish folklore. Riddling was popular in pre-modern society. Riddles lightened the strain of heavy, protracted work such as drying malt in the sauna or making liquor and helped to while away winter evenings. Boys enjoyed teasing girls with sexual riddles, but riddling was also a contest of wit. Most older riddles are true riddles—that is, the answer can be worked out using the question as a point of departure. They often referred to objects and phenomena in the surrounding environs. Youth once posed these riddles, but today riddles are popular only with children. The character of riddles has also changed. Many riddles are humorous, and the answer does not quite follow from the question. Riddles are still used to test ingenuity and knowledge, but the appropriate response is often difficult to guess. It has already to be known.

Pre-industrialized society required children to do their share of the farmwork, and after 1866 they had to attend school. What free time they had after these responsibilities could be spent playing games such as various forms of tag, hide-and-seek, ball games, and hopscotch. Counting-out rhymes were utilized to determine the role of participants in games. Some games are still played on Finnish-Swedish playgrounds. Adolescents preferred party games, ones with an erotic charge in particular—pawn games, for example—and these games provided them with an opportunity to find and test potential mates. Moreover, games were a form of amusement at festivals, especially Christmas, New Year's Eve, and Lent, as well as at weddings.

CALENDAR CUSTOMS

Finnish-Swedish festivals have been influenced by international, European, Scandinavian, and Russian customs. The festival of St. Lucia, celebrated on 13 December, is important for Finnish-Swedes. Since it is shared with Sweden, it highlights the Swedish dimension of Finnish-Swedish identity. It is observed with a public procession as well as in homes. The central figure of both public and domestic forms of the festival is the girl who represents St. Lucia. She dresses in a white gown and wears a crown of candles. In the official procession she is accompanied by maids, "star boys" with white conical hats ornamented with stars, and brownies dressed in red. The festival is celebrated in church, and singing is a crucial element. St. Lucia is appointed by vote. Thus, Finnish-Swedes choose the official "Lucias" on national, regional, and local levels. The honor of representing Lucia brings with it social responsibilities: visiting the old and sick and spreading light and happiness in the community. Domestic observance of Lucia Day has children offering their parents coffee and tea, gingerbread cookies, and special buns made with saffron and raisins.

Christmas customs exhibit influences from **Germany** and, more recently, the United States. The older equivalent of the modern Santa Claus once roamed the countryside at Christmas, begging at wealthier homes. In the nineteenth century Christmas was transformed into a family holiday, and the former beggar became the bringer of gifts for children. At the same time, Christmas decorations, food, songs, and trees were introduced. The festival of St. Knut of Denmark on 13 January marked the end of the Christmas season for Finnish-Swedes, while the nearby Finns regarded Epiphany (6 January) as the end of the season. In the nineteenth century the festive period was celebrated with dancing and mumming among the folk, while masquerades figured in bourgeois traditions. Nowadays St. Knut's Day is most important for children, since on this day they are allowed to strip the Christmas tree of the candy used to decorate it.

Runeberg Day, the birthday of Johan Ludvig Runeberg (1804–1877), Finland's national poet, on 5 February is another annual feast commemorating Swedish culture in Finland. Before the introduction of Kalevala Day, the festival of Finnish culture on 28 February, and Independence Day on 6 December, Runeberg Day was the unofficial national holiday. It is primarily a public festival, celebrated in the schools and in the towns where the poet lived at some point in his life. For most Finnish-Swedes Runeberg Day is the occasion for eating Runeberg pastries, almond cakes garnished with jam and icing.

Shrovetide was once an important festival, but it has declined somewhat in significance. Mumming, begging, sleigh rides, dancing, and copious eating characterized the traditions of the lower classes, while the bourgeoisie celebrated with balls and masquerades. At the beginning of the twentieth century, public processions arranged in Helsingfors (Helsinki) at Shrovetide were banned by the Russian authorities since they had a political edge. Under the cover of their masks participants felt free to comment on politics. Blinis were popular Shrovetide fare; all Russian influences were not excluded! Nowadays Shrovetide provides a pretext for outdoor activities among children and university students and for eating buns filled with cream and marzipan or jam.

Once a period of sorrow and abstinence commemorating the passion of Christ, Easter is now chiefly observed by children who dress as "witches" and beg for candy from their relatives and neighbors. Food is also of considerable significance. In addition to eggs and lamb, the fare includes the Finnish national dish, *memma*, made of rye meal, malt, and water. Finnish-Swedes have adopted this dish as well as Russian *pasha*, a sweet made of curds, cream, almonds, and candied peel. In some Swedish-speaking areas of Finland, bonfires were lit, and everyone tried to build the largest bonfire.

Midsummer's Eve, or the Feast of St. John the Baptist, is a popular festival in Scandinavia, and Finnish-Swedes spend the holiday in the company of friends, eating the first potatoes and strawberries of the season. In some areas the lighting of bonfires or dancing around the Maypole are indispensable components of the festival.

On the last Saturday in August, a genuinely Finnish-Swedish festival is celebrated: the End of the Summer House Season or the Venetian Evening. Summer houses are cherished by many Finnish-Swedes, and with this festival they bid farewell to their life in the summer house for that year. Fireworks, festive lighting, and bonfires illuminating the Ostrobothnian countryside dominate this festival, and those who do not have summer houses can take part in the celebration by watching these displays.

Swedish Day on 6 November, the date of the death of King Gustavus Adolphus of Sweden in 1632, is chiefly an official festival. Many Finnish-Swedes celebrate it only by wearing special Swedish Day pins, which are sold by schoolchildren, though some also attend official celebrations organized by the Swedish political party.

CHALLENGES OF THE MODERN WORLD

The impact of globalization on Finnish-Swedish folklore has not yet been the object of scholarly study. Nevertheless, it is obvious that the Internet, for instance, has changed the communications patterns of many people and that channels for the dissemination of folklore have been altered. The influence of international popular culture on Finnish-Swedish culture and folklore has increased, but folklore has always been affected by outside sources. The importance of Swedish television in shaping Finnish-Swedish culture and identity cannot be overlooked, particularly in Ostrobothnia, and some Finnish-Swedes know more about Swedish politicians and entertainers than about their Finnish counterparts.

The main concern among Finnish-Swedes today, however, is not globalization but their survival as an ethnic group. The threats posed by the Finnish language were an ingredient in the creation of Finnish-Swedish ethnicity in the late nineteenth and early twentieth centuries and are still perceived as a major problem. Meanwhile, the official ideology of an exclusively Swedish identity is difficult to adapt to the rising number of bilingual families, and it will probably have to be remolded in the near future to accommodate bilingual individuals.

STUDIES OF FINNISH-SWEDISH FOLKLORE

Unfortunately, little about Finnish-Swedish folklore has been written in English. Available sources in English include Asplund Ingemark's dissertation "On the Bible and Folk Belief" (2005); Häggman (1992); essays by Carola Ekrem and Lena Marander-Eklund in Honko (2000); and Wolf-Knuts (2003). Important non-English sources include Anne Bergman and Carola Ekrem (1992), which deals with Finnish-Swedish youth culture and traditions; Biskop (1990), a treatment of folk dance; Ekrem (1997), an account of Finnish-Swedish games; *Finlands svenska folkdiktning I-VIII* (1917–1975), which includes folktales, legends, proverbs, riddles, songs, dances, and folk beliefs; and Swahn (2000).

BIBLIOGRAPHY

Asplund Ingemark, Camilla. 2005. On the Bible and Folk Belief. Diss., Åbo Akademi University.

Bergman, Anne, and Carola Ekrem. 1992. *Fest och fritid: fyra studier i finlandssvenska festtraditioner och ungdomsseder*. Helsingfors: Svenska litteratursällskapet i Finland.

Biskop, Gunnel. 1990. *Folkdans inom folkdansrörelsen-folklig dans?* Helsingfors: Finlands svenska folkdansring r. f.

Ekrem, Carola. 1997. *"Vi leder en blindbock till kungens bord": Lekar från Svenskfinland*. Helsingfors: Svenska litteratursällskapet i Finland.

Finlands svenska folkdikting I-VIII. 1917–1975. Helsingfors: Svenska litteratursällskapet i Finland.

Häggman, Ann-Mari. 1992. Ballad Singing in an Ostrobothnian Village. *Arv: Scandinavian Yearbook of Folklore* 48:215–223.

Honko, Lauri, ed. 2000. *Thick Corpus: Organic Variation and Textuality in Oral Tradition*. Helsinki: Finnish Literature Society, 2000.

Swahn, Jan-Öjvind. 2000. *Folk i fest-traditioner i Norden*. Höganäs: Föreningen Norden.

Wolf-Knuts, Ulrika. 2003. Contrasts as a Narrative Technique in Emigrant Accounts. *Folklore* 114:91–105.

Camilla Asplund-Ingemark

GREENLAND

GEOGRAPHY AND HISTORY

The largest island of the world, situated in the Arctic Ocean east of Canada, Greenland is a mountainous land with deep fjords, some of which cut right into the edge of the inland ice, calving and allowing icebergs to slide through them to the sea. At intervals Greenland has been populated since 2500 B.C.E. by hunting societies and from the twelfth century C.E. onward by the Eskimo ancestors of the Greenlanders, the Inuit. Crossing Smith Sound from Ellesmere Island, they brought their Thule culture of skin boats, dog sledges, ingeniously made skin dresses, efficient gear for

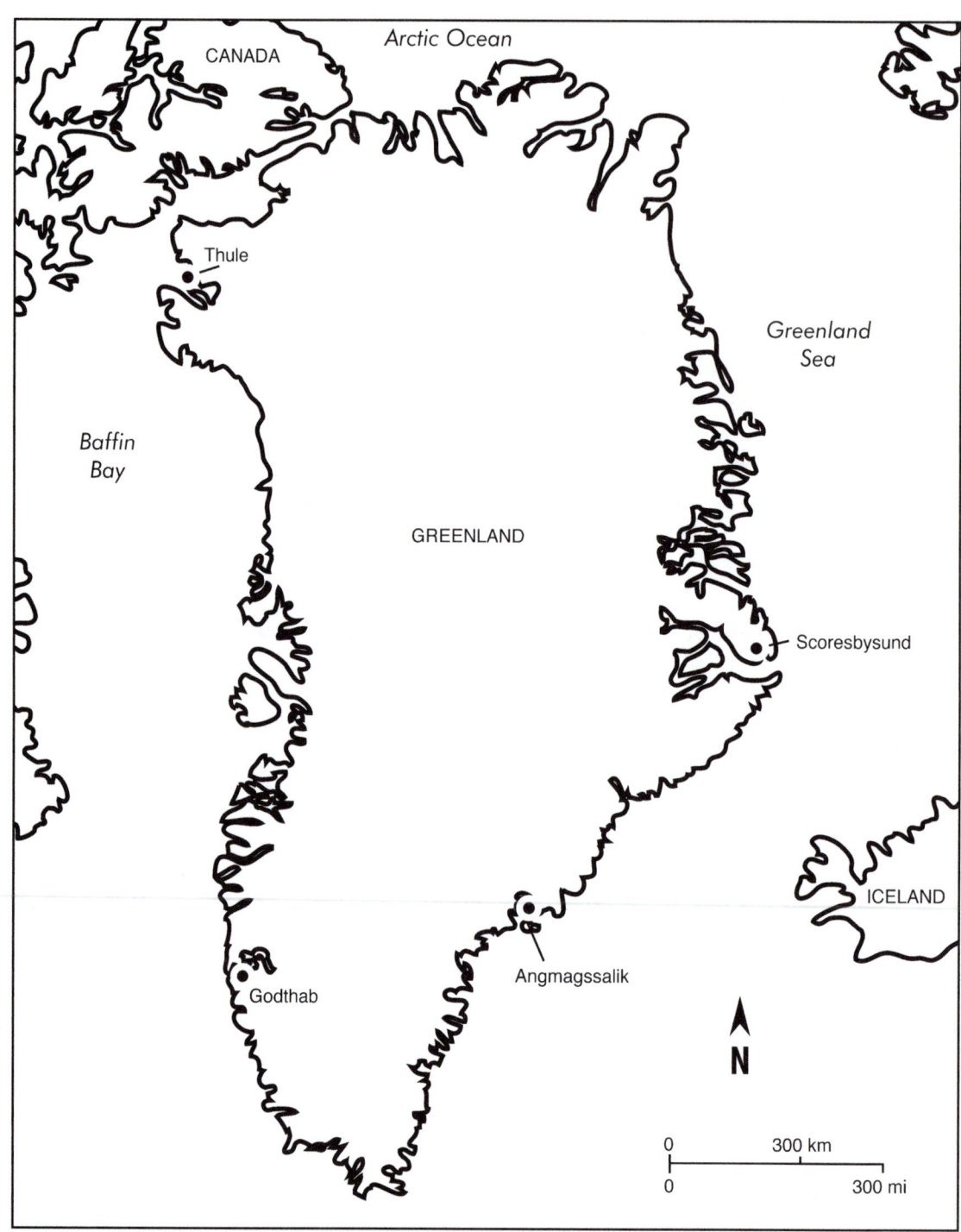

Greenland.

sealing, whaling, hunting, and fishing, and semi-subterranean winter houses with sunken tunnel entrances. Women looked after their children, kept their blubber lamps continuously burning in winter, and were busy converting the animals caught by their men into food, clothing, boat covers, and tents. Besides hunting, a strenuous occupation, the men made their own tools of wood, bone, and stone as well as dog sledges and the skeletons for kayaks and skin boats.

The migrations of faunal species arriving in spring and departing in autumn determined the annual round of wintering in settlements of an average fifty to seventy-five persons from late September to late April. The migrations also shaped summer activities: where to go, each family traveling on its own in the open skin boat (*umiaq*) rowed by the women with the men escorting in kayaks. The family, ten to twelve members constituting up to three generations, put up its skin tent at meeting places for fishing for capelin, on an island for hunting the bigger species of seals passing by in open waters, or at the bottom of fjords for hunting caribou in the inland. This way of life in societies based on kinship and alliances forms the background for stories about poor boys, deserted widows, and small girls attracting extra-human support, great hunting feats, impressive skills in kayaking, and heroic deeds in faraway mythic lands. Also in real life long-distance travels were popular, and at trade fairs storytelling, song duels, shamanic competitions, and competitive games ensured cultural exchange between differing locales. Colonization, beginning in 1721 in west Greenland, gradually took over trade and brought Christian missions that proscribed shamanism, all kinds of drum songs, and other "pagan" festivities, allowing only certain games, storytelling, and songs of reprimand, which survived until early modern times.

SUPERNATURAL LORE AND SHAMANISM

Shamans of either gender, who served as mediators between this world and the Otherworld, possessed an interior light for seeing the invisible realms. These comprised one on earth beyond ordinary sight, others below earth and sea and in Heaven, and still others within the dark interior of humans. It required solitary walks through the wilderness, repetitive movements, or drumming to enter the state of being able to use this sight, which at the same time cut off the view of the visible world. Only other shamans and the beings of the Other-world could see that interior light, which attracted spirits offering their beneficial services. The shaman would acquire that Otherworldly light when still a pupil going through a frightful experience of death and revival. Being devoured and thrown up again by a giant polar bear or a huge dog was the most common shamanic experience in east Greenland. A visit to Moon was another, provided the shaman apprentice got his entrails cut out by the bisexual Entrail-Snatcher and restored by Moon. Equally important as this second sight was the shaman's ability to traverse the Otherworld by flying, gliding across

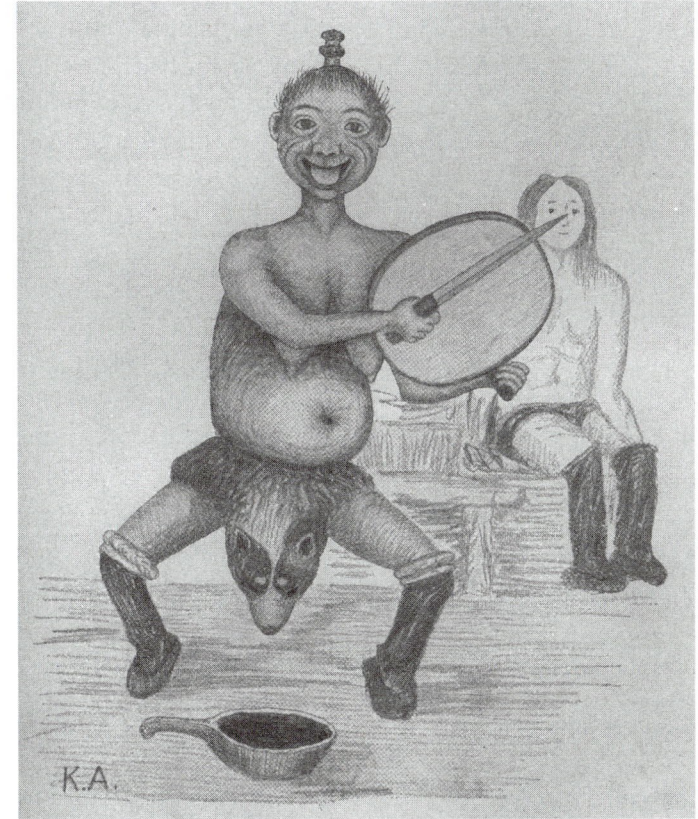

The Entrail-Snatcher en route to Moon. Among other figures, this one "with the large groin" (*Nalikkatteeq*) was represented at the masked dances (*uaajeerneq*). Drawing by Kârale Andreassen, ca. 1919. (From Knud Rasmussen, *Myter og Sagn fra Grønland* [Copenhagen: Nordisk forlag, 1921])

the open or ice-covered sea, or just walking. At the horizon of sea and sky access was available to either realms, the one below or that above, but a visit below could also be made by walking the bottom of the sea. Overcoming several dangerous passages, the walking shaman would reach the realm of death or farther away the giant house of Sea Woman. She was called "Mother of the Sea" among other names, because seabirds and sea mammals were reborn through the tunnel of her womblike house in spring unless taboo violations had polluted both her and the tunnel. In that case a shaman had to visit, fight, and clean the angry woman, comb her hair, and have it put up so that she would gratefully release the birds and animals. These changed from human to animal forms while leaping into the cleared river of the tunnel.

Visits to the realm of death below are uncommon in the older, documented stories, though they abound in tales of historical shamans, who wanted to ensure that this abode was not identical with the burning Hell of which the early missionaries preached. Also, tales of visits to the realm of death in Heaven were less frequently related in the older stories.

In myth, Moon was the primary goal of a shaman's visit to Heaven so that he might acquire the aforementioned light, additional helping spirits, or a baby for a childless woman. From the horizon steep steps or a rainbow led upward and farther on along a river, probably the Milky Way, right on to the house of Moon and his sister Sun. Another route went by the Northern Lights, believed to be deceased humans playing ball with the skull of a walrus. In possession of the seeing light himself, Moon watched to ensure that taboos were kept on earth. As engenderer of life on earth, causing both tide and menstruation as well as the breaking up of ice in spring, he could punish a wrongdoing woman by making her pregnant. In vain he would try to become the rightful father of the child, but Moon—like any being of the Otherworld—could not become integrated into human society. Once belonging to this society, Moon committed incest with his sister, Sun. Overwhelmed with shame, she cut off her breast and offered it to him to eat with the words, "Because I seem to be to your taste." She then lit a torch and spiraled up to Heaven. In myth Moon still pursues her with the much cooler light of his glowing torch. This is how time, the alternation of day and night and of the seasons, maintains its cycles. Meanwhile, Moon and Sun share a house with a partition between them. Sexually, they live apart and thus do not reproduce themselves. Having children meant also getting old, dying, and becoming reborn by name—that is, having one's name conferred on a newborn relative. Only by remaining outside this recycling of human life would Moon and Sun keep up the normal course of time, so eclipses made people panic. The game animals were part of the recycling of humans in that they had the same sort of souls as humans. Humans took care of their reincarnations through hunting rites and the observance of taboos. But in contrast to humans the animals had no names except that of their species.

The ordinary rites of passage of humans and animals were significant but not spectacular and rarely the shaman's business. Shamans were either called upon in situations of crisis like illness, hunger, and prolonged bad weather, or—quite often—for entertainment. A shaman might practice a simple way of making a diagnosis by lying covered up on the platform and getting into the right mood of "seeing" by tapping a round piece of skin stretched out in his hand. The more dramatic seances took place inside the darkened house, the shaman getting excited by singing, rhythmic contortions, and hitting the frame of his drum—the only musical instrument of the Inuit—and then summoning his helping spirits. The first to arrive could be rough, thrashing people around or chasing them out of doors with the threat of killing them. More communicative spirits admonished people to observe their rules, usually indirectly by singing, or they told gossip from the world of spirits. In case the shaman went traveling, they would accompany him in a shower of sparks, leaving one helping spirit behind as a farsighted reporter. When in danger the shaman received support by the audience calling him back by repeated shouts of *kiakkakkaa*. When, on the point of getting lost, the shaman eventually returned to his body, he would wake up with the cry of a baby and relate his own travelogue.

STORIES

Stories were transmitted freely at all times but especially in winter. Extensive collections initiated by farsighted Inspector H. J. Rink in 1858 and recorded by Greenlanders evince both their ongoing transmission and acculturative changes. The presence of the colonial authority and new knowledge of the world and Christianity left their stamp on the contents, and literacy inspired talented Greenlanders to transform their oral stories into charming pieces of prose. Illustrations of the stories in print meant the birth of Greenland painting. Regrettably, though, none of the existing translations into English pay justice to the rich art of Greenland storytelling. Today the telling of captivating experiences and of stories about ghosts and *qivittut* (singular: *qivittoq*) is still a favorite pastime. *Qivittut* are persons who, due to an insult or an unhappy love affair, have left human society for good. They are believed to survive by supernatural means in the mountains, and an encounter with such a transformed human is deeply feared. Today suicide among the young is at times diagnosed as the modern way out of similar psycho-social stresses.

In east and north Greenland traditions continued on a wider scale into the twentieth century due to their late colonization in 1894 and 1910, respectively. South and southwest Greenland received continuous input of less acculturated stories by immigrants from the east coast until 1900. Consequently, European and Inuit fieldworkers in these peripheries have enriched the museums and archives (including the National Museum and Archives of Greenland) with numerous pieces of delicate carvings and clothing, photos of daily life, drawings, and songs and stories on record, both historical or set in a timeless past. The native worldview is apparent in such stories and in biographies of the shamans.

In their spatial universe the Inuit were living at the coast of this world, the visible *sila*, in contrast to the inivisible *silap aappaa*, the "Otherworld." Numerous humanoid beings such as animals, deceased humans, dwarves, giants, or the so-called fire people lived their invisible lives in various realms of the Otherworld. The faunal species would show their animal forms in the visible world and let themselves be killed of their own free will in response to appropriate behavior of the hunter and his cohabitants. Life in one world was dependent on life in the other, meaning that humans were obliged to follow numerous rules, especially taboos in connection with birth, death, miscarriages, and the killing of big animals. Breaking a taboo, especially by eating a forbidden part of an animal, would disturb life in both worlds, causing forbidding weather (*sila*, meaning weather becoming "angry"), disappearance of game, sickness, and other misfortunes.

GAMES AND CELEBRATIONS

In full lamplight, ordinary people would play spiritlike figures at the New Year's feast and at other festivities in east Greenland. A song, a set of movements, and a humorous disguise were associated with each figure representing the character of a spirit, an animal, or a typical human action. The face would be either covered by a mask or blackened with soot and distorted by crossing strings and a small stick distending the mouth. Some of these figures might be just as rough in thrashing people as the frightening spirits of the shaman, but the tone of the play was less frightening. Most figures, especially men dressed as pregnant women, called forth roars of laughter. Today similarly disguised figures, *mitaartut*, pay mute visits at Epiphany to every house in their settlement, make laughable erotic gestures, and receive small gifts in a continuing mixture of west Greenland and former Scandinavian traditions.

Other pastimes, whether during visits, at fairs, or just for shortening the long, dark evenings in winter, were male competitions in physical capabilities and strength and the popular *ajagaq*, ring and pin game, played by everybody. An *ajagaq* consists of a stick connected by a string fastened at one end to a curved piece of bone having several drilled holes. The trick is to fling the *ajagaq* aloft on the string and catch it on the stick hitting one of the holes. Long series were played of hitting the holes, which might denote stages in, say, a boat race or the playful loss of one body part after another. A player having "lost his head," though, might win it back by improved throws. Another popular pastime was cat's cradle, some figures of which demanded a small story explaining the steps in the making.

Visits occasioned by a seance or a feast of masked dancers might lead to the "putting out of the lamps," in which one copulated with the first person of the opposite sex one happened to get hold of in the darkness. The same activity might also finish a happy visit from another settlement, beginning with a solid meal and continuing with individuals taking turns in drumming, singing, and dancing. Some songs were sung in chorus, and numerous individual songs, both inherited and recently composed, commemorated a personal experience

The seal ball game. Drawn and engraved by Aron of Kangeq. (From Bodil Kaalund, *The Art of Greenland* [Berkeley: University of California Press, 1983]. Original is in the National Library of Greenland)

of overwhelming emotion. Defending accusations against one's immoral behavior was another issue both within and outside the song duels. Such contests attracted numerous visitors and were performed by two persons of the same gender singing songs of derision, accompanied by drumming and supported by relatives singing the chorus. Song duels served as outlets for grievances in these small societies, while in everyday life nobody had the right directly to interfere with the decisions and behavior of members of another household. No public courts or councils existed for taking care of justice. Upbringing, joking, and circulating reprimands by singing made most people behave. In the numerous stories about feuds, song duels are generally occasions for committing acts of violence, even murder. This rarely happened in real life, where measures were taken to avoid such violence. People wintering in the same settlement could not engage in a duel, and usually the challenger would warn the opponent in time for him to compose a counter-song. Laughter from the audience revealed a song's success, and the duel would never result in any formal punishments.

SONGS AND SPELLS

Singing and composing songs took up a considerable part of life, starting with the pet song composed by one's mother or grandmother, such as this one to a small child, named after the mother's sister and sitting "up there" in the pouch of the mother's anorak:

> See her up there, the innocent coquette.
> No man has yet touched her,
> No man has yet stamped her—
> She is not my child's mother,
> She is not my child's brother—
> But she is mother's sister!
> Crook-backed (as she was),
> Stammering
> Restless in all her movements—
> From early morning wishing but to fall in with menfolk,
> She tries to outwit them, the little creature—
> See how she raps with her hands
> Hear how she whimpers—
> Hey! How she can run.

In stories, pet songs could serve magical ends—for instance, calling the owner back from the Otherworld to normal life. Of more general use and considered very efficient were secret songs and spells, *serratit*. Although muttered, a spell lost some of its efficacy when employed. Reciting it in public for everybody to hear made it useless thereafter. Selling or giving away a spell to another person had to take place in secrecy, after which it lost its power for the former owner. A spell had a defined end—for instance, to bestow dizziness, to further a talent for sewing, to strengthen the effect of an amulet, and to either ward off or practice sorcery. Amulets, similarly effective in a limited field, were small, made from part of a bird, an animal, a human

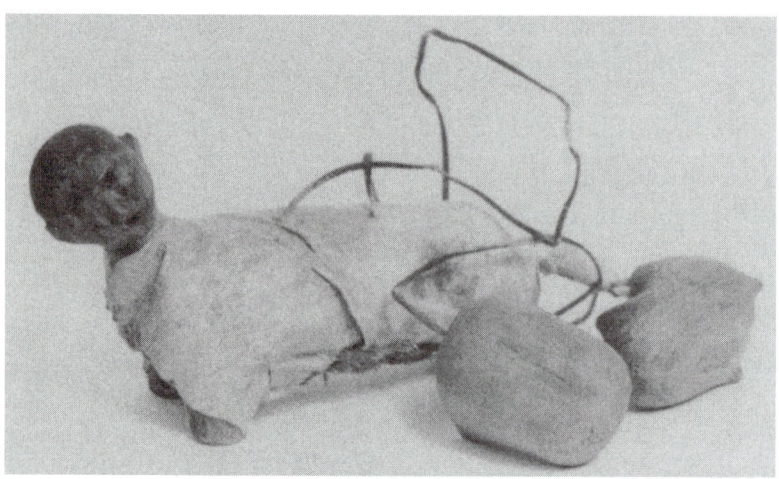

Harpooned *tupilak* with the seal bladders attached to the line. Made by Mitsuarnianga, ca. 1905.

being, or a tool, for example, and worn on the body, sewn into one's clothes, placed in one's kayak, or set close to one's lamp. A few amulets were carved objects, a doll, for instance. Carved faces on the handles of tools added to their value. Means for sorcery were varied: parts of human skeletons were considered particularly powerful, more so if combined with bones of various birds and animals, wrapped up in a skin, and stuffed with peaty soil. This *tupilak* was made alive by sucking the genitals of the sorcerer muttering a magic song. The *tupilak*, easily mistaken for a small seal, would ask the sorcerer where to go and whom to attack. A kayaker who became entangled in the harpoon line and who was drowned by the harpooned animal was occasionally thought to have met with a *tupilak*. A sudden case of insanity was diagnosed as the boomerang effect of sorcery, returned on the creator by the enemy's stronger magical means of defense. Confessing the failed attempt was a recommended cure because the effect of sorcery (as of magic songs and spells) depended on secrecy.

The famous *tupilaks* carved in bone for sale to tourists represent the composite nature of the former, generally bigger, and less elegant *tupilak*. Europeans asking for such representations initiated that industry. In choosing their motifs modern Greenland painters and sculptors still look to their rich past as made manifest, for instance, in the sculpture of the orphan Kaassassuk with the tail of a ferocious animal around his waist. This animal, "the lord of power," made Kaassassuk extremely strong by throwing him to the ground time and again. Having avenged himself on the entire settlement, which maltreated him all his life, he became an asocial brute. Yet according to acculturated versions, Kaassaassuk eventually met his superior in a wrestling match and, humiliated, stopped being a constant threat to everybody. This figure stands as the symbol of the Greenland home rule in front of its administrative buildings in Nuuk, the capital of a modernized country, celebrating its first twenty-five years of home rule in 2004.

BIBLIOGRAPHY

Hauser, Michael. 1984. *Greenland Music: A Discography through 1981.* Copehagen: Rosekilde.

———. 1992. *Traditional Greenland Music.* Copenhagen: ULO.

Holm, Gustav. 1914a. Ethnological Sketch of the Angmagsalik Eskimos. *Meddelelser om Grønland* 39:1–147.

———. 1914b. Legends and Tales from Angmagsalik. *Meddelelser om Grønland* 39:229–317.

Holtved, Erik. 1943. *The Eskimo Legend of Navaranâq: An Analytical Study.* Acta Arctica 1. Copenhagen: Ejnar Munksgaard.

Kaalund, Bodil. 1983. *The Art of Greenland: Sculpture, Crafts, Painting.* Berkeley: University of California Press.

Kleivan, Inge. 1960. *Mitârtut: Vestiges of the Eskimo Sea-Woman Cult in West Greenland.* Meddelelser om Grønland 161.5. Copenhagen: C. A. Reitzels Forlag.

———. 1971a. Song Duels in West Greenland—Joking Relationship and Avoidance. *Folk* 13:9–36.

———. 1971b. *Why Is the Raven Black? Acta Arctica* 17. Copenhagen: Ejnar Munksgaard.

Kleivan, Inge, and Birgitte Sonne. 1985. Eskimos: Greenland and Canada. *Iconography of Religions* 8.2:43–48.

Sonne, Birgitte. 1982. The Ideology and Practice of Blood Feuds in East and West Greenland. *Études/Inuit/Studies* 6:21–50.

———. 1988. In Love with Eskimo Imagination and Intelligence: The Work of Knud Rasmussen. *Études/Inuit/Studies* 12.1–2:21–44.

———. 2000. Heaven Negotiated: The Realms of Death in Early Colonial Westgreenland. *Études/Inuit/Studies* 24.2:65–87.

———. 2001. Sources to Greenland Shamanism: Survey and Ethnohistorical Implications. *North Atlantic Studies* 4.1–2:31–38.

Thalbitzer, William. 1914–1941. The Ammassalik Eskimo I-II. *Meddelelser om Grønland* 40:113–740.

Birgitte Sonne

ICELAND

GEOGRAPHY AND HISTORY

When considering the folklore of Iceland, a number of key factors that played central roles in shaping the culture and identity of the Icelandic people must be borne in mind. First, it must be remembered that Iceland is a volcanic island set at around 66 degrees north, just below the Arctic Circle, west of northern **Norway**, and northwest of the British Isles and the Faroes. The blessings of the nearby Gulf Stream and the hot water produced by volcanic activity are countered somewhat by the close proximity of the Arctic Circle and the northern pack ice. When settlers first arrived here in the late ninth century, the relatively young country was supposedly covered with birch forests. Nowadays, erosion has limited the areas of settlement to the coastal areas, especially the flat plains of the south and the wider fertile valleys of the southwest, as well as several other valleys and fjords in the far east (centering on Egilsstaðir and Seyðisfjörður), the north (around Akureyri), and the northwest (centering on Ísafjörður). While agriculture still plays a central role, the most important economic pursuit for centuries has been fishing. Until the late nineteenth century, however, Iceland was still a rural agricultural community. Few townships existed outside the small coastal villages of Reykjavík, Seyðisfjörður, Grindavík, Akureyri, Ísafjörður, and Vestmannaeyjar. The general pattern of settlement was very much like that of Orkney: outside the tighter valleys of the east and northwest, the population was relatively widely dispersed, possibly one of the main reasons that mumming traditions never really developed here as they did in neighboring countries.

The next main factor to bear in mind is the background and makeup of the population and other cultural influences on Iceland over history. Recent genetic surveys support the information provided by the sagas and the twelfth-century *Landnámabók* (The Book of Settlements) that the original Icelanders were a mixture of Nordic and

Gaelic people. It is now believed that 80 percent of the male settlers and 50 percent of the first female settlers were Nordic, the rest having their roots in the British Isles (especially Orkney, Shetland, north **Scotland**, the Hebrides, and **Ireland**). Most likely, many of these people with Celtic heritage came to Iceland as either slaves, wives, or concubines. Even though there are few signs of Gaelic in place-names or the Icelandic language (which is western Nordic), a number of essentially Gaelic motifs that appear in the sagas and later folktales of Iceland (such as the mention of "talking heads," supernatural bulls, and "eternal battles") suggest a high degree of Celtic influence in the first years. Alongside this, we have the early saga evidence of a ball game named *knattleikur*, not found elsewhere in Scandinavia, which offers strong parallels to modern Irish *hurling* and Scottish *shinty*. Other traditions, such as the use of edible seaweed—rare in Scandinavia—betray early connections with Ireland and Scotland. At the same time, it should never be forgotten that the Nordic world itself embraced a wide number of cultures. Several elements of northern **Sámi** belief present in Icelandic lore from early on (for example, the idea of dueling magicians) emphasize that early Iceland must have been one of the first truly multicultural societies.

Over time, however, the direct connections with Scotland and Ireland broke down, as did Iceland's formal connections with Norway. Initially a republic allegedly established by Norwegians who were escaping from the oppression of Norway's first overall king, Haraldur the Fair-Haired, Iceland later came under Norwegian rule and then became part of the Danish state along with Norway as an eventual result of the Kalmar agreement in 1387. It then remained part of **Denmark** until regaining independence in 1944. The Danish influences on Icelandic culture are particularly obvious in seasonal customs connected to Lent (the customs of children "thrashing" their parents with light, decorated sticks to earn cream buns on Shrove Monday and then knocking the "cat" out of a barrel and going to shops in costumes on Ash Wednesday—all of which are well known in Denmark).

In addition to these influences from Scandinavia and the Gaelic-speaking countries, a number of other potential foreign influences must be kept in mind when considering the background of Icelandic folk belief and tradition, especially that of the English and Germans (the Hanseatic merchants) who vied for fishing trade with Iceland during the later Middle Ages. Overseas trade was to continue until the Danes finally imposed a trade monopoly on the country in the seventeenth century, something that effectively cut Iceland off from much of the rest of the world. Indeed, this trade ban was to have devastating effects during the natural catastrophes of the eighteenth century (especially the volcanic eruptions at Laki and the resulting so-called *móðuharðindi*, or dust-cloud hardship), when the situation became so bad that the Danish state considered evacuating the country completely.

Considering the history of Iceland given above, it is not surprising that the folk beliefs and general worldview displayed in Icelandic legends and folktales are mainly Scandinavian with a few scattered Celtic notes. This was essentially an emigrant community with considerable interest in its past. Indeed, from the time of settlement, Icelanders were known for their fascination with family history and genealogy, an interest that actively continues to this day. Along with the Icelanders' early contact with writing through connections with Ireland and the Catholic Church (the Icelanders were officially converted ca. 1000), interest in family history produced hundreds of manuscripts written in the vernacular in Iceland during the Middle Ages. Commencing with translations of religious books and laws, Icelanders swiftly progressed to recording lives of the Norwegian kings and then histories of themselves, in the form of *Landnámabók* and the sagas. Both of these have roots, it is generally believed, in legendary material (both supernatural legends and family histories) long preserved in oral tradition. Here we find some of the earliest examples of legends concerning water horses, trolls, and mermen (*Landnámabók*), sacrifices to elves (*Kormáks saga*), nature spirits (*Barðar saga*), and even Christmas hauntings (*Eyrbyggja saga* and *Grettis saga*).

EDDIC POEMS

Most important of all works in this regard, however, are the Eddic poems and Snorri Sturluson's *Prose Edda* (often known as *Snorra Edda*). The former, preserved mainly in two manuscripts from the late thirteenth century, is a collection of poems dealing with the Old Norse gods and ancient Scandinavian heroes. It is generally accepted that most of these works also lived for some time in oral tradition before they were recorded. Many believe that they have their roots in pagan times and that in some form most originated in mainland Scandinavia. It has also been suggested that they contain some of the earliest dramatic works recorded in Northern Europe. Snorri Sturluson's *Prose Edda*, composed around 1220, is largely based on such poetic work. Often wrongly regarded as a kind of Bible of Old Nordic mythology, the *Prose Edda* is essentially a mythological and metrical handbook designed for poets. While containing invaluable information about early mythological beliefs in Iceland (as recorded by a Christian academic in the thirteenth century), it is questionable whether anyone can argue that these same myths represent a general Nordic corpus from pre-Christian times. Indeed, many contemporary commentators believe that there was considerable local variation over time in these matters.

After the time of Ari *fróði* (the Learned [1067/ 1068–1148]), the man behind *Landnámabók*, and Snorri Sturluson (1179–1241), little systematic collection of folk material seems to have taken place prior to the Enlightenment, when the manuscript collector Árni Magnússon (1663–1730) collected several folk legends along with other material. The home-educated farmers themselves, however, went on recording *rímur* verse, incantations, poems, and sagas by the hundred. Especially important in this regard are Jón Guðmundsson the Learned (1574–1658), Eiríkur Laxdal (1743–1816), and Jón Ólafsson frá Grunnavík (1705–1779). Much of this invaluable material still needs to be sifted through.

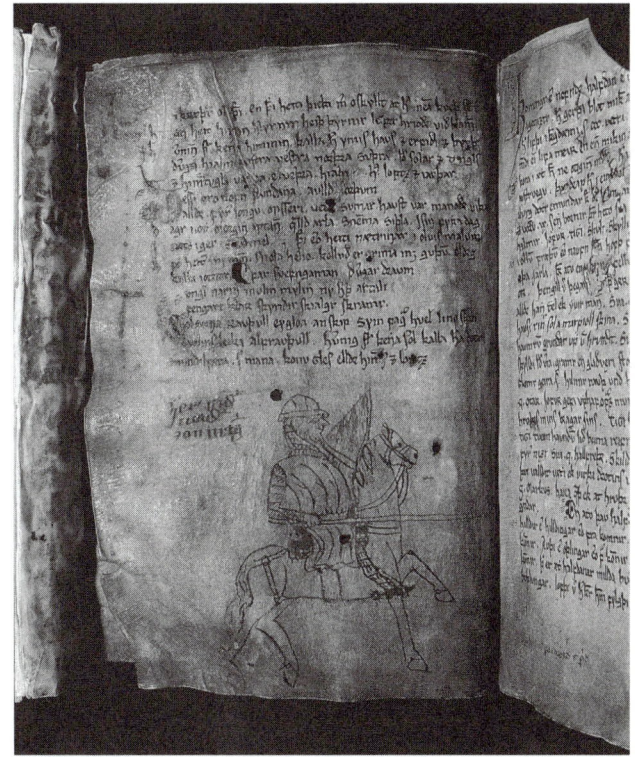

Illustration from a fourteenth-century manuscript of Snorri Sturluson's *Prose Edda*. The *Prose Edda* is essentially a mythological and metrical handbook designed for poets. (© 2004 Werner Forman/TopFoto/The Image Works)

FOLKTALES

The first real collections of Icelandic folktales in the mid-eighteenth century owe as much to the encouragement of four foreigners. After the initial example of the Grimm brothers, Englishman George Stephens (1813–1895) published a list of Icelandic folkloristic material that needed to be collected in July 1845. Then the German scholar Konrad Maurer (1823–1902), who visited Iceland in 1858, did fieldwork with storytellers throughout the country and published his results in 1860 in *Islandische Volkssagen*. By that time, the first small tentative collection of tales (*Íslenzk Æfintýri* [Icelandic Folktales]) had already been published by Magnús Grímsson (1825–1860) and Jón Árnason (1819–1888) in 1852. The encouragement that Mauer gave these two men during his visit eventually led to the appearance of the much larger *Íslenzkar þjóðsögur og Æfintýri* (Icelandic Folktales and Wonder Tales) in two volumes, which were published with Maurer's help in Leipzig in 1862 and 1864. This work provides the inspiration for all folktale collections to be published in later times, and almost all translations have been drawn from it. Several things must always be remembered about this material, however. First, like many other collections of the time, the contents were selected from a wider body of material (the complete collection was later published in six volumes in 1954–1961) with a particular agenda in mind associated with the romantic nationalist movements of the time. (For example, in Iceland, one notes an emphasis on those legends connected to saga heroes.) Second, like the Grimm brothers and unlike the real fieldworkers of the time such as Asbjörnsen and Moe in Norway and J. F. Campbell in Scotland, Jón Árnason and Magnús Grímsson (who died before the project was completed) did little collecting themselves. Tied down by jobs in the southwest of Iceland, they sent out a call for material to scholars and priests around the country. These men then wrote up the accounts they collected and sent them to Jón Árnason, who in turn dispatched them to be finally edited by others in Denmark and **Germany** before publication. The process means that the material contained in the collection is of varying style and quality. It nonetheless remains important for the invaluable information it contains about the worldview and beliefs of the Icelandic rural community in the nineteenth century and its role in forming Icelandic national identity.

The arrival of the Jón Árnason and Magnús Grímsson's collection of folktales opened the floodgates for a century of folktale collection and publication in Iceland by locally educated scholars from Ólafur Davíðsson (*Huld* in 1890–1898, compiled with others, and *Íslenzkar þjóðsögur* in 1895, compiled alone and published in complete form in 1945), to Rakel Pálsdóttir, who published the first collection of contemporary folk legends in 2001. Especially valuable are the collections made by Sigfús Sigfússon, Sigurður Nordal, and þórbergur þórðarsson, which closely reflect the improved recording techniques utilized by the collectors and then the more recent sound recordings of various kinds of folkloristic material made in both Iceland and the "western Icelandic" settlements of North America by Hallfreður Örn Eiríksson and others under the auspices of the Arnamagnean Institute in Iceland, where this material is still stored.

The main difficulty with working with this wealth of material, however, is that there have never been any central folklore **archives** in Iceland and, until recently, no overall archives or index of Icelandic folktales (except for Einar Ólafur Sveinsson's early index of wonder-tale types in 1929). Ethnological material concerning material culture and custom (including various national questionnaires about folk customs) is all kept in the Ethnological Department (*þjóðháttadeild*) of the National Museum (*þjóðminjasafn*), while material concerning folktales, ballads, and beliefs is stored in the Arnamagnean Institute at the University of Iceland (*Háskóli Íslands*) along with the early medieval manuscripts. Later manuscripts, including those of the earliest folktale collections, are kept in the National Library (*þjóðarbókhlaðan*). In the last few years, however, work has been progressing at the university on an overall Icelandic legend database (*Sagnagrunnur*), which will hopefully be opened on the Internet in 2005. (See the Web site at www.hi.is/~terry/database/database.htm.) At the moment, this material (over 10,000 published legends, which can be connected to the Arnamagnean Institute's own equally large database of sound recordings) is available only in Icelandic. However, translation is planned in the near future. Work is also proceeding on a similar complete database of Icelandic wonder tales.

LEGENDS

The wealth of legendary material collected in Iceland underlines, above all, the close connections between Icelandic and Nordic folk belief. As in Norway and Denmark, there are legends about water horses (*nykrar*) stealing children; wise mermen (*marbendlar*); dangerous mermaids; seal wives (similar to models known in northern Norway, Ireland, Scotland, and the Scottish Isles); lake monsters; man-threatening trolls; the ghosts of children left to die of exposure (*útburðir*, also well known across Scandinavia); priest-magicians who have studied at the Black School (very much a Scandinavian phenomenon); and cooperation and relationships between human beings and elves (known in Iceland as *álfar* or *huldufólk*, meaning "hidden people," similar to the Norwegian *huldre*). Meanwhile, the mainland Nordic figures missing in Iceland reveal an environmental influence. Here there is no *skogsrå* (forest spirit) like that known across Sweden, since there are no real forests for her to inhabit. Similarly, there is no fiddle-playing *fossegrim* (waterfall spirit) like that found in Norway. (Iceland has no similar fiddle tradition.) Especially interesting is the fact that the wide-ranging Nordic *nisse/gardvård*, a spirit that protects farms against evil spirits and bad luck and that reached Shetland and Orkney in the form of the brownie, never seems to have come to Iceland or the Faroes. As has been recently noted, this may be due to the fact that on the mainland this spirit was believed to be a forefather that lived in a farm grave mound. While ancient Bronze Age and early Iron Age grave mounds abounded in both mainland Scandinavia and the Scottish islands, Iceland had nothing of the kind when it was first discovered.

Equally worthy of research are those aspects of folk belief that exhibit subtle differences from the forms generally encountered in mainland Scandinavia. This applies especially to the Icelandic concepts of the elves. For example, unlike many of their Nordic kindred, the Icelandic elves do not live in the earth beneath our feet. Instead, they mainly live above the ground in rocks and cliffs (like many of their Celtic relations). Furthermore, unlike their semi-bestial, pagan Scandinavian kindred, they do not have animal tails. Many have obviously been converted to Christianity. Indeed, in most ways, they are like mirror images of the inhabitants of rural Iceland up until the time at which the legends first came to be recorded except for the fact that they seem richer and more powerful. They suffer few of the hardships encountered by the average Icelandic farmer of the time. In many ways, these legends reflect the dreams of those who told them.

Another interesting difference encountered in Iceland is the preponderance of outlaw legends found in the earlier collections. These stories, which often take on a wonder-tale structure of capture and escape similar to that defined for the Russian folktale by Vladimir Propp, also tell us much about the way in which the Icelanders viewed their world. To begin with, it is generally understood that the area inhabited by outlaws is the near uncharted (at the time) wilderness or highland area in the center of the country, an area that is "outside" the settlement, which people have to cross as they travel between different farms or areas. The outlaws thus have much in common with trolls and elves. Many of the outlaw legends also describe hidden outlaw settlements based in wonderful lost green valleys with their own laws and institutions—yet another expression of the storytellers' dreams of a better life (and something as far from the truth as one can imagine). Other legends, closer to the truth, show great sympathy for the criminal who has been forced to steal or been involved in adultery, perhaps even incestuous relations with his sister. The enemy in such legends is clearly the authorities, be they foreign officials with their over-harsh laws, the foreign merchants that controlled the local trade, or the landowning farmers (prior to the development of fishing villages in the nineteenth century, a high percentage of the population lacked farms of their own). This enmity is also reflected in many magician legends, where the magician (both a farmer and a priest) is seen as the friend of the little man against the authorities (and the Devil).

While many aspects of Icelandic folk belief have, of course, changed over time, many things remain. New stories are still told about the elves trying to prevent road building that is likely to disturb, if not destroy, their place of abode. While it is questionable whether many Icelanders would actually state any certainty about the existence of such figures, there are not many either who would emphatically deny their possible presence among us. The same belief in other planes and other sources of knowledge is seen in the Icelanders' continued belief in the existence of ghosts, some form of fate, and the power of dreams, all of which are also well reflected in the earliest accounts about the Icelandic people written in Iceland.

Besides the sagas, which provide a valuable insight into the daily lives of Icelanders at least during the thirteenth and fourteenth centuries (if not during the time at which they are supposed to take place: around 1000 C.E.), the earliest learned glimpses into ethnological detail regarding the lifestyle of Icelanders come from the sixteenth and early seventeenth centuries—first in Bishop Oddur Einarsson's *Qualiscunque descriptio Islandiæ* (*Íslandslýsing* [A Description of Iceland]) in 1588–1589 and then in the slightly more detailed and much more widely read description of the country, *Crymogea* (1609), written by Arngrímur Jónsson the Learned (1568–1648). The latter was deliberately designed to contradict the exaggerated accounts of the barbaric ways of the Icelandic people circulated by English and German authors of the time. Among other things, these works provide us with the first real information about certain Icelandic folk dances, games, and sports.

FOOD, CLOTHING, GAMES, AND CUSTOMS

Almost 200 years later, in 1772, two Icelandic students in Copenhagen, Eggert Ólafsson and Bjarni Pálsson, published *Reise igjennom Island* (Travels in Iceland [1772]), a wide-ranging scientific report on the country and its nature, customs, and inhabitants that had been commissioned by the Danish king. At around the same time, a number of travelogues written by foreign travelers started to appear. These reports contain valuable objective views of Icelandic housing, foods, clothing, and customs in the eighteenth and nineteenth centuries as well as individual accounts of *sagnaskemmtun* (storytelling evenings, similar to the Irish *ceilidh*), where the household would sit together in the main living/sleeping room doing household chores while others told stories, read from the Bible or saga literature, or chanted *rímur* during in the long Icelandic winter evenings. This particular feature of Icelandic rural society played a central role in the dissemination of folktales, worldview, and values. It also helps to explain why so many literary motifs (especially from the sagas) have come to blend with legendary material in oral tradition. Along with the regular church services, it might be seen as a form of schooling for the people of the farms.

The first Icelandic survey of riddles, games (especially chess), sports, rigmarole rhymes, and folk dramatic traditions (connected essentially with the communal *vikivaki* dance sessions of the sixteenth to late eighteenth centuries), *Íslenzkar gátur, skemtanir, vikivakar og þulur* (Icelandic Riddles, Games, Dances, and Rigmaroles) appeared between 1887 and 1903. Originating from Jón Árnason's collection of material, this was edited by Ólafur Davíðsson, a younger collector following in Jón's footsteps. It paved the way for a long series of books dealing with different aspects of rural life in Iceland in earlier centuries, running up into the present time. The real foundation of this work is *Íslenzkir þjóðhættir* (Icelandic Folk Ways [1934, 1945, 1961]) by Jónas Jónasson frá Hrafnagili (1856–1918), a locally educated and highly motivated parish priest from the north of Iceland. Like many of his predecessors in the field of folklore collection, Jónas did not have the benefit of studying abroad, but unlike most of them he endeavored to make up for this by extensive reading of foreign works on folklore and direct written contact with foreign scholars in the field, which enabled him to undertake a number of valuable comparative studies. It is with good reason that he has been dubbed the father of modern Icelandic folklore studies.

The cultural world that Jónas and those who follow in his wake describe has a number of individual features worthy of note. As mentioned above, the roots of this society are essentially Scandinavian, reflected in the old division of the year into two halves (winter and summer), with powerful liminal periods not only at the height of each season (midwinter and midsummer) but also in earlier times at their start and finish (especially the start of winter). The same connections can be seen in the remnants of the old Scandinavian system of months such as *þorri* and *Góa* and in the Danish influences on Lenten seasonal custom and many seasonal foods. Indeed, careful comparison always needs to be done with all Icelandic folklore before anything can definitely be classed as being uniquely Icelandic (something all too rarely done during the years when Iceland was fighting complicated legal battles for its independence from Denmark).

Of central importance for analyzing this society, however, is the necessity of realizing the nature of the social unit over time in Iceland. While there were few towns in the past and often long distances between farms, nowadays little evidence of regional dialect exists. This resulted from several factors. First, between the sixteenth and eighteenth centuries, only a limited number of people owned land. Others moved annually between farms where they were employed on yearly contracts. For men, part of the work during the wintertime involved fishing for the farmer and/or traveling to buy fish. Since the main winter fishing grounds were in the south and west of the country, this meant an annual mass migration of workers from the north to the south and back again (no small trip across the snow-covered, windswept desert highlands). Along with the comparatively high level of literacy and relatively easy access to books in Icelandic, this not only helped prevent the development of regional dialects but also led to the easy movement of belief, custom, and oral tradition throughout the country.

Furthermore, the fact that people tended to live and work together (largely for warmth) in large communal rooms on the larger farms rather than in small individual cottages or crofts (like those known in Scotland or Ireland) helped limit the creation of "outsider" figures in most of Iceland. While foreigners, outlaws, and the supernatural were natural outsiders, and while there were a number of well-known (and quite well-received) tramps, there was little space for the creation of "witch figures" in Iceland. Indeed, in the close-knit Icelandic family and social system, any woman left alone on a farm would usually soon be taken in by another farm or joined by other family members or workers. The witch-burning craze in Iceland, when it occurred, was thus limited both in area and in sex. Those most associated with magic and witchcraft in Iceland tended to be self-educated men living on the outskirts of society in the western fjords, where geographical conditions demanded closer "communities" with the resulting possibility of "outsiders."

In general, the shape of the Icelandic farm and the foods produced and eaten on it were also shaped by local conditions, among them the lack of larger trees such as oak, pine, and elm, the gradual disappearance of the birch forests, and the worsening of the climate from the thirteenth century onward, reaching an ultimate low in the disasters of the eighteenth century. The earliest houses were longhouses of wood, stone, and turf like those found in Norway, the Faroes, Shetland, and Orkney, and the same building materials continued to be used until early in the last century, wood being either imported or collected on the beaches (along with stranded whales). As time went on, however, the role of turf and stone increased, and rooms became smaller to make better use of heat. Extra rooms were added to the main living room, and then corridors connecting rooms (including a kind of sauna), leading back from the front of the house. In time, the sauna itself became the communal living/sleeping room, hence the use of the word *baðstofa* (bath room) for the main living quarters by the sixteenth century. Indeed, it is quite possible that J.R.R. Tolkien's image of the "hobbit hole" in *The Lord of the Rings* was based on his knowledge of Icelandic farms as they were at this time.

The worsening of the climate also played a key role in the shaping of those foods nowadays referred to as "traditional" in Iceland. The growing of cereal crops was soon abandoned in Iceland and replaced by an increasing dependence on domestic animals (especially sheep, then horses and cattle), fishing, the collection of mosses and herbs, and hunting wild birds. In general, everything available was utilized, and a number of key forms of preservation were employed, ranging from wind-drying to smoking and pickling (using whey). Pickled meats of this kind (including pickled sheep's head, whale blubber, and ram's testicles) are the central features of the annual *þorrablót* festivals nowadays celebrated in Iceland in January and February each year, where city people eat the preserved foods of their forefathers (a relatively new festival celebrating old ways). Other well-known, traditional foods are *skyr* (a form of curds), *hangikjöt* (smoked lamb), and skate and shark—allowed to rot in the ground for some time—the former being the traditional meal eaten in Iceland on 23 December.

When it comes to the question of music, dance, and national costume, it seems clear that much of the modern image is something deliberately created during the mid- to late nineteenth century. While the sagas make several references to harps and other instruments, musical instruments in Iceland were for many years largely limited to the *langspil* (closely related to the Norwegian *langspel*), simply because, as with so much else, local materials were limited. Regarding dance, which has early roots, the limited written source material makes it very difficult to reconstruct the precise steps of the communal so-called *vikivaki* dances that were so popular in Iceland between the sixteenth and eighteenth centuries until the church and the arrival of traditional pair dancing from abroad put an end to them. What is evident is that these were chain and circle dances similar (but not identical) to those still danced today in the Faroe Islands, involving both communal song (often ballad-related) and dance. The gatherings themselves seem to have been a forerunner to the modern "acid house" phenomenon, involving a great deal of drink and no small amount of "bonding."

Even more popular in Iceland for centuries was the singing or chanting of so-called *rímur*, long poetic cycles based on sagas, romances, and wonder-tale motifs, which would often form the central point of an evening's *sagnaskemmtun*. This tradition has roots in both the foreign ballad and the native skaldic and Eddic poetry tradition. Its popularity and the complexity of its poetic imagery underline the degree to which the poetic tradition has always played a central role in Icelandic culture, even today, when surprising numbers of poetry books are still published (and read) annually at Christmas.

In terms of other particularly Icelandic "entertainment" of the past, it is necessary to mention also Icelandic wrestling (*glíma*), which, while related to local forms of wrestling known elsewhere (for example, in the British Isles and Norway), also has rules and holds that are peculiar to Iceland. Its age as a popular sport in Iceland is testified to by both the sagas and the later folk legends where *glíma* contests not only demonstrate the manliness and skill of protagonists but also regularly provide an external poetic image of the clash between the mundane and the supernatural. Indeed, ghosts (or outlaws) and men commonly wrestle when they meet at borderlines between the two worlds.

CHALLENGES OF THE MODERN WORLD

Icelandic society today is, of course, very different from that of the past, more than half of the population of 280,000 living in the vicinity of the capital, Reykjavík, where speed, mobility, and the importance of keeping up with modern technology and global trends are central. Indeed, **globalization** and especially the influences of American media are visible everywhere in modern Icelandic urban culture. Alongside this, the range of folklore research in Iceland is also changing. Accompanying continued research into the nature of heritage, nostalgia and identity, and the changes that have recently occurred in belief, custom, and tradition, new work has been undertaken into various aspects of Icelandic urban culture, especially the development of school traditions (the school in a sense having a ritual year of its own); the role of folklore for immigrant identity (for example, among the Icelandic-Vietnamese); and the local forms assumed by global culture as it comes into contact with Icelandic conditions. In this sense, as with earlier folklore, Iceland still has a particular value for the study of folklore: it remains a naturally limited island community that imports ideas, traditions, and concepts from abroad and makes them its own by adapting them to a home environment that still has deeply rooted traditions of its own.

BIBLIOGRAPHY

Icelanders do not have surnames, the name Jónsson being merely a statement of a person's paternity. Hence, as in Icelandic phone books, authors are designated here by their Christian names rather than their surnames.

Agnar Helgason and others. 2000a. Estimating Scandinavian and Gaelic Ancestry in the Male Settlers of Iceland. *American Journal of Human Genetics* 67:697–717.

———. 2000b. mtDNA and the Origin of the Icelanders: Deciphering Signals of Recent Population History. *American Journal of Human Genetics* 66:999–1016.

———. 2000c. mtDNA and the Islands of the North Atlantic: Estimating the Proportions of Norse and Gaelic Ancestry. *American Journal of Human Genetics* 66:723–737.

Arngrímur Jónsson. 1985. *Crymogea,* translated by Jakob Benediktsson. Reykjavík: Sögufélag.

Árni Björnsson. 1993. *Saga daganna.* Reykjavík: Mál og menning.

———. 1995. *Icelandic High Days and Holidays,* translated by Anna Yates. Reykjavík: Iceland Review.

———. 1996. *Merkisdagar í mannsœvi.* Reykjavik: Mál og menning.

Bjarni þorsteinsson. 1906–1909. *Íslensk þjóðlög.* Siglufjörður: Siglufjarðarprentsiðja.

Bo Almqvist. 1991a. Dead Child Legends Westward Bound. In *Viking Ale: Studies on Folklore Contacts between the Northern and the Western Worlds,* edited by Éilís Ní Dhuibhne-Almqvist and Séamas Ó Catháin. Aberystwyth: Boethius Press. 155–165.

———. 1991b. Scandinavian and Celtic Folklore Contacts in the Earldom of Orkney. In *Viking Ale: Studies on Folklore Contacts between the Northern and the Western Worlds,* edited by Éilís Ní Dhuibhne-Almqvist and Séamas Ó Catháin. Aberystwyth: Boethius Press. 1–29.

———. 2000. The Dead from the Sea in Old Icelandic Tradition. In *Islanders and Water Dwellers: Proceedings of the Celtic-Nordic-Baltic Folklore Symposium Held at University College, Dublin, 16–19 June 1996,* edited by Patricia Lysaght, Séamas Ó Catháin, and Daíthi Ó hÓgáin. Dublin: University College. 1–18.

Boucher, Alan, trans. and ed. 1989. *The Iceland Traveller: A Hundred Years of Adventure.* Reykjavík: Iceland Review.

Craigie, William A. 1952. *Sýnisbók íslenzkra rímna: Frá upphafi rímnakveðskapur til loka nítjánda aldar, I–III*. London: Thomas Nelson.

DuBois, Thomas A. 1999. *Nordic Religions in the Viking Age*. Philadelphia: University of Pennsylvania Press.

Eggert Ólafsson. 1975. *Travels in Iceland by Eggert Ólafsson and Bjarni Pálsson*. Reykjavík: Örn og Örlýgur.

Einar Ólafur Sveinsson. 1929. *Verzeichnis isländischer Märchenvarianten*. FFC 83. Helsinki: Academica Scientiarum Fennica.

———. 1940. *Um íslenzkar þjóðsögur*. Reykjavík: Sjóður Margrétar Lehmann-Filhés.

———. 1971. Jón Árnason (1819–1888). In *Leading Folklorists of the North*, edited by Dag Strömbäck. Oslo: Universitetsforlaget. 419–435.

———. 2003. *The Folktales of Iceland*, translated by Benedikt S. Benedikz and others; edited by Einar G. Pétursson. London: Viking Society for Northern Research.

Erlendur Haraldsson. 1978. *þessa heims og annars: Könnun á dulrœnni reynslu Íslendinga, trúarviðhorfum og þjóðtrú*. Reykjavík: Saga.

Frosti F. Jóhannsson, ed. 1988–1991. *Íslensk þjóðmenning, I, and V–VII*. 1988–1991. Reykjavík: þjóðsaga.

Gísli Sigurðsson. 1996. þjóðsögur. In *Íslensk bókmenntasaga, III*, edited by Halldór Guðmundsson. Reykjavík: Mál og menning. 409–494.

———. 1998. Introduction. In *Eddukvæði*, edited by Gísli Sigurðsson. Reykjavík: Mál og menning. ix–lxiii.

———. 2000. *Gaelic Influence in Iceland. Historical and Literary Contacts: A Study of Research*. 2nd edition. Reykjavík: Háskólaútgáfan.

Gunnar Karlsson. 2001. *Iceland's 1100 Years: A History of a Marginal Society*. Reykjavík: Mál og menning.

Gunnell, Terry. 1995. *The Origins of Drama in Scandinavia*. Cambridge: D. S. Brewer.

———. 1998. The Return of Sæmundur: Origins and Analogues. In *þjóðlíf og þjóðtrú: Ritgerðir helgaðar Jóni Hnefli Aðalsteinssyni*. Reykjavík: þjóðsaga. 87–111.

———. 2001a. From Grímnismál to Graffiti: Themes and Approaches in 100 Years of Icelandic Folkloristics. In *Norden og Europa: Fagtradisjoner i nordisk etnologi og folkloristikk* (Den 28. nordiske etnolog- og folkloristkongress, Hankø, mai, 2000), edited by Bjarne Rogan and Bente Gullveig Alver. Oslo: Novus. 92–102.

———. 2001b. Mists, Magicians and Murderous Children: International Migratory Legends concerning the "Black Death" in Iceland. In *Northern Lights: Following Folklore in North Western Europe: Essays in Honour of Bo Almqvist*, edited by Séamas Ó Catháin. Dublin: University College Dublin Press. 47–59.

———. 2003. Waking the "Wiggle-Waggle" Monsters: Animal Figures and Cross Dressing in the Icelandic Vikivaki Games. In *Folk Drama Studies Today: Papers Given at the International Traditional Drama Conference 19–21 July, University of Sheffield*, edited by Eddie Cass and Peter Milligan. Sheffield: Traditional Drama Research Group. 207–224.

———. 2004. The Coming of the Christmas Visitors: Folk Legends concerning the Attacks on Icelandic Farmhouses Made by Spirits at Christmas. *Northern Studies* 38:51–75.

Hallfreður Örn Eiríksson (with Helga Jóhannsdóttir). 1974. *Recordings of Icelandic Folklore*. Reykjavík: Stofnun Árna Magnússonar á Íslandi.

Hallgerður Gísladóttir. 1999. *Íslensk matarhefð*. Reykjavík: Mál og menning.

Hannes þorsteinsson and others 1935–1936. *Huld, I–II*. Reykjavík: Sigurður Kristjánsson.

Helgi Guðmundsson and Arngrímur Fr. Bjarnason. 1933–1949. *Vestfirzkar sagnir I–III*. Reykjavík: Bókaverzlun Guðm. Gamalíelssonar and Bókaforlagið Fagurskinna.

Hermann Pálsson and Paul Edwards, trans. and eds. 1972. *The Book of Settlements*. Winnipeg: University of Manitoba Press.

Jón Hnefill Aðalsteinsson. 1987. Wrestling with a Ghost in Icelandic Popular Belief. *Arv* 43:7–20.

———. 1990. Folkloristik och etnologi på Island under 1980-talet. In *Tiden och historien i 1980–talets kulturforskning*, edited by Anders Gustavsson. Uppsala: Institutionen för kultur-antropologi och etnologi, Uppsala universitet. 279–289.

———. 1993. The Testimony of Waking Consciousness and Dreams in Migratory Legends concerning Human Encounters with the Hidden People. *Arv* 49:123–131.

———. 1994. Sæmundr Fróði. A Medieval Naster of Magic. *Arv* 50:117–132.

———. 1996. Six Icelandic Magicians after the Time of Sæmundr Fróði. *Arv* 52:49–62.

Jón Árnason. 1995. *Icelandic Legends*, translated by George E. J. Powell and Eiríkur Magnússon. Felinfach: Llanerch.

Jón Árnason and Ólafur Davíðsson. 1887–1903. *Íslenzkar gátur, skemtanir, vikivakar og þulur*, I–IV. København: Hið íslenzka bókmenntafélag.

Jón Árnason and Magnús Grímsson. 1852. *Íslenzk Æfintýri*. Reykjavík: E. Þórðarsson.

———. 1954–1961. *Íslenzkar þjóðsögur og œvintýri* I–VI. Reykjavík: Þjóðsaga.

Jón G. Friðjónsson. 1993. *Mergur málsins. Íslensk orðatiltæki, uppruni og notkun*. Reykjavík: Bókaklúbbur Arnar og Örlygs.

Jón Samsonarson. 1964. *Kvæði og dansleikir*, I–II. Reykjavík: Almennabókafélagið.

Jón Þorkelsson. 1956. *Þjóðsögur og munnmæli*. Reykjavík: Bókfellsútgáfan.

Jónas Jónasson and Oddur Björnson, eds. 1977. *Þjóðsögur og þjóðsagnir*. Akureyri: Oddur Björnsson.

Jónas Jónasson frá Hrafngili. 1961 (1934). *Íslenskir þjóðhœttir*. Reykjavík: Ísafoldarprentsmiðja.

Jónas Kristjánsson. 1988. *Eddas and Sagas: Iceland's Medieval Literature*, translated by Peter Foote. Reykjavík: Hið íslenska bókmenntafélag.

Larrington, Carolyne, trans. 1999. *The Poetic Edda*. Oxford: Oxford University Press.

Lúðvík Kristjánsson. 1980–1986. *Íslenskir sjávarhœttir* I–V. Reykjavík: Menningarsjóður.

Maurer, Konrad. 1860. *Isländische Volkssagen der Gegenwart*. Leipzig: J. C. Hinrichs'sche Buchhandlung.

Oddur Einarsson. 1971. *Íslandslýsing: Qualiscunque descriptio Islandœ*, translated by Sveinn Pálsson. Reykjavík: Menningarsjóður.

Ólafur Davíðsson. 1987. *Íslenzkar þjóðsögur* I–IV. Reykjavík: Þjóðsaga.

Ólína Þorvarðardóttir. 2000. *Brennuöldin: Galdur og galdratrú í málskjölum og munnmælum*. Reykjavík: Háskólaútgáfan.

Price, Neil. 2001. *The Viking Way: Religion and War in Late Iron Age Scandinavia*. Uppsala: Department of Archaeology and Ancient History, Uppsala.

Rakel Pálsdóttir. 2001. *Kötturinn í örbylguofninum og fleiri flökkusagnir úr samtímanum*. Reykjavík: Bjartur.

Sigfús Sigfússon. 1922–1958. *Íslenzkar þjóðsögur og sagnir* I–XVI. Seyðisfjörður and Reykjavík: Þjóðsaga.

Sigurður Nordal and Þorbergur Þorðarson, eds. 1962. *Gráskinna hin meiri*. Reykjavík: Þjóðsaga.

Sigríður Þ. Valgeirsdóttir. 1994. *Gömlu dansarnir í tvær aldir: Brot úr íslenskri menningarsögu*. Reykjavík: Sigríður Valgeirsdóttir.

Simpson, Jacqueline, ed. and trans. 2004. *Icelandic Folk Tales and Legends*. Revised edition. London: Batsford.

Snorri Sturluson. 2000. *Edda*, translated by Anthony Faulkes. London: Dent.

Sveinn Einarsson. 1991, 1996. *Íslensk leiklist*, I–II. Reykjavík: Hið íslenska bókmenntafélag.

Þorsteinn M. Jónsson. 1969. *Gríma hin nýja* I–V. Reykjavík: Þjóðsaga.

Valdimar Tr. Hafstein. 2000. The Elves' Point of View. *Fabula* 41:87–104.

Vésteinn Ólason. 1982. *The Traditional Ballads of Iceland*. Reykjavík: Stofnun Árna Magnússonar á Íslandi.

———. 1998. *Dialogues with the Viking Age: Narration and Representation in the Sagas of the Icelanders.* Reykjavík: Heimskringla: Mál og menning, Academic Division.

Terry Gunnell

NORWAY

GEOGRAPHY AND HISTORY

The narrow, mountainous strip of land that is Norway lies on the northern edge of Europe with almost a third of its length projecting above the Arctic Circle. Strongly influenced by the North Sea, its unpredictable weather played a significant role in the lives of pre-industrial inhabitants, who often competed directly with the elements for survival. Mountains, forests, lakes, rivers, and glaciers left the land less than 4 percent tillable, forcing farmers to supplement small yields with fishing, hunting, and forestry.

Pre-industrial Norway had few sizable cities and only one significant trade center, Bergen, whose population by the first half of the 1800s had barely reached 15,000. Except for exports of fish and timber, commerce played a minor role in the country's economy. The professional class (ministers, doctors, civil officials) accounted for a mere 2 percent of the population and were predominantly of Danish and German origin, the latter having come during the 1600s to develop newly opened copper and silver mines. By the 1800s Danish had long been the official language of Norway, which since 1536 had been ruled as a province of **Denmark**.

Independent and powerful throughout the Viking Age (ca. 800–1000 C.E.) and for almost 300 years thereafter, Norway was devastated by the Black Death (1349–1350) and subsequently became the weaker member of various unions with Denmark and **Sweden** before coming completely under Danish dominance. When the union with Denmark ended in 1814 as a result of the Napoleonic Wars, Norway obtained a liberal constitution during a brief period of independence before being turned over to Sweden. Norway shared a king with Sweden until 1905, when the Norwegian people voted for, and achieved, full independence and a constitutional monarchy.

These social and political realities underlie a favorite theme of Norwegian folk narrative: the lowly peasant prevailing over the greedy tax-collector, hard-hearted sheriff, or ungodly minister. While these authorities along with the entire professional class wrote and spoke Danish, the vast majority of the population continued to speak their local dialects. The rudimentary education received by most rural children seldom included writing, though they learned to read the Danish Bible, hymns, and catechism as they prepared for Confirmation in the Lutheran State Church around the age of fourteen. Once this obligatory rite had conferred adult status upon them, young people were expected to support themselves. Most left home to become manual laborers on more prosperous farms in the local parish, while others apprenticed themselves to tradesmen or went to sea. As the nineteenth century wore on, they increasingly sought employment in growing towns and cities as household servants or factory workers.

Norwegian carriage, Hardanger Fjord, Norway. Rugged landscape such as this afforded little arable land, so Norwegian farmers have been forced to supplement small crop yields with fishing, hunting, and forestry. (Courtesy Library of Congress)

Most of these workers were the sons and daughters of cotters (tenants of small-holdings who exchanged their labor for a portion of the farm's yield). As high taxes caused many property owners to forfeit their land, the cotter class grew rapidly in the 1800s until their number exceeded that of freeholders. Still the basic social unit remained a landowning family along with their cotters and various servants and laborers. Land ownership passed from father to son and traditionally stayed in the same family for generations. Life on the farm was stable and isolated, though new impulses came occasionally through contact with itinerant traders, craftsmen, soldiers, beggars, and visitors. The work of the farm, dictated by the soil and shifting seasons, proceeded in a rhythm recorded on the wooden calendar stick known as the *primstav*. Dividing the year into summer and winter halves, the *primstav* originated to mark the thirty-seven saints' days added to the year when Norway became a Christian country (ca. 1000). The symbols on the *primstav* indicated the days when the church expected workers to leave their chores and attend mass but soon became reminders of when to slaughter livestock, weed and harvest fields, shear sheep, weave cloth, and perform other needed chores.

This mixture of Christian piety and practical necessity accurately reflects the worldview shared by the majority of Norwegians between the Christian conversion and the Industrial Revolution. Beliefs taught by the church merged with those of ancient Norway as parishioners faithfully took communion and confessed their sins even as they continued to believe in the unseen spirits of forest, field, river, lake, and air, with whom harmonious relations must be maintained. While the church firmly condemned belief in, and tributes made to, these hidden beings, most pre-industrial Norwegians apparently found no contradiction between honoring the *gardvord* (the farm's guardian spirit) with a bowl of ale or porridge on Christmas Eve and attending church services on Christmas Day.

The Lutheran Reformation (1537) did little to suppress this mixture of beliefs. Coming to an unprepared Norway by royal edict of the Danish king, the Reformation introduced a century of unsettled conditions. In some parishes the last Catholic priest became the first Lutheran minister, and not until a new generation of trained Lutheran ministers entered the pulpit in the early 1600s did the change in worship form begin to take hold. Even then, pre-Christian beliefs in the hidden beings along with remnants of Catholicism persisted alongside official Lutheranism and did so well into the 1800s. Perhaps the most significant change brought by the Reformation was the requirement that ministers have a university degree to be ordained. Prospective ministers went to study in Denmark or **Germany** (Norway being without a university until 1813), where they acquired not only an education but also a Continental lifestyle and worldview that distanced them significantly from their parishioners.

MEDICINE AND SUPERNATURAL LORE

Because of their superior education and a lack of professionally trained doctors, ministers often tended to the physical ills of the parishioners, who otherwise relied on home remedies or consulted the *kloke* (wise—that is, folk healers). Actually, there was little difference in the remedies applied by any of these practitioners, who generally shared the view that disease was caused by bodily impurities, which had to be expelled by emetics, purges, blistering poultices, and bleeding. Some folk healers relied only on rational means, but those who believed the impurity had supernatural origins (projectiles shot by nature spirits or the magic of envious witches) held that only supernatural cures (magic words and rituals) would work. Since germ theory gained few adherents before the 1880s and nutritional deficiency diseases continued to elude explanation far into the twentieth century, doctors had little better to offer, and folk tradition shows self-trained healers succeeding where professionals failed.

Unusually skilled folk healers were said to "have the Black Book," a compendium of magical cures whose power, many believed, derived from the Devil himself, an image that suggests the ambiguous position (both needed and feared) that folk healers occupied. Fear of the folk healer climaxed during the sixteenth- and seventeenth-century witch trials, which saw some 350 Norwegians executed, many merely for using magical healing formulas. Examples of these formulas are preserved in the 150–200 *svarteböker* (Black Books) that remain in private collections, libraries, and museums, individual compilations of remedies and spells from oral and written sources made by various individuals during the 1700s and 1800s.

A number of Black Book formulas addressed English disease (rickets) as it raged in pre-industrial Norway. Though a few nineteenth-century folk healers achieved success and renown by using rational remedies such as cod liver oil, nutritious food, and outdoor exercise, doctors had no cure, and the folk belief persisted that the *huldrefolk* (hidden people) had kidnapped healthy babies and left behind the sickly "changelings." Parents put scissors or a Bible into the cradle and kept a candle burning day and night to ward off the *huldrefolk*, but permanent protection came only through the rite of baptism. The silver fastenings and cruciform embroidery applied to christening clothes originally functioned to protect the baptismal infant on the dangerous journey to the church (since it afforded the *huldrefolk* their last opportunity to steal the child) as did the six to eight baptismal sponsors.

Human vulnerability to abduction by the *huldrefolk* increased around all rites of passage, whose associated church ceremonies were similarly believed to remove the danger. New mothers were "churched" forty days after the birth, while marriage and funeral ceremonies featured protective metal (bridal crown and belt, cross-shaped amulet worn by the groom, and coins on the corpse's eyes). Burning candles as well as crosses woven into baptismal, wedding, and funeral tapestries provided extra protection before and during the ceremony.

Being alone in nature increased chances of being abducted by the *huldrefolk*, as did staying too long at the *seter* (summer mountain dairy). The *huldrefolk* owned the *seter* but permitted the human occupants to use it during the summer while the farm's small parcel of tillable land produced potatoes and barley. A dairy maid took the cows, sheep, and goats to graze on mountain pastures and converted their milk into the butter, cheese, and sour cream that would sustain the farm through the coming year. Belief that the *huldrefolk* reclaimed the *seter* in the fall helped ensure a safe return of the livestock.

The timely return from the *seter* exemplifies the mutual respect necessary for successful relationships with the *huldrefolk*. When asked to move a cowshed because manure was dropping on the *huldrefolk*, a wise landowner complied. So did his wife when called to be midwife to a *huldre* birth. Yet despite constant efforts to avoid trouble, the *huldrefolk* easily took offense and quickly avenged themselves by inflicting illness or causing the churn to yield no butter or the brewing to produce poor ale. Work-intensive processes of this sort that had uncertain outcomes seemed especially prone to *huldrefolk* interference. To guard against it, brewers drove a sheath knife into their beer barrels, and butter makers plunged hot pokers into their churns, utensils (along with milk strainers, butter boxes, cheese forms, and beer bowls) that were routinely incised with protective crosses.

Crosses, metal, and fire could also ward off witches, the other source of ill fortune. Witches profited at their neighbors' expense by sending their *hug* (minds or souls) into their churns to steal milk. (The witch was usually, but not exclusively, believed to be a woman since food preparation and health, the aspects of daily life most affected by witches, belonged on the woman's side of the gender-specific workload.) Witches could also steal milk by means of a *trollkatt* made from their own hair, fingernails, and blood that was then sent rolling from farm to farm to gather milk, a scenario that explained why some prospered while others failed.

A farm's prosperity also depended upon harmonious relations with the *nisse*, or barn spirit. As long as the farm inhabitants respected the *nisse* by practicing good animal husbandry, upholding traditions, and following established norms, all went well, but if they crossed the *nisse*, he took revenge by stealing from the landowner and causing illness or other misfortune. To appease and reward the *nisse*, a bowl of *römmegröt* (sour cream porridge) was left for him on Christmas Eve (a motif that lives on in Christmas store displays, greeting cards, and songs, though not in belief).

Other supernatural beings include the *nökk* (dangerous sprite of lakes and streams), the hypnotic *fossegrim* (demon of the waterfall), the *hulder* (beautiful temptress of men working alone), and the *oskorei* (terrifying riders of the Christmas sky). Some equated the *oskorei* with the dead, who haunted the living at other times of the year as well and occasionally brought disease and death. A child too fervently longed for by its dead mother became sickly and died, as did one whose mother refused to name it according to traditional rules. Ghost hauntings generally signaled unfinished business between the dead and the living, while certain categories of ghosts had a specific mission, such as the *utburd* (killed by its mother at birth and longing for baptism or burial in consecrated ground), the *draug* (souls of those who died at sea and appear to those about to meet the same fate), and the *deildegast* (who moved a property marker in life and for eternity must try to replace it).

A Norwegian *nisse* (barn spirit) fiddles while pigs dance. A farm's prosperity depended upon harmonious relations with the *nisse*. (© Mary Evans Picture Library/The Image Works)

LEGENDS AND FOLKTALES

Accounts of the dead, nature spirits, *huldrefolk*, and witches make up most of the *sagn* (legends), which along with *eventyr* (fairy tales) and *folkeviser* (ballads) constitute the verbal lore of pre-industrial Norway. Scholars identify three types of *sagn*, designating as *naturmytiske sagn* (nature-mythical legends) those accounts specifically concerned with supernatural beings. The *historiske sagn* (historical legends) provide a local perspective on actual events such as Norway's Christian conversion (the exploits of St. Olav), the Black Death (an old hag with a rake and a broom killing some or all in her path), and the Lutheran Reformation (the Black Book minister, trained in magic at Wittenberg and capable of making thieves return with stolen goods and forcing the Devil to do his bidding). *Opphavs sagn* (legends of origin) explain unusual natural phenomena, most often as the doing of St. Olav, trolls, or *jutuls* (giants). One popular legend explained a portal-like formation in the mountainside near Vågå in Gudbrandsdal through which a *jutul* disappeared after giving Johannes Blessom a magical ride on an airborne sleigh to bring him home (from Copenhagen, where he had gone to settle a legal dispute) in time for Christmas.

Unlike the *sagn*, *eventyr* (fictional folktales) portray no specific individual, place, or time. All tale types cataloged in the Aarne-Thompson index are well represented in Norwegian lore. "The Three Billy Goats Gruff," best known of the *dyre-eventyr* (animal tales), is the only Norwegian tale familiar to most Americans, though English translations often omit the essential element of the *seter* to which the goats are going when they meet the troll.

The *under-eventyr* (miracle tales), a sub-category of *vanlige eventyr* (the Norwegian equivalent of what folklorists more generally refer to as "ordinary folktales"), are the most common in Norwegian lore. Exciting, fantastic tales with multiple episodes, they typically feature the youngest and least promising of the cotter's children succeeding where others have failed. In "The Three Aunts" a poverty-stricken girl receives magical help to spin, weave, and sew such fine linen shirts that she wins the hand of the prince. *Legende eventyr* (religious tales) portray the Lord and St. Peter, who, while wandering the earth together, encounter individuals whose behavior they reward or punish. A greedy baker woman who refuses to give them bread, for example, becomes a woodpecker ("Gertrude Bird"), doomed to finding her food between bark and wood. *Novelle eventyr* (short story tales) rarely feature supernatural elements. The cotter's son silences "The Princess Who Wouldn't Stop Talking" simply by seeing the possibilities in things that others disdain. In the most familiar of the *eventyr om det dumme trollet* (tales about the dumb troll) a cotter's son wins an eating contest with the enormous troll by persuading it to cut a hole in its stomach. When the troll dies, the boy takes all its gold and silver and thereby pays off his family's debt.

Skjemte eventyr (jocular tales) make fun of human foibles, especially those of suitors and spouses, reflecting the central position of marriage in pre-industrial society. In "Stupid Men and Shrewish Wives" a woman convinces her gullible husband that he is dead and his neighbor comes naked to the funeral, convinced by his wife that his clothes are too fine for him to see. *Ramse eventyr* (listing tales) continually add new elements to a core story to achieve a comic effect, as in "The Pancake," who escapes a hungry family and rolls down the road, meeting and escaping from a series of comically named animals who would also like to eat him.

BALLADS

Several themes familiar from legends and fairy tales occur in the *folkeviser* (ballads). Rooted in the Middle Ages, when they accompanied chain dancing, these narrative songs use concrete images, exciting scenes, and dramatic dialogue to tell a story in verse stanzas of two or four lines plus repeating refrain. The repetition and fixed phrases that characterize ballad style aided the singer's memory and either moved the action forward ("Then he saddled his handsome, fleet steed") or advanced the time ("Now the sun rose over the valley"). The best known, "Dream Ballad," recounts a journey to the kingdom of the dead, where the dreamer sees virtues rewarded and sins punished.

Scholars classify ballads by their subject matter. *Legendeviser* (religious ballads) include the "Dream Ballad" as well as "Olav og Kari," in which Kari's envious mother-in-law convinces her son Olav that Kari is a witch whom he must kill. Yet Kari intercedes for both their souls in Heaven. *Ridderviser* (chivalric ballads) portray dramatic events among knights in a medieval setting. This type accounts for over half of Scandinavian ballads, including "Bendik og Årolilja," about a young couple whose love, forbidden during their lifetime, continues after death as two lilies growing from their graves on opposite sides of the church entwine above it. *Kjempeviser* (fighting ballads) portray battles among warriors or between humans and trolls such as the daring journey of "Åsmund Frægdegjeva" to Trollbotn, where he frees the king's abducted daughter. *Naturmytiske viser* (nature mythical ballads) portray supernatural beings in their encounters with mortals who either succumb to their power ("Margjit Hjukse") or prevail over them ("Villemann og Magnill"). Best known of the *skjemteviser* (jocular ballads) is the "Backward Ballad," whose narrator bridles his boot, saddles his sword, and ties his horse to his side. *Historiske viser* (historical ballads) recount well-known events involving high-standing persons ("Queen Dagmar," who died in 1212), bride stealing ("Falkvor Lommannsson," who abducted Ingrid in 1288), or Roland, who fought at the side of Charlemagne ("Roland og Magnus Kongjen").

During the 1800s, *skillingviser* (broadsides) put new texts to familiar melodies to comment on events of the day. The much shorter *stev* (four-verse lines sung in a fixed rhythm) have a far longer history. Sung in festive settings often in call-and-response, the spontaneously invented text addressed another person present who responded with an appropriate *stev*, also spontaneously composed.

Songs and Music

Religious folk melodies with texts based on old hymns were often played on the *langeleik* (zither), a sixteenth-century instrument whose oblong resonance box had a varying number of strings. The one nearest to the player passed over a series of frets where the melody originated.

Much of Norway's folk music derived from the work life of farm and *seter*, fishing boat and shanty, as did the *lokk* (song used to gather the livestock), the *bånsull* (lullaby), and the *lur* (long wooden horn used by dairy maids to call to distant *seters*). Shepherds originally used the *bukkehorn* (ram's horn) to scare away wild animals, but the addition of finger holes made it a musical instrument. Shepherd boys usually made themselves a *seljeflöyte* (willow flute) in the spring, when the bark easily left the tree to form a tube, and played it by overblowing and placing an index finger over the open end.

Like these instruments, almost all objects used and consumed on the preindustrial farm were produced there. The women made the food and textiles, while the men made the tools, containers, and utensils, including ladles and *tvarer*, porridge stirrers fashioned from a spruce trunk retaining the lowest round of shortened branches. As betrothal gifts, young men made *mangletrœr*, which were long, flat, highly decorated boards with a single handle used to roll the wrinkles from linen cloth wound around a cylinder. By accepting this gift, the young woman promised marriage and usually reciprocated with a gift that similarly demonstrated her suitability such as a pair of knitted stockings or gloves.

Arts and Crafts

The long, dark evenings of autumn, winter, and early spring afforded time for this handwork as farm inhabitants gathered in the one-room cabin around a single source of warmth and light to work, tell stories, and sing. While the men decorated surfaces with incising, *kolrosing* (powdered charcoal rubbed into an incised design), and chip carving, the women set up the loom to weave the wool and linen they had grown and combed, dyed, and spun. Their geometrical and floral weavings (*åklœr*) covered beds and walls to provide decoration and warmth. For use on fishing boats, coastal women wove shag carpet–like *ryer* better able to shed water.

The clothing that came from these looms was often further decorated with embroidery and drawn work. Inspired by contemporary European styles, festive garments varied by district and featured as much silver as the wearer could afford. Chains laced the women's bodices, and brooches covered their blouse fronts, while buttons brightened the men's vests and knee pants.

Silversmiths and other specialized craftspersons such as weavers, painters, and carvers traveled from farm to farm after the seventeenth-century rearrangement of the house (replacing the hearth with ceiling smoke hole at the center of the room with a corner fireplace and chimney that more effectively removed the smoke) paved the way for interior decoration. Professional weavers produced *billedvev* (picture weaving), while carvers and painters decorated the large floor-to-ceiling cupboard that now stood against the wall between the door and table. *Rosemaling* (decorative painting) was based on the curving acanthus vine and began in Norway around 1700. It varied in style by district and soon covered ale bowls, spoons, boxes, and chests along with the cupboards, walls, and ceilings of the more prosperous.

While *rosemaling* is relatively recent, carving has ancient roots in Norway (for example, on Viking ships and wagons and on stave church portals). Ale bowls and tankards were its favored arenas and items every family had in profusion since beer brewing was an essential part of celebrating Christmas (known as "drinking Christmas"), wakes (*gravöl*, "grave beers"), births (*barnsöl*, "child beers"), and other special occasions. The butter boxes (constructed of bent wood and laced with birch root) and porridge containers (of stave construction) that also proliferated were used to transport gifts of food, their richly carved and *rosemaled* surfaces decorating the festive table along with intricately carved wooden butter molds.

Geometrical, animal, and interlacing ribbon motifs produced by means of chip carving or incising predominated, but in mid-eighteenth-century Gudbrandsdal, acanthus carving developed into a luxuriant, highly modeled technique known as *döleskurd* (valley carving). Sometimes painted in rich greens and blues accented with gold and red in the local churches, *döleskurd* suited the manorial style of house characteristic of this fertile and well-traveled valley.

DANCE AND CELEBRATIONS

There as elsewhere people eagerly anticipated celebrations as a welcome break in the exhausting work routine. In addition to consuming beer and festive foods, celebrants chiefly told stories and danced to music provided by the fiddler, one of the most highly regarded members of the community. The ordinary violin arrived in Norway during the seventeenth century, when also the *hardingfela* (Hardanger fiddle), Norway's national instrument, developed. Richly ornamented with incised floral designs and mother-of-pearl inlays, the *hardingfela* has a shorter neck and flatter bridge than an ordinary violin along with four or five sympathetic strings that resonate in harmony when the upper strings are bowed. Folksongs and legends associate the *hardingfela* with the *fossegrim* (spirit of the waterfall), who would teach aspiring fiddlers to play in return for a suitable sacrifice.

The accompanying dancing (now known as *bygdedans*, rural dance) came to Norway around 1600. Done in pairs, it consisted of two types: the *springer* in 3/4 time (also known as the *pols*) and the *ganger* in 2/4 or 6/8 time (including the *halling* with its athletic kicks as the male partner tried to remove a hat from a pole suspended by the female partner). In general, couples moved around the room in a circle, each pair dancing independently of the others, not using the same movements at precisely the same time or with equal duration.

The fiddle continued to dominate Norwegian folk music until 1860, when the accordion began infiltrating rural areas to accompany the *runddans* (round dancing done in pairs, also known as *gammeldans*, old-fashioned dance), which by 1900 completely overshadowed *bygdedans*. *Runddans* originated in Germany and **Austria** in the 1700s and eventually developed Norwegian forms, including the *vals* (waltz) in 3/4 time, *reinlender* in 2/4 or 4/4 time, *polka* also in 2/4 time but much faster than the *reinlender*, and the *masurka* in 3/4 time.

SPORTS AND GAMES

Dancing and singing were often a part of pre-industrial games. In *hindeleiken* (dancing doe) the girls (does) danced and sang in a circle while waiting to be matched up with the watching boys (bucks). In *stubbedansen* (tree stump dance) a boy standing on a stump named one of the girls dancing in a circle around him and danced away with her, a process that repeated until all the children were paired off. In *stim* (contention) the girls waited outside a room while one of the boys was dressed up to look frightening. When the girls were then let in, one by one, those who could compose and sing a *stev* about the ugly apparition received a drink from the ale bowl.

Blindebukk, which included neither dancing nor singing, had one person sitting on a chair, blindfolded and with towel in hand, while the others poked, pinched, and grabbed him or her to see "if the roast is ready." The "roast," meanwhile, hit at the others with the towel, and the first one hit became the roast. Participants in *Å slå på ringen* stood in a circle while the one who was "it" walked around the perimeter before suddenly slapping the back of one of the players. Now both ran in opposite directions, trying to get back to that place first.

Of indoor games little is known except for *pinnespill* and *gnav*. *Pinnespill* involved sticks of wood or bone carved with eight different heads, six of each kind with values ranging downward from king through sledge, cow, spear, pitchfork, and grain, to peasant. Players sat around a table and took turns using a knitting needle to fish one stick out of the pile but lost their turn if they moved any of the other sticks. *Gnav* consisted of twenty-one different cards, two of each kind—thirteen with numbers and eight with pictures—their values ranging downward from cuckoo, dragon, cat, horse, house, the numbers twelve to one, the joker, pot, owl, and finally zero. Players aimed to get the most points by exchanging cards according to a set of intricate rules.

The games above belonged to the upper class, though ordinary cardplaying also flourished among the lower classes and was common at nineteenth-century house parties. In some settings drinking and gambling accompanied cardplaying, giving rise to a common legend motif concerning a player who drops a card and, while bending under the table to pick it up, catches sight of the Devil's cloven hoof. Games played with balls (made of the tarred and dried platelike polyporus tree fungus) numbered among pre-industrial sports, as did ice-skating on bone or wood. Skiing, on the other hand, was primarily a form of transportation.

For the masses, however, leisure was essentially unknown even for children, who from an early age worked alongside the adults. Though no work was allowed on Sundays, travel to church and prolonged devotions at home filled the time for many. Christmas provided the only prolonged break. After lengthy, work-intensive preparations (slaughter, candlemaking, brewing, cleaning, and baking a six-month supply of flatbread), both adults and children put aside all but essential chores for twelve days, beginning on Christmas Eve, when for once they could eat their fill. That night all the farm's inhabitants gathered to sleep on the straw-covered floor of the main house, seeking safety from the *oskorei*, as some believed, or leaving their beds for their returning dead ancestors. The next day they attended church services and on successive days held house parties and went *julebukk* (Christmas goat: masquerading). Following a leader who wrapped himself in a goatskin or blanket and held a pole topped with a goat's head (real or carved from wood) in place of his own, disguised participants proceeded noisily from farm to farm demanding food and drink.

A milder form of *julebukking* continues in modern Norway (though mostly among children instead of adults), and Christmas baking, cleaning, candle burning, brewing, and feasting on pork or mutton ribs also show traditional roots. *Lutefisk* (lye-soaked cod, an Advent fasting food in Catholic times, perennial yuletide fare in pre-industrial times but subsequently disdained as "peasant food") has recently regained popularity. Otherwise modern Norwegians have emphatically distanced themselves from pre-industrial folk belief and traditions. For this reason organizers of the 1994 Winter Olympics, while nevertheless choosing to base the opening program on Norwegian folklore, deliberately used the archaic term *vetter* (instead of *huldrefolk*) to emphasize the distance between modern Norwegians and this lore.

STUDIES OF NORWEGIAN FOLKLORE

Though modern folk music, jewelry, and clothing designs regularly draw upon tradition with great effect, verbal lore tends toward highly internationalized urban legends expressing the insecurities and frustrations of modern life, most notably the conflicts arising from the immigration of other ethnic groups to a once homogeneous society.

The traditional legends were first collected and studied in the nineteenth century starting with *Norske sagn*, published by Andreas Faye in 1833 as a resource for writers and to discourage lingering belief in the supernatural. Peter Christen Asbjörnsen followed in 1845 with *Norske huldreeventyr og folkesagn*, aiming to capture the legends' characteristic language and narrative situation. While early scholarship emphasized these legends' ties to Old Norse mythology, subsequent studies—Solheim

(1952), Bö (1955), and Alver (1971)—focused on their function within their own context. Christiansen (1977 [1958]) catalogs legends, and Kvideland and Sehmsdorf (1988) organize, analyze, and translate them.

Asbjörnsen together with Jörgen Moe produced Norway's pioneer and now-classic collection of fictional folktales, *Norske Folkeeventyr* (1841–1844, 1852). Transforming the written Danish of the time by introducing Norwegian syntax and vocabulary, the work significantly aided the ongoing effort to discover and define a national identity in the wake of the 1814 constitution. Asbjörnsen and Moe (1960) provides translations and classic illustrations of the tales, while Hodne (1984, 1998) catalogs and describes them.

Olea Cröger provided most of the material in *Norske Folkeviser* (1853), edited by M. B. Landstad and still the most complete edition of ballads and folksongs. Aiming to preserve faithfully the ballads as a literary and cultural heritage, Landstad emphasized their ties to medieval and Viking times. All these collections aimed to demonstrate the richness and quality of Norwegian culture, and they strengthened patriotic feeling as the nation prepared for independence. So did the efforts of Hulda Garborg and Klara Semb to preserve and cultivate *bygdedans* and Hardanger fiddle music in the 1890s. Additional folk music and dance resources include the Öystre Slidre Kulturskule Web site (home.online.no/~kgjetmun/index.html) and *Norsk visbebok. Norske vise- og sangtradisjoner gjennom 500 år* (1993).

Useful sources on other genres of Norwegian folklore focus on folk medicine (Bö 1986a, Holck 1996, and Stokker forthcoming), folk arts, crafts, and games (Stewart 1999 [1972], Nelson 1995, Larson 2001, and Enerstvedt 1982), and calendar and Christmas lore (Alver 1981, Scott 1998, Bö 1986b, Stokker 2000).

BIBLIOGRAPHY

Alver, Bente. 1971. *Heksetro og trolldom et studie in norsk heksevœsen* (A Study of Norwegian Magic and Witchcraft). Oslo: Universitetsforlaget.

Alver, Brynjulf. 1981. *Dag og merke: folkeleg tidsrekning og merkedagstradisjon* (Folk Calendar Traditions). Bergen: Universitetsforlaget.

Asbjörnsen, Peter Christen, and Jörgen Moe. 1960. *Norwegian Folk Tales*, translated by Pat Shaw and Carl Norman. New York: Pantheon.

Bö, Olav. 1955. *Heilag Olav i norsk folketro* (St. Olav in Norwegian Folk Belief). Oslo: Det Norske samlaget.

———. 1986a. *Folkemedisin og lœrd medisin: Norsk medisinsk Kvardag på 1800-talet* (Folk Medicine and Learned Medicine). Oslo: Det Norske samlaget.

———. 1986b. *Vår norske jul* (Our Norwegian Christmas). Oslo: Det Norske samlaget.

Bremnes, Olga, and others. 1993. *Norsk visbebok. Norske vise- og sangtradisjoner gjennom 500 år* (Norwegian Song Traditions). Oslo: Grøndahl Dreyer.

Christiansen, Reidar Th. 1977 (1958). *The Migratory Legends*. New York: Arno.

Cröger, Olea. 1853. *Norske folkeviser*, edited by M. B. Landstad. Christiana: C. Tönsberg.

Enerstvedt, Åse. 1982. *Tampen brenn: Norske barneleikar* (Norwegian Children's Games). Oslo: Det Norske samlaget.

Hodne, Örnulf. 1984. *The Types of the Norwegian Folktale*. Oslo: Universitetsforlaget.

———. 1998. *Det norske folkeeventyret: fra folkediktning til nasjonal kultur* (The Norwegian Folktale). Oslo: Cappelen.

————. 1999. *Norsk folketro*. Oslo: Cappelen.

Holck, Per. 1996. *Norsk folkemedisin: kloke koner, urtekurer og magi* (Norwegian Folk Medicine). Oslo: Cappelen.

Kvideland, Reimund, and Henning Sehmsdorf. 1988. *Scandinavian Folk Belief and Legend*. Minneapolis: University of Minnesota Press.

Larson, Katherine. 2001. *Woven Coverlets of Norway (with an Overview of Their Cultural Context)*. Seattle: University of Washington Press.

Nelson, Marion, ed. 1995. *Norwegian Folk Art: The Migration of a Tradition*. New York: Abbeville Press.

Scott, Astrid Karlsen. 1998. *Christmas in Norway: A Timeless Tradition* (film). Olympia, WA: Nordic Adventures.

Solheim, Svale. 1952. *Norsk sœtertradisjon* (Traditions of Norwegian Mountain Farming). Oslo: Aschehoug.

Stewart, Janice. 1999. (1972). *Folk Art of Norway*. Rhinelander, WI: Nordhus.

Stokker, Kathleen. 2000. *Keeping Christmas: Yuletide Traditions in Norway and the New Land*. St. Paul: Minnesota Historical Society Press.

————. Forthcoming. *Remedies and Rituals: Folk Medicine in Norway and the New Land*. St. Paul: Minnesota Historical Society Press.

Kathleen Stokker

SÁMI

GEOGRAPHY AND HISTORY

The Sámi are the indigenous population of northern Fenno-Scandia and the Kola Peninsula. For more than a thousand years this area was gradually colonized and populated by people from neighboring nations, and the Sámi today exist as an indigenous minority within the national borders of **Finland**, **Norway**, **Russia**, and **Sweden**. The existence of national borders through the Sámi area has, in turn, led to cultural differences based on different national policies regarding the indigenous population, making it impossible to speak of Sámi folklore as a homogeneous entity.

The Sámi today have rather specialized subsistence economies based upon fishing (Coastal and River Sámi) and reindeer herding and hunting (Mountain Sámi), and though the Sámi exist within all sectors of modern society, many can still be found in these traditional economies, with reindeer herding considered the "most Sámi." With its closeness to nature, reindeer herding has also become a symbol for a way of life characterized by traditionality, egalitarianism, harmony, spirituality, and ecological attitudes toward nature. These are new interpretations of old cultural descriptions of traditional Sámi ways of living that have generated the image of the "ecological" Sámi. This understanding of the Sámi as a "nature people" living in ecological harmony with nature is a newer version of the myth of "the Noble Savage." But the great symbolic value given to the reindeer-herding sector of Sámi life can also be interpreted as a continuation of outsiders' exoticization of the Sámi.

Early descriptions in written sources from antiquity onward depict a strange and "wild" hunting people in the northern areas of Europe. As an indigenous population with ways of living, language, and culture very different from those of most Europeans, the Sámi became "Europe's Ultimate Others." In this way, they were sought by missionaries, travelers, and adventurers, and their way of living, culture, and folklore were described and depicted in a series of comparatively trustworthy manuscripts and books.

Many earlier presentations of Sámi folklore, though, are biased. The researchers and collectors from neighboring nations represented various religious, economic, and political motivations in their enterprises of folklore documentation. Many of the written sources we have concerning Sámi belief and folklore must therefore be analyzed with this in mind. From this perspective, it is also crucial to understand contemporary Sámi folklore in the light of a history of collection, documentation, and research.

With its closeness to nature, reindeer herding has become a symbol for a way of life characterized by traditionality, egalitarianism, harmony, spirituality, and ecological attitudes toward nature. (Picture Collection, The Branch Libraries, The New York Public Library, Astor, Lenox and Tilden Foundations)

WITCHCRAFT

The earliest references to Sámi belief can be found in some of the old, Norse sagas, where the Sámi are described as particularly able in witchcraft. These sagas were put together in **Iceland** when Christianity had already been established as the religion of local chiefs, and they must be interpreted on the basis of this new worldview. They tend to assign elements from their pre-Christian Norse religion to the Sámi. But the texts show some ambivalence toward the Sámi. On one hand, they are demonized, and their use of magic is considered to be dishonorable and unmanly. At the same time their great power in these matters is acknowledged, and they are thus influential.

The Sámi reputation for ability in witchcraft seemed to continue. Witch hunts during the seventeenth century also hit the northern Sámi area hard, especially in Norway. Written documents from the witch trials against Sámi *noaidis* (shamans) give us some information on how government officials interpreted the indigenous religion of the Sámi. In 1627 the Sámi Qvive Baardsen was sentenced to death because he had used magic to produce favorable wind for sailing, with the unfortunate result that the boat had wrecked and the crew of eight lost their lives. The belief that the Sámi could raise the wind with the help of supernatural powers was widely spread throughout Europe. The trial, though, shows little interest in the actual content of Sámi beliefs. Instead, the records describe how this Sámi *noaidi* used a magical drum with some figures on it and place his actions within theories of demonology. This perspective gradually changed. A later witch trial accused Anders Poulsen, an old Sámi, of having used the shamanic drum, although there was no record of anyone being harmed. This resulted in a thorough description of the drum and its use, but the court was unable to decide whether this merited a death sentence. The description and the drum were sent to the central government in **Denmark** for consideration, thus signaling new interest in the documentation of Sámi beliefs.

RELIGION

Early descriptions of Sámi belief and religion are also found in reports from missionaries who worked to convert the Sámi to Christianity during the seventeenth and eighteenth centuries. But again, these writings cannot be viewed as impartial descriptions of Sámi beliefs. Instead, the missionaries wanted to know some details of these beliefs to make it easier to replace them with Christianity. The theological perspective led to a demonization of indigenous beliefs, and the Sámi "religion" that was constructed on the basis of their investigations became an inversion of Christian cosmology. This contributed to a focus on "their gods" at the expense of other aspects of the Sámi belief system. Moreover, often missionaries obtained information through force, threats, and even torture. But the missionaries also depended on the writings of earlier missionaries to uncover indigenous religious practices, for few apparently had firsthand knowledge of Sámi religion. Also, the geographical provenance of much of the material was extremely limited, for Sámi belief is not homogeneous and should be understood in terms of local variants.

Missionaries destroyed indigenous Sámi practices or forced them underground. Lutheran movements rooted in Sámi culture such as Laestadianism gained influence during the second half of the nineteenth century and further marginalized the older religious practices. While the old Sámi religion has been difficult to document, witnesses can still be found for the Sámi sacrificial stones, the *siedi*, hundreds of which have been identified. These stones are holy places, where sacrifices can be made to ensure good hunting, good fishing, good health, and other benefits. Dramatic narratives tell of disaster befalling people who did not show the right reverence for these places or who stole the sacrifices others had made. Evidence suggests that some of these stones are still used for sacrifices.

Later critical research stresses that Sámi belief practices should be documented and understood in their local contexts. Much work remains to be done along these lines. Elements of Sámi religion can still be found in folk belief, legends, and memorates and in Sámi healers' activities.

PRESERVATION OF SÁMI FOLKLORE

The most intensive collection and documentation of Sámi narrative folklore occurred from around 1870 through the first decades of the twentieth century. However, the general motivation for this documentation, closely tied to studies of the Finno-Ugric languages, was not folkloristic but linguistic. The field included Baltic, Finnish, Hungarian, Norwegian, and Swedish researchers, though Finland became the research center. Printed collections appeared in the series *Mémoires de la Société Finno-Ougrienne* covering the Sámi in Finland, Norway, and Russia. The largest

A Sámi family in Norway (ca. 1890–1900). (Courtesy Library of Congress)

collection is Eliel Lagercrantz's *Lappische Volksdichtung* I–VII (1957–1966), with material from the Norwegian Sámi area. Norwegian research also resulted in such important printed collections as J. A. Friis (1871a, 1871b) and Qvigstad and Sandberg (1887). J. Qvigstad also produced a four-volume collection (1926–1929). These collections allowed the Norwegian folklorist Reidar Th. Christiansen to maintain that very few ethnic groups in the world could match the comprehensive and rich materials from Sámi oral tradition.

These first collectors of Sámi folklore show how negative attitudes toward Sámi cultural products and Sámi narratives were emerging. A prominent folklorist—Qvigstad, for example, who in his lifetime collected and published many volumes of Sámi narratives—also expressed a very negative view of Sámi folklore. He believed that Sámi culture, language, and folklore would perish soon. He also maintained that most of what had been collected represented borrowings from neighboring people instead of distinctive Sámi lore. This view reflects the nationalism influencing academia at the time, reinforced by theories of cultural evolution.

Folklore research in the Nordic countries emerged with nationalism. An important motivation to investigate Sámi folklore was to learn how folklore related to other Scandinavian folklore in national archives. The area where the Sámi lived was a meeting place for currents from such national tradition areas as the Nordic, the Finnish, and the Russian. Qvigstad (1925b) argued that it was important to document Sámi folklore for this reason: "The Lapps [Sámi] are at the same time a receptive and conservative people. Apart from their reindeer herding culture, they have lived by borrowing from their neighbors as far as their vocabulary, religion, superstitions and material culture are concerned." Qvigstad held that the Sámi kept these "borrowings" with stubborn conservatism and that the collections in this way were an important source on Scandinavian folklore. The first Norwegian professor of folkloristics, Moltke Moe, wrote the introduction to the collection of folktales and legends that Qvigstad and Sandberg published in 1887, where he formulated the background for this theory of borrowing: "In this way the Lappish people have received a very rich supply of folktales from people that are superior to them in culture and cultural contacts. The rule is that it is the most advanced people who give and the lesser developed, who receive."

This idea of national influences in Sámi folklore had its theoretical and methodological foundation in the dominating research paradigm within folklore studies at this time: the "Finnish School," or the historical-geographical method of research as formulated by Julius Krohn and later elaborated by his son Kaarle. One characteristic of this folklore theory assigns much weight to the study of the stability of oral tradition in certain areas. The central hypothesis held that the transmission of folklore from one generation to the next within the same area is fairly stable, while more comprehensive changes occur when folklore migrates geographically. Politics and nationalism played a decisive role in the acceptance or rejection of narratives, and this would guarantee a homogeneous folklore heritage with defined national areas. In Finland, for example, the tendency was to look upon stability in variants within a certain area as virtually a sign of geographic and national unity—thus the close connection between nationalistic ideology and folklore research methods. From this angle the diffusionistic distribution maps, so important in this research tradition and showing information about where isolated folklore types had been collected, turned out to be mental maps of what could be considered areas of national influence.

Collecting folklore developed the romantic idea of saving a people's national, homogeneous spiritual heritage as a reflection of their authentic and common background. The homogeneity and authenticity of Sámi folklore were questioned on the basis of research methods and ideological ideas prevalent in folklore studies at the time, which stressed that much of the narrative material was shared with, and declared to belong to, the heritage of neighboring and more dominant cultures.

Researchers focused on collecting, organizing, and indexing folklore material that had been collected among living people seemingly without discovering that these narratives actually had a meaning for the people who told them. Instead, folk narratives were seen only as memories of the past, something that had to be collected and preserved to prevent its disappearance. The glorious past needed to be documented. While development toward assimilation into majority cultures was seen as inevitable, contemporary Sámi life was of very little interest. Folklore material was objectified and not tied to concrete historical contexts.

But there are alternative projects of documentation. The German physician and ethnographer Ludwig Kohl-Larsen (1884–1969) made extensive collections of Sámi folklore and had thorough knowledge of much of the Sámi area. He lived for a longer period in Finnmark from 1919 to 1924, working as a district physician in the Sámi area of Tana. During World War II he was transferred to Rovaniemi in Finland and later to Karasjok in Norway. As a representative of the German army, he had the opportunity to collect Sámi narratives in occupied Norway. The context of his work may be one of the reasons that this highly original collection of Sámi folklore is still little known and used in Norway.

NARRATIVES OF SIRI-MATTI

From a single person, the seventy-four-year-old, nearly blind Mathis Aslaksen Eira, or "Siri-Matti," who then lived in poverty south of Karasjok, Kohl-Larsen collected over 150 long, traditional stories. As both Siri-Matti and Kohl-Larsen spoke Norwegian, the narratives were told in this language and later translated to German. This collection has since been published in three rather conventional volumes in German (1971, 1975, 1982), all of them appearing after Kohl-Larsen's death.

Two other books completed by Kohl-Larsen have a different angle, since they contextualize the narratives to a much greater degree. During his stay in Karasjok, Kohl-Larsen also participated in a spring migration to the coast with the reindeer herd belonging to Siri-Matti's son. This resulted in a book that appeared in 1958, consisting of narratives that came to Siri-Matti's mind as they moved through the landscape. Kohl-Larsen took a great interest in the narrators and their personal stories. He recorded Siri-Matti's life history, and this large manuscript was published in 1994. Taken together, Kohl-Larsen's work with Siri-Matti gives us a thorough picture of a Sámi narrator, his repertoire, life history, worldview, environment, and life conditions.

Kohl-Larsen describes the half-blind Sámi narrator telling stories from his travels in this world and in the mythic world in an idealized way that almost takes on Homeric proportions. Mathis Aslaksen Eira was born in a tent on the Finnmark tundra in 1869. Although he spent most of his life herding reindeer, he was constantly on the move and had by the end of his life traveled extensively. He even went to Alaska to work among the "heathen Eskimos"—as Kohl-Larsen refers to them—under the auspices of a program to start reindeer herding there. This program, in fact, led to limited Sámi emigration to Alaska. Siri-Matti worked for some years in Alaska, but after his wife died, he returned to Finnmark and his mother's house with two small children. Here he occupied himself as a dealer in reindeer meat, then as a bootlegger. He also tried life as a fisherman among the Coastal Sámi for a couple of years. But the longing for the tundra and the life as a reindeer herdsman became too strong, and with the money he had earned in his last years, he was able to buy reindeer and resume this life.

Siri-Matti's narratives are part of a dialogue that he and his listeners use to understand their relationship to their surroundings and to "the Others" (both people and mythical beings). In his personal narrative, Siri-Matti often refers to contexts where narratives have been important in different parts of his life. He remembers his mother's and the old men's narratives when he was a child, and as he grew and experienced more, he came to think of himself as a narrator. This was especially true after he returned from his time in Alaska, which provided him with much narrative material. Siri-Matti's narratives are dialogical rather than representational, having emerged from heterogeneous and shared experiences as opposed to a monolithic and common heritage, and thus elude the simple folk narrative categorization.

Myths and Legends

Legends concerning historical incidents represent a very important part of Sámi folklore. Surrounded by more militarily powerful neighbors, Sámi often told of confrontations with them—especially with a legendary people called the Chudes (also called the Russian Chudes, the Russians, the Karelians, or the Kvens). These stories represent the genre of Sámi folklore with the widest distribution in the whole Sámi area.

The Finnish folklorist Lassi Saressalo has pointed to the "defensive" character of Sámi folklore: that the narratives represent "guerilla stories." They deal with the question of how a small, powerless population living in isolated places can defeat a much bigger and more powerful enemy with the help of smartness, cleverness, quickness, and a thorough knowledge of the local topography. One story, published in the second volume of Qvigstad's collection of Sámi folklore, tells of the pathfinder, who leads the enemy over a steep cliff:

> The Russian Chudes came to a farm and found a boy at home; they asked: "Where are the other people?" He told them: "They have gone to a wedding. I'll show you how to get there." So they went over a mountain. The boy says: "Where I am going first with a birchbark torch, you shall follow me." So he threw the torch over the edge of the mountain. The Russian Chudes jumped that way; they landed on fallen rocks, and were all half or completely killed. One was hanging on the edge of the cliff crying out, but then he also fell down the steep cliff. The next day people went to investigate. Then some of them were still half alive, and they ground their teeth at the boy, because he had betrayed them in this way.

Also the mythical and ambiguous character of the *Stállu* has been interpreted as a figure who represented something authentically Sámi in folklore. Folklorists as early as Læstadius in 1844 and Friis in 1871 understood this figure as a portrait of the enemies of the Sami, and they saw the *Stállu* as the Sámi depiction of roving Vikings or later tax collectors from neighboring states. The word *Stállu* means "the steel-armored." The most classical *Stállu* narratives concern a duel or a wrestling match between a *Stállu* and a Sámi. The *Stállu* is very dangerous, huge, and strong but also very stupid and gullible. Therefore, the Sámi outwits him with cleverness and slyness and so kills him, gaining all his wealth. But the *Stállu* is a multi-faceted character in Sámi folklore and can also appear as a Sámi ogre or even as a defender of Sámi norms used to frighten children who will not behave. This ambivalence has made the *Stállu* a very productive supernatural creature in Sámi folklore.

The Sámi philosopher Alf Isak Keskitalo has approached these stories in relation to the nation-building processes in the more powerful neighboring countries. This was an uneven power relation, where the Scandinavians gained greater power and pressed the Sámi to the margins. "The cognitive inheritance of this development is the folk legends," Keskitalo has written. But he maintains that these legends must be seen in connection with another important group of narratives in Sámi folklore, the stories about the unsuccessful Sámi religious revolt in Kautokeino in 1852, after which the Sámi leaders were sentenced to death. These narratives had not reached the attention of the folklore collectors, but they were told inside the Sámi communities as a warning about what might happen if violence should be used against the authorities. Keskitalo finds that this kind of folklore has had a fatalistic influence on Sámi mentality and that it has been an obstacle to the political organization and ethnic incorporation of the Sámi minority against the nation-states.

CHALLENGES OF THE MODERN WORLD

Some of the new interest in Sámi folklore seems to take as its point of departure a new "grand narrative," different from colonialism's idea of "culture death." Most of the research about the Sámi situation today is founded upon an understanding of the Sámi past as a history of suppression, with the present as an ethnic revival and struggle for rights. The future is something that should be politically defined by the Sámi people themselves but based on their own culture and traditions.

In the late 1980s the Sámi ethnic revival had begun to take place. The Norwegian government's decision to dam the Alta River and build a hydroelectric power station in 1978 was immediately met by organized protests from environmentalist organizations and local activists. The question of Sámi rights in the area very soon became a focus for these protests. A group of seven young Sámi performing a hunger strike in a *lávvu* (traditional Sámi herding tent) outside the Norwegian Parliament building in Oslo was the most visually potent symbol of the uneven fight between this indigenous population and the Norwegian government. As a result the Sámi parliament was established with the right to make pronouncements and give political advice to the Norwegian parliament in all political matters concerning the Sámi. These protests introduced the media to the plight of the Sámi and connected their problems to those faced by indigenous people the world over. Thus began public interest in traditional Sámi folklore and culture. Artists, musicians, and young researchers who wanted to work for a better political situation for the Sámi began to investigate Sámi culture to find material for a new and proud Sámi identity. Traditional Sámi folk costumes became more common among young people, traditional crafts were re-vitalized, and folklore material was investigated in the search for a common background.

The new perspective on Sámi folklore is apparent in the work of many younger Sámi researchers. For example, Gaski (1987) analyzes the epic poetry of the Sámi, which had been interpreted earlier as borrowings from the Finnish. Gaski clearly wants to raise the status of this epic poetry, but he also views this poetry as metaphorical comment on the colonization of the Sámi area by the more politically and economically powerful neighboring states. Gaski is not primarily trying to establish this folklore as a kind of "national epic" similar to the *Kalevala* in Finland. Rather, he is trying to understand what the texts actually meant to people who used them by combining methods from literary studies, linguistic studies, and cultural history. At the same time, he wants to turn this "internal" reading of the Sámi epic poetry into a criticism of the folklore research tradition, which dealt only with formal questions. Younger scholars are now following this and similar kinds of approaches to Sámi folklore.

The new interest in Sámi folklore has also expressed itself within art and literature. The Sámi film director Nils Gaup's *Ofelaš* (The Pathfinder; 1987) is based on the migratory legend about the pathfinder mentioned above. Gaup was able to transform the defensive and warning message of this story into a symbol for the ethno-political and cultural struggle that the Sámi recently have fought. This movie was an international success and was nominated for an Academy Award as Best Foreign Film.

Sámi musicians have found inspiration in the old Sámi *yoik*, a way of singing that the missionaries and the preachers of Laestadianism had characterized as heathen and connected to witchcraft. Nevertheless, it has survived in its original form in many Sámi areas. The Sámi multi-media artist Nils-Aslak Valkeapää helped to raise the consciousness of this singing as art. Later the Sámi musician Mari Boine created new musical forms inspired by Sámi music as well as music from other indigenous people around the world. This points to a new understanding of Sámi folklore in the age of globalization, in which people are inspired not only by their own folklore and history but by those of other indigenous people. This tendency is also obvious in the popular Sámi cultural festivals organized each summer (for example the Riddu Riddu festival), where artists from different indigenous areas meet and are inspired by each other.

STUDIES OF SÁMI FOLKLORE

Qvigstad authored a typology of Sámi folktales and legends in German (1925b), based on his own collections and those of others. Nesheim (1971) presents a short review in English of recurring elements in Qvigstad's printed collection of Sámi folklore. The largest collections of Sámi folklore are in Swedish (Læstadius 1997; Turi 1910; Tomasson 1988), in Norwegian (Friis 1871a and 1871b; Qvigstad and Sandberg 1887), in Sámi with Norwegian translations (Qvigstad 1926–1929), in Sámi with German translations (Qvigstad 1922, 1924, and 1925a; Lagercrantz 1957–1966), in German (Qvigstad 1920, 1932a, and 1932b; Kohl-Larsen 1971, 1975, 1982, and 1994), and in English (Billson 1918; Turi and Turi 1920). Earlier surveys of Sámi folklore research in Scandinavia can be found in Christiansen (1950) and Hultkrantz (1955). A new and valuable source to the field of Sámi folklore is Pentikäinen and others (2000). This book contains articles on Sámi folklore research and collection in Sweden (Hultkrantz 2000), Russia (Sergejeva 2000), Finland (Pentikäinen 2000), and Norway (Mathisen 2000).

BIBLIOGRAPHY

Billson, Charles J. 1918. Some Mythical Tales of the Lapps. *Folk-Lore* 29:178–192.

Christiansen, Reidar Th. 1950. Norwegian Research on the Language and the Folklore of the Lapps, Part II. Mythology and Folklore. *The Journal of the Royal Anthropological Institute* 80:89–94.

DuBois, Thomas A. 1996. *Seiðr*, Sagas, and Saami Religious Exchange in the Viking Age. In *Northern Peoples, Southern States. Maintaining Ethnicities in the Circumpolar World*, edited by Robert P. Wheelersburg. Umeå: CERUM, Umeå University. 43–66.

———. 2000. Folklore, Boundaries and Audience in *The Pathfinder*. In *Sami Folkloristics*, edited by Juha Pentikäinen and others. Turku: NNF. 255–274.

Friis, J. A. 1871a. *Lappisk Mythologi*. Christiania: Alb. Cammermeyer.

———. 1871b. *Lappiske eventyr og folkesagn*. Christiania: Alb. Cammermeyer.

Gaski, Harald. 1987. *Med ord skal tyvene fordrives: Om samenes episk poetiske diktning*. Karasjok: Davvi media.

Hultkrantz, Åke. 1955. Swedish Research on the Religion and the Folklore of the Lapps. *The Journal of the Royal Anthropological Institute* 85:81–99.

———. 2000. Fifty Years of Research on Sámi Folklore and Mythology. In *Sámi Folkloristics*, edited by Juha Pentikäinen and others. Turku: NNF. 75–101.

Keskitalo, Alf Isak. 1980. Om möjligheten av folklore som ett hinder i en etnisk inkorporasjonsprocess. *Tradisjon. Tidsskrift for folkeminnevitskap* 10:97–101.

Kohl-Larsen, Ludwig. 1958. *Der grosse Zug nach Mitternacht. Eine Fahrt mit den Lappen zum Nördlichen Eismeer*. Kassel: Erich Röth-Verlag.

———. 1971. *Reiter auf dem Elch. Volkserzählungen aus Lappland*. Kassel: Erich Röth-Verlag.

———. 1975. *Die steinerne Herde. Von Trollen, Hexen und Schamanen. Volkssagen aus Lappland*. Kassel: Erich Röth-Verlag.

———. 1982. *Das Haus der Trolle. Märchen aus Lappland*. Kassel: Erich Röth-Verlag.

———. 1994. *Das Leben des Rentierlappen Siri Matti - von ihm selbst erzählt. Aufgezeichnet von Ludwig Kohl-Larsen. Herausgeben von Erich Renner*. Frankfurt: Campus Verlag.

Læstadius, Lars Levi. 1997 (1844). *Fragmenter i Lappska Mythologien*. Åbo: NIF.

Lagercrantz, Eliel. 1957–1966. *Lappische Volksdichtung I–VII. (Suomalais-Ugrilaisen Seuran) Toimituksia 112, 115, 117, 120, 124, 126, 141*. Helsinki: Suomalais-Ugrilaisen Seuran.

Mathisen, Stein R. 2000. Changing Narratives about Sámi Folklore: A Review of Research on Sámi Folklore in the Norwegian Area. In *Sámi Folkloristics*, edited by Juha Pentikäinen and others. Turku: NNF. 103–130.

Moe, Moltke. 1887. Indledning. In *Lappiske eventyr og folkesagn, III–XXIX* by J. Qvigstad and G. Sandberg. Kristiania: Alb. Cammermeyer.

Moyne, Ernest J. 1981. *Raising the Wind. The Legend of Lapland and Finland Wizards in Literature*. Newark: University of Delaware Press.

Mundal, Else. 1996. The Perception of the Saamis and Their Religion in Old Norse Sources. In *Shamanism and Northern Ecology*, edited by Juha Pentikäinen. Berlin: Mouton de Gruyter. 97–116.

Nesheim, Asbjørn. 1971. J. K. Qvigstad (1853–1957). In *Leading Folklorists of the North*, edited by Dag Strömbäck. Oslo: Universitetsforlaget. 323–338.

Paine, Robert. 1994. Night Village and the Coming of Men of the Word: The Supernatural as a Source of Meaning among Coastal Saami. *Journal of American Folklore* 107:343–363.

Pentikäinen, Juha. 2000. Finnish Research on Sámi Folklore. In *Sámi Folkloristics*, edited by Juha Pentikäinen and others. Turku: NNF. 131–153.

Pentikäinen, Juha, and others, eds. 2000. *Sámi Folkloristics*. Turku: NNF.

Qvigstad, J. 1920. Lappischer Aberglaube. *Kristiania (Oslo) Etnografiske Museums Skrifter* 1:41–135.

———. 1922. Lappische Sprichwörter und Rätsel. *Kristiania (Oslo) Etnografiske Museums Skrifter* 1:137–251.

———. 1924. Lappische Erzählungen aus Hatfjelldalen. *Kristiania (Oslo) Etnografiske Museums Skrifter* 1:253–315.

———. 1925a. Lappische Texte aus Kalfjord und Helgøy. *Kristiania (Oslo) Etnografiske Museums Skrifter* 1:21–40.

————. 1925b. *Lappische Märchen- und Sagenvarianten.* (FF Communications 60). Helsinki: Suomalainen tiedeakatemia.

————. 1926–1929. *Lappiske eventyr og sagn I–IV.* (Instituttet for sammenlignende Kulturforskning. Series B: Skrifter III, X, XII, XV.) Oslo: Aschehoug.

————. 1932a. *Lappische Heilkunde.* (Instituttet for Sammenlignende Kulturforskning, Series B: Skrifter XX.) Oslo: Aschehoug.

————. 1932b. Lappische Wetterkunde. *Kristiania (Oslo) Etnografiske Museums Skrifter* 1:357–403.

Qvigstad, J., and G. Sandberg. 1887. *Lappiske eventyr og folkesagn.* Kristiania: Alb. Cammermeyer.

Rydving, Håkan. 1995. *Samisk religionshistoria. Några källkritiska problem* (Uppsala Research Reports in the History of Religions 4). Uppsala: Uppsala Universitet.

————. 2000. The Missionary Accounts from the 17th and 18th Centuries: The Evaluation and Interpretation of the Sources. In *Sámi Folkloristics,* edited by Juha Pentikäinen and others. Turku: NNF. 17–39.

Sergejeva, Jelena. 2000. The Research History of Kola and Skolt Sámi Folklore. In *Sámi Folkloristics,* edited by Juha Pentikäinen and others. Turku: NNF. 155–188.

Tomasson, Torkel. 1988. *Några sägner, seder och bruk, upptecknade efter lapparna i Åsele-och Lycksele Lappmark samt Herjedalen sommaren 1917. Red. av Leif Lindin och Håkan Rydving. Uppsala.* (Skrifter utgivna genom Dialekt- och folkminnesarkivet i Uppsala, series C:5.)

Turi, Johan. 1910. *Muittaalus sámid birra—En bog om lappernes liv.* Stockholm: I distribution Nordiska bokhandeln.

Turi, Johan, and Per Turi. 1920. *Lappish Texts.* With the cooperation of K. B. Wiklund, edited by Emilie Demant-Hatt. København: Bianco Lunos.

Wicklund, K. B. 1906. *Lapparnes sång och poesi.* Uppsala: N.p.

Stein R. Mathisen

<u>SWEDEN</u>

For centuries, Swedes have recorded the customs and traditions of the common people. In 1555, when he was exiled from his Protestant home country, Roman Catholic archbishop Olaus Magnus published a history of the peoples of the north, *Historia de gentibus septentrionalis.* He was particularly interested in the northern **Sámi.** A century later (when Sweden formed an empire that included **Finland,** Estonia, and **Latvia** as well as parts of today's **Germany, Russia,** and **Poland**), King Gustavus Adolphus II took initiatives to collect legends, poems, and heroic songs that could be used in the writing of a grandiose national history. During the eighteenth century, when the empire had shrunk considerably, official interest turned to agriculture and other peaceful pursuits. The "parish descriptions" written by ministers of the Lutheran State Church contain material of cultural historical value, as do naturalist Carl von Linné's descriptions of travels in the Swedish provinces. To him and his pupils it was important to record superstitions to weed them out.

FOLKLORE STUDIES IN THE NINETEENTH CENTURY

In the early 1800s, under influence from various Romantic movements, the esthetic accomplishments of the common people became even more interesting to researchers. Erik Gustaf Geijer and Arvid August Afzelius's three-volume collection of Swedish folk ballads, *Svenska folkvisor* (1814–1818), was important in furthering their appeal among the bourgeoisie. Some decades later, several collections of singing games, wonder tales, and legends appeared in print, many of them in the magazine *Runa*, edited by Rikard Dybeck (author of the Swedish national anthem). Other important texts appeared at midcentury, among them Nicolovius's reminiscences of "folk life" in the southern district of Skytt. From 1863 to 1868 Gunnar Olof Hyltén-Cavallius introduced a more theoretically oriented work concerning the district of *Wärend* and its inhabitants. In this book, the sub-title of which may be translated as "An Attempt at a Swedish Ethnology," he examines the beliefs, narratives, and material culture of the peasant folk to re-create ancient, in part pre-Christian, layers of culture.

By the end of the 1900s, the interest in peasant traditions increased even more. This was a period of intense nation-building and immense societal transformations: urbanization, industrialization, emigration, workers' movements, free religious movements, struggles to achieve universal suffrage, and the foundation of scholarly disciplines and museums. Artur Hazelius (1833–1901), who held a doctorate in Old Norse literature, was one of several scholars and museum builders who were deeply engaged in the concerns of his era. In 1873, he founded the Nordic Museum

In the seventeenth century, King Gustavus Adolphus II initiated a collection of legends, poems, and heroic songs that could be used in the writing of a grandiose national history. (Print Collection, Miriam and Ira D. Wallach Division of Art, Prints and Photographs, The New York Public Library, Astor, Lenox and Tilden Foundations)

(*Nordiska museet*), the aim of which was to exhibit the cultural history of all social classes and regions since the Protestant Reformation of the 1500s. However, peasant culture became the actual priority. This was even more the case with Skansen, the open-air extension of the Nordic Museum that opened in 1891 and was organized as a miniature of rural Sweden, containing animals, houses, people, and industry typical of different provinces from north to south.

The emphasis on peasant culture was, of course, entirely in keeping with the nationalistic Romanticism that still prevailed in Europe. According to it, peasants were closer to the spirit and soil of a nation than other social classes, and their ancient traditions constituted the base upon which the cultural repertoires and moral standards of a nation were to rest. Hazelius collaborated with historians, artists, crafts enthusiasts, and local historical movements in a massive effort to study, preserve, exhibit, celebrate, present, beautify, and promote the most pleasing and uplifting of the arts and customs of the country folk. All the efforts can be seen as part of a reform project aiming to prepare people to become citizens of a modern nation.

If Hazelius gave priority to material culture, other scholars and enthusiasts collected oral traditions, music, dance, and dialects. Dialect societies established at the universities of Uppsala and Lund had as their goal to record stories and songs and to describe the great diversity of regional customs. Eventually, the materials harvested by these societies became the basis for "folk memory" archives founded in Lund (1913), Uppsala (1914), and Göteborg (1919). In addition, a special state commission, established in 1908, became responsible for the documentation of folk music. Of particular interest were the fiddling traditions of Dalarna, a region that museum founders, writers, artists, and tourists helped elevate into the quintessence of Sweden.

FOLKLORE STUDIES IN THE EARLY TWENTIETH CENTURY

Thus, by the early 1900s, when a scholarly discipline concerned with folk culture was contemplated, the foundation was already in place for the development of two branches: a more broadly oriented "ethnological" one linked to history, geography, art history, technology, and architecture and a more "folkloristic" one connected to literature, philology, and the study of religion. Unlike in other Nordic countries, the two never turned into formally separated disciplines, and through the decades many scholars have been engaged in both. Nevertheless, it is of some advantage to discuss the two as separate entities.

The more broadly conceived branch, "Nordic and Comparative Folklife Research" (*Nordisk och jämförande folklivsforskning*), was constituted in 1909 because the leadership of the Nordic Museum recognized the need for studying the museum's vast collections. But it was not until 1918 that the museum, thanks to a private donation, could appoint a professor.

Nils Lithberg was the first holder of the position. But it was in 1934, when Sigurd Erixon (1888–1968) was invited to hold it, that folklife research became a true force in Sweden and abroad. Erixon created an Institute for Folklife Research, which was formally linked to both the Nordic Museum and Stockholm University. In 1937, he founded the journal *Folk-Liv*, in which articles in English, German, and French were published. Erixon continued the documentation and study of rural material culture initiated by Hazelius, paying particular attention to housing traditions. He conducted several of his numerous research projects in collaboration with geographers. The goal was to map out the distribution in Sweden of many phenomena—from barns and flails, to supernatural beings.

However, Erixon's visions and motivations differed from those of his predecessors in many ways. For one thing, the nation was not on his mind the way it had been for Hazelius. Rather, Erixon was convinced that folklife research was hampered by its ties to national boundaries and demonstrated that these often differed from the cultural ones. For another, more than his predecessors, Erixon emphasized that the core of ethnology was "man himself," not only "his" traditions and industry. Third, Erixon scrutinized such terms as *folk* and compounds with *folk* more carefully than earlier scholars. In this he and his students were, to a great extent, influenced by debates within German *Volkskunde*. But Erixon also read voraciously within British and North American social and cultural anthropology. Furthermore, he studied sociology, which at this time focused on social planning, an activity in which he and many other academics were involved during the 1930s and after World War II. This planning was part of a monumental effort to create a Swedish welfare state. It could be said that from the 1930s through the 1950s, the "folk" discipline, Nordic and Comparative Folklife Research, went hand in hand with political efforts to shape a "folk home" (*folkhem*). Erixon argued that folklife researchers could help planners avoid mistakes: for example, the documentation of traditional housing and village structures undertaken by him and his colleagues was potentially useful when new housing was to be built for the members of the growing rural proletariat who were flocking to the cities in search of jobs.

To increase and systematize the supply of data, Erixon and his collaborators began in 1928 to send out open-ended questionnaires on such topics as village organization, laundry methods, and festival celebrations to a network of lay respondents all over Sweden. Similar questionnaires calling for long essay answers are still being sent out not only from the Nordic Museum archives but also from other folklore and folklife archives in all the Nordic countries. However, many changes have taken place in the procedure. Some were instituted as early as the 1940s, when a young employee at the Nordic Museum, Mats Rehnberg (who was to head the Department of Ethnology in Stockholm during the 1970s), began collaborating with workers' unions in distributing questionnaires to urban and industrial workers. Such efforts contributed to making the study of working-class life a more self-evident component of folklife research than it had been before.

Also the disciplinary branch linked to literary studies and philology was long dominated by one forceful scholar, Carl Wilhelm von Sydow (1878–1952). In 1912, he was appointed to direct Folk Memory Research (*folkminnesforskning*) at Lund University in southern Sweden, and the following year he also became head of the Folk Poetry Archives (*folkdiktsarkivet*). In 1910, von Sydow had defended a dissertation entitled "*Två spinnsagor*" (Two Spinning Tales), and throughout his life he continued to study folk narratives and expressions of belief in supernatural beings and occurrences. He was awarded the title of full professor as late as 1938, and from 1940 until his retirement in 1946, he headed a department at Lund University, temporarily called Nordic and Comparative Folk Cultural Research (*Nordisk och jämförande folkkulturforskning*).

In many respects, von Sydow was ahead of his time. This is true of his critique of some, if not all, of the tenets of the "Finnish" historic-geographic method. He argued that this methodology left too little room for studies of individual narrators and their communities. His distinction between "active" and "passive" storytellers became highly influential, as did his coinage *oikotype*, by which he meant the distinct form a tale or other cultural item assumes in a specific cultural or natural environment. However, most of von Sydow's terminological innovations concern genre distinctions. On formal and stylistic grounds he devised a complex system of oral narrative genres. Particularly famous is the *memorate*, by which he meant people's stories about their own personal experiences. He underlined that, though untraditional, these stories are important as evidence of people's experiences and their evaluations of them. In many ways, the *memorate* is a precursor to the "personal experience story."

Von Sydow's thinking has had considerable impact on folkloristics internationally, as can be seen in the works of Lauri Honko and in the efforts of the Irish Folklore

Commission. Von Sydow's publications are particularly well known in English-speaking countries, in part due to the book *Selected Papers on Folklore* (1948), which contains some of his texts in translation, selected by Archer Taylor. Some of Sweden's best-known folklorists internationally—among them Sven Liljeblad, Anna-Birgitta Rooth and Jan-Öjvind Swahn—were von Sydow's students.

FOLKLORE STUDIES SINCE WORLD WAR II

In 1946, when von Sydow retired, Sigfrid Svensson was appointed professor of Nordic and comparative folklife research at Lund University, the discipline now called the same here as in Stockholm. The core of the department was von Sydow's archives. Renamed *Folklivsarkivet* (the folklife archives), they now covered all of folklife. Svensson, who had long worked at the Nordic Museum, was a well-known scholar at the time of his appointment. In his dissertation, "*Skånes folkdräkter*" (1935), he analyzes the folk costumes of the southern region of Skåne in a long historical perspective. In the 1600s, parts of Skåne experienced an economic boom, and peasants adopted features of aristocratic fashion in their clothing. But their fortunes did not last, and through a process of "cultural fixation" these Renaissance features became cemented during centuries of isolation and relative poverty. This is one of several works in which Svensson investigates stability and change in peasant communities, in particular in the form of acceptance or rejection of innovations emanating from urban centers. In *Bygd och yttervärld* (Neighborhood and the World Beyond, 1942) he analyzes changes in clothing, tools, customs, folk art, and popular iconography as complex cultural, social, and historical processes.

Svensson remained in charge of folklife research in Lund until 1967. During his tenure the archives expanded considerably, as did the number of students. For years, beginners in Lund as well as Stockholm studied his *Introduktion till folklivsforskningen* (Introduction to Folklife Research), which was first published in 1966. Actually, in the 1960s, the department in Lund had become as important as that in Stockholm. It could be said that Erixon and Svensson jointly shaped the discipline of folklife research and jointly presided over it during its classical period. But there were differences. For example, Erixon was probably more closely connected to British and American anthropology than Svensson, who was more clearly linked to German *Volkskunde*. Possibly, one can also say that Erixon's agenda was more international than Svensson's. In *Folk-Liv*, Erixon wrote broadly conceived articles in English on such topics as the future of a field to be called "Regional European Ethnology" and the connections between ethnology, sociology, and anthropology. There are no counterparts to these texts in Svensson's production.

Broad connections between disciplines continued to be highlighted after 1955, when John Granlund took over as head of the Institute for Folklife Research in Stockholm. Granlund introduced his students to the works of American anthropologists such as Kroeber and Redfield at the same time as he retained empirical focus on Swedish peasants. Such a focus was most important to the relationship between the institute and the museum of which it was a part. It was also important to some of the instructors at the institute who were also curators at the museum. One of them was Anna-Maja Nylén, author of a monumental book published in English as *Swedish*

Handcraft (1976) and curator of a celebrated permanent exhibition entitled *Tradition och nutid* (Tradition and Contemporary Life). This and other exhibitions were used in teaching folklife research. This was one of the ways in which ethnology students benefited from the links between the museum and the university.

At the same time, the influence from sociology and anthropology continued. Contributing to this was sociologist Börje Hanssen, whose book *Österlen* (1952) came to influence a whole generation of ethnologists. The book is a detailed, quantitatively based investigation of economic and cultural interactions between peasants and town dwellers in southeastern Skåne at the end of the eighteenth century.

At Uppsala University, folklife research developed along its own path. In lieu of a university department, the Dialect and Folk Memory Archives (*Landsmåls- och folkminnesarkivet*) or ULMA, which had been in existence since 1914, constituted a base for the study of verbal folklore. Another Uppsala institution became increasingly important: the Royal Gustavus Adolphus Academy for Swedish Folk Culture (*Kungl. Gustav Adolfs Akademien för svensk folkkultur*), established in 1932. Created as a foundation to commemorate the death of Gustavus Adolphus II in 1632, this academy has been central to the development of folklore and folklife studies in all the Nordic countries. This is due particularly to its economic support of young scholars and of such periodicals as *Arv* and *Ethnologia Scandinavica*.

In 1948, a formal Department of Folklife Research was established at Uppsala University when Dag Strömbäck was appointed to hold the chair of folklife research. At the time, Strömbäck also headed ULMA, and the new department remained closely linked to the archive. Trained as a philologist, Strömbäck was an expert in Old Norse literature, religious beliefs, and magical practices, as can be seen in his book *Sejd* (1935). Strömbäck retired in 1972, but the department long retained an interest in Old Norse culture. One of his students, Bo Almqvist, known for his book *Norrön niddiktning* (Old Norse Lampooning; 1974), eventually was invited to teach in Dublin, while another, ballad scholar Bengt R. Jonsson, became the head of the Archives of Folk Song and Folk Music (*Svenskt Visarkiv*), established in Stockholm in 1951.

Meanwhile, folkloristic studies were also conducted outside Uppsala during the 1950s and 1960s. A leading folklorist was Carl-Herman Tillhagen, who for a long time headed the Folk Memory section of the Nordic Museum archives. He reorganized this section, making it more accessible to scholars and journalists than it had been before. Two of his numerous books are particularly noteworthy. One is a major study of folk medicine, entitled *Folklig Läkekonst* (1958), and the other an enchanting collection of folktales told by Romani narrator Johan Dimitri-Taikon: *Taikon berättar* (1946). The book is one of several publications by Tillhagen on Romani culture. This research interest was rare among folklife researchers. Actually, with the exception of research devoted to Sámi culture, little was written by scholars in the field at this time about the culture of the ethnic groups in Sweden. Indeed, the 1950s constituted a peak period for the belief that Swedes were extraordinarily homogeneous with regard to culture, language, and religion.

In 1972, all folklife departments at Swedish universities were given a name that Erixon and others had championed, ethnology, in particular European (*Etnologi, särskilt europeisk*) or, in everyday speech, ethnology. It is somewhat ironic that the very same year, the Department of Folklore at the University of Pennsylvania, pointing to Sweden, added "Folklife" to its official designation.

The universal name change was part of governmental policies to give all universities a more unified profile at a time when increasing numbers of children of the welfare state demanded higher education. Like social anthropology, ethnology benefited from the concerns of many students at this time with economic injustices at home and abroad. Ethnology also benefited from a rising interest in rural life of the past. Within a few years, new departments were instituted at Göteborg and Umeå Universities. In the 1990s, these were followed by programs at other new universities and colleges. Thus, at the end of the twentieth century, ethnology was very well entrenched in the Swedish academic and intellectual landscape.

One scholar was especially important during the 1970s and 1980s: Åke Daun in Stockholm, whose master's thesis, *"Upp till kamp in Båtskärsnäs!"* (Get Up and Fight in Båtskärsnäs!; 1968), changed the course of ethnology in Sweden. Daun had studied in **Norway** with social anthropologist Fredrik Barth and applied Barth's interactionist theories to his analysis of politics and culture in the northern industrial community, Båtskärsnäs, where he had conducted participant observation. All this was new to ethnology. But it must be emphasized that Daun also followed up Erixon's and Hanssen's concern with social action and community planning. In the 1970s, he achieved great visibility as a frequently critical member of governmental committees and as a media personality. Later, in the 1980s and 1990s, he became one of the first of several European ethnologists to study national mentalities. His book, *Swedish Mentality* (1996), has become well known internationally. A few of Daun's students continued his concern with politics, among them Lena Gerholm, whose study of a failed cultural political project has won acclaim. The title *Kulturprojekt och projektkultur* (1985) can perhaps be translated as Culture Projects and the Culture of Project Makers.

Daun and his followers changed also some other basic assumptions of Swedish ethnology. In their opinion, ethnologists were not at all in the business of preserving and presenting folk culture or any other kinds of culture either in museums or elsewhere; ethnologists were in the business of describing social life in order to effect political change. To Daun, ethnology's links to national romanticism and cultural historical museums are heavy burdens to be discarded.

At Lund University, scholarly interests took somewhat different directions. In 1967, when Sigfrid Svensson retired, a prolific researcher named Nils-Arvid Bringéus took over. In many ways, he has continued Svensson's interests in change and innovation in peasant communities, not least with regard to foodways and the rituals of the life cycle and the annual cycle. Bringéus, who has a background in theology, has also contributed to the study of customs and rituals of religious life. Among his many books are a voluminous study of Gunnar Olof Hyltén-Cavallius as ethnologist (1966) and an analysis of the role of imagery in the lives of common people during the nineteenth century. Entitled *Bildlore* (Picture Lore; 1982), the latter takes up not only folk art but also other kinds of popular imagery, including the works of the Swedish "folklife painters" of the Düsseldorf school. From 1972 until 1992, Bringéus served as main editor of *Ethnologia Scandinavica*, the successor to Erixon's journal, *Folk-Liv*.

In the 1970s, Bringéus took part in the new ethnological debates concerning culture, a concept that was now of much more interest than "folk" or "tradition." The concept is central in Bringéus's introductory textbook, *Människan som kulturvarelse* (Man as Cultural Being), which has been reissued many times since it was first published in 1976. But culture theory is even more in focus in a seminal work published in 1979 by two young ethnologists in Lund: Jonas Frykman and Orvar Löfgren. Spirited and full of ideas, this book, which has been translated into English as *Culture Builders: An Historical Anthropology of Middle-Class Life* (1987), combines British anthropological structuralism, the thinking of Norbert Elias concerning the "civilizing process," and the sociological thought of Richard Sennett. The result is a fresh mixture in which the middle classes and the peasants at the turn of the century in 1900 are contrasted through a scrutiny of such cultural domains as hygiene and conceptions of nature.

Culture Builders inaugurated a distinctly ethnological brand of cultural analysis that has had a decisive influence on ethnology and other disciplines in Sweden. Crucial to this development was the collaboration between Orvar Löfgren in Lund and Billy Ehn in Stockholm, which resulted in a small book entitled *Kulturanalys* (Cultural Analysis; 1982). Here influence from the thinking of Clifford Geertz is spelled out more clearly than in *Culture Builders*. Also, Ehn's books published in the early 1980s based on fieldwork in day-care centers and other workplaces and Gösta Arvastson's studies based on fieldwork in car factories have been important in linking cultural analysis to ethnography and thereby to giving cultural analysis wide acceptance as a method suited to the analysis of contemporary life. During the 1980s and early 1990s, ethnography became central to many discussions about cultural analysis. This was the case in Stockholm, where Billy Ehn and Barbro Klein collaborated on the book *Från erfarenhet till text* (From Experience to Text; 1994).

CONTEMPORARY FOLKLORE STUDIES

The Swedish ethnological brand of cultural analysis continues to be influential, even on scholars whose professed theoretical interests lie elsewhere. This is true of some of the recent ethnological works on gender, sexuality, and fertility. A growing number of researchers are engaged in these areas—among them Britta Lundgren, Susanne Lundin, Lena Martinsson, and Birgitta Meurling. A learned study of lesbian culture in the 1930s was undertaken by Pia Lundahl (2001), and an intriguing investigation of how young people in a middle-class community talk about sexuality has been conducted by Maria Bäckman (2003). A few scholars devote themselves to masculinity studies, among them Bo Nilsson, who has investigated the lives of aging rural bachelors (1999).

Many contemporary ethnologists study migration, ethnicity, and the multiethnic society. In 2005, perhaps a fourth of the 9 million inhabitants of Sweden are immigrants or closely related to immigrants. By this time, most Swedes acknowledge that it is impossible to uphold a notion that their country is exceptionally homogeneous culturally, and ethnologists have contributed to changing this self-perception. One of these influential ethnologists is Beatriz Lindqvist, who has written *Drömmar och vardag i exil* (Dreams and Everyday Life in Exile; 1991), a study of the cultural adjustments of refugees from Chile. Another is Per-Markku Ristilammi, who has analyzed the stereotypes through which scholars and mass media created "immigrant suburbs" such as Rosengård outside Malmö (1994). In his latest book (2004), Magnus Magnus Berg compares multiculturalism in Namibia with its counterpart in Sweden. Berg's work exemplifies an increasing desire among young ethnologists to get away from the long concern of the field primarily with Swedish culture. In another important project (directed by Lena Gerholm in Stockholm) young ethnologists are investigating the role of Islam in contemporary Swedish life. One of them studies the impact of Islam on young Swedish women who are not Muslim: on bodily comportment, language, dress, and modes of thinking.

Other scholarly directions, more or less in the tradition of cultural analysis, concern consumer culture, the "new" economy, heritage politics, and tourism. Especially during the last few years, Orvar Löfgren's work has been important in all these respects, as can be seen in his book *On Holiday* (1999). Though increasingly criticized by some practitioners, especially for its vagueness and the lack of historical precision, cultural analysis has contributed to confirming ethnology's position within the humanities and social sciences. This has been particularly useful at a time when the discipline has increasingly distanced itself from its roots in cultural historical museums. This distancing was symbolically sealed in 2000, when the Department of Ethnology in Stockholm moved from the Nordic Museum to the campus of Stockholm University. At the same time, however, the museum hired Birgitta Svensson, a scholar oriented toward not only cultural history but also contemporary culture theory and discourse analysis. Svensson is now in charge of maintaining links between the museum and the universities.

What has happened to the disciplinary branch known as folkloristics since 1972? Once again, it must be emphasized that there have never been any impenetrable boundaries between folklorists and ethnologists. Although they have tended to emphasize different kinds of data, they have often followed parallel paths methodologically and theoretically. However, it is possibly true that the folklorists, more than their ethnological cousins, have been engaged in sustained cooperation with scholars in the other Nordic countries and beyond. This was certainly the case from 1959 until 1996, when the Nordic Institute of Folklore (NIF) flourished, first in Copenhagen and later in Turku, Finland, thanks to funding from the Nordic Council of Ministers.

But by the same token, the study of verbal traditions and beliefs was quite well represented also inside Sweden during the NIF period. In 1973, Anna Birgitta Rooth, a former student of von Sydow, was appointed to succeed Dag Strömbäck as chair of the Department of Ethnology in Uppsala. She had authored many books before accepting the position. Among them were the highly praised *The Cinderella Cycle* (1951), a book on the techniques of oral narrative art entitled *Folklig diktning* (1965), and several works on myths and animal stories she had collected in Alaska in the 1960s. During her years in Uppsala, Rooth added many entries to her list of publications, among them an analysis of the paintings of Hieronymus Bosch (1992) in relationship to medieval culture and mentality.

Another leading folklorist of the latter half of the twentieth century is Bengt af

Klintberg, who is known to wide audiences in all the Nordic countries also as a journalist, poet, and fiction writer. He began his scholarly career at Stockholm University in the 1960s, when he published an intriguing book on magical formulas, *Svenska trollformler* (1965). In the 1970s, when back-to-rural life movements were at the apex of their popularity, his folklore courses attracted large numbers of students. Af Klintberg has written extensively about *märchen*, legends, children's folklore, games, sayings, riddles, proverbs, and other genres. But more than anything else, his name is linked to contemporary, urban legends. He has written and spoken so extensively on these forms that in Sweden they are called *klintbergers*.

But also other folkloristic research tendencies can be discerned. One is a part of cultural analysis as it was shaped in Lund. Jonas Frykman's book, *Horan i bondesamhället*, which might be translated as The Whore in Peasant Society (1977), is an innovative study of folk beliefs, social avoidance, and stigma based on the thinking of British structuralists. Also Jochum Stattin's study of the water spirit of peasant belief, *Näcken* (1984), exemplifies this tradition, as does Lynn Åkesson's analysis of "the unusual," or the characters, in a small southern community (1991). All three books draw on the rich materials in the **archives** created by von Sydow.

An additional, prominent area of folkloristic research (sometimes linked to cultural analysis) is based on the minutes of seventeenth- and eighteenth-century legal proceedings concerning witchcraft and related accusations. Especially noteworthy is Inger Lövkrona's feminisistic analysis (1999) of the fate of Annika Larsdotter, a young, unwed, eighteenth-century mother who killed her newborn baby. Lövkrona has also written extensively on violence against women and on erotic humor in peasant society. A great deal of Lövkrona's work is close to that of historians who, like scholars of comparative religion and literature, have conducted a number of studies that might be labeled "folkloristic."

Other materials and themes remain prominent in contemporary folklore scholarship, particularly studies of peasant legendry. Important researchers include religion scholar Catharina Raudvere's investigation of narratives and beliefs concerning the *mara* (1993) and Ulf Palmenfelt's analysis of the performance of legends by peasants on the island of Gotland (1993), an analysis that is in part based on the diary kept by one nineteenth-century collector. As a whole, the study of oral narratives, including life stories, is currently undergoing something of a renaissance, as can be seen in the work of Alf Arvidsson, Barbro Klein, and Georg Drakos. The last has been particularly concerned with narration in the contexts of illness and suffering. An additional area that has lately attracted scholars of different persuasions is rituals and celebrations. Noteworthy are Barbro Blehr's analysis of the Norwegian Constitution Day (1999), Lotten Gustafsson's of the Medieval Week in the town of Visby (2002), and Lizette Gradén's of parades in a Swedish-American town (2003).

One folkloristic field that has remained significant is music and song. While some of the scholars in this field call themselves ethnologists or folklorists, others prefer to be identified as musicologists or ethnomusicologists. A great deal of the work— by Jan Ling, Märta Ramsten, Gunnar Ternhag, Annika Nordström, and others— concentrates on Swedish folksong and folk music in a more traditional sense, but an increasing amount is also devoted to music as it relates to the mass media, migrations, and **globalization**. A leading scholar with several areas of specialization is Owe Ronström, himself an outstanding musician. One of his books is an analysis of music and dance among immigrants from former Yugoslavia (1992). Testifying to the increasing importance of the study of music, song, and dance among immigrants and their descendants is also the fact that Dan Lundberg, the current head of the *Svenskt visarkiv* (Archives of Folk Song and Folk Music), is an expert on Turkish music in Sweden.

There are both drawbacks and benefits involved in the continuous and close alliance between the "broader" field of ethnology and the "smaller" specialization of folkloristics. One of the drawbacks is that in Sweden the study of narration and narrative traditions has never developed the close affinity with literary and linguistic methodologies that it has in countries where folkloristics is more closely linked to the study of literature and languages.

However, the benefits might outweigh the drawbacks. Together, the two branches constitute a fairly substantial discipline that has succeeded in maintaining a recognizable profile both inside and outside academia. Not only the sheer number of practitioners but also, above all, shared concerns have contributed to this. For example, although many ethnologists and folklorists conduct ethnography in contemporary settings, historical perspectives remain central to both—as does the use of the materials in the ethnological archives. Although the critique of the archives has periodically been lively, they have contributed to giving the entire discipline stability. Their existence has never really been questioned.

CHALLENGES OF THE MODERN WORLD

It is not easy to predict where these two deeply intertwined specializations are heading. That they are not, at least in the near future, going to fold into one seems clear. Nor do they seem to be on the road to dissolving into some generalized form of cultural studies, as some have feared. Nevertheless, there are "threats." One comes from the new field called "heritage studies," which takes an interest in topics that were once the province of ethnology and folkloristics. Another difficulty comes from inside the discipline. Unlike Swedish anthropologists, today's ethnologists and folklorists seldom publish their most substantial work in English or other foreign languages. This is an increasing problem for scholars who represent small languages but would like to compete in international arenas at the same time as they continue to address home audiences.

Some Swedes bemoan the disappearance of folklife research as it was shaped during its "classical" period, when material culture was at the center of attention. Given the necessary transformations of all scholarship, it is certain that ethnology's present concerns will turn into new pursuits. However, at the moment the discipline is strong and visible.

Important English-language journals representing Swedish folklore and ethnology are *Arv: Scandinavian Yearbook of Folklore*, founded in 1945 as a continuation of *Folkminnen och Folktankar*, founded in 1914 by Carl Wilhelm von Sydow (since 1952 most articles are published in English or German); *Folk-Liv: Journal of Nordic and Comparative Ethnology*, founded by Sigurd Erixonm, who served as editor from 1937 to 1972; and *Ethnologia Scandinavica*, the successor to *Folk-Liv* since 1972.

BIBLIOGRAPHY

Åkesson, Lynn. 1991. *De ovanligas betydelse.* Stockholm: Carlsson.

Almqvist, Bo. 1974. *Norrön niddiktning: traditionshistoriska studier i versmagi.* Stockholm: Almqvist and Wiksell.

Arnstberg, Karl-Olov. 1989. *Utforskaren: Studier i Sigurd Erixons etnologi.* Stockholm: Carlssons.

Arvidsson, Alf. 1999. *Folklorens former.* Lund: Studentlitteratur.

Blehr, Barbo. 1999. Sacred Unity, Sacred Similarity: Norwegian Constitution Day Parades. *Ethnology* 38: 175–189.

Bringéus, Nils-Arvid. 1966. *Gunnar Olaf Hyltén-Cavallius, som ethnolog: en studie kring Wärend och wirdarne.* Stockholm: N.p.

———. 1982. *Bildlore: Studiet av folkligabildbudskap.* München: Callwey.

———. 2000 (1976). *Människan som kulturvarelse. En introduktion till etnologin.* Stockholm: Carlssons.

Daun, Åke. 1968. *Upp till kamp i Båtskärsnäs: Ein etnologisk studie av ett samhälle inför industrinedläggelse.* Stockholm: Institutet för folklivsforskning vid Nordiska museet och Stockholms universitet.

———. 1996 (1989). *Swedish Mentality.* University Park: Pennsylvania State University Press.

Ehn, Billy, and Barbro Klein. 1994. *Från erfarenhet fill text: om kulturvetenskaplig reflexivitet.* Stockholm: Carlssons.

Ehn, Billy, and Orvar Löfgren. 1982. *Kulturanalys.* Lund: Liber.

Erixon, Sigurd. 1937. Regional European Ethnology I. *Folk-Liv* 1: 89–108.

———. 1938. Regional European Ethnology II. *Folk-Liv* 2: 263–294.

———. 1947. *Svensk byggnadskultur: studier och skildringar belysande den svenska byggnadskulturens historia.* Stockholm: Aktiebolaget Bokverk.

Frykman, Jonas. 1977. *Horan i bondesamhället.* Lund: Liber.

Frykman, Jonas, and Nils Gilje, eds. 2003. *Being There: New Perspectives on Phenomenology and the Analysis of Culture.* Lund: Nordic Academic Press.

Frykman, Jonas, and Orvar Löfgren. 1987 (1979). *Culture Builders: An Historical Anthropology of Middle Class Life,* translated by Alan Crozier. New Brunswick, NJ: Rutgers University Press.

Geiger, Erik Gustaf. 1814–1818. *Svenska folk-visor från fornidten.* Stockholm: Strinnholm och Häggström.

Gerholm, Lena. 1985. *Kulturprojekt och projektkultur: en fallstudie av en kulturpolitisk försöksverksamhet.* Malmö: LiberFörlag.

Gradén, Lizette. 2003. *On Parade: Making Heritage in Lindsborg, Kansas.* Uppsala: Studia Multietnica Upsaliensia, 15.

Gustafsson, Lotten. 2002. *Den förtrollade zonen: lekar med tid, rum och identitat under Medeltidsveckan på Gotland.* Nora: Nya Doxa.

Hammarlund-Larsson, Cecilia, Bo G. Nilsson, and Eva Silvén. 2004. *Samhällsideal och framtidsbilder. Perspektiv på Nordiska museets dokumentation och forskning.* Stockholm: Carlssons.

Hanssen, Börje. 1952. *Österlen; en studie över social-antropologiska sammanhang under 1600-och 1700-talen i sydöstra Skåne.* Stockholm: LTs förlag.

Hultkrantz, Åke. 1960. *International Dictionary of Regional European Ethnology and Folklore.* Volume I: *General Ethnological Concepts.* Copenhagen: Rosenkilde and Bagger.

Hyltén-Cavallius, Gunnar Olof. 1863–1868. *Wärend och widarne; ett försök i svensk ethnologi.* Stockholm: N.p.

Klein, Barbro, and Mats Widbom, eds. 1994. *Swedish Folk Art: All Tradition Is Change.* New York: Harry N. Abrams.

Klintberg, Bengt af. 1980 (1965). *Svenska trollformler.* Stockholm: FIBs lyrikklubb.

————. 1982. *Harens klagan. Studier i gammal och ny folklore.* Stockholm: P. A. Norstedts and Söners förlag.

————. 2000 (1972). *Svenska folksägner.* Stockholm: Pan/Norstedts.

Kvideland, Reimund, and Henning K. Sehmsdorf, eds. 1989. *Nordic Folklore: Recent Studies.* Bloomington: Indiana University Press.

Lindow, John. 1978. *Swedish Legends and Folktales.* Berkeley: University of California Press.

Lindqvist, Beatriz. 1991. *Drömmer och vardag i exil: om chilenska flyktingars kulturella strategier.* Stockholm: Carlssons.

Löfgren, Orvar. 1999. *On Holiday: A History of Vacationing.* Berkeley: University of California Press.

Lövkrona, Inger. 1999. *Annika Larsdotter barnamörderska: kön, magt och sexualitet i 1700-talets Sverige.* Lund: Historiska Media.

Lundahl, Pia. 1998. *Lesbisk identitet.* Stockholm: Carlssons.

Nylén, Anna-Maja. 1976 (1968). *Swedish Handcraft,* translated by Anne-Charlotte Hanes Harvey. Lund: Håkan Ohlssons.

O'Dell, Tom. 1997. *Culture Unbound: Americanization and Everyday Life in Sweden.* Lund: Nordic Academic Press.

Palmenfelt, Ulf. 1993. *Per Arvid Säves möten med människor och sägner: folkloristiska aspekter på ett gotländskt arkivmaterial.* Stockholm: Carlssons.

Raudvere, Catharina. 1993. *Föreställningar om maran i nordisk folktro.* Lund: Religionshistorika avdelningen, Lunds universitet.

Ristilammi, Per-Markku. 1994. *Rosengård och den svarta poesin: en studie av modern annorlundahet.* Stockholm: Symposion.

Ronström, Owe. 1992. *Att gestalta ett ursprung: en musketnologisk studie av dansande och musicerande bland jugoslaver i Stockholm.* Stockholm: Institutet för folklivsforskning.

Ronström, Owe, and Gunnar Ternhag, eds. 1994. *Texter om svensk folkmusik från Haeffner till Ling.* Stockholm: Kungl. Musikaliska akademien.

Rooth, Anna Birgitta. 1951. *The Cinderella Cycle.* Lund: Gleerups.

————. 1965. *Folklig diktning. Form och teknik.* Stockholm: Almqvist and Wiksell.

————. 1992. *Exploring the Garden of Delights: Essays in Bosch's Paintings and Medieval Mental Culture.* Helsinki: FFC 251.

Stattin, Jochum. 1984. *Näcken: spelman eller gränsvakt?* Malmö: Liber.

Strömbäck, Dag. 1935. *Sejd: textstudier i nordisk religionshistoria.* Stockholm: H. Geber.

Strömbäck, Dag, ed. 1971. *Leading Folklorists of the North.* Oslo: Universitetsforlaget.

Svennson, Sigfrid. 1935. *Skånes folkdräkter en drakthistorisk undersokning.* Stockholm: Nordiska museet.

————. 1942. *Bygd och ytterväld.* Stockholm: Fritzes kunl. hovbokhandel.

————. 1969. *Introducktion till folklivsforskning.* Stockholm: Natur o. kultur.

————. 1974. *Svensk etnologi: från forntidstolkning till samtidsforskning.* Revised edition. Stockholm: Natur och Kultur.

Sydow, Carl Wilhelm von. 1948. *Selected Papers on Folklore: Published on the Occasion of His 70th Birthday,* edited by Archer Taylor. Copenhagen: Rosenkilde and Bagger.

Tillhagen, Carl-Herman. 1958. *Folkig läkekonst.* Stockholm: Nordiska museet.

Barbro Klein

Western Europe

France: Peoples and Regions

FRANCE OVERVIEW

GEOGRAPHY

On 25 October 1792, the night sky was ablaze with gunfire in eastern France. Having declared war on **Austria** four days earlier, France found itself under immediate counterattack, and it summoned troops to defend its most vulnerable outposts. Soldiers poured into the barracks without delay, ready to fight for the glory of their country. Claude-Joseph Rouget de Lisle, an officer stationed in Strasbourg, composed a compelling national hymn that evening, one that would set even the most

France and Brittany.

apathetic heart alight with patriotic sentiment. The soldiers loved it, and by July of the following year, a regiment from Marseille sang it proudly while marching into Paris. The "Marseillaise" became the national anthem of France in 1795, and the story of its origin remains an important part of French folklore to this day.

Each province, city, and village in France maintains its own folk beliefs and regional customs, but a more cohesive, national folklore binds the country together. France believes that it is a land blessed by God and that its heroes have acted as God's representatives on earth in a quest for greatness. Many of its legendary figures are kings, emperors, popes, and saints, possessing divine approbation and extraordinary powers. French folklore is therefore intertwined with both the monarchy and the church, beginning at the point where the historical facts blur into myth.

In many ways, the landscape of the country contributes to France's identity. Its temperate climate, tending toward cooler temperatures in the north and warmer temperatures in the south, combines with favorable agricultural conditions to give France a long-standing reputation as a desirable place to live. Currently, 61.4 million people occupy the 551,000-square-kilometer landmass. France is one of the largest countries in Western Europe in terms of both population and area. The French refer to their country as the "Hexagon," an apt name considering that it serves as a six-sided gateway to other lands. The faces of France enable travelers to gain access to **England**, Belgium, and **The Netherlands**, **Germany** and **Switzerland**, **Italy**, Mediterranean Africa, and the Western Hemisphere. Consequently, military strategists throughout history have understood that control of France means control of Western Continental Europe and an unshakable right of entry to both Britain and Africa. Due to its geography, France has been thought of as a highly coveted prize for thousands of years: a boon to any conquering nation and an advantageous place for any political leader to live.

CELTS AND ROMAN GAULS

Around 600 B.C.E., colonists from the Greek city of Phocaea founded a settlement on the Mediterranean coast of France. Massalia, now Marseille, became an important trading post between Greek newcomers and indigenous Celts. The Greeks introduced olives and grapes to the region, founding two major industries that survive to this day in southern France. Greek goods were purchased by the Celts and then sold in northern France via the Rhone-Saone Valley. By the fifth century B.C.E., the Etruscans had also established trade colonies in France, further strengthening Greek influence in the country. Art and architecture during this period such as the tower at Mauressip adopted a decidedly Greek appearance, and the first religious temples appeared. Before the arrival of the Greeks, the Celts followed a spirituality that was firmly rooted in the natural world. They worshipped in groves of trees, celebrated the changing of the seasons, and considered certain elements such as rock and water to be holy. In general, the Celts avoided any direct pictorial depiction of their gods. Thus, when the Greeks arrived, the Celts did not embrace the Hellenistic pantheon of gods. Instead, they merely added Greek touches to their native religion. The Celts, for instance, did build Greek temples to house their own gods, but they incorporated treelike pillars and freestanding rock to mimic the ways of old.

Even as centuries passed, the names and attributes of the Celtic gods did not change. During the third and second centuries B.C.E., however, Celtic methods of worship underwent a slight process of Hellenization. Due to their exposure to Greek culture, the Celts began assigning specific human forms and distinctive poses to their individual gods. In other words, Celtic folklore and folklife adapted to Greek influence but did not undergo radical change.

This cooperative blend of Greek and Celtic religious traditions experienced a transformation when the Romans appeared. In 218 B.C.E., two Roman envoys used southern Gaul as a land bridge to join their homeland to Spain and as a battleground for the Second Punic War. Rome eventually conquered Gaul, and with Roman domination came imposed alterations to Gallic folk beliefs. The Romans transferred the names of their own gods onto those of the Gauls, diminished the role of local druids, and erected houses of worship in the Roman manner such as the Maison Carrée at Nîmes.

In addition to these modifications of the Gallo-Greek religion, the Romans introduced the concept of state worship to Gaul. Romans believed that their emperors were guided by divine influence and were thus extraordinary beings in their own right. Major temples such as the Maison Carrée honored the holy aspects of these earthly leaders, while minor temples paid tribute to their health or good fortune. Historians have loosely inferred certain details of the common religious practice from temple architecture. Most temples included a portico to serve as a gathering place, an inner room that contained a statue of the object of reverence, and a courtyard to perform required rites. In worshipping the sanctity of the emperor, the citizens of Gaul raised the state to something holy in their own consciousness—a belief that ultimately evolved into a firm conviction of the greatness of their own country.

Although Roman influence seriously eroded most of the original folklore and folklife of Gaul, it invariably facilitated the continuation of some early spiritual practices. Roman roads, for example, allowed for pilgrimages to water shrines like the one at Vichy, located in the outer reaches of the country. Some shrines turned into successful commercial centers. As a result, thriving towns emerged from former hamlets. The Celts believed that water contained magical properties, and in the days of Roman Gaul, pilgrims visited shrines to receive healing for their maladies. At the shrine of Sources-de-la-Seine, for instance, visitors purchased "ex-votos," or bronze statuettes of afflicted body parts, then washed them at the shrine to be cured. Associations of water with Otherworldly power only grew during the Gallo-Roman period. Pilgrimages, holy water, and ex-votos would later be incorporated into Christian rites.

During the second and third centuries, other religious practices arrived in Gaul from the east. These mystery cults focused neither on the divinity of the natural world nor on the divinity of the state. Rather, they centered their attention on the plight of humanity. Devotees met in relative secrecy to embark on a journey of self-improvement with the ultimate aim of salvation. Due to the clandestine nature of this type of worship, only a few generalities are known about individual cults. The Cult of Cybele, for example, was popular in the Lyon area of Gaul, and members were initiated by baptism in the blood of the bull. The bull was also a key motif in the Cult of Mithras, one that appealed primarily to soldiers. In this cult, the slain bull represented the unending cycle of birth, death, and rebirth. Mithraic art often depicts plant life springing from the bull's body as it dies. The cult's very temples were constructed to imitate the cave where the bull was killed. Followers of these and other cults in second- and third-century Gaul believed that they were learning secrets about the divine and that these secrets would help them obtain eternal life.

Christianity in Gaul began as one of these small, salvation-oriented mystery cults and proved popular among foreigners living in the south. Gallo-Romans viewed these Christians with a high degree of suspicion due, in part, to their refusal to participate in the widespread state-worship of the time and also to a popular perception that Christians were cannibals who endorsed incest. Gallo-Romans began a campaign of intolerance to stamp out Christianity, ranging from exclusion from public places to death sentences carried out in the amphitheater. In 177, a small group of Gallo-Christians in Lyon were sentenced to be eaten alive by wild animals in front of a crowd of spectators. One Christian, a slave woman named Blandina, stepped out in front of the animals to find that they would not touch her. Roman officials were horrified and killed her immediately, then burned her body and scattered her ashes in the river. Christians received cruel treatment from Gallo-Romans until the conversion of the Roman emperor himself.

In 313, Emperor Constantine promulgated the Edict of Toleration of Christian Worship. No Christian was to suffer discrimination, torture, or death on religious grounds. With the assurance that their followers were safe, Christian leaders began to worship more publicly. Cathedrals and churches filled the cities of Gaul, and by the end of the century Christianity became the normative religion. Places considered sacred by Celts, Greeks, and Romans were destroyed, and churches were built over temple ruins on the desecrated sites.

As the hierarchy of the Christian Church became more firmly established in Gaul, the folk view of bishops took on many of the characteristics of the former reverence for gods. When a bishop died, his grave would become a popular site for local veneration and cross-country pilgrimages. The grave of St. Just, bishop of Lyon during the fourth century, attracted so many visitors that the once-simple tomb evolved into a large church. The writer Sidonius reported that this building was not even large enough to hold all the pilgrims who attended mass there on the saint's birthday. With the advent of Christianity, nature worship gave way to saint worship.

The Gallic people formerly relied on water shrines to heal their sick, but now they sought a different cure. Shrines dedicated to saints quickly earned a reputation for similar restorative powers—especially if the venerable site contained a piece of clothing or body part of the saint in question. The number of pilgrimages to these sites increased dramatically in early Christian Gaul, and due to the limited number of relics per saint, the demand for more saints grew at about the same rate. For this reason, sainthood extended beyond bishops to priests and laypeople of strong belief.

Toward the end of the fourth century and throughout the fifth century, groups of Christians came together to form isolated communities under the direction of certain spiritual leaders. Some of these leaders, such as John Cassian, served as monks in the Holy Land before founding monasteries in France, while others—St. Martin of Tours, for example—were local bishops who saw in the monastic trend a way to eradicate the last vestiges of pre-Christian belief from the local countryside. Monasteries offered Christian guidance to those seeking salvation and earthly protection from the barbarian invasions that were beginning to plague Gaul. Gallo-Christians, then, had a dual incentive to embrace the monastic lifestyle, for it promised safety both in this world and in the hereafter.

THE FRANKISH KINGDOM

By the end of the fifth century, Gaul had died, and France was born. The Romans experienced defeat at the hand of the Franks, and in 486 the Frankish ruler Clovis became France's first king. In 507 he gathered thousands of warriors and proceeded to the Cathedral of Rheims, where he and his men submitted to a mass baptism performed by St. Remi. This defining moment confirmed Christianity as the official religion of the nation and instituted a new relationship between church and state. No longer would God and the emperor be worshipped separately, as was common practice in Gaul. In France the Catholic Church was the only religion, and the king served as God's representative to the country. According to the Divine Right of Kings, the monarch was infallible because he was chosen by God. Royal edicts carried the same weight as papal bulls, and, in fact, French kings were more highly regarded than foreign popes. The church and the monarchy developed an interdependent rule of France, each one validating the other's existence to the French people. The king was essential because he symbolized God on earth, and the church was vital because it provided a moral framework that ensured the salvation of all French citizens. The subtext of the resulting theocracy was that France was a nation of the elect, a noble land singled out by God to be governed under divine rule.

For various reasons, Clovis can be considered the first secular saint of France. His place in history as France's first king has made certain his prominence in the country's folklore. Furthermore, despite a convincing amount of evidence to the contrary, the French still believe Clovis to be an immense civilizing force: a benevolent conqueror who brought gentility and graciousness to a previously undignified people. Although the Franks were considered "barbarian" by Roman Gauls at the time of invasion, the French now hold the Franks as the more refined of the two tribes. Immortalized in Asterix comic books, the Gauls lived a rough, raucous life primarily driven by animal instinct. Their emblem is the rooster, whereas the Franks are symbolized by the fleur-de-lis. The French maintain that Clovis taught the Gauls to channel their aggression into strategic warfare, to restrain their appetites in appreciation of quality over quantity, and to submit to a highly structured social regime. Even in the modern view, Gallic elements are considered crude, whereas Frankish elements are considered sophisticated. The French credit Clovis with the creation of a superior culture and consider him to be the prototype of the ideal ruler.

The next saintly figure in French history is Charlemagne, a ruler whom many deem the true successor to Clovis. He became the king of the Franks in 768 and was declared Holy Roman Emperor on Christmas Day of the year 800. His personal biographer described him as a near giant for the time (standing at over six feet tall) with a heavy build and a flowing beard. Charlemagne believed that universal order was best achieved through academic study and devotion to God. To that end, he built the nation's first universities, free for all who chose to attend, at Tours, Metz, Paris, St. Denis, and Rheims. In addition, he repaired monasteries and castles razed to the ground by invading Saracens—Muslims from Spain who intended to overrun France from south to north. Due to Charlemagne's benevolent attitude toward his people, France has bestowed upon his memory the legacy of a wise and tender monarch.

Charlemagne furthered education and piety in France, but he is perhaps best remembered for his military exploits. After the year 1000, oral legends of his battles against the infidel provided inspiration for northern minstrels who sang the *chansons de geste*, or songs of war. Celebrated for his chivalry, skill in battle, and religious zeal, Charlemagne was a popular hero in this genre of epic poetry that tended to muddle historic facts. In 778, for example, Charlemagne attempted to invade **Spain** but was defeated in a surprise attack by the Basques. The incident, a colossal failure in Charlemagne's otherwise bright career, was transformed into a battle against the dreaded Saracens in the renowned *Song of Roland*. To add to the drama, the composer had a fictitious nephew of Charlemagne slain by a nefarious Saracen. Another legend tells of a nightly visitation by St. James, who ordered Charlemagne to rescue his tomb at Compostela from the Saracen infidels who now ruled the area. Even today, the trek to Santiago de Compostela is a popular pilgrimage. Other tales of Charlemagne recount his long journeys to the Orient to help oppressed Christians and his battles in Jerusalem to bring the holy city to Christian rule. (The real Charlemagne, of course, never came anywhere near the Holy Land.) Charlemagne's cousin and childhood companion, Guilhem, is also included in the national folklore. Guilhem reputedly fought off Saracens in Nimes, Orange, and Narbonne before heading to Rome. In Rome, he vanquished a Saracen giant who nevertheless cut off his nose, marking him for life. Guilhem won his last grand battle against the Saracens in Barcelona and retreated at age forty-eight to the south of France. He established a monastery there that housed a piece of the True Cross, then slew one last Saracen giant with a single blow of his sword, and spent the rest of his days in monastic contemplation. Wandering minstrels from the north carried the Charlemagne and Guilhem *mythos* to every corner of the land so that by the end of the eleventh century, Charlemagne was firmly established as the national inspiration for the Crusades.

In actuality, Christians and Muslims lived harmoniously in Jerusalem until the eleventh century, when the Fatimid dynasty destroyed the Church of Holy Sepulcher in Jerusalem and turned the Christian inhabitants into slaves. Peter the Hermit was outraged at this turn of events and embarked on a mission to Christianize Jerusalem. He preached his cause throughout France, Germany, and Italy, capturing the attention of Pope Urban II. The pope joined forces with Peter and declared that participation in the Crusade would count as full penance for all past and future sins, effectively guaranteeing the Crusader entry into Heaven. With Charlemagne as their folkloric role model, men from all walks of life left their stations in France to fight Muslims in the Holy Land.

MEDIEVAL FRANCE

Out of all the kings who reigned during this era, "St." Louis IX stands out in the French consciousness as the most iconic monarch. He ascended the throne at the age of twelve after his father died of dysentery in the south of France. Both his parents were extremely religious, and Louis centered his policies and practices on the teachings of the church. In a manner reminiscent of Jesus and the disciples, Louis could often be found sitting under trees, instructing large crowds of citizens in the ways of piety and virtue. A staunch supporter of religious artwork, he commissioned the construction of the celebrated Sainte Chapelle, one of the most beautiful churches in all of France. He fervently supported the Crusades, and although his gentility to Christians is well documented, his intolerance of Muslims and Jews cannot be ignored. Louis stated that any unbelievers should be met "with a sword in the belly," and the first burnings of the Talmud occurred under his direction. St. Louis is the figure who perhaps best embodies the Divine Right of Kings, and in the national folklore, he certainly holds the position of the country's most zealous monarch.

Households in France were largely dominated by women during the Crusades, a development that heavily influenced the artistic and literary tradition of the time. Wandering minstrels in the Early Middle Ages sang songs of war, but in the High Middle Ages, they began to sing of love. *Trouvères* from the north and troubadours from the south recited poems that expressed concern over husbands fighting in dangerous lands, the desire to remain faithful to an absent spouse, and liaisons with handsome young knights traveling through the country. Called *Fin amor*, or courtly love, a set of rules existed to govern the love shared between a knight and his usually married lady. Only after the knight had completed a series of tasks set out by the lady was any romantic favor given, and the lady had the right to withdraw her love if the relationship was ever made public. Restraint on both sides was vital to assure the secrecy of the match, so wandering minstrels habitually changed the names of characters in the love poems. Religious themes also appeared in the poetry of the time, and they, too, were oriented to women's interests. Particularly into the twelfth century, the Virgin Mary became a popular subject for the wandering minstrels. Her steadfastness, long-suffering, and gentle love were upheld as a model of virtue for lonely French *chatelaines* who might succumb to the temptations of courtly love. Each region of the country cultivated its own style of veneration and its own interpretation of her relationship with women on earth. The troubadours and the *trouvères* learned tales from many regions and carried them throughout the country. As a result, a lady in Provence would become intimately familiar with traditional stories from **Brittany**. The troubadours and *trouvères*, then, acted as a unifying force in homogenizing French folk culture at the time of the Crusades.

Wandering minstrels from the north transmitted yet another set of legends to all areas of France: the tales of Camelot. This mythology originated in the British regions of Devon and Cornwall as well as in Brittany and gradually trickled down from north to south. The stories of King Arthur, the Knights of the Round Table, and the Quest for the Holy Grail blended ancient Celtic beliefs with Christianity and were immensely popular in France during the Middle Ages. Arthurian knights embodied the chivalric virtues of gentility, honor, and valor so cherished at the time, which made them respectable to men and irresistible to women. Furthermore, the prominence of Christianity in the story cycle resonated with a nation embroiled in a Holy War against Jews and Muslims. The legends surrounding the Grail captured the French

It took the Catholic Church 500 years to canonize her officially, but Joan of Arc's loyalty to God and to France gave her a prominent place among the litany of saints in French folklore. (Courtesy Library of Congress)

imagination for two reasons. First, the Grail quest shared some striking similarities with the popular pilgrimages and Crusades of the time. It involved an arduous voyage to a sacred place, it tested the participant's piety with struggles and obstacles, and it resulted in redemption from the sins of the earth. Second, Breton folklore maintains that Anne, mother of Mary, came from the island of Ys off the coast of Brittany. She left Ys when it sank into the ocean, and she headed to Jerusalem, where she married Joachim. After giving birth to Mary, she then returned to her homeland. Arthurian legends, then, supported the widespread belief in the virtue of the Crusades and the supremacy of France.

Militarism and patriotism co-existed in the French folk mentality long after the Crusades were over. In 1412, near the end of the Hundred Years War, a little girl was born into a peasant family in the Lorraine region of the country. The archangel Michael visited Joan of Arc when she was just thirteen years old, instructing her to be a good girl and to help the king of France get rid of the English. St. Margaret and St. Catherine appeared to her soon afterward, speaking French to encourage her to fulfill her God-given destiny. She was to liberate France from the alliance between England and Burgundy, restoring governance to French monarchs alone. The saints avowed that God was on the side of the French and that the English had no business running God's country. Joan could not ignore this Heavenly plea. She left her village at sixteen, spoke earnestly with the crown prince, and led an army against British forces. By the time she was nineteen, opposing political forces succeeded against her. She was tried, found guilty of wantonness, sorcery, and blasphemy, and sentenced to be burned alive in Rouen. She cried out at the injustice of the decree, and in small recognition for her religious devotion, a compassionate Englishman handed her a small wooden cross to gaze at as her life went up in flames. It took the Catholic Church 500 years to canonize her officially, but her loyalty to God and to France gave her a prominent place among the litany of saints in French folklore.

From Clovis to Joan of Arc, medieval French folk belief asserted that the greatness of France originated in its privileged alliance with God. Political and religious leaders worked together to support this view, and folktales spread the message until it permeated the consciousness of the era. After the end of the Middle Ages, French folklore moved away from its religious emphasis and instead concentrated on the inherent superiority of the country itself.

THE FRANCE OF LOUIS XIV

In the seventeenth century, this attitude was most clearly demonstrated by Louis XIV, who famously declared, "I am the State." His parents, Anne of Austria and Louis XIII, despised each other and would never have had a child if it were not for a freak storm that kept the king from visiting his mistress twenty-three years into their marriage. The people of France had nearly given up hope of a natural successor to the aging king and were overjoyed at the birth of their new ruler. From the moment he was born, Louis XIV learned to expect adoration from court and country. To teach him penmanship, his tutor had him copy out, "Homage is due to kings. They do what they please."

Louis XIV was not five years old when he became king. He was clearly too young to rule, so a group of court advisers governed in his name until Louis reached a more appropriate age. Burning with resentment at his lack of real power, Louis watched helplessly as the court made decisions contrary to his wishes. When Louis was twenty-two, the prime minister, his most influential adviser, died, giving Louis the opportunity to depose the other court advisers and rule independently.

The reign of Louis XIV focused its energies on intensifying the glory of France. Louis understood in early childhood that other members of the Paris nobility were not to be trusted, so he constructed a new court that better matched his own ideology. Louis thought of himself as a latter-day Apollo and set out to create a suitable home for a Sun King. He built a breathtaking palace at Versailles, sparing no expense, and invited all prominent artists, writers, and musicians to take up residence.

Louis XIV focused his energies on intensifying the glory of France and forever changed the French folk mentality. (Courtesy Library of Congress)

The gardens alone contained over 1,200 imported orange trees, plants from the far corners of the country, an exquisitely beautiful network of fountains, and a zoo. At Versailles, a new nobility arose based entirely on personal merit and loyalty to the king. Versailles concentrated the splendor and brilliance of France into an eternal symbol—one based entirely on the adulation of an earthly leader rather than a spiritual one. Louis XIV, in fact, once commented that God must be infinitely jealous of his glory.

Louis XIV changed the French folk mentality forever. Although Catholicism remained the official religion of France, it ceased to pervade every element of French culture. The king was no longer God's divine representative on earth. Instead, he was a human object who was venerated because he created greatness out of nothing. Through the king, all things were possible: a flourishing artistic life, a palace of luxuries, and inevitably a debt large enough to force the people into abject poverty.

THE FRENCH REVOLUTION AND NAPOLEON

The French people could suffer in silence only for so long. When the people cried out during Louis XVI's reign that they had no more bread to eat, his wife, Marie Antoinette, naively replied, "Then let them eat cake." The angry peasants revolted, liberated prisoners from the Bastille on 14 July 1789, and declared the nobility to be the enemy of the people. In this spirit, leagues of French revolutionaries burned down the houses of the gentry. Aristocrats were duly executed in great numbers,

Burning the royal carriages at the Chateau d'Eu, 24 February 1848. During the French Revolution, the ideals of liberty, equality, and brotherhood invariably ended up empowering a people caught under a new kind of tyranny. (Courtesy Library of Congress)

then replaced by a new system of government supposedly founded on the principles of liberty, brotherhood, and equality. In truth, the new regime was just as tyrannical as the nobility it replaced.

Revolutionaries disagreed with both the monarchy and the church that supported it. However, French culture had been shaped by the Catholic Church for over 1,000 years, and Catholic ideology extended far beyond the Sunday masses. Indeed, every element of French folklore and folklife had its roots in Catholic Christianity. The new Republic, in response, attempted to abolish the folklore and folklife of the day and replace it with a new, entirely nationalistic folklore. It was as if France did not exist until that moment. The seven-day week was replaced by ten-day measures of time, new names were given to the days of the week and the months of the year, and all holidays were eliminated and replaced with special days that commemorated key events in the revolution. Marianne, newly created as the national goddess of Reason, was boldly depicted carrying the French flag, despite the absence of women at any level in the new government. Priests were no longer paid, some were even jailed for anti-revolutionary sentiment, and many were deported to far-off lands. Catholic rites were made illegal. In its place, a new state-religion called "Theophilanthropy" was introduced. Theophilanthropy acknowledged the existence of a Supreme Being, and the revolutionary government legislated a new set of quasi-religious practices as the official religion. The republicans soon discovered, however, that folk belief cannot be invented overnight.

A subversive folklife flourished in this period as never before. The ideals of liberty, equality, and brotherhood invariably ended up empowering a people caught under a new kind of tyranny. Parishioners who never would have dreamed of assuming the role of a priest now found themselves organizing "white masses" led by laypeople. Quite often, the local schoolteacher replaced the local priest—a fitting role for someone who had traditionally served as parish assistant. When the churches were closed, the devout would congregate in the woods and hold Catholic masses reminiscent of early medieval worship. Women were excluded from any role in official government but found warm acceptance in the underground Catholic revival. In fact, women were more likely to risk open defiance of government decree, for they would not be punished as severely as men would. A woman would only be chastised, whereas a man might be killed, and for this reason, nearly all of the Catholic riots at the time were led by women.

Though the revolutionaries acted in the name of liberty, they soon became oppressors themselves. The revolution had birthed a climate of intense fear and political unrest. During this time, the mere act of speaking out against the state's fabricated folk beliefs might endanger one's life. Citizens who remained loyal to the church or loyal to the monarchy found themselves fighting in defense of their beliefs for ten long years. The new Republic, then, guaranteed liberty, freedom, and brotherhood only for like-minded revolutionary republicans. The people cried out for new leadership, and in 1799 their prayers were answered.

Napoleon Bonaparte, a rising star in the military, modeled his leadership style on the great icons of old. Clovis and Charlemagne served as particular inspirations. After presenting a new constitution to the French Senate—one that was passed with an overwhelming majority—Napoleon positioned himself to rule France alone, much in the manner of Louis XIV. Just before he was made emperor, he arranged for Pope Pius VII to sign the Concordat, a document that reestablished the Catholic Church as the official state religion, reestablished Sunday observance and religious holidays into the French calendar, and offered absolution to priests who had married during the ten-year revolutionary republican government. He also invited the pope to his coronation, set to take place on 2 December 1804.

That day, a grand convoy of horse-drawn chariots made their way to the cathedral. The last one, blazoned with a golden "N" on each side, slowed down as it approached the doors of the church. Napoleon, dressed in his finest garb, stepped out of the horse-drawn carriage and with his wife, Josephine, joined the procession toward the altar. There stood the pope, a figure not seen in France since the days of the aristocracy. As he spoke the opening words of the ceremony, all eyes fell on Napoleon. Confident, refined, and ambitious, this was the man who would lead France out of ruin and restore it to former glory. Relics from the days of Charlemagne filled the cathedral, reminding all in attendance of the noble quest France was about to undertake. The pope lifted up a crown of golden laurel leaves to complete the ceremony but was stopped. In a symbolic move establishing a new relationship between church and state, Napoleon reached out and placed the crown on his own head.

Once his status was made official, Napoleon swiftly achieved what he had promised to do. He formed a new aristocracy in France, rewarding those who had served him well in the past with titles of nobility. He restored the university to prominence and established a new banking system that stabilized the insecure economy. Perhaps his most significant contribution to French life was the Napoleonic Code, passed after careful examination of every French law. Nearly 200 years old, the Code still serves as the basis of law in most Francophone regions of the world.

The defeat of Napoleon's army in **Russia**, subsequent forced abdication in 1814, return to Paris, and exile to the island of Elba round out the folklore of this shooting star in French history. Despite his demise, his place in the pantheon of French folk heroes is secure due to his role as the architect of post-revolutionary France. Napoleon rebuilt a crumbling nation, reaffirmed its greatness in the world, and successfully reworked the philosophical connection between church and state. The Concordat verified Catholicism as the true religion of France, but the act of self-coronation asserted the dominance of nationhood.

A boy wears the crown of the Three Wise Men at Epiphany. (© Mark Antman/The Image Works)

CALENDAR CUSTOMS

The French calendar, reworked by Napoleon to be inclusive of both religious and state holidays, is a good example of the presence of folklore in the country today. Ancient Celtic celebrations mingle with Roman Catholic observances and historic anniversaries to form a calendar that commemorates the rich history of French folk beliefs.

Early in the year, the French celebrate Epiphany, or the arrival of the wise men at the birthplace of Baby Jesus. The mother in each French household bakes a heavy marzipan cake with a bean or clay figurine inside. When it is time to serve the cake, the youngest person climbs under the table and announces the serving order of the dessert. Once everyone is served, the youngest person may rejoin the family. The lucky person who bites into the bean or figurine receives a paper crown and is said to have good fortune the whole year through.

In the spring, a day of feasting precedes a season of fasting. Mardi Gras, a holiday now celebrated worldwide, features parties and food-filled festivities. Mardi Gras takes place the day before Lent, the traditional forty-day period of fasting and contemplation that precedes Easter. In France, no church bells ring during Lent. It is said that they fly to Rome to be with the pope. They return to their home parishes on Easter Sunday, dropping chocolate coins into people's gardens in midflight. Some French Catholics attend mass on Easter, but as church attendance has dropped significantly in the twentieth and twenty-first centuries, this is no longer a national custom.

On 1 April, people play tricks on each other in a custom similar to that found in North America. For reasons long forgotten, however, the jokes in France revolve around fish. Children tape paper fish onto people's backs and cry out "*poisson d'avril*" or "April Fish." Real fish are hidden in all sorts of unsavory places, and chocolate fish are given as gifts.

One month later, all schools, banks, government buildings, and places of business close to usher in the month of May. Ceremonies harking back to Celtic times feature children dancing around Maypoles and springtime parades that fill the streets. During such celebrations, people tend to eat their meals outdoors. On 8 May, the French gather in town squares for a very different reason; every year, they mark the end of World War II with a more somber commemoration.

Another special day in France is 14 July, the anniversary of the capture of the Bastille. This holiday signals the end of aristocratic domination and is observed with exuberant celebrations involving demonstrations, fireworks, and reenactments.

The Virgin Mary reputedly ascended into Heaven in bodily form after the Resurrection of Jesus, and the French commemorate this day on 15 August. Women, in particular, go to Marian shrines and pray for loved ones or light votive candles in parish churches. Some towns named after Mary plan community festivities centered on the church.

Due to the impact of globalization, large urban centers in France have begun to celebrate the largely North American tradition of Halloween on 31 October. Children do not go door-to-door for candy, however. The French version of this holiday is more adult-oriented and features costume parties and dances in downtown clubs.

The next day, 1 November, is reserved for families to mourn the passing of their loved ones. Families place bouquets of daisies or chrysanthemums on family grave sites, then gather together for a solemn meal afterward. Devout Catholics may attend mass or light candles in the memory of those who have died.

On Christmas Eve, families participate in Reveillon, an all-night festivity that begins with a large dinner, followed by a midnight mass, gift opening, singing, and a family breakfast the next morning. In recent years, North American images of Christmas have started to infiltrate French culture, but the traditional practices remain largely intact.

Roman, Celtic, Catholic, and republican elements have combined to create the French calendar. Increasingly, globalization threatens to alter age-old customs or add new holidays (such as Halloween) to the well-established set of traditions. Globalization has impacted French folklore and folklife in a number of ways. The Nazi occupation during World War II, for instance, had a devastating effect on the morale of the country. It divided France in two, confirming the historical perspective that government cannot totally be trusted. It also shook the French belief in their own greatness severely. The Nazis often disregarded local folklore by transforming castles and other such storied buildings into offices or apartments. Religious practices were discouraged. In consequence, the French felt very unsure of their place in the world, causing them to question previously held beliefs and customs. Such existentialist thinking led to the student rebellions of the 1960s and, to some extent, the general culture of strikes and protest demonstrations so common in the country today. Further erosion of folklore and folklife is inevitable with the inclusion of France in the European Economic Union, the removal of French banknotes bearing the images of iconic leaders of the past, and the move toward a more homogeneous economic policy. These new threats, however, are unlikely to destroy French folk beliefs completely. As long as the statue of Joan of Arc remains in Rheims, Versailles is maintained in all its splendor, and the *Marseillaise* plays on 14 July, French folklore and folklife will carry on.

STUDIES OF FRENCH FOLKLORE

The interrelationship of French folklore with both history and religion has produced abundant resources. King (1990) provides a clear overview of the Celtic, Greek, and Roman periods in Gaul. Marks (1975) is a good general reference for artistic life in the French Middle Ages. *The Song of Roland* (Burgess 1990) and the romances of Chrétién de Troyes (Staines 1991) are excellent primary sources for a firsthand look at the Arthurian side of medieval culture, and Bernard de Ventadour may be the definitive troubadour of the era. Sackville-West's biography of Joan of Arc (1936) provides an accurate, detailed, and intimate account of its subject, and Ashley's biography of Louis XIV (1948) is equally informative. Desan (1990) is an especially helpful source for the study of folklore in the contexts of the Revolution and the church. Another useful reference for the interactions of folklore, history, and religion is Weber (1991).

BIBLIOGRAPHY

Ashley, Maurice. 1948. *Louis XIV and the Greatness of France.* New York: Macmillan.

Burgess, Glyn, trans. 1990. *The Song of Roland.* New York: Penguin.

Desan, Suzanne. 1990. *Reclaiming the Sacred: Lay Religion and Popular Politics in Revolutionary France.* Ithaca, NY: Cornell University Press.

Ippolito, Marguerit-Marie. 2001. *Bernard de Ventadour: Troubadour Limousin du xiie siècle, prince de l'amour et da la poèsie Romane.* Paris: L'Harmattan Édition.

King, Anthony. 1990. *Roman Gaul and Germany.* Berkeley: University of California Press.

Marks, Claude. 1975. *Pilgrims, Heretics, and Lovers: A Medieval Journey.* New York: Macmillan.

Sackville-West, Vita. 1936. *Saint Joan of Arc.* London: Cobden-Sanderson.

Staines, David, trans. 1991. *The Complete Romances of Chrétién de Troyes.* Bloomington: Indiana University Press.

Weber, Eugene. 1991. *My France: Politics, Culture, Myth.* Cambridge: Harvard University Press.

Naomi Brun

BRITTANY

GEOGRAPHY

When a Breton notices the first signs of deteriorating eyesight, he makes a pilgrimage to buy a statue of St. Jean du Doigt in the village of Plougasnou. With the relic in hand, he proceeds to the village well, dug thousands of years ago by the pre-Christian Celts. He then dips the statue in the holy water, washes his failing eyes, and takes a drink, praying to the saint all the while. This age-old ritual allegedly restores eyesight within one year unless the sufferer has displeased the saint in some way. He may then return to the well at Plougasnou, throw water on the saint's nose, and ask for a cure once more. If his vision remains poor, the outraged pilgrim may torture the statue out of frustration. Common techniques include drowning, burning, and cutting off appendages.

Traditions such as these continue to thrive in twenty-first-century Brittany. Time moves slowly on this rocky peninsula jutting northwestward from **France**, so its inhabitants have retained a fierce, nature-oriented spirituality often associated with isolated communities. Brittany, in fact, is relatively cut off from the rest of Europe. The Atlantic Ocean surrounds the land on three sides, and devastating storms are perhaps the greatest threat that Bretons face from day to day. To cope with such hardships, they rely on a faith that blends ancient Celtic and Roman Catholic religions. Both belief systems have roots in Breton history, and the emerging mixture provides the foundation for the relationship between the people and their landscape.

The former name of Brittany, "Armorica," means "the land facing the sea." Indeed, both land and sea define Breton geography. In a process that began over 700 million years ago, a cycle of sediment buildup and erosion created the layers of granite and slate that now form the coast. Much of Brittany consists of vast expanses of rock where very little can grow, so the Breton diet relies heavily on the bounty of the sea. However, crashing waves did penetrate some points of the shoreline to form river valleys, allowing fertile land and forest to develop in the Breton interior. Rocks, trees, caves, and riverbeds provide homes for the fairies of Breton folklore, and wells indicate shrines from long ago. To the Bretons, the places where rock and water meet are considered sacred, and there is an undeniable link between craggy cliffs and death for a seafaring people. Particularly jagged areas of the shoreline are believed to be doorways into the Otherworld, conceivably due to the abundance of shipwrecks in those regions. At any rate, the tempestuous climate and harsh landscape created a connection between Breton folklore and the rhythms of the natural world.

CELTIC LORE AND RELIGION

The ancient Celtic deity Cernunnos perhaps best embodies the Breton understanding of the life cycle. From November until April, Cernunnos lives in the Otherworld with Ana, the Great Mother Goddess. In early May, she takes another lover, and Cernunnos flees to the earthly realm, wearing the horns of the cuckold. He brings new, green growth to barren land, keeps forests safe from destruction, and protects animals that make their home among the trees. When he returns to Ana in the Otherworld at the end of October, he leaves behind his horns but removes his fruitfulness from the earth. Therefore, Bretons tend to associate Cernunnos with both life and death. Mesolithic (10,000–5000 B.C.E.) burial grounds near the village of Teviec reveal an allegiance to Cernunnos, for antlers were placed on the skeletons as if shed for the voyage to the Otherworld. Even the earliest inhabitants of Brittany expressed an environmental spirituality and a preoccupation with death. Bretons still mark the yearly departure of Cernunnos by baking little horn-shaped cakes called *kornigou*.

Cernunnos is not the only god associated with death. Ankou, a deity found strictly in Brittany, is the personification of death itself. Breton art depicts Ankou as a skeleton brought to life. The enormous brim on his hat keeps his face hidden from view, and he holds a scythe sharpened on human bone. He uses the scythe to harvest the dead, whom he then places in a wooden cart. Residents of the Finistère and Côtes du Nord regions claim that horses pull the cart, while inhabitants of Morbihan claim that two oxen and a half-starved horse must carry the burden. Bretons who have the misfortune to die on 31 December, however, must draw the cart themselves. In any event, the creaking of the wooden wheels

The ancient Celtic horned deity Cernunnos—pictured here—perhaps best embodies the Breton understanding of the life cycle. (© Mary Evans Picture Library/The Image Works)

is enough to strike fear into the heart of many Bretons, for a noisy cart announces imminent disaster.

When a Breton dies, friends and family gather around the fireplace to recount tales of Ankou and tell stories about the recently departed. The more glorious the tale, the better, for a well-lived life guarantees a place in the Otherworld for any soul. A Breton who died with unfinished business, on the other hand, remains somewhat tied to the earth and goes to Anaon, otherwise known as the Marsh of Hells. In Anaon, the spirit is trapped in "frozen torment" and can leave only to wander the earth in misery. Still others are transformed into menhirs, or standing stones. On Samhain, from sundown on 31 October to sundown on 1 November, all the dead return to visit their living relatives. Extra places are set at the dinner table in the evening, and the next morning, families eat a meal of pig's head and milky bread. Having spent time with loved ones, a departed spirit goes back to its ethereal realm, where it must reside until the following Samhain.

Although some Bretons consider menhirs to be petrified human beings, others think differently. Menhirs, upright stones ranging from three feet to thirty feet in height, often appear in large groups. From a distance, they resemble groves of trees, which the Celts considered to be holy. Consequently, some scholars believe that these Neolithic structures (5000–2000 B.C.E.) may have figured in nature celebrations, and the shadows they cast do help calculate the movements of the sun and the moon. Judging from existing rituals, menhirs may have been fertility symbols, for men who desire children will rub themselves on the oversized rocks. Then again, menhirs may have been used to identify burial grounds in the same manner as dolmens. Dolmens consist of a stone placed on top of two standing stones, and they mark entrances to communal graves. Like menhirs, dolmens are good examples of Neolithic carvings that are still readily found in Brittany.

Another good source of Breton carvings is metalwork dating from the Bronze Age (2400–600 B.C.E.). Highly detailed swords, torques, and axes suggest fine bronze craftsmanship, and remnants of these items can be found all over Europe. Breton metalwork, then, was well regarded, and trade flourished, especially between Brittany, **England**, and **Wales**. In fact, Bronze Age coins from all three nations feature Celtic deities such as rider goddesses and other symbols of fertility. Many of the sacred wells, shrines that combine the holy elements of rock and water, also date from this period. Celtic spirituality, therefore, became increasingly iconic in this time. Due to the fact that no firsthand written record of Celtic spiritual belief exists, scholars rely on these pictorial representations to glean an understanding of the Breton worldview.

Like Celts in other lands, the Bretons found divine inspiration in their surroundings. A sense of connection between the elements created a feeling of reverence in the Breton soul, so holy places joined one element with another. Fairies, or *korrigan*, reputedly dwelt in such locations and bestowed good or bad fortune on those who paid them a visit. People gathered around wells because they combined rock with water, and they met in the forests that linked earth with air. Trees of all types were held in high regard due to their downward stretching roots and upward reaching branches, but some trees were considered to be especially sacred. The oak was one of the most favored trees among the Celts, for it not only connects land and sky but also manifests the life cycle every year. Oak trees unfurl new leaves in the spring, deepen their hue in the summer, turn bright colors in the fall, and then lie dormant all winter, only to repeat the process the following spring.

The cycle of birth, maturity, decline, and regeneration, made visible in the animal and plant worlds, was applied to human life in Brittany. Every woman became a purveyor of magic when she gave birth, and every man proved himself to be divine after recovery from illness or battle wounds. Rituals marked the passage from one life stage to the next, sometimes made concrete in an icon or artwork. Still worn by women in modern-day Brittany, the *triskele* is a Celtic symbol of a woman's life as she moves from being a girl, to a woman, to a crone. Each point on the triangle is decorated with a concentric spiral, signifying the issues she will have to face before she can proceed to the next phase of her life.

Breton spirituality, focusing on nature, connection, and regeneration, survived remarkably well against the colonizing forces of the following centuries. The Romans, who successfully established themselves in western Gaul (present-day Brittany) by 51 B.C.E., did not diminish Celtic folk belief in any significant way. Rather, the Bretons assigned Roman names to their own Celtic deities. For them, the importance was not in the name itself but in the dominions of the gods. The Celtic sky-god, for instance, who represented the conflict between light and dark, became equally recognized under the name of Jupiter. At any rate, the Romans were more interested in urbanizing western Gaul than in eradicating its religion. The major cities of modern Brittany such as Rennes, Vannes, and Nantes originate in the Roman period, as do their excellent roads and political infrastructure.

During the tumultuous second and third centuries, western Gaul lost its appeal as a Roman stronghold. Assassinations, peasant revolts, and devastation wrought by North Sea raiders destroyed much of the peace and prosperity enjoyed during the first century. Coin values fluctuated wildly, so western Gaul ultimately reverted to a barter system. By the end of the fourth century, the people no longer trusted the efficiency of their Roman rulers. Consequently, they expelled the Romans and returned to self-government.

CELTIC MIGRATION FROM BRITAIN

As the Bretons began to re-establish themselves as an independent people, their Celtic brethren in southern England and Wales were looking for a place to call home. The scholars Ferdinand Lot and Nora Chadwick claim that these peoples left their homelands to escape the Pictish and Scottish raiders, who had been active since the late third century. Since Brittany was geographically accessible from southern Britain, and since the language and culture had grown in similarity due to a long history of trade, English and Welsh emigrants came to Brittany in large numbers. In fact, the medieval Welsh story cycle known as the *Mabinogion* recounts the tale of Conan Meriadec, who took his army to Brittany in 388 and founded a dynasty, intermarrying with Breton women. Although the legend is widely considered to have little historical basis, the influx of English and Welsh is fact.

Nowhere is the British influence more readily visible than in the traditional

Breton dress, seen on special occasions even in the twenty-first century. Like the British, each Breton family belongs to a specific clan, made evident in the details of one's clothing. All in all, there are sixty-six clans in Brittany, and a woman's *coiffe*, or lace headdress, identifies her clan to other Bretons. In general, men wear black suits with wide-brimmed hats, and women wear black dresses with white lace aprons and caps.

CHRISTIANITY IN BRITTANY

Shortly after the British arrived, missionaries, monks, and religious hermits also came to Brittany. The towns of St. Brieuc and St. Malo were named after the first and last missionaries to come to the Celtic land, arriving in 429 and 627, respectively. These religious newcomers helped to reconstruct a viable country after the destruction of the previous centuries and provided the foundation for the Breton understanding of sainthood. To the Bretons, a saint is an individual who lives in harmony with his or her surroundings and willingly provides aid to those in need. According to legend, Brittany has 7,777 saints, and churches dedicated to these saints are built over wells or in forests that served as the original shrine. Saints are local, and their icons are handed down from generation to generation. In fact, images of saints are believed to be somewhat alive and can be threatened or punished if they choose not to help those under their protection.

Brittany's original saints spread the message of Christianity all over the land and won many converts. Bretons did embrace Roman Catholicism, but they incorporated elements of their own Celtic belief system as well. The resulting spirituality was neither solely Celtic nor exclusively Catholic but a blend of both faiths that has survived to the present. Bretons probably became accustomed to assigning new names to old deities during the Roman period and then applied this practice to their Christian faith. For example, Roman Catholics believe that Jesus' grandmother was called Anne, a name similar to that of the Celtic mother goddess Ana. Bretons claim that Anne and Ana are the same being: a Breton woman who left the city of Ys when it began to sink into the ocean. Anne/Ana traveled to Judea, where she met Joachim and had a baby girl called Mary. After Mary gave birth to Jesus, Anne/Ana returned to Brittany, to be visited by her grandson years later. By incorporating some Celtic elements into Roman Catholicism, Bretons could remain true to both religions simultaneously. Local priests have bridged the gulf between the two faiths by representing Rome inside the church, then removing their shoes and stoles to lead nature worship outside the church. Perhaps this willingness to accommodate old beliefs has allowed Catholicism to flourish in Brittany, for it has been a strong presence in Breton society since the arrival of the first missionaries in the early Middle Ages.

MEDIEVAL AND EARLY MODERN BRITTANY

Medieval Breton folk literature provides good insight into the Breton worldview. Arthurian tales, for example, fuse England, Wales, and Brittany into one Celtic backdrop. The forests, lakes, and wells in the legends house fairies and other ethereal beings. Magic occurs in such sacred places, and it is not surprising that Sir Lancelot of the Lake was brought up by the fairy Vivien in a Breton forest. Broceliande, the name of this forest near Paimpont, contained the Fountain of Youth, the Fountain of Barenton—symbolic of poetry—and the Garden of Joy. Anyone with the fortune to be raised in such an auspicious environment would be bound to lead an extraordinary life, and Lancelot certainly did not disappoint his readers. The Arthurian stories were certainly Celtic, but they were also Christian. The knights, after all, traveled far and wide to find the Holy Grail, reputed to have touched Jesus's lips at the Last Supper.

After France annexed Brittany in 1532, folklore and folklife remained relatively unchanged. Brittany, like France, was a Roman Catholic land, and folk customs in France ranged so widely from province to province that the French saw no need to subsume Breton culture entirely. Moreover, French influences could enter the territory only along their one shared border. Life in Brittany, then, remained fairly constant until after the World War II, when globalization began to homogenize cultures all over the world. In fact, Brittany is still holding on to its way of life in the face of modernization.

CHALLENGES OF THE MODERN WORLD

As of the early twenty-first century, the introduction of high-speed technology and shopping malls has not yet done away with Breton traditions that date back thousands of years. Traditional Breton attire is no longer worn on a daily basis but is ritually donned for important church services and village weddings. Fishing still plays an important role in the Breton economy, but fishermen now abide by government regulations and use the Internet to sell their stock. Pilgrims still go to Plougasnou to dip a statue of St. Jean du Doigt in a holy well, but now they take a motorbike to get there. Undoubtedly, some aspects of Brittany have modernized. Throughout history, however, the Bretons have held on to their ancient beliefs and customs during frequent periods of change; the twenty-first century will likely prove no different. In short, Brittany possesses a resilient nature that will ensure its cultural survival long into the future.

STUDIES OF BRETON FOLKLORE

Anyone wishing further information about Breton folklore and folklife will find an abundance of excellent resources. A good general overview of the Breton worldview can be found in the Breton folklore article in the encyclopedia series *Man, Myth, and Magic*. In *The Bretons*, Patrick Gaillou and Michael Jones have compiled an archeological and social history of Brittany, which will be valuable to anyone wanting to learn about Breton anthropology. Reader's Digest and the French publishing house Larousse have compiled a book entitled *Pays et gens de Bretagne*, which provides commentary on the folklife of each region of Brittany. Paul-Yves Sebillot has cataloged Breton beliefs and customs in *Le folklore de la Bretagne I et II*.

BIBLIOGRAPHY

Gaillou, Patrick, and Michael Jones. 1991. *The Bretons*. Oxford: Basil Blackwell.

Le Scouezec, G. Brittany. 1997. In *Man, Myth, and Magic: The Illustrated Encyclopedia of Mythology, Religion, and the Unknown*, edited by Richard Cavendish and Brian Innes. New York: M. Cavendish. 2:284–285.

Pays et gens de Bretagne: Collections pays et gens de France. 1982. Paris: Librairie Larousse et Selections du Reader's Digest.

Sebillot, Paul-Yves. 1968. *Le folklore de la Bretagne I et II*. Paris: Editions G-P Maisonneuve et La rose.

Naomi Brun

Iberian Peninsula: Peoples and Regions

SPAIN OVERVIEW

GEOGRAPHY AND HISTORY

The westernmost country in Europe, Spain until 1492 had been considered the *fines terrae* or end of the known world. According to legend, Hercules inscribed the columns at Gibraltar and Ceuta with "*non plus ultra,*" establishing that point beyond which there was nothing more. Spain, roughly twice the size of the state of Oregon, covers 504,782 square kilometers with a population just over 40 million. As a peninsula, Spain's geography is characterized by natural borders: the Mediterranean Sea to the east, the Atlantic Ocean to the west, the Cantabrian Sea to the north, and the Pyrenees Mountains on the border with France to the northeast. Other mountain

Regions of Spain.

ranges like the cordillera Cantábrica, the Sistema Ibérico, the Sistema Central, and the Sierra Morena make Spain the most mountainous country in Europe after Switzerland. At the same time, however, an extensive, arid plateau known as the "*meseta*" lies in the central part of the country with an elevation of over 600 meters above sea level. Two groups of islands, the Balearics in the Mediterranean off the coast of Valencia and the Canary Islands in the Atlantic along the coast of Africa, also form part of Spain's geographical identity and contribute to its disconnected and diverse landscape. Likewise, Spain still maintains political sovereignty over two cities on the African coast, Ceuta and Melilla.

Four major rivers cut across Spain's landscape, creating key arteries that connect areas of the country and endowing the geography with character. The Ebro, the longest and most important river in the north, begins in the mountains on the Cantabrian coast and flows into the Mediterranean Sea south of Cataluña. In the south, the Guadalquivir (an Arabic name meaning "large river") extends throughout Andalucía to the Atlantic coast with Seville as its major port. Across the southern part of the *meseta* in Castilla-La Mancha, the Tajo flows through Toledo to Portugal, where it empties into the Atlantic at the port of Lisbon. In the Castilla-León, in the northern part of the *meseta*, the Duero also flows into the Atlantic on the coasts of Portugal.

Spain's geographical location and fragmentation foment a highly diverse climate and landscape that lead some to speak of Spain as a "small continent." The *meseta* creates a more Continental climate, elevated and isolated from the sea with high temperatures and scarce rainfall. To the north and northwest, the Atlantic or oceanic zone offers a very humid climate with moderate temperatures and large amounts of rain that create dense forests in the areas of Galicia, Asturias, Cantabria, and the País Vasco. Lastly, the Mediterranean climate extends along Spain's eastern coast from Levante through the southern region of Andalucía. Here, mild winters and hot summers make the beaches a prime tourist location while at the same time offering a perfect place for the cultivation of olives and oranges.

Spain's geographical diversity is mirrored by its sociocultural diversity. With Spain's 1978 constitution, the central government conceded political autonomy to different regions of the country that had inherently unique social, linguistic, cultural, and regional identities. These *autonomías* are Andalucía, Aragón, Canary Islands, Cantabria, Castilla-La Mancha, Castilla y León, Cataluña, the Comunidad Balear, the Comunidad Valenciana, Extremadura, Galicia, La Rioja, Comunidad Autónoma de Madrid, Comunidad Foral de Navarra, País Vasco, and Principado de Asturias y Región de Murcia. Though the constitution recognizes Spanish (*castellano*) as the country's official language, the geographic separation between distinct regions led to the evolution of other Romance languages from the original Latin: Galician (*gallego-portugués*) and Catalán. Catalán maintains a linguistic structure different from that of Spanish and has formed its own dialects in Spain, including *valenciano* and *balear*. The impenetrable mountain ranges surrounding the País Vasco prevented Roman influence on the Basque language, also known as *euskera*, whose mysterious origin is not related to any of the other languages spoken in Spain. In their respective autonomous communities, each of these languages is recognized as the region's official language along with Spanish.

Likewise, these areas are as diverse culturally as they are linguistically. On the Costa Brava to the south of the Pyrenees Mountains, Cataluña, with a historically solid middle class, is an important industrial and commercial center with Barcelona as its cultural and political capital. The País Vasco, famous for its independent spirit, is known for its hardworking people as well as its often-difficult relationship with the rest of Spain. With a history of labor movements and anarchist ideology, Asturias bases its economic livelihood on coal mining. The rainy climate in Asturias y Galicia often leads people to refer to these areas as the *España verde*. Both geographically and culturally, Galicia shares ties with the Celtic tradition of **Ireland** and depends economically on cattle and land grazing as well as fishing. The aforementioned *meseta* represents the political, geographic, linguistic, and cultural center of Spain, where Madrid, Spain's capital, can be found. In the south, Andalucía is the area most influenced by the Arab presence, especially noticeable in its architecture and the physical appearance of its people. Andalucía's hot climate makes it the ideal place for Spain's cultivation of olives and as a destination of millions of Spanish and European tourists. Valencia, to the northeast of Andalucía, is the peninsula's most fertile land, from which oranges are exported all over the world.

Spain's geographic borders have often contributed to its economic, political, and cultural isolation from the rest of Western Europe throughout history, leading Spanish thinker Miguel de Unamuno to characterize Spain's otherness from Europe with "Africa ends at the Pyrenees." While Spain's geographical isolation separated it from the social, political, economic, and religious events of Europe, many feel it also contributed to Spain's multicultural diversity. Spain's rich history of immigrants and cultural fusion begins with the Iberos, fierce warriors whose independent spirit is often perceived as the seed of an essential Spanish identity. Believed to have arrived in about 1600 B.C.E., the Iberos influenced contemporary Spain through the name given the Iberian Peninsula by the Greeks in 600 B.C.E.

Around 1000 B.C.E., Celtic peoples with a deep knowledge of ironworking moved into the peninsula and began mixing with the Iberos to create a culture known as *celtibero*. Soon seafaring groups such as the Phoenicians and the Greeks, attracted by the peninsula's natural resources such as tin (*estaño*), began to establish cities on the Mediterranean coast. The Phoenicians founded cities such as Cádiz and extended their presence past Málaga almost to Almuñecar. A peaceful culture, they did not engage the Iberos in battle but rather introduced coins, the alphabet, metalworking, and fabric weaving. Likewise, the Greeks dedicated themselves to commercial ends, increasing the cultivation of grapes and olives, introducing the preservation of fish through salt as well as the extraction of minerals from the soil, and founding schools and academies. From stories told and written by Phoenician and Greek sailors, the Iberian Peninsula became a mythical place for ancient cultures, a legendary land with an abundance of gold and silver.

Perhaps the wealth associated with the peninsula caught the attention of the Romans, who in 218 B.C.E. invaded the peninsula, defeated the Carthaginians (a colony of Phoenicians who settled on the northern coast of Africa in Carthage), and began their six-century domination of the area that would leave an indelible mark on the cultural, political, religious, and linguistic identity of Spain. The Romans "pacified" and "civilized" the peninsula and assimilated its cultures into their empire by renaming the peninsula *Hispania*, dividing the land into provinces, imposing linguistic unity through the use of Latin, establishing an organizational hierarchy privileging landowners, and constructing aqueducts, roads, theaters, and bridges. In 380 C.E. Christianity became the official religion of the Roman Empire and extended quickly and profoundly throughout the peninsula. It continues to this day to characterize the majority of Spanish religious beliefs.

In the middle of the third century C.E., a group of barbarous tribes from the north, known as the Visigoths, invaded Spain as the Roman Empire dwindled. While the Visigoths adopted Christianity, the Roman religion, and Latin, they imprinted the peninsula with a Germanic personality by imposing feudalism. Nevertheless, the influence of the Visigoths did not last long, nor did it enjoy a wide diffusion throughout the peninsula. In 711 C.E., the Moors invaded the Iberian Peninsula and extended their presence and influence to the Cantabrian mountains until 1492, when the military loss at Granada marked the end of the Christian *reconquista* (reconquest) of the peninsula and the beginning of modern Spain. With almost 800 years of Arab presence in the peninsula (which the Arabs renamed *Al-Andalus*), Spanish culture inevitably assimilated linguistic aspects (with words such as *ojalá*— May God/Allah grant that; *almohada*—pillow; and *zanahoria*—carrot) as well as gastronomic preferences for eggplants, sugar, spinach, and rice. Moreover, Arabic architecture continues to testify to the lasting impression left by the Moors in Spain in such cities as Seville, Toledo, and Granada, site of the imposing fortress the Alhambra. In science and philosophy, the Arabs introduced the concept of zero, and thinkers such as Averroes re-ignited Western interest in Aristotle. With the conclusion of Christian Spain's *reconquista*, a new era of intolerance emerged alongside a modern Spanish identity. In 1492, Arabs and Jews were expelled from the peninsula with the idea of establishing a "pure" Spanish racial and religious identity both within their own borders and across the ocean in the Western Hemisphere.

Today, Spain once again finds immigrants attracted to the wealth and promises it has to offer as people from underdeveloped areas such as Eastern Europe, Africa, and Latin America enter Spain (often called the *antesala a Europa* or "Europe's vestibule"). Often isolated from the political, economic, and cultural phenomena of other European countries, Spain now shares, for better or for worse, issues like immigration and confronts tensions common to developed countries of the modern world.

RELIGION

For nearly 800 years, Christians, Jews, and Muslims lived together peacefully in what is called *convivencia*. With the victory of the *reconquista*, the Christian holy war to regain the peninsula from the Moors, and the expulsion of the Jews and Muslims, Spain entered a new era of religious orthodoxy and conservative adherence to traditional Catholic values. With the infamous Inquisition (1478–1834), Spain sought to purge difference by rooting out heretics and non-Catholics. Likewise, the *conquista* in the New World was seen in the sixteenth century not only as an opportunity to extend the Spanish Empire by conquering land but as a way to fortify Catholicism by converting souls. Also, when Northern European countries felt the ripples of change as Protestantism swept through **Germany**, **The Netherlands**, and **England**, Spain resisted and became the leader for the Counter-Reformation.

Nevertheless, counter to the strict adherence to orthodox Catholic beliefs, Spain has a long history of mysticism and asceticism. Over 3,000 mystical works were written in Spain in the sixteenth century alone. Three major mystic writers were Teresa de Ávila (1512–1582), San Juan de la Cruz (1542–1591), and Fray Luis de Granada (1504–1588). In painting, the elongated, ethereal figures of El Greco likewise suggest a heterodoxical spirituality in the face of strict fanaticism, on the one hand, and a growing belief in secular humanism, on the other.

The tension between orthodoxy and heterodoxy acquired a new dimension as Spain slowly emerged from the Dark Ages and began to embrace the scientific attitude and secular beliefs espoused by Renaissance thinkers. The conflict between tradition and modernity in Spain has always had religion as a primary component. In the Enlightenment, Spanish writers and thinkers such as Fray Benito Jerónimo Feijoo (ironically, a Benedictine monk) attempted to dismantle the perceived opposition between religion and science in order to "modernize" Spain by educating the masses and eliminating superstitious thought. In the twentieth century, fanaticism once again appeared in Spain with Francisco Franco's dictatorship, which, allied with the Catholic Church, sought to revive Spain's Catholic empire by systematically eliminating any ideological elements perceived to be non-Spanish. One curious exception to the oppositional conflict between orthodoxy and heterodoxy, tradition and modernity, religion and secularism in Spain is the Opus Dei. An organization affiliated with the Catholic Church, it maintains an air of secrecy and mystery and has resisted many of the modernizing trends brought by Vatican II in the 1960s. However, unlike religious orders—for example, the Jesuits—members of this group occupy many secular positions in corporations, on editorial staffs, as directors of banks, and as government officials in Spain and around the world.

Although Catholicism still pervades Spanish identity and appears in everyday phrases such as *como Dios manda* ("as God demands," to assert something done correctly) or *va a misa* ("It goes to Mass," to certify something's validity), popular forms of belief often subvert or oppose traditional Catholic dogma. Swearing often acquires a tone of blasphemy as Spaniards often invoke scatological acts directed toward God, Jesus (including the crucifix), and the Virgin Mary. Furthermore, superstitions and pagan festivals retain a place in Spanish culture today. In such regions as Galicia, healers and witches (known as *meigas*) are common parts of daily life. In the summer, St. John's Day (*El día de San Juan*) celebrates a Catholic saint with bonfires and pagan rituals on the beach designed to harness the power associated with the summer solstice. Even traditional Catholic practices such as pilgrimages (also known as *romerías*), in which believers walk long distances to pay homage to a town's saint or the Virgin Mary, seem to forgo any strict adherence to official dogma. The most famous pilgrimage is the *Camino de Santiago* (St. James's Way), a 1,000-year-old trail that leads from France, across the Pyrenees Mountains, to the Cathedral in Santiago de Compostela. There pilgrims pay homage to the mythic Santiago, St. James, the Moorslayer. Spain's special brand of Catholicism is most evident during Holy Week, when hooded penitents walk barefoot in chains carrying an altar with their specific parish's statue of the Virgin Mary while onlookers yell "*Guapa!*" (Gorgeous!) to her.

MYTHS, POEMS, AND FOLKTALES

The *convivencia* of Jews, Christians, and Muslims in Spain planted the seeds for Spanish literature through an oral tradition that mirrored other kinds of cross-cultural influences from the era. The origins of Spain's literature are most commonly associated with *jarchas*, a lyric poem only a few lines long written in a mixture of Arabic and Hebrew called *mozárabe*. From the tenth century, these poems often concluded a larger text known as a *moaxaja* and told the story of a forlorn woman seeking advice from her mother while lamenting the absence of her lover, or *habib*. Later in the Middle Ages, similar themes of love and absence could be found in other lyric poems called *villancicos*. Another important part of Spain's oral tradition from the Middle Ages are the *romances* (ballads), which are forms of popular literature that entertained common folk. There were many types of *romances*, and they dealt with themes of love, historic figures and battles, allegories and fables, the Bible, and *fronterizo* (border) stories with Arab characters.

Rodrigo Díaz de Vivar, legendary Spanish figure. The poem "*Cantar de Mío Cid*" (The Song of My Cid) recounts the actions of Rodrigo Díaz de Vivar (El Cid) during his battles with both Arabs and Christians. (General Research Division, The New York Public Library, Astor, Lenox and Tilden Foundations)

With the Christian reconquest of Spain arose a Castillian oral tradition in which a *trovador* (troubador), also known as a *juglar*, would travel the country singing poems. Such poems were of one of two types: a *mester de juglaría* or a *mester de clerecía*. In the former, poets would recite popular anonymous poems about love or, more commonly, heroic adventures of legendary Spanish figures such as El Cid. The poem "*Cantar de Mío Cid*" (The Song of My Cid) represents a *cantar de gesta*, an epic influenced by the French *chanson de geste* that recounts the actions Rodrigo Díaz de Vivar during his battles with both Arabs and Christians. El Cid, a name of respect given to Díaz de Vivar by his Arab combatants, means "the Lord" and indicates the fear he instilled in his enemies. The poem depicts Cid, a historical figure, as a faithful Christian, loyal servant to king and country, dutiful husband and father, and vengeful enemy when wronged.

Mester de clerecía, on the other hand, focused on religious themes and imitated literary styles imported from **Italy**, namely, *cuaderna vía*. *Cuaderna vía* was composed of stanzas of four lines characterized by consonant rhyme, each containing fourteen syllables. Presenting a didactic message, the language combined formal and informal styles to address varying levels of education in its audience. The first well-known poet in this style is Gonzalo de Berceo, who wrote *Los milagros de Nuestra Señora* (Miracles of Our Lady), which describes different experiences individuals have with the Virgin Mary leading to their subsequent conversion to Christianity.

Myths that continue to influence and inform Spanish identity today speak of figures that represented social sectors and cultural archetypes while emulating some traditional Spanish value. The Celestina acquired her mythic status through Fernando de Rojas's tragicomedy *La Celestina* (1499), which became a centerpiece in Spanish literature. She acted as a *trotaconventos* (matchmaker) paid by a man to help him subvert a woman's resistance. Referred to in the work as the *vieja barbuda* (the whiskered old lady), she represents a Spain in transition from the theocratic feudalism of the Middle Ages to the mercantile Renaissance. Similarly, Don Quijote represents a singularly Spanish figure who embodies an era in transition and captures the essence of Spanish culture. Miguel de Cervantes's two volumes of *El Ingenioso Hidalgo Don Quixote de la Mancha* (1605, 1615) trace the adventures of the *caballero andante* (traveling knight) as he tries to make sense of a broken world by imposing the lessons he had learned from *novelas de caballería* (knightly novels). What starts as a parody of several literary styles from the seventeenth century ends as an enduring investigation of the truths of human existence and an exploration of the power of imagination. Lastly, Don Juan, perhaps the most recognizable Spanish archetype (now a stereotype), became famous through such plays as Tirso de Molina's *El burlador de Sevilla*, José de Zorilla's *Don Juan Tenorio*, and Mozart's *Don Giovanni*. Nevertheless, Don Juan's origins lie in a folk narrative called "*El convidado de piedra*" (The Stone Guest). In it a young womanizer, addressing a statue in a mausoleum, invites his lover's dead father for dinner. The "don Juan" figure most commonly identified is that of Zorilla, whose soul is saved through the love of the virginal doña Inés.

SONGS AND MUSIC

The most widely recognized song associated with Spain is the *cante jondo* or *flamenco*. A part of Spain's Romani culture, this music embodies the cultural fusion of Arabic, Indian, and European sounds into a uniquely Spanish rhythm. Literally meaning "deep song," the *cante jondo* combines guitar, male or female voice, and the staccato percussion of a dancer's heels with steady clapping to create a music of pain, despair, and lament. Such singers as Tomasito and Rosario Flores and groups like Azúcar Moreno, Ketama, and Ojos de Brujo combine these traditional flamenco elements with other types of music—rumba, rap, rock, and jazz—in what is known as "fusion flamenco."

Spain's traditional popular songs include the *copla* (cabaret song) and the *zarzuela* (theatrical song), while traditional instrumental music consists of the *tuna* and the *pasodoble*. Popularized in the first half of the twentieth century, early versions of the *copla* contained very provocative, erotic lyrics. But with the censorship of the Franco dictatorship in 1939, *coplas* became a means to express what were considered to be traditional Spanish values and what the regime considered to be essentially "Spanish." The *zarzuela*'s origins date back to the seventeenth century, but it became a highly popular form of song and performance in the late nineteenth century and into the twentieth century. A spectacle of music, song, and dance, the *zarzuela* is a type of Spanish operetta that presents scenes and situations from what is considered typically Spanish everyday life. Like the *copla*, the *zarzuela* became a means to articulate traditional Spanish values and express a sense of nationalistic pride during the Franco dictatorship. The *tuna* and the *pasodoble* do not include lyrics but are entirely instrumental compositions. *Tunas* are remnants of the roving bands of troubadors, usually students, who would wander the streets in the Middle Ages, offering songs. Finally, the *pasodoble* is a march usually associated with bullfights, but the term also refers to a type of music connected to a traditional dance for couples.

In the late 1960s, as foreign popular music infiltrated Spain and the seeds for mass media culture were planted, a series of protest singers, known in Spanish as *cantautores*, emulated the social messages of singers such as Bob Dylan. Spanish singers and songwriters like Ana Belén, Lluis Llach, and Joan Manuel Serrat used their music to denounce oppression, poverty, censorship, and injustice. In the 1970s Julio Iglesias, Miguel Bosé, Raphael, and the Duo Dinámico offered love ballads typically known as *canción ligera* or "light songs." In the early 1980s, the music scene (as well as other aspects of popular culture like film, fashion, and design) exploded with the *movida* in Madrid. Groups such as El gabinete Caligari, Los hombres G, Mecano, and Duncan Dhu combined marketing, performance, and style to revitalize Spain's music and culture scene.

DRAMA AND THEATER

The height of Spain's production of drama and theater occurred in the seventeenth century during a period of decadence in the Spanish Empire. In this period the predominant literary style was the baroque, which in theater manifested itself in the *comedia*. A uniquely Spanish theatrical form, the *comedia* presents a highly structured plot with little or no character development. Rather, characters represent archetypes, including the invention of the *gracioso* (comic character), who would provide moments of levity and comic relief, and their struggles articulate specific preoccupations plaguing Spanish society at that time. Specifically, these works focus on the traditional Spanish value of honor and its preservation.

Another Spanish theatrical invention is the *esperpento*, created by Ramón del Valle-Inclán in the 1920s with the work *Luces de bohemia*. In this play, Max Estrella wanders from café to café encountering all manners of deformities and distortions, revealing society's own degradation. During the dictatorship, such dramatists as Antonio Buero Vallejo, known for *Historia de una escalera*, and Alonso Sastre, author of *Escuadra hacia la muerte*, wrote social plays while fighting censorship. After the dictatorship, the elimination of censorship opened the way for performance groups like *Els Comediants* and *Els Joglars*, which, through a mixture of dance and body movement, presented non-linear, non-narrative forms of drama that brought into Spain the idea of post-modern theater.

DANCE

Dance in Spain varies according to region and often embodies a source of pride for individuals in that area. The *jota* is typical of Aragón, the *muneira* of Galicia, the *sardana* of Cataluña, and the *fandango* of Andalucía. Many dances accompany a specific type of music. The *pasodoble* describes both song and its dance, the *sevillana* accompanies *seguidillas*, and *flamenco*, perhaps the most famous dance associated with Spain, is both song and dance. The *flamenco* as dance usually occurs on a wooden stage called a *tablao* but can take place anywhere: concert halls, patios, or parks. Like the musical *fusión flamenca*, the dance style has undergone a revitalization in recent years with dancer-choreographer Joaquín Cortez's innovations. More traditional male flamenco dancers include Antonio Canales and the late Antonio Gades.

SPORTS AND GAMES

Bullfighting and football are the sports most widely practiced and followed in Spain today. The art of bullfighting (*tauromaquia*) likely began in some form around 711 C.E. Many artists and writers, for example, Francisco Goya, Federico García Lorca, and Ernest Hemingway, have painted or written about the bullfight (*corrida de toros*). Some view the bloody spectacle as a symbolic representation of human degradation and the struggle against death. Others have interpreted the bullfight as an explicit expression that flaunts the overt sexuality stereotypically associated with the Spanish male. Today, this sport is a source of controversy in which a dwindling number of supporters see bullfighting as a cultural symbol associated with a unique Spanish identity that deserves to be preserved. Many, however, feel the sport is a grotesque survival of humankind's brutality toward animals, and they advocate the elimination of what they consider a barbaric practice.

A bullfight in Barcelona, Spain. Today, bullfighting is a source of controversy in which a dwindling number of supporters see it as a cultural symbol associated with a unique Spanish identity that deserves to be preserved. (Courtesy Library of Congress)

The practice of bullfighting involves a *torero* (bullfighter) or *matador* (bull killer), the latter appearing only during the last stage of the bullfight. Each *corrida de toros* involves three bullfighters and six bulls known as *toros bravos*, a special breed specifically designed for the *corridas*. Each individual bullfight is broken down into three stages. First, the bulls face the *picadores*, who sit on horses and stab the bull with a lancelike weapon to weaken the bull. Then, the *banderilleros* attack the bull on foot, carefully timing their approach to the bull to stab long barbed darts into the bull's back. Lastly, the main bullfight takes place as the *torero* taunts the bull and steps aside as it charges. The bullfight ends when the *torero* makes one final pass at the bull and stabs it through the heart, killing it instantly. Only in very special circumstances when the bull has proven especially brave is the animal saved and put out to stud so his offspring may be part of a future *corrida*. The *toreros* are lauded for their bravery and become as famous as rock stars, sometimes passing into legend. Some of the most famous *toreros* are Manolete, Ignacio Sánchez Mejías (immortalized in a Lorca poem), and El Cordobés.

Whereas *tauromaquia* is seen by some as part of a traditional, authentic Spanish cultural identity, *fútbol* (soccer) is part of a mass media, consumer culture entertainment industry whose appeal stretches across geography, race, and social class. The teams that dominate the Spanish league are the Real Madrid, Barcelona FC, and the Atlético de Madrid. Soccer in Spain has become the arena in which strong sentiments of regionalism, manifested particularly during the championship tournament *Copa del Rey* (King's Cup), and nationalism are on display, especially during the European and World Cups. Spatial referents important in Spanish soccer are the stadiums Santiago Bernabeu, where the Real Madrid plays, and Nou Camp, where Barcelona FC plays. Currently, David Beckham is the highest paid soccer player in the world and plays for the Real Madrid alongside the legendary players Ronaldo, from Brazil; Figo, from Portugal; and the current team captain Raul González Blanco, from Spain.

ARTS, CRAFTS, AND ARCHITECTURE

Spanish artists—El Greco, Diego Velázquez, Francisco Goya, Salvador Dalí, and Picasso, among others—have produced works that have touched on universal values and have gained international recognition. Based in Toledo during the sixteenth century and known in **Greece** as Domenikos Theotokopoulos, El Greco exhibited a mystical style through his elongated, yet muscular, human figures, who were often portrayed with an ethereal light. Diego Velázquez, a court painter for Phillip IV, articulated the complexities of the baroque world and redefined art with his famous painting *Las meninas* (1656), in which the painter included himself. Goya, often referred to as the father of modern art, began his career as a court painter for Carlos IV, dedicating himself to portraits of nobility and their leisurely habits. Nevertheless, such paintings as *3 de Mayo* (1808) and *Saturno devorando a su hijo* (1821–1823) show scenes of brutality, war, and destruction with a sense of social protest. Salvador Dalí and Picasso are perhaps the two most famous Spanish painters of the twentieth century. Dalí, a surrealist, portrays fantastic scenes that attempt to break the limits of reality and incorporate the fragmented, intuitive logic of dreams. Picasso, founder of cubist painting, is most widely known for his painting *Guernica* (1937), whose fragmented, distorted forms decry the destruction of a civilian population bombed by German pilots during the Spanish civil war, transforming it, likewise, into the most powerful anti-war art ever made.

Architecture in Spain exemplifies many different styles and serves as remnants that embody and symbolize past eras and the values they espoused. Along the coast, one can still see Roman towers that served as outposts watching for enemy ships. Similarly, city centers such as Ávila maintain the Roman wall that once protected the city from invaders. In cities such as Toledo and especially in the Andalucian cities of Granada and Córdoba, Arabic-style buildings with keyhole entrances, colorful tiles, and refreshing fountains dominate the cultural scene. Imposing classical architecture can be seen in the straight lines and immense stature of El Escorial, designed by Juan Herrera, whereas the ornate decoration and design are visible in facades like the ones at the University of Salamanca and the University of Alcalá.

In Barcelona, the uniquely Catalán style of *modernisme* is apparent in the many buildings and parks designed by Antonio Gaudí at the beginning of the twentieth century. Perhaps Gaudí's most famous construction is the unfinished Sagrada Familia Cathedral, in which the architect integrated organic forms and resisted the straight lines associated with other kinds of modernist architecture. Since the death of Franco, Spain has seen a boom in urban design heralded by such architects as Rafael Moneo, Oriol Bohigas, and Santiago Calatrava. Buildings such as the Torre Picasso of Madrid, the Torre Mapfre of Barcelona, and the Guggenheim Museum of Bilbao reveal attempts to construct a more modern Spanish identity that imitates important European and American urban models.

In cities such as Granada, Arabic-style buildings with keyhole entrances, colorful tiles, and refreshing fountains dominate the cultural scene. (Courtesy Library of Congress)

Crafts in Spain include a wide range of materials—wood, metal, leather, tile, and glass—but perhaps the best known is the pottery from Talavera. Likewise, porcelain produced by Lladró has acquired international recognition. Inlaid wood and metalworking are most typically associated with Toledo, famous for its Damascan style.

CHALLENGES OF THE MODERN WORLD

Since the death of Francisco Franco in 1975, Spanish society has undergone tumultuous changes that have modernized the economic and technological infrastructure. Certain tensions have arisen between the values of Spanish post-modern consumer society and the traditional ideas considered to be typically Spanish. With the dictator's death, Spain quickly embraced democracy and eliminated censorship, while at the same time advancing rights for women, homosexuals, and other minorities.

Nevertheless, with an open, pluralistic, and democratic society, Spain now contends with problems that were before unknown or, at the least, unseen. Such problems common to other developed countries as delinquency, prostitution, drugs, and illegal immigration now also plague Spain. Moreover, issues such as Basque separatist terrorism and simply the diverse cultural identities that compose Spanish society prove contrary to the idea of a unified, national Spanish character.

Combined with these internal pressures, external infiltration of multi-national corporate identities combined with Spain's eager desire for a European identity have polemicized the idea of a pure Spanish identity. Visible icons such as McDonald's and Kentucky Fried Chicken appear in the plazas alongside typical Spanish cafés challenging them for the space of representation. Similarly, industries of cultural production—film, press, and television—are being bought by foreign businessmen (as in the case of Rupert Murdoch's ownership of Sogecable), making the notion of authenticity obsolete. Ironically, however, Spain has become an active player in a global consumer economy, and such Spanish banks as Banco Bilbao Vizcaya and Banco Santander as well as Spanish communications conglomerates like Telefónica are being exported throughout the world, especially to Latin America, where the effect on cultural production is similar to that in Spain.

BIBLIOGRAPHY

Barton, Simon. 2004. *A History of Spain*. New York: Palgrave.

Cowans, Jon, ed. 2003. *Modern Spain: A Documentary History*. Philadelphia: University of Pennsylvania Press.

Da Costa Fontes, Manuel. 2000. *Folklore and Literature: Studies in the Portuguese, Brazilian, Sephardic, and Hispanic Oral Traditions*. Albany: State University of New York Press.

Davies, Catherine, ed. 2002. *The Companion to Hispanic Studies*. London: Arnold.

Douglass, Carrie B. 1997. *Bulls, Bullfighting, and Spanish Identities*. Tucson: University of Arizona Press.

Gies, David T., ed. 1999. *The Cambridge Companion to Modern Spanish Culture*. Cambridge: Cambridge University Press.

Graham, Helen, and Jo Labanyi, eds. 1996. *Spanish Cultural Studies: An Introduction*. New York: Oxford University Press.

Hooper, John. 1986. *The New Spaniards*. London: Penguin.

Jordan, Barry. 2002. *Spanish Culture and Society: The Essential Glossary*. London: Arnold.

Jordan, Barry, and Rikki Morgan-Tamosunas. 2000. *Contemporary Spanish Cultural Studies*. London: Arnold.

Labanyi, Jo. 2002. *Constructing Identity in Contemporary Spain: Theoretical Debates and Cultural Practice*. Oxford: Oxford University Press.

Muñoz, Pedro M., and Marcelino C. Marcos. 2005. *España Ayer y Hoy*. Upper Saddle River, NJ: Prentice Hall.

Pereira-Muro, Carmen. 2003. *Culturas de España*. Boston: Houghton Mifflin.

Quesada Marco, Sebastián. 1987. *Curso de civilización española*. Boston: Houghton Mifflin.

Rodgers, Eamonn, ed. 1999. *Encyclopedia of Contemporary Spanish Culture*. London: Routledge.

Ross, Christopher J. 1997. *Contemporary Spain: A Handbook*. London: Arnold.

Sánchez-Romeralo, Antonio, and Fernando Ibarra, eds. 1972. *Antología de Autores Españoles Antiguos y Modernos I*. Englewood Cliffs, NJ: Prentice-Hall.

Spence, Lewis. 1985. *Spain: Myths and Legends*. New York: Avenel Books.

Stanton, Edward F. 1999. *Handbook of Spanish Popular Culture.* Westport, CT: Greenwood Press.

———. 2002. *Culture and Customs of Spain.* Westport, CT: Greenwood Press.

Ugarte, Michael, and Kathleen McNerney. 1999. *España y su civilización.* 5th edition. Boston: McGraw-Hill College.

Vincent, Mary, and R. A. Stradling. 1994. *Cultural Atlas of Spain and Portugal.* Oxford: Andromeda Oxford.

William J. Nichols

BASQUE

GEOGRAPHY AND HISTORY

The Basque Country is called Euskal Herria in Euskara, the language of the Basques. Part of the Basque Country lies in southern **France**, but most is found in northern **Spain**. The historical names of the seven provinces of the Basque Country are still used today: Lapurdi, Nafarroa Beherea, and Zuberoa in France; Araba, Bizkaia, Gipuzkoa, and Nafarroa in Spain. However, today the region is often referred to by other names. The provinces on the French side are called Iparralde (the north side), and the area in Spain is divided into two autonomous communities (similar to American "states"), one formed by Nafarroa and the other made up of Araba, Bizkaia, and Gipuzkoa. No matter what the region is called, it is known for its beautiful beaches, steep mountains, green valleys, and, farther inland, its golden plains. The climate is very damp, allowing for dry farming—that is, farming without irrigation.

Today the Basque communities in Spain are famous for industry (steel in the twentieth century, advanced technology in the twenty-first), and the idyllic landscape of Iparralde draws many tourists. But as little as a century ago, the majority of Basques made a living by farming or fishing. Many of the characters of Basque folklore are tied to those occupations. Basques today are very involved in their local politics and in the politics of the European Union, and yet Basque identity still draws much from the agricultural and maritime traditions of the region's past.

During the nineteenth century, many young Basque men migrated to the Western Hemisphere to find work and start new lives. Some of them came to North America around the time of the California gold rush in 1849 but soon learned that it was easier to earn a living by selling meat and wool to the miners than it was actually to be a miner. Thus began the decades-long history of Basques coming to the western United States to work with sheep. The most prominent aspect of their European heritage preserved among these Basque-Americans is the tradition of dance.

In the Basque Country, traditions have been shaped by the late arrival of Christianity (around the tenth century) and subsequently by the Catholic Church as well as by the Basque desire to hang on to their old ways and customs, even while surviving and thriving in the modern world. In the nineteenth century the Basques fought two wars, called the Carlist Wars, in an attempt to protect the old laws under which their ancestors had lived for centuries. Even though they lost those wars and the privileges associated with the old laws, modern Basques are still aware of them and keep their memory alive through their traditions. In the early twentieth century, the Spanish civil war (1936–1939) pitted many Basques against the forces of Francisco

Franco, who wanted to eliminate ethnic diversity and local languages in Spain in order to create a nation of Spaniards. Franco won that war, and during his long dictatorship (1939–1975) the Basques worked secretly to preserve their unique language. Euskara forms its own language family, and except for some borrowed words, it is not related to Spanish or any other Indo-European language.

THEATER AND OTHER ORAL ART FORMS

The struggle to save the language contributed significantly to the preservation of oral arts within Basque culture. One such art is the *pastorale*, a form of theater traditionally performed by amateurs from different villages in Iparralde who would learn the rhyming lines of the play by listening to others sing the parts. Many stylized characters appear in the traditional *pastorales*, and different colors represent the Moors and the Christians, for example. The Devil often plays a role and dances frantically across the stage when he appears. The *pastorales* are full of music, dance, and song. Modern *pastorales* are being created, using recent history for subject matter, but the performances are still held outdoors and are still preceded by a colorful parade. Today sound systems and microphones are also a part of the performance.

Bertsolaritza is the most famous Basque oral art form. It is prominent throughout the Basque Country but particularly promoted and organized in the provinces of Araba, Bizkaia, and Gipuzkoa. The *bertsolari*, a performer of this art form, is sometimes called a Basque troubadour, although the troubadours of other cultures do not necessarily do the same thing as the *bertsolari*. These artists create rhyming verses about a topic that is presented to them on the spot and then sing the verses a cappella before an audience, using a melody that has also been assigned. Most often today (but not always), these performances are organized as competitions in which *bertsolaris* attempt to outwit each other while creating the strongest possible verses according to the judgment of a panel of experts. These competitions are extremely popular and draw large crowds. They are also often broadcast on radio and television.

MYTHS, LEGENDS, AND FOLKTALES

Another positive result of efforts to save the language has been a renewed interest by scholars in the preservation of the old folktales and myths handed down for centuries in Euskara. The most common characters in Basque folklore are Mari, known by many names, including Anbotoko Anderea; Laminak (lamia); Sorginak (witches); Basajauna (lord of the forest); and Jentilak (wild men). Folklorists such as Caro Baroja are eager to discuss the existence of Mari the goddess, especially her powers as Queen of the Spirit World, holding her up as the reason for, and foundation of, a matriarchal aura that pervades Basque society. However, upon close examination it appears that Mari has been demoted several times down through the ages, though folklorists avoid talking in such terms. Other female characters in the mythic pantheon are discussed as contemporaneous with Mari, but external influences can easily be identified both in the *lamina* (with physical attributes reminiscent of the Greek lamia) and in the *sorgina* (the witch), who has been present in folklore and history in many parts of the world. It becomes apparent after examining the characteristics of the Basque *lamina* and *sorgina* that each one contains some of Mari, but in a diminished state.

Mari is one of the most ancient names of a feminine spirit who is generally thought to be capable of many of the functions attributed to diverse deities or spirits in the Basque Country. She is the leader of all the other spirits. In some parts of the Basque Country, Mari means "lady" and is used in conjunction with the name of the mountain or cave where she is thought to appear. Thus, we have a long list of names for Mari, including

Mari Muruko (in Elduayen)

Mariburute (in Udabe, Nafarroa)

Aldureko Mari (in Gorriti)

Marie Labako (in Ispaster)

Marije Kobako (in Markina)

Marimur (in Leiza)

Mariurraka (in Abadiano)

Mariburrika (in Garay and in Berriz)

Puyako Maya (in Oyarzun)

Andre Mari Muiroko (in Arano)

Muruko Damea (in Ataun)

Aralarko Damea (in Amezqueta)

Anbotoko Dama (in Zarauz)

Amuteko Damie (in Azcoitia)

Anbotoko Sorgina (in Durango)

The name Mari may be related to the words *mairi*, *maide*, and *maindi*, used to designate other legendary characters in Basque mythology, though the stories tied to these characters are different. The *mairi* were builders of dolmens. The *maide* are masculine spirits of the mountains who supposedly built the cromlechs (megalithic tombs) that dot the Basque landscape. Their feminine counterparts are the *laminak* or spirits of the fountains, rivers, and caves. The *maindi* may have been the souls of ancestors who visited their ancient homes at night.

According to legend, Mari is female. She appears in various shapes and forms, depending on the location:

a woman with the feet of a bird (Garagarza)

a lady seated on a cart crossing the sky pulled by four horses (Amezgueta)

the figure of a woman giving off flames (Zaldivia)

a lady mounted on a ram (Oñate and Cegama)

a woman whose head is encircled by a full moon (Azcoitia)

a half moon giving off flames (Escoriaza)

a white cloud (Durango, Ispaster)

a rainbow (Cerain)

a ball of fire (Oñate, Segura, Orozco)

a scythe of flame crossing the heavens (Ataun, Cegama, Zuazo de Gamboa)

The figures of animals such as the bull, ram, male goat, horse, serpent, and vulture represent Mari and her subordinates, the terrestrial spirits or forces who do her work in the world. Her usual dwelling place is inside the earth. Since the interior of the earth is connected to the surface by various means—caves, caverns, abysses—Mari makes appearances in these places much more often than in others.

It is generally believed that gold and precious stones richly adorn her dwellings. Often she is described as holding a gold comb, and stories tell of objects taken from her caves that turn into gold when the thief exits or, conversely, golden objects that turn into wood or stone upon leaving.

According to legend, Mari changes her dwelling from time to time, spending seven years in caves at various sites in the Basque Country such as Anboto, Oiz, Mugarra, Aralar, Aizkorri, and Murumendi.

In many Basque myths Mari is considered to be the queen of all the spirits that populate the world. Many of her characteristics are also attributed to the *laminak*, but differences between them support the theory that Mari pre-dates the *laminak* and that she was originally a more powerful being.

Laminak were thought by some to be like mermaids, having a woman's body from the waist up and a fish's body from the waist down. Others say their whole body is that of a woman except for the feet, which are often the feet of a duck, chicken, or some other bird. The concept of the *lamina* has changed from century to century.

The majority of legends about these spirits present them as female, but in Lapurdi and Nafarroa Beherea both genders are represented. In Zuberoa, they are called *lamina* or *maide*, depending on whether they are female or male.

In Lapurdi some people say *laminak* are little people who live underground. The tale told about the lamias of the Bazterretxea farm—reported by Jose Miguel Barandirán—would also suggest that they are small in stature.

Those who lived on the Bazterretxea farm used to leave a bowl of milk and pieces of toasted corn bread and bacon sprinkled with grease from a frying pan on one corner of the hearth every night before they went to bed. While everyone was sleeping, the lamias would slide down the chimney and have a party with the leftovers. Then, in greatest secrecy, they would disappear again up the chimney. The next day the Bazterretxea family would find the manure spread, the ditches cleaned, the fields plowed, and the cornfields weeded.

But one night the family forgot to leave the pieces of bacon and the crusts of corn bread on the corner of the hearth. After that, the resentful lamias moved to another neighborhood far away and never appeared again at Bazterretxea.

Today *laminak* are spoken of as imaginary beings from another time. However, when asked about the existence of such beings, clever Basques may respond, "Everything that has a name exists." Another phrase one often hears about the characters of Basque folklore is "One should not believe that they exist, but one should not say that they don't."

Laminak are famous for spinning, building dolmens, and constructing bridges. Like Mari, it is said that the *laminak* live off "no." For example, if a worker has twenty bushels of wheat but declares that he has only sixteen, the four bushels he does not declare are taken by the *laminak*. Both Mari and the *laminak* are reported to have been seen combing their hair with a gold comb.

Sorginak (witches) appeared in many cultures, but in the Basque Country many still feel their presence, and their influence is not considered entirely negative. A huge cavern near Sara, France, called Zagarramurdi is where witches were believed to have danced and held covens and festivals known as *akelarreak* long after the Basque Country was Christianized in the tenth century.

Basajaunak looked like men but were much bigger and taller than men were. They had incredible strength and were very energetic. They also had hair all over their bodies. They lived in the woods, and they worked the land for a living. They were very knowledgeable about these matters, and some Basques say that *basajaunak* taught humans how to make charcoal and how to forge iron. Often *basajauna* is spoken of in the singular, as if only one existed. According to legend, when the sheep bells ring in a flock, a *basajauna* is nearby. In some parts of the Basque Country people also talk of *basa anderea*, the lady of the forest, who is believed to be the daughter of the *basajauna*.

Jentilak were also big men with amazing strength, but they were not as hairy as the *basajaunak*. They had voices like a lion's roar or like thunder. All the animals ran from them in fear. Their bodies were very, very big, and the ground shook whenever they walked on it.

Today, of course, people do not report seeing the *laminak*, the *basajaunak*, and other spirits as often as they once did. Many claim that the presence of Christianity has driven these helpful spirits out of Basque Country. But some people still report seeing Mari fly from one mountain to another on a bolt of lightning.

MUSIC AND DANCE

For Basques and their descendants outside Basque Country, folklore is passed on less through legends and fables and more through music and dance. In the United States, the North American Basque Organizations, Inc. (NABO) sponsors music camps where children can learn to play instruments, sing songs, and study folk dances from Basque culture.

Three of the most interesting musical instruments associated with Basque culture are the *txistu*, the *ttun-ttun*, and the *txalaparta*. The *txistu* is a three-holed vertical flute

A dance troupe performs at the Boise Basque Festival. (© Larry Mangino/The Image Works)

played with one hand. The other hand is often playing the *ttun-ttun*, a drum worn on a strap over the shoulder. The *txistu* is the most popular Basque instrument, and American Basques learn to play it at NABO-sponsored annual music camps. The *txalaparta* consists of a board supported by chairs or benches on either end. Two players strike the board with four sticks, creating rhythms and tones that are remarkably musical and pleasant. Visiting players from Basque Country have inspired a growing interest in this instrument in Basque-American communities.

Almost every Basque club in the United States sponsors a dance troupe, and some have separate groups for different ages. The number of Basque dances performed by these groups is much too long to discuss here, but some of the more popular dances sport names such as *ezpata dantza* (sword dance) and *sagar dantza* (apple dance). A visit to the NABO Web site (www.basqueclubs.com) will provide a wealth of information on Basque dances and other aspects of Basque folk culture that are supported and maintained outside the Basque Country.

SPORTS AND GAMES

The two Basque games most widely known are *pelota* and *mus*. *Pelota* is an early form of handball that evolved into the highly popular jai alai, a game played on a court with a small ball and long baskets worn on the hand. *Mus* is a card game played with a deck that resembles tarot cards. The object of the game is to win by bluffing your opponents into believing you have a stronger hand than you actually do. Comparisons are often made between *mus* and poker.

STUDIES OF BASQUE FOLKLORE

Many of the principal works on Basque folklore are in Spanish (for example, Barandirán 1972; Caro Baroja 1985; Hornilla 1991; Urza 1994), but a few have been translated into English (for example, Barandirán 1991). Important English-language sources—some of which deal with Basque communities in the United States— include Gallop (1998), Henningsen (1980), and Totoricagüena (2002, 2004). The NABO Web site is the place to go for information on Basque dance, song, sports, language, cuisine, history, religion, and surnames as well as information on Basque Country in Europe and links to Basques around the world and to the Basque government.

BIBLIOGRAPHY

Barandirán, Jose Miguel. 1972. *Obras completas.* Vol. 1. Bilbao: La Gran Encicilopedia Vasca.

———. 1991. A *View from the Witch's Cave*, translated by Linda White. Reno: University of Nevada Press.

Caro Baroja, Julio. 1985. *Mitos vascos y mitos sobre los vascos.* San Sebastián: Txertoa.

Diccionario Enciclopédico Vasco. 1972. Vols. 4, 15, and 22. San Sebastián: Auñamendi.

Gallop, Rodney. 1998 (1930). *A Book of the Basques.* Reno: University of Nevada Press.

Henningsen, Gustav. 1980. *The Witches' Advocate.* Reno: University of Nevada Press.

Hornilla, Txema. 1991. *Los heroes de la mitología vasco: Antropología y psicoanálisis.* Bilbao: Mensajero.

Totoricagüena, Gloria. 2002. *The Basques of Boise: Dreamers and Doers*. Series Urazandi. Vitoria-Gasteiz: Eusko Jaularitza.

————. 2004. *Identity, Culture, and Politics: Comparing the Basque Diaspora*. Reno: University of Nevada Press.

Urza, Carmelo. 1994. *Historia de la pelota vasca en las Americas*. Donostia: Elkar.

Linda White

CATALAN

GEOGRAPHY AND HISTORY

The Catalan linguistic and cultural area in the western Mediterranean, currently known as the Catalan Countries, is part of four states: **Spain** (Catalonia, the autonomous community of Valencia, the Balearic Islands, the Aragon Fringe, and the Carxe); Andorra; **France** (the Northern Catalonia in the department of the Eastern Pyrenees); and **Italy** (the city of Alguer in Sardinia). All this territory shares a common culture, the most visible part of which is its language, Catalan, with some 7.2 million speakers.

Interest in Catalan folklore arose in the middle of the nineteenth century as a result of Romanticism. The first folklorists were primarily concerned with verbal art. This trend, which considers folklore to be literature, began in 1853 with the publication of Manuel Milà i Fontanals's collection *Observaciones sobre la poesía popular con muestras de romances catalanes inéditos*. Subsequently, Francesc Maspons i Labrós, Jacint Verdaguer, Valeri Serra i Boldú, Pau Bertran i Bros, i Sebastià Farnés, and others continued to collect and publish mainly folktales (*rondalles* in Catalan), traditions, legends, riddles, and proverbs. In Majorca, the most important publications were the *Romancer popular de la terra catalana* (1893) by Marià Aguiló, the *Rondaies mallorquines d'en Jordi des Recó* (1936–1972) by Antoni M. Alcover, and *Die Balearen in Wort und Bild geschildert* (1869–1891) by Archduke Louis Salvador of Austria-Tuscany. In the other Balearic Islands, Andreu Ferrer Ginard, Josep Roure Torent, and Joan Castelló i Guasch made important folktale collections. In the community of Valencia, the first anthologies of folktales were collected by Francesc Martínez, and Adolf Salvà. Enric Valor then published his *Rondalles valencianes* (1950–1958), now a highly popular collection. In Northern Catalonia, the collection by Esteve Caseponce, *Contes vallespirenchs replegats per En Mir y Nontoquis* (1907), is one of the best known.

In the final third of the nineteenth century, folklore understood as literature was supplemented by another approach: folklore from the perspective of hiking. The founding in Barcelona of the Catalan Association of Scientific Hiking in 1876 and the Catalan Hiking Association in 1878, which merged in 1891 to form the Hiking Centre of Catalonia, encouraged the creation of other hiking organizations in Catalonia. One of the main objectives of these organizations was to collect folkloric and ethnographic material. These hiker-folklorists were interested in both oral and material folklore, and they encouraged local and regional studies. A leading representative of this trend was Cels Gomis. Hiking folklore evolved into academic folklore largely due to Rossend Serra i Pagès, who taught folklore at the School of Governesses in Barcelona (1901 to 1917) and in several hiking and cultural centers in the country.

Among the group projects in Catalonia in the first third of the twentieth century, two of the most important were the Ethnography and Folklore Archive of Catalonia (1915–1929), connected to the University of Barcelona, and the Popular Songs of Catalonia, an ambitious project to collect Catalan songs that began in 1922 and that has given rise to the most important unpublished documentary source in the Catalan countries.

The Spanish civil war (1936–1939) interrupted this activity, and in the post-war period research into Catalan folklore was maintained only due to the individual efforts of three self-taught folklorists: Aureli Capmany (1868–1954), Joan Amades (1890–1959), and Ramon Violant (1903–1956). Aureli Capmany made some particularly interesting studies of music, dance, and traditional festivals, the most important of which were *La dansa a Catalunya* (1930–1953) and the *Calendari de llegendes, costums i festes tradicionals catalanes* (1951). Joan Amades is the most prolific and internationally best-known folklorist. Among his most important works is *Folklore de Catalunya I: Rondallística* (1950), a book that surprised the folklorists Paul Delarue and Walter Anderson for the large number of tales that it contained and that was referenced in the second edition of Antti Aarne and Stith Thompson's catalog, *The Types of the Folktale* (1961). Other important works are *Folklore de Catalunya II: Cançoner* (1951), *Folklore de Catalunya III: Costums i Creences* (1969), and the *Costumari Català* (1950–1956). *El món de Joan Amades* was published in 1990 to mark the centenary of his birth. It contained a chronology of his activity as a folklorist and summarized all his bibliography. Ramon Violant had an overall concept of folklore that in time led him to ethnography. His main contribution was to the Pyrenean culture, which he described in the book *El Pirineo español* (1949). With Joan Amades, he was curator of the Museum of Popular Industries and Arts, founded in Barcelona in 1940 (now part of the Ethnological Museum of Barcelona).

In the latter half of the twentieth century, folklore recovered its academic base. The leading figures in this area were Josep Romeu i Figueras, author of the book *Materials i estudis de folklore* (1993), which brings together his main contributions to the study of Catalan folklore, and Josep Massot i Muntaner, who has recently inventoried and published up to thirteen volumes of materials of the popular songs of Catalonia. Among others, the following authors have written about the history of Catalan folklore: Llorenç Prats, Joan Prat, Josep M. Pujol, Josefina Roma, and Ramon Violant.

In the final decades of the twentieth century, activity was especially significant in the community of Valencia, the Carxe, the Aragon Fringe, and Andorra. In the community of Valencia, the leading figures are Joaquim González Caturla, Josep Bataller, Tomàs Escuder, Francesc Gascon, and Pepa Guardiola. In the Carxe, Ester Limorti and Artur Quintana published the first collection of folk narratives *El Carxe: Recull de literatura popular valenciana de Múrcia* (1998), which was transcribed from tape recordings. Similar studies were made in the Aragon Fringe by the researcher Carlos González Sanz and the team led by Artur Quintana, who published the anthologies *Lo Molinar* (1995–1996) and *Bllat Colrat* (1997). In Andorra, the project *Estudi Etnogràfic de les Valls d'Andorra* (1993–1995) gave rise to various ethnographic and folkloric publications in the collection "Ethnography Archive of Andorra."

Since the late 1970s, which brought the end of the Franco dictatorship and the return of autonomous institutions, people have been eager to highlight identifying elements of Catalan culture. The most visible aspect of these efforts has been the revival of traditional festivals. Museums of ethnography and folklore have also been created: for example, in Catalonia, the Ecomuseum in Valls d'Àneu, the Museum of Rural Life in Espluga de Francolí, and the Museum of Montsià; and in Andorra, the museums of family life, Casa d'Areny-Plandolit and Casa Rull, and the Farga.

FESTIVALS AND CELEBRATIONS

Four major cycles of festivals are important: Carnival, Easter week, Corpus Christi and local festivals, and Christmas. Various festivals take place as part of the Carnival cycle. The *Santantonades* are typical of several towns in the north of the community of Valencia, Majorca, and the southern areas of Catalonia, and they are held around 17 January, the feast of St. Anthony. The three central elements of the festival are the blessing of the animals, the construction and burning of the so-called cabin of St. Anthony, and the performance of a popular play with satirical verses about the life of the saint. In some towns and villages in the Pyrenees, plays featuring bears and hunters are performed during Carnival. They are known as the *Ball de l'ós* (The Dance of the Bear) or simply as the *Óssa* (The She-Bear) in some towns in Andorra. Most towns and cities hold an urban Carnival that has the following structure: the arrival of the Carnival King, Carnestoltes; the reading of a satirical sermon that criticizes events that have occurred during the year; dances and processions of floats; and the death and subsequent burial of King Carnestoltes.

The Easter cycle consists of a series of acts that revolve around the Passion and the death of Jesus Christ. Among the most popular are the processions in which the participants parade through various streets of the town carrying *passos* (small floats with sculptures representing scenes from the Passion) on their shoulders or on wheeled platforms. In Verges, several mysteries of the Passion are acted out during the procession, and the popular and fascinating Dance of Death is performed. Passion plays, staged in theaters, are highly characteristic of this cycle. Particularly important are the ones held in Esparraguera, Olesa de Montserrat, and Ulldecona.

The most popular feature of the Corpus Christi cycle and the local festivals is the *seguici popular* (popular retinue), consisting of a set of festive and theatrical characters that go back to the Feast of Corpus Christi, established by the Roman Catholic Church in the fourteenth century. Particularly important are the figures that represent

A *gegante*, a giant statue carried as a parade float, moves through a crowd during the Patum festival in Burgas, Spain. (© Owen Franken/CORBIS)

creatures from bestiaries of both real and mythical beings and the *gegantes* (giants) and *capgrossos* (big heads), which represent humans. These figures are extremely popular, and there are estimated to be almost 2,000 giants and 10,000 big heads in Catalonia alone. The popular plays known as the *balls parlats* (spoken dances) are based on satirical dialogues and are a feature of numerous towns in central Catalonia. In many towns in the Catalan Countries around Corpus Christi, it is customary to cover the streets with carpets of flowers, which the carts and other participants in the festival pass over. These festivals are known as *Enramades*. Among the most characteristic celebrations of this cycle are the Corpus or Patum in Berga, the Corpus in Valencia, and the festivals of the Moors and Christians (extremely popular throughout the community of Valencia).

The Christmas festivities are characterized by popular plays that focus on the birth of Jesus and how he is worshipped by the shepherds and the wise men. The most popular are *Els Pastorets* (with the shepherds as the main characters) and the *pessebres vivents* (stable scenes with real people who act out the birth of Christ in the open air). The *pessebre vivent* in Engordany in Andorra has the longest tradition. In Alguer and Majorca on Christmas Eve night the song of the Sibyl is performed in church. A character representing the sibyl Eritrea sings some verses about the signs of the final judgment and the advent of Christ. On Epiphany (6 January) a procession is held to celebrate the arrival of the Three Wise Men, who bear gifts for the children. This tradition is extremely popular in all the towns and villages throughout the Catalan Countries. One of the most popular traditions throughout the Catalan Countries takes place in the heart of the family on Christmas Eve: the *tió* (Yule log), a pre-Christian survival of a tree cult, produces sweets and toys for the children.

As well as these major cycles, some other festivals should be mentioned. The Assumption of the Virgin Mary is celebrated on 15 August in Elx in the community of Valencia, and the main event is a popular play that dates to the Middle Ages. The feast of St. George, celebrated on 23 April in many towns in the Catalan Countries, is of a highly secular nature. Street stalls sell books and roses, which people buy to give to their loved ones.

MUSIC AND DANCE

The festivities include building *castells* and dancing *sardanes*. *Castells* are human towers, some of which are extremely complex. They originated in the human constructions built at the end of some old popular dances. One of these dances still survives in Muixeranga d'Algemesí in the community of Valencia, and it closely resembles the human towers because of its circular construction. Other human constructions, in this case open ones such as the Moixiganga of Sitges or the Falcons of Vilafranca del Penedès in Catalonia, are also part of this tradition.

The *sardana* is a dance that originated in the north of Catalonia. It is one of a group of dances performed by dancers who hold hands in a line and move about in a winding motion. At the beginning of the twentieth century it spread throughout Catalonia and adopted its current form—that is, with the dancers standing in a circle.

Another dance that is very popular is the *jota*. The dancers stand in twos, one in front of the other, while they execute the steps. Other dances are not so widespread and are restricted to particular towns and festivities: for example, the *ball de bastons* (stick dance), in which the dancers jump and strike the sticks that the other dancers are holding, and the *ball de cintes* (ribbon dance), in which the dancers plait their ribbons around a central pole as they dance.

Music is also an essential part of any festival. Bands of musicians accompany the *seguici popular*, groups of *gralla* players mark the beginning of the process of constructing a human tower (the *gralla* is a popular wind instrument, similar to an oboe), *xarangues* (brass bands) accompany the Carnival processions, and the *cobla* (small orchestra) performs the music for the *sardana*. In some places the activity of *rondar* is still very much alive. It consists of the singer improvising to the music of a group made up mainly of wind instruments, but with some string or percussion instruments.

Calendar Customs

Many now-Christian festivals contain elements of previous traditions. The summer and winter solstices, for example, correspond to two dates on the Christian calendar: the feast of St. John and Christmas. Both these festivals are extremely popular throughout the Catalan Countries, and the dominant traditions are related to fire.

On St. John's night (23 June) it is customary to make bonfires in the street. In some towns in the Pyrenees, the festivity of the *falles* is one of the most traditional. In the small village of Isil, the *falles* (splintered pine logs with a wedge driven into one end so that the wood can dry out better) are prepared and then left for months in the mountains. On 23 June, just when it is beginning to get dark, some men from the village, the *fallaires*, come down from the mountain with a burning *falla* on their backs. When they get to the village, they pile all the *falles* together to make a bonfire.

At Christmas the custom of lighting bonfires used to be very popular, though nowadays it is preserved only in a few places. For example, the people of Bagà, in Catalonia, celebrate the *fia-faia*. They light the *faies* (bundles of grass known as *faiera*), which can be up to four meters high, and make a communal bonfire.

Fire is also a part of many other traditions and is often connected with the beasts of the *seguici popular* or particular festivals such as the Patum in Berga, which takes place at Corpus, or the *falles* (complex figures sculpted from paper, cardboard, and wood that are burnt in public) in Valencia on St. Joseph's Day (19 March). Recently, *correfocs* (fire running) has become very popular in many local festivals. Groups of people dressed up as devils run through the town holding large flares that spray out sparks and let off fireworks.

In many towns in the Catalan Countries, festivals with bulls are also very popular. There are several different types: the *bou cappllaçat* festival (where the bull is led by ropes tied to its horns), the running of the bulls in the street (or sometimes in a ring), and the *bou embolat* festival (where the animal has burning torches tied to its horns), which takes place at night.

Food

Over the years, traditional Catalan cuisine has consolidated various dishes associated with the festivals held in the different seasons because family meals are prepared from the products that are most readily available at the time. In the spring, eggs were traditionally plentiful, which accounts for the popular St. Joseph's *crema* (custard) and the Easter *mona* (a cake decorated with hard-boiled eggs and, in more modern times, with chocolate figures), which godparents give their godchildren on Easter Monday. The typical product of the summer festivals is sweet *coca* or savory *coca*, made from a pastry of eggs and flour garnished with various sorts of vegetables (onions and peppers) in the case of savory *coca* (also known as *coca de recapte*) or sugar, pine nuts, or custard in the case of sweet *coca*. St. John's *coca* is particularly popular. It is garnished with preserved fruit, custard, and pine nuts and eaten on St. John's night. The traditional event of the autumn festivals used to be slaughtering a pig near St. Martin's Day (11 November). After slaughtering the pig and preparing the sausages, people would gather to cook and eat the parts of the pig that could not be easily preserved. Another typical autumn festival has to do with paying homage to the dead and is held on 1 November: the *castanyada*. On this day, people eat roasted chestnuts and *panellets* (small, sweet cakes made of sugar and almonds and garnished with pine nuts). The winter festivals are characterized by Christmas fare, the traditional dishes being *escudella* or *carn d'olla* (the main ingredients of which are mush and products from the slaughter of the pig) and roast turkey. The traditional dessert is *torró* (made from almonds and honey). The best types of *torró* are considered to be Agramunt, Alacant, and Xixona. As well as the gastronomy that is associated with the festivals, open sandwiches of bread rubbed with tomato and cold meats, and *paella* (made of rice, vegetables, and meat) are extremely popular.

STUDIES OF CATALAN FOLKLORE

The richness of Catalan folklore and the will to collect and study it have led to the creation of several archives in the twentieth century that contain important unpublished resources. The Ethnography and Folklore Archive of Catalonia is housed at the Milà i Fontanals Library, and the Popular Songs of Catalonia is at the Center for the Promotion of Popular and Traditional Catalan Culture, both in Barcelona. Part of Rossend Serra i Pagès' collection can be found at the Municipal Historical Archive, also in Barcelona.

In 1993, the Catalan government created the Center for the Promotion of Popular and Traditional Catalan Culture and succeeded in channeling many projects for compiling, preserving, and disseminating Catalan folklore and ethnography. The institution has made specialized studies readily available through the *Revista d'Etnologia de Catalunya* (Catalan Journal of Ethnology). It also has a library, where part of Joan Amades's collection is housed, and an audio library. The Folklore Research Group of Osona, the "Carrutxa" Centre for Documentation on Popular Culture in Reus, the Ethnography Archive of Andorra, and Alguer's Archive of Traditions— all founded fairly recently—also have considerable resources. The Rovira i Virgili University in Tarragona has the following collections: the Ethnography Archive of Catalonia belonging to the Department of Anthropology, the Folklore Archive belonging to the Department of Catalan Studies, and the Vidal-Capmany collection, which contains documents from the folklorists Aureli Capmany and Sebastià Farnés.

As far as bibliographical tools are concerned, in 2003 Carme Oriol and Josep M.

Pujol published the *Índex tipològic de la rondalla catalana* (Index of Catalan Folktales), which was produced in accordance with the guidelines of Antti Aarne and Stith Thompson's international catalog of tale types (1961). One should also consult these Web sites: www.etnocat.org, www.sardanes.net, and rondalles.uib.es.

BIBLIOGRAPHY

Aarne, Antti, and Stith Thompson. 1961. *The Types of the Folktale*. Revised edition. Folklore Fellows Communication, No. 184.

Aguiló, Marià. 1893. *Romancer popular de la terra catalana*. Barcelona: Llibrería d'Alvar Verdaguer.

Alcover, Antoni M. 1936–1972. *Rondaies mallorquines d'en jordi des Recó*. 24 volumes. Ciutat de Mallorca: Moll.

Amades, Joan. 1950. *Folklore de Catalunya I: Rondallística*. Barcelona: Selecta.

———. 1950–1956. *Costumari Català*. Barcelona: Selecta.

———. 1951. *Folklore de Catalunya II: Cançoner*. Barcelona: Selecta.

———. 1969. *Folklore de Catalunya III: Costums i Creences*. Barcelona: Selecta.

Capmany, Aureli. 1930–1953. *La dansa a Catalunya*. 2 volumes. Barcelona: Barcino.

———. 1951. *Calendari de llegendes, custums i festes tradicionals catalanes*. Barcelona: Dalmau I Jover.

Caseponce, Esteve. 1907. *Contes vallespirenchs replegats per En Mir y Nontoquis*. Perpinyà: Imprenta d'En Joseph Payret.

Fàbregas, X. 1979. *Tradicions, mites i creences dels catalans*. Barcelona: Edicions 62.

Limorti, Ester, and Artur Quintana. 1998. *El Carxe: Recull de literatura popular valenciana de Múcia*. Alicante: Instituto de Cultura Joan Gil-Albert.

Louis Salvador, Archduke of Austria-Tuscany. 1869–1891. *Die Balearen in Wort und Bild geschildert*. 7 volumes. Leipzig: Brockhaus.

Massot i Muntaner, Josep. 1993–2003. *Obra del Cançoner Popular de Catalunya Materials*. 13 volumes. Barcelona: Publicacions de l'Abadia de Montserrat.

Milà i Fontanals, Manuel. 1853. *Observaciones sobre la poesía popular con muestras de romances catalanes inéditos*. Barcelona: Narciso Ramirez.

Oriol, Carme. 2003. *Introducció a l'Etnopoètica: Teoria i formes del folklore en la cultura catalana*. Valls: Cossetània.

Oriol, Carme, and Josep M. Pujol. 2003. *Índex tipològic de la rondalla catalana*. Barcelona: Departament de Cultura de la Generalitat de Catalunya.

Prats, Llorenç. 1988. *El mite de la tradició popular*. Barcelona: Edicions 62.

Prats, Llorenç, Dolors Llopart, and Joan Prat. 1982. *La cultura popular a Catalunya: Estudiosos i institucions (1853–1981)*. Barcelona: Serveis de Cultura Popular.

Quintana, Artur, ed. 1995–1996. *Lo Molinar*. 3 volumes. Calaceit: Instituto de Estudios Turolenses.

———. 1997. *Bllat Colrat*. 3 volumes. Calaceit: Instituto de Estudios Altoaragoneses.

Romeu i Figueras, Josep. 1993. *Materials i estudis de folklore*. Barcelona: Alta Fulla.

Valor, Enric. 1950–1958. *Rondalles valencianes*. 3 volumes. Valencia: Torre.

Vidal I Gayolà, Joan, ed. 2000. *Quaderns de Cultural Popular*. 14 volumes. Barcelona: Ediciones Primera Plana, S. A.

Violant, Ramon. 1949. *El Pirineo español*. Madrid: Plus-Ultra.

Carme Oriol

GALICIA

GEOGRAPHY AND HISTORY

The somewhat isolated, semi-autonomous region of **Spain** located in the far northwestern corner of the country, Galicia juts out on the map to the west over Portugal and is bordered on the north by the Bay of Biscay, on the east by the mountain ranges of León and the Asturias, and on the west by the Atlantic Ocean. Its coastline, interspersed with sunken estuaries called *rías*, has been compared with the fjord-lined coast of **Norway**, and its rainy weather to that of **Ireland**. Because of the frequent rain, the earth is green, and the air cool and often misty.

Galicia is one of the least prosperous regions of Spain, but the last quarter century has brought a considerable increase in the prosperity due to economic assistance from the European Union. What Galicia has lacked in economic prosperity, however, is countered by its spiritual riches. For more than a millennium, pilgrims from across Europe have been wending their way along *el Camino de Santiago* (the Way of St. James), through formidable passes in the Pyrenees mountain chain dividing **France** and Spain, across the north of Spain, and on to Galicia's great Cathedral in Santiago de Compostela.

Since the death of the dictator Francisco Franco in 1975, Spain has been a parliamentary monarchy with the king as the head of state and an elected president as head of the government. As a semi-autonomous region within Spain, Galicia is governed by the elected Xunta de Galicia (Galician Assembly).

The people are called *galegos* or *gallegos*, depending on the language being used. For consistency, the following distinction will be followed here: references to the region are to "Galicia" or "Galician," but references to the people themselves will take the forms "Gallego" and "Gallegan." Most people in Galicia speak Castilian Spanish (*castellano*), but many also speak *galego* (which linguists refer to as Galician), a regional language akin to Portuguese.

Fishing and agriculture dominate the Galician economy. The small farms (*minifundios*) produce maize, potatoes, turnips, cabbages, small green peppers, apples, pears, and grapes. Although tractors are now common, plowing was until recently still done with a single blade or pointed prod pulled by oxen. Heavy wooden-wheeled carts (*carros chirriones*, screeching carts) are still seen, but they, too, are quickly disappearing.

Emigration was the traditional way of alleviating land pressure and keeping the region's problems within manageable proportions. Between 1911 and 1915, more than 230,000 emigrated to Latin America, especially **Cuba** and Argentina. There are also Gallegan communities in all the bigger cities of Spain, France, **Germany**, and **Switzerland**. Most such immigrants try to save money for a rapid return to Galicia. Some of the savings brought back by migrants go into land, but much more is invested in houses and businesses that sell food and drink. In the early years of the twenty-first century, however, the greater prosperity that occurred after Spain's entrance into the European Union is causing fewer people to emigrate. Thus, most verbal art of *moriña* (melancholy) brought on by being away from Galicia belongs to the parents and grandparents of Galicia's contemporary residents.

The name of the region is derived from the *gallatae*, the name for the people who lived there at the time of the arrival of the Romans in the second century B.C.E. There is, however, disagreement about the ethnic source of these people. Many authorities claim a Celtic origin and see traces of that origin in the presence of various folk traditions that include the use of a *gaita* (a small bagpipe) in almost all music groups as well as the dark hair and fair complexions of the inhabitants. There are also various archeological remains that speak to the Celtic presence in Galicia's past—for example, gold wrist and neck torques, stone sculptures, and menhirs. Other authorities assert that the Celtic claim is merely a romantic, nineteenth-century notion propagated by Gallegan nationalists.

The spiritual and governmental center of Galicia is the city of Santiago de Compostela, since the tenth century a pilgrimage site where there exists the legendary resting place of the bones of St. James the Greater (Santiago). A vast number of faith-promoting stories about St. James, creating in effect a St. James Cycle, permeate the beliefs of Galicia, and the symbols of St. James (cockleshells and the distinctive cross of St. James—often lizard-shaped and crimson-colored) are ubiquitous.

During the dictatorship of Francisco Franco (1936–1975), the Spanish government actively discouraged regional identities, except for the dominant Castilian one, as a way of uniting the country's disparate cultures. Ironically, Franco was born in El Ferrol, Galicia, and was raised speaking *galego*. Soon after Franco died in 1975, and with the constitutional establishment of regional autonomy in 1978, the Gallegos reasserted their cultural individuality. An important element in the resurgence of Galician culture was, and continues to be, the teaching in schools of not only the Gallegan language but also traditional folklore narratives written in that language.

SUPERNATURAL LORE

Roman Catholicism is overwhelmingly the central religious force in Galician society, though in general men tend to be less obviously religious than women. Catholic churches, cathedrals, monasteries, and various types of shrines—including, where two or more roads meet, distinctive and sometimes elaborate high stone crosses (*cruceiros*)—dot the landscape. Most Gallegan folktale collections contain one or more stories about the actions of the Santa Compaña (a nocturnal procession of souls in torment, figures akin to zombies) who are encountered at night, especially at crossroads.

The beliefs of most Galicians are also infused with a vigorous strain of supernaturalism. Fig symbol amulets (in the shape of a clenched fist with the thumb inserted between the index and middle fingers), scapulars, and objects to ward off the evil eye, for example, are often sold near a church when a religious holy day is being celebrated.

When illness occurs, the usual Galician pattern is to consult a medical doctor first. If the illness does not subside, then the person doubts that the illness is medical and may consult a healer (*curandero* or *curandera*), who may effect a cure with herbs or other non-medical remedies. Various other people are believed to possess supernatural powers: *meigas* (who provide love and curing potions), *barajeras* (who cast out evil and foretell the future), and *brujas* (who are believed to cause harm). A common saying is *"Eu non creo nas bruxas, pero habelas hainas!"* (I don't believe in witches, but they exist!).

ST. JAMES AND FRANCISCO FRANCO

The most frequently embedded narrative—in the form of visual images that are cut into granite walls and rendered in jet stone (*azabache*), sterling silver, and wood—is that of St. James the Greater. The traditional legend records that after Jesus's death, his apostles fanned out across the known world to evangelize people to the new faith. James, the son of Zebedee, chose to go to Spain. There, though hounded by Roman soldiers, James persisted and finally baptized a handful of converts, pouring water over their heads from a cockleshell. This artifact, seen in considerable variety throughout Galicia, is the standard symbol of St. James, and to commemorate their visit, pilgrims and other visitors to Santiago de Compostela have been buying shells (either actual shells or replicas) for at least 1,000 years. While "still a living woman" (as the formula goes), the Virgin Mary arrived in Galicia to encourage James to continue his efforts despite his dismal missionary results. Her boat turned to stone and still lies in pieces on the coast near the Galician town of Muxía. To commemorate her connection with St. James, a statue of the Virgin Mary dressed as a pilgrim stands in the cockleshell-shaped chapel of Our Lady the Refuge of the Divine Pilgrim (*Nuestra Señóra del Refúgio de la Divina Peregrina*) in the town of Pontevedra.

According to the cycle stories, James later returned to Judea, where Herod ordered his beheading. His body was turned over to two of his disciples, Teodoro and Atanásio, who were provided with a boat made of marble by angels who then guided them to the shores of cool, green Galicia, where they were to bury their leader. The grave site, however, was lost in the undergrowth until the ninth century, when Pelayo, a faithful Christian hermit, followed the light from a bright star and discovered the hidden sepulcher. Upon this spot was built a succession of churches culminating in the magnificent baroque cathedral that now stands over what is said to be the grave of St. James. A silver sarcophagus holding the bones of St. James as well those of his two disciples is located in a separate crypt below the main altar.

Some even say that Galicia's capital city, Santiago de Compostela, means "St. James of the Starry Field," thereby commemorating the miraculous sign given to Pelayo. One of the most popular stories concerns the pre-Christian Reina Lupa (the Wolf Queen), who ruled Galicia when Teodoro and Atanásio returned there with James's body. When they asked for her permission to bury James, she said, "I'll give you a cart for the coffin of your friend and some oxen to pull it. Take his body

Medieval pilgrim badges in the shape of scallop shells. The scallop shell is the symbol of St. James, and the site of Santiago de Compostela in northern Spain has been a pilgrim destination for hundreds of years. (© Museum of London/Topham-HIP/The Image Works)

to Monte Ilicino [now called Pico Sacro] and you can bury him there." She knew full well that the oxen were, in fact, wild bulls, and she hoped they would gore the two men to death when they tried to hitch them to a cart. She also knew that if by some miracle the bulls did not kill them, then the dragon that lived in the cave at the top of Monte Ilicino would. The mountain was dedicated to Jupiter, and she believed that Jupiter would not let this new religion take hold. But when she found out that upon seeing the crosses around the necks of the two men, the bulls became tame and the fire-breathing dragon fell down the bottomless cave, she needed no more proof of the power of St. James and his disciples.

Many years later, in 844, and at the precise time that the Spanish Christians needed a powerful hero to inspire them to defeat the Moors, Don Ramiro I dreamed of James on a white horse, sword in hand. The next day at the Battle of Clavijo, Ramiro and his troops won a decisive battle. Santiago soon became known as *Matamoros* (the Moor Killer) and subsequently was recognized as patron saint of all Spain. In folklore images, therefore, James is sometimes featured as the gentle pilgrim, with staff, cloak, scrip, and gourd, while at other times he appears as a warrior on horseback.

Far from pious and more contemporary are the jokes still being told about the Galician-born dictator Francisco Franco, whose name still sounds through the streets of Spain, though without the fear it once engendered. A favorite in Santiago de Compostela, probably because the joke is set in that historic Galician city, deals with a divine pronouncement from no less a figure than the apostle St. James himself:

One day, Francisco and his wife Carmen were in Santiago de Compostela for a visit. While he was talking with city officials in the City Hall, Carmen went across the plaza to the Cathedral to pray. As she was kneeling before the high altar's thirteenth-century statue of St. James, she heard the voice of the Apostle call out to her, "Carmen, I need a young horse to replace my old one so I can continue to do battle against the Infidel." Astonished, Carmen rushed out of the Cathedral and across the plaza to her husband and told him what she had heard. Together they went to the high altar to kneel in prayer when the voice of the Apostle boomed through the Cathedral: "*Qué vergüenza*, Carmen! What have you done? I asked you for a new horse, and instead you've brought me an old ass."

Rain, ubiquitous rain, is the frequent topic of folkloric sayings. People throughout Spain tease the Gallegans about it, but the Gallegans take the joking in stride and reply, "*Galicia, donde la lluvia es arte*" (Galicia is where the rain is art). In fact, when it rains, the dull gray granite of which most houses and city walls are made glistens like diamonds.

Various popular vocal and instrumental groups, with Gallegan names such as "Doa" and "Milladoiro," sing and play popular music accompanied by the skirl of bagpipes (*gaitas*) and a distinctive percussion drum held against the player's chest. Medieval hurdy-gurdies also have a place in several of these groups.

Another popular tradition, seen most frequently in Santiago de Compostela, is the *tuna*, a small band of male musicians and singers who roam the streets at night in colorful Renaissance costumes with long, multi-colored ribbons attached at the shoulder. Their job presumably is to serenade (for a price) the sweetheart of some young fellow to impress her or at least capture her attention. In fact, of course, they are equally happy to receive gratuities just for making music in the streets and cheering up the passersby.

CALENDAR CUSTOMS

As with people in other Mediterranean cultures, the daily lives of Gallegos living in northwest Spain are intertwined with events in their religious calendars. Galicians' faith is mixed with selective skepticism, yet they eagerly go to *romerías* (pilgrimages to local religious sites on designated religious holidays), where they ask for a saint's intercession in matters beyond their control, seek cures for illnesses, take a welcome break from their hard work, and be with family members. These religious holidays are almost always accompanied by secular activities such as picnicking, drinking wine, and listening to music.

A considerable number of purely non-religious observances are also threaded through the calendar of observances, such as the "Disembarking of the Vikings" in September at Catóira, where villagers, wearing sheepskin vests and horned helmets, vigorously re-enact the attack of a marauding Viking fleet in the tenth century. Other major folklore festivals are Carnival, when the wild Mardi Gras celebrants wear cross-dressing costumes; *Os Maios*, celebrating springtime by costuming schoolchildren as flowers and creating flowery floats; and in the autumn, the *Magosto* hog-butchering rituals in which families come together to slaughter and prepare their summer-fattened pigs for winter food.

Folk rituals containing both sacred and secular elements are numerous throughout the year. Five of these calendar rituals provide excellent examples.

In February, the Day of San Blas (St. Blaise) is celebrated with a series of Masses at each church holding an eponymous statue. The images of the saint are usually represented with him holding his hand to his throat, since he was martyred by having his throat slit. He came to be associated with throat illnesses, and in wet and rainy February coughs and colds are frequent, hence his popularity. In Santiago, following mass at the Collegiate Church of the Sar and at San Pelayo de Antealteras, the priest lights both upper ends of a Y-shaped candle, and as the faithful gather at the altar rail, he places the twin-lighted Y of the candle over the shoulders and around the neck of each person in line. The priest then pronounces a prayer for their health. The faithful, mostly women, subsequently brush their handkerchiefs and prayer cards against the statue of San Blas three or more times. At the conclusion of the ceremonies and with the noise of fireworks overhead, people stream by the kiosks set up in the churchyard to buy long, doughnutlike *churros*, anise-flavored cookies called *rosquitas*, and children's plastic toys.

In May many Gallegans make their way to the cool, rocky north coast and the sanctuary of San Andrés (St. Andrew) in Teixido. The traditional saying is that if you do not go to San Andrés while you are alive, then you must make the trip after you are dead (in Gallego: "*A San Andrés de Teixido, vai de morto quen non foi de vivo*"). Thus, no one bothers the bees that collect in great numbers on the sugary *rosquitas* for sale at one of the kiosks because one of the insects might contain the soul of someone who had not made it to Teixido while still living. The folklorist Antonio Fraguas Fraguas tells the story this way:

> If a family drives to Teixido, they save one seat for the dead relative who has not gone to Teixido when alive. On the way they may stop at a *milladoiro*, which is a pile of stones located near a sanctuary people travel to. These stones may have been placed there as symbols of troubles left behind, or perhaps they were handy sources of a weapon against thieves. When at last the pilgrims arrive at San Andrés de Teixido, they address the dead relative, saying, "Get out now, we are going to church." They go to Mass and after that they put out food for the dead, but of course the dead don't eat, so they give the food to one of the beggars who are always there. Then they go to the fountain. They say that one ought to throw some chunks of bread into the fountain to see if it floats or if it goes to the bottom. If it floats they will come back to Teixido. Some people put the fountain's holy water into a container and break off a piece of a yew tree branch because it is thought to encourage a love interest in another.

At the entrance of the sanctuary, pilgrims encounter another notable feature of this festival. Many of the local women bake small crude figures made of dough in the shape of the attributes of St. Andrew: fish, boats, hands, and the saint himself. These figures (*simulacra*) are painted with food coloring in pink, yellow, blue, and green, then strung on a string, and offered for sale as souvenirs.

Folk art follows folklore everywhere in Galicia. The Sargadelos ceramic factory (a Gallegan factory similar to the famous Spanish company Lladró) makes small ceramic figures of St. Andrew capable of holding holy water as well as small ceramic bowls to hold the broken-off yew branches.

To celebrate Corpus Christi in early June, many Gallegans travel to Redondela to see the flower carpets and the Coca. The narrow streets and plazas are everywhere covered with fresh flower carpets that have been put down petal by petal. They are spectacular and may include such elaborate scenes as the prophet Elias in his flaming chariot all set out in petals of many colors in front of the main church. Sand is used for faces, flowers for clothing. Water is sprinkled on the carpets to keep them from blowing away and gives a dewy, sparkling look to the carpets. Since the religious procession of the Holy Host (the Corpus Christi) in its monstrance, as well as the secular parade, marches over the flower carpets throughout the city streets, it is necessary to arrive early in the morning to see the flower carpets intact.

The Host is followed in the procession by young girls—*penliñas* (virgin angels)—carried on the shoulders of women dressed completely in white (*penlas*). Each *penliña*, as a representative of joy, waves white wrist ribbons as she "dances" on the shoulders of the *penla*.

Similar to other places in Spain, there are men wearing papier-mâché puppet heads called *cabezudos* (big heads) or walking on stilts as *gigantes* (giants) and boys carrying swords for mock battles are dressed in white shirts and pants with red or green waistbands. Then, pulled along by a "handler," appears what many audience members have come to see: a twenty-foot-long paper dragon called the Coca. The traditional story, which helps explain the dancing children and the sword-carrying boys in the parade, is that long in the past the people of the village, in order to propitiate a dragon (the Coca) living in a cave nearby, would send two of the most beautiful girls in Redondela to him each year. One year the boys in the town decided to get together to fight and kill the dragon because their most beautiful girls were being taken away. The green and white Coca, with children inside making the dragon's mouth move, is dragged around on wheels during the parade by his male "handler" to show that it was vanquished. Miniature versions of the Coca are created by the Sargadelos ceramic factory and sold in shops all over Galicia.

On 25 July, *el Día de Santiago* (St. James's Day) is celebrated throughout Spain, but nowhere with such fervor as it is celebrated in Galicia. In the cathedral at Santiago, the day is celebrated with multiple Masses, the swinging of the five-foot-high blazing censor from transept to transept in the cathedral, and parades through the streets. During the previous week, workers erect a wooden, false-front, Moorish-style palace across the entire front of the cathedral. Firecrackers are attached to this facade. In the evening before the saint's day, the firecrackers are lit, and the Moor's palace appears to burn away, reminding the audience of Santiago Matamoros. When the Day of St. James (25 July) falls on a Sunday, it is declared to be a Holy Year and is celebrated with extra exuberance and the rare opening of the Holy Door on the east side of the cathedral to welcome pilgrims.

The September celebration at Muxía, the place where the Virgin's stone boat landed, is growing in popularity with Gallegans. About 100,000 people went to the three-day event in 2003, and the number nearly doubled in 2004. The Muxía *romería* is held each year on the closest Sunday after 8 September (the date set by the Catholic Church to honor the birth of the Virgin Mary). Throughout the day, the area inside and outside the church is crowded with the faithful circulating through the building. Many pray inside the church, while others move about on, under, and around the enormous rocks forming the Virgin's boat. The rock-shaped tiller and huge stone, shaped like an overturned hull, are reputed to cure kidney problems if one crawls under them, allowing the area of the body near the kidneys to scrape against the underside of either of these rocks. To effect a cure, it is said one must crawl under the stone nine times plus one more (*nueve veces y una más*). In this way, Muxía offers to its visitants the same magic power of healing that is exhibited at the many other pilgrimage shrines—that is, the site possesses a touch of the divine provided by association with a holy personage. To partake of the divinity, the devout need only bring their faith and come into contact with the sacred object. This is, of course, the same significance bestowed on the sacred objects contained in innumerable reliquaries in church treasuries—objects that cover the gamut from bones, to thorns, to pieces of the true Cross.

ARTS AND CRAFTS

From folk art to fine art, the best representations of Gallegan folk interests have been created by the Sargadelos ceramic factory, whose origins stretch back to the eighteenth century. The ceramic pieces produced by this highly respected factory are primarily decorative pieces made of hard porcelain using raw materials found around the factory. The shapes, patterns, and colors are largely inspired by interpretations of the different cult and popular artistic styles from Galicia's folk artisan tradition. The popular blue, white, and brown figures represent such characteristic images as the typical Gallegan plow, a farm couple standing near their cow, the Coca, and the two pieces mentioned earlier as receptacles of fountain water and yew leaves from the shrine of San Andrés in Teixido. The Sargadelos factory also produces a number of traditional amulets (*colgantes*) thought to protect against injury or evil. Different shapes offer protection against a specific threat: for example, wolves, those who want to kill love, those who wish to hurt with words, those who cause others to lose things, those who want to catch one saying the wrong things, and thieves. The company maintains a Web site at www.sargadelos.com.

There is also an abundance of traditional household pottery made in Galicia. Water jugs, piggy banks, wine bowls, casseroles, flowerpots, and platters are all popular items. They are almost all wheel-formed and fired in a kiln that uses a direct flame. The bright terra-cotta colored pottery, often with a characteristic yellow-orange glaze, is frequently decorated with concentric circles. The popularity of these items is, however, decreasing, as they are being replaced by less rustic crockery.

A distinctive granary unique to Galicia, the *hórreo* is another popular folk artifact both in active use and as souvenir replicas, some even used as jewelry crafted from silver and gold. In the small villages (*aldeas*), the houses are generally single-family dwellings, behind which are their *hórreos*. These rodent-proof granaries resemble small houses built on short granite pillars and are used for storing maize and potatoes. It is not uncommon, too, for wet laundry to be hung under an *hórreo* to dry.

Now that Spain is a member of the European Union, emigration has lessened, and greater prosperity is evident. There is, however, an increasing emphasis in the public schools on the Gallegan language, Gallegan legends, and Gallegan authors, all contributing to some sense of separatism from Spain. Nevertheless, the new prosperity is making that option less and less appealing as time goes on.

STUDIES OF GALICIAN FOLKLORE

Essential information about Galician culture is briefly summarized in Valentine and Valentine (1992). Valentine and Valentine (1999) gives a good introduction to the role of oral traditions in Galicia. For insight into the Santiago pilgrimage, Turner and Turner (1978) offers anthropological insight into the meaning of Christian pilgrimages, including the one to Santiago. Simmons, Pierce, and Myers (1991) is especially useful because of its photographic representations of the figure of St. James in both Spain and the Western Hemisphere. Starkie (1965) is a highly readable, but dated, account of the history of the pilgrimage to Santiago de Compostela.

More specific to folklore is Ortiz (1999), which focuses on jokes about Spain's dictator Francisco Franco, and Valentín (1987), which recounts Franco jokes told in Galicia, where Franco was born and later vacationed during his reign. For a life history of a Galician woman from which are drawn generalizations of everyday life, see Buechler and Buechler (1981). Personal narratives of another hardworking woman's stories are presented in Valentine and Valentine (1992).

Studies dealing with specific cultural performances in Galicia, with their strong folkloric influences, can be found in Valentine and Valentine (1998), which discusses why Gallegos want to trek to the north coast of Galicia; Valentine and Valentine (1997), which describes Galicia's version of wild Mardi Gras activities; Valentine and Valentine (2005), which details the pilgrimage to Muxía; and Valentine and Valentine (2001), where their collaborator relates the story of the discovery of a small glass cylinder containing a two-sided image of the Virgin Mary and the subsequent religious and folklore events surrounding its twice-yearly celebrations in Galicia.

For those who wish to read folkloric works written in Spanish and/or Gallegan, the following citations make a good start. The first known folklorist in Galicia is Feijóo y Montenegro (1676–1764), who wrote of pilgrimages in Galicia in his "Peregrinaciones y sagrados romerias" (1984). Fraguas Fraguas (1988a) is the work of a master of the study of oral traditions. Fraguas was the first director of the *Museo Pobo Galego* in Santiago de Compostela and a knowledgeable contributor to Galician folklore for most of his ninety years.

For useful survey guides to various religio-folklore events in Galicia, see Mariño Ferro (1987), Sueiro and Nietos (1983), and Fraguas Fraguas (1988b). Also useful are Angeles Sanchez (1982) and Cebrián Franco (1982, 1989). For oral traditions on the topic of witches and the supernatural, see Liste (1981). For general collections of oral traditions, the classic source is Lisón Tolosana (1979), based on his **fieldwork** in Galician villages using important folklore sources. Bouza-Brey (1982) and Carré Alvarellos (1980) are also valuable resources. Useful, too, is Ramos (1988), where fifty-five stories by Gallegan men and women of all ages are printed in either Gallegan or Spanish, along with some paralinguistic cues.

BIBLIOGRAPHY

Angeles Sanchez, M. 1982. *Guia de fiestas populares*. Madrid: Viajar/Editorial Tania.

Bouza-Brey Trillo, Fermín. 1982. *Etnografía y folklore de Galicia*. 2 volumes. Madrid: Ediciónes Xerais de Galicia.

Buechler, Hans, and J. M. Buechler. 1981. *Carmen: The Autobiography of a Spanish Galician Woman*. Cambridge, MA: Schenkman.

Carré Alvarellos, Leandro. 1980. *Las leyendas tradicionales gallegas*. Madrid: Espasa-Calpe.

Cebrián Franco, Juan José. 1982. *Santuarios de Galicia*. Santiago de Compostela: Arzobispado de Santiago de Compostela.

———. 1989. *Guia para visitar los santuarios marianos de Galicia*. Madrid: Ediciones Encuentro.

Eade, John, and Michael J. Sallnow. 1991. *Contesting the Sacred: The Anthropology of Christian Pilgrimage*. New York: Routledge.

Feijóo y Montenegro, Benito Jerónimo. 1984. Peregrinaciones y sagrados romerías. In *Obra Selecta*. Santiago de Compostela: Sálvora.

Fraguas Fraguas, Antonio. 1988a. Estudio antropológico de la poplación. In *Enciclopedia temática de Galicia*. Volume 4: *Antropología*. Barcelona: Nauta. 12–81.

———. 1988b. *Romarías e santuarios*. Vigo: Galaxia.

Frey, Nancy Louise. 1998. *Pilgrim Stories: On and Off the Road to Santiago, Journeys along an Ancient Way in Modern Spain*. Berkeley: University of California Press.

Hitt, Jack. 1994. *Off the Road: A Modern-Day Walk Down the Pilgrim's Route into Spain*. New York: Simon and Schuster.

Howes, H. W. 1925. A Galician Rocking Stone. *Man* 25.7:108.

Kelley, Heidi. 1994. The Myth of Matriarchy: Symbols of Womanhood in Galician Regional Identity. *Anthropological Quarterly* 67.2:71–80.

Lisón Tolosana, C. 1979. *Brujería, estructura social y simbolismo en Galicia*. Madrid: Akal.

Liste, Ana. 1981. *Galicia: Brujería, superstición y mística*. Madrid: Penthalon.

Llorens Artigas, J., and J. Corredor-Matheos. 1974. *Spanish Folk Ceramics of Today*, translated by Martha Tennent. 2nd edition. Barcelona: Editorial Blume.

López-Gómez, Felipe Senen. 1982. *Arte popular en Galicia*. Madrid: Silex.

Mariño Ferro, Xosé Ramón. 1987. *Las romerías/peregrinaciones y sus símbolos*. Vigo: Xerais.

Ortiz, Carmen. 1999. The Uses of Folklore by the Franco Regime. *Journal of American Folklore* 112:479–498.

Ramos, Rosa Alicia. 1988. *El cuento folklórico: Una aproximación a su estudio*. Madrid: Pliegos.

Simmons, Marc, Donna Pierce, and Joan Myers. 1991. Santiago, Reality and Myth. In *Santiago: Saint of Two Worlds*, edited by Joan Myers. Albuquerque: University of New Mexico Press. 1–29.

Starkie, Walter. 1965. *The Road to Santiago: Pilgrims of St. James*. Berkeley: University of California Press.

Sueiro, Jorge-Victor, and Amparo Nieto. 1983. *Galicia: Romería interminable*. Madrid: Penthalon.

Turner, Victor, and Edith Turner. 1978. *Image and Pilgrimage in Christian Culture: Anthropological Perspectives*. New York: Columbia University Press.

Valentín, Uxío. 1987. Franco Jokes: The Spaniards Are Still Getting Even with the Generalissimo. *Journal of Popular Culture* 20.4:83–92.

Valentine, Eugene, and Kristin B. Valentine. 1992. Galicians. In *Encyclopedia of World Cultures*. Volume 4: *Europe*, edited by L. Bennett. New York: Hall. 118–121.

———. 1998. "Dead or Alive, You're Going to Teixido": The Teller and the Tale. In *Fiction and Social Research: By Ice or Fire*, edited by Anna Banks and Stephen Banks. Walnut Creek, CA: Altamira Press. 79–86.

———. Forthcoming. Healing at the Coast of Death in Spanish Galicia: The *Romería* to Our Lady's Boat. *Journal of American Folklore*.

Valentine, Kristin B., and Eugene Valentine. 1992. Performing Culture through Narration: A Gallegan Storyteller. In *Performance, Culture, and Identity*, edited by Elizabeth Fine and Jean Haskell Speer. Westport, CT: Praeger. 180–205.

———. 1997. Folklore Figures in Spanish Galician *Carnaval*. *Southern Folklore* 54.3:227–235.

———. 1999. Storytelling in Spanish Galicia. In *Traditional Storytelling Today: An International Sourcebook*, edited by Margaret Read MacDonald. Chicago: Fitzroy-Dearborn. 230–233.

———. 2001. Veneration of the Virgin of Crystal in Ritual and Narrative. *Iowa Journal of Communication* 33.1:9–21.

Eugene Valentine and Kristin B. Valentine

SEPHARDIM

GEOGRAPHY AND HISTORY

Sephardic Jews trace their origins to medieval **Spain** and Portugal. The term *Sepharad* comes from the biblical reference in Obadiah 1:20. "The exiles of Jerusalem who are in Sepharad will inherit the cities of the Negev." *Sepharad* has traditionally come to refer to the Iberian Peninsula. The Jews who lived there and their descendants have thus been referred to as Sephardim. Their ancestors were a part of the intellectual milieu of Jewish, Muslim, and Catholic thinkers, doctors, jurists, and religious leaders characterized as the Golden Age of Spain. From the late fourteenth century to the end of the fifteenth century, persecutions and expulsions led hundreds of thousands to leave their homelands. The Sephardic exile from Spain led in two geographical directions—to Northwestern Europe and to North Africa and the eastern Mediterranean.

Following the Edict of Expulsion against the Jews of Spain (1492), thousands found temporary refuge in neighboring Portugal, only to be forced to leave from there in 1497. Others went to culturally familiar southern France. Yet others established a well-respected community in Amsterdam, which to this day remains distinct as the Portuguese and Spanish Congregation. In Northwestern Europe—**the Netherlands, France, England**, and, ultimately by extension, the Americas—many Sephardic Jews eventually assimilated into the prevalent culture.

Exiles from the Iberian Peninsula seeking refuge in North Africa were initially rejected and mistreated by the indigenous Jews of Morocco and Algeria. Eventually, Sephardic communities were established and prospered there for centuries. The largest number of Spanish and Portuguese Jews were welcomed by the open arms of the rapidly expanding Ottoman Empire in the eastern Mediterranean. Communities were established in depopulated areas such as the capital, Istanbul, Thessaloniki, Smyrna, and Aleppo and in cities in what is now Bosnia, **Macedonia**, Bulgaria, Romania, and **Greece**. Other Sephardic Jews sought to re-establish themselves in the Levant in Jerusalem, Tiberias, and Safed. In these areas their special Iberian Jewish culture fostered and grew.

Despite the economic and intellectual stagnation of the eighteenth and part of the nineteenth centuries, Ottoman Sephardic culture survived until the eve of the Holocaust. Largely due to twentieth-century settlement of Sephardim in North America and Israel, Sephardic identity and culture enjoyed a revival around the time of the celebration of the 500th anniversary of the expulsions in 1992.

Commercially and professionally skilled, the Spanish Jews were seen as valued additions by the Ottoman authorities. Sephardic Jews held such distinguished positions as diplomats, physicians, and literary contributors. They enjoyed a period of prosperity and cultural efflorescence during the sixteenth century. Some 400 years later, the Ottoman Empire reached the end of a sociopolitical-economic downward spiral. With the rise of European nationalism and other factors, this once-strong multicultural superpower lost its role and potency. Rarely harassed under Muslim rulers, Jews and Christians sought new homes where they could carry on their businesses. Many Sephardic Jews found homes in Eretz Israel in the three ancient cities of Jerusalem, Tiberias, and Safed. Others made their way to European cities such as Paris and Rome. Thousands, however, journeyed to America during the so-called Great Wave of Migration between 1884 and 1924. They established Sephardic communities in Cincinnati, Indianapolis, Seattle, Los Angeles, and Atlanta, as well as the largest in New York City.

World War II dealt a strong blow to four centuries of Sephardic life in the eastern Mediterranean. Communities in Greece, Yugoslavia, and Romania were completely destroyed. Thousands were deported and found their end in the death camps. Sephardic Jews in North Africa fared better. In Morocco numerous individuals and families were imprisoned in detention camps. After the war, few survivors returned to their homes. Instead, they were drawn to proto-state Israel as well as the United States, other European nations, and South America.

Descendants of the Spanish Jews lived in a large number of social settings. Ottoman and North African Sephardim spent four centuries negotiating within pluralistic milieus. In fact, the particular nature of pluralism in medieval Spain led Sephardic Jews to assimilate cultural elements from the Muslims and Christians with whom they lived. This led to distinct modes of Sephardic expression within Jewish law (halakha) and tradition (minhag).

Within a generation of exile, Spanish-Jewish culture had been transplanted to many centers in the Ottoman Empire. Sephardic culture of Ottoman and North African Jews developed in different directions. However, they held onto a fierce pride in their Spanish origins, and over the centuries they placed emphasis on the purity of descent—two features of Spanish grandeza that have generally characterized the Sephardim. Sacred and secular traditions were steadfastly maintained and flourished in both locations. Sephardic histories, modes of religious expression, languages, and a large body of traditional culture reflect the considerable diversity of the Spanish heritage they carried as well as the cultures of the lands where they established residence. For over four centuries, this culture was preserved and maintained with a faithful and proud sense of loyalty.

While the Jews staunchly held on to the laws of Judaism, they adopted some of the customs of their neighbors. For example, like Orthodox Christians and Muslims, Jewish children were given the names of their living grandparents, the highest form of compliment to the forebearers. Daily and holiday festive foods made use of local ingredients while upholding the laws of kashrut. Judeo-Spanish and Hakatia, Sephardic vernaculars, included Turkish, Greek, Arabic, and Slavic words.

Jewish life is governed by two parallel sets of laws: halakha is codified in the official system; minhag is the customs and traditions particular to specific communities, reflecting their social, historical, and geographic setting. The Torah, the Talmud with associated commentary, and other writings are the basis of the faith of Sephardic Jews. Interwoven into the standard belief and practice are numerous customs that emerged from local influences.

Sephardic Jews have a rich tradition of folk belief and customs relating to curing that possibly have their roots in medieval Spain. This tradition strongly represents a reflection of culture contact and practices borrowed from, or shared with, non-Jewish neighbors. Informal belief activities were most frequently the realm of women. The beliefs in afflictions associated with the evil eye and the practice of cures for women's ailments were strongly held in the Ottoman Balkans. The mere presence of the evil eye could be determined through rituals such as pouring melted lead into water or other means of divination. The evil eye was counteracted with amulets (kameoth or alephs). They took many different forms and were most often used to protect newborn babies and their mothers.

Barrenness and other unnamed female illnesses were countered by concoctions called indulcos or endurcos, which included ingredients from the animal and vegetable world, including a piece of a mummy. Use of this type of charm was so wholeheartedly disapproved of by a group of rabbis in Jerusalem that in 1847 a little-heeded warning was issued against its continued use.

213

Until the thirteenth century, the Jews of Spain spoke Arabic. With the rise of the Christian Spaniards, Judeo-Spanish (also known as Ladino and Judezmo) developed as their vernacular. After the Sephardic Jews and their descendants integrated into existing Jewish communities in Northern Europe, they adopted the local languages. In northern Morocco and the Ottoman Empire, however, they retained an archaic, fifteenth-century Castilian and in a reverse assimilation imposed it on the resident Jews. Judeo-Spanish was one of the elements that anchored the Sephardic Jews of the Ottomans to their Spanish past. The language came to be considered specifically Jewish. It distinguished Jews from other residents of the eastern Mediterranean, though non-Jewish merchants used Judeo-Spanish in trade relations.

BALLADS, PROVERBS, AND FOLKTALES

In the nineteenth century a flowering of Judeo-Spanish secular and sacred literature occurred in the Ottoman Sephardic communities. By the late nineteenth century an increase of Westernization, especially with the introduction of modern education and French language through the schools of the Alliance Israelite Universelle, led to a decline in Judeo-Spanish expression in general. The retention of Judeo-Spanish is significant because of the wealth of traditional literature preserved in this language through the mid-twentieth century. The variety of forms of traditional literature expressed in Judeo-Spanish ranges from romantic poetry, to evocative proverbs (*refranes*) and to folktales with moralistic endings (*consejas*).

Much of the Balkan Sephardic oral literature was collected and documented in the late nineteenth and early twentieth centuries by Spanish-language scholars. They were attracted to a trove of archaic linguistic treasures in the Ottoman Empire. The focus of their collections was primarily the ballads and proverbs, though a number of folktales were also documented.

Proverbs, *refranes* or *reflanes* as pronounced in Judeo-Spanish, form a rich body of Judeo-Spanish traditional literature in daily use. They also are a piece of heritage that speaks to the Iberian origins of Sephardic Jews, as proverbs are an essential part of the verbal art everywhere in the Hispanic world. Daily speech was peppered with proverbs and sayings that spoke of their distant Spanish origins. They reflect the culture, thoughts, and distinctive philosophy of life of Balkan Sephardic Jews. Hundreds of Sephardic proverbs existed about numerous subjects touching all parts of human life. The themes varied from such subjects as Jews as seen by themselves and others, the figure of the rabbi, Jewish holidays, and behavior of Jews in their world. Usually a simple phrase, each describing a situation, elaborates, pokes fun at, or changes an idea. The function of Sephardic proverbs, like those of other communities, essentially is to instruct. They are direct to get across a crucial lesson: "*Seas bienvenido mal si vienes solo*" (Bad things never come alone); "*El querer es poder*" (To want is to be able). Other proverbs pointedly instruct about family and life-cycle occasions, especially marriage. Jewish society is a patriarchal society. Girl children are beloved, but sons are desired. The richness of traditional proverbs or *refranes* preserves these sentiments, as seen in the following:

Quien nino cria, oro fila; quien nina cria, lana fila; *a la fin del ano o puliada o podrida.*	Whoever raises a son spins gold; whoever raises a daughter spins wool; at the end of the year it will be moth-eaten.
La fija en la faxa, la axugar en la caxa.	The daughter still in diaper, the trousseau in the trunk.
Una fija, una gravina; dos, con savor; tres, mal es; cuatro, crevanto; cinco, suspiro; sex, sex fijas para la madre y mala vida por el padre.	One daughter, a carnation; two, a delight; three, it is bad; four, frightening; five, a sigh; six, six daughters for the mother and a rotten life for the father.
Quando sube el asno de la escalara *Se pasan el muera y esfuegra*	When the donkey goes up the ladder, Will daughter-in-law and mother-in-law make peace?

Samuel Armistead documented Judeo-Spanish proverbs that probably came from Spain with the exiles. The examples are followed below by their early counterparts, which were compiled in 1627 in the proverb dictionary of Gonzalo Correas. The translation is essentially identical in each case:

A gran' a grano, hinche la gayina el papo. *Grano a grano, hinche la gallina el papo.*	One seed at a time, a hen fills its craw.
Antes que te cazes, mira lo que hazes. *Antes ke te kases, mira lo ke hazes.*	Watch what you do before you get married.
Dime con quén andas; te diré quén sos. *Dime kon kién fueres i diréte kién eres.*	Tell me who you go around with, and I'll tell you who you are.

The early Hispanists who conducted research on Judeo-Spanish oral literature documented a wealth of folktales only after recording the ballads and proverbs. They considered the tales primarily as samples of the spoken language and transcribed them in close phonetic notation to create an important corpus. Some Sephardic folktales were taken into exile from the Iberian Peninsula. Some tales come directly from the Torah. Other folktales make use of globally recognized motifs such as the well-known Cinderella story. In the Balkans, the tale tradition was enriched by the diverse local traditions with which the Sephardim were in daily contact. In Morocco, certain stories show borrowings from the local Arabic or indigenous Berber traditions.

One of the pre-eminent characters whose adventures and interactions are related in the tales told in all communities is the Turkish trickster hero, the Hodja or Djoha. This quintessential character is at times a simpleton and at times clever and wise. On the one hand, he makes decisions based on clever observations of human nature, and, on the other hand, he represents nonsensical conclusions to life situations.

GOD'S WAY

One day four boys asked the Djoha, "We have a bag of walnuts, but we don't know how to distribute them among us. Can you help us?" Djoha asked them, "How do you want me to distribute them among you, God's way or man's way!"

"Of, course, God's way!" the boys answered in unison.

Djoha opened the bag and gave two handfuls to one boy, one handful to another boy, the two remaining walnuts to the third boy, and none to the fourth boy.

"What kind of fair distribution is this?" they asked.

The Djoha replied, "This is God's way. To some people He gives much; to some a little; and to others He gives nothing."

HOW CAN YOU PLEASE ANYONE?

One day, Djoha and his son went on a journey. Djoha let his son ride the donkey while he walked. Along the way, they passed some people who said, "Look at that healthy young boy on the donkey!"

The boy then let his father ride while he walked. Djoha rode and the boy walked by his side. Soon they met another group.

"Look at that! Poor little boy has to walk while his father rides the donkey." This time, Djoha climbed onto the donkey behind his son. Soon they met another group, who said, "Look at that poor donkey! He has to carry the weight of two people."

Djoha then told his son. "The best thing is for us to walk and lead the donkey. Then no one can complain." So they continued their journey on foot. Again, they met some others who said: "Just take a look at those fools. Both of them are walking under this hot sun and neither of them is riding the donkey." In exasperation, Djoha lifted the donkey onto his shoulders and said, "Come on; if we don't do this, it will be impossible to make people stop talking."

So intertwined in the Sephardic tradition is Djoha that he frequently appears in proverbs, such as *"El mazal de djoha"* (The luck [Hebrew] of Hodja) and *"A djoha le disheron amokote, se kito la nariz!"* (When Djoha wants to get rid of mucus, he cut off his nose!).

Among the most recognized and significant forms of Sephardic oral tradition are the narrative ballads or *romansas*. According to Armistead, they preserve the form and content of the Spanish ballad tradition from the Middle Ages and are part of the Pan-Hispanic ballad tradition. Like the other, the Pan-Hispanic *romancero*, the Judeo-Spanish ballad singers performed songs based on medieval Spanish and French epics and other European ballad traditions. The ballads concern events in Spanish, Portuguese, and Italian history; they retell biblical episodes, legends from classical antiquity, or details of medieval *romans d'aventure*.

Sephardic *romanceros* did not exist within a vacuum; they borrowed from the popular poetry of the peoples among whom they lived. Greek, Turkish, and Arabic influences are often present in the verses. A few Balkan *romansas* are adaptations of modern Greek ballads, while others translate French, Italian, and Catalan narrative songs. Others were invented by the Sephardim in exile, and some may have reached the Jewish communities well after 1492, brought by *converso*, or crypto-Jewish, emigrants. Over the centuries, the Balkan and North African traditions remained distinct, though Armistead has shown that a few ballad types have migrated from one tradition to the other. Because of continued proximity to Spain, the Moroccan tradition was influenced by modern Spanish traditional ballads brought by twentieth-century Spanish immigrants—particularly Andalusians—to the Spanish zone of Northern Morocco.

Some ballads and other song forms in the Sephardic repertoire are associated with life cycle events such as wedding songs, lullabies, and songs of mourning. The following excerpt from the well-loved ballad "The King Nimrod" tells the story of the birth of Abraham. It was sung at circumcision parties.

Quando el rey Nimrod, el campo salia,	When Nimrod the king went out to the field,
Miraba en el cielo y en la istrarla.	He looked to the sky and to the stars.
Vido luz santa en la judieria.	He saw a sacred light among the Jews,
Que avia de nacir Abraham avinu.	For our father Abraham was about to be born.

Lyric songs (*cantigas*) were sung in specific social contexts, often at the crucial moments of transition: births, weddings, and funerals. Like the ballads, the lyric songs trace their origins to the Iberian Peninsula. In the Balkans, many of the songs are very similar to songs from the major urban areas, Istanbul, and Thessaloniki. Furthermore, recorded music was a source of Spanish popular songs for singers in the Balkans. They were quickly learned by Jewish singers, who gradually came to consider them an authentic part of their own Sephardic repertoire. The following lyrics known throughout the Spanish world are also found in Sephardic repertoire replete with a reference to a Christian ritual: "*A la una nasí yo, / a las dos me baftizaron*" (I was born at one o'clock; / at two I was baptized).

Arts, Crafts, and Architecture

Jewish traditional material culture, Judaica, accompanies rituals within the synagogue and in the home. A large repertoire of objects, many of them produced by professional artisans and workshops, is utilized in worship service. Other items can be considered as folk art made by informally trained artists. When they went into exile, few Sephardim were able to carry with them the wealth of ritual Judaica they had used in Spain and Portugal. No more than a dozen pieces have survived to the present. Furthermore, few illustrations of ritual objects have survived to indicate their appearance. An illumination in the Sarajevo Haggadah showing the interior of an *aron ha'kodesh* with the dressed Sephardic Torah including a Torah crown provides a key to the forms used in Spain. A comparison of the embroidered cloth Torah scroll covers in the illumination shows similarities with nineteenth-century Turkish Torah scroll covers.

Sabbath lamp, to be lit before sundown on Friday. This nineteenth-century ceramic lamp is from North Africa, made and used by the Jews who inhabited the caves in Morocco or Libya. (Erich Lessing/Art Resource, NY)

Sephardim brought Spanish architectural influences showing the heritage of the *mudijar*, or Moorish, style of synagogues in Spain to the Ottoman Balkans. The curves and archways in synagogue interiors are evidence of this built heritage. Architectural references are evident in Sephardic bench-form Hanukkah lamps, especially Moroccan examples, with Moorish archways decorating the back walls above the oil wells. Other devices found on these objects include five-fingered hands, a protector against the evil eye, and birds and fish.

Material culture found in the home is part of a larger complex of expressions associated with holidays and life-cycle events. All forms of this expressive culture are rich with flavor and meaning. Life-cycle customs and holiday celebrations are highly localized and reflect the influences of Muslim and Christian neighbors. Judeo-Spanish culture is evident in all aspects of these customs. The Sephardic wedding is one of the richest examples of interplay between customary behavior and material culture. It is not a single ceremony but a prolonged period of ceremonies and customs. Marriages were arranged exclusively through the process of matchmaking. Girls were frequently promised at the young age of nine or ten and usually married somewhere between the ages of twelve and sixteen. It was not uncommon for girls to be betrothed and marry an uncle or a first cousin. The formal betrothal or engagement, or *desposorio*, was often celebrated on the same day as the wedding. The evening following this ritual was observed with joy and the exchange of gifts. The young man and his family came to the young woman's house with a tray of jewelry, perfume, and sugared almonds. At this time, the man gave his fiancée something of value, often a ring, as a token of betrothal. With the acceptance of the gift, the woman was considered the man's wife, though they did not yet live together. At the occasion of the engagement, the groom is usually given a *megillat Esther*, or scroll of Esther, finely written on parchment and encased in worked silver, which is read annually during the celebration of Purim.

The occasion of the engagement presents an event when the bride-to-be ritually serves her new in-laws a traditional sweet as a demonstration of her housewifely skills. The ritual of serving of *dulce* or *glyko* (Greek)—sweets made of preserved fruits such as orange peel, rose petal, pears, or quinces—showed the young woman's ability to serve with humility and graceful skills. She was judged on the presentation of her tray of sweets, *la tavla de dulces*, and her skill in serving.

Handworked textiles form an important part of every young Sephardic bride's trousseau, or *ashugar*. This collection of possessions that a bride brought into marriage could include handmade fine embroideries and pulled thread textiles for household use, clothes, a sewing machine, silver serving pieces, and wool-stuffed mattresses and pillows. The contents of the trousseau as well as the monetary dowry were enumerated in the marriage contract, *ketubah*, that accompanied every marriage. A day or two before the wedding ceremony, the value of the trousseau was appraised, *preciado d'el ashugar*, and then transported from the home of the bride to her new home with her husband's family. Traditional music usually accompanied this parade. It is said that without this finery and the dowry a Sephardic bride had a difficult time finding a suitable mate of the same or higher social level: "*Lo que no se hace a la boda, no se hace en ninguna hora*" (She who did not have it at the wedding will not have it any other time). After the transport of the trousseau, the groom's family sends to the bride a *bogcha* (Turkish) or cloth, filled with the items she will need to go the Turkish bath or *mikvah* prior to the wedding.

Many of the customs associated with the ceremony such as the canopy, or *huppah* (Hebrew), under which the couple stands and the breaking of the glass by the groom are universal to Jewish communities worldwide. Afterward, the couple is pelted with rice, sweets, and coins to ensure a sweet, rich life blessed with children. At the Sephardic ceremony, guests are given favors, or *bobonieras*, often made by the same ladies who make them for Christian brides. These fanciful items consist of a tulle sack with an odd number of sugared almonds. Lace handkerchiefs, silk flowers, silver boxes, or a ballpoint pen engraved with the name of the bride and groom adorn these items as remembrances of the event.

A week filled with festivities and company followed the formal ceremony. On the last day of that week, in preparation for the Sabbath meal, the groom went to the market to buy a fish, the traditional main course. The bride then jumped over a tub holding the fish three times so that she should "be blessed by as many children as the fish in the sea."

FOOD

Sephardic Jews strongly and proudly maintain food traditions. This is an area rich in symbolism and also expresses their Hispanic origins. Weekly on the eve of the Sabbath, fish dishes were customarily served as the main course. They symbolized the forward movement of the fish, thus indicating the prosperity desired by the head of household. The North African *dafina* is a meal cooked in one pot like Northern European *cholent* that can be kept warm all Saturday. The Saturday morning breakfast, or *desayuno*, included cheese or vegetable *borekas*, *boyos*, and *bolemas*, types of baked turnovers traced to pre-exile Spain, served with hard-cooked eggs, olives, cheeses, melons, grapes, and other fruits.

The Jewish New Year, *Rosh Hashanah*, and the series of holidays immediately following were also replete in symbolic meanings. For example, at the *Rosh Hashanah* meal in Sephardic homes, the head of a fish or the head of a sheep was served to the head of the household. By eating this food at this particular time, each person could be like the head and move forward in health in the New Year. A seasonal ingredient in a number of foods, including the *hallah*, was pumpkin (*calabaza*). It was used then because its thick rind symbolized the strength of God to protect and strengthen. This round fall vegetable also symbolized wishes for a well-rounded, full year.

Bimuelos, a fried dough delight almost identical to *bunuelos* made in Spanish-speaking countries, are made in Sephardic kitchens for the winter holiday, Hanukkah. It was said that Hanukkah, as celebrated by the Sephardic Jews, was *"El buen dia de la tripa"* (A good day for the stomach!).

The typically Sephardic *huevos haminados or enjaminados*, baked eggs, were central to the symbolically significant Passover *seder* plate. Like the white eggs used by Ashkenazi Jews, these browned, hard-boiled eggs represented one of the offerings in the ancient temple. After the Passover ceremony, family members played egg wars, as their Greek Orthodox neighbors did, to see whose egg was the last to crack. *Haminados* were served year-round at Jewish-owned coffee shops in the Balkans.

NAMING TRADITIONS

The Sephardic naming tradition, in contrast to that of Ashkenazi Jews, is to give their children names of living relatives. The first children—male and female—are named for the living paternal grandparents. The second child of either sex is named for the living maternal grandparent. This custom parallels naming traditions of the neighboring Greek Christians. It leads to a proliferation of first cousins with the same names. The custom of giving nicknames developed out of naming practices described above that resulted in the need to distinguish among numerous cousins with identical given names. This, too, is a practice common to both Jews and Christians in the Balkans. Nicknames are derived from different sources. Some, such as Moses "the burnt one," for one who was burned in an accident, or Joseph "red," a person with red hair, are given because of a physical feature. The naming model is not a hard-and-fast rule. Frequently, a child's name will be derived from circumstances of birth. For example, a son born during Hanukkah may be named Nissim, meaning "miracles," since it is a holiday that commemorates a miracle. A daughter born at the time of Purim will be named Esther, and a son is given the name Mordechai in honor of the protagonists of the story recalled at that season. When previous babies in the family had died, Sephardic parents gave a newborn the name Marcado or Marcada, meaning "one that is sold," and Judeo-Arabic speakers named the infant Makhlouf, meaning substitute or compensation. Such a baby was symbolically sold at birth and cared for by the "buyers" for the first three days.

STUDIES OF SEPHARDIC FOLKLORE

The literature on Sephardic history and folklore grew considerably in the last decades of the twentieth century. Díaz-Mas (1992) is an excellent and accessible source about the life and culture of Jews in Spain prior to the expulsions. Stillman and Stillman (1999) provides a well-rounded overview of the Sephardic experience throughout the Mediterranean basin. Essays are organized to address themes of Sephardic and Oriental Communities: Past and Present, Intellectual History, Literature and Folklore, Linguistic Studies, and Music and Art. Firestone (1962) discusses the continuity of folk beliefs and healing maintained by Sephardic women in Seattle, one of the significant early-twentieth-century communities in the United States. This work serves as a standard to which all following studies refer. Levy and Zumwalt (2002) is the result of many years of painstaking field research in the Balkans that documented contemporary practices and beliefs. The authors identify and follow a number of *buenas mujeres*, good women, who serve a needed role in their respective communities. Numerous works have been written about the history, variations, and future of Judeo-Spanish. Luria (1930) represents a career devoted to documenting the particular speech patterns in this significant southern Serbian community. Luria is one of the early Hispanists to compile extensive collections of oral traditions to study the language. Harris (1994) presents a much more current examination of a language dying because of cultural changes and drastic loss of populations. Molho (1950), a classic work by a rabbi and historian, remains an excellent compilation and discussion of the wide range of Sephardic traditional culture, including oral traditions and holiday and life-cycle customs. Haboucha (1992) has systematized a large body of texts scattered in often-obscure articles and has made it readily accessible, providing an indispensable starting point for subsequent research on Judeo-Spanish folktales. Sephardic proverbs have been steadfastly collected by scholars of Spanish language as well as folklorists since the early twentieth century. Levy (1969) is one of the earliest studies actually to access vast collections. It remains a seminal source for the study of this vast body of oral tradition. Armistead, Silverman, and Katz (1971, 1994, in press) represents the largest body of work on Sephardic musical traditions. They have also compiled impressive discographies. Armistead's Web site, www.sephardifolklit.org/flsj/sjjs/orallit/Oral_Lit_Sephardic.html, is an outstanding summation of years of concerted research and analysis of the entire realm of Sephardic oral literature. *Greek-Jewish Musical Traditions* (1978) provides an excellent sampling of sacred and secular songs sung in the Sephardic communities of Greece. Two exhibit catalogs provide discussions of Sephardic material culture and history: Juhasz (1990) consists of illustrated articles discussing objects such as costume, jewelry, marriage contracts, and occasions rich in objects such as marriage and childbirth, while *The Sephardic Journey 1492–1992* (1992) accompanied an exhibit to commemorate the Quincentenary of the Expulsion of the Jews from Spain. Not only topics relating to synagogues and ceremonial objects but also the rich topic of the Judeo-Spanish proverb are addressed. Roden (1997) provides historical notes along with recipes for Sephardic food in the entire Mediterranean basin by one of the most prolific writers on Jewish food. *See also* **Ashkenazim**.

BIBLIOGRAPHY

Armistead, Samuel G., Joseph H. Silverman, and Israel J. Katz. 1971, 1994, in press. *Folk Literature of the Sephardic Jews*. 3 volumes. Berkeley: University of California Press.

Díaz-Mas, Paloma. 1992. *Sephardim: The Jews from Spain*, translated by George K. Zucker. Chicago: University of Chicago Press.

Firestone, Melvin M. 1962. Sephardic Folk-Curing in Seattle. *Journal of American Folklore* 75:301–310.

Greek-Jewish Musical Traditions. 1978. Ethnic Folkways Records FE 4205.

Haboucha, Reginetta. 1992. *Types and Motifs of the Judeo-Spanish Folktales*. New York: Garland Folklore Library.

Harris, Tracy. 1994. *Death of a Language: The History of Judeo-Spanish*. Newark: University of Delaware Press.

Juhasz, Esther. 1990. *Sephardi Jews in the Ottoman Empire, Aspects of Material Culture*. Jerusalem: Israel Museum.

Levy, Isaac Jack. 1969. *Prolegomena to the Study of the "Refranero Sefardí."* New York: Las Américas.

Levy, Isaac Jack, and Rosemary Levy Zumwalt. 2002. *Ritual Medical Lore of Sephardic Women: Sweetening the Spirits, Healing the Sick*. Urbana: University of Illinois Press.

Luria, Max A. 1930. *A Study of the Monastir Dialect of Judeo-Spanish*. New York: Hispanic Institute.

Molho, Michael. 1950. *Usos y costumbres de los sefardíes de Salónica*, translated by Federico Pérez Castro. Madrid-Barcelona: C.S.I.C.

Roden, Claudia. 1997. *The Book of Jewish Food*. London: Viking.

The Sephardic Journey 1492–1992. 1992. New York: Yeshiva University Museum.

Stillman, Yedida K., and Norman A. Stillman, eds. 1999. *Essays in From Iberia to Diaspora, Studies in Sephardic History and Culture*. Leiden: Brill.

Annette B. Fromm

The Low Countries

FLANDERS (BELGIUM)

GEOGRAPHY AND HISTORY

Not an independent country, Flanders is the northern half of the Kingdom of Belgium, situated in Western Europe and surrounded by the North Sea, the Kingdom of **The Netherlands**, the Federal Republic of **Germany**, the Grand Duchy of Luxemburg, and **France**. The standard language in Flanders is Dutch, whereas in the south of Belgium, called Wallonia, it is French. The surface area of Flanders is 13,580 square kilometers. Flanders has a moderate, humid climate and is situated on the European Plain. Most of it is less than 100 meters above sea level. The most important city is Antwerp, which has one of the greatest harbors in the world. Other cities

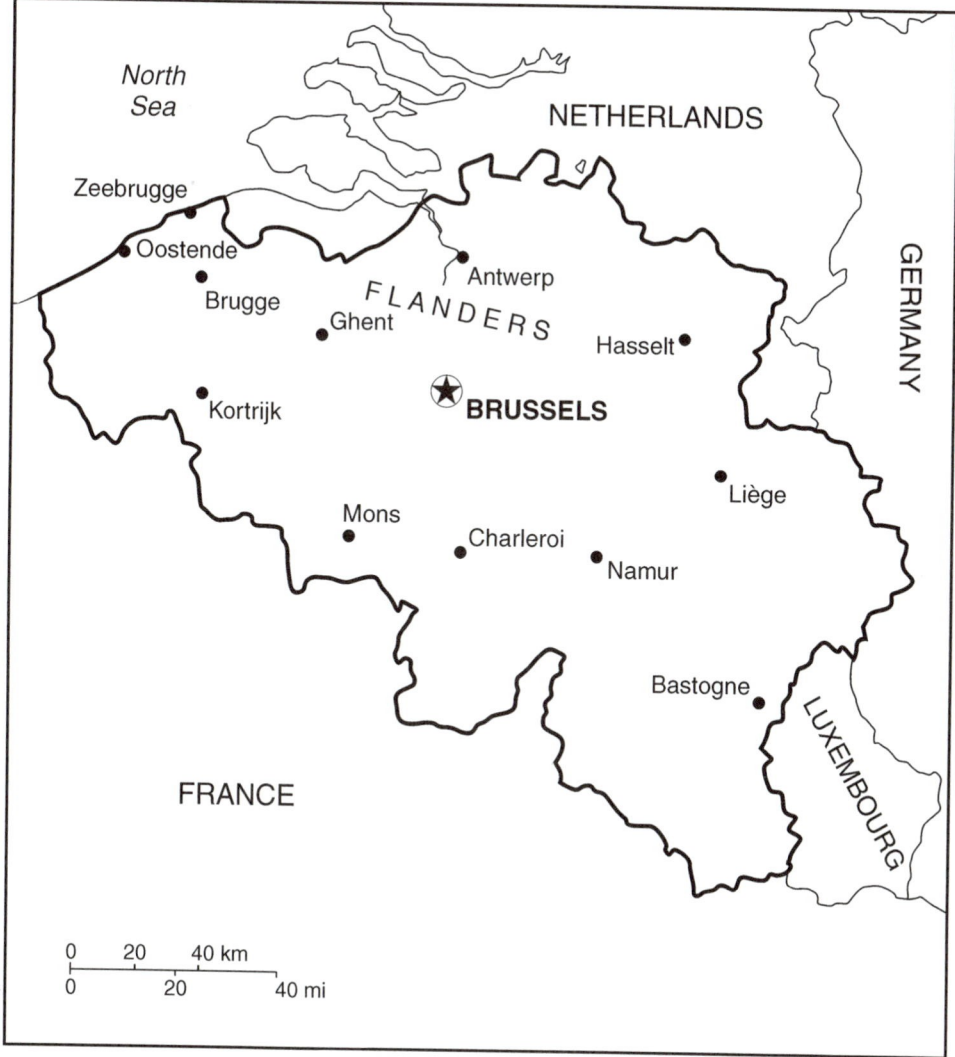

Flanders (Belgium).

include Ghent; Bruges, sometimes called the Venice of the North; Leuven, where the oldest university in the Netherlands is housed; Mechelen, once the capital of the Netherlands with the world-famous carillon school; and Hasselt. Flanders is also densely populated. More than 6 million people live in this fairly small region. Brussels, the capital of Belgium, is an enclave in Flanders and is mainly French-speaking. Since 1993 it has been a federal state in the kingdom with its own government responsible for culture, education, environment, public works, foreign trade, and other government operations.

To some extent, the name "Flanders" in an incorrect term. From the tenth century to the fourteenth century, this part of Europe consisted of a great number of virtually autonomous "principalities" such as the County of Flanders, to which belonged part of present-day France and the Kingdom of the Netherlands. Flanders—theoretically a fief of France—often fell out with other principalities such as the Duchy of Brabant, the counties of Hainault and Holland, and the prince-bishopric of Liège—in theory part of the Holy Roman Empire. In the fourteenth century most of these principalities were united by the dukes of Burgundy (present-day France). What is now called Flanders was one of the richest regions in the world. After the Burgundians the Habsburgs (the Spanish branch followed by the Austrian) had power, and at the end of the eighteenth century the whole "country" was annexed by the French Republic. After Napoleon's abdication these regions were added to the Kingdom of the Netherlands in 1815, but a revolution in the south resulted in the creation of the Kingdom of Belgium in 1831.

At that time the new country was bilingual. In Wallonia (the southern part) and in Brussels the upper class spoke French. In the North (present "Flanders") only dialects of Dutch were spoken, and people living only twenty-five or so kilometers apart could not understand each other. In that period politicians, trying to enforce a sense of nationhood, made French the official language. The Industrial Revolution spread into French-speaking Wallonia, while Flanders, with a moribund textile industry, sank quickly into poverty and became around 1850 one of the poorest regions in Europe. Efforts were made for a revival. In Flanders, where a great many Flemish, Brabant, and Limburg dialects were spoken, the so-called Flemish Struggle or Flemish Movement began. The struggle was primarily linguistic, as the Flemish people themselves decided upon standardizing their language, which would be the Dutch spoken and written in the Kingdom of the Netherlands. Minor differences of intonation, word stress, and vocabulary distinguish the Dutch in the North (Holland) and the Dutch used in northern Flanders. However, the differences are less marked than between the English of New York and the English used in London. Since language was the essence of the "struggle," much folklore material published in small, regional periodicals dealt with language (for example, fairy tales, legends, riddles, children's songs, game songs, proverbs, and popular vocabulary).

The southern border of Flanders is also the boundary between the Germanic part of Europe (Germany, **Austria**, Scandinavia, and **England**) and the Romance or Latin cultural world (France, **Spain**, and **Italy**). This boundary has not been altered—beyond two or three kilometers—for more than ten centuries. However, this does not change the fact that culture was exchanged between the Germanic and

Latin regions. As part of Western European tradition, Flemish folklore shares traditions with other societies. Moreover, increasing global influences in the form of travel, cinema, literature, and television has been accelerated by immigration from developing countries.

RELIGION AND RITUAL

Since the introduction of Christianity in the eighth and ninth centuries, Flanders has been, with the exception of some short periods in the sixteenth century, totally Roman Catholic. The very powerful clergy controlled private as well as public life from cradle to grave. However, since the secularization that began in the 1960s, people no longer abstain from meat on specified days, confessing to a priest has become a curiosity, and only about one-eighth of the Flemings, most of them elderly people, attend mass. The number of men who take holy orders has reached the lowest ebb. These trends have had significant consequences since religious popular culture was the principal part of Flemish folklore. Some decades ago, most Flemings were present in church at least four times in their lives in observance of certain rites of passage: baptism, confirmation, marriage, and the funeral service.

A minority of children born in Flanders are still christened. This happens in the presence of the parents and a godfather and godmother. The custom of dressing the baby with a christening dress used by the brothers or sisters or even by one of the parents still occurs. Friends and relatives are informed about the christening by colorful birth announcement cards, specially printed for that occasion. Since the 1960s a "birth-list," a page with addresses of shops where presents can be bought, is added. When the relatives or friends pay the mother and the baby a visit, they are given "sugarbeans." These candies, shaped like beans, are almonds or chocolate enclosed with white sugar. They are packed in specially designed boxes or cornets.

During the rite of transition from childhood to maturity at about twelve to fourteen years old, boys and girls are "confirmed" in church, that is, considered as adults. About thirty years ago, this ceremony took place at a younger age, about eleven years, following Holy Communion. The girls then wore a long, white dress as if they were young brides, while the boys wore trousers for the very first time in their lives. Nowadays, the participants look their best, but there is no uniformity anymore. What has not been altered is the festive meal or banquet that takes place in the family circle and that is followed by distribution of presents. Freethinkers in Flanders organize a festivity for the same age bracket, called simply the "Spring Festival."

Only a minority still marry in church. Many couples live together, though it must be said that the number of marriages is on the rise again, but not always with a religious ceremony. Some couples who marry in church keep to the old customs. In the country, it is still customary that neighbors let off fireworks on the eve of the marriage. Years ago this was said to drive off demons who might endanger the couple's life, but nowadays it is a hint to the newlywed couple that they must not forget to treat their neighbors well.

The funeral service as transition rite is mostly observed in church, since most deceased people belong to the older generations. Death is still informed by specially designed announcements. Since most people die in hospital and the whole organization of the funeral is arranged by morticians, the custom of hanging black cloth in and around the house of the dead person has vanished. The emphasis of the service is now on texts and/or songs, chosen by the relatives and read or sung by the children or grandchildren. Up to about five or six years ago, the relatives and friends bade the deceased farewell at the church gate and were not present at the burial or cremation. Now relatives and friends go to the cemetery or crematorium, where they throw flowers either on the coffin, in the grave, or on the cinerary urn. After this ceremony they have lunch—once known as "corpse-meal."

CALENDAR CUSTOMS

Strictly speaking, New Year's Day, 1 January, is no longer a religious festival, but it is still observed with many traditions. Relatives meet to exchange wishes, with drinking being the most important activity. The godson and/or goddaughter, pupils in primary school, read a specially written New Year Letter filled with best wishes to the godfather or godmother. Sending wishes with cards is a custom that has increased perceptibly. The more expensive these cards, the better. Another custom that is still vital is New Year's singing. Children go from door-to-door and sing New Year's songs in exchange for money or candy. The Flemish call this "begging-singing." The songs are centuries-old, but the repertory has dried up. Now the same three or four songs are sung each year.

An important festival is Epiphany, 6 January, which celebrates the meeting between Jesus and the Three Wise Men (called the Three Kings in Flanders). Nowadays it is a genuine family feast. Some decades ago, a cake was baked in which a bean had been hidden. The family member who found the bean on his plate became at once king, and he (not she!) then chose his queen, his court jester, royal doctor, lord chamberlain, and other members of court. That began the feast, and every "dignitary" had to play his or her part. Recent research has shown that this custom is increasing in popularity. What is more striking is the "begging-singing" on this very day. The children, dressed as kings with golden crowns on their heads, wear long robes. One of the three has a blackened face because one of the Wise Men was traditionally black. One of the Kings carries a golden star that can turn. Then the trio goes from door-to-door to sing and beg. Until about fifty or sixty years ago, this custom was also observed by adult men, and the money, not candies, collected was offered to the poor people of the parish or was handed over to the parish priest for missionary work. Now children go about in groups of five or six without dressing up. Only the songs have survived.

For generations, Lent has been the preparatory time for Easter, a period of mortification. The day before Lent begins—that is, Shrove Tuesday—was

The "king" wearing his Chain of Honor. (Photograph by Alfons Roeck)

an evening for thorough reveling and gorging. Since the nineteenth century, Carnival has been strongly influenced by German traditions. The Carnival fellowships, consisting mainly of men, start with their activities on 11 November at 11:11 A.M. They publish a weekly or monthly newsletter with most texts in the local dialect, compose a Carnival song for that specific year, and start preparing a Carnival ball party or, still more important, organize the Carnival pageant, an expensive affair. The fellowship elects a Prince-Carnival, who will be present at every occasion and who wears a seventeenth-century costume and headgear adorned with an immense pheasant feather. One of the characteristics of Carnival is making fun of the authorities and politicians. Carnival processions date to the Middle Ages. However, during the French Occupation (1795–1814) they were banned. A revival occurred in the nineteenth century, but during the two world wars the pageants were again forbidden by the German occupiers. At present, Carnival can be admired in many cities. The city of Aalst hosts the most famous procession today.

Prince-Carnival and his retinue. (Photograph by Alfons Roeck)

Palm Sunday (the Sunday before Easter) recalls Jesus's triumphal procession through Jerusalem. He was seated on a donkey and welcomed by a crowd waving palm branches. Since there are no palm trees in Flanders, people substitute box branches. These branches are consecrated in church, and the worshippers take some of them home to hang indoors

Penitential procession in Veurne (West-Flanders). (Photograph by Alfons Roeck)

since they protect against lightning. In many places, great and small, Palm Sunday donkey processions were organized in the Middle Ages. In one municipality (parish), Hoegaarden in the province of Brabant, this custom survives. Every year on Palm Sunday a waving crowd walks singing or praying through the city streets. In the middle of the procession a wooden donkey, on which a huge wooden Christ is sitting, is drawn through the parish.

Easter is celebrated after Lent. Once a year the houses are cleaned very thoroughly, and all the family members get new clothes. The Easter Hare, a German importation, and egg-hunts have become common sights. Church bells, which have been silent for three days, return from Rome and chime lustily.

Halloween has come to Flanders via France from the United States and for the past

St. Nicolas and Black Pete. (Photograph by Alfons Roeck)

several years has been mainly observed by youngsters. Not only hollowed-out pumpkins but everything horrifying gets involved in the festivities: witches, Dracula, werewolves, dragons, skeletons, and characters from television programs and horror stories.

On All Saints' Day, 1 November, people throughout Flanders visit the church to plant flowers—until recently only white ones—on the graves, tombs, or the columbarium or in the memory garden of their beloved deceased. The custom of lighting candles on the grave has not died out yet.

The Feast of St. Nicolas on 6 December honors the bishop of Myra who is buried in the cathedral of Bari (Italy) and has nothing to do with "Santa Claus" in the United States. For centuries, he has brought toys and candies on the night of 5 December. Sitting on a snow-white horse, he rides over the roofs and drops toys and other gifts through the chimneys. He is helped by Black Pete, who carries a rod to punish naughty children. Now, however, the bearded bishop arrives by boat from Spain and sits in an immense car that drives through the streets. His helper has turned into a respectable boy who means well for all children. Lately St. Nicolas has had fierce competition from Father Christmas, the American Santa Claus. Sometimes both of these children's friends operate at the same time in the same building.

On Christmas worshippers still go to church to attend midnight mass, but for most people it is a day for dining out. Putting up a Christmas crib, an idea elaborated by St. Francis in the thirteenth century, is still very popular. Moreover, many municipalities or cities build a genuine stable in the marketplace, and living animals such as sheep, donkeys, and oxen are stabled in it. The raising of a Christmas tree with presents lying beneath is a fairly recent custom. It was imported by German merchants in Antwerp, but it was the raising of the Christmas tree by German soldiers during World War I (1914–1918) that decided its popularity. Since 1945, raising a Christmas tree has been common throughout Flanders.

Until about forty or fifty years ago, religious processions occurred in most Flemish towns and villages on a Sunday in summertime. They were ambitious pageants, organized for the service or cult of a local saint, for reminding people of episodes in Mary's life, or for the representation of miracles that supposedly occurred in the very place. People from a variety of walks of life participated: dignitaries, schools, youth movements, brass bands, associations with flying colors, and even a unit of the army. A priest or a bishop, walking under a canopy, concluded the procession by holding up a monstrance containing the consecrated Host. When the priest with the monstrance passed by, all spectators knelt. In the streets where the procession passed, the houses were exquisitely decorated, and thousands of flowers or strips of gold and silvery paper were strewn on the paving stones. Most processions have disappeared, but in Scherpenheuvel, province of Brabant, the most important place of pilgrimage in

Flanders, the Candle Procession takes place on the first Sunday after All Saints' Day. The moment the procession walks by, pilgrims light thousands of candles planted in the ground. Other such processions throughout Flanders have a demonstrable impact on the tourist economy.

MEDICINE

When medical science still stood in its prehistory or when consulting a doctor was unaffordable for most people, sick people went to an herb doctor, the so-called green doctor, or they went to see a person who knew something about charms and spells. This person, man or woman, read some texts from a book or notebook, handed down for generations, many of which were written in archaic Dutch or in kitchen Latin or perhaps even contained nonsensical words or expressions. With alternative medicine now increasing in popularity, the visit to a "healing magician" has not fully come to an end yet.

Others, however, resorted to faith-based cures, often visiting a church or chapel where a specific saint is worshipped. For example, St. Apollonia, whose teeth had been broken out by her executioners, is approached by someone with a terrible toothache. She or he lights a candle, after it has been paid for, and prays for a rapid recovery. This religious custom persists throughout Flanders. There are as many saints as there are ailments. In churches or chapels where many people come flocking in, a notebook can be used to write the intention—for instance, "Holy Joseph, please cure my daughter" or "Mary, Mother of God, help me recover, please." These texts are called *vota scripta*, or written wishes.

MYTHS, LEGENDS, SONGS, AND FOLKTALES

Flanders also has a strong storytelling tradition, including fairy tales, legends, myths, and, in recent decades, jokes or urban legends. From the very beginning of the nineteenth century, folktales were noted down and published in Flanders, resulting in a corpus of a few thousand stories. However, after World War II students at the Catholic University of Leuven, under the directorship of K. C. Peeters and S. Top, and at the State University of Ghent, under the directorship of P. DeKeyser, were sent "on mission" to collect legends, record them on tape or cassette, classify them, and study them historically, geographically, and socially. This ambitious work has resulted in tens of thousands of folk legends. This collection is the pride of Flemish folklorists and the crowning glory of Flemish folklore studies.

What do these legends deal with? Some, presumably of pre-Christian origin, tell about demons living in the water, mermaids and nixes, wild huntsmen and dwarfs or goblins, and animals who talk. A second category deals with apparitions or ghosts. Some of these figures seek revenge, others come back to fulfill an unkept promise, while still others claim more prayers for the repose of their souls. The largest part of the collection deals with the Devil and his numerous friends and collaborators: sorcerers, werewolves, and freemasons—all avowed enemies of the Roman Catholic Church—as well as witches. A fourth category includes stories based on historical personages such as gangs of robbers, Napoleon, and Emperor Charles V.

A market-singer. (Photograph by Alfons Roeck)

Very few, if any, people still believe in the contents of all these legends. There is one exception. According to popular belief, witches are able to kill people and animals or commit arson at a distance with the help of the Devil, magical books, or methods they were taught by other witches. In short, all the misery and problems in the village community were the evil work of witches. Witch trials were conducted in the sixteenth and seventeenth centuries in Flanders, and some 200 women were executed, the last one in 1684. Legends about witches constitute the major part of the recent collection. We learn from these texts what evil they could do as well as ways to protect oneself against them—for instance, by making an appeal to the clergy, especially monks, who provide a printed prayer or a religious item (rosary or saint's medal) with which to ward off evil. Priests and monks are still regularly approached for these items.

Of the enormous collection of recent legends only a very small part, less than 3 percent, has been published. That is why scholars and students have been busy putting the legends on the Internet at www.volksverhalenbank.be. This Web site offers an extensive summary of 65,000 to 70,000 legends. The names of witches, wizards, and werewolves are replaced by initials to protect privacy. At present, 40 percent of the legend collection has been placed on the Web site.

Years ago, the University of Leuven began to collect folksongs. From the seventeenth century until about 1950 market-singers performed at the weekly markets. People coming to market delighted in the funny or horrifying songs and could even buy illustrated texts of them, though modern media have all but done away with that. Old-age songs, some of them dating to the Middle Ages, are still sung but mainly by elderly people when they meet or at special occasions. Nevertheless, some singers of popular songs have re-discovered the folksongs and have recovered part of the lost ground. Moreover, younger musical ensembles—some even playing with re-constructed ancient instruments—have had some commercial success with compact discs (CDs) and performances of folksongs.

TOWN RIVALRIES

Medieval towns were democratically organized much earlier in Flanders than in some other European regions or countries. Common burghers were granted social, economic, and even military rights. They founded militias to which the ruler or his representative could appeal in case of an emergency. Unfortunately, these towns were economic competitors with other towns even when the distance between them was only a few dozen kilometers. This resulted in many riots as well as real civil wars. The "others" were given nicknames that still exist. Inhabitants of Antwerp are "señores," people from Brussels are "chicken-gorgers," those of Ghent are "noose-carriers," the inhabitants of Turnhout (in the province of Antwerp) are called "Christian Jews," and those of Bruges are "the Bruges Madmen." Some years in many towns, magnificent secular-historical pageants strut through the streets. Sometimes the age-old rivalry between towns is readily apparent. This is the case between Aalst and Dendermonde (province of East-Flanders), between Ghent and Oudenaarde (province of East-Flanders), and between Antwerp and Mechelen (province of Antwerp). Man-made giants with biblical names (Goliath), classical-mythological ones (Poseidon), historical ones (Emperor Charles the Fifth), or even fictitious names (Tijl Uilenspiegel) are carried in most of these pageants. The Age of Giants has not yet come to an end. Even very recently, new giants have been built and carried in these pageants.

During the French occupation (1795–1814) the medieval militia were suppressed but were re-established after 1815. They had more a recreational than a military function. These associations are found primarily in the provinces of Antwerp and Limburg. During the season they set up shooting competitions, after which the winner is proclaimed "King." The shooter who wins the contest three times in a row is proclaimed "Emperor." The King has a small silver shield on which his name and the year of his victory are engraved, and this shield is then attached to a chain of honor. Some associations have chains with dozens of shields, some of which are more than four centuries old. The King always wears this chain of honor when he attends a ceremony. Apart from shooting, the archery-guilds also have picturesque parties or dinners where, in some instances, the same menu as three centuries ago is served. After dinner people dance. In the province of Antwerp the "brothers" use bow, crossbow, or handbow to shoot at a target, a "bird" hanging on a perpendicular pole twenty meters above ground. In Limburg, the short-rifle is used. Every year in this province or in the neighboring province of Dutch-Limburg the Old Limburg Marksmen Festival is organized, with Flemings and Dutch competing before some 25,000 spectators.

DRAMA, SPORTS, AND GAMES

Drama societies are active in all Flemish communities, no matter how small. However, age-old folk plays are never found on their programs. In Rutten near Tongeren, province of Limburg, an open-air mystery play, called *Evermarus-play*, is still performed on 1 May. According to some sources, it was written in the Middle Ages, though a more plausible estimate would be the seventeenth century. In Brussels, Antwerp, Ghent, and other towns puppet shows are very popular, though adults typically prefer plays with human actors. The repertory is more than 100, perhaps even 200 years old, rather lumpish of character, and sometimes characteristically vulgar.

Cardplaying and billiards are the most common games in pubs and bars. Many associations also engage in age-old ball games or bowling. After World War II *pétanque* came from France to become the most-watched ball game. Also, pigeon-flying is still very popular. Soccer and cycling are the two most popular spectator sports.

Part of the open-air museum, Bokrijk. (Photograph by Alfons Roeck)

ARCHITECTURE

Flanders is embedded in the Western European cultural world. This implies that construction of important buildings or monuments (for example, cathedrals, collegiate churches, city halls, city weighhouses, and clothmakers' halls) reflects the styles and artistic trends of Western Europe. On the other hand, for ages common people were badly housed in small wooden houses, covered with a thatched roof. In the country the hovel mainly consisted of a loamed beam-structure. Fire risk and security compelled people to build with stone or bricks. Half-timbered constructions, so popular in Germany, can be seen in the eastern part of Flanders. A great many houses in towns had a wooden frontage, but these disappeared over the course of time. When the Industrial Revolution influenced people to move from the countryside, masses of very cheap, unhygienic cul-de-sacs were built on the outskirts of towns. They still exist but are now lived in by immigrants. In the country the situation had not been altered for centuries: wattle-and-daub predominates. On fertile, loamy ground, large farms were squarely built with brick. However, on poor, sandy grounds the barn, stable, and farmhouse stood under one roof to form the so-called long-frontage farm. In the twentieth century booming prosperity caused everything that was "old" to be pulled down.

BREWING

Belgium (especially Flanders) is one of the most pre-eminent brewing countries of the world. Flemings are not the most prodigious beer-drinkers in the world, but more than 250 different beers are brewed in Flanders. First and foremost, beer is extremely important in this part of the world, and this does not apply to the number of bars or pubs. Flanders hosts beer-pageants, beer-festivals, beer-tasting contests, beer-cellars, beer-fountains, beer-guilds, beer-drinking contests, and waiter-races as well as other beer-related events. In some bookshops cookbooks, in which all the recipes stress beer as an important ingredient, are for sale.

STUDIES OF FLEMISH FOLKLORE

Folklorists realized that an age-old patrimony was about to vanish and succeeded in building an open-air museum (Bokrijk) in the province of Limburg. It officially opened in 1958. In all Flemish provinces, old valuable buildings were pulled down, all the parts were carefully numbered, and they were taken to Bokrijk to be meticulously rebuilt. Bokrijk includes dozens of large and small farms, a village church, chapels, a brewery, mills, country schools, inns, a smithy, and a carpenter's shop as well as other traditional buildings. In 1965, when the destruction of the old historical city center of Antwerp began, many houses of the sixteenth and seventeenth centuries—when Antwerp was the most important harbor in the world—were broken down in great haste and rebuilt in Bokrijk. This part of the Bokrijk Museum is called "the Old Town Quarter." During the tourist season the buildings in Bokrijk are lived in or used by people who actively practice crafts such as wickerwork, threshing, and making bobbin lace.

Much has been written about Flemish folklore, but most of it is in Dutch. Some fifty years ago, a tremendous work was started. Hundreds of periodicals (great and small, even those with very few subscribers) from 1683 onward were excerpted. Not only the titles of the articles and contributions but those of the reviews as well were published. Meanwhile, some important periodicals were excerpted up to 1990. This is the case for *Volkskunde*, founded in 1888 and presently in its 105th year of publication. Thirty-seven voluminous bibliographies have been published under the name of *Nederlandse Volkskundige Bibliografie*, issued by the Centrum voor Studie en Documentatie te Antwerpen. The *Vlaams Centrum voor Volkscultuur*, subsidized by the government, publishes a quarterly, *Mores*, as well as an annual in which all the titles of articles and reviews of hundreds of periodicals are listed. This center (www.vcv.be) provides useful information on Flemish folklore for folklorists anywhere in the world.

BIBLIOGRAPHY

Peeters, K. C. 1982. *Eigen Aard* (Our Culture). Antwerp: De Vlijt.

Roeck, A., J. Theuwissen, and J. Van Haver. 1982. *Vlaamse Volkscultuur* (Flemish Popular Culture). Amsterdam: Baert Deurne.

Top, S. 1986. *Kalender van de Vlaamse feesten* (Calendar of Flemish Feasts: Pageants, Festivals, Processions, etc.). Amsterdam: Helios, Kapellen.

Alfons Roeck

THE NETHERLANDS

GEOGRAPHY AND HISTORY

Situated on the northwestern corner of the European continent, the Netherlands are bordered on the east by **Germany**, on the south by Belgium, and to the north and west by the North Sea. They have a land area of 34,000 square kilometers (including 41,526 kilometers of inland waters). Several European rivers, which have always been important as trade arteries and as water supplies, discharge on the coastal side. The Rhine and the Maas bisect the land, and near its southern borders the Scheldt discharges into the estuary of the islands of Zeeland. As the name suggests, the Netherlands, or Low Lands, are largely flat and partially low-lying. The northwestern part of the country, roughly one-third of the total area (about 10,000 kilometers, even lies below sea level; most of the rest is only a few meters above sea level.

At the beginning of the Christian era the west of the Netherlands was still above water, but rising sea level and human interventions fundamentally altered this situation. Deforestation and the centuries-long cultivation and drainage of the soggy peat bogs caused the coastal region to subside, and regular flooding began to occur. This subsidence necessitated a structural program of drainage, which led to large-scale

The Netherlands.

impoldering and dike construction throughout the whole of the west and in a part of the northern Netherlands. This, in turn, led to continuing subsidence, until the land was sometimes as much as six meters below sea level. The land was protected against the sea by a natural row of sand dunes and by coastal defenses built in modern times and against internal water by polder dikes with windmills that constantly pumped the water toward the sea. A consequence of a devastating storm tide in 1953 inspired the building of massive defensive works (flood barriers and still higher dikes), which are intended to afford the whole country extra protection.

The continual confrontation with water is an important element in Dutch history, folklore, and tourism. As early as the twelfth century, the first local "democratic" governmental authorities in the county were the *waterschappen* and *hoogheemraadschappen*, organizations concerned with dike construction and drainage. The windmills, which drained the land, and the wooden shoes, which were highly practical footwear for country dwellers, thus became the pre-eminent symbols of Dutch identity to outsiders. The struggle against water ("God created the earth, and the Dutch created the Netherlands") is an established folkloristic and touristic image worldwide, perhaps reaching its narrative high point in the widely known book about Hans Brinker, the little boy from Haarlem who saved the Netherlands from a catastrophic flood by sticking his finger in a hole in a broken dike. This apocryphal story was invented by American writer Mary Mapes Dodge in her book *Hans Brinker, or, The Silver Skates* (1865), and it is thus generally most familiar in the English-speaking world, particularly among Americans. The story is known in the Netherlands only on a secondhand basis as a consequence of marketing to tourists.

In the seventeenth and eighteenth centuries the need to control the often-turbulent inland waters and the search for new land for raising livestock and growing crops in the densely populated Netherlands turned farmers to the lakes in the west of the country. In the twentieth century large areas of a former arm of the sea that reached deep into the country—the Zuiderzee, now the IJsselmeer—were turned into polders and pumped dry for large-scale agriculture. The latter intervention has led to the disappearance of fishing villages along the shores of the Zuiderzee. The low-lying polders that are kept pumped dry are still characteristic of the structure of the rural West Netherlands. In the late twentieth century the egalitarian and communal efforts that previously had been necessary to maintain the polders even became a metaphor for the socioeconomic and political organization of modern Dutch society. The British press coined term "polder model" in 1997 to refer to a society in which the people literally and figuratively seek to keep their feet dry on the basis of mutual consultation and consensus.

In part because of its location, economic activities, and liberal politics, the composition of the Dutch population has always been subject to considerable growth and change through immigration and emigration. Dutch folklorists of the nineteenth century hypothesized that the "Ur-population" consisted of a mix of Germanic and Celtic tribes, influenced by Roman rule until the third century C.E. Archeological finds since the seventeenth century in ancient burial mounds, megalithic tombs and forts, and peat bog tracks with the bog bodies have served to confirm the importance of these Batavian forebears. After the great Western European mass migrations of the fourth and fifth centuries the population of this river delta region would have comprised primarily Saxons, Frisians, and Franks.

Beginning in the late Middle Ages the flourishing economic and cultural situation and the often tolerant political climate regularly attracted groups of immigrants, whose presence changed the composition of the population. For example, after the fall of Antwerp in 1585 many Flemings moved north, followed in the seventeenth century by Sephardic Jews (see **Sephardim**) from **Spain** and Portugal. After 1685 French Huguenots sought out the tolerance of the Dutch Republic, and in the nineteenth century German tradesmen and merchants saw Holland as an attractive place to establish themselves. The modern years of prosperity from 1960 to 1970 attracted guest workers from Turkey (now 300,000) and Morocco (now 250,000) to fill vacancies in industries and for unskilled and semi-skilled jobs. The dismantling of the Dutch colonial empire led to the migration of large groups of East Indian Dutch (now 440,000) from Indonesia after its independence in 1949, and nearly half the population of Surinam left that former colony in the period around its independence in 1975 (now 300,000). In contrast, the Dutch Antilles are still part of the Kingdom of the Netherlands, but there has been a major economic flight from these six islands, particularly among the young, in the years since 1990. In combination with the arrival of relatively large numbers of refugees seeking asylum and economic refugees from all corners of the world in the years since 1980, a multicultural society has now emerged, particularly in the urban centers. Of its 16 million population in 2004, about 2.7 million were not of Dutch ancestry, including about 1 million from other European Union countries and America. The attitude of the Dutch government—condemned by some as too tolerant—has contributed to a situation in which the integration of non-Western immigrants, particularly Muslims, is being regarded as unsuccessful. Large numbers have not adopted the language and culture for themselves and live within their own traditionally oriented sub-cultures.

PRESERVATION OF DUTCH FOLKLORE

An interest in the peculiar cultural identity of the Netherlands arose as early as the sixteenth century. The process of forming an independent state, influenced by the struggle against Spanish domination in the sixteenth century, created a consciousness regarding the origins of the country and its population. The country was asserted to have grown from an amalgam of Germanic tribes, among whom the "Batavians" were regarded as the most important, not least because of the symbolic analogy with the Batavians' revolt against Roman colonization. Thus arose a "Batavian myth," a literary and academic theme and genre that sought and defined the origin of the Dutch people. Its foundations rested on a text by the Roman historian Tacitus about the "origin, morals, and customs of the Germans." This "Germans" theme would remain an unwavering benchmark for the practice of ethnology in the Netherlands until into the twentieth century. The folklorists of the nineteenth and early twentieth centuries attempted to derive an important part of Dutch popular culture from customs that were practiced in pre-Christian or "pagan" times and that ultimately remained unchanged or were only superficially altered when they were "Christianized." This was typical of the current approach to ethnology, which proceeded from a static concept of cultural continuity. In general, European ethnologists held onto the idea that specific population groups, particularly farmers and fishermen, were still the bearers of a "pure" culture of the "folk," preserved in an "authentic" form.

Joannes Le Francq van Berkhey (1729–1813) offered an early ethnographic expression of this concept of continuity and authenticity focusing on the folk culture of the

Cover of *Zeeland* magazine (1927), with a romantic drawing of the city hall of Middelburg and "Zeeuswe Meisjes," Zeeland girls in traditional dress.

Dutch countryside. In his *Natuurlyke Historie van Holland*, this "first" Dutch ethnographer sketched the nature of the Dutch people and their customs and attitudes. It was not until the end of the nineteenth century that the founding of the Flemish journal *Volkskunde* in 1888 stimulated a more scientific ethnology. It became a serious forum for the first generation of new ethnologists working in Dutch. The priest Jos Schrijnen (1869–1938) subsequently laid the scientific basis for the discipline with his manual *Nederlandsche volkskunde* (1915–1917). The National Open Air Folkmuseum, which encouraged the systematic collection of material folk culture, was established in 1912. The folklorist Dirk Jan van der Ven (1891–1973) dedicated himself to popularizing folklore, wishing to make the Dutch conscious of their own identity on the basis of their regional traditions and customs. He stimulated the practice of the "reenactment" of these usages through historical popular celebrations and folk dances as a cultural and political strategy for moral rearmament. In the meantime the Germanist Jan de Vries (1890–1964) emerged on the national and international stage as the most prominent Dutch ethnologist. He devoted his energy to stricter scientific practice of the discipline and took a more critical attitude toward the still-prevailing continuity thinking and essentialist approaches. However, he seriously compromised himself by cooperating in the abuse of ethnology for the National Socialist ideology during World War II.

The establishment of a national center for ethnology in 1934 under the leadership of P. J. Meertens (1899–1985) meant the institutionalization of the discipline. It focused on gathering ethnographic data by means of questionnaires in various fields of ethnology, with the goal of assembling a *Volkskunde-Atlas voor Nederland en Vlaams-België* and with the hope of arriving at new insights on the basis of this ahistorical, cartographic approach. In 1965 a new phase of research was ushered in with the appointment of J. J. Voskuil as research director. He devoted himself to introducing historical and serial data into the cartographic approach. Although this historicizing method was the impetus for important renewal, he also continued to stress the study of classic ethnological themes and resisted the new forms of neo-folklore and their study that responded to **modernization**. For him, changes in the culture of everyday life under the influence of the modernizing world and the related need for public folklore around old traditions that in turn flowed from this were not an object for study. Under his leadership some overinvestment in the past and historical ethnology occurred.

Compared to Germany, ethnology acquired little or no status in the universities in the Netherlands. Despite the presence of several extraordinary professors of ethnology during the twentieth century, the discipline achieved no fixed place in university education and still cannot claim this. As a consequence, research has remained almost purely limited to what after 1985 was renamed the Meertens Institute, an independent organization within the Royal Netherlands Academy of Arts and Sciences, where researchers, trained in various academic disciplines, give shape to the discipline as ethnologists.

RELIGION

Religion plays a key role in Dutch culture. The religious history of the Netherlands has been one of conflict. The arrival of Anglo-Saxon missionaries in the

Mary in the Holy Oak at the pilgrimage shrine of Meerveldhoven in the southern part of the Netherlands. The oak has the miraculous statue of Mary in the middle, and the branches are filled with silver votive offerings. (Photograph by Peter Jan Margry, 1981)

seventh and eighth centuries meant a first confrontation with the existing population. Nevertheless, a rapid and effective process of Christianization began, and pre-Christian beliefs receded into the background. Because of the lack of historical sources, the degree to which non-Christian elements continued to exist in the culture will always remain unclear. Whatever the case, the Catholic Church developed a virtual monopoly on religion. With regard to the devotions and veneration of saints, the pattern of religion among the people was very similar to that elsewhere in Western Europe with a large number of Marian shrines and cults of the Sacrament, which often developed from an apparition or miraculous event. When the critique within the church began to take on sharper forms, changes occurred within that devotional pattern. From within the church came the fourteenth-century movement Modern Devotion, which focused on a more inward religious life, and the humanist Erasmus of Rotterdam. From outside Menno Simons, Luther, and Calvin were the most important figures in introducing the new, Protestant views. Calvinism was the dominant current in the Netherlands, while Lutheran and Anabaptist Protestants were minorities. For the Dutch the movement of religious reformation in part ran parallel with a process of political partition. The revolt of the northern Netherlands against King Philip II of Spain in 1576, the separation of this region from the southern section (the later Belgium and Luxembourg), which followed in 1579, and the creation of the Dutch Republic, the seven United Provinces of the Netherlands (roughly equivalent to the present country), resulted. Among other important consequences were an economic flight of southern Netherlanders to the north and a religious upheaval through which the Netherlands entered a long history of Protestantization. The state remained a collection of rather autonomous provinces, so that particularism continued to exist, with consequences for language, religion, morals, and customs that remained as regional identity markers.

With the creation of this Republic in 1579, Calvinism in the form of the Reformed Church acquired the status of a state church, and a Dutch Calvinist spirituality developed that focused on the Word, daily reading of the Bible, preaching, and hymn-singing. The majestic and, in time, archaic language of the *Statenbijbel*, the official Dutch translation introduced in 1637, has left its mark on Dutch language and culture. Visitors to the Netherlands during that time were struck by the simplicity of life and aversion to the public display of wealth as well as the openness and tolerance of the populace, qualities that they saw as connected with Calvinism. These are, to a large extent, superficial images, part of a tradition of descriptions of the Dutch by foreign visitors.

After the Reformation, Catholicism was suppressed and its expression no longer tolerated in public. This meant that the Catholic cultural landscape was gradually destroyed as chapels were closed and images destroyed or hidden from sight. Public rituals such as processions, saints' days, ringing of bells, pilgrimages, Carnival, and other immaterial expressions of the religion were forbidden. This Protestantization was not total. The population of the southern provinces of North Brabant and Limburg remained almost entirely Catholic, and elsewhere, particularly in North and South Holland and Gelderland, large concentrations of Catholics could also be found. In total about a third of the population continued to practice Catholicism out of public sight.

For the rest, it took a long time for Protestants to relinquish all their old Catholic customs. Until into the eighteenth century they continued to celebrate certain saints' feasts and tolled church bells at funerals in the expectation that this was good for the salvation of the deceased's soul. During this period there were increasing rationalist denunciations of the "superstitions" associated with Catholic belief. For instance, the 1691 book *De betoverde Weereld* by the preacher Balthasar Bekker characterizes many forms of necromancy and magic as illusion and deception. Such a climate contributed to the Netherlands being the first place in Western Europe where, already in the seventeenth century, the burning of witches ceased. (The last death sentence was in 1608, the last witchcraft trial in 1659.) Although widespread belief in, and accusations of, witchcraft declined sharply in the seventeenth century, they did occur occasionally, particularly in rural areas, even into the twentieth century. A particular focus of ethnographic research was the practice of folk magic and divination.

In the seventeenth century the pilgrimage culture at shrines in the Netherlands had almost disappeared. With the exception of several highly private saints' cults, it was displaced to adjoining regions. Large groups of Catholics traveled to neighboring countries, often on foot, in order to evade the ban on their devotions. These long journeys gave pilgrimage an element of penance and resulted in an increased internalizing of faith. Moreover, such pilgrimages and the miracles with which they were connected began to function as factors that defined Catholic identity and symbolized hope for this minority's future.

After the Dutch or Batavian Republic of 1795, the Netherlands obtained its first constitution, which guaranteed freedom of religion. This anticipated a thorough emancipation process for Catholics, who after two centuries of religious repression and political discrimination could again freely exercise their faith. For this they reached back to the "Golden Age of Catholicism," the late Middle Ages. Old devotions to saints were revitalized, and former shrines were reconstructed. Saints' cults and confraternities were reintroduced. The importance of comfort and healing was expressed in the reintroduction of the practice of votive gifts, in which metal objects or human or animal figures were offered.

During the eighteenth century the conflict between Calvinists and Catholics gradually weathered into peaceful co-existence, in the course of which, to a great extent because of geographic differences but also through social and religious differences, a divided society emerged. During the nineteenth century this intensified, as an almost complete separation in all realms of Dutch society arose between Protestants and Catholics. This situation, termed "pillarization," endured until the second half of the twentieth century. It remained the almost universal ordering factor in all segments and aspects of Dutch life from about 1850 to about 1965. From the end of the nineteenth century a social-democratic faction joined the two religious groups to become a third major pillar.

The modernization of society since World War II has sidelined the role of the churches. Church membership and attendance have fallen to under 10 percent of the population, making the Netherlands one of the most secular countries in the West. Meanwhile with more than 1 million Muslims, the visible presence of Islam in public space has grown steadily, with the construction of traditional mosques with minarets and the increasing practice of wearing head scarves and other traditional clothing.

Concurrent with the emptying of the churches, interest in alternative spirituality and healing practices has increased enormously. The growth of a multicultural society has introduced new types of religious healers (winti doctors from Surinam, Islamic healers, African healers) and their practices. One of the most popular faith healers ever in the Netherlands is, however, the Dutch medium Jomanda, who is able to mobilize hundreds of thousands of often-desperate people in either a medical or social respect for her healing services. "New Age" beliefs and practices enjoy intense interest. A wide cross-section of the population still has a cultural-historical connection with the religious tradition in which they were raised, but religion has been marginalized as a factor in politics and society. A large proportion of the public will admit to a religious feeling that has been characterized as "something-ism": no faith in a personal god but acknowledgment that there must be "something." The ritual and religious vacuum in society in the past decades has led to the rediscovery or invention of rituals, both in the religious and ecclesiastical realm and in rites of passage. Funeral culture has especially undergone vigorous growth and innovation. One reflection of this is the spontaneous creation

Spontaneous shrine created after the murder of Dutch film director Theo van Gogh on 2 November 2004. (Photograph by Peter Jan Margry)

of memorial monuments ("spontaneous shrines") by the public at the sites of major disasters, for individual victims of senseless violence, and, in the form of roadside memorials, for traffic victims.

CALENDAR CUSTOMS

A country's religious culture can define its festival culture. In the Netherlands, however, the Reformation swept away almost all of the existing public celebrations of Catholic holy days and saints' days. Fairs, in the Middle Ages the annual markets that coincided with the celebrations for the patron saint of a church or city, continued to exist, but in altered form. From the seventeenth century they became more opportunities for recreation, where a variety of attractions such as plays, lotteries, gambling, puppet shows, and musicians was available. The Netherlands still has hundreds of itinerant fun fairs and traveling carnivals. In addition, several feasts such as Epiphany (6 January) and St. Martin's Day (11 November) remain popular as occasions when children clothed as beggars go from door-to-door with lanterns or singing in hope of receiving small change, baked goods, or candy. The Easter Cycle begins with *Palmpassen* (Palm Sunday), when palm leaves are blessed in the Catholic churches, taken home, and hung up as a means of averting external danger. The more general secular custom of painting and hiding Easter eggs (or chocolate eggs), which the children then find and eat, is connected with Easter itself.

With the disappearance of the medieval Catholic feasts, the celebration of birthdays and anniversaries involving members of the House of Orange, the Protestant royal family, emerged. They have been the pre-eminent sovereign power in the Netherlands, first as *stadhouders* and, from 1814, as monarchs. The struggle for independence from Spain at the end of the sixteenth century also brought the tradition of celebrating the liberation of various cities such as Leiden's *Ontzet*, Alkmaar's *Victorie*, and the rebels' capture of Den Briel, where, according to a popular ballad, "the Duke of Alva lost his glasses" (Den Briel "Bri[e]l[le]"; "his glasses"; "*zijn bril*"). Since 1817, the Reformed Church's privileged position has permitted it to celebrate 31 October as Reformation Day.

During the "bourgeois" nineteenth century the festival culture in general grew strongly. For instance, it was then customary to celebrate Christmas both in the church and with family festivities at home. Around the middle of the nineteenth century the decorated Christmas tree entered from neighboring Germany, especially among the urban middle class. It was, however, only between 1960 and 1980 that Christmas became a general family celebration involving gift-giving. At present about 75 percent of the Dutch celebrate Christmas, and about half of this group exchange gifts. But the most important children's feast in the Netherlands, the celebration of Sinterklaas (St. Nicholas), the aged bishop from Spain with his black helpers (*Zwarte Pieten*), comes not long before Christmas, on 5 or 6 December. On this occasion, called *pakjesavond* (package evening), people exchange gifts, accompanied by a teasing poem and/or a handmade item relating specifically to the receiver. Aspects of this celebration came under threat some years ago from ideological assertions that the Black *Pieten* were racist caricatures and politically incorrect, but such objections are seldom heard anymore. Although ethnological research indicates that families not native to the Netherlands rarely adopt Dutch customs, now and then, when the Sinterklaas feast and the Muslim Sugar Feast, which marks the end of Ramadan, coincide, schools will hold collective celebrations. Because of the depth of the attachment to the Sinterklaas tradition among the population, the threat from the increasing importance of Christmas through globalization and commercialization does not appear to be serious.

In the southern, Catholic provinces the forbidden feast of Carnival was kept alive in memory, thanks to its continued celebration in neighboring Belgium and Germany. In the nineteenth century it was revived somewhat as an elite celebration in the cities of the Catholic south, but only after 1945 was there a massive celebration of Carnival, which extended to areas outside the cities and for which public life would stop for several days. The great parades with floats characterize these events, not only providing amusement but also delivering satirical critiques of society, local and beyond. As a result of the breaking down of the pillarized social structures, growing mobility, commercialization, and media coverage, since the 1980s Carnival has also been introduced here and there in the "Protestant" Netherlands, and numbers of celebrants travel from that region to participate in Carnival in the southern cities.

In the nineteenth century, the Netherlands had no true national holiday except for the annual commemoration of the Battle of Waterloo in 1815 and the "heroic deeds" performed there by the later king Willem II. The birthdays of members of the royal family were causes for national celebration, but only after 1887 did this become concentrated in one holiday, the Queen's Birthday. It was instituted for the first female sovereign, Wilhelmina (1880–1962), and intended to emphasize the idea of national unity in a society split by religious divisions and pillarization. It was celebrated with public festivities such as parades with brass bands, performances by folklore groups, and barbecues. Along with the organization of national historic folk events, this contributed to the folklorization and historicization of "traditional" Dutch folk traditions and popular culture.

Since she ascended the throne in 1980, Beatrix, the present queen, has celebrated her birthday officially on the holiday, 30 April, by visiting her subjects in two Dutch towns or cities, accompanied by several other members of the royal family. On the "free" Queen's Birthday anyone in the country can sell things, play music, and sing or perform street theater without having to obtain the usual permits. The "free market," where secondhand goods are hauled out of attics and offered for sale on the streets, draws hundreds of thousands to city centers. There is also singing, quantities of beer are consumed, and people dress up in orange clothing with orange crowns or wigs and carry orange mascots—orange being the color of the Royal House of Orange. On 4 May, Dutch Memorial Day, the victims of World War II are honored. Liberation Day (5 May) marks the end of World War II for the Netherlands, an occasion again recognized with free markets and music festivals.

Dutch festival culture is being affected by outside influences from North America and general globalization. An example from the 1930s is the observance of Mother's Day. Since the end of the 1980s, Halloween has also been celebrated on 31 October as a children's feast. Television coverage of this holiday in America and the production of Halloween-themed films introduced this event to Europe, at least in its outward forms, both as something for children and as a theme for parties in the flourishing disco and club culture. Actively promoted by florists, greeting card companies, and the postal service, Valentine's Day also arrived in the Netherlands at about the same time.

The massive increase in the number of feasts and festivals in the Western world since the 1980s and the equally massive increase in attendance at them have been termed "festivalization." This development is connected with the expansion of free time, greater prosperity, and the increasing need for mass expressions in which people do not observe passively by means of television but in which they can actually participate. Festivals and feasts can be an attractive means of gaining publicity and developing public image. This is true for cities, for which festivals are often developed for commercial purposes (for example, Amsterdam's Queen's Birthday and Rotterdam's Antillean Carnival) as well as for minority groups (the Surinamese Kwakoe Festival; Gay Pride in the canals of the "Gay Capital," Amsterdam; and the Indonesian Pasar Malam market festival in The Hague).

SPORTS AND GAMES

As a collective form of recreation and sport, ice-skating and sledding have always been important social events in the Netherlands. One sees this in the seventeenth-century paintings of Hendrick Avercamp. The nineteenth century saw a blossoming in special associations founded to establish winter ice rinks where there was too little natural water. Since the end of the nineteenth century, the national skating event, the Elfstedentocht (Eleven Cities Tour), has been held over a distance of about 200 kilometers through eleven cities in the province of Friesland, sometimes under severe conditions. This "tour of tours" can occur only after a deep frost, because the ice must be thick enough to support the 16,000 skaters who participate. Mild winters lately have forestalled the event. So that the "tradition" will not be lost, each year an alternative skating marathon is held on frozen lakes in Canada or Scandinavia.

SONGS AND FOLKTALES

Dutch oral narrative culture is part of the European stock of stories, rooted in, or shaped by, Indo-European, classic, medieval, and Arabic sagas, legends, fairy tales, and other folk stories. Research into this tradition was inspired by the pioneering work of the Grimms in the early nineteenth century, when the importance of each language's characteristic oral culture and its centrality to national identity became recognized. Pioneers in collecting oral narratives included Henri Welters for Limburg, Cornelis Bakker for Waterland, Dam Jaarsma for Friesland, and Gerrit Jan Boekenoogen for all the Netherlands. Through the efforts of volunteers, over 30,000 Dutch folktales have been written down for the Meertens Institute. Likewise, its use of questionnaires enabled the institute to record oral traditions regarding such figures as werewolves, gnomes, will-o'-the-wisps, and supernatural animals. Now the questionnaires deal more with modern themes such as urban legends, UFO accounts and crop circles, jokes, and tear-jerking songs.

The Dutch language has had an extensive song culture. Thousands of folksongs have been preserved. Through the centuries many new song texts have been set to existing melodies. Efforts to collect this material began in the nineteenth century, and many songs were written down by Ate Doornbosch in the first half of the twentieth century. Characteristic genres were seamen's chanteys and street songs. Although the Netherlands originally had no regional folk music styles, toward the end of the twentieth century music in specific regional dialects developed as a part of the dialect renaissance.

ARCHITECTURE

Foreigners generally know the Netherlands as "Holland." This comes from the centuries-long dominance of the province of Holland within the seven United Provinces. It was in the important cities of Holland that the seventeenth-century Golden Age took form: the expansion of the canal cities, the economic prosperity through trade, and painting. With regard to architecture and urban design, the Netherlands has long had a special claim to notability. Because of the lack of hard stone and the ample supply of river clay, already in the Middle Ages a transition was being made from wooden construction to brick. By the seventeenth and eighteenth centuries brick had become the characteristic look of the Dutch city of the Golden Age. The economic significance of the many waterways and trade was further reflected in their refined canal structure. These were an urban feature absent from the Eastern Netherlands, where the influence of the Hanseatic League is much more visible. Depending on the wealth of the region and the use of the land, the countryside also had varying types of farmsteads. Such regional identities also can be discovered in research into the probate inventories from the seventeenth and eighteenth centuries. While in the east of the country the utility value of the domestic material culture is more central, the prosperous fishing towns of the west were attached to their local costumes and lifestyle, and the use of objects was more related to their significance for the local community. Delft blue pottery, which was then found not only everywhere in the Netherlands but around the world, had a special place among the household goods. It was made and decorated in two genres: with imitation Chinese motifs, which had become familiar through imports by the Dutch East India Company, and with typical Dutch decorations based upon local folk culture. Delft blue, in all its neo-styles, is still a best-selling souvenir for tourists.

Dutch painting of the seventeenth century is world-famous and valued for its genre pieces of daily life, portraits, depictions of urban culture, and landscapes. Later, the influence of nineteenth-century nationalism and romanticism effected a revival of interest in local and regional folk culture through painting. Once again painters were attracted to the picturesque quality of Dutch fishing and farming towns. Towns such as Volendam, Marken, Domburg, Scheveningen, Hindelopen, and Laren became idealized icons of Dutch society. As an ultimate development, paintings and small souvenirs became export products. In both **Japan** and **China** precise copies of complete old Dutch villages—such as the 1992 Holland Village near Nagasaki—have been constructed for tourists.

While in the Far East historic Dutch buildings are still highly esteemed, in the

West the new Dutch architecture and urban design of the early twentieth century are highly admired. This period once again found a characteristic architectural style in brick. The buildings of the Amsterdam School and H. P. Berlage are the best-known examples. After World War II both the population and the need for dwellings grew explosively, leading to modernization, standardization in architecture, and large-scale, socially financed residential neighborhoods in which pre-fabricated concrete construction methods were employed. Ultimately, this architecture proved to be insufficiently strong esthetically, qualitatively, and in terms of social structure. Since the 1990s the tendency has been to reach back to historic, regional, and traditional architectural forms.

CHALLENGES OF THE MODERN WORLD

Along with an inclination toward innovation and ready acceptance for new trends and developments, the Netherlands' role as a trading nation, which in principle welcomed immigrants and divergent opinions, has contributed to the globalization of Dutch culture. This passion for innovation has sometimes been so rapid and radical that it provokes nostalgic reactions. For instance, by the mid-1980s the thorough abandonment of various ecclesiastical rituals in the 1960s and 1970s created a need to fill the "ritual vacuum" that had arisen, though this was often more about form and sentiment than content.

Globalization has also led to increased interest in what is specifically Dutch about Dutch culture, a situation not unique for the Netherlands. In reaction to the threat of losing their own identity, over the past three decades a deeper interest has grown up among the Dutch in their own history and national and cultural traditions. Not only on the national level but also at the local and regional levels, old customs, rituals, and language variants are again being positively valued and cultivated. As a form of leisure activity, these usages are being artificially brought to life as neo-folklore, as dialect renaissance, and in the form of historical reenactments.

This also plays a role in commerce and tourism, where new images of the Netherlands are being created. The Miss Windmill contest, for example, promotes this one icon of Dutch culture, while "Frau Antje," a "milkmaid" with blond hair and blue eyes and clothed in Volendam's local costume, specifically targets the German cheese market. It is a stereotypic symbol intended to emphasize the traditional processes and authenticity of Dutch dairy products as a counter to industrialization and globalization. On the other side, there is also a modern "black" folklore variant. Many foreign visitors to Amsterdam are attracted by the flip side of the liberal and tolerant Dutch society in the world of legal window prostitution on the Wallen and the "coffee shop" circuit, with its tolerated sale and use of soft drugs.

STUDIES OF DUTCH FOLKLORE

Historiography of twentieth-century Dutch ethnology and ethnologists is available in Dekker (2002) and (in English) in Vermeulen and Kommers (2002). The only existing bibliography in English is the very much outdated *Folklore* (1932). The best overview of modern research in Dutch ethnology and folklore studies is Dekker,

Roodenburg, and Rooijakkers (2000). The results of modern Dutch folklore studies were published in *Volkskundig Bulletin. Tijdschrift voor Nederlandse cultuurwetenschap* (1975–2000). The successor to this journal is *Kleine c. Etnologisch tijdschrift* which began publication in 2005. The Belgian journal *Volkskunde* is also important to Dutch ethnological studies.

The only national scientific institution working in ethnology and folklore in the Netherlands is the Ethnology Department of the Meertens Instituut in Amsterdam. Its Web site gives information on the specific research programs and gives direct access to some major ethnological databases on such topics as folksongs, folktales, pilgrimages, and festivals (www.meertens.nl). The National Open Air Folkmuseum (Nederlands Openluchtmuseum) has a Web site that provides a good impression of its important material culture collections and regional housing styles as well as the museum's temporary exhibitions (www.openluchtmuseum.nl). Another open-air museum is located at Enkhuizen and offers a good impression of the village and fisherman culture around the former Zuiderzee. See its Web site at www.zuiderzeemuseum.nl. The Public Folklore Center (Nederlands Centrum voor Volkscultuur) in Utrecht deals mainly with public folklore and the dissemination of ethnological knowledge for educational purposes and for a broader public. It publishes three periodicals: *Traditie, Levend Erfgoed. Vakblad voor Public Folklore & Public History*, and *Alledaagse Dingen*. Its Web site is www.volkscultuur.nl.

BIBLIOGRAPHY

Abraham-Van der Mark, E. E., ed. 1994. *Successful Home Birth and Midwivery: The Dutch Model.* Westport, CT: Bergin and Garvey.

Barnouw, Adriaan J. 1940. *The Dutch: A Portrait Study of the People of Holland.* New York: Columbia University Press.

Bergen, C., and others, eds. 2002. *The Mysterious Bog People.* Zwolle: Waanders.

Boissevain, Jeremy, and Jojada Verrips. 1989. *Dutch Dilemmas: Anthropologists Look at the Netherlands.* Assen: Van Gorcum.

Bouchakour, Morad. 2002. *Party! in the Netherlands.* Amsterdam: Artimo.

Caspers, Charles, and Peter Jan Margry. 2003. Cults and Pilgrimage Sites in the Netherlands. In *Saints of Europe: Studies towards a Survey of Cults and Culture*, edited by Graham Jones. Donington: Shaun Tyas Publishing. 29–42.

Dekker, Ton. 2002. *De Nederlandse volkskunde. De verwetenschappelijking van een emotionele belangstelling* (Dutch Folklore Studies: The Professionalization of an Emotional Interest). Amsterdam: Aksant.

Dekker, Ton, Herman Roodenburg, and Gerard Rooijakkers, eds. 2000. *Volkscultuur. Een inleiding in de Nederlands etnologie* (Popular Culture: An Introduction to Dutch Ethnology). Nijmegen: Sun.

Efting Dijkstra, Marjolein. 2004. The Animal Prop: Animals as Play Objects in Dutch Folkloristic Games. *Western Folklore* 63:169–188.

Frijhoff, Willem. 2002. *Embodied Belief. Ten Essays on Religious Culture in Dutch History.* Hilversum: Verloren.

Galema, A., and others, eds. 1993. *Images of a Nation: Different Meanings of Dutchness, 1870–1940.* Amsterdam: Rodopi.

Gelderblom, Arie-Jan, Jan L. de Jong, and Marc Van Vaeck, eds. 2004. *The Low Countries as a Crossroads of Religious Beliefs.* Leiden: Brill.

Gijswijt-Hofstra, Marijke, and Willem Frijhoff. 1991. *Witchcraft in the Netherlands from the Fourteenth to the Twentieth Century.* Rotterdam: University Press.

Gijswijt-Hofstra, Marijke, and others. 1999. *Witchcraft and Magic in Europe: The Eighteenth and Nineteenth Centuries.* London: Athlone Press.

Ginkel, Rob van. 1997. *Notities over Nederlanders. Antropologische reflecties* (Notes on the Dutch: Anthropological Reflections). Amsterdam: Boom.

Haan, H. de. 1994. *In the Shadow of the Tree: Kinship, Property and Inheritance among Farm Families.* Amsterdam: het Spinhuis.

Hermans, Theo, and Reinier Salverda, eds. 1993. *From Revolt to Riches: Culture and History of the Low Countries, 1500–1700: International and Interdisciplinary Perspectives.* London: Centre for Low Countries Studies.

The Holland Handbook. 2003. The Hague: X-Pat Media.

Hooker, Mark T. 1999. *The History of Holland.* Westport, CT: Greenwood Press.

Horst, Han van der. 2001. *The Low Sky: Understanding the Dutch. The Book That Makes the Netherlands Familiar.* Schiedam/The Hague: Scriptum/Nuffic.

Huizinga, Johan. 1924. *The Waning of the Middle Ages.* Harmondsworth: Penguin.

———. 1968. *Dutch Civilisation in the Seventeenth Century and Other Essays.* New York: Harper and Row.

Ishwaran, K. 1959. *Family Life in the Netherlands.* The Hague: Van Keulen.

Jong, Ad de. 2001. *De dirigenten van de herinnering. Musealisering en nationalisering van de volkscultuur in Nederland, (1815–1940)* (The Conductors of Memory: "Museumization" and "Nationalization" of Folk Culture in the Netherlands). Nijmegen: Sun.

Kers, Martin. 1988. *Hollandbook: Photographic Impressions.* Zutphen: Terra.

Kossmann, Ernst H. 1978. *The Low Countries 1780–1940.* Oxford: Oxford University Press.

Lijphart, Arend. 1968. *The Politics of Accommodation. Pluralism and Democracy in the Netherlands.* Berkeley: University of California Press.

Margry, Peter Jan, and Charles Caspers, eds. 1997–2004. *Bedevaartplaatsen in Nederland* (Lexicon of Places of Pilgrimage in the Netherlands). 4 volumes. Verloren: Hilversum. (Internet version: www.meertens.knaw.nl/bol/.)

Marland, H., and M. Pelling. 2004. *The Task of Healing. Medicine, Religion and Gender in England and the Netherlands 1450–1800.* Rotterdam: Erasmus Publishing.

Matter, Fred, ed. 1990. *Toverij in Nederland, 1795–1985. Bibliografie* (Bibliography on Magic and Sorcery). Amsterdam: P. J. Meertens-Instituut.

Meder, T. 2004. "There were a Turk, a Moroccan, and a Dutchman . . .": Narrative Repertoires in the Multi-ethnic Neighbourhood of Lombok in the Dutch City of Utrecht. In *Erzählen zwischen den Kulturen,* edited by Sabine Wienker-Piepho and Klaus Roth. München: Waxmann. 237–258.

Meder, T., and E. Venbrux. 1999. Anders Bijma's Folktale Repertoire and Its Collectors. *Fabula* 40.3–4:48–61.

Meertens, P. J., and Maurits de Meyer. 1959–1969. *Volkskunde-Atlas voor Nederland en Vlaams-België* (Folklore Atlas of the Netherlands and Flemish Belgium). 4 volumes. Amsterdam and Antwerp: Standaard Boekhandel.

Nieuwhoff, Constance. 1985. *The Costumes of Holland.* Amsterdam: Elsevier.

Palm, C.H.M. 1964. Costumes of Staphorst, a Village in the Eastern Netherlands. *International Archives of Ethnography* 50:43–59.

Post, Paul, and others. 1998. *The Modern Pilgrim: Multidisciplinary Explorations of Christian Pilgrimage.* Leuven: Peeters.

Roodenburg, Herman W. 1991. "The Hand of Friendship": Shaking Hands and Other Gestures in the Dutch Republic. In *A Cultural History of Gesture from Antiquity to the Present Day,* edited by J. N. Bremmer and H. W. Roodenburg. Cambridge: Polity Press. 152–189.

————. 2002. Making an Island in Time: Dutch Folklore Studies, Painting, Tourism and Craniometry around 1900. *Journal of Folklore Research* 39:173–200.

Schama, Simon. 1987. *The Embarrassment of Riches: An Interpretation of Dutch Culture in the Golden Age*. New York: Knopf.

Stott, Annette. 1998. *Holland Mania: The Unknown Dutch Period in American Art and Culture*. Woodstock: Overlook Press.

Vermeulen, Han, and Jean Kommers, eds. 2002. *Tales from Academia: History of Anthropology in the Netherlands*. 2 volumes. Saarbrücken: Verlag für Entwicklungspolitik.

Verrips, Jojada. 1973. The Preacher and the Farmers: The Church as a Political Arena in a Dutch Community. *American Anthropologist* 75:852–868.

White, Colin, and Laurie Boucke. 2001. *The Undutchables: An Observation of the Netherlands: Its Culture and Its Inhabitants*. 4th edition. Lafayette, CO: White Boucke.

Peter Jan Margry (Translated from the Dutch by Don Mader)

Central Europe

AUSTRIA

GEOGRAPHY AND HISTORY

A federal republic in Central Europe with nine provincial states, Austria (*Österreich*) borders on eight countries: **Germany**, **Switzerland**, Liechtenstein, **Italy**, **Slovenia**, **Hungary**, **Slovakia**, and the Czech Republic. With a landmass of 83,855 square kilometers, it is about the size of the American state of Maine, has a population of just over 8 million, and is one of the smaller countries of Europe. It has always been a major transit land between Northern Europe and Italy to the south and the Balkan countries to the southeast. More than two-thirds of the Italian province Alto Adige (South Tyrol) is culturally and linguistically Austrian-German and thus included in any treatment of the folk culture of Austria.

Austria.

The country can be divided into three regions. In the north the Danube Valley is generally flat with hills in the east, where large vineyards are found. The center, roughly two-thirds of the country, is mountainous, a larger percentage than in Switzerland, and the numerous high mountain valleys have produced distinctive folk cultures—for example, the Zillertal and the Öztal. The foothills of the Alps in the southeast lead down to the plains of Hungary. In present-day Austria there are ninety people per square kilometer, compared to 247 in Germany, and one-third of the populace lives in one of the five major cities, Vienna, Graz, Linz, Salzburg, or Innsbruck. Nearly one-fourth of Austrians live in Vienna, a city of 1.7 million inhabitants, while only about 16 percent live in towns or villages of less than 1,000. The population is 98 percent German-speaking, but six minorities are recognized: Slovenian, Croatian, Hungarian, Czech, Slovak, and Romany or Sinti (Gypsies), found largely in Vienna or in the southeastern and southern states. Most Austrians speak a variety of German derived from the Bavarian dialect.

Austria has been populated continually since the Paleolithic age. From 800 to 400 B.C.E. Celtic tribes inhabited much of present-day Austria with the exception of the extreme west, where river and place-names still reflect pre-Celtic settlements. During the Roman Empire the provinces of Raetia, Noricum, and Pannonia were established as border regions, and Christianity arrived as early as the second century. With the collapse of the Roman Empire continuous settlement began with Bavarians who came into contact and conflict with Slavs and Avars advancing from the east. Karl der Grosse (Charlemagne) established a Carolingian march, a boundary province, on present-day Austrian territory in the ninth century, but this collapsed in 907 through defeat at the hands of the Magyars (Hungarians). The region was reclaimed in 976 by Leopold von Babenberg, the descendant of a noble Bavarian family that would rule for nearly 300 years. The Babenbergs, with the permission of Emperor Friedrich Barbarossa, transformed their territory, first called Ostarrichi in 996, into a duchy of the Holy Roman Empire of the German Nation in 1156. In 1282, the newly elected emperor of the empire, Rudolf von Habsburg, gave his sons two duchies, Austria and Styria, thus laying the foundations for a Habsburg dynasty that lasted for 600 years, with Vienna as the primary residence of the family.

Throughout this era the Habsburgs increased their territory to include the Duchy of Carinthia, the Earldom of Tyrol, Bohemia, Hungary, and large portions of northern Italy. Through marriage the House of Habsburg eventually included Spain and its Western Hemisphere colonies as part of the empire. The Imperial Riding School in Vienna is a remnant of this alliance, and the performances (*Dressur*) of the white Lipizzaner stallions still reflect bullfighting traditions from horseback in the Hispanic world. The Ottoman Empire attacked Austria on two different occasions, in 1529 and again in 1683, leaving behind foodways and even Turkish memories. Bundt cakes with swirls of chocolate are called *Gugelhupf*, resembling a turbaned head, and corn is called *Türken* or *Kukuruz*, the Turkish word for maize. As a result of the Napoleonic invasions, wars, and severe defeats of the early nineteenth century, the Holy Roman Empire of the German Nation broke apart in 1806. Austria, however, had already become an independent empire (*Kaiserreich*) by 1806. In South Tyrol a folk hero would emerge in 1809. Andreas Hofer was able to assemble a fighting force because the *Tiroler Bauernfreiheit* (Tyrolean Peasant Freedom) permitted the bearing of arms. During much of that century the Austrian-Hungarian Monarchy lost more territory than it gained, and following World War I its territory was reduced in 1918 to the German-speaking country that we now know. In 1938 Austria was annexed by National Socialist Germany but became independent again following World War II. This long history of a multicultural empire has left distinct traces throughout Austrian culture from its costumes to its customs, from its speech to its stories.

All Austrian folk culture reveals a constant interplay between Christian traditions and what many think of as survivals of an ancient and pagan past. Christian calendar customs abound: Christmas, Easter, Pentecost, Corpus Christi, St. Martin's Day, All Saints' Day, and many more. Interspersed are seasonal customs such as *Sonnenwende* (solstice), *Fastnacht* or *Fasching* (Shrovetide), and *Silvester* (New Year). Parades, processions on horseback (*Umritte*), and pilgrimages are still very much a part of these calendar customs, as are bonfires (*Jahresfeuer*) on the mountains. The *Strettweger Kultwagen*, a cult cart from 700 B.C.E., displayed in a museum in Graz allows for the assumption that such processions reach deep into Austria's past.

The *Vierbergerwallfahrt* (four-mountain pilgrimage) in Carinthia was considered for a long time as proof of the

Austrian folk hero Andreas Hofer. (Print Collection, Miriam and Ira D. Wallach Division of Art, Prints and Photographs, The New York Public Library, Astor, Lenox and Tilden Foundations)

pre-Christian origin of such processions. It begins at midnight on the second Friday after Easter, and participants climb four mountains, covering forty kilometers in seventeen hours. Along the way pilgrims pick foliage and place it in the brims of their hats, and grain is consecrated so that the harvest in Carinthia will be good. Because the procession encircled the "holy" region of the pre-Christian divinity Isis Noreia, whose name was used by the Romans for the region, Noricum, it was believed that this traditional pilgrimage was 2,000 years old. Recent folklore and historical research during the last thirty years, however, has clearly documented that the procession as we now know it arose around the year 1500 C.E.

Prior to industrialization Austrian peasant culture was divided into *Körndlbauern* (grain farmers) found mostly in the Danube basin and the hill country, *Hörndlbauern* (cattle farmers) primarily in the mountainous regions and the high valleys, and *Weinbauern* (vintners) along the eastern portion of the Danube and on the southern foothills of the Alps in Styria and South Tyrol. Because Austria is about 47 percent forested, there were *Holzknechte* and *Zimmerleute* (woodcutters and carpenters), and due to the large iron ore reserves in the east, there were *Hüttenwerker* (iron foundry workers). As a predominantly Catholic country, the sacred landscape is also of great significance in Austria. One finds, for example, a *Kalvarienberg* (Mount Calvary) in some particularly religious communities such as St. Radegund in Styria, where the Stations of the Cross are found in small wayside chapels along a hillside. There are numerous monasteries and cloisters—seventeen in Upper Austria alone. The large number of pilgrimage churches and saints indicates the importance of Catholicism for the traditional culture of Austria. Religious motifs also play a role in handwork, for example, among the painters of reverse-glass pictures (*Hinterglasmalerei*) or the production of painted peasant furniture (*Bauernmöbel*). In general, Christian holidays and seasonal customs remain an important part of the calendar customs in Austria.

CALENDAR CUSTOMS

Throughout Austria numerous customs reflect the interplay between Christian and non-Christian elements of the society. *Weihnachten* (Christmas) and *Fastnacht* (Shrovetide) are but two. The Christmas season begins with Advent, the first Sunday after 26 November, and continues for the next four Sundays. The custom of the *Adventkranz*, a green wreath with four candles, of which one is lit on successive Sundays, came from Protestant Germany in the 1920s and thus was initially rejected by Catholic Austria. Since 1945, however, it has been accepted by the Catholic Church and is today found throughout Austria. Advent calendars are traditional in households with children, with little windows that are opened on each day until Christmas. Inside are pictures representing the gifts, food, and drink that can be anticipated when the holiday finally arrives. Traditionally, Advent is a time of fasting. No weddings and no dances or other such festivities are celebrated in strict communities. In Vorarlberg there is a 6 A.M. mass, called *Engelmesse* (Angels' Mass), where candles supply the only light, and dark clothing is still common in more remote regions. During Advent *Krippen* (crèches), small and large, are displayed. These nativity scenes present the birth of Christ in the stall in Bethlehem. The Christ child, Mary and Joseph, oxen, and donkeys are accompanied by shepherds, the Three Kings, and the star that guided their way. Other biblical and secular scenes include handworkers and peasants and are generally in an Alpine landscape. The figures are carved, but some are of clay or papier-mâché. Some of the crèches—for example, in Upper Austria's Salzkammergut—fill the entire room and have more than 1,000 pieces. In almost all churches such nativity scenes can be seen after 24 December, and some localities still present them and other sacred folk dramas live. Joseph and Mary seek shelter (*Herbergsuchen*) in Upper Austria, while in Salzburg and Styria nine families meet and hold devotionals before an altar with a picture of the Holy Family, preferably depicting their search for housing in Bethlehem. For each of nine nights one family would host the devotional, always taking the picture with them to the next house (*Frautragen*). Widespread in the south of Germany and in Austria and Switzerland, a *Klöpfelnacht* (Night of Knocking) is traditional. Boys wearing masks and carrying noisemakers move from house to house on the last three Thursday evenings of Advent, knocking on doors and windows, scattering peas and beans, and playing pranks on the local residents. In Tyrol they are accompanied by a donkey, an *Anklopfesel* called a *Zuselmandl*. They are often given food and even gifts at the houses where they pause. Some have interpreted the noisemakers as evidence of antiquity, a midwinter frightening of dead spirits, and the food as examples of fertility symbols.

Christmas itself consists of Christmas Eve followed by a two-day holiday, the first for the family and the second for visiting relatives and friends. Traditionally, the house and the church are cleaned for the celebration. Gifts are said to be left by the *Christkindl*, the Christ Child, but in earlier times St. Nikolaus was the one who gave the gifts on 6 December. Demonic figures are frequently associated with the gift-giver—for example, the *Krampus*, a horned and ugly figure whose role is to discover if children have been good during the year. Small *Krampus* figures, made of dates and nuts, are found at Christmas

Austrian children with toys under a Christmas tree, 1923. (Courtesy Library of Congress)

markets throughout Austria today. The *Christbaum* (Christmas tree) itself is most likely a nineteenth-century innovation. Today the Christmas tree is put up and decorated on Christmas Eve and is usually not taken down until Epiphany, 6 January, the end of the *Zwölften* (Twelve Days) when merrymaking and celebrations are common. This period may be a continuation of the Roman celebration of the Saturnalia, which also covered twelve days. The long-standing practice of bringing evergreen branches into houses suggests that this was a midwinter celebration in anticipation of spring. Branches of evergreens were hung on gates, and some were brought inside and hung from the windows or the ceiling. In 1494 the German moralist Sebastian Brandt tells of such customs in his *Narrenschiff* (Ship of Fools), and depictions show Martin Luther celebrating Christmas with his family under a tree with lights attached to the branches. In the Gailtal in Carinthia farmer-peasants traditionally brought fir trees into their farmyards and placed them there with no decorations. In Aussee it was customary to cut out the crown of the tree and divide it into three parts to be burned on *Rauchabend* (Christmas Eve or incense evening, 24 December), *Silvester* (New Year's Eve, 31 December), and the evening of *Dreikönig* (Epiphany, 6 January). For a while Christmas trees were placed on graves, but Advent wreaths, now common in cemeteries, replaced them. Some traditions even had people *feeding* outdoor trees by placing dumplings and cakes at their roots and coins, apples, ivy, or mistletoe in the branches—offerings to the dead souls who are active.

The customs of *Dreikönig* (Three Kings, Epiphany) exemplify the combining of Christian and pagan, ancient and new traditions in Austria. This occasion was celebrated as the day of the presentation (*Erscheinung*) of Christ, but it was also the traditional date of the birth of the Greek god of wine, Dionysus. When the birth of Christ was changed to the night between 24 December and 25 December, the early

January date continued to be celebrated, particularly as the beginning of the New Year. In Montafon, in the state of Vorarlberg, people wish someone a Happy New Year up until Epiphany. The custom, referred to as *Sternsingen* (Star Singing), is found throughout the German-speaking world and is particularly popular in the village of Heiligenblut in Carinthia. Today the baptismal water in the church, salt, and chalk are blessed. The salt, when placed in a butter tub, wards off sickness, and the consecrated chalk is used to place a blessing on households. Young people, dressed in white shirts or blouses, wearing crowns and wigs of flax, carry burning incense and poles with illuminated stars attached from one house to the next. They sing and offer blessings in verse, and they write 20 C+M+B 06 on the sill above the door, indicating that the house has been blessed for the coming year by the Three Kings, Caspar, Melchior, and Balthasar. In some remote agricultural regions the threshing floor of the barn is cleaned for dancing, and bread and water are laid out for the Three Kings. Non-Christian beliefs, many of which are oracular in nature, are also associated with 6 January. Weather is forecast by peeling an onion into twelve pieces and leaving it overnight on a table. The amount of moisture on each peel indicates which months will be dry and which wet. Divining rods are cut and then letters carved on them, "C" (for Caspar) if one is searching for gold, "B" (Balthasar) for silver, and "M" (Melchior) for water. In some portions of Austria and reaching into Bavaria, the date is also referred to as *Berchtentag* (Berchta Day). The mysterious figure Berchta moves about in the night, followed by an army of dead souls, checking on wool spinners, and frightening adults. She was also particularly dangerous for children and would do them harm. Sometimes children were laid under a crib to deceive Berchta. In some areas where people believe that Berchta and the evil spirits of dead souls accompany the Three Kings, a good bit of noise-making, firing of weapons, banging on drums or cymbals, singing, and shouting occurs. In Tyrol people once ate fatty dumplings so that the knife of Berchta, who was known for cutting open the stomachs of humans, would slip off and cause no harm. A Styrian custom had people place noodles on the roof to feed the wind caused by the passing of Berchta and the dead spirits. It is interesting that Berchta, known in some locations as *Butzenberchta* or *Budlfrau*, was also someone who brought gifts, much as the *Christkindl*, the Christ Child, does at Christmas.

At the end of winter, it has long been customary to celebrate the coming of spring and summer at the time called *Fastnacht* (Shrovetide) in Western Austria and *Fasching* in the east. Not exclusively but especially in South Tyrol the custom of *Pflugumziehen* (plow procession) serves as a preliminary to *Fastnacht* celebrations. Some scholars have associated this custom with all Aryan people, and undoubtedly it represents, or at least precedes, the awakening

Fastnacht celebration in South Tyrol. (© Oliver Bolch/HAGA/The Image Works)

of spring and the fertility of the fields, while also demonstrating the strength of the men and the difficulty of their work. Men are dressed in costumes suggestive of demonic spirits. This plow-procession often ends with the hunting down and driving out of "Wild Men," who are giant figures with long hair and clubs. Such forest people (*silvani*) are well known in the legends of mountain folk, especially in south Germany, Austria, and Switzerland. These "Wild Men" from the forest are also said to be winter demons and are to be driven out of the forest, conquered, and victoriously paraded about. Sometimes they are tried and symbolically killed by spilling animal blood poured into a pig's bladder. On occasion, in the place of the Wild Man, a bear will appear, and sometimes it is a *Schnappviecher* (snapping creature). This practice is still seen in various forms in contemporary urban *Fastnacht-Karneval* versions found mostly in village celebrations in the southwestern part of the German-speaking world.

During the *Fastnacht* season, groups mostly of men parade around the village, behave foolishly, and often make an effigy, which they then burn. The custom is reflected in a folk festival in Tyrol, where an *Egethansel*, a large figure of rags and straw, is brought into the house after being tried for various happenings in the recent past. Masked figures during Shrovetide are said to represent dead spirits (similar to the plow procession), demons and animals (resembling the bear), and caricatures (like the *Schnappviecher*). Precautions must be taken to warn the populace about the spirits that are moving around during this time. Particularly dangerous is the sudden appearance of an unknown and unexpected and mysterious figure (*Überzähliger*), thus increasing the expected number (as occurs with the Thirteenth Wise Woman in "Sleeping Beauty"). During one such procession (*Hudlerlaufen*), runners (*Schleicher*) and even the Devil were to carry something sacred in their shoes so that the demons could not harm them (a practice paralleling that of weddings: carry something in one's shoe for good luck). Even though Shrovetide is a favorable time for marrying, one should not marry on specific days, for on the dance floor "the devil is afoot." What remains today are begging processions (*Heischegänge*), noise-making, and burning, drowning, or burying of effigy figures, sometimes in a manure pile. One folklorist points to the village of Ostermiething near Laufen on the Salzach River, where one sang on Fat Tuesday of a *Sommer- und Winterstreit* (Summer and Winter Battle), clearly suggesting that in antiquity *Fastnacht* was a seasonal celebration and in its beginnings had no relationship to current pre-Lenten practices.

In contemporary Austria the tradition of driving cattle up to the high meadows for the summer is still common. This rather festive occasion takes place on 3 May (*Kreuz-Auffindung*), and the cattle remain until 14 September (*Kreuz-Erhöhung*). Thereafter the Alps are said to belong to bogeymen and night people, and no one should spend the night in Alpine huts without their permission. It is also commonly believed that a black cow should not lead the way. The lead cow(s) are decorated with a crown of sorts with much greenery and a small piece of cloth embroidered with the Christian IHS, that is, a contraction of the Greek IHΣους (Jesus). While the Cross symbolizes sacrifice in the Christian world, it was certainly found in ancient pre-Christian graphic presentations as a decorative form. In folk belief, it is a symbol used for magically fending off evil and, according to Erich and Beitl (1974), is "one of the oldest protective symbols in the Germanic cultural circle." The crown/wreath itself is a well-known symbol: a sign of triumph (laurel wreath), the Christian crown of thorns, and even as a crown of stars on the Queen of Heaven, the Virgin Mary, but it was pre-figured by the Germanic crown made of green twigs, still seen in Virgin Crowns (*Schäppel*). Here the wreath was interpreted as a symbol for growth, fertility, and female chastity.

The *Maibaum* (Maypole) is found particularly in Southern Germany, but also in Austria and Switzerland. It is commonly interpreted as a larger version of the *Lebensrute* (life branch) or *Segenszweig* (blessing branch) and as a fertility symbol found in the spring customs of many people. It is placed in a central location of honor and left standing for a considerable period of time. When it is erected in honor of a wedding, it remains standing until the first child is born. If the bride is already pregnant, the saying goes that the groom "put up his own pole." A uniquely Austrian version of decorating trees is found in Salzburg. The so-called *Prang(er)stangen* are richly flower-decorated and rounded trees that are part of processions on *Dreifaltigkeitssonntag* (Trinity Sunday), celebrated eight days after Pentecost. Children born on the last day of Pentecost celebrations are considered to be particularly lucky. The main celebration of the year, however, is *Fronleichnam* (Corpus Christi Day), the seventh Sunday after Easter.

LEGENDS

Traditional narrative in Austria is particularly rich in historical legends, including those told about the miracles of local saints. The young woman Radegund, married against her will, was nevertheless a good and faithful wife who died at a young age. When thieves tried to take the golden wedding ring from her skeleton, she is said to have folded her hands into a fist to keep them from removing her ring. This was the miracle that led to her sainthood, and the small village of St. Radegund near Graz is named in her honor. The legend of the Austrian flag is also well known, though mostly likely not factual. The flag is red with a white stripe running vertically across the middle one-third, and it is also found in the crest of the Babenbergs. According to legend, it was Duke Leopold V who gave the country its colors. In 1187, while on a Crusade from Austria and Styria, Leopold arrived in Styria at the same time as the English monarch Richard the Lionhearted. After many battles to take the harbor city of Akkon, the Christians were finally victorious. Duke Leopold was said to have fought so bravely that his white tunic was covered in blood. Only where his belt had been was there a white stripe, whereupon Leopold declared that red-white-red would become the colors of his country. A second well-known legend continues this story with one about King Richard. Even though Leopold was the first to reach the fortress of Akkon, the hotheaded English ruler tore down the Austrian flag and replaced it with his own. When King Richard was returning home, his trip took him through Austria, where Leopold promptly arrested and imprisoned him in the castle at Dúrnstein. When Richard did not return to **England**, a singer from his court, Faithful Blondel, was sent to seek and free his lord. He traveled from castle to castle, singing the favorite song of the king, only to be repeatedly disappointed. When he reached Dúrnstein, he had just finished the first verse when Richard continued with the next. The English had to pay a high ransom to free their king.

MUSIC AND DANCE

Today traditional Austrian music and dance are most often heard and seen as part of a *Heimatabend* (homeland evening), when chorus and dance associations perform. In the past numerous musical instruments—including the *Wurzhorn* (alphorn), fiddles, particularly the Viennese *Schrammel* (small fiddle), dulcimers, and harps, and in South Tyrol the zither and the *Raffle* (rattle)—were used. The *Schweglpfeife* (flute) was found in Salzburg and the Salzkammergut, and the small *Maultrommel* (Jew's harp) is still produced in Molln in Upper Austria and sold worldwide. Traditional folk music contributed to the works of such composers as Joseph Haydn and Anton Bruckner. Yodeling and Alpine calls have also played a role in Austrian folk music. Quite common still today are the so-called *Gstanzl*, four-line rhyming verses more popularly known as *Schnaderhüpfel* and found throughout Alpine regions. These songs have a number of well-known verses but may be subject to spontaneous and amusing additions. They have a long history, including examples in Martin Luther's *Tischreden* (Table Talk).

Ist der Apfel rosenrot,	If the apple is red as a rose,
so ist ein Würmlein drinnen;	there is a little worm within;
ist das Maidlein säuberlich	if the young maiden is clean [as a whistle],
so hat es krause Sinnen.	she [surely] has confused senses.

In more recent times the humorous nature of the songs continues in verses like:

Ich steh auf der Brücke	I stand on the bridge
und spuck in den Kahn,	and spit into the boat [below],
da freut sich die Spucke,	and the spittle is so happy,
dass sie kahnfahren kann.	that it can go for a boatride.

Folk dance clubs still perform some traditional dances—for example, the *Schwerttanz* (sword dance) and the *Reiftanz* (ring dance). Traditional children's songs and chain dances have disappeared almost completely. *Werbetänze* (courtship dances), which formed the basis for the Viennese waltz, consist of three types. In the *Steirische*, found throughout central and eastern Austria, the interplay is between young men and women. In Upper Austria a group dance, the *Landlerische* (rural dance), is danced on the grain threshing floor of a barn by a *Burschenschaft* (boy's association) who are dancing for the female audience. The accompanying music has both a regular and an irregular rhythm, and the singing is in several voices. The best-known dance in the entire Alpine region is the *Schuhplattler*, a rapid dance where the feet are raised and slapped with the hands in an increasingly fast and rhythmic beat. This dance has spread through costume and dance clubs and has developed many new steps that were performed also with female participants.

ARCHITECTURE AND CLOTHING

The vernacular architecture, particularly of the farmsteads, varies from region to region. In the Austrian Open Air Museum in Stübing near Graz, all of the different regional house styles are represented. Outbuildings for grain storage are raised above the ground to keep rodents out, and Alpine huts for herders or hikers are typically low to the ground to avoid strong mountain winds. Roof lines are steeper as one moves east, and there is often a cupola with a bell for signaling mealtimes. In Styria this bell is called a *Sterzglocke* (hominy bell), because hominy is a staple food in the region. To some degree farms are similar to those of central and southern Germany with living quarters and animal stalls all under one roof. Still there are notable differences. Some cattle, hay, and grain storage buildings are separated from the living quarters, a so-called *Paarhof*. Building with wood or stone reflects the region, forest, or mountain landscapes, but in some cases—for example, in the north of Tyrol—the lower portion of the house is of stone and the upper portions of wood, with large balconies wrapping around the house. The most dramatic style is the four-sided farmstead of Upper Austria, a *Vierkanthof*, with an inner farmyard, sometimes referred to as a *Bauernburg* (peasant's fortress). The outer walls often include samples of *sgraffito*, a decoration made by scratching off a design on an outer wall surface to reveal an underlying colored representation of nature or human activities. Traditional farms in the mountains were called *Rauchhäuser* (smokehouses) because of the open fire in the center of the house, sometimes with openings high up to allow smoke to escape. The smoke was intended to dry the grain and meat stored in the attic. In the eighteenth century about 70 percent of the houses were "smokehouses," and in the first half of the twentieth century more than 1,500 were still documented in Carinthia and Styria, though most were no longer used as originally intended. Clearly reflective of the Roman Catholic regions of Austria is the *Herrgottswinkel* (God's Corner), a small religious corner shrine in farmhouses, found traditionally in the room where the family dines. There is always a carved crucifix, with a dove representing the Holy Ghost hanging from the ceiling as well as occasionally oil paintings of Jesus and Mary with hearts aflame, that is, *Herz Jesu* and *Herz Mariae*. The head of the household, the peasant farmer, occupied the place closest to the corner. Today these small shrines are seen in private houses, apartments, restaurants, and elsewhere even in large cities.

Traditional costumes in Austria feature *Loden* coats and jackets, made of heavy combed wool in various colors depending on the region. They are traditionally green or gray, but brown is also found in Carinthia, perhaps a Slavic influence. In Salzburg the coat-jacket is green with a black collar; in Styria it is gray with green cuffs and stitching. The colorful sheepskin coats with elaborate stitching may have come to Styria from contacts with Hungary and Slovakia. Traditional trousers are of leather, *Lederhosen*, and feature black, green, or white stitching. While the *Dirndl* dress is found throughout the German-Alpine regions, there are also other styles with long skirts, crocheted blouses, and elaborate headdress. For the most part, red is not found in traditional costumes since this was a color associated with nobility, but red is often seen in Tyrolean costumes, for example, worn by *Schützen* (marksmen). These are groups of men who wear historic costumes and carry arms reminiscent of the battles against Napoleon under Andreas Hofer and reflecting their sense of independence and the historical *Bauernfreiheit*. Virtually every region of Austria still has *Trachtenvereine*, associations or clubs where traditional costumes are worn for festive occasions. It is not uncommon to see these costumes in modern venues, the opera, a ball, and particularly occasions when individuals are recognized by state or local authorities for homeland preservation activities.

STUDIES OF AUSTRIAN FOLKLORE

Austria has recorded its traditions in a folklore atlas, the *Österreichischer Volkskunde Atlas (ÖVA)*. Included are detailed maps and extensive texts accompanying the graphic presentations primarily of material culture but also including language and customs. Several studies review the history of folklore in Austria: Schmidt (1951), Jacobeit and others (1994), and Dow and Bockhorn (2004). Handbooks include Haberlandt (1953) and Erich and Beitl (1974). Wolfram (1963) is the latest, but perhaps the most comprehensive, summary overview of folklore in Austria. In 2002 the *Salzburger Landesinstitut für Volkskunde* (Salzburg State Institute for Folklore) issued a CD entitled *Im Winter und zur Weihnachtszeit. Bräuche im Salzburger Land* (In the Winter and at Christmas Time: Customs in the State of Salzburg). The CD presents ninety-one multi-media short texts, 124 longer texts by sixty well-known authors, 650 photographs, thirty videos, eighty sound recordings, and over 200 Internet links. Two other CDs have followed this format: *Vom Frühling bis zum Hebst* (From Springtime to the Fall) and *In Familie und Gesellschaft* (In the Family and in Society). All three CDs include numerous links to Web sites dealing with Austrian folklore.

BIBLIOGRAPHY

Dow, James R. 1992. Austrian *Volkskunde*: A Contemporary Sampler. *Journal of American Folklore* 105:368–373.

Dow, James R., and Olaf Bockhorn. 2004. *The Study of European Ethnology in Austria.* Aldershot, UK: Ashgate.

Erich, Oswald A., and Richard Beitl. 1974. *Wörterbuch der deutschen Volkskunde.* Dritte Auflage (Kröners Taschenbuchausgabe Bd. 127). Stuttgart: Kröner.

Haberlandt, Arthur. 1953. *Taschenwörterbuch der Volkskunde Österreichs: Der andere Teil.* Wien: Österreichischer Bundesverlag.

Jacobeit, Wolfgang, Hannjost Lixfeld, Olaf Bockhorn, and James R. Dow. 1994. *Völkische Wissenschaft: Gestalten und Tendenzen in der deutschen und österreichischen Volkskunde in der ersten Hälfte des 20. Jahrhunderts.* Wien: Böhlau Verlag.

Jeggle, Utz, and Gottfried Korff. 1986. On the Development of the Zillertal Regional Character: A Contribution to Cultural Economics. In *German Volkskunde*, edited by James R. Dow and Hannjost Lixfeld. Bloomington: Indiana University Press. 124–139.

Johler, Reinhard. 2000. *Die Formierung eines Brauchs: Der Funken-und Holepfannsonntag.* Wien: Veröffentlichungen des Instituts für Europäische Ethnologie der Universität Wien. Bd. 19.

Luidold, Lucia, and Ulrike Kammerhofer-Aggermann. 2002. *Im Winter und zur Weihnachtszeit: Bräuche im Salzburger Land.* Salzburg: Salzburger Beiträge zur Volkskunde 13.

Schmidt, Leopold. 1951. *Geschichte der Österreichischen Volkskunde.* Buchreide der Österreichischen Zeitschrift für Volkskunde. N. S. Bd. 2. Wien.

Wolfram, Richard. 1963. Österreich. In *Volkskunde: Beharrung und Wandel der europäischen Volkskultur in der Gegenwart.* München: JRO-Verlag.

Wolfram, Richard, and Ingrid Kretschmer. 1959–1979. *Österreichischer Volkskundeatlas.* 6 map fascicles with commentary. Wien: Böhlau.

James R. Dow

GERMANY

GEOGRAPHY AND HISTORY

A Central European federal republic, Germany borders nine countries: **Austria**, **Switzerland**, **France**, Luxemburg, Belgium (see **Flanders**), Holland (see **The Netherlands**), **Denmark**, Poland, and the Czech Republic. With a landmass of 357,000 square kilometers, it is a little smaller than the American state of Montana and has a population of 84 million. Including those in Austria, Switzerland and parts of **Italy**, Belgium, and France, more than 94 million people speak German, making it the second most spoken language in Europe after Russian (115 million) and far ahead of French (62 million) and English (58 million). Germany is one of the most technologically advanced countries of Europe and has always been a major transit zone between north and south, east and west. Since the fall of the former German Democratic Republic in 1989, Germany has been reunited into one country.

Germany can be divided into several major regions geographically, linguistically, and culturally. The entire north is flatland, while the middle section consists of a series of low mountain ranges. In the south the land rises toward the Continental Divide, to the Black Forest in the southwest, and in the southeast to the Alps. About 81 percent of Germany today is covered by fields, forests, or meadows. Its population density of 247 people per square kilometer reflects its many large cities as well as relatively sparsely inhabited rural areas. The largest cities are Berlin, Hamburg, Munich, Frankfurt, and Cologne. The entire population is German-speaking, with only one recognized minority, about 70,000 Sorbians, also called Wends, in and around the city of Bautzen in the state of Saxony. While all Germans speak a standard variety of German, many dialects, divided primarily into Low German in the north and High German in the south, exhibit significant differences. Within these major divisions are regional and local dialects, for example, Alemanic in the southwest and Bavarian in the southeast. The major dialect regions are divided still further. The climate in Germany is affected in the

Germany.

north and west by the Gulf Stream and in the south by the Alps. Summers are warm but not extremely hot, and winters are mostly rainy and cloudy with significant snow accumulations in the mountains.

Germany has been populated continually since prehistoric times. Neandertal man takes its name from a valley near the modern city of Wuppertal. Celtic tribes inhabited much of the western and southern portions of present-day Germany during the pre-Christian millennium, and the ancient Romans established numerous colonies along much of the Rhine River (*Colonia agrippinensis*, named after Nero's mother, is now Cologne) and throughout the southern half of the country. The first detailed information on the Germans comes from commentaries written by Romans such as Julius Caesar's *De Bellum Gallico* (ca. 58 B.C.E.) and an ethnography by Tacitus, *Germania* (98 C.E.). In 800 C.E., Karl der Grosse (Charlemagne) was crowned *Kaiser* (emperor) of the Holy Roman Empire of the German Nation, an empire that lasted more than 1,000 years, until 1806. Even though the primary residence of the emperor for centuries was in Vienna, Germany made up the largest portion of the empire with kingdoms, duchies, archbishoprics, free cities, and even free knights. The variety of political entities is responsible for the many castles found throughout Germany as well as the wide variety of customs. Each of the modern states of Germany has a shield, which reveals the colors of the original city or state (Bavaria: white and blue), the animals representing their regal nature (Berlin: bear), or objects reflecting local trade or commerce (Rhineland: ship's wheel).

In the seventh century an Irish monk named Winifried brought Christianity to Germany, where he was called Bonifatius (Boniface). He successfully replaced the symbolic oak tree with the Christian Cross, but forests are still thought of as a sacred place of worship, and knocking on wood is equivalent to calling forth a god from within the tree. The *Wünschelrute* (divining or dowsing rod) has long been used to locate underground treasures, including gold, silver, and water. In the middle of the fifteenth century Johannes Gutenberg, a goldsmith in Mainz, produced the first Bibles printed with movable type. It was not long before *Volksbücher* (chapbooks) offered published versions at city and regional fairs of stories that had previously been known only in oral tradition, for example, "Reineke the Fox" and the legend of Dr. Faustus. At the beginning of the sixteenth century Martin Luther countered the Roman Catholic Church with his Protestant Reformation and divided Germany into two confessions, which would result in parallel Christian cultural traditions. Finally, in the nineteenth century Germany industrialized and became a highly advanced technological country, which would play havoc with its old traditions but would introduce new ones. Secondhand or

Chapbook of Reineke the Fox, published in Lübeck in 1498.

revived traditions, called *Folklorismus* in Germany, would begin to play a role in modern folk culture. In the latter half of the twentieth century, Germany contributed to the development of the European Union and took millions of "guest workers" into the economy and into an evolving multicultural scene. Today the Federal Republic of Germany is democratic, officially Christian, and increasingly multicultural. The population is roughly 40 percent Catholic and 40 percent Protestant, with the rest claiming no religious confession or belonging to Judaism, Islam, or other religions.

CALENDAR CUSTOMS

Calendar customs and official holidays in German folk culture are numerous. Many exhibit a significant element of Christian traditions, for example, Christmas, Easter, and Corpus Christi. Seasonal customs such as *Fastnacht* (Mardi Gras) and *Weihnachten* (Christmas) also reveal ancient roots, but one must be careful in seeking survivals from prehistoric times in such traditions. Parades, church processions, and re-enactments of past legends are, however, quite common throughout Germany. In more remote regions pilgrimages are still very much a part of these calendar customs, as are bonfires (*Jahresfeuer*) on the mountains at such times as *Sonnenwende* (summer solstice). Wine festivals are celebrated in the Rhine and Mosel Valleys, and the famous *Oktoberfest* in Munich, now little more than a beer-drinking circus, is celebrated at the same time as *Kirmes* (church dedication [Mass]), the time for harvest festivals.

Two Christian holidays, Christmas and Easter, are central to an entire series of traditional customs and practices. Christmas is preceded by Advent, a four-week period when wreaths with candles are found in most homes, both Catholic and Protestant. One candle is lit on each of four Sundays preceding Christmas. During this time St. Nikolaus, accompanied by Knecht Ruprecht, a somewhat frightening figure, traditionally visits homes to determine if children have been well behaved. Before the door, children leave a shoe, in which a small gift or a switch is found the next morning, depending upon how good or bad the children in the household have been. On Christmas Eve the *Christbaum* (Christmas tree) is set up and decorated, and gifts are placed there by the *Christkind* (Christ child). The season lasts until 6 January, called *Dreikönig* (Three Kings, that is, Epiphany), when children in the village or the neighborhood go from house to house carrying poles with illuminated stars on them, singing, begging, making noise, and leaving a sign marked in chalk over the door 20 C+M+B 06, indicating that the house has been blessed for the coming year (in this case, 2006) by the Three Kings, Caspar, Melchior, and Balthasar. This same custom is widely practiced in Austria.

Easter is preceded by the forty days of Lent, but the dates differ each year, affecting pre- and post-Easter celebrations. Easter is celebrated on the first Sunday after the first full moon following the spring equinox on 21 March. Thus, one of the major German festivals, *Fastnacht*, virtually always falls in February. In Germany the celebration has different names, depending on the region. The common term, *Fastnacht*, indicates that this is the eve of fasting, as is the practice in the Catholic Church during Lent. In the Rhineland, which has traditionally been Catholic, it is called *Karneval*, a term borrowed from the Latin *carne vale*, meaning "goodbye to meat" and clearly referring to the custom of food denials during Lent. In Bavaria the season is called *Fasching*, a term found in written texts as early as 1204, and refers to the heavy drinking of the season (*-sching* comes etymologically from *schenken*, meaning to pour, for example, wine or beer). Throughout southwest Germany, however, where the festival is widely practiced, both in larger cities such as Freiburg im Breisgau and in numerous villages such as Elzach, Rottweil, Bahr, Villingen, and many more, it is called *Fasnet*. The core word *fas* has two different meanings in German, both still in contemporary usage. The verb *faseln*, when used in everyday folk speech to describe someone, makes reference to nonsensical talk and behavior such as a *Fasel-Hans* or a *Fasel-Liese*, the male and female versions of such individuals. The same verb, when used with animals, carries the meaning of breeding. For example, a *Faselhengst* is a stud horse, and a *Faselschwein* is a brood sow. This interpretation of the season as a time of nonsense and frivolity, including procreation, reflects the actual happenings of the season today: nonsense and sexual promiscuity. The earliest usage of the word is found in Wolfram von Eschenbach's *Parsival* of 1206, spelled *vasnat*, and only later do we find it written *vastenaht*. The nineteenth century, which for the most part was mythology-friendly, looked for ancient meanings and survivals in the custom, seeing the core word as *fas* with its various meanings and not *fast*, indicating a Christian period of fasting.

The wide variety of *Fastnacht* costumes found throughout Germany, with the most colorful attire and the most frightening masks found in the Black Forest region, suggests an overlay of old and new, traditional and folklorized elements. Elzach provides perhaps the best example of the complexity of the old and the new. On *Schmutziger Donnerstag* (Dirty Thursday), children have their own parade, but they are accompanied by a host of *Schuddig* (*Schaurtag*, dialect *Schurtig*, that is, "day of horror"), men dressed in bright-red costumes with triangular hats covered by snail shells and worn upside down in mockery of a bishop's hat. Some carry poles for the *Sprung* (springing) and others an inflated *Saublodere* (sow's bladder) used to slam against the pavement to make a loud noise like a gunshot. Still others carry a *Streckschere* (extensor claw) used to reach out and pinch or otherwise harass onlookers, particularly women. At noon on *Fasnet* Sunday, a town crier calls forth the celebration, and at 3 P.M. the costumed figures spring with their poles through the streets and slam the pig's bladders on the street. At 8 P.M. a dance includes the *Teufelsschuddig* (Devil *Schuddig*), dressed in black, as well as the *Rägemolli*, men dressed in yellow costumes with black spots that depict the sun and the moon. All dance and spring with their poles around a huge bonfire. On Monday at 5 P.M. the crier, now accompanied by night watchmen, musicians, and the ever-present *Schuddig*, once again calls for a celebration. On Tuesday a *Latschariverein* (slipper [shoe] association) meets in a local tavern and holds forth with humorous verses, drinking, and general merriment. In the afternoon a major

Schuddig with a sow's bladder. (Photograph by Hannjost Lixfeld)

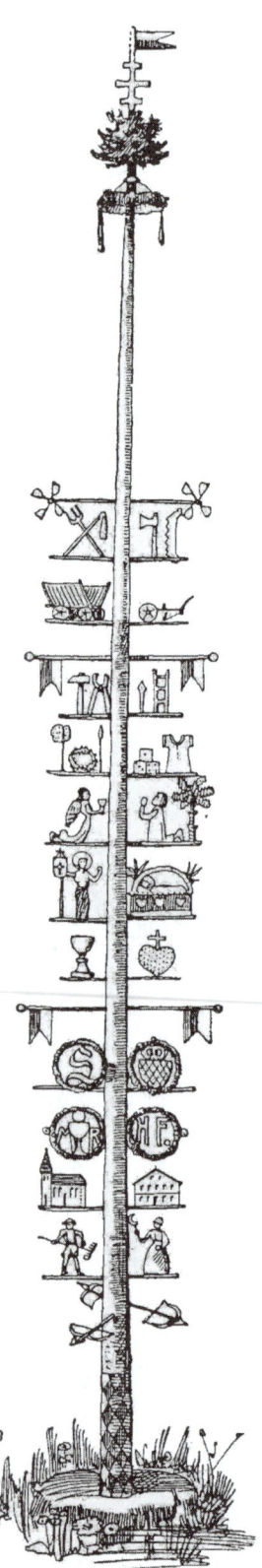

parade with everyone participating takes place again. Individuals are "tried" for sins of the last year, political events are reviewed and praised or condemned, verses new and old are quoted, and the general merriment continues until midnight, at which time the *Larve* (mask) and the costumes are put away until the next year.

Other processions, some of which clearly indicate the end of winter and the coming of spring, lead up to Easter Sunday during Lent. In the Rhineland-Palatinate, children, some dressed in straw suggesting the barrenness of winter and others covered with flowers indicative of the reawakening of spring, go from house to house chanting:

Stri, stra, stro, der Summerdag is do!	Stri, stra, stro, summer day is here!
Der Sommer und der Winter des sind Geschwisterkinder,	Summer and Winter those are siblings.
Summerdag, Staab aus,	Summer day, [get your] staff out,
Blost dem Winter die Aaga aus,	Blow Winter's eyes out,
Stri, stra, stro, der Summerdag is do!	Stri, stra, stro, summer day is here!

The children then receive small gifts from each household.

The Easter season itself begins then with Palm Sunday, a procession through the streets with large palm leaves covered with flowers and ribbons. Egg decorating, hiding, and rolling are common, as are egg trees and egg chains made with emptied and colored eggshells. In the village of Vogelsberg in Baden young boys go crowing, clucking, and laughing to houses where young girls live, and the boys beg for eggs. The booty is taken to an inn, where they are blown out and the contents used to make an egg-cake, while the shells are strung on a cord to be hung across the street of the village. After church on Easter Sunday, the young boys return and throw rocks at the string of eggs until all are broken, with younger children looking on and anticipating the day they can join the fun.

In May the well-known *Maibaum* (Maypole) is erected in a conspicuous place in the center of a city or village. Traditionally, there are three kinds of Maypoles. The most typical is one cut down by young men and decorated with carved scenes of local trades. This tradition most likely reaches back to the time of handworkers of the past, showing both their physical strength and their skills at woodwork. A second type of Maypole is the *Wirtshausmaien* (inn Maypole), placed in front of an inn or tavern and paid for by the innkeeper with drinks. The *Liebesmai* (love Maypole) comes from the tradition of a young man placing a small tree in front of a young woman's house to indicate his love for her. In some locations a king and queen are chosen, a dance around the pole is performed, and branches of greenery are brought into the house (*Mai ins Haus*).

Forty days after Easter is *Himmelfahrt* (Ascension Day), ten days after that *Pfingsten* (Pentecost) occurs, and *Fronleichnam* (Corpus Christi) takes place on the Thursday after Whitsunday, the seventh Sunday after Easter. This last day concludes the Easter season with a procession, sometimes on horseback, with *Prangstangen*

Maypole. (From Georg Buschan, *Das deutsche Volk in Sitte und Brauch* [Stuttgart: Union Deutsche Verlagsgesellschaft, 1922]) (trees decorated with flowers) and flowers strewn on the ground to form a carpet of color. On the way selections from the Gospels are read at four altars, placed in the four directions of the compass, and prayers for good weather are offered.

Late summer and fall are filled mostly with harvest festivals that include food, drink, and dancing. The *Schwerttanz* (sword dance) is still practiced by some dance groups, but more common are the Munich *Metzgersprung* (butchers' leap) and the *Schäfflertanz* (coopers' dance), the Nürnberg *Schembartlaufen* (bearded mask procession), the Furth *Drachenstich* (dragon spearing), and the Ulm *Fischerstechen* (fishermen's spearing), all of which come from seasonal celebrations by the guilds and the handworkers of the past. In the south and in Austria cattle, decorated with crowns and wreaths, are brought down from the mountains in the *Almabtrieb* to stalls for the winter. November begins a period of remembrance with All Saints' Day on the first day of the month and the Protestant *Totensonntag* (Death Sunday), introduced in 1816 by King Friedrich Wilhelm III of Prussia in memory of nine fallen soldiers. In 1926 the *Volkstrauertag* (People's Memorial Day) was instituted to memorialize those who died in World War I. St. Martin's Day falls on 11 November. It is the day to remember the knight who shared his cloak with a beggar, only to learn later that the man was none other than Jesus himself. Traditionally, 11 November represents the end of the old year and the beginning of a new one. On this day in the past workers received their pay for the summer labors, and in celebration the new wine could be tasted. At 11:00 A.M. on 11 November (*am 11.11. um 11 Uhr*), the opening sessions to plan the next *Fastnacht* take place, with much drinking and with the blessing of the patron saint of drinking and gluttony, St. Martin. December brings Advent, St. Nikolaus Day, Christmas, and finally *Silvester* (New Year's Day), named for Pope Silvester I in 335 C.E., the date on which Christianity became the Roman state religion. When the Gregorian calendar replaced the Julian calendar in 1582 and a leap year was included, New Year's Day was moved to 1 January, but the traditional date of 6 January (Epiphany) is still celebrated in rural areas as the beginning of the year. *Silvester* in the German-speaking world as elsewhere is celebrated with noise-making and fireworks. On every 31 December since 1925 in Berchtesgaden a *Verein der Weihnachtsschützen* (Association of Christmas Marksmen) has been meeting in a tavern, where they eat, drink, and then go out to shooting grounds to fire their guns. They see this as a "sacred duty," and they fire their guns on other occasions such as *Kirmes* (church dedication [Mass]), St. John's Day, in memory of fallen soldiers, or as a salute to one of their fellow marksmen. Customs in Germany represent not only formalized recognition of various occasions, with individuals playing specific roles, but also a place and a time to continue verbal, musical, costume, and dance practices, some of which are old, if not ancient, and some of which are relatively new.

MYTHS, LEGENDS, AND FOLKTALES

Germany is perhaps best known around the world for its folktales, legends, and myths. Indeed, the fairy tale collection of the Brothers Grimm is still second only to the Bible in number of sales per year in Germany. Between 1812 and 1815, when the Grimms published the first version of their *Kinder- und Hausmärchen* (Children and

The Brothers Grimm by Ludwig Emil Grimm (1843).

Household Tales), they produced a model that would be copied by many countries, especially in Northern and Eastern Europe. Their collection grew from the original 156 stories in the first version to a total of 211 in the final edition. Many stories were included and later removed, so that we now know that another thirty-two tales were part of the canon at one time but were deleted for a number of reasons. One famous tale, "Bluebeard," was most likely dropped from the collection since there were two other stories with the same plot, motifs, and message: "Virgin Mary's Child" and "Fitcher's Bird." The Grimms also published a smaller edition of fifty selected tales, beginning in 1825 and continuing through ten editions until 1858. This smaller collection always included the most popular tales, for example, "Little Red Riding Hood," "Cinderella," "Hansel and Gretel," "Snow White," and "The Bremen Town Musicians." Interest in the antiquity of the tales has paralleled similar concerns regarding German customs, but most research suggests that they did not originate in antiquity but rather in the Middle Ages and many even later. The tales were collected by the Grimms from middle-class friends, neighbors, and relatives who visited the brothers and told their stories, learned perhaps as a result of fieldwork among the German peasantry. Since some of these informants came from a French Huguenot background, some stories bear a clear relationship to well-known French stories, particularly the collection *Contes du Temps passé* by Charles Perrault in 1697. Perrault was perhaps the one who first removed many of the vulgar and crude elements from the stories, meanwhile making significant additions. In the case of "Little Red Riding Hood," for example, the cannibalistic devouring of the grandmother's blood and bones by the title character, found in numerous variants of the oral tale, is no longer in the Perrault and Grimm versions. Missing also is the ruse that the child needs to defecate after eating parts of her grandmother, a trick thought up by the child to escape the wolf. The "little red cap" was most likely added by Perrault to indicate the social status of the young girl and is not found in any of the oral variants other than those directly influenced by Perrault. The Grimms made significant changes in "Cinderella," for example, the omission of the pumpkin-coach found in Perrault's version. The patriarchal Grimms also reduced the ability of the main character to speak, while retaining the two jealous stepsisters chopping off their heels and toes so that their feet will fit the slipper. In earlier versions of the Grimm tales, Cinderella participates in the discussion with her stepsisters regarding the young prince and her desire to be allowed to try on the slipper also, but by the final version she does not speak at all, even though she is quickly recognized by the prince. In the last scene pigeons peck out the eyes of the two stepsisters because of their mistreatment of Cinderella. The core and basis of the story "Hansel and Gretel," the famine, is also an addition by the Grimms to the 1843 fifth edition of their collection. The "Virgin Mary's Child" is one of the few stories for which we have variants throughout the seventeen editions, both the small and the large ones, as well as handwritten copies as early as 1808, several years prior to their publication. The test, not to open one forbidden door in Heaven, leads to curiosity and transgression, which the "Child" denies. The Virgin Mary punishes her with muteness and restores her ability to speak only when she admits her sin. This test is the same as in "Fitcher's Bird" as well as in the deleted "Bluebeard," with the secret chamber now located in a castle and the punishment being death by dismemberment. "The Bremen Town Musicians" is the only story in the Grimm collection to feature a city by name and is today the logo of the city of Bremen. It is the story of aging animals, a donkey, dog, cat, and rooster, who are making their way to the city to earn their keep as musicians when they encounter robbers. When they decide to stay in the robbers' house, the animals are able to frighten them away with their braying, barking, meowing, and crowing. They then receive the house as their reward and live out their old age there. Contrary to the 1937 Walt Disney version, the wicked witch of "Snow White" is killed in the end not by falling from a cliff but by dancing herself to death in red-hot iron shoes, which she must wear at the wedding of Snow White. Other well-known stories such as "The Frog King" and "The Juniper Tree" have often been interpreted psychoanalytically or mythologically. The fear of the frog by the young princess is seen as a disguised version of fear of sex, here symbolically represented by a slimy frog, while the juniper tree is interpreted as a survival from antiquity of the world tree *Yggdrasil* in Germanic mythology. Since most of these stories were created or at least made popular by telling and enhancing them during the late Middle Ages, such suggestions have limited credence among scholars. It is important to note that the Grimms worked on their tales consistently throughout their entire adult lives, from around 1808 until their final version in 1858. Their goal was to create an ideal type for the literary fairy tale, and they used two tales sent to them by the artist Philipp Otto Runge as their model. "The Fisherman and His Wife" and "The Juniper Tree" were written in Low German dialect, but in structure, tone, and content, they represented what the Grimms wanted to produce in their other tales.

When the Brothers Grimm published their collection of *Deutsche Legenden* (German Legends) in two volumes in 1816 and 1818, a flood of similar collections appeared both in the German-speaking world and in other European countries. In Germany alone more than 600 collections were published between 1858, the date of their final edition, and 1960. This collection was just as wide-ranging as the fairy tale collection had been and included a total of 585 legends. The stories treat fate, revenants, omens of death, ghosts, and predictions about the end of the world. There are also stories of incest, human sacrifice, shape-shifters, plagues and epidemics, and nature spirits as well as magical plants (mandrake root) and animals (dragons). Some of these legends have become familiar far beyond Germany. Perhaps the best known is that entitled "The Pied Piper of Hamelin" in English, though called simply "*Die Kinder von Hameln*" (The Children of Hameln) in German. As with all legends, a historical element forms the core of the story. We read that in the year 1284 a man dressed in a coat of many colors appeared in the village of Hameln on the Weser River. He proclaimed himself a rat-catcher and promised to rid the town of rats for a fee. When the amount was agreed to by the local residents, the man produced a fife and walked through the streets playing his instrument. The rats came out of the houses and gathered around him, whereupon he led them down to the Weser and marched right into the water, followed by the rats, who then drowned. When the villagers refused to pay the large sum previously agreed to, the man disappeared, only to return dressed in a strange red hat, again playing his fife. This time 130 children joined in and followed him to a nearby mountain, where they disappeared. Only three escaped, one who was blind and could tell where the children had been taken, one who was mute and could point the way, and a third who was dressed only in a nightshirt and returned home to fetch a coat. A later variant of the story gives 26 June (loosely associated with St. John's Day on 24 June and St. Paul's Day on 29 June) as the exact date on which the children disappeared, a degree of temporal precision quite common in legendry. The term "Pied Piper" itself comes from a 1634 English version of the story, and Robert Browning's poem is certainly the most popular version. Today, inscribed on the City Hall of Hameln, we read:

> In the year of our Lord 1284
> from Hameln were led away,
> 130 children who here were born,
> lost by a piper inside the mountain.

The motif of someone ridding a town of rats or other vermin, sometimes with a magical musical instrument, is well known in folklore. For example, St. Patrick drove the snakes of Ireland into the sea. While clear evidence indicates exactly what happened to the children, there is reason to believe that some young people actually did disappear. Perhaps they were part of a Children's Crusade in the thirteenth century, perished during the St. Vitus Dance epidemic of the Middle Ages, or were recruited to migrate to another area of the German-speaking world. The bishop of Olmütz sought families in the thirteenth century to colonize his Bohemian diocese, and the city records of Hameln and Olmütz reveal a striking number of the same family names.

One of the best-known legends from the Grimm collection is the story of "Barbarossa at Mt. Kyffhausen" in Thuringia. It is said in the legend that Emperor Barbarossa did not die and that he will live until Judgment Day, concealed in an underground palace inside Mt. Kyffhausen. On occasion a peasant or a shepherd has been led by a dwarf into the mountain, where he saw the emperor. In his underground palace he sits on a stone bench at a round table, resting his head in his hands, asleep but nodding his head and blinking his eyes. His beard has grown long, right through the table (or, according to some, around the table), and when it has encircled the table three times, he will wake up. It has already grown two times around the table. When he finally emerges, he will hang his warrior's shield on a leafless tree, which will then send forth green leaves, heralding a better age. The motif of a famous leader waiting in an underground palace for a better time is also told of Arminius, the German who defeated three Roman legions under Varus in the Battle of the Teutoburger Forest in 9 C.E. as well as Friedrich II, Wittekind, the chief of the

Saxons, *Karl der Grosse* (Charlemagne), and King Arthur. In fact, Emperor Barbarossa drowned in a river while participating in a Crusade in 1190, but the legend has remained popular, and today a monument and a cave considered to be the entrance to the underground chambers can be found on Mt. Kyffhausen.

The one set of legends that has led to the most interest from scholars of antiquity and myth is the story of the ghostly rider, found as an isolated theme in the "Wild Huntsman" and as part of a more elaborate narrative in "Faithful Eckhart." The theme tells of a demonic hunter, a lost soul who is accompanied on his ride by spectral hounds. In some variants the ghostly rider leads a host of lost souls across the night sky to the barking of dogs, the wild raging of the wind, and the sound of galloping horses. Austrian scholars attempted to associate this wild horde with presumed death cults of antiquity and worship of the Germanic god Wotan, but evidence does not sufficiently support this assertion.

Still other German legends are popular outside the cultural region, including stories of shape-shifting "werewolves" and "revenants," those who return from the dead. Closely related are stories of ghosts and others who are condemned to wander the earth searching eternally for home or family members. The mysterious figure of Bertha—in Austria and southern Germany, Perchta—recalls *la llorona* of the American Southwest, the mother who wanders along the shores of lakes and rivers, wailing and searching for her lost child. The "Eternal Jew," known in most folk cultures throughout the Western world, must wander the earth for all eternity, never finding his home.

German heroic legendry has long been associated with Scandinavian mythology, the assumption being that a proto-Germanic corpus of myths and gods existed even in prehistory for the entire Germanic world. It was then recorded in the Nordic epics and sagas. The Grimms also posited a time when the past was unspoiled, genuine, and in tune with the laws of nature. The myths were a primary source for this assumption, as we can see in Jacob Grimm's introduction to his *Teutonic Mythology*:

> History teaches us to recognize in language, the farther back we are able to trace it, a higher perfection of form, which declines as culture advances. . . . Now, if such inferences as to what is nonextant are valid in language, if its present condition carries us far back to an older and oldest, a like proceeding must be justifiable in mythology too, and from its dry watercourses we may guess the copious spring, from its stagnant swamps, the ancient river.

The stories found in the heroic legends of Siegfried in the thirteenth-century German epic the *Nibelungenlied* were, for the Grimms, "[f]ragments of a belief dating back to the most ancient times, in which spiritual things are expressed in a figurative manner, [and] are common to all stories." Far more important was their belief that the "farther we go back, the more the mythical element expands: indeed it seems to have formed the only subject of the oldest fiction." It was thought that if we read and reconstruct the fairy tales, legends, and other German stories, we will arrive at the original myths that were the common property of the Germanic world. When Siegfried sets out to find the beautiful woman Kriemhilde, he provides us with information on a

"Siegfried Kills the Dragon Fafnir." Drawing on the Cliff Ramsundfelsen in S'dermanland, Sweden.

common motif in the fairy tales, the ability to understand the language of animals—in this case birds—but the motif is buried in the plot of the story. Siegfried defeats a dragon named Fafnir by digging a trench and penetrating him from below with his sword. He is bathed in dragon's blood, making him invincible like a Germanic god except for one spot between his shoulders where a linden leaf fell. Siegfried takes a treasure horde from the dragon Fafnir, then roasts his heart. When he tests the heart to see if it is done, he burns his finger and places it in his mouth. Suddenly he hears and understands birds in the tree above him who are talking about Regin, Fafnir's brother, who will kill anyone who takes the treasure. Just where the treasure came from is not clarified in the *Niebelungenlied,* since it was assumed that listeners to the oral epics were already familiar with the background of the story.

Following the Grimms' suggestion, when we look to Germanic mythology, particularly the Icelandic epics, the *Eddas* of the early thirteenth century, we are able to fill in the details of Siegfried's newly found and cursed treasure. Three Germanic gods, Odin (the Nordic name for Wotan), Loki, and Hoenir, were out exploring the world when they came to a beautiful waterfall where they found an otter who had been eating a salmon and was now half-asleep. Loki, the evil god, threw a stone and struck the otter on the head, killing him. The gods took the otter and the salmon with them and soon came to a farm owned by a man named Hreithmar. They asked him for a night's lodging and offered to pay him. When they showed him their catch, the otter and the salmon, Hreithmar called his sons Fafnir and Regin and told them that their brother, Otter, had been killed. The father and the two remaining sons attacked the gods, bound them up, and made them prisoners. The gods then offered to pay a ransom for their release, whereupon the otter was flayed and Hreithmar told them that they must fill it and completely cover it with gold. The gods agreed to the demands. Odin sent Loki out to the World-of-Dark-Elves, where he met a dwarf named Andvari, disguised as a fish in a pool of water. Loki seized him and demanded all the gold he had collected in his rocky dwelling. The dwarf produced the gold demanded of him but kept a small golden ring, which Loki then noticed. When the god asked for the ring, the dwarf pleaded to keep it so that he could become wealthy again. Loki refused and took the ring, and as he was walking away, the dwarf placed a curse on the ring saying that it would destroy anyone who owned it. The story continues with the gods returning to Hreithmar, who frees them after receiving the gold, but he and his sons now possessed a treasure that had been cursed. The sons kill their father and take the gold.

Thus, when Siegfried takes the treasure from Fafnir, who had changed himself into a dragon, he became the owner of a cursed treasure. The birds had also warned Siegfried about Regin, whom he then kills. Siegfried himself is later murdered by being pierced with a sword in exactly the spot where the linden leaf had left him vulnerable. His murder takes place in the Odenwald (Odin's Forest) near the modern-day city of Heidelberg. This story forms the basis for much of the German epic the *Nibelungenlied* and later the operas of Richard Wagner.

SONGS AND MATERIAL CULTURE

German folksongs are well known through performance in choral concerts around the world. German drinking songs such as "*In München steht ein Hofbräuhaus*" or the ubiquitous "*Ein prosit der Gemütlichkeit*," sung as a toast on almost any drinking occasion, are especially well known. Regional songs are popular: for the Rhineland, "*Einmal am Rhein*," or for Lüneberg, "*Auf der Lüneburger Heide*." Other songs includes those to be sung while hiking, such as "*Mein Vater war ein Wandersmann*," or playful songs using the names of birds, as in "*Vogelhochzeit*," in which birds are named and then words are used that rhyme with the bird's name. Serious songs reflect the many wars that have taken place on German soil: "*Ich hatt' einen Kameraden*" and even "*Ach du lieber Augustin*," now sung as a drinking song but originally composed to reflect the loss of almost everything during the Thirty Years War of 1618–1648. Much later the song "*Lily Marleen*" became the song of the soldiers during World War II. One song written by the poet Heinrich Heine has become a popular folksong. "*Die Lorelei*" tells the legend of a beautiful maiden who sits atop a cliff that juts out into the Rhine River, right at its narrowest point. Boatmen are taken with her beauty, watch her as she combs her long blond hair, and fail to pay attention to the rocks submerged under the surface of the river. Many have lost their lives here, and many ships lie at the bottom of the river. In the 1960s, Elvis Presley made a regional Swabian song popular by using the melody to "*Muss i denn, muss i denn zum Städtle hinaus*" and writing new words for the song, creating "Cause I Don't Have a Wooden Heart."

In Germany several open-air museums present in living history the vernacular architecture, material culture, and regional customs and practices. Here one can also see some of the traditional costumes, foodways, and local farming and industry practices as well as enactments of local traditions, for example, *Ringreiten* (ring riding), where a mounted horseman must capture a ring hanging from an arch or a tree. Such museums are located near Bad Homburg (*Hessenpark*), Hagen (*Westfälisches Freilichtmuseum*), and Kommern (*Rheinisches Freilichtmuseum*).

GERMAN FOLKLORE UNDER THE NAZI REGIME

One final chapter in German folklore must be mentioned. During the time of National Socialism the study of German and Germanic traditions was placed at a high level in two ideological umbrella organizations, the Rosenberg Office and the SS Office of Ancestral Inheritance. These competing offices had in common their search for Germanic antiquity and insistence on the continuity of traditions in all forms, whether customs, narratives, songs, or material culture (for example, the infamous swastika). An Institute for German Folklore was established, made up of six "research posts": "Peasant Life Structures," "Peasant Handicrafts," "German Farmsteads," "Folk Speech," "Mythology," and "Games and Sayings." The results of field investigations carried out by these posts were to be delivered to the central **archives** in Berlin, where everything was to be evaluated, "foreign" materials were to be removed, and the purified traditional items were to be returned to the German folk and used by scholars to educate the military on the uniqueness of German folk cultures for the world. While the institute itself was disbanded as the war came to an end, the **fieldwork** carried out by numerous scholars continued to surface through the latter half of the twentieth century. We have collections of folksongs, folk narratives, vernacular architecture, and folk speech, for example, that are still being located and published by the directors of the research departments of the two umbrella organizations. The Nazi regime invested large funds and manpower in the study of traditions, much of which was kept by the investigator in charge and used for decades and multiple publications following the war and even into the present century.

STUDIES OF GERMAN FOLKLORE

German folklore is quite accessible through numerous collections and scholarly studies. The history of folklore in Germany is recorded in several studies, for example, Jacobeit and others (1994) and Dow and Lixfeld (1986). An evaluation of the modern research interests in the field is found in the collection by Brednich (2001), a study of the question of "authenticity" was prepared by Bendix (1997), and a study by Röhrich (1991) looks at "reality" in folktales. German folktales have also been assembled in a single volume as part of the University of Chicago Press series *Folktales of the World* (Ranke 1966). There are handbooks by Erich and Beitl (1974), a ten-volume study of superstition by Bächtold-Stäubli and Hoffmann-Krayer (1987 [1927–1942]), and a two-volume set of German folk speech, particularly proverbial sayings and everyday speech (Röhrich 1977). The household tales of the Grimms have been translated into many languages on numerous occasions, most recently into English by Zipes (1987). However, Ward's translation (1981) represents the only time that the legends have been translated into English. During the 1930s and 1940s an attempt was made to assemble an atlas of German folklore, but this work was never completed. Austria did complete its portion of the Pan-German atlas and covers a few south German regions. Perhaps the most complete work on German folklore is the *Enzyklopädie des Märchens* (Encyclopedia of the Fairy Tale), which is devoted primarily to folktales but in fact covers a much wider range of materials than just fairy tales. This massive work is still being assembled and will most likely not be completed for another decade. Finally, there are many Web sites devoted to German folklore directly or indirectly. For customs, festivals, and celebrations it is easy to consult a city's home page and look for details, for example, Elzach at www.elzach.de and the story of the "Pied Piper" at www.hameln.de. Several sites in the United States are devoted exclusively to fairy tales: www.fln.vcu.edu//grimm/grimm_menu.html and www.pitt.edu/~dash/folktexts.html. German and German-American customs can be found at www.serve.com/shea/germusa/customs.htm.

BIBLIOGRAPHY

Bächtold-Stäubli, Hanns, and Eduard Hoffmann-Krayer, eds. 1987 (1927–1942). *Handwörterbuch des deutschen Aberglaubens*. 10 volumes. Berlin: de Gruyter Verlag.

Bausinger, Hermann. 1990. *Folk Culture in a World of Technology*, translated by Elke Dettmer. Bloomington: Indiana University Press.

Bendix, Regina. 1997. *In Search of Authenticity. The Formation of Folklore Studies*. Madison: University of Wisconsin Press.

Brednich, Rolf Wilhelm, ed. 2001. *Grundriss der Volkskunde. Einführung in die Forschungsfelder der Europäischen Ethnologie*. 3rd edition. Berlin: Reimer Verlag.

Dow, James R., and Hannjost Lixfeld. 1986. *German Volkskunde (A Decade of Theoretical Confrontation, Debate and Reorientation—1967–1977)*. Bloomington: Indiana University Press.

Erich, Oswald A., and Richard Beitl, eds. 1974. *Wörterbuch der deutschen Volkskunde*. 3rd edition. Stuttgart: Kröners Taschenbuchausgabe Bd. 127.

Grimm, Jacob. 1966. *Teutonic Mythology*, translated by James Steven Stallybrass. 3 volumes. New York: Dover.

Grimm, Jacob, and Wilhelm Grimm. 1981. *The German Legends of the Brothers Grimm*, translated by Donald Ward. Philadelphia: Institute for the Study of Human Issues.

———. 1987. *The Complete Fairy Tales of the Brothers Grimm*, translated by Jack Zipes. 2 volumes. New York: Bantam Books.

Jacobeit, Wolfgang, Hannjost Lixfeld, Olaf Bockhorn, and James R. Dow. 1994. *Völkische Wissenschaft. Gestalten und Tendenzen in der deutschen und österreichischen Volkskunde in der ersten Hälfte des 20. Jahrhunderts*. Wien: Böhlau Verlag.

Ranke, Kurt, ed. 1966. *Folktales of Germany*, translated by Lotte Baumann. Chicago: University of Chicago Press.

Röhrich, Lutz. 1977. *Lexikon der sprichwörtlichen Redensarten*. 2 volumes. Freiburg: Herder Verlag.

———. 1991. *Folktales and Reality*, translated by Peter Tokofsky. Bloomington: Indiana University Press.

James R. Dow

HUNGARY

GEOGRAPHY AND HISTORY

Situated in the southeastern part of Central Europe, the Hungarian Republic encompasses about 93,000 square kilometers with 10.5 million inhabitants. Until the end of the World War I the country was larger, containing the whole area of the Carpathian Basin, with more than twice the post-war population (including millions of Romanians, Germans, Slovaks, Croatians, Serbians, and Slovenes within its boundaries). Today about 5 million Hungarians live abroad: in traditional Hungarian territories in **Austria**, **Slovakia**, **Ukraine**, Romania, **Serbia**, **Croatia**, and **Slovenia**;

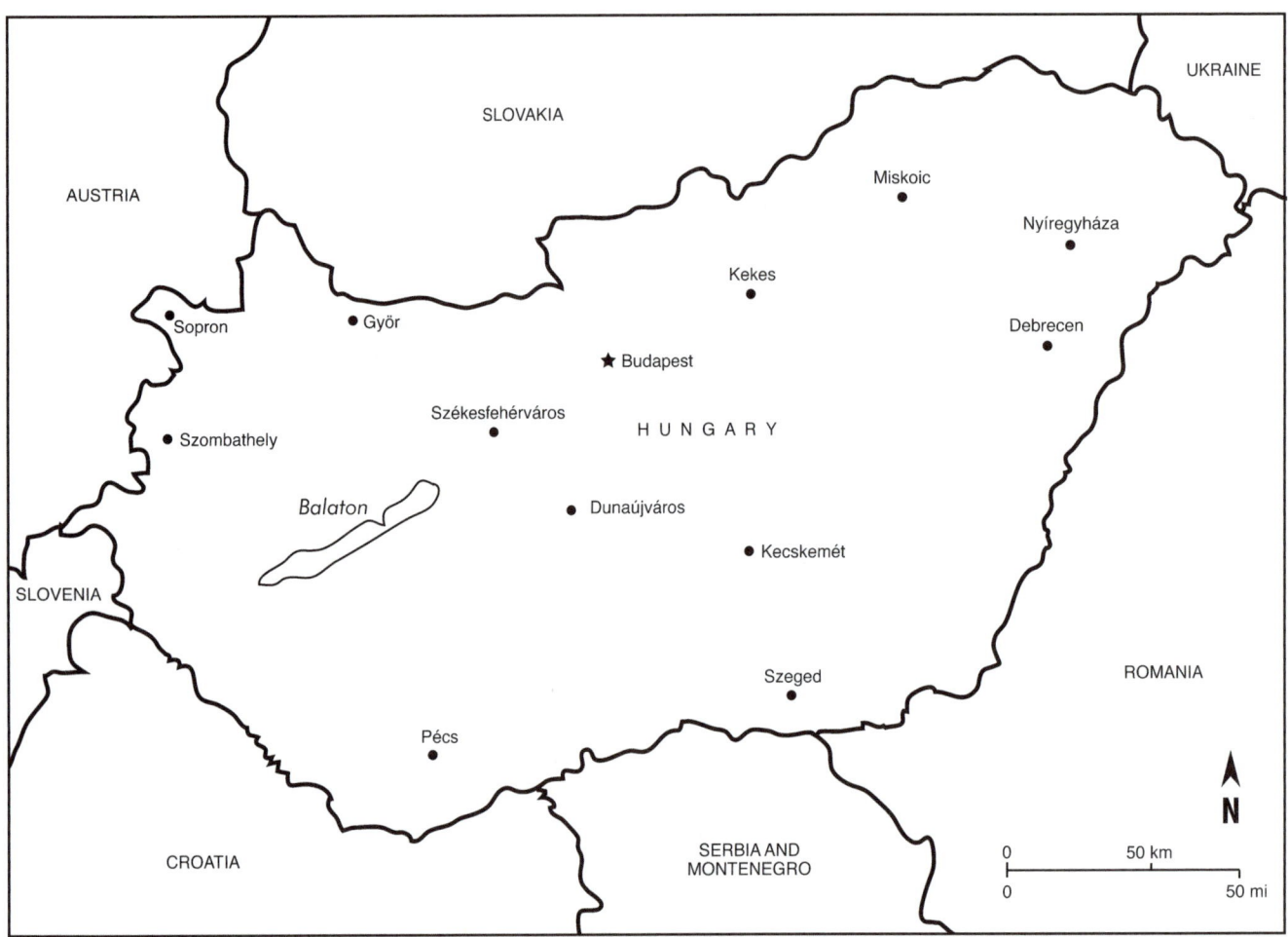

Hungary.

and as immigrants (mostly from the last quarter of the nineteenth century) in the United States, Canada, Brazil, Argentina, South Africa, **Israel**, **Russia**, and elsewhere. The maintenance of their mother tongue and of traces of their traditional culture varies widely in these enclaves. In present-day Hungary the number of ethnic minorities is relatively small: Germans, Slavs, Romanians, and other minorities form about 7–8 percent of the population. Due to the low birthrate, their number is decreasing. The only exceptions are the **Roma**, whose number is still growing and today is above half a million. (Many Roma were also among the Holocaust victims from Hungary.) The Jewish community in Hungary radically increased during the nineteenth century, reaching more than 1 million persons. Between the two world wars forced emigration was significant. Among the remaining persons the number of Holocaust victims from Hungary was above half a million. Only a fragment of the Budapest Jews survived, while village Jews were wiped out. Because compulsory ethnic identification does not occur in the Hungarian official statistics, it is hard to guess the actual number of Jews in the country. It might be about 100,000. For the last three to four generations Hungarians have had a negative birthrate, both in Hungary and in the surrounding countries. The rates of suicide and divorce among Hungarians are among the highest in Europe.

The traditional way of life of Hungarians during the past centuries was based on agriculture, and the typical settlement was the village. In the western part of the country small villages (with a few hundred inhabitants) were typical, while the central part sported larger villages of many thousands of people. Scattered settlements and hamlets were also known. Hungarians liked to live on the lowlands, and high mountains remained unsettled. Extensive cattle breeding was well known on the *puszta* (empty plains without permanent settlements), which became the symbol of Hungary for Europeans.

The ecohistory of the common people in Hungary can be divided into four phases. Before the "land taking" (*honfoglalás*)—that is, the conquest of the Carpathian Basin by the Hungarians (896 C.E.)—the people lived in a semi-nomadic society with some forms of agriculture and wine-growing. During the next hundred years they were forced to settle in villages and were converted to Christianity. A typical East European feudalism arose with characteristics of the "first serfdom." The Ottoman invasion (after the defeat at Mohács in 1526) ended the independent Hungarian kingdom, and then the Austrian Habsburgs ruled the western and northern parts of the country. Until the end of the seventeenth century, south and central Hungary was ruled by the Turks. A nominally independent principality of Transylvania was separated from Hungary and was reunified only in the second half of the nineteenth century. For three centuries the "second serfdom" was dominant. Citizens rose against the Habsburgs several times, and finally the Liberty War (1848) freed the serfs. The third phase lasted until about the end of the World War II. It was characterized by the rapid, capitalistic development of the country, which left millions of peasants without their own land or capital. After 1945 a communist takeover nationalized and socialized not only industry but agriculture as well. This fourth phase gradually became more and more acceptable to the common people. The collapse of the Soviet system (1989) has reopened the capitalistic economy with an enormous inner migration from the villages. Officially, Hungary joined the European community on 1 May 2004, but social problems such as unemployment both in villages and in towns, crises in agriculture and industry, and an aging society still plague Hungary.

Hungarians are a very pessimistic people with a good sense for criticism. They are also very individualistic, forming small groups and parties who fight against each other. In the past the image of the "brave, fighting, fiery" Hungarian was predominant. Among the different ethnic groups in Hungary conflicts and cooperation were as frequent as in other countries. Among the peasant revolts the "Crusade" movement (1514) was particularly violent. It was put down by the noblemen with extreme cruelty. The idea of Hungarian supremacy—that is, "we are the only state-forming entity" in the country, who, as "the shield of Christianity" has saved Europe from the Turks—was popular in the upper class for centuries. Today traces of such ideology survive in the vocabulary of some politicians. There is a strong feeling of solidarity with Hungarians outside the country, but this is tinged with a touch of reproach.

With its forests, rivers, and gold mines medieval Hungary was one of the richest and most powerful countries in Europe. Though destroyed by the Tartar (Mongolian) invasion of 1241, it was soon rebuilt as a number of small nomadic peoples such as the Petchenegs, Uz, Kumanians, and Jász (related to the Ossetians) were assimilated into Hungarian society. The Turkish invasion was devastating to the central parts of the country. By the end of the seventeenth century colonists from the west (Germans) and from the north (Slovaks) migrated to the empty areas, making the culture quite diverse, as evidenced by the languages and churches. The construction of canals through the lowland rivers and the moors during the first half of the nineteenth century changed the landscape. Railways opened new routes to markets and doomed some of the old ones. Self-governance of village communities developed only in some parts of the country, especially Transylvania.

Hungarians still speak their old and isolated Finno-Ugric (Uralic) language. According to the conventional model of the language families, the Uralic peoples separated from each other 5,000–6,000 years ago. The Ugric group (Voguls and Ostyaks living today in West Siberia as well as the Hungarians) split later into two groups at least 4,000 years ago. Then the Hungarians migrated westward, absorbing influences from the peoples on the Great Russian Steppe and from Iranian, Caucasian, and early Turkish peoples. Among the oldest loanwords in Hungarian, the terms of agriculture, religion, culture, and learning date to that time. Arabic and Byzantine sources indicate that Hungarians by the eighth and ninth centuries C.E. lived on the steppe, north of the Black Sea. They were organized in a federation of seven tribes, with various other allied tribes. Most probably they were taking over the institution of the Sacred Ruler versus a military commander from the Khazar Empire. Just before the Conquest (896 C.E.) the head of the family of Prince Árpád became the supreme ruler, but their dynasty (with many kings and Christian saints) ended in 1301. Judging by their personal names, the early Árpáds spoke an Old Turkish vernacular at home.

Among the conquering Hungarians were Christians, Jews, and Muslims. The conversion of the Hungarians was initiated from different centers: today's Germany, Austria, Moravia, Italy, and Byzantium. However, medieval Hungary followed Rome and the Latin Church (not the Eastern Church). Some heathen revolts, mostly by people in rural areas, occurred until about 1061, but they had no long-lasting results. Among the medieval heretics only the Hussite movement was popular in Hungary. The Renaissance and humanism influenced Hungary, especially at the court of the king Matthias Corvinus.

The Reformation arrived very soon in Hungary, and both Lutheranism and Calvinism had an impact on Hungarian Christianity. In Transylvania even the extreme anti-trinitarian movement became strong. The Counter-Reformation in Hungary, directed by the Jesuits with the help of the Habsburgs, finally achieved success by the first third of the seventeenth century. Today one-third of Hungarians follow the reformed churches, who consider themselves the most ardent group in keeping alive traditional Hungarian values in contrast to the cosmopolitan and "Austrophile" Roman Catholic Church. Only a small number of Hungarians converted to Islam between the sixteenth and eighteenth centuries. There are several Catholic Uniate (Eastern Rite) churches for ethnic Romanians and Ukrainians (Ruthenians). The small Greek, Serbian, Armenian, and other minorities have kept alive their own churches. Meanwhile, the first "free churches" (for example, Adventists) date in Hungary to the first part of the nineteenth century. By the end of the same century the Orthodox and Reformed Jewish communities were separated from one another. Already before the World War I new sects (for example, Nazarenites, Salvation Army, and Jehovah's Witnesses) made successful missions in Hungary. In some socialist agrarian movements of the late nineteenth century we find a religious vocabulary, too. During the years of communism in Hungary the church was oppressed. Even today there is a paucity of priests, nuns, monks, and other religious professionals. During the last thirty years "new religions" such as Hare Krishna, Bahái, several Buddhist groups, and Scientology have penetrated into Hungary. Their practitioners are mostly young urban people. However satanism, neo-paganism, and neo-shamanism have remained insignificant in Hungary.

The peasant population consisted of ethnic Hungarians, while miners were originally Germans and salesmen were Jews. The Industrial Revolution in the nineteenth century absorbed first the Germans, then the Hungarians, Slovaks, and others. The emancipation of the Jews paved the way for their integration into Hungarian society. The nineteenth century produced political nationalism, which featured bloody conflicts between native Hungarians and other ethnic groups. Before then only the 1784 uprising of Romanian serfs in West Transylvania against Hungarian noblemen can be described as a bloody ethnic and social revolt. From 1820 to about 1870 many highwaymen (known by the Hungarian term *betyár*) were active in central Hungary, but only as criminals, lacking organization or social ambitions. The most famous person among them, Sándor Rózsa, served with his fellow bandits in the Hungarian Liberty War (1848–1849). In Slovak, Romanian, and Ruthenian folklore in Hungary, the earliest traces of highwaymen date to the beginning of the eighteenth century.

Hungarian peasants dancing. (Courtesy Library of Congress)

Traditionally, the majority of Hungarian peasants were unschooled. Only after World War II was primary education extended to everyone. Today elderly Hungarians in some areas outside Hungary are illiterate in their mother tongue. Among the Roma the same situation is fostering the survival of their oral traditions, word of mouth being even today the primary means by which their traditions are passed along.

RELIGION AND FOLK BELIEF

According to common assumption, the forefathers of the Hungarians once had a belief system similar to that of the much later forms of West Siberian shamanism. Terms for persons with supranormal knowledge (*táltos, tudós*) and a curious term (*reg, rejtõzik*) originally perhaps meaning "trance" might have originated with that ancient lore. Important Hungarian terms in the basic religious vocabulary (for example, *isten*, "god," *ördög*, "devil," later *imád*, "adores," *bûn*, "sin," *bocsájt*, "forgives," and *id/egy*, "holy, saint") pre-date the conquest, and in many cases the loanwords in Hungarian came from hitherto-unknown languages.

Early legal texts from the eleventh century explicitly define punishments for certain heathen habits—eating raw meat, performing sacrifices at stone altars and wells, and more—but in some cases the Latin texts of early Hungarian law are copies of earlier Carolingian decrees. Witch trials proliferated in Hungary from the late sixteenth century until the end of the eighteenth century, with many motifs paralleling general European traditions (for example, the Black Sabbath, seals of the Devil, riding on broomsticks, and rank order of the witches). There are cases when witch accusations clearly had a political motivation. Most of the witchcraft legends in modern folklore tell about everyday conflicts in villages. The historical data concerning the seer of the dead (*halottlátó*) increased during the last two centuries. It is still a well-known practice among the common people. The visions have a clearly Christian aspect, and they were common not only among Roman Catholics but among Hungarians of all faiths.

Conceptions about souls, dualistic origin legends, old names for sickness (for instance, *beteg*, "ill," *fene* or *íz*, "names for disease") have a long history in Hungarian. A few first names could also be explained by old taboo semantics.

Medieval Hungarians soon became good Christians, regularly praying and undertaking pilgrimages and vows. The common Hungarian name for the Virgin Mary, *boldogasszony* (literally, "happy woman") dates to before the conquest. Both old and recent Christian vocabularies retain vestiges of an earlier religious terminology.

The Reformation stressed the importance of the mother tongue and also the education of all the people. Thus, we have gathered in the sixteenth and seventeenth centuries more descriptions of the religious life of the common people. The Counter-Reformation forced a baroque-style folk religiosity, with dynamic forms of representation such as new churches, chapels, road crosses, cemeteries, pilgrimages, saints' pictures, chapbooks, prayer books, miracle legends, and rosaries.

Hungarian folklorists distinguish between folk belief (*néphit*), a primitive way of thinking, and folk religion (*népi vallásosság*), the way in which Hungarians express their religiosity or how they celebrate religious events. Until recently at funerals there was a place for laments performed by the widow or by paid professional keeners.

There are some Hungarian traces of brides' laments, too. From the sixteenth century we have texts for incantations of magic healing. They are close to the "layman's prayers," a genre that has been collected during the last ten years. Their baroque imagery has European parallels and can be dated from the Middle Ages. Another success story in Hungarian folklore was the recent collection of para-biblical folklore: stories about the creation of the world, Noah's life and deeds, Jesus Christ and St. Peter on the roads, and signs of the Last Judgment, for example. In some cases the texts can be compared with European apocryphal sources.

The common worldview in Hungary is a simple Christian one: Heaven, Earth, Hell. According to some folklorists, in Hungarian folktales and origin legends we find reminiscences of an older three-part world (upper world/our world/lower world), perhaps interconnected with a tree of life. But scholars who have tried to reconstruct the "original Hungarian" religion and mythology have been unable to do so. Attempts to compare Hungarian beliefs and customs with Persian, Aryan, Sumerian, and other mythologies have yielded few results regarded as credible by scholars.

BALLADS AND FOLKTALES

Collecting folktales, folksongs, ballads, and other texts began about 200 years ago. A recently published, almost complete type index of Hungarian folktales (*mese*) is based on about 20,000 texts. The type index of Hungarian belief and historical legends (*monda*) is in preparation. Several thousand legend texts have been collected. Folksongs (*népdal*) in Hungary can be traced back centuries. Their music, rhythm, and poetics can be divided into two strata: "old style" and "new style." Recently, the critical edition of Hungarian popular songs from the eighteenth century was begun. Typical folksongs in Hungary have a lyrical theme, and their form is strophic, often with concatenation of stanzas with different content. Ritual songs, on the other hand, are not strophic and have a ritual thematic sequence within the text.

According to Lajos Vargyas, Hungarian folk ballads (*népballada*) are the oldest ones in East Europe, and they may derive, according to some scholars, from French ballads prior to the fourteenth century. More likely the Hungarian folk ballad arose gradually during the sixteenth century. It has many parallels with folk ballads of neighboring peoples. Collectors have reported about 200 "old style" ballad themes, and there are also 100 "new style" ballad themes, mostly about local accidents or moralizing criminal stories. A special group of ballads, devoted to the most famous *betyárs* (highwaymen), was popular by the second half of the nineteenth century.

SONGS, RIDDLES, AND PROVERBS

In spite of the industrious search for a "naive *epos*" in Hungary throughout the nineteenth century (similar to the Finnish *Kalevala*), folklorists could not find any traces of Hungarian heroic epic songs. As among many other European peoples, they perhaps were never extant in Hungarian folklore.

Genres such as riddles and proverbs were not completely neglected by the folklorists, but there is no summary work about them. Only recently, Gyula Paczolay compared the most important Hungarian proverbs with their European parallels. He is preparing a critical edition of the oldest printed Hungarian bilingual (Latin—and in some cases Greek—and Hungarian) proverb collection (from 1598) with many thousands of texts.

The riddle is one of the oldest genres of Hungarian folk literature. The term for "tale," *mese*, originally meant "riddle," and the word is clearly Finno-Ugric. But this does not mean that our riddles are 4,000 years old.

Hungarian folklorists have paid special attention to the best storytellers. Gyula Ortutay initiated this trend, the "Budapest school" of folk narrative studies, and his pupils (especially Linda Dégh) have developed the idea into a successful methodology, which is gaining international acceptance.

MUSIC

In the country of Béla Bartók, Zoltán Kodály, and other world-famous composers, the status of ethnomusicology is very high. Folklore archives contain about 1 million musical items. Béla Bartók began the classification of tunes, and the generations of scholars after him have further developed his system. Five regional "dialects" of Hungarian folk music have been identified: Transdanubia, Upper Hungary, the Great Hungarian Plain, Transylvania, and that of the Hungarian *csángós*, who live in Romania east of the Carpathians. As for the historical development, Zoltán Kodály compared the "old style" with the "new style." Both are four-line stanzas, with a system of melodic and textual variations: for example, AAA (variant A for the "old style") and ABBA for the "new style," with the "couple construction" of the shift of the fifth in the melody. According to Kodály, even the "shift of fifth" is older than the Hungarian conquest and can be found among the Finno-Ugric Cheremis, who live along the Volga River. Recently, several Hungarian ethnomusicologists have tried to fix the time of the origin of the new style. Their suggestions run from the sixteenth century to the end of the nineteenth century.

Instead of such purely morphological systematization, a more historical approach has recently been suggested. Accordingly, the most simple Hungarian folk tunes are very old. They occur in refrains or in key motifs of ritual songs and among the children's songs. There are also folksong melodies that originated in medieval music, especially during the Gregorian period. Only a few Hungarian folk melodies can be traced directly to Renaissance music in Europe. Late Renaissance and early baroque dance melodies were very popular in Hungary. The first hints of a new style were registered in the melodies from the end of the eighteenth century. The common religious hymns in Hungary (for both Catholics and Protestants) can be traced to the seventeenth century. The melodies are inseparable from the common European tradition. Hungarian music in the nineteenth century was following the elitist musical styles and that of the societal dances, too. Vienna-originated *csárdás* (similar to waltz or polka in other countries) and the virtuoso recruiting song, *verbunkos* (from German *Werbung*, meaning "recruiting the soldiers"), were very popular in the entire country.

The study of the instrumental folk music was neglected in Hungary for a long time. It was a common opinion that only Romani bands could play instrumental music. It is true that relatively good descriptions of traditional or popular music played by Romani quartets exist from the end of the eighteenth century. But also shepherds or peasants can play on simple musical instruments. There is no typical Hungarian musical instrument. The dulcimer (*cimbalom*) or the clarinet-like *tárogató* in their actual forms were manufactured in factories by the end of the nineteenth century.

The great Hungarian composer Ferenc Liszt stressed the view that the music of the Hungarian people is the Romani band music. It was a false premise. Roma usually play all kinds of music for their audiences. Today in Transylvania the best virtuosi play both old Hungarian and old Romanian folk music. The first Hungarian folk music orchestras (usually with Roma playing in them) started their "grand tours" of Europe during the first half of the nineteenth century. They ventured from St. Petersburg to London, visiting all the important musical metropolises. Meanwhile, the famous *klezmer* music (so popular today in Europe) was played only for Jews and not for a wider audience in Hungary.

The great Hungarian composer Ferenc Liszt. Hungarian folk music inspired Liszt as well as composers like Haydn, Beethoven, and Brahms. (Courtesy Library of Congress)

Hungarian folk music inspired Haydn, Beethoven, Liszt, Brahms, and practically all the Hungarian composers of the last 100 years. It was played on stages, especially for the *népszínmû* (musical play about the life of the people). From the first folklore festivals in Hungary in the 1930s groups of village people, dressed in local costumes, have performed traditional songs, dances, and folk customs. By the end of 1970s young urban people were organizing *táncház* (dance-house) evenings, when amateurs could sing and dance in accord with Hungarian traditions as close to the original form as was possible. Some songs from these venues became known the world over. Hungarian folksong and folk dance ensembles are excellent cases for folklorism, and they have often received awards both in Hungary and abroad. Genuine folk music and folk dance are important elements in Hungarian school programs, and schools follow the Kodály model of teaching folk music.

Hungarian ethnomusicologists have usually been less appreciative of another kind of popular music, *magyar nóta* (Hungarian song), which was created and performed from the second half of the nineteenth century until about the time of World War I by personally known and usually amateur artists. Both text and melody are sweet, often dull, and melancholic. Though not Hungarian folk music, it is still much cherished among the petty bourgeois and among Hungarians abroad.

Music for entertainment in Hungary has even today some ties with old, popular music. Workers' songs in Hungary are not very numerous, and in most cases they are translations from international trade union or political party songs.

CALENDAR CUSTOMS AND DRAMA

Folk customs in Hungary follow the common European pattern. Either they are calendar customs, occurring throughout the year, or they celebrate the special days of one's life: birth, baptism, engagement, marriage, death, funeral, and memorial days. As they are observed today, they recall baroque or later traditions. Of course, in all celebrations and ceremonies there are several historical strata. For winter customs (*regölés*), scholars have found a number of different reasons that people over the last 1,000 years have undertaken these celebrations.

The forms of folk drama are less spectacular. Mostly in winter or at Carnival time, village youth make their own amusements dressing up and performing tricks, jokes, and animal skits. These rites may have a magical background, and they serve to bind young people together.

Elaborate masks are rare in Hungary, but masks and long fur coats as costumes were known among the easternmost groups of Hungarians. The most famous masked Carnival, the *busó* in Mohács, with large carved wooden masks (typical in Europe from Bulgaria to the Alps), harks back to South Slavic contacts and is said to celebrate the withdrawal of the intruding Turks in the seventeenth century.

Nativity plays (*betlehemezés*) take two forms, either with actors representing the Holy Family, the Magi, and the shepherds or with children carrying from house to house a small model of a church with the infant Christ lying in it. A third form of nativity play is a very primitive puppet theater.

Elaborated puppet theater was not well known in Hungarian folklore. But German marionette theaters visited Hungary in the nineteenth century. They performed common European pieces, though usually in the Hungarian language. Shadow theater (common among Turks and Greeks) was not at all present in Hungary. On the other hand, some plays (mostly miracle plays) were performed in schools for centuries.

Hungarian playwrights in the nineteenth century as well as movie screenplay writers of the twentieth century have often focused on village life with great success. Peasants have organized for themselves amateur theater groups, and they usually perform "village life" plays.

Fairs, circuses, and other shows were very popular in Hungary, and very good descriptions of them exist from about 1800 until World War I. Later, wandering movie projectionists visited the villages, too.

Folk festivals are a new phenomenon in Hungary, not dating back more than seventy years, when the *Gyöngyösbokréta* movement was organized. Village ensembles, which sing and dance and enact traditional customs in folk costumes, usually perform on national holidays. Hungary is a member in the chain of international folklore festivals as well. The worldwide *Folkloriada* was organized in August 2004 in Hungary. In the 1970s, for the International Danubian Folklore Festival in Kecskemét, Hungarian folklorists organized international symposia on folklorism. According to the Hungarian theory, folklorism is not a negative or "out-of-date" phenomenon but one that covers all forms of folklore. Folklore tourism has also flourished in Hungary.

DANCE, GAMES, AND ARTS AND CRAFTS

According to György Martin's system, Hungarian folk dances can be grouped into two strata: old-style dances (maidens' round dances, herdsmen's dances, leaping and lads' dances, and old couples' dances) and new-style dances (recruiting dances

and *csárdás*). As one would expect, dance forms coincide with
those of the folk music. Martin
studied the comparative aspects
of the dances and wrote monographs on the best performers of
dances.

Children's games are still alive
in Hungary. There are good collections and archives storing this
material. Modern sports have replaced traditional sports. The
same situation is true for toys
and dolls. A special museum of
children's old and traditional
games and toys is located in
Kecskemét.

Hungarian folk art includes
such forms as pottery, furniture,
carved wood tools and decorative objects, textiles, and folk architecture. Both the technique
and the forms follow historical

Woman shopping for textiles at a market in Hungary. Other forms of Hungarian folk art include pottery, furniture, carved wood tools, and decorative objects. (Courtesy Library of Congress)

styles. There are only a few specimens of folk paintings or folk graphics. Cemeteries
were fully decorated only in some places. Folk religion encouraged folk art, using
even genres that were not made by, but rather for, peasants (for example, glass pictures, saints' sculptures, church relics, tomb inscriptions, and memorial verses).

CHALLENGES OF THE MODERN WORLD

Globalization is a dangerous phenomenon today, but thanks to the relatively isolated situation of the Hungarian culture, traditional values have not yet disappeared
completely. Traditional Hungarian values are an important factor in the nation's
cultural policy. The more than 200-year-old tradition of Hungarian folklore research
has contributed much to that. Hungarian folklore research stands on a very high
scholarly level. Its foundations include esthetics (János Erdélyi), comparative philology (Lajos Katona), psychoanalytic folklore (Géza Róheim), phenomenology (János
Honti), social aspects (Gyula Ortutay), folk religiosity (Sándor Bálint), and study of
the folk customs (Zoltán Újváry). There are two academic research institutes of folklore and ethnography in Budapest. The Ethnographic Museum is situated at the
main square, opposite parliament. The Open Air Ethnographic Museum in Szenten-
dre has an excellent and rich collection. Folklore and **ethnography** are subjects of
study at five universities in Hungary (Budapest, Szeged, Debrecen, Pécs, and
Miskolc) as well as at Cluj/Kolozsvár (Romania) and Novi Sad/Újvidék (Serbia).
These institutions have hundreds of graduate students conducting their own studies.
The most important studies of Hungarian immigrants' folklore have been conducted
in the United States and Canada by Linda Dégh. It seems there will be a future not

only for Hungarian folklore but for Hungarian folklore research, too. *See also* **Ashkenazim, Roma**.

BIBLIOGRAPHY

Balassa, Iván, and Gyula Ortutay. 1984. *Hungarian Ethnography and Folklore*. Budapest: Corvina.

Dégh, Linda. 1995. *Narratives in Society: A Performer-Centered Study of Narration*. Folklore Fellows Communications 255. Helsinki: Academia Scientiarum Fennica.

Dömötör, Tekla. 1982. *Hungarian Folk-Beliefs*. Bloomington: Indiana University Press.

———. 1988. *Hungarian Folk Customs*. Budapest: Corvina.

Fél, Edit, and Tamás Hofer. 1969. *Proper Peasants*. Budapest: Corvina.

Fél, Edit, Tamás Hofer, and Klára K. Csilléry. 1969. *Ungarische Bauernkunst*. Budapest: Corvina.

Hofer, Tamás, and Edit Fél. 1979. *Hungarian Folk Art*. Budapest: Corvina.

Honti, János. 1975. *Studies in Oral Epic Tradition*. Budapest: Akadémiai Kiadó.

Hoppál, Mihály. 2000. *Studies on Mythology and Uralic Shamanism*. Budapest: Akadémiai Kiadó.

Klaniczay, Gábor. 2002. *Holy Rulers and Blessed Princesses: Dynastic Cults in Medieval Central Europe*. Cambridge: Cambridge University Press.

Kodály, Zoltán. 1982. *Folk Music of Hungary*. Budapest: Corvina.

Kósa, László. 2000. The Age of Emergent Bourgeois Society from the Late 18th Century to 1920. In *A Cultural History of Hungary in the Nineteenth and Twentieth Centuries*, edited by László Kósa. Budapest: Corvina-Osiris. 7–100.

Martin, György. 1988. *Hungarian Folk Dances*. Budapest: Corvina.

Ortutay, Gyula. 1972. *Hungarian Folklore: Essays*. Budapest: Akadémiai Kiadó.

———, ed. 1977–1982. *Magyar néprajzi lexikon* (Encyclopedia of Hungarian Ethnography). 5 volumes. Budapest: Akadémiai Kiadó.

Paládi-Kovács, Attila, ed. 1988–2001. *Magyar néprajz nyolc kötetben* (Handbook of Hungarian Ethnography). 8 volumes. Budapest: Akadémiai Kiadó.

Pócs, Éva. 1989. *Fairies and Witches at the Boundary of South-Eastern and Central Europe*. Folklore Fellows Communications 243. Helsinki: Academia Scientiarum Fennica.

Róheim, Géza. 1966. *Hungarian and Vogul Mythology*. 2nd edition. Seattle: University of Washington Press.

Sárosi, Bálint. 1986. *Folk Music. Hungarian Folk Music Idiom*. Budapest: Corvina.

Scheiber, Alexander. 1985. *Essays on Jewish Folklore and Comparative Literature*. Budapest: Akadémiai Kiadó.

Vargyas, Lajos. 1983. *Hungarian Ballads and the European Ballad Tradition*. Budapest: Akadémiai Kiadó.

Voigt, Vilmos. 1975. Aspects of the Examination of Acculturation in Hungarian Folk Culture. *Acta Ethnographica* 24:295–330.

———. 1999. *Suggestions towards a Theory of Folklore*. Budapest: Mundus Hungarian University Press.

———. 2000–2004. *Történeti folklorisztikai tanulmányok* (Historical Studies on Folklore). 3 volumes. Budapest: Universitas Könyvkiadó.

———. 2004. A Brief Account of More Than Two Hundred Years of Teaching Folklore and Ethnography (Including Cultural Anthropology) at Hungarian Universities. *Acta Ethnographica Hungarica* 49:181–210.

———, ed. 1988. *A magyar folklore* (University Handbook of Hungarian Folklore). Budapest: Osiris.

Voigt, Vilmos, and Mihály Hoppál. 2003. *Ethnosemiotics © Hungary*. Budapest: European Folklore Institute.

Vilmos Voigt

SLOVAKIA

GEOGRAPHY

Situated in Central Europe, Slovakia consists of two large geographical zones: the lowlands mainly in the south and the mountain ranges of the Carpathians in the central, north, northwest, and northeast of the country. The climate of Slovakia is the mild, Continental type, with hot summers (as hot as 30–35 degrees Celsius or 85–95 degrees Fahrenheit) and cold winters (as cold as –20 degrees Celsius or 0 degrees Fahrenheit) with considerable snow and frost.

HISTORY

The historical development of Slovakia and its culture was influenced by its geographical position at the heart of Europe as a territory across which numerous migrations can be traced. Western European cultural influences were intensified by colonists mostly from Germanic countries in several waves from the twelfth to the nineteenth centuries. They exerted considerable influence on the growth of an urban way of life as well as on the development of law and the evolution of crafts. Mining and winemaking reached high standards also thanks to their influence. Beginning in the fourteenth century but mainly in the next two centuries, colonization based on what was called "Walachian Law" reached Slovakia and had a strong cultural impact.

Ethnically, this colonization consisted mostly of Ruthenians and Poles, even though the migration had started during the expansion of the Ottoman Empire into the Balkans and was named after the Romanians and Walachians. According to this law, newly founded villages or settlements as well as already established German

Slovakia.

villages were not so strongly tied to a feudal landlord but had some freedom of self-government. In addition, economic progress came in the form of a new way of grazing sheep by utilizing pastures situated high up in the forests and mountains (in Slovak, *hole*, meaning "naked"). The production of sheep's milk as well as new products prepared from this milk such as *žinčica* (a sour milk drink), *bryndza* (a soft, fermented cheese), sweet cheese, and smoked cheese became an inevitable part of Slovak cuisine, and *bryndzové halušky* (small dumplings served with *bryndza* and fat) reached the symbolic position of a "national dish." This Walachian type of sheep-breeding and its seasonal rhythm had an impact on Slovak culture. Shepherds routinely stayed in the highland pastures with their flocks from spring until autumn. A group of shepherds lived in a wooden hut, called a *koliba*, and were supervised by a man called a *bača*. The *bača* supposedly was a good manager of the group as well as the sheepfold (*salaš*). He was also perceived as a wise man, a healer of people as well as animals, because he knew much about the surrounding natural world, including its medicinal herbs. Very often the *bača* was also a well-known and admired storyteller.

The modernization of Slovak society began in the eighteenth century during the reign of the Habsburg rulers, who introduced economic, educational, and administrative reforms. Nonetheless, prolonged feudal relations together with unfulfilled nation-building demands created tensions and slowed the process of modernization. However, this lag in progress meant that research into folklore and **ethnography**, which began at the end of the eighteenth century and flourished in the nineteenth century, could focus on genuinely archaic phenomena within the culture and everyday lives of the people.

Constant poverty and a bad economic situation in the country prompted emigrations. In the seventeenth century, fueled by economic and religious reasons, Slovaks colonized the Hungarian Lowlands (the Great Hungarian Plain). The end of the nineteenth and the beginning of the twentieth centuries witnessed a strong wave of emigration to the United States and Canada. Initially, this emigration consisted primarily of men motivated by the need to earn money for the improvement of the economic situation of the family, who stayed home in Slovakia. Only later, beginning in the 1920s, did most Slovak emigrants to the United States and Canada decide to stay there permanently.

RELIGIOUS AND FOLK BELIEFS

Slovakia's belief system is grounded in Western Christianity but was influenced by the pre-Christian beliefs it absorbed. The ancestors of present-day Slovaks inhabited a powerful kingdom known as the Great Moravian Empire. The rulers of this empire asked the Byzantine Church to send representatives to preach Christianity to the people in a language they could understand. Two missionary brothers, Cyril and Methodius, recently proclaimed the patron saints of Europe by the Catholic Church, came to the region in the ninth century C.E. They brought literacy, a Slavic translation of the Bible, and the Eastern Orthodox or Byzantine type of Christianity. Later, the followers of Cyril and Methodius were expelled from the country, and beginning in the tenth century, as Slovakia gradually became a part of the Kingdom of **Hungary**, Western Christianity became dominant in the country. In the sixteenth century the country was very strongly influenced by the Lutheran Reformation movement, thanks especially to the German urban population and the nobility, which turned to Protestantism out of opposition to the House of Habsburg. The already mentioned Walachian colonization also had a religious impact by advancing Orthodoxy from the eastern borders of the country westward. The Habsburgs reacted with a strong countermovement, causing regional wars as well as local conflicts throughout Slovakia during the entire seventeenth century. Most people gradually turned back to the Catholic Church, and nowadays more than 80 percent of those who claim to be believers identify themselves as Roman Catholic. The emigration of Slovaks to the Hungarian Lowlands during the eighteenth century was motivated by their desire to remain true to their Protestant beliefs. In present-day Slovakia approximately 10 percent of believers identify themselves as Protestant (most of them Lutherans). The Orthodox Church was also gradually expelled by the Habsburgs, in part through the "Unity Treaty" of the seventeenth century after the Greek-Catholic or Byzantine Church was established in Hungary, which at the time also included Slovakia. Currently, about 5 percent of Slovaks belong to this church. Individual denominations and churches in general had a sad and sometimes cruel history of oppression during the second half of the twentieth century. Nevertheless, according to the latest census, 80 percent of Slovaks identify themselves as believers or as members of one of the eleven denominations.

In spite of church dominance, folk beliefs are still alive. Some are practiced unconsciously, such as knocking on wood or wooden furniture to prevent further speech and ensure a positive result or good luck. It is a tradition, and nobody thinks anymore of the evil spirits of the wood who would sabotage happy plans if they heard them. There was, and still is, a wide range of practices, seasonal and magical, related to healing animals or people. The use of aromatic plants such as garlic and various herbs having medicinal properties (some considered sacred) is well known, as is purification with water and/or smoke.

AGRICULTURAL CRAFTS AND PRACTICES

Historically, Slovakia has been predominantly an agricultural country. Agrarian culture originated in early medieval times and remained the prevailing occupation of the people until the first half of the twentieth century. Different crafts, closely connected with agriculture, developed to provide goods and services for everyday use as well as luxury items to meet the demands of more sophisticated customers. Industrialization came to Slovakia relatively late—at the end of the nineteenth century. The most developed industries included the manufacture of textiles and linens, leatherworking, and the processing of lumber. Less prominent industries were the manufacture of machines and chemicals and food-processing. The heavy metal industries were "forced" on Slovakia only in the second half of the twentieth century. Mining, especially ore mining, has been of special importance since medieval times.

Many archaic agricultural practices could be found in Slovakia even into the second half of the twentieth century, especially in the border areas of the country. These included using a wooden plow to cultivate the land and using the ashes of burned bushes as fertilizer. The survival of some outdated practices, however, did not mean that agricultural practices throughout the country were outdated, since agricultural enterprises employing machinery and a specialized agricultural labor force also flourished. The production of cereals and grains dominated, along with potatoes in the northern regions (beginning in the eighteenth century) and maize (beginning in the nineteenth century). Vineyards were planted, and the production of wine for personal use became common throughout the country. Specialized wine-producers, making wine for the market, could be found in the villages and small towns of the southwest and southeast. Raising livestock was an important part of agrarian culture and included animals used for transportation (horses and oxen), those used for the production of dairy products (cows, goats, and sheep), and those used for meat (pigs) and eggs (chickens and geese). The maintenance of cows and sheep depended on the availability of pastureland in the summer and sufficient fodder for the winter. In Slovakia at the end of the nineteenth century, pastureland accounted for approximately one-fifth of all land devoted to agriculture. Buildings used for hay storage during the winter and located in mountain meadows have always been part of the landscape. Nowadays those wooden structures are often remodeled and used for recreational purposes.

The slow development of agriculture related in large measure to the ways in which family property was inherited and divided. Statistics from the first half of the twentieth century indicate that people working in agriculture were not differentiated much socially. Most belonged to the class of small producers and landowners, those with five to ten hectares of land. This situation was a consequence of long-lived feudal traditions, especially those that required fulfilling the legal claims of all the sons of a family to equal parts of the family property. Sons often continued to live with their parents, even after marrying, because only those who worked on the family property had the right to inherit. Family property (in Slovak *otcovizeò*, *dedovizeò*—that is, the land of the fathers, forefathers) was divided when the father, who was, in fact, not the owner but the manager of the property, died or, being old and weak, decided to retire. This could happen even when the sons themselves had reached the age of grandfathers.

In fact, a family could continue to grow larger and larger. When a young woman married, she received a dowry from her father's family. Daughters inherited only in the rare case when there were no male heirs. For a married woman her husband's family became most important because her children were brought up in that family and were the potential heirs of their father's property. Even when women became equal heirs by law in the first half of the nineteenth century, they usually did not exercise this right in the hopes that their sisters-in-law also would follow suit and not join the heirs of the property their children might claim from their husbands' families.

The equality of shares is evident not only from the appearance of the countryside but also in values practiced in everyday life. The importance of the family as protector of the individual is obvious in Slovak traditions. Within this close-knit type of family all members were important, including aging relatives. Old parents stayed within a family, and the sons and daughters-in-law were obliged to care for them. A family took care of all its members, including the handicapped ones. This kind of family structure was most evident in rural areas. It differed within the community of craftsmen because a craft was passed on "from father to son." When there were many children in a craftsman's family, some had to leave the family and earn their living in some other profession.

Crafts were also a very important way of earning a living in Slovakia. They were highly specialized and from the fifteenth to the nineteenth centuries were associated with guild production. Guilds required journeymen to travel. Thus, journeymen became mediators of news and fashion. Crafts produced at home existed alongside the work of artisans. Weekly, monthly, or seasonal markets were held for the exchange of products as well as of news and information. Outside Slovakia a frequent stereotype of "Slovaks" was that of wandering tinkers or bricklayers who worked abroad on a seasonal basis.

CALENDAR CUSTOMS

The rhythms of peasant life and work form the basis for annual customs, as do the celebrations of Christian holidays. The winter and summer solstices were two important times of the year. During the winter solstice, which came to include Christmas, some archaic traditions continued to live on. For example, on St. Lucy's Day, 13 December, masked figures visited houses, where they swept the room with a goose wing for purposes of purification. Various magical practices were also used to foresee one's future husband. For example, on St. Andrew's Day, 30 November, a girl could put a piece of man's clothing under her pillow at night, and she would see her future husband in a dream. Good wishes from young boys, who were associated with potency and a positive male principle, were thought to provide good health and good crops for the members of a household and a good future husband for the maiden in the house.

Nowadays the Christian celebration of Christmas is mostly observed with the Baby Jesus bringing presents to the children in a family. On Christmas Eve, presents, mainly for children, are put in secret under the Christmas tree. The decorated evergreen tree became the dominant Christmas decoration during the twentieth century, replacing older types of decorations made from hay. After Christmas a time of Carnival is celebrated. Enjoyable activities and magical ways for gaining prosperity form the roots of many of the practices of Carnival time involving masked creatures. Phallic symbols and coats with the fur turned inside out contributed to the masks' appearance.

The vernal equinox was also an important magical time, especially in connection with starting work. On St. George's Day, 24 April, it was traditional to send livestock out to the pastures. It is expressed by the words of a folksong:

> Saint George gets up,
> opens the field
> for the grass to grow
> green, grass-blue, violet.

The most important church holiday of the spring is Easter. In traditional folk culture decorated eggs symbolizing rebirth are given as gifts. On Easter Monday young men are allowed to throw water on young girls and "beat" them with a switch made of

In Slovakia, the rhythms of peasant life and work form the basis for annual customs, such as Spring Festival. (© Jaroslav Kubec/HAGA/The Image Works)

willow. This custom is still widely observed, though nowadays perfume is used instead of water, and not only young men but also small boys accompanied by their fathers visit girls' homes. Instead of decorated eggs, chocolates and money are given as gifts to the boys.

The celebration of May Day in some regions of Slovakia is characterized by young men giving traditional tokens of affection to their sweethearts. This gift is a small Maypole decorated with ribbons and fixed to the roof of a girl's house. Much more widespread is the custom of erecting a Maypole in the center of a village or town, in a park, or in front of a village office, church, local pub, or football stadium. Dances are organized and held there as well. The Catholic Church celebration of Corpus Christi and in some places also of Pentecost Week is observed with a village procession to decorated outdoor altars.

The summer solstice is not celebrated anymore in a traditional way. It used to be celebrated on the feast of St. John the Baptist, 24 June, by burning fires outside the village. Meetings around such fires were recently resurrected by populist and nationalist political parties, but they have not generated much support or interest among the general public.

The celebrations that followed harvest have shown surprising vitality. Traditionally, such a celebration occurred within the peasant household and was centered on the working group, but it was adopted by the cooperative farm system in the second half of the twentieth century and outgrew its previous form to become a celebration involving the whole village, including a parade, dinner, and dance.

No special traditions were connected with the autumn equinox except those of shepherds coming back from the pastures around St. Michael's Day, 30 September, and those associated with the grape harvest festival. Perhaps the most elaborate and important celebrations taking place during the autumn were, and continue to be, All Saints' Day, 1 November, and All Souls' Day, 2 November. Both of these holidays are devoted to the memory of the dead and of one's ancestors. People visit cemeteries and decorate graves with flowers and candles.

LIFE-CYCLE CUSTOMS AND RITUALS

Customs associated with the life cycle—that is, rites of passage—have survived in both stable and transformed versions, sometimes elaborated on, or controlled by, church and civic institutions over the centuries. Customs associated with the birth of a child started at the wedding, when care was taken, if only in a magical way, to ensure that the newly married couple would have children. For example, the bride was given a baby boy to hold on her lap. Since the second half of the twentieth century women have been delivering their children in hospitals. Nonetheless, some customs associated with delivery and birth continue, including those meant to protect the mother and child from any possible evil and those meant to ensure good health and a happy future for the child. The birth celebration was connected with baptism, when the child was given a name. In Catholic villages names were usually taken from the calendar of saints and their feast days, while in Lutheran communities names were mostly taken from the Old and New Testaments or Slavic tradition. In addition to a new name, a new relationship was established between the newborn child and its chosen godparents and between the parents and the godparents, especially the godmother. These artificially constructed relationships copied real relationships and brought certain rights and obligations to all those involved.

Selecting a husband or wife in traditional village society was often a matter of free choice based on friendship and love. However, the approximately equal financial situation of the families involved also mattered. Most marriages were endogamous— that is, a partner was chosen within a given community. If there was some problem with a choice concerning the financial situation or religious affiliation of the young man or woman, the parents decided who would be their child's future spouse. Cases of children born out of wedlock were quite rare since usually there were no serious obstacles to a marriage.

A number of customs were associated with the marriage ceremony itself. For example, to make it difficult for the bridegroom to obtain his bride, he often had to pay other young men in the village to "steal" her from the wedding party. To ensure prosperity for the young couple, grain or rice was poured on them. In addition, because it was believed that the bride had positive magical power, she gave out sweets and coins to the people, mostly children, who were standing around. Because marriage meant the beginning of the socially accepted sexual life of the newlyweds, songs with erotic undertones might be sung at the wedding celebration. Some customs emphasized the importance of the bride's becoming a part of her new family. She had to prove her skills as a housewife, for example, by sweeping up a broken bowl. There are, in fact, many layers of customs, some influenced by established institutions and some the result of current fashion. Some customs are observed nationwide, while others are typical of a certain region only.

Customs connected with death emphasized the departure of the deceased, separation from those who remained alive, and defense against any possible bad influence of the deceased on the living. A wide range of superstitions concerned portents of death. These included, for example, dreams about a white goose or a white dog or hearing the hoot of a small owl (*kuvik*). Some special customs, such as those suggesting a belated wedding, followed when a young, unmarried person died. Many of the customs associated with death have been lost over time, since now people often die in hospitals, where they are excluded from the family circle. The memory of ancestors and other departed family members is kept alive through regular visits to the cemetery. These visits take place on All Saints' Day and All Souls' Day as well as on Christmas and on the anniversary of the deceased's birth and death.

FOLKTALES AND POETRY

Folk literature and folksongs were the two main areas of research when folklore studies began in Slovakia in the early nineteenth century. The activity of collecting, editing, and publishing texts was connected to ideas of nation-building, activities of revivalists, and Romanticism. Myths and legends received most attention, even though these were not the most common genres found in folk literature, which also included fairy tales, animal tales, humorous tales, and anecdotes. Examples of myths include the story of the hero who goes to visit the sun to ask him some questions or the tale of the hero who must fight a dragon to liberate a captive princess. A legend is a story that the narrator and the listener believe—or at least believe could have happened. In legends, real as well as mythical creatures can appear, and real as well as fantastic feats can occur. Legends are often tied in some way to the narrator's surroundings from the near or distant past. For example, the legend cycle recounting the exploits of Juraj Jánošík, a noble bandit of the early eighteenth century, has a central position in Slovak folklore. Fairy tales pick up on many situations reflecting the structure and activities of family life. For example, in fairy tales it is usually the youngest brother who is expected to look after aging parents, which was the case in real life. Also the frequent motif of the stepmother in fairy tales reflects the reality that young women did often die in childbirth, making second marriages common. The memoir, in which the narrator recalls events from his life, is still a vital genre. These narratives are usually quite current and reflect the narrator's individual point of view.

Folk poetry is mainly represented by various kinds of folksongs. Huge collections of Slovak folksongs have been published or archived since the nineteenth century. These include ballads, lullabies, carols, "meadow songs" (sung by girls when collecting hay in the mountain meadows), soldiers' songs, and bandits' songs. Some songs are functionally tied to certain happenings. For example, wedding songs include those reflecting the departure of the bride from her parents' home as well as those sung while the bride's veil is removed and replaced by a kerchief or bonnet. Other songs are free of any connection to a specific event. There is also an apparent regional division in terms of musical form between songs from the northern mountain regions and those from the southern lowland regions.

MUSIC AND DANCE

Music has played an important role in folklife and was an integral part of dance, song, and drama. Some songs such as Christmas carols and meadow songs were sung a cappella. However, most songs were accompanied instrumentally, often by a solo musician playing a bagpipe. Over time the bagpipe player came to be replaced by the button-box accordion player, who often accompanied performances of dance as well as song. Solo performers also included shepherds playing various kinds of pipes. The best-known and most characteristic Slovak folk musical instrument is the *fujara*, composed of two pipes bound together. Groups of musicians who played similar instruments often formed bands, the most common types being the string band and the brass band. Brass bands were more recent and were influenced by military music.

Most of the folk music played in Slovakia belongs to the "new Hungarian style" with its characteristic syncopated rhythm and well-defined musical form.

Folk dance is closely connected to folk music. Magical ritual dances probably form the oldest layer in the historical and musical development of dance. Those dances performed during Carnival retained their original function of ensuring the fertility of the land. Dances performed by girls in rows or circles in early spring featured throwing away a straw doll, an effigy of winter called a *morena*. There were also separate dances for girls and for boys, pair dances, shepherds' dances, and bandits' dances (*odzemok*). Like folksongs, dances were also strongly influenced by the new Hungarian musical style. The *čardáš* and the *verbunk* (a dance mimicking the recruiting of men into the army) were added to the dance tradition and became dominant, in fact. For the most part, folk dances are no longer performed in the villages or countryside where they originated. However, these dances are preserved in the activities of folk ensembles, amateur and professional groups of dancers, singers, and musicians who perform traditional dances in a more or less stylized way onstage. In fact, Slovakia has witnessed a folk dance revival in recent years. People across the country come together socially to learn traditional ways of dancing.

Young man playing a *fujara*, Detva, Slovakia. (© Jaroslav Kubec/HAGA/The Image Works)

DRAMA

Dramatic performances occur in Slovak folklife most frequently in connection with rituals. Actors are often masked and act as if they are the characters they are portraying. An example is the "burial of a contrabass," a dramatic game full of joy and erotic meaning. The Carnival is over, the music is finished, and the "priest" gives a farewell speech to a "deceased" contrabass. By pretending to be sorrowful members of the family, the audience is also involved in the burial. Somewhat more serious, though not always, is a dramatic presentation re-enacting the story of the shepherds who see the light over Bethlehem and bring gifts to the Baby Jesus. This performance often includes numerous jokes and comic dialogue. The bases for these dramatic performances can be found in medieval mystery plays and in the school dramas of the Renaissance. In addition, folk drama has definitely had a strong influence on puppet theater and on amateur theater traditions, still evident in many of the villages and small towns of Slovakia.

GAMES, ARTS, AND CRAFTS

Folklore studies never paid much attention to sports or games within traditional Slovak culture. Sports such as wrestling as well as other physical activities were practiced mostly by young men. Card games were played in a social context, just as they are today, with one change. While, traditionally, card games were part of the world of men, nowadays families and even children on their own play cards to relax.

Visual art does not exist in isolation. It coexists with other cultural phenomena. Historically, traditional folk art was created by peasants or by specialists and artisans, and it was accepted in the community. Its artistic features were often copied from art produced in higher social strata. Thanks to the conservative nature of rural society and also to its economy, some of these borrowed artistic features remained alive for a long time in peasant art. The highest development of decorative folk art dates to the nineteenth century. Folk art had many different functions, among which the esthetic did not necessarily dominate. In fact, the origins of folk art can probably be found in utilitarian, magical, or ritual functions. A great deal of artistic creativity could be seen in folk costumes, especially in women's dress, including embroidered blouses, bonnets decorated with lace, hand-woven aprons, and colorful leather applications on fur coats. Blueprint production as well as other crafts accommodated the demands of customers. Except for different kinds of silver buttons and pins made of brass worn by men as well as women, jewelry was rare in Slovak folk costumes.

Decorative art could also be found in architecture. Most of Slovakia exhibits wooden folk architecture, typical of Northern Europe. A small portion of southern Slovakia features architecture that uses clay and stone, typical of Southern Europe. The most decorative parts of wooden houses were the roof and front facing of the house. In southern Slovakia gate columns made from soft stones and reaching artistic quality could often be found. In both parts of the country artistically decorated or carved gravestones and wooden crosses could be found in old cemeteries. Later, beginning in the twentieth century, crosses made of iron, products of ironworks and mills, appeared as well. Some villages were well known for their stone carvers, specialists who created plastic art, including crosses, small chapels, and statues of saints, which were situated at crossroads or by roadsides either in or outside villages.

CHALLENGES OF THE MODERN WORLD

Culture constantly undergoes the process of change. **Modernization** in the forms of urbanization and industrialization began in Slovakia in the nineteenth and twentieth centuries. Migration accelerated this process. In the second half of the twentieth century politics and ideology also influenced change. The forced collectivization of agriculture and denial of private property had consequences that became evident in social changes to family and community life. These changes coincided with the trend of the early 1960s to get rid of everything old and traditional. For example, new buildings of new materials were built in the villages, and traditional dress was worn only by old village women. The strong influence of **globalization** has been felt in Slovakia since the 1980s, when the disappearance of many traditions and customs was already nearly complete. Some traditions are still preserved in everyday life, though changed in form and function. These include some family celebrations (like weddings), relations within a family (for example, the necessity of caring for aged parents), knowledge of folktales (if not told, then read to children), and songs, dances, and costumes preserved in folk ensembles.

STUDIES OF SLOVAK FOLKLORE

The bibliography of Slovak folklore goes back to the nineteenth century, when collections of songs, folktales, and literature were widely edited and published. The beginning of the twentieth century saw the publication of village monographs, which presented an overview of the lifestyle and traditions of specific villages or regions. Books devoted to more general topics, such as fishing and vine cultivation, were published mostly in the second half of the twentieth century. Additional publications available in Slovak include an ethnographic history of Slovakia, an overview of Slovak folklore, ethno-cartographic publications, and an encyclopedia of folk culture in Slovakia. For those who are interested in learning more, some publications are available in English or with expanded English summaries.

BIBLIOGRAPHY

Botiková, Marta, ed. 1997. *Tradície slovenskej rodiny* (Slovak Family Traditions). Bratislava: Veda Publishing House.

Cooper, D. L., ed. 2001. *Traditional Slovak Folktales Collected by Pavol Dobšinský*. Armonk, NY: M. E. Sharpe.

Etnografický atlas Slovenska (Ethnographic Atlas of Slovakia). 1990. Bratislava: Veda Publishing House.

Gašparíková, V., ed. 2002. *Heroes or Bandits: Outlaw Traditions in the Carpathian Region*. Budapest: European Folklore Institute.

Habáňová, G., ed. 1998. *Folk Architecture in Slovakia*. Bratislava: Academic Electronic Press.

Stoličná, R., ed. 2000. *Slovakia: European Contexts of Folk Culture*. Bratislava: Veda Publishing House.

Marta Botiková

SLOVENIA

GEOGRAPHY AND HISTORY

Slovene is the westernmost language in the South Slav branch of the Slavic languages group and has played a special role throughout Slovene history. It is still considered one of the foundations of national identity. Spoken by about 2.2 million people in at least thirty-two main dialects in and near Slovenia as well as in immigrant communities elsewhere, it uses a modified Latin alphabet with twenty-five characters and employs dual number, a very rare linguistic phenomenon, which is used for two people or objects in all inflected parts of speech.

Four major European geographic regions meet in Slovenia: the Alps, the Dinaric area, the Pannonian Plain, and the Mediterranean. Four cultural regions correspond to them: Alpine region (on the north), the Littoral (on the west), Pannonian region (on the east), and the central Slovene region. Alpine mountains cover some 40 percent of the entire nation. Triglav, the highest mountain peak in Slovenia, is the country's national symbol. Most of Slovenia has a Continental climate with cold winters and warm summers. Forests cover half the territory, making Slovenia the third most forested country in Europe.

Slavs first appeared and inhabited the territory between the Alps, the Adriatic Sea, and the Pannonian Plain in the sixth century C.E. and occupied at first a much

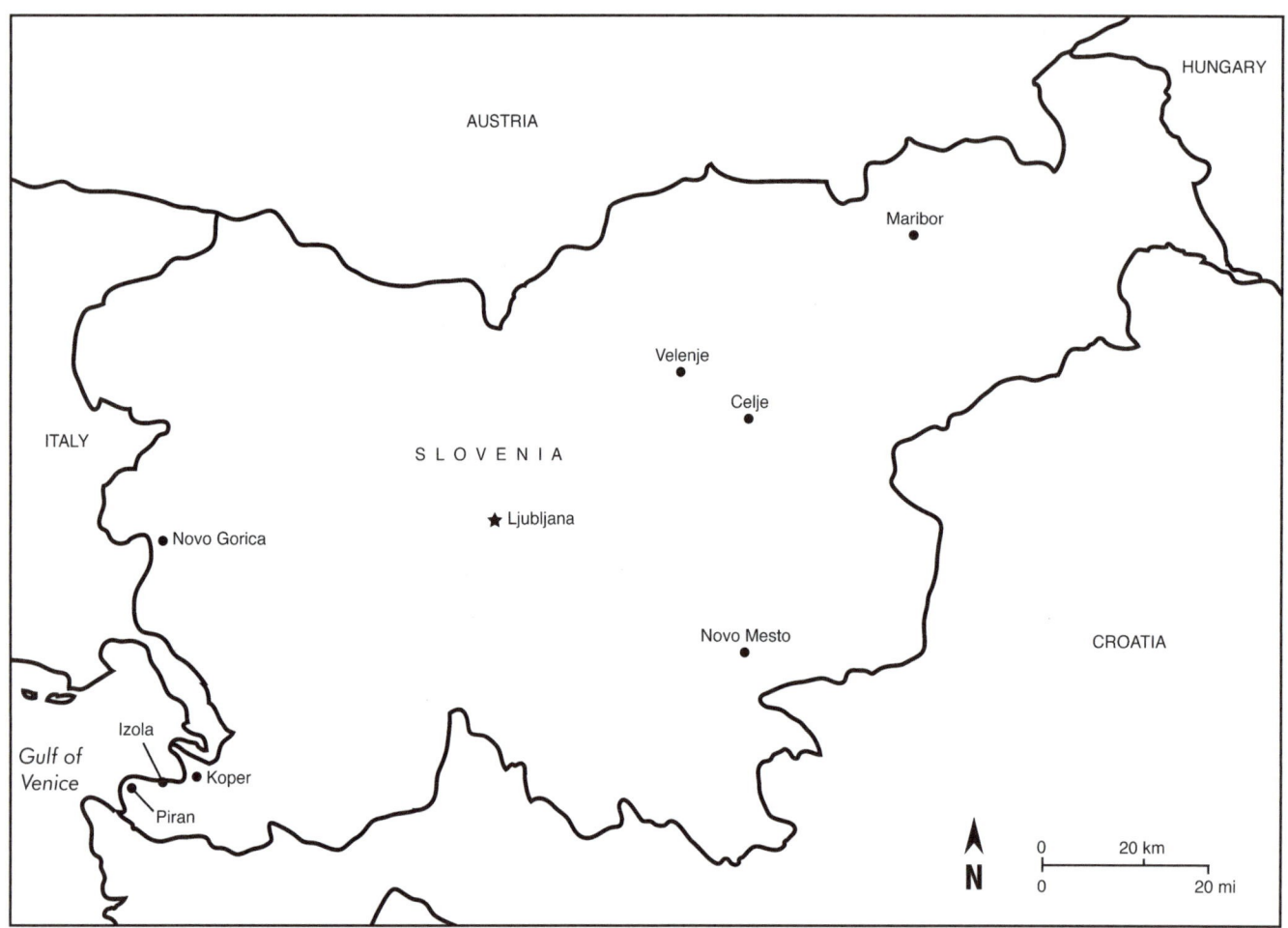

Slovenia.

larger territory than at present. The first Slovene state was the Slavic Duchy of Carantania in the seventh century. It lost its independence in 745 and became a part of the Frankish Empire. The Slavs gradually converted to Christianity. During the fourteenth century most of Slovenia's regions belonged to the Habsburg Empire and later to the Austro-Hungarian Empire. After the collapse of the latter in 1918, Slovenes joined the Kingdom of Serbs, Croats, and Slovenes—renamed the Kingdom of Yugoslavia in 1929. After World War II Slovenia became a part of the Federal People's Republic of Yugoslavia, later the Socialist Federal Republic of Yugoslavia. The modern state of Slovenia dates to 1991 with the dissolution of that nation. In 2004 it joined the European Union and the North Atlantic Treaty Organization (NATO). Approximately 50 percent of the total population lives in urban areas such as the capital, Ljubljana, and the majority of Slovenes are Roman Catholic, though other religious communities are represented as well.

CALENDAR CUSTOMS

Today's calendar customs include primeval remains of pre-Christian annual customs, usually transformed into Christian holidays. In addition, there survive a number of pre-Christian customs such as magical protective and supplicative customs, through which people tried to elicit the well-being upon which their survival depended more deeply in pre-industrial times. Ancient traditions based upon notions of magic are seen most clearly in Shrovetide and Easter customs (magic of water and greenery and painted Easter eggs), traditional bonfires (magic of greenery), Christmas celebrations (magic of fire), birching customs (*tepežkanje*), and the custom of going from door to door (*koledovanje*). Traditional bread, connected with everyday life, also had a central role in pre-Christian customs. Among the most colorful customs seen today are parish festivals and blessings (*žegnanje*).

Rural and urban trade in Slovenia was always linked to blessings. These provided a special opportunity to hold a fair. Every fair would start with a church ceremony, often a procession. Gatherings of relatives, friends, and acquaintances followed the religious celebrations. Tradesmen would arrange their stalls around the church, offering decorated honey-bread (*lect*), which resembled gingerbread and appeared in many shapes, in bright colors, and with decorations (often inscriptions). Young men gave girls dolls and hearts made out of honey-bread with inscriptions expressing their love. Those with more money chose rings, chains, and silk scarves. Between the two world wars the popularity of honey-bread hearts started to wane, and young men began to prefer to take girls to *tombola* (lotteries). Girls thanked them with bunches of flowers, and then some went to dance at an inn. Thus, blessings were once the best opportunity for meeting one's future spouse. In addition to traditional religious meetings, local heritage festivals are particularly interesting since they include folklore performances as well as samplings of traditional cuisine and displays of typical peasant occupations such as charcoal burning and haymaking in order to preserve the memory of previous generations. Of course, local heritage also manifests itself in processions and parades. During the 1980s in particular, historic exoticism in tourist performances attracted much public attention. Sociability and good cheer are important elements of celebrations.

Some of the post-war calendar holidays determined the calendar rhythm of life and replaced the former annual agrarian magic festivals. For example, Republic Day (29 November) was once the day for butchering pigs, while Labor Day (1 May) was the time for planting potatoes. Today's younger generation prefers the carnival festivities and holidays imported from abroad such as St. Valentine's Day and Halloween. Cultural celebrations multiplied during the post-socialist 1990s, when religious holidays were revived, tourism became economically viable, and local communities sought to emphasize their identity in the face of encroaching globalization.

The custom of celebrating spring by making a sheaf of greenery and plants (*butara*) reaches back to pre-Christian times. With the advent of Christianity the custom changed to incorporate the commemoration of Christ's entry into Jerusalem and the palm fronds that were strewn before him as he walked in the city. Today, this custom is still celebrated throughout Slovenia with making the sheaf and taking it to church for blessing. The size of the sheaf varies in different areas of Slovenia. In some regions it may be several meters long. Sheaves are adorned with greenery such as box, twigs of heather, honeysuckle, spring flowers, and colored strips of wood shavings, though in recent times oranges and apples have become acceptable adornments.

The components are gathered in the winter months as soon as available. In the areas where large sheaves are made, they must consist of seven different types of wood: hazelwood, flowering dogwood, juniper, elder, box, ivy, and pussy willow. Ancient customs associated with the *butara* have been preserved. After the blessing in church, the *butara* was kept at home for the rest of the year for good fortune and to ward off ills. In many regions of Slovenia, the boys would rush home with the *butara* after church on Palm Sunday, remove the leaves, and offer them to the farm animals for good health. Whoever in the village was first to offer from the blessed *butara* would have healthy livestock for the rest of the year. Then the mother took the leaves to the attic and placed them between the rafters to protect the home against fire and lightning. In the north the boys returned home with the blessed sheaves and circled the home three times to protect the home from fire and lightning. In the east, the custom was to burn some branches of the sheaf upon returning home from church to protect the house against evil.

Easter eggs (*pirhi*) are colored and decorated hard-boiled or blown chicken eggs. They date among the Slovene peasantry from the seventeenth century, though the oldest surviving example dates from the end of nineteenth century. They are known in different regions of Slovenia as *pisanice*, *pisanke*, *remenke*, and *remenice*. Traditionally, eggs have been an essential part of Slovene Easter celebrations. They are taken in a basket of traditional Easter foods to church on Easter Saturday to be blessed and later set out on the table for the Easter meal. Easter eggs were given as gifts from one person to another, distributed as part of the Easter celebration, and used in traditional Easter games such as chopping on Easter Monday. The method of decorating the eggs has varied from region to region. In the regions of Bela Krajina, Prekmurje, Primorska, Beneèija, and Notranjska, the eggs were decorated with *pisalka* (pencil) and wax. In the region surrounding Ljubljana, in Gorenjska, and in Štajerska, the eggs were decorated with pen and ink. In Dolenjska, Notranjska, Štajerska, and Prekmurje the designs were scratched with a knife. In Škofja Loka, a distinctive variation of the Easter egg was the baked egg formed from dough, made into a little loaf, and decorated with gold leaf and other ornaments. In Bela Krajina and Prekmurje geometric and stylized designs—lines, crosses, spirals, triangles, hearts, circles, dots, and the sun—decorate the eggs. Christian symbols—especially the monograms of Mary (M) and Christ (IHS: *Isus Hristi Salvator*)—are incorporated. In the western regions of Slovenia, Gorenjska, and Primorska, the eggs are decorated with naturalistic forms: clover, daisies, grapes, and birds. Inscriptions are a more recent phenomenon. They may include Easter greetings, sayings, verses, and love messages from girls to boys. Nowadays men and women continue the tradition of egg decoration, particularly in Bela Krajina and Prekmurje. These traditional Easter eggs are greatly valued and exhibited as products of Slovene folk art. There is great interest in reviving this traditional art. Children are encouraged to learn the techniques of egg decoration, and considerable creativity and excitement are generated during the weeks preceding Easter. The Easter egg was originally colored with natural colors from plants. Today chemical dye is usually used. After coloring or decorating the egg, it is polished with either the skin from bacon or an oiled cloth. With eggs, which are colored with at least two colors, the whole process may be repeated at least twice.

Christmas (*Božič*) is the most popular religious and family holiday in Slovenia. It has a long tradition of veneration and celebration, filled with elements of the archaic Indo-European heritage interwoven with later Christian practices. The term "Christmas" means "little god" in Slovene. Set at the time of the winter solstice, when the old sun dies and is re-born, the holiday is connected with the celebration of the sun god and his son. The period around 25 December is when the Indo-European peoples celebrated the New Year, the start of a new cycle on the birthday of the invincible sun god (*Dies natalis Solis invicti*). Many customs, beliefs, superstitions, traditions, and magical events are connected with Christmas in Slovenia. The majority is part of the common European heritage: the cult of greenery, fire, and water, fortune-telling and giving presents, caroling, and Christmas baking. A later Christian addition replaces the sun's light with Christ's eternal light, represented by the fir tree. The Christmas fir arrived here only in the middle of the nineteenth century from German-speaking lands, while the Christmas crèche came to Ljubljana in 1644 with the Jesuits.

In addition to Christmas decorations, the oldest Christmas tradition is the baking of bread, which also extends back to the pre-Christian period. The Christmas loaf differs from region to region. Three types are normally baked: wheat, rye, and buckwheat. These formerly ceremonial breads have magical properties and bring both people and animals health, strength, and energy. Carolers have also been connected to Christmas for some time now. Primož Trubar, the author of the first book printed in Slovene (1550), mentioned carolers. The successors to ancient pagan singers, carolers brought blessings and luck to the house for the coming year.

Slovenes speak of three Christmases: that on 25 December and two "little Christmases" (on New Year's Day and Epiphany). On these days, every family burned incense, the smoke of which brought magic power and expelled demons.

Since the fourteenth century Slovenes have made mass pilgrimages every seven years to Cologne (Köln, Germany). The same time period was also one of flourishing pilgrimages to churches in Slovenia. Pilgrimage holidays and benediction Sundays were special kinds of festivities, which provided opportunities for confession, prayer, and thanksgiving; purchases and encounters; meeting new people; visits to dentists; and gaining indulgences by dispensing alms to beggars.

The role of the patron saints was also very important in the Slovene belief system. Saints were, and still are, seen as protectors against diseases of the body (in the past saints were primarily protectors against the plague and other contagious diseases) and natural and other disasters. In return for received or expected pardon, pilgrims donated paper and wax votive pictures, figurines, or gifts such as salt. This ritual, known at least since the Middle Ages, reached its heyday among broad masses of peasants in the nineteenth century, when the nobility and the middle classes had already begun to abandon it. It almost disappeared in the second half of the twentieth century.

WITCHCRAFT AND FOLK MEDICINE

Folk traditions concerning witchcraft and folk medicine are rich and diverse. According to some older sources, wizards and witches were mythological and demonic creatures such as *kresnik*, *vedomec*, *lamija*, and fairies. Other sources maintain that ordinary people could learn witchcraft as a trade. According to data from Slovene folk traditions, magic was performed by analogy, observing the rule of a part representing the whole. Magic might aim to prevent evil through the use of water, medical herbs, and potions. Wizards and healers knew spells and how to conjure and adjure spirits. They might rely on books about black magic and various magical objects such as sticks, goat horns, and bells, which were sometimes considered to be the seat of the beneficial spirit. Of special interest is the fact that, according to folk tradition, the magic acts performed by wizards differ from those of witches. Since the beginning of the twentieth century, a relatively high number of witchcraft incidents as well as cures performed by folk healers have been recorded.

Incantations are the most archaic element in the treasury of folk medical knowledge. In the first half of twentieth century they were used in folk medicine by only 15 percent of Slovenes. Other folk medical practices were based on traditional and empirical knowledge about the curative effects of plant and animal substances. To some extent incantations resemble prayers, the main difference being that in incantations one usually addresses the deity by personifying a particular disease and requests it to go away. Nowadays the relation between the magical and religious approaches to treating disease, on the one hand, and the scientific approach, on the other, is probably identical, but what has changed is that the magical and religious component has been replaced by alternative medicine. Evidence suggests that many ideas, methods, and techniques belonging to alternative medicine are rooted in Slovene tradition, but this tradition was discontinued for some time before being revived recently.

SONGS AND MUSIC

The majority of folksongs collected during the nineteenth century consisted only of verbal texts. The first collection of Slovene folksongs by Karel Štrekelj was an exemplary edition of the song texts, with a systematic classification of the entire material. But, to his own regret, Štrekelj was able to publish only some 200 tunes compared to many thousands of song texts. Systematic collection of songs with tunes began in 1905. By 1914 it yielded nearly 13,000 songs with tunes. In 1956 this unpublished material was handed over to the Institute for Ethnomusicology (today part of the Scientific Research Center of the Slovene Academy of Sciences and Arts in Ljubljana), which at the same time started the field research and collecting throughout the Slovene ethnic territory that still continue. By 2003 approximately 55,000 items of folk music had been recorded on tape. On the basis of this material it has been possible to prepare a new, comprehensive, critical edition of songs with tunes.

Slovene folksongs and tales often depict persons destined for special missions. One is the tenth male (*desetnik*) or female (*desetnica*) child. Also the ninth, twelfth, or thirteenth child of the same sex was thought to be a deity, demonic creature, clairvoyant, or wizard, yet simultaneously also a victim—a tithe destined for a certain deity. As an ordained person, the tenth child is the one who sacrifices everything to attain wisdom. In Slovene folksongs, the tenth daughter has to roam the world. The tenth brother appears only in recent songs.

Characteristics of Alpine folk music predominate in most of Slovenia. The major mode is now used almost exclusively, and all singing is basically part-singing. On the periphery of Slovene ethnic territory, however, three regions exhibit different musical characteristics: Prekmurje in the northeast, Rezija (Val di Resia, Italy) in the northwest, and Bela krajina in the southeast. In Bela krajina, Slovene and Croatian traditions (including ancient ceremonial summer-solstice songs sung antiphonally) are interspersed with other South Slav elements. Various groups of refugees, fleeing from the Turks, settled there from the fifteenth century onward. In the central regions the chief performers of part-songs were the young men in the villages. Until World War II they gathered regularly in the evenings on an open central area to sing before they dispersed to visit their girls. Girls' and women's singing in three or more parts was modeled on this style. Since World War I a style of singing in three parts has become predominant. A more complex style of four- or five-part-singing was regarded as a specialty of Slovenes in South Carinthia. The same style was found in many parts of Slovenia, either still in practice or remembered by older people. In the eastern peripheral region of Prekmurje, however, singing in diaphony is the rule. If men join the women in singing, their voices duplicate the women's part an octave lower. In Rezija, an isolated valley in the Western Julian Alps, the music has generally maintained a pronounced archaic character. All music, either vocal or instrumental (for a violin and a small, three-string double bass), is based on a drone.

The Alpine character of the western and central parts of Slovenia is also apparent in some musical instruments. Playing on homemade alphorns in two pairs was described during the seventeenth century as common in two central regions. Besides the most recent standard form of the *citra* (zither), until recenty a homemade variety of the instrument with rectangular form was used. In the late eighteenth century a most popular dance-music trio consisted of a violin, an *oprekelj* (a dulcimer), and a small double bass. The portable cymbal (*cimbale*) was played especially in the eastern regions of Slovenia and was one of the most important instruments of village ensembles until World War I. In the small region of Rezija, the violin and the violoncello were the only musical instruments played to accompany folk dances. The *tamburicas*, imported from **Croatia** at the end of the nineteenth century, are still played as a folk orchestra only in the region of Bela krajina. In the twentieth century the accordion became the dominant instrument in Slovene village dance music. It may be played alone to accompany the dance or as the leading instrument in an ensemble.

The largest group of musical instruments in Slovenia consists of aerophones. In the eastern part of Slovenia some shepherds' instruments, not intended for dance music, are still found. In addition to a family of locally made side-blown flutes (*žvegle*), the panpipe (*orglice*) is notable. Of special interest is the *klopotec*, a wind rattle formerly set out in the vineyards in eastern Slovenia to frighten birds. People like its sound, and imitations of the sound occur in short song texts, for in the minds of the people the wind rattle is singing. The same is also said for bells.

DANCE

Folk dances characterized the Slovene ethnic area until just before World War II. They exist now only in the rural areas, where most Slovenes lived until recently. By comparison with other aspects of the culture, the dance tradition is basically quite uniform, considerable differences being discernible in some outlying areas (such as

Rezija in Italy) or where history contributed to changing the composition of the populace (as in Bela krajina). Original dances of the Slovenes became extinct very early but were eventually replaced by dances spread throughout the entire area of Slovenia, mostly from German-speaking countries, less often from the Romanic countries and neighboring Croatia. The process of extinction was applauded by the Catholic Church, which did not approve of dancing and at many times even forbade it. Foreign dances were mostly brought to Slovenia by *frentarji*, young artisans who went abroad according to the custom of the time to complete their training. Soldiers doing military service in different countries of the Austrian Empire also acted as agents for the introduction of foreign traditions.

Transmission of dances produced considerable variations. Folk musicians did not read music but remembered the tunes by ear. If something escaped their memories, they improvised. The dances were subject to more profound changes. Usually, only the essential elements of the dances were remembered, and for this reason they were simplified and adapted by dancers.

The Slovene dance tradition is divided into two strata. The earlier stratum consists of the remnants of ancient rites expressed in dance and game, which were not particularly Slovene in character since they were also known by other European people. They are characterized by the simplest of movements such as walking, running, and leaping, all freely intermingled. The earliest dance traditions are connected with Shrovetide masques and customs. The later stratum consists mostly of dances for pairs. Almost all are of foreign origin, some completely adapted to Slovene gestures, while others retain their foreign aspects both in melody and in choreography. Among these the earliest and most popular is *štajeriš*, which spread from the region of Štajersko. Song and dance, characteristic of the earliest forms of *štajeriš*, are also features of the *prvi rej* of the Zilja Valley of Koroška (Carinthia, **Austria**). This dance is related to a competitive game played by boys, *štehvanje*, which was the opening event at the *žegen* (kermess). Among other generally known dances are *zibenšrit*, *šotiš*, and *mazurka*, which began to disappear from memory by the beginning of the twentieth century. The leading place among the new dances was taken by the polka and the *valèek* (waltz).

Remnants of group dances in Slovenia include *ka èo zvijat* (snake coiling), *èindara, kolo* (round dance), and *gredo Abrahama* (going to Abraham). "Going under the bridge," formed by the upheld joined hands of a pair, is danced in *metlšiko kolo* (round dance from Metlika), *vreèo šivat* (bag sewing, dance from Bela krajina), and *dreto šivat* (twine sewing), a children's dance from Gorenjska.

SPORTS AND GAMES

Once residents of the Bloke plateau skied during winter through the otherwise impassable terrain on skis of special shape and size. Usually, these were made of beech wood, hewn and smoothed into narrow planks approximately 160 centimeters long, 8–12 centimeters wide, and 1.5 centimeters thick. They had curved tips. Bindings were made from braided horsehair or leather. To prevent slipping, old felting was nailed to the bottom of the skis. Bindings were placed nearer the front tips so that the rear of the ski remained on the ground during the stride. The inhabitants of

Bloke ordinarily glided on flat terrains freehand. Only when they traveled for long distances, especially if they were carrying heavy burdens, did they use a staff. Staffs were not usually used for movement along slightly inclined surfaces, but for downhill skiing and side-to-side steering and braking. The bottom of the ski was waxed with melted tallow or beeswax to keep the snow from sticking. Skis were used for hunting, woodcutting, traveling for business, going to mass, visiting, and various other activities requiring travel during the winter, including burials. One family in each village kept a pair of specially designed, longer and wider skis for the transport of the coffin. People also skied for recreation. They zigzagged skillfully down steep slopes near the village. They also played games and had competitions on skis. Skiing did not spread beyond the plateau because of the extreme geographic and social isolation of the region. With the appearance of modern skiing, the kind of skiing characteristic of Bloke began to decline. It ultimately died away in 1942, when the Italian occupying authorities forbade the use and possession of skis in order to paralyze partisan movements. From a technical viewpoint Bloke skiing did not have an influence on the development of modern skiing in Slovenia, but it did have a popularizing effect and is one of the factors behind the popularity of skiing in the country.

FARM ARCHITECTURE

Many Slovene boroughs and towns developed in the twelfth and thirteenth centuries, when a number of villages were granted municipal authority. Villages were founded and grew, acquiring their final form usually by the end of the nineteenth century. In Slovenia the following types of settlements can be found: solitary farm, scattered settlement, chain village, long village, hamlet, cluster village, and complex village. Four types of farm buildings more or less correspond to the four cultural regions of the country. For example, the area of the Alps, being primarily forest, is covered with wooden houses, while stone was the primary construction material along the coast. Likewise, shingles covered the roofs in more arboreal regions, while in the flatlands, people used thatch for roofs. Since the seventeenth century a growing number of houses are covered with tiles. Apart from the Kras regions, the first houses built of stone and/or brick were constructed in the sixteenth century, while brick finally became an important material when a new building code was adopted in the nineteenth century.

A special farm outbuilding once seen throughout Slovenia

Klopotec, a device for frightening birds, in the Slovenske gorice. (Photograph by Mojca Ramšak, July 1996)

was the hayrack, a simple wooden construction for drying hay. Some thirty different types can be distinguished by their construction. The hayrack developed in construction and functionality together with farming methods during the eighteenth and nineteenth centuries, but it was described and recorded as a well-established, distinctively Slovene farming structure in the middle of the seventeenth century by Matevž Merian and Janez Vajkard Valvasor. Hayracks have horizontal bars on which the hay or grain is hung to dry. The bars are fastened to strong wooden poles or stone pillars. These give the structure its stability, while the roof partially shelters the drying crops from rainfall. It is found in the major part of the highland and Alpine regions, but it is also situated in the fields, meadows, and highland pastures in the vicinity of peasant settlements. Hayracks are being replaced by more modern means of hay production such as hay rolls. Honey production has a long tradition in Slovenia. The beehive panel paintings are a unique Slovenian phenomenon and one of Slovenia's most important forms of folk art. Beekeeping has been an integral part of Slovenian agriculture since the sixteenth century. Originally, bees were kept in hollow logs or in woven baskets. By the eighteenth century, the *kranjiè* hive was developed. The wooden bee-house (*èebelnjak*) incorporated removable boxes that resembled a chest of drawers, thus creating individual hives. The *kranjiè* hives have panels (*panjske konènice*) above the entrance of the beehive. At the end of the eighteenth century the Vienna court apiarist, Slovene Anton Janša, bred a native species of Carniolian bee.

ARTS AND CRAFTS

Traditional handicrafts such as lace-making, woodcarving, pottery, basket-weaving, oil-producing, gingerbread- and candle-making, and pipe-making can still be found in many rural areas of Slovenia, though a rapid decline in individual domestic crafts began after World War II. In the late 1970s an organized preservation of domestic crafts was initiated, and today Slovene craftsmen successfully display their products in many exhibitions abroad. Domestic crafts form a basis for the development of new designs and inventiveness on the basis of re-evaluation of models already tested by history.

STUDIES OF SLOVENE FOLKLORE

Slovene ethnology was officially born with the Seminar for Ethnography, established in 1919 in Ljubljana, though lectures did not begin until 1940–1941. In 1923, the Slovene Ethnographic Museum was established and was followed in 1947 by the Institute for Slovene Ethnology. The Slovene Ethnological Society was established in 1975 and now consists of more than 200 members. The main focuses of Slovene ethnology are traditional and contemporary aspects of Slovene culture in Slovenia and surrounding countries (**Austria, Italy,** and **Hungary**) where Slovene minorities are found. This interest in Slovene culture also extends to migrants in more distant European countries as well as in America and Australia. Several professional journals publish articles on Slovene folklore, for example, *Traditiones* (1972–present), *Etnolog* (1926–1944,

1991–present), *Slovenski etnograf* (1948–1990), *Glasnik Slovenkega etnološkega društva* (1975–present), and *Časopis za zgodovino in narodopisje* (1904–present).

BIBLIOGRAPHY

Badjura, Rudolf. 1956. *Bloško starosvetno smučanje in besedje* (Old Bloke Skiing and Terminology). Ljubljana: Državna založba Slovenije.

Bogataj, Janez. 1989. *Domače obrti na Slovenskem* (Domestic Crafts in Slovenia). Ljubljana: Državna založba Slovenije.

Brancelj Bednaršek, Andreja. 1993. *Belokranjske pisanice* (Decorated Eggs of Bela krajina). Metlika: Belokranjski muzej.

Čop, Jaka, and Tone Cevc. 1993. *Slovenski kozolec* (Slovene hay-Rack). Žirovnica: Agens.

Guček, Svetozar. 1989. *Slovenija, zibelka smučanja v srednji Evuopi* (Slovenia: Cradle of Skiing in Central Europe). Ljubljana: Kmečki glas.

Koželj, Zvezdana. 1994. Slovenia. *Second Report on Historical Centers*. Ljubljana: Mladinska knjiga. 381–409.

Kropej, Monika. 2000a. Magija in magično zdravljenje v pripovednem izročilu in Ijudsko zdravilstvo danes (Magic as Reflected in Folk Traditions and in Contemporary Folk Medicine). *Etnolog* 10:75–84.

———. 2000b. The Tenth Child in Folk Tradition. *Studia Mythologica Slavica* 3:75–88.

Kumer, Zmaga. 1983. *Ljudska glasbila in godci na Slovenskem* (Folk Music Instruments and Musicians in Slovenia). Ljubljana: Slovenska matica.

Kuret, Niko. 1989. *Praznično leto Slovencev* (The Festive Year of the Slovenes). Ljubljana: Družina.

Makarovič, Gorazd. 1981. *Slovenska ljudska umetnost: zgodovina likovne umetnosti na kmetijah* (Slovene Folk Art: The History of Fine Art on Farmhouses). Ljubljana: Državna založba Slovenije.

———. 1991. *Votivi* (Votives). Ljubljana: Slovenski etnografski muzej.

Ovsec, Damjan. 1993. *Velika knjiga o praznikih: Praznovanja na Slovenskem in po svetu* (The Big Book of Holidays: Holidays in Slovenia and around the World). Ljubljana: Domus.

Peršič, Magda. 2003. *Šege na Pivškem. Praznični časi in praznovanja v koledarskem letu* (Customs in Pivka Region. Festivity Time and Holidays in the Calendar Year). Postojna: Nostranjski muzej.

Ramovš, Mirko. 1992. *Polka je ukazana, plesno izročilo na Slovenskem* (Polka Is a Request: Dance Tradition in Slovenia). Ljubljana: Kres.

Slovenske ljudske pesmi 1–4 (Slovene Folksongs, volumes 1–4). 1970, 1981, 1992, 1998. Lujbljana: Slovenska matica.

Tomažič, Tanja. 1988–1990. Nekatera bistvena dogajanja in pojavi na področju družbene kulture v 19, stoletju na Slovenskem (Some Essential Developments and Phenomena in the Sphere of Social Culture in Slovenia in the Nineteenth Century). *Slovenski etnograf* 33–34:389–431.

Vodušek, Valens. 2003. Folk Music: Slovenia. *Etnomuzikološki članki in razprave* (Ethnomusicological Articles and Papers), edited by Marko Terseglav and Robert Vrčon. Ljubljana: ZRC SAZU. 215–219.

Židov, Nena. 2000. Ali so metode alternative medicine v Sloveniji res nekaj povsem novega? (Methods of Alternative Medicine—Are They Really Quite New in Slovenia?). *Etnolog* 10:139–159.

Zupanič Slavec, Zvonka. 2000. Zagovori—magične korenine medicine (Incantations—The Magic Roots of Medicine). *Etnolog* 10:85–94.

Mojca Ramšak

SWITZERLAND

GEOGRAPHY

Also known as the Swiss Confederation, Switzerland is a federal state, consisting of twenty-six cantons, which lies in southwestern Central Europe. To the west it borders on **France**, to the south and southeast it shares a border with **Italy**, to the east with **Austria** and Liechtenstein, and in the north it borders on the Federal Republic of **Germany**. With an area of 41,290 square kilometers Switzerland is among the small countries of Europe (comparable to **The Netherlands**). In spite of its small size the country has great variety.

The central Alps traverse the country in two chains with a length of approximately 300 kilometers from Lake Geneva in the southwest to the country's border in the east. Two significant European rivers find their sources in the central Gotthard massive. The Rhone cuts its path between the Wallis and Bernese Alps to the west, and the Rhine makes its trek to the east. Besides this main axis numerous side valleys lead from the northern and southern alpine foreland into the Swiss alpine region, which encompasses almost two-thirds of the entire surface area of the country. Only a small part of this region—mainly valley floors and sunny terraces—is settled and used productively. The alpine meadows, which are used seasonally, constitute a considerable part of the mountainous regions. Wide parts of the Swiss alpine area are uninhabitable because of the cliffs, scree, ice, and snow. The Alps form an important weather and climate division. The northern alpine foreland and the north side of the Alps are characterized by much precipitation (over 400 centimeters per year), while the interior of the Alps is known for its dry weather conditions (about 51 centimeters annually). The Alps are a part of the European watersheds between the

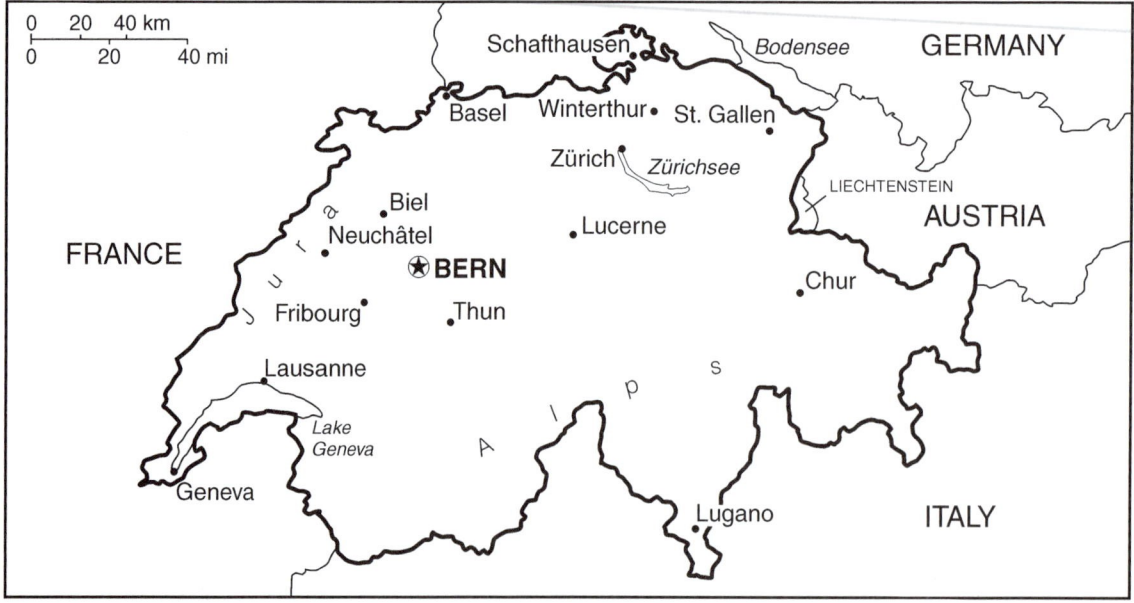

Switzerland.

Mediterranean and the North Sea. In spite of, or even because of, the passage from Northern to Southern Europe being hindered by the transverse barrier of the Alps, Switzerland is an important country for passage, for passes not only bind individual valleys but also cross the main mountain ridges of the Alps.

Other prominent features of the Swiss landscape include the Jura, a limestone mountain range of medium altitude, with parallel chains running from northwest of Lake Geneva into the region of Basel. The Jura highlands, whose maximum altitude is around 1,700 meters, form the border with France in the northwest. Between the southern foot of the Jura and the northern slope of the Alps as well as between Lake Constance and Lake Geneva lie the Swiss midlands, a hilly moraine land crossed by many river valleys. As a whole, Switzerland can be designated as a mountain and hill country, more than half of it lying over 1,000 meters above sea level. This landscape as well as cultural influences from outside over the course of history account for the variety of languages and dialects.

LANGUAGE

German is spoken north of the Alps as far west as the rivers Saane and Sense. However, it is a variety of German known as "Schwizerdütsch," with dialectical forms differing greatly from the written language of high German. Since the second half of the twentieth century Swiss German has been the colloquial language of choice in all areas: school, church, politics, and the mass media. Consequently—and also through internal migration—local and regional language forms have increasingly given way in their importance to a Pan-Swiss German colloquial language. West of the two rivers Saane and Sense French is spoken. Almost 20 percent of all Swiss have French as their mother tongue. In wide regions of French-speaking Switzerland the local dialects have practically died out.

The relationship between the German-speaking majority and the French-speakers, or Romands, is traditionally somewhat tense. Political developments in recent years in Switzerland seem, however, to have strengthened rather than lessened the opposition between the German- and French-speaking people. Especially in questions of the entrance of Switzerland into the United Nations (UN) or other international organizations Francophones have shown themselves to be more open than the more nationalistic and conservative-thinking German speakers. For some time now people have designated this language border as the "Roestigraben" (Roesti ditch). (*Roesti* refers to a favorite potato dish popular in the German Swiss region—and in other areas of Switzerland as well.) Many Romands even speak of the "Riddeaux de Roesti"—that is, the Roesti Curtain—in imitation of the Iron Curtain. Nevertheless, it would be wrong to claim to see here a serious language conflict between the two language groups. Indeed, folklore studies have shown that the decisive cultural border between west and east Switzerland does not run along the Saane and the Sense Rivers but farther to the east with the rivers Reuss and Aare—thus indicating that the old political borders as well as religious or denominational borders can be more important than language borders.

South of the Alps in Tessin and in the southern valleys of Graubünden, Italian is spoken by 6.5 percent of Swiss citizens. The canton of Graubünden is multilingual.

Though it is a part of the Italian-language area, the majority of people there speak German. In addition to these two languages there exist different forms of Romansch. Only 0.5 percent of the entire Swiss population speaks Romansch, which is subdivided further into Ladin, Puter, Jauer, Sursilvan, Sutsilvan, and Surmirn. These in part differ strongly from one another. For a few decades Rumantsch Grischun has established itself as the compromise, or bridge, and as the written language. Because of immigration from abroad since the 1950s there now live many people in Switzerland who have a mother tongue that is different from the languages of the country.

RELIGIOUS AND CULTURAL DIVERSITY

Switzerland is also diverse in its religions and denominations. Already before the establishment of the Confederation, Jews lived in the region of present-day Switzerland. For a long time they were citizens with lesser rights and did not receive full citizenship until 1866. According to the census of 2000, barely 18,000 Swiss men and women belonged to the Jewish faith, accounting for 0.2 percent of the total population. Since the Reformation and well into the present, the opposition of Catholic and Protestant regions has significantly impacted Swiss political and cultural life. The old denominational borders have been dissolved increasingly through such factors as reduction in religious affiliation in general, geographic mobility, and mixed marriages. Today 42 percent of the population of Switzerland belongs to the Roman Catholic Church, while 36.5 percent belongs to a Protestant-Reformed state or free church. In 1950 about 60 percent of the Swiss were Protestant and 40 percent Catholic; today Catholics are the majority. Even in Zürich, the city of reformer Huldrych Zwingli, the number of Catholics is today higher than the number of Protestants.

Switzerland thus has a multiplicity of folk cultures, dependent on the climate and the composition of the soil, which determined the predominant economic system and the political and legal conditions that developed. Traditional folk cultures were greatly influenced by existing economic systems. The heterogeneity of the natural and spatial conditions between and within the main regions—midlands, Alps, Jura Mountains, and the regions on the south side of the Alps—led to the development of numerous regional economic systems. In the midlands there was already an emphasis on agriculture with the production of grains. In addition, wine was produced in the climatically favorable areas. In the alpine region the people were mostly self-reliant, being equipped with a small farm and a few cattle. From the late Middle Ages on, a regional specialization in agriculture grew, and from that developed the four agricultural zones in old Switzerland: grain land, field grassland, herdsmen land, and the interior alpine zone.

HISTORY AND FOLKLORE

The founding of the Confederation began in the herdsmen land. The myths of the founding of old Switzerland are widely known. William Tell, who is more a mythological than historical character, came from the village of Bürgeln and is said to have rebelled against the despotism of Governor Gessler, who had been put into power by the Habsburgs. After being taken prisoner and making a spectacular escape, Tell is said to have killed Gessler with his crossbow in a narrow pass near Küssnacht after Gessler had earlier demanded that Tell shoot an apple from the head of his son with the very same crossbow.

The actual myth of the founding of Switzerland tells of a secret meeting of outstanding citizens of Uri, Schwyz, and Unterwalden on the Rütli meadow above Lake Lucerne. Even the names of those who are said to have sworn the oath always to stand together in times of desperate straits in the battle against the tyrants are found in the myth: there were said to be among the delegations from the inner Swiss valleys a Walter Fürst from Uri, a Werner Stauffacher from Schwyz, and an Arnold from Melchtal.

This myth achieved worldwide fame through Friedrich Schiller's interpretation in his *William Tell*, which was published in 1804, and also through Gioacchino Rossini's opera, which was performed for the first time in 1829. It continues today to affect the Swiss, who, despite the urbanization and industrialization of their country, like to see themselves as strong, courageous, and visionary mountain people connected to nature. At the end of the eighteenth and the beginning of the nineteenth centuries the Swiss as well as the wide circle of educated Europeans were fascinated with the Alps. Although modern Switzerland had its origins in the discussions between liberals and conservatives that led to the compromise constitution of 1848, many Swiss prefer to view the historically inexact date of the Rütl compact, assigned to 1 August 1291, as the founding act of the country.

Schiller characterized the old Swiss as a small group of herdsmen who took up the fight against one of the large powers of the time, the House of Habsburg—at that time dukes of Austria—and were victorious. Many Swiss see themselves as descendants of these herdsmen folk, though the region of the alpine herdsmen culture, the herdsmen land, was only part of Switzerland. Hans Georg Wackernagel stated in 1936 in a speech about "The Historical Significance of the Herdsmen Culture" that through the middle of Switzerland ran an old cultural border between warring, self-certain cattlemen, who after independence thought that they could depend on the aid of relatives, and the clan in legal disputes (even including blood revenge) against the farmers, who were bound to village laws and were also bound to their feudal leaders in performing their required tasks. Richard Weiss also spoke of a conscious opposition between the politically active herdsmen and the neighboring farmer. According to Weiss, the herdsmen were inclined to engage in athletic training and warring forays. He traces this back to the fact that the work of herdsmen, tending the cows and making cheese, demanded, on the one hand, great strength but, on the other, gave them considerable free time for playing and conversing, while the farmers had to work constantly.

Above all, the traditional alpine games belonged to the alpine festivals, which occurred at the summer solstice or when the cows were brought down from the mountains to the valleys in the fall: *Schwingen* (a form of wrestling), stone tossing, and other exercises of strength. These combat games were framed with displays of flag waving, alphorn performances, and yodeling.

Folk game from the *Lucerne Chronicle of Diebold Schilling* (1513).

Early-nineteenth-century engraving of a stone-tossing competition.

Representations of such kinds of power sports in old chronicles, such as the *Lucerne Chronicle of Diebold Schilling* of 1513, show just how old these alpine customs are. Alpine customs were early demonstrated outside the region. In 1517 an alpine boy from the Hasli Valley demonstrated stone tossing for Duke Karl of Savoy, who was staying in Bern at the time. In the city of Basel in 1526 a man from Frutigen in the Kander Valley in the Bernese highlands was paid from the city coffers with a piece of cloth in the city's colors (black and white) for his alphorn performance. Even today alpine customs, especially games, represent the essence of traditional Swiss folklife in Switzerland as well as abroad.

At the end of the nineteenth century, at a time when the relationship of economic forces between the "herdsmen land" and the "grain land" was to the advantage of the latter, considerable evidence indicates that the alpine games, which had been closely bound with the professional pride of the alpine people, had been largely forgotten. It was not the inhabitants of the alpine regions but rather noble and middle-class circles in the cities of the midlands who revived the alpine customs. After all, at different times and in many places—in ancient Greece and Rome, for example—herdsmen were deemed to represent an earlier, seemingly better time, a more natural and therefore happier stage of nature.

This fascination with the Alps at the end of the eighteenth century and through the nineteenth century goes back to the natural scientist and poet Albrecht von Haller (1708–1777), who depicted in his poem "The Alps" (1729) the simple life of the alpine inhabitants and elevated it above the decadence of the courts of the nobility and in the cities. The Swiss herdsman, separated from the baseness of the world through the wall of the Alps, lives, according to Haller, poorly yet purely. He drinks spring water and milk and lives on the lap of nature, accompanied by the song of the nightingale. Without knowledge of social barriers, he loves truly. Each season brings him corresponding work and simple joys. By the end of the eighteenth century "The Alps" had gone through a good dozen different editions and thirty translations into five languages. The "Idylls" of the Zürich painter and poet Salomon Gessner received even greater acclaim between 1756 and 1772. The work was translated into twenty-one languages and made Gessner the most read author of his time. Also the famous Jean Jacques Rousseau had a part in this alpine glorification with his novel *The New Heloise*, which is set in the Alps. A few years after the appearance of these works alpine enthusiasts from throughout Europe came to the places supposedly described by these literary pieces. The stories of these poems and novels moved a large number of foreigners from all of Europe, among whom Germans were the majority, to such an extent that one can truthfully speak of a Swiss and alpine fascination among the Germans in the last quarter of the eighteenth century. Numerous travel publications about Switzerland appeared in response to this early "mass tourism" in the Bernese highlands. Aside from the dangers that lay in wait for the travelers in the high mountains, these works contained descriptions of the life of herdsmen and cheese-makers.

The invasion of the French in 1798 interrupted this development of the early tourist trade, which was especially favorable for the Bernese highlands. The confusion of war that spread over Europe as a result of the French Revolution led very quickly to an almost complete cessation of educational and pleasure travel. Not until several years later could tourism return to life again after the peace compacts of Luneville and Amiens. Attempts to make Switzerland attractive again to foreigners and to elevate their own culture and morale climaxed in 1805 in a grand Festival of Herdsmen and Cheesemakers in Unspunnen, which lies near Interlaken. This festival marks the beginning of the development and consolidation of a series of stereotypes that seem even today to determine for Swiss and foreigners the "true Swiss being."

Attendance at the first alpine herdsmen festival was very large. According to the report by Wagner about the "Course of Events of the Herdsmen Festival in Unspunnen," one can enumerate such attendees as a "Prince . . . , who remains incognito, Prince Esterhazy, Prince Schönburg," five counts, five barons, many Bernese patricians, and "more than a hundred other foreign gentlemen and ladies of distinction." On the day of the festival the participants—the alphorn players, the wrestlers, the stone tossers, the singers—all assembled at 8 A.M. in front of the Castle Interlaken and formed a parade, in which the judges "and the rest of the upper leaders of this region, the supporters of the festival, . . . foreigners and other private persons" joined. The games began with the stone toss. Afterward the wrestlers entered the ring. Between their bouts the two alphorn players at the festival competed for victory. The organizers of the first herdsmen festival in Unspunnen had obviously ranked alphorn blowing as the outstanding event, and thus they had medals made with the inscription "To the Honor of the Alphorn" and declared the

Early-nineteenth-century engraving of the festival at Unspunnen, which first occurred in 1805.

winner of the contest as the "King of Unspunnen." The participation of only two horn players at the first Unspunnen Festival shows that the organizers had overestimated by far the significance of alphorn playing for the herdsmen and cheese-makers as well as their willingness to demonstrate this talent.

It is clear from contemporary reports about the development and execution of the first herdsmen and cheese-makers' festival in Unspunnen that this Olympics of the mountain inhabitants derived from the wishes of intellectuals, who were expressing their romantic ideas about the life of the alpine folk. Seemingly archaic, yet genuine, alpine customs and sporting events of strength—such as wrestling and the stone toss—as well as the sounds of the alphorns, all of which were unfamiliar to the city dwellers and foreigners, formed the nucleus of the festival. Thereby the originally primary function of this activity stepped into the background. Stone tossing and wrestling served to develop the strength and dexterity of the cheese-makers, who certainly had hard physical work to do in moving about large blocks of cheese. Yodeling and the alphorn were originally means for communicating between the mountain and the valley, signaling between different mountains, and calling in the cattle. The citizens, artists, and foreigners of the upper class, though, did not witness the demonstrations as forms of communication and hard work. Rather, they saw as always the work of the cheese-makers and herdsmen as a happy activity, as a passage from the travel report of the German poem Wilhelm Heinse reveals: "They do nothing except milk the cows and make cheese and cut and gather the hay." So apparently one saw in these activities an expression of exuberant power and joy in life, which in its naturalness had a certain esthetic appeal and which thereby could entertain the ladies and gentlemen of refined society. Furthermore, these activities gained an exclusive significance in the realm of the alpine herdsmen festival. Moreover, they were also elevated to a position of significance in patriotism and nationalism: the customs of the cheese-makers were quite simply styled as the "customs of the fatherland."

A continual development can be shown in the growing Swiss enthusiasm for the belief that one found in the herdsman and cheese-maker of the Bernese highland the "Noble Savage." This development lasted from the Unspunnen festivals of 1805 and 1808 until the time when the Swiss saw their culture represented best through the cheese-makers and herdsmen. That corresponded fully with foreigners' expectations. As the backers had hoped, this image was successful in directing tourism into the Bernese highlands again. The travelers, however, did not want just to admire the cheese-makers and herdsmen and their unspoiled life; they also wanted the "genuine customs," which had been described so frequently and fully in connection with the Unspunnen festivals, to be actually demonstrated for them. Expectations had been awakened; these had to be satisfied.

SONGS, YODELING, AND MUSIC

Reports about trips through Switzerland emphasize that the German romantics had considerable interest in the legends, customs, language, and folksongs. The major collectors of songs—such as Achim von Arnim and Clemens Brentano, Friedrich Heinrich von der Hagen, and Ludwig Uhland—worked in Switzerland or had friends who were traveling through Switzerland to collect song texts for them. Furthermore, they had an active correspondence with Swiss collectors, researchers, and librarians. Achim von Arnim possessed the *Series of Eight Swiss Herdsman Songs*, which originated in the estate of the song collector G. S. Studer and which had been published in 1805 by Sigmund von Wagner. Research on folksongs in Switzerland began with this song collection, which appeared in expanded editions in 1812, 1818, and 1826 and which ultimately contained seventy-six songs with their melodies. Very quickly, numerous songbooks and collections of songs appeared: in 1825 the *General Swiss Song Book*, the *Confederate Song Chronicle* by E. L. Rochholz around 1835, the *Little Alpine Rose: Swiss Pocketbook of Songs* in 1849, and *Swiss Folksongs* by Ludwig Tobler (1882–1884). The systematic collection of Swiss folksongs began with the founding of the Swiss folksong archive in Basel in 1906, first in the German- and then in the French-speaking regions. A little later people turned their attention to the wealth of songs in the Romansch regions and then to the region of the Tessin. Between 1908 and 1925 the Bernese Germanist and song researcher Otto von Greyerz published the six-volume collection *Swiss Folksongs, in the Röseli Garden.*

Yodeling is a form of song in which the sound changes quickly between high falsetto and deep chest tones. Furthermore, many visitors to the Catholic alpine cantons were, and are today, fascinated by a special song, denominated "prayer call" (*Betruf*) or "alp blessing" (*Alpsegen*). The literature often refers to this song as "psalmody" or compares it to a litany. It is an evening prayer that the herdsmen on the mountain pasture calls out from an open spot to the valley below after completing a day's outdoor work. To increase the volume, he usually uses a kind of megaphone, which is a wooden funnel called a *Folle*, once used for straining milk. This is important because of the belief that the power of the prayer extends as far as the sound carries. In order to include the entire alpine locale, the prayer caller turns to all sides. He sings his prayer in four to five recitation tones in order to ask Mary and the saints to protect and preserve the mountain and everything that is on it.

Along with folksongs the alphorn found great respect in the nineteenth century among foreigners, though at the first Unspunnen festival there were only two and at the second only one performer. In 1814 Franz Niklaus König, who had already begun in 1809 to support the revival of alphorn playing, wrote: "One hears and sees almost nothing of the alphorn. A major purpose of the folk festival organized at Unspunnen was to awaken again this authentic alpine music."

The efforts of the Bernese patricians and artists to rejuvenate the alphorn as well as the interest generated in Unspunnen led to the appearance of alphorn players in the areas whose points of interests and overlooks of the Bernese highlands were heavily visited by tourists. Thus, the teacher

Early-nineteenth-century engraving of an alphorn player.

Kehrli of Brienz, who had appeared as an alphorn player in 1805 and 1808 in Unspunnen, performed on the instrument at the Giessbach waterfalls. There he also sang "Swiss folksongs" with his children for such prominent tourists as Ludwig Uhland and Lord Byron. Soon there arose complaints among the foreigners, whose romantic view of the unsophisticated simplicity and modesty of the Swiss mountain people conflicted with the performer's need to earn a living. Since it contradicted their tendency to poeticize the country life, they did not see, and did not want to see, that earning the daily bread by the country people was becoming increasingly difficult because of the growing population. The reality of the mountain population in the transition from the eighteenth century to the nineteenth century had little to do with the idyll described by Haller, and it is understandable that under the prevailing economic conditions the natives made use of these possibilities afforded by tourists to market their customs. Soon laws were made against the so-called beggar's performance, the playing of the alphorn for money.

CALENDAR CUSTOMS

Not only the mountain population but increasingly the inhabitants of the Swiss midlands took over in following the ideas of "genuine Swissness" that were formed abroad. But in no way can it be claimed that the "myth of origin" and the "traditional customs" were foisted on the Swiss by foreigners. Rather, the romantic views from abroad and especially from Germany—in part through the reporters such as those who wrote about the Unspunnen festival—had an effect on the Swiss self-image. The phenomena, which were already in decline but which some are inclined to view today as "ur-Swiss," received new life through the demand from abroad. An example of this has been shown with the alphorn performances. In the course of such revitalization the original function was almost completely forgotten, and new meanings and connotations assumed the foreground. Even the instrument as such changed in that it became increasingly longer. Yodeling, alphorn performances, and many other folk activities became so stylized beyond their association with the life of the herdsmen and cheese-makers that they became the symbols of the alpine inhabitants and finally the trademarks of the "fatherland."

Thus, alpine folklore goes back in its present-day form to the nineteenth century rather than to the older times, as is sometimes claimed. This holds true also for several of the most important city festivals such as the Bern Onion Market, the Geneva Escalade, or the Zürich *Sechseläute* (6 P.M. bell ringing).

According to one report, the Bern Onion Market is said to date indirectly from the city fire of 1405, in which 650 houses burned down and many people died. At that time fire departments from the neighboring city of Freiburg (Fribourg) in Uechtland came to the aid of the Bern citizens. To show appreciation for their help, they were offered the right to bring their farm products (apparently there were already lots of onions) once a year to the market in Bern. The market must have developed from the widely dispersed markets of Martini. It can be traced back in its present form only to the nineteenth century. Onion farmers came at that time to the Onion Market from the Bern lake region and presumably also from the neighboring regions of Fribourg. For this market as well as for the related folk festival the stands are erected after midnight, and sales begin as early as 4 A.M. or 5 A.M. the next day. Special trains bring people to the Bern old city, in which huge crowds have already gathered. The onions that are offered for sale are artistically bound in wreaths, braids, chains, and other designs and are meant more for display than for consumption. The high point for many of the market visitors, especially the youth, is the confetti battle in the late afternoon.

The people of Geneva celebrate the Escalade in memory of the successful defense against the attack that the Catholic Karl-Emanuel, count of Savoy, had undertaken with his superior forces against Calvinistic Geneva in the night of 11 December 1602. With the aid of ladders Savoy soldiers climbed (French *escalade*, "ascent") the city walls to open the gates for the main forces. However, a shot fired by a dying watchman alarmed the city population, who bravely grabbed their weapons and were able to drive off the invaders. Women also had their part in the defensive battle. Catherine Royaume is said to have thrown a heavy soup kettle, including its contents, at the invaders or perhaps poured it over them. Thus, the *Marmite* (kettle, pot) plays an important role in the annual festival. In the narrow streets of the old city a vegetable soup is sold from the *Marmite*, and the confectioners produce little chocolate soup pots filled with marzipan vegetables. The sponsors of the festival are the approximately 2,300 members of the Compagnie 1602, which was founded in 1926. Before then the Patriotic Association of Geneva for the Renewal of the Escalade, founded in 1898, had celebrated the memorial festival annually. The high point of the Escalade is the parade of riders, musketeers, and crossbowmen in historic uniforms on Sunday afternoon.

Likewise, the Zürich *Sechseläuten*, which is actually a spring custom and today a "historical, patriotic" event, is a creation of the nineteenth century. The name goes back to a time when an early Zürich trade law required that crafts apprentices had to work after the beginning of spring until the ringing of the evening bell at 6 P.M. Later, the festival of the vernal equinox (21 March) was moved to the second half of April. It now takes place on the third Monday in April. Should this occur during the week before Easter or on Easter Monday, then it takes place a week later. Dressed in historical costumes, members of the twenty-five guilds and of the Society of the Constaffel, with some on horseback and accompanied by music groups, march through downtown to the *Sechseläuten*-Square on the lake in front of the opera house. There, under the sound of the bells and the playing of the "*Sechseläuten*-March," the huge bonfire is ignited at 6 P.M. Atop the bonfire is a "snowman," called *Böögg*, made from cotton, who symbolizes winter. Groups of riders gallop around the fire, which gradually reaches the "snowman." The spectators are eager to see how long it lasts until the "snowman" catches fire and the petards inside explode and how long it lasts until the snowman is burned up or falls to the ground. One determines the weather for the coming summer from whether it is a long or brief time until the *Böög* meets its end. This festival, in which the guilds play a central role, first developed when the historical guilds, which had determined the government of the city from 1336 until the invasion of the French Revolution troops in 1798, had long lost their power. Since 1866 the guilds have played absolutely no part in politics. They are much more significant in the social life in the city. It is considered an extraordinary honor to be accepted by one of the guilds because one becomes thereby a part

Fasnacht at Basel. (Photograph by Astrid Matter)

of an important economic, political, and social network.

The central city festival in Basel is the *Fasnacht*, which occurs on the Monday after Ash Wednesday during the Catholic Lenten season. It begins at 4 A.M. with the *Morgestraich*. Formerly, all lights downtown were extinguished. At the strike of 4 A.M. the march of the members of the *Fasnacht* societies with their illustrated lanterns and lantern wagons to the accompaniment of drums and piccolos begins its way to the central marketplace. The pictures on the lantern wagons humorously depict people and events of public life worthy of ridicule. In the previous fall organizers decide on a theme to be presented at the next *Fasnacht*. In general, the subject is based on local events. In the restaurants the celebrants eat the traditional *Mehlsuppe* (soup made of roasted flour) and sheet cake with a cheese or onion topping (*Chäswäie, Zibelewäie*). On Monday and Wednesday afternoons the large *Fasnacht* parades, which in Basel bear the somewhat elegant name "Cortège," take place. In the evening they listen in restaurants to the verses of the *Schnitzelbängler*. For about 150 years singers have been appearing with their *Schnitzelbängg*, comic four-line verses, in which they mock the events of the year. Since the *Schnitzelbängg* have been broadcast by the media for years, more and more of the singers have opted for all-Swiss or even international themes rather than Basel themes, which would be understood only there. For example,

Im Bush sy Frau isch blaich und schreit	Bush's wife is pale and screams,
Dr George sig kurz in Oonmacht gheit	George has just fainted.
Am Brätzel isch är fascht verstiggt	He almost choked on a pretzel,
So n'es Dail hän mir em Blocher gschiggt.	So we sent some to Blocher.

The Blocher referred to in the last line is Christopf Blocher, Dr. jur., a politician and right-wing conservative of the Nationalist Swiss People's Party (SVP), who is considered a demagogue by many. Since 1 January 2004, he has been a member of the state government, the Federal Council.

Early records of the Basel *Fasnacht* go back to the fourteenth century, but this festival also experienced an expansion into its present-day form in the nineteenth century. An official *Morgestraich* occurred for the first time in 1835. In 1910 a *Fasnacht* committee was established, which discreetly directs the *Fasnacht* behind the scenes. To finance the *Fasnacht*, badges (*Blaggette*) are created for different prizes in gold, silver, and bronze and then sold. The Carnival societies do not just take care of the *Fasnacht* tradition. All year long they attend weekly courses in drumming and piping. Membership in one of the well-known clubs raises the status of a Basel citizen in the same fashion that membership in a guild lends prestige to a citizen of Zürich.

In addition to Basel, which is exceptional as a Protestant locale, one finds in the Catholic regions of Switzerland, especially in the rural areas, numerous villages and regions that are known for *Fasnacht* celebrations. For example, in Kriens, which lies near Lucerne, masks carved from linden wood are worn during *Fasnacht*. Wooden masks are also known in Lachen, in the canton of Schwyz, in Sarganserland, in some regions of Graubünden (Grison), and in the Lötschen Valley of Wallis. Those are by no means all, but they represent the most important *Fasnacht* regions of Switzerland.

STUDIES OF SWISS FOLKLORE

The *Schweizerische Gesellschaft für Volkskunde*, SGV (Swiss Society for Folklore, SSF) was founded in 1896. A year later the *Schweizer Archiv für Volkskunde* (Swiss Archive for Folklore) was founded as a professional journal, whose first publisher was Eduard Hoffmann-Krayer, one of the founding members of the society. He also created the *Internationale Volkskundliche Bibliographie*, IVB (International Folklore Bibliography) (issued since 1917) and played a significant role in bringing about the *Handwörterbuch des Deutschen Aberglaubens* (Dictionary of German Superstitions; 1927–1942). In 1937 a Swiss Institute for Folklore was established in Basel as the permanent site of the Swiss Society for Folklore, which deals with folk music and folksong, houses and settlements, religious folk art and medicine, legal customs, and other folklore genres. In the course of its history the organization has carried out a number of projects. In the 1930s the collection of comprehensive materials about folklore with the aid of a survey (*Enquete I*) containing 1,585 questions began. Since the material that was gathered was very heterogeneous and considered the parts of the country quite differently, folklorists decided, after having tested the work with other folklore studies, to develop a questionnaire with considerably fewer, yet deeper, questions. This survey was conducted by trained interviewers in 387 communities (of a total of approximately 3,000). The answers that were obtained became the foundation for the work in the *Atlas der schweizer Volkskunde*, ASV (Atlas of Swiss Folklore). This large work, which was begun by Paul Geiger and Richard Weiss and continued after their death by Walter Escher, Elsbeth Liebl, and Arnold Niederer, tries to present Swiss folk culture as it was shortly before World War II with the aid of maps and extensive commentary. The atlas, which contains 292 maps, was completed in 1995. In addition to this largest work of the *ASV*, the research on the Swiss farmhouse up to 1945 should be mentioned. Currently, there are available respectable volumes about farmhouse research, in which the history and function of individual and regionally distinctive house types are extensively described, along with their construction, habitation, and husbandry. Earlier, Richard Weiss's small, but very instructive, work about Swiss house landscapes had appeared (1959). Max Gschwend's *Swiss Farm Houses* (1970) also offers a good overview of the subject. Already in 1942 a department for film had been founded by the Swiss Society of Folklore. Directed by Paul Hugger, who took over the leadership in 1962, the film work concentrated on the documentation of handicrafts that were dying out.

In 1913 Eduard Hoffmann-Krayer first published his "Small Handbook of Swiss Folk Culture of the Present" under the title *Festivals and Customs of the Swiss People* (1940). However, a first overview that dealt with all of Swiss folk culture appeared first in 1946 with *Folklore of Switzerland* by Richard Weiss, who emphasizes the social functions of the cultural phenomena that he presents and shows the relationships among them. This work was seen as a model for a long time even beyond the borders of Switzerland and went through three editions (1946, 1978, 1984). In 1992 the Swiss Society brought out in three volumes, the *Handbook of Swiss Folk Culture: Life between Tradition and Modernity, a Panorama of the Swiss Daily Life*.

For a long time folklore was taught at Swiss universities in the framework of other disciplines. Since 1900 Hoffmann-Krayer had taught Phonetics, Swiss Dialect and Folklore at the University of Basel in connection with German studies. The first Professorship for Folklore was established in 1946 and was occupied by Richard Weiss, who remains the most dominant personality in Swiss folklore. A Special Professorship for Folklore has existed at the University of Basel since 1962; it was changed to a regular professorship in 1965. The famous researcher of the Walser (a German-speaking ethnic minorty in the romance Alps), Paul Zinsli (1906–2001), taught Swiss German Language, Literature, and Folklore at the University of Bern from 1946 to 1971. Since Zinsli's retirement folklore has been taught only on the side. The narrative researcher and fairy tale specialist Max Lüthi became well known far beyond the borders of Switzerland. He has taught the course Comparative European Folk Literature at the University of Zürich since 1968. The French-speaking part of Switzerland follows the French example in the division of the university disciplines. Therefore, folklore is taught under the discipline of general ethnology or social anthropology.

In addition to publications, Swiss folklore may be researched at these Web sites: www.drg.ch (Dicziunari Rumantsch Grischun [Rhätoromanisches Wörterbuch, Forschungsstelle]); www.hls.ch (Historisches Lexikon der Schweiz); www.sagw.ch/dt/kommissionen/woerterbuch (Schweizerdeutsches Wörterbuch, Schweizerisches Idiotikon); www.musee-suisse.com/e/index.html (Swiss National Museums, Schweizerisches Landesmuseum); www.fasnachts-comite.ch/english.html (Carnival in Basel).

BIBLIOGRAPHY

Atlas der schweizerischen Volkskunde (ASV). 1950–1995. Erlenbach-Zürich: Eugen Rentsch.

Bachmann-Geiser, Brigitte. 1981. *Die Volksmusikinstrumente der Schweiz (Handbuch der europäischen Volksmusikinstrumente, Bd. 4)*. Zürich: Atlantis.

———. 1999. *Das Alphorn. Vom Lock- zum Rockinstrument*. Bern: Paul Haupt.

Bärtsch, Albert Holzmasken. 1993. *Fasnachts- und Maskenbrauchtum in der Schweiz, in Süddeutschland und Österreich*. Aarau: AT Verlag.

Baumann, Max Peter. 1976. *Musikfolklore und Musikfolklorismus. Eine ethnomusikologische Untersuchung zum Funktionswandels des Jodels*. Winterthur: Amadeus.

———. 1977. Funktion und Symbol. Zum Paradigma "Alphorn." In *Studia instrumentorum musicae popularis*. Bd. V., edited by Erich Stockmann. Stockholm: Musikmuseet, Statens Musiksamlingar. 27–32.

———. 1981. *Bibliographie zur ethnomusikologischen Literatur der Schweiz*. Winterthur: Amadeus.

Baumann, Walter, and Michael Wolgensinger. 1979. *Folklore Schweiz. Brauchtum, Feste, Trachten*. Zürich: Orell Füssli.

Bremberger, Bernhard, and Stefanie Döll. 1984. Der Betruf auf dem Urnerboden im Umfeld von Geschichte, Inhalt und Funktion. *Jahrbuch für Volksliedforschung* 29:65–96.

Gschwend, Max. 1970. *Schweizer Bauernhäuser*. Bern: Paul Haupt.

Haller, Albrecht von. 1998 (1729). *Die Alpen*. gutenberg.spiegel.de/haller/gedichte/alpen.htm.

Hoffmann-Krayer, Eduard. 1940. *Feste und Bräuche des Schweizervolkes*. Zürich: Atlantis.

Honegger, Andreas. 2003. *Zürcher Sechseläuten*. *Constaffel und die 25 Zünfte*. Zürich: Verlag Neue Zürcher Zeitung.

Hugger, Paul, ed. 1992. *Handbuch der schweizerischen Volkskultur. Leben zwischen Tradition und Moderne. Ein Panorama des schweizerischen Alltags*. 3 volumes. Zürich: Offizin.

König, Franz Niklaus. 1814. *Reise in die Alpen*. Bern: gedruckt bei Ludwig Albrecht Haller.

Lüthi, Max. 1966. *Volksmärchen und Volkssage. Zwei Grundformen erzählender Dichtung*. Bern: Francke.

———. 1968. *Das europäische Volksmärchen. Form und Wesen*. Bern: Francke.

———. 2004. *Märchen*. 10th edition. Stuttgart: Metzler.

Niederer, Arnold. 1968. Folklore Studies in Switzerland. *Journal of the Folklore Institute* 5:236–240.

———. 1970. Zur volkskundlichen Forschung in der Schweiz 1955–1970. *Hessische Blätter für Volkskunde* 61:221–235.

Schweizerisches Idiotikon. Wörterbuch der schweizerdeutschen Sprache. 1881–1999. Frauenfeld: Huber.

Spreng, Hans. 1946. *Die Alphirtenfeste zu Unspunnen 1805 und 1808*. Bern: Schmid. (Internet version: edbessrv6.unibe.ch/digibern/de/Engine/DirektSprung/DirectView.asp?KatalogID'3& RecordNum'2345.)

Staël, Anne Louise Germaine de. 1985 (1814). *De l'Allemagne. Über Deutschland*. Frankfurt a. M.: Insel.

Thalmann, Rolf. 1981. *Das Jahr der Schweiz in Fest und Brauch*. Zürich: Artemis.

Weiss, Richard. 1946. *Volkskunde der Schweiz*. Erlenbach-Zürich: Eugen Rentsch.

———. 1950. *Einführung in den Atlas der schweizerischen Folkskunde*. Erlenbach-Zürich: Eugen Rentsch.

———. 1959. *Häuser und Landschaften der Schweiz*. Erlenbach-Zürich: Eugen Rentsch.

Wyss, Johann Rudolf, ed. 1979 (1826). *Schweizer Kühreihen und Volkslieder. Ranz de Vaches et Chansons nationales de la Suisse*. Zürich und Freiburg i. Br.: Atlantis.

Zinsli, Paul. 1968. *Walser Volkstum in der Schweiz, in Vorarlberg, Liechtenstein und Piemont. Erbe, Dasein, Wesen*. Frauenfeld und Stuttgart: Huber.

Max Matter (Translated from the German by Scott Darwin)

Eastern Europe

ALBANIA

GEOGRAPHY AND HISTORY

As an ethnic people, Albanians live separated in several political states on the Balkan Peninsula in Southeast Europe. The focal state is Albania, which has approximately 3.5 million inhabitants. To its north and northeast border lies Kosova, a region that until 1999 was under Serbian state administration in the former Yugoslavia. Kosova has more than 2 million inhabitants, 90 percent of whom are Albanian. On Albania's eastern border lies **Macedonia** with 800,000 Albanians, constituting 30 percent of the population of that country. Montenegro lies northwest of Albania and is inhabited by 42,000 Albanians, or 8 percent of the population. On the northern and eastern borders of Kosova is **Serbia**, where nearly 100,000 Albanians live. Albanians also inhabit an Albanian-populated area in **Greece** called Çamëria. To the west Albania borders on the Adriatic Sea, while the Ionian Sea lies to its southwest. Albania is connected to **Italy** and at the same time reaches the Ionian Sea through the Otranto Channel.

The land surrounding the political entity of Albania is Albanian land, and Albanians are its native inhabitants. Yet throughout history, the borders of the central state have been fractioned and truncated several times, and, consequently, the people have lived under several foreign state administrations. These historical circumstances have had tremendous impact on the shaping of the spiritual culture and oral tradition of this people. Nonetheless, despite life under other political states, Albanians have been able to preserve their ethnic and cultural values, which mark them as a national integral group. It is these ethnic and cultural features that form the identity of their nation.

The land where Albanians live has great natural beauty and is referred to in early antique times. In Homer's poems *The Iliad* and *The Odyssey* and in the poetic writings of Hesiod are references to fertile land, rich pastures, and great herds from Epyrot and some other Illyrian tribes, which lived within the boundaries of the territory currently inhabited by Albanians. They were separated from the neighboring areas by mountains or sea. This region encompasses a range of landscape features: from coastal areas to wild rivers and waterfalls, fields, mountains, and unending valleys. Foreign visitors who visited this land called it "the Balkan's Switzerland" or "the rocky garden of Southeast Europe." What is more, the natural beauty and enchantment have often served as a source of inspiration for creators of folklore. The mountainous landscape has had its impact on the shape and motives that decorate traditional costumes. For example, a characteristic dress for women in mountainous areas is *xhubleta*, though it cannot be found along the coast. Likewise the white *fustanella* dress, which is common for men in the south, is not worn by men living in the north.

The hydrography of this region is rich and derives from the mountainous landscape. Water, mainly in rivers, is sufficient in quantity. Rivers pour into the Adriatic, Ionian, Aegean, and Black Seas. The landscape and the climate, Continental and

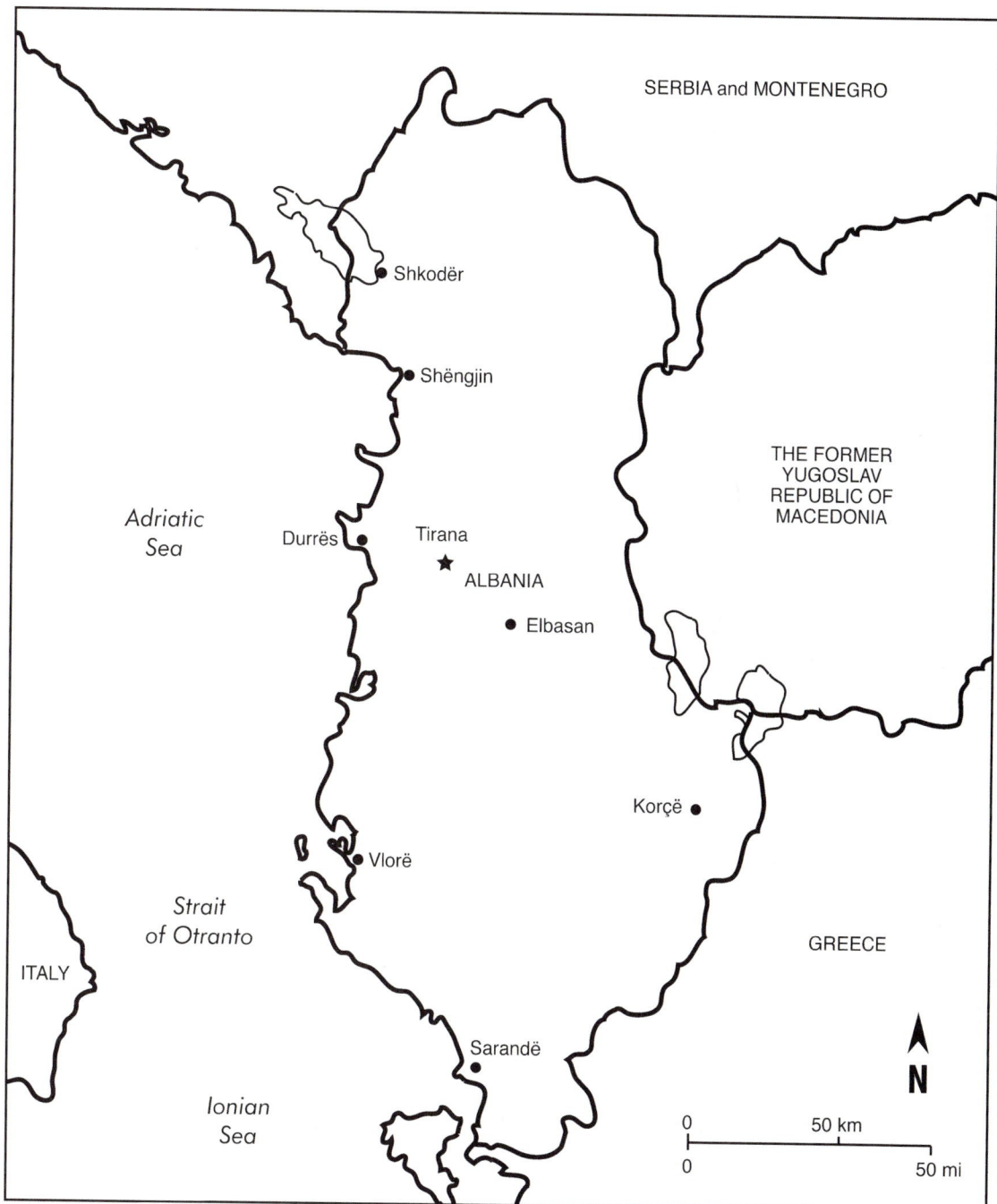

Albania.

coastal, have affected the shaping of traditional culture in general. The rough mountainous climate has contributed to the creation and long life of heroic epics, long
verses associated with the sounds of an age-old traditional instrument, the *lahuta*
(lute). The colors of nature have had an impact on such compositions, and it is noticeable that the folk costumes of Albanians, especially women, are of bright and
lively colors.

The *lahuta* (lute) is used to accompany performances of Albanian epic songs. (From *Zymer Ujkan Neziri, Epika Legjendare e Rugovë V* [Pristinë: IAP, 1997])

Albanians are the oldest group of people in Southeast Europe. All indicators show that they are the descendants of early Aryan paleo-Balkan inhabitants, known in history as Illyrians, Macedonians, or Epyrots. According to many ethnologists and historians, Illyrians constituted the Tyrrhenopelasgian population of pre-Hellenic origin, which lived in the southern part of the Balkan Peninsula and extended its borders to Thrace and Italy. Illyrians and Greeks are the oldest people of the Balkans, and Homer himself in his writings mentions Illyrian tribes such as the Paons and Thesprots. The first to write about Illyrians was Herodotos, who even mentions their music in the Illyrian state of Dardania. The predecessors of Albanians, the Illyrians, lived in tribes. Some of these tribes even had statelike organization, regular administration, political and administrative boundaries, chancelleries, army and regular recruitment, money, and other trappings of modern civilizations. Illyrians are even known as the people who constructed many of the old cities along the Adriatic coast. The first Illyrian state recognized by history emerged at the end of the fifth century B.C.E., while the last Illyrian state was that administered by King Genc. It was conquered by the Romans in the year 168 B.C.E. During the time of Illyrian kingdoms, history also refers to a woman who governed the Illyrian state of the Ardian tribe. That was Queen Teuta, wife of King Agron. Illyrians were pagan, and traces of such belief can still be found in many traditional rituals.

As a result of dynamic ethnic and social movements as well as superfluous historical and political events in the central part of the Balkan Peninsula, other people infiltrated this region, leaving their marks in the ethnic and religious structure of this people. As history shows, this territory was first infiltrated by the Romans, then the Slavs, and then the Turks. The arrival of these ethnic communities in the Balkans, mostly as invaders, conditioned the withdrawal of autochthonous ethnic Illyrian institutions as well as Thracian and Macedonian ones. With the penetration of the Romans, the Illyrian tribes, once inhabitants of the whole Balkan Peninsula, would become Romanized. With the arrival of the Slavs in the Middle Ages, another large portion of Albanians would become Slavic. This is how the geographic borders surrounding Illyrians and their descendants closed down. However, traces of the Illyrians survive throughout the Balkan Peninsula. In the central and western Balkans, Albanians continued to remain in the ethnic-geographic boundaries set forth by the Illyrians, despite facing pressure from foreign invasions and dominion for centuries.

Nowadays, Albanians have three religions. Their strategic geographical position placed them at an appealing meeting point for the world's three largest civilizations: Roman civilization based on Western Christianity, the Byzantine civilization based on Orthodox Christianity, and the Ottoman civilization based on Islam. The Ottomans exercised hegemony over the Balkan Peninsula, especially Albanian-inhabited land, from the fourteenth through nineteenth centuries. Muslim Albanians live in Kosova, most parts of Albania (especially central Albania), Macedonia, and East Serbia. Catholic Albanians live in north Albania and some parts of Kosova. Orthodox Albanians live mostly in south Albania and in Albanian-populated Greece as well as south Italy: the Arbëresh (Albanesi).

Because of the frequency of wars, pressures from different invaders, difficult economic situations, or desire for a better life, Albanians have often migrated. Illyrian migrations occurred at the time of Roman invasion, during Byzantine rule, upon the arrival of Slavs in Albania, and during the Ottoman rule and that of the Albanian Pashas in the eighteenth and nineteenth centuries. Significant migration took place during the Ottoman invasion in the fifteenth century. To avoid rape and other forms of abuse, part of the population moved to the more protected highland areas, while others left for Greece or southern Italy. The number of people who left to avoid Ottoman depredations is believed to be about 200,000. Albanians, who left for Italy at this time, are known as the Arbëresh (or Albanesi in Italy), and they continue to live in Calabria and **Sicily**. Five centuries after leaving their ancestral land, they preserve their knowledge of the Albanian language, customs, and traditions as a way of maintaining national identity. Besides these earlier waves of migration, other mass movements of population such as those that took place between 1913 and 1923, when many Albanians (30,000 to 40,000) left Kosova, Montenegro, and west Macedonia for İsmir and other parts of Anatolia in Turkey, have left their mark in folklore. Many historical folksongs relate to the subject of exile.

MYTHS, LEGENDS, AND FOLKTALES

Besides state organizations and historical-political circumstances, folklore as a form of expression of the people's spirit has undergone the same challenges as the people themselves. Folklore shapes human awareness and is manifested in every human creation and activity. The Albanian belief system represented a continuation of the paleo-Balkanic culture, which established itself in this region long ago. The most ancient forms of belief among Albanians include fetishism, animism, totemism, and paganism. Traces of fetishism occur when, for example, a rock with a hole or other items for personal use were believed to have the power to heal or bring luck. Totemism, which refers to belief in the first mythical predecessors of the tribe, characterized Illyrian beliefs. A contemporary survival of totemism involves the snake: necklaces that are shaped like snakes, the motif in clothing designs and traditional architecture depicting shapes and movements of the snake, and the belief that snakes as protectors of households should not be killed and that every house should have such a guardian. Paganism relates convictions of the existence of supernatural forces, often highly enigmatic, that impact the fate of people for better or worse. The best way to turn these forces to the benefit of people was to honor them by giving them presents, sacrificing people and animals, and building monuments. In Albanian folklore, one renowned composition is the ballad of human sacrifice, "The Ballad of the Walled-in Woman," which is dedicated to the destructive forces that at night destroyed a bridge built by people during the day. In Albanian tradition, cult monuments built atop mountains meant being closer to God. This practice has survived alongside rites and sacrifices dedicated to the forces of nature. Animal sacrifices might be offered as pleas for rain, or people might wake up early on specific days and climb high into the mountains to pray to the sun. Pilgrimages may also recall practices designed to influence spiritual beings in the pre-Christian past. The symbol of the sun can be found in all Albanian folk costumes. Belief in the forces of nature is also expressed in the phrases with which stories and old songs begin—"By Land and by Heaven," "By Moon and by Sun," "For the Sun That Kills and Absolves"—which had the intention of strengthening the truth value of the story about to be told. Fairy tales, too, have a relevant figure, the "Daughter of the Sun and the Moon." Some pre-Christian cults existed to honor fire, whose use brought good for humankind. Other cults focused on families, ancestors, land fertility, many elements of flora and fauna, and other phenomena related to human life. An important pagan cult related to mothers' breasts as a source of the milk used to feed people in the first months of their lives. Symbols of women's breasts can be found carved into the wood used for making doors of Albanian houses, a practice that was thought to bring good luck to the house and wealth to its residents. One of the strongest oaths or vows of Albanian highlanders is "By my mother's breast milk, from which I drank."

The struggle between the forces of nature and between what is good and what is bad is also expressed by using different mythological figures, which had their place in legends passed orally through generations. Some of these Albanian mythological figures include *Ora*, which at times implies the guardian snake of a household and otherwise refers to the guardian angel that every person, family, clan, and province was believed to have. It could be wicked as well as good. When a person suffered from some misfortune or encountered a series of unfortunate events, it was said that *"I ka vdekë Ora"* (His *Ora* died) or *"E mori Ora e ligë"* (He was taken over by his wicked *Ora*). Albanians also have a blessing that goes, *"Të gjetshin Orët e mira"* (May good *Oras* await you, or May good times be ahead of you), and a curse that warns, *"Të marrshin Orët e liga"* (May bad *Oras* await you, or May bad times be ahead of you). Another important legendary figure is the *Zana* (fairy), often mentioned in epic songs and tales. She is often thought of as a very beautiful woman with long hair and supernatural power who lives in a cave. There is often one *Zana* or a company of three of them. Her power rests within the golden horns of three wild goats. If a man was to do something good for *Zanas*, they would reward him. On the contrary, they were believed to be able to be quite wicked if offended. *Zana* plays a major role in the heroic story-songs about the hero Muji, who was initially a shepherd. Muji helped get *Zana's* children to sleep, and she rewarded him by letting him drink from her milk, giving him supernatural powers, and making a brave and invincible hero out of him.

The *Kuçedra* (serpent-dragon) is a mythological figure of Albanian folklore, to which is always attributed negative forces of nature. It is usually represented as a great monster with many heads that lives in caves, on mountains, and near springs. It prevents people from accessing their water supply, causes droughts, and produces general fright. The *Kuçedra* can be killed by another mythological figure, the *Dragoi*. This being is a man who is born with wings, has supernatural power, and can fly. Moreover, he can kill the monster. People still praise men whom they admire for their power by saying, "He is brave like a *dragua.*" While *Dragoi* is male, *Kuçedra* is female. These figures are believed to originate from patriarchal times, when there was considerable belief in the cult of men's power or strength.

One of the most frequently mentioned figures in Albanian fairy tales is *E bukura e Dheut* (Beauty of the Land). This is a woman who always symbolizes beauty and perfection and lives in the underground world, in the air, or beyond the sea. She possesses the elixir of immortality. To reach her, fairy tale heroes must pass through great challenges and sacrifices. Marriage with her implies the integration of the personality and fulfillment of the greatest ideals of the fairy tale hero. She is also present in Greek fairy tales and is reminiscent of sorceress Kirkê in *The Odyssey.*

LIFE-CYCLE RITUALS

Ritual practices often figured in the lives of Albanians. The most basic ones are the rituals of birth, marriage, and death. In the tradition of the patriarchal communities in the not very distant past, especially of ones living in the rural areas, a childless family could not even be imagined—especially one without sons who would inherit the wealth, the memories, and the name of the ancestors. Hence, in these traditions, the family of a young man who was of marrying age would seek a bride for him from a family with a history of births, especially of male children. Furthermore, the bride had to come from a well-respected family so that she could bring well-being and children to the family that would ensure the survival of the family name. When the bride was pregnant, the whole family would make sure that she did no hard work and that she ate well so that she could give birth to healthy children. When she would be about to give birth, she would have the women from her husband's family near her. They were supposed to know much about the ritual of birth. If she gave birth to a baby boy, the husband's father or the husband himself would fire shots from a shotgun to let the village know that "the house was rejoicing." No such practice happened for births of baby girls. After the birth, the baby was subjected to a number of rituals, prayers, and practices in order to protect it from the evil eye. The bride who could not give birth to any children would be called ill-fated; men were never blamed for a marriage without children, despite the fact that they, too, could have been sterile. The fault would always be the woman's. A family that had only daughters would declare one of them a sworn virgin. This always happened after the chosen daughter agreed to it and after the approval of the family and the village. This meant that she could never marry, would wear men's clothing, and would sacrifice herself for the family in order to preserve its name and the tradition. This "sex change" was always social and never biological.

The wedding was the most important moment in the lives of young Albanian men and women. In the past Albanian young women spent much of their time as girls in preparation for marriage, and their families usually determined their fate. Today, almost nothing of this practice remains. The wedding was a joyful event not only for the new couple but also for both families and their relatives. Many rituals took place in the house of the bride before the wedding, and these were performed with lyrical songs, which wished luck and prosperity in the lives of the young couple. As a wedding song recorded in 1980 says,

O Bali, t'u gzoftë tërvesa	O Bali, may your table be joyful
Qi na i mlodhe gjithë kto mesa!	For bringing all these nieces together.
O Bali, t'u gzoftë sinija	O Bali, may your tray be joyful
Qi na i mlodhe gjithë kto bija!	For bringing all these daughters together.
Sofra jote gjithmonë koftë,	May your sofra always be alive;
Shpija jote u zgjanoftë!	May it get bigger.

The rituals of death are related to the moment of death itself but also to the afterlife. Albanians believe that a human being does not die and disappear but "changes life." That is why they try to maintain the spiritual links with the dead. It is believed that the dead can hear, see, eat, and drink, and families mourn their dead by singing songs. Women usually mourn by singing praise to the good qualities of the deceased and giving the deceased messages to send greetings to the other deceased members of the family. Sometimes, men also perform the mourning—usually referred to as wailing. Men mourn in groups by singing and shouting ritual songs, pulling at their hair, and scratching their faces. Such types of mourning are also found among other people of the Balkans, and some believe that they have a Paleo-Balkan source. Illyrians mourned their dead this way, and we find similar mourning practices in the northern mountainous region of Albania.

CALENDAR CUSTOMS

Seasonal rites are always linked to the cult of nature. Many of these rites originated in pre-Christian times or even earlier, even though some of them were later embedded in Christianity and Islam. Such rites begin with the period that lasts from 22 December until 6 January. The winter solstice was called "the day of the return of the sun for the summer" and is the time of year when the daylight period begins to lengthen. The date 24 December was the "Night of Buzm," later known as Christmas. Albanians of Muslim faith refer to it as the Snow Feast. The rites at this feast were marked with bonfires, believed to give light to the sun and prayers to encourage fertility of the land and women. The "Day of Blessed Water" on 6 January was the occasion for rites performed on this day related to the pre-Christian water cult. "Summer Day" occurred on 1 March, and its observance symbolized the revival of nature. It was believed that plants had said good-bye to the earth and would now re-surface. The day of 25 March was also a feast of nature. Albanians of Christian Orthodox faith called it *Vangjelizmoi*, those of Muslim faith called it *Sultan Nevruz*, and Catholics called it the St. Mary's Day. It is believed that this feast is linked to the ritual of death and revival of the god of fertility. Many magical rites are performed on this day. On 23 April or 6 May another celebration, the *Shëngjergji* (St. George's Day), is celebrated by Albanians of all faiths. It is believed that it honors livestock breeding. Other celebrations marking seasonal changes have survived but are now celebrated as religious occasions.

EPICS AND BALLADS

All Albanian cults, rites, beliefs, and other types of manifestations of the soul involved oral traditions. Albanian verbal folklore is very rich and exists in a range of genres. Epic refers to the traditional recital of verses, ballads, and epic songs. The older legends or ballads are related to such cultural phenomena as the myth of sacrifice, revival, and *besa* (vows). The most commonly known is the "The Ballad of the Walled-in Woman," based on the myth of sacrifice, which deals with a woman who was sacrificed by being built into a wall of a structure so that the structure would stand. Many bridges, castles, and churches are related to this myth. Some of these structures still survive. Songs of sacrifice have also been encountered among Serbians, Montenegrins, and Greeks. The ballad says that the woman who was built into a wall asked that part of her body be left out of the wall so that with the right breast she could feed her little boy and caress him with the right hand.

The ballad of revival derives from the story of a dead man who rises from the dead in order to keep a promise that he gave while alive. This ballad was found among the Albanians throughout the Balkans, with slight changes, usually as a result of religious beliefs. However, the structure is always the same. What makes this ballad an autochthonous one is *besa*, the keeping of a promise, an important Albanian value. Albanians believe that if you do not keep your *besa*, even the soil will not dissolve you. In this ballad, a mother, mourning over her dead son's grave, tells him: "Kostandin, my son, where are you? / Where is the *besa* you gave me?"

The epic is the richest oral tradition of the Albanians. The long epic verses are of two types depending on the theme: the cycle of heroic epic songs (or the Songs of Frontier Warriors) and the historical epic songs. The Cycle of the Songs of Frontier Warriors is built on heroic deeds of the brothers Muji and Halili and their friends as well as the sons of Muji during wars with invaders from outside who came over land and sea to take their lands and their women. The cycle of heroic epics may be compared to Homer's *The Iliad*, to the Robin Hood ballads of **England**, the epic of the Spanish Cid, *Le Chanson de Roland*, the *Niebelung* among the Germans, and other European heroic traditions. This epic is related to cultural events of the medieval age of the twelfth through the fourteenth centuries before the period of the Ottoman Empire. It has a rich mythological layer, augmented later with elements coming from the Ottomans. The heroes of the *epos* are valiant with supernatural powers and deeds. Throughout their lives they are surrounded by mythological figures and giants. The features assigned to these characters are heroism, maturity, courage, altruism, patience, and other heroic virtues. These songs provide the source for much cultural data on early Albanians. This *epos* is also found among the Slavs and the Bosnians, but studies of the songs show that these types of songs among the Albanians have more pre-Christian elements as compared to the monotheism that pervades Slavic examples. It is thus believed that the Albanian variant of the heroic *epos* is the oldest. This *epos* was created in the mountainous region of today's northern Albania and southwestern Kosova and is sung by rhapsodists. The position of the mountains made it possible to preserve a culture distinct from that in the plains and was a suitable context for the development of the epic. It is believed that the battles of the epic heroes took place in the *Bjeshkët e Nemuna* (The Damned Mountains), and toponyms related to the events of the *epos* may be found in the region. This *epos* was later disseminated to many places inhabited by Albanians.

SONGS

The songs of the historical epic tradition treat the heroic deeds of real heroes who were part of Albanian history. Through this tradition, the popular memory built a chronicle of major historical events and immortalized the bravery of those who died fighting against the invaders. The most renowned songs of the historical epic tradition are those sung about Skanderbeg, the national **hero** who fought the Ottoman sultans in the fifteenth century and for twenty-five years kept all the Albanian lands united. This is known as the Golden Age of the nation. These songs also passed on a feeling of patriotism that is characteristic of Albanians. The subject most often treated in the historical epic cycle is migration. A phenomenon characteristic throughout Albanian history, it inspired many folksingers.

Folk lyric encompasses all those short, usually rhyming songs that are sung during calendar rites, at family rites, for love, and on other occasions. They are sung to the accompaniment of instruments or without them both by soloists and by ensembles. The most beautiful ones are the lyrical songs of love. They are rich in figures of speech describing the beauty of the girl, the feeling of love, and other conventions of romance. The songs of the cradle or lullabies include the following from 1983:

Nina nana po të përkundi	Nina nana, I am rocking the cradle;
Ti m'u bofsh plak katundi	May you become a village elder.
Nina nana sheqer n'letër	Nina nana, sugar on paper;
Ti m'u bofsh plak i vjetër!	May you grow to be a very old man.

FAIRY LORE, PROVERBS, AND RIDDLES

Oral prose encompasses long stories, fairy tales, short stories, anecdotes, animal tales, riddles, and proverbs. Fairy tales were told to children in the past, usually by their grandmothers. The main components of the fairy tale were the characters (usually mythological) and the mythical means that justify the actions of the characters. The space in which the action takes place is never constrained and includes the sky, the land, and the underground. The structure of the fairy tale is usually formed throughout generations. The mythological elements found in

Albanian folk dances are usually divided into men's dances and women's dances, though mixed-gender dancing also occurs. (From the Archive of the Institute of Albanology)

the Albanian fairy tale testify to a layering of beliefs from fetishism to monotheism. In their descriptions and actions, the different characters of the Albanian fairy tales resemble those found in the fairy tales of the other people of the Balkans.

Other genres of Albanian oral prose include anecdotes, short stories with an educational purpose that always end with a lesson. They were created out of practical experience and are often related to specific people and places. The lesson given in the end is always moral and educational. Proverbs are idioms that usually lose their meaning in translation since they have lexical components characteristic of a particular language and people.

MUSIC AND DANCE

The oral tradition of the Albanians would not be complete without the music, both vocal and instrumental. Albanian vocal music is characterized by encompassing both monophonic and polyphonic songs. Monophonic songs are mostly a feature of the northern parts, whereas polyphonic songs are found farther south in the plains and along the coastal areas. The instruments that accompany Albanian songs are stringed, wind, and percussive. The songs of the legendary epic were sung to the accompaniment of ancient instruments such as the *lahuta* (lute) and the *çifteli*. Both of these instruments are stringed instruments made of wood and animal skin.

A traditionally made Albanian carpet. (From the permanent ethnographic exhibit at the Institute of Albanology)

Oral tradition is also accompanied by dances, usually performed in two, three, and four steps as well as in free steps. They are usually danced in closed circles, semi-circles, and two facing lines. The dances are usually divided into men's and women's dances, but there are also mixed dances.

ARTS, CRAFTS, AND ARCHITECTURE

Albanians are very creative in their handicrafts. The handicrafts and the clothing are made by Albanian women with crochet hooks, needles, or various techniques using wood. The colors and the motifs in Albanian clothing originate from nature. The folk clothing is also made by men, who process the materials from the skin and the wool of animals as well as from cotton and silk. Other folk arts are carpetmaking; the making of dishes from clay, wood, and metals; manufacturing ornaments from precious metals such as gold, silver, and bronze; and making weapons.

Architecture is also of a folk character, and traditionally constructed houses and the *kulas* (turrets) are still used for shelter by Albanians. They were built to be very resistant, which explains why they still stand. Additional information on Albanian folklore can be found at the useful Web site: www.albanian.com/information/history/origins.html.

The *xhubleta*, the characteristic dress worn by women in mountainous areas of Albania. (From the permanent ethnographic exhibit at the Institute of Albanology)

BIBLIOGRAPHY

Akademia e Shkencave të RPS të Shqipërise. 1990. *Gjeografia fizike e Shqipërise, I.* Tiranë: Qendra e studimeve gjeografike.

Balada dhe legjenda. 1974. Prishtinë: IAP.

Berisha, Anton Nikë. 1998. *Qasje poetikës së letërsisë gojore.* Prishtinë: Rilindja.

Bogdani, Ramazan H. 2003. *Visare etnokoreografike.* Tiranë: Akademia e Shkencave e Republikës së Shqipërise.

Elsie, Robert. 2001. A *Dictionary of Albanian Religion, Mythology, and Folk Culture.* London: Hurst.

Fetiu, Sadri Fetiu. 2000. *Balada popullore shqiptare.* Prishtinë: IAP.

Grup autorësh. 1994. *Gjeografia e Kosovës.* Prishtinë: ETMMK.

Historia e Shqipërise. 1959. Tiranë: UT.

Këngë dasme I. 1980. Prishtinë: IAP.

Mustufa, Myzafere. 2003. *Përralla shqiptare (poetikja dhe mitikja).* Prishtinë: IAP.

Ninulla. 1983. Prishtinë: IAP.

Sejko, Veis. 2002. *Mbi elemente të përbashkëta në epikën shqiptaro—arbëreshe dhe serbokroate.* Tiranë: Bargjini.

Selimi, Yllka. 2004 (2001). *Praktika kalendarike dhe funksione të tyre.* Pristinë: Gjurmime Albanologjike, seria folklore-etnolgji 31.

Tirta, Mark. 1999. *Migrime të shqiptarëve.* Tiranë: në Etnografia Shqiptare, Sh.B. Shkenca.

———. 2003. *Etnologjia e shqiptarëve.* Tiranë: GEER.

Vlahovic, Petar. 1967. *Neki problemi slovenizacije ranobakanskog stanovnistva u polimlju i potarju.* Beograd: Etnolosko drustvo Jugoslavije.

Xhemaj, Ukë. 1984 (1983). *Relikte të kultit të gjarpërit në traditën popullore shqiptare.* Prishtinë: Gjurmime Albanologjike, seria folklor-etnologji, 13.

Young, Antonia. 2000. *Women Who Become Men.* Oxford: Berg.

Arbnora Dushi

ASHKENAZIM

HISTORY

The name "Ashkenaz," which first occurs in Genesis 10:3 as the name of one of Noah's great-grandsons, came to be applied by Jews in the Middle Ages to the Rhine Valley of **Germany**. From at least the sixteenth century the term "Ashkenazim" (or "Ashkenazic Jews") has been used to refer to Jews from Germany and also more generally from Central and Eastern Europe as well as to their descendants. This is in contrast to the **Sephardim** (or Sephardic Jews), who trace their ancestry to the Iberian Peninsula. (The term "Sephardim" is sometimes applied more loosely to encompass as well other non-Ashkenazic Jews, for example, those from North Africa, the Near East, and **India**.) From the partitions of **Poland** in the late eighteenth century until World War I, most Ashkenazim lived within the boundaries of the Russian Empire, primarily in the so-called Pale of Settlement, those western territories in which Jews were allowed to live without special permission. After the territorial changes resulting from World War I and until the Nazi exterminations of World War II, the majority of Ashkenazic Jews lived in Poland and the Soviet Union, but sizable populations also existed in North and South America, Western Europe, **Palestine**, and **Australia**.

The everyday vernacular of most Ashkenazim well into the twentieth century was Yiddish, a Germanic language written in the Hebrew alphabet and containing lexical and grammatical elements derived from Semitic (Hebrew and Aramaic), Slavic (especially Polish, Ukrainian, and Belarusian), and Romance (Old French and Old Italian) in addition to its Germanic base. Ashkenazic folklore is thus usually understood as the folklore of Yiddish-speaking Jews. Like all languages, Yiddish was not uniform in time and space, and, similarly, Ashkenazic folklore is not chronologically or geographically homogeneous: old customs, for example, die and are replaced by new ones, and the foods, songs, and proverbs of, say, Lithuanian Jews are not necessarily the same as those of Ukrainian Jews. (Limitations of space generally prevent consideration of the verbal folklore of Ashkenazim who abandoned Yiddish for Hebrew or for the languages of the local co-territorial majority such as German, Polish, Russian, Hungarian, or in the Americas, English, Spanish, or Portuguese. The fluctuation between present and past tense in the discussion that follows, however, reflects the persistence of elements of Ashkenazic folklore among non-Yiddish-speaking Jews and also among the minority of present-day Jews who continue to speak Yiddish.)

A group of Ashkenazic Jews from the early twentieth century. (Courtesy Library of Congress)

While maintaining a religious and linguistic separation from their non-Jewish neighbors, Ashkenazim creatively borrowed from those neighbors' folklore. Yiddish words were set to Slavic melodies, and sometimes the texts of Slavic folksongs were paraphrased or reworked in Yiddish. A Ukrainian song about an unnamed woman going into town to buy buckwheat flour to make pancakes, for example, becomes a Yiddish song about Yakhne-Dvoshe going to town to buy flour to make *homentashn*, the pastry associated with the spring holiday of Purim. A genre of songs about the birth and naming of Jesus provides the basis for a song about the birth and naming of the prophet Samuel. Proverbs and folktales are translated or paraphrased, often with a Jewish "twist" added: the Yiddish adaptation of a German proverb asserting that "poverty is not shameful" points out that "poverty is not shameful, but it is no great honor either."

In the English-speaking world being Jewish is generally taken as a religious identification: a Jew is someone who practices Judaism. In the Old World, however, being Jewish was understood also in ethnic or national terms, and Polish spelling, for example, distinguishes two words for "Jew": the capitalized Żyd to refer to someone of Jewish nationality and the lowercase żyd to refer to someone of Jewish religion. Nonetheless, almost all Jews in general and Ashkenazim in particular have some connection with Judaism either as current practice or as family tradition, and much of Ashkenazic folklore is informed by elements of the canonical Jewish religious texts (the Hebrew Bible; the Talmud and other later rabbinical commentaries; the daily, Sabbath, and holiday prayer books) and religious practice.

The boundary between "official" religious practice and "folk religion" is permeable, and indeed a Yiddish proverb (derived from a Talmudic maxim) states that "a custom may overrule a law." For example, the widespread *tashlikh* ritual of symbolically casting off one's sins into a body of water on the first day of the Jewish New Year (Rosh Hashanah, Yiddish *rosheshone*) survived the opposition of some medieval rabbis who viewed it as a relic of propitiating water spirits. It also acquired a folk etymology: the Hebrew word *tashlikh* ("Thou wilt cast [all their sins into the depths of the sea]," Micah 7:19) was associated with the Yiddish word *tashn* (pockets), and so those performing the ritual often empty out their pockets, allowing the contents to fall into the water. In the twentieth century the tossing of crumbs became a centerpiece of the ritual, and at the end of the century a joking enumeration of the kinds of bread crumbs to be used for different sins (originally due to an American rabbi, the late Richard J. Israel) became Internet folklore.

CALENDAR CUSTOMS AND LIFE-CYCLE CELEBRATIONS

Each of the holidays in the yearly cycle is accompanied by both religious rituals and folkloric practices. Slices of apple, for example, are traditionally dipped in honey on Rosh Hashanah to assure a sweet year, and at the same holiday cooked carrots (*mern*) were seen as a guarantor of fertility in the coming year since the Yiddish verb *mern* means "to multiply." The potato pancakes fried in oil (*latkes*) that are served during the winter holiday of Hanukkah (Yiddish *khanike*) are said to commemorate the vial of consecrated oil that miraculously burned for eight days when the Temple in Jerusalem was re-dedicated after the Macabbees expelled the Syrian Hasmoneans. In the spring, on Purim, the Book of Esther is read, and tradition requires those present to react with noise-making every time they hear the name of Haman, the evil royal minister. At the Passover meal and ritual (*seder*), when unleavened bread (*matzah*) is specified by religious law, one piece required to complete the seder is hidden at the beginning of the meal, and children compete to find it and hold it for ransom. For the holiday of Shevuot (Yiddish *shvues*) it is traditional to decorate the home with elaborate designs cut out of paper.

Similarly, the various stages in the life cycle are marked both religiously and folklorically. The room of an expectant mother or of the mother of a newborn child was traditionally hung with paper amulets with Hebrew inscriptions to protect her and her child from evil spirits, especially from Lillith, according to legend the rebellious first wife of Adam, who steals children. Such amulets were known as *shiramayles*, from the first words ("a song of ascents") of Psalm 121, a frequent component of the amulets. Fear of the evil eye militated against buying or making anything for the expected child before childbirth, and the custom continues even if belief in malevolent forces is not now widespread. Children are normally named after family members, but among Ashkenazic Jews (in contrast to Sephardim) only deceased relatives are honored in this way. The child is given a Hebrew name identical or related to that of the ancestor, which is used in religious contexts such as being called to read from the Torah, in the marriage contract (*ketube*), and in memorial prayers. For everyday purposes, however, he or she is called by the Yiddish equivalent or diminutive of that name (for example, Hebrew *Shelomoh*, Yiddish *Shloyme, Shloymke* [Solomon], or Hebrew *Malkah*, Yiddish *Malke, Malkele* [literally "queen"]) or a Russian, Polish, English, or other vernacular name that begins with the same letter as the Hebrew name or translates it (*Sam, Regina* [the Latin word for "queen"]).

At weddings it was traditional (and remains so in some communities) for the groom to veil the bride himself, explained as a way of assuring him that he was marrying the right woman (unlike the biblical Jacob, who was tricked into marrying Leah instead of her sister, Rachel). The final (non-religious) element of the wedding ceremony, the breaking of a glass by the groom, is often interpreted as commemorating the destruction of the Temple in Jerusalem. Instrumental folk music accompanies different parts of the wedding procedure (for example, greeting the guests, veiling the bride, and leading the guests home) as well as traditional wedding dances.

Among the customs associated with death is that of covering all mirrors in the home where the religiously prescribed week of mourning (*shive*) is observed either to avoid seeing the spirit of the deceased in the mirror or to avoid the vanity of looking at oneself. Traditional religious law requires the presence of a quorum of ten males (*minyen*) for the mourners' prayer (*kaddish*) to be recited, while custom dictates that visitors bring food for the mourners. The need for a ten-man quorum for the *kaddish* and certain other prayers conflicts with biblical and Talmudic precepts against counting people (later interpreted by the folk as being simply unlucky). The creative folk solution was to count "not one, not two, . . . not ten" or to use the words of a ten-word biblical verse (often Psalms 28:9) instead of numbers. German Jews borrowed the German word for "anniversary," *Jahrzeit*, a word that also referred to a memorial church service on the anniversary of someone's death. The Yiddish term *yortsayt* became associated with the custom of lighting a memorial candle (*yortsayt-likht*) on the anniversary (according to the Jewish calendar) of a relative's death.

MAGIC AND FOLK MEDICINE

Various beliefs and practices connected to magic and folk medicine existed alongside official and folk religious practices. Portents of good fortune included having a cricket in the house, finding a nut with a double kernel, seeing a stork, or dreaming about roses, while bad luck should be expected if a cat (of any color) or a hare crossed one's path, if a horse neighed at the outset of a journey, or if one dreamed about geese or beans (beans mean going to jail). If a fly falls into your glass of tea, you are going to get a letter, but if you dream about catching flies, it means that your enemies will be defeated.

Certain activities were viewed as dangerous or protective. A schoolboy, for example, should not play with a cat because he will forget his lessons or have a weak memory in general (perhaps a parallel to the English expression "cat got your tongue?"). One can protect oneself from an angry dog by showing it a "fig" (the thumb placed between the index and middle fingers) or by reciting a rhymed formula that includes the words, "I am Jacob's child, you are Esau's child." One can also recite Exodus 11:7: "But against any of the children of Israel shall not a dog move his tongue." (A Yiddish proverbial expression suggests that more protection is provided by *a posek mit a shtekn*—a biblical verse together with a stick.)

Cures for both physical maladies and evil spells could be effected by an *opshprekherke*, a woman knowledgeable about the appropriate anti-spells or by a variety of magic procedures. Warts, for example, could be cured by rubbing them with the two halves of a sliced apple, binding the two halves together so the apple would look whole, throwing it into the sewer pipe, and proclaiming, "Just as I don't know where the apple is going, so may I not know where my warts are going." To alleviate the pain of teething, a dog's or horse's tooth should be hung around the child's neck and its throat smeared with butter or chicken fat.

MYTHS, LEGENDS, AND FOLKTALES

Ashkenazic verbal art has both religious and secular elements. Some of the many legends from oral tradition about biblical and post-biblical personalities recorded in the Palestinian and Babylonian Talmud (third to fifth centuries C.E.; before that transmitted orally) were also preserved in European oral tradition. King Solomon is a popular figure in such legends, as is the prophet Elijah, who often appears as a miracle worker. Later legends involve the Baal Shem Tov (Master of the Good Name), Israel ben Eliezer (ca. 1700–1760), founder of the religious and spiritual revival movement known as Hasidism, and his disciples, the dynastic spiritual leaders of the movement. There are also secular legends about such historical figures as Napoleon, Emperor Franz Josef, Russian tsars, or Rothschild as well as legends about the *golem*, a creature brought to life by the use of the divine name or other magical means in order to protect Jewish communities against persecution.

Folktales include both Jewish versions of international tale types and original Jewish tales. The former, adapted to the conditions of Jewish life, have been described as *di zelbe Yente, nor andersh farshleyert* (the same [woman named] Yente, but veiled differently). Parables and morality tales co-exist with fairy tales (*vundermayses*, wonder stories); tales for children (including animal tales and nonsense stories); tales about supernatural creatures (*sheydim* [devils], *shtretelekh* [elves], and *dibukim* [dybbuks, the souls of dead people who have possessed living people]); and humorous tales (including stories about such trickster figures as Hershele Ostropolyer and Motke Khabad and stories about the "wise men" [that is, fools] of Khelm). Related to the humorous tales is the still-productive genre of Jewish jokes, many of which are Jewish adaptations of international types. The Israeli folklorist Dov Noy has suggested that the only purely Jewish type consists of such joking, riddle-like interpretations of traditional religious texts as the following, which is based on the fact that both the name "Cain" and the verb "to chew" are pronounced *kayen* in Yiddish: How do we know that Eve had no teeth? Because she had a son Cain (that is, she had a son chew [for her]).

PROVERBS AND RIDDLES

Ashkenazic culture is particularly rich in proverbs, for example, *Patsh zikh nisht in baykhele ven fishele iz nokh in taykhele* (Do not pat yourself on the belly when the fish is still in the river; that is, do not count your chickens before they are hatched). Proverbial expressions include comparisons such as *shiker vi Lot* (drunk as Lot) or *sheyn vi Ester hamalke* (beautiful as Queen Esther). (Note also the parodic *sheyn vi Ester hamalpe* [beautiful as Esther the monkey].) Like these comparisons, many proverbs are derived from the Bible or other religious sources. They are sometimes quoted in the original Hebrew or Aramaic, sometimes translated or paraphrased in Yiddish. (Nearly 10 percent of the 4,000 proverbs in Ignacy Bernstein's 1908 collection of Yiddish proverbs and proverbial expressions are of biblical or Talmudic origin.) Often such quotations are used for humorous ends, with the Hebrew or Aramaic original followed by a parodic Yiddish or even Slavic paraphrase, for example, *vayavoy homon* (and Haman came); *makht Rashe* (Rashi [a famous commentator] comments): *chort ego prines* ([in Russian:] the Devil brought him). Parodic quotations of this type play a prominent role in a classic work of Yiddish literature, Sholem Aleichem's *Tevye the Dairyman.*

Related to proverbs are riddles such as *Flit on fligl, moyert on tsigl, ligt zikh vi a har, shteyt uf vi a nar* (Flies without wings, builds without bricks, lies down like a lord, gets up like a fool); the answer is "snow." Variants include more philosophical riddles such as "What do you do to get rid of someone?—If he is rich, you ask him for a loan; if he is poor, you give him a loan" and joking riddles like "Why does a rooster close its eyes when it crows?—Because it can do it by heart." There is also a genre of riddles with which schoolboys challenged one another, for example, "How many sons did Jacob have? Twelve. And how many children did Isaac have? Two. Then why did Abel kill Cain?" (The one challenged to come up with the explanation is supposed to miss the fact that it was Cain who killed Abel.)

Also related to proverbs are what James Matisoff has called "psycho-ostensive expressions," especially formulas used to protect oneself or others or to wish good or harm to others. Saying something positive about someone or mentioning something good that has happened to oneself should be accompanied by the protective formula *keynehora* (no evil eye). Mention of someone's misfortune makes it necessary to say *nisht do gedakht* (it should not happen here) or *af mayne sonim gezogt* (it should happen to my enemies). To strengthen one's credibility, one can say *oyb ikh zog lign, zol ikh krank lign* (if I am telling a lie, may I lie sick [in bed]).

SONGS

Unlike Yiddish proverbs, a major collection of which was published as early as 1860 by Abraham Tendlau, Yiddish folksongs began to be collected seriously only at the turn of the twentieth century, with the first major collection of texts without melodies published in **Russia** in 1901 and collections with melodies published in Russia and Poland in the second decade of the twentieth century. Even these early collections contained both "true" folksongs and folklorized versions of songs by known authors and/or composers. The 1901 volume, for example, included a lullaby written by Sholem Aleichem, "Shlof, mayn kind" (Sleep, My Child), which collectors in the field submitted to the editors as an anonymous folksong and which was accepted by them as such.

These and later collections included both religious and secular songs. Particularly distinctive among the former is the *nign*, or song without text, which has its origins in the Hasidic movement. That movement also gave rise to songs about wonder-working rabbis, which in turn provoked parodies created by opponents of Hasidism. Songs about returning to the ancestral homeland, the Land of Israel, are often couched in terms of the divine promise of redemption from exile. Another striking category of religious songs is the *mishshprakhike lider* (mixed-language songs). Some combine Slavic, Yiddish, and Hebrew linguistic material, while others provide a religious exegesis of an overheard sentence in a Slavic language. In one such song a rabbi interprets the Ukrainian sentence meaning "Catherine, young woman, come here" in terms of similar-sounding Hebrew words that mean "A sect rejoicing in song, full of glee; Lord, Thou hast redeemed us." These songs illustrate the Hasidic doctrine of finding religious content in all the elements of the surrounding world, even in non-Jewish languages. (In some secular songs, however, language mixture is used purely for comic effect.)

Holiday songs may be primarily religious in orientation, retelling, for example, the biblical story of Passover, or may stress celebratory aspects such as eating potato pancakes and playing games at Hanukkah. The purely secular songs cover the entire range of Jewish (and human) experience: lullabies and other songs sung to, and with, children, love songs, songs about getting married and songs sung at weddings (including those by the traditional wedding jester or *badkhn*), songs about family life and about work, songs about emigration and about immigrant life, songs about military life, and songs of protest. There are also songs of the underworld, dance and riddle songs, humorous and satirical songs. Ballads deal with unrequited love, betrayal, murder, or historical events such as pogroms or war. The twentieth century brought both lyrical and narrative songs created and sung in Nazi ghettos and concentration camps as well as a variety of Soviet folk and pseudo-folk songs.

MUSIC, DANCE, AND DRAMA

Jewish folk instrumentalists (*klezmers* or *klezmorim*) created and performed music for celebrations, primarily weddings (both Jewish and non-Jewish). Their compositions accompanied the ritual components of the traditional wedding as well as the dancing that followed it. Wedding dances included both those in which any guest could participate like the *freylekhs* or *sher* (although men and women danced separately) and certain dramatized dances limited to specific participants, such as the *broyges-tants*, which simulated a quarrel between the two mothers-in-law.

Aside from such dances, the other main element of dramatization in traditional Ashkenazic folklore was the *Purim-shpil* (Purim play), the folk-theatrical versions of Bible stories performed on the holiday of Purim. These included the *Akhashverosh-shpil* (the story of Purim itself, based on the Book of Esther), *The Wisdom of Solomon, David and Goliath, The Binding of Isaac, Jacob's Blessing, The Selling of Joseph,* and others as well as occasional secular subjects. Such performances, which included words and music, were allowed only on Purim, a holiday when it was permissible to break many rules: students chose their own rabbis, who gave mock sermons, and men were supposed to get so drunk that they could not distinguish between "blessed is Mordechai" and "cursed is Haman."

SPORTS AND GAMES

Some rules were also relaxed for Hanukkah. The general hostility to gambling was suspended, and there developed a custom of playing cards on Hanukkah and also on Christmas Eve, the latter sometimes explained as a way of keeping people indoors and away from potentially hostile Christian neighbors. Children, too, gambled on Hanukkah, if only for nuts or buttons, with the aid of a top (*dreydl*), the four sides of which each bore one of the Hebrew letters *nun, giml, hey,* and *shin*. These letters were interpreted in a common variant to mean *nisht* (nothing; that is, pass), *gants* (everything, meaning to take the whole pot), *halb* (half, allowing one to take half the pot), and *shtel* (put; that is, add to the pot). A religious interpretation was also superimposed, namely, that the letters stood for the Hebrew words *neys godol hoyo shom* (a great miracle [that of the long-burning oil] happened there).

Children's play included both "quiet" and "active" games. Among the former were paper-and-pencil games like *iks-miks-driks* (tic-tac-toe) and games based on finding symbols, letters, or words in the Hebrew text of the Bible or Talmud. Active games ranged from circle games (sometimes with dances modeled on adult wedding dances), to hide-and-seek, to "war" games, to a kind of "cops and robbers" in which the "king," responding to the complaint of the "peasant" about having been robbed, ordered the "sheriff" to mete out punishment to the "thief" (slaps and punches, each of which had a specific name). There were also swimming and skating games. The latter had names connected with religious practice. For example, skating with one's eyes closed was called *shma-yisroel-glitsh* because during the *shma-yisroel* (Hear, O Israel) prayer it was traditional to cover one's eyes. Some games required counting-out rhymes to choose sides or to choose "it":

Af dem beymele	On the tree
shteyt a feygele,	stands a bird.
kukt es, kukt es	It looks, it looks
mit an eygele.	with its eye.
Kukndik aher, kukndik aher,	Looking here, looking here,
zogt shoyn yo, zogt shoyn yo,	it says "yes" already, it says "yes" already,
yo, yo, yo.	"yes, yes, yes."

ARTS, CRAFTS, AND ARCHITECTURE

Ashkenazic folk art was often connected with religious practice. The biblical prohibition on making "graven images," usually understood as a ban on making images of humans, especially in the form of sculpture because of the danger of idolatry, was enforced at different times with varying degrees of strictness. Decorative motifs included geometric figures such as the *mogn-dovid* (the Star or literally Shield of David), the menorah or candelabrum, the Tablets of the Law, floral patterns, and depictions of animals as well as Hebrew calligraphy. Although most ritual objects were made by professional craftsmen, there were also—especially in poorer communities—folk versions of such items as mantles for the scroll of the Torah, curtains for the Ark where the scrolls were kept, and the pointers used when reading from the Torah during religious services. The folk versions of the *yad*, the arm-shaped pointer ending in a hand with pointed index finger, were often wooden imitations of those made by professional silversmiths. To keep the Torah scroll from unwinding, the two halves are bound with a long strip of embroidered linen called a *mappah* or *vimpl*. Among Jews in the German and Czech lands it was traditional for the parents of a baby boy to present to their synagogue a Torah binder cut from the swathing sheet used at their son's circumcision and then embroidered by the mother.

Although synagogues in larger towns and cities were usually the work of professionally trained architects and builders, the many synagogues in smaller towns (both wooden and masonry) were often manifestations of folk art and architecture. The wooden synagogues, which were numerous in Poland, **Ukraine**, Belarus, and Lithuania, frequently shared structural and decorative elements with other sorts of local buildings, both Jewish and Christian. The wall and ceiling decorations included both traditional texts (prayers, blessings, quotations from the Bible—especially from the Book of Psalms—and from the Talmud) and traditional images. Scenes of the biblical Land of Israel included representations of the graves of the matriarchs and patriarchs near Hebron and of Jerusalem, which sometimes looked like a small town (*shtetl*) in Eastern Europe, complete with onion-domed Russian Orthodox churches.

Birds and animals, both real and mythical, were frequently used images. The latter included the Leviathan and the *shorabor*, the sea and land creatures, respectively, upon whose meat the pious would feast at the coming of the Messiah. The former, too, had symbolic or allegorical significance: a stork, for example, could stand for the pious sages since its Hebrew name (*hasidah*, the feminine form of the adjective "pious") is thought to come from its reputation for piously taking care of its young. Depictions of such seemingly exotic creatures as leopards, eagles, deer, and lions might allude to the Talmudic injunction: "Be bold as a leopard, swift as an eagle, fleet as a deer and strong as a lion to do the will thy Father who is in Heaven" (*Pirkei avot* 23:5).

Folk art for individual and family use was represented in the decoration of the embroidered bags used to protect and carry tallis or prayer shawl and phylacteries (*tfilin*) as well as in decorated skullcaps (*yarmulkes*) and bags for Passover matzah, Sabbath tablecloths, and covers for the challah (Yiddish *khale*), the Sabbath and holiday bread. Various types of papercuts, made by schoolboys and their teachers, students of yeshivas (higher religious schools), and old men, were used as window decorations (*reyzelekh* or *shvuelekh*) or were hung on the wall as protective amulets (*kameyes*). Another type, the *mizrekh* (plural *mizrokhim*), was hung on the eastern wall of the home or synagogue to indicate the direction of Jerusalem, which one was supposed to face when praying. The *kameyes* and *mizrokhim* were also done in other media: watercolor, pen and ink, and embroidery, for example. Before the era of mass-produced toys, the Hanukkah top (*dreydl*) and the Purim noisemaker (*groger*) were also folk craft objects.

FOOD

Traditional foods also exemplified folk art. The Sabbath and holiday challah could be braided or decorated with symbolic figures: a bird for Rosh Hashanah so that prayers would fly up to Heaven like a bird or a ladder for the eve of Yom Kippur, the Day of Atonement, in order that prayers might ascend to God. More generally, the traditional culinary arts of cooking and baking yielded foods associated with particular holidays as well as regional specialties. Mentioned earlier were the Purim pastries called *homentashn* and the potato pancakes (*latkes*) served during Hanukkah. A traditional part of the Friday-night Sabbath meal was, and is, *gefilte fish* (literally "stuffed fish," from the original manner of preparation, which involved stuffing the ground fish back into the fish skin before cooking, but now usually served as the stuffing alone). The fish was typically flavored with sugar in Poland and with pepper in Lithuania, Belarus, and Ukraine. The line separating these two culinary "dialect" areas corresponded to the boundary between Central (Polish) and Eastern (Lithuanian and Ukrainian) Yiddish dialects.

One area of traditional cuisine that was particularly extensive was the repertoire of dough-based dishes: in 1959 Uriel and Beatrice Silverman Weinreich recorded some forty recipes from a woman born in Ukraine around 1870 and analyzed them according to kind of flour, type of dough, shape, method of cooking, fillings, accompaniments, and functions. The list included different kinds of bread and pastry as well as blintzes, *homentashn*, *latkes*, noodles (including Passover noodles made from potato flour), *varenikes* (boiled dumplings filled with cherries, cheese, potatoes, kasha [buckwheat groats], or cabbage), knishes (baked yeast pastry filled with cabbage, cheese, potatoes, or kasha with *grivns* [cracklings] and fried onions), and others.

STUDIES OF ASHKENAZIC FOLKLORE

The serious study and publication of Ashkenazic folklore began at the turn of the twentieth century. Materials were published throughout the twentieth century in Yiddish-language collections and in Yiddish-, Hebrew-, and German-language folklore journals such as *Filologishe shriftn fun YIVO* (Wilno, 1926–1938), *Yidisher folklor* (New York, 1954–1959), *Reshumot* (Odessa/Berlin/Tel Aviv, 1922–1953), *Yeda'-'am* (Tel Aviv, 1948–   ), and *Mitteilungen der Gesellschaft für jüdische Volkskunde* (Hamburg/Berlin/Vienna, 1898–1929). Important work was also done in the Soviet Union by Moshe Beregovski (1982, 2001) and others, some of which has been published only recently. The works by Noy (1971), Schwarzbaum (1968), Slotnick (1976), Weinreich and Weinreich (1959), and Yassif (1986) provide useful bibliographical details on studies and collections of Ashkenazic folklore. Significant contributions to the study of Ashkenazic folklore have been made in recent decades by Shifra Epstein, Olga Goldberg-Mulkiewicz, Galit Hasan-Rokem, Barbara Kirshenblatt-Gimblett, Dov Sadan, Mark Slobin, Chava Weissler, Jacob Weitzner, and Sarah

Zfatman, among others. See also the bibliographies, syllabi, and other materials published in the *Jewish Folklore and Ethnology Review*. Zborowski and Herzog (1995 [1952]) provides much useful ethnographic detail but overlooks variations over time and space.

BIBLIOGRAPHY

Ben-Amos, Dan, and Jerome R. Mintz, eds. and trans. 1972. *In Praise of the Baal Shem Tov (Shivhei ha-Besht): The Earliest Collection of Legends about the Founder of Hasidism*. Bloomington: Indiana University Press.

Beregovski, Moshe. 1982. *Old Jewish Folk Music: The Collections and Writings of Moshe Beregovski*, edited and translated by Mark Slobin. Philadelphia: University of Pennsylvania Press.

———. 2001. *Jewish Instrumental Folk Music: The Collections and Writings of Moshe Beregovski*, translated and edited by Mark Slobin, Robert A. Rothstein, and Michael Alpert. Syracuse, NY: Syracuse University Press.

Bernstein, Ignacy. 1908. *Jüdische Sprichwörter und Redensarten*. Frankfurt: J. Kauffmann.

Ginzberg, Louis. 1909–1938. *The Legends of the Jews*. 7 volumes. Philadelphia: Jewish Publication Society.

Kumove, Shirley. 1985. *Words like Arrows: A Collection of Yiddish Folk Sayings*. New York: Schocken.

———. 1999. *More Words, More Arrows: A Further Collection of Yiddish Folk Sayings*. Detroit: Wayne State University Press.

Lowenstein, Steven M. 2000. *The Jewish Cultural Tapestry: International Jewish Folk Traditions*. New York: Oxford University Press.

Matisoff, James A. 1979. *Blessings, Curses, Hopes, and Fears: Psycho-Ostensive Expressions in Yiddish*. Philadelphia: ISHI.

Mintz, Jerome. 1968. *The Legends of the Hasidim: An Introduction to Hasidic Culture and Oral Tradition in the New World*. Chicago: University of Chicago Press.

Mlotek, Eleanor Gordon, comp. 1977. *Mir trogn a gezang: Favorite Yiddish Songs of Our Generation*. 2nd ed. New York: Workmen's Circle.

Mlotek, Eleanor Gordon, and Joseph Mlotek, comps. 1988. *Pearls of Yiddish Song: Favorite Folk, Art and Theatre Songs*. New York: Workmen's Circle.

———. 1997. *Songs of Generations: New Pearls of Yiddish Song*. New York: Workmen's Circle.

Noy, Dov. 1971. Folklore. In *Encyclopaedia Judaica* 6. Jerusalem: Encyclopaedia Judaica/New York: Macmillan. 1374–1410.

Pollack, Herman. 1971. *Jewish Folkways in Germanic Lands (1648–1806): Studies in Aspects of Daily Life*. Cambridge, MA: MIT Press.

Roskies, Diane K., and David G. Roskies. 1975. *The Shtetl Book*. N.p.: KTAV.

Rubin, Ruth. 1973. *Voices of a People: The Story of Yiddish Folksong*. 2nd ed. New York: McGraw-Hill.

Schwarzbaum, Haim. 1968. *Studies in Jewish and World Folklore*. Berlin: Walter de Gruyter.

Slotnick, Susan A. 1976. *The Contributions of the Soviet Yiddish Folklorists*. New York: YIVO.

Tendlau, Abraham. 1860. *Sprichwörter und Redensarten deutsh-jüdischer Vorzeit*. Frankfurt: M. Keller.

Trachtenberg, Joshua. 1939. *Jewish Magic and Superstition: A Study in Folk Religion*. New York: Behrman.

Ungerleider-Mayerson, Joy. 1986. *Jewish Folk Art from Biblical Days to Modern Times*. New York: Summit.

Weinreich, Beatrice Silverman, ed. 1988. *Yiddish Folktales*. Translated by Leonard Wolf. New York: Pantheon.

Weinreich, Uriel, and Beatrice Weinreich. 1959. *Yiddish Language and Folklore: A Selective Bibliography for Research*. The Hague: Mouton.

Wischnitzer, Rachel. 1964. *The Architecture of the European Synagogue*. Philadelphia: Jewish Publication Society of America.

Yassif, Eli. 1986. *Jewish Folklore: An Annotated Bibliography*. New York: Garland.

Zborowski, Mark, and Elizabeth Herzog. 1995. *Life Is with People: The Culture of the Shtetl*, with a new introduction by Barbara Kirshenblatt-Gimblett. New York: Schocken.

Robert A. Rothstein

CROATIA

Ethnologists often assign Croatian folklore to three cultural zones—the Adriatic, the Dinaric, and the Pannonian—or four geographical regions—Littoral, Mountainous, Central, and Lowland Croatia.

LITTORAL CROATIA

In Littoral Croatia (or the Adriatic cultural zone) the way of life has emphasized fishing, cultivation of vineyards, olive groves, figs, and almonds, and shipbuilding and trade. The inhabitants grew vegetables in small fields located on terraces. They also collected wild plants and kept sheep and goats. The Mediterranean types of animal-yokes were used. Animal skins served for storage of water and wine and for making musical instruments. Wool was stamped with the feet. The clothing was simple but embellished with considerable jewelry. Traditional stone houses were often built close together in townships on defensible hillsides with stables located nearby. Stone slabs and later cylindrical tiles called *kupa* covered the roofs. People used open hearths and large earthenware or stone vessels for water and oil. There were also small houses with round floor plans made of stone without the use of mortar. Some of these remain in use. With their husbands away at sea—or in foreign countries as economic emigrants—women often undertook the work of men.

The traditional music of the northern Adriatic areas is characterized mainly by chromatic modes with successive approximate semi-tones or with an approximate whole tone between two semi-tones. Two-part singing in pairs—of the same or mixed genders—is realized by movement in parallel, somewhat narrower, minor thirds with a delayed unison ending at which the parts arrive by contrary motion. The inversions of these intervals—somewhat wider major sixths and octave ends—appear when the lead part is performed by the male singer accompanied by a female. Singers often insert vocables. Sometimes, the entire refrain—or the whole tune—is performed in this way. This manner of singing is called *tarankanje*.

Dances are frequently accompanied by two *sopila* or *roženica*, double-reed wind instruments that produce two-part music with the same tonal characteristics as singing. It is also customary to dance to the accompaniment of a *šurle* (a single-reed instrument with two separate chanters) or of a *mih* or *meh* (similar to the *diple na mješinu* bagpipe from the mountainous regions). In the inland northern part of Istria, an instrumental group called *gunjci* (made up of violin, clarinet, and two-stringed bass) or the *(h)armonika* (a diatonic accordion) may accompany dancing. The older

Croatia.

traditional music of the central and southern Adriatic is marked mainly by diatonic two-part singing of smaller range with delayed unison endings, while fifth endings (*na bas* singing) were added in the mid-1900s. In the south, around Dubrovnik, one-part singing is more common. More recent songs have characteristics of the major mode. Gradual descent from the seventh to the third degree is typical for the lead melody, which is in the upper part of these songs. They are performed in two parts (in parallel thirds) or as multi-part harmonics. The latter is known as *klapsko pjevanje* (*klapa* singing) because it is performed by a male group called a *klapa*, consisting of between four and eight singers. In the mid-nineteenth century this style of singing was practiced in urban centers, whence it was introduced into the villages during the twentieth century. Wide popularization of *klapa* singing is linked to the Dalmatian Klapa Festival in Omiš (established in 1967), where every year adaptations of traditional *klapa* songs as well as new compositions in this style are performed.

In the Dalmatian hinterland (particularly in the villages in Ravni Kotari), mute circle dances are performed with a six-part step structure. These also predominate in the dance repertoire of the islands in the Zadar and Ŝibenik archipelago. In the villages, dances are accompanied by the *mih* or *mišnjice* (bagpipe). The *lirica* or *lijerica*, found in the southern Adriatic region of Croatia and throughout the eastern Mediterranean, is a bowed instrument with a short neck and three strings, two for the melody and an open third string for the drone. The seated musician rests the *lirica* on his left knee while stamping out the beat with his right foot. The instrument is usually played to accompany the *poskočica* dance—also known as the *linđo*. In towns, mandolin ensembles accompany dances: the *šotić* (the *schottische*), *kvatropaše* (*Siebenschritt*), *furlana*, *valcer*, *manfrina*, *kvadrilja*, and *polka šaltina*.

The *tanac* dances are found on the islands along the entire Croatian coast as well as on the mainland near Dubrovnik. They are usually danced to *mijeh* (bagpipe) accompaniment. Dancing in a circle alternates with dancing in two lines facing each other and with dancing in couples around the circle. Various figures are performed by couples: the female dancers often rotate intensively, while the male dancers make fast, mincing steps, sometimes clapping their hands. The island *tanac* is similar to the *balun* dance in Istria and to the *hrvatski tanac* or *mišnjača* in the Lika region.

Reports from the fifteenth century describe the dances performed by shoemakers with arches, staves, and kerchiefs in Dubrovnik. These were similar to the chain sword dances that were fashionable throughout Europe during the sixteenth and seventeenth centuries and that were also performed in Dalmatian towns. They have survived on the Pelješac Peninsula and on the islands of Lastovo and Korčula. Another sword dance from the Mediterranean past, the *Moreška* (*moresca*), is also performed in the town of Korčula.

MOUNTAINOUS CROATIA

Mountainous Croatia (or the Dinaric cultural zone) has a stony terrain partly covered with forests. The highland livestock-raising was of the Alpine type: during the winter, the entire population moved to lowland villages with their animals. Along with this Alpine type, the transhumant method of stock-raising was also known. It was characterized by extensive sheep-rearing, without collection of hay, at only a single location—not two as in the Alpine type. Only the shepherds and the sheep went high into the mountain meadows in summer or to the warm, coastal areas during the winter. The inhabitants also made their living by tilling small plots of land with the aid of simple implements or by cutting timber and carting the logs from the forests. In the past they were mostly graziers, shepherds, and warriors on the long Turkish border. In mountainous Croatia, lambs were grilled on the spit for the major holidays. The houses were made of logs with steep roofs covered with shingles, and the social organization was more patriarchal than in other Croatian regions. Wool cloth was used for making clothing. Typical head-covers were small, round, flat red caps with a tassel. Women wore woolen aprons woven on the vertical looms, while the men tucked their weapons into wide leather belts. There was considerable leisure time for music-making, woodcarving, and knitting.

The older traditional music of the Dalmatian hinterland and the Lika region is characterized by a narrow-interval style: tunes are based on chromatic modes of narrow range, with intervals that deviate from the tempered system. In two-part singing, drone accompaniments and intervals of the second frequently appear. The parts also conclude in the interval of the second. Short songs in ten-syllable couplets are performed in a style of singing usually known as *ojkanje* and characterized by performing longer or shorter melisma, sometimes with sharp and prolonged shaking of the voice on "*oj*," "*hoj*," "*voj*," "*ej*," or "*aj*" syllables (pronouncing the "j" as "y" in English). *Ojkanje* is practiced outdoors and is considered to have pre-Slavic origins. It appears as the solo singing of lone travelers (*putničko*) or in two-part tunes (*vojkavica*, *treskavica*, *rera*, *ganga*, and *rozgalica*). *Ojkanje* is also known in Bosnia, and similar singing styles exist in the mountainous regions of **Albania**, Bulgaria, **Greece**, and **Turkey**.

Heroic deeds are extolled in songs and in epic poems—sung or recited. Narrative songs (epics and ballads) are performed by individual singers who often direct their gaze at a handheld book as an aid to concentration, since the songs are long and sung from memory. The most famous performers of epic songs are the *guslari*, singers who accompany themselves on the *gusle*, a bowed single-stringed chordophone found widely throughout the Balkans. The *guslari* perform all the verses, improvising two basic recitative melody sections. The instrumental melody is similar to the vocal one. In the past, the *guslari* were privileged and highly respected members of their communities.

The *diple* is a widely distributed single-reed instrument with a double chanter, the older type of which produced one-part music. Newer *diples* can produce two-part music. It is frequently attached to a bellows and is then called *diple na mješinu* or *mih*. This kind of bagpipe without a drone is also found all along the Adriatic coast and on the islands. It is played by shepherds, but also at parties and sometimes as an accompaniment to dancing.

Newer layers of music, especially in the Lika region, are characterized by diatonic tunes using the *na bas* singing style. Musicians also use the solo-*tambura*, called the *danguba*, to accompany their own singing. The old mute circle dance (*nijemo kolo*) without musical accompaniment is typical of the dance repertoire of the mountainous region. The *nijemo kolo* has a six-part dance pattern. In step structure, this dance is almost identical to the *kolo* from the Faroe Islands, which is performed to the singing of ballads, and to the Arab dance, the *dabke*. The dance is performed in large steps and leaps. The main accompaniment is the clanging of the women's jewelry and the deep breathing of the dancers. The circle dance can be open or enclosed, and couples can separate from the group. The circle form has been almost completely lost in some areas so that what is, in fact, dancing by couples has retained only the *kolo* name.

CENTRAL CROATIA

The landscape of Central Croatia (which corresponds to the western part of the Pannonian cultural zone) consists of hilly areas and river valleys with larger villages and small towns along the roads and many smaller hamlets. Along the Kupa and Sava Rivers, pile-dwellings once prevailed. The influence of Central Europe as well as that from other Croatian regions is strong. Corn and hemp are grown, cattle and horses are raised, and the region is known for its viticulture of the Continental type. Poultry was the usual choice for the roast meat prepared for the festivities in the past. This is still seen in the popularity of turkey on such occasions. In Central Croatia textile production and other craft activities occurred. Family unity was more pronounced in this region than elsewhere.

In music, diatonic tunes prevail, mainly in tetrachordal to hexachordal tone ranges, sometimes with changeable degrees (for example, a major and minor third above the root tone). Melodies usually conclude on the second degree, which can also be the root tone. Apart from unison tunes—mainly in ritual songs—there are two-part songs with unison endings in the older tradition or in the interval of the major third and perfect fifth in the newer tradition. The newer repertoire includes tunes that tend to be, or already are, in major mode. There are various wind instruments of the flute type: the *žvegla* or the *frula* (the duct flute), the *dvojnice* or *dvojke* (the double-duct flute), and various others made as souvenirs and toys in the shapes of birds, fish, hammers, and walking sticks. In the nineteenth century and at the beginning of the twentieth century, dances in the Bilogora and Moslavina areas were accompanied by the *dude* bagpipe with a triple chanter. The *guci* instrumental groups consisting of two *gusle* (violins in this case) and a *bajs* (a bass played with a bow), sometimes together with a *cimbal* (dulcimer), were typical of the entire region. In the first half of the twentieth century they were joined and/or replaced by various kinds of *tambura*, which spread from eastern Croatia (Slavonia).

In the performance of dances with obvious Central European influences, dancers tend to rotate quickly. The couples spin intensively, even in not exclusively couple dances but also, for example, in the *drmeš*. The *drmeš* is often done in smaller or larger circles. This is the best-known and most popular dance in northwestern Croatia, and two basic dance figures are performed. The first is done in small steps with relatively little movement through the dance area but with marked vertical shaking of the entire body. In the second figure, the dancers rotate at unusual speed. It is believed that *drmeš* adopted some elements of an older dance, the *tanac*, which was widely performed in the nineteenth century and is similar in some details to the Hungarian *czardas*.

The *dučec*, *kozatuš*, and *staro sito* are performed in northwestern Croatia and are characterized by energetic jumping. In the past they were connected with fertility cults and had parallels in other European countries. These dances are performed on the stage, as part of festival performances, or during Carnival. Circle *kolo* dances (usually at Easter and during the customs of the spring cycle, around bonfires, and around the tables at weddings) accompanied by the singing of ballad verses were well known as the older layer of dance repertoire until the end of the nineteenth century in Hrvatsko Zagorje and Međimurje. With the penetration of couple dances from the northwest, circle dances lost popularity, though they predominate among the dances of the Pannonian part of Croatia.

LOWLAND CROATIA

Lowland Croatia is situated in the eastern Continental part of the country and is the richer, eastern part of the Pannonian cultural zone. Great plains with very fertile soil and lowland forests watered by the Danube, Drava, and Sava Rivers dominate the landscape. The agriculture is based on wheat, corn, and sunflowers, and the people raise pigs, cattle, and horses. As in Central Croatia, houses were built at ground level and made of clay or unbaked bricks, though one-story log cabins are also common. They had three rooms: a main room, a kitchen, and a storage room. Sometimes there was a covered porch at the entrance on the broader side of the house. The roofs were usually covered with thatch. The villages were large with laid-out streets. Clothing was made largely of white hemp or linen cloth (later of cotton), and rich decorations were either woven, embroidered, or appliquéd onto it. People wore *opanci* (moccasins) or boots. Weaving on horizontal looms was a domestic craft, along with pottery made on foot-operated wheels. The mandatory roast meat prepared for the major festivities throughout the year was pork.

The music of the western part of the region is characterized by unison tunes with melodies of wide range, often based on medieval modes and on anhemitonic pentatonic scales. These tunes provide settings for various lyrical texts, with romantic love being the predominant theme. Until the beginning of the twentieth century, the *gajde*, a single-reed bagpipe with a double chanter and a drone pipe fixed to a bellows, and the *dude*, a bagpipe with a triple chanter, were the main instruments for dance accompaniment. In the western and northern regions, typical instruments include the *citura* in Podravina or the *trontolje* in Međimurje (bourdon box zithers) and the *cimbal* (dulcimer). Violins are preferred in the western parts, joined by the *cimbal* and *tambura* for chording accompaniment. The *tambura* ensembles predominate in the east. The *tambura* (or *tamburica*), a long-necked lute, came to the Balkans with the Turks in the fourteenth and fifteenth centuries. It was brought to the Slavonian areas in the seventeenth and eighteenth centuries. There it was gradually adopted as a folk instrument. It had transformed by the end of the nineteenth century into a Croatian national symbol, spread among the Croatian emigrant groups in Europe and elsewhere. At first it was played as a solo instrument (the *samica*), but from the mid-nineteenth century *tamburas* were also brought together in small groups. Today *tamburas* are widespread throughout Croatia, existing in various shapes with varying numbers of strings—usually four—and in various tunings. Twentieth-century *tambura* ensembles have prevailed in providing music for *kolo*-dancing, which was the center of village life even up to the 1950s. With its liveliness, song, and shouting dancers, it became the trademark of Slavonia—a symbol of regional identity.

In the eastern part of Lowland Croatia, diatonic two-part singing in tetrachordal to hexachordal tone ranges prevails. In addition to lyrical songs and ballads with longer texts, short songs are also typical. They are based on ten-syllable couplets, mostly of jocular character, and are performed in various contexts to various types of tunes (the *svatovac*, *bećarac*, and *poskočnica*). The relative prosperity of this region can be seen in the costume and jewelry, cuisine, and house furnishings and is reflected in the generous hospitality of the people and in the costly celebration of weddings, church holidays, and other festivities.

History

All these zones and regions are merely analytic categories: there are many transitional areas with no fixed boundaries. The intensive migrations, particularly during the Turkish conquests in Europe from the fifteenth century until the nineteenth century, have been the main contributor to the interweaving of types, the existence of transitional forms, and the high number of variants in Croatian folk culture. Moreover, Croatian oral literature cannot be framed by zones due to the uncertainty of the origins of the tales and motifs. One can speak only conditionally of the greater or lesser popularity of the individual oral literary genres in the various Croatian regions during a particular period. For example, epic poetry is encountered much more rarely in the Central and Lowland regions than in the Littoral and Mountainous regions. Although the types and motifs of fairy tales and other stories were largely international, the narrators gave them a personal, local, or national stamp. Historical and local particularities are found within internationally known narrative topics in Croatian stories. Actual historical characters appear—for example, Emperor Diocletian, Empress Maria Theresa, Emperor Joseph II, and Emperor Franz Joseph, along with Miho Pracat, a rich, transoceanic merchant from Dubrovnik. The narrator's actual experiences intertwine with fictitious elements drawn from the stories, particularly those about maritime adventures, sirens of the sea, monsters of the deep, and wonders seen in distant lands, all of which are retold in coastal Croatia. Actual historical events (for example, the sixteenth-century Peasant Uprising and wars conducted on Croatian territory) are seen and interpreted through the eyes of the folk narrator.

Theories abound as to the origin of the Croatian people. *De administrando imperio*, a work by the Byzantine emperor Constantine VII Porphyrogenitus from the tenth century, speaks of the arrival of the Croats from "White Croatia" (today's **Poland**) in Dalmatia in the seventh century. The oldest known stratum of the Croats is a group of militarily organized pastoralists and equestrians in the steppes between the Caspian Sea and the Sea of Azov. They joined Slavic tribes and adopted their language as they migrated to the shores of the Adriatic and mixed with the indigenous peoples, who were the inheritors of a culture brought by Greek and Roman colonists as well as by the Huns, the Langobardians, and the Avars who passed through the area and left remnants of their own lives as they pillaged the Roman Empire. These events divide

Zagreb Folk Festival, Zagreb, Croatia. (© Hideo Haga/HAGA/The Image Works)

Croatian history into three phases: their nomadic, non-Slavic life; their movement westward; and their integration into militarily superior native alliances. One of these tribes identified as Croatian emerged during the fifth century and settled from the Carpathian foothills to almost as far as Prague. The population was mainly Slavic peasants with a highly developed grain-growing culture, who were familiar with a complex plow and the enclosed stable livestock-raising methods. They lived in villages in houses of various types and wore white linen clothing, decorated with interwoven and stitched-on ornamentation.

During the seventh century, a large group broke away from the Carpathian Croats and moved south to the former Illyrium. As allies of the Byzantine emperor against the Avar tribes, they were permitted to settle along the coast of the Adriatic Sea. A tenth-century legend about the migration of the Croats to their present homeland, led by five brothers and two sisters, is the oldest written testimony to Croatian oral traditions. Legends about the origin and names of individual settlements date from very early times (the twelfth century to the fourteenth century), and the continuity of these legends has been preserved. Medieval chronicles of the Dalmatian towns and religious tracts in Latin, Italian, and Croatian present legends about the miracles of the patron saints of the Dalmatian towns.

Due to their conversion to Christianity, the indigenous pagan worldview of the Croats is difficult to reconstruct. Old myths lost their contextual links and began to be transformed into traditional poems and narratives. The world of mythic creatures has survived, however, and is very much alive and present in Croatian oral narratives, with notable regional variations. The *coprnice* (enchantresses) and *grabancijaši* (sorcerers' apprentices) of northwestern Croatia differ from the *vještice* (witches), *svećice* (will-o'-the wisps), *more* (hobgoblins), *dobrice* (fairies), *sudenice* (fairy godmothers, well intended and not so well intended, who appear at a baby's birth), and *vijori* (evil wind spirits) from Slavonia. To cite another example of regional distinctiveness, the Istrian and coastal *krsnici* (elves) usually conduct their nocturnal battles with the *štriguni* (goblins) only in the northern part of the Adriatic.

Pagan rituals were given Christian or historical explanations and transformed into contemporary folk customs. In the stock-raising regions we still find at Carnival groups of masked men in costumes made of animal skins with bells tied to their belts (for example, *zvončari*, *buđe*, *naphanci*, and *didi*). Although the details differ, particularly in the head masks made of leather, wood, and sometimes animal horns, these archaic, noisy, and aggressive Carnival personages have many relatives throughout the Mediterranean region. Sometimes two men dressed in shabby clothing, imitating the sexual act—*djed/did* and *baba* (Grandpa and Grandma)—appear with them.

Magical beliefs are connected with birth. A host of fantastic creatures influence the fate and health of a baby and hamper its sleep at night. Many important moments connected with the good health or illness of a small child, the loss of a child's milk teeth, and so on were accompanied with words, rhythmical sentences, and verses, likely preserving remnants of magical formulas. Likewise, the various games, songs, and stories of children, many of them akin to theater, are believed to be remnants of ancient initiation rituals, though these games are today disappearing. Songs, toasts, and dialogues connected with the conclusion of marriages originated in part from pre-Christian ritual. Games and dramatic performances reflecting local, regional, and national identity might be incorporated into traditional weddings. In the twentieth century, this resulted in the public staging of weddings, thus creating a popular theater genre. Death requires certain rules of behavior. Laments, dirges, and graveside eulogies are common, as are wakes, which provide an opportunity for stories, games, and jokes.

The Carnival season includes processions, the wearing of masks, acting, and song and dance as well as the judgment and sentencing of the dummy and messages written on the sides of carts in the parades. In some places, a group of men in costume act out the guarding of Christ's tomb. Still today in many places in the Adriatic region, members of the processions perform *Gospin plač* (Our Lady's Weeping) as a continuation of the tradition of medieval dialogical poems and sacred drama.

Songs and performances in processions are often connected with specific days throughout the year, particularly patron saints' days. Croatians hold a particular affinity for Sts. George, Philip, and James, John the Baptist, Luke, Martin, Nicholas, Andrew, Barbara, Lucia, and Stephen. St. Martin's Day, traditionally the day on which must transforms into wine, still includes the parodic scene of the baptism of the wine. Songs sung in the processions are sometimes called *koleda*-songs, but this term is usually limited to those sung in the processions between Christmas Eve and Epiphany. All *koleda*-songs praise members of the households where they are being sung and wish them fertility and prosperity. In addition to the verbal magical formulas connected with Christmas Eve, Christmas Day, and Epiphany, northern areas of Croatia observe *koleda* drama performances such as *Adam i Eva*, *Betlehemari*, and *Kriskindli*, which today are largely performed only by children in house-to-house processions.

After the Schism in 1054, the Croats sided with the Western Church, accepted the Latin script, and participated in the development of feudal society. An upper class of feudal lords also developed, adopting the aristocratic court culture of the European West and that of the clergy. Many legends and stories recorded from the Middle Ages until the late Baroque period were designed to stimulate religious piety among priests and laity. The contents of many of these stories were first heard as sermons, which were then adopted and passed on largely in oral form. *Plačevi*, passion poems and dramas, poems about conflicts of the soul and the body, or those about the final, terrible Judgment Day continue to echo through oral performances.

During the fifteenth century, the humanist movement gained strength in urban cultural circles and brought the Renaissance to the coastal cities of Croatia. Data on Croatian oral lyrical poems exist from that time. A court document about the trial of witches in Öibenik in 1443 contains a Latin translation of oral formulas associated with love spells, while the first known notations of oral lyric verses in the Croatian language are found on the fragment of a mocking poem in a complaint made by the Gučetić family to the city judges of Dubrovnik in 1462. Some twenty years later, Juraj Šižgorić, a Šibenik humanist, was one of the first scholars in Europe to collect sayings and translate them into Latin. However, at that time the Turkish forces began to penetrate into Croatian territory. It was only with the victory of the Christian army near Sisak in 1593 that the Ottoman advance was halted, and this was followed by a century of uncertain peace. Some of the Croats living in the occupied regions adopted the Islamic faith, while around a third of the Croatian inhabitants left their homes. They were replaced by the Turkish army with Orthodox *Vlasi*, or Wallachs, who had originally been Romanized Balkan settlers. Some of the Croats migrated to **Italy**, some to what is now **Slovenia**, and others to **Hungary**, **Slovakia**, Lower **Austria**, and Moravia. Descendants of these refugees live throughout these parts of Europe, and they still speak a variant of the Croatian language. The first *bugarštica*—as the specific 15/16 syllabic line in medieval balladry is called—was noted down in Croatian colonies in the south of Italy in 1497.

Croatian Renaissance literature drew its verses and motifs from oral tradition. The popular poems written in the *canzoniere* collections have been preserved, and they included poems in the folk style. The works of the leading Croatian writers of that time included inserted sayings, riddles, conundrums, toasts, homages, and *bugarštica* ballads all borrowed from oral tradition. We find echoes of legends, most of which explain the origins of localities and their names. Many themes and motifs in the living oral literature of that time were transferred to writing and thus preserved and often re-entered oral tradition. In this sense, the slave-girl motif is especially interesting. More recent literary and historical research has uncovered the motif of the female captive (typical for the old Mediterranean sword dance, the *moresca*) in early Croatian literature. The slave-girl character resembles that of the fairy and of men dressed as women in the Carnival and spring processions. This hints at a pre-Christian ritual stratum and the influence of Slavic *koleda* customs and medieval *Kalendae Januariae* customs, while also demonstrating the merging of the cultures of the landed gentry and of the masses, particularly in southern Croatia.

Other seventeenth- and eighteenth-century documentation of Croatian folklore includes the work of the Italian travel writer Alberto Fortis, who influenced the European literary fashion of *Morlacchism* by describing customs and writing down poems he encountered. Andrija Kačić Miošić's work *Razgovor ugodni naroda slovinskoga* (The Pleasant Conversation of the Slavic Folk), written in 1756, was inspired by oral ten-syllable epic poetry. Some of his poems appeared in several important European publications of that time.

Croatian epic poetry cannot be easily distinguished from the body of southern Slavic epics with which it shares many formal characteristics as well as some of the epic heroes (for example, Janko of Sibinj, Prince Marko, Ban Derenčin, and Ivo of Senj). Croatian epic poetry thrived in the period from the seventeenth to the nineteenth centuries and for a long time was the favored genre of the Southern Slavs, as it dealt with their struggle against the Turks.

Turkish influence in Croatian folk culture is more visible in the eastern part of the Pannonian zone and in the Dinaric zone. It is evident in *lexis*, crafts, costume, foodways, and the appearance and equipment of houses and villages. During the Turkish occupation, part of Istria and the coastal strip of Dalmatia (the Dubrovnik Republic) were free and independent areas, while some parts were under the authority of the Venetian Republic. The western part of the Pannonian region was within the Habsburg Monarchy. Christian authorities set up the so-called Military Border—the *confinium militare*. Rather than being serfs, the rural population there was organized along military lines, and even today one can see differences between "border" and "civil" villages.

At the end of the seventeenth century, withdrawal of the Turkish army from Slavonia (the Pannonian zone) caused another wave of migrations. The Islamic Croatian inhabitants of Slavonia pulled back into Bosnia, while the Roman Catholic Croatian population from Bosnia settled in Christian countries, mainly in the Danube Basin region. Austrian authorities modernized education and improved agricultural methods first in the Military Border and then in Civil Croatia and Dalmatia. They organized colonization of the fertile flatlands of eastern Croatia by Germans, Czechs, and Slovaks. After the Croatian *ban* (governor), Josip Jelačić, abolished serfdom in the Croatian countryside in 1848, large extended family households (*zadruga*) and their properties began to disintegrate. Throughout Slavonia, foreign interests, primarily Germans and Hungarians, bought up this property. Gradual industrialization began. The peasants had to move into the towns or emigrate. In 1878 the Habsburg Monarchy occupied Bosnia-Herzegovina, and in 1881 the territory of the former Military Border was restored to Civil Croatia. At the end of the nineteenth century, rural production became oriented toward the market. Traditional costume was worn only on special occasions. New buildings on many smaller farms changed the structure of settlements. Peasants went to work in the factories and mines, while their families continued to live on small village properties, leading to a new distribution of roles within families. There were also changes in dance **repertoire** in the second half of the nineteenth and the twentieth centuries. Central European influences are now most obvious in the couple dances (*mazurka*, *valcer*, *polka*, *schottische*, *siebenschritt*, *rašpa*, *štajeriš*, *furlana*, and *palaisglais*) in northwestern, northern, and central Croatia and in Istria and the Gulf of Quarnero region. These dances are also readily recognizable under their local names in other parts of Croatia.

At the end of World War I, Croatia became part of the newly created Serbian-dominated state of Yugoslavia. The new borders separated Croatia from Central Europe and opened the way to powerful cultural and political influences from the Balkans. The efforts at "Serbinization" created strong opposition in Croatia, led by the Croatian Peasant Party. Croatian politicians found the symbols of national identity in the Croatian peasantry. Therefore, a cultural movement developed among the peasants to preserve—and sometimes revive—the visible features of traditional peasant culture. All regions organized "authentic" Croatian festivals. However, political gains disappeared during World War II, which raged in Croatia from 1941 until 1945. After the war, the revolutionary nature of the new order was expressed in the destruction of the old system of values. The attempt at collectivization of villages according to the Soviet model was a failure. Despite the slogans about the unity of the peasants and the industrial workers, the peasants, who were attached to tradition, came under constant suspicion. The stance of the authorities toward religion deprived people of numerous symbols and festivities. There was a popularization of Balkan foods and music. The process of abandoning the traditional rural culture continued with the introduction of electric power, motor vehicles, and electronic media. From the 1970s, people were permitted to go abroad as "guest workers," and this brought additional changes. Events during the last decade of the twentieth century such as the independence of Croatia and the liberation from totalitarian ideologies also produced new migrations and changes. Almost one-quarter of Croatian territory was completely devastated during the war between 1991 and 1995. The cultural response to the new situation is visible in the change of symbols, in a gradual return to traditional values, and in a clear emphasis on religious, national, and regional identity. To gain independence and to enter the period of transition in the era of globalization is a challenge for Croatia. However, the traditional way of life and the traditional rural culture cannot be renewed. Today's scholars do not focus exclusively upon the past but do research in the urban centers, too, examining graffiti, music, poems, and songs based on traditional models, echoes of early and contemporary legends, rumors, life stories, tales about local events, jokes, accounts from, and responses to, topics from the mass media, and the tragic stories of the very real experiences of internally displaced persons and refugees.

BIBLIOGRAPHY

Bezić, Jerko. 1974. Hrvatska muzika. Narodna. In *Muzička enciklopedija 2*. Zagreb: Jugoslavenski leksikografski zavod. 168–175.

Bošković-Stulli, Maja. 1978. Usmena knjiæevnost. In *Povijest hrvatske knjiæevnosti*. Zagreb: Liber-Mladost. 325–335.

Freudenreich, Aleksandar. 1972. *Kako narod gradi napodručju Hrvatske*. Zagreb: Republički zavod za zaštitu spomenika kulture.

Gavazzi, Milovan. 1939. *Godina dana hrvatskih narodnih običaja, I. od poklada do jeseni*. Zagreb: Matica hrvatska.

———. 1988 (1939). *Godina dana hrvatskih narodnih obiËaja, II. Oko Božiča*. Zagreb: Matica hrvatska.

Radauš-Ribarić, Jelka. 1975. *Narodne nošnje Hrvatske*. Zagreb: Jugoslavenska akademija znanosti i umjetnosti.

Rihtman-Auguštin, Dunja. 1988. *Etnologija naše svakodnevice*. Zagreb: kolska knjiga.

———. 1996. *Christmas in Croatia*. Zagreb: Golden Marketing.

Vitez, Zorica. 2000. *Croatian Folk Culture at the Crossroads of Worlds and Eras*. Zagreb: Gallery Klovičevi dvori.

Ivan Lozica

GEORGIA

GEOGRAPHY AND HISTORY

Bounded on the west by the Black Sea, on the north by the Caucasus Range, on the east by the Caspian lowland, and on the south by the Lesser Caucasus Range, Georgia has a rugged landscape, two-thirds of it mountainous. The climate is marked by diversity. Georgian territory includes almost all climatic zones of the planet, ranging from humid subtropical to the belt of eternal snow and glaciers. Thus, the geography of Georgia has naturally made for the complex character of the country's social, economic, and cultural structure.

From its geographic situation, cultural and economic potential, and mode of life, Georgia was from the beginning perceived as a constituent part of ancient European civilization. In fact, in his *History* Herodotos set the northern boundary of the world settled by human beings at the mountains of the Greater Caucasus Range.

Georgia.

In the Georgian language, "Georgia" is called *Sakartvelo*, which means literally "the land of *Kartvels*," or Georgians. The word *Kartvel* was early used to denote a group of people who inhabited part of what is present-day Georgia. Later, as a result of the political changes occurring in the country, the term came to denote the peoples residing in the territory of the same country united to form a common culture. The term "Kartvelian languages" refers to genetically related languages: Georgian, Svan, and Zan (Megrelian and Laz). These languages stem from a single parent language called proto-Kartvelian. The genesis of the proto-Kartvelian language is related to the problem of the provenance of the Georgians. Many scholars consider Georgians to be the ancient indigenous population of the Caucasus. Bearing in mind that the most ancient remains of humans have been discovered in present-day Georgia, it makes sense to view the Georgians as the cultural inheritors of the early inhabitants of the Caucasus.

Ushguli village, Svaneti.

Comparative analysis of Kartvelian languages shows that the group initially considered to be predecessors of current Svan-speakers must have been the first to settle the northwestern region of Georgia. This may have occurred as early as the second millennium B.C.E. The separation of the Zan and Georgian languages probably occurred in the first millennium B.C.E. The Zan tribes settled in the western and northwestern Black Sea lowlands as well as in nearly mountainous areas. Other ethno-geographical entities who settled in Georgia include the Imereti, Guria, Racha, Lechkhumi, Inner and Lower Kartli, Khevsureti, Pshavi, Tusheti, Khevi, Mtiuleti, Ertso-Tianeti, Kakheti, Saingilo, Samtskhe, Javakheti, Trialeti, Achara, and Klarjeti. Their territories correspond to where their languages and dialects are spoken. In addition to their contributions to Georgian national identity, each group has preserved its distinctive culture to some degree. Topographical and climatic factors such as isolation due to heavy winter snowfalls in mountainous areas have contributed to the preservation of cultural distinctiveness.

SCOPE AND THEMES OF GEORGIAN FOLKLORE

The scope of Georgian folklore depends on whether one is referring to a nation or a linguistic entity. If we compare Georgian-language materials with those of other languages, then the meaning of the concept "Georgian" becomes narrower, denoting only folklore created in the Georgian language. From another perspective, the concept "Georgian folklore" might encompass the folklore of the Megrels, the Laz, and the Svan, as well as that of other Georgian peoples. In this case consideration is given not only to linguistic relationships but also to the genetic and typological connections between the folklores created in the languages in question.

Following the proclamation of Christianity as the official religion in the fourth century, indigenous religions became the target of persecution. Historical sources report belief in gods whose names have, for the most part, not survived in popular memory. Some of these deities have been assimilated by Christianity. Most scholars assume, for example, that the god of the moon, whose worship must have been spread throughout Georgia, was subsequently supplanted by St. George, the foremost Christian saint of the Georgians.

Ancient beliefs and notions based on pre-Christian thought have survived as a relatively ordered system among the mountain population of Eastern Georgia (chiefly in Pshavi and Khevsureti). However, according to one view, these beliefs must have taken shape in these regions as a result of the weakening of the role of the official church, automatically leading to Christianity "turning folk" and closer to indigenous belief systems. According to beliefs current in the mountain region of Eastern Georgia, everything in the world is ruled by an ordaining god. He has his royal tent pitched above the Gergeti, one of the peaks of the Caucasus Range, in the seventh heaven. The god-ordainer sends his sons to earth, entrusting their guidance and help to Kviria, the steward of land who is hierarchically one step lower. Thus, while the other sons of the god are communal and tribal gods, Kviria—along with the father god—is a common god for all. The god's children are charged with protecting their serfs from the *devis* (ogres). According to Georgian mythology, the ogres are zoomorphic beings who abduct humans or force the population to give them tribute in the form of a beautiful woman. They are characterized by crude physical force, possess considerable treasure, especially cattle, and know the secret of blacksmithing. After a long fight the god's children finally force the ogres to leave the habitation of humans and to settle in the netherworld.

The storming of Kajaveti, a chthonic world populated with mythical beings and inaccessible to people, is also linked with the name of the god's children. The raid resulted in carrying away a treasure—cultural values—from Kajaveti. According to different versions, these included such items as silver cups, a measuring vessel, gold *panduri* (a stringed musical instrument), anvil and hammer, razor, and pearls.

Individual elements of pre-Christian belief have survived abundantly in cultic life. Distinctive among them is the belief in mythical creatures, some of which function as branch deities. In various regions of Georgia, different beings are named as shepherds of beasts. They differ in both name and external features as well as sex. Most perfect among them is the image of the goddess Dali, preserved in Svan oral traditions. According to these stories, Dali is of extraordinary beauty; her appearance is accentuated by her long golden hair. She dwells among high rocks. A hunter who encounters Dali by chance becomes especially privileged. He slaughters many animals, receives from her a valuable present in the form of a ring or bead, and enjoys her support. However, the hunter is bound to observe the taboo of not revealing the real cause of his success at risk of being punished with death. In Megrelian folklore Dali has her counterpart, Tqashmapa ("queen of the woods"). Her outward features are beauty, long hair, and nudity. Usually, she asks a hunter to sleep with her, promising him permanent lucky hunting as a reward. The situation is the same here: the hunter must not betray the secret of his liaison with Tqashmapa. A hunter who fails to keep his word is turned into stone together with his hounds. According to some traditions, if the hunter's wife or some other member of his family bathes Tqashmapa in milk, she will relinquish her claims on the hunter.

Megrelian folklore also has traditions of the Mesepis. According to these stories, the chief function of the Mesepis is to allot a beast to a hunter. This is the animal eaten by the Mesepis the previous year and then restored from its bones and skin. Once a year, the Mesepis come out of the sea for one week: one year female Mesepis, and the next year male Mesepis. Besides Svaneti and Samegrelo, oral traditions about patrons of beasts occur throughout Georgia. In Kakheti and Khevsureti, for example, the guardian of beasts is called Ochopintre or Ochopinte. At some places, other mythical creatures combine the same function. Such are the *eshmaki* (demons) that, according to some legends, first devour the beast and then restore it from the bones and skin, allotting it to a particular hunter for slaughter. Besides Dali, the male Apsati also appears in Svaneti folklore. The Christian St. George may also fill the role of guardian of beasts.

Among traditions of mythic content are short, simple stories about various evil spirits such as the Ochokochi, whose name is a compound corresponding in Megrelian to "he-goat" and "man." According to the existing stories, the Ochokochis have no special function. They wander in the woods, scaring the hunters or shepherds they encounter with their appearance. According to some traditions, the Ochokochi chases the Tqashmapa in order to have sexual intercourse with her. Often, a Tqashmapa, harassed by the Ochokochi, is protected by a hunter. The Georgian Ochokochi finds clear parallels with Pan in Greek mythology.

Alongside gods protecting animals, other names of specialized gods are known in Georgia, together with short, ritual texts performed in their honor. Among them are Boseli, protector of domestic animals, and Aguna, guardian of wine and vine-growing.

Amirani has special significance in Georgian mythology. According to the Svan version, Amirani is the son of Dali, the goddess of beasts, and an unknown hunter. The hunter meets Dali in a cave and falls in love with her. The hunter's wife learns the story and kills Dali by cutting her hair while she sleeps. At Dali's death, the hunter extracts from her womb a boy whom he calls Amirani. This child bears marks of his divine origin: representations of the sun and the moon on his shoulder blades and a golden tooth. Amirani is stalwart and physically strong.

Amirani fights against evil beings, giants, and dragons. In these battles he is aided by his sworn brothers Badri and Usup. One of the important episodes of the legend treats Amirani's love for Kamar, daughter of the master of the sky, and their elopement or her abduction by Amirani, which mirrors the theft of fire from Heaven. Kamar lives in a crystal tower suspended from Heaven, surrounded by magic objects. The master of skies learns about the elopement of Amirani and Kamar from the tower by means of the fragments of a magic bowl broken by Amirani. Amirani fights the master of skies, who is in pursuit, and defeats him. He is aided by Kamar, who identifies the part of her father's body where Amirani can deliver a mortal wound. Ultimately, Amirani challenges God (or, according to the Christianized versions, Jesus) to single combat. For this God chains him to an iron stake in a cave in the rocks of the Caucasus Mountains. God orders an eagle to tear daily at his liver. Amirani's faithful dog never leaves him, licking the chain permanently. Through this licking the chain grows so thin during the year that it is on the point of breaking. But then the smiths strike the anvil with their hammer, healing the chain. This recurs annually on Holy Thursday.

THEMES AND MOTIFS IN FOLKTALES AND FAIRY TALES

Georgian folklore is rich in fairy tales. This genre is especially popular in lowland Georgia, both in its western and eastern parts. In the high mountain zone except for Svaneti, fairy tales are seldom told. But the fairy tale continues to live on actively in Georgian folklore. Quite a few storytellers, especially in the countryside, have fairly rich repertoires of fairy tales. Telling a fairy tale has not always been dictated by gratifying one's literary interests, and in some cases performance of a fairy tale is of a ritual character. Thus, in Svaneti a tradition called *lipanali* survives to the present day. For the duration of a week, each family hosts the ghosts of dead relatives, entertaining them by telling them fairy tales. The ghosts are said to enjoy listening to fairy tales, thus favorably disposing them toward the living.

Scholars have noted 176 original fairy tale types and sub-types in Georgia. In general, Caucasia—like other mountainous areas such as the Carpathians and the Alps—is a region distinguished for its ethnic pluralism. The variety of ethnic groups probably contributes to the diversity in the Georgian fairy tale repertoire. It is also significant that its geographical location as intermediary between east and west has made Georgia an area of contact between different cultures. Whether these contacts involved cooperation or confrontation may be revealed through comparative analysis of fairy tales.

Georgian folklore is rich in such themes as hospitality, heroism, chivalry, and love. Traditions of Georgian kings hold a significant place in the folklore repertoire, for Georgia has a long-standing history as a state. The oldest folklore dealing with Georgian royalty is the legend of King Parnavaz (third century B.C.E.). The legend tells of the king's miraculous dream, his hunting, and the discovery of a treasure hidden in a cave. A historical source of the same period contains a legend on the provenance of the Georgian royal dynasty from the biblical King David. The legend of the bringing of Jesus's tunic to Georgia and its burial there is also recorded in the same period.

Especially popular and varied are the legends of Queen Tamar—a reflection of Georgia's unprecedented development during her reign (1178–1213). Furthermore, her position as a female monarch is itself extraordinary in the world of her times. Her status is reflected thematically in the folklore about her. For example, she keeps the star that brings winter in custody, and hence it is always spring in her kingdom. Similar motifs surround David the Builder (1089–1125), who imprisoned the Devil and forced him to aid in building churches. Georgian folklore assigns miraculous features to other Georgian kings as well. Thus, King Vakhtang Gorgasali (fifth century C.E.) hears the bells tolling from Heaven, while King Solomon (1752–1784) is given the crown directly by God from Heaven because of his Christian modesty and love for his neighbors.

Owing to its geopolitical situation, Georgia was forced to wage continuous warfare with its near or distant neighbors, and an appreciation of the fatherland's defenders resulted in the predominance of the heroic-chivalrous theme in Georgian folklore. The ideal of Georgian heroic poetry is a brave "good warrior" whose foremost duty is to defend his fatherland, his neighborhood, widows, and orphans—in general, victims of violence. Such a hero often devotes his entire conscious life to the service of this ideal. This is reflected in his voluntary refusal to marry since marriage may inhibit his performing his knightly mission. However, one martial song says:

> He is glad to go to war who has a good horse;
> Returning home gladdens him who has a good wife.

Taking part in chivalrous single combat and dying honorably rather than shamefully compromising to save one's life are the principal motif of Georgian heroic folk poetry. This motif is most pronounced in the ballad "The Tiger and the Hunter." A young hunter encounters a tiger. Neither wants to give way, and in an uncompromising fight they slaughter each other. In the second part of the ballad, considered to be a later addition, the mother of the hero equally mourns her son and his adversary, offering condolences to the tiger's mother for the loss of her worthy offspring.

Georgian folk lyrics assign special place to amorous and philosophical themes. The philosophical lyrics deal particularly with the theme of life and death. Although songs on this theme are often poles apart in their mood, according to Georgian folklore, preference is given to optimism and building:

> This fleeting world is like this: night is lighted by day.
> What hostility has destroyed is built up by love.

The chief purpose of living in this world is to win fame or to do good. One needs fame both to bequeath to posterity and as a basis for entering Heaven. However, it should be noted that, according to folk poetry, a Georgian man, notwithstanding his Christian faith, does not spend much time thinking about heavenly bliss. Moreover, he calls Heaven "land of blackness"—a place where there is no joy. This attitude becomes more pronounced in epitaphs, which often offer reminders of the futility of life. Such inscriptions are found abundantly on gravestones adorned with relief representations in all parts of Georgia.

Examples of Georgian folk poetry on the theme of love are inexhaustible. According to the tradition, pre-marital sex was strictly forbidden in Georgia. Besides, although the free choice of the boy and the girl largely formed the basis of establishing a home, more often than not if the parents opposed the marriage because of economic or other considerations, the young couple was forced to give up their choice. This likely contributed to the power and ardor of feeling in songs created on the theme of love.

The legend of Abesalom and Eteri, a monument of Georgian folk love epics, attracts attention by its delicacy of feeling, the complexity of its characters, and its developing tragedy. The prince Abesalom and his vizier Murman simultaneously fall in love with beautiful Eteri, a common girl. She and Abesalom swear eternal love for each other. The chagrined Murman sells himself to the Devil to gain the hand of the desired Eteri. During the wedding Murman throws the millet given to him by the Devil at Eteri. As a result the girl becomes infected with lice. Only Murman, using powers given him by the Devil, can heal Eteri. Although he gains possession of her, he fails to win Eteri's love. Abesalom, left alone, falls mortally sick. Neither the water of immortality or Eteri's visit can save him. Abesalom is unable to avoid fate as he quietly dies. Eteri, who has no link left with this world after Abesalom's death, commits suicide. Abesalom and Eteri are buried together. But even after death, the evil Murman interferes with the lovers, burying himself alive in a grave dug between them.

Songs and Poetry

The harsh attitude of rulers toward the simple folk—shown first by local feudal rulers, then by tsarist Russia, and finally by Soviet authorities—evoked a bitter protest among a population burdened with social problems. Periodically, strong individuals or groups emerged to oppose the oppressive authorities and attempt to restore justice on their own. Episodes in the lives and struggles of such dissidents constitute a favorite theme in Georgian folklore. Epic song texts created about a nineteenth-century folk hero, Arsena, enjoyed widespread popularity, spread by vagrant musicians and bagpipers. The epic of Arsena resembles legends throughout world folklore on the theme of a hero who protects the poor. Principal episodes include conflict with the feudal lord, going to the woods as a robber, expropriation of property from the rich and its distribution among the poor, easy victory in the struggle against government detachments, being captured through perfidy, escape from prison, conflict with oneself and seeking danger, and death.

Performance of poetic texts is closely linked with singing. The dialects of Georgian musical folklore largely coincide with the language dialects. The general peculiarity of Georgian folk music is a varied song of one through four voices divided into two principal branches: East Georgian and West Georgian. Choral monophony is mainly characteristic of the mountain dialects of Eastern Georgia as well as the singing of the Samtskhe-Javakhetians and the Laz. Solo monophonic songs are known throughout Georgia. These include lullabies, oxcart drivers' songs, and songs sung while plowing. Georgian folk music covers all spheres of social life, resulting in a large number of work, ritual, drinking, lullaby, war, and mourning songs.

Georgian polyphony is represented in considerable variety in Guria and Achara. Especially specific is the so-called *krimanchuli*, demanding an unusually high register of voice from the male and the skill of performing involved ornamentation with a pharyngeal sound. A third voice also takes part in the song's refrain, while the second voice sings the verse. East Georgian three-part songs are characterized by homophonic and homophonic-polyphonic structure. In the former case the higher voice develops the melody by parallel movement, and in the latter case the first voice sings and the second is a refrain, or vice versa, creating a contrapuntal relationship between them.

From the viewpoint of versification, the verbal texture of the Georgian folksong reflects various stages of development of verse. Alongside verses fully ordered in terms of rhythm and rhyme, we find examples whose only poetic component is a refrain. Parallelism between stanzas, segmentation into strophes, and other necessary elements of rhythmic organization are neglected. Ritual songs and worksongs are characterized by such texts. Significant flaws from the viewpoint of organization of verbal subject matter are characteristic of Gurian songs that stand out for their polyphony, with melody being clearly dominant. The opposite is the case in Pshav-Khevsuretian poetry. Here the expressive power of words is raised to the highest rank, while melody performs the function only of an outward ornament. Hence, it is monotonous and undeveloped. The improvised contest of two poets should be considered the highest manifestation of Pshav poetic skill. Such a tournament is usually held during a feast. A Pshavian intones to another Pshavian mostly satirical and humorous lines fitting the situation. In most cases there are two mutually unrhymed lines, to which the opponent must respond in song in order to round out the verse both structurally and in terms of content. Then the person who began the song must answer, and so the interchange continues. The contest lasts until one of the contestants cuts the opponent short, that is, sings something to which he has no answer.

DRAMA

Elements of drama—fused with magic rituals—occur often in Georgian folklore. An example is the magic rituals for controlling the weather. The participants in the ritual carry a specially made doll to every household, calling upon the residents, through a special song, to donate eggs, flour, cheese, and wine. Then, to cause rain, the doll is thrown into the river, and the participants themselves splash in the water and then eat the food they have gathered.

Spring mysteries connected with the cult of propagation and fertility constitute an embryonic stage of drama. The Svan *murqvamoba* (*koshkoba*) stands out among them with its phallic attributes, imitation of sexual acts, and round dance—as preserved in a description from the 1910s. According to that description, a snow tower

Berikas in the streets of Tbilisi. (Photograph by Goga Chanadiri)

is made in the village square, with a flag hoisted on its top (according to another description, a wooden image of the phallus). The participants of the ritual are chosen: the "caesar," queens, one who personifies phallic power (*sakmisai*), and his attendants. They are attired in appropriate garments and attributes such as wooden swords and phallic symbols. First comes the scene of the love relations between the caesar and his queens, which is followed by the abduction of the queens by *sakmisai*. The caesar wrestles with his adversary. Ultimately, the participants in the festival destroy the tower to ensure a better harvest.

Of the ancient spring carnivals only the *berikaoba* has survived. As an improvised spectacle of a theater of masks, it occurred in all regions of Georgia. The principal motif of such performances is death and revival as well as marriage and marital relations, represented in different cases by various animals, usually the bear and the wild boar. Today the *berikaoba* is represented by a procession in the streets of the capital by masked performers arriving from nearby provinces, dances, and gathering money from passersby. In addition to the tradition losing some of its earlier significance, the costumes and masks of the participants have become impoverished. The time of holding the *berikaoba* remains unaltered, traditionally coinciding with Shrovetide.

Syncretic coexistence of melody, word, and plasticity is an ordinary phenomenon in Georgian folklore. However, in individual cases one of these elements may assume a leading role. Viewed in this way, it will not be difficult to single out Georgian folk dance, the best examples being hunter, war, and cultic round dances. These dances have been cultivated and are the adornment of Georgian folk ballet.

Sports and Games

Sport contests and games have always been an indispensable attribute of traditional Georgian life. Varieties of sport archery, fencing, spear throwing, riding, polo, a variety of modern rugby, and wrestling have been widespread in Georgia since early times. Among these, contests in wrestling and weight lifting—including contests to judge who could throw a heavy boulder or wooden beam the farthest—were widespread until recently. Racing horses at short and long distances is also popular. Such contests are held jointly by transhumance herdsmen and people resting at alpine zone resorts (for example, Guria or Achara). This sport is highly popular in Megrelia, too. Contests in polo survive to the present day. In Megrelia as well as in Guria and Achara, these contests are held during folk festivals. In some regions of Georgia, the earlier ritual function of such racing contests has survived. Thus, in Pshavi and Khevsureti, racing is an obligatory component at divine service. In the mountainous region of Eastern Georgia horse-racing contests are held in honor of a deceased person.

ARTS, CRAFTS, AND ARCHITECTURE

The material arts in Georgia include making everyday objects as well as constructing bridges, churches, fortifications, economic facilities, or dwelling-houses; treatment of wood and stone; processing wool, flax, and cotton; goldsmithing; pottery; and other branches of artisanship. The existence of old traditions of these arts in Georgia is attested by remains of material culture discovered during archeological excavations as well as by written sources. For example, numerous items of goldsmithing have come to light in Georgian territory, some being 3,500 to 4,000 years old.

Folk architecture in Georgia is fairly diverse, which is accounted for by differing natural conditions and the unequal level of social development in different regions. In mountain areas the peasant's house performed economic and defensive functions. Fort-house types developed. In Svaneti, Khevsureti, Pshavi, Tusheti, Khevi, and Mtiuleti a square stone tower is frequently part of the dwelling complex. Villages with many towers have survived in Svaneti to the present day. The entirely fortified village of Shatili is preserved in Khevsureti. The *darbazi*-type dwelling was widespread in ancient times in Kartli, Samtskhe, and Javakheti. The determining element of *darbazi* is its stepped roof, creating a domelike space, and the solid wooden *deda-bodzi* ("mother-pillar"), adorned with carved ornament. In the humid, subtropical climate of the West Georgian lowland, wooden houses, characterized by artistically treated wooden balconies, are still popular.

Traditions of decorative treatment of clay and wool as well as withes and wood are preserved at present, too, such activity being one of the principal sources of income for some villages. Over the last 100 years Georgia has experienced radical changes. Especially notable were the changes following Sovietization with its

Megrelian wooden house. (Photograph by Goga Chanadiri)

Earthenware market on the road in the village of Shrosha, Imereti. (Photograph by Goga Chanadiri)

destructive impact on traditional relations and modes of life. In this period migration of the population from villages to cities assumed a mass scale, causing the desertion of whole villages, especially in mountainous regions (Racha, Svaneti, Khevsureti, Pshavi, and Tusheti). With authority imposed from outside, Georgia significantly deviated from natural development. For example, the construction in the countryside of urban-type houses proved totally incompatible with the natural conditions and the infrastructure. Attempts at modernizing traditions have resulted in a cultural mix-and-match that violates their ancient uniqueness, paralleling the inclusion of absolutely inappropriate music, garments, and food in Georgian weddings. The dismantling of the USSR has brought about a new wave of change due to globalization, though attempts have been made to integrate Georgian cultural traditions with modern life and more global cultural trends.

BIBLIOGRAPHY

Gabunia, Leo, and others. 2000. Earliest Pleistocene Hominid Cranial Remains from Dmanisi, Republic of Georgia: Taxonomy, Geological Setting, and Age. *Science* 288:1019–1025.

Hunt, D. G., trans. 1999. *Georgian Folk Tales*. Tbilisi: Merani Publishing House.

Kurdovanidze, T., comp. 2000. *The Index of Georgian Folktale Plot Types. Systematic Directory, according to the System of Aarne-Thompson*. Tbilisi: Merani Press.

Lang, D. M. 1966. *The Georgians*. London: Thames and Hudson.

Rayfield, D. 1994. *The Literature of Georgia. A History*. Oxford: Clarendon Press.

Tuite, K., trans. and ed. 1994. *An Anthology of Georgian Folk Poetry*. London: Associated University Presses.

———. 1994–1996. Highland Georgian Paganism—Archaism or Innovation? *The Annual of the Society for the Study of Caucasia* 6–7:79–91.

Urushadze, V., trans. 1958. *Anthology of Georgian Poetry*. Tbilisi: State Publishing House.

Elguja Dadunashvili

GYPSY. *See* Roma

LATVIA

LATVIAN FOLKLORE ARCHIVES

The study of folklore in Latvia is part of the European tradition, historically defining folklore in general and specific folklore genres in standard terms and following similar methods of collecting and publishing as those used in neighboring states such as **Germany, Denmark, Finland,** and Estonia. The contents of the Latvian Folklore Archives (founded on 2 December 1924) suggests the scope of available materials: fairy tales (35,971 items), legends (57,722), anecdotes or short humorous tales (33,438), miscellaneous narratives (19,488), descriptions of recent traditions (802), riddles (44,538), proverbs and sayings (309,121), folksong texts (1,042,530), *zinge* texts—that is, songs of more recent origin (75,825 items)—children's songs and rhymes (72,614), album rhymes (14,350), choreography (24,348), beliefs and explanations of dreams (foreseeing) (388,275), customs (46,267), animal language and onomatopoetic sound imitations (8,194), melodies (30,375), place-names and

Latvia.

nicknames (10,943), names of animals and plants (3,329), farm signs and tombstone inscriptions (435), special names and sayings, word puzzles (54,258), descriptions of historical places and persons of interest (2,428), drawings and photographs (1,140), incantations and magic (54,923), traditional healing (78,646), essays on folklore (366), folklore from other nations (21,467), descriptions of folklore performances (34), and miscellanea (77). The **archives** also contain the papers of nineteenth-century collectors, among them the manuscript collection of the greatest Latvian folklorist, Krišjānis Barons, his card catalog, and his "Dainu Skapis" (Cabinet of Folksongs), which includes more than 200,000 folksongs gathered in one middle-sized wooden cabinet. On 4 September 2001, the Cabinet of Folksongs became part of the United Nations Educational, Scientific, and Cultural Organization (UNESCO) Memory of the World Register.

While collecting and interpreting folklore in Latvia has followed mainstream European tradition, folk poetry has received particular emphasis. The archives contain more than 1 million four-lined verses, Latvian classical quatrain texts, together with more than 30,000 melodies. When did these songs originate? Before answering this question and considering the reasons for the popularity of quatrains in Latvian tradition, it is necessary to examine the process of folksong performance.

Singing continues to be an important part of Latvian spiritual life. In 1914, Krišjānis Barons wrote, "In modern times the singing of folksongs is waning everywhere, in some areas it has disappeared altogether. In the past, each season, each celebration, festivity, work, and time of rest not only had their own songs, but also different ways of singing of songs, different tunes." This suggests the impact of late-eighteenth-century German philosopher J. G. Herder's influence on Latvian folklore studies. He viewed folklore as a historical artifact, a survival from the past transmitted through an oral tradition that was rapidly giving way to "higher" stages

Sigulda Mid-Winter Festival, Kiekatas, Latvia. (© Hideo Haga/HAGA/The Image Works)

of contemporary European culture. Moreover, Herder held that folklore—though vanishing—could provide insights into national character and reveal a people's real cultural heritage, an idea adopted by Latvian scholars. Singing folksongs had special significance during the periods of heightened national consciousness such as the Neo-Latvian movement of the 1850s through 1870s, when the spiritual property of Latvian folksong served as evidence that Latvians had their own history and consequently rights to their own future. This idea served as a basis for Latvian (as well as Estonian and Lithuanian) song festivals, which, begun in 1873, have continued uninterrupted till the present (the twenty-third occurring in 2003) and are now recognized in the UNESCO Register of Intangible World Culture Treasures. Between 1918 and 1940, the years of Latvia's first national independence, Herder's idea that folk poetry reflects the spirit of a nation was used to provide a cultural foundation for the new political entity, which was perceived as a unified nation integrated by an ancient folklore heritage. During this period the Archives of Latvian Folklore was established, and serious collecting began. More than 2.5 million items became part of the archives' holdings. Between 1924 and 1940 the archives published twenty-eight books: collections of folklore compiled by the archives' employees; scientific works and collections of folklore; and melodies. A third period of particular interest in folksongs occurred during Singing Revolution (which peaked between 1989 and 1991). Singing folksongs became a ritual of identity.

GEOGRAPHY AND HISTORY

Latvia's geographical position and history suggest why folksong has figured so largely in its sense of identity. Latvia lies in Northeastern Europe on the coast of the Baltic Sea and the Gulf of Riga. It borders Lithuania, Byelorussia, **Russia**, and Estonia and faces **Sweden** across the Baltic. The landscape is mainly level, with almost half of it covered with natural forests. Lakes and small rivers abound. Providing trading potential, navigable waterways—the Daugava River (Zapadnaja Dvina in Byelorussia and Russia) and ice-free expanses of the Baltic Sea—have contributed to the country's development.

The history of Latvia as a state is short (from 1918 till 1940 and beginning again in 1991), yet complex and rich in contrasting interpretations, especially during the Soviet period between 1940 and 1991. The spiritual values that afford a basis for the nation, though, are time-honored. Since Latvians do not have their own ancient chronicles or other written sources (even the recorded history of the Latvian language is relatively short because the first books did not appear until the 1580s), archeological excavations are the main source for knowledge about the history of this land. Historians also recommend the importance of folklore as a source for folk history.

During the emergence of Latvian language, culture, and nationhood, some complicated consolidation and assimilation processes were taking place. The coast of the Baltic Sea became habitable at the end of the Ice Age, approximately 12,000 years ago. During the first phase of development (9000–4000 B.C.E.) Mesolithic culture changed to Early Neolithic culture (3500–2500 B.C.E.), which overlay an existing local way of life. Starting from the Middle Neolithic (2500 B.C.E.), intensive changes both within inhabitants and cultures began: (1) localized culture survived; (2) bearers of Comb Ware culture (predecessor of Finns and Estonians) reached the coast of the Baltic Sea (2500–2000 B.C.E) from the northeast; (3) then the bearers of Battle (Boat) Axes and Corded Ward culture (predecessor of Latvians and Lithuanians) came from the south and southeast (2000–1700 B.C.E.). During the next millennium Baltic tribes spread over a wide expanse of territory from the Volga to the Vistula (possibly even to the Rhine). The territory of modern Latvia was at a crossroads of ancient trading routes. The Daugava Basin, linked with the Dnieper River, tied ancient Balts with the Black Sea; the Baltic Sea connected with the territory of Old German and Celtic peoples; and the Amber Route through the Danube Basin connected with the Mediterranean area. During this period (1700–500 B.C.E.), the Baltic language split into two groups: East Baltic (ancestor of Latvian and Lithuanian) and West Baltic (ancestor of Old Prussian). More than a millennium has elapsed since the disintegration of East Baltic occurred. Ancestors of Latvians and Lithuanians then developed differences in language and culture. The future Latvian language assumed stresses on words' first syllables and lost vowels from word ends. Latvian words became at least one syllable shorter. Most likely, the distinctive features of Latvian folk poetry emerged. These peculiarities were sufficient to consider East Baltic speakers being split into different peoples between 500 B.C.E. and 500–700 C.E. Ancestors of the Latvians (700–1200 C.E.) split into four large groups: Latgallians on the east and north, Cours (Curonians) on the west, Semigallians and Selonians between them, and Livs (posterity of Baltic Finns) along the shore of the Gulf of Riga. Starting from the tenth century, chronicles present some information about the Latvians' predecessors, while the written history of Latvia begins with the introduction of Christianity.

The first encounter between the inhabitants of Latvia and Christian Europe happened in the east. Contacts with the Russian Orthodox Church were established in the second half of the twelfth century. Consequently, the basic Christian terminology in Latvian is loanwords from Old Russian. Representatives of the Roman Catholic Church from Germany appeared on the shores of the Baltic Sea and the Gulf of Riga near the mouth of the Daugava in the 1180s. At this time, the total ethnic region was divided in "provinces," as they were called in the chronicle written in 1227 by the priest Henry (*Heinrici, chronicon Livoniae*). At the beginning of the century, the pope declared a Crusade against these provinces, even those in the east, whose inhabitants had been baptized by the Orthodox Church. During the thirteenth century German Crusaders conquered territories in today's Latvia and Estonia. As a result of this Crusade a new state, Livonia, appeared, ruled by the Order of the Crusaders and a Catholic bishop. Riga, founded in 1201 as a bishop's seat, became the biggest city of this region.

This defeat was crucial for the continuing development of Latvian native culture as Latvians suffered violent exploitation from the Crusaders and the bishop's followers. Natural social and cultural development ceased, and stagnant cultural preservation took its place. Probably this was a reason contributing to further specification and individualization in Latvian folk poetry. During the next 700 years, Latvia became a battlefield for a chain of invaders endeavoring to control this highly profitable trading crossroad. Livonia, ruled by German nobility, was conquered and apportioned between **Poland** and Sweden and later occupied by the Russian Empire, which split the territory into three provinces. At the conclusion of World War I, the first Latvian independent state, the Republic of Latvia, was established on 18 November 1918.

SONGS AND POETRY

It is hard to overestimate the place of songs and singing during the fight for national sovereignty. Herder's idea that folksongs offered a distinctive national voice among the various traditions of the world generated widespread folksong collecting by Latvian scholars and patriots. Beginning in the mid-nineteenth century, hundreds of Latvians began to collect songs, fairy tales, and other folklore genres. Meanwhile, songs and other folklore became weapons for protesting the subjugation of one nation by another. Folklore collecting was perceived as an honorable task because the existence of a rich national cultural heritage allowed Latvians to assume equality with other European nations. Soon it became clear that folksong collections afforded material for a multi-volume publication. Particularly noteworthy was the work of Krišjānis Barons, who compiled and edited *Latvju Dainas* (1894–1915), the first extensive publication of Latvian folksongs. It included 217,996 texts in six volumes. Barons offered tangible evidence of Latvian culture's uniqueness. His catalog of handwritten folksong texts remains a national treasure. Meanwhile, a vast collection of tales and legends was gathered and published by Ansis Lerhis-Puškaitis between 1894 and 1903, and Fricis Treilands-Brīvzemnieks collected and published customs and beliefs during the 1880s.

The most numerous and distinctive genre in Latvian folklore is 4-lined verses, classical quatrains. From the point of view of folklore scholars, Latvian traditional folk poetry is divided into two categories—the more remarkable being these quatrains, 4-lined verses polished and crystallized with extreme care over centuries, perhaps even millennia. About 80 percent of Latvian songs consist of 4 lines. Another 10 percent, which consist of poems of between 6 and 24 lines, are considered to be short classical songs. The remainder of the songs are long classical songs with line numbers fluctuating between 26 and 100. The second category of folk poetry includes folk romances, songs of literary origin, "zinges," popular songs, and "table songs." These are believed to be of more recent origin and resemble the folksongs of neighboring societies in texts and melodies.

Rhythmically, about 90 percent of the Latvian quatrains are in trochaic folksong meter: four-foot trochees, each line consisting of two feet with a caesura in the middle (- u / - u // - u / - u). The placement of the caesura and the number of syllables are strictly regulated. A one-syllable word at the end of a foot may be prolonged with an additional meaningless sound (mainly *i*, sometimes *a* or *e*). If the last word has three syllables, it may be shortened by omitting the last vowel. Meanwhile, if the third syllable of a foot is a long vowel, a diphthong, or a short vowel plus a consonant, the fourth syllable is not mandatory. About 10 percent of the quatrains are dactylic: a two-foot dactyl (- *u u* // - *u u*). Possibilites for variation are greater than with the trochee line. Songs using both meters are very rare and are found mainly in specified sub-genres such as dandling songs, which are recited or sung while dandling a child on one's knees (about 3,000 items in the archives).

Contemporary Latvian words are stressed on the first syllable, while in folksongs the stressed syllable is determined by the rhythm of the song. For example, *tādzīvuot* in a verse line becomes "*Tādzī-vuo-ti // mei-ti-ņām.*" This kind of change may be a survival of an ancient, freely moved stress similar to that of contemporary Lithuanian. While Latvian classical verses are rarely rhymed, rhymed lines appear in the latest sub-groups of popular songs, especially in "*ziņģes.*"

From the point of view of text structure, these short songs are highly formularized. Many of them are built on the principle of analogous parallelism, for example, "*Šorīt // sarkana / Saulīte // lēca; / Šorīt // mūs' māsa / Sieviņa // tapa*" (This morning // the red / Sun // rose; / This morning // Our sister / Became // a wife). Usually, the first two lines present some kind of an exposition, while the second part reflects the idea in connection with people's lives as a summary and gives some solution or synthesis of a problem.

This linguistic sub-group of folk poetry also has a specific "grammar." This includes diminutive forms: among its nine words the quoted song has two diminutives (*saulīte* and *sieviņa*). Their expression in folksongs may replace more ancient longer word forms. Another specific grammatical trait of folksongs is using verbs in the past tense instead of the present or future. Latvian past tenses regularly have an additional syllable. The distinctive feature of quatrain verse is its rhythm pattern, which renders many grammatical elements meaningless and as a consequence not essential to translate. Quatrains are very hard to translate, for many forms and phenomena have no equivalents outside the Latvian language.

The whole corpus of traditional quatrains constitutes a linguistic sub-system. Meanings of individual words emerge mainly through the semantics of the whole quatrain, thematically connected songs, or all the texts with similar formulas. For example, the complete spectrum of meanings of the word *sun* is seen through analyzing about 3,000 songs about the sun. As part of the formula "*Sarkana saule,*" or varying with diminutive form "*Sarkana saulīte,*" "red" (the color) changes its meaning to "fierce" or "aggressive." Moreover, the quatrains preserve ancient language forms, expressions, and meanings. Therefore, in the quatrain quoted above *māsa* does not mean "sister" as in modern Latvian, but "kinswoman." Both of these meanings are activated when the song is sung or recited, though. Similarly, the ten or more meanings the word *sun* can have in folksong texts afford an enormous wellspring of denotations that cannot be grasped outside these texts. This special word power expressed in folklore consists of "marked" words, which have a special sense for Latvian traditional culture; "mythemes" connected with pre-Christian religion; poetic words and parallelisms, linking items (or half-lines or lines or two lines) without prescribing the logical nature of their linkage. So the quatrains are self-contained, and chains of quatrains have developed around thematic motifs or key words (for example, "sun songs" or "oak songs"). Reciting or singing folk poetry is a creative process. The performer must select quatrains and construct sequences because the number of songs and their order may be modified by any performer anytime.

Deeply rooted in the past, folk poetry is the most reliable source for data about Latvian mythology as a functioning phenomenon of everyday life. Narratives such as fairy tales and legends provide less reliable data due to their more international character. Instead of being a system introduced from outside, indigenous Latvian mythology's relevance to the whole nation or part of it finds reinforcement in its use in folksong. The traditional Latvian pantheon has no system of clear subordination, but each deity has his or her own sphere of independent activities. Some gods and goddesses are found in folksong texts only, for example, *Saules meitas* (the Daughters of the Sun) and *Dieva dēli* (the Sons of the God).

Tautasdziesma has two meanings. On one hand, it refers to a song text being recited, and, on the other hand, it also indicates the text and the melody to which it is sung. The melodies of folksongs are divided into two principal categories: *teicamās dziesmas* (recitative-like or "spoken" songs) and *dziedam s dziesmas* (songs to be sung). Performing the first category, the leading singer recites the first section of the melody, and the second part is sung by a group of singers. The melodies have a narrow melodic range of three to five tones. Another type of melody is used if the song has a more or less constant sequence of verses pre-determined by plot. Long classical songs, folk romances, and *ziņģes* exemplify this. These melodies have a wider range of five to eight tones. The first publication of a quatrain and its melody appears in the tractate of the scientist Fridericus Menius, *Syntagma de Origine Livonorum* (About the Origin of Livonians), in 1632. Andrejs Jurjāns collected a significant body of music during the 1880s. His materials were published between 1894 and 1926, and materials gathered during the first part of nineteenth century were published by Jēkabs Vītoliņš between 1953 and 1986.

MUSIC

In addition to manuscripts, the Latvian Folklore Archives has a number of sound recordings, the oldest ones recorded on phonograph cylinders. They date from 1926 through 1947 and total 168 cylinders. Since 1951, tape recordings are made every fieldwork season, and the oldest ones are re-recorded. Video recording started in the 1980s and is widely used in recording song materials now.

Many song texts and music materials are found in the files of choreographers.

Latvian folk dances and games are popular as a kind of folk art. Folk dance ensembles perform at folk dance festivals and sometimes at song festivals.

During the Soviet period, when folklore was used as propaganda, some performing ensembles were officially sponsored by the government to show the "happy life" under the communists. In 1980s a confrontation between this official Soviet folklorism based on stylized tradition and authentic performance of traditional art occurred. This contributed to the Singing Revolution, when folk art became Latvia's only weapon in the struggle for independence.

STUDIES OF LATVIAN FOLKLORE

During the Soviet period (1945–1991) the work of the Latvian Folklore Archives, based mainly on pre-war models, had continued. The most important publication began in 1979: a full scientific edition of classical folksongs in fifteen volumes. By early 1985 five volumes in six books had appeared. After 1991, Latvian folklorists continued this project. The three next volumes were published between 1994 and 2003. The ninth volume is now being prepared for print. In collaboration with European and American researchers and research centers, some new research directions have begun.

BIBLIOGRAPHY

Arājs, Kārlis, and Alma Medne. 1977. *Latviešu pasaku tipu rādītājs* (The Types of the Latvian Folktale). Rīga: Zinātne.

Archives of Latvian Folklore. 1979–1985, 1994–2003. *Latviešu Tautasdziesmas* (Latvian Folksongs). 8 volumes. Rīga: Zinātne.

Barons, Krišjānis. 1894–1915. *Latvju Dainas* (Latvian Folksongs). 6 volumes. Jelgavā: H. I. Drawiņ-Drawneeka.

Birkerts, Pēteris. 1929–1930. *Latvju tautas anekdotes* (Latvian Folk Anecdotes). 4 volumes. Rīga: Vaitera un Rapas akc. sab. tzdevums.

Jurjāns, Andrejs. 1894–1926. *Latvju tautas mūzikas materiāli* (Latvian Folk Music Materials). 6 volumes. Rīga: N.p.

Lerhis-Puškaitis, Ansis. 1894–1903, 2002. *Latviešu tautas teikas un pasakas* (Latvian Folk Legends and Fairy Tales). 7 volumes. Rīga: Atēna.

Melngailis, Emilis. 1951–1953. *Latviešu mūzikas folkloras materiāle* (Materials of Latvian Music Folklore). 3 volumes. Rīga: Latvijas valsts izdevniecība.

Šmits, Pēteris. 1925–1937. *Latviešu pasakas un teikas* (Latvian Fairy Tales and Legends). 15 volumes. Rīga: N.p.

———. 1940–1941. *Latviešu tautas ticējumi* (Latvian Folk Beliefs). 4 volumes. Rīga: Latviešu folkloras krātuves izdevums ar kulturas fonda pabalstu.

Sūna, Harjs. 1966. *Latviešu Rotaļas un Rotaļdejas* (Latvian Games and Dances). Rīga: Zinātne.

Švābe, Arveds, Kārlis Straubergs, and Edīte Hauzenberga-Šturma. 1952–1956. *Latviešu tautas dziesmas* (Latvian Folk Songs). 12 volumes. Kopenhāgenā: Imanta.

Vikis-Freibergs, Vaira, and Imants Freibergs. 1988. *Saules Dainas* (The Sun Songs). Rīga: Grāmata.

Vītoliņš, Jēkabs. 1953–1986. *Latviešu tautas mūzika* (Latvian Folk Music). 5 volumes. Rīga: Zinātne.

Beatrise Reidzane

MACEDONIA

GEOGRAPHY AND HISTORY

Its contemporary geographical and multicultural character, nestled in the heart of the Balkan Peninsula, bordered by **Serbia** and Montenegro to the north, Bulgaria to the east, **Greece** to the south, and **Albania** to the west, reflects a Macedonia that has existed from biblical times, through the reign of Alexander the Great, and to the Byzantine era, when it occupied a larger territory. The geography and history of

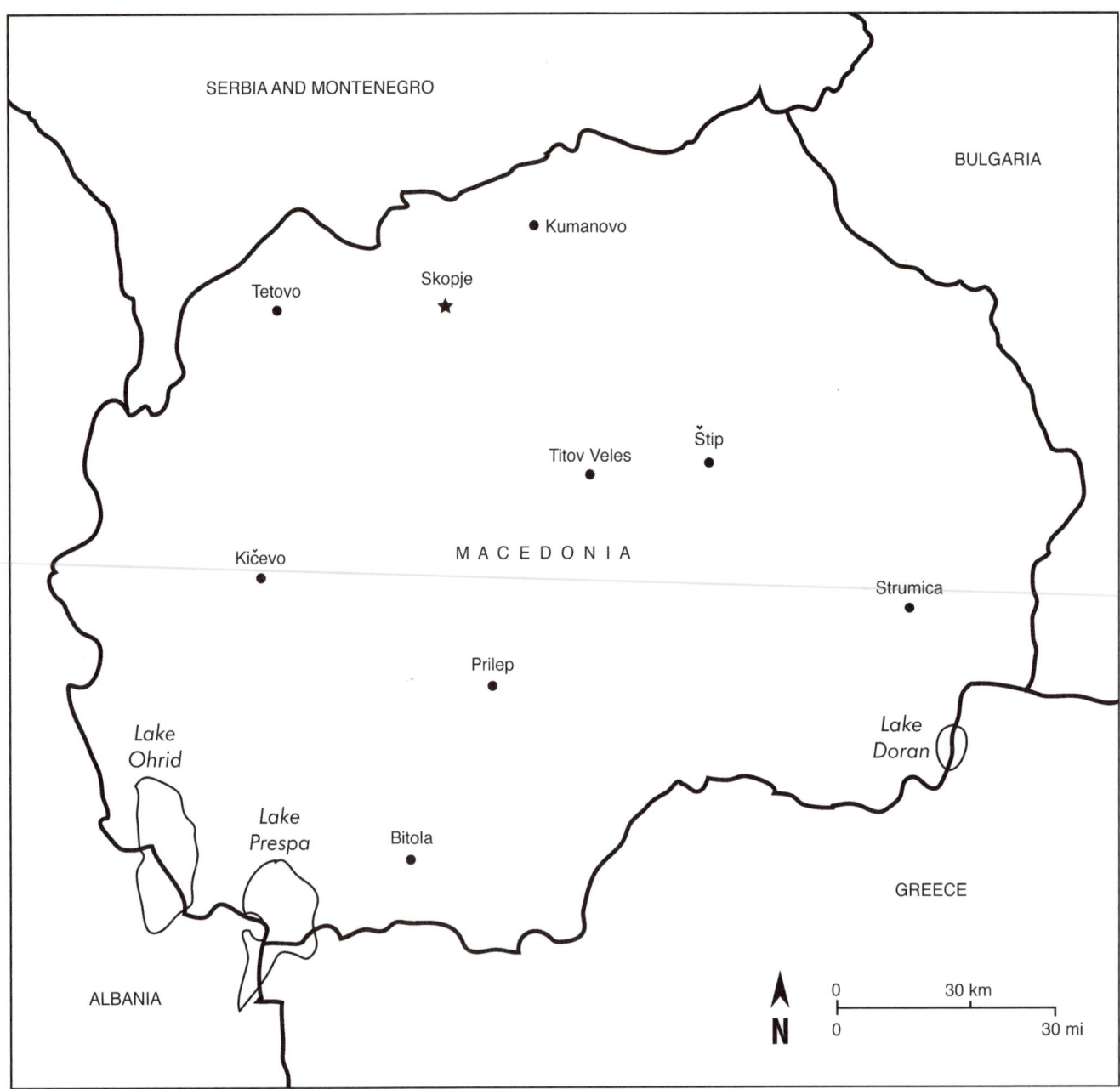

Macedonia.

migration, trade, and cultural exchange have resulted in a territory characterized by a variety of languages and religious, ethnic, and cultural traditions. However, the base of the ethno-cultural Macedonian zone lies in the sixth-century settlement of the Slavs in the Balkans and the resulting mixture of the traditions of the natives with those of the conquerors.

The Christianization of Macedonia occurred during the time of the Byzantine Empire. The Slavic culture survived this turbulent era, though somewhat modified. A greater change in Macedonian culture and tradition took place during the Ottoman Empire, which lasted from the fourteenth century until 1913. It was under Ottoman rule that Macedonia took on its modern multicultural identity, becoming home to Serbs, Bulgarians, and Greek-speaking Christians as well as Turkish and Albanian Muslims, Vlachs, Jews, and Gypsies. After the Balkan Wars and the breakup of the Ottoman Empire, Macedonia was occupied by Serbs and Bulgars. From 1944 to 1991, Macedonia was established as one of the states of the Yugoslav nation, becoming independent again only after the dissolution of Yugoslavia.

In the mid-twentieth century, a tremendous effort was made to collect folklore from ethnic Macedonians as well as other minorities within the country. In 1950, the Institute of Folklore was founded for the study of the customs and traditions of all Macedonians. Even after Macedonian independence in 1991, the institute has remained active in fostering consciousness of the nation's diverse culture.

The majority of the inhabitants of Macedonia are Slavs and adherents of the Eastern Orthodox faith. They accepted Christianity in the ninth century from the disciples of Cyril and Methodius, two monks from Thessaloniki who created the Slavic alphabet. However, evidence of pre-Christian paganism survives in religious and folk tradition. Especially in the Middle Ages, when the Bogomil heresy emerged in the Balkans, did this become obvious. Exhibiting strong anti-feudal and anti-clerical tendencies, the Bogomils challenged church authority. In fact, their cosmological myths exhibit a kind of dualism, which holds that the Devil was responsible for the creation of the world and people. Traces of such ideas are still discernible in contemporary Macedonian legends. Such gaps between official belief systems and those of the folk are obvious in almost all narrative forms, which have integrated very ancient Near East religious motifs with medieval elements.

The modern scholarly interest in Macedonian folklore began when the earliest manuscript of folk poetry from the surroundings of Kostur (from the sixteenth century) was published in Paris in 1958. However, Europe's first fascination with the folklore of Macedonia took hold with the mid-nineteenth-century rise of Romanticism.

Statue of Sts. Cyril and Methodius, two monks from Thessaloniki who created the Slavic alphabet, Ohrid, Macedonia. (© Sean Sprague/The Image Works)

Consequently, a national Romanticism developed in the country itself, leading many collectors such as the Miladinov brothers, Stefan Verkovich, Kuzman Schapkarev, and Marco Cepenkov, to publish their collections. However, the first publications on Macedonian folklore came from the Serbian ethnographer Vuk Stefanovik Karadžić (1815 and 1822) and the Russian Slavonic scholar V. I. Grigorovich (1844 and 1845). The first published collection was one of the two tales collected by Konstantin Miladinov in 1863 in the Zagreb literary almanac *Biser*. In 1885 Kuzman Shapkarev published the first collection of Macedonian folktales. Among the most prominent twentieth-century folklorists are K. Penushliski, Filip Kavaev, Blaze Konevski, and Vasil Iljovski.

MYTHS, LEGENDS, AND FOLKTALES

Macedonian folktales are well known for their great antiquity, anthropomorphized animal characters, and recurrent supernatural aspects. For example, the fable "The Lion and the Mouse" is among the oldest of Macedonian animal tales. It contains a motif known from 3000 B.C.E. The similarity between Macedonian and other folktales results from similar conditions in which these nations once existed as well as their cultural and historical interrelations.

There are also many folktales based on more realistic events with realistic characters and environments. In Macedonian narrative folklore they are known as novellas and anecdotes. Sometimes it is a problem distinguishing between the two genres. The major characteristic dividing them is the structure of the narrative as well as motifs and content. For example, novellas (short stories) are known as realistic tales with diverse themes that deal with all aspects of popular life. Macedonian *novellas* contain many international motifs that are transformed into domestic ones by the addition of regional elements. The longest recorded novella is *Silyan the Stork*.

Macedonian anecdotes date from the same time period as *novellas*—the feudal period. This view is supported by their themes, for they deal, for the most part, with class relationships and conflicts characteristic of the feudal order. Macedonian folk anecdotes contain many general international motifs, transformed by their tellers into localized versions with domestic characters and plots. The most popular characters are Iter Peyo (Clever Peter) and Nastradin Hodja, while the most popular stories are "How Peyo Took the Donkey to the Judge," "Iter Peyo," and "Nastradin Hodja and Iter Peyo Exchange Lies."

Legends (*Legendi*) and historical oral traditions (*Predanija*) are among the oldest genres of Macedonian folk literature. They are separate genres due to their content and themes. They have also developed in different ways. Both genres are artistic blends of real historical data and poetic imagination. Characteristic of oral traditions are historization (the relating of the action to some historical event or person) and localization (making a connection between the setting of the tale and some definite real territory). Macedonian legends and traditions are characteristically full of archaisms. Since the narrator has frequently forgotten the exact circumstances under which his story took place, if he ever knew them, names of characters and places may often be confused, a phenomenon known as contamination. The most famous Macedonian legends are "About the Sun and the Moon," "The Godfather and the

Straw," "King Pharaon and the Gypsies," "On the Jews, Fairies, and Whirlwinds," "Christ and the Gambler," and a group of legends that explain the origin of plants, animals, and natural phenomena (wind, lightning, and thunder).

Historical traditions (*Predanija*) may be further divided into traditions concerning historical persons (for example, "St. Kliments's Footsteps") and those of historical events (for example, "The Taking of Constantinople and the Judgment of the Turks"). They are the result of supplementary, imaginative material being added to recollections of a real, concrete event or person. The events preserved in traditions are those that left a deep impression on the common people, and the characters immortalized in them are those who were important in defending or liberating their fellows. Such traditions are created and preserved because of a strong sense of curiosity about the past. Historical traditions contain not only the relevant facts about the event or character about which they were composed but also popular interpretations—collective rather than individual. In traditions about historical personages, the heroes are highly idealized and legendary in character.

Macedonian historical traditions (*Predania*) date primarily from the fourteenth century onward, the time of the Turkish occupation. Many deal with the occupation itself, the history of the Balkan Slavs, and the last of the decisive battles against the Turkish conquerors. Parts of the historical traditions concerning historical personages are integrally related to traditions about historical events, such as those dealing with Alexander the Great and Marko Krali. Even these characters are typical not only for the Macedonian oral narratives but also for those of other peoples in and around the Balkans such as the Serbs, Bulgarians, Greeks, and Turks. Some of these oral traditions and legends as well as others about prominent characters in local Macedonian history (such as Kliment and Naum) show that this genre existed even before the arrival of the Turks in Macedonia.

POETRY

Folk poetry tends to be more popular than narratives because of its application in song. The first collections of Macedonian folk poetry were published by Vuk Karadžić, Croatian poet Stanco Vraz, and Stefan Verkovich. In the collection of the brothers Dimitri and Constantine Miladinov, lyric poetry is grouped in the following categories: fairy, religious, heroic, shepherd, *haiduk*, laments, humorous, amorous, wedding, Lazar Day, harvest, and city songs. Kuzman Shapkarev divides his songs into similar categories: fairy, dragon, religious, ritual (with the sub-groups Christmas, Lazar Day, New Year's, marriage or wedding, funeral), and songs from political, social, family, and private life (with sub-groups brigand or *haiduk*, shepherd, harvest, humorous, and other). In recent times a few noteworthy publications of Macedonian folksongs in which lyric poetry is predominant have appeared. Of particular interest is the work of the greatest recorder of Macedonian folk literature, Marko Tsepenkov, whose collection of folksongs is found in the first volume of his ten-volume edition of collected works. Significant among the larger anthologies of Macedonian folk poetry is the outstanding ten-volume edition by Kiril Penushliski. The oldest lyric folksongs may be considered to be the ritual songs, especially the ones related to the calendar: New Year's Day, Christmas, Lazar Day, Gyorguovden (St. George's Day), and Easter. The oldest recorded examples of Macedonian folksongs are the versions of three love songs written down by the Austrian high priest Sylvester in Kostur in the sixteenth century. Over the ages some of these genres of Macedonian folksongs changed in respect to subject as well as versification, composition, and style. Ritual and worksongs abandoned mythological and religious motifs, replacing these with elements from family and other everyday life, whereas the songs of shepherds, farmers, and craftsmen often came to deal with social issues. There were, of course, new political genres as well. The appearance of *haiduks* (outlaws fighting against the Turks) in Macedonia in the seventeenth and eighteenth centuries resulted in the appearance of *haiduk* song, primarily epic but with many lyric passages.

SONGS AND MUSIC

The interpretation of Macedonian folk poetry was one of the most popular aspects of Macedonian folklore. Combined with Macedonian music and accompanied by specific Macedonian folk instruments, Macedonian folksongs have been, and still are, very popular among the people. The most popular traditional musical instruments are the *kaval* (an end-blown, vertical flute), *gaida* (bagpipe), *tambura* (plucked string instrument of the lute family with pear-shaped body and long fretted neck), and *tapan* (a type of drum). These instruments are part of what typically is known in Macedonian as the "folk orchestra."

Compared to other kinds of bagpipes in the Balkans, the *gaida* has retained authentic and individual characteristics stemming from the Macedonian traditional practice. What makes the *gaida* impressive is its style of playing, which eschews dynamic nuances and emphasizes a constant mezzo forte volume. Its style is also marked by the impossibility of repetition of tones without using ornamentation. One must also play in staccato, a product of the need for permanent air pressure to sustain the instrument's sound. Macedonian *gaida* melodies are pronounced and exhibit rhythmic mobility in wavy contour, enthusiasm, and power. The short melodies are easy to remember.

The *supelka* is a small, labial, aerophonic musical instrument made of wood, bone, and recently of other material in the shape of a small cylindrical tube 250–300 millimeters long. The inner part of the *supelka* is completely hollow (the source of its name). Since the *supelka* has been a favorite instrument, people have always enjoyed its beautiful melodies. Usually, most *supelka* makers are not musically educated people. Since the *supelka* was mainly made and used by shepherds, it gained the epithet of being a cattle breeder's musical instrument, but it did not belong exclusively to a particular social group. Religious and national differences did not influence the use of this musical instrument. Macedonians as well as Turks, Albanians, and Muslims played it, though **Roma** and Vlachs do not.

DANCE AND DRAMA

Macedonian folklore is known for its dramatic and very attractive *oro* dance. Dances are performed during religious holidays (Bozik, Vodici, Veligden, Gjurgjovden, Spasovden, and Petrovden), state holidays, and weddings, usually in the center of the village in front of churches, schools, and houses. Today they are mostly performed by the professional folk groups (KUD) or by average people, particularly at weddings. The most popular Macedonian folk dances are Teskoto, Nevestinsko, Camce, Komitsko, Masko, Kavardarka, and Tikvesko, which take their names from their region of origin or the symbolic aspects of their movements. Dancers form a circle and hold each other in several ways: by hands, by shoulder, or by the waist, for example. Each dancer performs the same movements and steps, usually counterclockwise except in certain dances performed clockwise. The dance melodies are played on traditional instruments: *gajda*, *zurla*, *tapan*, *kaval*, *tambura*, *tarabuka*, *ut*, and *dajre*. The *chalgii* ensemble (which consists of a violin, clarinet, *ut*, *lauta*, *kanon*, and *dajre*) often accompanies dancing.

The dramatic dimensions of Macedonian folksong and folk dance evince traces of very old dramatic performances from the pre-Christian period, about which little is known. Macedonian folk drama has disappeared from contemporary life, but an effort to revive this genre is currently occurring. This revival derives from motives and elements that are visible in other folklore genres. Recent folkloristic scholarship agrees that, as in the many other parts of the Balkans, the folk rituals, *Rusalii* (a kind of ritual trance) and *Babary*, are the most specific evidence of theatrical forms.

ARTS, CRAFTS, AND ARCHITECTURE

Macedonian folk art has not yet been sufficiently explored. Nor is there a clear general distinction between material culture and folk art. For example, Macedonian engraving may be perceived as either craft or art because the work serves both practical and esthetic purposes. Folk art consists of many components, including embroidery, barrel making, quilt work, costume design, and egg coloring.

Macedonian folk embroidery has a rich cultural heritage going back many centuries. Peasant women passed on their skill and art from generation to generation, though with variations in techniques, coloring, and ornamentation. Embroidery provides the major decoration of folk costumes throughout the country. Besides the wide regional variation in embroidered ornamentation, Macedonian folk embroidery has developed and formed within the framework of traditional stylistic characteristics due, above all, to the nature of Macedonian costumes. In particular, women's dresses and head scarves, which are the main objects for embroidery, shaped the methods of decoration. Wool, silk, and silver thread, prepared in a traditional way, are the most important materials used in embroidery—the latter two especially for festival costumes. The dominant color in Macedonian embroidery is red in its rich register. In combination with red and black, yellow, green, and blue provide special effects.

Folk architecture is the most basic aspect of traditional material culture. Research on Macedonian architecture includes such traditional building types as houses, cabins, churches and monasteries, sacred buildings, privies, stables, agricultural outbuildings, and barns. The main characteristic of the Macedonian house is the architectonic link between the Asian and European house—between two different civilizations. Dusan Grabrijan has listed several characteristics of the Macedonian house in its transition from Oriental to modern Europe:

> The Macedonian house has a cellar, which is on a slope, is partly subterranean, and is part of the ground floor. . . . A porch opens on one or two sides. "Cardak" [balcony] is usually located in one corner of the upper floor. Due to the climate, the Macedonian house has winter quarters on the massive ground floor, which is constructed of stone and also often includes the cellar and a summer dwelling framework construction. In winter the portable cooking stove is placed in the living room and winter room. . . . [T]he Macedonian house consists of a "potom," comprising the cellar, woodshed, and stable, a courtyard enclosing the summer kitchen washroom, a ground floor, mezzanine with the winter kitchen and living room, and an upper floor where summer living and sleeping quarters are organized around the "cardak."

Most representative traditional houses in Macedonia are in the region of Ohrid, Titvo Veles, and Štip.

CHALLENGES OF THE MODERN WORLD

Over the last five decades, Macedonian life has been shaped by socialism, which distorted awareness of the folk tradition. Meanwhile, Macedonian popular culture has been subjected to various pressures. Macedonian folklore and ethnology did not study the domain of popular culture because of political pressure, lack of theoretical interests, and preconceptions about the influence of church and religion on popular culture. This period was also marked by new customs such as various celebrations of revolutionary anniversaries and battles, the ceremony surrounding Youth Day, city holidays, enterprise holidays, and Women's Day. Performances by folk groups were well received in connection with these. Increasing political decentralization showed a tendency to spark national folklore symbols. National flags at the wedding celebration are a normal phenomenon in contemporary folklife and in folklore presentations onstage as well. Simultaneously, increasing demands for a market orientation in the economy encourage the commercialization and instrumentalization of folklore in entertainment (for example, newly composed folk music). It is more than obvious that today folklore in Macedonia has changed and has little in common with traditional norms. Even though there are still folklore *reservats* (enclaves) in the mountain villages, they are in the process of totally disappearing. One of the reasons is, of course, the great migration (from rural to urban) that took place over the past fifty years due to the socialistic collectivization in the former Yugoslavia, when the land was industrialized and the village people moved to the cities for factory work. Thus was the cultural heritage of the Macedonian village almost completely destroyed.

But the last decade—especially after the dissolution of Yugoslavia and the formation of Macedonia as a separate state—has witnessed the reinvigoration of Macedonian folklore. First of all, with the independence of the Macedonian state came a need to enhance the cultural identity of Macedonians not only in Macedonia but also in their relations with other nationalities. In these circumstances folklore was one of the most important markers of cultural identity.

It is obvious that the authority of selected tradition is used to glorify ethnocentric consciousness and self-values in relation to another culture and another identity. Folklore symbols and models are often the most charged elements in the contemporary dismembering of culture. But generally each culture has a distorted consciousness of self in relation to other cultures. Because of the need of other nationalities to express their culture and traditions, a new multiculturalism in understanding Macedonia occurred and offered a new challenge to folklore studies.

Recently, a new phenomenon connected with Macedonian folklore, ethnotourism, has emerged. Many folklore festivals take place in the summer to take advantage of the tourist industry. Ethnotourism emphasizes the modification and stylization of tradition and the appearance of new traditions.

BIBLIOGRAPHY

Borivoe, Dzimrevski. 2000. *Gajdata vo Makedonija*. Skopje: Institut za folklor.

Cuckow, Mane. 1959. Folklore in Macedonia. *Viltis* 18:10–11.

Cvetkovska, Danica, and others, trans. 1988. *The Moon in the Well and Other Macedonian Folk Tales*. Greenfield Center, NY: Greenfield Review.

Cvetkovski, Vladimir. 1982. Constantine the Great and Helena in Macedonian Folk Literature. *Revue de etudes sud-est europeennes* 20:277–280.

Dimoski, Mihailo. 1977. *Makedonski narodni ora*. Skopje: Institute of Folklor.

Escher, Wolfgang, ed. 1972. *Mazedonische Volksmärchen*. Düsseldorf: Diederich.

———. 1975. The Macedonian Folk Tale. *Macedonian Review* 5:167–171.

Grabrijan, Dusan. 1985. *Bosensko orientalska architektura*. Ljubljana: Založba Partizanska Knjiga.

Hadzimanov, Vasil. 1963. The Dvodelnik, a Macedonian Folk Instrument. *Journal of the International Folk Music Council* 15:82–83.

Hadzimanov, Vasil, and Zivko Firfov. 1961. Instruments folkloriques en Macedoine. *Journal of the International Folk Music Council* 13:77–78.

Harvey, Andrew, and Anne Pennington, trans. 1978. *Songs from Macedonia*. Oxford: Mid-Day Publications.

Holton, Milne, ed. 1974. *The Big Horse and Other Stories of Modern Macedonia*. Columbia: University of Missouri Press.

Iliovski, V. 1954. O maskedonskim narodnim pripovjetkama. *Makedonske narodne pripovjetke*. 5–37.

Jenkins, Nancy. 1947–1948. People in Macedonia: Notes and Photographs. *The Geographical Magazine* 20:477.

Klickova, Vera. 1973. The National Dresses of Macedonia. *Viltis* 32.2:9–12.

Krsteva, Angelina. 1975. *Macedonian Folk Embroidery*. Skopje: Institut za folklor.

———. 1976. Macedonian Folk Embroidery. *Macedonian Review* 6:303–307.

Landauer, Lindy. 1956. The Costume of Macedonia. *Let's Dance* 13.10:13–15.

Lunt, Horace C. 1986. On Macedonian Nationality. *Slavic Review* 45:728–734.

Martin, George S. 1956. *Mazedonische Märchen und Fabel*. Wiesbaden: Greif.

Mazon, Andre. 1923. *Contes slaves de la macedonie sud-occidentale: Etude linguistique, texts et traduction, notes de folklore*. Paris: Champion.

Obrebski, Joseph. 1977. *Ritual and Social Structure in a Macedonian Village*. Program in Soviet and East European Studies, Occasional Papers 1. Amherst: University of Massachusetts.

Penushliski, Kiril. 1966a. Macedonian Revolutionary Folk Poetry and the National Consciousness of the Macedonian People. *Journal of the Folklore Institute* 3:250–266.

———. 1966b. Macedonian Local Traditions of Prince Marco. *Journal of the Folklore Institute* 3:331–340.

————. 1989. Dramatic Elements in Macedonian Folklore. *Macedonian Review* 18:61–64.

Petrushevski, Ilija. 1976. Macedonia and the Macedonians on the Geographical and Ethnographical Map. *Macedonian Review* 6:166–171.

Popovich, Ljubica D. 1976. Some Folkloristic Elements in Medieval Art in the Territories of Serbia and Macedonia. *Balkanista* 3:91–144.

Rice, Timothy. 1960. The "Surla" and "Tapan" Tradition in Yugoslav Macedonia. *Galpin Society Journal* 35:122–137.

Sazdov, Tome. 1971. Marko Cepenkov and His Work as a Collector. *Macedonian Review* 1:198–201.

————. 1972. The Brothers Miladinov in Foreign Literature. *Macedonian Review* 2:161–165.

————. 1974. Foreign Collectors of Macedonian Folk Art. *Macedonian Review* 4:52–56.

————. 1975a. King Mark. *Macedonian Review* 5:136–141.

————. 1975b. Kuzman Shapkarev and the Macedonian Revival. *Macedonian Review* 5:157–159.

————. 1979. Stephan Verkovin Verkovicch (1821–1893) and the Affirmation of Macedonian Culture. *Macedonian Review* 9:46–55.

————. 1983a. Balkan Festival of Folk Songs and Dances in Ohrid. *Macedonian Review* 13:220–222.

————. 1983b. Work of Marko Tsepenkov. *Macedonian Review* 13:51–57.

————. 1984. Macedonian Proverbs and Sayings. *Macedonian Review* 14:214–220.

————. 1987. *Macedonian Folk Literature*. Skopje: Macedonian Review Editions.

————. 1988. Origins and Classification of Macedonian Folk Prose. *Macedonian Review* 18:144–156.

Tilney, Philip V. R. 1970. The Immigrant Macedonian Wedding in Ft. Wayne. *Indiana Folklore* 3.1:3–34.

Tomev, Foto S. 1971. *Short History of Zhelevo Village, Macedonia*. Toronto: Zhelevo Brotherhood.

————. 1980. *Macedonian Folktales*. Toronto: Multicultural History Society of Ontario.

Tomov, George. 1973a. Macedonia. *Viltis* 32.2:5–9.

————. 1973b. Macedonian Folk Dances. *Viltis* 32.2:12–13.

————. 1973c. Macedonia Folk Songs. *Viltis* 32.2:14–15.

Tomovski, Krum. 1970. Architecture in Macedonia in the Nineteenth Century. In *La Macedoineet les Macedoniens dans la passe: Recueil d'articles scientifiques*. Skopje: Institut de l'histoire nationale. 505–520.

————. 1976. Islamic Architecture and Art in Macedonia. *Macedonian Review* 6:244–249.

————. 1980. Architecture in Ohrid and the Ohrid Region. *Macedonian Review* 10:388–343.

Traerup, Birthe. 1970. *East Macedonian Folksongs: Contemporary Material from Malesevo, Pijanec, and the Razlog District*. Copenhagen: Akad, Forlag.

Tselakovski, Naum. 1973. Folk Tradition of St. Clement of Ohrid. *Macedonian Review* 3:226–233.

Tsepenkov, Marko. 1983. Christ's Cross, Czar Constantine, and Czarina Helena. *Macedonian Review* 13:63–69.

Ermis Lafazanovski

POLAND

HISTORY

Two distinct, though interdependent, traditions characterize the 1,000-year history of Polish culture: the major tradition and the minor tradition. The major tradition is high-level, scholarly, consciously cultivated by philosophers, writers, theologians,

Poland.

and other scholars, and passed on both directly (in schools and other institutions) and indirectly (through writing, images, and print). The minor, non-scholarly tradition is characterized by indirect, largely automatic, oral, intergenerational transmission. The major tradition is linked to the culture of the ruling strata: initially, feudal knights, subsequently, the landowning nobility (*szlachta*) as well as, marginally, urban-dwellers. The minor tradition was located outside those milieus: a peasant culture inherited from the Slavs, subsequently developed within the Polish ethnos, and considered the main tendency in proto-Polish ethnic culture. It included folklore, that is, the verbal forms of this tradition (various genres and microforms) as well as multi-coded forms (the ritualized behaviors of social groups).

Rural communities provided a natural setting for the creation and cultivation of Polish traditional folklore. It has never been monolithic, nor has a single national folklore ever existed. It varied among ethnographic regions, social groups, occupations, and settings.

Historically, the main outlines of Poland's ethnographic diversity, reflecting early tribal divisions—Wielkopolska (Great Poland), Małopolska (Little Poland), Pomerania, Silesia, and Mazovia—took shape with the emergence of the Polish state and its conversion to Christianity in the tenth and eleventh centuries.

The foundation of the worldview of Polish traditional folklore, the recorded sources of which date from the nineteenth and early twentieth centuries, is molded by the religious system of Western Christianity (Catholicism) with assimilated pre-Christian beliefs. It is a magical, naturalistic, religious worldview characterized by the conviction of the oneness of life in nature (a person is a microcosm, part of the larger cosmos) and a lack of distinction between religion and magic. Its main network of meanings was defined by a dualistic cosmogonic myth (syncretic, structurally common to other Slavic peoples, and partly formed from elements of the Book of Genesis), ascribing the creation of the earth to God (personifying fire) and the Devil (personifying cosmic waters). The resulting dichotomy within individual elements of the structure of the world (for example, time, space, numbers, colors, flora, and fauna) has also taken on an unequivocally value-laden nature: God is good; the Devil is evil.

FOLKTALES

Within the range of Polish oral folk prose we may distinguish fiction (animal tales, magical fairy tales, sequential fairy tales, tales of unusual events, short-story tales) as well as nonfiction (cosmogonic myths and etiological tales; legends: historical, local, and belief-based; anecdotes; microforms such as proverbs, riddles, rhymes, and spells; reminiscences). Polish verse folklore is subject to classifications diversified by its form of transmission (spoken or sung), its context (context-free or context-sensitive), the environment where it is performed (ritual, habitual, or occasional), whether or not it is connected with dancing, and the properties of the poetic genre as determined by the performer's intention.

Polish songs—mostly ritual, universal, and occupational—are typically associated with music abounding in repetitions and parallelisms reflecting a symbiosis between nature and peasant life and characterized by rhymes due to the influence of Latin and church poetry. They are typically versified as follows: four-line—that is, the so-called three-rhyme arrangements mainly in couplets and five-line arrangements, especially well known in Western Poland, including Silesia—and tri-, tetra-, penta-, and hexasyllabic combinations, which add up to fourteen or even seventeen syllables. The ritual songs are the oldest, and they matter only within their ritual contexts. Universal songs are governed by the principles of pattern and typicality concerning characters, situations, elements of landscape, and language formulas. Ballads fall on the boundary between lyric and epic, being thematically "chronicles of crime." They are recorded from all regions of Poland, mostly from Southern Poland and Silesia. The most popular Polish ballads include *"Pani pana zabiła"* (A Lady Killed Her Husband), *"Petulance"* (A Girl from Podole), *"Pan karze żonę ja zdradę"* (A Man Punishes His Wife for Infidelity), *"O dzieciobjczyni wójtównie"*

(The Infanticidal Village Mayor's Wife), and *"Jasio konie poił"* (Jasio Watered the Horses).

Animal tales were less frequent in Poland, though three types were known: Aesopian fables (from literary influences); the tricks of the cunning fox and the misfortunes of the gullible bear (recorded almost exclusively in Silesia and Pomerania); and the animal tale proper (the most numerous and the richest in all regions of Poland). *Märchen*-type fairy tales have no distinctively Polish or regional features but consist of a vast number of international motifs. Krzyżanowski's categorization of these stories in 1962, based on the Aarne-Thompson index of tale types, also encompasses other prose genres.

Polish *Märchen*-type fairy tales differ from their East Slavic counterparts by their lack of opening, middle, or closing formulas and their hefty dose of realism and rationalism. The following fairy tale migratory types have a large number of Polish regional variants: *"Szklana góra"* (The Glass Mountain) (AT 530), *"Ptak złotopióry"* (The Bird with the Golden Feathers) (AT 550), *"Sezamie, otwórz się"* (Open Sesame) (AT 676), *"Rybak i jego żona"* (The Fisherman and His Wife) (AT 555, known particularly in Kashubia as *"O rybaku i rybce"* [The Fisherman and the Little Fish]).

Many concepts, patterns, and current migratory motifs in the folklore of various European peoples have humorous renditions in Polish folklore, as comic tales have considerable potential for adaptation to such features of various ethnic settings as local heroes, scenes of action, social and moral realities, and use of dialect. These migratory motifs include, for example, patterns involving peasants' bets with the Devil (AT 1091), the defeat of the Devil during division of the harvest (AT 1030), Godmother Death (AT 332), and tales about mountain caves and great chieftains and kings. Regional types of anecdote such as Silesian and Tatra Highlander may also be distinguished.

Much Polish traditional folklore consists of historical and local tales, forming a type of microhistory. They have etiological overtones, explaining, for example, the origins of place-names from the names of their founders (such as Kraków from Krak). They assume the character of national tales as preserved by chroniclers: the Wielkopolska Cycle (Popiel and Piast) by Gallus Anonymus and the Małopolska Cycle (Krak and Wanda) from the Chronicle of Wincenty Kadłubek. The heroes of these tales were extraordinary figures or historical personalities: kings (Casimir the Great, John III Sobieski), queens (Jadwiga, Bona Sforza), national heroes (Kościuszko), renowned robbers (Dobosz in the Hucul area and Janosik in Slovakia and Podhale), and figures popularized through literature (Wernyhora, the wizard Twardowski). Another variety is tales recording folk beliefs whose heroes are supernatural beings such as nymphs, fairies, water spirits, ghosts, changelings, witches, and hobgoblins.

A related genre is the religious tale with didactic intent. It has many legendary Pan-European plots involving Christ and St. Peter's travels on earth: Wishes Fulfilled (AT 750 A), The Greedy Woman (Changed into an Animal) (AT 751 A), Threshing by Fire (AT 752 A), and Christ and the Blacksmith (Rejuvenation) (AT 753). The Bed of Suffering (AT 756 B) has the largest number of Polish versions.

RIDDLES, PROVERBS, CHARMS, AND SPELLS

Microforms—riddles, proverbs, charms, and spells—have the most stability of form and content. Riddles provided speed training for the mind and memory and were a source of amusement and information about the world. They constituted a type of metalanguage. The oldest Polish riddle is preserved in the Gotard Manuscript of 1406 and refers to events from the New Testament: "A good man came to a bad man and asked him for something better than the Kingdom of Heaven, and he gave it to him" (answer: Joseph to Pilate: *Corpus Christi*). The oldest printed collection of Polish riddles was published in Kraków in 1552. Folk riddles may also be encountered in Polish folksongs, mainly those connected with the ritual year (midsummer songs and Christmas carols), as well as in folktales, where they function as "difficult tasks."

Proverbs and proverbial sayings serve to reinforce values. A vast number of them, for almost every eventuality, are critical statements, warnings, and recommendations as to how things should be, for example, *"Jak Kuba Bogu, tak Bóg Kubie"* (As James treats God, so should God treat James). They involve folk wisdom, though double-edged: "Fortune favors the brave" (encouragement), but "Dogs bite the brave" (caution). Some Polish proverbs are of Latin or Greek provenance, which connects them with proverbs well known in other countries where Latin is used: "What you don't know can't hurt you" or "A new broom sweeps clean" (medieval Latin). Proverbs derived from the medieval church calendar were of immediate practical significance for a peasant society. They occurred in the form of weather forecasts (communication from Nature to Mankind, the "voice" of Nature): *"Św. Barbara po lodzie, Boże Narodzenie po wodzie"* (St. Barbara with ice, Christmas with water); *"Suchy kwiecień, mokry maj, będzie żyto niby gaj"* (Dry April, rainy May, the rye will grow like a grove); and *"Przyszedł św. Bartek; żytko na zimę siej"* (St. Bartholomew came; sow the rye for the winter).

Charms and spells were also characterized by stability of structure and content in accordance with the conviction that errors or changes might cause them to be ineffective. These were verbal formulas used for the magical protection of health, good harvests, and other desirables. They might accompany acts of a magical and ritual nature, for example, while baking bread: *"Rośnij chlebie, jak słońce na niebie"* (Grow, bread, like the sun in the sky); while picking a magical herb to ensure good luck in love: *"Nasięrzale / rwę cię śmiale, / pięcią palcy, szóstą dłonią / niech się ja mną chłopcy gonią"* (Nasięrzał, I pick you bravely, with my five fingers and my hand, let the boys run after me) (an example from the Poznań region). The Roman Catholic Church attempted to eradicate spells and charms as remnants of paganism, and therefore few of them have been preserved. Those that do remain are very Christianized. (Eastern Christianity was less restrictive—hence the rich resources of Russian magical folklore.) These formulas most often constituted the core of a complex magic act. A folk healer might use them to strengthen his or her remedies, for example. Figures from Christian supernaturalism, including Jesus, the Mother of God, and saints, and the precedents of sacrosanct history fixed in the structures of these formulas were an important source of power.

In addition to charms and spells, *modlitewki* (non-canonical prayers) were another form of individual magical protection. These were private, Christianized, magical invocations of God and the saints, mostly recorded in Southern Poland. Contact formulas (prayers of welcome), directed at the new moon, well known among other Slavs, and including requests for health or wishes for crops to grow, also provide examples of relics of former cults. Prayer formulas directed at the sun and at dawn are of a similar relic nature. They substitute Christian deities, especially the identification of the Morning Star with the Virgin Mary, who is noted as the "healer of sins."

LIFE-CYCLE CELEBRATIONS

Polish folk tradition included family rites linked to the human life cycle and annual ceremonies, originally determined by the rhythm of nature and, under the influence of Christianity, by the liturgical calendar of the Catholic Church. Polish folk rituals were a form of communication between an individual and the local community and between a person and the Sacred. They constituted a raft of archaic beliefs, opinions, concepts, and practices with strong magical overtones, mixed with religious requirements, notions, and practices introduced during the Christianizing process. The resulting bans, imperatives, symbolic gestures, words, and accessories were meant to protect a man (and his household) in times of change (rites of passage) and represented a projection of the future.

In family customs and rites three main ritual complexes may be distinguished: birth, marriage, and funereal. These were complemented by social, occupational, and occasional customs. In Polish tradition the institution of the family has always stood at the pinnacle of the hierarchy of values.

In marriage the principle of equality in property, with feelings and outward appearance pushed to the background, was paramount and universal. The parents, especially fathers, played a decisive role in the selection of spouses for their children. Spinsterhood and bachelorhood were generally condemned and led to loss of social prestige. The rich complex of ritual wedding customs characteristic of traditional rural Poland falls into the following sequence: formal discussions with the parents of the bride-to-be; researching the matrimonial qualifications of the suitor and his property status (with the crucial role of matchmakers for the conclusion of the marital agreement); the engagement (contracting a marriage), encompassing the customs connected with the nuptials. The wedding was preceded by the reading of banns in church every Sunday for three weeks; invitations to guests; the virgins' night before the wedding when the bridesmaids made a wedding crown and a *rózga* (wedding twig) and the bride's tresses were unbraided to the accompaniment

A Polish bride on the eve of her wedding, near Minsk, Poland; 1841 engraving by Lewicki. (The Art Archive/Bibliothèque des Arts Décoratifs Paris/Dagli Orti)

of unbraiding songs; and baking a wedding cake (*kołacz; korowaj* in Eastern Poland). The subsequent scenario, formally identical in principle, varied according to ethnicity, region, and locality as well as socioeconomic class and occupation. Going to church was preceded by *przeprosiny* (apologies) and blessings, accompanied by songs. Wedding processions usually encountered obstacles to and from the marriage ceremony, and offering vodka or beer to those who hindered the procession was among the duties of the senior best man or the wedding-host. Seating procedure at the wedding banquet was also determined by regional and local traditions, as were the repertoires of songs for the occasion directed at specific addressees and of dances during the party. The wedding ceremony culminated in placing a bonnet on the new bride's head (*oczepiny*), replacing the crown of flowers with a bonnet as the young woman sat on an overturned kneading-trough (symbolizing fertility), and consummating the final change in the young woman's status by marking her entry into the class of married women. This was accompanied by widely known old-time ritual songs, for instance, about hops, characteristic of Southern Poland, and the crown of flowers in Northern Poland. The placement of the bonnet was followed by a traditional schedule of events: the "women's dance," then "collecting money for the bonnet," the purchase of the bride from the women, the bride's so-called *kulawy* (lame) dance, other wedding guests' dances with the bride for a fee, and sharing out the *kołacz* among the wedding guests. The final phase of the wedding was the *poprawiny* (the party held on the day after a wedding) and then moving to the husband's house. This was also accompanied by ritual songs and by customary, playful masquerade scenes (for example, the magical provision of abundance and breaking pots with ashes behind the departing guests). Folk practice after arriving at the new household required the welcome with bread and salt on the threshold and a tour by the bride around the table and corners of the room.

Remaining childless after marriage was believed to be punishment for sins. Birth customs were aimed at protecting expectant mothers, women in labor, and newborns from a range of material and supernatural dangers, while protecting the surroundings from the harmful influence of expectant mothers, especially women in labor, and accepting newborns and including them in the family and the community at both group and territorial levels. The cycle of birth customs began from the moment of conception. An expectant mother held a privileged position. (Pregnancy out of wedlock was stigmatized.) She was said to be both "blessed" and "unclean," which caused a number of bans and rules of isolation. For example, she could not perform ceremonial functions at weddings, or the bride would have a "hard life." Nor could she bake bread or draw water from a well for fear it would dry up. If she cared about proper childbirth and the good of the child, she should avoid passing over ropes or chains, wearing beads, sewing (hindering the birth), and bad company in case the child were subject to these evil influences as a result of sympathetic magic. Meanwhile, she should look at beautiful and nice objects. Childbirth took place in the home with the help of a rural midwife (*babka*). The magical practices applied in childbirth included opening drawers and cupboards and taking rings from the fingers of a woman in labor. Relics of archaic reception rituals survived in some places in the custom of placing newborns or newly baptized children on the table, threshold, stove, or ground, where their fathers would pick them up. A newborn's first bath was of a ritual nature, and silver coins and blessed herbs were dropped into the water. Mothers and children were affected by numerous bans during delivery, which were of an isolating and protective nature. It was believed that a woman in labor (vulnerable to demons and dangerous actions) should stay at home with the child. Numerous tales recording nymphs (*dziwożony*) and witches stealing children and substituting their own "changelings" strengthened this ban. Baptism replaced the original reception ritual. The formula uttered in various dialect versions before making one's way to church, "We take a pagan (Jew or Turk), and we bring back a Christian," was repeated on return from baptism in the past perfect tense. The post-Christening feast was called *krzciny*. The godparents (*kumowie*) played a substantial role. It was believed that their qualities were passed on to the children. Considerations of magic restricted choices of children's names. Most frequently, the name placed in the church calendar on the day of the child's birth was chosen.

The passing of an individual from the material world to the supernatural (or Other) world was also accompanied by rituals analogous to customs specific to the Western Slavs. Their main social purpose was the complete exclusion of the deceased from the household, family, and community. Their individual purpose was to ease the soul's departure for the land of the dead, for it was believed that dying involved the separation of the non-material soul from the body (the idea of anthropological dualism). The soul was identified with breath, and thus it was said of the dying that they had breathed their last. In funeral rites the coexistence of magic and religion may also be observed, as seen in Christian-based customs that have emerged from pre-Christian traditions. There was a general belief in prophetic omens foreshadowing death. For example, animals and birds would behave oddly: dogs howling with lowered muzzles, and owls (*Strix noctua*) hooting at night. Portents could also appear in dreams of teeth falling out, turbid water, and white horses. A long, agonizing death was generally interpreted as the result of an evil life. Behavior in one's dying hours was regulated by etiquette, which required total adherence to the sacraments of the church—confession, Holy Communion, and the final anointing—as well as external practices of a symbolic nature: lighting the blessed candle, sprinkling with holy water, and especially setting one's worldly affairs in order through reconciliation, forgiving grudges and wrongs, thereby restoring equilibrium and obliterating the borders that could pose an obstacle to the soul's passage to the Otherworld and making peace with God in the end. After death customary acts were performed: clocks were stopped, and mirrors were covered. The funeral was governed by rules suspending certain household and farming activities. In Kashubia, Masuria, Kujawy, and the Poznań region, especially the nightly prayers and chants—called *puste noce* (empty nights)—sending off the deceased were of a ritual, communal nature, while in Southern Poland this tradition was lost more rapidly. When carrying out the coffin, care was taken to ensure that the corpse was placed feet forward to prevent it coming back to life and terrorizing the members of the household. Subsequent stages in funeral rituals were also affected by a number of protective bans, especially the passage from the house to the church and thence to the cemetery. Conveying a dead man across the fields was forbidden, for fear he might harm the growth of plants. The ritual exclusion of the deceased from the local community took place at the edge of the village, while the rituals performed over an open grave were supposed to ensure him eternal peace. The ritual cycle was ended with a banquet in honor of the deceased (*stypa*).

CALENDAR CUSTOMS

Annual folk rites constituted an expanded set of religious and magical customs, beliefs, fortune-telling, and musical and dance formulas as well as verbal formulas (prayers, wishes, orations, songs, tales, legends, and pageants). They include both remnants of the pagan rituals of the Slavs honoring deities and ancestors and newer Christian elements. The oldest relics include, for example, the ritual of *dziady* (visitations of the souls of the dead) and the spring ritual of going around the village with a *gaik* (decorated small green tree) or with a rooster and being sprinkled with water. Polish annual rituals may be divided into several function-based groups: those through which people have repeatedly attempted to influence natural phenomena; those involving household, cultivation, and animal husbandry; others that were supposed to bring good harvests, health, increased numbers of domestic animals (also protecting them from spells), and good fortune in all trades; those guaranteeing life, health, success, favorable marriages, and riches; those of reception, intertwined in the annual cycle of rituals, such as acceptance of young women as married women; religious and cult practices; and those of a recreational nature. The cycle was composed of winter, spring, summer, and autumn rituals. The winter rituals commenced with *Gody*, the feast lasting from Christmas Eve until Epiphany. Originally, they were based on *dziady*, the festival honoring the souls of the dead, which was commemorated before the coming of Christianity during the winter solstice. Although it was maintained among the Eastern and Western Slavs, in Poland it mainly persisted in Christmas Eve rituals in a Christianized form and might involve leaving an empty place at the table on Christmas Eve or (especially in Southern Poland) inviting the wind, wolf, or fox to the Christmas Eve supper. Customs transferred from ancient Rome's joyful, boisterous Saturnalia may be found in the New Year's Eve festival. At the New Year people made wishes and performed magical practices, especially agrarian, in order to provide health, good harvests, and prosperity in the household for the whole year. These customs included having twelve meatless Christmas dishes (regionally differentiated) to ensure a good harvest of all crops for the following year and wishes made while sharing the wafer at the start of the Christmas Eve ritual supper. Commonly, the predictions involving the weather, harvest, and marriage came after the Christmas Eve supper all over Poland (and in Southern Poland also on New Year's Day). Carolers would also come around with wishes: carrying a star and/or a homemade crèche and presenting Nativity scenes, singing carols (especially the farmers' Christmas carols, which date at least to 1544), and announcing them to the landlord and his family. The carolers' repertoire included folk and church carols: "*Przybieżeli do Betlejem*" (Shepherds Came Running to Bethlehem) and "*W żłobie leży*" (Infant Holy), for example. In Southern, Northern, and Eastern Poland caroler groups also included people disguised as **Roma**, Jews, *turoń*, a she-goat, a bear, or a horse. *Herody* (rural itinerant theaters presenting plays about King Herod) were also common during the Christmas period. Biblical plots were mixed with elements of regional folklore in their performances. On St. Szczepan's Day (26 December) oats that were thrown upon people were usually blessed. The Christmas season ended with the Epiphany, when the sign of the Cross was written on the doors as well as the date of the current year after the dedication of the incense and the chalk (K + M + B) as magical-religious protection of the house.

The blessed candles were dedicated on Candlemas (2 February). They gave protection from thunderstorms and were also lit during death. The Carnival period (Old Polish *zapusty*) lasted from Epiphany until Ash Wednesday. The peasants' Carnival was a period of entertainment but also of various ritual and magical practices serving fertility and the harvests. The last Tuesday of Carnival is called *tłusty* (fat). This is when the most is eaten and drunk before the fast that anticipates the Easter rituals, which incorporate ancient pagan spring rituals.

Marzanna, the folk image of the death of winter.

Early spring marked the start of a new year for both nature and the household. Many rituals and customs in this period had as their aim the destruction and expulsion from the village of all the evils of winter—for example, the expulsion, burning, and drowning of death and winter, personified in *Marzanna*, a doll dressed as a woman, well known in Poland since the fifteenth century, usually on the third Sunday of Lent. Various country festivals magically summoned spring, vegetation, and fertility: girls bringing *gaik* or *maik* (a decorated small green tree, a treetop, or a pine or spruce branch) into the village and walking around with a rooster accompanied by a song about Christ's suffering.

The Easter period opened with Palm Sunday. Palms were blessed and then used in rituals to protect people and domestic animals from diseases and evil spells and animals from natural disasters. Water blessed by a priest on Holy Saturday also had protective power, as did river water. Washing oneself in such water on Good Friday (Easter Sunday in Northern Poland) guaranteed health and beauty. Food blessed on Holy Saturday (*święconka*), including painted eggs (*pisanki, kraszanki*), were symbols of life. Blessed Easter eggs were divided up during the Easter breakfast while people made wishes. The scope of life symbolism also included ritualized magical practices performed on Easter Monday: pouring water upon others (the so-called *lany poniedziałek, śmigus-dyngus*), sprinkling with water (common in Southern and Central Poland), or scourging with green branches (Northern Poland). These were relics of pre-Christian cleansing procedures to bring rain and guarantee health and fertility.

Agrarian customs and rituals were very much at the forefront in celebrating Pentecost, commonly considered a shepherds' feast. People lit torches in the evening and ran around the fields in order to bring good harvests. They also lit a bonfire, danced around it, and jumped over it.

St. John's fires (*sobótki*) were the main element of the rituals on St. John the Baptist's Eve, the night of 23–24 June. The earliest mentions of women's ring dances around bonfires date from the thirteenth century. Midsummer rituals trace their origins to archaic pagan rituals honoring the sun, love, and fertility during the summer solstice, the shortest night of the year. It was a time of happy amusement, singing, jumping through and around bonfires, professions of love, courtship, launching wreaths into the water by marriage-age girls, fortune-telling about marriage, searching for the crock of gold that could reveal treasures hidden in the earth, and free lovemaking, permitted by custom and tradition but condemned by the church. The ban on bathing in rivers and lakes "until St. John baptizes the water" is still in force. Geographically, the most widespread summer ceremony was the Feast of the Assumption (15 August). Blessing medicinal herbs, ears of corn, poppy heads, and garden flowers as well as other harvest festivities crowned the year's work of the peasant family. Previously in Poland, manorial and farmer harvest festivities were organized. Richer landowners arranged them for their families and the laborers hired for the duration of the harvest. The local lord or farmer, to whom the crown was brought, treated the reapers to food and drink, and people danced far into the night. Harvest songs expressed joy at the gathering of an abundant harvest and praised the wisdom of the farmers. The refrain *"Plon niesiemy plon / jaśnie panu w dom"* (Harvest, we're bringing in the harvest / to the house) was repeated many times.

On All Souls' Eve (1 November) the souls of the dead were believed to walk the earth. Marital fortunes were foretold on the eve of *Andrzejki* (St. Andrew's Day, 30 November). Boys told fortunes in a less widespread practice on *Katarzynki* (St. Catherine's Day, 25 November). Other fall and early winter customs occurred on *Barbórka* (St. Barbara's Day, 4 December), when a miners' feast and entertainment was held, and on the feast of St. Nicholas (6 December), in Poland the patron saint of beasts of prey (especially wolves), shepherds, and cattle. On that day in Mazovia offerings were made on the saint's altar. Gift-giving by persons dressed as St. Nicholas is a more recent custom.

MUSIC

The properties of Poland's folk music are mainly determined on the basis of local nineteenth-century materials (the Kolberg, Konopka, Lipiński, Gloger, Chałubiński, and Kleczyński collections) and a twentieth-century collection of 75,000 recordings in the Polish Academy of Sciences Art Institute, on which the series of publications *Polish Folk Song and Music: Sources and Materials* is based. Pan-Polish features include equal-half-tone twelve-note scales, major-minor scales, syllabic song (one sound per syllable of text), cadenza and glissando (mainly in slow song from Central Poland), and the predominance of monodic song (polyphony is characteristic only of the Carpathian zone). The melodies of songs fit seconds or thirds best, rarely greater intervals. The overall contour of the tune undulates with a descent at the end, and the melodic periods are essentially covered by dividing the text into verses and stanzas. The syllabic or syllabotonic versification system is most common: dodecasyllabic and hexosyllabic verse predominates in Podhale, while octosyllabic and tetrasyllabic verse is characteristic of Central Poland. Songs are usually formed from rhyming two- or four-verse phrases, though these are also heterosyllabic stanzas, and the lyrics tend to be padded with interjections (exclamations; for example, *hej*) or nonverbal refrains. The rhythms that gave rise to Polish national dances are particularly frequent in these songs. The mazurka (performed at a three-beat, fast tempo, with rhythmic compression in the first part of the bar) is encountered all over Poland but as a dance rhythm occurs only in Central Poland in dances with mazurka rhythms, for example, *kujawiak*, *mazur*, and *obertas*. The *krakowiak* (which is rapid, two-beat, and dodecasyllabic) predominates in the Kraków and Rzeszów regions. It has a syncopated rhythm. The *polonaise* (three-beat, slow) is rhythmically similar to the mazurka. Other features of Polish folksong include a lack of grace notes. The medium-toned natural voice from the chest predominates in vocalic articulation. Wedding songs are sung with a lower tone, and dance songs with a higher one. The slowest tempos may be heard in ritual songs in the open air, and the fastest in dance songs. Tunes are usually formally structured in stanzas, songs usually have eight or sixteen bars (or more due to repetition or refrains), and the division of musical periods is usually symmetrical $(4 + 4, 8 + 8, 2 + 2)$.

Most commonly, traditional ensembles included violin, tambourine, double-bass, or pipes and were later expanded by adding a second violin (playing the accompaniment in two simultaneous musical notes). Compositions were performed by multiple repetition of identical melodies, and fragments of the stanza were gradually enriched with ornaments, variants, transpositions, and repetitions.

Five major regions in Poland may be distinguished according to their music. The Central Polish complex (dominated by the three-part mazurka), which includes the Wielkopolska sub-region, exhibits many songs with polonaise and waltz rhythms, cheers (two- or three-part dances), figure dances, and repeated melodies. Typical instruments are the *mazanki*, pipes, *kozioł*, and double-bass. Characteristic of Kujawy is the *kujawiak* (slow dance with mazurka rhythms) as well as a rich violin-playing technique. Silesia has many polonaises, figure dances, and dance games, and wind instruments are included in bands. Mazovia is characterized by long, wooden advent and pastoral pipes (*ligawki*).

In the Northwest music has two- and three-beat meters, calm tempos, low tones of voice, and two-meter wooden pipes (*bazuny*), while music in the Northeast is characterized by two-, three-, five-, and eight-beat meters, the silencing of final syllables and sounds, and rich cadenzas in woodland songs.

The Eastern region is noted for many archaized, leisurely, non-metrical ritual chants and a three-beat dance repertoire, and in the South folk music is marked by a clear preponderance of two-beat melodies (also functioning as dance couplets) and widespread *krakowiak* rhythms. The Beskids are characterized by chromatic harmony and such instruments as the *trąbita* (long, wooden pastoral pipes) and *gajdy* (a kind of bagpipes), and Podhale and the Pieniny Mountains by non-harmonic polyphonic chant and such instruments as the *złóbcoki* (*gęśliki*, a kind of fiddle). Two dance cycles are typical only of Podhale: *góralski* (highlander, performed by men and women) and *zbójnicki* (highland robbers' folk dance, performed by men only). The men sing with their voices at a high pitch and at great tension, and the women with low, clear voices. Bands in the Rzeszów area include dulcimers.

Polish musical folklore shows links with Western European traditions as well as with that of the Eastern and Southern Slavs and Wallachians. Its influence outside Poland came with the spread of mazurka rhythms to the repertoire of European national dances during the Renaissance and baroque periods.

DANCE

The oldest Polish folk dances were unnamed ritual capers. Dances were defined by the type of movement involved, for example, "chase" or "jump." The accompaniment strengthened the rhythm. A major section of wedding dances was non-ritual dances in which every invited guest could participate. Ritual dances have become part of the roles of the persons performing certain functions. Other ceremonies were also occasions for midsummer rituals, harvest festivities, the *posiady* (social get-togethers in private houses) among the mountain people (*górale*), and the common dances organized several times a year. Five major "dance dialect" zones may be distinguished. In the Northwestern zone were dances named after their respective regions: Silesia, the area around Kalisz, Wielkopolska, *pałuckie*, Kujawy, Kashubia, Warmia, and Masuria. They comprised a large number of dances accompanied by playing and singing with a deliberate dancing style. Slow polonaise rhythms may be encountered in all regions in that zone. The range of the Central zone includes dances from the regions located round the mid-Vistula Basin: Kurpie, various parts of Mazovia around Warsaw, Western Podlasie, the areas around Łęczyca, Sieradz, Kielce, Powiśle (along the Vistula), and, to some extent, the Sandomierz area. These dances (for example, mazurkas, *oberki*, and *kujawiaki*) are dominated by mazurka rhythms, predominantly performed in a fast-paced whirl, yet evenly and smoothly. The Eastern zone sees the performance of dances currently called *podlaskie* (Northern and Eastern Podlasie), *lubelskie* (Lublin region), and *rzeszowskie* (Rzeszów region). They are a dynamic, joyful reflection of the dancers' sincerity and carefree amusement, resolution, boldness, and self-assuredness. The Southern zone encompasses Małopolska (Kraków region). Its dances have a dual beat, characterized by syncopated rhythms and swift tempos. They are full of dynamism and jesting, with men and women mostly dancing in pairs. The

Oberek dance from the Lowicz region, performed by the Folk Dance Ensemble of Maria Curie-Skłodowska University, Lublin, 2002. (From the archives of the Folk Dance Ensemble of UMCS)

Highland zone encompasses all mountain areas in Southern Poland, where folk traditions were linked to the shepherd culture. The *góralski* and *zbójnicki* as well as dances from all over the Beskids and Podtatrze (the Tatra highlands) characterize the region. They contrast starkly with the dances of the other zones in interaction among the dancers and the structure, choreographic technique, types of accompaniment, musical instruments used in the accompanying ensemble, and how songs are begun by dancers before the dance to affirm the rhythm. These forms of dance are further differentiated inside every region. For instance, about forty dances occur within the Lublin area. Several originally folk dances have been ennobled by passing into Polish culture to become national dances: the walking polonaise, *krakowiak*, *mazur*, *oberek*, and *kujawiak*. They were distinctive expressions of patriotism, especially when Poland was a nation without a state.

CHALLENGES OF THE MODERN WORLD

Three types of folklore may be distinguished in modern Polish culture: traditional folklore (now disappearing, though a vital phenomenon as recently as World War II), reconstructed traditional folklore, and spontaneous contemporary folklore. The classical verbal genres of traditional folklore are still living or only just remembered, the traditional ritual forms are undergoing gradual reduction and secularization, and the vocal, musical, and choreographic forms rarely occur. Almost all varieties of adult fairy tale have completely disappeared, and since the late nineteenth century they have become an exclusively children's genre. Riddles have lost their traditional everyday rural content and biblical themes and have become abstract, aiming at amusement (for example, "What flies around and glitters?—A fly with a gold tooth"; "What walks along the walls and taps?—A spider with its foot in a cast"). In numerous travesties and parodies of traditional proverbs it is not their core but their allegorical context that is transformed—traditional: "Hit the table and the scissors will reply"; modern: "Hit the table and it will fall to pieces." Short jokes, updated with strongly articulated punch lines, and enjoying massive popularity, have replaced longer comic stories. They are based on traditional prototypes such as relationships between ourselves and other people, stupid neighbors, and obscene topics. Nowadays, living traditional forms of folklore may be observed, especially in the regions that are resisting homogenization, mainly Podhale, Silesia, and Kashubia. It is important that immigrants from these regions who settle in multicultural states such as the United States and Canada also maintain their cultural continuity.

Reconstructed traditional folklore, or staged folklore, is frequently encountered today. It consists of both the intentional maintenance of authentic traditional folk genres, plots, and contents (the individual outputs of storytellers, writers, and poets writing in their local dialects, plus performances by rural musicians, bands playing traditional instruments, local customs and rituals) and the reconstruction of ritual forms that have already disappeared (such as weddings), which are relearned and stylistically elaborated along with their frequently expanded vocal, instrumental, and choreographic sides. This form of contemporary folklore is called derivative folklore or folklorism. It involves the reproduction in intentionally arranged situations of selected contents, plots, and forms of folklore. Customs and rituals related to former household tasks (such as spinning, plucking birds, and pickling cabbage) and to the annual cycle (for example, *Andrzejki* [marriage-related fortune-telling on St. Andrew's Eve], *Katarzynki* [fortune-telling for boys on St. Catherine's Day], caroling, homemade Nativity creches, *dyngus* [the ritual pouring of water on Easter Monday], Carnival mummers and scarecrows, weathercocks, rural spring festivals [*Marzanna, gaik*], midsummer bonfires and harvest festivities) occur most frequently. The most widespread form of reconstructed folklore is the traditional wedding. Here the natural multi-functional nature of genuine folklore (magical-religious, socio-ritual, economic-legal, and esthetic-recreational) focuses on a single function: spectacular-recreational. For the spectators, though, the tradition-based wedding is an esthetic experience.

The activities of various cultural and educational institutions serve to maintain these forms and thereby nurture tradition on the local, provincial, and national levels as well as through numerous folklore festivals, competitions, and reviews of folk groups. Important events encourage storytelling (*Sabałowe bajania* in Bukowina Tatrzańska), folk music (*Festiwal Kapel i Śpiewaków Ludowych* in Kazimierz Dolny), and dance (*Festiwal Folkloru Ziem Górskich* in Zakopane and *Światowy Festiwal Polonijnych Zespołw Folklorystycznych* in Rzeszów). In staged folklore primary stress is laid on culturally and regionally identified content, especially in the so-called authentic folkloristic groups that are active over most of rural Poland. Post-folklorism is another tendency for a contemporary form of national folklore to emerge. Little by little, the folklore of the individual ethnographic regions is becoming a symbol of national folklore, an expression of conventionalized popular patriotism, and a protection against destructive uniformity, especially in response to European integration processes.

Spontaneous contemporary folklore is an unrestrained, constantly changing creation of various settings ranging over the whole of society. It is multi-form in nature, depending on the situation in which it is created. It may be expressed in occupational-environmental and intersocial settings. The first includes the folklore of children, youth, tourists, laborers, prisoners, and sailors. It is a manifestation of microcultures' "philosophy" of life and creative activity, the material for which may also come from the mass media (especially television). Currently, intersocial folklore is very much alive and is being spread rapidly both directly through oral transmission and indirectly through transmission (writing, print, Internet, and other examples of derivative orality). Such forms of folklore as rumors, gossip, anecdotes, urban legends, jokes, social and sociopolitical satires, stereotypical toasts and formularized wishes such as wedding formulas, situational proverbs, and love and erotic phrases may be distinguished.

A "folk" trend is also developing in music in contrast to folklorism, represented by ethnographic museum song-and-dance groups, which reproduce traditional patterns (for example, the representative *Mazowsze* and *Śląsk* folklore groups). Discopolo songs, an example of this new musical-vocal folklore, may include ballad conventions, travesties, or the modernization of traditional common and convivial songs. They are "collectivized"—deprived of authorship—and their main function is entertainment. This type of music (recently disappearing) dominates traditional wedding dances, especially in rural, small-town, and work-related settings.

STUDIES OF POLISH FOLKLORE

The first programmatic interest in Polish folklore and folk culture emerged in the second half of the eighteenth century during the Enlightenment and flowered during the Romantic period (1822–1863), which emphasized authentic folk material as the supposed first, pre-historic stage of national literature. These interests took on two forms: collecting folklore (including the work of Doęga-Chodakowski, Pauli, Wacław from Olesko, and most eminently Kolberg) and adapting folklore material to literary contexts (for example, the work of Mickiewicz and Słowacki). In the second half of the nineteenth century collecting was put on a scholarly footing, and **ethnography** and folklore studies emerged as separate fields of study. Scholarly journals began publication: *Zbiór Wiadomości do Antropologii Krajowej* (1877–1895) and its successors: *Materiały Antropologiczno-Archeologiczne i Etnograficzne* (1896–1919), *Wisła* (1887–1916), and *Lud* (1895–1939, 1945–present). They belong to the basic canon of folkloristic sources along with Kolberg's monumental work *Lud, jego zwyczaje, sposób życia, mowa, podania, przysłowia, obrzędy, gusła, zabawy, pieśni, muzyka* (Folk, Its Customs, Way of Life, Speech, Tales, Proverbs, Rituals, Sorcery, Games, Songs, Music). Monographs on individual regions began to be published after 1865.

In 1895 Polskie Towarzystwo Ludoznawcze (Polish Ethnographical Association [PTL]), which included folklorists, was founded in Lwów. Since 1945 it has been headquartered in Wrocław. The PTL's publications include the annual *Lud* and the main folklore journal *Literatura Ludowa* (1957–1970, 1972–present). Since 1961 it has also been editing and re-editing in Poznań the collected works of Kolberg, totaling over eighty volumes, from manuscript materials. In 1910 the first department of ethnography in Poland was established at Jan Kazimierz University in Lwów. After Poland gained independence in 1918, five Polish universities had such departments.

Since World War II, folklore researches have been conducted in many institutions and university centers, including Opole, Warsaw, Wrocław, Lublin, Cieszyn, and Łódź. Important contributors to modern Polish folklore studies include Krzyżanowski (the founder of the Polish school of comparative studies in literature and folklore), Simonides, Hernas, and Sulima.

BIBLIOGRAPHY

Bartmiński, J. 1990. *Folklor—Język—poetyka* (Folklore—Language—Poetry). Wrocaw: Ossolineum.

Benet, S. 1996. *Song, Dance, and Customs of Peasant Poland.* 2nd edition. New York: Hippocrene Books.

Bryk, A., and St. Leszczyński. 1970. *Pieśni i tańce lubelskie* (Songs and Dances from the Lublin Region). Lublin: Wydawnictwo Lubelskie.

Brzozowska-Krajka, A. 1998. *Polish Traditional Folklore: The Magic of Time*, translated by W. Krajka. New York: Columbia University Press.

———. 1999a. Pan-European Proliferation of Folk Motifs: A Cure for Fragmentation? In *East-Central European Traumas and a Millennial Condition*, edited by Z. Biaas and W. Krajka. New York: Columbia University Press. 5–18.

———. 1999b. Polish Folklore Studies at the End of the Twentieth Century. *SEEFA Journal* 4.1:7–10.

————. 1999c. Time, No Time and Pure Potency in Folk Medicine. In *Proceedings of the International Congress. Shamanism and Other Indigenous Spiritual Beliefs and Practices*. Moscow: Russian Academy of Sciences Institute of Ethnology and Anthropology. 315–322.

Brzozowska-Krajka, A., and A. Monies-Mizera. 1999. Select Annotated Bibliography of Polish Folkloristics for the Period: 1990–98. *SEEFA Journal* 4.1:11–21.

Burszta, J. 1974. *Kultura ludowa—kultura narodowa. Szkice i rozprawy* (Folk culture—National Culture: Sketches and Debates). Warszawa: Ludowa Spółdzielnia Wydawnicza.

————. 1985. *Chłopskie źródła kultury* (Peasant Sources of Culture). Warszawa: Ludowa Spdzielnia Wydawnicza.

Dąbrowska, G. 1981. Taniec ludowy (Folk Dance). In *Etnografia Polski. Przemiany kultury ludowej* (Polish Ethnography: Changes in Folk Culture), Volume 2, edited by M. Biernacka and others. Wrocław: Ossolineum. 285–326.

Jagiełło, J. 1975. *Polska ballada ludowa* (Polish Folk Ballad). Wrocław: Ossolineum.

Kasjan, J. M. 1983. *Polska zagadka ludowa* (Polish Folk Riddle). Wrocław: Ossolineum.

Kolberg, O. 1977. *Przysłowia* (Proverbs), edited by St. Świrko. Warszawa: Ludowa Spłdzielnia Wydawnicza.

Krzyżanowski, J. 1962. *Polska bajka ludowa w układzie systematycznym* (The Taxonomy of the Polish Folktale), Volume 1. Wrocław: Ossolineum.

————. 1971. Folklorystyka polska (Polish Folklore Studies). In *Dzieje folklorystyki w Europie* (The History of Folklore Studies in Europe), edited by G. Cocchiara, translated by W. Jekiel. Warszawa: Państwowy Instytut Wydawniczy. 629–638.

————. 1980. *Szkice folklorystyczne*. Volume 3: *Wokół legendy i zagadki. Z zagadnień przysłowioznawstwa* (Folklore Sketches, Volume 3: On Legends and Riddles, Problems of Proverb Studies). Kraków: Wydawnictwo Literackie.

————, ed. 1965. *Słownik folkloru polskiego*. Warszawa: Wiedza Powszechna.

Kwaśniewicz, K. 1981. *Zwyczaje i obrzędy rodzinne* (Family Customs and Rites). In *Etnografia Polski. Przemiany kultury ludowej*, Volume 2 (Polish Ethnography: Changes in Folk Culture), edited by M. Biernacka and others. Wrocław: Ossolineum. 89–126.

Moszyński, K. 1967. *Kultura ludowa Słowian*. Volume 2: *Kultura duchowa* (Slavic Folk Culture. Volume 2: Spiritual Culture). Warszawa: Wiedza Powszechna.

Ogrodowska, B. 1996. *Święta polskie: Tradycja i obyczaj* (Polish Festivities: Tradition and Custom). Warszawa: Alfa.

Pełka, L. J. 1987. *Polska demonologia ludowa* (Polish Folk Demonology). Warszawa: Iskry.

Pokropek, M. 1978. *Atlas sztuki ludowej i folkloru w Polsce* (The Atlas of Folk Art and Folklore in Poland). Warszawa: Arkady.

Simonides, D. 1981. *Folklor słowny* (Verbal Folklore). In *Etnografia Polski: Przemiany kultury ludowej* (Polish Ethnography: Changes in Folk Culture), Volume 2, edited by M. Biernacka and others. Wrocław: Ossolineum. 327–343.

Stęszewski, J. 1981. *Muzyka ludowa* (Folk Music). In *Etnografia Polski: Przemiany kultury ludowej*, Volume 2, edited by M. Biernacka and others. Wroclaw: Ossolineum. 245–284.

Thomas, W. I., and F. Znaniecki. 1974. *The Polish Peasant in Europe and America*. Volume 1. New York: Octagon Books.

Tomicki, R. 1978. Religious Dualism in the Slavic Cosmogonic Myth. In *Poland at the Tenth International Congress of Anthropological and Ethnological Sciences*, edited by M. Frankowska and others, translated by J. Sehnert. Wrocław: Ossolineum. 59–67.

Anna Brzozowska-Krajka (Translated from the Polish by Robert A. Orr)

ROMA

GEOGRAPHY AND HISTORY

The Romani (Gypsy) people number about 10 million and live in diasporic communities throughout the world, primarily in Europe and the United States. Terminology for Romani groups is problematic. Most of the standard ethnonyms stem from false historical connections and are considered derogatory. The English "Gypsy" and its cognates (Spanish *Gitano* or French *Gitan*) derive from the mistaken notion that Romani people were Egyptians. Moreover, European derivatives of *Tsingani*—*Țigan* (Romanian) or *Zigeuner* (German)—erroneously indicate Romani descent from the *Atsingani*, a Byzantine heretical sect. To reflect the current practice of Romani organizations, "Rom" (plural: Roma) is used here as a noun to replace "Gypsy." The largest Romani communities in the world are in Southeast Europe, and this survey focuses largely on the Balkans.

Comparative linguistic evidence points to the origins of Romani society in northern India. Sometime after 1000 C.E., Romani communities migrated northwest, making their way through Persia and Armenia and eventually arriving in the Balkans by the fourteenth century. Within 100 years they were spreading across Europe. Wherever Roma have journeyed or settled, they have met with negative attitudes on the part of majority ethnic populations due to their dark features, distinctive culture, and non-mainstream way of life. Typically surviving on the margins of society, Romani people are perceived as a distinct "other" in relation to the mainstream world and, indeed, sometimes cultivate this image themselves. Two events stand out in the long and bitter history of the Romani: slavery and the Holocaust. As Roma moved into Romania in the late fourteenth century, they were systematically enslaved by the Romanian nobility, clergy, and state. This continued for five centuries, until 1864, when emancipation was legislated, and the following years of transition were extremely difficult. Emancipation spurred waves of emigration both eastward and westward from Romania in the late nineteenth century, especially to the United States; Seventy years later, between 1933 and 1945, Romani citizens throughout Europe were targeted alongside others for annihilation as "undesirable" members of society. Hundreds of thousands perished in Nazi death camps.

Roma traditionally have been craftsmen and laborers for local populations as well as specialists in various skills serving and/or performing for dominant society. Many of the occupations Roma engaged in demanded that they be itinerant: music-making, fortune-telling, bear-training, horse-dealing, woodworking, and basketry, for example. A nomadic way of life, adopted over the years as Roma migrated and traveled (both for their work and due to expulsion), was at one time widespread. At present, however, nomadism is relatively uncommon since most Romani groups have long been settled or are only seasonally or semi-peripatetic.

Romani society is extremely diverse and complex. No single experience unites worldwide or even localized Romani communities. Roma have no exclusive territorial base, nor do they share a way of life or religious faith. Physical characteristics are not universal. Some—but not all—speak Romani (which encompasses numerous local dialects), and other languages employed are as diverse as the countries in which Roma have settled. Degrees of traditionalism and levels of assimilation also vary greatly between groups. Despite this heterogeneity, three general principles underlie Romani social organization. The first is the centrality of the family, which, including the extended family, is the fundamental social unit among Roma. Critical to the culture of the family, Romani society is patrilocal (a bride moves to her husband's family's household and becomes a source of labor there). Second is a strong sense of group identity. Romani communities are internally organized according to groups and sub-groups that intersect and overlap. They are based primarily on regional, occupational, linguistic, and/or religious distinctions. In some Romani communities in the United States and Europe, social categories reflect family, clan, and tribal structures, termed (in Romani) *familia*, *vitsa*, and *natsia*, respectively. By contrast, Romani group identity in much of East Europe is based on traditional economic activities. Group designations such as *fierari* (blacksmiths) and *rudari* (woodcarvers) in Romania or *kalaidzhii* (tinsmiths) and *koshnichari* (basket makers) in Bulgaria mirror occupational identity and the primary terms of self-ascription by specific groups. While there is a strong sense of cohesion within internal tribal and other Romani social groups, they have little contact with each other. Relations between diverse groups and sub-groups are typically minimal and even hostile at times. As a third general principal of Romani life, boundaries between Roma and non-Roma (termed *gadzhe*, sg. *gadzho*) starkly demarcate social structure. Roma are the underprivileged and powerless in society, while non-Roma are privileged and powerful. A recognition of this divide is embedded in a collective Romani understanding of the world. Much of the Romani worldview is informed, then, by social boundaries and perceived distinctions between "us" and "them": in the context of the family, intra-Romani group dynamics, and Romani/non-Romani relations.

It is difficult to speak of a single belief system among Roma. Religious faith varies since Romani groups usually adopt the dominant religion of the region in which they live (and are thus Christian or Muslim). Formerly, however, in much of traditional Romani society, a belief system rooted in pollution taboos was operative. In its most rigid form, this system prescribes the strict separation between Roma (pure) and non-Roma (polluting). Violation of this code results in being defiled (*maxrime*) and potentially expelled from the community. Ritualized rules also concern the upper and lower parts of the body—viewed as clean and unclean, respectively—and inform taboos pertaining to menstruating women, childbirth, sexual relations, contact with the lower part of the body, and food preparation. Some American and English communities maintain strict adherence to pollution rules, while more moderate beliefs are observed in varying degrees in parts of Europe. At the same time, large numbers of Roma, such as in East Europe, no longer follow or even recognize these prescriptions.

Whether or not Romani folklore is simply the borrowed folklore of the dominant population among whom Roma live or their own indigenous traditions is much debated. Undoubtedly, Romani folklore shares much in common with that of surrounding communities. It is a commonplace that Roma often preserve dominant-populace folklore longer than its own members do. But Romani folklore—even in the context of shared traditions—also has its own imprint. This does not mean that there is a universal "Gypsy" folklore. Rather, it means that while related to the adjacent traditions, folklore among Roma also reveals distinctive elements in terms of content, performance, and style. Thus, folklore genres often reflect Romani themes such as grief (for example, due to estrangement, imprisonment, or aging) or conflict between Roma and non-Roma. Furthermore, Romani folklore is typically performed with an expressive, demonstrative style and is frequently embellished through improvisation and ornamentation (especially in music, song, and dance).

LIFE-CYCLE CELEBRATIONS

Romani folklore takes place on two performance stages: the first is for Romani in-group events, and the second for out-group, non-Romani consumption. Romani in-group folklore takes place at family celebrations (for example, baptisms or circumcisions) or private gatherings of relatives and close friends. By contrast, folklore for out-group audiences or consumers happens in public settings such as non-Romani festivities (mainly weddings). The practitioners of most out-group folklore are traditional male Romani musicians—customarily instrumentalists (though many sing as well)—who earn their living by performing. Where there are female musicians, they are usually vocalists. The instruments and genres that such musicians employ are distinctive to the regions where they reside. In East Europe, they pass on their skills and occupation through the male kin line and have been performing for mainstream—as well as Romani—society in some cases since the fourteenth century. In certain areas, these are entire groups or clans, such as the *lăutari*, Romani musicians in Romania, who were formerly slaves, or *muzikanti* (musicians) in Bulgaria. Genres that *lăutari* play for non-Romani audiences include lyric, epic, and ritual wedding songs as well as dance music. The best-known Romani professional musicians are from **Hungary**, the Balkans, and **Spain**. In all of these cases, the music they play for non-Roma overlaps significantly with Romani repertoire.

Customs that accompany childbirth in many Romani communities guard against pollution and complications. Sympathetic magic is commonly evoked in the folklore of birth. Prohibitions surrounding the activities of pregnant women among traditional Bulgarian Roma include not jumping over ropes or chains and the rejection of certain foods (rabbit, fish, or snails) for the protection of the child. Men are not permitted to associate with women during and after birth. Once a baby is born, it is washed and purified (in salted water), and both mother and child are separated from the community for a period of three, seven, or forty days on account of her being considered polluted, though she is occasionally visited by other women, especially those who wish to become pregnant. The baby is carefully protected until its christening. In **Poland**, a newborn baby is shielded from the evil eye with talismans. In Hungary, mirrors are covered in homes in which a baby has been born so that its soul does not escape through the "passageway" provided to the Otherworld. Traditional practices among American Roma are comparable. When the baby is three days old, it is dressed in newly made clothes and wears an amulet until its baptism to ensure good luck (*baxt*).

Among Orthodox Christian and Catholic Roma, church christening is a ritual of purification. It is performed by a priest and attended by the godparents and guests. The godparents, chosen at this time, share in a lifelong ritualized bond with the child that includes mutual obligations: gift-giving and services to each other. Women later sprinkle holy water throughout the household to shield the baby from impurities. If a baby becomes sick after it is christened, a second baptism may occur in order to cure the illness. In some East European communities, the child also undergoes a "Romani baptism." Among Romani-speaking Hungarian Vlach Roma (the second-largest Romani group in Hungary), the Romani baptism entails a festive celebration for men, who sing and drink through the night as the baby's father and godfather cement their new relationship. In Balkan Romani communities, professional Romani musicians are typically hired for baptism celebrations, in which music, dancing, and feasting take place.

For Muslim Roma in **Macedonia** and Bulgaria, male circumcision is also a festive family celebration. Professional Romani musicians provide the music for such events in traditional ensembles consisting of the *zurla* (an oboe-like, conical-bore instrument with a double reed) and *tapan* (a cylindrical, double-headed drum).

Weddings are the most celebrated events of the life cycle among Roma. The attention and festivities accorded weddings reflect the significance of marriage within the Romani community, since it provides, through the potential for children, the basis for the family and the principal means for transmitting Romani culture. Most Roma practice in-group (endogamous) Romani marriage. Endogamy within smaller groups and sub-groups also is preferred and quite frequent, though in no way universal. Among very traditional Roma such as the *spoitori* (tinsmiths) and *căldărari* (coppersmiths) in Romania, some adolescents marry in their early teens; many, however, marry later. At times betrothals are arranged by parents between young children, who then wait some years to marry. Although brideprice has died out among many Roma (for example, by the mid-twentieth century in Poland), it still survives in some communities where marriages are arranged. The bride's father asks for a given amount for his daughter when betrothal plans are made. Engagement parties are sometimes held at this time (lamb is typically served). Balkan Romani weddings traditionally occur after St. George's Day—in late April or early May. In the past, weddings took place over an entire week; now they usually last one to three days.

Rituals preceding the wedding banquet underscore the economic nature of marriage as well as traditional gender roles, purification, the couple's separation from childhood and entry into adulthood, and fertility. Many of the rituals parallel wedding practices in dominant society. The bride customarily brings a dowry to her new home. Among some Roma (in Bulgaria and **Greece**), the dowry is exhibited at her parents' home for several days before the wedding. In Bulgarian and Macedonian Muslim Romani communities, on the day before the wedding the bride takes a ceremonial public bath accompanied by women and musicians, who play ritual music on the *zurla* and *tapan*. Invoking the purifying power of the color red that imbues Romani wedding symbolism, the bride dons a red kerchief to guard against pollution and the evil eye. A henna ritual is also performed. Henna, a brown dye, is rubbed into the fingers and palms of the bride while coins pressed into them leave imprints. It is said that the longer the traces of henna remain on the bride's hands, the longer she will be loved by her husband. Throughout these rituals, the bride ritually weeps as she prepares to leave her family. Following the henna ceremony, a procession with music and dancing passes through the bride's neighborhood.

On the day of the wedding, a banner is displayed for the groom—an emblem decorated with tokens of fertility and purity such as pieces of fruit and popcorn strung on red thread. In a male ritual that marks his passage into manhood, the groom is then "shaved for the first time" while professional Romani musicians perform ritual songs. Indeed, music pervades the events of the wedding day. The bride is dressed in special attire (usually white) in the morning. Her veil is then ceremoniously placed on her head by her godmother and female kin while musicians sing to her, articulating the separation she is making from her girlhood. The bride is often offered a mirror at this time to view her own maidenly

Romani musicians perform as the bride is veiled and regards herself in the mirror in her home. Piteşti, Romania, 25 August 2002. (Photograph by Margaret H. Beissinger)

beauty before she becomes a wife. Meanwhile, the groom and his party make their way with music and dancing through the streets to the bride's house, where he joins her and is met by her parents. In Bulgaria, the bride's mother greets the couple with bread dipped in honey (representing fertility), which she puts in their mouths, expressing hopes that a year henceforth they will also hold a baby—preferably male—in their arms. The wedding guests typically celebrate for some time in front of the bride's home with music, dancing, and food. The bride, groom, and guests then proceed on through the neighborhood. Occasionally, the bride is displayed seated on the top of a car in which the groom rides. Following this, the couple sometimes attends a religious wedding ceremony. While traditional weddings often take place without a service, among more assimilated Romani groups such as Orthodox Christian Roma in **Russia** and the Balkans, a church wedding is fully part of the day's sequence.

The key event of the wedding day is the banquet, where feasting and dancing continue late into the evening or all night. At rural weddings, banquets occur under a large tent; in cities, they are often in restaurants. In southern Romania, music during the banquet includes song and dance played by professional Romani musicians (*lăutari*) on traditional instruments (violin, accordion, cimbalom, and bass viol) or electrically amplified instruments (accordion, synthesizer, clarinet, and drums). Dance music includes traditional Romani in-group genres (for example, the *lăutar* or "Gypsy" *hora*) as well as a solo improvised dance (*manea*, plural *manele*), which is among the most popular dance forms at weddings throughout the Balkans. Its music reflects regional and Middle Eastern influences. While formerly a female Romani

Lăutar ("*Gypsy*" *hora*) at a Romani wedding banquet, Bucharest, Romania, 26 May 2001. (Photograph by Margaret H. Beissinger)

in-group genre, it is now also danced by mixed-gender groups and non-Roma. In traditional Russian and Ukrainian Romani communities, men and women are seated separately at the wedding feast, as if to underscore the profound contrasts between gender roles in traditional Romani marriage. Later in the evening, among East European Roma guests present the couple with money, the standard wedding gift, which is publicly announced (often by one of the musicians). The newly married bride's veil is then removed, and she dons a kerchief, typically weeping at this time and gazing in the mirror as she bids farewell to her maidenhood. As her godmother and other women hover around her to place the kerchief on her head, the musicians continue to sing from the ritual wedding repertoire. In the bridal song printed below—which was performed by a *lăutar* in Mârşa, Romania, in 2002—the vocalist sings to the bride, whose "voice" then addresses her mother. The "foreign home" is her husband's, where she will soon move. The "flower" is her maidenhood.

> "Bid, oh bride, farewell
> To your father, to your mother,
> To you brothers, to your sisters,
> To your garden full of flowers,
> To the neighbors
> Whom you grew up with."

> "Weep, oh Mama, weep with pity,
> For I was your child
> And now I leave you behind
> And go alone to a foreign home.
> You don't find at your mother-in-law's
> Love from your daddy.
> You don't find at your father-in-law's
> The good times like before.
> When I was mama's little girl;
> I knew how to wear a flower,
> I knew how to wear a flower."

Following the banquet, the couple, their family, and their close friends proceed to the groom's home, where the bride is met by her new mother-in-law, often with bread and honey and a small child—reiterating the underlying message of fertility. Another feast is served, followed among traditional Roma by the nuptial consummation as the newlyweds retire and re-emerge later with evidence, it is hoped, of the bride's virginity: blood on her nightgown or sheets. In Bulgaria, the groom's mother and sisters exhibit the blood-stained cloth as they perform a traditional dance. The color red is a potent symbol expressed throughout Romani weddings of the purity that the virginal blood represents and the power of fire as a purifying element. The next day, another meal is served for the in-laws and close friends. Elopement—viewed as a type of betrothal—also occurs at times, sometimes as an alternative to a costly wedding or when either family evinces resistance to the marriage. In this case, plans are sometimes made for a later wedding celebration.

Weddings among American Roma are grand, costly affairs often held in rented halls. People travel long distances to attend them. The wedding arrangements are made by the fathers of the couple, and wedding sponsors (a married couple) are then chosen. The female sponsor helps the bride as she dresses for the wedding. Her red veil (*diklo*) is then placed, along with a red rose, on a stick and wielded by unmarried girls, who dance in a circle while the men remain separate. The bride joins the dance but later is led away while the female sponsor and other women place the veil on her head. This is a crucial ritual juncture since from this time on, the bride is considered married. The bride is then blessed by her family, and they ritually bid farewell to each other while the bride predictably sobs. Sometimes dramatic opposition and wailing express resistance to this moment of social rupture. The feast and collection of cash for the couple, conducted by the male sponsor, follow, as does subsequent merrymaking, which lasts for three days. On the second night, the newlyweds sleep together, followed by the requisite display of bridal honor (virginal blood). As a final symbolic gesture, the two mothers braid the bride's hair, interweaving her veil in the braids.

Death rites in traditional Romani communities focus on pollution and the soul of the deceased (*mulo*). The corpse—considered contaminated—is prepared soon after death. It is bathed in salted water, dressed in new clothes, and placed in a coffin by female kin. Coins are placed on the closed eyes of the dead so that the "traveler" will have money to pay for his or her journey to the afterlife. Other objects deposited in the coffin include the deceased's comb (a possession regarded as polluted that must be removed from the living) and scissors (to defend the dead from evil spirits). Mirrors in the home of the deceased are covered since they represent an unnatural portal for the soul to reach the land of the dead. The deceased is mourned for up to three days. During this time, the corpse is closely guarded, and candles are kept lit nearby. Underscoring the polluted state in which the corpse and mourners find themselves, it is initially forbidden for the mourners (for example, among Polish and Hungarian Roma) to comb their hair or bathe. Mourners often grieve through ritualized lament. Laments include the "voice" of the deceased, who "speaks" to the mourners, as well as the mourners' voices addressing the deceased. In Vlach Romani communities in Hungary, laments are performed mainly by older men (sometimes older women) and center upon themes of the agony of fate, death as a painful departure from one's family, and the inescapable plight of Romani life, including the metaphor of wandering. As a lament recorded in Hungary in the late 1980s has it,

> That one has to go to the cemetery?
> . . . .
> To die, to die, one has to die.
> I have to leave my family behind.
> Unfortunate as I am,
> I must perish this way.
> . . . .
> I am wandering and cannot find a place
> Where I can put my head down.
> I put my head on the soil.
> Look how much I am suffering!
>
> I live, I live, but for what?
> When I do not have a single happy day?
> Oh, my God, it is so bad for me.
> My life is full of mourning.

A funeral is a communal event in Romani society, attended by many. Afterward, a feast is held for the mourners. Strict mourning is demonstrated by abstaining from merrymaking, wearing dark attire, leaving beards unshaven for men, and cutting off hair for women. The mourning is formally demarcated at regular intervals by a remembrance feast (*pomana*). The length of time one mourns reflects the degree of relatedness to the deceased and religious conventions. Once the final remembrance feast takes place in Polish Romani communities, a celebration is held with singing and dancing to usher the mourners back into normal routines.

Beliefs concerning the soul of the departed (*mulo*, pl. *mule*) play a significant role in Romani death rites. In East Europe, a coffin is typically removed from a house through a window so that the deceased does not return through the front door to haunt the living. If an unmarried person dies, a mock wedding is held to guard against the return of the unfulfilled dead soul (*mulo*) to torment the living. Slovak Romani communities believe that *mule* return to haunt the living but can be averted with food offerings placed on windowsills, in corners, or on thresholds (particularly at Christmas). In the past among Roma in **England**, Romania, and Poland, the deceased's belongings were burned or destroyed. Among the *Mānuš* (*Manouches*), a longtime Romani community in central **France**, burning and disposing of the possessions of the departed as well as refraining from speaking about him or her are central to the belief system. In this way, the *Mānuš* find a silent "place" for the deceased in their spiritual collective. A mourner may also pay respect by abandoning a habit or preferred activity of the dead. Later that loss is resurrected in the life of the mourner, and in this way, a full circle of recognition, honor, and respect for the departed is completed.

CALENDAR CUSTOMS

Romani calendrical-cycle folklore consists of seasonal-religious holidays that for the most part have been adopted and adapted by Roma from the surrounding population. Most of them have pagan roots in agricultural folklore, and even those ostensibly related to religious holidays are secular celebrations among most Roma. While concerns expressed during these holidays are fertility, prosperity, foretelling the future, and mutual forgiving, socializing and partying among relatives and friends take center stage.

Over time, many seasonal holidays have merged with Christian holidays, a good number of them Orthodox and Catholic saints' day celebrations as well as Christmas and Easter. Christmas among Roma centers on feasting and making merry. The proverbial "Christmas pig" graces the table among Romanian Roma. The *slava*, a saint's-day celebration feast, is the central event at Easter among Roma in the United States. Relatives and friends open their doors, sharing food and drink and wishing each other well. They also exchange green- and red-dyed eggs, a tradition practiced by Muslim Roma as well. Indeed, Balkan Muslim Roma celebrate Easter in addition to various saints' days as secular holidays. In East Europe, St. Elijah's Day (or Ali Baba's for Muslims), St. Lazarus's Day among rural Roma, St. Theodore's Day (with its "brides' fair"), and many more that coincide with seasonal thresholds or junctures provide occasions, both large and small, for celebration among Roma. During the late spring and early summer, peasants sprinkle water on young Romani girls dressed in greenery who go from house to house singing the *paparuda* in Romania or *peperuda*, as it is called in Bulgaria, a ritual song to induce rain, the performance of which has been preserved only by Roma.

The most prominent saint's day holiday among Southeast European Roma is St. George's Day (23 April or 6 May in the Orthodox Church calendar). It is observed by Christians and by Muslims, who call it the Day of the Cauldrons or Erdelezi. Festivities last up to three days and signal the beginning of spring and the first time that animals are taken to pasture. The centerpiece is a copious feast with roast lamb, the quintessential sacrificial animal. Indeed, among Macedonian Muslim Roma, butchering the lamb is itself a ritual accompanied by music on the *zurla* and *tapan*, played by Romani musicians. According to legend, young boys used to be offered as victims on this day until St. George pitied them and substituted lambs from his own flock instead, thus saving the boys' lives. Themes of fertility, including love and marriage, are associated with St. George's Day. Among Bulgarian Roma, future events, including marriages, are foretold at this time in a custom called "singing the rings": girls place their rings in a container; someone tells a fortune and then pulls out a ring whose owner is the person to whom the future is told. In Romania, Romani girls bake cakes with an herbal aphrodisiac, which they distribute. Thus, St. George's Day serves to bring quarreling lovers or even spouses back together. Bride capture (elopement) is even sanctioned by some Roma on this day, while the traditional wedding season commences directly following it.

St. Basil's Day is the other major saint's day observed by south and east Slavic Roma, who merge three days of celebration (13–15 January on the Orthodox calendar) with New Year's festivities. In Russia and **Ukraine**, celebrants go from house to house visiting relatives and neighbors and singing carols. A legend holds that at one time people obliterated all the Roma in the world except for a little boy, whom St. George saved, and a little girl, rescued by St. Basil. Once all the other Roma were eradicated, people got bored since there was no one left to entertain them. Then the two Romani children were brought forth and began to sing and dance. They made everyone happy and went on to perpetuate all the subsequent generations of Roma.

In France on 24–25 May, a spring pilgrimage of thousands of Catholic Roma from throughout Europe celebrates and ritually purifies the statue of "Black Sara," adopted as a Romani patron saint but never canonized by the church. Sara was the maid of Jesus's aunts, believed to have been miraculously washed up in the French Camargue after the Crucifixion. Music, especially flamenco (a traditional Spanish Romani genre), figures prominently in this festival.

SONGS AND MUSIC

Non-professional Romani musicians perform in-group, non-ritual music at informal gatherings in private. Both men and women sing but do so chiefly without traditional instruments. This is the case among rural Vlach Roma in Hungary and **Slovakia** as well as some Romani groups in Romania. They distinguish two categories of song: slow songs, expressing grief, nostalgia, and longing (including some performed at wakes), and fast or dance songs. Heartache and suffering are common themes in the slow songs, though cheerier topics are also expressed. The following, sung by a member of the Romanian *ursari* (bear trainers), conveys a representative Romani theme—the agony of prison life, which breaks family ties and frustrates hope:

> The wind blows through the leaves;
> Letters no longer arrive.
> Perhaps the mail service is down,
> Or my mama-dear has forgotten me.
> My brother doesn't visit me;
> He's abandoned me like a dog.
> Oh world, what woe!
> . . . .
> May the prison guards fall asleep [oh mama]
> So that I can escape from here, oh God!

Romani non-ritual songs express hardship in many forms, for example, lovesickness, loss, poverty, and injustice. The following song from Slovakia makes reference to the Nazi camps in which Roma were interred during World War II:

> In the concentration camp,
> The Gypsies work hard;
> They work hard
> And they go barefooted.

Do not beat me, do not beat me
Or you will murder me.
I have children at home.
Who will bring them up?

Dance songs are also sung at Romani in-group gatherings (as well as at weddings or celebrations for which professional musicians have not been hired). Clapping, snapping fingers, stomping feet, and percussive effects on household objects such as spoons, pots, or pans typically accompany a lead singer. Female family members customarily dance to this music.

Professional musicians also perform non-ritual, in-group songs. They likewise sing of heartache and grief (from passion, infidelity, envy, drinking, or growing old) as well as of the pleasures of family life, especially their children and material well-being. Professional Romani musicians in southern Romania often sing such *lăutar* or "Gypsy" music, songs accompanied by traditional instruments typically interpreted in a distinctive vocal style marked by vibrato, falsetto, and emotional expression. The voice in the following song from Romania is that of a parent who expresses love for his or her children and willingness to make sacrifices for them. The female Romani vocalist sings professionally with her husband's family's village ensemble.

For whom did I work
All of my life?
For my son, for my daughter,
For my house and home.
All my life I worked
Just for my children,
To raise them in happiness
To bring them much joy.

I have lost entire nights [working]
And entire days as well
Just for you, my child,
To raise you [my dear one].

FOLKTALES

Romani folktales are told among family members and friends. Storytellers are non-professionals, either male or female, adults or children. Accomplished performers engage and entertain their audiences sometimes for hours on end. Although storytelling happens when people gather casually, it also transpires in more formal settings such as at funerals or baptisms. Among Greek Roma, storytelling takes place during death rites, often providing, as it does for Vlach Roma in Slovakia, levity from the intensity of mourning. Storytelling by Vlach Roma in Hungary occurs in gendered groups. When men tell tales, they perform for mixed-gender or all-male audiences. Their deliveries are intense, marked by elaborate formulas and lively audience participation. By contrast, female storytellers perform only for other women and children and adopt a less demonstrative style. Prose narrations are sometimes combined with intermittent, slow songs in a type of *chant-fable* form.

Romani folktales include three large categories: legends, anecdotes, and wonder tales. The most numerous are legends—termed *svati* (sg. *svata*)—which are believed to contain some amount of truth. Legends evoke Romani themes and are remarkably down-to-earth. A frequent topic is origins, as in the Hungarian Romani tale that relates how "the devil helped God create the world" or the Spanish narrative that tells how God meted out destinies to all people except the "Gypsies, who have no real assigned place in the world and live or eat by their own wits." In Greece, legends explain why Roma "don't have an alphabet" and why they eat hedgehog. A Russian legend tells how Roma dispersed throughout the world (a "Gypsy traveled right around the earth, and everywhere he went he left a child behind"), while Serbian legends answer why so many Roma are musicians (God and St. Peter willed it) and why they have no church (it was made of cheese, and they ate it). Many legends account for the Romani way of life. Generosity and hospitality are represented, but so are less flattering aspects such as the alleged aversion to the mainstream work ethic; the blessing by a Spanish Christ concludes that Roma "will eat but not work." Another legend (also found among other minorities) holds that Roma fashioned the nails for Christ's Crucifixion. Legends about the *mule* or dead souls are common as well, for example, the tale of the Balkan "Vana," a young mother who dies soon after the birth of her baby but whose dead soul cannot rest until she has repossessed the child and taken him with her to the land of the dead.

Romani storytellers also tell humorous anecdotes, including bawdy tales and jokes that, like legends, concern the Romani world and are told with directness and simplicity. A tale from Bosnia pokes fun at the proverbial Romani love of eating, describing hyperbolic amounts of food in a dreamed-of "Gypsy paradise," while an American anecdote mocks the Romani super-wedding, an event so overwhelming that the bride chokes on an egg yolk at her own nuptials (but later is revived). A common character is the Romani trickster who outwits non-Roma, often giving serious topics an amusing spin. In a Greek allegorical tale, a "little Gypsy" defeats a giant, while in a Czech narrative, a Romani woman beats a prison guard in a riddling contest, thus freeing her husband from jail.

Finally, Romani storytellers tell wonder tales or *Märchen* (*paramichi*, sg. *paramicha*), which in contrast to legends and anecdotes are virtually all generic and rarely include Romani characters or themes. Many instead find parallels in the international corpus of wonder tales. Narratives of magic, initiation, quests, and journeys to the Otherworld are routine. Thus, tales circulating among Greek Roma include fearless heroes, magic belts, and golden birds in golden cages—classic wonder-tale motifs. Moreover, Polish Roma tell a male Cinderella narrative, and a Czech Romani tale of "two children" is a stirring, familiar narrative of triumph over misfortune and the loss of parents. While these wonder tales do not explicitly refer to Romani content, Romani readings of them invariably render poignant, meaningful sub-texts: the unlikely and downtrodden succeed, justice triumphs over injustice, and the virtues of generosity and kindness overcome selfishness and wrongdoing. Of course, these same tales also have immense universal appeal.

STUDIES OF ROMANI FOLKLORE

A general introduction to Romani history is found in Fraser (1995). Works that treat Romani culture by country include Sutherland (1975) for the United States, Marushiakova and Popov (1997) and Tomova (1995) for Bulgaria, Ficowski (1989) for Poland, Stewart (1997) for Vlachs in Hungary, and Williams (2003) for the *Mānuš* of France. A fine survey of Romani traditional music is Carol Silverman (2000). Volume 38.1 (1996), a special issue of *The World of Music*, titled *Music of the Roma: Ethnicity, Identity, and Multiculturalism*, contains articles devoted to Romani music, and Baumann (2000) contains essays on Romani traditional culture, especially music. Monographs on Romani music and musicians include Kovalcsik (1985). For Hungary, Sárosi (1978) and Lange (2003) are informative, as is Starkie (1933), though it is somewhat dated. Beissinger (1991) treats professional traditional Romani musicians in southern Romania. Keil and Keil (2002) is a descriptive account of Romani music in Greece, with photos by Dick Blau. Flamenco as a traditional Romani genre is treated in Schreiner (1990). The best anthology of Romani folktales is Tong (1989). Yates (1995 [1948]) includes tales but little commentary.

Several videotapes present traditional Romani music. Gatliff (1993) is a musical travelogue with eight portraits of Romani musicians and their performances from northern India to France and Spain. Marre (1992) also provides an overview of Romani music as the film treats India and then travels through East Europe featuring performers. Erdevicki-Charap (1999) offers a view of the female Czech Romani singer Ṽra Bílá and her ensemble of accompanying musicians.

Sound recordings of Romani music are far more numerous. Anthologies include *Latcho Drom* (1993), *Road of the Gypsies* (1997; notes by Weber), *World of Gypsies Vol. 1–3* (2000–2003; notes by Heller), and *Gypsy Caravan* (2001). Many other recordings feature Romani music from specific countries and culture areas.

BIBLIOGRAPHY

Baumann, Max Peter, ed. 1996. *Music of the Roma: Ethnicity, Identity, and Multiculturalism*. The *World of Music* 38.1 (special issue).

———. 2000. *Music, Language, and Literature of the Roma and Sinti*. Berlin: VWB, Verlag für Wissenschaft und Bildung.

Beissinger, Margaret. 1991. *The Art of the Lăutar: The Epic Tradition of Romania*. New York: Garland Publishing.

Erdevicki-Charap, Mira. 1999. *Black and White in Colour* (film). London: Arcimboldo.

Ficowski, Jerzy. 1989. *Gypsies in Poland*. Warsaw: Interpress Publishers.

Fraser, Angus. 1995. *The Gypsies*. 2nd edition. Oxford: Blackwell Publishers.

Gatliff, Tony. 1993. *Latcho Drom* (film). Ken Eisen, Shadow Distribution.

Gypsy Caravan. 2001 (sound recording). Putumayo World Music.

Heller, Diz, ed. 2000–2003. *World of Gypsies Vol. 1–3* (sound recording). Arc Music, Catalog Nos. 1613, 1633, and 1848.

Hübschmannova, Milena. 1975. Gypsy Folk-Poems from Czechoslovakia. *Studies in Indo-Asian Art and Culture* 4:35–48.

Keil, Charles, and Angeliki Vellou Keil. 2002. *Bright Balkan Morning: Romani Lives and the Power of Music in Greek Macedonia*. Middletown, CT: Wesleyan University Press.

Kertész-Wilkinson, Irén. 1997. Song Performance: A Model for Social Interaction among Vlach Gypsies in South-eastern Hungary. In *Romani Culture and Gypsy Identity*, edited by Thomas Acton and Gary Mundy. Hatfield, Hertfordshire: University of Hertfordshire Press. 97–126.

Kovalcsik, Katalin. 1985. *Vlach Gypsy Folk Songs in Slovakia*. Budapest: MTA, Institute for Musicology of the Hungarian Academy of Sciences, Zenetudomány.

Lange, Barbara Rose. 2003. *Holy Brotherhood: Romani Music in a Hungarian Pentecostal Church*. Oxford: Oxford University Press.

Latcho Drom. 1993 (sound recording). Caroline Records 1776-2.

Marre, Jeremy. 1992. *The Romany Trail, Part II: Gypsy Music into Europe* (film). Koch Vision/ Shanachie Video.

Marushiakova, Elena, and Vesselin Popov. 1997. *Gypsies (Roma) in Bulgaria*. Frankfurt am Main: Peter Lang.

———. 2003. Field Notes from Russia and the Ukraine. In *Ethnic Identities in Dynamic Perspective: Proceedings of the 2002 Annual Meeting of the Gypsy Lore Society*, edited by Sheila Salo and Csaba Prónai. Budapest: Gondolat. 123–127.

Sárosi, Bálint. 1978. *Gypsy Music*. Budapest: Corvina Press.

Schreiner, Claus, ed. 1990. *Flamenco: Gypsy Dance and Music from Andalusia*. Portland, OR: Amadeus Press.

Silverman, Carol. 2000. Rom (Gypsy) Music. In *Garland Encyclopedia of World Music*, edited by James Porter and Timothy Rice. New York: Garland Publishing. 8:270–293.

Starkie, Walter. 1933. *Raggle-Taggle: Adventures with a Fiddle in Hungary and Romania*. New York: E. P. Dutton.

Stewart, Michael. 1997. *Time of the Gypsies*. Boulder, CO: Westview Press.

Sutherland, Anne. 1975. *Gypsies: The Hidden Americans*. London: Tavistock.

Tomova, Ilona. 1995. *Gypsies in the Transition Period*. Sofia, Bulgaria: International Center for Minority Studies and Intercultural Relations.

Tong, Diane. 1989. *Gypsy Folk Tales*. New York: Harcourt Brace Jovanovich.

Weber, Alain, ed. 1997. *Road of the Gypsies* (sound recording). Network Medien GmbH.2 No. 24756.

Williams, Patrick. 2003. *Gypsy World: The Silence of the Living and the Voices of the Dead*. Chicago: University of Chicago Press.

Yates, Dora. 1995 (1948). *Gypsy Folk Tales*. New York: Barnes and Noble.

Margaret H. Beissinger

RUSSIA

PRESERVATION OF RUSSIAN FOLKLORE

Russian folklore constitutes an immense field that includes, in the broad understanding, popular beliefs, rituals, oral utterances, tales, songs, and material arts such as regional architecture, woodcarving, and embroidery. The bulk of this survey concerns the beliefs, sayings, and songs of the peasants in the nineteenth and early twentieth centuries. In Russia, the verbal art of the people is often referred to as "oral literature" and regarded as folklore in the narrow sense of the term.

Folklore was integral to the life of the Russian peasants, who were almost totally illiterate and stood at a cultural-linguistic distance from the educated classes. The effect of Tsar Peter the Great's enforced Westernization of Russia at the beginning of the eighteenth century was to split the masses from the upper crust. By the reign of

Russia.

Catherine the Great in the late eighteenth century, the members of the aristocracy were barely distinguishable from their French counterparts: they emulated Western dress, manners, and architecture; they read European literature in French translation; and, of course, they spoke French among themselves. By contrast, the peasants maintained their ancient village traditions with their oral narratives, rituals, belief system, and patriarchal domestic order. Their isolation from the mainstream of Russian cultural and political life explains, to a good extent, why their folklore remained so well preserved into the twentieth century.

Though frowned on by the church, folklore was always a popular entertainment among the various strata of Russian society. Ivan the Terrible and other tsars kept *skomorokhi* (ancient Russian minstrel-buffoons) at court in the sixteenth and seventeenth centuries. Peasant storytellers were a common phenomenon in upper-class households in the eighteenth and nineteenth centuries. The most famous of these was Alexander Pushkin's nurse Arina Rodionovna, who narrated folktales for the great poet during his house arrest on his mother's estate in Pskov Province in the mid-1820s. Though notebooks

Ivan the Terrible—pictured here—and other tsars kept *skomorokhi* (ancient Russian minstrel-buffoons) at court in the sixteenth and seventeenth centuries. (Courtesy Library of Congress)

containing epics, religious songs, and proverbs circulated from hand to hand in the seventeenth and eighteenth centuries, the first recorders of Russian folklore were the Englishmen Richard James and Samuel Collins, who lived in Moscow in the seventeenth century. Some tales, often considerably changed from the village variants, appeared in print in the second half of the eighteenth century in the collections of M. D. Chulkov and V. A. Levshin, and Kirsha Danilov's collection of epics (*Drevnie rossiiskie stikhotvoreniia, sobrannye Kirsheiu Danilovym*) was published in 1804. Significant interest in village life on the part of educated classes dates from the early decades of the nineteenth century and was prompted largely by the Romantic urge to discover the Russian national spirit. Yet the erratic censorship policies under Tsar Nicholas I made it difficult for anyone but the staunchest supporters of the government to publish, and much of the material collected during the 1830s and 1840s entered print only after the ascendancy of Alexander II to the throne in 1855.

In the late nineteenth and early twentieth centuries, collecting activity and folklore scholarship flourished in Russia. During the 1860s and 1870s much of the oral literature that remains foundational for the study of Russian folklore today was first published. A. N. Afanas'ev's *Russian Folktales* (*Narodnye russkie skazki*), a compilation that included materials gathered much earlier from numerous sources, appeared between 1855 and 1866. P. V. Kireevskii's multi-volume collection of *Songs* (*Pesni, sobannye P. V. Kireevskim*) began to appear posthumously in 1860. In 1861 V. I. Dal's *Proverbs of the Russian People* (*Poslovitsy russkogo naroda*) appeared, and publication began on P. V. Bessonov's four volumes of spiritual songs, *Wandering Pilgrims* (*Kaleki perekhozhie*). The profusion of folklore works during this period was a result not only of a relaxation in censorship but also of an amazing new discovery in the backwoods of northern Russia. During an administrative exile in 1860, the government official P. N. Rybnikov found by chance that the ancient epic tradition, which educated Russians had thought extinct, was thriving. In the middle of the night on an island in Lake Onega, Rybnikov heard a peasant chanting a song that proved to be the epic (*bylina*) of the merchant Sadko of Novgorod. Rybnikov persuaded the singer to repeat what he had sung and then perform more epics. Over the next several years Rybnikov collected over 200 texts of *byliny*, which he published between 1861 and 1867 as *Songs Collected by P. N. Rybnikov* (*Pesni, sobrannye P. N. Rybnikovym*).

A decade later, A. F. Gilferding sought *byliny* in the same region and sometimes from the same singers as Rybnikov. Before he caught typhus and died in 1872, Gilferding had collected over 300 texts, which were published posthumously in 1873 under the title *Onegin Byliny Transcribed by A. F. Gilferding in the Summer of 1871* (*Onezhskie byliny, zapisannye A. F. Gil'ferdingom letom 1871 goda*). Gilferding organized his songs by region and performer rather than by theme and included a biography for each singer. This arrangement, which paid tribute to the artistry of the peasant bearers of songs and tales, became the model for future publications of Russian folklore. Russian folklorists were thus among the earliest to pay close attention to the creative peculiarities of the peasant-artists in the transmission of traditional songs and narratives.

In 1872 the first volume of E. V. Barsov's *Laments of the Northern Region*

(*Prichitaniia severnogo kraia*) appeared, introducing the Russian public to the great North Russian wailer Irina Fedosova. P. V. Shein collected lyric and ceremonial poetry throughout the second half of the nineteenth century; his monumental *Great-Russian in His Ceremonies and Songs* (*Velikorus v svoikh obriadakh i pesniakh*) appeared in 1898. A. I. Sobolevskii's multi-volume collection of folk lyrics, *Great Russian Folk Songs* (*Velikorusskie narodnye pesni*), appeared between 1895 and 1902. A multitude of other seminal collections appeared in the second half of the nineteenth and early twentieth centuries. In addition, at the turn of the century the thick journals *Ethnographic Review* (*Etnograficheskoe obozrenie*) and *Living Antiquity* (*Zhivaia starina*) published a variety of folklore and ethnographic material.

HISTORY

Russian folklore should be viewed both in its general relation to other Indo-European and Slavic folklores and to Russia's own distinctive past. Prince Vladimir is credited with the baptism of Kievan Rus according to the Eastern Orthodox rite in 988. Unfortunately, we lack detailed written descriptions and myths that might elucidate the pre-Christian religion of the ancient East Slavs. Much of our information comes from medieval church documents, which inveigh against the sway of pagan practices among the populace and the lower clergy. These documents suggest that during times of crop failure and drought in ancient Russia a line of division existed between the church and princes, on the one hand, and the lower classes, on the other. Around 1071 two *volkhvi* (priest-magicians, similar to Finnish shamans) murdered a priest and some noblewomen during a famine. About the same time a *volkhv* created an uprising in Novgorod, where the prince and his retainers stood with the bishop for the Christian faith while the people followed their pre-Christian leader. The church viewed oral poetry and narratives as remnants of paganism and upbraided the people for tale-telling and encouraging the performances of the *skomorokhi*. In the seventeenth century, Tsar Alexis banished the *skomorokhi* from Moscow to the northern wilderness, where they passed on their art to the local peasants.

Chronicles, sermons, and the twelfth-century literary epic "The Song of Igor's Campaign" (*Slovo o polku Igoreve*) contain the scattered names of supernatural personages and partial descriptions of rituals. Along with archeological finds, they help reconstruct to a certain extent the life and belief system of the ancient East Slavs, who during the Tatar Yoke of the thirteenth and fourteenth centuries evolved into three separate nationalities—Russians, Ukrainians, and Belarusians. The *Primary Chronicle* notes that in 980 Prince Vladimir set up statues of six deities outside the palace yard. Their names were Perun, Khors, Dazhbog, Stribog, Simargl, and Mokosh. Significantly absent from this list was Volos (Veles), the god of cattle, commerce, and, possibly, the dead, whose veneration was widely attested in ancient Kiev. Perun was the chief deity of Vladimir's pantheon and represents an East Slavic variant of such Indo-European atmospheric gods as Zeus, Indra, and Thor. Khors was a sun god. Dazhbog seems to have been a deity of blessings. He, too, may have been connected to the sun and seems to have been the offspring of Svarog, another ancient East Slavic personage who was a divine smith on the order of Hephaistos. Stribog may have been connected to the wind. Simargl was represented as a winged dog and served as the guardian of seed and new shoots. Mokosh, the only female personage in Vladimir's pantheon, is probably associated with Mother Earth and with the occult.

It is likely that Vladimir's pantheon did not fully represent rural practice. Medieval documents give us a number of other names as they berate orgiastic celebrations in honor of Koliada, Kupalo, and Iarilo and meatless meals in honor of Rod and Rozhanitsy. In ancient times Koliada and Kupalo were no doubt agrarian spirits of particular holidays. In the nineteenth and twentieth centuries, these names signified the spirits of the Yuletide season and of the summer solstice. Iarilo seems to have been a deity of male potency represented by a phallus. Rod and Rozhanitsy are a bit harder to identify. Judging by their names, some scholars have connected them with the power of reproduction in general (*rod* signifies "kinship") and the specific mistresses of individual birth and destiny (*rozhanitsa* signifies "one who gives birth"), but this interpretation is not universally accepted. General agreement exists that the ancient East Slavs worshipped a great Mother Goddess (perhaps Mokosh) and that, through the intermediary of the *volkhv*, they supplicated their dead ancestors for help in the harvest, healing, and divination. Most likely the belief of later centuries in a house spirit (*domovoi*) that assumes the form of a dead master reflects the pre-Christian cult of ancestors. In addition, the later belief in a wide array of spirits of nature, including a forest spirit (*leshii*), a water spirit (*vodianoi*), and a field spirit (*polevoi*), indicates that the prehistoric East Slavs' perception of the world was animistic.

In the nineteenth and twentieth centuries, ancient modes of thinking and ideas about particular saints and unclean spirits stamped the peasants' day-to-day lives, their birth, marriage, and death customs, and the elaborate ceremonials that defined their agricultural year. Although the vast majority of peasants were baptized into the Orthodox Church and prided themselves on being Christians, their actual practice represented a synthesis of Christian and pagan notions and rites and was often termed a "dual faith" (*dvoeverie*). Throughout the nineteenth century the Russian intelligentsia engaged in a heated debate about whether the peasant was in essence Christian or prone to atheism, and supporters of the religious nature of the peasant liked to point out that the word for "peasant" (*krest'ianin*) was close to that for "Christian" (*khristianin*). Of course, the peasants themselves did not acknowledge the Christian/pagan dichotomy in their belief system. For them the crucial distinctions were "one's own" or "kin" (*rodnoi*) versus "alien" (*chuzhoi*), "clean" (*chistyi*) versus "unclean" (*nechistyi*), and, of course, "male" versus "female." They regarded Christ, Mary, the saints, Mother Earth, and their own *domovoi* as clean and helpful, while devils, nature spirits, sorcerers and witches, and someone else's *domovoi* were unclean and harmful.

WITCHCRAFT AND MAGIC

Notions about the unclean force pervaded all aspects of Russian popular life, and the peasants lived in continual fear of malefic magic (*porcha* or "spoiling") from witches and sorcerers. A limitless number of gestures, amulets, and charms (*zagovory*) were employed for protection from the evil eye and other forms of "spoiling" and from the ever-present Devil. The peasants made the sign of the Cross over their mouth when they yawned to keep away devils, who, it was believed, were always looking for an opening through which to enter an unsuspecting human; they protected water buckets by covering them with splinters in the form of the Cross; they uttered prayers and turned clothing inside out when entering the forest to avert harm from the *leshii*. For help in time of need they might turn to St. Nicholas "the Wonderworker," the peasants' most beloved saint, or they might call on Mother Damp Earth. In some areas of rural Russia during periods of epidemics peasants practiced a rite of "plowing around" (*opakhivanie*), in which women harnessed themselves to a plow and made a furrow around the village to release the healing power of Mother Earth.

Protective measures were an integral part of rituals connected with birth, death, and marriage since, peasants believed, such transitional times were fraught with danger from the unclean force. Pregnant women and babies were kept out of the sight of strangers to protect them from the evil eye. In northern Russia women typically gave birth in the bathhouse, and the newborn child, regarded as especially vulnerable to attacks of the unclean force, was baptized very shortly after birth. Russians distinguished between the "clean" dead or "parents" (*roditeli*) and the "unclean" or "unquiet" dead (*zalozhnye pokoiniki*). The latter category consisted of great sinners or anyone who suffered premature or unnatural death. It included drunkards, victims of murder, those believed to be sorcerers or witches, and suicides. On the matter of suicides, church practice concurred with popular beliefs in refusing them burial in consecrated ground. The peasants believed that Mother Damp Earth did not accept the unclean dead and that such corpses were prone to leave the grave and inflict harm on the living. Even in the late nineteenth century, newspapers reported instances when peasants dug up the bodies of drunks or supposed sorcerers buried in the village cemetery because they believed them responsible for drought or poor harvest.

Cemeteries were also the sites of special commemorations of dead relatives. Days set aside for rites connected with the dead in the ancient calendar were readily taken over by the church as occasions for remembering the deceased. Particularly important were the autumn celebration of the Saturday of St. Demetrius and spring Ancestors' Days occurring during Shrovetide, the week after Easter (*Radunitsa*), and Trinity Week (*semik*). Some medieval church documents bewailed the revelry in the cemeteries during these days, suggesting that these celebrations retained much of their pre-Christian nature among the larger populace.

LIFE-CYCLE CELEBRATIONS

The wedding was one of the most significant events in the life of the Russian village. Marriage was regarded primarily as an economic enterprise, and since the extended patriarchal family was gaining a worker and childbearer, the groom's family incurred the greater part of the expense. Normally, ceremonies did not take place during peak agricultural seasons but after the harvest in autumn or between the Yuletide holidays and Lent. Russians spoke of "playing the wedding," and, in fact, village weddings consisted of a series of "scenes" in which each participant had a certain role to enact. Typically, a family council might decide to marry a son and would send the matchmakers to a suitable girl. The matchmakers were to conduct themselves courteously

A Russian country wedding, 1865. (Print Collection, Miriam and Ira D. Wallach Division of Art, Prints and Photographs, The New York Public Library, Astor, Lenox and Tilden Foundations)

and arrange the business largely in euphemisms and riddles. They might, for example, speak about themselves as "purchasers" and the girl as "goods." Such avoidance of direct statement or of using the name of the bride was one of many ways of protecting the young couple from evil spirits, who presumably would not understand what was occurring. Peasants also gave "known" sorcerers honored places at weddings to defend themselves from the harm they might unleash and to solicit their aid against other sorcerers who might "spoil" the young couple. On occasion, frightened villagers were known to kill suspected witches and sorcerers who harmed weddings or crops.

Following matchmaking, a typical peasant wedding included a small drinking party (*malyi zapoi*), a large drinking party (*bol'shoi zapoi*), and then the wedding itself. At the small drinking party the groom would "inspect" the bride for defects, while she and her party, consisting of several girlfriends, would express hostility toward him and his attendants. Generally, the final arrangements would be made for the dowry and "purchase" of the bride at the small drinking party, and the bride would now be "veiled" by placing a large scarf over her head. Tradition mandated that she chant laments expressing her unwillingness to get married and protesting that her father was selling a "white swan," as the bride was termed in wedding poetry, to "strange people" or "geese," as in-laws were termed. Sometimes a professional wailer was also hired. Barsov includes the following lament of a bride on her mother's grave in his *Laments of the Northern Region*:

A flock of swans has flown down;
The swans indeed are all standing by,
All white and cheerful.
Only one white swan,
Suffers pain in her ardent heart. . . .
Tell me, my beloved mother,
Me, a grieving, poor orphan,
Did my father come to you,
Did he consult you, inform you
That he is giving me in marriage to strange people,
To an alien, distant land? . . .
Oh, ransom me, save me
From this great loss of freedom.

The evening before the wedding a gathering occurred at the bride's house, where much of the poetry and playacting concerned the removal of the "red beauty" (*krasota*), a ribbon symbolizing her maidenly state. The bride took a ritual bath, and her friends were sprinkled with the bathwater for good luck and fertility. If she was an orphan, tradition required her to visit her mother's grave. She was dressed, blessed, and seated under the family icon. In their procession to the bride's house the groom and his party encountered obstacles that the best man, who was master of ceremonies (*druzhko*), was expected to overcome. The *druzhko* also gained entrance to the bride's house by solving riddles or purchasing seats. At a certain point, the bride's father would bless the young couple with an icon and lead his daughter around the groom three times. Now the bride ceased lamenting, whips were cracked and guns were fired to deceive the evil spirits, and the young couple set off for the church to be married. As a sign of her married status, the bride's hair was now parted and woven into two braids, sometimes by her father-in-law, and her head was covered.

Returning from the church, the young couple might stop first at the bride's house, where they would be greeted by bread and salt, the traditional Russian symbols of hospitality. Or they might proceed directly to the groom's house for several days of partying and merrymaking. For much of this period, the bride and groom would remain silent and abstain from food, a tradition regarded as protective magic against evil spirits. Other rites of this period included the bride's removing her husband's boot as a sign of her submission, the young couple's offering vodka to the guests in exchange for coins (gilding), and placing a young boy on the bride's lap to ensure that she would have male children. In some areas the custom of leading the bride and groom to bed and then inspecting her shift for signs of her virginity existed. The bride was not allowed to join in the merrymaking until her veil was removed.

CALENDAR CUSTOMS

The agricultural cycle of the Russians, like that of most Europeans, represented a grafting of Christian feasts and liturgical seasons onto the pre-Christian calendar. The most elaborate celebrations occurred during Yuletide, Shrovetide (*Maslenitsa*), and Trinity Week (also known as "Green Week" and "Rusal'naia Week"). Ritual poetry and foods reflecting the peasants' concern for fertility and abundance accompanied these holidays. The church's feasts of the Nativity and Baptism of Christ coincided with the ancient celebrations of the winter solstice, which marked the turn from darkness toward light. In the Russian village the festivities had an almost exclusively agrarian character. Mummers went about singing songs (*koliadki*) that welcomed the spirit of the feast (*Koliada*), wished the hosts bounty and fertility, asked for handouts such as little pastries in the shape of cows (*korovki*) or goats (*kozuli*), sausage, and other treats, and sometimes warned of what would happen if there were no handouts. Shein includes the following *koliadka* in his collection:

> *Koliada* came
> On the eve of Christmas.
> Give a *korovka*,
> A buttery head.
> And may God grant
> To the person in this yard
> That his rye be thick,
> That his rye be abundant
> From an ear a whole bin,
> From a grain a whole loaf,
> From a half-grain a pie.
> May the Lord endow you
> With good life and luck
> And riches,
> And may the Lord give you
> Even more.

New Year was a time when girls engaged in divination rituals to find out if they would marry during the coming year.

In ancient times Shrovetide, the counterpart to European Carnival, occurred near the spring equinox. But with the superimposition of the Christian cycle of Lent and Easter, it was pushed to an earlier date and became a rowdy, gluttonous feast characterized by winter games and sliding. Motifs associated with the sun were preserved in actions such as building bonfires, pushing a wheel with a torch on it around the village, and riding around the village on horseback carrying a torch. An effigy called *Maslenitsa* was ritually welcomed and then burned at the end of the celebration. Spring was celebrated during the seven weeks following Easter, with the greatest festivities concentrated in Trinity Week. At this time, peasants honored the birch tree as the harbinger of new vegetation by decorating it and dancing the circle dance (*khorovod*) around it. They welcomed and then banished the *rusalka*, a female spirit of water, forest, and field often imagined as a suicide by drowning. All three great seasonal celebrations included funereal rites, which took the form at Yuletide of playing dead and then rising; at Shrovetide, of visiting the cemetery and offering pancakes (*bliny*) to the dead; and on the Thursday of Trinity Week (*semik*), of holding a service for those who had not yet received proper burial that year. A few weeks after Trinity came the holiday of Ivan Kupalo, which marked the summer solstice and coincided with the liturgical feast of John the Baptist. Throughout Russia the belief existed that on Midsummer's Eve a miraculous fern blossomed in the forest over the site of buried treasure.

Anthropologists have long suspected that pagan deities stood behind the veneration of many Christian saints to whom the peasants assigned agricultural functions. Elijah the Prophet, whose feast on 20 July was rigorously observed to avoid crop damage from thunder, lightning, and hail, assumed the function of Perun, while St. Vlas, a patron of cattle, took the place of the ancient Volos. The peasants seem to have attributed some of the functions of Mokosh to St. Paraskeva, a third-century virgin martyr whose name means "Friday" and whose cult was connected with healing springs. As "Mother Friday" she was a patroness of women's work, and women refrained from spinning and other household tasks on cer-

Celebrated on the verge of winter and spring, Shrovetide celebrations are accompanied by loads of pancakes and other delicious dishes. The last Sunday of the Shrovetide Week is marked by the ritual burning of a straw doll, the symbol of Shrovetide. (© Topham/The Image Works)

tain Fridays to avoid angering her. The deities standing behind St. George and many other saints are less clear. The people revered George as a protector of livestock and of wild animals, and they turned their cattle out to pasture for the first time in the spring on his feast day (23 April). On the Intercession of the Mother of God (*Pokrov*, 1 October), they placed their cattle on winter rations. This feast was also the usual beginning of the wedding season, and its name, "*Pokrov*," which signifies cover, was often reinterpreted to mean the head-cover obligatory for a married women. In central Great Russia haymaking often began after the feast of Sts. Peter and Paul (29 June), while the major church feast of the Assumption of Mary (15 August) became an occasion for blessing the first fruits of the field.

LEGENDS, FOLKTALES, AND OTHER ORAL GENRES

In addition to ceremonial poetry, an extensive and varied oral literature enriched peasants' daily life and leisure hours. Most scholars classify this material in terms of literary genres: proverbs, riddles, charms, folk drama, laments, lyrics, ballads, epics, legends, and tales. But certain qualifications must be remembered when comparing folklore with written literature. In oral literature there is no canonical text, and performance is key. Each new performance is a new creation, and the artistic quality can vary considerably depending on the bearer. The comparison with literature becomes even more problematic when one takes into consideration that in the Russian tradition all poetic folklore genres are sung or chanted. One needs to hear a song, and analysis becomes as much the province of ethnomusicologists as of literary scholars.

Russia's rich storehouse of proverbs and sayings comes from multiple sources, including the Bible, everyday life, and Russian literature. Proverbs tend to sum up aspects of popular wisdom in a succinct fashion: "If you fear the wolf, / Keep out of the forest"; "A word is not a swallow; / You can't catch it once it flies away." Priests, judges, and women come in for especially harsh treatment, reflecting prevalent social attitudes: "Priests feed on dead men, / And bedbugs feed on the living"; "What judges find useful / Is what climbs into their pockets"; "When the devil can't manage things, / He sends a woman." Some proverbs serve in the folktale or epic as *loci communes*: "Morning is wiser than evening"; "A woman's hair is long, / But her wit is short." In former times, riddles existed for almost every aspect of Russian domestic life, agriculture, and hunting. By the nineteenth century they were used ritually in situations where one must avoid using the name of the enterprise or person (for example, the wedding ceremony), and they served as entertainments or tests of wit. Innumerable folktales highlight the riddle-solving abilities of poor peasants and wise maidens.

Russian folklore scholarship refers to such genres as memorates, fabulates, and legends as "non-folktale prose" (*neskazochnaia proza*) because in the nineteenth and early twentieth centuries these narratives expressed the actual belief of most peasants. The line separating belief narratives and folktales can be blurry, and a fabulate or legend presented as an anecdote or with elements of satire can easily slip into a folktale. Memorates tell of brief encounters with supernatural personages such as the *domovoi*, *leshii*, *vodianoi*, *rusalka*, and, of course, the Devil. Fabulates are more complex narratives than memorates and are generally related by someone other than the person who experienced the supernatural encounter. For example, a peasant may recount how his great-grandfather came upon a *rusalka* in the forest, captured her with a Cross, and took her home. Many stories about the activities of village witches and sorcerers or of buried treasure seem best regarded as fabulates, though the line between fabulates and legends is not always clear. Legends tend to be set in the fairly distant past and often treat biblical personages and saints or historical figures and events. Perhaps the major hero of the Russian religious legend is Christ, who walks the Russian countryside in the guise of a beggar and tests the charity of the peasants. Other religious personages figuring prominently in legends include St. Nicholas, whose dominant trait is compassion and willingness to help; St. Elijah the Prophet, who is punitive and can destroy a peasant's fields; St. Paraskeva/Friday, who punishes women for spinning on her Fridays; and the dreaded and uncompassionate leap-year saint Cassian. Here one also finds narratives about great sinners who seek forgiveness, priests who "punish" the icon of St. Nicholas, and satirical narratives about drunkards arguing their way into Heaven. One of the most significant collections of legends, A. N. Afanas'ev's *Russian Folk Legends* (*Narodnye russkie legendy*), created a sensation when church authorities banned it after it had already appeared in print in 1859 on the grounds that it contained blasphemous material.

Folktales flourished in Russia. For the most part, they fall into three sub-types: animal tale, magic tale (better known in English as fairy tale), and the tale of everyday life, though this classification is not exhaustive. The animal tales tend to resemble fables, and the actors are generally animals that embody certain human traits.

The fox (who is always female in the Russian tale) is cunning, the wolf stupid, the hare cowardly, the bear clumsy, and the nanny goat unscrupulous. These tales are often structured around a meeting of two or more animals and their ensuing dialogue. Thus, the fox attempts to coax a lascivious cock to confess his sins to her, or a fox convinces a wolf to catch fish by sticking his tail in a hole in the ice. Some animal tales have a chain structure, with each repetition adding another element. One very popular tale describes pulling a gigantic turnip out of the ground by adding grandmother to grandfather, a grandchild to grandmother, a puppy to the grandchild, and then a series of beetles until finally the turnip emerges. Tales with a chain structure were often highly rhythmic and sometimes in verse.

Russian magic tales share many common subjects with other European tales. Considerable ceremonialism accompanied their telling, and good narrators tended to pay close attention to the requirements of trebling (three sons, three episodes) and the inclusion of multiple rhythmic formulas ("Speedily a tale is spun, not so speedily a deed is done"). Some outstanding tellers, however, stamped their own personalities on the tale, as in the case of the Siberian narrator Natal'ia Vinokurova. As M. K. Azadovskii has shown in a paper included in Oinas and Soudakoff's anthology of Russian folklore studies (1975), her interest in psychological and social detail outweighed her attention to the ceremonial requirements of the genre. The defining feature of the magic tale is plot, and, as Vladimir Propp established in his groundbreaking *Morphology of the Folktale* (completed in Russian in 1928), all share basically the same structure. The tale begins with some harm or the desire to obtain something (the firebird, an abducted mother or bride, light) and involves the departure of the hero, a journey to a distant land termed "the thrice tenth kingdom" (which, in tales with a female protagonist, is often the neighboring forest or field), the meeting of a donor, who tests and then gives the hero a magic agent, the procurement of the desired object or person often through combat with a villain, and a return. Sometimes on the return home a male protagonist is killed or thrown into a pit. He then must be revived and perform new tasks before he can claim his bride and his kingdom. Propp defined this structure succinctly in his book *Historical Roots of the Wondertale*, published in Russian in 1946 and included in an English translation of Propp's work in 1984. The male hero is most often the third son of a tsar, though he may be the son of a merchant or peasant, or he may be a fool. His name is usually "Ivan." The female hero is a girl "more beautiful than a tale can tell or a pen can describe" who is persecuted by her evil stepmother. In the very popular story "Vasilisa the Beautiful," for example, the stepmother sends Vasilisa into the forest to the witch Baba Iaga for light, and Vasilisa succeeds, aided by a doll that her mother bequeathed her on her deathbed. The tale's movement from the breakup of the hero's childhood home to marriage seems to replicate symbolically the maturation process. The hero, especially in the masculine tales, is typically weak and passive yet encounters friendly powers that aid him in obtaining the object of his quest. Gray Wolf, for example, helps Ivan Tsarevich in his quest for the firebird, the horse with the golden mane, and Elena the Fair, and he revives him with the water of life after he has been hacked to death by his older brothers. Among the more colorful villains in the Russian magic tales are multi-headed dragons and the great lady-snatcher

The folktale about Prince Ivan, the Firebird, and the Gray Wolf. (Print Collection, Miriam and Ira D. Wallach Division of Art, Prints and Photographs, The New York Public Library, Astor, Lenox and Tilden Foundations)

Koshchei the Deathless. The witch Baba Iaga the Bony-legged, who lives deep in the forest in a hut on chicken legs and moves about with the aid of a mortar and pestle, sometimes serves as a villain, but she is equally prone to function as a donor whose aid the hero may solicit.

Tales of everyday life and anecdotes constitute by far the largest sub-category of Russian folktales. These tales are usually set in the village and sometimes note specific place-names and local customs. They tend to glorify the clever peasant, and often the plot turns on a reversal of fortune: a poor, downtrodden peasant gets the better of such negative personages as his rich brother, a priest, a judge, a nobleman, or his wife. Unlike the belief genres where the Devil is awesome and destructive, the Devil of these tales is typically stupid and easily outwitted by a peasant. Other memorable personages include Ivanushko the Fool and a personification of grief and bad luck called "Misery" (*Gore*).

SONGS

An inexhaustible number of lyric songs existed among the Russian people, and in contrast to such genres as spiritual songs and epics, which tended to be performed by special singers, lyrics were the property of everyone. Their range of themes was broad and included love (especially the end of a love affair due to marriage) and the hard life of married women, house serfs, barge-haulers, drivers, soldiers, bandits, and others. One important structuring device was the use of substitute terms from nature for people and emotional states. A swan stood for a bride; a quail, swallow, or nightingale for a young girl; a falcon or hawk indicated a young man or a groom; a duck a married woman and a drake a married man; a river stood for separation; an oak tree for manly strength; a poplar, birch, or ash tree for a young girl; the bending of trees and the end of vegetation signaled sorrow; and a red bush stood for a young girl entering marriage. The following excerpt from a folk lyric builds on such nature symbolism:

> Down the little river, down the rapid river,
> There a duck is swimming, and with her is a drake.
> Out in front is swimming the fine drake,
> The fine drake, dove-colored and splendid,
> And after him swims the little gray duck.
> "Wait a minute, wait a minute, you dove-colored, splendid one,
> Oh, surely it would be better for us to swim together.
> Yes, to swim together, not to drift apart.
> Between us has flowed a swift river,
> The swift river, my successful rival."

By the end of the nineteenth century, the most popular folksongs in the Russian villages were *chastushki*, or "folk rhymes," which were often performed to the accompaniment of an accordion. These consisted of four-line rhymed verses and accommodated a range of contents including love, social discontent, obscenity, and, in Soviet times, political propaganda.

Spiritual songs (*dukhovnye stiki*) carried a clear Christian stamp. Their subjects were based on biblical themes, lives of saints, and various apocryphal materials. By the nineteenth century they were generally performed by pilgrims who wandered from shrine to shrine seeking alms, were often organized into professional guilds, and sang at fairs, monasteries, and churches. Some spiritual songs might also be included in the repertoire of epic singers. Among the favorite subjects were "The Book of the Dove" (*Golubinaia kniga*), a discussion about the origins of things that had its source in apocrypha; "The Dream of Mother of God," which presents the passion of Christ through a dream of Mary before his birth; the "Two Lazaruses," based on the story of Lazarus the beggar from the gospel of Luke; and songs about St. George (Egor), St. Alexis "Man of God," and St. Mary of Egypt.

EPICS

The epic, along with the folktale, is one of the most popular and most-studied Russian folklore genres. Folk epics are divided into *byliny*, which took shape between the tenth and sixteenth centuries, and historical songs, which developed after the sixteenth century. The *byliny* are normally divided into three cycles. The oldest and most fantastic is often termed "shamanistic" or "magical," and its songs recount the

Ilia Muromets—pictured here in this Russian folk art—is the central figure of the Russian epic tradition. (Print Collection, Miriam and Ira D. Wallach Division of Art, Prints and Photographs, The New York Public Library, Astor, Lenox and Tilden Foundations)

adventures of the giant Sviatogor ("Holy Mountain"), who is too heavy for Mother Damp Earth to carry; Volkh, a magician who obtains victory through the use of his occult powers; and the revered plowman Mikula "the Villager's Son," whom Mother Damp Earth loves.

Most *byliny* belong to the Kievan Cycle and center on a mythologized Prince Vladimir and the epic heroes (*bogatyri*) who feast at his court, seek brides, collect tribute for him, engage in contests of various types, and, of course, fight the enemies of Holy Russia. Ilia Muromets is the central figure of the Russian epic tradition and the folklore personage who best represents the embodiment of courage, self-sacrifice, and patriotism for many Russians. He was the great champion of widows and orphans, the protector of the Orthodox Church, and the defender of the Russian land from monsters and foreign invaders. *Byliny* about him and other heroes of the Kievan Cycle probably originated within the princely circles of Kievan Rus between the eleventh and fourteenth centuries. A very popular *bylina* relates Ilia's journey to Kiev and his struggle with Nightingale (Solovei) the Bandit. Songs about his combat with the "Great Idol" (Idolishche) and his own son "Falconer" (Sokolnik) are also ancient and probably took shape around the theme of the struggle of Kievan Rus with its nomadic neighbors, the Pechenegs and Polovetsians. As the epic tradition evolved, it assimilated motifs connected with the Tatars, whom, contrary to historical fact, the Russians defeat in the *byliny*. The song about Ilia Muromets and Kalin Tsar reflects the struggle with the Tatars and sometimes includes another widespread motif: the enmity of Prince Vladimir and other Kievan nobility toward Ilia because of his peasant origin. When popular ideas about social justice arise in the epic, Ilia Muromets can always be found on the side of the poor and downtrodden. One late *bylina* tells of Ilia's miraculous healing by Jesus Christ after sitting home as a cripple for thirty years.

Many other heroes appear in *byliny* of the Kievan Cycle. Dobrynia Nikitich is the great diplomat of the epic. He serves as Vladimir's right-hand man who helps procure a wife for his prince and defeats the Dragon of the Puchai River. Alesha Popovich is a priest's son who, though brave, can be deceitful. He defeats the dragon Tugarin, but he also attempts to marry Dobrynia's wife, Nastasia, in the latter's absence. Churilo Plenkovich is the Don Juan of the folk epic who meets his death at the hands of a jealous husband, while Stavr is saved from a dungeon by his clever wife, Vasilisa, who dresses as the man "Vasilii" and courts Vladimir's daughter. Dunai is one of the few tragic heroes of the epic. Jealous of his wife, who betters him in a shooting contest, he slays her and then commits suicide. The women of the Kievan Cycle are as colorful as their male counterparts. Vasilisa is smarter and shoots better than all the men in Prince Vladimir's palace, and only his daughter recognizes that she is a woman; Vladimir's wife, Apraksia, is promiscuous; Maria the White Swan, whom Mikhailo Potyk marries and later brings back from the grave, is a sorceress who runs away with a foreign king and then poisons her husband and imprisons him in a stone; the sorceress Marinka turns Dobrynia into an aurochs. The third cycle of *byliny* centered on the northern trading city of Novgorod, which was spared from the assaults of the Tatars. Its heroes are the merchant Sadko, who charmed the sea king with his playing on the *gusli* (similar to a psaltery), and the rabble-rouser Vasily Buslaevich.

Many *byliny* treat subjects that are widespread in other epic traditions, such as the battle with a monster, the struggle between father and son, and the rivalry in arms between husband and wife. At the same time, they reflect actual conflicts of Kievan Rus (with nomadic neighbors or the Tatars) and the struggle between Christianity and paganism. But it is almost impossible to identify specific personages and events in them. In the historical song, by contrast, actual events and personages are immediately recognizable, though in a popular re-interpretation that often distorts the details. Many historical songs are grouped around the person of Ivan IV ("The Terrible"), whose struggle against the boyars and battles against the Tatars enhanced his popularity among the common people. The period between the end of the Riurikid dynasty and the election of Mikhael Romanov to the Russian throne (1598–1613), known as "The Time of Troubles," was captured in songs about Boris Godunov's supposed murder of the Tsarevich Dmitrii at Uglich and the ascension to the throne of Grishka Otrepev ("The False Dmitrii"). Other songs focus on Stenka Razin and Pugachev, two Cossack rebels who gathered armies that threatened tsarist power in the seventeenth and eighteenth centuries, respectively. The Russian folk ballad stands apart from the epic in its dramatic quality and its tragic representation of individual fate. Singers often included them along with epics and occasionally spiritual songs in their repertoires and termed them collectively "old songs" (*stariny*).

The epic was the most demanding folklore genre to perform, and many of the best singers were old men and women who spent many years learning their art. Sung without instrumental accompaniment in northern Russia, epic performance consisted in transmission of traditional plots through building up lines in which the metric requirements were fulfilled at a fairly rapid pace of narration, in part through the use of fixed epithets (for example, "good youth," "knightly horse," "white hands," "stone palace," and "evil Tatar") and *loci communes* (such as formulaic expressions for entering a palace or choosing a steed). Among the great singers encountered by Rybnikov and then Gilferding, Trofim Riabinin of the Onega region stands out. He passed his art on to his son Ivan, who passed it down to his stepson, who in turn transmitted it to his son, P. I. Riabibin-Andreev, a well-known performer of the Soviet era. Trofim Riabinin and others had learned songs from Ilia Elustafev, who died in the 1830s at ninety. Some epic performers were skilled in other genres as well. Ivan Riabinin was a gifted teller of folktales, and the well-known performer from the

Olonets Region Nastas'ia Bogdanova, who lived into the 1930s, was known for her laments, tales, and spiritual songs as well as her *byliny*. The folk epic became extinct somewhere in the middle of the twentieth century.

STUDIES OF RUSSIAN FOLKLORE

Expeditions for collecting songs and folktales as well as major interpretive studies continued into the Soviet period. But after the relative freedom of the 1920s, the Stalinist regime restricted folklorists who did not adhere to a Marxist-Leninist line. In addition, understanding the value of popular traditions in transmitting the ideas of socialism to the masses, the Soviets encouraged the creation of a hothouse folklore that glorified the Revolution, Lenin, and Stalin while attacking such class enemies as the *kulak* and the priest. The study of genres implying that the people were still religious or superstitious and challenging the official image of them as enlightened and atheistic was discouraged. Yet, in spite of the hostile political climate, Russian folklorists made tremendous achievements during the Soviet era in collecting, performance studies, and interpretations. After Stalin's death and, especially, during the Gorbachev years and post-Soviet period the restrictions on folklorists were eased, and the recording and study of folklore today continues to be a robust enterprise that is once again, as in its initial years, often connected with questions of national identity.

BIBLIOGRAPHY

Afanas'ev, Aleksandr. 1945. *Russian Fairy Tales*, translated by Norbert Guterman. New York: Pantheon.

Aleksander, Alex E. 1975. *Russian Folklore: An Anthology in English Translation*. Belmont, MA: Nordland.

Bailey, James, and Tatyana Ivanova. 1998. *Russian Folk Epics*. Armonk, NY: M. E. Sharpe.

Fedotov, G. P. 1935. *Stikhi dukhovnye* (Spiritual Songs). Paris: YMCA Press.

———. 1960. *The Russian Religious Mind: Kievan Christianity: The Tenth to the Thirteenth Centuries*. New York: Harper.

Haney, Jack V. 1999–2003. *The Complete Russian Folktales*. 5 volumes. Armonk, NY: M. E. Sharpe.

Hilton, Alison. 1995. *Russian Folk Art*. Bloomington: Indiana University Press.

Ivanits, Linda J. 1989. *Russian Folk Belief*. Armonk, NY: M. E. Sharpe.

Oinas, Felix. 1985. *Essays on Russian Folklore and Mythology*. Columbus, OH: Slavica.

Oinas, Felix, and Stephen Soudakoff, eds. and trans. 1975. *The Study of Russian Folklore*. The Hague: Mouton.

Olson, Laura J. 2004. *Performing Russia: Folk Revival and Russian Identity*. London: Routledge Curzon.

Propp, V. Ia. 1968. *The Morphology of the Folktale*, translated by Laurence Scott. 2nd edition. Austin: University of Texas Press.

———. 1984. *Theory and History of Folklore*, translated by Ariadna and Richard Martin; edited by Anatoly Liberman. Minneapolis: University of Minnesota Press.

Reeder, Roberta, ed. and trans. 1993. *Russian Folk Lyrics*. Bloomington: Indiana University Press.

Ryan, W. F. 1999. *The Bathhouse at Midnight: Magic in Russia*. University Park: Pennsylvania State University Press.

Sokolov, Y. M. 1950. *Russian Folklore*, translated by Catherine Ruth Smith. Detroit: Folklore Associates.

Wizgell, Faith. 1998. *Reading Russian Fortunes: Print Culture, Gender, and Divination in Russia from 1765*. Cambridge: Cambridge University Press.

Linda J. Ivanits

SERBIA

GEOGRAPHY AND HISTORY

A part of the federal republic of Serbia and Montenegro, Serbia is situated on the Balkan Peninsula of Southeastern Europe. Flanked by **Hungary** on the north, **Macedonia** and **Albania** on the south, Romania and Bulgaria on the east, and **Croatia** and Bosnia-Herzegovina on the west, the nation covers 39,518 square miles.

Serbia.

Serbia is defined by a variety of landforms, ranging from fertile plains drained by rivers such as the Danube, the Sava, the Drina, the Morava, the Ibar, and the Western and Southern Morava, to ancient mountains, limestone basins, and forested hills. Mountain ranges and spurs run in various directions, especially along the eastern Bulgarian border and in Montenegro. The climate is as varied as the land, with bountiful rain in the plains and heavy snows in the mountainous regions.

Of Serbia's some 10.5 million residents, about half live in urban areas. Belgrade, the capital and densest city, is home to over 1.5 million. The population of Serbia is 70 percent Serbian, but a significant number (17 percent) claim Albanian descent. Most ethnic Albanians live in the southwestern province of Kosova, one of Serbia's two autonomous provinces. The second province, Vojvodina, located in the northeast, includes among its population many ethnic Hungarians (about 3 percent of Serbia's total population). **Roma** (Gypsies), a recognized ethnic group with historical ties to Serbia, reside throughout Serbia proper. Gypsies settled among the Serbs beginning in the fifteenth century, often living a communal life on the outskirts of existing towns. These settlements were known as *Tsiganska Mala* (Gypsy mahalla) and are still found in parts of Serbia.

Most Serbs speak Serbo-Croatian, the official language, but other languages such as Albanian, Hungarian, Macedonian, and Slovenian are spoken within those ethnic communities. Accordingly, the majority of Serbs adhere to the Serbian Orthodox Christian religion (65 percent). Another 19 percent are Muslim, and 4 percent are Roman Catholic. The remaining population includes Jewish, Protestant, Christian, and other religious minority groups. During the fifteenth century, after being expelled from **Spain**, many Sephardic Jews settled in Serbia and thrived in their new home.

Thousands of years before the ancestors of the Serbs appeared on the Balkan Peninsula, their Slavic forebears had established a homeland north of the Black Sea in the region between the Vistula and Dnieper Rivers (in present-day **Poland**, **Russia**, and Western **Ukraine**). When a migrant Asian people (the Avars) penetrated the area, migrations began southward into the Pannonian Plains (now part of Hungary and Serbia). Other Slavic tribes joined the movement, and by the early seventh century, at the invitation of Emperor Heraclius (610–664 C.E.), the lands south of the Danube were settled by considerable numbers of Slavs.

By the end of the seventh century, the Slavic tribes dominated the Balkan lands. Until the twelfth century, these autonomous clans and tribes resisted attempts to create any semblance of a national state. Territorial defensive units, called *župa*, provided governance and protection. *Župa* were sub-divided into extended communities called *zadruga*, essentially family clans. Led by the oldest and most experienced family member (usually male), the *zadruga* functioned as the principal social and economic unit and in some regions managed to survive into the twentieth century.

The Slavs were Christianized by the end of the tenth century, primarily through the missionary work of St. Cyril and St. Methodius, and the Slavic language, now known as Old Slavonic, became the official church language, adopting the Glagolitic and later the Cyrillic scripts. The Slavs retained their identities as regional, extended tribes and clans until the twelfth century, when a series of strong rulers, most notably Stevan Nemanya and St. Sava, led a successful effort to establish a national state. By the time of the Serbian emperor Dušan the Mighty (1331–1355), Serbia's role extended throughout Serbian territory, Bulgaria, and vast portions of Albania and **Greece**. After Dušan's death, the empire disintegrated into dozens of smaller states and principalities that were eventually absorbed into the Ottoman Empire. With minor exceptions, Montenegro in particular, the South Slavic population (Bulgarians, Serbs, Macedonians, and Bosnians) lost their properties, national institutions, and governing systems. The Ottomans, however, did not forbid their subjects from practicing their beliefs, which allowed the Orthodox Church in Serbia to survive, though with a severely suppressed status. Throughout the next five centuries of Ottoman domination, the church transmitted and preserved Serbian culture, art, literary language, and history as well as Orthodox religious beliefs and values.

Significant features of Serbian folklore and traditional ways became highly developed during the Ottoman period and continued to influence current history, especially with regard to the status of the province of Kosova. By the nineteenth century, Turkish rule had become oppressive, and the desire for revolution permeated the Balkans. In 1878, the Treaty of Berlin established Serbia as an independent kingdom. After the Balkan Wars in 1913, Serbian boundaries were extended to include former territories and Macedonia. The Kingdom of the Serbs, Croats, and Slovenes was established when the Austro-Hungarian Empire dissolved after World War I. The kingdom incorporated the provinces of Croatia, Dalmatia, Bosnia, Herzegovina, Slovenia, Vojvodina, and Montenegro. (Kosova province at that time was part of Serbia proper.) In 1929, the name "Yugoslavia" was adopted.

In 1941, Nazi **Germany** invaded Yugoslavia. Following World War II, Yugoslavia was ruled by the communist resistance fighter Marshal Tito (Josip Broz), who declared the nation a non-aligned, independent republic, rejecting orders from the Stalinist government in the Soviet Union and accepting economic and military aid from the West. With the death of Tito in 1980, a collective presidency governed the country, and in 1990 the Communist Party collapsed. Soon thereafter, **Slovenia**, Croatia, and Bosnia-Herzegovina declared their independence, and in 1993 Serbia and Montenegro became a new Federal Republic of Yugoslavia. The conflict triggered by the political reorganization of the former Yugoslavia, especially in Bosnia and Croatia, has cost thousands upon thousands of human lives. Ethnic hatreds and religious animosity fueled the warfare, and political rivalries extended them. In 1995 Serbia, under President Slobodan Milošević, Bosnia, and Croatia signed a peace agreement. In 2000, Vojislav Kostunica was elected president. Milošević initially refused to accept the results, but mass demonstrations forced him to resign. Milošević surrendered to Serbian authorities in 2001 and was extradited to The Hague later that year to be tried for war crimes by a United Nations Tribunal. In 2003, Yugoslavia was reconstituted and renamed "Serbia and Montenegro."

SOCIAL STRUCTURE

Serbian traditions and folkways reflect the turbulent history of the Serbs, the lands where they live, and the reliance on family and clan for protection and support. The *zadruga*, or extended family household, is still considered the "traditional" social structure, even though it has almost disappeared as an official form in the current era. Nonetheless, understanding the *zadruga* clarifies the traditional values of the Serbs and rural life in Serbia until the latter half of the twentieth century. Even though the term *zadruga* was incorporated into legal codes, the term *kuča* (household or, literally, "hearth") was more commonly used among the people. Kinship was the primary basis for the legal definition of the *zadruga*, even though non-family members could become members. The *zadruga* was not exclusively patrilineal, since both men and women could marry into it. In most instances, members lived in the same household compound, which contained a single hearth as well as various types of outbuildings. A typical *zadruga* could include four or five nuclear families, as many sleeping quarters (*vayats*) as there were families, and a main house, which was used for communal eating and as sleeping quarters for the elderly. A prosperous *zadruga* would consist of several *vayats* and several outbuildings (corn cribs, grain storage sheds, a main house with a porch) and look much like a small settlement.

Every *zadruga* had a *stareshima* (headman) who governed and guided the household and the property. The *stareshima* was not always the oldest male. The headship could be given to the most able son, brother, or nephew, even if the youngest. If the *stareshima* did not perform well, the *zadruga* would choose another. This system of home governance allowed adult men to be absent for long periods of time, perhaps seeking work or engaging in trade, knowing that their affairs were being overseen back home.

Common property holdings were the foundation of the *zadruga* structure. Major holdings were usually in land, although *zadruga*-type organizations also existed among some town merchants. Not all property was held collectively: clothing, bedding, and small items for personal use could be owned individually or by the nuclear unit. Minor economic enterprises could also be carried out separately. It was through these means that mothers amassed their daughters' dowries.

The Serbian language reflects the importance of kinship and the *zadruga* system with a vocabulary that provides explicit terms for the many types of familial relationships. For instance, instead of the single, generic term "uncle," the brother of one's father is referred to as *strits*, while the brother of one's mother is *uyak*. A male cousin on the father's side is called *brat od strits*, and a male cousin on the mother's side is *brat od uyaka*. The term for cousin is *brat*, literally "brother," but one's true brother, that is *rodjeni brat*, is identified by adding the modifier *rodjeni*, which means "born." At least sixty terms are used to specify as many family relationships, including generational links and those established by marriage. For example, a man's mother-in-law is a *tashta* and his father-in-law a *tast*, while a woman's mother-in-law is a *svekrva* and her father-in-law a *svekar*.

The cohesiveness of families is reflected in two other traditional relationships, that of *probratimstvo / posestrimstvo* (blood brotherhood/sisterhood) and that of *kumstvo* (godparent). *Probratimstvo* established a tie between two individuals of similar age who promised to assist one another in times of need for the rest of their lives. In earlier times, the ritual establishing this relationship was performed in a cemetery where the ancestors' spirits would be present. The custom of blood brotherhood has all but disappeared, but the tradition of *kumstvo*, or godparent, persists. The position of the *kum* (or *kuma* for a woman) is usually inherited along the male line. *Kumstvo* is a kinship link created through ritual and deeply honored by the participating families. Intermarriage is not permitted between households tied to one another by *kumstvo*. The *kum* or *kuma* is a principal player in all family holidays and rites, acting as best man or maid of honor in weddings and christening children of the adopted family. The *kum* is also present at the *slava*, a social and religious celebration that has been at the core of Serbian life for over 1,000 years.

SLAVA CELEBRATION AND CALENDAR CUSTOMS

Krsna Slava honors the patron saint of the family, chosen at the time of the family's conversion to Christianity in the ninth century, and it honors the family's patrilineal ancestors. The word *slava* means "glory" as a noun and "to celebrate" as a verb, and its history goes back to the time of the Balkan missionaries Sts. Cyril and Methodius. Balkan ethnographers agree that the rites observed as part of the *slava* celebration were part of an ancient religion honoring household gods and that they originated long before the Christian conversion of the Slavs, Greeks, Romans, and other Indo-European peoples. The early Christian Church forbade belief in, and veneration of, household gods, but efforts to extinguish the older faith were for a long time unsuccessful. After repeated failures, the missionaries recognized the futility of forcing people to abandon old beliefs and customs and supported efforts to Christianize by providing analogous Christian protectors. Thus, Sts. Nicholas, John, George, and Elijah, the Archangel Michael, and others replaced the household gods. Each family adopted the name day of a saint as its family *Krsna Slava* (literally, "the celebration of becoming Christian"). In general belief and practice, the *slava* is inherited along patrilineal lines and transfers to the female when the male line ceases. In many regions of Serbia even today, those families who have inherited the same saint consider themselves spiritually related. In fact, in several locales in the past, marriages were traditionally forbidden between families under protection of the same saint. The *slava* is always observed on the same day: for instance, St. John the Baptist on 20 January, St. Nicholas on 19 December, and St. George on 6 May. (The Julian calendar is followed for religious holidays.) Besides honoring the patron saint, the protector of the family, the *slava* is understood to be a feast day when the family reunites and the home is open to all. The activities always include a traditional blessing ceremony, vast quantities and varieties of food and drink, music, dance, and laughter.

Prominently displayed in the home at the *slava* celebration is a table bearing an icon of the patron saint, a lighted, decorated candle, a special bread, a glass of wine, and a bowl of cooked wheat. During the ceremony honoring the saint and the living family, its faith, and its ancestors, a priest—or designated representative—begins by censing the table and those present. He then reads the names of the extended family members, offers prayers for them, and blesses a special cake-bread (*kolač*), asking each immediate family member to place a hand on the *kolač*. The *kolač* is turned at least three times by those holding it while the priest chants a prayer. The underside of the *kolač* is then cut in the shape of the Cross and partially broken open so that each quarter can be blessed with a drop of wine. The priest and family members then each kiss the *kolač* and each other, while the priest repeats, "Let Christ be among us." Each family member responds, "So be it." The now-blessed *kolač* is then placed in the center of the table next to the *slava* candle, which burns throughout the day.

A wheat dish, called *koljivo* (literally, "a sacrifice cut by knife while alive"), also honors the life of the family—specifically, ancestors and the recently departed. To prepare the *koljivo*, wheat berries are soaked overnight, cooked, ground or left intact, and mixed with sugar, crushed walnuts, and spices, and then shaped into a dome-shaped cake. It is variously decorated, most often with raisins arranged as a Cross. After being blessed with wine and after the names of the recently departed family members are recited, the *koljivo* is served to each family member and visitor.

Each aspect of the *slava* ceremony carries with it specific Christian symbolism as well as meanings that pre-date Christianity. Ethnographic descriptions indicate little change in the *slava*'s acknowledged purpose: the affirmation of family ties within the context of a sacrificial feast of thanksgiving. Considerable regional and familial variations exist, but the celebration as a commemoration of the family persists. The secular aspects of the festivities, which emphasize good food, good drink, good company, music, and dance, vary more widely and do not appear to need guidance by established models. Even so, unwritten rules of tradition determine the atmosphere and organization of these festivities. The quality of the wine, the order and types of food served, the hospitality exhibited by the hosts, the appearance of the surroundings, the degree of respect shown for the occasion by family and guests, the generosity of the family, and other aspects of the event are regulated, tempered, and judged by the participants according to traditional values and esthetic principles.

Many traditional Serbian foods are prepared and served at the *slava*: *schlivovitz* (traditional plum brandy); hors d'oeuvres that include delicate slices of smoked ham; spicy sausage; chunks of a white and salty farmer's cheese; *ayvar*, a relish made by grinding roasted peppers and eggplant; *sarma*, ground pork rolled in marinated cabbage leaves and cooked for many hours; roast lamb and pork; and an assortment of desserts, including *baklava* and various strudels.

In the spring, many Serbs honoring St. George as their patron saint observe on their *slava* a number of customs associated with the arrival of spring. Formerly, flowers and a variety of other plants would be gathered and immersed in buckets of water overnight. In the morning, women would bathe in this water, believing that it would bring them good health. Even into the late twentieth century, spring rites could be observed in much of Serbia. On the eve of St. George's Day, young—and even some older—people would meet in the moonlight in a meadow or grassy field where they would dance and sing folksongs, often accompanied by flute players, a bagpipe, or an accordionist. Later, they would gather branches of willow, dogwood, beech, and hawthorn. The women would twist some of these branches into wreaths to wear around their waists and then carry armloads back to the village to decorate their homes. Each type of branch had symbolic significance—fertility, health, and growth, for example. In the morning before sunrise, people would wash their faces in the dew of the grass and flowers. Wreaths of field flowers were woven and then attached to wells or hung over doors, on gateposts, or from the eaves of the cottages. Today these wreaths are most often found above doorways.

Additional spring customs are associated with Lazarus's Saturday, the day before Palm Sunday. Referred to as *Vrbitsa* (The Day of Willows), the rite honors Lazarus, whom Jesus raised from the dead, but probably pre-dates Christianity. Children wear little bells hung around their necks and form a procession that circles the church three times. The children then either gather pussy willows in nearby fields to be blessed in the church or distribute already collected ones to the congregation.

In June, around the day called *Duhovi* (Souls' Day), groups of young girls would dance and sing on the streets of the village, stopping at every house. The songs focused on love, marriage, selecting a husband, and wishing for a happy married life with healthy children. In July around *Ivandan* (John the Baptist Day), herders burned birch bark as an offering for the health of flocks of sheep or herds of cattle.

One of the oldest folk customs described by many ethnographers and memorialized in lyrics still sung today is the rain dance known as *dodola*. A rain dance was performed to ward off natural calamities such as drought. Young girls, dressed only in grasses, flowers, and other plants, were named *dodole* (rain maidens) and would go from household to household dancing and singing a traditional song that was hoped would bring the needed rain. When the *dodola* appeared on the doorstep, she would be drenched with buckets of water and given small gifts. The version of the chant collected in the village of Orashats by Joel Halpern in the late 1960s closely resembles versions collected by V. S. Karadžić in the early 1800s:

> Let the gentle rains come!
>   Oh Dodo, Dodole!
> So we can harvest white wheat!
>   Oh Dodo, Dodole!
> And in the fields, grape vines!
>   Oh Dodo, Dodole!
> And meadow lands and grasses!
>   Oh Dodo, Dodole!

Folk customs associated with Christmas abound. Variations of such customs observed in the mid-nineteenth century in rural areas persist even today. On Christmas Eve, the father of the family goes into a wooded area and cuts a straight oak sapling, which he brings into the house, offering a traditional salutation. As he enters the house, he is showered with mixed grain, usually held in a small bag or mitten. He places the sapling, called a *badnyak*, upon the embers in the fireplace. In the morning, a pre-arranged visitor arrives and, tossing mixed grains through the doorway, calls out, "Christ is born!" Someone inside the house responds by calling out, "Indeed, He is born!" and, in turn, showers him with grain. Another person in the group stirs up the embers and the *badnyak* with a poker, trying to revive the fire. As the sparks scatter, someone exclaims, "As many sparks, so many oxen, cows, horses, goats, sheep, swine, beehives; so much good fortune and happiness." The visitor is then covered with a blanket and showered with gifts and coins. The remains of the *badnyak* are carried outside accompanied by those present, who sing and bear lighted candles. A variation of this tradition, especially today, involves using a *badnyak* with a few remaining leaves and decorating it with dried fruit, nuts, and vegetables. The *badnyak* is ceremonially burned at the end of Christmas festivities.

In addition, many families placed straw on the floor of their homes and under table linens on Christmas Eve, probably to commemorate the stable in which the Christ child was born. Neither table nor floor would be cleared for three days.

Preparation of a special Christmas dish, the *Chesnitsa*, and various other secondary customs are still observed today. The *Chesnitsa* is an unleavened loaf of bread with a special coin kneaded into it. When the bread is broken, the person who finds the coin is expected to have an especially fortunate year. It is also customary on *Badnje Veče* (Christmas Eve) to prepare special foods that do not contain animal fat or dairy products. Everyone who shares this meal needs to eat at least a small portion of each of the seven foods for good health and good fortune. The traditional foods often served include roasted fish; boiled rice or a vegetable; *ayvar*, a roasted pepper salad; soup; a salted bread with no eggs or butter called *zdravlje* (literally, "health"); stewed dried fruit (such as apples, peaches, pears, raisins, figs, and dates); and assorted nuts. A living wreath of wheat often decorates the table. Approximately two weeks before Christmas Eve, wheat berries are soaked overnight and left to sprout on a glass dish. The berries must be kept moist, and a place for a candle is preserved in the center. The resulting green, living wreath of wheat symbolizes new life in the dead of winter. On Christmas morning many families prepare a basin of water, adding a piece of oak, an apple, and a libation of wine. Family members dip their fingers into the water on Christmas morning and anoint their faces for good health in the coming year.

At some point during the Christmas, *slava*, or Easter festivities as well as on other family feast days, stories are told, traditions remembered, and history recounted. Such narrations cover a range of folklore material from old legends about a wood nymph called a *vila* and epic ballads about the Battle of Kosovo (1389), to adventures of the folk hero Prince Marko (Marko Kraljević) and epics about outlaw heroes called *haiduks*.

SONGS, FOLKTALES, AND POETRY

When Vuk Stefanovich Karadžić organized his vast collection of Serbian folksongs and poems in the early nineteenth century, he presented "Women's Songs" first, suggesting that these lyrics, short tales, and beliefs constituted the earliest Serbian folk poetry. He devoted a section to lyrical songs and fragments that alluded to mythological beliefs and ideas. The pre-Christian religious beliefs that permeated the lives of the South Slavs, including the Serbs, featured aspects of nature worship and the veneration of ancestors. A natural phenomenon was often anthropomorphized; that is, the forest, fields, and animals had spirits that protected them, and these spirits were not always benign. One such spirit, the *vila*—sometimes described as a fairy or wood nymph, at other times as a creature to be feared—was variously depicted as swift as the wind, with long hair and silky veils waving in the wind as she flew the skies, as beautiful and eternally young, robed in white gauze, and with shimmering golden hair. The *vila* had the sweetest imaginable voice, but at the same time she was armed with bow and arrows. These creatures were believed to live by lakes or in meadows hidden deep in forests or on high mountain peaks beyond the clouds. They liked to dance and possessed supernatural powers.

Perhaps the most famous *vila* plays an Athena-like role in the Prince Marko heroic ballads. She is his *posestrima* (blood sister), granting him protection and aid when he needs it most. She binds his wounds and repeatedly heals his pierced heart. This *vila*, named Ravioyla, could foretell the future, control storms, and change herself into a snake or a swan. Another famous *vila* figures prominently in an old legend about the building of a fortress town (Skadar). In this poem she demands a human sacrifice before she will allow the walls of the fortress to be built. Her demands, however, occur only after she is ignored and deceived.

Such folktales and oral epic poems preserved Serbian ethnic history, ethical values, and religious beliefs throughout the Ottoman domination, a period of nearly 500 years. The epic songs, perhaps more than any other folk narrative, instilled hope and courage in the Serbian people and simultaneously preserved folk history. Throughout the centuries, epic songs were either recited or accompanied by a *gusle*, a one-stringed, bowed instrument. The *gusle* seems to be of Asian origin, but it has a long history among the Slavs. A woodblock from a species of maple is scooped out and covered with sheepskin or sometimes donkey or rabbit skin. It has a short neck, which often ends in a stylized scroll. Horsehair is fixed to a large peg and stretched over a high bridge. Three *gusle* shapes predominate: the trapezoid (Serbian), the hexagonal (Bosnian), and the pear-shaped (Montenegrin). The player rests the instrument upon his knees and plays—much as one does a violoncello—using an arc-shaped bow, which is also strung with horsehair and has a straight handle.

While the rhythms of the folk lyric vary freely, those of the folk epic are predominantly trochaic. The lines are usually decasyllabic with a caesura (or pause) after the fourth syllable. Recent studies of Serbian oral traditions often present the *gusle* as the guiding muse and its muscial line as the basic rhythmical line for Serbian oral narrative. This idea provides one of the building blocks in the thory of oral composition developed by Milman Parry and Albert B. Lord. Many of the epics collected by Parry and Lord belong to the Muslim traditions of Bosnia and flourished in the context of Ramadan observance. For a month Muslims fast from sunrise to sunset. Then men gather in coffeehouses to eat, talk, and listen to epic performances. The Muslim oral epic is a lengthy, *gusle*-oriented composition. These epics do not function in the same ways as do the Serbian epics because they do not have as didactic a purpose. Audiences depended upon the Serbian oral epic to preserve history, religious beliefs, and rituals, to unify the group as an ethnic and religious community against a common oppressor, and to teach moral and social values to the young. Throughout the Ottoman period, Serbs feared extinction. Consequently, the oral epics of the Orthodox Serbs are shorter, less elaborate, and often recited without musical accompaniment. Matija Murko, a Czech ethnographer who provided detailed descriptions of epic singing (or chanting) from his field trips in the 1930s, reported the collective singing and reciting of epics as a widespread, non-specialized practice. The reciting of the narrative accompanied work and travel and occurred during festivities as well as in solitude. The epic songs could be recited, chanted, sung to a *gusle* by an individual (sometimes a professional *guslar* such as Filip Višnjić), sung by a duo in unison or parts, or sung collectively in unison or parts.

Vuk Stefanović Karadžić (1787–1864), pioneer folklorist, ethnographer, and linguist, is responsible for recognizing the value of Serbian folk literature, collecting thousands of versions of lyrics, proverbs, songs, heroic ballads, and epic poems, and meticulously recording information about the informants and the circumstances under which the material was collected. His work has become the foundation of the literary culture of the Serbs. Vuk is also responsible for standardizing the vernacular language, producing a grammar, and promoting the language of the people as the literary language. After preparing a small collection of Serbian oral poems based on his own memory and finding receptive audiences in Germany, in **Austria**, and among Serb scholars, Vuk began his field collections by transcribing songs from refugee *guslars* and *haiduks*. Filip Višnjić, a blind *guslar*, provided him with dozens of songs, while Tešan Podrugović, a Bosnian Serb freedom fighter, recited thousands of lines for Vuk. Vuk's monumental collection was published between 1824 and 1866. The oral heroic poems Vuk collected were primarily decasyllabic pieces recited or sung in the villages of the Serbian hill country.

EPICS

The earliest heroic songs do not have a clear historical foundation. Instead, they refer to a mythical past and unknown events. A much larger number recount historical events and can be grouped according to subject into cycles. The oldest of these historically based heroic narrative poems recount events associated with the history of Old Serbia in the twelfth through fourteenth centuries. They are referred to as the Nemanya Cycle. Among the most memorable and powerful heroic poems are those that belong to the Kosovo Cycle and describe events before, during, and after the 1389 Battle of Kosovo, the most celebrated battle of Serbian history. Many generations of Serbs grew up learning most of their history through folk epics and poetry. Because it was presented by *guslars* and reciters with passion and artistry, this folk history became immeasurably more influential than it would have been had it been learned from books.

The Battle of Kosovo marked the end of an epoch not only in Serbia but also in European history. This tragic battle was deeply and permanently etched in people's memory and can be traced in contemporary chronicles, in medieval literature and frescoes, and in legends and ballads. The battle is the central event in Serbia's struggle to preserve its independence. Within the epic cycle, it is interpreted as that watershed moment when the Serbs, in a monumental effort to protect European Christendom from the invading Ottomans, lost their empire and a whole generation of men. In this historic battle, the Serb hero, Miloš Obilić, killed the leader of the Turkish forces, Sultan Murad I, in his tent. Likewise, a Turkish warrior beheaded the Serbian ruler Prince Lazar. Both armies were vanquished, but in the years that followed, the Turks succeeded in overpowering the Balkans. In the epic poems that describe the massacre, motifs of treason and betrayal, prophecy, irony, human frailty, and valor occur, but the principal emphasis is on heroism and the foreordained defeat of the Serbs. In one of the epic songs, "The Fall of the Serbian Empire," St. Elijah brings a message from the Mother of God to Prince Lazar asking him to choose one of two empires. If he chooses an empire on earth, he will triumph over the Turks; if he chooses an empire in Heaven, he will lose the battle and die with all his men. Lazar's decision is to forfeit earthly rewards because "what is earthly is all fleeting, vain, and unsubstantial; heavenly things are lasting, firm, and eternal." This decision to win the grace of God is at the core of the Kosovo myths among the Serbs and has influenced subsequent generations to assume the same values. The aftermath of the battle, its horrors, and its impact on the survivors at home appear in several poems of the Kosovo Cycle. One of the most loved is "The Maiden of Kosovo." Here a young girl walks the bloody battlefield giving aid to the wounded. She happens to find one of the dying heroes, Pavle Orlovich, who describes to her the horrifying events of the battle. He then asks her for whom she is searching, and she names another hero, Milan Toplica, to whom she was promised as a bride. Pavle tells her then of Milan's tragic death and sends the weeping maiden home.

The third prominent cycle in the epics collected by Vuk Karadžić is known as the Prince Marko Cycle. A historical figure, Prince Marko Kraljević (1335?–1394) was the son of King Vukashin and became a Turkish vassal after the defeat of the Serbs at Kosovo. The legends and epics extolling his feats are among the most popular folk narratives of Serbia. A fighter for the Orthodox faith, Prince Marko achieved prominence because of his courage and incredible feats while fighting for freedom. His kind and just heart, physical prowess, strategic cleverness, and loyalty to his piebald steed, Sharatz, are identifying traits of his legend. His close relationship to the beautiful *vila* Radivoiyla, his mentor and protector, his rescue of a Turkish princess, and his clever strategies for outwitting the enemy established him as a true folk hero.

In the same vein, other epics about outlaw heroes called *haiduks* and *uskoks* developed and spread during the Ottoman period. The general unhappiness and misery among the population increased over the centuries. Oppressive practices such as the blood tax (the enforced seizure of young Serbian boys to become janissaries in the Turkish army, never to see their families again) continued unabated. As the economy began to fail, taxes became exorbitant, and the government became more and more corrupt, the *haiduks* (literally, brigands) began to take matters into their own hands. They led heroic lives—short, brutal, and secret—and like Robin Hood figures in other cultures, they became folk heroes because they fought for the people. If caught by the Turks, *haiduks* suffered a tortuous death: impalement. Early descriptions of the *haiduks* point out that they were simple, good folk—honorable men who initially would steal back only tax money collected by the Turks from peasants. Later, however, the bands of *haiduks* behaved less honorably, becoming brigands in the usual criminal sense, inspiring fear and loathing. Nevertheless, their reputation as bold, fearless, and unyielding rebels against the Turks won for them a place in folk history.

The traditional songs and epics of the Serbs contributed in significant ways to the shaping of the culture and have been accepted by Serbs not only as interesting descriptions of historical events but also as symbolic expressions of intense experiences shared by a whole nation. When the social identity of a group is threatened, as it was for centuries for the Serbs under the Ottomans and later Austro-Hungary, the need to maintain, validate, and preserve history, social values, and beliefs becomes more and more urgent. At such times, folklore becomes instrumental in efforts to unify and define the group. With freedom, the fear of cultural extinction disappears. Strict control over the transmission of historical and cultural heritage, especially in oral traditions and customs, is no longer necessary. An underground society is now aboveground, so language, history, and culture can be openly taught and realized. As people's interest in their traditions diminishes, audience control and the ability to "correct" those traditions probably decrease steadily. Traditions, consequently, gradually change from being an essential educational and political tool to becoming a source of entertainment and a nostalgic reminder of a nation's past. Given a new threat to social identity, however, folk traditions will once again assume their role of preserving, validating, and shaping culture.

BIBLIOGRAPHY

Butler, Thomas. 1980. *Monumenta Serbocroatica*. Ann Arbor: University of Michigan Press.

Ćosić, Dobrica. 1989. Traditions and Ideologies in the Historical Fate of the Serbian People. In *Battle of Kosovo*, edited by Vladimer Savić. Belgrade: Matice Isljenika Srbije. 10–11.

Čubelič, Tvrtko. 1963. *Lirske Narodne Pjesme*. Zagreb: Školska Knjiga.

Grubačić, Bratislav, and Momir Tomić. 1988. *Srpske Slave*. Belgrade: Litera.

Halpern, Joel M., and Barbara Kerewsky Halpern. 1972. *A Serbian Village in Historical Perspective*. New York: Holt, Rinehart, and Winston.

Hammel, E. A., Robert S. Ehrich, Radmila Fabijanović-Filipović, Joel M. Halpern, and Albert B. Lord. 1982. *Among the People—Native Yugoslav Ethnography: Selected Writings of Milenko S. Filipović*. Ann Arbor: University of Michigan Press.

Karadžić, Vuk Stefanović. 1987. *Srpske Narodne Pjesme* (Serbian Folksongs). 4 volumes. Belgrade: Prosveta-Nolit.

Koljević, Svetozar. 1980. *The Epic in the Making*. Oxford: Clarendon Press.

Kotur, Kristivoj. 1977. *The Serbian Folk Epic*. New York: Philosophical Library.

Laffan, R.G.D. 1989. *The Serbs: The Guardians of the Gate*. New York: Dorset Press.

Lodge, Olive. 1944. Folk Festivals in Yugoslavia. *Folk-Lore* 55:59–68.

Lord, Albert. 1968. *The Singer of Tales*. New York: Atheneum.

Maxwell, Grant. 1891. Slava. *Folk-Lore* 2:65–72.

Mihailovich, Vasa D. 1983. *Landmarks in Serbian Culture and History*. Pittsburgh: Serbian National Federation.

Murko, Matija. 1951. *Tragom Srpske-hrvatske narodne epike (1930–32)* (Tracing the Serbo-Croatian Folk Epic [1930–32]), translated by Jelka Arneri and Ljubomir Jonke. Zagreb: NP.

Nedić, Vladan. 1969. *Antologija Narodnih Lirskih Pesama*. Belgrade: Srpske Kniževna Zadruga.

Pavlovich, Paul. 1983. *The Serbians: The Story of a People*. Toronto: Serbian Heritage Books.

Pennington, Anne, and Peter Levi. 1984. *Marko the Prince: Serbo-Croat Heroic Songs*. New York: St. Martin's Press.

Popović, Tatyana. 1988. *Prince Marko: The Hero of South Slavic Epics*. Syracuse, NY: Syracuse University Press.

Radenković, Ljubinko. 1982. *Narodne Basme i Bajanje*. Kragujevac: NRIO Svetlost.

Resanović, Emilija. 1983. Serbian Folk Poetry. In *Landmarks in Serbian Culture and History*, edited by Vasa Mihailovich. Pittsburgh: Serbian National Federation. 62–75.

Schneeweis, E. 1961. *Serbocroatische Volkskunde.* Berlin: Walter De Gruyter.

Soulis, George Christos. 1984. *The Serbs and Byzantium during the Reign of Tsar Stephen Dušan (1331–1355) and His Successors.* Dumbarton Oaks: Harvard University Press.

Von Ranke, Leopold. 1853. *The History of Servia and the Servian Revolution.* London: Henry G. Bohn.

Vuković, Milan T. 1985. *Narodni Obiœaji i Verovanja i Poslovice Kod Srba.* Belgrade: Slobodan Jovich.

Wilson, Duncan. 1970. *The Life and Times of Vuk Stefanović Karadžić 1787–1864.* Oxford: Clarendon Press.

Zimmerman, Zora Devrnja. 1979a. The Changing Roles of the Vila in Serbian Traditional Narrative. *Journal of the Folklore Institute* 16:167–175.

———. 1979b. Moral Vision in the Serbian Folk Epic: The Foundation Sacrifice of Skadar. *Slavic and East European Journal* 23:371–379.

———. 1985. The Serbian Krsna Slava. *The Great Lakes Review* 11:21–37.

———. 1986. *Serbian Folk Poetry: Ancient Legends, Romantic Songs.* Columbus, OH: Kosovo Publishing Company.

Zora D. Zimmerman

UKRAINE

GEOGRAPHY AND HISTORY

Once known as the breadbasket of Europe, Ukraine is a rich and fertile land with a temperate climate. As the root of its name (*krai*; border) would indicate, it is located on the border. It is between Europe and Asia, and it is also between the land and the sea. The Black Sea is to the south of Ukraine, and battles with the Turks and Tatars, many of which took place on the Black Sea and on rivers flowing into it, mark Ukraine's history. Ukraine's natural wealth and location have been both a blessing

Ukraine.

and a curse. Ukrainians love their land. Nature imagery abounds in songs and stories. Embroidery designs are rich with flowers. Trees or branches are used in rituals that mark the turning points in the calendar year such as the summer solstice rite, Ivan Kupalo, and they are used in weddings and funerals. Ukrainians see themselves as one with their land, returning to it at death and becoming a part of it as their remains rejoin the soil. Yet many neighboring powers have coveted this land and its bounty, and the territory of Ukraine has been highly contested, enjoying few periods of political independence, a fact that has colored verbal lore and possibly material culture.

Whether in spite of, or because of, its history of subjugation, Ukraine has developed a distinctive culture that has retained a recognizable core even as the political powers controlling the area have changed. The earliest known cultural artifacts date back to 5000 to 3500 B.C.E. and resemble items produced today. Today's clay pots used for baking buckwheat, for example, are almost identical with pots from the earliest digs. The prehistoric culture is called Trypillian after a major excavation site. Items from the digs include pottery with distinctive swirling designs and terra-cotta female figurines, often with a rhombic pattern incised on the abdomen. The prevalence of the female figure in prehistoric statuary has led scholars such as Gimbutas and Rybakov to speculate that this area was once goddess-worshipping and possibly also matriarchal. While very early religious belief and social structure must remain matters for speculation, we do know about the gods and goddesses worshipped by the Slavs, the Ukrainians among them, at the time that Christianity was introduced. They include Perun, a deity of fire whose sacrificial stone, amber, is prized to this day; Dazhbog, the god of plenty; Berehynia, the protectress; and Rozhanytsia, the birth goddess.

Christianity came to Ukraine in 988. Prince Volodymyr of Kyiv, as legend has it, examined numerous religions and chose Orthodox Christianity for its beauty and emotional power. Eastern Ukraine has remained Orthodox, while Western Ukraine became Roman Catholic when it came under the Polish-Lithuanian Commonwealth. The church in this part of Ukraine falls within the jurisdiction of the pope but celebrates its service according to the Eastern rite, an arrangement negotiated at the Treaty of Brest (1596). During the Soviet period, efforts were made to eradicate all religion, both Orthodox and Catholic, though many believers continued to worship in secret, allowing for a successful reintroduction of religion in the post-Soviet period.

Historical narratives tell us that Volodymyr baptized the people of Kyiv in the river Dnipro

The icon corner in a house in Iavorivka, Drabiv Region, Cherkasy Province. (Photograph by Peter Holloway, 2001)

and then cast the idols that they had worshipped into the same river. The site where the Perun idol surfaced was considered a sacred place by the populace and is now the location of the Vydobyche monastery. While Christianity became the official religion of Ukraine, it did not obliterate earlier beliefs, and as monasteries such as Vydobyche were founded on sites already considered blessed, so Christianity and paganism mixed in all spheres of folk belief. Goddess worship continues in the veneration of Mary Theotokos, who appears as a central figure both in official religious practice such as church decoration and in folkongs and prayers. Ukrainian legends are richly peopled with religious figures: God, Christ, and saints, especially Nicholas and Peter. They walk the earth and explain the nature of the world. Nicholas's kindness toward a peasant and Cassian's haughtiness explain why the former saint has two feast days a year, while Cassian is cursed with being the saint of 29 February, thus having his day only once every four years. Other legends tell why people must die, why they cannot know the hour of their death, and why it is best not to try to alter fate. Legends speak of devils and pagan place spirits such as the spirit of the house (*domovyk*) as often as they tell about saints. These beings of the unclean force (*nechysta syla*), however, uphold the tenets of official religion, such as going to church on Sunday, by punishing people who do not behave as they should.

WITCHCRAFT AND FOLK MEDICINE

An interesting aspect of belief is folk medicine and witchcraft accusations. Herbalism is not associated with witches. Herbs and berries are widely used by everyone, urban as well as rural, and plant knowledge is not considered witchcraft. Rather, the specialized knowledge associated with witchcraft focuses on fear sickness and on illnesses produced by maleficence, such as those caused by the evil eye (*prysrit*). Children are believed to be most susceptible to fear sickness, though it can also affect adults, especially those in love. The cure involves diagnosis and removal. In Eastern Ukraine, this is done by passing an egg over the body while reciting prayers and then breaking the egg into a glass of water. The egg removes the malaise from the body, and the shapes that it takes in the water indicate the nature and the severity of the problem. In Western Ukraine a similar ritual is performed using melted wax. A folk healer, usually called a *babka*, was, and is, both a valued and respected member of the community and a person susceptible to persecution. From the point of view of the *babky* themselves, the words they speak are not incantations but prayers (*molytvy*), and their services are God's work, for they are merely conduits for divine power. The views of others are mixed and can be extremely negative. Folk healers suffered a great deal under the Soviet system, being accused of exploiting superstition for personal gain. Folk healing is currently experiencing a revival because Soviet strictures against this genuinely valued form of medicine are gone. This does not mean that the folk healer is above suspicion and concomitant accusation. As before Soviet rule, a woman with the power to heal is suspected of having equal power to cause illness. An active belief in witches feeds such suspicions.

Witchcraft beliefs are as widespread now as they were when extensive ethnographic work first began in the late nineteenth century. Presumably, they merely went unarticulated during the Soviet period. A witch (*vid'ma*) need not be a person who makes a contract with the Devil, and a person can be born a witch if she is the seventh daughter of seven daughters or a baby born with a tail. Witches go to church and take communion and need not misbehave in any way. If they do, they are most often suspected of stealing milk from cows belonging to other people, though accusations of causing fear, sickness, or other ailments in people are also possible. Most witch stories are attested in legend form. Few people proclaim themselves to be witches, and actual accusations are far less common than stories about witchcraft. Whether the fear of female power that these legends express is a survival of earlier matriarchal beliefs is another matter for speculation.

LEGENDS

Legends are currently the most widely circulated oral genre. Traditional stories flourish, and, in addition to the topics already mentioned, people frequently tell how the *domovyk* comes at night and oppresses the dreamer, foretelling impending disaster. Stories about the return of the dead abound. In them, the dead come back to help the living, or they seek help from them, requesting flat shoes, for example, to walk more comfortably in the Otherworld. Currently, common legends deal with topics close to home. Historical topics, such as stories about rulers of the past, are not now popular. New legends are being generated in response to new events, and stories that derive from American disaster movies have recently been collected. Other prose genres include folktales of various types. Many tales that began as oral folklore are now disseminated by television, the movies, and the publishing industry. Still, there are recognized masters of oral storytelling, many known beyond their native villages. Less skilled narrators also transmit folktales orally, if only in their immediate circle, and the presence of television in almost every home has not destroyed storytelling.

EPICS AND MINSTRALS

Ukrainian folklore is very rich in legend and other prose genres. However, the best-known Ukrainian verbal art form is epic poetry (*dumy*). *Dumy* were performed by professional blind minstrels called either *kobzari* or *lirnyky* after the instruments that they played. The *kobza* no longer exists, and *kobzari* now play the *bandura*. This is an asymmetrical plucked and strummed string instrument that developed out of the *kobza*, a lute. While the *kobza* was played like a lute, the *bandura* is played more like a harp, though three distinct playing styles are attested. Because it is unique to Ukraine, it is often seen as emblematic of this country and its folk music. The *lira* is not a lyre, as its name and legends linking it to David would imply, but a hurdy-gurdy that sounds very different from the *bandura*. Other important instruments, not peculiar to minstrels, include the *sopilka* (flute), *tsymbaly* (zither), *trembita* (long horn), the accordion, the violin, and the ocarina.

Kobzari and *lirnyky* were among the few folk performers who were recognized as professionals. They belonged to guilds and went though apprenticeship and initiation. They had to be blind because minstrelsy was a social welfare institution open only to those who could not do normal work, meaning farm labor. Because minstrelsy was a form of begging, a stigma was attached to it, and neither minstrels nor their songs, with the exception of *dumy*, were extensively studied. *Dumy* did receive a great deal of attention because of the prestige of epic, with scholars often presuming that these songs originated among literate poets, later "sinking" to the folk milieu.

There are three cycles of *dumy*: those that describe the battles against the Turks and the Tatars from the fourteenth to the sixteenth centuries, those connected to the uprising against the Poles led by Bohdan Khmel'nyts'ky, and the so-called everyday life songs that tell of family conflict precipitated by the hardships of war. Most *duma* content is sad. These are not songs of glorious triumphs in battle; rather, *dumy* tell how all three sons of a family die together on the battlefield, or they lament a brash young fighter giving in to hubris, drinking too much, and fighting more of the enemy than he can handle—with predictably disastrous results. In the everyday life songs, wives

Pavlo Suprun (right), a blind minstrel, sings and begs outside the Lavra Monastery in Kyiv. (Photograph by Natalie Kononenko, 1999)

deal with the prolonged absence of their husbands, and sisters lament brothers riding off to war or dying far from home. There are no happy plots. The songs make no nationalistic assertions, yet they are so much connected with Ukraine that they have been considered a threat to tsars and Soviet rulers alike. Although documentary evidence is sparse, the most extreme action against *dumy* was taken by Stalin in 1939, when he summoned the minstrels of Ukraine to a conference and then had all but a few executed.

Although far less studied than *dumy*, the other parts of minstrel repertory are more indicative of folk preferences. These include begging songs (*zhebranky*) invoking Mary Theotokos, historical songs, and religious songs (*psal'ma*). Historical songs are a shorter, more melodramatic version of *dumy*. In the song about Morozenko, for example, the hero watches the removal of his own beating heart. *Psal'my* were the most popular songs in minstrel repertory. They are not psalms but songs that warn against gluttony, excessive indulgence in sex, or failure to attend church on Sunday. Some present a folk interpretation of biblical themes. The *psal'ma* about St. Barbara tells of her refusal to marry a pagan prince, despite the tortures to which she is subjected. Lazarus tells about two brothers, both named Lazar, one poor and ill and the other rich and miserly. After death, the poor brother sits on the right hand of God, while the rich one is sent to Hell for failing to help his sibling.

Although only minstrels could perform for pay, their songs, begging songs excluded, were known and sung by non-professionals. The general populace also sang many other genres, either solo or in chorus, with one person leading and the others picking up the refrain. Lyric songs express emotions from loneliness to apprehension about the unfaithfulness of a lover. Ballads are especially popular and, when courtship rituals still existed, were the song of choice among the young. The ballad of a young woman who is jilted by her lover and drowns the baby conceived in the unfortunate union, for example, has been popular since early folksong collecting and has remained so, becoming a popular recording in the late 1990s.

LIFE-CYCLE CELEBRATIONS

Songs and other verbal arts accompany every ritual. Weddings are elaborate affairs that include a pre-wedding phase, the wedding proper, and a post-wedding carnival. Once a couple has decided to wed, the groom's family initiates a formal request for the bride, which requires special encoded speech by an elder (*starosta*) who represents the groom. The *starosta* must speak in traditional metaphor, for an outright statement of intent is considered bad luck. If the proposal is accepted, the parents of the couple meet to make wedding arrangements, negotiating the gifts to be given and the number of guests to be invited by each side. The wedding itself varies from region to region but typically includes a ritual preparation of the wedding bread (*korovai*). Songs accompany this part of the ritual. Bride and groom then walk the village with small breads (*shyshky*), inviting people to the celebration. The night before the wedding, the bride's friends gather at her home to prepare a wedding tree (*hil'tse*) and to say good-bye to the bride and her maidenhood. Songs, many of which are sad and express fear of married life, characterize this part of the wedding. A church ceremony seals the marriage, but then the bride and groom separate and go to their own homes for partying and the folk part of the wedding. A formal procession (*poizd*) sets out from the groom's home to pick up the bride. There are mock impediments to the *poizd*, and the teasing songs exchanged between the groom's entourage and the bride's are still especially popular. Gift-giving (*daruvannia*) takes place at the groom's home or at both houses and also requires special metaphorical speech, which can be erotic. The rebraiding of the bride's hair, signaling her loss of virginity, is an important ritual, as is the rite performed on the morning after the wedding. The bride's parents do not participate in the party at the groom's home but go there the next morning to acknowledge that their daughter is now part of the groom's household. Either later that day or the following day, a carnival (*tsyhanshchyna*) begins. Some features of the carnival include pranks and thievery: the people who continue to party take gates off hinges or steal chickens from their neighbors, for example. Either the parents of the couple or the godparents are cross-dressed and pulled through the streets in a cart. They are then either thrown in the river or forced to treat the wedding guests to sweets and alcohol.

Contemporary village weddings have many of the features listed above and typically last four days. During the Soviet era, church weddings were rare, and the church ceremony was

A church wedding in Mryn, Nosiv Region, Chernihiv Province. (Photograph by Natalie Kononenko, 2000)

replaced by a civil one. The post-wedding carnival was prohibited, and drinking was frowned upon. Nevertheless, both took place in most villages discreetly, out of sight of the village head. In the post-Soviet period, most villagers choose to have both civil and religious ceremonies. In the urban setting, the civil ceremony is preferred, weddings last only one day, and there are far fewer guests.

A special form of the wedding is the death wedding or *pokhoron-vesillia*. If a young person dies unmarried, her or his funeral is celebrated as a wedding, with the boyfriend or girlfriend of the deceased acting as the groom or bride. The deceased is dressed in wedding clothes and given a ring. Other wedding features typically include the *korovai* and the *hil'tse*. After the ceremony, the person who had acted as groom or bride is free to marry another. Though still practiced, the death wedding is losing popularity, and legends tell about death weddings going wrong, especially if a photograph is placed in the coffin. The deceased, it is said, then returns to claim his or her sweetheart.

Funerals in the rural setting are elaborate. After a person dies, post-menopausal women wash the body and lay it out in the icon corner. This duty falls to neighbors and friends, for relatives should not touch the deceased. The women who prepared the body, now joined by the family, keep vigil, discuss the virtues of the deceased, and read the Psalter. Ideally, the vigil continues for three days and nights, but having the deceased spend one night in the home is considered sufficient. At the funeral, a service may be held in the home. A procession follows. The coffin, its lid, a Cross, an icon, and a portrait of the deceased are carried down village streets by family, friends, and anyone else who wishes to honor the deceased. During the procession, relatives lament. Traditional laments are still performed in Ukraine, and good singers can go on for hours. Laments chide the deceased for abandoning the living and ask them to return, eventually admitting that this is impossible. The procession takes the coffin to the cemetery, and once the coffin is lowered into the grave, lamentation must cease. Interment is followed by a meal that begins with a dish made of grain or bread called *kanun* or *kolivo*. The meal ends with a fruit

Wedding banquet in Krut'ky, Chornobai Region, Cherkasy Province. (Photograph by Natalie Kononenko, 1998)

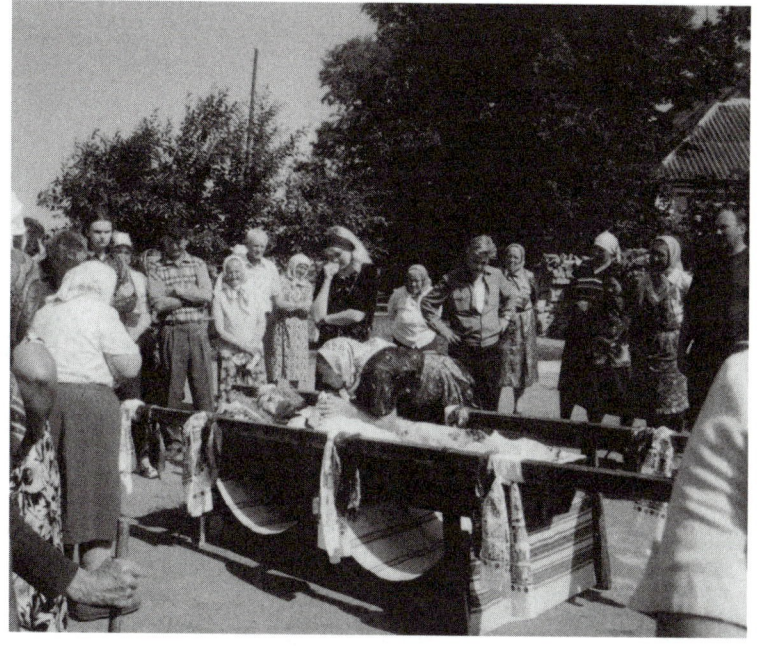

Funeral in Iavorivka, Drabiv Region, Cherkasy Province. The funeral procession has stopped at a crossroads and the widow of the deceased sings laments. (Photograph by Natalie Kononenko, 2000)

pudding (*kysyl'*), and when this is served, the church choir (*pivchy*) sings songs called *psal'my*. These differ from minstrel *psal'my* in that they speak on behalf of the deceased, usually in the first person, and deal with the inevitability of death. Folklorists have overlooked funeral *psal'my* because they have assumed them not to be oral. However, *psal'my* exhibit variation and form a dialogue with laments, making them an integral part of the funeral.

Soviet efforts to take religion out of the funeral entailed replacing the church service with an oration by a state-trained worker that took place on a dais in the cemetery. This practice has not survived into the post-Soviet era, and in general, Soviet influence on funerary customs has been minimal. When Psalters were banned, they nevertheless were hand-copied and read, and there are rumors of Crosses hidden inside the pyramids and obelisks favored as Soviet grave markers.

Many folk beliefs are associated with death and dying. A person who has trouble dying is thought to be a witch or a sorcerer. His or her sufferings are relieved by breaking a hole in the roof above the bed to release the soul. The water used to wash the deceased must be disposed of with care because it can make plants wither. It is especially important that "dead" water be poured where no living creature will inadvertently step on it, for that will cause illness and possibly death. Conversely, "dead" water is reputedly sought by witches. It can be used for good (to deaden pain) and for ill (to cause paralysis).

Birth and baptism do not have many oral forms associated with them. Many taboos apply to pregnancy. For example, a pregnant woman must not steal lest the body of her baby carry a birthmark shaped like the stolen item; she cannot become frightened for the same reason. Once she has given birth, she and the infant should not leave the farmstead for forty days because they are especially susceptible to the evil eye. Until recently, birth took place at home with the assistance of a midwife. The midwife could be the local healer, and she, too, was called *babka*, though usually with an adjective such as *povival'na* (swaddling). She had many ceremonial functions throughout the lives of the children she delivered, and when midwives were replaced by clinics in Soviet times, many regions instituted the *nazvana* (designated) *babka*, a woman who did not deliver the baby but performed the ritual functions of the midwife.

The most important rite connected to birth is baptism, a church ritual, and it is considered so important that during the Soviet era it was often performed in secret and on older children. As for folk birth rituals, many are connected to cloth and to fiber. When a baby was born, the midwife was supposed to tie the umbilical cord with unspun hemp. In some regions, it was considered important that the hemp be taken from a female, seed-bearing plant, lest the child become infertile. It is common to stage a mock attack on the child's paternal grandmother, ripping her clothes, ostensibly to provide diapers. At baptism, the godmother provides a three-meter length of cloth (*kryzhma*) and accepts the infant from the priest with this cloth.

ARTS AND CRAFTS

Cloth plays an important role in Ukrainian ritual, and one of the hallmarks of Ukrainian culture is embroidery both on clothing and on strips of fabric called ritual towels (*rushnyky*). These have a strictly symbolic function. They are draped around icons, for example, to protect the home, much as the icons themselves do. During the marriage ceremony, whether civil or religious, the couple stands on a *rushnyk* spread by their mothers. After the service, a *rushnyk* is used to tie their hands together. *Rushnyky* are tied around the *korovai*, draped over the icon used to bless the couple, and held over the head of the bride when she enters her new home for the first time. A *rushnyk* decorates the lid of a coffin during a funeral, and *rushnyky* are typical gifts for people who help a family celebrate a ritual. They are given to *starosty* during a wedding, and after a funeral they are distributed to those who carry the coffin and dig the grave. *Rushnyky* can help those who might become unquiet dead, unable to rest in peace. If a soldier dies on the battlefield, as happened so often during World War II, his sister embroiders a *rushnyk*, which is not displayed but kept in a trunk (*skrynia*).

There is a complex traditional symbolic system for *rushnyky* and other embroidered items. The tree of life motif offers protection and fertility and can be used on almost any item. A wedding *rushnyk* must have an open wreath, signaling life ahead, while the wreath on a funeral towel must be closed. Wedding *rushnyky* typically have birds to indicate the migration of the bride to a new home. Skill with a needle is considered the mark of a good woman. A girl was expected to fill a *skrynia* with embroidered items by the time she was ready to wed, and a display of her handiwork at the groom's home was frequently part of the marriage rite. Embroidery is so closely associated with Ukrainian culture that diaspora groups practice and teach embroidery to assert Ukrainian identity.

Other important fiber arts include the weaving of rugs (*kylymy*) that are used on whitewashed walls where coverings near beds and benches are a must. In Western Ukraine, an intarsia weaving technique, similar to the one used for *kylymy*, produces *lyzhni*, multi-colored blankets with a long, warm nap. Also characteristic of Western Ukraine are vests with the fur on the inside and with the outside leather richly ornamented with embroidery and appliqués. Seed beads are used to make *gerdany*, intricate necklaces as wide as a collar, which exhibit complex designs akin to those found in embroidery.

Pottery is an important craft. There are pockets of top-quality clay in Ukraine, and pots of great delicacy and beauty have been produced at these sites for millennia. The prestige of archeological digs has made pottery a craft that Ukrainians treasure and associate with their culture.

CALENDAR CUSTOMS

Ukrainian agrarian ritual has been heavily influenced by the church calendar, though folk religion preserves many pre-Christian elements. Thus, vegetation is honored throughout the calendar, and fortune-telling and prophylactic magic abound. Songs accompany yearly cycle rites: from the welcoming of spring, to the marking of the summer solstice, to the celebration of Christmas and the New Year. Of all the yearly cycle rites, the one most associated with Ukrainian culture and folklore is Easter (*Paskha*). This is the time when people make *pysanky*, decorated eggs that, like embroidery, are presented by Ukrainians to outsiders as emblematic of

Plate of *pysanky* from the collection of Natalie Kononenko. (Photograph by Peter Holloway, 2003)

Girls dancing around the tree called Marena at an Ivan Kupalo celebration in Berlozy, Kozelets Region, Chernihov Province. (Photograph by Natalie Kononenko, 2001)

their culture. *Pysanky* are batiked eggs. Designs are made in molten wax on the raw egg with a stylus (*kystka*). The egg is then dipped into a light-colored dye, such as yellow, the artist then drawing an additional pattern on the dyed surface. Dyeing and drawing progress to increasingly darker shades, the last color often being black—at which point the wax is removed, and the egg becomes a talisman. It is not eaten.

From the point of view of verbal arts, some of the most interesting calendar items are Christmas plays. Live actors stage several types of plays. The most basic is a mock funeral where actors bring in a coffin and lament with humorous, often erotic songs. The "funeral" concludes with the "resurrection" of the "deceased." The play most associated with Ukraine was a puppet show called *vertep* (crèche) staged by semi-professional actors. The *vertep* is performed on a two-tier stage with the puppets on top acting out a religious scene such as the Nativity while the lower stage exhibits slapstick routines. At *Malanka*, performed at the New Year, people dress as Death and as stock comic or political figures and behave as the character they personify. Some participants act out small scenes. *Hahilky*, a spring activity, resembles an athletic contest with a young man sitting on another's shoulders and trying to unseat another such pair.

As songs accompany all rituals, so does dance. People dance at weddings, and dances go with virtually all agrarian calendar rites. Many are circle dances around a central object such as the decorated tree and bonfire used at Ivan Kupalo. During the Soviet period, dance became a popular spectacle performed on stages in cities and later on television. Based loosely on folk forms, staged dance featured acrobatic moves and colorful, often matching costumes. In the diaspora, dance, often the showy variety, was a way of attracting young people to Ukrainian activities and showcasing Ukrainian culture to outsiders.

ARCHITECTURE

Folk architecture is important, and the thatched cottage is as emblematic of Ukraine as *pysanky* and embroidery. In villages, houses are still constructed following the traditional layout and using ancient techniques such as wattle-and-daub. The entryway of the house should be protected and must face away from the street. Inside, the icon corner should first catch the visitor's eye. It is considered the male part of the house, and men are responsible for the flame in the icon lamp. Guests are entertained at the table set beneath the icons. Diagonally across from the icons is the female part of the house where the stove is located. The stove takes up as much as one-quarter of the home, and the back of it—reserved for elders—is considered the best sleeping place in the house. Urban apartments, while not built by hand, have many traditional layout features. Typically, doorways are protected by an entryway, and the icon corner is in the main room with the table beneath it. Door protection may be a symbolic remnant of the country's efforts to shield itself from invading neighbors.

Stove with sleeping area in Iavorivka, Drabiv Region, Cherkasy Province. (Photograph by Natalie Kononenko, 2000)

CHALLENGES OF THE MODERN WORLD

Ukraine's political situation has influenced both folklore itself and the study of folklore. Folk materials were sporadically recorded in the early nineteenth century, and the first collection of *dumy* might well have been inspired by the work of the Brothers Grimm. Intense folklore work, however, began in the later 1800s. At this time, Ukraine was part of **Russia**. It was labeled Little Russia (*Malorossiia*), terminology designed to incorporate it into the Russian fold as a lesser entity. The Ukrainian language and other marks of independence were suppressed. It may seem ironic that folklore flourished under such circumstances, but this suited tsarist policies of belittling Ukraine. Folklore was associated with the unsophisticated and the rural, implying that Ukraine, as a country rich in folklore, was backward. Thus, while high culture artistic expression was discouraged, folklore collecting and scholarship were not. As a result, archival repositories of Ukrainian folk material are unusually rich.

When the Soviets came to power, they first sought to eliminate folklore, assuming that there would be no need for it in a progressive state. Later, realizing folklore's power, Soviets tried to use it for political ends. A Commission on Soviet Traditions, Festivals, and Rituals was established to formulate Soviet rituals and disseminate them to the populace, while academic institutions like the Folklore Institute of the Academy of Sciences were charged with helping folk artists create appropriately Soviet songs, stories, and other folk art. *Dumy* about Lenin were created, baptism was replaced with the star ceremony, Christmas was replaced by New Year observances, and Soviet elements were added to weddings and funerals. New items such as holidays commemorating the Soviet Socialist Revolution and marking the first and last days of school were created, and there was an effort to eliminate items incompatible with Soviet ideals such as religious and openly erotic songs.

In the post-Soviet period, efforts to influence folklore are fewer, though not absent. Because the Soviet system did try to manage folklore, Ukrainian intellectuals and Ukrainians in the diaspora try to undo Sovietization, though they often disagree on the proper course of action. The goals of the folk themselves are efficacy and beauty. They try to conduct rituals that will effectively cement a marriage and to produce *rushnyky* that are a delight to the eye and songs that please the ear. Many pre-Soviet forms have returned. While minstrelsy as a social welfare institution is gone, *psal'my* are back, and so is erotic folklore. The effect of seventy years of Soviet power is the addition of elements such as the ceremony marking the beginning and end of the school year rather than any large-scale elimination of genres or topics. The fall of the Soviet Union also opened up Ukraine to globalization. Ukraine declared independence in 1991. Since then, television and toys from abroad have begun to enter this formerly closed country, and Barbie clones can now be found in the most remote villages. Politically, Ukraine is seeking to use its natural riches and its traditional liminal position to become more active in the global arena. Time will tell how this affects Ukrainian folklore. A useful Web site on Ukrainian folklore may be accessed at www.arts.ualberta.ca/uvp/.

BIBLIOGRAPHY

Antonovych, V., and Mykhailo Drahomanov. 1874–1875. *Istoricheskie pesni malorusskogo naroda* (The Historical Songs of the Little Russian People). 2 volumes. Kyiv: Izdatel'stvo russkogo imperatorskogo geograficheskogo obshchestva.

Borysenko, V. K. 1988. *Vesil'ni zvychaii ta obriady na Ukraiini: istoryko-etnohrafichne doslidzhennia* (Wedding Customs and Practices in Ukraine: A Historico-Ethnographic Study). Kyiv: Naukova dumka.

Britsyna, O., and I. Holovakha. 2004. *Prozovyi fol'klor sela Ploske na Chernihivshchyni* (The Prose Folklore of Ploske, Chernihiv Region). Kyiv: IMFE.

Chubinskii, P. P. 1872. *Narodnyi dnevnik, Trudy etnografichesko-statisticheskoi ekspeditsii v zapadno-russkii krai* (The Folk Calendar: Studies of the Ethnographic and Statistical Expedition into the South-West Russian Region). Volume 3. St. Petersburg: N.p.

———. 1877. *Obriady: Rodiny, krestiny, svad'ba, pokhorony* (Customs: Birth, Baptism, Wedding, Funeral). Volume 6. St. Petersburg: N.p.

Gimbutas, Mariya. 1982. *Goddesses and Gods of Old Europe: Myths and Cult Images*. Berkeley: University of California Press.

Hasiuk, O. O., and M. H. Stepan. 1989. *Khudozhne vyshyvannia* (Art Embroidery). Kyiv: Vyshcha shkola.

Havryliuk, N. K. 1981. *Kartografirovanie iavlenii dukhovnoi kul'tury (po materialam rodil'noi obriadnosti ukrainstev)* (Mapping Spiritual Culture Using Ukrainian Birth Customs). Kyiv: Naukova dumka.

Hnatiuk, V. 1904, 1912. *Znadoby do halyts'ko-rus'koi demonolohii* and *Znadoby do ukraiins'koi demonolohii; Etnohrafichnyi zbirnyk* (Materials on Galician and Rusyn Lower Mythology; Materials on Ukrainian Lower Mythology). Volumes 15, 32, and 34. L'viv: Naukove tovarystvo im. Shevchenka.

———. 1912. *Pokhoronni zvychai i obriady. Etnohrafichnyi zbirnyk* (Funeral Customs and Rituals). Volume 32. L'viv: Naukove tovarystvo im. Shevchenka.

Hrushevs'ka, Kateryna. 1927–1931. *Ukraiins'ki narodni dumy* (Ukrainian Folk Epic). 2 volumes. Kharkiv/Kyiv: Derzhavne vydavnytstvo ukraii'ny.

Hrushevs'kyi, Marko. 1906. *Dytyna u zvychaiakh i viruvanniakh ukraiins'koho naroda* (The Child in the Customs and Beliefs of the Ukrainian People). L'viv: Naukove tovarystvo im. Shevchenka.

Kalynets, Ihor. 1968. *Ukraiins'ki pysanky* (Ukrainian Easter Eggs). Kyiv: Mystetstvo.

Kolessa, Filiaret. 1983. *Ukraiins'ka usna slovesnist'* (Ukrainian Oral Literature). Edmonton: Canadian Institute of Ukrainian Studies.

Kononenko, Natalie. 1998. *Ukrainian Minstrels: And the Blind Shall Sing*. Armonk, NY: M. E. Sharpe.

Kylymnyk, Stepan. 1994. (1957). *Ukrains'kyi rik u narodnykh zvychaiakh v istorychnomu osvitlenni* (The Ukrainian Year in Folk Custom and in Historical Perspective). Kyiv: Oberehy.

Odarchenko, Petro, and Halyna Carynnyk. 1992. *Ukraiins'kyi narodnyi odaih* (Ukrainian Folk Costume). Toronto: World Federation of Ukrainian Women's Organizations.

Rybakov, B. A. 1994. *Iazychestvo drevnikh slavian* (The Paganism of the Early Slavs). Moscow: Nauka.

Shubravs'ka, M. M., and O. A. Pravdiuk, eds. 1970. *Vesillia u dvokh knyhakh* (The Wedding; in Two Volumes). Kyiv: Naukova Dumka.

Speranskii, M. N. 1904. *Iuzhno-russkaia pesnia i sovremennye ee nositeli (po povodu T. M. Parkhomenka)* (The South-Russian Song and Its Contemporary Performers [on the Topic of T. M. Parkhomenko]). Kyiv: N.p.

Sventsits'kyi, I. 1912. *Pokhoronni holosinnia. Etnohrafichnyi zbirnyk* (Funeral Laments). Volume 31. L'viv: Naukove tovarystvo im. Shevchenka.

Voropai, Oleksa. 1963–1966. *Zvychaii nashoho narodu* (The Customs of Our People). Munich: Ukrains'ke vydavnytstvo.

Zakovich, N. M., P. I. Kosukha, and V. A. Perunov. 1986. *Sotsialisticheskaia obraidnost'* (Socialist Ritual). Kyiv: Vyshcha shkola.

Natalie Kononenko

The Mediterranean

Italy: Peoples and Regions

ITALY OVERVIEW

GEOGRAPHY AND HISTORY

The Italian peninsula begins in the Alps and extends for 1,300 kilometers to the southeast into the Mediterranean Sea. Its geographical configuration contrasts the north and the south—a divide that characterizes much of Italian history, economy, and culture. There exists a basic dichotomy between Continental and Mediterranean Italy, between the "modern" north and "backward" south. Northern Italy comprehends the regions of Piedmont, Aosta Valley, Ligury, Lombardy, Trentino–Alto Adige, Veneto, Friuli–Venezia Giulia, and Emilia Romagna; middle Italy encompasses Tuscany, Marches, Umbria, and Latium; and southern Italy includes Abruzzi, Molise, Campania, Puglia and Salento, Lucania, Calabria, and the islands of Sicily and Sardinia. This north-south split has roots in the distant past. With the depopulation and agricultural regression at the end of the Roman Empire, the activity of sheep-rearing in uncultivated land dominated the middle-south, while a hunter-gatherer economy developed in northern areas. However, during the Lombard domination (from the sixth and seventh centuries) northern Italy and Tuscany revived agricultural activities, which later would provide the basis for a closed feudal economy called *curtense* (mainly based on barter). Meanwhile, sheep-farming continued in the Byzantine middle-southern area.

From the eleventh century to the thirteenth century the northern and middle areas re-populated and developed agriculture, thanks to the monasteries—which reclaimed and cleared uncultivated land—the resumption of commerce, and the new urban/countryside relationship established during the age of the city-states. The autocratic system declined under increasing non-feudal contractual relationships with the urban bourgeoisie (*mezzadria*). In the south, on the other hand, the rural immobility prevailed with the Norman and Aragonese re-feudalization of the territory.

The fifteenth and sixteenth centuries witnessed an important agricultural transformation in the north. Subsidized by commerce, there developed massive production of linen, hemp, and silk as well as cultivation of rice, maize, and fodder. In the middle-south, the Papal State and the Kingdom of Naples preserved a feudal economy where agriculture integrated with transhumant sheep-farming. The capitalistic transformation of the countryside and the consequent development of the farm economy (farms run by tenants who exclusively employed wage-earning workers) during the eighteenth and nineteenth centuries affected only the north. In the nineteenth century, industry significantly expanded in most of northern Italy and developed only sporadically in the south in the twentieth century. As a result, the south came to be marked by the following characteristics: widespread poverty, associated with a meager economy, archaic culture, and political immobility; isolated and

Italy, Piedmont, and Sicily.

overpopulated, built-up areas that developed in accord with environmental constraints; strong endogamy with a deep sense of family and strict social control; and a population with a profoundly rooted rural culture even in urban areas. The dichotomy between north and south is recognizable in all cultural aspects of Italy, with regional distinctions making the nation appear even more fragmented.

In the north and in Tuscany, the city-states, the Renaissance towns, and the middle-class cities have created rural areas thanks to their investment in agriculture, the products of which were sold back to the cities and industrial areas. In the south, however, the cities grew from the countryside. Large landowners used the profits earned from agricultural activities to build their own palaces in the cities, never investing to improve agriculture. As a consequence, the rural spirit has continued to imbue the southern city and its urban configuration, creating a continuum between city and countryside where, unlike in the north, urban values have never been accepted.

PEASANT CULTURE

The study of folk culture in Italy has often been mistakenly interpreted as the study of "peasant culture," which is mostly related to farmers' life; that is, folk culture has been identified exclusively with agricultural life. This misinterpretation has prevented a full understanding of the different existing folk cultures and traditions and their relationships, which are sometimes in conflict with each other.

Italian peasants, 1897. The study of Italian folk culture has often been mistakenly interpreted as the study of "peasant culture." The peasant's vision of the world was based on tradition and continuity with the past, often eschewing innovation. (Courtesy Library of Congress)

Essentially, peasant economy is pre-modern, feudal in its structure. The farm tends to be autonomous, self-sufficient, and linked to the domestic economy. The products of the land are consumed within the family without passing into the market, though part of them may be owed to an external figure or authority who controls the access to the land (the baron, city, or nation).

The stereotype of the peasant economy in the south is one of immutability from the Neolithic age up to the present day. Southern folk culture actually developed between the seventh and thirteenth centuries, following a radical redistribution of the population that determined a total reorganization of the ethnic composition of the territory. Pre-historic or pagan survivals are present in southern peasant culture. However, these are only elements of a more complex historical mosaic—at all appearances fragmented, chaotic, and contradictory—that may be understood only by examining the cultural changes, including cultural stratifications (from paganism to Christianity), the influence of hegemonic culture, and the consequent resistance and syncretisms experienced by southern peasant culture.

Particularism and tradition are two fundamental aspects of peasant culture. Particularism emerged from the cultural isolation faced during the high Middle Ages, which contributed to the fragmentation of the past unified culture. The amazing variety of folklore, however, reflects some uniformity. Every community has its own traditions, songs, and dialect, which may be similar to those of its neighboring villages, while presenting some variations.

The peasant's vision of the world was based on tradition and continuity with the past, often eschewing innovation. In Italy peasants include small landowners, farmers, and sharecroppers. Anthropologists have examined the particular composition of southern peasants, the so-called peasant/farmhand class, which comprehended country people (small landowners and day laborers) who worked the land by hand, in contrast to higher classes (masters and civilians) who did not perform any manual work. Farmhands were not just wage laborers, as in northern Italy, but farmers or very small landowners with insufficient land who had to work for large agriculture barons to make a living. The values of southern traditional culture primarily originated among the peasantry. However, other social classes participated in various degrees in the formation process. The values emphasize hierarchy and social inequality (the peasant is not a free producer but subordinated to a master); ethics of honor (personal and sexual); and fatalism, which recognizes the impossibility of change or improvement. For peasants, history is something that has been received. They can do nothing to change it. As a consequence, peasants tend to exhibit a melancholic view of life.

Peasants usually turned to magic-religious practices. Their poor living conditions usually translated into a sense of precariousness, uncertainty over the future, and constant sense of pressure from natural and social forces that seemed to be impossible to confront and dominate. Magic practices and religious-magic beliefs developed within this context of fear and instability. The belief that an entity is motivating or actually guiding people's actions constitutes the main principle of magic. The following *strambotto* (an old Italian verse form) from the Lucania area (Basilicata region) exemplifies this sense of hopelessness and loneliness: "*Quanne nascett'ie mamma non c'era / Era sciute a lave' l'ambassature*" (When I was born, my mother was not there. / She left to wash the wraps).

Familism (a complex cultural value that centers on the belief that everything revolves around the family) and particularism (divisiveness, splitting into factions) substitute for national values and institutions such as the state and political groups, thus keeping the peasant from larger historical movements. Edward Banfield, in his research and fieldwork on the Lucania area, theorized the interpretive category of "amoral familism," which speaks to an ethnic trend to put the family above everything. Essentially, the immediate family takes precedence over individual needs. Banfield articulated its ethos as a desire to maximize the immediate, material situation of the nuclear family and the belief that others will do likewise. In commenting on this value, Carlo Tullio-Altan said that the family is at the summit, followed by the company and then by friends/customers. He traced this emphasis on family as far back as 1443, when it was noted by Leon Battista Alberti. Frederik Friedmann defined the southern question as a condition of "extreme poverty" (*miseria*), which includes more than loss of material possessions. Poverty represents for southern peasants a way of life, a philosophy pervading all society. It manifests as desperation among poorest classes and as cynicism and *abulia* among higher classes (illustrated by Tomasi di Lampedusa's novel, *The Leopard*). The peasants' compulsive desire to possess (the so-called *roba*—possessions—in the novels of Giovanni Verga) is an expression of their existential instability, their need to create artificial supports for their vacillating personality, which is constantly susceptible to crisis.

MOUNTAIN DWELLERS AND OTHER NON-PEASANT CULTURES

Existing somewhat in opposition to peasant life were those not involved in agriculture, for instance, fishermen, shepherds, and mountain dwellers, none of whom exhibited the same tendency toward stability, frugality, and caution as did farmers. They could often be disdainful of farm life. The mine workers from Pezzaze (Valtrompia, in the mountainous area of Lombardy) used to sing:

Contadino non voglio sposar	I do not want to marry a farmer.
polenta e patate mi tocca mangiar	It would mean eating potatoes and polenta
e invece i minatori	[boiled corn meal] every day;
	while mine workers,
mangiano e bevono come signori	if they have money, eat and drink like rich
se ne hanno [di soldi].	people.
Minatore voglio sposar	I want to marry a miner
perche' il mondo mi fa girar	because he would let me travel around the
	world,
e invece il contadin	while a farmer
dove nasce ti fa morir	would make me die where I was born.

The song underlines the ideology of freedom, mobility, and power of money that belonged to certain categories of workers. Miners, according to folk belief, lived an unconstrained life and could eat at the tavern like "rich people."

Particularly interesting was the situation of mountain dwellers. The original Paleolithic economy of hunter-gatherers, transformed in the Mesolithic epoch into a hunting and pastoralist economy (with men as nomadic hunters and women as seminomadic gatherers and breeders of herbivores), ultimately developed a mountain pasture economy, in which men looked for seasonal work outside the village as woodcutters, charcoal-burners, mine workers, traveling artisans, and transhumant shepherds. Meanwhile, women stayed in the villages and were occupied in the domestic mountain pasture system, which included breeding livestock, grassland farming, and horticulture.

The individual mountain pasture, intended to support the family, was managed by women (particularly unmarried girls). It represented the archaic form of mountain pasture economy (while the collective mountain pasture, intended for the market, was handled by men), which preserved the traditional practice of bundling (nocturnal courtship that allowed intimacy without the possibility of sexual intercourse). The cultural system of the mountain pasture is well summarized in the following lullaby from Premana (a mountainous area of Lombardy), in which a bride recalls her mountain pasture when she was picking heather. Now, she laments that with marriage she has lost the "good old days":

ol mè bontémp do è 'l mo mài andà	My good time, where did it go?
mi l'ò perdú e j òltri a i l'à troà	I have lost it, and the other girls have
	found it.
mi l'ò perdú sü scì da Prómanìghe	I lost it when I went to Premaniga [the
	name of her alpine pasture],
a i l'à troà 'l tofsìn che 'ndàve a	and the girls, who were picking heather,
fà la vrìghe.	found it.

The agricultural activity in the mountain is fairly poor due to the hostile conditions of the environment. Therefore, the figure of the farmer is almost non-existent. Animals such as cows, goats, or sheep are more important than the land or the final agricultural products. As a proverb reports, it is the cow that sustains the family and the goat that supports the widow.

Although the mountain economy is archaic, it is not necessarily obsolete. During the Middle Ages, the immigrant who left for the mountains soon became an outcast who, after being urbanized, might end up as an artisan, trader, or worker. As for shepherds, there is a difference between herders of cattle (*malgari*); northern shepherds, who are also known as "jargon outcasts" (individuals who commonly speak jargon); and Apennine shepherds (from Ligury to Sicily and Sardinia), who are part of the Mediterranean transhumant sheep-farming culture. There is a history of opposition between shepherds and farmers for the use of the territory. Shepherds are typically represented as proud and aggressive (for instance, the Sardinian *balente*—the valiant shepherd) and inheritors of a "bellicose culture" from ancient warriors' groups.

OUTCASTS

Outcasts (*marginali* in Italian) are people who, economically speaking, are marginal or absolutely extraneous to productive activities. From a social point of view, outsiders are merely tramps whose own language is jargon. They normally are not engaged in any industrious occupation but are involved in parasitic activities (begging), crime (robbery, fraud), outdoor performances or other entertainment (such as the circus), small businesses (barkers and traveling haberdashers), or services associated with fraud and solicitation (knife grinders, chimney sweeps, individuals who made umbrellas or repaired copper cookware and tins). Outcasts do not have a home or a fixed residence within the territory in which they operate because they constantly travel. They describe themselves as "sly" (*furbi*), "right" (*dritti*), "men of law" (*leggera*), "men on the street" (*bianti*), "men on the road" (*calcanti*), and "walking men" (*camminanti*, in opposition to people who live a sedentary life—*fermi*).

The jargon usually has its own lexicon, quite common to all jargons in Italy. For instance, in Italian jargon "bread" is *artone* or *moròcco* (which means "hard") and becomes in the Venetian jargon *artón* or *maròco*, words that in the local jargon of Bergamo are pronounced as *artù* or *maròch*.

Outcasts, who were manifestly urban people, even though originally rural, have initiated working-class culture. This is evident in the huge diffusion and use of the outsider's jargon within the proletarian and urban sub-proletarian classes as well as in the lifestyle of the

The *lazzaroni* (homeless beggars), as they live in the streets of Naples, Italy (1902). Outcasts are involved in begging, crime, outdoor performances, or services associated with fraud and solicitation. (Courtesy Library of Congress)

working class, particularly in the nineteenth century, which reproduced the existential Paleolithic working rhythm (or jolted work)—an alternation of occasional work and squandering of money in taverns.

Outcasts' culture is ideological. It expresses a strong identity, based on a radical opposition to productive society (represented by farmers—*gagi*, which means in Romani terminology, "the others, the non-Rom") and on the inversion of values: outsiders work on holidays (on Sundays, at festivals and fairs) while resting on weekdays. Furthermore, outcasts prefer waste and ostentation. They are typically associated with mythical themes of the upside-down world, including the "Paese di Cuccagna" (the Land of Cockaigne, or the legendary land of plenty); the term *cuccagna* comes from the jargon verb *cuccare*, which means "to take" or "to earn."

Though poor, they show a strong sense of superiority toward others and trust their own intelligence, astuteness, and love of risk and novelty, which are for them sources of income (for instance, the song sold by the storyteller or the new product sold on the streets). Outcasts were generally skilled. They could read and write. Essentially, they mediated between the written urban culture and the illiterate country environment. For instance, songs and tales were preserved by farmers but written and circulated by outcasts who made their own living from them. They composed the songs, wrote them down on broadsides, and sold them to the public. They were also invited during evening watches at the cowsheds to tell stories or fairy tales in exchange for a place to stay and some food, as the ending formulas—usually explicit requests—of some tales such as this example from Tuscany suggest: "*A tutti i poeri della citta', diedono pane, vino e carne: / e se ne stettero / e a me nulla mi dettero*" (People gave bread, wine, and meat to all the poor in the city, / but they gave nothing to me). Another example comes from Sicily: "*Iddi arristaru filici e cuntenti / Ma a nui un ni desinu nenti*" (They [the audience] were happy and satisfied / but did not give anything to us).

The following ending formula of a fairy tale from Tuscany is particularly attention-grabbing because the performer, besides asking for food (expressed with an inversion typical of the upside-down world), also begs for shoes, a fundamental garment for vagabonds:

Se ne stettero e se ne godettero	They [the audience] stayed and enjoyed
E a me nulla mi dettero	and gave nothing to me.
Mi dettero un panierino di vino	They only gave me a small basket of wine
Un fiaschettino di pane	And a small flask of bread,
Un paio di scarpette rosse	A pair of red shoes.
Andetti a casa e eran tutte rotte.	I arrived home, and they [the shoes] were ripped up.

WORKING-CLASS CULTURE

The analysis of working-class culture initiated by Gianni Bosio has been mistakenly approached in terms of continuity with peasant culture. On the other hand, the research conducted by Danilo Montaldi on the urban and rural sub-proletarian classes shows that the transition has not been linear. Moreover, Montaldi's study has demonstrated that outcasts actually shaped the historical core of the new working class. As long as the farmer owned some land, he did not become a factory worker. He might have gone through phases, including the dayworker experience on other farms, or if evicted from his land, he might have eventually wound up an outcast. During periods of crisis farmers supplemented the family income with some wage-work by young members of the family or the womenfolk (wife and daughters), who were generally employed in domestic factories (spinning and weaving), industry (textile mills), or as dayworkers or rice pickers. The participation of some family members in work outside the farm was part of the common peasant's strategies. They helped establish the industrial economy. Essentially, the transition from agriculture to industry started within the peasant economic system.

The working-class mentality, which in the industrial environment was constantly challenged by a highly modified reality, appeared radically different from the peasant perspective. Instead of honoring values like tradition and safety typical of the peasant's world, the new environment privileged the ideals of innovation and risk. Moreover, factory workers as well as artisans valued manual skills and technical knowledge.

Farmhands were not farmers at all. Instead they represented the working class of the land. They had the attitude of the working class, mostly expressed in abhorrence for the land. Moreover, it was thanks to farmhands that political and union revolts, copying working-class models, were organized in the countryside in both north and south.

RELIGIOUS BELIEFS AND RITUALS

Religious life shows strong continuity. In fact, prehistoric places of worship became first pagan temples and then Christian sanctuaries; fertility or orgiastic cults were transformed in celebrations of saints (for example, the feast of St. John on the summer solstice or a New Year's Eve pagan rite becoming Christmas). Syncretism has progressively been promoted by the cultural politics of the church in Italy.

Feminine and agricultural ceremonies (such as the *benandanti* from Friuli examined by Carlo Ginzburg) have been forgotten, while the worship of the dead has been Christianized. The witches' Sabbath is an inquisitorial creation, more heretical than folkloric, as suggested by the representation of the Devil, which is not traditional but Christian. The only rituals that have resisted the antithesis between suppression and Christianization are Carnival and funeral lamentations.

The Counter-Reformation in the sixteenth century opposed the widespread use of folk rituals. Jesuits largely contributed to indoctrinating people at that time. For instance, the reading of sacred scriptures in vernacular language was forbidden. In its place catechism and pamphlets with images describing the lives of saints, prayers, miracles, and lauds grew extensively.

In the seventeenth century, the Jesuits committed themselves to the re-evangelization of southern Italy. Relying on a significant propaganda apparatus, which included processions similar to Carnival folk parades and religious theater fashioned after folk festivals, they created a baroque folk culture that still exists. In the country the church defeated witchcraft as an alternative and autonomous cultural model. Sorcery now survives only as superstition or as syncretistic residual. The figure of the rural priest replaced the witch even in the abilities that were generally attributed to the sorcerer, including the power to stop storms.

The division between north and south is also present in the religious history of Italy. The north was associated with European heretical movements and with the Reformation, while the south was connected with magic. Religion in the south is fundamentally syncretistic, positioned between official religion and folk magic. It manifests itself in many superstitions and rituals in which the cosmos has been reduced to human dimension, for instance, worshipping the Virgin Mary, venerating saints and the dead, purging souls, pilgrimages to sanctuaries, extra-liturgical worship, funeral lamentation, tarantism, Carnival rituals, and magic practices such as the evil eye, envy, spells, and possession.

SONGS AND BALLADS

Folksongs reflect the same division between northern and southern Italy. Costantino Nigra has associated this partition with the Italian dialectal division. On the one hand, in northern Italy, there are dialects with truncated endings: *pane* (bread) becomes *pan*. Consequently, ballads have truncated verses. On the other hand, in middle and southern Italy dialects include flat words—"bread" (*pane*) is pronounced *pane*—and as a result songs are lyrically monostrophic with flat verses (*strambotto*, *stornello*, and octave).

In northern Italy folksongs are typically of North European derivation, exemplified in ballads with epic-lyrical verses, truncated rhymes, polystrophic texts, often with refrains, rigid rhythmic structures, the presence of a chorus, and polyvocality as well as the European modal basis with dominance of a major key. The local version of the ballad "*Il figlio del conte*" (The Earl's Son), from the mountainous area of Lombardy-Santa Croce of Pellegrino, is an example of a northern folksong:

El fiol del signor conte—vuleva to moèr	The son of the earl // wanted to get married.
El fiol del signor conte—vuleva to moèr	The son of the earl // wanted to get married.
E voleva sposar l'inglesa—i era figlia d'un cavalier	He wanted to marry an English girl. // She was the daughter of a knight.
E voleva sposar l'inglesa—i era figlia d'un cavalier	He wanted to marry an English girl. // She was the daughter of a Knight.
La sera la dimanda—e la notte la sposò	One evening he proposed to her // and at night he married her.
La sera la dimanda—e la notte la sposò	One evening he proposed to her // and at night he married her.
E la mattin bonora—per la Francia se ne andò	Early in the morning // he left for France.
E la mattin bonora—per la Francia se ne andò.	Early in the morning // he left for France.

In middle and southern Italy, folksongs have a Mediterranean origin, which results in flat-hendecasyllabic-lyrical songs (*strambotto* and *stornello*), monostrophic texts, free rhythmic structures, prevalence of solos, powerful melismas, and eastern modal bases with a predominance of minor key. Here is an example of a folksong from Tuscany:

STORNELLO

Fiore di canna	Flower of cane,
Tutta la notte co' piedi alla culla	all night by the cradle
Non ho marito e son chiamata mamma.	I do not have a husband but they call me mother.

STRAMBOTTO

Il porto di Livorno è traditore	The port of Livorno is treacherous.
Ci stanno le belle donne che fan l'amore.	There are beautiful women who make love to men.

OCTAVE

Cosa t'ho fatto vedova maligna	What did I do to you, perfidious widow,
Che la tua figlia a me tu non vuoi dare?	that you do not want me to have your daughter?
Io non t'ho chiesto né campo né vigna	I have asked you for neither land nor vineyard
Nemmeno un par di buoi per lavorare	nor a couple of oxen to work in the field.
Io non t'ho chiesto né oro né argento	I have asked you for neither gold nor silver.
Dammela la tua figlia son contento	Give me your daughter, and I will be happy.
Io non t'ho chiesto né argento né oro	I have asked you for neither silver nor gold.
Dammela la tua figlia se no moro [muoio].	Give me your daughter, or I will die.

Lyrical monostrophic folksong from middle-south Italy (particularly from Tuscany and Sicily) appears sophisticated, modern, and popular. It seems to derive from literary forms of urban song. An archaic example of it may be found in the lullabies and ritual songs of southern Italy.

The northern ballad is directly related to European balladry. The content of the narrative songs is feudal, while their structure is Renaissance and their music baroque. Actually, they seem to be an extraordinary example of literary and musical stylization, a sort of pseudo-feudal revival, as suggested by their narratives, which might have been rearranged by professionals according to the Romantic style or to a neo-medieval reconstruction not too different from the false Romantic medieval style. This hypothesis suggests that the ballad, like fairy tales, may date from the

Romantic period of the late eighteenth and early nineteenth centuries. Professionals, creators, and promulgators of both genres could be identified with outcasts, including ballad singers and traveling storytellers (beggars and vagrants) for fairy tales. They rapidly appropriated the new and successful Romantic style of literary and urban derivation, elaborated upon it, and spread it out in the country through narratives, which folklorists would have collected and credited to a remote medieval past. Storytellers (examined by Roberto Leydi and Bruno Pianta) have had the primarily function of creating and circulating folksongs. They adapted former songs according to the technique known as "*parodia*" (the text is re-written while maintaining the original music). Storytellers together with outcasts who once performed during fairs and in village open markets while selling folksongs on broadsides or discs disseminated the ballad, the lyrical monostrophic chant, and the social song. Moreover, they created the typical storyteller's repertoire, which in northern Italy comprehended the "*canzone*" (folksong), quatrains of brief verses of seven- to ten-syllable lines with narrative content (*faits divers* and news items) ending in a truncated verse. An example is the opening lines of "*Mamma perche' non torni*" (Mother, Why Don't You Come Back), a *canzone* by the Lombard storyteller Adriano Callegari from Pavia:

L'amor di mamma non ha più Renato	Renato does not have his mother's love anymore.
Un grave male l'ha paralizzato	A serious illness has paralyzed him.
Si trova il piccolo in cattivo stato	The little boy is ailing.
Giace infermo in tenera età.	So young, he lies infirm.

On the other hand, in the middle-south, the repertoire included folk stories in sestinas and octaves of hendecasyllables. Here is an example—the story of the bandit Salvatore Giuliano—taken from the collected works of the Sicilian storyteller Cicciu Busacca:

Mortu truvau a Turiddu Giulianu	She found Salvatore Giuliano dead,
E ccu lu pettu di purtusa chinu	His chest perforated.
Fici na schigghia, si turcìu la manu	She let out a yell and twisted her hands
Malidicennu lu malu distinu	while cursing the bad fate.
Po supra di ddu corpu tantu amatu	Then on his beloved body
S'abbandunau sviluta e senza ciatu.	She let herself abandon while breathlessly fainting.

Social folksongs originated and became popular for several reasons, including the crisis of traditional society, the transformation of the rural areas, and the gradual emergence of the proletariat. Their themes included historical events, military issues, work, war, immigration, labor unions, and politics. These songs related not to farmers but to factory workers, artisans, farmhands, mountain dwellers, and outcasts. The metrics were based on the typical storyteller's song. The following examples show different genres, first, a verse from a historical song, "Lamento di Napoleone"

(Napoleon's Lament), which in a later version from Cologno al Serio (Lombardy) became a military song (A Soldier's Lament):

Napoleone comincia a dire	Napoleon said,
Porté 'na penna e un carimaio	"Bring me a pen and an inkpot
Che voglio scrivere la mia vita	Because I want to write about my life.
Che l'è diciott'anni che faccio	It has been eighteen years since I have
'l soldà.	been a soldier."

Next is a song from the *montanini*—Tuscan seasonal workers who periodically left the mountains to work in the flat and swampy areas of the *maremma* (in Tuscany):

Tutti mi dicon Maremma Maremma	Everybody keeps talking about the *maremma*.
Per me l'è stata una Maremma amara	As for me, that was a vicious place.
L'uccello che ci va perde le penne	The bird that flies over there loses its feathers,
Il giovin che ci va perde la dama	While the young man loses his woman.
Tutto mi trema il cor quando ci vai	All my heart trembles whenever you go there
Per lo timor che più non tornerai	because I am afraid you will not come back anymore.
Tutto mi trema il cor quando ci andate	All my heart trembles when you go there
Per lo timor che voi più non tornate.	Because I am afraid you will not come back anymore.

Finally, here is a famous union song in defense of the eight-hour workday, sung by the Lombard female farmhands in paddy fields:

Se otto ore vi sembran poche	If eight hours seem too few,
Provate voi a lavorare	Why don't you try to work yourselves?
E sentirete la differenza	You will understand the difference
Di lavorare e di comandar	Between working and ruling.
E sentirete la differenza	You will understand the difference
Di lavorare e di comandar.	Between working and ruling.

MUSIC

Ethnomusicological **fieldwork**, begun in the 1950s with the fieldwork of Alan Lomax and Diego Carpitella, has documented the existence of other forms of folksongs, including the alpine choral chant, polyvocal songs (Liguria: *trallalero*, Tuscany: *bei*, Lombardy: *tir*), the descant (*vatoccu* or clapper song from Umbria and Marches, *la longa* song and *pera* or pear song from Istria), and finally the octaves recited by extemporizing poets. Remaining culturally significant were ritual songs and lullabies, widespread all over Italy. Here are two examples of ritual songs. The first one, *"Maggio delle ragazze"* (May of Girls) is a May song from Riolunato (Emilia):

Ecco il ridente maggio	Here is the cheerful May.
Ecco quel nobil mese	Here is that fine month
Che viene a dare imprese	Which gives
Ai nostri cuori.	Our hearts expectations.
. . . .	. . . .
Io son venuto per ambasciatore	I am here as a messenger
Innanzi a voi magnifica donzella	In front of you, lovely lady.
Qui mi ha mandato il vostro caro amore	Your dear lover sent me to you.
Per lui io canto per lui ho una favella	I sing for him, and I speak for him.
Qui mi ha mandato il vostro caro aiuto	Your dear companion sent me to you.
Per lui io parlo e per lui io vi saluto.	I speak for him, and I bring greetings from him.

The second example is a verse taken from the "Passion" usually performed on Good Friday at Stornarella (Apulia):

te benedéice o figlio li tretatré ganne	My son, may He bless you and your thirty-three years of age.
li nouve mese ca t'éite purtéite nel séine	May He bless the nine months I carried you.
te benedéice le fasce e li panne	May He bless the garments
o quann'io ti mbascévo trimilanne	in which I, still trembling, used to wrap you.
o quanno ti mbascévo trimilanne.	in which I, still trembling, used to wrap you.

Preserving archaic musical structures, lullabies have privately expressed the woman's condition and mother's frustrations. They have been means by which women could freely express their true feelings. The following is an example of a cradlesong from Ripalta Nuova (Lombardy):

Nina ninà ninà la cüna	Swing the cradle,
Bagaióla o bagaióla bèla.	Beautiful baby.
O maritàs o 'ndà monachèla.	You either get married or become a nun.
Öna de le dó bisogna fare.	One of the two you must do.
O maritàs o monachèla andare,	You either get married or become a nun.
O maritàs o monachèla andare.	You either get married or become a nun.

Lullabies could also express love and affection. This type of song was usually attributed to the baby's sisters (though all women of the family used to sing them).

The following song, "O mio ben" (My Beloved One), comes from Cigole (Lombardy):

En co de l'era gh'è un camì che föma.	At the end of the farmyard there is a smoking chimney.
L'amor del mio ben che 'l si consöma.	It is my love for my beloved one that is consuming.
El si consöma a pòco a pòco	It is consuming little by little
Come la lègna érda 'nsöma 'l fuòco-oi siò.	Like green wood on a fire.

Repertoires of instrumental music, typically played by traveling professionals or local semi-professionals, were performed only to accompany traditional folk dances (*saltarello*, *trescone*, and *giga*), which frequently bore geographical names (*monferrina*, *bergamasca*, *polesana*, *alessandrina*, *veneziana*, *furlana*, and *resiana*) from the area in which they originated. Some of the instruments used by the musician included violin, bagpipe (later replaced by the accordion and concertina), *ciaramella* (fife), tambourine, guitar, *chitarra battente* (Renaissance guitar), Pan's flute, and harp and *ghironda* (Italian hurdy-gurdy or turning device)—the last no longer employed. Among well-known archaic instruments was the *torototéla*, a musical bow that, until quite recently, has accompanied begging.

DANCE AND DRAMA

The most popular southern traditional dance is the *tarantella*. It is a typical courtship dance accompanied by tambourine and *tammorra*. The *tarantella* has been mostly employed in the Salento area to heal people suffering from tarantism (extensively examined by Ernesto de Martino), a psychological malady or cultural disease believed to result from the bite of the mythical tarantula. Tarantism was also recorded in Sardinia, where it is known as *argia*, and Campania.

Folk theater essentially plays a ritual function. That is why it is often associated with the calendar cycle of festivals and ceremonies. The New Year's Cycle, for instance, includes *zingaresche* (Gypsy-like shows where performers attempt to predict the future for the participants), representations of the months, and rituals of the middle of Lent

Neapolitan *tarantella*, eighteenth century. (The Art Archive/Museo Nazionale di San Martino, Naples/Dagli Orti)

463

(*segalavecchia*; literally: "saw the old woman"). The Spring Cycle comprehends May representations, armed dances (sword dance and mimed and costumed dances called *Moresche*), and the *Maggio Drammatico* (literally, dramatic recited or sung performance based on texts written by folk poets). The Holy Week Cycle mostly includes Passions and sacred representations.

Until quite recently, puppet theater in northern Italy and the marionette theater (*Opera dei Pupi*) in southern Italy were very popular and frequently staged. Noteworthy to remember also is the "cowshed theater" of the mid-twentieth century, the main characteristic of which was performing lays, usually peasant representations, in cowsheds.

FESTIVALS AND RITUALS

Festivals, sacred or secular, are still predominant folk expressions in Italy. Under the pressure of pervasive mass culture, they might have been transformed, renewed, and adapted, sometimes with questionable results. However, they have resisted the changing times, as proved by many unexpected revivals.

The major secular festivity is Carnival, very popular all over the nation. In big cities such as Venice and Viareggio (Tuscany) it survives in an urbanized fashion. Carnival still preserves some traditional authenticity in smaller communities such as Ivrea (Piedmont), Bagolino and Schignano (Lombardy), Palu'del Fersina (Trentino), Sappada (Veneto), Valli del Natisone (Friuli), Tufara (Molise), and Montemarano (Campania). Towns' festivals such as the *palio of Siena* (a horse race in Siena, Tuscany), based on competition among city wards or administrative districts, still generate considerable enthusiasm and massive participation.

Religious and social ceremonies usually involve the transportation on urban streets of heavy monuments such the *Gigli di Nola* (Lilies of Nola) in a town near near Naples, *Corsa dei Ceri* (big wooden pillars) at Gubbio (Umbria), and the *Macchina di S. Rosa* (a sort of tower borne by porters) at Viterbo (Latium). The counterpart of these urban ceremonies is represented by rural folkloristic customs so widely practiced in many parts of Italy, like the carrying of the village May-tree or Maypole.

The most prominent religious events, particularly in southern Italy, consist of pilgrimages to major sanctuaries, including Madonna of Caravaggio (Lombardy), Madonna of Loreto (Marches), Saint Rita of Cascia (Umbria), Madonna of Divine Love in Rome (Latium), St. Gennaro in Naples and Madonna of Pompeii (Campania), St. Michael Archangel of Monte Sant' Angelo and St. Nicola of Bari (Apulia), and St. Francis from Paola (Calabria). Minor pilgrimages and sanctuaries include Madonna of Caravaggio at Fanzolo (Veneto), SS. Trinity of Vallepietra (Latium), Madonna of Montevergine (Campania), Madonna of Pollino (Lucania area), and Madonna of Polsi (Calabria). Well known and very well attended are the powerful and moving processions of the *battenti* (flagellants) in Campania and Calabria regions.

Sardinia deserves a different approach because it is the only Italian region that shows a radically distinctive culture. Due to their historical background, people from Sardinia are different from the rest of Italians. Their history emphasizes their diversity. The island was colonized by Phoenicians, Greeks, and Carthaginians and eventually by Romans. When the Roman Empire fell, Sardinia became Byzantine. Then the territory became a colony of Genoa and later of Pisa, until the Crown of Aragon conquered it. In the eighteenth century, it was handed over to the dukes of Savoy, and in 1861 the kingdom of Sardinia was transformed into an Italian state. The main activities are sheep farming using the system of *vidazzone* (alternation from seeding to pasture), agriculture in the Campidano area, and mining in the vicinity of Iglesias. The archaic nature of Sardinian culture is evident in the language, which retains more Latin sounds compared to those of other Romance languages. Other peculiar Sardinian cultural forms include the shepherd's code of honor (particularly in the Barbagia area), tarantism (*argia*), the circle dance (*ballu tondu*), polyphonic reed instruments (*launeddas*), polyphonic music and multi-voiced songs (*tenores* and *tasgias*—male vocal ensembles), and lyrical metrics (*mutu* and *mutettu*) especially used for extemporized poetic contests. Here are two verses of a funeral lament (*attitu*) from Ossi (vicinity of Sassari):

e fizu oi fizu meu,	Son, my dear son,
chelzo a ti nde pesare.	I want you to get up,
sa prenda valorosa.	My precious rock.
E fizu oi fizu meu,	Son, my dear son,
mi chi mama no chere.	Your mother does not want [you to be dead].
no b'andese a sa losa.	Do not go to that grave.

The stanza that follows is very famous, usually sung to accompany the circle dance (*ballu tondu*):

Procurad' e moderare,	It would be better
Riccones, sa tirannia.	for you, rich people,
Si non pro vida mia	to moderate your tyranny.
Torrades a ped' in terra	Otherwise, I believe
Declarada es già sa gherra	you will fall to the ground
Contra de sa prepotenzia,	because war has been declared
E cominza sa passenza	upon arrogance,
In su populu a mancare.	and people start losing their patience.

STUDIES OF ITALIAN FOLKLORE

Important journals for the study of Italian folklore are *Archivio per lo studio delle tradizioni popolari* (1882–1909); *BRADS Bollettino del Repertorio dell'Atlante Demologico Sardo* (1966–present); *Lares* (1912–present); *Il Nuovo Canzoniere Italiano* (1962–1968); and *La ricerca folklorica* (1980–present).

BIBLIOGRAPHY

Aime, M., S. Allovio, and P. P. Viazzo. 2001. *Sapersi muovere*. Roma: Meltemi.

Alasia F., and D. Montaldi, eds. 1960. *Milano, Corea*. Milano: Feltrinelli.

Angioni, G. 1976. *Sa laurera*. Cagliari: EDES.

———. 1989. *I pascoli erranti*. Napoli: Liguori.

Arata, G. V., and V. Biasi. 1935. *Arte sarda*. Milano: Treves.

Atti del Primo Congresso di Etnografia Italiana. 1912. Perugia: Unione tipografica cooperativa.

Banfield, E. C. 1958. *The Moral Basis of a Backward Society*. Glencoe, IL: Free Press.

Barbieri, G., and L. Gambi. 1970. *La casa rurale in Italia*. Firenze: Olschki.

Barozzi, G. 1976. *Ventisette fiabe raccolte nel mantovano*. Milano: Regione Lombardia.

Basile, G. B. 1995. *Lo cunto de li cunti*. Milano: Garzanti.

Bermani, C. 1970. *L'altra cultura*. Milano: Edizioni del Gallo.

———. 1991. *Il bambino è servito*. Bari: Dedalo.

Bertolotti, G., and others. 1979. *Premana*. Milano: Silvana.

Bonomo, G. 1959. *Caccia alle streghe*. Palermo: Palumbo.

Bosio, G. 1975. *L'intellettuale rovesciato*. Milano: Bella Ciao.

———. 1981. *Il trattore ad Acquanegra*. Bari: De Donato.

Bravo, G. L. 2001. *Italiani*. Roma: Meltemi.

Bronzini, G. B. 1956–1961. *La canzone epico-lirica nell'Italia centro-meridionale*. 2 volumes. Roma: Signorelli.

———. 1961. *Vita tradizionale in Basilicata*. Matera: Montemurro.

Burke, P. 1980. *Cultura popolare nell'Europa moderna*. Milano: Mondadori.

Buttitta, A. 1961. *Cultura figurativa popolare in Sicilia*. Palermo: Flaccovio.

Cagnetta, F. 1975. *Banditi a Orgosolo*. Rimini-Firenze: Guaraldi.

Calderini, E. 1953. *Il costume popolare in Italia*. Milano: Sperling and Kupfer.

Calvino, I., ed. 1956. *Fiabe italiane*. Torino: Einaudi.

Camporesi, P. 1976. *La maschera di Bertoldo*. Torino: Einaudi.

———. 1980. *Il pane selvaggio*. Bologna: Il Mulino.

———. 1985. *Il paese della fame*. Bologna: Il Mulino.

———. 1989. *La terra e la luna*. Milano: Il saggiatore.

———. 1990. *La miniera del mondo*. Milano: Il saggiatore.

———, ed. 1973. *Il libro dei vagabondi*. Torino: Einaudi.

Carpitella, D. 1973. *Musica e tradizione orale*. Palermo: Flaccovio.

———, ed. 1975. *L'etnomusicologia in Italia*. Palermo: Flaccovio.

Catalogo della mostra di etnografia italiana in Piazza d'armi. 1911. Bergamo: Istituto italiano d'arti grafiche.

Cirese, A. M. 1973. *Cultura egemonica e culture subalterne*. Palermo: Palumbo.

———. 1976. *Intellettuali, folklore, istinto di classe*. Torino: Einaudi.

———. 1988. *Ragioni metriche*. Palermo: Sellerio.

Cirese, A. M., L. Serafini, and A. Milillo, eds. 1975. *Tradizioni orali non cantate*. Roma: Ministero dei Beni culturali e ambientali.

Clemente, P., ed. 1987. *Pittura votiva e stampe popolari*. Milano: Electa.

Cocchiara, G. 1966. *Le origini della poesia popolare*. Torino: Einaudi.

———. 1981. *Storia del folklore in Italia*. Palermo: Sellerio.

Cole, J. W., and E. R. Wolf. 1974. *The Hidden Frontier*. New York: Academic Press.

Corio, L. 1885. *Milano in ombra*. Milano: Civelli.

Corrain, C., and P. L. Zampini. 1970. *Documenti etnografici e folkloristici nei sinodi diocesani italiani*. Bologna: Forni.

Corso, R. 2001 (1914). *La vita sessuale nelle credenze, pratiche e tradizioni popolari italiane*. Firenze: Olschki.

D'Ancona, A. 1891. *Origini del teatro italiano*. 2 volumes. Torino: Loescher.

———. 1906. *La poesia popolare italiana*. Livorno: Giusti.

de Martino, E. 1949. Intorno a una storia del mondo popolare subalterno. *Società* 5:411–435.

———. 1958. *Morte e pianto rituale nel mondo antico*. Torino: Einaudi.

———. 1959. *Sud e magia*. Milano: Feltrinelli.

———. 1961. *La terra del rimorso*. Milano: Il saggiatore.

di Nola, A. 1976. *Gli aspetti magico-religiosi di una cultura subalterna italiana*. Torino: Boringhieri.

———. 1983. *L'arco di rovo*. Torino: Boringhieri.

Documenti dell'Archivio Etnico Linguistico-Musicale 1–3 (sound recording). N.d. Roma: Discoteca di Stato.

Etnografia e folklore del mare. 1957. Napoli: L'arte tipografica.

Falassi, A. 1985. *Italian Folklore. An Annotated Bibliography*. New York: Garland.

———, ed. 1988. *La festa*. Milano: Electa.

Fara, G. 1920. *L'anima musicale d'Italia*. Roma: Ausonia.

———. 1940. *L'anima della Sardegna*. Udine: Idea.

Favara, A. 1957. *Corpus di musiche popolari siciliane*. 2 volumes. Milano: Maestri arti grafiche.

Friedmann, F. G. 1953. The World of "La miseria." *Partisan Review* 20.2:218–231.

Frizzi, A. 1912. *Il ciarlatano*. Mantova: Frizzi.

Galasso, G. 1982. *L'altra Europa*. Milano: Mondadori.

Gallini, C. 1967. *I rituali dell'argia*. Padova: CEDAM.

———. 1970. *Il consumo del sacro*. Bari: Laterza.

Ginzburg, C. 1966. *I benandanti*. Torino: Einaudi.

———. 1972. Folklore magia religione. In *Storia d'Italia*, volume 1, edited by R. Romano and C. Vivanti. Torino: Einaudi. 601–676.

———. 1976. *Il formaggio e i vermi*. Torino: Einaudi.

———. 1989. *Storia notturna*. Torino: Einaudi.

Gramsci, A. 1975. *Quaderni del carcere*. 4 volumes. Torino: Einaudi.

Guidoni, E. 1980. *L'architettura popolare italiana*. Bari: Laterza.

Hennig, W. 1956. *Folk Music from Italy* (sound recording). 2 volumes. Folkways FE 4520.

Imbriani, V. 1877. *La novellaja fiorentina*. Livorno: Vigo.

Lanternari, V. 1955. La politica culturale della Chiesa nelle campagne: la festa di S. Giovanni. *Società* 11:64–95.

———. 1976. *Crisi e ricerca d'identità*. Napoli: Liguori.

Levi, C. 1945. *Cristo si è fermato a Eboli*. Roma: Einaudi.

Leydi, R. 1963. *Canti sociali italiani*. Milano: Avanti!

———. 1973. La canzone popolare. In *Storia d'Italia*, volume 5, edited by R. Romano and C. Vivanti. Torino: Einaudi. 1181–1249.

———. 1973. *I canti popolari italiani*. Milano: Mondadori.

———, ed. 1959. *La piazza*. Milano: Avanti!

———. 1970–1971. *Italia* (sound recording). 3 volumes. Albatros VPA 8082, 8088, 8126.

———. 1990. *Canti e musiche popolari*. Milano: Electa.

———. 1995. *Canté bergera*. Vigevano: Diakronia.

———. N.d. *Italia 1–4* (sound recoriding). Albatros.

Leydi, R., and R. Mezzanotte Leydi. 1958. *Marionette e burattini*. Milano: Avanti!

Lomax, A. 1955–1956. Nuova ipotesi sul canto folkloristico italiano. *Nuovi argomenti* 17–18: 108–135.

Lomax, A., and C. Bianco, eds. 1965. *Italian Folk Songs* (sound recording). Folkways FE4010.

Lomax, A., and D. Carpitella, eds. 1957. *Italia* (sound recording). 2 volumes. Columbia KL5173.

———. 1973. *Folklore musicale italiano* (sound recording). 2 volumes. Pull QLP 107–108.

———. 1999. *Italian Treasury* (sound recording). 10 volumes. Rounder 1801–1805, 1807, 1808, 1811, 1816, 1817.

Magrini, T., ed. 1992. *Il maggio drammatico*. Bologna: Analisi.

Montaldi, D. 1961. *Autobiografie della leggera*. Torino: Einaudi.

Nerucci, G. 1880. *Sessanta novelle popolari montalesi*. Firenze: Le Monnier.

Nigra, C. 1888. *Canti popolari del Piemonte*. Torino: Loescher.

Ostermann, V. 1940. *La vita in Friuli*. 2 volumes. Udine: Idea.

Pansa, G. 1924–1927. *Miti, leggende e superstizioni dell'Abruzzo*. 2 volumes. Sulmona: Caroselli.

Pasolini, P. P. 1955. *Canzoniere italiano*. Parma: Guanda.

Pasqualino, A. 1977. *L'opera dei pupi*. Palermo: Sellerio.

Perusini, G. 1961. *Vita di popolo in Friuli*. Firenze: Olschki.

Pianta, B. 1982. *Cultura popolare*. Milano: Garzanti.

Pigliaru, A. 1975. *Il banditismo in Sardegna*. Milano: Giuffrè.

Pitré, G. 1894. *Bibliografia delle tradizioni popolari d'Italia*. Torino-Palermo: Clausen.

———. 1941. *Novelle popolari toscane*. 2 volumes. Roma: Soc. ed. del libro italiano.

Plomteux, H. 1980. *Cultura contadina in Liguria*. Genova: Sagep.

Pola Falletti di Villafalletto, G. C. 1939–1942. *Associazioni giovanili e feste antiche: loro origini*. 4 volumes. Milano: Bocca.

Pratella, F. B. 1941. *Primo documentario per la storia dell'etnofonia in Italia*. 2 volumes. Udine: Idea.

Revelli, N. 1977. *Il mondo dei vinti*. 2 volumes. Torino: Einaudi.

Romano, R., and C. Vivanti, eds. 1972–196. *Storia d'Italia*. 6 volumes. Torino: Einaudi.

Rossi, A. 1969. *Le feste dei poveri*. Bari: Laterza.

Rossi, A., and R. Simone. 1977. *Carnevale si chiamava Vincenzo*. Roma: De Luca.

Rubieri, E. 1877. *Storia della poesia popolare italiana*. Firenze: Barbera.

Sanga, G. 1979. *Il linguaggio del canto popolare* (with sound recordings). Milano-Firenze: ME-DI Sviluppo—Giunti-Marzocco.

———. 1984. *Dialettologia lombarda*. Pavia: Dept. of Scienze della letteratura dell'Università.

———. 1997. Un modello antropologico dell'emigrazione alpina. *La ricerca folklorica* 35:121–128.

———, ed. 1986. L'abbigliamento popolare italiano. *La ricerca folklorica* 14:1–120.

———. 1989. La piazza. *La ricerca folklorica* 19:1–134.

Santoli, V. 1968. *I canti popolari italiani*. Firenze: Sansoni.

Sarnelli, P. 1962. *Posilecheata*. Firenze: Sansoni.

Sassu, P., D. Carpitella, and L. Sole. 1974. *La musica sarda* (sound recording). 3 volumes. Albatros VPA 8203.

Schenda, R. 1986. *Folklore e letteratura popolare*. Roma: Istituto della Enciclopedia Italiana.

Scheuermeier, P. 1980. *Il lavoro dei contadini*. Milano: Longanesi.

Sciama, L. D. 2003. *A Venetian Island*. New York: Berghahn.

Scotellaro, R. 1954. *Contadini del Sud*. Bari: Laterza.

Šebesta, G. 1973. *Fiaba-leggenda dell'alta Valle del Fèrsina*. S. Michele all'Adige: Museo provinciale degli usi e costumi della gente trentina.

Seppilli, T., ed. 1983. La medicina popolare in Italia. *La ricerca folklorica* 8:1–136.

———. 1989. *Medicine e magie*. Milano: Electa.

Sereni, E. 1968. *Il capitalismo nella campagne 1860–1900*. Torino: Einaudi.

Silvestrini, E. 1982. *Ceramica popolare del Lazio*. Roma: Quasar.

———, ed. 1988. *La Piazza Universale*. Milano: Mondadori-De Luca.

Sordi, I. 1991. *Teatro e rito*. Milano: Xenia.

Straparola, G. F. 1927. *Le piacevoli notti*. Bari: Laterza.

Tassoni, G. 1973. *Arti e tradizioni popolari*. Bellinzona: La Vesconta.

Tommaseo, N. 1841–1842. *Canti popolari toscani, corsi, illirici, greci*. 4 volumes. Venezia: Tasso.

Toschi, P. 1946. *Bibliografia delle tradizioni popolari d'Italia dal 1916 al 1940*. Firenze: Barbera.

———. 1955. *Le origini del teatro italiano*. Torino: Einaudi.

———. 1960. *Arte popolare italiana*. Roma: Bestetti.

———. 1962. *Guida allo studio delle tradizioni popolari*. Torino: Boringhieri.

Trinchieri, R. 1953. *Vita di pastori nella campagna romana*. Roma: Palombi.

Tullio-Altan, C. 1986. *La nostra Italia*. Milano: Feltrinelli.

Venturelli, G. 1983. *Documenti di narrativa popolare toscana*. Lucca: N.p.

Viazzo, P. P. 1990. *Comunità alpine*. Bologna: Il Mulino.

Wagner, M. L. 1996. *La vita rustica della Sardegna riflessa nella lingua*. Nuoro: Ilisso.

Glauco Sanga (Translated from the Italian by Francesca M. Muccini)

PIEDMONT AND VAL D'AOSTA

GEOGRAPHY AND HISTORY

The Piedmont territory acquired its modern configuration under Emmanuel Philibert of Savoy, who regained the family's possessions in 1559 as a result of the Treaty of Cateau Cambrésis, which ended a long war between **France** and **Spain**. He achieved an institutional order that was more centralized, socially stable, and juridically definite. The decision to regulate the license to carry arms, granting it only to individuals belonging to a territorial, non-mercenary military force set up by him, established the modern public monopoly over the right to practice violence. Emmanuel Philibert also defined the first outline of the provinces, including that of Aosta. The latter did not acquire an independent administrative structure until 1945. Subsequently, it became a self-governing region within the Italian state.

Piedmont and Val d'Aosta are the northwestern part of **Italy**. To the west they border on France, and to the north on **Switzerland**. To the east and south are, respectively, the regions of Lombardy and Liguria. The capital of Piedmont is Turin. The region is divided into eight provinces and in 2001 had 4,166,442 inhabitants in an area of 25,399 square kilometers. It is the largest Italian region after **Sicily**. The morphology of the territory includes mountains (43.3 percent), hills (30.3 percent), and plains (26.4 percent). The capital of Val d'Aosta is Aosta, and in 2001 the region had 119,356 inhabitants in an area of 3,263 square kilometers. It is the smallest region in Italy and also the highest, being entirely situated in mountains.

Piedmont and Val d'Aosta are surrounded to the west and north by the Alps, which here contain the highest peaks in Europe. The flatland is the beginning of the

Po Valley. The barrier of the mountains protects the plains and hills from the north winds, so the climate is a temperate, Continental one. The Po, the largest river in Italy, begins in Piedmont. This region was one of the poles of Italian industrial development and is now characterized by transformation and deindustrialization processes. The agricultural and food production sector is becoming more important, with the typical cultivation of hillside vineyards. In Val d'Aosta the main activities are tourism and winter sports, though the traditional economic sectors of animal husbandry and dairy production still play an important role.

Since the 1970s the local governments in Piedmont and Val d'Aosta have been promoting research and museum activities relevant to popular traditions. Piedmont is the Italian region that has the most ethnographic museums (more than 200) and eco-museums (seventeen).

Until the last quarter of the twentieth century, the population of the hilly areas and of the plains spoke Piedmontese, a Gallo-Italian dialect, in everyday life. This dialect also had an urban, cultured version and had produced various genres of literature. Cultural associations now endeavor to maintain this dialect, which is disappearing, particularly among young people, and several regional laws promote its being taught. An Alpine Provençal or Occitanian ethnolinguistic minority is present in the valleys of the provinces of Cuneo and Turin up to the Susa Valley. On the northern side of this valley, toward the north and throughout Val d'Aosta, Franco-Provençal is spoken. Both these minorities are active in revitalizing their language. There is less vitality in the Alemannic German of the Walser population, who are scattered in enclaves in the Piedmontese provinces of Novara and Vercelli and in Val d'Aosta.

Piedmont and Val d'Aosta have undergone considerable population movement. The main flows included migrations from the poorest rural areas toward Turin and the other areas of industrial development, large migrations to America in the nineteenth and early twentieth centuries, and seasonal migrations to France, in which the men left the upland areas to find various types of work and then returned to their villages for summer farming work. Moreover, the period of intense industrial expansion of the late 1950s and 1960s, when a major role was played by the automobile industry, brought to Piedmont and Val d'Aosta a large wave of migrants from southern Italy. These migrants' main goal was work in the big factories. At present a new type of immigration is taking place: these immigrants come from the Southern Hemisphere and from Eastern European countries and take the most insecure, manual, and difficult jobs. Most of them come from the Maghreb, **Albania**, and Romania.

RELIGION

Popular religion has left its mark on the territory of Piedmont and Val d'Aosta. The most important folkloric saints are those who preside over the fate of production activities (mainly agropastoral ones) and protect families, family-owned firms, and local communities. One of the most popular saints was St. Anthony the Abbot, whose most significant task was to protect farm animals. On his feast day (17 January) the most current ritual practice was the blessing of the animals. Nowadays this practice has reappeared in cities, where household pets, cars, and trucks are blessed.

The feast of St. Anthony the Abbot is one of the canonical dates that open the period of the traditional Carnival. At Bellino in the mountains near Cuneo, an old Carnival quest has recently been revived: on 17 January two men—one dressed as St. Anthony, the other as a piglet (this animal is an attribute of the saint)—visit the cattlesheds of the village where nighttime parties are being held. After the piglet has played some mischievous tricks, such as stealing eggs and chickens or teasing the women, the saint blesses all the bystanders.

A cult widespread, particularly in the Alpine and Pre-Alpine areas, was that of the Christian soldier martyrs of the *legione tebea*, who, according to an ancient *Passio*, refused to obey the order of the emperor Maximianus Herculeus to persecute other Christians. Despite their being an elite force, they were all slaughtered. This large group of martyrs includes two folkloric patron saints of animals, particularly cattle: St. Magnus, whose shrine is at Castelmagno in the mountains near Cuneo, and St. Bessus, whose shrine is in the Soana Valley between the Canavese area and Val d'Aosta.

The feast day of St. John the Baptist occurs on 24 June, around the time of the summer solstice. During the previous night, bonfires were lit on the hills and mountains, and herbs and dew, which acquired particular therapeutic and magic properties, were gathered.

In popular iconography, St. Martin (11 November) is a knight who cuts his cloak in two parts and gives half to a poor man. In the traditional conception, this act symbolized the division of the farming year into two halves: the harvesting period was over, the new wine was being drawn, and plowing began the next production cycle. Moreover, sharecroppers moved to a new owner's farm. From that day on, the products that had not been harvested by their owners were at the disposal of whoever wished to appropriate them, particularly poor people.

An ex-voto from the church of St. Anthony, Mogardino, 1988. (Photograph by Piercarlo Grimaldi)

MYTHICAL ANIMALS

The traditional calendar is also marked by the presence of several mythical animals. The bear is a figure about which an elaborate lore has developed, expressing itself in legends, proverbs, iconography, and ritual practices. Its importance is confirmed by the Catholic Church's acknowledging a St. Ursus (bear), who was bishop of Aosta in the sixth century and was a protector of animals and of the countryside. His feast falls on 2 February. The folkloric bear opens springtime work and makes it possible to predict its success. Exactly during the night between 1 and 2 February, the bear looks up at the moon and, depending on whether it is full or new, decides whether to return to hibernation for forty days more or to emerge from its den and resume active life. In the former case the computation of the lunar calendar predicts a "low" Easter, whose latest possible date is 25 April, whereas in the latter case there will be a "high" Easter, whose earliest possible date is 22 March. This corresponds to an early spring and a mild year. Like the mythical bear, during that night farmers looked at the moon to ascertain its phase and make similar predictions about the beginning and progress of their work. The Carnival bear mask that appeared in the village streets at the beginning of February helped farmers enter this observation in their oral diaries. This mask is still present in some Carnival festivals (for instance, at Mompantero in the mountains of the province of Turin and in some villages of the valley that leads to the Great St. Bernard Pass). It has been re-introduced recently into other festivals after a period of disappearance, for instance, in Volvera, a village near Turin.

The bear figure is also linked to hibernation, whose alternation with the active period serves as a model for the stages of agropastoral life in Piedmont and Val d'Aosta. The intensely exhausting months of production activities are followed by a period in which consumption and comparative inactivity prevail. During the late autumn and winter, the accumulated supplies are used for the survival of the family and its animals. In the same way, hibernating animals consume the reserve they have stored in their bodies. Besides the bear, other hibernating animals mark this pattern. For example, folk wisdom holds that the marmot feeds on its own fat by inserting its snout into its anus, thus expressing in its posture and physiology the circularity of agropastoral time.

Other animals appeared in the Carnival rites in the role of scapegoats for the evil that had marked the life of the local community during the year. They were usually fowls, in most cases turkeys, geese, and cocks, which, after the reading of a mock testament that exposed the sins and eccentricities committed in the village, were beheaded in various ways by young people. This rite is still performed at Tonco in the wine-producing hills near Asti. After the reading of the testament, the turkey (which in recent years has been killed beforehand) is hung up in the main square. Then young people with sticks come galloping on horseback through a passage in the crowd and strike it until one of them breaks its neck and seizes its head.

A character halfway between the animal world and the humanized one appears in the tales that nourish imagination during the nighttime gatherings in the cattlesheds: the wild man who once appeared also in Carnival. He is known throughout Italy and elsewhere in Europe and is present in medieval sacred and profane imagery. He is usually represented covered with hair and leaves and lives in the woods and in caves. In his rare contacts with humans, he imparts information that is priceless for survival, such as dairy techniques, and pieces of wisdom, such as proverbs and sayings. People take advantage of this knowledge but end up by offending and mocking him, thus driving him back to seclusion.

FOLK MEDICINE, MAGIC, AND WITCHCRAFT

Techniques of popular medicine had a place in religious cults, magic-symbolic practices and beliefs, and empirical knowledge and competence. Images and sanctuaries of the Virgin Mary that encouraged lactation in new mothers such as the Romanesque church of San Secondo in Cortazzone in the province of Asti were well known. However, in the traditional agropastoral society, where the diet was so meager that it approached malnutrition, the work was exhausting, and the heating was insufficient, it was therapeutic to grant a sick person richer and lighter food, more rest, and a warm environment. Honey was used like medicine, particularly for cough. Wine was a tonic frequently added to soup or coffee or boiled with sugar and spices and served hot. When children were infested with intestinal parasites, the cure consisted in "marking the worms," a symbolic technique. The healer dipped into a plate full of water three, seven, or nine hemp threads, causing them to cross each other, and uttered prayers and other, often secret formulas. If the threads floated, became twisted, or straightened out, this meant that the child was infested with parasites, while if the threads moved to the sound of the prayers, the worms were stopped. At the end of the twentieth century, many traditional healers, especially herbalists and chiropractors, were active in Piedmont and Val d'Aosta.

Purely evil practices were attributed to witches. In most of the Piedmontese territory a witch is known as a *masca* (plural: *masche*). Witches and sorcerers are important figures in the tales told in cattlesheds but are also perceived as an actual presence in the community and sometimes in the family. In most cases the *masca* is an old, lonely, marginal woman, but she may also be your mother-in-law or neighbor. People are afraid of her envy and threats, and she is regarded as a danger for children and animals. Children's clothes are not left to dry outdoors after sunset because in the dark they are threatened by the possible evil influence of witches. The *masca* is believed to be able to turn into an animal such as a horse, sheep, lamb, cat, or even a fly and to float in the air, abandoning her body to a sleeplike state. She can also turn into a bramble bush and bar the frightened wayfarer's path, but if she is struck or cut with a pruning knife while in that form, on the next morning the wound will be visible on her body. Among the witch's instruments is also the "book of command," a collection of formulas and invocations used for magic operations. When the witch dies, it must be given to her heir, who will take on her functions as a *masca*. In rural areas, the priest, who read the "book," was sometimes regarded as a *masca*, or at least considered capable of "*fare la fisica*," that is, performing operations halfway between magic and conjuring tricks. Sometimes, on the contrary, he was regarded as a protection against witches and their spells.

FOLKTALES AND SONGS

The main occasions for handing down oral narrations were the nighttime gatherings in cattlesheds, particularly during the winter, an important period of community and family interaction, which also allowed exchanges of news and meetings between young men and women. Though the *masche* were an important topic, they were not the only one. People drew also from the traditional stock of fables such as "The Braggart" and "The Devil's Bride." It was also an occasion for singing a vast and varied repertory of songs. Sometimes, to be allowed to take part in the party in the cattleshed and to meet the girls, young men sang a dialogue-song in which they asked to be admitted. After some exchanges of wisecracks, the women let them in. Other occasions for singing occurred during work in the fields and vineyards, during quest rites, and in taverns. A particular importance is attributed to the extensive corpus of epic-lyric songs. In the late nineteenth century Costantino Nigra produced an important collection of them and defined their metric, linguistic, and narrative features. Nigra believed that Piedmont shared these songs with other parts of Europe such as France, Catalonia, and Portugal, where a Celtic linguistic sub-stratum can be detected. He held that Piedmont was their center of diffusion in Italy.

CALENDAR CUSTOMS

Traditional agropastoral life is marked by a yearly calendar that reflects the cyclic time of nature and farming activities as well as community and liturgical feasts. A group of beginning-of-the-year rites clusters around the cycle of Christmas and New Year's Day. This is a period of prognostication, when traditional procedures are used to predict the weather for the new year. One practice requires careful observation of the twelve days after Christmas or after New Year's Day. The conditions on each day are regarded as a forecast of the climatic conditions for each of the twelve months. Some women actually used to mark on their calendar the weather conditions at each hour of the day in the hope of predicting the daily weather for the year to come. Many divination practices referred to marriage. A well-known one had a marriage-age girl place a soup plate full of water outside her window with one of her hairs in it. On the next morning, she might see that the hair had "written" the future bridegroom's name in the frozen water.

The Carnival period lasted from the Epiphany or St. Anthony's Day to Mardi Gras. There were many widespread, persistent Alpine Carnival festivals characterized by the presence of masks with costumes, bright-colored ribbons, little mirrors, and floral ornaments. Every five years during Carnival the feast of the *abaìo* occurs at Sampeyre in the Valle Varaita in the province of Cuneo. Three hundred characters appear in it, including the *abbà*, the treasurer, the *sapeurs* (sappers), Harlequin, and a couple of old people (masks that reappear in other European Carnivals). They perform parades, overthrow ritual barriers, put the treasurer on trial, and—after he has drawn up his testament—execute him. Celebrations of this type are also carried out in a modified form in some cities. The most famous of these festivals is that of Ivrea, where an intricate ceremony with masks and Napoleonic costumes combines with a "battle of oranges," in which gangs of *aranceri* (orange men) run wild in a riotous, heated contest that leaves enormous heaps of crushed oranges on the pavement.

During Carnival, a "knight" gallops to behead a suspended turkey with his "lance." Tonco, 1991. (Photograph by Piercarlo Grimaldi)

During Lent, several quest rites were practiced; many of these have been revived. In the hills of Lower Piedmont, the "egg singing" consisted of a nighttime tour of the village and farms, during which young people sang and begged for eggs and wine, which were consumed by the community on the day after Easter. If some people did not give any, the songs ended with verses that cursed them and wished them sterility. During Holy Week, some adolescents, carrying a rough cross, traveled through the countryside in order to sing a Passion in dialect (for which there is documentary evidence in Provence in the fifteenth century) and to carry out a quest. Holy Week was also the period when miracle plays were concentrated. This is a type of popular drama that for centuries has marked liturgical time, both at Christmas and, even more, before Easter. Although during the first decades of the twentieth century this theatrical practice seemed to be disappearing, it is now being unexpectedly revived. Once more, people are playing the roles of Christ, the apostles, Judas, Pilate, the Judeans, and the Roman legionnaires to enact the canonical stages of the Passion, in many cases with the addition of traditional or popular characters such as the bear and devils. An important popular Christmas drama is *Gelindo*, whose title comes from its protagonist, one of the shepherds who appear with the canonical characters of the Nativity. The shepherd meets St. Joseph and the pregnant Virgin Mary, is deeply moved by her beauty, and shows them the refuge in the cave. Afterward, with a group of other commoners, he tries to return to the place where the Savior was born, but he is worried about the fate of his farm and family and repeatedly returns home for a last errand and a last check. Thus, he embodies one of the traits attributed to Piedmontese farmers. The text, whose origin is uncertain, comes from Monferrato, as reflected in the dialectal part in some versions. It was performed in cattlesheds and church recreation centers and, recently, in local theaters, for instance, in Alessandria, where it is very successful.

The flourishing of spring was celebrated by the feasts of *calendimaggio* (May Day) or *maggio* (May). This is often the name of the ceremony but also denotes a symbolic tree or leafy branch. Contrary to the custom of similar ceremonies in the rest of the country, in many parts of Lower Piedmont the celebrants are girls (in the past they were little girls), and the presence of a tree is represented by a fir branch or a small fir. At Magliano in the province of Cuneo in 1972, the girls revived the itinerant rite of the May quest. One of them is the "May bride" and carries the fir branch, decorated with bright ribbons, flowers, and a small doll. Perhaps the doll is a reference to maternity and fertility, for the girls who perform the quest call it *bambin* (baby) and wish the bride another one. Or the doll may be the last trace of the icon of a rural spirit. The girls come into the farmyard and sing the ritual verses that present them as embodiments of spring. They announce the coming of May and springtime, praise the house that is giving them hospitality and the handsome young men around them with various matrimonial hints, and ask the mistress of the house to give them a present that they will put in the basket they carry.

The fir branch is only a variant in the rich symbolism of the tree, which includes an extensive series of ceremonial objects. All of them, though having different features, can be traced back to a complex characterized not only by the branch but also by a tapered, elongated, or spindlelike shape and by the presence of bread, colorful ribbons, and floral ornaments. The area of diffusion of these ceremonial objects covers an extensive part of the Piedmontese mountains, pre-Alps, and hills, which may

An oxen race in honor of the feast day of St. Victor, usually on 8 May or the Sunday closest to the holiday. The wagon carries blessed bread. (Photograph by Piercarlo Grimaldi)

The traditional dance by the Spadonari on the feast day of St. Vincent. Giaglione, 2004. (Photograph by Piercarlo Grimaldi)

almost be regarded as an area of a shared tree cult.

Within this typology, an object called *bran* in the dialect of the Susa Valley is formed of a long, spindle-shaped wooden structure containing a loaf of bread and decorated with flowers, multi-colored ribbons, and bunches of grapes. It connects the tree cult and the local sword dances. In the villages of Giaglione, Venaus, and San Giorio in the Susa Valley at the patron saints' feasts during the winter and spring, three dances with swords are performed in which the *bran* appears (or its presence in the past is documented). These dances have their own patterns and figures, which differ from the others known in Piedmont or the rest of Europe. Their pace is fluid and moderate, stately rather than warlike. Their movements (and their local names, still in use) recall agricultural work such as harvesting or plowing. The costumes worn by the dancers, who are called *spadonari* (sword carriers), are rich in floral elements and colors. They wear a tall, oval hat covered with multi-colored plastic or fabric flowers and ribbons in brilliant colors hanging over their backs and a colored jerkin rich in embroidery, decorations, and fringes. Counting the dances that are still in use (six) as well as those documented from the past (twenty) identifies Piedmont as the region with the most sword dances in Italy.

Particularly during the summer in many patron saints' festivals, ceremonial floats are still used, chiefly in the province of Asti and in the Piedmont area near Cuneo (approximately 20 occurrences active out of 100 documented ones). The float is drawn by oxen and follows a processional route. In some cases it is used as a stage for displaying for auction goods that have been given to the saint or for reciting sonnets in dialect. The only extant cases of actual races of the carts with animals at full speed are from the province of Vercelli at Caresana and Asigliano.

In the autumn on All Souls' Day (2 November), the calendar cycle overlaps the rites that mark stages in human life. Women cover graves with flowers, achieving a short-lived springtime. During the night between 1 and 2 November after having recited the rosary, women once left the table set with wine and chestnuts for the refreshment of dead relatives returning to their houses. In order to allow them to rest, sometimes even the beds were left empty.

CELEBRATION FOR DRAFTEES

Another rite of passage is still very important in the territory: that of celebrations for draftees. The young men who have been drafted into the military play leading roles in the ceremonial scenario of banquets, parades, and outdoor or indoor dances. A sort of ceremonial license allows them to eat and drink to excess and to break the customary rules of polite behavior in public. The purpose is to show off their newly attained manliness. Reference to the army and their country is made by means of neckerchiefs, forage caps, and flags, but the main component is that of a publicly legitimated and acknowledged virility.

From the late Middle Ages to the modern era, the *badie*, young men's associations that fulfilled essential functions in the community, organized young men's activities. Besides acting sometimes as an armed militia and as an agent for the socialization of young people, the *badie* carried out the task of organizing, managing, and interpreting the holiday periods, during which maintenance of law and order was under their control. As an expression of community and cult independence, they were thwarted by the Counter-Reformation and in many cases were disbanded or transformed into brotherhoods. Some of them, however, are still present and active in rituals, particularly in the Alpine area and in Val d'Aosta, under the name of *badoche*.

SPORTS, GAMES, AND HANDICRAFTS

Many traditional popular games are included in local festivals or form festive events themselves. In Lower Piedmont, for example, the "elastic ball game" involves two teams of four players with bound fists. In the main square of the village, they pass to each other a small, very heavy ball that must not fall outside the boundaries. This game requires considerable speed and energy and is occasionally still played. The Palio of Asti is an exclusively urban event that has been recently revived. This race is held in September and has been imitated in several other places. It is parodied by the donkey race that occurs in Alba and in some villages of the province of Asti. In Val d'Aosta the *bataille des reines* (battle of queens) is a traditional game connected with transhumant cattle-raising. During the winter, young cows are reared in small groups in individual cattlesheds in the valley. Around 16 June (St. Bernard of Menton's Day), they are brought to the summer pastures on the mountainside and kept separated from the bulls. In the mountain pastures, the cows that acquired a dominant role in the little cattlesheds confront each other in order to determine which of them will be the "queen" of the larger herd in which they have all been gathered.

Various festivals that occur in the countryside near Asti feature a donkey as the central figure of a race that burlesques the well-known Palio, which occurs in Asti on the third Sunday of September. Castiglione Tinella, 1993. (Photograph by Piercarlo Grimaldi)

The *reine* will also have an important practical role because she will help the herders direct and gather the other animals, which will follow her as leader. Throughout a long summer afternoon, the cows engage in a series of bloodless duels, in which they push each other vigorously with their horns until one of the two gives way and surrenders. At the end, the strongest is recognized. A country feast accompanies these duels. Cattlebreeders, herders, and onlookers eat, drink wine, chat, and make bets. At present the duels of the *reines* on the summer pastures are regarded as the semi-finals of a grand tournament that will take place with all the ceremony of mass sports in a large stadium near Aosta, crowded not only with local spectators but also with many tourists. The *bataille des reines* is becoming an element in the identity of Val d'Aosta.

In Aosta, at the end of January, a large fair is dedicated to St. Ursus. Its most significant expression consists of wooden sculptures whose shapes reflect the persistence and revival of a tradition. Throughout Piedmont and Val d'Aosta there is a renewal of interest in traditional handicrafts, ranging from ancient festive costumes and lace to wooden sculptures and toys. These products have found new venues of presentation at fairs and calendar feasts.

CHALLENGES OF THE MODERN WORLD

The last quarter of the twentieth century, particularly in Piedmont, saw a strong renewal of interest in the region's heritage of popular tradition, belying some people's belief that popular tradition was about to disappear forever in the context of urbanization and industrial (and tertiary-sector) development. This interest has the particular feature of not being concentrated in metropolitan areas or research institutions but of being widespread all over the territory. It is supported by associations, local leaders and intellectuals, entrepreneurs, administrators, politicians, and teachers. The continuity (or revitalization) of the elements of local tradition now passes through these people's interpretation and research and is influenced by their goals and interests. At present, attention is focused on some particular sectors. One is that of the calendar feasts and farmers' feasts, whose revival is expanding very quickly and in some cases actually reinventing ceremonies based on traditional or allegedly traditional models. Examples include the previously described "egg quests" (which were revived at Magliano, then regained their territory) and the proliferation during the last decade of miracle plays, which were retrieved from the past with varying degrees of philological accuracy. It is interesting to notice that nowadays many girls take part in these ceremonies, even the ones in which the leading roles once belonged to men. Another area of interest focuses on local ethnographic **museums**, which chiefly provide information about crafts and farming activities. The interest in "ancient trades" appears also in exhibitions that are held at many local fairs. Other aspects include singing, dialectal theater, and music. Popular tunes and songs are variously reinterpreted with both acoustic and electronic instruments in a way that is meant to be traditional.

In the context of **globalization** with its attendant homogenization of consumption and recently also of the confrontation with newly immigrated ethnic groups, the reintroduction of popular tradition and references to it are an instrument not only for defining the population's sense of belonging and local roots but also and increasingly for gaining access to financial resources and to the media, for creating a marked, colorful image of the territory, and for attracting Italian and foreign tourists.

STUDIES OF PIEDMONTESE FOLKLORE

The first history of Piedmontese folklore studies has recently been published (Grimaldi 2005). Studies prior to scientific specialized research can be found in the reports of diocesan synods (Corrain and Zampini; 1970) and in the mid-nineteenth-century *Corografie*, which consist of geographic, historic, and economic reports on Piedmont. Of particular interest, among the *Corografie* is that written by Zuccagni-Orlandini (Galanti 1979), which contains much ethnographic information on Piedmont. Costantino Nigra was the most important scholar in the nineteenth century, and his scholarship was recognized by the European scientific establishment.

During the first half of the twentieth century, G. C. Pola Falletti Villafalleto became well known for his reconstruction of the calendar of festivities with particular attention to the *badie* (1939–1942). During the second half of the century, Roberto Leydi (1995) became renowned for his ethnomusicological research and fieldwork. In the 1970s and 1980s, the writer Nuto Revelli (1977, 1985) contributed to Piedmontese folklore with his collections of biographies recorded in the mountainous area of the province of Cuneo.

In the 1970s, the Laboratorio Etnologico per l'Italia Nord-Occidentale (LEINO), directed by Gian Luigi Bravo, was established at the University of Turin. The Laboratorio aims to research traditions of Piedmont and Aosta Valley, while framing them in the wider context of revitalization as well as in the sociocultural dynamic of a complex society. The work will continue to develop at the University of Turin and the University of Eastern Piedmont, focusing on themes of festivals, sacred representations, folkloric imagery, and local museums as well as technology for audiovisual communication and electronic archiving.

BIBLIOGRAPHY

Artoni, Ambrogio, Gian Luigi Bravo, and Piercarlo Grimaldi. 1987. *Il gioco della tradizione* (film). Cuneo: Produzione Casati.

———. 1989. *Cambio della guardia per il Carnevale* (film). Torino: Centro Linguistico ed Audiovisivi dell'Università di Torino.

———. 1990. *La bataille di reine: dall'alpeggio all'arena* (film). Torino: Centro Linguistico ed Audiovisivi dell'Università di Torino.

Artoni, Ambrogio, Gian Luigi Bravo, Piercarlo Grimaldi, Renato Grimaldi, and Sergio Zoppi. 1991. *Il tempo contadino. Feste, riti e cerimonialità nella campagna astigiana* (film). Torino: Produzione Cassa di Risparmio di Asti e Centro Linguistico ed Audiovisivi dell'Università di Torino.

Beccaria, Gian Luigi, ed. 1982. *Fiabe piemontesi*. Milano: Mondadori.

Bolgiani, Franco. 1997. Storia, leggenda e culto dei martiri tebei. In *Rivoltare il tempo*, edited by Piercarlo Grimaldi. Milano: Guerini. 107–119.

Bravo, Gian Luigi. 1983. *Festa contadina e società complessa*. Milano: Franco Angeli.

———. 1989. La medicina popolare/Piemonte e Valle d'Aosta. In *Medicine e magie*, edited by Tullio Seppilli. Milano: Electa. 120–125.

———. 2001. *Italiani. Racconto etnografico*. Roma: Meltemi.

———. 2003. Orso e capra a nuova vita. In *Bestie, santi, divinità. Maschere animali dell'Europa tradizionale*, edited by Piercarlo Grimaldi. Torino: Museo Nazionale della Montagna "Duca degli Abruzzi." 35–43.

———. 2005. *Feste, masche, contadini*. Roma: Carocci.

Bravo, Gian Luigi, and Paolo Quaregna. 1982. *Bal do sabre. Rito antico, rito moderno* (film). Torino: Rai, Sede Regionale per il Piemonte.

Corrain, Cleto, and Pierluigi Zampini. 1970. *Documenti etnografici e folkloristici nei Sinodi diocesani italiani*. Bologna: Forni.

Galanti, Bianca Maria. 1979. *Mondo popolare nella corografia di A. Zuccagni-Orlandini*. Roma: Bulzoni.

Grimaldi, Piercarlo. 1993. *Il calendario rituale contadino. Il tempo della festa e del lavoro fra tradizione e complessità sociale*. Milano: Angeli.

———. 1996. *Tempi grassi, tempi magri. Percorsi etnografici*. Torino: Omega.

———. 2001. *Le spade della vita e della morte. Danze armate in Piemonte*. Torino: Omega.

———. 2003. *Pasqua, Natale, Santissimo Carnevale. La messa delle maschere di Saint-Rhémy en Bosses* (film). Verzuolo: Sabbatini Multimedia, Università del Piemonte Orientale.

———. 2005. *Parlandone da vivo*. Torino: Omega.

Leydi, Roberto, ed. 1995. *Cantè bergera. La ballata piemontese dal repertorio di Teresa Viarengo*. Vigevano: Diakronia.

———. 2001. *Gelindo ritorna. Il Natale in Piemonte*. Torino: Omega.

Nigra, Costantino. 1988 (1974). *Canti popolari del Piemonte*. Torino: Einaudi.

Pola Falletti Villafalleto, G. C. 1939–1942. *Associazioni giovanili e feste antiche: loro origini*. 4 volumes. Torino: Comitato di difresa dei fanciulli.

Porporato, Davide, ed. 2001. *Archiviare la tradizione. Beni culturali e sistemi multimediali*. Torino: Omega Edizioni.

Revelli, Nuto. 1977. *Il mondo dei vinti*. 2 volumes. Torino: Einaudi.

———. 1985. *L'anello forte*. Torino: Einaudi.

Gian Luigi Bravo and Piercarlo Grimaldi
(Translated from the Italian by Francesca M. Muccini and Marta Innocenti)

SICILY

GEOGRAPHY AND HISTORY

Thanks to its geographical location, Sicily has constituted for centuries an intersection of various cultures. In addition to the indigenous population, many other peoples, including Sicilians, Carthaginians, Greeks, Romans, Byzantines, Arab-

Berbers, Normans, Svevis, Angevins, and Spanish, overlapped over the years. The processes of acculturation and their values in the Mediterranean context have obviously developed differently according to the diverse historical epochs. Sicily, for instance, was considered the "center of the world" in ancient times. Then, in the ninth century C.E. it became a crucial factor in the diffusion of Arab-Islamic culture in Europe. Sicily became a multicultural laboratory during the Norman epoch while constantly remaining a frontier between Continental and Mediterranean cultures. When the center of gravity of political and economic interests began to shift toward the heart of Europe and the Americas, the vital role Sicily played in the relationships between East and West increasingly weakened until it finally faded away. This progressive marginalization, together with the perpetuation of archaic productive structures, has not, however, resulted in the impoverishment of its complex cultural identity. Moreover, despite transformations on the surface, Sicilian cultural identity has remained consistent with its deepest expressive and ideological forms, becoming an example of cumulative cultural history characterized by different stratifications of cultures that have never totally disappeared.

An example is the Sicilian dialect with its numerous local variations. Toponomastics and onomastics, specific phonetic traits and grammatical forms, and the close relationship between "words" and "things" allow us to understand the system of borrowings, transformations, and innovations following the merging of the several languages of the various historical inhabitants of the island: from the Greek substratum, still recognizable in the toponomastics, to the development of modern Sicilian idiom during the Norman epoch, which has gradually enriched its vocabulary with contributions from Angevin, Catalan, and Castilian languages.

The character of traditional culture in contemporary Sicily originated in the nineteenth century. During this period the main industries on the island were extensive agriculture, animal husbandry, sulfur and rock salt mining, fishing, and the production of marine salt. The homogeneous economic condition was borne out by analogously uniform social and cultural circumstances. The majority of people were either day laborers, shepherds, craftsworkers, sharecroppers, or small landowners whose activities responded to a group of noblemen who owned the majority of farmland as well as industries such as tuna canneries and mines. This class of noblemen did not personally take care of their businesses but entrusted the management to middlemen, *gabelloti*, who were the actual supervisors. The landowners resided in the most important urban areas. Between them and the rest of people was a minuscule middle class consisting of lawyers, notaries, accountants, and those who provided services to the local urban aristocracy. During this time of broad political and historical changes, including the growth of Romantic ideology and the development of independent European states, the careful, rigorous study of Sicilian folklore began.

Giuseppe Pitrè (1841–1916), a Palermitan, is the major scholar acknowledged for his work on Sicilian folklore. His enormous commitment was manifest in the *Biblioteca delle Tradizioni Popolari Siciliane* (Library of Sicilian Folklore), a work of twenty-five volumes published between 1870 and 1913. It includes songs, tales, legends, habits, customs, beliefs, festivals and performances, material culture, folk medicine, and more. Pitrè's work can be accessed in a recently published bibliography (D'Anna 1993).

AGRICULTURAL FOLKLORE

Seasonal cycles have for centuries dominated Sicilian life "from the cradle to the grave" and guided cultural codes and behaviors. The island's primary economic activity was extensive grain farming. Until the beginning of the 1950s, one-third of the land on the island belonged to approximately 1,000 families, and the agricultural practices were still very archaic. Plowing, for instance, was performed with the use of animal-drawn plows, while tools were made by local artisans. Harvest involved groups of farmers, mostly seasonal, recruited to work in the island's vast inland fiefs. The organization of work was almost identical everywhere, save for a few local variations. Before sunrise a group of harvesters gathered at the workplace (*antu*). The team was typically composed of eight men with scythes for cutting wheat, followed by a man with the specific tasks of picking piles of wheat, wrapping them, and heaping them up in shocks. The cutters, lined up in a row, preceded the binder. The various stages of harvesting were accompanied by devotional phonic-rhythmic formulas or songs that corresponded to the pace of work. Once the field was harvested, sheaves were brought from the field on muleback to where they would be threshed. The threshing floor was generally located in an airy and high location.

When the sun was high in the sky, farmers opened the shocks on the threshing floor and started the beating action. The beating was performed by one or several mules (donkeys, horses, and oxen were hardly ever used) led by the farmer, who beat out the wheat from the straw while walking on the shocks. During the beating the farmer might encourage the animals to maintain a steady pace. He might also recite precise devotional expressions or sing songs that lasted throughout the duration of work in order to alleviate the tedium. Next came the winnowing, which farmers generally reserved for a windy day. They used a several-pronged pitchfork to toss the wheat against the breeze to free it from chaff and crushed straw (*spagghiata*). Then, the farmer sifted the wheat in a large shallow sieve placed on a wooden tripod until he had filtered out the remaining weeds, dust, and chaff. He then took his wheat to the local mill. Mills were typically watermills whose style dated from the Middle Ages.

Farmers' songs could be performed either in monodic form, sometimes accompanied by a plucked idiophone such as the Jew's harp (*marranzanu, mariolu*), or in polyphonic style, which emphasized the middle and final cadences. Similarly performed songs also accompanied grape harvest, olive picking, and other collective working activities.

Along with these agricultural occupations the island was also noted for sheepraising. Today, in certain marginal areas of Sicily sheep farming still preserves some characteristics unchanged from the past. This is evident in small-scale farms, where farmers continue to use free pasture, milk and sheer manually, and make cheese and ricotta. The continuation of sound communication systems—voiced and whistled calls—among farmers or for farmers to manage their cattle are still of particular interest. Farmers continue using bagpipes and cane flutes. The actual sheep-shearing is usually performed between the months of May and June and marks the beginning of the annual cycle. It comprises a series of collective ritual activities including dances, songs, and contests between the shepherds and their families as well as consumption of meat as a propitiatory symbol.

FISHING FOLKLORE

In addition to the land, the sea has represented another important theater for major economic activities and an accompanying rich oral, expressive **repertoire**. Up to the 1960s, fishing for swordfish was practiced in the Straits of Messina in accordance with an archaic procedure, employed since the days of Polibio (third–second century B.C.E.). In the summer, between July and September, the swordfish appears on the surface to mate. The swordfish was sighted from the tall mast of a boat. Then, a signal indicating the presence of the fish was given to the crew of a swift rowboat four or five meters in length (*luntru*). The *luntru* was equipped with a tall mast from which a crew member directed the chase. The area of the sea where the boats operated was divided into sectors previously assigned to each fishing crew. Communication between the oarsmen and the lookout occurred through precise gestures and sounds. When the fish was within reach, the lookout gave the harpooner, who stood at the boat's prow, a signal to prepare the harpoon. Every launch that hit the target was accompanied by a thankful praise to a saint (normally St. Nicholas, to whom fishers, particularly from the area of Messina, are especially devoted). Ritual phrases of goodwill and thanksgiving were usually recited at the beginning and end of the expedition. Traditionally, when a fish was caught, a double cross was carved by fin-

gernail next to its eye, while some parts of it were consumed raw. During the 1960s the introduction of boats with engines and other devices did not substantially change some aspects of the traditional fishing, including the use of signals and the kind of tools employed. However, nowadays the old style of fishing is mainly a sport or recreational activity, having been replaced by modern efficiency.

Coastal fishing activity is still practiced with nets and *nasse* cages (or fish pots), and in many small fishing communities in the area of Palermo and a few other places on the island the only other existing method, which resists innovation, is represented

A Sicilian fisherman. (Courtesy Library of Congress)

by tuna fishing. The term *tonnara* refers either to the establishments along the island that serve as shelter for boats, nets, fishing tools, and fish or to the complex series of dense nets that are commonly laid in the sea off the Sicilian coasts between May and June, when the tuna swim past the coast. A series of vast nets called *cura* (tail) are lowered perpendicularly to the coast toward the open sea, thus directing the tuna to a sequence of "rooms" made of net. The tuna are captured in these successive nets, which are gradually restricted in size and raised toward the surface, where the fish are attacked (*mattanza*) with what might be described as large spears in a sophisticated trap system. The network of net chambers is called an *isola* (island). An interesting feature of the *mattanza* is the team effort of the fishermen involved in each catch. From his boat, the *raisi* (head fisherman of the *mattanza*) directs the work of the men in the other small boats. Because a *mattanza* involves an entire school of fish, dozens of tuna may be captured. The fish struggle as they are herded into ever smaller, shallower net chambers (the final one is called *coppu*, "the chamber of death") and finally lifted onto the boats for the *mattanza*. Indeed, the term *mattanza* has found its way into the Italian vernacular as a synonym for "massacre." The *raisi* decides where and when to put the nets and when it is time for the *mattanza*. The fishermen, about 100 people, are called *tonnaroti* (men of the tunas). When it is time to catch the fish, the *tonnaroti* carry out the *mattanza*. At the *raisi*'s order all the *tonnaroti* exult in shouts and archaic songs (*cialoma*) as they lift the floor net of the death room. As the bottom of the net lifts the tuna to the surface, the frantic fish flail about on the surface of the sea. The expression *"aiamola"* and invocations to Jesus Christ and saints are alternately repeated by the *raisi* and the crew. When the crew start to lift the big net, a faster *cialoma* called *u Gnanzu* is alternately performed by the crew and the *raisi*.

Salt-making

Salt extraction encompasses much of the history of the Western Sicilian coast (from Trapani to Marsala) and of the Eastern coast (from Augusta and Capo Passero). Records documenting salt-making date to the Middle Ages in the reports of the Arab geographer Muhammed al-Idrisi. Water was drained by pumps activated by windmills into a complex system of basins where salt, in successive phases of evaporation, was formed and harvested. The picturesque windmills still characterize the landscape of these areas. Some of them have been restored and are still employed for salt-making. At Paceco, in the province of Trapani, a small salt museum, Museo del Sale, has been set up in a saltworks, Salina Culcasi. The museum recounts the different stages involved in collecting salt, a process that until the mid-twentieth century was still done by hand. Salt-making involved three harvest cycles, with a fifteen-day break between them, during the months of July and August. Salt-making was piecework. Seasonal workers (*a stagghiu*) gathered in teams (*venna*) of eight or more (up to sixteen), depending on the extent of the saltworks, supervised by a *curatolo* or *mastru i salina* (supervisor), who controlled the state of the basins and of the water throughout the year. In his turn, the *curatolo* appointed a foreman (*capuvenna, capurali*) and a fiduciary (*signaturi*) to verify the amount of harvested salt. The harvest usually started around 2 or 3 A.M. and continued until 4 P.M. Every team established shifts for their workers, who were alternately employed in loading and carrying the baskets of salt to the designated gathering point. Essential for this activity was the reckoning of the baskets, which was conducted by the fiduciary of the supervisor. Workers were paid according to the quantity produced and counted the baskets themselves in order to assure the accuracy of the fiduciary. Closely related to salt harvest is the vast repertoire of saltworkers' songs. The songs kept the rhythm of the hard work. They represented a sort of counting method for the baskets. The complicated lyrics include vernacular expressions and jargon, which refer to the number of collected baskets of salt—from one to twenty-four—intermixed with extemporaneous lines of reproach, mockery, and incitement as well as recriminations against work conditions, erotic innuendos, and invocations of saints. Twenty-four baskets formed a unit. Every unit was marked on a wooden stick fastened to the worker's hip. Acclamations of the Virgin Mary and saints were mandatory when 100 units were reached during the workday or before the end of it. Although the methods used have changed as processes have become mechanized, thus separating lyrics from their previous function, those folksongs are still remembered by the older saltworkers (*salinari*), who occasionally perform them during convivial meetings.

Songs

Although rich and abundant, the heritage of folksongs associated with work environments does not represent the whole musical universe of Sicilian cultural tradition, for there are other folksongs connected to life-cycle events or ceremonies and feasts. The most popular folksong is the *canzuna*. The *canzuna* is a monostrophic song in alternate rhyme, commonly formed of eight verses, sometimes four or six, but rarely exceeding twelve. The *canzuni* were performed for different occasions of social and working life. They were executed either solo or by a group, with or without musical instruments. Melodies typically rely on the use of a two-part formula; the melodies divide the poetic text in two distichs. They are presented in modal form with a descendant rhythm, often enriched by melismas. Among the most refined monodic-style executions are the folksongs of charioteers. The chariot has been used as a vehicle for transporting goods in Sicily since the 1830s, when the Bourbons initiated the transit system. Before then supplies were usually carried on muleback (*retini*) or via maritime routes. The chariot had been the commonest means of transportation up to the 1960s, when it began to be supplanted by automobiles. The charioteer normally owned his wagon and horse (or mule) or worked with those of someone else when employed by another charioteer. He transported loads on behalf of a third party, landlords, merchants, and manufacturers, seldom buying and selling supplies on his own. Sometimes journeys were quite long for charioteers. However, they represented an opportunity to meet with others in the *fondaci* (from the Arabic *funduq*, "shelter, lodge"). Usually located in the countryside, the *fondaci* were shelters where charioteers gathered to spend the night or rest a few hours, eat, and feed the animals before going back on the road. During these meetings charioteers challenged each other to singing contests. Essential qualities in the song *alla carrettiera* (charioteer's style) were the cadence (*carienza*) and the sincerity in the performance; textual beauty and vocal talent were secondary. The ending lines of each *canzuna* included the *chiamata* (call)—two decasyllabic lines freely introduced by the performer to invite or challenge his fellows to continue the song. At times, verses that expressed appreciation for listeners or apologies for a poor performance and lines that indicated the place of origin of the song or the name of the people from whom the song had been acquired substituted for the call. Charioteers have now disappeared and have been replaced by truck drivers. However, they have preserved their sense of higher status over peasants, with whom they nevertheless shared the same cultural horizon. This self-representation is distinctly noticeable when they speak about their own songs by distinguishing them, with some deprecation, from those "*viddanisca* songs" (*viddanu*, peasant). The folksong repertoire has been passed on from father to son. To carry on the technique of performing these songs, ex-charioteers still get together sometimes to re-create the singing contests and challenges peculiar to their own cultural universe. Some still preserve their horse carts, which are truly works of art. The tradition of painting the cart initially responded to the necessity of protecting the wood from premature deterioration. Later it became a form of art that developed specialized schools at several centers on the island. Workshops within each major region—Western and Eastern Sicily—show their own distinctive characteristics and styles. Each part of the cart would be decorated and divided into panels. Each panel would usually depict scenes—*scacchi* (squares)—inspired by the epicknightly repertoire, including the adventures of Charlemagne's knight Roland (Orlando in Italian) and other French paladins, whose legends had been very popular in Sicily since the middle of the nineteenth century.

Also abundant is the repertoire of narrative folksongs (*storie*). Storytellers performed the *storie* on the street, selling cheap printed and illustrated versions of the songs in flyers or pamphlets. The stories told of local legends or present and past events often related to crimes and politics. Sometimes the storyteller, usually accompanied by a guitar, did not narrate the whole story but only a few episodes from it illustrated on painted display boards. Although representations of events have undergone considerable change thanks to modern media, storytellers have continued their activity. The facts they narrated represented exemplary accounts and models that individuals converted into paradigms of behavior consistent with their conceptions of the world. Further, storytellers and their audience shared the same ideological structure. The events, albeit taken from ordinary life, when dramatically narrated and illustrated by the storyteller, became myth. An example is the vast repertoire of folk epic songs dedicated to the bandit Salvatore Giuliano (1922–1950), an outlaw folk **hero**, a real-life Robin Hood, the "king of bandits" whose adventures are very much present in every recent storyteller's collection. Giuliano's transformation from outlaw to hero mirrors a mythical-symbolic mechanism that tends to redeem the past by transfiguring it. Among legends in verses (maybe narrative folk poems), the most popular is *La Storia della Baronessa di Carini* (The History of the Baroness of Carini), inspired by a sixteenth-century historical event. The poem tells of the ferocious murder of the baroness by either her father or her husband on account of an illicit relationship.

On religious feast days such as Christmas and Easter, tales of the Nativity and the Passion or stories of saints were usually sung by the *orbi* (blind storytellers), true experts in that genre who frequently accompanied themselves with a violin or other stringed instruments. Although the activity of storytelling has gradually died out, since many of its professionals have died, the persistent vitality of devotional and religious practices characteristic of folk religion has sustained fascinating customs and rituals. Among them are the *lamentanzi* (or *lamenti, ladate, parti*), songs performed during Holy Week and Easter in several towns on the island. The *lamentanzi* are polyvocalic songs of Byzantine origin that alternate solo and choral performances. Narrative folksongs of the Nativity continued to be performed, accompanied by two different kinds of bagpipes: the *zampogna a paro* and the *zampogna a chiave*. The names suggest that in the first the chanters are of equal length, while in the second the two divergent chanters are of unequal length, with the longer one having a key.

CALENDAR CUSTOMS

Folk ceremonies have largely survived the changes connected to a different organization of production activities and the consequent transformations in social life. Generally speaking, Christian calendar holidays have not lost their pre-Christian affiliation with agricultural cycles. For instance, Easter rituals represent the death and resurrection of a god to ensure the cyclical rebirth of time and nature. In Sicily this phenomenon, however common throughout Catholicism, is particularly marked by the abundance of natural elements during the summer rituals and the production and consumption of breads and cakes whose shapes reproduce elements of the vegetable kingdom. Especially eloquent in this regard are rituals during Easter from Palm Sunday to Resurrection Sunday. Cities—including Trapani, Marsala, Enna, Caltanisetta, and other minor centers—stage performances of elaborate ceremonies. St. Joseph festivals are included within this archaic system of rituals. Officially, St. Joseph's Day is 19 March. However, this date only initiates a larger festival sequence that extends from March to May and from August to September, with dates varying according to place. Numerous Sicilian towns are involved in the cult of the saint, whose most significant ritual sequences include donations, bonfires, banquets, religious representations, processions, and the auction of donated goods. Together with the public dimension of the festival, mostly carried on by men, a more private, domestic side exists that depends almost exclusively on women. As fulfillment of a vow, women prepare imposing structures resembling altars or chapels decorated with myrtle, laurel, flowers, fruits, *lavureddi* (wheat grown in darkness), and, above all, breads of different sizes shaped to represent phenomena from the vegetable and animal kingdoms. On these tables or altars—called *tavuli, artari,* or *ceni* depending on the local dialect—are other kinds of food such as cooked, salted, and sweet food; food made of early fruits and vegetables; vegetables cooked in an omelet style; and soups. The preparation lasts several days. On the day of the festival, food is offered to some "official" guests (in the past these were the poor people of the town; today they are children) who represent the Holy Family (Jesus, Mary, and Joseph), the apostles, and the *Virgineddi* (the young virgins). The rest of the food is usually distributed among relatives, friends, and casual visitors assembled for the occasion. Particularly rich are the "tables" prepared in some centers of the provinces of Trapani, Palermo, and Agrigento.

The theme of regeneration is also expressed in the laurel festivals that focus

Carnevale di Aci Reale float, Sicily, Italy. In Sicily, the Carnival celebration retains clear connections to the pastoral culture with which it was originally associated. (© Yashiro Haga/HAGA/The Image Works)

on the central role of the aromatic essence, from its communal harvesting, to its display during local processions, to the offering of its leaves to the saint to whom the feast is dedicated. Laurel festivals are widely diffused in the Nebrodi Mountains. It is common in Sicily to name the festival after the saint being honored: St. Cathald at Gagliano Castelferrato, St. Vito at Regalbuto, St. Sebastian and Madonna of the Lavina at Cerami, and St. Silvester at Troina in the province of Enna; or St. Sebastian at Tortorici, St. Basil and St. Marc of Alunzio, St. Anthony at Capizzi, the Madonna of the Graces at Naso, and Holy Mary Annunziata at Ficarra in the province of Messina.

The Carnival celebration retains clear connections to the pastoral culture with which it was originally associated. Through such activities as pantomimes, dancing and masquerade, contests and games, playing pranks, and gluttonous eating, Carnival represents the rupture and reconstruction of cosmic and social order, the passage from the old to the new life cycle, and the affirmation of cosmos over chaos. In many places, the conclusion of Carnival includes the burning of an effigy called *u Nannu* (grandfather), often accompanied by the *Nanna* (grandmother). The bonfire is usually preceded by the representation of a funeral that includes various phases: the testament, the wake, the funeral cortège, and the funeral lament (in the cities of Palermo, Cinisi, and Mezzojuso, for instance). The causes of death are usually explained as excessive eating and sexual activity, both symbols of the regenerating value of orgy. Masks are used in pantomimes, games, and contests. On Carnival Sunday, at Mezzojuso (in the province of Palermo), there takes place a pantomime called *Mastru ri campu* (Master of the Field). Up to the second half of the nineteenth century, this type of representation also took place in the poorest areas of the city of Palermo.

The competitive (or conventional conflict) model informs the folk dramatic representation known as *Tenzone dei Mesi*, which was quite popular in the past but is less well known and sporadically performed nowadays except for the community of Barrafranca (in the province of Enna), where the drama is regularly staged. This folk drama tells of the conflict among the Months, who, armed with a sword or another weapon, ride horses and declaim in verses their own contributions to the fertility of nature. No one wins because prosperity is provided by each of them, as the Year—denominated the King of Months—aims to represent symbolically. At Novara of Sicily (a town in the province of Messina) during the period between Epiphany and Ash Wednesday people practice the *lucu da maiurca* (game of the *Maiorchino*—a seasoned pecorino cheese), in which players roll a cheese weighing about ten to fifteen kilograms down a two-kilometer trail, which goes from the main square of the town to its suburbs. The team that arrives first at the finish line wins the contest.

On Fat Thursday in some areas of the province of Messina, there are parades that involve masked princesses, knights, and ladies. However, the central character of the parade remains the masked bear (*Ussu*), an intriguing figure covered with animal skins and carrying heavy bells hanging from its belt. Guards would lead him in chains under the supervision of hunters and beaters. The latter would perform a rhythm with shell trumpets (*brogni*) and drum (*tammurinu*). While groups of women perform extemporaneous dances accompanied by musicians, the bear would attempt to chase them. One of the most interesting examples of this ritual takes place in the town of Saponara.

ARTS AND CRAFTS

Another important aspect of Sicilian folklore is represented by folk art and artifacts of a utilitarian nature. The figurative art of Sicilian tradition, based upon collectively shared esthetic norms, responds to precise needs and will continue to be passed on as long as it is functional. Religious beliefs are central and recurrent themes in Sicilian folk art. Until recently, many cities on the island have been centers for printed sacred images whose dimensions depend on their use and what the purchasers can afford. In the past, these images were attached behind houses' front doors, on the doorjambs, on the beams supporting the roof, or on the trunk containing the trousseau and family linen; in the barns or cowsheds; on barrels, on the *cannizzi*—special cylindrical containers made of intertwined canes for preserving wheat, on animals, in the workplace, or on means of transportation. Images of saints associated with healing specific diseases or protecting body parts were always carried. These sacred images represented tangible signs of the mediation between individuals and the Otherworld. They had clear apotropaic, therapeutic, and protective values, all essential characteristics in an existence marked by destitution and precariousness. Eventually, objectification of the sacred produced sacralization of the object.

To the same magical-religious domain belong other popular practices in Sicily as well as other areas of the Catholic world such as the ex-voto—an offering to a saint or the Madonna in fulfillment of a vow. Ex-votos are generally placed in a church that contains a shrine to the patron saint to whom the prayer is offered to commemorate the recovery of the donor from some grave danger. Many sanctuaries in Sicily keep collections of ex-votos; for example, the church of Sts. Alfio, Filadelfo, and Cirino at Trecastagni (in the province of Catania), the Madonna of Loreto at Altavilla Milicia (in the province of Palermo), and the Holy Annunziata in Trapani. Ex-votos painted in Sicily are usually referred to as *miracula* (miracles), a term that reveals linguistic correspondence between the object and the divine intervention concretized in the experience of the "miracle." Until recently, the production of ex-votos was assigned to specialized workshops that skillfully illustrated through symbolic and stereotyped designs the circumstances of the cure or rescue from incurable diseases, dangerous childbirths, shipwrecks, workplace accidents, or assaults by bandits or pirates. The artist in charge of painting the ex-voto usually focused on just one narrative element associated with the miraculous event, while portraying the image of the saint or Madonna to whom the prayers were offered. Ex-votos were meant to be displayed at major pilgrimage sites as public testimonies for graces received.

Another kind of ex-voto included representations of body parts. The anatomical votives represented diseased body parts healed or expected to be cured by a deity. They were made from a variety of materials from silver to wax and in a variety of forms (relief, sculpture in the round, painting). The practice of offering anatomical votives (even though donors nowadays tend to give a heart as symbol of recovery) still continues as attested by items sold in jewelry stores (for instance, in downtown Palermo near the Church of Saint Dominic, historically known as the headquarters of silver craftsmen) and at the most popular sanctuaries on the island. In the province of Catania, painted ex-votos, particularly related to the cult of Sts. Alfio, Filadelfo, and Cirino, continue to be produced, though on a much smaller scale than in the past.

Another form of art that belongs to the devotional domain is painting on glass. The complex technique requires producing a design on one side of a piece of glass that is to be viewed from the other side. Creations made using this technique appeared in the houses of wealthy farmers toward the end of the eighteenth century. However, the most significant production of paintings on glass began in the 1830s by specialists known as *pincisanti* (saints' painters). These paintings, the subjects of which mostly concern saints and the Madonna, were considered less vulgar and more sophisticated than, for instance, devotional prints. Although the general artistic value of devotional folk art was secondary to its religious meaning, the production of paintings on glass was perceived as closer to religious art and therefore became more popular among the richest groups of farmers.

CHALLENGES OF THE MODERN WORLD

Starting in the 1950s, the agricultural environment considerably changed due to a different organization and mechanization of work, to different harvesting and irrigation systems, and to the disappearance of certain crops such as cotton, linen, and sugarcane. Along with the transformation in rural areas, the sociocultural setting has changed mostly due to a progressive depopulation of the countryside and other areas depending on an agropastoral economy and to the resulting growth of urban areas. The phenomenon has partially modified the cultural setting of Sicily. However, practices of natural folk medicine and magical-religious folk medicine, though less common than before, are still performed by *ciarmavermi* and *maari* or *magari* (literally, magicians). The *ciarmavermi* is perceived by the community as a sort of empirical healer from whom people seek treatment for lesser diseases or ailments, including intestinal infestation with worms—from which the name *ciarmavermi* derives. This type of healing in its commonest form is domestic and generally performed by women. It excludes any relation to the "beings" (*esseri*)—"restless souls of dead individuals who wander in the air." Conversely, the magico-religious branch of folk medicine relies almost exclusively on the supernatural power of the practitioners (*magari*) and on their connection with the *esseri*. In most cases the healer attempts ritually to cure a range of supernaturally induced ailments, including *fattura* (possession).

Traditional children's games and recreational activities (*pisula* and *marredda*) are progressively disappearing as well as oral narratives, fairy tales, novellas, and legends whose themes and motifs derive from either European or Eastern sources. Of Arab origin, for instance, is the fictional character Giufà, a well-known Sicilian comic figure and protagonist of many anecdotes. On the other hand, food habits seem to be more resistant to changes. Some regional dishes have been revived and reintroduced in Sicilian cooking, including *couscousu* (couscous), a coarsely ground semolina pasta originating in North Africa prepared with fish, vegetables, or meat as well as *cannolu* (stuffed pastry shells), *cassata* (ricotta cream cake), and *gelo di mellone* (watermelon ice), which in the past were prepared only for certain occasions but now are consumed all year round.

Following a temporary crisis after World War II, there has been a significant resurgence of interest in puppet theater (*opera dei pupi*) in recent decades. It emerged in Sicily in the early nineteenth century and remained popular until the 1950s. Typically, the marionettes depict medieval characters and legendary events based loosely on history, including the stories of Charlemagne's knights. There are differences between the Palermo and the Catania puppet theaters: the shape and size of the puppets, the way puppets are controlled by puppeteers, and the signs used to advertise the shows. A very important institution in this field is the Antonio Pasqualino International Museum of Puppets Antonio Pasqualino in Palermo (*Museo Internazionale delle Marionette Antonio Pasqualino*). UNESCO has recently honored the Sicilian Puppet Theater as a "masterpiece of intangible heritage."

Many museums in Sicily are engaged in the preservation and appreciation of heritage. These include the Sicilian Ethnographic Museum in Palermo, founded by, and dedicated to, the anthropologist and ethnologist Giuseppe Pitrè, the House-Museum "Antonio Uccello" at Palazzolo Acreide in the province of Siracusa, and the Ibleo Museum of Art and Folk Traditions "Serafino Amabile Gustella" at Modica in the province of Ragusa. Some ceremonies, festivals, and celebrations are experiencing a revival, and the number of such commemorated festivities in Sicily has increased considerably. The confraternities, which were traditionally in charge of organizing festivals and ceremonies, have been revitalized and, in some cases, revived. Religious reasons have contributed to some revivals. Another important motivation is that a celebration represents for a community the acknowledgment of its own identity. Patterns of migration have often produced replicas of patron saints' festivals, which may be held in summer, when emigrants return to Sicily on vacation, as well as on the actual dates officially recognized by the church. In this way the festivals can retain their religious significance, while the replica events afford a focus for community identity.

BIBLIOGRAPHY

Bonanzinga, Sergio. 1992. *Forme sonore e spazio simbolico*. Palermo: Archivio delle tradizioni popolari siciliane—Folk Studio, n. 31–32.

———. 1993. Introduzione. In *Musiche popolari siciliane raccolte da Giacomo Meyerbeer*, edited by F. Bose. Palermo: Sellerio.

———. 1995. Etnografia musicale in Sicilia (1870–1941). In *Suoni e culture. Biblioteca dell'Archivio Etnomusicale Siciliano*, volume 1. Palermo: CIMS.

———. 1996. *I suoni delle feste. Musiche e canti, ritmi e richiami, acclamazioni e frastuoni di festa in Sicilia* (sound recording with booklet). Palermo: Folkstudio.

———. 2002–2004. Suoni e gesti voci della Pasqua in Sicilia. *Archivio Antropologico Mediterraneo* 5–7:181–190.

Buttitta, Antonino. 1957–1959. Cantastorie in Sicilia. Premessa e testi. *Annali del Museo Pitrè* 8–9:149–236.

———. 1961. *Cultura figurativa popolare in Sicilia*. Palermo: Flaccovio.

———. 1982. Introduzione. In *Le immagini devote del popolo siciliano* by G. Cocchiara. Palermo: Sellerio.

———, ed. 1990 (1988). *Le forme del lavoro. Mestieri tradizionali in Sicilia*. Palermo: Libreria Dante.

Buttitta, Ignazio E. 1992. *Feste dell'alloro in Sicilia*. Palermo: Archivio delle tradizioni popolari sicil-iane—Folk Studio, n. 29–30.

Cocchiara, Giuseppe. 1982 (1939). *Le immagini devote del popolo siciliano*. Palermo: Sellerio.

D'Agostino, Gabriella, ed. 1991. *Arte popolare in Sicilia. Le tecniche, i temi, i simboli*. Palermo: Flac-covio.

———. 1996. *Segni e simboli nell'arte popolare siciliana*. Palermo: Studi e materiali per la storia della cultura popolare—Associazione per la conservazione delle tradizioni popolari, n. 22.

———. 2002. *Da vicino e da lontano. Uomini e cose di Sicilia*. Palermo: Sellerio.

D'Anna, Giuseppe. 1993. *Bibliografia degli scritti di Giuseppe Pitrè*. Roma: Bulzoni.

Giallombardo, Fatima. 1981. *La festa di San Giuseppe in Sicilia. 1*. Palermo: Archivio delle tradizioni popolari siciliane—Folk Studio, n. 5.

———. 1990. *La festa di San Giuseppe in Sicilia. 2. L'Area del Trapanese*. Palermo: Archivio delle tradizioni popolari siciliane—Folk Studio, n. 23.

———. 2003. *La tavola l'altare la strada. Scenari del cibo in Sicilia*. Palermo: Sellerio.

Guggino, Elsa. 1974. Canti di lavoro in Sicilia. In *Demologia e folklore. Studi in memoria di Giuseppe Cocchiara*. Palermo: Flaccovio.

———. 1980. *I canti degli orbi. I Cantastorie ciechi a Palermo*. Palermo: Archivio delle tradizioni popolari siciliane—Folk Studio, n. 4.

———. 1986. *Un pezzo di terra di cielo. L'esperienza magica della malattia in Sicilia*. Palermo: Sellerio.

———. 1993. *Il corpo è fatto di sillabe. Figure di maghi in Sicilia*. Palermo: Sellerio.

———. 2004. *I canti e la magia*. Palermo: Sellerio.

———, ed. 1978. *I carrettieri*. Palermo: Archivio delle tradizioni popolari siciliane—Folk Studio, n. 3.

Macchiarella, Ignazio. 1993. *I canti della Settimana Santa in Sicilia*. Palermo: Archivio delle tradizioni popolari siciliane—Folk Studio, n. 33–34.

Napoli, Alessandro. 2002. *Il racconto e i colori. "Storie" e "cartelli" dell'Opera dei Pupi catanese*. Palermo: Sellerio.

Pasqualino, Antonio. 1977. *L'opera dei pupi*. Palermo: Sellerio.

Ruffino, Giovanni. 1991. *Dialetto e dialetti di Sicilia*. Palermo: Cusl.

———. 1995. *I pani di Pasqua in Sicilia*. Palermo: Centro di Studi Filologici e Linguistici Siciliani ("Materiali e Ricerche," n. 2).

———. 2001. *Profili linguistici delle Regioni. Sicilia*. Roma-Bari: Laterza.

Gabriella D'Agostino (Translated from the Italian by Francesca M. Muccini)

Other Mediterranean Countries

GREECE

GEOGRAPHY AND HISTORY

The Greek word for "folklore" is *laografia*, a composite of the noun *laos*—meaning "nation, people"—and the verb *grafo*—meaning "to write." Throughout Greece several foundations and museums exist that focus on the research, preservation, study, and presentation of Greek folklore. They publish books and scholarly journals such as *Ethnographica*, issued by the Peloponnesian Folklore Foundation. Their activities include the production of recordings of Greek folk music, usually from field recordings. In the field of research, they try to add to the understanding of the ethnographic

Greece.

wealth of Greece. They promote traditional cultural events and ethnographic interests by the revival of folk rituals and customs.

Awash by the Mediterranean Sea, Greece serves as a crossroads for three continents: Europe to the west and north, Asia to the east, and northern African across the sea to the south. Its climate, typical of the Mediterranean, is marked by warm summers and relatively mild winters, though variations occur between the north and south and between the mainland and the islands. The Greek economy relies mostly on agriculture. Greece produces cereal grains (maize, millet, rice, and wheat), olive oil, grapes, wine, and tobacco. Its animal husbandry consists mostly of cattle, goats, and sheep. Settlements are compact, relatively permanent, densely populated, usually nucleated villages or towns. Local prefects and mayors rule them. Squares and neighborhoods constitute sociopolitical networks, where Greeks gather to socialize, discuss, and gossip.

ROOTS AND THEMES OF GREEK FOLKLORE

The performative character of Greek folklore varies depending upon age and gender. The traditional ritual protocol of group activities usually calls upon the participation of elderly men first, then younger men, followed by elderly women and then younger women, with children coming in last of all. In addition, different traditions exist for men, women, and children. Regionalism is strong in the country, as individual communities create and celebrate traditions that reflect their own understanding of "being Greek." Everything is local. However, the study of folklore developed as Greece was trying to establish itself as an independent nation after years of foreign domination by Slavs, Franks, and—for the longest period—Turks. Yet **nationalism** and regionalism do not compete as much as they inform each other. Traditional heritage and historical remembrance are often identical. Looking in from the outside, we might view the Greek people as simultaneously ancient and modern.

Greece has an extraordinarily ambiguous, complex historical relationship with the idea of Europe itself and, more generally, with the stereotyped entity commonly called "Western culture." Western Europe asks Greeks to be European, while lovers of Greek culture from elsewhere ask them to be their own ancient counterparts. Only in the early nineteenth century did Greece enter the modern world as an independent nation, freeing itself from 400 years of Turkish rule. What followed was a debate over what exactly it meant to be Greek.

The "father" of the Greek nation is an ancient, strong, heroic guy, something like a classical statue of Zeus, in white marble, with fine details and precise dimensions. Its "mother," on the other hand, seems relaxed, magical, erotic, a belly dancer in the blurred harem of fate. The father's image captures what Michael Herzfeld terms the "Hellenic thesis." This thesis, based on Western Europe's perception of ancient Greece, views modern Greek culture—especially folk culture—as the survival of ancient Greek ideals and denies Oriental influences. On the other hand, the "Romeic thesis" is represented by the mother's image, most characteristically exemplified by linguistic demoticism and reflecting the familiar self-image that Greeks entertain about themselves when conversing with each other.

Greece is symbolically both holy and polluted. It is holy in that it is the mythic ancestor of all European culture, and it is polluted by the taint of Turkish culture, a taint that late medieval and Renaissance Europe viewed as the embodiment of barbarism and evil. The history of European culture is permeated by references to its sacred roots in ancient Greece. In other words, as a modern nation-state, it encourages an identity with the West, which represses connections to all things stereotypically non-Greek, especially the Turkish and the female.

The early Greek folklorists saw their task as establishing a discipline based on the undeniable cultural continuity between the modern Greeks and their linguistic ancestors. Using folklore as the vehicle for political nationalism, Greek folklorists tried to define cultural identity. In this spirit the first students of modern Greek folklore demonstrated continuity in the Greekness of the inhabitants of Greece from antiquity to modern times. In the same sense, Greek folklore attempted not only to preserve a tradition but also to defend it against everybody who doubts its indissoluble unity with its ancient predecessors. Folklorists' ultimate goal was consolidation of a nation-state while creating a national discipline of folklore studies. Specific ideology was transmitted through literature, while philosophical nationalism was interpreted as patriotism. Oratory allowed no words of Turkish origin, for example. Instead, ancient Greek terms were used to express imported ideals (usually labeled as neoclassical purism). The folklorists supported the demotic Greek, the language of the people.

Today the ancient Greek tradition seems still to be very prominent. Television shows, games, and toys based upon ancient Greek mythical heroes are quite popular with children. Tourists from all over the world visit famous Greek antiquities and come to meet the marvelous ancient Greek world. "Modern" Greeks, however, still suffer a crisis of identity; as novelist Nikos Kazantzakis put it: "What has the double-descended modern Greek taken from his father, what from his mother? He is clever and shallow, with no metaphysical anxieties, and, yet, when he begins to sing, a universal grieving leaps up from his oriental bowels and breaks the crust of Greek logic."

Being Greek Orthodox is the secular lifestyle for most Greeks. Religiously based events, such as weddings, baptisms, and feast days, define many annual festivities lasting for days, even months, where folklore is being performed at its best. Many pagan elements become prevalent at those occasions, a very peculiar characteristic that can certainly be traced to the Greek past. For example, Hyacinth is an ancient Greek god who, when hit by Apollo's discus by mistake, was transformed into a flower. He is also a contemporary Christian saint, who in 98 C.E. was martyred for his love for Christ and who symbolizes eternal youth. Today, particularly on the island of Crete, his double-faced presence is celebrated on 3 July in something akin to a Greek Valentine's Day. Many rituals take place during Carnival, Easter time, and around 15 August (Feast of the Assumption of the Virgin Mary) as well as during the Christmas holidays. On 21 May, during the celebrations for St. Constantine and St. Helen in northern Greece, possessed participants walk on live coals.

In Greece, naming procedures are also religiously defined. Greeks get their first names by actually being baptized. "Name days" are more important celebrations than birthdays. Greeks traditionally carry religious names derived from those of saints. Other important categories of names are those related to ideals such as freedom and democracy or to ancient Greece (for example, Demosthenes and Socrates).

Superstitions are prevalent, though not dominant, in Greek culture. Particularly important is the evil eye. Both prayers and spells may keep it away. People carry or decorate their belongings with folk objects, usually in the shape of a blue eye, a pomegranate, or garlic, which they believe will protect them. To exorcize the evil eye, they spit three times.

Many herbs used as folk remedies grow on the Greek slopes and plains. Local drinks, usually white, alcoholic, distilled spirits such as the Cretan *raki* or the Macedonian *tsipuro*, are the best cure for sore throats, stomach trouble, and toothaches. In local markets one finds a variety of medicinal herbs, each one prescribed for different medical conditions. Bookstores sell books that explain their therapeutic properties.

The Greek language belongs to a sub-family of the Indo-European linguistic family. Regional dialects such as the Cypriot, the Pontic, and the Cretan exist as well as many varieties of folk speech. Predominant in the language are hand gestures and facial expressions. After all, Greek is a high-touch culture. Well known is the expression, "It's all Greek to me," which suggests the difficulty particularly of the ancient form of the Greek language.

MYTHS, LEGENDS, AND FOLKTALES

Ancient Greek mythology elicits universal admiration. Greek myths constitute core narratives of a larger ideological system set outside historical time. The Aesopian fables educate youth and are expected to mold their ethos and character. Myths about Greek gods and demigods are popular themes for even contemporary television shows and films worldwide.

At the same time, legends also prevail, as Greeks like to narrate them artfully in regular conversations to reflect many of the hopes, fears, and anxieties of our time. Older legends refer to episodes considered miraculous and bizarre, such as enclosing in the foundation of a bridge the master builder's wife in order to prevent the structure from crumbling. Common legends also refer to miraculous situations involving saints, such as specific Byzantine icons weeping.

Greek children grow up with not only myths and legends but also folktales. Telling them is traditionally the grandmother's task, the grandfather usually being the one to tell stories from the wars or the older times. Tales are related and received as fiction or fantasy. As is true of other cultures, famous tales from the international **repertoire** have been adopted by the Greeks and thus have obtained "Greek" **motifs** and patterned figures of speech.

"What walks on four legs in the morning, two legs at noon, and three legs in the evening?" The riddle posed to Oedipus by the Sphinx is perhaps the first wisdom question Greeks have an account of. In Greece riddles are used to educate youth, who particularly enjoy testing each other's abilities in answering them. Certainly, many riddles are blended into folk narratives as well.

PROVERBS AND JOKES

In addition, proverbial speech is very common in Greece. On specific occasions such as in the village of Olympus on the island of Karpathos, everyday communication may be based on the exchange of such expressions. Often locals organize contests that test the inhabitants' abilities to stretch their improvisatory skills by composing and performing proverbs. In the Cretan village of Anoya, for example, a lively tradition of *madinada* (proverbial distich) contests, known as *kontaromahies*, which translates as "joust," occurs. Certain formulas, poetic devices, and rules are at play in these contests, and performers use those compositional strategies to gain authority and recognition.

Jokes take the form of fictional narratives and end in unpredictable and surprising outcomes for humorous effects. Greeks enjoy ethnic jokes, which may refer to their neighboring countries such as **Turkey** or to local communities such as jokes about Cretans and Pontics. Many such jokes are based on stereotypes. Joke-telling is an entertaining activity. Popular, too, are jokes that play with the etymology of specific Greek words.

MUSIC AND DANCE

Mythology places the birth of music and dance in Greece. A legend says that the Kourites, the ancient inhabitants of Crete, danced and played instruments loudly to cover the crying of the infant Zeus so that his father, Kronos, who ate his own children, could not find him. Moreover, Theseus, on his return from Crete, performed a dance with his companions that resembled the turns and the curves of a labyrinth. Even the famous shield of Achilles was, according to Homer, decorated with a scene from a feast at the palace of Knossos.

In Greece, music remains an important social activity in many rural communities. Music-making is still very much alive. Singing, playing instruments, and dancing are central activities. Elaborate collective rituals and celebrations punctuate the peasant calendar. Greek community feasts such as weddings, baptisms, and saints' days belong to a category of events (*gledia*) that include dancing, drinking, singing, eating, talking, and, more generally, people in high spirits (*kefi*) who are willing to share these moments with others in their community. In those events, music, dance, and song constitute a triad. Thus, the researcher of Greek folk music should not observe only the music per se but also the lyrics of the songs and the dances that accompany them. As a result, music is not separated from dance and song in the Greek folk tradition.

Since the 1930s, many Greek and foreign researchers have investigated Greek songs. Some recorded and transcribed folksongs. Many recordings have also been, and are still being, produced for public use. Among the first to distinguish folksongs into cycles for the purpose of easier study and presentation was Nikolaos Politis. In a 1914 book he categorizes them as follows: historical, *kleftika* (of the klephts, or brigands), *akritika* (of the borders), *paraloges* (Byzantine ballads), love songs, bridal songs, lullabies, carols, of the exile, *mirologia* (mourning songs), songs of the netherworld and the angel of death, gnomic, work and *vlahika* (rural songs), and *perigelastika* (mocking) songs.

As for Greek folk music, one could certainly distinguish between the music of the mainland and the music of the islands. Within those two very broad zones, however, many more distinctions exist. So, for instance, one may talk of the music of the island of Crete and within it distinguish between a western and an eastern musical style. In all cases, however, the functions of folk music are similar: to be performed during traditional, ritual contexts and for the community.

Throughout Greece playing instruments is an almost exclusively male activity (as mourning is strictly female). In different parts of Greece we find different instruments. The basic instrumental music family consists of two components, the melodic and the rhythmic. Traditionally, the most popular Greek wind instruments are the *klarino* (type of clarinet), the *gaida* (type of bagpipe), and the *zournas*. String instruments are the *laouto* (type of lute), the *violi* (violin), the *lira* (different from the lyre, three-stringed), and the *kanonaki* and the *santouri* (plucked and struck zithers, respectively). Usually, the *defi* (tambourine) and the *daouli* (two-headed drums) are used as percussion. Depending on the part of Greece, different combinations of the above create various folk music idioms.

The third member of the triad, dancing, is an integral part of Greek life. An event may not be considered proper if dance is not a basic component. During those events dancing improvisation may follow the music, but song lyrics might provoke a dancer's emotions. Spectacular dancing figures carry meaning relating to something communal or personal. Everyone who dances holds a specific role as part of the group to which she or he belongs. She or he speaks through dancing and without words. Greek dances are mostly taught informally, through observation and participation. Usually, before each dance takes place during a feast, the person who expects to lead it throws a bill or two in front of the musicians. One of the musicians, basically the leader of the group, picks up this money. This practice is not considered payment. It is called "gifting money" for "ordering a dance." Most of the time only men are culturally allowed to do that, and every man has to do that in order to represent his name, family, and clan.

Through these music and dance events, both public and social in nature, the people of Greece articulate their community beliefs, while also representing their identity. Because music and dance are languages, forms of communication through which Greek people express ideas about their culture and society, their analysis provides another mode through which to understand social processes.

FOOD AND CELEBRATIONS

We listen to Greek music, and we see Greek dances. At the same time, we taste drinks and foods from the traditional Cretan cuisine. CNN promotes the Cretan diet through documentaries that show how Greeks, especially Cretans, enjoy lengthy life spans (a product of the well-known "Mediterranean diet"). Musicians in Crete perform live music in combination with freshly made local variations of traditional foods at various events that take place outdoors during the summer and indoors during the winter.

Specific foods such as bread, a symbol of continuity and healthy life, mark Greek events. Specific sweet breads are made during Easter (*tsoureki*) and Christmastime (*vasilopita*). At weddings in Crete, round bread (*koulouri*) is "embroidered" to look like a traditional piece of cloth. It is as important and as necessary for life as weddings are. Serving massive amounts of meat and other food at feasts signifies health and prosperity.

Festivals and celebrations may as well be wine feasts. At the sounds of traditional music, Greeks open their wine barrels to honor saints (such as St. George the Inebriant) or merely to socialize and have fun. Women from the village offer Greek cuisine, and specialists talk about wine and its history. The many wine presses found by archeologists point to the presence of wine throughout Greek civilization.

Famous all over Greece are wedding feasts, because marriage is considered of supreme value, a necessary condition of procreation and therefore of the continuation of life and, in a more metaphysical sense, of the self through the perpetuation of family names and the persons of the parents. All in all, Greek weddings are arenas within which aspects of social identity are represented and reflected. They are "big" and "fat." The preparations for these events start months before the specific day of the actual religious wedding ceremony. An important custom in traditional weddings is the dowry exchange and the decoration with money of the couple's soon-to-be marriage bed. Mothers either mourn in anticipation of separation from their daughters or perform wedding songs.

Greek costumes, mostly worn today by men and women on special occasions, are very elaborate. They vary from place to place, even within a specific region. Their basic colors are black, red, and white. A visit to the museum of the history of the Greek costume (Lyceum of the Greek Women) is worthwhile. Kerchiefs and scarves as well as jewelry, usually gold coins, spread all over the female chest are important paraphernalia.

SPORTS AND GAMES

In 776 B.C.E., Hercules, the older Kouritis, moved to Olympia, where he began the first Olympic Games. (According to others, the originator was Pelops, from whom Peloponnese takes its name.) The modern Olympic Games, however, date from 1896. The Olympic folk culture consists of various folk items such as logos, advertisements, and songs that are especially designed to please the participants and spectators. More importantly, they wish to emphasize the inherent Greekness of the sporting ideal. Delegates to the contemporary games are two children, Phoebus and Athena, the god of music and light and the goddess of wisdom and protector of the city of Athens. An ancient Greek doll inspired the creation of the 2004 mascots, since dolls have been perhaps the most desirable toys since antiquity. In them we see two children who, through the joy of playing, reveal that the real value of participating in the games is the sole enjoyment of competition, not necessarily winning. Two siblings, a boy and a girl, are the ambassadors of collaboration, equality, and brotherhood.

Children in rural Greece still play on the streets, devising games based on the materials they have at their disposal: perhaps tree branches, balls, and rope. They enjoy playing pranks and impersonating legendary heroes. Often they perform songs— vocally only—most of which are associated with a specific game such as finding a hidden ring or kerchief. Teasing is always at the center of their activities, which also include competitions and acting.

They favor *Karagiozis*, a form of shadow theater usually performed in open-air theaters on large white screens erected at the far side of the place, overhung by the dark blue sky and the shadows of trees. Often a small orchestra of musicians sits in front of the screen. Among them is the singer who is going to perform folk poetry and songs. In some cases, though, the singer and the puppet player are the same person. The puppets used in *Karagiozis* are usually made from animal skin and represent figures of history and romance, of nature and fantasy. They are designed, constructed, and mechanically operated by human beings. Like the stage upon which they perform, they are usually limited in size but not in imaginative quality. They can be anything their creator desires: people, animals, pieces of furniture, rocks, or legendary monsters. Thus, objects become animated on the stage as well. Puppets tend to be far more plausible than human actors, costumed and made up to represent them. Today the repertory of *Karagiozis* is being renewed. It brings children into contact with tradition. As folk comedy, *Karagiozis* portrays the essence of life. The performers express themselves with originality. They create their own stories and characters upon folk roots. They mingle elements of tradition with those of their era. Occasionally, at the Children's Museum in Athens, Plaka, one can experience bits of such performances.

ARTS, CRAFTS, AND ARCHITECTURE

Greek folk architectural style depends on landscape, so there are island and mainland, sea and mountain house styles. White and blue are the prominent colors of island houses, while contours of ocher, claret, and brown dominate the mainland. Roofs may be tile-red, traditionally with a chimney. Island houses are whitewashed, while those in the mountains are paved with stones. Cobblestone roads are a marvel in both the Aegean and mainland Greece. Iron doors in bright colors, such as the ones at the village of Koskinou on Rhodes, are remarkable. So also are Greek pottery and woodcraft products. Churches exist everywhere in Greece. On the mainland the Byzantine architectural style—that is, basilica with cupola—is prominent. Inside these churches we find many decorations and Byzantine iconography. On the islands churches are plain, white buildings with a blue sea in the background and with a few icons and a candelabrum. Mainly in Thrace, Crete, and the islands across the western coast of Turkey, many examples of Islamic architecture exist. On the Ionian islands, Crete and Rhodes, on the other hand, are many Venetian-style buildings. The maritime provinces have ports of specific character, functioning as poles for socializing and strolls.

Natural threads, used in the making and elaborating of regional costumes and household textiles (such as carpets, blankets, and curtains), are produced in Greece. Young girls learn orally, often through their grandmothers, how to embroider and knit. Laces decorate many households. Knowing how to make them is considered a very special artistry. Looms may be used in specific regions such as Cretan mountain villages.

CHALLENGES OF THE MODERN WORLD

In Greece one comes across villagers relaxing in chairs in front of picturesque coffee-houses, whiling away their time, enjoying their coffee at their own pace. Between fingers calloused from years of farmwork, they click their worry beads (*komboloi*), ever faithful companions through the years. Today Greek folklore is circulated, for instance, through folksong books with accompanying CDs. It is also officially taught by folk dance troupes (such as the Lyceum of the Greek Women) and other cultural associations. In addition, folklore is produced for outside consumption. Representations of folk events take place for tourists. Greek immigrants abroad perform their own folklore. Multi-media folk productions are also taking place, such as a CD-ROM created for the Music Library by Lilian Voudouri on Greek folk music instruments, available to schools and educational institutions.

Yet the identity question is still prominent for Greeks. The dream of a unified Europe, which started officially in 1980, finds Greeks once more puzzled and confused. The present era of globalization very intensively asks Greeks for a brave look into the mirror, where they are supposed to see not only the heroes of the past but the present reality.

STUDIES OF GREEK FOLKLORE

Resources in Greek folklore are rich and varied. A look through the journal *Laografia* and at articles published in the journal of the Modern Greek Society Association (MGSA) affords a sense of the scope of available materials. Video and audio sources are also extensive. A good example of videotapes on Greek folk dance is *I Hori tou Topou Mas* (The Dances of Our Country), produced by Dora Stratou. Among the many recordings of Greek folk music, especially noteworthy are the archival resources and official radio broadcasts presenting various traditional Greek music styles. A good example is *Cretan Traditional Music: Radio Broadcasts* (1996). The Academy of Athens has a Web page worth browsing (www.academy ofathens.gr), and several Greek folklore museums can also be found on-line, for example, www.culture.gr/2/21/toc/hist_mus.html.

BIBLIOGRAPHY

Anoyanakis, Fivos. 1991 (1976). *Greek Folk Music Instruments*. Melisa: Athens.

Baud-Bovy, Samuel. 1984. *Dokimio yia to Elliniko Tragudi* (Essay for the Greek Folksong). Nafplio: Peloponnisiako Idrima.

Beaton, Roderick. 1980. *Folk Poetry of Modern Greece*. Cambridge: Cambridge University Press.

Cowan, Jane. 1990. *Dance and the Body Politics in Northern Greece*. Princeton, NJ: Princeton University Press.

———. 2000. Greece. In *The Garland Encyclopedia of World Music*, edited by Tim Rice, James Porter, and Chris Goertzen. New York: Garland. 2:1007–1032.

Dimou, Nikos. 1997. *Apoloyia enos Anthelina* (Apology of an Anti-Hellene). Athens: Opera.

Dubisch, J., ed. 1986. *Gender and Power in Rural Greece*. Princeton, NJ: Princeton University Press.

Herzfeld, Michael. 1982. *Ours Once More: Folklore, Ideology and the Making of Modern Greece*. Austin: University of Texas Press.

―――. 1987. *Anthropology through the Looking-Glass: Critical Ethnography in the Margins of Europe*. Cambridge: Cambridge University Press.

Holst-Warhaft, Gail. 2000. Dance; Music. In *Greece in Modern Times: An Annotated Bibliography of Works Published in English in Twenty-Two Academic Disciplines during the Twentieth Century*, edited by Stratos E. Constantinidis. Lanham, MD: Scarecrow Press. 61–68, 241–243.

Kazantzakis, Nikos. 1969. *Taxidevontas: Italia, Egyptos, Sina, Ierusalim, Kipros, O Morias* (Traveling: Italy, Egypt, Jerusalem, Cyprus, Morias). 6th edition. Athens: Ekdosis El. Kazantzaki.

Kochilas, Diane. 2001. *The Glorious Foods of Greece*. New York: HarperCollins.

Lambraki, Myrsini. 2001. *Herbs, Greens, Fruit: The Key to the Mediterranean Diet*. Iraklio: MKS Metaxaraki Advertising.

Loukatos, Dimitrios. 1977. *Introduction to Greek Folklore*. Athens: MIET (Educational Foundation, National Bank of Greece).

Myrsiades, Linda Suny. 1988. *The Karagiozis Heroic Performance in Greek Shadow Theater*. Hanover, NH: University Press of New England.

Politis, Nikolaos. 1914. *Ekloye apo ta Traghoudhia tou Ellinikou Laou* (Some Songs of the Greek People). Athens: Estia.

Psilakes, Maria, and Nikos Psilakes. 1995. *Cretan Cooking: The Miracle of the Cretan Diet*. Iraklio: Karmanor.

Raftis, Alkis. 1995. *Encyclopedia of Greek Dance*. Athens: Theater of Dora Stratou.

Sifounakis, Nikos. 1998. *Cobblestone Roads of the Aegean and Mainland*. Athens: Kastaniotis.

Slesin, Suzanne, Cliff Stafford, and Daniel Rozensztroch. 1988. *Greek Style*. New York: C. N. Potter.

Maria Hnaraki

MALTA

GEOGRAPHY AND HISTORY

The country of Malta is at the center of the Mediterranean Basin, a region composed of lands in Europe, Asia, and Africa that cluster around the Mediterranean inland sea. With a population of approximately 383,600 people, the three inhabited islands of the country are the island of Malta with a maximum length of only seventeen miles and ninety-five square miles of territory, Gozo with twenty-six square miles of territory, and Comino with barely one square mile. This means that Malta, though tiny, is one of the most densely populated countries anywhere. With much variety from locality to locality and many influences from throughout the Mediterranean, Malta is rich in contrasts. One of the few natural resources with which it is richly endowed is sandstone, which is the major building material throughout the nucleated settlements where the masses live.

Since many Maltese believe that their islands emerged early from the Mediterranean Sea and will one day soon be swallowed by it, it is not surprising that the Maltese tend to be proud and fatalistic. That much Maltese folklore shares elements with folklore from neighboring countries even across religious differences suggests that many of these similarities are very ancient, even pre-Christian.

Above the ground floor on many especially large mansions in Malta that date between the sixteenth and early eighteenth centuries are demonic-looking faces with bulging eyes and extended tongues that have been sculpted in sandstone in partial or full relief either into the gallery brackets or above the many entrances. Paul Cassar (1995) has theorized that these decorative, but grotesque, figures were perhaps intended to ward off a malevolent force called the evil eye, a belief that Maltese share with almost all peoples of their region. The evil eye is a malevolent spirit that one person can cast upon another or even upon animals, houses, or fields to cause harm. While it is believed that almost anyone can be victimized by the evil eye, children and pregnant women are among those believed to be particularly vulnerable. Coupled with this belief that one is under constant threat of being harmed by the evil eye is a trust in the efficacy of perpetual vigilance and certain charms, talismans, manual gestures, and devotional actions that can neutralize the potential harm. At sea, where Maltese frequently encounter danger, they hope that the pair of eyes with which they often decorate their boats, the so-called eyes of Osiris (a god originating in Egypt and Nubia), will offer them protection. Similarly, they find solace in the

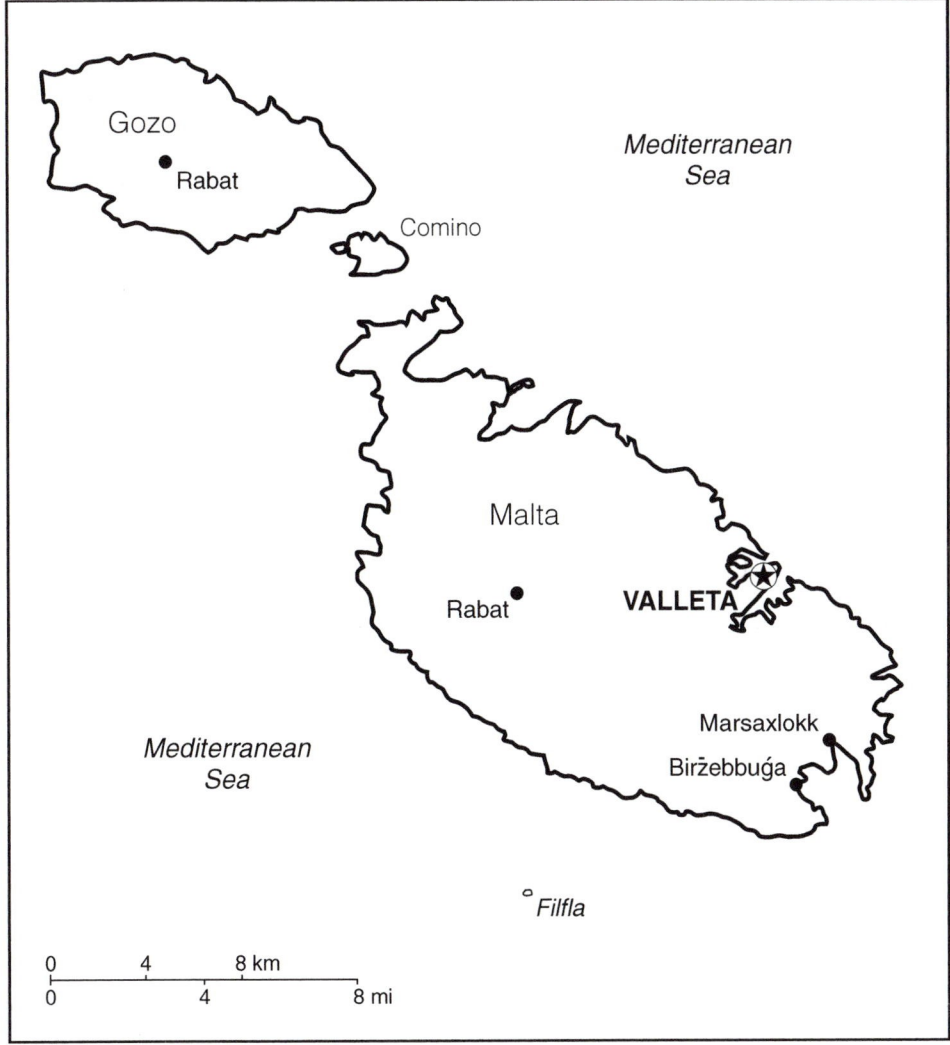

Malta.

fact that many Maltese churches have two clocks that are deliberately set to show different times, one to supply correct information and one to confuse the Devil.

Malta is home to some of the earliest megalithic monuments ever constructed, including many that even pre-date pyramid-building in Egypt. While the Maltese are very proud of this legacy, another legacy in which they manifest even more pride is biblically based. It emerges from the belief that in 59 or 60 C.E., St. Paul was shipwrecked in Malta while he was aboard a ship traveling from Alexandria to Rome. Catholicism is a core part of Maltese nationalism, and they take pride in the belief that it was via this fortuitous apostolic connection with St. Paul that Christianity first arrived in Malta.

Since Malta is located on the edge of southernmost Europe and was ruled for two and one-half centuries beginning in 1530 by a religious order of knights who waged battles with Muslims well after most other parts of Europe were no longer concerned with Crusades, Maltese folklore reflects an intense siege mentality, which is reinforced by strong identification with both Christianity and Europe. It is also reinforced through Maltese consciousness that Malta is a country in a region that has often known conflict. Materially, the siege mentality is reflected in the extraordinary fortifications surrounding key parts of the country that are masterpieces of Baroque military architecture. The Knights of St. John (also known as the Knights of Malta) were members of European royal families, and the fortifications they commissioned have counterparts in magnificent palaces, mansions, churches, and squares designed and constructed by master builders and town planners throughout the islands.

Before winning its independence from Britain in 1964, Malta was for long periods colonized by a number of peoples from Asia, Africa, and Europe, but those from Asia and Africa (including Phoenicians, Berbers, and Arabs) most influenced the Maltese language. Beginning in the 1800s, however, Italian and, to a much lesser degree, English have also been spoken in Malta. That tiny Malta was able to maintain a Semitic linguistic heritage long after being reclaimed by Indo-European-speaking rulers reflects both a strong sense of self-confidence and one way in which Malta is a microcosm of Mediterranean civilization.

LIFE-CYCLE CELEBRATIONS AND CUSTOMS

Each year in Malta, many special processions take place in fulfillment of religious vows. In the city of Senglea, for example, a procession with the statue of the Redeemer occurs on the first Sunday in June in keeping with a historic vow made by the people of this locality when long ago it was virtually the only place in Malta spared from the ravages of two cholera epidemics. In some processions, people endure great suffering (for example, by walking or crawling long distances without shoes) to manifest their religious devotion. Maltese in general devote much time to participating in religious events. Though both genders follow this pattern, expectations tend to be more demanding for females, and non-conformity by females can easily besmirch the reputation of an entire family.

The veneration of saints has an ancient history in Catholicism, and since saints and angels are typically associated with miracles and the ability to intervene for good, they play important roles in day-to-day life in Malta. Days associated with various saints are especially important in terms of how people conceptualize and refer to time, seasonality, and many patterns of behavior.

Being born on the days of some saints was considered lucky. A man born on St. Mary's Day in August was thought likely to become a jockey. But being born on days associated with other saints was deemed to carry liabilities. Despite being a major holiday, Christmas was traditionally considered an unlucky day on which to be born. Through the 1800s, it was believed by many that a person born on this day would annually be transformed into a frightful ghost and that the only way that relief could come would be if they sat up each night on 24 December counting the holes in a sieve.

In the town of Birgu (also known as Vittoriosa), some mothers even in the late 1900s used to pay the sexton to toll "a bell of thanksgiving" after the successful delivery of a child. Church bells also furnish important time indications in Malta and traditionally have been rung to announce various liturgical functions and sometimes to emphasize the most salient parts of these observances. When bells are used to call people to religious functions, they usually are rung a half hour earlier in rural areas since people require more time for traveling from their scattered farms. During most *festas*, celebrations associated with particular saints, bells are rung more often and more joyously than usual. The way bells ring to indicate the time of day is very different from the way they ring to announce a death.

Long ago, Maltese families reacted to the death of their members by hiring paid weepers (called *newwietra*) who, after a corpse had been placed on a stretcher or bier with a cushion full of laurel and orange leaves under its head, would accompany the procession from the church to the grave loudly lamenting while bagpipes or *zagg* played. Later they smashed flower pots against the ground, cut off a horse's tail, cut down trellis vines, and painted over windows and doors in black, while men ceased to shave for extended periods. Long after the paid beggars and weepers were no longer used, funeral cortèges continued to be noisy and emotional, and bagpipes were largely replaced by string and brass instruments.

During the early 1900s, some villagers reacted to death by completely removing the blinds and replacing them with sheets, while some families in villages and towns removed knockers and knobs from the front doors of their residences. Even after this last custom gradually began disappearing among the upper-class families and in the capital city of Valletta, some families attached a black crepe sash to their front door and lowered the curtains or blinds of the balcony windows.

Malta's rather "high-tech" culture of today no longer provides for these customs or for the processions of relatives and friends following behind sumptuous, horse-drawn hearses, the last such procession taking place in Gozo in the 1970s. In keeping with the central role of families in mortuary customs, however, bodies are usually washed and prepared for burial in homes rather than in public facilities. As is true in northern Africa, it is customary to make certain that a deceased person's eyes are closed in this process.

Maltese married couples consider becoming parents a great blessing, and folk belief holds that in the months of January, April, and August conception is easiest because "the blood" of both sexes is especially fertile. As late as World War I, Malta had a high infant mortality rate, and mothers in particular spent much time trying to maximize their chances of having successful births that would not be too difficult and that would allow children to prosper through childhood. In keeping with such concerns, some couples planned their weddings on autumn or winter days associated with particular saints (for example, St. Lucy's Day on 13 December or St. Ursula's Day on 21 October) in hopes that being married on such a day might bring heavy rain, a frequent predictor of an easy first birth. In contrast, some other mothers invoked the protection of particular saints (for instance, St. Blaise and St. Ludgarda) or made vows to do certain things in gratitude if various saints would assist them in having an easy or safe delivery. It was for this reason that many Maltese mothers after delivering children presented votive offerings in the form of paintings or items of infant clothing in thanksgiving; these are still on public display in many parts of Malta in chapels, churches, or other holy places. Some expectant mothers made special pilgrimages in hope of achieving the same ends while carrying around a particular statue or item that was considered especially blessed. It was even a custom for expectant mothers in the town of Naxxar to drink water containing powder made from the bones of St. Victor.

With varying degrees of efficacy, people in various societies sometimes use religious and various medicinal practices that are ancient and not necessarily scientific to protect themselves from sickness and other forces believed to be harmful. In Malta, for example, many people believe that egg whites can cure dysentery or that not consuming ice cream in winter is a way to lessen the likelihood of catching a cold. In addition, they sometimes place graffiti on the walls of churches to request protection from danger or to express thanksgiving for having avoided a misfortune. Over time, not only do beliefs having to do with illness change, but normative patterns having to do with dress also change.

An item of female clothing that ceased to be worn even by elderly women belonging to some religiously conservative groups in the mid-1900s was the *faldetta*. Usually in black but occasionally in dark blue or even white for weddings, the *faldetta* was a very large head covering made of satin or silk, stiffened with whalebones, which hid much of a woman's face, especially from the sides. Similar customs whereby females in various degrees hide their faces have a long history in the Mediterranean Basin.

Social Structure

Maltese reference seasons not only by their formal secular names but also by religious names in terms of various winds and rainfall that occur seasonally and also in terms of the days that are associated with saints at these various times. As statues of St. Bartholomew usually show him holding keys and his feast day on 24 August occurs about the time when the rainy season begins, a Maltese proverb states that St. Bartholomew holds the keys to the rainy season. Maltese tend to retire for a long siesta in the middle of the day, and commercial activities are more restricted on Sundays than on other days. During the Lenten period, festive occasions, including weddings, are not held. Moreover, on Good Friday, cinemas are generally closed.

As only minimal religious diversity exists in Malta, it has been traditional in folklore to equate non-Christians with infidels. Because Malta is located on the extreme margins of Europe and experienced a relatively long and late occupation by Muslims that left a strong linguistic legacy, the Maltese tend to be among the most militantly Christian and European, even by standards current elsewhere in Europe. Malta has the highest number of religious specialists (priests and nuns) per capita of any country classified as a part of the European Continent, and these specialists have a tremendous influence in society. Additionally, numerous para-religious groups exist in Malta.

Although a new family law approved in 1993 has leveled the playing field for males and females, it has been traditional to consider females as inferior to males in status. According to one Maltese proverb, "Seven women in their right senses are surpassed by a mad man." Despite the recent emphasis on the legal equation of motherhood and fatherhood, children are traditionally considered to be the wards of the mother in the sense that she has a greater responsibility for their day-to-day raising.

A significant degree of segregation in schools and in adulthood separates males and females in public. Even in churches, males tend to have more options to sit where they wish and to visit certain sacred areas of churches than do females. A long tradition has women leaving the workforce when they marry. As in many societies, a double sexual standard is operative, with more restrictions imposed on females. Since the use of contraception is illegal, women fear becoming pregnant before marriage.

It was once customary in Malta for a father to display a pot containing basil on a ledge outside his home to indicate that he had a daughter for whom he wished to find a husband. Well into the late twentieth century, it was not uncommon for some families to employ marriage brokers to improve their chances of contracting good marriages. The best months for a wedding were considered to be January, April, and August (the last two ironically since there was almost never rain despite the belief that a rainy wedding day meant an easy first delivery). A marriage is considered a relationship between two families as well as between two spouses. Married couples typically have especially frequent contact with the relatives on the wife's side.

RELIGION

When one thinks of church in Malta, one thinks primarily of the Roman Catholic Church, to which approximately 98 percent of all Maltese belong. As neither state nor church allows divorce, marriage is undertaken with great seriousness. Traditionally, marriages require that the families of the wives furnish them with dowries, and families are not shy about displaying items in bridal dowries in order to enhance family status.

As in other status-conscious Mediterranean societies, families are much concerned about honor, shame, and saving face, and gossip is widely used as a means of social control. Though of lesser importance, social avoidance is also used in this way. Homes are not considered public gathering places for casual visiting, and problems within families are generally dealt with in private.

In Malta, a locality is largely recognized as such by its religious status, and no locality of significance is without a number of churches and chapels, the most important of which is typically the parish church. When most Maltese think of the history

A crowd gathers for a *festa* in Malta. Each town or village church in Malta is dedicated to a saint. During *festa* season, each village holds a five-day festival for its saint, culminating in a feast day on which a statue of the saint is carried about the streets. (© Paul Almasy/CORBIS)

of a locality, they reflect largely upon its history as a parish. Similarly, pride in one's locality is largely manifested in the extent to which one supports the parish church and pays homage to its patron saint.

A *festa* consists of a series of activities and performances associated with the celebration of the feast day of a particular saint, and many include festive as well as somber elements that are strictly religious in tone and purpose. Although a few *festa* commemorations are celebrated at the same time nationwide, the vast majority are parish commemorations planned and carried out in a spirit that is both devotional and competitive as compared with that of other parishes. Special religious services, the decoration of churches, special ringing of church bells, parading statues, cleaning houses, decorating streets, good band music, and displays involving fireworks and confetti are important elements in a typical *festa* commemoration. Even male members of para-religious confraternities with origins that go back to the Middle Ages often march in uniforms during *festa* processions.

While the ways that these events are organized can differ considerably depending on the occasion, the locality, and the season, most parish *festas* are periods when it is almost obligatory for relatives and friends associated with the place where a *festa* is held to come together. The principal *festa* in Floriana is the feast of St. Publius and is celebrated in spring. In Siggiewi, by contrast, the patron saint is St. Nicholas, whose feast day is in December. Since December is a rainy and somewhat cold season in Malta, however, the people of Siggiewi celebrate his feast in June and hold only small-scale December festivities in his honor. In addition to the principal *festa* of every parish, it is common for various parishes also to sponsor a number of secondary *festas* annually.

FOOD

The *lampuki* (or dolphin fish) is extremely popular, and its preparation for eating has an impact on Maltese culinary traditions. Apart from the fact that this fish is delicious, it has long been a Christian symbol. For some the dolphin symbolizes resurrection, salvation, and the bearer of souls across water to Heaven. The doors of many houses use a brass fixture in the form of a dolphin that is always kept brightly polished.

Rabbit stew is the national dish of Malta and is often served with pasta of many types. A Paschal lamb, symbolic of Christ, is for many people a favorite food at Easter. The Maltese consume bread in large quantities and many varieties. Before cutting a new loaf, some Maltese used to kiss it and make the sign of the Cross on it with the knife, thereby emphasizing its association with the Holy Mass and its central role in the local diet. Winemaking from local grapes is as old as history in Malta.

It was common for shepherds to lead their goats and sheep from home to home where they could be milked and the fresh milk sold on the spot. Maltese fever and some other illnesses finally caused this custom to be outlawed. Beekeeping is an ancient activity, and many scholars theorize that Malta gets its name from a word that means honey. Wax from beehives has long been used to make candles for churches as well as for homes.

MALTESE CROSS

The Maltese Cross is associated with the Knights of St. John (also known as the "Hospitallers of St. John of Jerusalem" or simply as the "Knights of Malta"). This Cross's eight points are said to symbolize the eight Beatitudes and their associated obligations. The Order of St. John ran hostels and hospitals for Christian pilgrims to Jerusalem before the Crusades.

The flower *Lychnis chalcedonica* is also known as a Maltese Cross or Jerusalem Cross because of the arrangement of the petals in the shape of the Cross adopted by the Knights of Malta. All Saints' Day is a time when Maltese like to decorate graves with fresh flowers. However, they so strongly associate the chrysanthemum with funerals and All Saints' Day that they generally do not like to keep it indoors—a common European avoidance even as far away as Paris.

MUSIC

For centuries after the Berbers and Arabs were no longer present in large numbers, Maltese peasants cultivated and kept alive a musical genre known as *ghana*. It focuses on topics ranging from historical sagas to recent happenings, love, social comedy, politics, relationships, and so on. *Fatti, kanzunetti,* and *makkjetti* are pre-composed songs. *Spirtu pront,* sung in quatrains, is extemporaneous singing, performed by two or more singers who cleverly compose their lyrics on the spur of the moment, often with double and triple entendres so as to challenge other singers with subtle insults as they respond to each other's lyrics. This type of folksinging is made especially difficult because the second and fourth lines of the quatrains have to rhyme even as the words build on a continuing theme. A singer of this type of music is called a *ghannej*, and the guitarists are called *kitarristi*.

Prejjem are instrumental performances in which one guitarist typically plays the lead and two other guitarists play the rhythm, one note lower than the lead guitarist. The most traditional instruments used to perform this genre of music include flute, open drum, bagpipes, guitar, and *zufzafa* or friction drum, a sort of drone instrument consisting of a reed that passes through a membrane stretched over an open drum. On the friction drum the player wets his fingers and rubs the reed to produce a special sound. In bars where women concerned about their reputations never venture, women sometimes sing an impromptu, ancient type of folk music called *bormliza* with lyrics similar to those of haiku poetry. With accompaniment supplied by two or three guitarists, this type of music requires a strong voice capable of sustaining long phrases. When occasionally performed by a male, *bormliza* must be sung in a very high register.

OTHER CUSTOMS AND PRACTICES

As in most societies, Maltese tend to idealize their culture and history. For example, Maltese tend without historical justification to view Malta's participation in piracy and slavery as less lengthy than that of its Muslim neighbors. Maltese folklore is particularly rich in proverbs, many of which have parallels in other Mediterranean societies. Nicknames of two types have been used over at least several centuries in Malta, some inherited through the father and applied to all his offspring and some attributed to a particular person. While some of these names are humorous or even neutral, others are insulting ways of demeaning others through verbal aggression. One of the most frequent exclamations that one hears in Malta is "Madonna!"

The small size of Malta presents few opportunities for hunting except for birds and rabbits. However, hunting is surrounded by much ritual and ceremony. Almost 6 million birds are killed or netted each year, and in the rustic town of Siggiewi, for example, a special mass is celebrated as early as 2:45 A.M. for hunters. Though many Maltese raise rabbits for food domestically, others hunt them with ferrets and dogs.

It is not uncommon in some parts of Malta to see a diapered horse pulling a fancy carriage known as a *karozzin* with tourists as passengers. In contrast, mules and donkeys are in more frequent use for hawking and for transporting farmers between their homes and fields.

A festive boat race pits teams of racers from cities bordering Malta's historic Grand Harbor against each other. This regatta takes place annually on 8 September. In addition to competition among localities, it involves fireworks, band marches, and much merrymaking—traditional elements in some greater or lesser degree present on most holidays in Malta. With a past history of sometimes vying with each other to influence public celebrations, both church and state are much involved in ceremonies that take place on this national holiday when the Regatta, a secular competition, takes place. From the perspective of the church, this day is Il-Bambina or the feast day of Our Lady of Victory. Both government and church recognize this most important holiday as commemorating the time in 1565 when Malta successfully defended itself against a major Turkish aggression called the Great Siege. Expressing national pride and thanksgiving for this victory of tiny Christian Malta against a giant Muslim aggressor, officials lay wreaths at the monument in Great Siege Square. Emphasizing this contest between good and evil, parades that take place on this occasion depict Malta's Turkish opponents by people who wear masks that are unrealistically dark, though in reality Maltese and Turks are not much different in complexion.

Among the non-elite adult masses, traditional leisure activities for men include participating in band clubs, visiting bars, boating, promenading, chatting in a church piazza, and playing soccer, darts, draughts (i.e., checkers), dominos, or *brilli*. Tending to have smaller non-kin networks than men, women spend more time with family members and on domestic chores, which for some include multiple shopping trips and church visits daily. It has been traditional for many women to sew, weave, knit, promenade, and play *tombla* (also known as bingo or "*housie housie*"). Occasionally, women even go on a *xalata*, for which they hire a bus and guitarist for a picnic outing where they sing and entertain each other.

Though the country has no rivers and few trees and sometimes suffers from periodic droughts, its agreeable climate, many beaches, friendly people, and vast tourist infrastructure make it appealing to visitors. Four types of globalization impact Malta significantly. One derives from the centrality of its location and multiplicity of past colonial influences. A second is that a long history of emigration means that more people of Maltese heritage live abroad than in Malta. A third is tourism, which is the single most important economic resource and annually brings into the islands an overseas population in excess of its residents. A fourth influence comes through Malta's membership in the Commonwealth and numerous Mediterranean organizations and most recently its admission into the European Community. For this small country to profit from globalization while protecting the integrity of its indigenous language, traditions, and values is a continuing challenge.

STUDIES OF MALTESE FOLKLORE

General resources on Maltese folklore include two periodicals: *Maltese Folklore Review* (1962–present) and *Melita Historica* (1952–present). The Gharb Folklore Museum (located at Gharb on Gozo in Malta) is another important resource.

BIBLIOGRAPHY

Aquilina, Joseph. 1972. *A Comparative Dictionary of Maltese Proverbs*. Msida, Malta: Royal University of Malta.

Boissevain, Jeremy F. 1969a. *Hal-Farrug: A Village in Malta*. New York: Holt, Rinehart and Winston.

———. 1969b. *Saints and Fireworks: Religion and Politics in Rural Malta*. London: Athlone Press of the University of London.

Camenzuli, Anthony. 2002. Defamatory Nicknames and Insult in Late Eighteenth-Century Malta: 1771–1798. *Melita Historica* 13:319–327.

Camilleri, George. 1992. *Realms of Fantasy: Folktales from Gozo*. Victoria, Malta: Gozo Press.

Cassar, Paul. 1995. The Tongue Symbol in Maltese Architecture to Ward Off the Evil Eye. *Melita Historica* 11:337–346.

Cassar Pullicino, Guze. 1966. Notes for a History of Maltese Costume. *Maltese Folklore Review* 1:149–225.

Cassar Pullicino, Guze, and Charles Camilleri. 1998. *Maltese Oral Poetry and Folk Music*. Msida, Malta: Malta University Publishers.

Cassar Pullicino, Joseph. 1992. *Studies in Maltese Folklore*. Msida, Malta: Malta University Press.

Cremona, Anton. 1973. Death, Mourning and Funeral Customs. *Maltese Folklore Review* 1: 301–304.

Galley, Micheline, ed. 1994. *Maria Calleja's Gozo*. Logan: Utah State University Press.

Goodwin, Stefan. 2001. Malta. In *Countries and Their Cultures*, edited by Melvin Ember and Carol Ember. New York: Macmillan Reference USA. 3:1400–1407.

———. 2002. *Malta, Mediterranean Bridge*. Westport, CT: Bergin and Garvey.

McLeod, Norma, and Marcia Herndon. 1975. The Bormiliza, Maltese Folksong Style, and Women. In *Women and Folklore: Images and Genres*, edited by Claire R. Farrer. Austin: University of Texas Press. 81–100.

Mitchell, Jon P. 2002. The Devil, Satanism and the Evil Eye in Contemporary Malta. In *Powers of Good and Evil: Social Transformations and Popular Belief*, edited by Paul Clough and Jon P. Mitchell. Oxford: Berghahn Books. 77–103.

Mizzi, Sibyl O. Reilly. 1981. Women in Senglea: The Changing Role of Urban, Working-Class Women in Malta. Diss., State University of New York at Stony Brook.

Wettinger, Godfrey. 1980. Honour and Shame in the Late Fifteenth Century Malta. *Melita Historica* 8:65–77.

Wilhelmsen, Finn. 1976. Marsaxlokk: An Ethnography of a Maltese Fishing Village. Diss., Wayne State University.

Zarb, Tarcisio. 1998. *Folklore of an Island: Maltese Threshold Customs*. San Gwann, Malta: Publishers Enterprises Group.

Stefan Goodwin

Cumulative Index

1: Topics & Themes, Africa, Australia & Oceania
2: Southeast Asia & India, Central & East Asia, Middle East
3: Europe
4: North & South America

Aarne, Antti, **1:**23, 94

Abaìo feast, **3:**474

Abantu Bandi ne Fikolwe Fyandi (My People and My Ancestors), **1:**235

Abanyole, **1:**123–131; drama, music, poetry, **1:**127–130; geography and history, **1:**123; song and dance, **1:**125–127; stories and tales, **1:**123–125; studies of Abanyole folklore, **1:**130

Abesalom and Eteri legend (Georgia), **3:**358

Aborigines. *See* Australian Aborigines

Abrahams, Roger, **1:**29, 67

Abu El-Abed stories and jokes (Lebanon), **2:**392–394

Abu Nuwas (Swahili), **1:**155

Acacia Seek Women's Ceremony (Australian Aborigines), **1:**297

Academia Mexicana de Folklore, **4:**280

Accouche, Samuel, **1:**149

Acculturation, **1:**24, 65

Achebe, Chinua, **1:**195

Achulean culture, **1:**194

Adaptation and modernization, **1:**52

Adenaike, Tayo, **1:**201

Adriatic cultural zone, Croatia. *See* Croatia, Littoral

Advent (Austria), **3:**252

Adventure tales: Croatia, **3:**347; Cuba, **4:**313; Guam, **1:**335–336; Ijo, **1:**206; Ireland, **3:**29; Lakota, **4:**71; Malay, **2:**143; Nez Perce, **4:**100, 103; Samoa, **1:**389; Sephardim, **3:**215; Spain, **3:**182, 183; Tuareg, **1:**115; Uttar Pradesh, **2:**90; Western Inuit and Yupik, **4:**135, 136

Aeneid (Virgil), **1:**44

Aesop's tales: Greece, **3:**496; Poland, **3:**381; Swahili, **1:**158

Afanas'ev, A.N., **3:**410, 418

Africa: Eastern Africa, **1:**123–162; map of peoples, **1:**102; North Africa, **1:**101–122; Southern Africa, **1:**234–276; Western and Central Africa, **1:**163–233

African Americans, **4:**143–156; architecture, **4:**153–154; arts and crafts, **4:**154–155; blues, rap, and hip-hop, **4:**152–153; diaspora of, **1:**19–20; dozens, **4:**150; field hollers and worksongs, **4:**151–152; proverbs, **4:**150–151; roots of African American folklore, **4:**143–145; rumor stories, **4:**151; slavery and spirituals, **4:**145–148; Suriname Maroons, **4:**237–238; toasts, **4:**148–150; trickster tales, **4:**148

Africanisms, **1:**20

African National Congress, **1:**269

Afro-Asiatic languages (Berber), **1:**101

Afro-Cuban myths, **4:**313–314

Afzelius, Arvid August, **3:**144

Agriculture and farming: Ainu, **2:**286–287, 291; Appalachia, **4:**163–164; Armenia, **2:**366; Bali, **2:**157–158; Bangladesh, **2:**99; Baule, **1:**163; Benin, **1:**170; Bhutan, **2:**106; Bihar, **2:**25, 29; Cherokee, **4:**9, 19; Ga, **1:**182; Gaddi, **2:**31; Haryana, **2:**39; Hawai'i, **1:**369; historical monument farms, **1:**59; Hopi, **4:**46–47; Iban, **2:**172; Ijo, **1:**204; Iroquois, **4:**51; Italy, **3:**452, 482; Japan, **2:**272, 279; Kaingang, **4:**194; Korea, **2:**303; living history farms, **1:**59; Lunda, **1:**234; Navajo, **4:**83; Nepal, **2:**113; New Caledonia, **1:**311; Palestine, **2:**404; Peru, **4:**200; Poland, **3:**387; Rarámuri, **4:**299; Russia, **3:**415–417; Semai, **2:**145–146; Seminole, **4:**111–112; Sertão, **4:**216–217; Shona, **1:**254–255; Shuar, **4:**222; Sibundoy, **4:**230; Sicily, **3:**482–483, 487, 490; Slovakia, **3:**287–289; Sri Lanka, **2:**124; Swahili, **1:**156; Taiwan, **2:**260; Tajik, **2:**329; Ukraine, **3:**445–446; Wolof, **1:**209, 210, 213; Zulu, **1:**270

Agron (King), **3:**322

Aguiló, Marià, **3:**195

Ahupaua'a (Hawai'i), **1:**376

AIDS: Shona, impact on, **1:**254–255; Tuareg, **1:**118, 120

Ainu (Japan), **2:**285–294; geography and history, **2:**285–287; modernization, challenges of, **2:**290–293; and nationalism, **1:**63; religious beliefs and rituals, **2:**287–290; studies of Ainu folklore, **2:**293–294

Aishwarya (Queen of Nepal), **2:**114

Ait Atta (Berber), **1:**106

Ait Menguellet, Lounis, **1:**108

Ajagaq game (Greenland), **3:**108

Aji dress, **1:**7–8

Akanandun tales (Karnataka), **2:**62

Akan cultural complex and Baule, **1:**163

Akan (Twi) language (Ga), **1:**181

Åkesson, Lynn, **3:**153

"Akono and Silimala" (Kaliai), **2:**183, 188

Alaska: Haida, **4:**38–39; Tlingit, **4:**117; Western Inuit and Yupik, **4:**128–131

Albania, **3:**320–330; arts, crafts, and architecture, **3:**329; calendars, **3:**326; cults, **3:**324; epics and ballads, **3:**326–327; fairy lore, proverbs, and riddles, **3:**328–329; geography and history, **3:**320–323; life-cycle rituals, **3:**325–326; music and dance, **3:**329; myths, legends, and folktales, **3:**323–325; religion and beliefs, **3:**322–323; songs, **3:**328

Alberti, Leon Battista, **3:**453

Alcheringa: Ethnopoetics (Tedlock & Rothenberg), **1:**31, 85

Alcover, Antoni M., **3:**195

Aleichem, Sholem, **3:**335, 336

Alevi Muslims (Turkey), **2:**430

Alexander I (Tsar), **3:**91

Alexander II (Tsar), **3:**410

Alexander the Great, **3:**370, 373

Alexis (Tsar), **3:**411

Alha epic tale (India), **2:**91

Alien and Sedition Acts (U.S. 1798), **1:**65

"Aligermaa" story (Mongol), **2:**256

Aligouran (Tuareg), **1:**115

Ali ibn Zayid stories (Yemen), **2:**439

Allegories. *See* Stories and tales

All Right, Vegemite! (Australia [British]), **1:**284

All Souls' Day: Ireland, **3:**34; Mexico, **4:**271; Piedmont and Val d'Aosta, **3:**477

al-Mahdi, Muhammad, **2:**415–416

Almqvist, Bo, **3:**149

Alp er Tunga legend (Turkey), **2:**432

Alphorn playing, **3:**312, 313

Alpine Carnival festivals (Piedmont and Val d'Aosta), **3:**373

Alpine influence: Croatia, Mountainous, **3:**343; Slovenia, **3:**300–301; Switzerland, **3:**308–312

"The Alps" (poem), **3:**310

Amades, Joan, **3:**196

A Mau a Mau (Hawai'i), **1:**376

"Amazons" (Nagaland), **2:**76

American Ethnologist (Robarchek), **2:**146–147

1: Topics & Themes, Africa, Australia & Oceania
2: Southeast Asia & India, Central & East Asia, Middle East
3: Europe
4: North & South America

American Folklife Preservation Act, 1:77

American Folklore Scholarship: A Dialogue of Dissent (Zumwalt), 1:13

American Folklore Society (AFS), 1:5, 6, 13, 30, 84

American Indians, 4:1–142

American Romani weddings, 3:401

Amirani (Georgia), 3:356

Amulets: Ashkenazim, 3:332, 338; Berber, 1:103–105, 107, 109; Denmark, 3:83; England, 3:1; Galicia, 3:203; Greenland, 3:109–110; Israel, 2:380; Kiribati, 1:343, 347; Kurds, 2:385; Russia, 3:412; Sephardim, 3:213; Tajik, 2:333; Tlingit, 4:118; Tuareg, 1:117, 119; Wolof, 1:211

"Analog" copies, 1:4–5

Analytical Survey of Anglo-American Traditional Erotica (Hoffmann), 1:56

Anansi (Jamaica), 4:341

Anatsui, El, 1:201

Ancestors and dead: Ainu, 2:288, 290, 291–292; Albania, 3:326, 327; Ashkenazim, 3:333, 334; Australian Aborigines, 1:293–294, 297, 298; Austria, 3:253–255; Bali, 2:159–160; Baule, 1:164; Benin, 1:174–176, 178; Brittany, 3:171, 172; Caribs of Dominica, 4:332–333; Catalan, 3:200; China, 2:213; Chinese living abroad, 2:235, 238–239; Duna, 2:166; Ecuador, 4:197–198; England, 3:1, 6, 13, 19; Ga, 1:181–182; Gaddi, 2:36; Galicia, 3:206–207; Germany, 3:269; Guam, 1:337–338; Haiti, 4:318; Hawai'i, 1:368; Hopi, 4:45–46; Hungary, 3:278; Iban, 2:173, 174–175; Igbo, 1:199; Ireland, 3:27, 34; Isaan, 2:132–134; Israel, 2:377, 379; Japan, 2:273, 276; Kadazandusun, 2:176; Kaingang, 4:194; Kaliai, 2:183–184, 186; Kashmir, 2:61; Khasi-Jaintia, 2:67, 72–73; Kiribati, 1:342; Korea, 2:296–298, 302, 303; Lunda, 1:235–236, 239; Madagascar, 1:139; Maluku, 2:202; Manchu, 2:250; Maroons of Jamaica, 4:339–340; Marquesas Islands, 1:380; Marshall Islands, 1:351; Mexico, 4:271–273; Nepal, 2:117; New Caledonia, 1:311, 312; Norway, 3:127, 128, 132; Orissa, 2:83, 87; Palestine, 2:407; Persia, 2:423; Piedmont and Val d'Aosta, 3:477; Poland, 3:385–386, 388; Roma, 3:401, 402, 406; Russia, 3:412, 413, 416; San, 1:242–246; Semai, 2:148; Shona, 1:251; Sibundoy, 4:230–231; Sicily, 3:490; Slovakia, 3:290; Tairora, 2:206, 207; Taiwan, 2:261, 266; Tlingit, 4:122–123; Ukraine, 3:440, 445; Vanuatu, 1:327, 328; Xavante, 4:247; Yoruba, 1:224, 225; Zande, 1:229, 232. *See also* Funerals and burials

Andersen, Hans Christian, 3:12, 85

Anderson, Benedict, 2:278

Anderson, Hugh, 1:285

Anderson, Walter, 3:196

Andes: Quechua, 4:208–209; Sibundoy, 4:229–230

Andrew, Saint, 3:206, 289, 349, 388

Anecdotes: Albania, 3:328, 329; Australia (British), 1:286, 287; Bali, 2:163; Cheyenne, 4:29; China, 2:222; England, 3:6, 9, 10, 13; Guam, 1:337, 339; Ireland, 3:38–39; Kashmir, 2:61; Latvia, 3:362; Macedonia, 3:372; Manchu, 2:248; Marshall Islands, 1:351; Maya, 4:259; Poland, 3:380, 392; Roma, 3:406; Russia, 3:420; Siberia, 2:322; Sicily, 3:491; Slovakia, 3:292; Tajik, 2:326; Turkey, 2:432; Uyghur, 2:339, 340; Wales, 3:75, 76–77; Western Inuit and Yupik, 4:133; Xhosa, 1:259, 260

Anglicanism in Australia, 1:278

Aniakor, Chike, 1:201

Animal dances: Cherokee, 4:15; Cheyenne, 4:28; Choctaw, 4:33

"The Animal Languages" (Mascarene Islands), 1:146

Animism and animal tales, 1:94; Ainu, 2:287–288; Australian Aborigines, 1:293–296; Bali, 2:152, 160; Bangladesh, 2:96, 103; Benin, 1:177; Caribs of Dominica, 4:332–333; Cherokee, 4:12–13; Cheyenne, 4:26–27; China, 2:213; Ga, 1:184; Guam, 1:335–336; Haiti, 4:320; Hawai'i, 1:368; Iban, 2:173; Igbo, 1:195–196; Iroquois, 4:55–56; Italy, 3:472; Lakota, 4:71–72; Lunda, 1:237–238; Malaita, 1:302; Malay, 2:142; Maya, 4:259; Mongol, 2:256–257; Nahua, 4:283–284; Nez Perce, 4:100–101; Nuer, 1:153; Palau, 1:360–361; Peru, 4:202; Poland, 3:381; Quechua, 4:210; Rarámuri, 4:301; Russia, 3:418–419; Samoa, 1:394; San, 1:242–247; Shona, 1:250, 253; Siberia, 2:316–319; Sibundoy, 4:232; Suriname Maroons, 4:238; Tlingit, 4:121–123; Trobriand Islands, 1:317; Western Inuit and Yupik, rapport with, 4:134; Wolof, 1:216; Xavante, 4:250; Yanomami, 4:253–254; Yoruba, 1:219, 223–224; Zande, 1:230–231. *See also specific types of animals*

Ankou (death, Brittany), 3:171–172

Ankrah, Roy, 1:186

Anne of Austria, 3:164

"Annual Bibliography," 1:5

"Annual Folklore Bibliography," 1:5

Anthony the Abbot, Saint, 3:470–471

Antiquarianism, 1:1–3; and museums, 1:57

Antiquitates Vulgares (Bourne), 1:1, 2

Antiquities, 1:1–3

The ANZAC Book (Australia [British]), 1:285

Apache, 4:1–8; arts and crafts, 4:6; geography and history, 4:1–3; modernization, challenges of, 4:6–7; rituals and ceremonies, 4:5–6; stories and tales, 4:3–4; studies of Apache folklore, 4:7

Apache Wars, 4:3

Apartheid: Xhosa, 1:258, 262; Zulu, 1:269

ap Nudd, Gwyn, 3:74

Apollonia, Saint, 3:229

Appadurai, Arjun, 1:42

Appalachia, 4:156–166; architecture, 4:163–164; arts and crafts, 4:164; dance and drama, 4:161–162; festivals and celebrations, 4:161; food, 4:164; geography and history, 4:156–158; and invented tradition, 1:51; modernization, challenges of, 1:79, 4:165; myths, legends, and folktales, 4:159–160; and race, 1:79; religious beliefs, 4:158–159; songs, ballads, and music, 1:79, 4:160–161; sports and games, 4:162–163; studies of Appalachian folklore, 4:165

"Applied folklore," 1:77

Aqa Jamal, 2:425

Arabian Nights, 3:12

Arabic language (Berber), 1:101

Arabs: Berber influenced by, 1:101–103; Spain influenced by, 3:180, 182. *See also* Palestine

Archaisms in Macedonian legends, 3:372

Architecture: African Americans, 4:153–154; American southwest, 1:39; Appalachia, 4:163–164; Ashkenazim, 3:338; Australia (British), 1:282–283; Austria, 3:257–259; Bangladesh, 2:102; Benin, 1:176; Bhutan, 2:111–112; Caipira, 4:180; Cherokee, 4:18–19; China, 2:226–228; Chinese living abroad, 2:242; Flanders (Belgium), 3:232; Igbo, 1:200–201; Jamaica, 4:337; Japan, 2:278; Kazakh, 2:313; Maluku, 2:201–202; Mississippi Delta, 4:167; Moorish, 3:218; The Netherlands, 3:244–245; Shona, 1:253–254; Slovenia, 3:303–304; Sri Lanka, 2:128–130; Ukraine, 3:446–447; Uyghur, 2:344; Vanuatu, 1:330–331. *See also* Housing

Archives, 1:3–5; Latvia, 3:364; and modernization, 1:52; and repertoire, 1:82

Arctic region: Western Inuit and Yupik, 4:128–131

Arendt, Hannah, 1:29–30

Arhuaran (son of Oba Ozolua), 1:177

Ari fróði (the Learned), 3:113

Arizona: Apache, 4:1–3; Hopi, 4:44–45; Navajo, 4:82–83

Arjuna, 2:40

Armenia, 2:357–372; epics and historical narratives, 2:359–362; geography and history, 2:357–359; modernization, challenges of, 2:369; songs and legends, 2:362–369

Armes Prydein (poem), 3:73

Arminius, 3:268

Armor. *See* Weapons and armor

Arnamagnean Institute, 3:114, 115

Arngrímur Jónsson the Learned, 3:116

Arnim, Achim von, 3:312

Árni Magnússon, **3**:113

Arochukwu and British colonialism, **1**:9

Árpád, Prince, **3**:276

Arsena epic (Georgia), **3**:358

Arshak and Shapuh (Armenia), **2**:363

Artashes and Artavazd (Armenia), **2**:361

Artashes and Satenik (Armenia), **2**:360

Arthur (King), **1**:45; Finland, **3**:95; France, **3**:163–164; Germany, **3**:269; Wales, **3**:71, 72

Arts and crafts: African Americans, **4**:154–155; Ainu, **2**:291, 292; Albania, **3**:329; Apache, **4**:6; Appalachia, **4**:164; Armenia, **2**:365; Ashkenazim, **3**:337–339; Assam, **2**:23; Australia (British), **1**:282–283; Australian Aborigines, **1**:294, 296–299; Bangladesh, **2**:100–102; Baule, **1**:167–168; Benin, **1**:176; Berber, **1**:109–111; Bhutan, **2**:111; Bihar, **2**:29; Caipira, **4**:180; Cherokee, **4**:17–18; Cheyenne, **4**:28; China, **2**:226–228; Chinese living abroad, **2**:242; Choctaw, **4**:32; The Comoros, **1**:143; Ecuador, **4**:192; and ethnicity, **1**:26; Galicia, **3**:208–209; Georgia, **3**:361–362; Greece, **3**:500; Guam, **1**:339; Haida, **4**:43; Haiti, **4**:324–325; Haryana, **2**:44–45; Hawai'i, **1**:374; Hopi, **4**:49–50; Hungary, **3**:282–283; Igbo, **1**:201; Ijo, **1**:204–206, 208; Iroquois, **4**:56–57; Japan, **2**:278; Kadazandusun, **2**:180–181; Kazakh, **2**:312–313; Khasi-Jaintia, **2**:73; Kiowa, **4**:65–66; Kiribati, **1**:346–347; Lakota, **4**:75; Lebanon, **2**:397; Macedonia, **3**:375–376; Malaita, **1**:306; Malay, **2**:143–144; Maluku, **2**:201–202; Marquesas Islands, **1**:383–384; Marshall Islands, **1**:354–355; Mongol, **2**:258–259; Nagaland, **2**:77–78; Navajo, **4**:90–92, 94; Ojibwe, **4**:108–109; Orissa, **2**:84–85; Palau, **1**:364; Palestine, **2**:408; Peru, **4**:207; Quechua, **4**:214; Rarámuri, **4**:303–304; Seminole, **4**:114; Sephardim, **3**:217–219; Sertão, **4**:219; Shona, **1**:253–254; Shuar, **4**:227–228; Siberia, **2**:323; Sicily, **3**:489–490; Slovenia, **3**:304; Spain, **3**:186–187; Sri Lanka, **2**:128–130; Suriname Maroons, **4**:241; Tairora, **2**:208; Taiwan, **2**:264–265; Tajik, **2**:330–331; Tlingit, **4**:125–126; Tonga, **1**:402–403; Trobriand Islands, **1**:324–325; Tuareg, **1**:109–111, 119–120; Turkey, **2**:436–437; Tuvalu, **1**:409–410; Ukraine, **3**:444–445; Uttar Pradesh, **2**:94; Uyghur, **2**:344; Uzbek, **2**:353–354; Vanuatu, **1**:330; Western Inuit and Yupik, **4**:138–139; Yoruba, **1**:225–226; Zande, **1**:233. *See also* Carving and sculpture; Jewelry; Textile arts

Arts and Crafts of Hawai'i, **1**:375

Arurhan, **1**:178

Arútam (Shuar), **4**:222–223

Arvastson, Gösta, **3**:151

Arvidsson, Alf, **3**:153

Asad, Talal, **1**:91

Ash, John, **1**:87

Ashantis, **1**:187

Ashima (China), **2**:220

Ashkenazim, **3**:330–341; arts, crafts, and architecture, **3**:337–339; calendars, **3**:332–333; and diaspora, **1**:20; food, **3**:339; history, **3**:330–332; life-cycle celebrations, **3**:332–333; magic and folk medicine, **3**:333–334; music, dance, and drama, **3**:336–337; myths, legends, and folktales, **3**:334; proverbs and riddles, **3**:335; songs, **3**:335–336; sports and games, **3**:337

Ashliman, D.L., **1**:94

Asian Folklore Studies, **2**:231

Asian Music: Journal for the Society of Asian Music, **2**:231

Assam, **2**:17–24; arts and crafts, **2**:23; cultural tradition, **2**:3, 4; geography, **2**:17–18; modernization, challenges of, **2**:23–24; music and dance, **2**:22–23; oral tradition, **2**:21–22; people and language, **2**:18–19; society and religion, **2**:18–19

Astrology: Appalachia, **4**:177; Armenia, **2**:359; Denmark, **3**:84; Nepal, **2**:116; San, personification of stellar bodies by, **1**:243; Sri Lanka, **2**:126; Taiwan, **2**:262; Tajik, **2**:333; Zande, **1**:231

Atatürk, Mustafa Kemal, **2**:432

Atheism (Tajik), **2**:325

Atlas de la Nouvelle-Calédonie et dépendances, **1**:314

Audience participation in storytelling. *See* Call-and-response stories

Augers. *See* Diviners and divination

Aura Poku (Queen Poku) (Baule), **1**:165

Australia (British), **1**:277–299; arts, crafts, and architecture, **1**:282–283; collectors of Australian lore, **1**:287; Duna, influence on, **2**:166; English heritage, **1**:278–280; folktales and superstitious lore, **1**:286; food and sports, **1**:290; historical roots of Australian folklore, **1**:288–289; Irish heritage, **1**:280–281; modernization, challenges of, **1**:290; modern legends and tales, **1**:287; music, **1**:288; oral traditions, **1**:283–285; post-war immigration and Englishness, **1**:281–282; preservation and study of Australian folklore, **1**:290–291; Scottish heritage, **1**:281; song, **1**:285–286

The Australian (Australia [British]), **1**:287

Australian Aborigines, **1**:292–299; Dhuwa moiety in central Arnhem Land, **1**:295–296; Dreamtime verbal and material arts, **1**:297–298; geography and diversity, **1**:292–293; moieties, authority, and power, **1**:294–295; mythology, **1**:293–294; and race, **1**:80; Tiwi culture, **1**:98, 296–297; Tjukurrpa (or Dreamtime), **1**:293; translation of language, **1**:90; Wandjina, **1**:298–299

Australian Broadcasting Commission, **1**:286

Australian Folklore: An Annual Journal of Folklore Studies, **1**:278, 291

Australian Folklore Society, **1**:291

"Australianisms," **1**:283

The Australian language (Australia [British]), **1**:284

The Australian Legend (Australia [British]), **1**:281

The Australian National Dictionary (Australia [British]), **1**:284

The Australian Yarn (Australia [British]), **1**:287

Austria, **3**:249–259; architecture and clothing, **3**:257–259; calendars, **3**:252–256; geography and history, **3**:249–252; legends, **3**:256; music and dance, **3**:257

Austrian flag legend, **3**:256

Autobiographies: Bali, **2**:163; Dakota and Lakota, **4**:73–74, 77; Maya, **4**:265

Autoethnography, **1**:30

Avercamp, Hendrick, **3**:243

Averroes, **3**:180

Awale (Baule), **1**:166–167

Awul Chand (spiritual leader, Bangladesh), **2**:103

Ayurvedic system, **2**:90

Azadovsky, Mark, **1**:35–36, **3**:419

Azande. *See* Zande

Azúcar Moreno, **3**:183

Baal Shem Tov, **3**:334

Baardsen, Qvive, **3**:135

Babka (folk healer, Ukraine), **3**:439

Bäckman, Maria, **3**:151

Badie (young men's associations), **3**:477

Badnyak (sapling, Serbia), **3**:431–432

BAE. *See* Bureau of American Ethnology

Bagpipes: Croatia, **3**:341, 343, 344, 346; Macedonia, **3**:374; Malta, **3**:505; Scotland, **3**:63; Sicily, **3**:487

Baha'is (Tuvalu), **1**:405

Baird, James, **1**:74

Baissac, Charles, **1**:146

Bakánowa (Rarámuri), **4**:305

Baker, S.J., **1**:284

Bakhtin, Mikhail, **1**:48

Bakker, Cornelis, **3**:243

Balance, concept of: Cherokee, **4**:9; Navajo, **4**:85; Tlingits, **4**:118

Baldensperger, Phillip, **2**:411

Bali, **2**:152–165; folk theater, **2**:161–163; geography and history, **2**:152–155; modernization, challenges of, **2**:163–164; music, **2**:161; religious and folk beliefs, **2**:156–157; rules, rituals, and customs, **2**:157–160; social and family structure, **2**:155; spirits, **2**:160–161; studies of Balinese folklore, **2**:164; and worldview, **1**:98

Bálint, Sándor, **3**:283

Balkan Peninsula, **3**:322

"Ballad of the Walled-in Woman" (Albania), **3**:323, 327

1: Topics & Themes, Africa, Australia & Oceania
2: Southeast Asia & India, Central & East Asia, Middle East
3: Europe
4: North & South America

Ballads: Albania, 3:327; Appalachia, 4:160; Croatia, 3:344; European, 1:94; Hungary, 3:279; Italy, 3:459; Italy, northern, 3:459; Mexico, 4:273; Norway, 3:128–129; scholars collecting, 1:2; Scotland, 3:57–62; Sephardim, 3:216–217; Sicily, 3:486. *See also* Music and dance

Balys, Jonas, 1:56

Bamba, Cheikh Ahmadou, 1:212

Banfield, Edward, 3:453

Bangladesh, 2:95–105; architecture, 2:102; arts and crafts, 2:100–102; dance and drama, 2:99; festivals and markets, 2:99–100; folk medicine, 2:102–103; geography and history, 2:95–96; music and songs, 2:96–98; myths and folktales, 2:99; religious beliefs and customs, 2:103–105; social structure, 2:98

Banjos, Appalachia, 4:160–161

Bàn Macintyre, Duncan, 3:61

Banshee, 3:33–34

Bantu language: Shona, 1:248; Xhosa, 1:257

Bantu Studies (Zulu), 1:272

Baptism: Denmark, 3:88; Flanders (Belgium), 3:225; France, 3:159, 161; Isle of Man, 3:47; Marquesas Islands, 1:380; Norway, 3:126; Palestine, 2:406; Peru, 4:201; Poland, 3:385; Rarámuri, 4:301–302; Roma, 3:397, 398, 405; Russia, 3:411; Sertão, 4:216; Shona, 1:250; Sibundoy, 4:233; Slovakia, 3:291; Ukraine, 3:444

Barabaig's worldview, 1:97, 98

Barandirán, Jose Miguel, 3:192

Baraza la Mwaka (Swahili), 1:159

Barbara, Saint, 3:349, 388, 441

Barbarossa, Friedrich, 3:250, 268, 269

"Barbarossa at Mt. Kyffhausen," 3:268–269

Barber, Benjamin, 1:43

Bargen, Doris, 2:274

Barghash (Sultan), 1:155

Baring-Gould, Sabine, 3:13

Barns (Appalachia), 4:163–164

"The Barnyards o Delgatie" (song), 3:60

Baron, Robert, 1:77

Barons, Krišjanis, 3:363, 366

Barrow, Nathaniel, 4:155

Barry, Phillips, 1:23

Barsov, E.V., 3:410, 414

Barth, Fredrik, 3:150

Bartholomew, Saint, 3:506

Bartók, Béla, 3:280

Bar-Yohai, Shimon, 2:374

Basil, Saint, 3:403, 404

Basketry: Apache, 4:6; Cherokee, 4:17; Choctaw, 4:34–35; Iroquois, 4:53–54; Navajo, 4:91; Western Inuit and Yupik, 4:139

Basque, 3:189–195; geography and history, 3:189–190; music and dance, 3:193–194; myths, legends, and folktales, 3:190–193; sports and games, 3:194; theater and other oral art forms, 3:190

Basseri and worldview, 1:98

"The Bastard from the Bush" (Australia [British]), 1:284

Basur (Bali), 2:157

Bataille des reines traditional game, 3:477–478

Bataller, Josep, 3:196

Batiked eggs as Ukrainian identity, 3:445–446

Battlefield Band, 3:66

Battle of Culloden (Scotland), 3:54

Battle of Kosovo, 3:432, 434

Baughman, Ernest W., 1:94

Baule, 1:163–169; arts and crafts, 1:167–168; games and recreation, 1:166–167; geography, history, and social structure, 1:163–164; housing, 1:168; modernization, challenges of, 1:168; music and dance, 1:165–166; religion, 1:164; stories, myths, and proverbs, 1:164–165

Bauman, Richard, 1:27, 68, 69–70

Bausinger, Hermann, 1:37, 52

Beadwork: Cherokee, 4:18; Haiti, 4:324; Iroquois, 4:56–57; Seminole, 4:113; Tlingit, 4:125–126

Béaloideas (folklore journal), 3:40

Bean, C.E.W., 1:285

Bear Butte (Cheyenne), 4:22, 25

"The Bear's Son" (Nahua), 4:285

Bear stories and rituals: Ainu, 2:285, 286, 288–292; Korea, 2:295–296, 304; Piedmont and Val d'Aosta, 3:471–472; Siberia, 2:316, 318, 319, 321, 323; Sicily, 3:489

Beatrix (The Netherlands), 3:242

Beckham, David, 3:186

Beckwith, Martha Warren, 1:41

Beekeeping: Malta, 3:509; Slovenia, 3:304

Beer: Candoshi, 4:185; Rarámuri, 4:304

Begging songs (Ukraine), 3:441

Beitl, Klaus, 1:52

Bekker, Balthasar, 3:239

Belau. *See* Palau

Belén, Ana, 3:184

Beliefs. *See* Religion and beliefs

Belize: Maya, 4:256–257

Belle Highwalking (Cheyenne), 4:26, 27

Bell-tolling (Malta), 3:505

Bemba language (Lunda), 1:234–235

Ben-Amos, Dan, 1:29, 68

Bendix, Regina, 1:37

Benedict, Ruth, 1:27

ben Eliezer, Israel, 3:334

Benfrey, Theodor, 1:22

Benin, 1:169–180; ancestor worship, divination, and the supernatural, 1:174–176; arts, crafts, and architecture, 1:176; celebrations and rituals, 1:178; games and sports, 1:178; geography and history, 1:169–172; modernization, challenges of, 1:179; proverbs, folktales, and music, 1:176–177; religious beliefs, 1:172–173; witchcraft, 1:174

Bennett, Martyn, 3:66

Ben-Yehudah, Eliezer, 2:376

Beowulf, 1:45, 3:1

Berber, 1:101–112; arts and crafts, 1:109–111; beliefs and folklore, 1:103–107; geography and history, 1:101–103; modernization, challenges of, 1:111–112; music, 1:107–108. *See also* Tuareg

Berceo, Gonzalo de, 3:182

Berg, Magnus Magnus, 3:152

Berikoaba drama (Georgia), 3:360

Berkhey, Joannes Le Francq van, 3:236

Berlage, H.P., 3:245

Bernard, Saint, 3:477

Bern Onion Market (Switzerland), 3:314

Bernstein, Ignacy, 3:335

Bertran i Bros, Pau, 3:195

Bessonov, P.V., 3:410

Bessus, Saint, 3:471

Bhabi (Goddess of Fortune, Nepal), 2:116

Bhagavadgita (India), 2:40

Bhojpuri language (Mauritius and Rodrigues), 1:145

Bhutan, 2:105–112; architecture, 2:111–112; arts and crafts, 2:111; cultural tradition, 2:3; folk medicine, 2:107; folktales, 2:107–108; folk theater and dance, 2:110; geography and history, 2:105–106; lozey and tsangmo, 2:108–109; modernization, challenges of, 2:112; music, 2:109–110; religious beliefs, 2:106–107; songs, 2:109; sports and recreation, 2:111

Biatu (bear) story (Siberia), 2:323

Bibi mushkilkusho (Miracle-worker granny) stories (Tajik), 2:328

Bibliography, 1:5–7

Biblioteca delle Tradizioni Popolari Siciliane (Library of Sicilian Folklore), 3:481–482

Big Book of Australian Folk Song, 1:286

Bihar, 2:24–30; ballads and folksongs, 2:28; cultural tradition, 2:4; geography, language, and religion, 2:24–25; Muslim refugees from Bangladesh, 2:95; myths, legends, and folktales, 2:25–27; popularity of folklore, 2:29–30; proverbs and riddles, 2:28–29; studies of Bihar folklore, 2:30

Bill Bowyang's Bush Recitations (Australia [British]), 1:285

binti Saad, Siti, 1:157, 160

Bird, S. Elizabeth, 1:72

Birendra (King of Nepal), 2:114

Birth beliefs. *See* Childbirth

Bislama language (Vanuatu), 1:326

Biyela, Umhle, 1:273–274

Bjarni Pálsson, 3:117

Black Book magic, 3:125–126

Black Culture and Black Consciousness (Levine), 4:144

Black Dogs (shapeshifters), England, 3:8

Black English dialect, **4**:143

Blackening ritual (Scotland), **3**:56–57

"Black Sara," **3**:404

Blacksmithing: African Americans, **4**:154; Australia (British), **1**:283; Benin, **1**:173; Guam, **1**:339; Haiti, **4**:324; Igbo, **1**:201; Navajo, **4**:90–91; Tuareg, **1**:102, 104, 105, 108, 113–115, 117, 119; Zande, **1**:233

Blaise, Saint, **3**:206, 506

Blame poetry: Shona, **1**:250; Yoruba, **1**:222

"Blancaflor" (Nahua), **4**:287

Blanco, Raul González, **3**:186

Blankets: Navajo, **4**:90. *See also* Textile arts

Blátand, Harald, **3**:83

Bleek, W.H.I., **1**:271

Blehr, Barbro, **3**:153

Blessingway ceremony (Navajo), **4**:86

Blessom, Johannes, **3**:127

Blocher, Christof, **3**:316

Blood brotherhood/sisterhood (Serbia), **3**:428–429

Blood sacrifices. *See* Sacrifices

Blues: African Americans, **4**:151, 152–153; Mississippi Delta, **4**:169–171

Boas, Franz: and cultural relativism, **1**:14–15; and diffusion, **1**:22; and ethnography, **1**:27; and fieldwork, **1**:34; and text, **1**:84

Boas, George, **1**:73

Boasting (Shona), **1**:250

Boats and boating: Malta, **3**:510; Swahili maritime imagery, **1**:156. *See also* Canoes

Bob, Victor, **4**:173

Body markings. *See* Tattoos and body markings

Body painting: Bangladesh, **2**:101; China, **2**:224; Hopi, **4**:48; Ijo, **1**:205; Malaita, **1**:303, 306; Nepal, forehead dots in, **2**:121; Palestine, **2**:407; Xavante, **4**:215, 246

Boekenoogen, Gerrit Jan, **3**:243

Bogdanova, Nastas'ia, **3**:424

Bogle, Eric, **1**:288

Bogomils, Macedonia, **3**:371

Bogue Chitto, **4**:32

Bohigas, Oriol, **3**:187

Boine, Mari, **3**:142

Bokwe, John Knox, **1**:260

"Bold Jack Donahue" (Australia [British]), **1**:284

Boleyn, Anne, **3**:11

Bona Sforza (Queen), **3**:381

Bonfires: Catalan, **3**:199; Denmark, **3**:87; Poland, **3**:387–388; Sicily, **3**:488

Bonifatius (Boniface), **3**:261

Bon (pre-Buddhist faith) in Bhutan, **2**:107

Book of Changes (China), **2**:213, 262

Book of Songs (China), **2**:218

Bormliza (singing style, Malta), **3**:510

Borneo Mail, **2**:182

Bosch, Hieronymus, **3**:152

Bosè, Miguel, **3**:184

Bosio, Gianni, **3**:456

Bosque Redondo (Navajo), **4**:83

Bothy ballads (Scots Scotland), **3**:59–60

Botkin, Benjamin, **1**:36

Bourne, Henry, **1**:1, 2

Bowl games (Iroquois), **4**:57

Boxing: Quechua, **4**:213–214; Tonga, **1**:397; Vanuatu, **1**:330

"The Boy Who Jumped to Rota" (Guam), **1**:336

Bozkurt (Gray Wolf) legend (Turkey), **2**:432

Brahmans (priestly class): Gaddi, **2**:32; India, **2**:2, 3, 13; Isaan, **2**:131–132; Kashmir, **2**:60, 61; Nepal, **2**:115; Orissa, **2**:81

Brand, John, **1**:2

Brandt, Sebastian, **3**:253

Bran structure (Piedmont and Val d'Aosta), **3**:476

Braveheart (movie), **1**:50

Brazil: Caipira, **4**:177; Cantomble in, **1**:79; Kaingang, **4**:193; Sertão, **4**:216–217; Xavante, **4**:243; Yanomami, **4**:251–252

Bread-baking tradition (Slovenia), **3**:299

Breathnach, Breandán, **3**:26

"The Bremen Town Musicians," **3**:267

Brennan, William, **3**:36

Brentano, Clemens, **3**:312

Brer Rabbit tales: African American, **4**:148; Wolof, **1**:209

Bricolage, **1**:47–48

Bridal customs. *See* Marriage

Bride-of-the-rain ceremonies (Berber), **1**:105–106

Brideprice, Roma, **3**:398

Brieuc, Saint, **3**:174

Briggs, Charles, **1**:34, 70

Bright Sheng, **2**:220

Brigit, Saint, **3**:30

Brihatkatha (India), **2**:60–61

Bringéus, Nils-Arvid, **3**:150, 151

British Broadcasting Corporation, **3**:14

British Columbia: Haida, **4**:38–39; Tlingit, **4**:117

British Folklore Society, **1**:13

The British Folklorists (Dorson), **1**:13

British rule and influence: Africa, **1**:8–9; Assam, **2**:17; Australia (British), **1**:278–282, 291; Benin colonization by, **1**:172; Gaddi, **2**:32; Iban, **2**:173; India, **2**:4; Kadazandusun, **2**:179; Kiribati, **1**:341, 345; Malaita, **1**:300; Mauritius and Rodrigues, **1**:144; Palestine, **2**:401, 406; Semai, **2**:150; Shona, **1**:249, 253; Sri Lanka, **2**:124; Tonga, **1**:403; Trobriand Islands, **1**:316; Tuvalu, **1**:405; Vanuatu, **1**:325; Xhosa, **1**:257

Brittany, **3**:170–176; Celtic lore and religion, **3**:171–173; Celtic migration from Britain, **3**:173–174; Christianity, **3**:174; geography, **3**:170–171; life-cycle customs, **3**:171–173; medieval and early modern, **3**:174–175; modernization, challenges of, **3**:175; nature worship, **3**:172–173

Broadwood, Lucy, **3**:13

Brooke, James, **2**:173

Brothers Grimm. *See* Grimm brothers, influence of

Browning, Robert, **3**:268

Bruckner, Anton, **3**:257

Brunvand, Jan Harold, **1**:71, 95

Buddhism: Australia (British), **1**:290; Bali, **2**:152, 154; Bangladesh, **2**:96; Bhutan, **2**:106–107; Bihar, **2**:25; China, **2**:213, 216, 223; Chinese living abroad, **2**:236, 239; Gaddi, **2**:31; Isaan, **2**:131–136; Japan, **2**:274, 275–276; Karnataka, **2**:48; Kazakh, **2**:308; Korea, **2**:296, 299, 300–301; Manchu, **2**:249; Mongol, **2**:255, 257, 258; Orissa, **2**:80; Siberia, **2**:316, 320; Sri Lanka, **2**:124–126; Taiwan, **2**:261, 262; Uttar Pradesh, **2**:88; Uyghur, **2**:336; Uzbek, **2**:348

Buffalo as theme (Swahili), **1**:155

Buffalo Dance (Cheyenne), **4**:28

Buggane (Isle of Man), **3**:46

Bulletin ("Bushman's Bible") (Australia [British]), **1**:285

Bullfighting: Ecuador, **4**:192; Maya, **4**:264; Spain, **3**:185–186

Bundling tradition (Italy), **3**:454

Bungee jumping (Vanuatu), **1**:327

Bunyan, Paul, **1**:36

Bureau of American Ethnology (BAE), **1**:76, 84

Burials. *See* Funerals and burials

Burn, Adrian, **1**:88

Burns, Allan, **4**:260

Burns, Robert, **3**:57, 59, 66

Busacca, Cicciu, **3**:460

"The Bush Christening" (Australia [British]), **1**:285

Bushmen. *See* San

Bush Negroes. *See* Suriname Maroon

Bush spirits (Ijo), **1**:204, 207

Butterbean game (Cherokee), **4**:17

"Butterfly Spring" stories (China), **2**:217

Bwebwenato (Marshall Islands), **1**:352

Byliny (epic, Russia), **3**:410, 421–423

Byrne, Joe, **3**:38

Byrnes, Dan, **1**:288

Byron, Lord, **3**:314

Byzantine Empire, **3**:371

Cabinet of Folksongs, **3**:363

Caesar, Julius, **3**:261

Caipira, **4**:177–181; arts, crafts, and architecture, **4**:180; food, **4**:179–180; games, **4**:179; geography and history, **4**:177–178; music and festivals, **4**:180; religious beliefs and rituals, **4**:179

Calatrava, Santiago, **3**:187

Calendars: Albania, **3**:326; Apache, **4**:5; Ashkenazim, **3**:332–333; Austria, **3**:252–256; Bali, **2**:153–154, 161; Catalan, **3**:199; China, **2**:213; The Comoros, **1**:142; Cuba, **4**:311; Ecuador, **4**:191; England, **3**:17–20; Finnish-Swedish, **3**:101–102; Flanders (Belgium), **3**:226–229; France,

1: Topics & Themes, Africa, Australia & Oceania
2: Southeast Asia & India, Central & East Asia, Middle East
3: Europe
4: North & South America

3:168–169; Galicia, 3:206–208; Germany, 3:262–265; Hopi, 4:47; Hungary, 3:281–282; Ireland, 3:26–27; Isle of Man, 3:47–51; Kiowa, 4:66; Korea, 2:301; Maya, 4:257; Mexico, 4:272; Navajo, 4:89; Nepal, 2:120; The Netherlands, 3:241–243; Palestine, 2:404; Persia, 2:423; Peru, 4:204–205; Piedmont and Val d'Aosta, 3:474–477; Poland, 3:386–388; Quechua, 4:211–212; Rarámuri, 4:299; Roma, 3:403–404; Russia, 3:415–417; Scotland, 3:64–66; Serbia, 3:429–432; Sicily, 3:487–489; Slovakia, 3:289–290; Slovenia, 3:296–299; Switzerland, 3:314–317

Calendimaggio (May Day feast), 3:475

California: Australia (British) social influence by, 1:278; Proposition 187 to limit public services to non-citizens, 1:66

Call-and-response stories: Ga, 1:185, 191; Guam, 1:338; Igbo, 1:196; Lunda, 1:236; Shona, 1:250, 253; Wolof, 1:216; Yoruba, 1:218, 221; Zande, 1:233

Callaway, Henry, 1:270, 271, 273

Callegari, Adriano, 3:460

Calvin, 3:238

Camayd-Freixas, Erik, 1:74

Camés (Kaingang myth), 4:195–196

Campbell, J.F., 3:114

Campos, Rubén, 4:279

Cana'an, Tawfiq, 2:411

Canada: Haida, 4:38–39; Iroquois, 4:50–51; Ojibwe, 4:103–105; Tlingit, 4:117; Western Inuit and Yupik, 4:128–131

Canales, Antonio, 3:185

Candoshi, 4:181–187; geography and history, 4:181–182; religious beliefs, rituals, and celebrations, 4:182–185; songs and music, 4:185–187; studies of Candoshi folklore, 4:187

Cannibalism: Haiti, 4:318; Yanomami, 4:253, 254

Canoes: Ainu (Japan), 2:291; Benin, 1:174; Hawai'i, 1:373, 375; Ijo, 1:207, 208; Kaliai, 2:183; Kiribati, 1:342, 343, 347; Malaita, 1:306; Maluku, 2:202; Marshall Islands, 1:355; Palau, 1:361, 363; Seminole, 4:115; Tlingit, 4:126; Trobriand Islands, 1:321–322, 324; Tuvalu, 1:409

Cantomble (Brazil), 1:79

Canzuna (folksong, Sicily), 3:485

Capitalism, 1:42

Capmany, Aureli, 3:196

Capping (African American), 4:150

Captain Cook Chased a Chook: Children's Folklore in Australia, 1:284

"The Captain of the Push" (Australia [British]), 1:285

Caracalla, Abdel Halim, 2:397

Card games: China, 2:226, 242; Persia, 2:424; Rarámuri, 4:305; Slovakia, 3:293, 294

Caribs of Dominica, 4:329–336; folk medicine, 4:333–334; folktales, 4:331–333; geography and history, 4:329–331; witchcraft and magic, 4:334–336

Carlos IV, 3:186

Carlyle, Thomas, 1:46

Carnival: Catalan, 3:197; Croatia, 3:348, 349; Cuba, 4:311; Flanders, 3:227; Galicia, 3:206; Georgia, 3:360; Hungary, 3:282; Italy, 3:457, 464; Piedmont and Val d'Aosta, 3:471, 472, 474; Poland, 3:387; Quechua, 4:210–211, 213; Sibundoy, 4:234–235; Sicily, 3:488; Slovakia, 3:289. *See also* Mardi Gras

Carnival societies (Switzerland), 3:316

Carolina Sea Islanders, 1:20

Caroline Islands, 1:333, 339

Carpenter, Inta Gale, 1:82

Carpitella, Diego, 3:461

Carribean, 4:309–347

Carucci, Laurence, 1:353

Carving and sculpture: Australian Aborigines, 1:297; Baule, 1:164, 167; Cherokee, 4:18; Ecuador, 4:192; Guam, 1:339; Haida, 4:42; Haiti, 4:324, 325; Hawai'i, 1:374; Igbo, 1:201; Ijo, 1:205; Marquesas Islands, 1:378, 383–384; Navajo, 4:91–92; Palau, 1:359–360, 364; Shona, 1:253, 254; Suriname Maroons, 4:241; Tlingit, 4:126; Tonga, 1:402; Trobriand Islands, 1:320, 324; Western Inuit and Yupik, 4:138; Wolof, 1:213; Yoruba, 1:225; Zande, 1:233

Caseponce, Esteve, 3:195

Casimir the Great, 3:381

Cassian, John, 3:160, 439

Castelló i Guasch, Joan, 3:195

Caste system. *See* Social structure

del Castillo, Bernal Díaz, 4:275

"The Castle of Dimdim" (Kurds), 2:387

Catalan, 3:195–201; calendars, 3:199; festivals and celebrations, 3:197–198; food, 3:199–200; geography and history, 3:195–197; music and dance, 3:198–199

Catherine, Saint, 3:164, 388

Catherine the Great, 3:409

Catholicism: and Afro-Cuban myths, 4:314; anti-Catholic nativism in U.S., 1:65; Australia (British), 1:278, 280–281, 289; Caribs of Dominica, 4:331–332; Chinese living abroad, 2:239; France, 3:161, 166, 167; Haiti, 4:318–319; immigrants to U.S., 1:66; Kewa, 2:189; Kiribati, 1:341, 348; Latvia, 3:365–366; Maluki, 2:198; Marquesas Islands, 1:380; Mauritius and Rodrigues, 1:145; Mexico, 4:269–271; Otomí, 4:290; Peru, 4:200–202, 206; Quechua, 4:209; Rarámuri, 4:297–300, 302; Réunion, 1:148; Sertão, 4:217, 218; The Seychelles, 1:149; Shuar, 4:220–221;

Sibundoy, 4:230, 234–235; Spain, 3:180–182; Sri Lanka, 2:125, 126, 128; Taiwan, 2:261; Tonga, 1:401; Turkey, 2:430; Tuvalu, 1:405. *See also* Christianity

Cattle: India, sacredness of, 2:13; Jie, importance to, 1:132–135; Nuer, importance to, 1:150, 153

"The Cattle-Killing" (Xhosa), 1:264

Cattleshed as community gathering-place, 3:473

Cauld Blast Orchestra, 3:66

Cautionary tales, Isle of Man, 3:46–47

Cayurucrés (Kaingang myth), 4:195–196

Céilidh (visiting house), 3:26, 57, 117

Celebrations. *See* Festivals and celebrations

Celtic influence, 3:70; Brittany, 3:171–173; England, 3:4–5; France, 3:158–159; Galicia, 3:203; Iceland, 3:112; Ireland, 3:23, 34; Piedmont and Val d'Aosta, 3:474; Spain, 3:179; Wales, 3:72, 75

Cemetery rites. *See* Funerals and burials

A Centennial Index (American Folklore Society), 1:6

Central Africa. *See* Western and Central Africa

Central America, 4:256–308

Cepenkov, Marco, 3:372

Ceramics: Australian Aborigines, 1:297; Baule, 1:163; Berber, 1:109, 111; Caipira, 4:179; Candoshi, 4:186; Cherokee, 4:17–18; Hopi, 4:49–50; Igbo, 1:201; Iroquois, 4:52; Lakota, 4:75; Mexico, 4:272; Navajo, 4:91, 92; Shona, 1:253; Tajik, 2:330–331; Turkey, 2:436–437; Uzbek, 2:354; Vanuatu, 1:330; Yoruba, 1:226

Ceremonies. *See* Rituals and ceremonies

Cernunnos, 3:171

Cervantes, Miguel de, 3:183

Cetshawayo (Zulu king), 1:269

Cha cha cha (Cuba), 4:312

Ch'a-don Lee, 2:299

Chadwick, Nora, 3:173

Chagnon, Napoleon, 4:251–252

Chain structure, tales (Russia), 3:419

Chameleon as theme (Yoruba), 1:222

Chamisso, Adelbert von, 1:350

Chamorros. *See* Guam

Chamula and worldview, 1:98

Changeling, fairy, 3:47

Chant of Urdmau (Palau), 1:362

Chants: Assam, 2:29; Benin, 1:178; Bhutan, 2:109; Ga, 1:191; Gaddi, 2:35, 36; Haryana, 2:40; Hawai'i, 1:366, 369–371, 375; Iban, 2:174, 175; Igbo, 1:197; Isaan, 2:134, 136–137; Kadazandusun, 2:178; Kashmir, 2:64; Kiribati, 1:344; Marquesas Islands, 1:381–382; Marshall Islands, 1:352; Palau, 1:360, 361–362; Samoa, 1:394; Shuar, 4:226; Yoruba, 1:222–223

Charioteers' folksongs, Sicily, 3:485–486

Charlemagne, 3:161–162, 167, 250, 261, 269

Charles II (England), 3:3, 15, 19

Charles, Thomas, 3:74

Charms and spells: England, **3:**9; Greenland, **3:**109–110; Jamaica, **4:**343; Poland, **3:**382; Shuar, **4:**226. *See also* Incantations

Chaseworld: Foxhunting and Storytelling in New Jersey's Pine Barrens (Hufford), **1:**30

Chastushki (Russia), **3:**421

Cherokee, **4:**8–21; architecture, **4:**18–19; arts and crafts, **4:**17–18; festivals and ceremonies, **4:**15–16; food, **4:**19; geography, **4:**8; history, **4:**9–10; modernization, challenges of, **4:**20; music and song, **4:**14–15; myths, legends, and folktales, **4:**12–14; religious beliefs, **4:**11–12; social structure, **4:**9–10; studies of Cherokee folklore, **4:**20–21; writing system of, **1:**24, **4:**14

Cherokee Nation of Oklahoma, **4:**8

Cheyenne, **4:**21–30; arts and crafts, **4:**28; geography and history, **4:**21–23; modernization, challenges of, **4:**29; myths, legends, and folktales, **4:**25–26; religious beliefs and rituals, **4:**23–25; songs and dance, **4:**26–28; sports and games, **4:**28; studies of Cheyenne folklore, **4:**29–30

Chiang Kai-shek, **2:**260

Chickee (Seminole), **4:**114

Child, Francis James, **1:**94, **3:**13, 59

Childbirth and birth rituals: Abanyole, **1:**125; Albania, **3:**325; Ashkenazim, **3:**332–333; Bali, **2:**156; Chinese living abroad, **2:**236; Croatia, **3:**348; Gaddi, **2:**36; Igbo, **1:**196; Jie, **1:**134; Kashmir, **2:**61; Korea, **2:**298; Malaita, **1:**305; Malta, **3:**505–506; Nepal, **2:**115–116; Orissa, **2:**83; Palestine, **2:**404, 406; Persia, **2:**418–421; Poland, **3:**384–385; Roma, **3:**397; Samoa, **1:**393; Seminole, **4:**114; Tairora, **2:**204; Taiwan, **2:**263; Tajik, **2:**333; Ukraine, **3:**444; Vanuatu, **1:**329; Yoruba, **1:**223. *See also* Baptism; Circumcision

Child naming: Abanyole, **1:**125; Ashkenazim, **3:**333; Bangladesh, **2:**104; Benin, **1:**177; Berber, **1:**104; and ethnicity, **1:**26; Greece, **3:**495–496; Khasi-Jaintia, **2:**71; Malaita, **1:**306; Nagaland, **2:**78–79; Nepal, **2:**116; Samoa, **1:**387; Sephardim, **3:**220; Shona, **1:**250; Slovakia, **3:**291; Tuareg, **1:**104, 108; Yoruba, **1:**222

Children's Crusade, **3:**268

Children's games: Ashkenazim, **3:**337; Croatia, **3:**348; Denmark, **3:**86, 87; Greece, **3:**499–500; Haiti, **4:**325; Jamaica, **4:**341; Norway, **3:**131; Western Inuit and Yupik, **4:**133, 139–140; Xavante, **4:**244–245. *See also* Games, sports, and recreation

Children's songs, stories, and verses: Albania, **3:**328; Armenia, **2:**366; Australia (British), **1:**284; England, **3:**20; Finnish-Swedish, **3:**100–101; Ga, **1:**187–190; Italy, **3:**462; Jamaica, **4:**341; Malaita, **1:**301; Nagaland, **2:**77; Nez Perce, **4:**101–102; Palestine, **2:**409; Tuvalu, **1:**407; Uzbek, **2:**352; Vanuatu, **1:**330; Western Inuit and Yupik, **4:**133, 139–140

CHIME, **2:**231

China, **2:**211–233; arts, crafts, and architecture, **2:**226–228; clothing styles and food, **2:**228–229; drama, **2:**224–225; folksongs, **2:**218–221; folktales and legends, **2:**216–218; geography and history, **2:**211–213; India, comparison with, **2:**9; modernization, challenges of, **2:**229–231; music, **2:**222–223; myths, **2:**215–216; narrative poems, **2:**216; opera, **2:**224; oral folklore traditions, **2:**214–215; paper cutting, **2:**228; preserving Chinese folklore, **2:**214; religious beliefs, **2:**213–214; sports and games, **2:**225–226; storytelling and musical performance, **2:**221–222; studies of Chinese folklore, **2:**231

Chinese Exclusion Act (U.S. 1882), **1:**65

Chinese living abroad, **2:**233–245; anti-Chinese nativism, **1:**65; arts, crafts, and architecture, **2:**242; food and medicine, **2:**240–241; history, **2:**233–235; Mississippi Delta, **4:**173; modernization, challenges of, **2:**243; myths and folktales, **2:**241–242; religious beliefs, **2:**235–236; rituals, festivals, and celebrations, **2:**236–240; sports and games, **2:**242; studies of overseas Chinese folklore, **2:**243

Chingisizm, **2:**308

Chinoperl Papers, **2:**231

Chinyanta Shadrack Nankula (Mwata Kazembe XIV), **1:**235

CHIPAWO (Children's Performing Arts Workshop), **1:**254

Chippewa. *See* Ojibwe

Chivalrous combat in Georgian folktales, **3:**357

Choctaw, **4:**30–38; arts and crafts, **4:**32, 34–35; dance, **4:**33–34; geography and history, **4:**30–32; modernization, challenges of, **4:**37; myths, legends, and folktales, **4:**35–36; studies of Choctaw folklore, **4:**37–38; supernatural lore, **4:**36–37

Choctaw Fair, **4:**32–33

Choeten Zangmo, **2:**110

Chomsky, Noam, **1:**69

Choris, Louis, **1:**350

Christening ritual. *See* Baptism

Christian V, **3:**83

Christianity: African American, **4:**145; Armenia, **2:**357, 363, 368; Assam, **2:**18; Australia (British), **1:**289, 290; Bangladesh, **2:**95, 96; Baule, **1:**164; Benin, **1:**179; Bihar, **2:**25; Caipira, **4:**180; Candoshi, **4:**182; Caribs of Dominica, **4:**331–332; Cherokee, **4:**11; Cheyenne, **4:**24; China, **2:**213; Chinese living abroad, **2:**236, 239; Choctaw, **4:**37; Duna, **2:**166, 167; Ecuador, **4:**191–192; Guam, **1:**333, 337; Haiti, **4:**317–319, 321; Iroquois, **4:**59; Israel, **2:**372, 374; Jamaica, **4:**343; Kadazandusun, **2:**177, 181; Karnataka, **2:**48; Kazakh, **2:**308; Kewa, **2:**189, 196; Khasi-Jaintia, **2:**66, 73; Kiowa, **4:**62–63; Kurds, **2:**385, 389; Lakota, **4:**69;

Lebanon, **2:**392, 398, 399; Lunda, **1:**236; Malaita, **1:**301–303; Maluku, **2:**197, 198–199; Marquesas Islands, **1:**378, 380, 381; Maya, **4:**261; Mexico, **4:**269–270; Mongol, **2:**253; Navajo, **4:**87, 88; Nepal, **2:**114–115; New Caledonia, **1:**313; Ojibwe, **4:**109; Otomí, **4:**290–292; Palestine, **2:**401, 406; Peru, **4:**200–201, 205–206; Quechua, **4:**209; Rarámuri, **4:**297–298, 301–302; Samoa, **1:**394–396; Seminole, **4:**112; Shona, **1:**249, 252; Shuar, **4:**220, 224; Siberia, **2:**320; Sri Lanka, **2:**125, 126; Tairora, **2:**209; Taiwan, **2:**261; Tlingits, **4:**119; Tonga, **1:**399–401; Trobriand Islands, **1:**319–320; Turkey, **2:**430; Tuvalu, **1:**405; Vanuatu, **1:**325, 326–327; Western Inuit and Yupik, **4:**131–132; Xhosa, **1:**258, 260, 263, 266–267; Zande, **1:**228; Zulu, **1:**272

Christianity, early: Brittany, **3:**174; Denmark, **3:**83; England, **3:**4; Finland, **3:**90; France, **3:**160–161; Georgia, **3:**354; Germany, **3:**261; Hungary, **3:**279; Latvia, **3:**365–366; Macedonia, **3:**371; Malta, **3:**504; Poland, **3:**380; Russia, **3:**411–412, 415–417; Sámi, **3:**136; Scotland, **3:**55; Serbia, **3:**426, 429, 430; Slovakia, **3:**286–287; Ukraine, **3:**438; Wales, **3:**73

Christiansen, Reidar, **3:**137

Christmas customs: England, **1:**2; Jamaica, **4:**338; Russia, **3:**416; Serbia, **3:**431–432

Christmas tree (Austria), **3:**253

Chronological primitivism, **1:**73

Chulkov, M.D., **3:**410

Chunkey game (Cherokee), **4:**16–17

Churchill, Winston, **3:**38

Church of England, **1:**1–2

Ciarmavermi (magician, Sicily), **3:**490

"Cinderella," **1:**22, 95; England, **3:**12; Germany, **3:**266; Ireland, **3:**29; San, **1:**241

Circumcision: Abanyole, **1:**125; Bangladesh, **2:**104; Berber, **1:**108; and ethnicity, **1:**26; Palestine, **2:**406; Roma, **3:**398; Tajik, **2:**329, 333; Vanuatu, **1:**329; Wolof, **1:**211

Civilization and Its Discontents (Freud), **1:**74–75

Civil rights (Tlingits), **4:**126

Civil wars. *See* Wars and conflicts

Clans: Australian Aborigines, **1:**295; Brittany, **3:**174; Hopi, **4:**45–47; Iroquois, **4:**51; Japan, **2:**273, 275, 276; Jie, **1:**136; Kazakh, **2:**309; Kewa, **2:**189, 191; Khasi-Jaintia, **2:**67; Kiribati, **1:**341, 342; Malaita, **1:**301; Manchu, **2:**246; Marshall Islands, **1:**350; New Caledonia, **1:**310; Roma, **3:**397; Serbia, **3:**426; Tlingit, **4:**117; Trobriand Islands, **1:**316, 317; Tuareg, **1:**114; Wolof, **1:**214. *See also* Family relationships

Classes of society. *See* Social structure

The Classic of Mountains and Seas (China), **2:**215

Clavie (Scotland), **3:**65

Clavijero, Francisco, **4:**276

Cleansing ritual (Isle of Man), **3:**48

1: Topics & Themes, Africa, Australia & Oceania
2: Southeast Asia & India, Central & East Asia, Middle East
3: Europe
4: North & South America

Cleverness. *See* Trickster

"The Clever Peasant Girl," **1**:95; Mascarene Islands, **1**:146

"Click Go the Shears" (Australia [British]), **1**:286

Clifford, James, **1**:48

Clinton, Bill, **2**:381

Clothing: Austria, **3**:258–259; Berber, **1**:106; Cherokee, **4**:18; China, **2**:227, 228–229; and colonialism, **1**:7–8; Gaddi, **2**:35; Greece, **3**:499; Hawai'i, **1**:371–372; Iceland, **3**:117–119; Igbo, **1**:201–202; Ijo, **1**:207; and invented tradition, **1**:50; Kazakh, **2**:312; Kiribati, **1**:347; Lumba, **1**:240; Malaita, **1**:303, 304; Malta, **3**:506; Manchu, **2**:246, 250, 251; Marquesas Islands, **1**:379, 384; Maya, **4**:262–263; Norway, **3**:130; Palestine, **2**:407, 408; Seminole, **4**:112–113; Siberia, **2**:316, 323; Sibundoy, **4**:234; Slovakia, **3**:294; Tairora, **2**:205, 208; Tajik, **2**:331–332; Trobriand Islands, **1**:324; Tuvalu, **1**:409; Wales, **3**:77; Western Inuit and Yupik, **4**:130; Wolof, **1**:212; Yoruba, **1**:224–225

Clottey, Attuquaye, **1**:186

Clovis, **3**:161

Club War (Finland), **3**:91

Coal miners and mining. *See* Miners and mining

Cockfighting: Bali, **2**:161; Ecuador, **4**:192; Iban, **2**:175; Kadazandusun, **2**:180. *See also* Games, sports, and recreation

"Codding" (expressive lying, Ireland), **3**:37

Cohen, Erik, **1**:86

Coleman, Simon, **1**:86

Colenso, J.W. (bishop of Natal), **1**:271, 274

Collier, Michael, **3**:36

Collins, Samuel, **3**:410

Colmcille, Saint, **3**:30–31

Colombia: Sibundoy, **4**:229–230

Colonialism, **1**:7–10; and diaspora, **1**:19; and ethnicity, **1**:25; and Ga, **1**:181; and globalization, **1**:42; and Shona, **1**:248; and Swahili, **1**:154, 159, 160; and Zande, **1**:228. *See also* British rule and influence; France; Spanish exploration and conquest

Comedia (Spanish drama), **3**:184

Comedy. *See* Humorous stories, skits, etc.

Communication and translation, **1**:89

The Comoros, **1**:142–143; beliefs and folklore, **1**:142–143; geography and history, **1**:142

A Comparative Study of Kashmiri and Hindi Folksongs (Handoo), **2**:62

Competence and performance, **1**:69–70

Competition as theme (Swahili), **1**:158, 159

Confucianism: China, **2**:212–213; Chinese living abroad, **2**:235, 236; Japan, **2**:275, 276; Korea, **2**:300; Taiwan, **2**:261

"Confusion of Tongues" (Nagaland), **2**:76

Conjuring. *See* Incantations

Conspiracy rumors (African American), **4**:151

Constantine (Emperor), **3**:160

Constantine VII Porphyrogenitus, **3**:347

Constellation stories. *See* Astrology

Constitution (Mexico), **4**:269

Contes du Temps passé, **3**:266

Contests. *See* Games, sports, and recreation; Races

Contrary Dance (Cheyenne), **4**:28

Cook, James, **1**:309, 366, 374, 378

Cooking. *See* Food customs and beliefs

"The Coon in the Box" (African American), **4**:144

Corn (Cherokee), **4**:19

Coronado, Francisco Vásquez de, **4**:1; and Hopi, **4**:44

Corridos (Mexico), **4**:273

Cortés, Hernán, **4**:275–276

Cortés, Martín, **4**:275–276

Cortez, Joaquín, **3**:185

Corvinus, Matthias, **3**:276

Cosmogonic myth (Poland), **3**:380

Cosmology. *See* Worldview

Costumes. *See* Clothing; Masks and masquerades

Cotters, Denmark, **3**:134

Council of Forty-Four (Cheyenne), **4**:22–23, 25

Counter-Reformation (Italy), **3**:457

Courtship: Appalachia, **4**:161; Choctaw, **4**:34; France, **3**:163; Italy, **3**:454; Kewa, **2**:194; Lakota stories, **4**:72; Scotland, **3**:56; Shona, **1**:250; Tlingit, **4**:124

Coyote tales (Nez Perce), **4**:100–103

"Cracker Night" (Australia [British]), **1**:290

Cradleboards (Apache), **4**:6

Crafts. *See* Arts and crafts

Crang, Mike, **1**:86

Creation stories: Apache, **4**:3–4; Armenia, **2**:357; Australian Aborigines, **1**:293–294, 297, 298; Bangladesh, **2**:99; Cherokee, **4**:11, 12; Cheyenne, **4**:25–26; China, **2**:215; Chinese living abroad, **2**:235; Duna, **2**:166, 168–169; Equador, **4**:198–199; Gaddi, **2**:32–34; Guam, **1**:335; Haida, **4**:40–42; Hawai'i, **1**:366, 370; India, **2**:5; Iroquois, **4**:54, 56; Isaan, **2**:135; Japan, **2**:274; Kadazandusun, **2**:177, 178; Kazakh, **2**:307–309; Kewa, **2**:191; Khasi-Jaintia, **2**:67–68; Kiribati, **1**:342; Korea, **2**:295–296; Lakota and Dakota, **4**:72; Malaita, **1**:302; Malay, **2**:142; Maluku, **2**:198–199; Manchu, **2**:247–248; Mescalero Apache, **4**:4; Mongol, **2**:255; Nagaland, **2**:75, 77; Navajo, **4**:85; Orissa, **2**:80–81; Otomí, **4**:290–293; Palau, **1**:360–361; Palestine, **2**:404; Persia, **2**:414–416; Roma, **3**:406; Samoa, **1**:388–389; San, **1**:242; Seminole, **4**:115;

Siberia, **2**:317–318; Tairora, **2**:206–207; Tonga, **1**:397, 400; Turkey, **2**:432; Tuvalu, **1**:406; Vanuatu, **1**:328; Xavante, **4**:249–250; Xhosa, **1**:259–260; Yanomami, **4**:252, 254; Zulu, **1**:269–270

Creoles, **1**:10–12; and Dominica, **4**:330, 335–336

Creolization, **1**:10–12; and Caribbean, **1**:10; and globalization, **1**:42; and hybridity, **1**:47; and Indian Ocean, **1**:10; and Latin America, **1**:10; and Louisiana, **1**:10; and Madagascar, **1**:10; and Mascarene Islands, **1**:144; and Mauritius and Rodrigues, **1**:144, 146; and nativism, **1**:65; and race, **1**:78

Crick, M., **1**:86

Criollos (Mexico), **4**:275–276

Croatia, **3**:341–352; Central, **3**:345–346; history, **3**:347–352; Littoral, **3**:341–343; Lowland, **3**:346–347; Mountainous, **3**:343–344

Croatian Peasant Party, **3**:351

Cromwell, Oliver, **3**:3, 15, 36

Crooked Mick of the Speewah, **1**:286

Crops. *See* Agriculture and farming

Crosh cuirns (Isle of Man), **3**:47, 48

Cross-dressing. *See* Transvestites, transsexuals, cross-dressing

Crusades, **3**:162–164, 365–366, 509

Cruz, San Juan de la, **3**:181

Cuba, **4**:309–315; and diaspora, **1**:20; fusion of cultures, **4**:315; geography and history, **4**:309–310; music literature, **4**:312–313; myths, legends, and folktales, **4**:313–315; sacred music and dance, **4**:310; secular music and dance, **4**:311–312

Culin, Steward, **2**:241–242

Cultural absolutism, **1**:15

Cultural and Natural Areas of Native North America (Kroeber), **1**:16

Cultural continuity of Greece, **3**:494, 495

Cultural creolization, **1**:10–11

Cultural evolution, **1**:12–14; geology as influence, **1**:12; and translation, **1**:91

Cultural exceptionalism. *See* Nationalism

Cultural imperialism, **1**:38

Cultural primitivism. *See* Primitivism

Cultural relativism, **1**:14–16; Boas, Franz, **1**:14–15; and cultural evolution, **1**:14; and Plato, **1**:14; and religion, **1**:14

Cultural studies tradition, **1**:72

Culture area, **1**:16–18; and motif, **1**:54, 55; and museum, **1**:57. *See also* Geography

Cunning. *See* Trickster

Cunningham, Allan, **3**:59

Cures. *See* Medicine and cures

Curutons (Kaingang myth), **4**:196

Customs and Traditions of Palestine, **2**:411

Cycles of life. *See* Life-cycle rituals and beliefs

Cyfarwyddiaid (storytellers, Wales), **3**:72

Cyril, Saint, **3**:371, 426, 429

Dabke dance (Lebanon), **2**:395, 396–397

Dadié, Bernard, **1**:168

Dainihonkoku Hokekyokenki (Buddhist tales, Japan), **2:**274

Dakota: "as-told-to" stories, **4:**73–74; geography and history, **4:**67–70; modernization, challenges of, **4:**75–76; music and songs, **4:**74, 77; myths, legends, and folktales, **4:**70; storytelling, **4:**73–74; vision talks, **4:**73; war stories, **4:**73

Dal, V.I., **3:**410

Dalí, Salvador, **3:**186

Damatian Klapa Festival (Croatia), **3:**343

Danaher, Kevin, **3:**23

Dance. *See* Music and dance

Danilov, Kirsha, **3:**410

Da-ño're (Xavante), **4:**246–248

Dansk Folke Museum, **1:**58

Daoism, **2:**217; China, **2:**213, 223; Chinese living abroad, **2:**236, 241; Japan, **2:**276; Taiwan, **2:**261, 268

Darcy, Les, **1:**286

Darkness khan (Mongol), **2:**255

Darwin, Charles, **1:**12

Das, Tulsi, **2:**92

Daun, Åke, **3:**150

Davenport, William Henry, **1:**353

David (Biblical King), **3:**357

David (Dewi), Saint, **3:**73–74

Davidson, Alan, **1:**11

David the Builder, **3:**357

Davies, Owen, **3:**10

Da-wawa (Xavante), **4:**248–249

Day of the Dead (Mexico), **4:**271, 272–273

Dayworkers, Italy, **3:**457

Dead. *See* Ancestors and dead

"Dead" water (Ukraine), **3:**444

Death and mourning rituals: Ashkenazim, **3:**333; Bhutan, **2:**110; Brittany, **3:**172; Croatia, **3:**349; Kiribati, **1:**343, 346; Madagascar, **1:**140; Malta, **3:**505; Marshall Islands, **1:**351; Nepal, **2:**116, 121; Réunion, **1:**148; Roma, **3:**401–402; Vanuatu, **1:**329; Yoruba, **1:**222; Zande, **1:**232. *See also* Funerals and burials

Death wedding (Ukraine), **3:**441

Décima (Cuban song form), **4:**312–313

Decolonization and diaspora, **1:**19

Deep Benin language (Benin), **1:**171

"Defiant girl" story (Mauritius and Rodrigues), **1:**146–147

Dégh, Linda, **1:**68, **3:**280, 283

Deities. *See* Gods and goddesses

DeKeyser, P., **3:**229

Delafosse, Maurice, **1:**165

Delargy, James, **3:**28

Delarue, Paul, **3:**196

Demographics: Assam, **2:**18–19; Bangladesh, **2:**95–96; Israel, **2:**278; Malta, **3:**506–507; Serbia, **3:**426; Swahili, **1:**158; Taiwan, **2:**260. *See also* History

Denmark, **3:**80–89; calendars, **3:**85–88; celebrations, **3:**88; geography and history, **3:**80–82; music and dance, **3:**85; religion

and beliefs, **3:**83; supernatural lore, **3:**83–85

Dennis, C.J., **1:**285

"The Derby Ram" (Australia [British]), **1:**285

Derwêshê Ebdî story (Kurds), **2:**388

A Description of the Isle of Man, **3:**43

Deutsche Gesellschaft für Volkskunde (German Folklore Society), **1:**6

Deutsche Legenden, **3:**267

"The Devil's Riddle," **1:**95

Devotional art, Sicily, **3:**489–490

Dhlomo, H.I.E., **1:**261

Dhola tale (Uttar Pradesh), **2:**91

Dhuwa (Australian Aborigines), **1:**295–296

Dialects: Assam, **2:**21; Bihar, **2:**30; Haryana, **2:**44. *See also* Creolization; Language

Diamondback rattlesnake motif (Choctaw), **4:**35

Días de los Muertos, **1:**7

Diaspora, **1:**18–22; Australia (British), **1:**281; and globalization, **1:**19, 21, 42; and hybridity, **1:**47; Jewish Diaspora, **1:**18–20; and race, **1:**78; Shona, **1:**254; Swahi, **1:**158; Vlach, John Michael, **1:**20

Díaz, Porfirio, **4:**278–279

Dice games: Cherokee, **4:**17; Peru, **4:**207. *See also* Gambling

Dickens, Charles, **3:**13

Diddley bows (Mississippi Delta), **4:**172

Diffusion, **1:**13, 22–24; and modernization, **1:**53; and motif, **1:**54

Digitalization, **1:**5

Dikes and drainage, **3:**234–235

Dilemma stories: Abanyole, **1:**123; Bhutan, **2:**108; Bihar, **2:**26–27

Dimitri-Taikon, Johan, **3:**149

Dinaric cultural zone. *See* Croatia, Mountainous

Dingane (Zulu king), **1:**269

Dinka, **1:**151

Dinnsenchas ("place lore"), **3:**35

Dinuzulu (Zulu king), **1:**273

Diocletian (Emperor), **3:**347

Dipendra (Crown Prince of Nepal), **2:**114

Diple musical instrument, **3:**344

Dirges. *See* Laments; Poetry

Discrimination and racism, **1:**79; African American, **4:**149; Haiti, **4:**318; Mauritius and Rodrigues, **1:**145

Diseases: effects on frontier, **1:**37–38; Hopi, **4:**44–45

"Dismantling Local Culture" (Shuman), **1:**43

Disney, Walt, **3:**267

Disobedience tales: Mauritius and Rodrigues, **1:**146; Nez Perce, **4:**101–102; San, **1:**244

"Disobedient Boy" (Nez Perce), **4:**101

Dispute settlement: Marshall Islands, **1:**350; Nuer, **1:**151; Tairora, **2:**209

Divani Lugat-at-Tiurk (Collection of Turkik Language), **2:**310

Divination. *See* Diviners and divination

Divine Right of Kings, **3:**161, 163

Diviners and divination: Baule, **1:**166, 167; Benin, **1:**171, 174–176, 179; China, **2:**213; Duna, **2:**167; Finnish-Swedish, **3:**99; Ga, **1:**191–192; Iban, **2:**172; Igbo, **1:**197; Isle of Man, **3:**48–49; Japan, **2:**273; Kaliai, **2:**187; Kewa, **2:**189; Kurds, **2:**386; Madagascar, **1:**139; Malaita, **1:**305; Nuer, **1:**152; Persia, **2:**419; Piedmont and Val d'Aosta, **3:**474; Russia, **3:**416; Shona, **1:**252; Siberia, **2:**319, 320; Tairora, **2:**206; Tuareg, **1:**114; Vanuatu, **1:**327; Yoruba, **1:**222; Zande, **1:**229, 230. *See also* Prophets and prophecies

"Doctor Know-All" (African American), **4:**144

Doctors. *See* Healers; Medicine and cures

Dodge, Mary Mapes, **3:**235

Dodola (rain dance, Serbia), **3:**431

Dolls: Hopi, **4:**49; Western Inuit and Yupik, **4:**139, 140

Dolphins as Christian symbol (Malta), **3:**509

Dominica. *See* Caribs of Dominica

Donohoe, Jack (Australian folk hero), **1:**286

Don Ramiro I, **3:**205

Doornbosch, Ate, **3:**244

Dorson, Richard, **1:**13, 36, 67, 83

Dorst, John, **1:**30, 48

Dotson, Louis, **4:**172

Dough-based cuisine, **3:**339

Douglas, Mary, **1:**28

"The Dowie Dens o Yarrow" (song), **3:**58–59

Dowry system: Bangladesh, **2:**104; Greece, **3:**499; Roma, **3:**398; Russia, **3:**414; Sephardim, **3:**219; Slovakia, **3:**288; Tuareg, **1:**119; Uttar Pradesh, **2:**93; Uzbek, **2:**354

The dozens (African Americans), **4:**150

Dragoi (Albania), **3:**324–325

"The Dragon Slayer," **1:**94–95

Drakos, Georg, **3:**153

Drama and theater: Abanyole, **1:**124–130; Appalachia, **4:**162; Ashkenazim, **3:**336–337; Bali, **2:**161–163; Bangladesh, **2:**99; Basque, **3:**190; Bhutan, **2:**110; China, **2:**214–215, 224–225; England, **3:**16–17; Flanders (Belgium), **3:**231–232; Ga, **1:**192; Georgia, **3:**359–360; Haiti, **4:**321; Haryana, **2:**44; Hungary, **3:**281–282; Igbo, **1:**198–199; Iroquois, **4:**58; Japan, **2:**276–277; Kaliai, **2:**187; Karnataka, **2:**53–54; Kashmir, **2:**63–64; Kiribati, **1:**344; Lakota and Dakota, **4:**74; Macedonia, **3:**374–375; Malay, **2:**143; Manchu, **2:**251; Marquesas Islands, **1:**383; Maya, **4:**261; Mongol, **2:**256; Orissa, **2:**83–84; Quechua, **4:**212–213; Sertão, **4:**219; Shona, **1:**252–253; Shuar, **4:**227; Sicily, **3:**488; Slovakia, **3:**293; Spain, **3:**184; Sri Lanka, **2:**128; Taiwan, **2:**264; Tajik, **2:**329–330; Tlingits, **4:**124–125; Turkey, **2:**435–436; Ukraine, **3:**446; Uttar Pradesh, **2:**92–93; Vanuatu, **1:**329–330

Dramitse Nga Cham dance (Bhutan), **2:**110

"Dream Ballad," **3:**128

Dreamcatchers (Ojibwe), **4:**108

Dream of the Red Chamber (China), **2:**222

1: Topics & Themes, Africa, Australia & Oceania
2: Southeast Asia & India, Central & East Asia, Middle East
3: Europe
4: North & South America

Dreams: Australian Aborigines, **1:**292–299; Denmark, **3:**84; Iceland, **3:**116; Israel, **2:**373, 380; Kewa, **2:**196; Lakota, **4:**74; Malaita, **1:**304–306; Nepal, **2:**118; Nez Perce, **4:**98; Rarámuri, **4:**304; Suriname Maroon, **4:**238; Xavante, **4:**247–249

Dresses. *See* Clothing

Drinking songs and rituals: China, **2:**214, 219; Ga, **1:**191–192; Germany, **3:**271; Khasi-Jaintia, **2:**69; Mongol, **2:**258; Russian wedding, **3:**414; Shuar, **4:**225–226

Drinks: Candoshi, **4:**185; Kariri, **4:**217. *See also specific types*

Drmeš dances (Croatia), **3:**345

"Droll-tellers" (Cornish), **3:**13

Drums: Cherokee, **4:**14; Cuba, **4:**310; Haiti, **4:**322; Iroquois, **4:**59; Maroons of Jamaica, **4:**340; Nahua, **4:**283; Navajo, **4:**87; Shuar, **4:**226; Western Inuit and Yupik, **4:**136–137

Dual faith belief system (Russia), **3:**411, 412

Dube, Violet, **1:**271

Duendes (Guam), **1:**338

Duhovi (Souls' Day, Serbia), **3:**431

Dukhovnye stiki (Russia), **3:**421

Dumy (epic poetry, Ukraine), **3:**440

Duna, **2:**165–170; folktales, **2:**168–169; geography and history, **2:**165–167; medicine and ritual, **2:**167; songs and ballads, **2:**169–170

Duncan Dhu, **3:**184

Duneier, Mitchell, **1:**80

Dunlop, Weary, **1:**286

Duo Dinámico, **3:**184

Dušan the Mighty, **3:**427

Dwellings. *See* Housing

Dybeck, Rikard, **3:**145

Dylan, Bob, **2:**220, **3:**184

"Eagle Catches the Chicks" game (China), **2:**226

Eagle clan (Haida), **4:**39

Easter ceremonies (Rarámuri), **4:**302–304

Easter eggs: Slovenia, **3:**298; Ukraine, **3:**445–446

Eastern Africa, **1:**123–162

Eastern Band of Cherokee Indians, **4:**8, 15–16

East Indian culture (Jamaica), **4:**344–345

East Slavs (Russia), **3:**411, 412

E bukura e Dheut (Beauty of the Land, Albania), **3:**325

Ecuador, **4:**187–192; arts and crafts, **4:**192; festivals and celebrations, **4:**191–192; medicine and magic, **4:**191; poetry, **4:**188–189; religious beliefs and rituals, **4:**197–199; roots of Ecuadorian folklore, **4:**187–188; Shuar, **4:**219–221; songs and

narrative games, **4:**189–190; studies of Ecuadorian folklore, **4:**188

Eddas, **3:**270

Eddic poems (Iceland), **3:**113

Edict of Expulsion (1492), **3:**212

Edo people. *See* Benin

Edward I (England), **3:**71

Edward I (Scotland), **3:**55

Edwards, Ron, **1:**286, 287

Eemut (Jie), **1:**131

Eggert Ólafsson, **3:**117

Eggs: as cure for illness, **3:**439; Slovenia, Easter eggs, **3:**298; Ukraine, Easter eggs, **3:**445–446

Egudu, **1:**197

Ehn, Billy, **3:**151

"Eight Immortals" stories (China), **2:**217

Einar Ólafur Sveinsson, **3:**115

Eira, Mathis Aslaksen. *See* Siri-Matti

Eiríkur Laxdal, **3:**113

Eisteddfod (Wales), **3:**75

"Elastic ball game" (Lower Piedmont), **3:**477

El bosta ("The Bus") song (Lebanon), **2:**394–395

El Cordobés, **3:**186

"Elder Cuckoo" story (Semai), **2:**146

Elders: Shona, **1:**249; Western Inuit and Yupik, **4:**133; Xavante, **4:**249

Elegiac poetry (Igbo), **1:**197

El Greco, **3:**181, 186

Eliade, Mircea, **1:**73

Elias, John, **3:**74

Elias, Norbert, **3:**151

Elijah (prophet), **3:**334, 417

Elijah, Saint, **3:**403, 418

Elizabeth I (Queen of England), **3:**54

Ellamma (Hindu goddess), **2:**50–51

El-Shamy, Hasan, **1:**56

Elustafev, Ilia, **3:**423

Emancipation from slavery: African American, **4:**146; Jamaica, **4:**339. *See also* Slavery

Embree, Ella, **2:**277

Embroidery: Greece, **3:**500; Macedonia, **3:**375; Ukraine, **3:**444–445. *See also* Textile arts

Emeneau, Murray, **2:**3

Emergence mythology. *See* Creation stories

Encyclopedia of a Malay History and Culture (Lumpur), **2:**145

Engiro (Jie), **1:**135, 136

England, **3:**1–21; calendars, **3:**17–20; celebrations, **3:**20; Celtic influence, **3:**4–5; children's folklore, **3:**20; drama, **3:**16–17; geography and history, **3:**1–4; ghost lore, **3:**10–11; life-cycle customs, **3:**20; music and dance, **3:**13–15; myths and legends, **3:**11–13; religion and beliefs, **3:**4; stories and tales, **3:**11–13; storytelling, **3:**11–13; superstition and fairy lore, **3:**5–8; witchcraft and popular magic, **3:**8–10. *See also* British rule and influence

The English and Scottish Popular Ballads (Child), **1:**94

English Anglicanism in Australia, **1:**289

English Civil War, **3:**3

English Folk Dance Society, **3:**14

English language: Ga, **1:**181; Guam, **1:**339; Hawai'i, **1:**371; Kiribati, **1:**348; Malaita, **1:**300; Mascarene Islands, **1:**144; The Seychelles, **1:**149; Vanuatu, **1:**326, 327

Englynion y Beddau (poem), **3:**71

Entrada (Quechua), **4:**213

Environmental determinism, **1:**16–17

Epic of El-Zir Salem (Palestine), **2:**404

Epic of Kajoor (Wolof), **1:**215

Epic stories, tales, poetry: Ainu, **2:**287; Armenia, **2:**359–362; Australian Aborigines, **1:**293, 297; China, **2:**215–216; Croatia, **3:**350; Iban, **2:**174; India, **2:**8–9; Japan, **2:**275; Karnataka, **2:**49, 50; Kazakh, **2:**312; Malaita, **1:**302; Manchu, **2:**246, 247–248; Mexico, **4:**280; Mongol, **2:**254–255; Nahua, **4:**285; Ojibwe, **4:**105; Persia, **2:**415; Russia, **3:**423–424; Siberia, **2:**317–318, 323; Turkey, **2:**432; Ukraine, **3:**440, 441; Uttar Pradesh, **2:**90–91; Uyghur, **2:**337; Uzbek, **2:**350; Wolof, **1:**215; Xhosa, **1:**264; Yemen, **2:**442. *See also* Hero

An Epoch of Miracles (Burns), **4:**260

Epos (heroic songs), **3:**327

Erasmus, **1:**57, **3:**238

Erdélyi, János, **3:**283

Erinmwin (Benin), **1:**172, 174

Erixon, Sigurd, **3:**146–148, 154

Escalade festival (Switzerland), **3:**315

Eschenbach, Wolfram von, **3:**263

Escuder, Tomàs, **3:**196

Esigie, Oba, **1:**178

Eskimos. *See* Western Inuit and Yupik

Es Safi, Wadih, **2:**396

Ethical concepts: Madagascar, **1:**139. *See also* Taboos

Ethiopia's influence in Israel, **2:**381

Ethnic cleansing and romantic nationalism, **1:**62

Ethnicity, **1:**25–27; Caucasia, **3:**356; and diaspora, **1:**19; and globalization, **1:**42; Lumba, importance of assertion, **1:**240; Mexico, **4:**270; Sri Lanka, **2:**124–126; Swahili, **1:**158

Ethnocentrism and nativism, **1:**64

Ethnography, **1:**27–31; and fieldwork, **1:**27, 33; and gender, **1:**39–41; Haiti, **4:**319–320, 326–327; Maya, **4:**256–257; and museums, **1:**59; and performance theory, **1:**69; Peru, **4:**200–201; and public folklore, **1:**76; and race, **1:**81; Sibundoy, **4:**229; and text, **1:**84; and translation, **1:**91; Western Inuit and Yupik, **4:**129; and worldview, **1:**98, 99; Yanomami, **4:**251

Ethnography and Folklore Archive of Catalonia, **3:**196

Ethnology (Sweden), **3:**146–151

Ethnomusicology (Hungary), **3:**280

Ethnopoetics, **1:**31–32; and translation, **1:**91

Ethnotouism, Macedonia, **3:**377

Etiological tales: Abanyole, **1:**123; Duna, **2:**168; Kashmir, **2:**61; Khasi-Jaintia, **2:**71; Lunda, **1:**236; Mongol, **2:**255. *See also* Creation stories

Eulogies. *See* Funerals and burials

Euro-Americans, contact with: Cherokee, **4:**10; Iroquois, **4:**52; Kiowa, **4:**61–62; Navajo, **4:**82; Nez Perce, **4:**99; Ojibwe, **4:**104–106; Western Inuit and Yupik, **4:**130–132

Europaeus, David, **3:**93

European folklore: and African-American tales, **4:**143–144; and Afro-Cuban myths, **4:**314; and Jamaican tales, **4:**341–342; and Nahua tales, **4:**284–286

Evans, Ivor, **2:**178

Evans-Pritchard, Edward Evan, **1:**150, 151, 228, 229–230

Evil eye, **1:**26; Berber, **1:**103–104; Greece, **3:**496; Malta, **3:**503–504; Sephardim, **3:**213; Wolof, **1:**211. *See also* Supernatural beliefs

Evil spirits (Sertão), **4:**217–218

"Evil Spirits, Evil Humans" (Igbo), **1:**197

Evolution. *See* Cultural evolution

Ewedo, Oba (Benin ruler), **1:**171

Eweka I (Benin ruler), **1:**171

Ewi (Yoruba), **1:**223

Ewuare, Oba (Benin ruler), **1:**173, 175

Exceptionalism, **1:**62–63

Exempla. *See* Stories and tales

Exile and diaspora, **1:**19

Exorcism: Lunda, **1:**236; Nuer, **1:**152–153; Shona, **1:**252. *See also* Spirit possession

Ex-voto (Sicily), **3:**489–490

Eyes of Osiris (Malta), **3:**503

"EzikaSarili" (Praises of Sarili) (Xhosa), **1:**262–263

Faatele (Tuvalu), **1:**407–408

Fables. *See* Stories and tales

Fabulates (Russia), **3:**418

Factor, June, **1:**284

Fafnir, **3:**270

Fairouz (singer, Lebanon), **2:**394

Fairs (Navajo), **4:**89

Fairy Bridge (Isle of Man), **3:**44–45

"A Fairy Husband" (Nagaland), **2:**76

Fairy lore, **1:**95; Albania, **3:**328–329; England, **3:**5–9; European, influence on Nahua tales, **4:**284–286; Finnish-Swedish, **3:**99; Georgia, **3:**356–358; Ireland, **3:**32–34; Isle of Man, **3:**44–47; Poland, **3:**381, 391; Roma, **3:**406; Scotland, **3:**55–56

"A Fairy Wife" (Nagaland), **2:**76

Fakelore, **1:**36

Faldetta (female clothing, Malta), **3:**506

Fall, Cheikh Ibra (Wolof ruler), **1:**212

Family relationships: Armenia, **2:**366–367; Assam, **2:**28; Bali, **2:**155; Bangladesh, **2:**98; Candoshi, **4:**181; China, **2:**212; The Comoros, **1:**142; eating flesh of relative unwittingly, motif of, **1:**56; Guam, **1:**334; Hawai'i, **1:**366–368; Hopi, **4:**46; Iroquois,

4:51; Israel, **2:**377; Italy, **3:**453; Kaliai, **2:**183; Kewa, **2:**189–191; Khasi-Jaintia, **2:**66; Lakota and Dakota, **4:**68, 72; Lebanon, **2:**395; Madagascar, **1:**139; Malta, **3:**507; Marshall Islands, **1:**350; Navajo, **4:**84; Nepal, **2:**115; New Caledonia, **1:**309–311; Peru, **4:**200; San, **1:**243; Seminole, **4:**116; Serbia, **3:**428; Shuar, **4:**221–222; Tlingit, **4:**117–118; Trobriand Islands, **1:**316–318; Turkey, **2:**430; Uttar Pradesh, **2:**91; Western Inuit and Yupik, **4:**132–133; Yoruba, **1:**225. *See also* Clans

Far from the Madding Crowd (Hardy), **3:**18

Farming. *See* Agriculture and farming

Far Out, Brussel Sprout! (Australia), **1:**284

Fastnacht festival: Austria, **3:**251; Germany, **3:**262–263; Switzerland, **3:**316–317

Fate: Chinese living abroad, **2:**235; Italy, **3:**453; Nepal, **2:**116; Palestine, **2:**407; Taiwan, **2:**262; Uttar Pradesh, **2:**90; Zande, **1:**229–230

"Father" image of Greek nation, **3:**494

"Fatherland" trademarks, Switzerland, **3:**314

"Father of Foolishness" tales (Iban), **2:**174

Fawkes, Guy, **3:**19

Feast of Saint Barbara (Lebanon), **2:**399

Feast of the Shaman (Ecuador), **4:**198

Feasts, calendar and farmers, revival of, **3:**478

Federal Writers Project (WPA), **1:**76

Fedosova, Irina, **3:**411

Feijoo, Benito Jerónimo, Fray, **3:**181

Feng shui (geomancy): Chinese living abroad, **2:**235, 237–240; Taiwan, **2:**263

Fenian Cycle, **3:**28–30

Ferrer Ginard, Andreu, **3:**195

Fertility: Albania, **3:**326; Armenia, **2:**367; Ashkenazim, **3:**333; Australian Aborigines, **1:**294, 295; Austria, **3:**252, 256; Bangladesh, **2:**100, 104; Baule, **1:**167; Benin, **1:**173, 175; Berber, **1:**104–106, 110; Bihar, **2:**29; Brittany, **3:**172; Croatia, **3:**345, 349; Denmark, **3:**86; Duna, **2:**166; England, **3:**17; Georgia, **3:**359–360; Haryana, **2:**42; Hopi, **4:**48; Isaan, **2:**132, 138; Isle of Man, **3:**47; Israel, **2:**372; Italy, **3:**457; Karnataka, **2:**50, 55; Kashmir, **2:**62; Manchu, **2:**250; Orissa, **2:**86; Otomí, **4:**293; Palestine, **2:**406, 408; Piedmont and Val d'Aosta, **3:**475; Poland, **3:**384, 387, 388; Roma, **3:**398–401, 403; Russia, **3:**415, 416; Samoa, **1:**389; Shuar, **4:**226; Siberia, **2:**317; Sweden, **3:**151; Ukraine, **3:**445; Uttar Pradesh, **2:**89; Zulu, **1:**270

Festa (Malta), **3:**508–509

Festival of Herdsmen and Cheesemakers, **3:**311–312

Festivals and celebrations: African American, **4:**146; Ainu, **2:**291–292; Appalachia, **4:**161; Assam, **2:**20–21; Australia (British), **1:**290; Bali, **2:**155, 159; Bangladesh, **2:**99–100; Benin, **1:**172, 174, 178; Caipira, **4:**180; Candoshi, **4:**185–186; Catalan, **3:**197–200;

Cherokee, **4:**15; China, **2:**218–219; Chinese living abroad, **2:**236–240; Choctaw, **4:**32–33; Cuba, **4:**311; Damatian Klapa Festival, Croatia, **3:**343; Denmark, **3:**88; Ecuador, **4:**191–192, 198; England, **3:**20; Ga, **1:**186, 192; Gaddi, **2:**36–37; Germany, **3:**265; Greenland, **3:**108–109; Haiti, **4:**323; Haryana, **2:**43–44; Hawai'i, **1:**366; Hungary, **3:**282; Igbo, **1:**199; India, **2:**11–13; Isaan, **2:**134; Israel, **2:**372, 376, 380; Italy, **3:**464–465; Ivan Kupalo (Ukraine), **3:**446; Jamaica, **4:**338–339, 344–345; Kadazandusun, **2:**179–180; Kashmir, **2:**64–65; Kazakh, **2:**313–314; Khasi-Jaintia, **2:**68–69; Kiribati, **1:**342, 344; Korea, **2:**301–303; Kurds, **2:**386; laurel, Sicily, **3:**487–488; Lebanon, **2:**399–400; Lunda, **1:**236, 239–240; Malaita, **1:**302; Malta, **3:**508–509; Marquesas Islands, **1:**379–381, 383; Marshall Islands, **1:**353, 355; Mexico, **4:**271; Mongol, **2:**258–259; The Netherlands, **3:**241–243; New Caledonia, **1:**313; Norway, **3:**130–131; Ojibwe, **4:**109; Orissa, **2:**85–87; Otomí, **4:**290, 291–292; Palau, **1:**362–364; Palestine, **2:**406–408; Persia, **2:**422–424; Peru, **4:**204–206; Piedmont and Val d'Aosta, **3:**474–478; Quechua, **4:**210–214; Roma, **3:**397–402; Russia, **3:**413–416; Samoa, **1:**393–394; Scotland, **3:**64–65; Serbia, **3:**429–430; Sertão, **4:**218–219; Shuar, **4:**223; Sibundoy, **4:**234–235; Sicily, **3:**487–489; Slovakia, **3:**290; Switzerland, **3:**311–312, 314–317; Taiwan, **2:**266–269; Tajik, **2:**332–334; Tlingits, **4:**127; Tonga, **1:**399; Turkey, **2:**434–435; Vanuatu, **1:**327; Western Inuit and Yupik, **4:**138; Yoruba, **1:**224–225; Zande, **1:**232; Zulu, **1:**270. *See also* Carnival; Harvest rituals; Mardi Gras

Feudal motifs in anecdotes (Macedonia), **3:**372

Fiber arts. *See* Textile arts

Fiddles (Appalachia), **4:**160–161

Field hollers: African Americans, **4:**151–152; Mississippi Delta, **4:**168–169

Fieldwork, **1:**32–35; and archives, **1:**3; and ethnography, **1:**27, 33; and ethnopoetics, **1:**32; and performance theory, **1:**68; and race, **1:**80; and repertoire, **1:**82

Fieldwork reflexivity, **1:**34

Fiestas. *See* Festivals and celebrations

Figo, **3:**186

Figures of speech. *See* Language; Simile and metaphor

Fillmore, Millard, **1:**65

Finding the Center (Tedlock), **1:**31, 85

Fine, Elizabeth C., **1:**85, 91

Finland, **3:**90–97; geography and history, **3:**90–92; German influence, **3:**91–92; *Kalevala*, **3:**92–96; Russian influence, **3:**91–92; Sámi (Lapps), **3:**90; Swedish influence, **3:**90–91

Finnish Literature Society, **1:**3

1: Topics & Themes, Africa, Australia & Oceania
2: Southeast Asia & India, Central & East Asia, Middle East
3: Europe
4: North & South America

Finnish National Museum, **1**:58

Finnish School, **1**:22–23

Finnish-Swedish, **3**:97–103; calendars, **3**:101–102; children's lore, **3**:100–101; geography and history, **3**:97–98; language, **3**:97, 102–103; medicine and cures, **3**:99; music and dance, **3**:100; storytelling, **3**:99–100; supernatural lore, **3**:98–99

Finsch, Otto, **1**:354

Firdausi (Tajik-Persian poet), **2**:326

Firebird: Armenia, **2**:365; Russia, **3**:419

Fisher, Archie, **3**:66

"Fisher's Ghost" (Australia [British]), **1**:286

Fishing: Ga, **1**:182; Ijo, **1**:204; Kaingang, **4**:194; Lunda, **1**:234; Marquesas Islands, **1**:379; New Caledonia, **1**:309; Seminole, **4**:114; Sicily, **3**:483–484; Western Inuit and Yupik, **4**:129–130; Wolof, **1**:209

Fishponds (Hawai'i), **1**:376

Fiske, John, **1**:72

Flags and nationalism, **1**:63

Flamenco, **3**:183, 184–185

Flanders (Belgium), **3**:223–233; architecture, **3**:232; brewing, **3**:232; calendars, **3**:226–229; drama, sports, and games, **3**:231–232; geography and history, **3**:223–225; medicine, **3**:229; myths, legends, songs, and folktales, **3**:229–230; religion and ritual, **3**:225–226; town rivalries, **3**:230–231

Flanders, Helen Hartness, **1**:41

"The Fleeing Pancake," **1**:95

Flood, Bo, **1**:339

Floods: Kaingang, **4**:195–196; Mississippi Delta, **4**:170–171; Yanomami, **4**:252, 254

Flores, Judy S., **1**:339

Flores, Rosario, **3**:183

Flores, Tomasito, **3**:183

Florida: Seminole, **4**:111–112

"Flower of Scotland" (song), **3**:57–58

Flower symbolism: Isle of Man, **3**:47–48; Malta, **3**:509

Flutes (Quechua), **4**:211, 212

Flying Canoe myth (Trobriand Islands), **1**:321–322

Folk Arts Program, **1**:77

Folk high schools (Denmark), **3**:82

Folk idioms. *See* Language

The Folk Literature of a Yucatecan Town (Redfield), **4**:259

Folk Literature of the South American Indians, General Index (Wilbert & Simoneau), **1**:56

Folklore Fellows, **1**:94

Folklore Handbook (Japan), **2**:279

Folklore Institute of Indiana University, **1**:161

Folk-lore Journal (Zulu), **1**:272

Folklore of the Holy Land (Hanauer), **2**:411

Folk-lore of Yucatán (Brinton), **4**:278

Folk-Lore Society (Bangladesh), **2**:95

The Folklore Text from Performance to Print (Fine), **1**:85

Folklorism, **1**:35–37; and modernization, **1**:52

Folklorism Bulletin, **1**:37

Folk medicine. *See* Medicine and cures

Folksong. *See* Music and dance

Folk Songs of Australia (Australia [British]), **1**:285

Folk Songs of Australia and the Men and Women Who Sang Them (Australia [British]), **1**:285

Folk Song Style and Culture (Lomax), **1**:17

Folktales. *See* Stories and tales

Folk Traditions of the Arab World (El-Shamy), **1**:56

Food customs and beliefs: Appalachia, **4**:164; Ashkenazim, **3**:332; Australia (British), **1**:290; Australian Aborigines, **1**:297; Bali, **2**:159; Bangladesh, **2**:101, 104; Caipira, **4**:179–180; Catalan, **3**:199–200; Cherokee, **4**:19; China, **2**:213, 228–229; Chinese living abroad, **2**:239, 240–241; and creolization, **1**:10–11; Denmark, **3**:87; Duna, **2**:167; and ethnicity, **1**:26; Greece, **3**:498–499; Haida, **4**:42–43; Iceland, **3**:118–119; Igbo, **1**:201–202; India, **2**:5, 13–14, 64; Iroquois, **4**:56; Israel, **2**:379; Kaingang, **4**:193–194; Kaliai, **2**:187; Kiribati, **1**:340, 343; Korea, **2**:296, 304; Lebanon, **2**:395; Malta, **3**:509; Marquesas Islands, **1**:379; Marshall Islands, **1**:349, 355; Nepal, **2**:116–118; Nez Perce, **4**:103; Palestine, **2**:410; Persia, **2**:419, 423; Seminole, **4**:113–114; Sephardim, **3**:219–220; Serbia, **3**:430; Sertão, **4**:216–218; Sicily, **3**:487, 491; Taiwan, **2**:261–263, 266; Trobriand Islands, **1**:316; Uyghur, **2**:345; Wales, **3**:77; Western Inuit and Yupik, **4**:129–130; Zande, **1**:228

Footwear (Western Inuit and Yupik), **4**:130

Foragers: Apache, **4**:1; Cherokee, **4**:19; and cultural shift, **1**:16–17; Kaingang, **4**:193

Ford Foundation, **2**:15, 58

Fortis, Alberto, **3**:350

Fortune-telling: Chinese living abroad, **2**:235; Korea, **2**:303. *See also* Diviners and divination

Forty Day Party (Tlingit), **4**:120

Foster, George, **1**:97

Founding myth of Switzerland, **3**:308–309

Four Sacred Mountains (Navajo reservation), **4**:84

"Fox as Nursemaid for Bear" (Mascarene Islands), **1**:144

Fraguas Fraguas, Antonio, **3**:207

France, **3**:157–170; Baule colonization by, **1**:164; calendars, **3**:168–169; Celts and Roman Gauls, **3**:158–161; ecomusées in, **1**:60; Frankish kingdom, **3**:161–162; French Revolution and Napoleon, **3**:165–167; geography, **3**:157–158; globalization, **3**:169; Greek influence, **3**:158–159; Louis XIV, **3**:164–165; Madagascar occupation by,

1:138; Marquesas Islands annexation by, **1**:377, 380; medieval era, **3**:162–164; nationalistic folk beliefs, **3**:166–167; New Caledonia colonization by, **1**:308–309, 314; open-air museums in, **1**:60; Réunion, as overseas department of, **1**:147; Sahara colonization by, **1**:103, 111, 114, 117; The Seychelles occupation by, **1**:149; storytelling, **3**:163–164; Vanuatu colonization by, **1**:325; Wolof colonization by, **1**:209, 211

Franciscans and Rarámuri, **4**:297

Franco, Francisco, **3**:181, 183, 187, 190, 203, 205

Frankish kingdom, **3**:161–162

Franz Joseph (Emperor), **3**:347

Frazer, James George, **1**:96, **3**:17

Freedom celebrations (African American), **4**:146

Freeman, Derek, **2**:176

French Guiana: Maroon, **4**:236–237

French language: The Comoros, **1**:142; Mascarene Islands, **1**:144; Mascarene Islands, creolization of, **1**:144; The Seychelles, **1**:149; Vanuatu, **1**:326, 327

French Revolution, **3**:165–167

Freney, James, **3**:36

Freud, Sigmund, **1**:74–75

Friedmann, Frederik, **3**:453

Friedrich II, Wittekind, **3**:268–269

Friedrich Wilhelm III (King), **3**:265

Friis, J.A., **3**:137, 140

Frontier, **1**:37–39; Australia (British), **1**:288–289; cultural imperialism, **1**:38; and diffusion, **1**:22; and invented tradition, **1**:50; and nationalism, **1**:37, 38, 62; Roman frontier, **1**:38; Zulu Difaqane, **1**:38

Frybread (Seminole), **4**:114

Frykman, Jonas, **3**:151, 153

Fudoki compilations (Japan), **2**:274

Fundamentalism, **1**:65

Funerals and burials: Abanyole, **1**:128–130; Armenia, **2**:368–369; Australian Aborigines, **1**:294; Baule, **1**:164, 168; Benin, **1**:174; China, **2**:228; Chinese living abroad, **2**:235, 237, 238; Duna, **2**:170; Haiti, **4**:325; Igbo, **1**:196; Ijo, **1**:205, 207; Kadazandusun, **2**:179; Kazakh, **2**:311, 313; Kewa, **2**:191–192; Khasi-Jaintia, **2**:71, 72; Korea, **2**:296–298; Kurds, **2**:386, 387, 389; Lebanon, **2**:398–399; Lunda, **1**:238; Madagascar, **1**:139; Malaita, **1**:303–304; Maroons of Jamaica, **4**:339–340; Marshall Islands, **1**:355; Nepal, **2**:116–117; New Caledonia, **1**:311; Palau, **1**:362; Peru, **4**:201–202; Poland, **3**:385–386; Roma, **3**:402; Russia, **3**:413; Samoa, **1**:393; Shona, **1**:250, 252–254; Suriname Maroons, **4**:239–240; Tairora, **2**:206; Taiwan, **2**:263; Tajik, **2**:329; Tlingit, **4**:120; Ukraine, **3**:443–444; Uzbek, **2**:351; Yoruba, **1**:224; Zande, **1**:232. *See also* Death and mourning rituals; Potlatches

Furniture: Appalachia, **4**:164; Zande, **1**:233

Fürst, Walter, **3**:309

Fur trade: Ojibwe, **4:**104–105; Western Inuit and Yupik, **4:**131

Ga (Gamei), **1:**180–193; children's songs, poems, and lullabies, **1:**187–189; drama, **1:**192; games and "playground verses," **1:**189–190; geography and history, **1:**180–181; housing and major occupations, **1:**182; proverbs and riddles, **1:**182–183; religion, **1:**181–182; rituals, **1:**191–192; songs and poems, **1:**185–187; stories and legends, **1:**184–185

Gaddi, **2:**30–39; festivals and fairs, **2:**36–37; geography and history, **2:**30–32; pilgrimage to Mani Makesh, **2:**34–35; *Saveen* healing chant, **2:**35–36; Shiva folklore, **2:**32–34

Gadeau, Germain Coffi, **1:**168

Gades, Antonio, **3:**185

Gaelic Royal National Mòd, **3:**63

Gaelic songs, **3:**60–62

Gaida (Macedonia), **3:**374

Galicia, **3:**202–211; arts and crafts, **3:**208–209; calendars, **3:**206–208; geography and history, **3:**202–203; St. James and Francisco Franco, **3:**204–206; supernatural lore, **3:**203–204

Gambhira (Bangladesh), **2:**96

Gambling: Ashkenazim, **3:**337; Iroquois, **4:**57; Malaita, **1:**306. *See also* Games, sports, and recreation

Games, sports, and recreation: Apache, **4:**5–6; Appalachia, **4:**162–163; Ashkenazim, **3:**337; Australia (British), **1:**284, 290; Bali, **2:**161; Basque, **3:**194; Baule, **1:**166–167; Benin, **1:**178; Bhutan, **2:**111; Caipira, **4:**179; Cherokee, **4:**16–17; Cheyenne, **4:**28; China, **2:**225–226; Chinese living abroad, **2:**242; Choctaw, **4:**33; Denmark, **3:**86; Ecuador, **4:**189–190; and ethnicity, **1:**26; Finnish-Swedish, **3:**101; Flanders (Belgium), **3:**231–232; Ga, **1:**189–190; Georgia, **3:**360–361; Greece, **3:**499–500; Greenland, **3:**108–109; Haiti, **4:**325; Hawai'i, **1:**373; Hopi, **4:**48; Hungary, **3:**282–283; Iceland, **3:**117; Igbo, **1:**196; Ijo, **1:**207–208; Iroquois, **4:**57; Isaan, **2:**138–139; Jamaica, **4:**341; Japan, **2:**277–278; Kadazandusun, **2:**179–180; Karnataka, **2:**55–56; Kazakh, **2:**312, 313–314; Khasi-Jaintia, **2:**72; Kiowa, **4:**65–66; Kiribati, **1:**342, 346; Kurds, **2:**390–391; Lakota, **4:**74–75; Malaita, **1:**306; Malay, **2:**144; Malta, **3:**511; Marquesas Islands, **1:**380, 384; Marshall Islands, **1:**354; Maya, **4:**263–264; Mongol, **2:**258; Navajo, **4:**89–90; The Netherlands, **3:**243; Norway, **3:**131–132; Nuer, **1:**153; Persia, **2:**424–425; Peru, **4:**207; Piedmont and Val d'Aosta, **3:**477–478; Quechua, **4:**213–214; Rarámuri, **4:**305–306; Samoa, **1:**390, 393; Shona, **1:**253; Siberia, **2:**319; Sicily, **3:**488–489; Slovakia, **3:**293–294; Slovenia, **3:**302–303; Spain, **3:**185–186; Sri Lanka, **2:**126–127; Switzerland, **3:**309–310; Taiwan, **2:**267, 269; Tajik, **2:**330; Tuareg, **1:**118; Turkey, **2:**435–436; Tuvalu, **1:**409; Uttar Pradesh, **2:**93; Vanuatu, **1:**327, 330; Western Inuit and Yupik, **4:**138, 139–140; Wolof, **1:**215; Xavante, **4:**244–245; Zande, **1:**232–233

Games of chance. *See* Gambling

Gamio, Manuel, **4:**279

Gans, Herbert, **1:**71

Gardens. *See* Horticulture

Garland Folklore Bibliographies, **1:**6

Garvey, Keith, **1:**286

Gascon, Francesc, **3:**196

Gaski, Harald, **3:**141

Gates, Henry Louis, Jr., **1:**79

Gathering foods. *See* Foragers

Gaudí, Antonio, **3:**187

Gaup, Nils, **3:**142

Gay folklore, **1:**41

Geertz, Clifford, **1:**48, **3:**151

Geijer, Erik Gustaf, **3:**144

Gelindo Christmas drama, **3:**475

Genc (King), **3:**322

Gender, **1:**39–41; gay folklore, **1:**41; Hopi, **1:**41; male-female duality as theme (Igbo), **1:**195; Sweden, studies on, **3:**151. *See also* Women's roles

Genealogy: Ainu (Japan), **2:**285; Hawai'i, **1:**366–367, 369, 372; Iceland, **3:**112; Kiribati, **1:**341; Marquesas Islands, **1:**382; New Caledonia, **1:**312; Palau, **1:**360; Samoa, **1:**386–387, 390; Tlingit, **4:**120, 124, 126; Tonga, **1:**401; Wolof, **1:**213–214; Zande, **1:**231

Genghis Khan. *See* Khan, Chingis

Genocide and nativism, **1:**64

Geography: Abanyole, **1:**123; Ainu, **2:**285–287; Albania, **3:**320–323; Apache, **4:**1–3; Appalachia, **4:**156–158; Armenia, **2:**357–359; Assam, **2:**17–18; Australian Aborigines, **1:**292–293; Austria, **3:**249–252; Bali, **2:**152–155; Bangladesh, **2:**95–96; Basque, **3:**189–190; Baule, **1:**163–164; Benin, **1:**169–172; Berber, **1:**101–103; Bhutan, **2:**105–106; Bihar, **2:**24–25; Brittany, **3:**170–171; Caipira, **4:**177; Candoshi, **4:**181; Catalan, **3:**195–197; Cherokee, **4:**8; Cheyenne, **4:**21–22; China, **2:**211–213; Choctaw, **4:**30–32; The Comoros, **1:**142; Cuba, **4:**309–310; and culture area, **1:**16–18; Denmark, **3:**80–82; Dominica, **4:**329; Duna, **2:**165–167; Ecuador, **4:**187; England, **3:**1–4; Finland, **3:**90–92; Finnish-Swedish, **3:**97–98; Flanders (Belgium), **3:**223–225; Ga, **1:**180–181; Gaddi, **2:**30–32; Galicia, **3:**202–203; Georgia, **3:**352–354; Germany, **3:**260–262; Greece, **3:**493–494; Greenland, **3:**103–111; Guam, **1:**333–334; Haida, **4:**38–39; Haiti, **4:**316–317; Haryana, **2:**39–40; Hawai'i, **1:**366; Hopi, **4:**44–45; Hungary, **3:**273–278; Iban, **2:**171–173; Iceland, **3:**111–113; Igbo, **1:**193–194; Ijo, **1:**204; India, **2:**1; Ireland, **3:**22–26; Iroquois, **4:**50–51; Isaan, **2:**131; Isle of Man, **3:**41–43; Italy, **3:**450–452; Jamaica, **4:**336; Japan, **2:**271–273; Jie, **1:**131; Kadazandusun, **2:**176–177; Kaingang, **4:**193; Kaliai, **2:**183–184; Karnataka, **2:**46–47; Kashmir, **2:**58–65; Kazakh, **2:**306–308; Kewa, **2:**189–190; Khasi-Jaintia, **2:**65–66; Kiowa, **4:**60–61; Kiribati, **1:**340–341; Korea, **2:**294–296; Kurds, **2:**383–392; Lakota and Dakota, **4:**67–69; Lebanon, **2:**392; Lunda, **1:**234–235; Macedonia, **3:**370–372; Madagascar, **1:**137–138; Malay, **2:**141–142; Malta, **3:**502–504; Maluku, **2:**197–198; Manchu, **2:**245–246; Marquesas Islands, **1:**377–380; Marshall Islands, **1:**349–350; Mauritius and Rodrigues, **1:**144–146; Maya, **4:**256–257; Mexico, **4:**268–269; Mississippi Delta, **4:**166–167; Mongol, **2:**252–254; Nagaland, **2:**73–74; Nahua, **4:**282–283; Navajo, **4:**82–83; The Netherlands, **3:**233–248; New Caledonia, **1:**308–309; Nez Perce, **4:**97; Norway, **3:**123–125; Nuer, **1:**150–151; Ojibwe, **4:**103–105; Orissa, **2:**79–80; Otomí, **4:**288–290; Palau, **1:**358–359; Palestine, **2:**400–403; Persia, **2:**413–414; Peru, **4:**199; Piedmont and Val d'Aosta, **3:**469–470; Quechua, **4:**209; Réunion, **1:**147–148; Roma, **3:**395–397; Sámi, **3:**134–135; San, **1:**240–242; Scotland, **3:**52–55; Semai, **2:**145–146; Seminole, **4:**111–112; Sephardim, **3:**211–214; Serbia, **3:**425–437; The Seychelles, **1:**149; Shona, **1:**248–249; Shuar, **4:**219–221; Siberia, **2:**315–316; Sibundoy, **4:**229–230; Sicily, **3:**480–482; Slovakia, **3:**285–286; Slovenia, **3:**295–296; Spain, **3:**177–180; Sri Lanka, **2:**123–124; Suriname Maroon, **4:**236–237; Swahili, **1:**154–155; Switzerland, **3:**306–307; Tairora, **2:**203–205; Taiwan, **2:**260–261; Tajik, **2:**325–326; Tlingit, **4:**117; Tonga, **1:**397; Trobriand Islands, **1:**316; Tuareg, **1:**101–103; Turkey, **2:**429–432; Tuvalu, **1:**404–405; Ukraine, **3:**437–439; Uttar Pradesh, **2:**88–90; Uyghur, **2:**335–337; Uzbek, **2:**348–350; Vanuatu, **1:**325–326; Wales, **3:**69–72; Western Inuit and Yupik, **4:**128–131; Wolof, **1:**208–209; Xavante, **4:**243; Xhosa, **1:**257–258; Yanomami, **4:**251–252; Yemen, **2:**439–442; Zande, **1:**227–228; Zulu, **1:**267–269. *See also* Culture area

Geology as influence on cultural evolution, **1:**12

George, Saint, **1:**45; Croatia, **3:**349; Georgia, **3:**354, 355; Isle of Man, **3:**50; Roma, **3:**403, 404; Russia, **3:**417; Serbia, **3:**429; Slovakia, **3:**289

Georgia, **3:**352–362; arts, crafts, and architecture, **3:**361–362; drama, **3:**359–360; fairy tales and folktales, **3:**356–358; folklore themes, **3:**354–356; geography and history, **3:**352–354; songs and poetry, **3:**358–359; sports and games, **3:**360–361

1: Topics & Themes, Africa, Australia & Oceania
2: Southeast Asia & India, Central & East Asia, Middle East
3: Europe
4: North & South America

Gerald of Wales, 3:70
Gerholm, Lena, 3:150, 152
"German Charlie" (Australia [British]), 1:286
German Folklore Society, 1:6
Germanic National Museum, 1:58
Germany, 3:260–273; Australia influenced by, 1:278, 279; calendars, 3:262–265; folklore under Nazi regime, 1:62, 3:272; geography and history, 3:260–262; Marshall Islands colonization by, 1:350, 356; myths, legends, and folktales, 3:265–271; Palau colonization by, 1:360; songs and material culture, 3:271
Geronimo, 4:3
Gesamtregister, 1:6
Gesellschaft für Volkskunde, 1:6
Geser epic (Mongol), 2:254–255
Gessler, Governor, 3:308–309
Gessner, Salomon, 3:310
Gherip-Sänäm story (Uyghur), 2:339
Ghiglier, Michael, 4:251–252
Ghost Dance (Kiowa), 4:63
Ghost stories: England, 3:10–11; Ireland, 3:34; Iroquois, 4:59; Karnataka, 2:51; Norway, 3:127; Seminole, 4:115. See also Supernatural beliefs
Ghul (ghoul) tales and superstitions (Persia), 2:418
"Gifting money" practice (Greece), 3:498
Gilbert, Thomas, 1:349
Gilferding A.F., 3:410
Ginzburg, Carlo, 3:457
Girls' Puberty Ceremony, 4:5, 6–7
Giuliano, Salvatore, 3:486
Glasgow Missionary Society, 1:258
Glassie, Henry, 1:70, 3:35
Globalization, 1:42–44; Australia (British), 1:290; Brittany, 3:175; Croatia, 3:352; and culture area, 1:18; and diaspora, 1:19, 42; and diffusion, 1:24; Finnish-Swedish, 3:102–103; France, 3:169; Georgia, 3:362; Guam, 1:339; Hungary, 3:283; and hybridity, 1:42, 47; Madagascar, 1:141; Malta, 3:511; Marquesas Islands, 1:384; and nationalism, 1:42, 62; The Netherlands, 3:240–242, 245; Piedmont and Val d'Aosta, 3:479; Samoa, 1:390–392; San, 1:240; Slovakia, 3:294; Swahilization, 1:158; and tourism, 1:86; Ukraine, 3:448; Wales, 3:77; Wolof, 1:216
Glyndŵr, Owain, 3:71–72
Gods and goddesses: Baule, 1:164; Caipira, 4:178; Cuba, 4:310, 313; Hawai'i, 1:369; Igbo, 1:195; Ijo, 1:204; Japan, 2:272; Malaita, 1:301; Rarámuri, 4:300–301; Russia, 3:411–412; Sámi (Lapps), 3:136; Serbia, 3:429–430; Yoruba, 1:222. See also specific religions and deities

Godunov, Boris, 3:423
Goetz, Herman, 2:32
Goldbert, David Theo, 1:79
The Golden Bough (Frazer), 1:96, 3:17
"Goldilocks and the Three Bears," 1:55
Gold rushes: Australia (British), 1:289; and Western Inuit and Yupik, 4:132
Goldstein, Kenneth S., 1:27, 68, 82
Goldwater, Robert, 1:74
Golem, 3:334
Gombrich, Ernst, 1:74
Gomis, Cels, 3:195
Gomme, Alice Bertha, 3:20
González, José Edwardo, 1:74
González Caturla, Joaquim, 3:196
González Sanz, Carlos, 3:196
Good fortune, portents of (Ashkenazim), 3:333
Goombeh (Maroons of Jamaica), 4:340
Gordimer, Nadine, 1:270
Gordon, Adam Lindsay, 1:284–285, 288
Gorgasali, Vakhtang (King), 3:357
Gossen, Gary, 1:98
Gourd dances (Kiowa), 4:65
Gow, Nathaniel, 3:63
Gow, Niel, 3:63
Gowdy, Bob, 3:34
Gowlett, Derek F., 1:274
Goya, Francisco, 3:185, 186
Grabrijan, Dusan, 3:375
Graburn, Nelson, 1:87
Gradén, Lizette, 3:153
Grain-growing culture, 3:348
Granada, Luis de, Fray, 3:181
"Grandfather's Clock," 1:55
"Grandmother Samsin" stories (Korea), 2:298
Granlund, John, 3:148
Grant, E.W., 1:272
Graphic arts. See Arts and crafts; Painting
"The Grateful Dead," 1:95
Graven images: animals as decorative elements, 3:338; ban on making, 3:337–338
Great Britain. See British rule and influence; England
Great Lakes region: Ojibwe, 4:103–105
Great Moravian Empire (Slovakia), 3:286
Great Plains: Lakota, 4:67–69
Great Siege (Malta), 3:511
Greco-Roman antiquity, 1:5
Greece, 3:493–502; arts, crafts, and architecture, 3:500; food and celebrations, 3:498–499; geography and history, 3:493–494; music and dance, 3:497–498; myths, legends, and folktales, 3:496; proverbs and jokes, 3:497; roots and themes of folklore, 3:494–496; sports and games, 3:499–500
Greek mythology, 3:496, 497, 499
Green Corn Ceremony (Cherokee), 4:15
Green Corn Dance ceremony (Seminole), 4:115
Greenland, 3:103–111; celebrations, 3:108–109; games, 3:108–109; geography

and history, 3:103–105; shamanism, 3:105–107; spells and songs, 3:109–110; storytelling, 3:107–108; supernatural lore, 3:105–107
Greig, Gavin, 3:58
Greyerz, Otto von, 3:313
Grigorovich, V.I., 3:372
Grimm, Jacob, 1:94, 3:269
Grimm, Wilhelm, 1:61, 94
Grimm brothers, influence of, 1:2, 55, 61, 3:12, 114, 243, 265–271; and Nahua tales, 4:285
Grots-Brots (Servandztiants, Armenia), 2:364
"Gruagach òg an fhuilt bhàin" (Fair-haired Young Girl), 3:60
Grundtvig, N.F.S., 1:76, 3:82
Grundtvig, Svend, 3:82
Gstanzl (verse form), 3:257
Guam, 1:333–340; geography and history, 1:333–334; Kantan Chamorrita, 1:338; magical and adventure tales, 1:335–336; modernization, challenges of, 1:339; myths and pourquoi tales, 1:334–335; spirits and the supernatural, 1:337–338; tales of social instruction, 1:336–337
Guam Council on the Arts and Humanities Agency (KAHA), 1:339
Guarani and Caipira, 4:177–178
Guardiola, Pepa, 3:196
Guatemala: Maya, 4:256–268
"The Gucci Kangaroo" (Australia [British]), 1:287
Gugga Chauhan (Rajput warrior), 2:41
A Guide for Fieldworkers in Folklore (Goldstein), 1:27
A Guide to Folktales in the English Language (Ashliman), 1:94
Guilds (Switzerland), 3:315
Guilhem, 3:162
Gunaddhya (early writer, Kashmir), 2:60–61
Gunner, Elizabeth, 1:272
Guru Padmasambhava (Indian Buddhist saint), 2:106, 107, 110
Gusle musical instrument, 3:344
Gustafsson, Lotten, 3:153
Gustavus Adolphus II, 3:102, 144, 149
Guy Fawkes Night (Australia [British]), 1:290
Gwala, Mafika, 1:272
Gyanendra (King of Nepal), 2:114
Gypsy. See Roma

Habsburg, Rudolf von, 3:250
Habsburg monarchy, 3:309, 350, 351
Hagen, Friedrich Heinrich von der, 3:312
Hagiographies (Ireland), 3:30–31
Haida, 4:38–44; geography and history, 4:38–39; myths, legends, and folktales, 4:40–42; potlatches, 4:42–43; social structure, 4:39–40; studies of Haida folklore, 4:43–44
Hainteny (Madagascar), 1:140
Hairstyles and head coverings: Berber, 1:104, 107; Igbo, 1:201; Maya, 4:262; Tuareg,

1:104, 107, 114; Wolof, 1:212; Yoruba, 1:226; Zande, 1:233

Haiti, 1:10, 4:316–329; arts and crafts, 4:324–325; and diaspora, 1:20; folktales, 4:320–321; geography and history, 4:316–317; Jean Price-Mars and Haitian ethnography, 4:319–320; modernization, challenges of, 4:325–326; music and dance, 4:321–323; proverbs, 4:320; religious beliefs, 4:317–319; sports and games, 4:325; studies of Haitian folklore, 4:326–328

Hakka Mountain songs (Taiwan), 2:263

Haller, Albrecht von, 3:310, 314

Hallfreður Örn Eiríksson, 3:114

Halliwell, J.O., 3:20

Halloween, 2:399–400

Halpern, Joel, 3:431

Halpert, Herbert, 1:84

Hamlet (Shakespeare), 3:17, 18

Handbook of North American Indians, 4:76

Hand game: Cheyenne, 4:28; Kiowa, 4:65

Hannerz, Ulf, 1:42

Hans Brinker or the Silver Skates, 3:235

"Hansel and Gretel": Germany, 3:266; and Nahua tales and, 4:285–286

Hanssen, Börje, 3:149

Hapiapo stories (Duna), 2:168–169

Haraldur the Fair-Haired, 3:112

Hardanger fiddle, 3:130–131

Hardy, Frank, 1:286

Hardy, Thomas, 3:14, 18

Harney, W.E. (Bill), 1:286

Harris, Joel Chandler, 4:143

Hartigan, Patrick, Fr., 1:285

Harvest rituals: Ainu, 2:288; Assam, 2:21; Bali, 2:155, 157–158; Bangladesh, 2:98, 99; Gaddi, 2:37; Iban, 2:172; Isaan, 2:134; Japan, 2:277; Jie, 1:135–137; Kadazandusun, 2:178, 179–180; Khasi-Jaintia, 2:70; Korea, 2:300, 302–304; Kurds, 2:389; Malaita, 1:304; Malay, 2:144; Marshall Islands, 1:355; Palestine, 2:409; Poland, 3:388; Swahili, 1:156; Tajik, 2:329; Tonga, 1:399; Uttar Pradesh, 2:89; Uzbek, 2:351; Vanuatu, 1:329; Wolof, 1:210; Zulu, 1:270. See also Festivals and celebrations

Harvey, Cloddagh Brennan, 3:28

Haryana, 2:39–46; arts and crafts, 2:44–45; cultural tradition, 2:4; drama, 2:44; festivals and celebrations, 2:43–44; geography and history, 2:39–40; modernization, challenges of, 2:45–46; myths, legends, and historical narratives, 2:40–41; songs, music, and dance, 2:42–43; studies of Haryana folklore, 2:46

Hasidism, 3:334, 336

Haughey, Tommy, 3:33

Hausa language (Ga), 1:181

Hawai'i, 1:366–377; arts and crafts, 1:374; chants, 1:369–370; dance and the hula, 1:371–372; games and sports, 1:373; geography and history, 1:366; lei, 1:372; modernization, challenges of, 1:374–375;

religious beliefs, 1:368–369; social structure and family, 1:366–368; studies of Hawaiian folklore, 1:375–376

The Hawaiians of Old, 1:376

Hay, George Campbell, 3:66

Haydn, Joseph, 3:257

Hayk and Bel (Armenia), 2:359

Haykian Aram (Armenia), 2:360

Hayrack (Slovenia), 3:304

Hazelius, Artur, 1:57, 58, 76, 3:145–146

Head coverings. See Hairstyles and head coverings

Headhunting (Maluku), 2:200

Healers: Abanyole, 1:127; African Americans, 4:146–147; Assam, 2:20; Bangladesh, 2:102–103; Caribs of Dominica, 4:333–334; Cherokee, 4:11; Choctaw, 4:36–37; Denmark, 3:84; Finnish-Swedish, 3:99; Iroquois, 4:57; Mexico, 4:270; Navajo, 4:86; The Netherlands, 3:240; Piedmont and Val d'Aosta, 3:473; Quechua, 4:209–210; Seminole, 4:115; Siberia, 2:320; Slovenia, 3:300; Tonga, 1:399–400; Ukraine, 3:439; Uyghur, 2:338; Vanuatu, 1:327. See also Medicine and cures

The Heather in the South (Australia [British]), 1:281

Hebrew Bible, 2:372, 374, 379, 381

Heine, Heinrich, 3:271

Heinrici, chronicon Livoniae (Latvia), 3:365

Heinse, Wilhelm, 3:312

Hemingway, Ernest, 3:185

Henderson, Hamish, 3:58, 66, 67

Henna ceremony, Roma, 3:398–399

Henry, Priest, 3:365

Herbal medicine. See Medicine and cures

Herder, Johann Gottfried, 1:2, 27, 35, 61, 76, 78, 3:363, 364, 366

Herdsman culture (Switzerland), 3:308–310

Heritage studies, 1:51

Heritage-tourism, 1:87

Hermes, 1:91, 92

Hero, 1:44–47; Ainu, 2:287; Albania, 3:327; Apache, 4:5; Australia (British), 1:291; Bangladesh, 2:99; Cherokee, 4:12; Cheyenne, 4:22–23, 25; China, 2:216, 222; and diffusion, 1:22; Georgia, 3:357; Iban, 2:174; India, 2:8–9; Inuit, 4:135; Ireland, 3:27–29; Jie, 1:132; Kadazandusun, 2:178–179; Karnataka, 2:50; Kazakh, 2:310; Kurds, 2:387–388; Malay, 2:143; Marquesas Islands, 1:381; Marshall Islands, 1:352; Mongol, 2:254–255; Nagaland, 2:75; Nepal, 2:119; Ojibwe, 4:105–106; Persia, 2:415; Peru, 4:202; Poland, 3:381; Russia, 3:422–423; Serbia, 3:433; Sibundoy, 4:231; Tlingit, 4:122; and trickster, 1:45–46; Tuareg, 1:115; Uyghur, 2:337, 340; Uzbek, 2:348–349; Vanuatu, 1:328; Yoruba, 1:224. See also Epic stories, tales, poetry

Hero Combat Play, 3:16

Herodotus, 2:403, 3:322, 352

Heroic tales. See Epic stories, tales, poetry; Hero

Herrera, Juan, 3:187

Herrick, Robert, 3:8

Herskovits, Melville, 1:47

Herzfeld, Michael, 3:494

Hesiod, 3:320

Hibernating bear pattern (Piedmont and Val d'Aosta), 3:472

"Hickory Stick Vic" (Mississippi Delta), 4:173

Hidalgo, Miguel, 4:277

Highland Games, 3:64

"Highlandism," 1:50, 65

Highways (Mississippi Delta blues), 4:170

Hiker-folklorists, 3:195

Híkuri (Rarámuri), 4:305

Hilley, Paddy, 3:37–38

Hinatini (Marquesan priest), 1:381

Hinduism: Assam, 2:19–21; Australia (British), 1:290; Bali, 2:152, 154; Bangladesh, 2:96; Bhutan, 2:107; Bihar, 2:25; Gaddi, 2:31; Haryana, 2:39, 40–41; India, 2:3, 4, 6–7, 11–13; Jamaica, 4:344; Kashmir, 2:59, 60, 64–65; Malay, 2:142–143; Nepal, 2:114; Orissa, 2:80; Sri Lanka, 2:124–125; Uttar Pradesh, 2:88, 90, 93

Hip-hop (African American), 4:153

Historia erdadera de la Conquista del la Nueva España (del Castillo), 4:275

Historical monument farms, 1:59

Historical narratives: Australia (British), 1:288–289; Kiribati, 1:344; Lunda, 1:236, 238; Macedonia, 3:372–373; Tuvalu, 1:406; Zande, 1:231; Zulu, 1:270

Historical Roots of the Wondertale, 3:419

Historic-geographic method and diffusion, 1:22–23

History: Abanyole, 1:123; Ainu, 2:285–287; Albania, 3:320–323; Apache, 4:1, 3; Appalachia, 4:157–158; Armenia, 2:357–359; Ashkenazim, 3:330–332; Austria, 3:249–252; Bali, 2:152–155; Bangladesh, 2:95–96; Basque, 3:189–190; Baule, 1:163–164; Benin, 1:169–172; Berber, 1:101–103; Bhutan, 2:105–106; Caipira, 4:177–178; Candoshi, 4:181–182; Caribs of Dominica, 4:329–331; Catalan, 3:195–197; Cherokee, 4:9–10, 13; China, 2:211–213; Chinese living abroad, 2:233–235; Choctaw, 4:30–32; The Comoros, 1:142; Croatia, 3:347–352; Cuba, 4:309–310; Denmark, 3:80–82; Duna, 2:165–167; Ecuador, 4:188; England, 3:1–4; Finland, 3:90–92; Finnish-Swedish, 3:97–98; Flanders (Belgium), 3:223–225; Ga, 1:180–181; Gaddi, 2:30–32; Galicia, 3:202–203; Georgia, 3:352–354; Germany, 3:260–262; Greece, 3:493–494; Greenland, 3:103–111; Guam, 1:333–334; Haida, 4:38–39; Haiti, 4:316–317; Haryana, 2:39–40; Hawai'i, 1:366; Hopi, 4:44–45;

1: Topics & Themes, Africa, Australia & Oceania
2: Southeast Asia & India, Central & East Asia,
   Middle East
3: Europe
4: North & South America

Hungary, 3:273–278; Iban, 2:171–173; Iceland, 3:111–113; Igbo, 1:193–194; Ijo, 1:204; Ireland, 3:22–26; Iroquois, 4:52–54; Isle of Man, 3:41–43; Israel, 2:372, 375–378; Italy, 3:450–452; Jamaica, 4:336–338; Japan, 2:271–275; Jie, 1:131–137; Kadazandusun, 2:176–177; Kaingang, 4:193; Kaliai, 2:183–184; Karnataka, 2:46–47; Kashmir, 2:58–65; Kazakh, 2:306–308; Kewa, 2:189–190; Khasi-Jaintia, 2:65–66; Kiowa, 4:60–62; Kiribati, 1:340–341; Korea, 2:294–296; Kurds, 2:383–392; Lakota and Dakota, 4:69–70, 73; Lebanon, 2:392; Lunda, 1:234–235; Macedonia, 3:370–372; Madagascar, 1:137–138; Malay, 2:141–142; Malta, 3:502–504; Maluku, 2:197–198; Manchu, 2:245–246; Marquesas Islands, 1:377–380; Marshall Islands, 1:349–350; Mascarene Islands, 1:144; Mauritius and Rodrigues, 1:144–146; Maya, 4:256–257; Mexico, 4:268–269, 278–279; Mississippi Delta, 4:166–167; Mongol, 2:252–254; Navajo, 4:82–83, 85; The Netherlands, 3:233–248; New Caledonia, 1:308–309; Nez Perce, 4:97–98; Norway, 3:123–125; Nuer, 1:150–151; Ojibwe, 4:103–105, 107–108; Orissa, 2:79–80; Otomí, 4:288–290; Palau, 1:358–360; Palestine, 2:400–403; Persia, 2:413–414; Piedmont and Val d'Aosta, 3:469–470; Poland, 3:378–380; Quechua, 4:208–209; Rarámuri, 4:297–298; Réunion, 1:147–148; Roma, 3:395–397; Russia, 3:411–412; Sámi, 3:134–135; Samoa, 1:387–388; Scotland, 3:52–55; Semai, 2:145–146; Seminole, 4:111–112; Sephardim, 3:211–214; Serbia, 3:425–437; The Seychelles, 1:149; Shona, 1:248–249; Shuar, 4:220–221; Siberia, 2:315–316; Sibundoy, 4:229–230; Sicily, 3:480–482; Slovakia, 3:285–286; Slovenia, 3:295–296; Spain, 3:177–180; Sri Lanka, 2:123–124; Suriname Maroon, 4:236–237; Swahili, 1:154–155; Switzerland, 3:308–312; Tairora, 2:203–205; Taiwan, 2:260–261; Tajik, 2:325–326; Tlingit, 4:117–118, 120–121, 123; Tonga, 1:397; Trobriand Islands, 1:316; Tuareg, 1:101–103, 113–114; Turkey, 2:429–432; Tuvalu, 1:404–405; Ukraine, 3:437–439; Uttar Pradesh, 2:88–90; Uyghur, 2:335–337; Uzbek, 2:348–350; Vanuatu, 1:325–326; Wales, 3:69–72; Western Inuit and Yupik, 4:128–132; Wolof, 1:208–213; Xavante, 4:243; Xhosa, 1:257–258; Yanomami, 4:251–252; Yemen, 2:439–442; Zande, 1:227–228; Zulu, 1:267–269
History of the Kingdom of Wei (China), 2:273

History of the Ojibway People (Warren), 4:107
Hitler, Adolf, 3:91
Hitopadesha tales (India), 2:7
Hobsbawn, Eric, 1:49
Hofer, Andreas, 3:250
Hoffmann, Frank, 1:56
Hogmanay (Scotland), 3:65–67
Holidays: Ecuador, 4:191–192; Roma, 3:403–404; Russia, 3:415–417. See also Festivals and celebrations; specific holidays
Holo Mai Pele (Hawai'i), 1:376
Holy Week Cycle plays (Italy), 3:464
Home governance system (Serbia), 3:428
Homer, 1:44–45, 3:320, 322
Home remedies. See Medicine and cures
Homogenization and globalization, 1:43
Honko, Lauri, 3:147
Honti, János, 3:283
Hoodoo: creation of, 1:79; doctors, 4:147
Hoop game (Lakota), 4:74
Hopi, 1:41, 4:44–50; agriculture, 4:46–47; arts and crafts, 4:49–50; geography and history, 4:44–45; katsina season, 4:47–48; language, 4:46; origins and ancestors, 4:45–46; social structure, 4:46; studies of Hopi folklore, 4:50
Hopkins, Matthew, 3:8
Hop tu naa (Isle of Man), 3:48–49
Horse carts (Sicily), 3:486
Horse racing (Georgia), 3:360–361
Horses and Kiowa, 4:61
Horticulture: and cultural shift, 1:16–17; New Caledonia, 1:309; Shuar, 4:222
Housing: African American, 4:153–154; Apache, 4:1; Appalachia, 4:163; Assam, 2:23; Australia (British), 1:282–283; Bangladesh, 2:102; Baule, 1:168; Benin, 1:176, 179; Berber, 1:110; Bhutan, 2:111; Bihar, 2:29; Caipira, 4:180; Caribs of Dominica, 4:331; Cherokee, 4:18–19; Ga, 1:182; Gaddi, 2:33, 36; Georgia, 3:361–362; Greece, 3:500; Haida, 4:39, 40; Haryana, 2:39, 45; Iceland, 3:118; Igbo, 1:200–201; Ireland, 3:25, 26; Iroquois, 4:53; Isaan, 2:135; Karnataka, 2:51–52, 56; Kazakh, 2:313; Korea, 2:298; Lebanon, 2:397; Macedonia, 3:374–375; Madagascar, 1:142; Malaita, 1:301; Maluku, 2:201–202; Mississippi Delta, 4:167; Nepal, 2:113; New Caledonia, 1:310; Orissa, 2:85; Scotland, 3:53; Seminole, 4:114; Sertão, 4:219; Shona, 1:253–254; Siberia, 2:318–319; Tairora, 2:204, 209; Tuareg, 1:109, 119–120; Tuvalu, 1:409; Ukraine, 3:446–447; Uttar Pradesh, 2:89; Vanuatu, 1:330–331; Western Inuit and Yupik, 4:132; Xhosa, 1:257
"How the Young Maidens Saved the Island of Guam" (Guam), 1:335
Hózhǫ' (Navajo) , 4:85
Hsuan-tang (Chinese Buddhist pilgrim) stories (Haryana), 2:40
Huayno folksongs (Peru), 4:204

Hufford, Mary, 1:30
Hula dance (Hawai'i), 1:371–372
Huldrefolk (Norway), 3:126
Hultz, D., 1:291
Human behavior as theme: Ga, 1:184; Yoruba, 1:219
Humanist movement (Croatia), 3:349
Humorous stories, skits, etc.: African Americans, 4:148–150; Australia (British), 1:284; Berber, 1:107; Choctaw, 4:36; Ga, 1:185; Lakota, 4:72; Maya, 4:261; Samoa, 1:393–396; Tuareg, 1:117, 118; Western Inuit and Yupik, 4:136; Wolof, 1:215. See also Jokes and joking rituals; Punning; Tall tales
Hungarian Ethnographic Society, 1:6
Hungary, 1:6, 3:273–284; ballads and folktales, 3:279; calendars and drama, 3:281–282; dance, games, and arts and crafts, 3:282–283; geography and history, 3:273–278; music, 3:280–281; religion and beliefs, 3:278–279; songs, riddles, and proverbs, 3:279–280
Hunger as theme (Jie), 1:132
Hungilisk game (Kurds), 2:390–391
Hunting: Ainu, 2:288; Appalachia, 4:164; Duna, 2:165; Kaingang, 4:193; Kaliai, 2:183, 187; Kurds, 2:389; Malta, 3:510; Marquesas Islands, 1:379; New Caledonia, 1:309; San, 1:246–247; Seminole, 4:114; Siberia, 2:315; Swahili, 1:156; and symbolic world, 1:30; Tairora, 2:205; Vanuatu, 1:330; Western Inuit and Yupik, 4:129–130, 135; Yoruba, 1:222
"Hunt the Wren" (song), 3:50
Hurston, Zora Neale, 1:31, 41, 48
Hutu massacre of Tutsi, 1:64
Hyacinth, Saint, 3:495
Hybridity, 1:47–49; and diffusion, 1:24; and globalization, 1:24, 42, 47; and race, 1:78
Hyde, Douglas, 3:22
Hyltén-Cavallius, Gunnar Olof, 3:14, 150
Hymes, Dell, 1:31, 32, 69–70, 84
Hymns: African American, 4:152; Cherokee, 4:14; Gaddi, 2:36; Haryana, 2:43; Hungary, 3:280; Igbo, 1:197; Iroquois, 4:59; Kiowa, 4:62–63; Kiribati, 1:345; Kurds, 2:391; Lunda, 1:236; Madagascar, 1:138, 141; Malaita, 1:303; Nagaland, 2:77; Navajo, 4:88; Norway, 3:123, 129; Tuvalu, 1:408, 409; Xavante, 4:249
Hyperbole. See Language

Iban, 2:171–176; chants, 2:175; geography and history, 2:171–173; oral folklore, 2:173–174; principles of Iban folklore, 2:173; rules and rituals, 2:174–175; studies of Iban folklore, 2:175–176
Iblis (the Devil) (Tuareg), 1:117
Iceland, 3:111–123; British influence, 3:112; Danish influence, 3:112; Eddic poems, 3:113; folktales, 3:114–115; food, clothing, games, and customs, 3:117–119; geography

and history, **3:**111–113; legends, **3:**115–117; music and dance, **3:**119; Norwegian influence, **3:**112; Sámi influence, **3:**112; travelogues, **3:**117

I Ching. See Book of Changes

Ichumar (Tuareg), **1:**116–117

Idaho: Nez Perce, **4:**97

Idamen iru (Tuareg), **1:**115

Idir, **1:**108

al-Idrisi, Muhammed, **3:**484

"Idylls" (poem), **3:**310

Igala, **1:**178

Igbo, **1:**193–204; arts and crafts, **1:**201; clothing and food, **1:**201–202; and colonialism, **1:**9; dance, **1:**198–199; folk gesture, **1:**197–198; folktales and proverbs, **1:**195–196; geography and history, **1:**193–194; oratory and poetry, **1:**196–197; rituals, **1:**199; village structure and layout, **1:**200–201. *See also* Benin

Iglesias, Julio, **3:**184

Igue festival (Benin), **1:**172

Ijo, **1:**204–208; games, canoes, and crafts, **1:**207–208; geography and history, **1:**204; music and song, **1:**207; religious beliefs and art, **1:**204–206; stories and proverbs, **1:**206–207

I-Kiribati. *See* Kiribati

Ile-Ife creation story (Yoruba), **1:**218–219

"*Il figlio del conte*" (ballad, northern Italy), **3:**458

Iljovski, Vasil, **3:**372

Illyrians, **3:**322, 323

Imam Hoseyn passion plays (Persia), **2:**416, 424

Imayen (Tuareg), **1:**114–115

Imazighen. *See* Berber

Imbongi tradition (Xhosa), **1:**261–267

Immigrants: Mississippi Delta, **4:**173–174; and nativism, **1:**64–65

Immolation (Nepal), **2:**117

Immortality as theme: Cherokee, **4:**13; San, **1:**244; Yoruba, **1:**222

The Immovable East (Baldensperger), **2:**411

Imvo Zabantsundu (newspaper) (Xhosa), **1:**262, 264

Inafa'maolek (Guam), **1:**334–338

Incantations: Assam, **2:**21; Bangladesh, **2:**102; Benin, **1:**173; Cherokee, **4:**11; Ga, **1:**185, 191–192; Hungary, **3:**279; Iceland, **3:**113; Igbo, **1:**197; Isaan, **2:**135; Khasi-Jaintia, **2:**72; Latvia, **3:**363; Malay, **2:**143; Manchu, **2:**251; Piedmont and Val d'Aosta, **3:**473; Slovenia, **3:**300; Tonga, **1:**399; Trobriand Islands, **1:**319, 320; Tuvalu, **1:**406–407; Uyghur, **2:**338; Uzbek, **2:**351, 352

Indaba (newspaper) (Xhosa), **1:**258, 260

Indentured laborers: Assam, **2:**19; Mauritius and Rodrigues, **1:**144; Réunion, **1:**148

Independence movement in Mexico, **4:**277–278

India, **2:**1–17; caste system, **2:**5–6; ethnographic factors shaping folklore, **2:**1–5;

festivals and celebrations, **2:**11–13; folk epics, **2:**8–9; folktales, **2:**7–8; food customs and beliefs, **2:**13–14; gender, **2:**6; genres in folklore, **2:**7; geography, **2:**1; Hinduism, **2:**6–7; Kashmir, influence on, **2:**59; modernization, challenges of, **2:**14–15; music and dance, **2:**9–11; studies of Indian folklore, **2:**15–16. *See also* individual states

Indian Antiquary, **2:**30, 57

Indians, American, **4:**1–142. *See also specific tribes*

Industrialization: and cultural relativism, **1:**15; and popular culture, **1:**72

Infanticide, **1:**15

Inheritance: Japan, **2:**273; Jie, **1:**134; Khasi-Jaintia, **2:**66; Slovakia, **3:**288–289; Tairora, **2:**205. *See also* Patrilineal societies

Initiation (rites of passage) ceremonies, **1:**26; Apache, **4:**1, 5, 6–7; Bangladesh, **2:**104; Croatia, **3:**348; Haiti, **4:**318; Igbo, **1:**196, 199; Israel, **2:**378; Japan, **2:**272, 277; Kashmir, **2:**61, 63; Malaita, **1:**304–305; Maluku, **2:**202; Nepal, **2:**116; Nuer, **1:**152; Palestine, **2:**406; Peru, **4:**201; Roma, **3:**406; Shuar, **4:**223, 224, 226; Siberia, **2:**319; Tairora, **2:**206, 207; Trobriand Islands, **1:**318; Ukraine, **3:**440; Vanuatu, **1:**329; Wolof, **1:**211; Xavante, **4:**247

Inkululeko (Xhosa), **1:**264

Inquisition (Spain), **3:**180

In Search of Authenticity (Bendix), **1:**37

Installation songs (Igbo), **1:**196

Institi Kreol, **1:**149–150

Institute of Research for Development (IRD), **1:**314

Institute of Swahilia and Foreign Languages, **1:**161

Insults: African American, **4:**150; Peruvian folklore, **4:**203

International Council of Museums, **1:**58

Internationale und Nationale Volkskundliche Bibliographien (Beitl & Kausel), **1:**6–7

International Folklore Bibliography (IFB), **1:**5

International Society for Folk Narrative Research, **1:**291

Interpreting Legend (Tangherlini), **1:**82

Inuit. *See* Greenland; Western Inuit and Yupik

Invented tradition, **1:**49–51; and nativism, **1:**65

Inversion of values by outcasts (Italy), **3:**456

Investiture ceremonies: Lunda, **1:**239; Samoa, **1:**393; Wolof, **1:**210

Iran. *See* Persia

Iranian Folklore Quarterly, **2:**426

Ireland, **3:**22–41; anecdotes and jokes, **3:**38–39; Australia (British) influence by, **1:**278–281; calendars, **3:**26–27; fairy lore, **3:**32–34; geography and history, **3:**22–26; ghost lore, **3:**34; hagiographies, **3:**30–31; heroic tales, **3:**27–29; legends, **3:**34–37; migration, **3:**23–24; modernization,

challenges of, **3:**39; music and dance, **3:**27–29; stories and tales, **3:**30–31, 34–37; storytelling, **3:**37–39; supernatural lore, **3:**31–34; tall tales, **3:**37–38

Irish Folklore Commission, **3:**40

Irish Potato Famine, **3:**24

Iron Teeth Woman (Cheyenne), **4:**26

Ironwork: African Americans, **4:**154; Haiti, **4:**324

Iroquois, **4:**50–60; arts and crafts, **4:**56–57; cultural history, **4:**52–54; drama, **4:**58; European contact, **1:**15, **4:**52; geography, **4:**50–51; herbalism, **4:**58; mask making, **4:**55–56; music, **4:**59; myths, legends, and folktales, **4:**54–55; rituals and celebrations, **4:**56; social structure, **4:**51; sports and games, **4:**57; studies of Iroquois folklore, **4:**59–60; supernatural lore, **4:**58–59

Irving, Washington, **3:**3

Isaan, **2:**131–141; geography, **2:**131; modernization, challenges of, **2:**139; music, **2:**137–138; myths and legends, **2:**135; proverbs and riddles, **2:**135–136; religious beliefs and rituals, **2:**131–135; songs, **2:**136; sports and games, **2:**138–139; *waikhuu* chant, **2:**136–137

Islam: Bali, **2:**154; Bangladesh, **2:**96; China, **2:**213; Chinese living abroad, **2:**236; Gaddi, **2:**31; Haiti, **4:**319; India, **2:**4; Israel, **2:**372, 374; Jamaica, **4:**344; Kadazandusun, **2:**177, 181; Karnataka, **2:**48; Kazakh, **2:**308; Kurds, **2:**385, 386; Lebanon, **2:**392, 398, 399; Malay, **2:**142, 150; Maluku, **2:**197, 198–199, 201; Palestine, **2:**401; Persia, **2:**424; Tajik, **2:**328, 334; Turkey, **2:**430; Uyghur, **2:**336–340; Uzbek, **2:**348, 349, 354; Yemen, **2:**440. *See also* Muslims

Islam, Mazharul, **2:**99

Island Caribs. *See* Caribs of Dominica

Isle of Man, **3:**41–52; calendars, **3:**47–51; fairy lore, **3:**44–47; folklore, **3:**43; geography and history, **3:**41–43; migration, **3:**43; smuggling, **3:**42

Israel, **2:**372–383; biblical, rabbinic, and early Christian texts, **2:**372–373; folklore in contemporary Israel, **2:**378–381; holy land for three religions, **2:**373–375; and Jewish Diaspora, **1:**21; and nationalism, **1:**63; Zionist settlements, World War II, and the Jewish state, **2:**375–378

Israel, Richard J., **3:**332

Italian immigrants in Mississippi Delta, **4:**173

Italian Switzerland, **3:**307–308

Italy, **3:**450–469; Australia (British) influence by, **1:**278; dance and drama, **3:**463–464; festivals and rituals, **3:**464–465; geography and history, **3:**450–452; mountain dwellers, **3:**453–455; music, **3:**461–463; outcasts, **3:**455–456; peasant culture, **3:**452–453; religious beliefs and rituals, **3:**457–458; songs and ballads, **3:**458–461; working-class culture, **3:**456–457

1: Topics & Themes, Africa, Australia & Oceania
2: Southeast Asia & India, Central & East Asia, Middle East
3: Europe
4: North & South America

Ivandan (John the Baptist Day, Serbia), **3**:431

Ivan Kupalo (summer solstice), **3**:417

Ivan the Terrible, **3**:409

Ivrea, festival (Piedmont and Val d'Aosta), **3**:474

Izaga nezimo zikukhuluma (Zulu), **1**:274

Izibongo, **1**:272–274

Izibongo: Zulu Praise-Poems, **1**:272

"The Izibongo of the Zulu Chiefs," **1**:272

Izibongo ZamaKhosi, **1**:272

Izwi Labantu (newspaper) (Xhosa), **1**:262, 264

Jaarsma, Dam, **3**:243

Jabavu, John Tengo, **1**:263, 264

"Jack and the Beanstalk," **3**:12

Jack in Two Worlds (McCarthy), **1**:85

"Jack the Giant-Killer," **3**:12

Jadwiga, Queen, **3**:381

Jae-hyo Shin (early writer, Korea), **2**:300

Jaguar stories (Yanomami), **4**:253–254

Jainism: Bihar, **2**:25; Gaddi, **2**:31; Haryana, **2**:39; Karnataka, **2**:48; Orissa, **2**:80

Jakobson, Roman, **1**:90, 91

Jamaica, **4**:336–347; children's songs and games, **4**:341; and diaspora, **1**:20; East Indian culture, **4**:344–345; festivals and celebrations, **4**:338–339; folktales, **4**:341–342; geography and history, **4**:336–338; Maroon culture, **4**:339–341; religious beliefs, **4**:343–344; spells and magic, **4**:343; studies of Jamaican folklore, **4**:345–346

James I (England), **3**:54

James II (England and Scotland), **3**:54

James IV (Scotland), **3**:54

James VI (England and Scotland), **3**:54

James VII (England and Scotland), **3**:54

James, Saint, **3**:204–206, 349

James, Richard, **3**:410

Jánošík, Juraj, **3**:292

Janša, Anton, **3**:304

Japan, **2**:271–284; arts, crafts, and architecture, **2**:278; folk religion and performing arts, **2**:276–277; geography and history, **2**:271–273; Marshall Islands influence by, **1**:350; medicine, **2**:278; modernization, challenges of, **2**:278–279; modern studies of Japanese folklore, **2**:279–281; and nationalism, **1**:63; Palau influence by, **1**:360; periods of cultural history, **2**:273–275; religious beliefs, **2**:275–276; sports and games, **2**:277–278; Taiwan, influence in, **2**:261, 265. *See also* Ainu

Jataka tales (birth stories of the Bodhisattva): Bhutan, **2**:108; India, **2**:7; Isaan, **2**:135; Sri Lanka, **2**:127

Jean du Doigt, Saint, **3**:170, 175

Jelacic, Josip, **3**:351

Jenkins, J. Geraint, **3**:78

Jenn tales and superstitions (Persia), **2**:417–418

Jewelry and personal adornments: Baule, **1**:167; Benin, **1**:176; Berber, **1**:106; Hawai'i, **1**:372; Igbo, **1**:201; Kiribati, **1**:347; Marquesas Islands, **1**:381, 384; Navajo, **4**:91; Tlingit, **4**:125–126; Tuareg, **1**:107, 119; Wolof, **1**:211. *See also* Amulets; Beadwork

Jews: Diaspora, **1**:18–20; folklore of, **1**:20, 62; immigrants to Mississippi Delta, **4**:174; immigrants to U.S., **1**:66; Nazi genocide of, **1**:64

Jhangar epics (Mongol), **2**:254–255

Jicarilla Relay Race (Apache), **4**:5–6

Jie, **1**:131–137; geography, **1**:131; social structure, beliefs, and historical tradition, **1**:133–137; stories, tales and historical tradition, **1**:131–133

Jingoism and nativism, **1**:64

Jinx as theme (Wolof), **1**:213

Jnoun (Berber), **1**:103–104, 111

Joan of Arc, **3**:164

John, Saint, **3**:199, 200, 265, 268

John Frum movement (Vanuatu), **1**:327

John III Sobieski (King of Poland), **3**:381

Johnson, Robert, **4**:170

Johnson, Samuel, **3**:38, 63

John Stands in Timber (Cheyenne), **4**:22

John the Baptist, Saint, **3**:290, 349, 388, 417, 429, 471

Jokes and joking rituals: Albania, **3**:328, 329; Ashkenazim, **3**:334; Greece, **3**:497; Ireland, **3**:38–39; Latvia, **3**:362; Malaita, **1**:302, 304; Roma, **3**:406; Shona, **1**:249, 250; Slovakia, **3**:292; Swahili, **1**:158; Wolof, **1**:214–215; Yoruba, **1**:224–225

Jolobe, J.J.R., **1**:262

Jolted work system, **3**:456

Jón Árnason, **3**:114, 117

Jónas Jónasson frá Hrafnagili, **3**:117

Jones, Mary, **3**:74

Jones, Michael Owens, **1**:77

Jones, Stephen, **2**:222

Jón Guðmundsson the Learned, **3**:113

Joning (African American), **4**:150

Jonkunu (Jamaica), **4**:338–339

Jón Ólofsson frá Grunnavík, **3**:113

Jonsson, Bengt R., **3**:149

Jordan, A.C., **1**:261

Joseph II (Emperor), **3**:347

Joseph, Saint, **3**:199, 200

Journal of American Folklore, **1**:5

Journal of Asian American Studies, **2**:243

Journal of Folklore Research, **1**:95

Journal of Palestine Oriental Society, **2**:412

Journal of the Royal Anthropological Institute, **2**:178

Journal of the Royal Asiatic Society, **2**:30

Judaism: Australia (British), **1**:290; Haiti, **4**:319; Israel, **2**:372; Jamaica, **4**:337; Palestine, **2**:401; Turkey, **2**:430. *See also* Jews

Juju music (Yoruba), **1**:223, 225

Julius Caesar, **3**:261

Jung, C.G., **1**:92

Junjappa stories (Karnataka), **2**:50

Jurjans, Andrejs, **3**:368

Júrjenson, Kaarjel, **1**:81

Just, Saint, **3**:160

"Just-so" stories (Nuer), **1**:153

Kabua the Great (Marshall Islands leader), **1**:350

Kabyle (Berber), **1**:108, 110

Kadazandusun, **2**:176–182; arts and crafts, **2**:180–181; celebrations and games, **2**:179–180; geography and history, **2**:176–177; modernization, challenges of, **2**:181; music, **2**:179; myths, legends, and folktales, **2**:178–179; religious beliefs and rituals, **2**:177–178; studies of Kadazandusun folklore, **2**:181–182

Kadoazi, **4**:183

Ka'ililauokekoa (Hawai'i), **1**:376

Kaingang, **4**:193–199; food, **4**:193–194; geography and history, **4**:193; symmetry in myths and folktales, **4**:194–197

Kairus (Kaingang subgroup), **4**:194–195

Kakárma (Shuar), **4**:222–223

Kalabari, **1**:204, 208

Kalákaua (Hawaiian king), **1**:371

Kalevala, **3**:92–96

Kaliai, **2**:183–188; geography and history, **2**:183–184; modernization, challenges of, **2**:188; myths, legends, and folktales, **2**:184–186; songs and music, **2**:186; storytelling, **2**:187; themes in folktales, **2**:188

Kalila Wa Demna (animal) tales (Palestine), **2**:405

Kamahualele (foster son of Hawaiian chief), **1**:370

Kambule, Mpondo, **1**:270

Kamehameha (Hawaiian king), **1**:367, 374

Kamês (Kaingang subgroup), **4**:194–195

A *Kammu Story-Listener's Tales* (Lindell, Swahn & Tayanin), **1**:81

Kammu traditions, **1**:81

Kanak people. *See* New Caledonia

Kanaval festival (Haiti), **4**:323

Ka Niam Khasi, **2**:66–67

Kantan Chamorrita (Guam), **1**:338

Kanyembo Lutaba, Paul (Mwata Kazembe XVII), **1**:238, 239

Kapchan, Deborah A., **1**:47, 48

Karadžić, Vuk Stefanovik, **3**:372, 373, 431, 432, 434

Karagiozis (shadow theater, Greece), **3**:500

Karimov, Islam, **2**:349

Kariri culture (Sertão), **4**:217

Karl-Emanuel, count of Savoy, **3**:315

Karl of Savoy, Duke, **3**:310

Karma, **2:**90

Karnataka, **2:**46–58; architecture, **2:**56; cultural tradition, **2:**4; drama and folk performance, **2:**53–54; games and recreation, **2:**55–56; geography and history, **2:**46–47; modernization, challenges of, **2:**57; social structure, religious beliefs, and folklore, **2:**47–51; studies of Karnataka folklore, **2:**57–58; Tulu-speaking region, **2:**47, 51–53

Kartvel (Georgia), **3:**353

Kartvelian languages, **3:**353–354

Kashghari, Mahmud, **2:**310, 336–338

Kashmir, **2:**58–65; cultural tradition, **2:**4; dance, **2:**62–63; drama, **2:**63–64; festivals and celebrations, **2:**64–65; geography and history, **2:**58–65; oral folk narratives, **2:**61; songs, **2:**61–62; studies of Kashmir folklore, **2:**65; written folk narratives, **2:**60–61

Kasibwaibwaireta's story (Trobriand Islands), **1:**322–323

Kathasarasagar tales (India), **2:**7

Kathasaritasagara (The Ocean of Story, India), **2:**60

Katona, Lajos, **3:**283

Katsina season (Hopi), **4:**47–48

Kausel, Eva, **1:**6

Kavaev, Filip, **3:**372

Kazakh, **2:**306–314; architecture, **2:**313; arts and crafts, **2:**312–313; festivals and celebrations, **2:**313–314; geography and history, **2:**306–308; modernization, challenges of, **2:**314; music, **2:**311–312; myths and legends, **2:**308–309; songs, **2:**310–311; sports and games, **2:**312

Kazantzakis, Nikos, **3:**495

Kearney, Michael, **1:**96, 98

Keawe (Hawaiian chief), **1:**370

Kehrli of Brienz, **3:**314

Kelly, Ned, **1:**279

Kel Seghsegh (Tuareg), **1:**118

Kel Tamajaq. *See* Tuareg

Keskitalo, Alf Isak, **3:**140–141

Ketama, **3:**183

Kewa, **2:**189–196; geography and history, **2:**189–190; modernization, challenges of, **2:**195–196; myths, **2:**190–191; songs, **2:**191–195

Khan, Chingis (Mongol leader), **2:**253, 308, 337

Khani, Ehmed, **2:**388

"Khan Zhaksy Ma?" (Is He a Good Khan?) (Kazakh), **2:**314

Khasi-Jaintia, **2:**65–73; ancestor cult, **2:**72–73; dance, **2:**69–70; festivals and celebrations, **2:**68–69; geography and history, **2:**65–66; modernization, challenges of, **2:**73; myth and legend, **2:**67–68; social structure and religious belief, **2:**66–67; tales, proverbs, and poetry, **2:**70–72

Khmel'nyts'ky, Bohdan, **3:**441

Khorenatsi, Movses, **2:**359, 361, 362

Khumalo, Asilita Philisiwe, **1:**272

Kidson, Frank, **3:**13

Kievan Cycle epic, **3:**422, 423

Kievan Rus, **3:**411, 422, 423

Kikikoi festival (Ecuador), **4:**198

Kindaichi, Kyosuke, **2:**293

"Kind and Unkind Girls," **1:**23

Kinder- und Hausmärchen (Grimm), **1:**94, **3:**265–266

Kinship. *See* Clans; Family relationships

Kinship festivals (Lunda), **1:**239

Kiowa, **4:**60–67; arts and crafts, **4:**65–66; games, **4:**65; geography and history, **4:**60–62; religious beliefs and practices, **4:**62–63; storytelling, **4:**66; studies of Kiowa folklore, **4:**66; and trickster, **1:**92

Kiowa War Mothers, **4:**64

Kireevskii, P.V., **3:**410

Kiribati, **1:**340–348; arts and crafts, **1:**346–347; games and sports, **1:**346; geography and history, **1:**340–341; modernization, challenges of, **1:**347–348; *mwaneaba:* the village meetinghouse, **1:**343–344; religious beliefs and rituals, **1:**342–343; signs, omens, and taboos, **1:**343; social structure, **1:**341; stories, songs, music, and dance, **1:**344–346

Kirk, Robert, **3:**56

Kirkpatrick, John Simpson, **1:**286

Kittredge, George Lyman, **1:**27

Kivas (Hopi), **4:**48

Klapa singing, Croatia, **3:**342–343

Klein, Barbro, **3:**151, 153

Kleinman, Arthur, **2:**278

Klezmer music, **3:**336

Klintberg, Bengt af, **3:**153

Knights of Malta, **3:**504, 509

Knights of St. John (Malta), **3:**509

Knives (Western Inuit and Yupik), **4:**136

Know-Nothings (U.S.), **1:**65

Knut, Saint, **3:**101

Kobzari (blind minstrels, Ukraine), **3:**440–441

Kodály, Zoltán, **3:**280

Kohl-Larsen, Ludwig, **3:**139

Kojiki origin myths (Japan), **2:**274

Kolac (cake-bread, Serbia), **3:**429–430

Kolberg, Oskar, **1:**61

Koleda songs (Croatia), **3:**349, 350

Koliada (spirit of the feast, Russia), **3:**416

Koljivo (wheat dish, Serbia), **3:**430

Kolo dances (Croatia), **3:**344–346

Konevski, Blaze, **3:**372

König, Franz Niklaus, **3:**313

Korea, **2:**294–305; ancestor worship and funeral rituals, **2:**296–298; dance, **2:**300–301; festivals and celebrations, **2:**301–303; food, **2:**304; geography and history, **2:**294–296; music, **2:**299–300; religious beliefs, **2:**298–299

Kosovo Cycle, **3:**434, 435

Kotzebue, Otto von, **1:**349, 353, 354, 356

Kourites (Greece), **3:**497

Krali, Marko, **3:**373

Kraljevic, Marko, **3:**432, 435

Krimanchuli singing (Georgia), **3:**359

Krishna: Bangladesh, **2:**97; Uttar Pradesh, **2:**94

Kristensen, Evald Tang, **3:**82, 85

Kroeber, Alfred E., **1:**16, 27

Krohn, Julius Leopold, **3:**96, 138

Krohn, Kaarle, **1:**22, **3:**138

Krsna Slava celebration (Serbia), **3:**429–430

Kuanyin (Taiwan), **2:**261

Kubodera, Itsuhiko, **2:**293

Kuçedra (serpent-dragon, Albania), **3:**324–325

Kuenkhen Longchen Rabjam (Buddhist saint-scholar), **2:**107

Kuenzang Dechen, **2:**108

Ku Klux Klan, **1:**66

Kula (Trobriand Islands), **1:**321–325

Kumina (Jamaica), **4:**343–344

Kumulipo creation chant (Hawai'i), **1:**370

Kurds, **2:**383–392; dance, **2:**390; geography and history, **2:**383–392; modernization, challenges of, **2:**391; music, **2:**389–390; myths, legends, and epics, **2:**387–389; poetry, **2:**386–387; religious beliefs, **2:**385–386; sports and games, **2:**390–391; studies of Kurdish folklore, **2:**391

Kuru (founder Haryana), **2:**39

Kwaio and worldview, **1:**96–97

Kwakwaka'wakw ceremonies, **1:**7

Kwa languages (Igbo), **1:**194

Kwoth (Nuer), **1:**151–152

Laale, Peder, **3:**85

Lacerda, F.J.M. de, **1:**235

Lacrosse: Iroquois, **4:**57; Rarámuri, **4:**305–306

Laestadianism (Sámi), **3:**136, 142

Lafleur, Jacques, **1:**314

Lagercrantz, Eliel, **3:**137

Lakota, **4:**67–81; arts and crafts, **4:**75; "as-told-to" stories, **4:**73–74; geography and history, **4:**67–70; modernization, challenges of, **4:**75–76; music and songs, **4:**74, 77; myths, legends, and folktales, **4:**70–72; sports and games, **4:**74–75; storytelling, **4:**73–74; studies of Lakota folklore, **4:**76–78; Vision talks, **4:**73; War stories, **4:**73

Lakshmi or Laxmi (goddess of wealth), **2:**100, 121

La Llorona legend (Mexico), **4:**271

Laments: Malta, **3:**505; Roma, **3:**401–402; Russia, **3:**414–415; Sardinia, **3:**465; Sicily, **3:**487; Tlingits, **4:**124; Ukraine, **3:**443–444. *See also* Death and mourning rituals; Poetry

Lampedusa, Tomasi di, **3:**453

Lamu Museum, **1:**161

Landlord system (Ireland), **3:**24

Lang, Andrew, **1:**2

Language: African-American, **4:**143; Ainu, **2:**285, 290–293; Apache, **4:**7; Armenia, **2:**357; Ashkenazim, **3:**331; Assam, **2:**18–19; Australia (British), **1:**278, 283–285, 289; Australian Aborigines, **1:**293; Bali, **2:**154, 163; Bangladesh, **2:**95; Basque, **3:**189, 190; Baule, **1:**165; Benin, **1:**171; Berber, **1:**101,

1: Topics & Themes, Africa, Australia & Oceania
2: Southeast Asia & India, Central & East Asia, Middle East
3: Europe
4: North & South America

103; Bihar, **2**:25; Caipira, **4**:177; Candoshi, **4**:182; Cherokee, **4**:10, 13; China, **2**:212–213; Chinese living abroad, **2**:234, 243; and colonialism, **1**:8; Creole, **1**:10; Denmark, **3**:81; Duna, **2**:165; Finland, **3**:90; Finnish-Swedish, **3**:97, 102–103; Flanders (Belgium), **3**:223, 224; Ga, **1**:180, 181; Gaddi, **2**:31; Galicia, **3**:202; Georgia, **3**:353–354, 358; Germany, **3**:260; Greece, **3**:496; Guam, **1**:334, 338; Haida, **4**:43–44; Hawai'i, **1**:374–375; Hopi, **4**:46; Hungary, **3**:273–274, 276; Iban, **2**:171–172; Igbo, **1**:194, 195–196; Isle of Man, **3**:42, 43, 50; Israel, **2**:372, 376, 377, 379, 381; Italy, **3**:455–456, 458; Jamaica, **4**:336–337; Kaliai, **2**:183; Karnataka, **2**:47; Kashmir, **2**:59–61; Kazakh, **2**:307, 308, 310, 314; Khasi-Jaintia, **2**:66; Kiribati, **1**:344, 348; Kurds, **2**:384, 391; Lakota, **4**:67–68; Latvia, **3**:365, 367–368; Lebanon, **2**:393; Lunda, **1**:234, 238; Malaita, **1**:301; Malay, **2**:141; Malta, **3**:504; Maluku, **2**:198; Manchu, **2**:245; Marquesas Islands, **1**:378; Marshall Islands, **1**:351; Mauritius and Rodrigues, **1**:144; Maya, **4**:256–257, 264; Mexico, **4**:268; Mongol, **2**:252–253; Nagaland, **2**:73–74, 76; Nahua, **4**:282–283; Navajo, **4**:83; Nepal, **2**:115; The Netherlands, **3**:244; Norway, **3**:123; Nuer, **1**:151; Ojibwe, **4**:104, 107; Orissa, **2**:79–80; Otomí, **4**:288; Palau, **1**:359, 361–362; Persia, **2**:415; Piedmont and Val d'Aosta, **3**:470; Quechua, **4**:208–209; Roma, **3**:395–396; Sámi (Lapps), **3**:136; San, **1**:241; Sardinia, **3**:465; Scotland, **3**:53–54, 58–62; Semai, **2**:145; Sephardim, **3**:214; Serbia, **3**:426, 428, 434; Seven Council Fires, **4**:67–68; The Seychelles, **1**:149; Shona, **1**:248; Siberia, **2**:315; Sibundoy, **4**:229; Sicily, **3**:481; Slovenia, **3**:295; Spain, **3**:178; Sri Lanka, **2**:124–125; Swahili, **1**:155; Switzerland, **3**:307–308; Tairora, **2**:203; Tajik, **2**:325; Tlingit, **4**:118; Tonga, **1**:403; and translation, **1**:89; Tuareg, **1**:101, 112; Turkey, **2**:430–431; Tuvalu, **1**:404–405, 408; Uttar Pradesh, **2**:88; Uzbek, **2**:348; Vanuatu, **1**:326–327; Wales, **3**:70, 76; Western Inuit and Yupik, **4**:129, 140; Xhosa, **1**:259; Yemen, **2**:440–441; Zulu, **1**:268, 269. *See also* Creolization; *specific language*

L'année philologique, **1**:5

Lapps. *See* Sámi

Lasseter's Reef (Australia), **1**:286

Læstadius, Lars Levi, **3**:140

"*Latha dha'n Fhin am Beinn Iongnaidh*" (song), **3**:61

Latvia, **3**:362–369; folklore archives, **3**:362–364; geography and history, **3**:364–366; music, **3**:368–369; songs and poetry, **3**:366–368

Latvian Folklore Archives, **3**:362–363, 368

A Latvian Storyteller (Carpenter), **1**:82

Latvju Dainas (Latvia), **3**:366

Lau, **1**:300

Laughlin, Robert M., **4**:259–260

Lauïc (Lauan) languages (Malaita), **1**:301

Laurel festivals (Sicily), **3**:487–488

Laval, Père, **1**:146

Lawgoch, Owain, **3**:71, 72

Lawless, Elaine, **1**:30

Lawson, Henry, **1**:285, 286, 288

Lazar, Prince, **3**:434, 435

Lazarus, Saint, **3**:403

Learning How to Ask (Briggs), **1**:34

Lebanon, **2**:392–400; celebrations, **2**:399–400; dance, **2**:396–397; folksongs, **2**:394–395; funeral rituals, **2**:398–399; geography and history, **2**:392; modernization, challenges of, **2**:400; poetry and music, **2**:395–396; stories and jokes of Abu El-Abed, **2**:392–394

Legacy of Excellence (Hawai'i), **1**:376

Legendi (Macedonia), **3**:372

Legends: Basque, **3**:190–193; England, **3**:11–13; France, **3**:163–164; Germanic-Scandinavian-Icelandic, **3**:269–271; Haryana, **2**:40–41; Ireland, **3**:34–37; Roma, **3**:404, 406; Russia, **3**:418. *See also* Stories and tales

Legris, Michel, **1**:147

Leisure activities. *See* Games, sports, and recreation

Lenin, Vladimir I., **2**:316

León, Nicolás, **4**:278

Leopard-skin priests (Nuer), **1**:151

Leopold V, Duke, **3**:256

Lerhis-Puškaitis, Ansis, **3**:366

Lévi-Strauss, Claude, **1**:47

Levshin, V.A., **3**:410

Leydi, Roberto, **3**:460

Lhuyd, Edward, **3**:78

Libation rituals. *See* Drinking songs and rituals

Life-cycle rituals and beliefs: Albania, **3**:325–326; Ashkenazim, **3**:332–333; Brittany, **3**:171–173; China, **2**:227; Chinese living abroad, **2**:236; England, **3**:20; Flanders (Belgium), **3**:225–226; Iban, **2**:173; India, **2**:5, 6; Kashmir, **2**:61; Korea, **2**:296; Malta, **3**:504–506; Nepal, **2**:121; Palestine, **2**:404; Persia, **2**:419; Peru, **4**:201; Poland, **3**:383–386; Quechua, **4**:210; Roma, **3**:397–402; Russia, **3**:413–415; Sephardim, **3**:218–219; Siberia, **2**:321; Slovakia, **3**:290–291; Somali, **1**:25–26; Ukraine, **3**:442–444; Uttar Pradesh, **2**:92–93; Uzbek, **2**:351. *See also* Initiation (rights of passage) ceremonies

Life token motif, **1**:55

Light of Yara (Cuba), **4**:314–315

"The Lights of Cobb and Co" (Australia [British]), **1**:285

Lika region (Croatia), **3**:344

Lili'uokalani (Hawaiian queen), **1**:375

Liljeblad, Sven, **3**:148

Lillith, **3**:332

Limerick, Patricia Nelson, **1**:38

Limorti, Ester, **3**:196

Lindell, Kristina, **1**:81

Lindqvist, Beatriz, **3**:151

Ling, Jan, **3**:153

Linné, Carl von, **3**:144

Linton, Ralph, **1**:65

"The Lion and the Mouse" (Macedonia), **3**:372

Liongo Fumo (Swahili), **1**:155, 156, 158, 161

Lipanali, fairy tale tradition (Georgia), **3**:356

Lipan Apache, **4**:3

Lipsitz, George, **1**:72

Liszt, Ferenc, **3**:281

Lithberg, Nils, **3**:146

The Little Hat (Ecuadorian song-game), **4**:189–190

"The Little Mermaid," **3**:12

Little people: Basque, **3**:192; Cherokee, **4**:13; Choctaw, **4**:36; Isle of Man, **3**:44

"Little Red Riding Hood" (Germany), **3**:266

Livestock: Navajo, **4**:83; Rarámuri, **4**:299

Living history farms, **1**:59

Livonia, **3**:366

Llach, Lluis, **3**:184

Llywelyn I (Wales), **3**:71

Llywelyn II (Wales), **3**:71

Lo'au (Tonga), **1**:401

Localization and oikotypification, **1**:67

Lock, Margaret, **2**:278

Löfgren, Orvar, **3**:151, 152

Log races (Xavante), **4**:245–246

Lo'i (Hawai'i), **1**:376

Lomax, Alan, **1**:17, **3**:14, 461

Lomax, John, **1**:27

Long, Long Ago (Zulu), **1**:272

Long-distance running (Rarámuri), **4**:296–297, 305–306

Longhouses (Iroquois), **4**:53

Lönnrot, Elias, **3**:92–96

Lorca, Federico García, **3**:185

Lord, Albert B., **3**:433

"*The Lore and Language of Schoolchildren,*" **3**:20

"*Die Lorelei,*" **3**:271

Lorik-Chanda (Uttar Pradesh), **2**:91

Los hombres G, **3**:184

Lot, Ferdinand, **3**:173

Louis IX (France), **3**:162–163

Louis XIII (France), **3**:164

Louis XIV (France), **3**:164–165

Louis XVI (France), **3**:165

Louis Salvador (Archduke of Austria-Tuscany), **3**:195

Lovejoy, Arthur O., **1**:73

Love songs: Armenia, **2**:366; Bangladesh, **2**:98; Caipira, **4**:180; China, **2**:214; Finnish-Swedish, **3**:100; Igbo, **1**:196; Ireland, **3**:27; Kurds, **2**:389; Lebanon, **2**:395; Macedonia, **3**:374; Manchu, **2**:248; Mongol, **2**:256;

Palau, **1:**362; Tlingits, **4:**124; Tonga, **1:**401, 402; Uyghur, **2:**341

Lövkrona, Inger, **3:**153

Lowenthal, David, **1:**51

Lowie, Robert, **1:**27

Luba language (Lunda), **1:**238

Lucerne Chronicle, **3:**310

Lucia, Saint, **3:**101, 349

Lucy, Saint, **3:**289, 506

Ludgarda, Saint, **3:**506

Luke, Saint, **3:**349

Lullabies. *See* Children's songs, stories, and verses

Lunda, **1:**234–240; festivals and ceremonies, **1:**239–240; geography and history, **1:**234–235; religious beliefs, **1:**235–236; verbal folklore, **1:**236–239

Lundahl, Pia, **3:**151

Lundberg, Dan, **3:**154

Lundgren, Britta, **3:**151

Lundin, Susanne, **3:**151

Luther, Martin, **3:**238, 253, 257

Lutheran Reformation, **3:**125

Lyric songs: Italy, middle and southern, **3:**459; Russia, **3:**420–421

Mabinogion (Wales), **3:**173

Macaulay, Donald, **3:**66

MacCannell, Dean, **1:**86

MacCumhail, Fionn (Finn MacCool), **3:**27, 28–29, 57

Macdonald, Mrs. Archie, **3:**61

Macdonald, Duncan, **3:**57

Macdonald, Dwight, **1:**71

MacDonald, Margaret Read, **1:**56

Macedonia, **3:**370–378; arts, crafts, and architecture, **3:**375–376; dance and drama, **3:**374–375; geography and history, **3:**370–372; myths, legends, and folktales, **3:**372–373; poetry, **3:**373–374; songs and music, **3:**374

Mackintosh, Iain, **3:**66

Maclean, Sorley, **3:**66

Macleod, Neil, **3:**59

MacNamara, Francis ("Frank the Poet"), **1:**284

Macpherson, James, **3:**95

Madagascar, **1:**137–142; beliefs and folklore, **1:**138–139; geography and history, **1:**137–138; housing, **1:**142; music and dance, **1:**141–142; poetry and proverbs, **1:**140–141; stories and tales, **1:**139–140

Madela, Laduma, **1:**269

Mafeje, Archie, **1:**262

Magellan, Ferdinand, **1:**333

Magic: Albania, **3:**326; Ashkenazim, **3:**333–334; Caribs of Dominica, **4:**335–336; Denmark, **3:**83–84; Ecuador, **4:**191; England, **3:**9–10; Georgia, **3:**359–360; Guam, **1:**335–336; Italy, **3:**453, 458; Jamaica, **4:**343; Malaita, **1:**303, 306; Marquesas Islands, **1:**381; Palau, **1:**360–362; Poland, **3:**380, 382–385, 387; Russia,

3:411–415, 419; Sicily, **3:**489, 490; Slovenia, **3:**300; Tuvalu, **1:**406–407; as type of tales, **1:**94; Vanuatu, **1:**327; Zande, **1:**228–231

Magical cures. *See* Medicine and cures

Magnus, Olaus, **3:**144

Magnus, Saint, **3:**471

Magnús Grímsson, **3:**114

Mahabharata epic: Bali, **2:**152; India, **2:**8, 39–40, 53–54, 62, 91

Mahsuri legend (Malay), **2:**143

Makahiki festival (Hawai'i), **1:**373

Malagasy language: The Comoros, **1:**142; Madagascar, **1:**139

Malaita, **1:**300–308; dance, **1:**303–304; games and sports, **1:**306; making of myth, **1:**300–301; music, **1:**304; narratives and myths, **1:**302–303; other Malaitan practices, **1:**306; rites, rituals, and dreams, **1:**304–306; society and beliefs, **1:**301–302; songs and riddles, **1:**303

Malay, **2:**141–145; arts and crafts, **2:**143–144; domination of Semai, **2:**145–146, 150; geography and history, **2:**141–142; modernization, challenges of, **2:**144; myths, legends, and folktales, **2:**142–143; poetry and folk theater, **2:**143; studies of Malay folklore, **2:**145

Malcolm, D. McK., **1:**274

Malebe, Chief (Bwilile), **1:**235

Male-female duality as theme (Igbo), **1:**195

Maleya Madeswara (Lord of the Mountain), **2:**48–49

Malinowski, Bronislaw, **1:**84, 96, 320, 321

Malo, Saint, **3:**174

Malta, **3:**502–512; food, **3:**509; geography and history, **3:**502–504; life-cycle customs, **3:**504–506; Maltese Cross, **3:**509; music, **3:**509–510; religion, **3:**507–509; social structure, **3:**506–507

Maltese Cross, **3:**509

Maluku, **2:**197–203; arts, crafts, and architecture, **2:**201–202; geography and history, **2:**197–198; modernization, challenges of, **2:**202–203; music, song, and dance, **2:**200–201; myths, **2:**199–200; religious belief, **2:**198–199

Mambo (Cuba), **4:**312

Mami (Mamy) Wata: Benin, **1:**179; Wolof, **1:**209

Mampong Oki (king of Ga), **1:**184

Manchu, **2:**245–252; dance and drama, **2:**251; epics and folktales, **2:**247–248; folksongs, **2:**248; geography and history, **2:**245–246; poetry and proverbs, **2:**248–249; preserving Manchu folklore, **2:**247; shamanism, **2:**249–251

"Manchu Odyssey" (Manchu), **2:**246

Mandela, Nelson, **1:**258

"The Man from Ironbark" (Australia), **1:**285

Manichaeism (Kazakh), **2:**308

Mani Mahesh pilgrimages (Gaddi), **2:**34

Manolete, **3:**186

Manx Christmas, **3:**49–50

Manx culture. *See* Isle of Man

Manx fairy, **3:**44–46

Mao Zedong, **2:**218

Map, Walter, **3:**10

Mapfumo, Thomas, **1:**252

Maps: Australia and Oceania, **1:**277; Carribean, **4:**309; North American native peoples, **4:**2; peoples of Africa, **1:**102; South American regions and peoples, **4:**178

Marble games (Cherokee), **4:**16

Marco Polo, **2:**253

Mardi Gras: Baule, **1:**168; France, **3:**168; Galicia, **3:**205, 209; Germany, **3:**262; Piedmont and Val d'Aosta, **3:**473; Samoa, **1:**394

Margaret, Saint, **3:**164

Mari (Basque goddess), **3:**190–193

Mariachi music (Mexico), **4:**273

Maria Theresa (Empress), **3:**347

Marie Antoinette, **3:**165

Marijuana (Jamaica), **4:**344

Marital relations as theme: Ga, **1:**184; San, **1:**243

Maritime imagery (Swahili), **1:**156

Marmite, **3:**315

Maroons of Jamaica, **4:**339–341

Maroons of Suriname. *See* Suriname Maroon

Marquesas Islands, **1:**377–386; arts and crafts, **1:**383–384; geography and history, **1:**377–380; modernization, challenges of, **1:**384; oral tradition: stories, legends, and chants, **1:**381–382; religion and ritual, **1:**380–381; song, dance, and music, **1:**382–383; studies of Marquesan folklore, **1:**385

Marriage: Assam, **2:**21; Bali, **2:**156; Bangladesh, **2:**104; Bihar, **2:**28; Candoshi, **4:**181–182; Chinese living abroad, **2:**237; Ecuador, **4:**190; Gaddi, **2:**35; Haida, **4:**39–40; Haryana, **2:**42, 43–44; Jie, **1:**135, 137; Kaliai, **2:**183; Karnataka, **2:**48; Kashmir, **2:**61; Kewa, **2:**190; Khasi-Jaintia, **2:**71; Lunda, **1:**234; Maluku, **2:**200; Nagaland, **2:**74; Nepal, **2:**115; New Caledonia, **1:**310, 313; Nez Perce, **4:**98; Orissa, **2:**83; Palestine, **2:**406–407; Roma, **3:**400; Samoa, **1:**387–388, 393; Siberia, **2:**318; Slovakia, **3:**291; Tairora, **2:**205, 207; Uttar Pradesh, **2:**89, 91, 93; Vanuatu, **1:**329; Western Inuit and Yupik, **4:**133; Wolof, **1:**215; Yoruba, **1:**222; Zande, **1:**228. *See also* Polygyny; Weddings

Marriage (Malta), **3:**507

Marriage brokers (Malta), **3:**507

"Marseillaise," **3:**158

Marshall, John, **1:**349

Marshall, William, **3:**63

Marshall Islands, **1:**349–358; arts and crafts, **1:**354–355; canoe building, **1:**355; food, celebrations, and ceremonies, **1:**355; games and sports, **1:**354; geography and history,

1: Topics & Themes, Africa, Australia & Oceania
2: Southeast Asia & India, Central & East Asia, Middle East
3: Europe
4: North & South America

1:349–350; modernization, challenges of, 1:356; oral folklore types, 1:353; social structure and religion, 1:350–351; song and dance, 1:353–354; stories and storytelling, 1:351–352; studies of Marshall Islands folklore, 1:356–357

Martial arts (Hawai'i), 1:373

Martin, Saint, 3:200, 241, 265, 349, 471

Martin, György, 3:282–283

Martínez, Francesc, 3:195

Martino, Ernesto de, 3:463

Martin of Tours, Saint, 3:160

Martinsson, Lena, 3:151

Mary, Saint, 3:505

Mary Theotokos (Ukrainian goddess), 3:439, 441

Mascarene Islands, 1:144–150; history, 1:144. *See also* Mauritius and Rodrigues; Réunion; The Seychelles

Mashrab, Rahim, 2:340

Masks and masquerades: Baule, 1:164, 165, 167; Benin, 1:175; Igbo, 1:198–199; Ijo, 1:205–207; Iroquois, 4:55–56; Jamaica, 4:338–339; Malaita, 1:303; New Caledonia, 1:311; Peru, 4:207; Yoruba, 1:222, 224, 225

Maspons i Labrós, Francesc, 3:195

Massada legend (Israel), 1:63, 2:377–378

Massaum (Cheyenne), 4:28

Massot i Muntaner, Josep, 3:196

Matchmakers (Russia), 3:413–414

Matisoff, James, 3:335

Matoub, Lounès, 1:108

Matrilineal societies: Australian Aborigines, 1:295, 297; Baule, 1:163; Cherokee, 4:9; Guam, 1:333; Hopi, 4:46; Khasi-Jaintia, 2:66, 67, 71; Lunda, 1:234; Marshall Islands, 1:350; Palau, 1:359, 360–361; Seminole, 4:116; Suriname Maroons, 4:239; Tuareg, 1:103, 114; Vanuatu, 1:326

Matrilocality: Cherokee, 4:9; Haida, 4:39; Hopi, 4:46; Shuar, 4:221–222

Matsu pilgrimage and stories (Taiwan), 2:261, 267–268

Mattanza (Sicily), 3:484

Maui Kisikisi (Tonga), 1:400–401

Maurer, Konrad, 3:114

Mauritius and Rodrigues: geography and history, 1:144–146; Madagascar, 1:138; music and dance, 1:147; stories and tales, 1:146–147

Maximianus Herculeus, 3:471

Maya, 4:256–268; clothing, 4:262–263; drama, riddles, and wordplay, 4:261; dumb priest stories, 4:261; folktales, 4:258–261; modernization, challenges of, 4:264; music, 4:263; space and time, notions of,

4:257–258; sports and games, 4:263–264; studies of Mayan folklore, 4:264–265; Zapatista rebellion, 4:258

May Day, 3:17, 18

Mayotte. *See* The Comoros

Maypole: Austria, 3:256; England, 3:1; Germany, 3:264; Italy, 3:464; Slovakia, 3:290

Mayr, Fr., 1:274

Mazurka dance rhythm, 3:389

Mbata, Alban Hamilton, 1:271

Mbaye Trambwe (King of The Comoros), 1:142

McCarthy, William Bernard, 1:85

McElhill, Patrick, 3:39

McEwan, Frank, 1:254

McGrath, Billy, 3:38

McGrath, Dennis, 3:33

McGrath, Patrick James, 3:33, 34, 37

McHugh, Willie, 3:37–38

McKenry, Keith, 1:291

McSorley, "Ribbonman," 3:34

Mdhladhla, Garland Clement S., 1:271

Mdunga, Guaise, 1:270

Mead, Margaret, 1:40

Mecano, 3:184

Medea, 1:56; and Nahua tale, 4:287

Medicine and cures: Abanyole, 1:127; African American, 4:146–147; Armenia, 2:357; Ashkenazim, 3:333–334; Bali, 2:156; Bangladesh, 2:102–103; Baule, 1:165–166; Benin, 1:171, 179; Bhutan, 2:107; Bihar, 2:27; Caipira, 4:179; Caribs of Dominica, 4:333–334; China, 2:213; Chinese living abroad, 2:240–241; Denmark, 3:84; Duna, 2:167; Ecuador, 4:191; Finnish-Swedish, 3:99; Flanders (Belgium), 3:229; France, 3:159; Ga, 1:191–192; Gaddi, 2:35–36; Galicia, 3:203; Greece, 3:496; Guam, 1:338; Haryana, 2:41; Hawai'i, 1:369; Iban, 2:172, 174–175; Igbo, 1:197, 201–202; Iroquois, 4:58; Israel, 2:372; Japan, 2:278; Kadazandusun, 2:178; Kazakh, 2:314; Kiribati, 1:343; Kurds, 2:385–386; Madagascar, 1:138; Malaita, 1:306; Malta, 3:506; Marquesas Islands, 1:381; Marshall Islands, 1:351; Mexico, 4:270; Mississippi Delta, 4:171; Navajo, 4:85; The Netherlands, 3:240; Norway, 3:123–125; Nuer, 1:152; Palestine, 2:407, 408; Persia, 2:417, 418, 420–421, 424; Peru, 4:202; Piedmont and Val d'Aosta, 3:472–473; Rarámuri, 4:304–305; Réunion, 1:148; Samoa, 1:392; San, 1:242; Semai, 2:148; Seminole, 4:115; Sephardim, 3:213; Sertão, 4:217–218; Shona, 1:252, 254; Siberia, 2:320, 322; Sibundoy, 4:231–232; Slovakia, 3:287; Slovenia, 3:299–300; Taiwan, 2:265–266; Tajik, 2:327–328; Tonga, 1:399–400; Tuareg, 1:114; Tuvalu, 1:406; Ukraine, 3:439–440; Uttar Pradesh, 2:90; Uyghur, 2:338; Uzbek, 2:351–352; Vanuatu,

1:327; Western Inuit and Yupik, 4:134; Wolof, 1:211; Zande, 1:229

Medicine Lodge Treaty of 1867, 4:62

Medicine man. *See* Healers

Meertens, P.J., 3:237

Meertens Institute, 3:237, 243

Megalithic stones: Basque, 3:191; Brittany, 3:172; Malta, 3:504; Scotland, 3:53

Meghalaya. *See* Khasi-Jaintia

Megrelian folklore (Georgia), 3:355

Mejías, Ignacio Sánchez, 3:186

Melanesia, 1:17, 300–332

"Melting pot," 1:49

Memê Alan, romantic epic (Kurds), 2:388

Memela, Nsukuzonke, 1:269

Memorates (Russia), 3:418

Memorials. *See* Funerals and burials; Potlatches

Mem û Zîn, romantic epic (Kurds), 2:388

Menarcheal theme: Hawai'i, 1:368; Kiribati, 1:343; San, 1:243, 246

Mendaña, Alvaro de, 1:378

Menius, Fridericus, 3:368

Meredith, John, 1:285

Mermaids: Finnish-Swedish, 3:98; Guam, 1:336; Iceland, 3:115; Wolof, 1:209. *See also* "The Little Mermaid"

Merton, Ambrose. *See* Thoms, William J.

Mesepis (Georgia), 3:355

Mestizos (Mexico), 4:276

Metalworking: Benin, 1:176; Igbo, 1:201; Wolof, 1:213; Yoruba, 1:226

Metaphor. *See* Simile and metaphor

Methodists (Australia), 1:279

Methodius, Saint, 3:371, 426, 429

Meurling, Birgitta, 3:151

Mexican immigrants in Mississippi Delta, 4:174

Mexican Revolution, 4:278–279; and Rarámuri, 4:298

Mexico, 4:268–282; ethnic composition, 4:270; folk beliefs, 4:270–273; folklore, 4:275–277; folklore studies in contemporary Mexico, 4:280–281; geography and history, 4:268–269; independence movement, 4:277–278; Maya, 4:256–257; music and songs, 4:273; nineteenth- and twentieth-century studies of Mexican folklore, 4:278–280; Rarámuri, 4:296–298; religion, 4:269–270; Virgin of Guadalupe, 4:273–275

Mexico and Central America, 4:256–308

Mfengu, 1:263

Mhòr non Oran, Màiri (Mary Macpherson), 3:61

Michael, Saint, 3:290

Microcosmic historical tradition, 1:132

Micronesia, 1:333–365

Micronesian Endowment for Historic Preservation, 1:365

Micronesian languages: Palau, 1:359; Tuvalu, 1:405

Midrash texts (Israel), 2:373

A Midsummer Night's Dream, 3:7

Midwives: Abanyole, **1:**125; African Americans, **4:**147; Norway, **3:**126; Persia, **2:**417, 420; Poland, **3:**384; Ukraine, **3:**444. *See also* Childbirth and birth rituals

Migration: Albania, **3:**322, 323; Armenia, **2:**367–368; Australia (British), **1:**286; Austria, **3:**250; Basque, **3:**189; Baule, **1:**165; Benin, **1:**170–171; Brittany, **3:**173–174; Croatia, **3:**347, 350–352; Denmark, **3:**81; Finland, **3:**90; France, **3:**158–159; Galicia, **3:**202–203; Georgia, **3:**362; Germany, **3:**261; Greenland, **3:**103–105; Hopi, **4:**45–46; Hungary, **3:**275–276; Iceland, **3:**111–112, 118; Ireland, **3:**23–24; Island of Man, **3:**42, 43; Jie, **1:**131–132; Kadazandusun, **2:**179; Lunda, **1:**235; Macedonia, **3:**376; Malta, **3:**504; Nagaland, **2:**74, 75, 77; The Netherlands, **3:**235–236; Norway, **3:**126; Palau, **1:**359–360; Palestine, **2:**404–405; Persia, **2:**417, 420; Piedmont and Val d'Aosta, **3:**470; Poland, **3:**381, 384; Roma, **3:**395; Sardinia, **3:**465; Scotland, **3:**54; Sephardim, **3:**212–213; Serbia, **3:**426; Sicily, **3:**480–482; Slovakia, **3:**285–287; Slovenia, **3:**296; Spain, **3:**179–180; Ukraine, **3:**444; Wales, **3:**70

Milad, myth of (Palau), **1:**359, 364

Miladinov, Dimitri, **3:**372, 373

Miladinov, Konstantin, **3:**372, 373

Milligan, Jean, **3:**63

Milošević, Slobodan, **3:**427

Mime: Ga, **1:**192; Lunda, **1:**237; Malaita, **1:**303; Samoa, **1:**394

Miners and mining: Ainu (Japan), **2:**286, 293; Appalachia, **4:**165; Australia (British), **1:**279; Duna, **2:**168; Finland, **3:**91; Isle of Man, **3:**42; Italy, **3:**454, 465; Ojibwe, **4:**105; Rarámuri, **4:**290; Scotland, **3:**53; Shona, **1:**252, 255; Sicily, **3:**481; Slovakia, **3:**285, 287; Spain, **3:**179; Suriname Maroon, **4:**238

"Min Min Lights" (Australia [British]), **1:**286

Minnesota: Lakota, **4:**67–69

Minstrels (Ukraine), **3:**440–442

Miošić, Andrija Kačić, **3:**350

Miracle plays (Piedmont and Val d'Aosta), **3:**475

Mishnah (Israel), **2:**373

Missionaries: Benin, **1:**171; Candoshi, **4:**181–182; Hawaiʻi, **1:**374; Kiribati, **1:**341; Madagascar, **1:**138, 140, 141; Malaita, **1:**303, 306; Marquesas Islands, **1:**378, 380, 385; Marshall Islands, **1:**354; Mascarene Islands, **1:**146; Navajo, **4:**87; New Caledonia, **1:**314; Quechua, **4:**212; Rarámuri, **4:**297; Samoa, **1:**391–393, 395, 396; Shona, **1:**252; Tonga, **1:**400, 401; Trobriand Islands, **1:**316, 319–320; Tuvalu, **1:**405, 408; Vanuatu, **1:**327, 329; Xhosa, **1:**258; Zande, **1:**228, 233; Zulu, **1:**266, 271

Mississippi: Choctaw Indians, **4:**30–38. *See also* Mississippi Delta

Mississippi Delta, **4:**166–175; field hollers and worksongs, **4:**168–169; folk medicine,

4:171; folktales, **4:**171–172; geography and history, **4:**166–167; musical instruments, **4:**172–173; non-African American folklore, **4:**173–174; spirituals and blues, **4:**169–171; studies of Mississippi Delta folklore, **4:**174

"Mixed breed," **1:**48

Moccasin Game (Navajo), **4:**89–90

Moddey Dhoo (Black Dog), **3:**43

Modernization, challenges of, **1:**52–54; Ainu, **2:**290–293; Apache, **4:**6–7; Appalachia, **4:**165; Armenia, **2:**369; Assam, **2:**23–24; Australia (British), **1:**290; Bali, **2:**163–164; Baule, **1:**168; Benin, **1:**179; Berber, **1:**111–112; Bhutan, **2:**112; Brittany, **3:**175; Cherokee, **4:**20; Cheyenne, **4:**29; China, **2:**229–231; Chinese living abroad, **2:**243; Choctaw, **4:**37; and cultural area, **1:**18; Dakota, **4:**75–76; and diaspora, **1:**19; Guam, **1:**339; Haiti, **4:**325–326; Haryana, **2:**45–46; Hawaiʻi, **1:**374–375; Ijo, **1:**208; India, **2:**14–15; Ireland, **3:**39; Isaan, **2:**139; Japan, **2:**278–279; Kadazandusun, **2:**181; Kaliai, **2:**188; Karnataka, **2:**57; Kazakh, **2:**314; Kewa, **2:**195–196; Khasi-Jaintia, **2:**73; Kiribati, **1:**347–348; Kurds, **2:**391; Lakota, **4:**75–76; Lebanon, **2:**400; Madagascar, **1:**138; Malay, **2:**144; Maluku, **2:**202–203; Marquesas Islands, **1:**384; Marshall Islands, **1:**356; Maya, **4:**264; and nationalism, **1:**61; Navajo, **4:**86–87, 92–93; The Netherlands, **3:**240, 245; New Caledonia, **1:**313–314; Nuer, **1:**153; Palestine, **2:**409–410; Peru, **4:**207; Quechua, **4:**214–215; and race, **1:**79; Sámi (Lapps), **3:**141–142; Semai, **2:**149–150; Shona, **1:**254; Siberia, **2:**324; Sibundoy, **4:**235; Slovakia, **3:**286; Slovenia, **3:**294; Suriname Maroons, **4:**238, 241–242; Tairora, **2:**208–209; Tajik, **2:**334; Tlingits, **4:**126–127; and tourism, **1:**86; Tuareg, **1:**111–112, 120; Uttar Pradesh, **2:**94; Uyghur, **2:**345–346; Vanuatu, **1:**331; Western Inuit and Yupik, **4:**139–140; Wolof, **1:**216; Xavante, **4:**250; Xhosa, **1:**258, 261–267; Zande, **1:**233

Modern Language Association International Bibliography (MLAIB), **1:**5–6

Modlitewki (prayers), **3:**382–383

Moe, Moltke, **3:**138

Mohammed, Prophet, **1:**115, 212

Mohammedan Saints and Sanctuaries in Palestine (Cana'an), **2:**411

Moieties: Apache, **4:**5–6; Haida, **4:**39; Iroquois, **4:**51; Tlingit, **4:**117–119, 124, 125; Xavante, **4:**243–245

Molina, Tirso de, **3:**183

Moluccas. *See* Maluku

Monasteries (France), **3:**160–161

Moneo, Rafael, **3:**187

Money transaction stories (Palau), **1:**360

Mongol, **2:**252–259; dance, crafts, and festivals, **2:**258–259; geography and history,

2:252–254; heroic epics and folktales, **2:**254–255; proverbs and riddles, **2:**258; religious beliefs, **2:**256–258; songs and poetry, **2:**255–256

Monsters and creatures: Abanyole, **1:**124; Bali, **2:**160; Cherokee, **4:**13; Croatia, **3:**348; Georgia, **3:**354; Iceland, **3:**115; Mauritius and Rodrigues, **1:**147; Navajo, **4:**85; Nez Perce, **4:**103; Piedmont and Val d'Aosta, **3:**471–472

Montaldi, Danilo, **3:**456

Montana: Cheyenne, **4:**21–22; Lakota, **4:**67–69

Montanini song, Italy, **3:**461

Montefiore, Judith, **2:**375

Mooinjer Veggey (Isle of Man), **3:**44

Moonlight rituals: Benin, **1:**177; Igbo, **1:**196; Shona, **1:**253; Zande, **1:**230

Moorish architecture, **3:**218

Morality lessons: Haiti, **4:**320; Ijo, **1:**206; Nez Perce, **4:**100–101; Rarámuri, **4:**301; Shona, **1:**250; Shuar, **4:**225; Wolof, **1:**216; Yoruba, **1:**222

Morant, Harry, **1:**285

Morelos, José María, **4:**277

Morgan, Louis Henry, **1:**15

Morganwg, Iolo, **3:**75

Morgon Kara legends (Siberia), **2:**321

Mori, Yoshiro, **1:**63

Morphology of the Folktale, **3:**419

Morris dance, **3:**15

Morrison, Toni, **1:**79

Morrisseau, Norval, **4:**108–109

Moser, Hans, **1:**36, 37

Mother Damp Earth (Russia), **3:**413, 422

Mother Friday (Russia), **3:**417

Mother Goddess (Russia), **3:**412

"Mother" image of Greek nation, **3:**494

Motif, **1:**11, 54–57; and type, **1:**54, 94, 95

Motif-Index of Folk-Literature (Thompson), **1:**55, 56, 286

Mounds (Cherokee), **4:**19

Mt. Graham (Apache sacred site), **4:**7

Mountain dwellers (Italy), **3:**453–455

Mountain pasture system (Italy), **3:**454–455

Mountain Spirits (Apache), **4:**5

Mourides, **1:**212

Mourning. *See* Death and mourning rituals

"Mouse oracle" (Baule), **1:**167

Mpande (Zulu king), **1:**269

Mqhayi, Samuel Edward Krune, **1:**261–264, 267

Mugabe, Robert, **1:**249

Mules and Men (Hurston), **4:**143

"Mulga Bill's Bicycle" (Australia [British]), **1:**285

Mullen, Patrick B., **1:**80

Mummers' Play: England, **3:**16–18, 20; Isle of Man, **3:**50

Murad I (Sultan), **3:**434

Murals. *See* Painting

1: Topics & Themes, Africa, Australia & Oceania
2: Southeast Asia & India, Central & East Asia,
   Middle East
3: Europe
4: North & South America

Murdoch, Rupert, 3:188

Murdock, George Peter, 1:17, 18

Muromets, Ilia, 3:422

Murqvamoba drama (Svan, Georgia),
   3:359–360

Murray, Margaret, 1:50

Museo del Sale (salt museum, Sicily), 3:484

Museum for German Folklore, 1:58

Museum of Popular Industries and Arts
   (Barcelona), 3:196

Museums, 1:57–60

Musho! Zulu Popular Praises (Zulu), 1:272

Musical instruments: Albania, 3:321, 329;
   Apache, 4:6; Appalachia, 4:160–161;
   Armenia, 2:369; Assam, 2:22; Bali, 2:161;
   Bangladesh, 2:97, 102; Baule, 1:165; Benin,
   1:177; Bhutan, 2:108–109; Cherokee, 4:14,
   15; China, 2:222–223; Croatia, Central,
   3:345; Croatia, Littoral, 3:341–343; Croatia,
   Lowland, 3:346; Croatia, Mountainous,
   3:344; Duna, 2:170; Ga, 1:191; Gaddi, 2:36;
   Greece, 3:498; Haiti, 4:322; Haryana, 2:42;
   Hawai'i, 1:371–372; Iban, 2:175; Igbo,
   1:197; Ijo, 1:207; India, 2:9; Iroquois, 4:59;
   Isaan, 2:137–138; Italy, 3:463; Jamaica,
   4:345; Kadazandusun, 2:179; Karnataka,
   2:49, 54; Kashmir, 2:64; Kazakh, 2:309–312;
   Khasi-Jaintia, 2:72; Kiribati, 1:345; Kurds,
   2:389–390; Lakota and Dakota, 4:74; Lunda,
   1:236; Macedonia, 3:374, 375; Madagascar,
   1:141; Malaita, 1:304; Malay, 2:143; Malta,
   3:510; Manchu, 2:251; Maroons of Jamaica,
   4:340; Marquesas Islands, 1:381, 383;
   Marshall Islands, 1:355; Mauritius and
   Rodrigues, 1:145, 147; Maya, 4:263;
   Mississippi Delta, 4:172–173; Mongol,
   2:258; Navajo, 4:87; Nepal, 2:118; Norway,
   3:129, 130–131; Ojibwe, 4:108; Orissa, 2:83,
   84; Peru, 4:205; Quechua, 4:211, 212;
   Roma, 3:399; Scotland, 3:62–63; Semai,
   2:148; Serbia, 3:433; Shona, 1:251; Shuar,
   4:226; Siberia, 2:319, 321; Sicily,
   3:482–483; Slovenia, 3:301; Tairora, 2:208;
   Tajik, 2:328–329; Tlingits, 4:124; Tonga,
   1:402; Tuareg, 1:108, 115–117; Turkey,
   2:433–434; Tuvalu, 1:408; Ukraine, 3:440;
   Uttar Pradesh, 2:92; Uyghur, 2:341; Uzbek,
   2:352–353; Vanuatu, 1:329; Wales, 3:76;
   Western Inuit and Yupik, 4:136–137; Wolof,
   1:214; Zande, 1:231–233; Zulu, 1:274–275.
   See also specific instruments

Music and dance: Abanyole, 1:125–130;
   African Americans, 4:145–148, 151–153;
   Ainu, 2:287, 291, 292; Albania, 3:328, 329;
   Apache, 4:5; Appalachia, 4:160–162;

Armenia, 2:362–369; Ashkenazim,
   3:335–337; Assam, 2:22–23; Australia
   (British), 1:285–286, 288; Australian
   Aborigines, 1:293, 294, 296–298; Austria,
   3:257; Bali, 2:161; Bangladesh, 2:96–99;
   Baule, 1:164, 165–166; Benin, 1:176–177;
   Berber, 1:107–108; Bhutan, 2:109–110;
   Bihar, 2:28; Caipira, 4:180; Candoshi,
   4:185–187; Catalan, 3:198–199; Cherokee,
   4:11–12, 14–15; Cheyenne, 4:26–28; China,
   2:218–223; Choctaw, 4:33–34; and
   colonialism, 1:8–9; The Comoros, 1:143;
   country dances, England, 3:14–15; and
   creolization, 1:10–11; Croatia, Central,
   3:345; Croatia, Littoral, 3:341–343; Croatia,
   Mountainous, 3:344; Cuba, 4:310–312;
   Dakota, 4:74, 77; Denmark, 3:85; Duna,
   2:169–170; Ecuador, 4:189–190; England,
   3:13–15; and ethnicity, 1:26; and
   ethnopoetics, 1:32; Finnish-Swedish, 3:100;
   and folklorism, 1:36; Ga, 1:185–187, 192;
   Georgia, 3:358–359; Germany, 3:271;
   Greece, 3:497, 498; Guam, 1:338, 339;
   Haida, 4:43; Haiti, 4:321–323, 326;
   Haryana, 2:42–43; Hawai'i, 1:368, 371–372;
   Hopi, 4:48; Hungary, 3:280–283; Iban,
   2:174; Iceland, 3:119; Igbo, 1:196–199; Ijo,
   1:207; India, 2:9–11; Ireland, 3:27–29;
   Iroquois, 4:53, 55, 59; Isaan, 2:136,
   137–138; Israel, 2:381; Italy (middle and
   southern), 3:459, 460; Jamaica, 4:338, 341,
   344; Japan, 2:276–277; Kadazandusun,
   2:179; Kaliai, 2:186; Karnataka, 2:49,
   52–53; Kashmir, 2:61–63; Kazakh,
   2:310–312; Kewa, 2:191–195; Khasi-Jaintia,
   2:69–70; Kiowa, 4:61–65; Kiribati, 1:342,
   344–346, 348; Korea, 2:299–301; Kurds,
   2:386, 389–390; Lakota, 4:74, 77; Lebanon,
   2:394–397; Lunda, 1:236; Macedonia,
   3:374–375; Madagascar, 1:140, 141–142;
   Malaita, 1:302, 303–304; Malta, 3:509–510;
   Maluku, 2:200–201; Manchu, 2:248, 251;
   Maroons of Jamaica, 4:340–341; Marquesas
   Islands, 1:378, 380, 382–383; Marshall
   Islands, 1:352–356; Mauritius and Rodrigues,
   1:145, 147; Maya, 4:263; Mexico, 4:273;
   Mississippi Delta, 4:168–172; and
   modernization, 1:52–53; Mongol,
   2:255–256, 258–259; Navajo, 4:87–89; The
   Netherlands, 3:243–244; New Caledonia,
   1:313; northern Italy, 3:458, 459–460;
   Norway, 3:129–131; Nuer, 1:152–153;
   Ojibwe, 4:108, 109; Orissa, 2:82–83; Palau,
   1:360–364; Persia, 2:422–424; Peru,
   4:203–205; Poland, 3:380, 388–391;
   Quechua, 4:210–212; Rarámuri, 4:302;
   Réunion, 1:148; Roma, 3:404–405; Samoa,
   1:394–396; San, 1:241, 246; Scotland,
   3:57–63; Seminole, 4:115; Sertão,
   4:218–219; The Seychelles, 1:149–150;
   Shona, 1:251–253; Shuar, 4:225–227;
   Siberia, 2:316, 323; Sicily, 3:482, 485–486;

Slovakia, 3:292–293; Slovena, 3:300–302;
   Slovenia, 3:300–302; Spain, 3:183–185;
   Suriname Maroons, 4:240–241; Swahili,
   1:155, 157–158; Sweden, 3:146;
   Switzerland, 3:312–314; Taiwan, 2:263;
   Tajik, 2:328–329; Tlingit, 4:124–125;
   Tonga, 1:401–402; Trobriand Islands, 1:320;
   Tuareg, 1:108, 111–112, 116–118; Turkey,
   2:433–435; Tuvalu, 1:407–408, 410;
   Ukraine, 3:441–442; Uttar Pradesh,
   2:91–92; Uyghur, 2:341–344; Uzbek,
   2:351–353; Vanuatu, 1:328–330; Wales,
   3:76; Western Inuit and Yupik, 4:128–129,
   136–138; Wolof, 1:212, 213, 215; Xavante,
   4:245, 246–248; Yoruba, 1:224–225; Zande,
   1:230, 231–232; Zulu, 1:274–275. *See also*
   Children's songs, stories, and verses; *specific
   types of songs and dances*

Muslims: Assam, 2:18–20; Australia (British),
   1:289, 290; Bangladesh, 2:95; Baule, 1:164;
   Berber, 1:101, 103; Bihar, 2:25; The
   Comoros, 1:142; Haryana, 2:39, 41; Israel,
   2:375; Karnataka, 2:49; Kashmir, 2:59, 60,
   64; Orissa, 2:80, 81; Sri Lanka, 2:124, 125;
   Swahili, 1:154–155, 157, 160; Tuareg,
   1:114; Turkey, Alevi, 2:430; Tuvalu, 1:405;
   Uttar Pradesh, 2:88; Wolof, 1:210–212. *See
   also* Islam; Shi'ite Muslims; Sunni Muslims

Mutomboko celebration (Lunda), 1:239–240

Mvingana (bard of Zulu king), 1:273

Mwaka festival (Swahili), 1:159

Mwaneaba (Kiribati), 1:343–344

Mwata Kazembe, 1:235, 236

Mysore. *See* Karnataka

Mysterious housekeeper motif, 1:55

Mystery cults, 3:159–160

Mythical creatures. *See* Monsters and creatures

Myth of the Negro Past (Herskovits), 4:144–145

Mythological Cycle (Ireland), 3:30, 31

Myths. *See* Stories and tales

Myths and Legends of Palau, 1:364

Myths of origin. *See* Creation stories

Naath. *See* Nuer

Nagaland, 2:73–79; arts and crafts, 2:77–78;
   cultural tradition, 2:3; geography and
   language, 2:73–74; myths, legends, and
   folktales, 2:74–76; names, symbols, and
   meanings, 2:78–79; songs, 2:76–77

Nahua, 4:282–288; European trickster tales,
   4:287; geography and history, 4:282–283;
   roots of Nahua folklore, 4:283–284; tales and
   songs of European origin, 4:284–287

Naipaul, V.S., 1:145

Nairne, Lady, 3:59

Name days (Greece), 3:496

Naming: Tlingit, 4:120. *See also* Child naming;
   Nicknames

Namunai folklori tojik (Examples of Tajik
   Folklore, Tursunzoda), 2:326

Nanny of the Windward Maroons of Portland
   and St. Thomas, 4:340

Napoleon, 3:167
Napoleonic Code, 3:167
Ṇara (Kaingang myth), 4:196–197
Narratives. *See* Stories and tales
Narrative songs. *See* Ballads
National Dance Company (Shona), 1:252
Nationalism, 1:60–64; and antiquarianism, 1:1; and culture area, 1:17; and diaspora, 1:19; and ethnicity, 1:25; and frontier, 1:37, 38, 62; and globalization, 1:42, 62; Mexico, 4:274–278
Native American Church: Cheyennes, 4:24; Kiowa, 4:63
Nativism, 1:64–67; and diffusion, 1:24
Natural phenomena as theme: Igbo, 1:199; Palau, 1:359; Russia, 3:421; Serbia, 3:432–433
Nature spirits: Ijo, 1:205–207; Lunda, 1:236
Navajo, 4:81–97; arts and crafts, 4:90–92, 94; balance, concept of, 4:85; ceremonies, 4:85, 86; cosmology, 4:85; dance, 4:88–89; and gender, 1:40; geography and history, 4:81–83; language, 4:83; medicine, 4:86–87; modernization, challenges of, 4:86–87, 92–93; music and song, 4:87–88; religion, 4:87; reservations, 4:82–84; sports and games, 4:89–90; studies of Navajo folklore, 4:93; translation of language, 1:90
Nazis. *See* Germany
Negro Folktales in Michigan (Dorson), 1:67
Nemanya, Stevan, 3:427
Nemanya Cycle, 3:434
Nenabozho (Ojibwe), 4:105–106
Nepal, 2:113–123; arts, crafts, and architecture, 2:119–120; cultural tradition, 2:3; dance and games, 2:119; festivals and celebrations, 2:120–121; folktales and beliefs, 2:117–118; geography and history, 2:113–115; modernization, challenges of, 2:121; music, 2:118; social and family structure, 2:115–117; songs, 2:121; studies of Nepalese folklore, 2:121–122
Nèpballada (ballad, Hungary), 3:279
Néprajzi Hírek, 1:6
Nestorian Christianity: Kazakh, 2:308; Uzbek, 2:348
The Netherlands, 3:233–248; architecture, 3:244–245; Bali, influence on, 2:154–155, 163–164; calendars, 3:241–243; geography and history, 3:233–236; Maluku, influence on, 2:197, 198, 202, 203; modernization, challenges of, 3:240, 245; preservation of Dutch folklore, 3:236–237; religion, 3:237–241; songs and folktales, 3:243–244; sports and games, 3:243; Taiwan, influence on, 2:261
New Caledonia, 1:308–315; geography and history, 1:308–309; modernization, challenges of, 1:313–314; music and dance, 1:313; myths, legends, and oratory, 1:312–313; social structure and kinship, 1:309–311; spirits and ancestors, 1:312; studies of New Caledonian folklore, 1:314

New Guinea and culture area, 1:17
The New Heloise (Rousseau), 3:310
New Mexico: Apache, 4:1–3
New Year's Cycle plays (Italy), 3:463
New York: Iroquois, 4:50–51
Nez Perce, 4:97–103; bravery, tales of, 4:103; coyote tales, 4:100–103; disobedience tales, 4:101–102; food, tales of, 4:103; geography and history, 4:97–98; myths, legends, and folktales, 4:98–103
Ngcobo, Sondoda, 1:272
Ngiracheungel (chief of Imeiong), 1:361–362
Nguni language (Zulu), 1:268
Nibelungenlied, 3:269–270
Nicholas, Saint: Croatia, 3:349; Flanders, 3:228; Malta, 3:508; Netherlands, 3:241; Poland, 3:388; Russia, 3:418; Serbia, 3:429; Sicily, 3:483
Nicholas I (Tsar), 3:410
Nicholson, Annie, 3:62
Nicholson, Kate, 3:61
Nicknames: Malta, 3:510; Shona, 1:249
Niger-Benue confluence hypothesis (Igbo), 1:193–194
Niger-Congo Kwa language (Ga), 1:180
Nigeria and European colonialism, 1:8
Nigerian Folklore Society, 1:226
Nightmares: Denmark, 3:84; Nepal, 2:118; Persia, 2:417. *See also* Dreams
Nigra, Constantino, 3:458, 474
Nihon ryoiki (Buddhist) tales (Japan), 2:274
Nihon shoki chronicles (Japan), 2:274
Nikitich, Dobrynia, 3:422
Nilsson, Bo, 3:151
Nilotic languages (Nuer), 1:151
"Nine [or Five] Miles to Gundagai" (Australia), 1:285
"Nino Culotta" (Australia), 1:286
Ni-Vanuatu. *See* Vanuatu
Njajaan Njaay, prince, 1:210
Nkuba, Chief (Shila), 1:235
"Noble Savage," 3:312
Nogqopoza, 1:270
Nolan, Hugh, 3:35, 36
Nomadism (Roma), 3:395
Nonconformists: Australia, 1:278; religious, 3:74–75
Nongqawuse episode of 1857 (Xhosa), 1:262, 264–266
Nonviolence (Semai), 2:146–149
Nordic Museum (Sweden), 1:57, 3:145–147
Nordström, Annika, 3:153
Norman Conquest of 1066, 3:1
Norteña music (Mexico), 4:273
North Africa, 1:101–122
North America, 4:1–175
North Dakota: Lakota, 4:67–69
Northeastern U.S.: Iroquois, 4:50–51
Northern Cheyennes, 4:21, 22
Northern Mariana Islands, 1:333
Norway, 3:123–134; arts and crafts, 3:129–130; ballads, 3:128–129; celebrations, 3:130–131;

geography and history, 3:123–125; legends and folktales, 3:127–128; medicine and cures, 3:125–127; music and dance, 3:129, 130–131; sports and games, 3:131–132
Novellas, Macedonia, 3:372
Noy, Dov, 3:334
Noyes, Dorothy, 1:29
Nozugum stories (Uyghur), 2:340
Nsugbe, Philip, 1:200
Ntsikana (Xhosa prophet), 1:260
Ntuli, F.L., 1:271
Nuer, 1:150–154; geography and history, 1:150–151; modernization, challenges of, 1:153; music and recreation, 1:153; poems, songs, and wordplay, 1:152–153; religion, 1:151–152
Nugent, Walter, 1:38
Numbers: Cherokee, 4:11; Navajo, 4:84; Seminole, 4:115; Tajik, 2:334
Nursery Tales, Traditions, and Histories of the Zulus, 1:271
Nwa-iba dress, 1:7–8
Nyasaye, 1:123
Nyembezi, Cyril Lincoln Sibusiso, 1:271, 272, 274
Nylén, Anna-Maja, 3:148

OAM (open-air museum), 1:57, 58
Obeah: Caribs of Dominica, 4:334–335; Jamaica, 4:343
"Oberon's Palace" (England), 3:8
Obilic, Miloš, 3:434
Observations on Popular Antiquities (Brand), 1:2
The Ocean of Wise Sayings (Mongol), 2:258
Ochokochi (Georgia), 3:355
O'Connell, Daniel, 3:36
Oddur Einarsson, 3:116
Odjig, Daphne, 4:108, 109
The Odyssey (Homer), 3:320, 325
Oghuz Nama (Uyghur), 2:337
Ogibe, Olu, 1:201
Ogilvie, Will, 1:285
Ogodo dress, 1:7–8
"The Ogre Blinded," 1:95
Ogre stories. *See* Monsters and creatures
O'Hanlon, Redmond, 3:36
Ohen, Oba, 1:175
O-ho-mah Lodge (Kiowa), 4:64–65
Oikotypification, 1:23, 67–68, 95
Oil exploration (Shuar), 4:221
Óí'ó club fights (Xavante), 4:244–245
Ojibwe, 4:103–111; arts and crafts, 4:108–109; festivals and celebrations, 4:109–110; geography and history, 4:103–105; history, 4:107–108; music and songs, 4:108; myths, legends, and folktales, 4:105–107; oral histories, 4:107–108; punning, 4:107
Ojkanje singing (Croatia), 3:344
Ojos de Brujo, 3:183
Okaikoi (son of Queen Dode Akaibi), 1:184
Oka Masao, 2:272–273
Okara dress, 1:7–8

1: Topics & Themes, Africa, Australia & Oceania
2: Southeast Asia & India, Central & East Asia, Middle East
3: Europe
4: North & South America

Okeke, Uche, 1:201

Okhuaihe (attendant to Oba Ewuare), 1:174

Oklahoma: Cherokee, 4:8; Cheyenne, 4:21–22; Choctaw, 4:30–32; Kiowa, 4:60–61; Seminole, 4:111–112

Ólafur Daviðsson, 3:114, 117

Olav, Saint, 3:127

"The Old Man and the Birds" (Mongol), 2:256

"Old Master Eats Crow" (African American), 4:147

"Old Woman from Paste" game (Kazakh), 2:313

Olney, Marguerite, 1:41

Olokpo dress, 1:7–8

Olunyole (Abanyole), 1:123

Olympic Games: Greece, 3:499; World Eskimo Indian Olympics, 4:138

Omens: Ainu, 2:288; Kiribati, 1:343; Nepal, 2:118; Uttar Pradesh, 2:90. *See also* Diviners and divination

Oñate, Juan de, 4:1

One Thousand and One Nights (*The Arabian Nights*), 2:404

Ontario: Iroquois, 4:50–51; Ojibwe, 4:103–105

On the Origin of Species (Darwin), 1:12

Open-air museums, 1:57–61

Opera: Austria, 3:259; China, 2:224; Chinese living abroad, 2:241; Italy, 3:464; Sicily, 3:491; Switzerland, 3:309, 315; Taiwan, 2:263–264

Opland, Jeff, 1:261

Oracles. *See* Diviners and divination

The Oral and Written Literature in Nguni (Zulu), 1:271

Oral Repertoire and World View (Pentikäinen), 1:82

Oral Tales of India (Balys), 1:56

Oral tradition: African American, 4:145, 146, 151; Ainu, 2:287; Appalachia, 4:159–160; Assam, 2:21–22; Australia (British), 1:283–285; Australian Aborigines, 1:297–298; Basque, 3:190; Baule, 1:164–165, 168; Benin, 1:170–171, 176–177; Bhutan, 2:112; Cherokee, 4:13; China, 2:214–215, 221–222; Choctaw, 4:35–36; and colonialism, 1:9; Croatia, 3:350; and folklorism, 1:35; Ga, 1:181; Guam, 1:338; Haides, 4:40, 41–42; Hawaiʻi, 1:366, 370; Iban, 2:173–174; Igbo, 1:193; Jamaica, 4:342; Jie, 1:131; Kadazandusun, 2:178–179; Kaliai, 2:183–184; Kashmir, 2:61; Kiribati, 1:344–346; Kurds, 2:391; Lakota, 4:77; Lunda, 1:236–239; Madagascar, 1:140; Malaita, 1:302; Malay, 2:142; Marquesas Islands, 1:381–383; Marshall Islands, 1:349, 353; Mauritius and

Rodrigues, 1:146; Maya, 4:260; and modernization, 1:53; Nahua, 4:283–284, 287; New Caledonia, 1:312–313; Ojibwe, 4:105–108; Palau, 1:360–361; Poland, 3:380; and popular culture, 1:72; and public folklore, 1:76; as public folklore, 1:76; Rarámuri, 4:301; Serbia, 3:433–434; Shuar, 4:225; Siberia, 2:322; Spain, 3:182; Sri Lanka, 2:127–128; Swahili, 1:161; Tairora, 2:203, 206, 209; Tlingit, 4:120–121; Tonga, 1:400–401; Turkey, 2:432–433; and type, 1:95; Vanuatu, 1:327–328; Western Inuit and Yupik, 4:128–129, 140–141; Wolof, 1:214–215; and worldview, 1:98; Yoruba, 1:218–223; Zande, 1:230; Zulu, 1:267

Oral Tradition (University of Missouri), 2:231

Oranmiyan, 1:171

Oratory: Greece, 3:495; Igbo, 1:196–197; Marquesas Islands, 1:380; Marshall Islands, 1:351; Nuer, 1:152; Rarámuri, 4:300–301; Sibundoy, 4:233–234; Tlingits, 4:123–124; Tuvalu, 1:406; Xavante, 4:249–250

Orbi (blind storytellers, Sicily), 3:486–487

Ordinary citizens as heroes, 1:46

Oregon: Nez Perce, 4:97

Original sin as theme (Malaita), 1:301–302

Origin myths. *See* Creation stories

"Origin of Corn" (Nahua), 4:284

"The Origin of the Fifth Sun" (Nahua), 4:284

Orikuchi, Shinobu, 2:279–280

Orissa, 2:79–88; arts and crafts, 2:84–85; cultural tradition, 2:4; dance, 2:82–83; festivals and celebrations, 2:85–87; folk theater, 2:83–84; geography and history, 2:79–80; myths of Lord Janannath, 2:80–81; myths of the Konark temple, 2:81–82; studies of Orissa folklore, 2:87

Orlovich, Pavle, 3:435

Oro dances (Macedonia), 3:374

Ortaoyunu ("play in the middle") puppet shows (Turkey), 2:435

Ortutay, Gyula, 3:280, 283

"Orwakol and His Seven Wives" (Jie), 1:135

Osceola (Seminole), 4:111–112

Ossianic ballads (Scotland), 3:61, 62

Österreichische Volkskundliche Bibliographie (ÖVB), 1:6

Oswald, James, 3:63

Otomí, 4:288–296; celebrations for the crosses, 4:290; geography and history, 4:288–290; origin myth, 4:290–293; Studies of Otomí folklore, 4:293–294

Otrepev, Grishka, 3:423

Ottoman Empire, 3:427, 433, 434

Ottoman influence: Albania, 3:327; Macedonia, 3:371

Our Father (Rarámuri deity), 4:300

Our Mother (Rarámuri deity), 4:300

Outcasts (vagabonds), Italy, 3:455–456, 460

Outlaw legends: Iceland, 3:116; Ireland, 3:36–37

Outline of World Cultures (Murdock), 1:17, 18

Ovia (Benin king's favorite wife), 1:175

Owen, Elias, 3:78

Owen, Robert, 3:53

The Oxford Companion to Australian Folklore (Australia [British]), 1:286

Ozidi (Izutu) tale (Ijo), 1:206–207

Ozolua, Oba, 1:172, 177

Pacific Arts Festival, 1:410

Paczolay, Gyula, 3:279

Pagan elements: England, 1:2; Greek religion, 3:495; and invented tradition, 1:50; Russia, 3:411–412. *See also* Gods and goddesses

Painting: Assam, 2:23; Australian Aborigines, 1:293, 296, 298, 299; Bali, 2:163; Baule, 1:168; Bhutan, 2:111; Bihar, 2:29; Dutch, 3:244; Greenland, 3:107; Haiti, 4:324; Haryana, 2:44; Hopi, 4:49; Igbo, 1:201; India, 2:6, 7; Japan, 2:277; Karnataka, 2:57; Nepal, 2:120; Netherlands, 3:241, 244; Norway, 3:130; Ojibwe, 4:108–109; Sicily, 3:486, 489–490; Spain, 3:181, 186–187; Sri Lanka, 2:128; Taiwan, 2:265; Tajik, 2:331; Turkey, 2:436; Wolof, 1:212. *See also* Arts and crafts

Palatkwapi (Hopi), 4:46

Palau, 1:358–365; ancient structures and artifacts, 1:359–360; arts and crafts, 1:364; geography and history, 1:358–359; language and chants, 1:361–362; political rhetoric and proverbs, 1:361; rituals, celebrations, and society, 1:362–364; stories and songs, 1:360–361; studies of Palauan folklore, 1:364–365

Palauan Legends, 1:364

Paleo-Balkanic belief system, 3:323–324

Pale of Settlement, 1:62, 3:330

Palestine, 2:400–413; geography and history, 2:400–403; modernization, challenges of, 2:409–410; Palestinian identity and folklore, 2:403–406; poetry, 2:408–409; religious beliefs, customs, rituals, and ceremonies, 2:406–408; studies of Palestinian folklore, 2:410–412

Palio of Asti festive race (Piedmont and Val d'Aosta), 3:477

Palles, Anne, 3:83

Palmenfelt, Ulf, 3:153

Palo Monte (Cuba), 4:310

Pancharaksha tales (Mongol), 2:255

Panchatantra (animal) fables (India), 2:7, 26, 60, 135

Pandits: Karnataka, 2:64; Kashmir, 2:60. *See also* Hinduism

Pandit Vishnu Sharma, 2:26

Pannonian cultural zone. *See* Croatia, Central; Croatia, Lowland

Panpipes (Quechua), 4:211

Papuans, 1:17

Parables. *See* Stories and tales

Parades: Quechua, 4:213. *See also* Processions

Paraskeva, Saint, 3:417, 418

Paredes, Américo, **1**:68

Paris Expo (1867), **1**:57

Parker, Mathew, **1**:2

Parnavaz (King), **3**:357

Parry, Milman, **3**:433

Parsons, Elsie Clews, **1**:27, 41

Particularism in peasant culture (Italy), **3**:452–453

"Pass the Fire" (Samoa), **1**:394

Pastorales (Basque), **3**:190

Paterson, A.B. (Banjo), **1**:285, 288

Patmutiun Hayots (History of Armenians, Khorenatsi), **2**:359

Patriarchal societies: Abanyole, **1**:123; Xhosa, **1**:266

Patrick, Saint, **3**:23, 30–31, 268

Patrilineal societies: Australian Aborigines, **1**:294, 296; Guam, **1**:333; Kiribati, **1**:341; Malaita, **1**:301; New Caledonia, **1**:309; Nuer, **1**:151; Shona, **1**:249; Vanuatu, **1**:326; Zande, **1**:228

Patriotism and nationalism, **1**:62

Patron saints: Malta, **3**:507–508; Piedmont and Val d'Aosta, **3**:470–471; Serbia, **3**:429–430; Slovenia, **3**:299

Pattini halle (Sri Lanka), **2**:127

Patton, Charley, **4**:170

Paul, Saint, **3**:268, 417, 504

Paz, Octavio, **1**:74

Peace Policy (American Indians), **4**:62

Peach Pit Game (Lakota), **4**:75

Peasant culture: Germany, **1**:61, 78; Italy, **3**:452–453; and public folklore, **1**:76; Russia, **3**:409; Sweden, **3**:144–146

Peate, Iorwerth C., **3**:78

Peeters, K.C., **3**:229

Pelicans and Chihuahuas and Other Urban Legends (Australia [British]), **1**:287

Pema Lingpa (Buddhist saint-scholar), **2**:107

Pentecostal religions (Benin), **1**:179

Pentikäinen, Juha, **1**:82

Penushliski, Kiril, **3**:372, 373

Peony Pavilion (China), **2**:224

The People of the Bat (Laughlin), **4**:260

Pepys, Samuel, **3**:17, 18

Percy, Thomas, **3**:13

Peregrino, F.Z.S., **1**:263

Performance art: Abanyole, **1**:127–130; and creolization, **1**:11; and diffusion, **1**:23–24; and ethnography, **1**:27–28; and ethnopoetics, **1**:32; and fieldwork, **1**:33; Guam, **1**:339; Madagascar, **1**:140; Marshall Islands, **1**:353; and modernization, **1**:53; and text, **1**:83; and translation, **1**:91; Tuareg, **1**:118; Western Inuit and Yupik, **4**:136–138; Wolof, **1**:216; Xhosa, **1**:261. *See also* Drama and theater; Music and dance; Storytelling

Performance theory, **1**:68–71

Perrault, Charles, **3**:266

Persia, **2**:413–429; folk beliefs surrounding pregnancy and labor, **2**:419–421; folksongs and festivals, **2**:422–424; folktales, proverbs, and jokes, **2**:422; geography and history, **2**:413–414; religion, **2**:414–416; sports and games, **2**:424–425; studies of Persian folklore, **2**:425–426; supernatural lore, **2**:416–419

Personal expression, importance to San, **1**:241

Personification of animals. *See* Animism

Personification of concepts (Benin), **1**:173

Peru, **4**:199–208; arts and crafts, **4**:207; Candoshi, **4**:181; festivals and celebrations, **4**:205–206; games, **4**:207; geography and history, **4**:199–201; life-cycle rites and folk medicine, **4**:201–202; modernization, challenges of, **4**:207; myths, legends, and folktales, **4**:202–203; poetry and folksongs, **4**:203–205; proverbs and ritualized insults, **4**:203

Peter, Saint, **3**:417

Peter the Great (Tsar), **3**:408

Peter the Hermit, **3**:162

Peyotism: Kiowa, **4**:63; Navajo, **4**:87

Phadaeng Nang Ai (Isaan), **2**:133

Phantoms. *See* Ghost stories

Phar Lap (Australia [British] racehorse), **1**:286

Philibert, Emmanuel, **3**:469

Philip II, **3**:238

Philip, Saint, **3**:349

Philosophical themes in Georgian folktales, **3**:357–358

Phra Ubali-kunuupamajan, **2**:134

Phynnodderee (Isle of Man), **3**:46

Pianta, Bruno, **3**:460

Picasso, Pablo, **1**:74, **3**:186–187

Piedmont and Val d'Aosta, **3**:469–480; calendars, **3**:474–477; celebration for draftees, **3**:477; folktales and songs, **3**:473–474; geography and history, **3**:469–470; medicine, magic, and witchcraft, **3**:472–473; mythical animals, **3**:471–472; religion, **3**:470–471; sports, games, and handicrafts, **3**:477–478

"Pied Piper of Hamelin," **3**:267–268

"Pig dance" (Marquesas Islands), **1**:383

Pike, Kenneth, **1**:28

Pikono nane songs (Duna), **2**:169–170

Pilgrimages: Austria, **3**:251; Bhutan, **2**:108; Brittany, **3**:170; France, **3**:160; Gaddi, **2**:34–35; Galicia, **3**:202, 203, 206–207; India, **2**:11, 14; Israel, **2**:373–374; Italy, **3**:464; Kurds, **2**:385; Malta, **3**:506; Orissa, **2**:84; Palestine, **2**:407; Quechua, **4**:212; Roma, **3**:404; Slovenia, **3**:299; Spain, **3**:181; Sri Lanka, **2**:126; Taiwan, **2**:267–268; Wolof, **1**:212

Pitrè, Giuseppe, **3**:481–482

Pius VII (Pope), **3**:167

Pixies. *See* Fairy lore

Plains tribes, myths of, **4**:26

Plantation houses (Cherokee), **4**:19

Plantation policy (Ireland), **3**:24, 25

Plantations: African Americans, **4**:146–147, 151; Jamaica, **4**:338; Mississippi Delta, **4**:167; Suriname Maroon, **4**:237

Plato, **1**:14

Playground verses. *See* Children's songs, stories, and verses

Playing in the Dark (Morrison), **1**:79

Plenkovich, Churilo, **3**:422

Plog, Stanley, **1**:88

Plough or Wooing Play (England), **3**:16

Podrugovic, Tešan, **3**:434

Poetry: Abanyole, **1**:127–130; Austria, **3**:257; Bhutan, **2**:108–109; China, **2**:214, 216; Croatia, **3**:350; Ecuador, **4**:188–189; and ethnopoetics, **1**:31–32; Ga, **1**:185–189; Georgia, **3**:358–359; Igbo, **1**:196–197; Isaan, **2**:135; Israel, **2**:377; Kazakh, **2**:310–311; Khasi-Jaintai, **2**:70–72; Kurds, **2**:386–387; Latvia, **3**:366–368; Lebanon, **2**:395–396; Lunda, **1**:236; Macedonia, **3**:372–374; Madagascar, **1**:140–141; Malay, **2**:142, 143; Manchu, **2**:248–249; Marquesas Islands, **1**:382–383; Mongol, **2**:255–256; Nuer, **1**:152–153; Palestine, **2**:408–409; Peru, **4**:203–205; Shona, **1**:249–251; Spain, **3**:182; Swahili, **1**:157, 159–161; Tonga, **1**:400–402; Tuareg, **1**:108, 115; Turkey, **2**:432; Tuvalu, **1**:407; Uyghur, **2**:340; Wolof, **1**:212, 214–215; Xhosa, **1**:261–267; Yemen, **2**:442–444; Yoruba, **1**:222–223; Zulu, **1**:270, 272–274. *See also* Ethnopoetics

Pokrov (Russia), **3**:417

Poland, **3**:378–394; calendars, **3**:386–388; dance, **3**:390–391; folktales, **3**:380–381; history, **3**:378–380; life-cycle celebrations, **3**:383–386; music, **3**:388–390; and nationalism, **1**:61; riddles, proverbs, charms, and spells, **3**:382–383

Polibio (Sicily), **3**:483

Political organization, politics, and political activism: and antiquarianism, **1**:1; Berber, **1**:108, 111; Ga, **1**:186; Igbo, **1**:196; Marquesas Islands, **1**:378; Mexico, **4**:269; New Caledonia, **1**:314; Palau, **1**:361; Samoa, **1**:387, 390; Shona, **1**:249, 252; Swahili, **1**:154, 159; Tuareg, **1**:116–117; Wolof, **1**:214; Yoruba, **1**:220

Polygyny: Bangladesh, **2**:98; Chinese living abroad, **2**:237; Lunda, **1**:234; Nepal, **2**:117; Shuar, **4**:222; Tairora, **2**:205; Wolof, **1**:213; Zande, **1**:228

Polynesia, **1**:366–411

Popular culture, **1**:71–73

þórbergur þórðarsson, **3**:114

Portugal: Benin, trading with, **1**:171, 173; Maluku, influence on, **2**:198, 201; Shona, trading with, **1**:249

Possession. *See* Spirit possession

Possession rites: Guam, **1**:338; Lunda, **1**:236

Potato cultivation (Ireland), **3**:24

Potlatches: Haida, **4**:42–43; Tlingits, **4**:119–120, 125

Pottery. *See* Ceramics

Poulsen, Anders, **3**:135

Pourquoi tales (Guam), **1**:334–335

1: Topics & Themes, Africa, Australia & Oceania
2: Southeast Asia & India, Central & East Asia, Middle East
3: Europe
4: North & South America

Powell, John Wesley, 1:84

Power, Richard, 3:36

Powwows: Cherokee, 4:15; Cheyenne, 4:25, 28; Ojibwe, 4:109

Pracat, Miho, 3:347

Praise poetry and songs: Igbo, 1:196; Lunda, 1:235, 238; Shona, 1:250; Wolof, 1:212, 214; Xhosa, 1:261–267; Yoruba, 1:222–223

Prat, Joan, 3:196

Prats, Llorenç, 3:196

Pratt, George, 1:396

Prayers: Alpine, 3:313; Lakota, 4:68–69; Poland, 3:383; Xavante, 4:249. *See also* Incantations

"Prayer to the Death of Creation, Chi-na-Eke" (Igbo), 1:197

"Prayer to Ulaasi, River Deity of Ihembosi" (Igbo), 1:197

Pre-Christian belief (Georgia), 3:354–356

Predanija (Macedonia), 3:372

Predictions. *See* Diviners and divination

Prenting (Maroons of Jamaica), 4:340

Prentis, Malcolm, 1:281

Preservation: and archives, 1:3–5; of Dutch folklore, 3:236–237; of Russian folklore, 3:408–411

Presley, Elvis, 1:11, 3:271

Presbyterianism in Australia, 1:278, 281

Price-Mars, Jean, 4:319–320

Priests: Maya dumb priest stories, 4:261. *See also* Brahmans (priestly class)

Primeros Memoriales (de Sahagún), 4:275

Primitive Art (Boas), 1:34

Primitive Culture (Tylor), 1:12

Primitivism, 1:73–75; and invented tradition, 1:51

Primitivism and Identity in Latin America (Camayd-Freixas & González), 1:74

Primitivism and Related Ideas in the Middle Ages (Boas), 1:73

"*Primitivism*" *in 20th Century Art* (Rubin), 1:74

Prince Marko Cycle (Serbia), 3:435

"The Prince of the Shining Countenance" (Madagascar), 1:140

Prithyi Narayan Shah (King of Nepal), 2:114

Processions: Austria, 3:255, 264–265; Croatia, 3:349; flagellants, Campania and Calabria, 3:464; Galicia, 3:207; Italy, 3:464; Malta, 3:504, 508; Poland, 3:384; Roma, 3:399; Sicily, 3:489; Ukraine, 3:442

Property holdings (Serbia), 3:428

Prophets and prophecies: Choctaw, 4:36, 37; Karnataka, 2:49. *See also* Diviners and divination

Propp, Vladimir, 1:82, 3:116, 419

Prose Edda (Snorra Edda), 3:113

Protestantism: Australia (British), 1:279; Kiribati, 1:341, 348; Marquesas Islands, 1:380; Tuvalu, 1:405. *See also* Christianity

Proverbs, 1:95; Abanyole, 1:130; African Americans, 4:150–151; Appalachia, 4:159; Ashkenazim, 3:335; Australia (British), 1:284; Baule, 1:164–165; Benin, 1:176–177; Bihar, 2:28–29; China, 2:214; Chinese living abroad, 2:234, 242; Ga, 1:182–183; Greece, 3:497–498; Haiti, 4:320, 326; Hungary, 3:280; Iban, 2:174; Igbo, 1:193, 195–196; Ijo, 1:206–207; Isaan, 2:135–136; Israel, 2:372, 373, 379, 380–381; Kazakh, 2:310; Khasi-Jaintia, 2:70–72; Kurds, 2:388; Lunda, 1:236, 237; Madagascar, 1:140–141; Malay, 2:142, 143; Manchu, 2:248–249; Marshall Islands, 1:352; Mongol, 2:258; origins of, 1:2; Palau, 1:361; Palestine, 2:403; Persia, 2:422; Peru, 4:203; Poland, 3:382; Russia, 3:418; Sephardim, 3:214–215; Shona, 1:249–251; Swahili, 1:155, 156, 159; Tajik, 2:326–327; Turkey, 2:432; Uyghur, 2:336; Yoruba, 1:218, 221–222; Zande, 1:231; Zulu, 1:270, 274

Pshav poetic contests (Georgia), 3:359

Puamana (Hawai'i), 1:376

Puberty. *See* Initiation (rights of passage) ceremonies

Public folklore, 1:75–78; and culture area, 1:17

Public Folklore (Baron & Spitzer), 1:77

Publius, Saint, 3:508

Pueblos: art forms, 4:49; Navajo, 4:82

Pujol, Josep M., 3:196

Punning: Balinese, 2:154; Ojibwe, 2:107; Sri Lanka, 2:127; Taiwan, 2:264; Turkey, 2:433, 435

"*Puntan Dos Amantes*" (Guam), 1:337

Punto (Cuban song form), 4:312

Puppet theater: Greece, 3:500; northern Italy, 3:464; Sicily, 3:490

Purdah (Uttar Pradesh), 2:89

Purgatory doctrine (England), 3:10

Purification ceremonies: Lunda, 1:239; Malaita, 1:304; Russia, 3:412–413, 439

Purim dramas (Ashkenazim), 3:336–337

Pushkin, Alexander, 3:409

Putta Kin Kai (Grandpa eats chicken) game (Isaan), 2:139

Putting Folklore to Use (Jones), 1:77

Pysanky (decorated eggs, Ukraine), 3:445–446

Q'assayids (Wolof), 1:212

Qivittut (Greenland), 3:107

Quatrain verses and songs (Latvia), 3:363, 366

Quechua, 4:208–216; arts and crafts, 4:214; drama and the *entrada*, 4:212–213; folktales and riddles, 4:202, 204, 210; geography and history, 4:208–209; life-cycle rituals, 4:210; modernization, challenges of, 4:214–215; religious beliefs, 4:209–210; songs and music, 4:202, 204, 210–212; sports and games, 4:213–214; studies of Quechua folklore, 4:215

Quest rites (Lenten), 3:474–475

Quilting. *See* Textile arts

Quintana, Artur, 3:196

Qvigstad, J., 3:137, 138

Rabghuzi, Nasiruddin, 2:338–339

"The Rabid Red Hero with One Hair" (Mongol), 2:255

Rabin, Yitzhak, 2:381

Rabon, Francisco, 1:339

Race, 1:78–81. *See also* Demographics; Discrimination

Races: Apache, 4:5–6; Rarámuri, 4:305–306; Tuareg, 1:119; Xavante, 4:245–246

Racism. *See* Discrimination and racism

Radio: Abanyole, 1:124; Australia (British), 1:286, 288; Baule, 1:168; Kiribati, 1:348; Navajo, 4:89; Shona, 1:252; Shuar, 4:226–227; Swahi, 1:158, 161; Tuareg, 1:118; Vanuatu, 1:329

Rahbani, Assi, 2:394

Raids: Apache, 4:3; Western Inuit and Yupik, 4:132–133

Rainbows (Sibundoy myths), 4:235

Rainmaking: bride-of-the-rain ceremonies (Berber), 1:105–106; Igbo, 1:197; Shona, 1:252; Wolof, 1:210

Rakel Pálsdóttir, 3:114

Ralámuli. *See* Rarámuri

Rama (Haryana), 2:41

Ramadam observances (Serbia), 3:433

Ramayana stories: Assam, 2:22; Bali, 2:152; India, 2:8, 11, 14; Karnataka, 2:53–54; Kashmir, 2:62; Uttar Pradesh, 2:92

Ramnarine, Tina Karina, 3:95

Ramsay, Allan, 3:59

Ramsten, Märta, 3:153

Ranavalona I (queen of Madagascar), 1:138

Ranchera music (Mexico), 4:273

Rangda stories (Bali), 2:157, 160–162

Raphael, 3:184

Rap music (African American), 4:153

Rara festival (Haiti), 4:323

Rarámuri, 4:296–308; cultural variation, 4:299–300; festivals and celebrations, 4:302–304; folk medicine, 4:304–305; folktales, 4:301; foreign cultural practices, adoption of, 4:298–299; geography and history, 4:296–298; maize beer, 4:304; oratory, 4:300–301; religious beliefs, 4:301–302; sports and games, 4:305–306; studies of Rarámuri folklore, 4:306–307

Rashi, 3:335

Rastafarianism (Jamaica), 4:343

Rattles: Benin, 1:174; Iroquois, 4:55, 59; Malaita, 1:304; Mascarene Islands, 1:147; Rarámuri, 4:302

Raudvere, Catharina, 3:153

Ravaton, Alphonse, 1:147

Raven clan (Haida), 4:39

Raven myths and songs: Haides, **4:**40–42; Tlingit, **4:**121, 122, 124; Western Inuit and Yupik, **4:**135

Rawjaa, Dulduitiin, **2:**256

Razin, Stenka, **3:**423

Rebirth. *See* Reincarnation

Rechuodel, **1:**365

Recipes. *See* Food customs and beliefs

Recommendation on the Safeguarding of Traditional Culture and Folklore (Australia [British]), **1:**291

Reconstructed folklore (Poland), **3:**391–392

Recreation. *See* Games, sports, and recreation

Redfield, Margaret Park, **4:**259–260

"Red Riding Hood," **3:**12

"Reedy River" (Australia [British]), **1:**285

Reformation, England, **3:**1

Regatta, national holiday (Malta), **3:**510–511

Region. *See* Culture area

Rehnberg, Mats, **3:**147

Reincarnation: Bali, **2:**156; Benin, **1:**172; Bihar, **2:**25; Edo, **1:**172; Greenland, **3:**106; Haida, **4:**41; Isaan, **2:**133; Orissa, **2:**80; Siberia, **2:**317, 318, 322; Trobriand Islands, **1:**319; Uttar Pradesh, **2:**88; Western Inuit and Yupik, **4:**133

Reindeer herding: Sámi (Lapps), **3:**134, 139; Siberia, **2:**316, 319

Religion and beliefs: Abanyole, **1:**123; Ainu, **2:**287–290; Albania, **3:**322–323; Appalachia, **4:**158–159; Assam, **2:**18–19; Australia (British), **1:**278; Bali, **2:**156–161; Bangladesh, **2:**103–105; Baule, **1:**164; Benin, **1:**172–173, 179; Berber, **1:**103–107; Bhutan, **2:**106–107; Bihar, **2:**25; Brittany, **3:**4; Caipira, **4:**179; Candoshi, **4:**182–185; Cherokee, **4:**11–12; Cheyenne, **4:**23–25; China, **2:**213–214; Chinese living abroad, **2:**235–236; The Comoros, **1:**142–143; and cultural relativsm, **1:**14; Denmark, **3:**83; Ecuador, **4:**197–199; England, **3:**4; Ga, **1:**181–182; Haiti, **4:**317–319; Hawai'i, **1:**368–369, 371, 374; Hungary, **3:**276–279; Iban, **2:**173, 174–175; Igbo, **1:**197–198; Ijo, **1:**204–206; India, **2:**6–7; and invented tradition, **1:**50; Ireland, **3:**23–24; Isaan, **2:**131–135; Israel, **2:**373–375, 380; Italy, **3:**457–458; Jamaica, **4:**343–344; Japan, **2:**275–277; Jie, **1:**133–137; Kadazandusun, **2:**177–178; Kaliai, **2:**188; Karnataka, **2:**47–53; Khasi-Jaintia, **2:**66–67; Kiowa, **4:**62–63; Kiribati, **1:**342–343; Korea, **2:**298–299; Kurds, **2:**385–386; Lunda, **1:**235–236; Madagascar, **1:**138–139; Malaita, **1:**301–302; Malta, **3:**507–509; Maluku, **2:**198–199; Manchu, **2:**249–251; Marquesas Islands, **1:**380–381; Marshall Islands, **1:**350–351; Mauritius and Rodrigues, **1:**145; Mexico, **4:**269–270; Mongol, **2:**256–258; Navajo, **4:**87; The Netherlands, **3:**237–241; Nuer, **1:**151–152; Ojibwe, **4:**109; Palestine, **2:**406–408;

Persia, **2:**414–416; Piedmont and Val d'Aosta, **3:**470–471; Quechua, **4:**209–210; Rarámuri, **4:**301–302; Réunion, **1:**148; Roma, **3:**396; Sámi, **3:**136; Semai, **2:**146–149; Seminole, **4:**115; Sertão, **4:**217–218; The Seychelles, **1:**149; Shuar, **4:**224–225; Siberia, **2:**316–317; Sicily, **3:**489–490; Slovakia, **3:**286–287; Spain, **3:**180–182; Sri Lanka, **2:**124–126; Suriname Maroons, **4:**238–240; Switzerland, **3:**308; Tairora, **2:**206; Taiwan, **2:**261–263; Tlingit, **4:**118–119, 126; Tonga, **1:**398–400; Tuareg, **1:**103–107; Tuvalu, **1:**405–406; Uttar Pradesh, **2:**90; Uyghur, **2:**337–338; Vanuatu, **1:**326–327; Wales, **3:**72–75; Western Inuit and Yupik, **4:**134–135; Wolof, **1:**210–213; and worldview, **1:**96; Xhosa, **1:**259; Yanomami, **4:**252; Zulu, **1:**269–270. *See also* Worldview

The Religious System of the Amazulu (Zulu), **1:**271

Reliques of Early English Poetry (England), **3:**13

Remedies. *See* Medicine and cures

Remi, Saint, **3:**161

Removal policy: Choctaw, **4:**31; Ojibwe children, **4:**105; Seminole, **4:**111–112

Renuka myth (Karnataka), **2:**51

Repertoire, **1:**81–83

Reservations: Cheyenne, **4:**21–22; Hopi, **4:**44; Kiowa, **4:**63; Lakota, **4:**69–70; Navajo, **4:**82–84; Seminole, **4:**116; Sioux, **4:**76

Réunion, **1:**147–148; geography and history, **1:**147–148; music and dance, **1:**148; stories and tales, **1:**148

Revitalization movements, **1:**65

Rhymes: Appalachia, **4:**159; Manchu, **2:**248; Russia, **3:**421; Yoruba, **1:**223. *See also* Poetry

Rhys, John, **3:**78

Rhythm: Haiti, **4:**322; Latvian poetry, **3:**367. *See also* Drums

Riabibin-Andreev, P.I., **3:**423

Riabinin, Ivan, **3:**423

Riabinin, Trofim, **3:**423

"The Rich and Poor Peasant" (Mascarene Islands), **1:**146

Richard the Lionhearted, **3:**256

Riddles, **1:**95; Abanyole, **1:**130; Appalachia, **4:**159; Armenia, **2:**359; Ashkenazim, **3:**334; Bangladesh, **2:**99, 100; Bihar, **2:**28–29; Finnish-Swedish, **3:**100; Ga, **1:**182–183; Greece, **3:**496; Iban, **2:**174; Igbo, **1:**195; Iroquois, **4:**53; Isaan, **2:**135–136; Israel, **2:**373; Karnataka, **2:**49; Kurds, **2:**388; Lunda, **1:**237; Malaita, **1:**303, 306; Malay, **2:**142, 143; Marshall Islands, **1:**352; Mauritius and Rodrigues, **1:**145; Maya, **4:**261; Mongol, **2:**258; Nepal, **2:**119; Poland, **3:**382, 391; Quechua, **4:**210; Russia, **3:**418; Shona, **1:**250; Tajik, **2:**326–327; Tlingits, **4:**125; Uttar Pradesh, **2:**91; Yoruba, **1:**218, 221–222; Zande, **1:**233; Zulu, **1:**270, 274

Rímur (poetic cycles), **3:**119

Rink, H.J., **3:**107

Rip Van Winkle stories (Siberia), **2:**322–323

Ristilammi, Per-Markku, **3:**152

Rites of passage. *See* Initiation (rites of passage) ceremonies

Rituals and ceremonies: Albania, **3:**325–326; Apache, **4:**5–6; Caipira, **4:**179; Candoshi, **4:**183–185; Cherokee, **4:**15–16; Cheyenne, **4:**24; Cuba, **4:**310; Ecuador, **4:**198–199; Haida, **4:**42–43; Igbo, **1:**197; Iroquois, **4:**56; Isle of Man, **3:**48; Italy, **3:**462; Jamaica, **4:**344; Latvia, **3:**364; Malta, **3:**510; Maroons of Jamaica, **4:**339–340; Mexico, **4:**271–273; Navajo, **4:**85, 86; Quechua, **4:**210; Rarámuri, **4:**299, 302–305; Scotland, **3:**56; Shuar, **4:**222–224, 226, 227; Sibundoy, **4:**233–234; Sicily, **3:**483–484, 487–488; Suriname Maroons, **4:**239; Western Inuit and Yupik, **4:**134–135; and worldview, **1:**96; Xavante, **4:**244–246, 248–249. *See also* Festivals and celebrations; *specific event (e.g., childbirth, marriage)*

Rivière, George Henri, **1:**60

Robarchek, Clayton A., **2:**146–147

Robert, Shaaban, **1:**158

Roberts, John W., **1:**79

Robertson, Jeannie, **3:**59

Robin Goodfellow, **3:**6, 7

Robin Hood, **3:**11, 13

Rochholz, E.L., **3:**313

Rock and roll, **1:**11

Rodeos: Australia (British), **1:**288; Navajo, **4:**90

Rodionovna, Arina, **3:**409

Roesti Curtain (Switzerland), **3:**307

Róheim, Géza, **3:**283

Rojas, Fernando de, **3:**183

Rojek, Chris, **1:**87

Roma, **3:**274, 278, 280–281, 395–408; calendars, **3:**403–404; folktales, **3:**405–406; geography and history, **3:**395–397; life-cycle celebrations, **3:**397–402; and nationalism, **1:**62; Nazi genocide of, **1:**64; Serbian, **3:**426; songs and music, **3:**404–405; wedding rituals, **3:**398–401

Roma, Josefina, **3:**196

Roman Catholics. *See* Catholicism

Romand (French Switzerland), **3:**307

Roman Gaul, **3:**159–160

Romani group identity, **3:**396

Romani professional music, **3:**397

Romanov, Mikhael, **3:**423

Romanticism, **1:**61; Macedonia, **3:**372

Romantic nationalism. *See* Nationalism

Romeu i Figueras, Josep, **3:**196

Ronaldo, **3:**186

Rooth, Anna-Birgitta, **3:**148, 152

Rose, Doudou Ndiaye, **1:**214

Ross, William, **3:**59

Rossini, Gioacchino, **3:**309

Rothenberg, Jerome, **1:**31, 85

1: Topics & Themes, Africa, Australia & Oceania
2: Southeast Asia & India, Central & East Asia, Middle East
3: Europe
4: North & South America

Rouget de Lisle, Claude-Joseph, 3:157
Round dance: Georgia, 3:359, 360; Hungary, 3:282; Kiowa, 4:64; Siberia, 2:319; Slovenia, 3:302
Roure Torent, Josep, 3:195
Rousseau, Jean Jacques, 1:74, 3:310
Royal House of Orange, 3:242
Royal Institute of Amazingh (Berber) Culture, 1:111
Royal Scottish Country Dance Society, 3:63
Royalty: Georgian folktales, 3:356–357; Igbo, 1:8; Lunda, 1:235, 236; Nagaland, 2:77; Wolof, 1:210; Zande, 1:228. See also specific names of kings, queens, etc.
Royaume, Catherine, 3:315
Rózsa, Sándor, 3:277
Rubin, William, 1:74
Rudd, Steele, 1:286
Rugs. See Textile arts
Rumba (Cuba), 4:311
Rumor stories (African American), 4:151, 169
Runeberg, Johan Ludvig, 3:101
Runge, Philipp Otto, 3:267
Rupayan Sansthan (Rajasthan), 2:15
Rushnyky (ritual towels, Ukraine), 3:444–445
Russia, 3:408–425; calendars, 3:415–417; epics, 3:421–424; history, 3:411–412; Israel, influence on, 2:376–377; legends, folktales, and other oral genres, 3:417–420; life-cycle celebrations, 3:413–415; preservation of folklore, 3:408–411; Siberia, influence on, 2:316; songs, 3:420–421; Tajik, influence on, 2:325–326; Uzbek, influence on, 2:349, 350; witchcraft and magic, 3:412–413
Ryan, John S., 1:291
Rybnikov, P.N., 3:410

"Sabour" (Mascarene Islands), 1:146
Sacred Arrows (Cheyenne), 4:23–24
Sacred Buffalo Hat (Cheyenne), 4:23–24
Sacred Cross of Calderón Pass (Otomí), 4:290–293
The Sacred Remains: Myth, History, and Polity in Belau, 1:365
Sacred story archives (Vanuatu), 1:328
Sacrifices: Albania, 3:324; Baule, 1:166; Benin, 1:172, 173; Bihar, 2:27; Chinese living abroad, 2:237, 238; Duna, 2:166–167; Gaddi, 2:35–36; Iban, 2:175; Jie, 1:135–137; Kadazandusun, 2:178; Karnataka, 2:51; Kazakh, 2:307; Khasi-Jaintia, 2:69; Korea, 2:297; Malaita, 1:304; Manchu, 2:250, 251; Marquesas Islands, 1:381; Maya, 4:265; Mongol, 2:258; Nepal, 2:121; Nuer, 1:152; Palestine, 2:408; Sámi (Lapps), 3:136; Semai, 2:146, 148; Siberia, 2:321; Taiwan,

2:261–262; Tajik, 2:334; Tonga, 1:399; Yoruba, 1:224
Sagyrbayev, Kurmangazy, 2:312
Sahagún, Fray Bernardino de, 4:275
"Said Hanrahan" (Australia [British]), 1:285
Saint cults: Brittany, 3:174; France, 3:160; Sicily, 3:487
Saint's day holidays: Greece, 3:497; Malta, 3:504–505, 508–509; Roma, 3:403–404; Sicily, 3:488
Saivism, 2:20
Saktism, 2:20
Salam,sina (Samoan chief), 1:388
Salesians (Shuar), 4:220–221
Sálote (queen of Tonga), 1:401
"Salsa" music (Cuba), 4:311
Salt making: Lunda, 1:234; Sicily, 3:484–485
Salvà, Adolf, 3:195
Sámi (Lapps), 3:90, 112, 134–144; geography and history, 3:134–135; modernization, challenges of, 3:141–142; narratives, 3:139–140; preservation of folklore, 3:136–139; religion and beliefs, 3:136; Russian influence, 3:140; stories and tales, 3:140–141; witchcraft, 3:135
Samoa, 1:386–397; ceremonies and rituals, 1:393–394; genealogical stories, 1:386–387; history, 1:387–388; origin tales, 1:388–389; spirit lore, 1:392–393; stories of humans and spirits, 1:389–390; theater and dance, 1:394–396; Tonga in Samoan folklore, 1:388; Western-influenced folklore, 1:390–392
Samuelson, R.C.A., 1:272
San, 1:240–248; animals and hunting lore, 1:246–247; geography and society, 1:240–242; the mythological Early Times, 1:242–244; stories, myths, and legends, 1:242; studies of San folklore, 1:247; transformation of the Early Times, 1:245–246; trickster tales, 1:244–245
San Carolos Apache, 4:6
Sand drawings: Navajo, 4:86, 92; Vanuatu, 1:330
Sandile (Xhosa chief), 1:260, 266
Sankaradeva (spiritual leader of Assam), 2:19–20
Sanskrit: Assam, 2:17; Bali, 2:152, 154; Bihar, 2:26; forerunner of other languages, 1:22; India, 2:3; Isaan, 2:135; Karnataka, 2:51, 53; Kashmir, 2:60; Manchu, 2:247; Nepal, 2:115
Santéria myths (Cuba), 4:313
San Vitores, Luis Diego de, 1:333
Sardana (dance), 3:198–199
Sardinia, 3:464–465; circle dances, 3:465; funeral lament, 3:465; poetic contests, 3:465; shepherd's code of honor, 3:465
Saressalo, Lassi, 3:140
Sargadelos ceramic factory (Galicia), 3:208–209
Sassoontsi Davit (Davit of Sassoon, Armenia), 2:364

Sastre, Alonso, 3:184
Sather, Clifford, 2:176
Satire: Bangladesh, 2:99; Igbo, 1:196, 197; Nepal, 2:119; Russia, 3:418; Sri Lanka, 2:128; Wolof, 1:214; Yemen, 2:444; Yoruba, 1:223
Sava, Saint, 3:427
The Savage Mind (Lévi-Strauss), 1:47
Saveen (Gaddi), 2:35–36
Sayrami, Mulla Musa, 2:341
Scarves. See Hairstyles and head coverings
Scéalaíocht (Ireland), 3:27–28, 30, 31, 37
Schapkarev, Kuzman, 3:372
Scheub, Harold, 1:272
Schiller, Friedrich, 3:309
Schilling, Diebold, 3:310
Schnitzelbängler (poems), 3:316
Schoolcraft, Heny Rowe, 4:105
School of Oriental and African Studies of London University, 1:161
Schools: Navajo children, 4:92; Western Inuit and Yupik, 4:131–132, 140–141
Schreiner, Olive, 1:270
Schrijnen, Jos, 3:237
Schwizerdütsch language, 3:307
Scotland, 3:52–69; Australia (British) influence by, 1:278, 279, 281; ballads, 3:57–62; calendars, 3:64–67; geography and history, 3:52–55; music and dance, 3:57–64; political autonomy, 3:55; regional divisions, 3:53–54; sports and games, 3:64; storytelling, 3:57; supernatural lore, 3:55–57
The Scots in Australia (Australia [British]), 1:281
Scott, Bill, 1:278, 287
Scott, Walter, 3:3, 59
Sculpture. See Carving and sculpture
Seal, Graham, 1:291
Seanchas (Ireland), 3:27–28, 30, 31, 34–35, 37
Sea stories: Croatia, 3:347; Marshall Islands, 1:352; Swahili, 1:156
Sechseläuten festival (Switzerland), 3:315
Secola, Keith, 4:108
Second sight (Ireland), 3:55
The Secret History of the Mongols (Mongol), 2:253–254
Secret societies (Japan), 2:272
Seers. See Diviners and divination
Sega (Mascarene Islands), 1:148, 150
Self-mutilation (Karnataka), 2:49
Sellmann, James, 1:334
Semai, 2:145–151; geography and history, 2:145–146; modernization, challenges of, 2:149–150; religious and folk beliefs and Semai peaceability, 2:146–149; social structure and Semai democracy, 2:149
Seminole, 4:111–116; arts and crafts, 4:114; clothing, 4:112–113; food, 4:113–114; geography and history, 4:111–112; housing, 4:114; social structure, 4:116; Studies of Seminole folklore, 4:116

Séndé (Kiowa trickster), 1:92–93

Sennett, Richard, 3:151

The Sentimental Bloke (Australia [British]), 1:285

Sephardim, 3:211–222; arts, crafts, and architecture, 3:217–219; ballads, proverbs, and folktales, 3:214–217; and diaspora, 1:20; food, 3:219–220; geography and history, 3:211–214; naming traditions, 3:220

Sequin art (Haiti), 4:324–325

Sequoyah, 4:14

Serbia, 3:425–437; calendars, 3:429–432; epics, 3:434–436; geography and history, 3:425–427; *slava* celebration, 3:429–432; social structure, 3:427–429; songs, folktales, and poetry, 3:432–434

Serra i Boldú, Valeri, 3:195

Serra i Pagès, Rossend, 3:195

Serrat, Joan Manuel, 3:184

Serratit (secret songs), 3:109

Sertanejo, 4:216

Sertão, 4:216–219; arts and crafts, 4:219; folktales, 4:218; food, 4:218; geography and history, 4:216–217; housing, 4:219; Kariri culture, 4:217; music and festivals, 4:218–219; religious beliefs, 4:217–218

Servandztiants, Garegin, 2:364

Seselwa (The Seychelles), 1:149

Seven Council Fires, 4:67–68

Seventh-Day Adventists and Tuvalu, 1:405

"Seventy Liar" stories (Mongol), 2:255

Sex and Temperament in Three Primitive Societies (Mead), 1:40

Sexual acts: Croatia, 3:348; Haryana, 2:44; Jie, 1:136; Malaita, 1:302; Maya, 4:260–261; Nahua, 4:283; Orissa, 2:83; Samoa, 1:393–396; Trobriand Islands, 1:316; Tuareg, 1:117–118; Yanomami, 4:253, 254

Sexual morality tales: Bangladesh, 2:98; Denmark, 3:84; Duna, 2:169; Haryana, 2:41, 44; Jamaica, 4:341; Karnataka, 2:51; Nahua, 4:285

Sexual symbols and innuendo: Bali, 2:163; Georgia, 3:355, 359–360; Isaan, 2:132; Kewa, 2:195; Mississippi Delta, 4:170; Nez Perce, 4:100; Spanish bullfighting, 3:185

The Seychelles, 1:149–150; geography and history, 1:149; stories, tales, and music, 1:149–150

Shadow theater (Greece), 3:500

Shahnama epic (Persia), 2:415, 423

Shaivism: Kashmir, 2:64; Orissa, 2:80

"Shaka" (Zulu), 1:272

Shaka (Zulu king), 1:268, 273–274

Shakespeare, William, 1:56; 3:7, 17, 72

Shamanism: Ainu, 2:287; Armenia, 2:357; Bhutan, 2:107; China, 2:213, 223; Ecuador, 4:198; Greenland, 3:105–107; Hungary, 3:278; Iban, 2:172–175; Japan, 2:272–273, 276; Kazakh, 2:307, 308–309, 314; Korea, 2:297–301; Malay, 2:143; Manchu, 2:247, 249–251; Mongol, 2:256–258; Nepal, 2:118;

Russia, 3:411, 421–422; Sámi, 3:135–136; Semai, 2:148; Seminole, 4:115; Shuar, 4:225; Siberia, 2:317, 319–321; Tairora, 2:206; Taiwan, 2:268; Tajik, 2:327; Tlingits, 4:118; Turkey, 2:430; Uyghur, 2:337–338, 343; Uzbek, 2:351–352; Western Inuit and Yupik, 4:134

Shapeshifting (Piedmont), 3:473

Shapkarev, Kuzman, 3:373

Sharp, Cecil, 3:13–15

Shasekishu compilation (Japan), 2:274

Shaw, George Bernard, 3:38

Shaw, R. Daniel, 1:90

"The Shearer's Dream" (Australia [British]), 1:285

Sheepherding and sheep farming: Italy, 3:455; Navajo, 4:83; Slovakia, 3:286

Shein, P.V., 3:411

Shi'ite Muslims: Kurds, 2:385; Persia, 2:415; Yemen, 2:440

Shikibu, Murasaki, 2:274

Shining Rock (Cherokee), 4:13

Shinto (Japan), 2:273

Shiva: Bangladesh, 2:96; Gaddi, 2:32–37; Haryana, 2:43; India, 2:13; Karnataka, 2:48, 49; Semai, 2:147

Shoe Game (Navajo), 4:89–90

Shoh-noma (The Book of Kings, Firdausi), 2:326

Shona, 1:248–257; architecture and arts, 1:253–254; dance and drama, 1:252–253; games and sports, 1:253; geography and history, 1:248–249; modern changes to and studies of Shona folklore, 1:254–255; modernization, challenges of, 1:254; music and song, 1:251–252; stories, poems, and proverbs, 1:249–251

Shooglenifty (Scotland), 3:66

Shotgun houses: African American, 4:153–154; Mississippi Delta, 4:167; in southern United States, 1:10, 20

Shrewdness tales. *See* Trickster

Shrovetide: Denmark, 3:86; Russia, 3:416–417

Shrunken heads (Shuar), 4:223, 226

Shuar, 4:219–228; arts, crafts, and trade, 4:227–228; folktales and narratives, 4:225; geography and history, 4:219–221; music, drama, and dance, 4:226–227; power and ritual, 4:222–224; religious beliefs and shamanism, 4:224–225; social structure, 4:221–222; songs, spells, and chants, 4:225–226

Shukha anumpa (Choctaw), 4:36

Shuman, Amy, 1:28, 43

Siberia, 2:315–325; animals, nature, and the spiritual world, 2:317–319; arts and crafts, 2:323; geography and history, 2:315–316; modernization, challenges of, 2:324; music and songs, 2:323; religious beliefs, 2:316–317; rituals, 2:321; shamanism, 2:319–321; storytelling, 2:322–323

Sibundoy, 4:229–236; ceremonial speaking, 4:233; festivals and celebrations, 4:233–235;

geography and history, 4:229–230; modernization, challenges of, 4:235; myths, legends, and folktales, 4:230–232

Sicilian Puppet Theater, 3:491

Sicily, 3:480–492; agricultural folklore, 3:482–483; arts and crafts, 3:489–490; calendars, 3:487–489; fishing folklore, 3:483–484; geography and history, 3:480–482; songs, 3:485–487

"The Sick Stockrider" (Australia [British]), 1:285

Sidonius, 3:160

Siege mentality in Malta, 3:504

Siegfried, 3:269–271

Sigfús Sigfússon, 3:114

Sigging (African American), 4:150

"The Significance of the Frontier in American History" (Turner), 1:38

Signifying (African American), 4:150

"The Signifying Monkey" (African American), 4:148

Sigüenza y Góngora, Carlos de, 4:276

Sigurður Nordal, 3:114

Sikhs: Assam, 2:18; Bihar, 2:25; Gaddi, 2:31; Haryana, 2:39; Kashmir, 2:59, 60

"The Silence Wager," 1:95

Silversmithing (Navajo), 4:90–91

Simile and metaphor, 1:29; African Americans, 4:153; Australian Aborigines, 1:294; Bali, 2:164; Bhutan, 2:108; China, 2:220; Ga (Gamei), 1:185; Hawai'i, 1:369; Igbo, 1:195, 197; Jie, 1:136; Kazakh, 2:311; Kewa, 2:190; Madagascar, 1:139; Marshall Islands, 1:351, 353; New Caledonia, 1:309; Nuer, 1:153; Palau, 1:361; Quechua, 4:204; Roma, 3:402; Samoa, 1:390; Swahili, 1:156; Taiwan, 2:263; Tlingit oratory, 4:120, 123–124; Ukraine, 3:442; Zande, 1:230

Simoneau, Karen, 1:56

Simons, Menno, 3:238

Sims, Paddy Japljarri, 1:298

Sinbad the sailor: England, 3:12; Swahili, 1:155

Singer, Milton, 2:14

Singing: Croatia, Littoral, 3:341–343; Croatia, Lowland, 3:346; Croatia, Mountainous, 3:344; Georgia, 3:358–359; Latvia, 3:364, 366–368; Malta, 3:509–510. *See also* Music and dance

Singing contests (Sicily), 3:485–486

Singing Revolution (Latvia), 3:364, 369

Sinhala people. *See* Sri Lanka

Sinxo, Guybon Bundlawa, 1:261

Sioux. *See* Lakota

Siri-Matti, 3:139–140

Siri Paddana myth (Karnataka), 2:52

Siu (Swahili), 1:158

Siwa-Lima moiety system (Maluku), 2:197, 199

Sižgoric, Juraj, 3:349

Skanderbeg (hero), 3:328

1: Topics & Themes, Africa, Australia & Oceania
2: Southeast Asia & India, Central & East Asia, Middle East
3: Europe
4: North & South America

Skiing (Slovenia), **3**:302–303

Skinner, James Scott, **3**:63

Skirts. *See* Clothing

Skomorokhi (minstrels, Russia), **3**:409, 411

Skulls (Mexico), **4**:271–272

Slava: Roma, **3**:403; Serbia, **3**:429–430

Slavery: African Americans, **4**:143–148, 151, 154; and African diaspora, **1**:78; Benin, involvement in, **1**:172; Haiti, involvement in, **4**:316, 323; Ijo, involvement in, **1**:204; Jamaica, involvement in, **4**:338–339, 342; and loss of native culture, **1**:79; Madagascar, involvement in, **1**:138; and Maroons of Jamaica, **4**:339; Mascarene Islands, involvement in, **1**:144, 146; Réunion, involvement in, **1**:147–148; Seminole, involvement in, **4**:111; and Suriname Maroon, **4**:236–237; Swahili, involvement in, **1**:154, 160

Slavic alphabet, **3**:371

"Sleepy Toon" (song), **3**:60

Slovakia, **3**:285–295; agricultural crafts and practices, **3**:287–289; calendars, **3**:289–290; drama, **3**:293; family inheritance structure, **3**:288–289; folktales and poetry, **3**:292; games, arts and crafts, **3**:293–294; geography and history, **3**:285–286; life-cycle customs, **3**:290–291; modernization, challenges of, **3**:286; music and dance, **3**:292–293; religion and beliefs, **3**:286–287

Slovenia, **3**:295–305; arts and crafts, **3**:304; calendars, **3**:296–299; dance, **3**:301–302; farm architecture, **3**:303–304; geography and history, **3**:295–296; modernization, challenges of, **3**:294; songs and music, **3**:300–301; sports and games, **3**:302–303; witchcraft and folk medicine, **3**:299–300

Šmidchens, Guntis, **1**:37

Smiles, Samuel, **1**:46

Smith, Iain Crichton, **3**:66

Smith, S.L.J., **1**:86

Smith-artisans. *See* Blacksmithing

Smithsonian Institution (Washington D.C.), **2**:15

Smuggling (Isle of Man), **3**:42

Snakes: Australian Aborigines, **1**:295–296; Choctaw, **4**:35

Snorri Sturluson, **3**:113

Snowsnake (Iroquois), **4**:57

"Snow White," **1**:55, 95; England, **3**:12; Germany, **3**:266, 267; San, **1**:241

Sobolevskii, A.I., **3**:411

Soccer in Spain, **3**:186

Social evolution. *See* Cultural evolution

Social instruction as theme (Guam), **1**:336–337

Socialism influence (Macedonia), **3**:376

Social problems as theme: Guam, **1**:336–337; Shona, **1**:250–251

Social Statics (Spencer), **1**:12

Social structure: Ainu, **2**:285–286; Armenia, **2**:366–367; Assam, **2**:19; Australia (British), **1**:278–280, 282; Australian Aborigines, **1**:294–295; Bali, **2**:153–156; Bangladesh, **2**:98; Baule, **1**:163–164; Benin, **1**:170; Cherokee, **4**:9–10; China, **2**:212; Gaddi, **2**:34; Guam, **1**:334; Haida, **4**:39–40, 42; Hawai'i, **1**:366–368; Hopi, **4**:46; Iban, **2**:172–173; India, **2**:5–6, 13; Iroquois, **4**:51; Israel, **2**:377, 378; Japan, **2**:272–275; Jie, **1**:133–137; Karnataka, **2**:47–49, 51, 52; Kashmir, **2**:60; Kazakh, **2**:308–309; Kewa, **2**:189, 190–191, 194; Khasi-Jaintia, **2**:67; Kiribati, **1**:340, 341, 347; Kurds, **2**:384–385, 388–389; Lebanon, **2**:393, 398; Madagascar, **1**:139; Malaita, **1**:301–302; Maluku, **2**:197; Manchu, **2**:245–246; Marquesas Islands, **1**:380; Marshall Islands, **1**:350–351, 356; Mongol, **2**:253; Nagaland, **2**:74, 77–78; Nepal, **2**:114–118, 121; New Caledonia, **1**:309–311; Orissa, **2**:81, 84; Palau, **1**:359, 360; Palestine, **2**:403–406; Persia, **2**:415, 423, 424; Peru, **4**:200; Roma, **3**:396; Samoa, **1**:389; San, **1**:240–242; Semai, **2**:149; Seminole, **4**:116; Serbia, **3**:427–429; Shuar, **4**:221–222; Swahili, **1**:156, 159; Tairora, **2**:205; Tonga, **1**:397–399; Trobriand Islands, **1**:316–318; Tuareg, **1**:102–103, 113–114; Tuvalu, **1**:405; Uttar Pradesh, **2**:89; Uzbek, **2**:354; Western Inuit and Yupik, **4**:132–133; Wolof, **1**:212, 213–214; Xavante, **4**:243–246; Yemen, **2**:439–440; Zande, **1**:228

Sociocultural evolution. *See* Cultural evolution

Sofki (Seminole), **4**:114

Soldier martyrs cult, **3**:471

"A Soldier's Lament" (military song, Italy), **3**:461

Solomon (King), **3**:334, 357

Son (Cuban dance), **4**:311–312

Song and dance. *See* Music and dance

The Song of Hiawatha (Longfellow), **4**:105

Song of Roland, **3**:162

"Song of Saada" (Swahili), **1**:156

Sorcerers at weddings (Russia), **3**:414

Sorcery. *See* Witchcraft

Sorghum, importance to Jie, **1**:133–137

Soul of the departed, beliefs (Roma), **3**:402

Soungala (The Seychelles), **1**:149

Source language (SL), **1**:89, 90

South African Journal of Science (Zulu), **1**:272

South African Spectator (newspaper) (Xhosa), **1**:262

South America, **1**:17, **4**:177–255

South Dakota: Lakota, **4**:67–69

Southeastern U.S.: Cherokee, **4**:8

Southern Africa, **1**:234–276

Southern Cheyennes, **4**:21, 22

Southern Folklore Quarterly, **1**:5

Soviet Union: changes to Georgia, **3**:362; folklorism, **1**:35, 82; influence in Ukraine, **3**:447–448; and Latvia, **3**:369

Spain, **3**:177–188; Arab influence in, **3**:183; arts, crafts, and architecture, **3**:186–187; dance, **3**:184–185; drama and theater, **3**:184; geography and history, **3**:177–180; Guam influenced by, **1**:333, 336–337; myths, poems, and folktales, **3**:182–183; Palau influenced by, **1**:360; religion, **3**:180–182; songs and music, **3**:183–184; sports and games, **3**:185–186

Spanish exploration and conquest: and Apache, **4**:1, 3; Cuba, **4**:309; and Ecuadorian folklore, **4**:188–189; Haiti, **4**:316; Jamaica, **4**:337; Mexico, **4**:272, 274, 275–276; Nahua, **4**:284–285; Otomí, **4**:289; Peru, **4**:201; Rarámuri, **4**:297–298; Sibundoy, **4**:229–230

Spatial symbolism and worldview, **1**:99

Spears. *See* Weapons and armor

Specimens of Malagasy Folklore, **1**:140

Speeches. *See* Oratory

Spells. *See* Charms and spells

Spencer, Herbert, **1**:12

Spengler, Oswald, **1**:73

"The Spider from the Gwydir" (Australia [British]), **1**:284

Spider tales: Baule, **1**:164–165; Zande, **1**:230

Spies, Walter, **2**:163

Spirit House (Samoa), **1**:395, 396

Spirit possession: Gaddi, **2**:35; India, **2**:7; Jamaica, **4**:343; Japan, **2**:274; Kadazandusun, **2**:178; Karnataka, **2**:49, 52–53; Korea, **2**:299; Kurds, **2**:386; Maluku, **2**:200–201; Manchu, **2**:251; Samoa, **1**:392–393; Semai, **2**:148; Shona, **1**:251; Sri Lanka, **2**:126; Suriname Maroon, **4**:237–239; Swahili, **1**:157, 158; Taiwan, **2**:268; Tuareg, **1**:108, 114; Uttar Pradesh, **2**:90; Uyghur, **2**:338

Spirits. *See* Supernatural beliefs; *specific type of spirit*

Spirit Sickness (Samoa), **1**:392, 393, 395

Spirituals: African Americans, **4**:145–148; Mississippi Delta, **4**:169; Russia, **3**:421; Yoruba, **1**:222

Spitzer, Nicholas, **1**:11, 77

Sports. *See* Games, sports, and recreation

Spring Cycle plays (Italy), **3**:464

Spring rites and customs (Serbia), **3**:430–431

Sri Lanka, **2**:123–130; arts, crafts, and architecture, **2**:128–130; ethnic groups and religions, **2**:124–126; folk rituals, **2**:126–127; folk theater, **2**:128; geography and history, **2**:123–124; written and oral folktales, **2**:127–128

"Stackerlee" songs and tales, **4**:171–172

Stair, John (missionary to Samoa), **1**:391

Stállu (Sámu), **3**:140

Stands in Timber (Cheyenne), **4**:23, 26

Stanley, John, 3:42

Stareshima (headman), 3:428

"The Star Husband Tale" (Thompson), 1:23

Stars. *See* Astrology

State-worship concept (Roman), 3:159

Stattin, Jochum, 3:153

Stauffacher, Werner, 3:309

Stephen, Saint, 3:50, 349

Stephens, George, 3:114

Sternsingen (Star Singing), 3:254

Stevenson, Robert Louis, 1:395

Steward, Julian, 1:16

Stickball game: Cherokee, 4:16–17; Choctaw, 4:33, 34–35

Stick dance (Swahili), 1:155

Stimulus diffusion, 1:24

Stivens, Dal, 1:286

Stocking, George W., Jr., 1:12

Stomp Dance Ceremony (Cherokee), 4:15

Stone Boy (Lakota story), 4:71

Storey, John, 1:71

Storia antica del Messico (Clavijero), 4:276

La Storia della Baronessa di Carini (narrative folk poem, Sicily), 3:486

Storie (narrative folksongs, Sicily), 3:486

Stories and tales: Abanyole, 1:123–125; African American, 4:143–144, 147–148; Albania, 3:323–325; Anansi, 1:10; Apache, 4:3–4; Appalachia, 4:159–160; Armenia, 2:359–362; Ashkenazim, 3:334; Assam, 2:21–22; Australia (British), 1:286–289; Australian Aborigines, 1:293–294, 296; Austria, 3:256; Bangladesh, 2:99; Basque, 3:190–193; Baule, 1:164–165; Benin, 1:176–177; Bhutan, 2:107–108; Bihar, 2:25–27; Caribs of Dominica, 4:331–333, 335; Cherokee, 4:12–14; Cheyenne, 4:25–26; China, 2:215–218; Chinese living abroad, 2:241–242; Choctaw, 4:35–37; Cuba, 4:313–315; Duna, 2:168–169; Finnish-Swedish, 3:99–100; Flanders (Belgium), 3:229–230; Ga, 1:184–185; Georgia, 3:356–358; Greece, 3:496; Guam, 1:334–338; Haida, 4:40–42; Haiti, 4:320–321; Haryana, 2:40–41; Hungary, 3:279–280; Iban, 2:173–174; Iceland, 3:114–115; Igbo, 1:195–196; Ijo, 1:206–207; India, 2:7–8; Ireland, 3:27–31, 34–37; Iroquois, 4:54–55; Isaan, 2:135; Israel, 2:372–373, 378–381; Jamaica, 4:341–342; Japan, 2:274; Jie, 1:131–133; Kadazandusun, 2:178–179; Kaingang, 4:194–197; Kaliai, 2:184–186; Karnataka, 2:49–51; Kashmir, 2:60–61; Kazakh, 2:308–309; Kewa, 2:190–191; Khasi-Jaintia, 2:67–68, 70–72; Kiribati, 1:344–346; Kurds, 2:387–389; Lakota and Dakota, 4:70–72; Lebanon, 2:392–394; Macedonia, 3:372–373; Madagascar, 1:139–140; Malaita, 1:300–303; Malay, 2:142–143; Maluku, 2:199–200; Manchu, 2:247–248; Marquesas Islands, 1:381–382; Marshall Islands, 1:351–352;

Mauritius and Rodrigues, 1:146–147; Maya, 4:258–261; Mexico, 4:273–277; Mississippi Delta, 4:171–172; and modernization, 1:52–53; Mongol, 2:254–255; Nagaland, 2:74–76; Nahua, 4:283–284; The Netherlands, 3:243–244; New Caledonia, 1:312–313; Nez Perce, 4:98–103; Ojibwe, 4:105–107; Orissa, 2:80–82; Palau, 1:360–361; Palestine, 2:403–406; Persia, 2:422; Peru, 4:202–203; Piedmont and Val d'Aosta, 3:473–474; Poland, 3:380–381; Quechua, 4:210; Rarámuri, 4:301; Réunion, 1:148; Roma, 3:405–406; Russia, 3:417–420; Sámi, 3:140–141; Samoa, 1:388–393 (*See also* Samoa); San, 1:242–247; Scotland, 3:57; Sephardim, 3:215–216; Serbia, 3:432–436; Sertão, 4:218; The Seychelles, 1:149–150; Shona, 1:249–251, 254–255; Shuar, 4:224–225; Sibundoy, 4:230–232; Slovakia, 3:292; Slovenia, 3:300; Spain, 3:182–183; Sri Lanka, 2:127–128; Suriname Maroons, 4:239–240; Swahili, 1:155–157, 160; Tairora, 2:206–208; Tlingit, 4:120–123; Tonga, 1:400–401; Trobriand Islands, 1:319–325; Tuareg, 1:114–115; Turkey, 2:432–433; Tuvalu, 1:406; Ukraine, 3:440–442; Uttar Pradesh, 2:90–91; Uyghur, 2:338–341; Vanuatu, 1:327–328; Wolof, 1:216; Xhosa, 1:258–261; Yanomami, 4:252–254; Yemen, 2:442; Yoruba, 1:218–220, 223–224; Zande, 1:230–231; Zulu, 1:270–272. *See also* Anecdotes; Proverbs

"Story boards" (Palau), 1:363–364

Storyknifing (Western Inuit and Yupik), 4:136

"The Story of Gavu" (Kaliai), 2:183, 184, 188

"The Story of the Nishan Shamaness" (Manchu), 2:249–250

The Storyteller's Sourcebook (MacDonald), 1:56

Storytelling: Abanyole, 1:123–125; Albania, 3:323–325; Apache, 4:4; Australia (British), 1:287; Australian Aborigines, 1:294; Bihar, 2:29–30; China, 2:214–215; Croatia, 3:349, 356; England, 3:11–13; Finnish-Swedish, 3:99–100; France, 3:163–164; Ga, 1:183, 184–185, 192; Galicia, 3:204–205, 207; Germany, 3:262–265; Greece, 3:496; Greenland, 3:107–108; Guam, 1:334; Haiti, 4:320–321, 327; Hungary, 3:280; Ijo, 1:206–207; Ireland, 3:26–27, 37–39; Iroquois, 4:54–55; Italy, 3:460; Jamaica, 4:342; Jie, 1:131; Kaliai, 2:187; Kiowa, 4:66; Kiribati, 1:344; Kurds, 2:388; Lakota and Dakota, 4:68, 73–74; Lunda, 1:237; Malaita, 1:301; Marquesas Islands, 1:380, 382, 383; Marshall Islands, 1:351–352, 356; Palau, 1:363–364; Piedmont and Val d'Aosta, 3:473; repeoire of storyteller, 1:81–83; Russia, 3:417–420; Samoa, 1:386–396; San, 1:240–247; Scotland, 3:57; Shona, 1:249, 250; Siberia, 2:322–323; Sibundoy, 4:230–231; Sicily, 3:486–487; Trobriand

Islands, 1:320; Tuareg, 1:114–115; Turkey, 2:435; Ukraine, 3:440; Wales, 3:75–76; Western Inuit and Yupik, 4:140; Wolof, 1:216; Yoruba, 1:218, 222; Zulu, 1:270–272

Strack, Adolf, 1:5

Štrekelj, Karel, 3:300

String stories (Western Inuit and Yupik), 4:136

Strobach, Hermann, 1:35

Strömbäck, Dag, 3:149

Strömberg, Bernt, 1:82

Strong, Pauline Turner, 1:47

Stuart, James, 1:272

Studer, G.S., 3:313

Studies of Ethnic Literature, 2:231

Sudan, 1:150–151

Sufism: Bangladesh, 2:97; Kashmir, 2:62; Kazakh, 2:308; Kurds, 2:385, 386; Uyghur, 2:337, 339, 342, 343

Sugpiaq. *See* Western Inuit and Yupik

Suharto (President, Indonesia), 2:198

Suh'tai (Cheyenne), 4:22

Suicide: Duna and women accused of witchcraft, 2:167; Kaliai, 2:187; Orissa and taboo attached to, 2:79; Xhosa national suicide, 1:260, 262

Sultan and *jinn* stories (Swahili), 1:158

Summer houses (Cherokee), 4:19

Sun Dance: Cheyenne, 4:24, 27; Kiowa, 4:61

Sunkutu Muonga (Kazembe VIII), 1:239

Sunni Muslims: Kurds, 2:385; Palestine, 2:406; Turkey, 2:430; Yemen, 2:441

Supelka (Macedonia), 3:374

Supernatural beliefs, 1:26; African American, 4:147; Apache, 4:5; Australia (British), 1:286; Australian Aborigines, 1:293–294; Benin, 1:173, 174–176; Caribs of Dominica, 4:332–333; Cheyenne, 4:23; Choctaw, 4:36–37; Denmark, 3:83–85; Ecuador, 4:197; England, 3:6, 10–11; Finnish-Swedish, 3:98–99; Ga, 1:182; Galicia, 3:203–204; Greenland, 3:105–107; Guam, 1:337–338; Haiti, 4:318; Igbo, 1:197–198; Ireland, 3:31–34; Iroquois, 4:54, 58–59; Kiribati, 1:345; Lakota, 4:70–71; Nez Perce, 4:98; Otomí, 4:290–292; Peru, 4:201–202; Russia, 3:418; Samoa, 1:388–396; Scotland, 3:55–57; Sertão, 4:217–218; Suriname Maroons, 4:238–239; Tlingit, 4:118, 122–123; Tonga, 1:399–400; Tuvalu, 1:406; Western Inuit and Yupik, 4:134; Wolof, 1:216. *See also* Fairy lore

Superstitions: Appalachia, 4:177; Australia (British), 1:286; Austria, 3:254; Bangladesh, 2:103–104; England, 3:5–8; Igbo, 1:197–198; Japan, 2:277; Persia, 2:421; Slovakia, 3:291; Spain, 3:181; Tajik, 2:334; Xhosa, 1:266. *See also* Vodou

Suriname Maroon, 4:236–243; arts and crafts, 4:241; and diaspora, 1:20; folktales, 4:240; geography and history, 4:236–237; modernization, challenges of, 4:238, 241–242; music, 4:240–241; religious beliefs

1: Topics & Themes, Africa, Australia & Oceania
2: Southeast Asia & India, Central & East Asia, Middle East
3: Europe
4: North & South America

and rituals, 4:238–240; roots of Maroon culture and folklore, 4:237–238; studies of Maroon folklore, 4:242

Surrallés, Alexandre, 4:185–186

Survivalist narratives (Igbo), 1:195–196

"Survivals," study of, 1:2–3, 50

Suryamati (Kashmir Queen), 2:60

Svensson, Birgitta, 3:152

Svensson, Sigfrid, 3:148, 150

Swahili, 1:154–162; class and competition, 1:159; dance, 1:157–158; elements of Swahili folklore, 1:156–157; geography and history, 1:154–155; myths, legends, and folktales, 1:155; outside influences, 1:158; proverbs, 1:159; race and demographics, 1:158; sources of Swahili folklore, 1:160; studies of Swahili folklore, 1:161; urban and rural, 1:160–161

Swahn, Jan-Öjvind, 1:81, 3:148

Swamp cabbage (Seminole), 4:114

Swan maiden motif, 1:56; Manchu, 2:247; Tairora, 2:208

Sweat lodges (Choctaw), 4:37

Sweden, 3:144–156; cultural anthropology studies, 3:146–148; cultural theory studies, 3:151; early twentieth-century folklore studies, 3:146–148; ethnology studies, 3:146–150; folklore scholarship, 3:152–154; late twentieth-century folklore studies, 3:148–151; Lund University folklife archives, 3:148, 150; multiethnic studies, 3:151–152; music and dance, 3:146; nineteenth-century folklore studies, 3:144–146; peasant culture, 3:144–146; Stockholm, Institute for Folklife Research, 3:146, 148; storytelling, 3:147; Uppsala University studies, 3:149

Sweet Medicine (Cheyenne), 4:23, 25

Switzerland, 3:306–319; calendars, 3:314–317; festivals, 3:311–312; founding myth, 3:308–309; geography, 3:306–307; history and folklore, 3:308–312; language, 3:307–308; religion, 3:308; songs, yodeling, and music, 3:312–314

Sword-Dance Play (England), 3:16

Sword dances: Basque, 3:194; Croatia, 3:343; England, 3:15; Piedmont and Val d'Aosta, 3:476

Swordfish fishing traditions (Sicily), 3:483

Sy, Cheikh Ahmadou, 1:212

Sylvester (high priest), 3:374

Symbolism. See Simile and metaphor; specific types of symbols

Symmetry, concept of (Kaingang), 4:194–197

Synagogues, 3:338

Syncretism, 1:47. See also Hybridity

Syv, Peder, 3:85

Taarab (Swahili), 1:155, 157–159

"The Table, Ass, and the Stick," 1:95

Taboos: Australian Aborigines, 1:297; Bali, 2:158; Bangladesh, 2:103–104; Chinese living abroad, 2:239; Greenland, 3:107–108; Hawai'i, 1:374; Kadazandusun, 2:178–179; Khasi-Jaintia, 2:70; Kiribati, 1:343; Madagascar, 1:139; Malaita, 1:302, 303; Nagaland, 2:79; Nez Perce, 4:98; Roma, 3:396; Samoa, 1:393–394; Siberia, 2:318; Tlingit, 4:118; Tonga, 1:399

Tacitus, 3:261

Tagore, Rabindranath, 2:95

Táin Bó Cualige (The Cattle Raid of Cooley), 3:28

Taíno: Haiti, 4:316; Jamaica, 4:337

Tairora, 2:203–210; arts and crafts, 2:208; geography and history, 2:203–205; modernization, challenges of, 2:208–209; myths and folktales, 2:206–208; religious beliefs and rituals, 2:206; studies of Tairora folklore, 2:209–210

Taiwan, 2:260–270; arts and crafts, 2:264–265; festivals, 2:266–269; food, 2:266; geography and history, 2:260–261; medicine and folk arts, 2:265–266; opera, 2:263–264; puppet performances, 2:264; religious beliefs and rituals, 2:261–263; songs, 2:263; studies of Taiwanese folklore, 2:269

Tajik, 2:325–335; arts and crafts, 2:330–331; clothing styles, 2:331–332; drama, 2:329–330; drama and theater, 2:329–330; festivals and celebrations, 2:332–334; folksongs and dance, 2:329; geography and history, 2:325–326; medicine and rituals, 2:327–328; modernization, challenges of, 2:334; music, 2:328–329; proverbs and riddles, 2:326–327; sports and games, 2:330

Taj Mahal, 2:11

The Tale of Genji (Japan), 2:274, 275

The Tale of the Heike (Japan), 2:275

Tales. See Epic stories, tales, poetry; Stories and tales

Tales of Gods and Spirits (China), 2:218

Tales of the Bewitched Corpse (Mongol), 2:255

Talismen: Madagascar, destruction of, 1:138; Siberia, 2:318; Ukraine, 3:446

"Talking Turtle" (African American story), 4:147–148

Tall tales (Ireland), 3:37–38

Tamajaq language (Tuareg), 1:112

Tamar (Queen), 3:357

Tamazgha (Berber), 1:101

Tambor (Cuba), 4:310

Tamil people. See Sri Lanka

Tanac dances (Croatia), 3:343, 345

Tanahill, Reay, 1:11

Tangherlini, Timothy R., 1:82

Tangun mythology (Korea), 2:295–296, 304

Tannahill, Robert, 3:59

Tantrism, 2:80

Taoism. See Daoism

Taotaomo'na (Guam), 1:337–339

Tarahumara. See Rarámuri

Tarankanje singing style (Croatia), 3:341

Tarantella (dance, southern Italy), 3:463

Tarantism (Italy), 3:463

"Tar Baby" (African American), 4:148

"The Tar Baby and the Rabbit," 1:94; Mascarene Islands, 1:144, 146; Réunion, 1:148; The Seychelles, 1:149

Target language (TL), 1:89, 90

Tartit, 1:112, 120

Tatars, 3:422, 423

Tattoos and body markings: Australian Aborigines, 1:297; Bangladesh, 2:101; Benin, 1:173; Berber, 1:104–105; Bihar, 2:28; Igbo, 1:201; Ijo, 1:207; Kiribati, 1:347; Lumba, 1:240; Malaita, 1:300, 303, 306; Maluku, 2:202; Marquesas Islands, 1:380–381; Marshall Islands, 1:354; Nagaland, 2:77–78; Siberia, 2:317; Tairora, 2:202, 203; Trobriand Islands, 1:324; Wolof, 1:215; Yoruba, 1:226

Taufa'ahau (King George Tupou, Tongan chief), 1:399

Tautasdziesma (Latvia), 3:368

Tayanin, D., 1:81

Taylor, Archer, 1:27, 3:148

Teaching spirits (Nez Perce), 4:98

Tea drinking: Appalachia, 4:164; Candoshi, 4:185; China, 2:221, 227; Finnish-Swedish, 3:101; Gaddi, 2:36; Korea, 2:296; Taiwan, 2:262; Wales, 3:77

Teatro de virtudes políticas (Sigüenza y Góngora), 4:276

Tebutalin (Manchu), 2:247

Technicians of the Sacred (Rothenberg), 1:31

Tedlock, Dennis, 1:31, 32, 85

Television: Baule, 1:168; Marquesas Islands, 1:384; Swahi, 1:161; Wolof, 1:216

Tell, William, 3:308–309

Tendlau, Abraham, 3:335

Tenzone dei Mesi (folk drama, Sicily), 3:488

Teresa de Ávila, 3:181

Terms of address (Shona), 1:250

Ternhag, Gunnar, 3:153

Terton Pema Lingpa, 2:110

Teuta (Queen), 3:322

Teutonic Mythology, 3:269

Text, 1:11, 83–85; and diffusion, 1:23; and ethnography, 1:27, 84; and ethnopoetics, 1:31; and translation, 1:83, 91

Textile arts: African Americans, 4:154; Australia (British), 1:283; Baule, 1:167–168; Benin, 1:176; Berber, 1:110; Cherokee, 4:18; Croatia, 3:345; Ecuador, 4:192; Guam, 1:339; Hawai'i, 1:374; Hopi, 4:49; Igbo, 1:201; Italy, 3:457; Kiribati, 1:346–347; Marquesas Islands, 1:378; Marshall Islands, 1:354; Navajo, 4:90; Quechua, 4:214; Samoa, 1:387; Shona, 1:253; Suriname Maroons, 4:241; Tlingit, 4:126; Tonga, 1:402; Tuareg, 1:119; Tuvalu, 1:409;

Ukraine, 3:445; Uzbek, 2:353; Wolof, 1:213; Yoruba, 1:226; Zande, 1:233

Thanksgiving, as example of invented tradition, 1:50

Thatcher, Charles, 1:284

Thatcher, Elaine, 1:28

Theater. *See* Drama and Theater

Themselves (Isle of Man), 3:44–46

Theodore, Saint, 3:403

Theorizing the Hybrid (Kapchan & Strong), 1:47

Thérèse, Allah, 1:168

Theunnissen, S.B., 1:274

Things Fall Apart (Achebe), 1:195

Third Sister Liu (China), 2:220

Thomas, Nicholas, 1:49

Thompson, Laura, 1:338

Thompson, Stith, 1:23, 27, 55, 56, 94, 286

Thoms, William J., 1:1, 13, 52

Thor, cult of, 3:83

"The Three Billy Goats Gruff" (Norway), 3:128

Three Kingdoms (China), 2:224

"The Three Oranges," 1:55

Three-part singing (Georgia), 3:359

Three Teachings (China), 2:213

Tifinagh (Tuareg), 1:103, 114

Tigran and Azhdahak (Armenia), 2:361–362

Tillhagen, Carl-Herman, 3:149

Time, concept of: Maya, 4:257. *See also* Calendars

Timur: Uzbek, 2:348–349

Tinariwen, 1:112

Tír na nÓg (Land of the Young), 3:34

"The Titanic" (African American), 4:149

Tito, Josip Broz, 3:427

Tiwi (Australian Aborigines), 1:98, 296–297

Tiyo Soga, 1:258–261, 266

Tjibaou, Jean-Marie, 1:314

Tjukurrpa (Dreamtime) (Australian Aborigines), 1:292–299

Tlingit, 4:117–128; arts and crafts, 4:125–126; dance, 4:124–125; geography and history, 4:117–118; history, 4:120–121, 123; modernization, challenges of, 4:126–127; music and songs, 4:124; myths, legends, and folktales, 4:120–123; oratory, 4:123–124; potlatch, 4:119–120; potlatches, 4:125; religious beliefs, 4:118–119

"Toad King" myth (Isaan), 2:132

Toasts (African American), 4:148–150

Tobacco: Cuba, 4:309; Iroquois, 4:58; Seminole, 4:113; Sertão, 4:217

Tobler, Ludwig, 3:313

Tolkien, J.R.R., 3:93, 118

"Tom Thumb": England, 3:12; San, 1:241

Tonga, 1:387, 388, 397–404; arts and crafts, 1:402–403; geography and history, 1:397; music, song, and dance, 1:401–402; oral tradition: stories and poetry, 1:400–401; religious beliefs, 1:399–400; social structure and worldview, 1:397–399; studies of Tongan folklore, 1:403

Tonga Traditions Committee, 1:403

Tongue-twisters (Igbo), 1:195

Tonkonga (Kiowa), 4:63–64

Tonyuquq, 2:336

Tools: Australia (British), 1:283; Benin, 1:173; Bhutan, 2:111; Denmark, 3:81; Duna, 2:168; Greenland, 3:104–105; Hungary, 3:283; Iroquois, 4:52; Isaan, 2:134, 136; Seminole, 4:114; Sicily, 3:482; Tuareg, 1:119; Western Inuit and Yupik, 4:130

Top, S., 3:229

Topan, Farouk, 1:157

Toplica, Milan, 3:435

Torgovnick, Marianna, 1:78

Torito de Pukara (Peru), 4:207

"Tortoise and No Argument Town" (Yoruba), 1:219–220

"Tortoise as Watchman for the King's Well" (Réunion), 1:148

Totem and Taboo (Freud), 1:74–75

Totems: Australian Aborigines, 1:294; Haida, 4:39, 43; Kiribati, 1:347; Malaita, 1:302; New Caledonia, 1:311; Shona, 1:250; Tlingits, 4:117, 126; Trobriand Islands, 1:317

Tourism, 1:85–89; Apache, 4:7; Baule, 1:168; Dominica, 4:330; and folklorism, 1:36; Greece, 3:501; Malta, 3:510, 511; Mauritius and Rodrigues, 1:147; Mayan clothing, impact on, 4:263; Rarámuri, 4:303–304; The Seychelles, 1:149; Switzerland, 3:311, 312; Vanuatu, 1:325, 330; Wolof, 1:209

"Tourist art": Benin, 1:179; Marquesas Islands, 1:379, 384; Marshall Islands, 1:354; Shona, 1:253; Tuareg, 1:119; Vanuatu, 1:330

"The Tower of Babel" (Nagaland), 2:76

Town rivalries (Flanders), 3:230–231

Toynbee, Arnold, 1:73

Toys: Appalachia, 4:164; Lakota, 4:75. *See also* Dolls

Trade: Benin, 1:172; Cherokee, 4:10, 17; and colonialism, 1:9; Ijo, 1:204; Navajo, 4:90, 92; Ojibwe, 4:104–105; Shuar, 4:227–228; Western Inuit and Yupik, 4:130–131; Zande, 1:228

Trading posts (Navajo), 4:83

Trading songs (Navajo), 4:87–88

Traditional Music and Song Association, 3:63

Tradition and Change (Singer), 2:14

Trail of Tears: Cherokee, 4:10, 11, 14, 16; Seminole, 4:112

Trains as theme (Australia), 1:288

Trances: Bali, 2:156, 161–163; Baule, 1:166; Gaddi, 2:35; Hungary, 3:278; Kadazandusun, 2:178; Karnataka, 2:49; Macedonia, 3:375; Maluku, 2:200; Samoa, 1:392; San, 1:242, 246; Semai, 2:148

Transformation (Lakota), 4:71

Transhumant culture (Wales), 3:70

Translation, 1:89–91; and text, 1:83, 91

Transvestites, transsexuals, cross-dressing: Bangladesh, 2:98, 99; Kashmir, 2:63;

Madagascar, 1:141; Orissa, 2:83; Samoa, 1:396; Uttar Pradesh, 2:91–92; Wolof, 1:215; Yoruba, 1:226

Traveler singing tradition (Scotland), 3:55, 58–59

Trdat and Grigor (Armenia), 2:362–363

Treasure buried in Jamaica, 4:337

A Treasury of American Folklore (Botkin), 1:36

Treaties: Cateau Cambrésis, 3:469; Lakota and Dakota, 4:69

Tree cult: Brittany, 3:172–173; Piedmont and Val d'Aosta, 3:475–476

Treilands-Brivzemnieks, Fricis, 3:366

Trevor-Roper, Hugh, 1:50

Trickster, 1:92–94; Abanyole, 1:123–124; African Americans, 4:147, 148; Apache, 4:4; Baule, 1:164–165; Benin, 1:177; China, 2:217; and creolization, 1:10; Duna, 2:168; England, 3:6, 7; Haida, 4:40–42; Hawai'i, 1:369; and heros, 1:45–46; Iban, 2:174; Igbo, 1:196; Ijo, 1:206; Jamaica, 4:341; Kewa, 2:196; Kiowa, 1:92–93; Lakota, 4:71, 72; Lunda, 1:237–238; Malay, 2:142; Marshall Islands, 1:352; Mascarene Islands, 1:144, 146; Maya, 4:282; Nagaland, 2:76; Nahua, 4:287; Nez Perce, 4:100, 102–103; Ojibwe, 4:105–106; Persia, 2:422; Rarámuri, 4:301; Réunion, 1:148; San, 1:241–246; Séndé, 1:92; The Seychelles, 1:149–150; Shona, 1:250; Swahili, 1:155; Tlingit, 4:122; Tonga, 1:400; Tuareg, 1:115; Uyghur, 2:340; Western Inuit and Yupik, 4:134, 135; Yoruba, 1:219–220; Zande, 1:230–231, 233; Zulu, 1:272

Trilochan Mahadev (Gaddi ancestor), 2:34

Trinity Week (Russia), 3:416

Trobriand Islands, 1:315–325; folktales and narratives, 1:319–320; geography and history, 1:316; kula, 1:321–324; kula art, 1:324–325; social structure, 1:316–318; songs, chants, and incantations, 1:96, 320; worldview, 1:96

Trubar, Primoz, 3:299

Truck driving as theme (Australia (British)), 1:288

Tsangpa Gyare, 2:105

Tsantsa feasts (Shuar), 4:223–224

Tsepenkov, Marko, 3:373

Tsistsistas (Cheyenne), 4:22

Tuareg, 1:112–122; arts and crafts, 1:109–111, 119–120; beliefs, folklore, stories, and poems, 1:103–107, 114–115; geography, 1:101–103, 112–113; history and social structure, 1:101–103, 113–114; modernization, challenges of, 1:111–112, 120; music, 1:107–108, 116–118; plays and theater, 1:118; sports and recreation, 1:118; studies of Tuareg culture and society, 1:120–121

Tuatha Dé Danann (Ireland), 3:31

Tudor, Owen, 3:72

Tuiteleleapaga (Samoan chief), 1:395

Tullio-Altan, Carlo, 3:453

1: Topics & Themes, Africa, Australia & Oceania
2: Southeast Asia & India, Central & East Asia, Middle East
3: Europe
4: North & South America

Tumba francesa (Cuba), 4:311
Tuna fishing traditions (Sicily), 3:484
Tupi-Guarani culture and Caipira, 4:177–178
Tupilaks (amulets), 3:110
Tupinikim and Caipira, 4:177
Turkey, 2:429–439; arts and crafts, 1:26, 2:436–437; dance, 2:434–435; geography and history, 2:429–432; music, 2:433–434; sports, games, and puppet theater, 2:435–436; studies of Turkish folklore, 2:437; verbal arts, 2:432–433
Turkish influence or occupation: Croatia, 3:350; Greece, 3:494–495; Macedonia, 3:373; Malta, 3:511
Turner, Frederick Jackson, 1:38, 39
Turner, George, 1:393
Turner, Louis, 1:87
Turner, Othar, 4:172–173
Turner, Patricia, 4:151
Turriff, Jane, 3:58
Tursunzoda, M., 2:326
Tuvalu, 1:404–411; arts and crafts, 1:409–410; games and sports, 1:409; geography and history, 1:404–405; magic and ritual, 1:406–407; music and dance, 1:407–408; oratory, myths, and legends, 1:406; religion, 1:405–406; studies of Tuvaluan folklore, 1:410
Tu Wei-ming, 2:234
"The Two Brothers," 1:55
Two-part singing (Croatia), 3:341–346
Tyabashe, Mdukiswa, 1:267
Tylor, Edward Burnett, 1:2, 12, 71
Type, 1:11, 94–96; and cultural area, 1:18; and diffusion, 1:23; and motif, 1:54, 94, 95; and translation, 1:91
Type and Motif Index of the Folktales of England and North America (Baughman), 1:94
The Types of Folktale (Aarne), 1:23, 94

uBaxoxele (Zulu), 1:272
Udechukwu, Ada, 1:201
Udechukwu, Obiora, 1:201
Udo dress, 1:7–8
Uhland, Ludwig, 3:312, 314
uHlangakula (Zulu), 1:272
Újváry, Zoltán, 3:283
Ukraine, 3:437–449; architecture, 3:446–447; arts and crafts, 3:444–445; calendars, 3:445–446; epics and minstrals, 3:440–442; geography and history, 3:437–439; legends, 3:440; life-cycle celebrations, 3:442–444; witchcraft and folk medicine, 3:439–440
uKulumetule (Zulu), 1:272
Ulster Cycle, 3:28–30

Ulster Folklife (folklore journal), 3:40
umkaSethemba, Lydia, 1:270, 271
Unamuno, Miguel de, 3:179
Unani system (Uttar Pradesh), 2:90
Uncle Remus (African-American), 4:143
UNESCO: Committee of Government Experts on the Safeguarding of Folklore, 1:291; Memory of the World Register, 3:363; recommending founding of open-air museums, 1:58; Register of Intangible World Culture Treasures, 3:364
Union song (Italy), 3:461
Unison singing (Croatia), 3:346
United Keetoowah Band, 4:8
United States: Australia (British) influenced by, 1:290; and globalization, 1:43; Guam influenced by, 1:334; Hawaiʻi influenced by, 1:374–375; Marshall Islands influenced by, 1:350, 356; Palau influenced by, 1:360
Unity of opposites as theme (Yoruba), 1:224
"Universal Declaration of Human Rights" (1948), 1:15
University of Dar es Salaam, 1:161
Unspunnen Festival (Switzerland), 3:311–313
"Untombi-yaphansi" (Zulu), 1:271–272
Urban II (Pope), 3:162
Urban legends (African American), 4:151
Urban life: Armenia, 2:369; Australia (British), 1:287, 290; Australian Aborigines, 1:293; China, 2:119; Denmark, 3:82; Haryana, 2:45; Kiribati, 1:348; Korea, 2:296; Marshall Islands, 1:349, 356; Nepal, 2:119; New Caledonia, 1:313; Piedmont and Val d'Aosta, 3:478; Shona, 1:254–255; Swahili, 1:154, 157, 160–161; Sweden, 3:145; Switzerland, 3:309; Uttar Pradesh, 2:89; Vanuatu, 1:325–326, 329, 331; Wolof, 1:216; Xhosa, 1:261; Yoruba, 1:220, 221
Urry, John, 1:86, 87
Ursula, Saint, 3:506
Ursus, Saint, 3:471, 478
U.S. Food and Drug Administration, 2:440
Uttar Pradesh, 2:88–94; arts and crafts, 2:94; cultural tradition, 2:4; folk beliefs and medical practices, 2:90; folk theater, 2:92–93; geography and history, 2:88–90; modernization, challenges of, 2:94; songs and music, 2:91–92; sports and recreation, 2:93; stories and epics, 2:90–91
uTulasizwe (Zulu), 1:272
uVusezakiti (Zulu), 1:272
Uyghur, 2:335–348; arts, crafts, and architecture, 2:344; dance, 2:343–344; folktales and folksongs, 2:339–341; food, 2:345; geography and history, 2:335–337; modernization, challenges of, 2:345–346; music, 2:341–343; myths and legends, 2:338–339; religious beliefs, 2:337–338; shamanism, 2:338
Uzbek, 2:348–355; arts and crafts, 2:353–354; epics, 2:350; geography and history, 2:348–350; music, 2:352–353; performance

arts, 2:353; songs, 2:351–352; studies of Uzbek folklore, 2:354

Vaishnavite sects: Karnataka, 2:48; Orissa, 2:80
Valdemar the Victorious, 3:81
Valkeapää, Nils-Aslak, 3:142
Valle-Inclán, Ramón del, 3:184
Vallejo, Antonio Buero, 3:184
Valor, Enric, 3:195
Van Gennep, Arnold, 2:296
Vanuatu, 1:325–332; architecture, 1:330–331; games, sports, arts, and crafts, 1:330; geography and history, 1:325–326; language and religion, 1:326–327; modernization, challenges of, 1:331; music and plays, 1:329–330; oral tradition: stories and myths, 1:327–328; song and dance, 1:328–329; studies of Vanuatu folklore, 1:331
Vargyas, Lajos, 3:279
Vasa, Gustav (King), 3:90
Vave (Swahili), 1:155, 156
Velázquez, Diego, 3:186
Ven, Dirk Jan van der, 3:237
Venezuela: Yanomami, 4:251–252
Verbal folklore. *See* Oral tradition
Verdaguer, Jacint, 3:195
Verga, Giovanni, 3:453
Verkovich, Stefan, 3:372, 373
Verse. *See* Children's songs, stories, and verses; Poetry
Vetalapanchavingshati (Bangladesh), 2:99
Vèvè (Haiti), 4:324
Vico, Giambattista, 1:73
Victoria (Queen), 3:65
Victorian Anthropology (Stocking), 1:12
Victorian period (England), 3:3
Vidyapiti (Indian poet), 2:30
Viennese Expo (1873), 1:57
Vierbergerwallfahrt (Austria), 3:251
Viking period (Denmark), 3:81
Vila (fairy, Serbia), 3:432–433
Vilakazi, Benedict Wallet, 1:261, 271, 272–273
Vinokurova, Natal'ia, 3:419
Violant, Ramon, 3:196
Violins: Apache, 4:6; Croatia, 3:346; Mongol, 2:258; Norway, 3:130, 131; Sicily, 3:486; Slovenia, 3:301
Virgil, 1:44
Virginity: Berber, 1:105, 110; Kiribati, 1:348; Roma, 3:401; Russia, 3:415; Samoa, 1:390, 393, 396; Shona, 1:252; Ukraine, 3:442
Virgin of Guadalupe, 4:273–275
Visionary poets, 1:31–32
Vision quests: Cheyenne, 4:22, 26; Iroquois, 4:55; Nez Perce, 4:98; Shuar, 4:222–223, 226
Vision talks (Lakota and Dakota), 4:73
Višnjic, Filip, 3:434
Vitoliņš, Jekabs, 3:368
Vitus, Saint, 3:268
Vizenor, Gerald, 1:93

Vlach, John Michael, 1:10, 20
Vladimir (Prince), 3:411, 422
Vlas, Saint, 3:417
Vodou in Haiti, 4:317–319, 321, 323, 324, 327
Vodoun, 1:47
Volkhvi (priest-magicians, Russia), 3:411, 412
Volkskultur in der technischen Welt (Bausinger), 1:52
Volkskundliche Zeitschriftenschau, 1:5
Volodymyr of Kyiv (Prince), 3:438–439
von Sydow, Carl Wilhelm, 1:23, 67, 3:147, 148, 154
Voskuil, J.J., 3:237
Voudouri, Lilian, 3:501
Vraz, Stanco, 3:373
Vrbitsa (Day of Willows, Serbia), 3:431
Vries, Jan de, 3:237

Waan Ailin Kein (Canoes of These Islands), 1:355
Wackernagel, Hans Georg, 3:309
Wagner, Richard, 3:271
Wagner, Sigmund von, 3:313
Waikhuu chant (Isaan), 2:136–137
Wailing: Russia, 3:411, 414; Xavante, 4:248–249. *See also* Funerals and burials
Wakwatshange, Ngqeto, 1:270
Waldron, George, 3:43, 46
Wales, 3:69–79; Celtic influence, 3:72; *eisteddfod*, 3:75; English influence, 3:71–72, 76–78; geography and history, 3:69–72; poetry, 3:75; religion and beliefs, 3:72–75; songs, 3:76; storytelling, 3:75–76
Walking sticks (Mississippi Delta), 4:173
Wallace, William, 1:50
"Waltzing Matilda" (Australia [British]), 1:285
Wandjina (Australian Aborigines), 1:298–299
Wangchuck, Jigme Dorji, 2:106
Wangchuck, Jigme Singye, 2:106
Wan language (Baule), 1:165
Wannan, Bill, 1:281, 287
Ward, Russel, 1:281
Warren, William, 4:107
Wars and conflicts: Australia (British), 1:289; Benin, 1:172; Candoshi, 4:181–182; Cheyenne, 4:23, 26; Comanches, 4:61–62; Hawai'i, 1:366, 374–375; Hopi, 4:45; Kiowa, 4:61–64; Kiribati, 1:341; Lakota, 4:69, 73; Marquesas Islands, 1:377, 380; Marshall Islands, 1:350; Mexico, 4:278–279; Ojibwe, 4:107–108; Otomí, 4:288–289; Palau, 1:360; Rarámuri, 4:297; Seminole, 4:111–112; Shuar, 4:223; Vanuatu colonization by, 1:325; Western Inuit and Yupik, 4:132–133; Wolof, 1:209; Xhosa, 1:257, 262; Yanomami, 4:251; Zande, 1:231; Zulu, 1:269
War songs and dances: Baule, 1:166; Hawai'i, 1:366; Igbo, 1:196; Ijo, 1:207; Kiowa, 4:65; Kiribati, 1:344–345; Lunda, 1:239; Malaita, 1:303; Marshall Islands, 1:352; New Caledonia, 1:313; Palau, 1:360

Washington (state) Nez Perce, 4:97
Water drumming: Malaita, 1:304; Zande, 1:232
Waters, Edgar, 1:285, 286
Water shrines: Brittany, 3:170; France, 3:159, 160
Water spirits: Ijo, 1:204, 207; Wolof, 1:209, 210
Waulking songs (Gaelic Scotland), 3:59, 61–62
Wealth: Bangladesh, 2:100; Benin, 1:170, 172, 176, 177; Berber, 1:106; Chinese living abroad, 2:239; England, 3:20; Finnish-Swedish, 3:99; Haryana, 2:43; Ijo, 1:205, 206; Ireland, 3:28; Jie, 1:135; Kazakh, 2:312; Khasi-Jaintia, 2:66; Nahua, 4:285, 286; Navajo, 4:83, 91; Nepal, 2:121; Netherlands, 3:238, 244; New Caledonia, 1:310–311; Orissa, 2:86; Quechua, 4:208–216; Spain, 3:179, 180; Tonga, 1:402; Trobriand Islands, 1:317, 318, 321, 322; Uttar Pradesh, 2:89, 92; Uyghur, 2:344; Wales, 3:71; Wolof, 1:209
Weapons and armor: Cherokee, 4:18; China, 2:227; Haiti, 4:324; Hawai'i, 1:374; Ijo, 1:205; Karnataka, 2:55–56; Kiribati, 1:347; Lunda, 1:239; Maluku, 2:200–201; Seminole, 4:114; Switzerland, 3:315; Tairora, 2:205, 208; Tuareg, 1:113; Western Inuit and Yupik, 4:130
Weaving. *See* Textile arts
Weddings: Abanyole, 1:127–128; Albania, 3:325–326; Armenia, 2:367; Ashkenazim, 3:333; Bali, 2:156–157; Berber, 1:105, 108; China, 2:228; Chinese living abroad, 2:236–237; The Comoros, 1:143; Croatia, 3:348–349; Greece, 3:499; Haryana, 2:43–44; Israel, 2:378–379; Kadazandusun, 2:180; Kazakh, 2:311, 314; Kiribati, 1:345; Kurds, 2:386; Lebanon, 2:396–398; Malaita, 1:304; Malta, 1:505–507; Marshall Islands, 1:355; Palestine, 2:403; Poland, 3:383–384; Roma, 3:398–401; Russia, 3:413–415; Shona, 1:252; Tairora, 2:206; Taiwan, 2:262; Tajik, 2:328, 329, 332; Tuareg, 1:105, 120; Ukraine, 3:442–443; Uzbek, 2:351; Vanuatu, 1:329
Weepers (Malta), 3:505
Weeping Woman legend (Mexico), 4:271
Weiers, Michael, 2:247
Weinreich, Beatrice Silverman, 3:339
Weinreich, Uriel, 3:339
Weiss, Richard, 3:309
Welcoming ceremonies: Candoshi, 4:184–185; China, 2:218
Welters, Henri, 3:243
Western and Central Africa, 1:163–233
Western Inuit and Yupik, 4:128–142; arts and crafts, 4:138–139; dance, songs, and music, 4:136–138; festivals and games, 4:138, 139–140; geography and history, 4:128–132; religious beliefs and rituals, 4:134–135; social structure, 4:132–133; studies of Yupik and Inuit folklore, 4:140–141

Whaling and Western Inuit and Yupik, 4:131
Wheel Game (Cheyenne), 4:28
White, Richard, 1:39
White Boys (Isle of Man), 3:50
White Buffalo Calf Woman (Lakota story), 4:70
Whiteman tales: Apache, 4:4; Western Inuit and Yupik, 4:135–136
White Painted Woman (Apache), 4:5
Whiting, Robert, 2:277–278
Wicca, 1:50
Wilbert, Johannes, 1:56
"The Wild Dog" (Nagaland), 2:76
Wild Hunt (England), 3:8
"Wild Huntsman" (Germany), 3:269
Wild man imagery: Austria, 3:255; Italy, 3:472
Wilhelmina (The Netherlands), 3:242
Willem II (Netherlands), 3:242
William of Newburgh, 3:10
William of Orange, 3:54
Williams, John (missionary to Samoa), 1:391
Williamson, John, 1:288
Williamson, Roy, 3:57
"Willy Reilly" (Australia), 1:285
Wilson, William A., 1:78
Windmills (Sicily), 3:484
Wine feasts (Greece), 3:499
Winifried (Germany), 3:261
Winter activities: Haida, 4:39; Iroquois, 4:58; Lakota, 4:68; Russia, 3:413; Slovenia, 3:302–303
Winter houses (Cherokee), 4:18–19
Wintu Indians (northern California), 1:97
Wisdom question (Greece), 3:496
Witchcraft: Bali, 2:155–157, 160–161; Baule, 1:164; Benin, 1:171, 174; Caribs of Dominica, 4:334–335; Choctaw, 4:36–37; Denmark, 3:83–84; Duna, 2:166, 167; England, 3:8–10; Flanders (Belgium), 3:230; Ga, 1:184; Hungary, 3:278; and invented tradition, 1:50; Italy, 3:457–458; Kewa, 2:189; Malaita, 1:306; Norway, 3:126; Palestine, 2:408; Piedmont and Val d'Aosta, 3:473; Russia, 3:412–413; Sámi, 3:135–136; Slovenia, 3:299–300; Tairora, 2:205, 209; Tlingits, 4:118–119; Trobriand Islands, 1:315, 324; Tuvalu, 1:406–407; Ukraine, 3:439–440, 444; Wolof, 1:211; Zande, 1:228–230
Witchcraft Act (England), 3:8
The Witch-Cult in Western Europe (Murray), 1:50
Witches' Sabbath (Italy), 3:457
Witch trials: Denmark, 3:83; England, 3:8–9; Norway, 3:125; Sámi, 3:135–136
Wolof, 1:208–217; caste system, 1:213–214; change and tradition, 1:216; economy and society, 1:209; folktales, 1:216; geography and history, 1:208–209; oral traditions: poems, epthets, and epics, 1:214–215; religious history, beliefs, and performances, 1:210–213; songs, games, and performances, 1:215

1: Topics & Themes, Africa, Australia & Oceania
2: Southeast Asia & India, Central & East Asia, Middle East
3: Europe
4: North & South America

"Women's Beliefs and the Mirror of Fools" (Aqa Jamal), 2:425

Women's movement, 1:40

Women's roles: Abanyole, 1:127; Australia (British), 1:279, 283; Australian Aborigines, 1:295–297; Baule, 1:166; Benin, 1:170, 174; Berber, 1:105, 106, 109, 110–111; Guam, 1:335; Hawai'i, 1:368; Igbo, 1:195; Jie, 1:134; Kiribati, 1:347; Lunda, 1:234; Malaita, 1:301, 303, 304; Malta, 3:507; Marquesas Islands, 1:379, 382; Marshall Islands, 1:350, 355; Samoa, 1:387, 392, 394–396; San, 1:240, 243–244, 246; Swahili, 1:157, 158; Tonga, 1:398; Trobriand Islands, 1:316, 322, 324; Tuareg, 1:103, 108, 109, 114, 116–120; Wolof, 1:210, 212, 214, 215; Xhosa, 1:257; Yoruba, 1:225, 226; Zande, 1:232. See also Fertility; Gender

Wonder tales. See Fairy lore

Wood carving. See Carving and sculpture

Woodworking: Appalachia, 4:163–164; Caipira, 4:180; Choctaw, 4:34; Ecuador, 4:192; Haiti, 4:325; Iroquois, 4:52, 55; Suriname Maroons, 4:241

Woofing (African American), 4:150

Wordplay: Lunda, 1:238; Maya, 4:261; Nuer, 1:152–153. See also Punning; Simile and metaphor

Words, Earth, and Aloha (Hawai'i), 1:376

Working Committee of the Sourth African Folk-lore Society, 1:272

Worksongs: Abanyole, 1:125; African Americans, 4:151–152; Armenia, 2:366; Bangladesh, 2:98; China, 2:214; Georgia, 3:359; Igbo, 1:196; Japan, 2:281; Kurds, 2:389; Macedonia, 3:374; Mississippi Delta, 4:168–169; Navajo, 4:88; Palau, 1:362; Palestine, 2:409; Scotland, 3:59; Siberia, 2:316; Swahili, 1:155; Uzbek, 2:351, 352; Wolof, 1:210; Zande, 1:232

World Eskimo Indian Olympics, 4:138

Worldview, 1:51, 53, 62, 96–100; Ainu (Japan), 2:287; Chinese living abroad, 2:240; Croatia, 3:348; and diffusion, 1:24; Ecuador, 4:198; Finland, 3:96; Greenland, 3:107; Hungary, 3:279; Iban, 2:174; Iceland, 3:112; and invented tradition, 1:51; Ireland, 3:31; Isaan, 2:131, 133; Kadazandusun, 2:178; Kaingang, 4:195–196; Kewa, 2:190; Kiowa, 4:62; Macedonia, 3:371; Malaita, 1:302; and modernization, 1:53; and nationalism, 1:62; Navajo, 4:85; Norway, 3:125; Poland, 3:380; Rarámuri, 4:300–301; and repertoire, 1:82; Roma, 3:396; Sámi (Lapps), 3:136; San, 1:242, 246; Trobriand

Islands, 1:96; Wales, 3:72; Western Inuit and Yupik, 4:134. See also Religion and beliefs

World War II and Western Inuit and Yupik, 4:132

Wrestling: Benin, 1:178; Cherokee, 4:16; Cheyenne, 4:28; China, 2:225, 230; Ga, 1:189; Georgia, 3:360; Greenland, 3:110; Hawai'i, 1:373; Iceland, 3:119; Ijo, 1:207–208; Kiribati, 1:346; Marshall Islands, 1:354; Mongol, 2:259; Sámi (Lapps), 3:140; Seminole, 4:113; Slovakia, 3:293; Switzerland, 3:309, 312; Tajik, 2:330, 333; Tonga, 1:397; Turkey, 2:435–436; Uttar Pradesh, 2:93; Western Inuit and Yupik, 4:138; Wolof, 1:215; Xavante, 4:245

The Written Suburb (Dorst), 1:30

Wubuxiben Mama (Manchu), 2:247, 250, 251

Wu Song outlaw stories (China), 2:222

Xavante, 4:243–251; ceremonial wailing, 4:248–249; geography and history, 4:243; hymns, 4:249; men's councils, 4:249; modernization, challenges of, 4:250; oratory, 4:249–250; social structure and rituals, 4:243–246; songs and dance, 4:245, 246–248

Xenophobia, 1:64

Xhosa, 1:257–267; geography and history, 1:257–258; S.E.K. Mqhayi and the Imbongi tradition, 1:261–264; Tiyo Soga and Xhosa folklore, 1:258–261; Yali-Manisi and the Imbongi tradition, 1:264–267

Xoklengs and Kaingang, 4:193

X-tabay (Mayan folktale), 4:258–259

Xúchiles (Otomí), 4:292

Yali-Manisi, David Livingstone Phakamile, 1:262, 264–267

Yama (Lord of Death), 2:121

Yams: Benin importance to, 1:178; Ga importance to, 1:192; Igbo importance to, 1:199; New Caledonia importance to, 1:309–313; Trobriand Islands importance to, 1:317, 320, 324; Vanuatu importance to, 1:327

Yanagi, Muneyoshi, 2:278, 279–281

Yanagita, Kunio, 2:279–280

Yang Yi, 2:220

Yanomami, 4:251–255; geography and history, 4:251–252; myths, legends, and folktales, 4:252–254; sorcery and rituals, 1:98; studies of Yanomami folklore, 4:254–255

Yanomamo: The Fierce People (Chagnon), 4:251

Yaravi folksongs (Peru), 4:204

Yehl, 4:40–42

Yellow Earth (China), 2:220

Yemen, 2:439–444; geography and history, 2:439–442; poetry, 2:442–444

Yeti (abominable snowman), 2:108

Y Gododdin (poem), 3:71

Yiddish language, 3:331–332

Yih-yuan Li, 2:234–235

Yijing (I Ching). See Book of Changes

Yodeling, 3:312, 313

Yoik (Sámi singing), 3:142

Yolina's story (Trobriand Islands), 1:323–324

Yolngu people, 1:294–296

Yoruba, 1:218–227; anthropomorphic figures in myth and legend, 1:223–224; arts and crafts, 1:225–226; chants and poetry, 1:222–223; riddles and proverbs, 1:221–222; rituals and performances, 1:224–225; studies of Yoruba folklore, 1:226–227; tales, myths, and legends, 1:218–220. See also Benin

Youth initiations. See Initiation (rights of passage) ceremonies

Yucatec Maya, 4:256–257

Yugoslavia, 3:351, 427

Yukon, Canada: Tlingit, 4:117

Yuletide. See Christmas customs

Yupik. See Western Inuit and Yupik

Zadruga (family clans, Serbia), 3:426, 428

Zajal poetry (Lebanon), 2:395–396

Zana (fairy, Albania), 3:324

Zande, 1:227–233; arts and crafts, 1:233; folktales, trickster tales, and animal fables, 1:230–231; games and sports, 1:232–233; geography and history, 1:227–228; historical narratives and proverbs, 1:231; magic and witchcraft, 1:228–230; modernization, challenges of, 1:233; music and song, 1:231–232

Zapatista rebellion (Maya), 4:258

Zarzuela, 3:183

Zenani, Nongenile Masithathu, 1:270, 274

Zhabdrung Ngawang Namgyal, 2:106, 110

Zhang, Qisheng, 2:217

Zhang Yimou, 2:220

Zhong, Jingwen, 2:216

Zimmerman, Georges Denis, 3:28

ZINATHA (Zimbabwe National Traditional Healers Association), 1:254

Zionism, 2:375–376

Zondi, Nolala, 1:270

Zorilla, José de, 3:183

Zoroastrianism: Persia, 2:414–416; Tajik, 2:328, 334; Uzbek, 2:348

Zulu, 1:267–276; geography and history, 1:267–269; music, 1:274–275; poetry, 1:272–274; proverbs, 1:274; religious beliefs and origin myths, 1:269–270; stories and storytellers, 1:270–272; studies of Zulu folklore, 1:275

Zulu Legends, 1:271

Zulu Proverbs, 1:274

Zulu Proverbs and Popular Sayings, 1:274

Zumwalt, Rosemary Lévy, 1:13

Zungu, Nombhonjo, 1:273

Zuni narratives, performance style of, 1:85

Župa (tribes, Serbia), 3:426

Zwingli, Huldrych, 3:308